SPECIAL EDITION

USING Microsoft® Office® Project 2003

Tim Pyron

800 East 96th Street
Indianapolis, Indiana 46240

CONTENTS AT A GLANCE

Introduction

I Getting Started with Microsoft Project 2003

1 The Power of Microsoft Project 2003 .15
2 Learning the Basics of Microsoft Project .29
3 Setting Up a Project Document .55
4 Managing Project Files .95

II Scheduling Tasks

5 Creating a Task List .115
6 Entering Scheduling Requirements .175
7 Viewing Your Schedule .231

III Assigning Resources and Costs

8 Defining Resources and Costs .277
9 Understanding Resource Scheduling .321
10 Assigning Resources and Costs to Tasks .359
11 Resolving Resource Assignment Problems .401

IV Reviewing and Distributing the Project

12 Reviewing the Project Plan .467
13 Printing Views and Reports .489

V Tracking and Analyzing Progress

14 Tracking Work on a Project .519
15 Analyzing Progress and Revising the Schedule .555

VI Coordinating Projects and Sharing Data

16 Working with Multiple Projects .603
17 Exporting and Importing Data with Other File Formats .631
18 Copying, Pasting, and Inserting Data with Other Applications .691

VII Using and Customizing the Display

19 Using the Standard Views, Tables, Filters, and Groups .735
20 Formatting Views .775
21 Customizing Views, Tables, Fields, Filters, and Groups .833
22 Using and Customizing the Standard Reports .877
23 Customizing Toolbars, Menus, and Forms .921

VIII Using Project Server and Project Professional

24 Introduction to Microsoft Office Project Server 2003 .965
25 Enterprise Project Administration .985
26 Enterprise Project Management .1029
27 Enterprise Resource Management .1069
28 Enterprise Collaboration .1119

Index

CD

CD1 Publishing Projects on the Web
CD2 Using Visual Basic with Project 2003
CD3 Customizing and Administering Project Server Access

Special Edition Using Microsoft® Office® Project 2003

International Standard Book Number: 0-7897-3072-3

Library of Congress Catalog Card Number: 2003114781

Printed in the United States of America

First Printing: February 2004

07 06 05 4

Trademarks

Warning and Disclaimer

Bulk Sales

Que Publishing offers excellent discounts on this book when ordered in quantity for bulk purchases or special sales. For more information, please contact

U.S. Corporate and Government Sales
1-800-382-3419
corpsales@pearsontechgroup.com

For sales outside the U.S., please contact

International Sales
1-317-428-3341
international@pearsontechgroup.com

Associate Publisher
Greg Wiegand

Acquisitions Editor
Stephanie J. McComb

Development Editor
Mark Cierzniak

Managing Editor
Charlotte Clapp

Project Editor
Tonya Simpson

Production Editor
Benjamin Berg

Indexer
Erika Millen

Proofreader
Wendy Ott

Technical Editor
Brian Kennemer

Publishing Coordinator
Sharry Lee Gregory

Multimedia Developer
Dan Scherf

Interior Designer
Anne Jones

Cover Designer
Anne Jones

Page Layout
Eric S. Miller

Graphics
Tammy Graham

TABLE OF CONTENTS

Introduction 1

Why You Should Use This Book 1

Why You Should Use Microsoft Project 1

What's New in Microsoft Project 2003 3

Two Editions of Microsoft Project 2003 3

File Compatibility 3

Ease-of-Use Features 4

Project Server 2003 4

How This Book Is Organized 5

Part I, "Getting Started with Microsoft Project 2003" 5

Part II, "Scheduling Tasks" 6

Part III, "Assigning Resources and Costs" 6

Part IV, "Reviewing and Distributing the Project" 7

Part V, "Tracking and Analyzing Progress" 7

Part VI, "Coordinating Projects and Sharing Data" 8

Part VII, "Using and Customizing the Display" 8

Part VIII, "Using Project Server and Project Professional" 9

Web Elements 9

Special Features in This Book 9

Visual Aids 9

Keyboard Conventions 10

Formatting Conventions 11

I Getting Started with Microsoft Project 2003

1 The Power of Microsoft Project 2003 15

Exploring Project Management 16

Projects Are Temporary 16

Project Objectives Are Specific and Measurable 16

Projects Are Constrained by Time, Cost, and Scope and Quality 17

What Microsoft Project 2003 Can Do for You 18

Some General, Common-Sense Guidelines for Project Managers 19

A Checklist for Using Microsoft Project 22

Preliminaries 22

Planning 22

Managing the Project 23

Project Management Scheduling Techniques 24

You Must Provide the Raw Data 24

The Calendar Used for Scheduling 25

How Project Calculates the Schedule 25
How Resource Assignments Affect the Schedule 26
Troubleshooting 27

2 Learning the Basics of Microsoft Project 29

Starting and Exiting Microsoft Project 30
Exploring the Microsoft Project Window 32
The Menu Bar 35
The Toolbars 35
The Entry Bar 37
The View Bar 37
The Project Guide Toolbar and Sidepane 38
The Status Bar 38
ScreenTips 38
NEW Using Learning Aids 39
Working with Project Guide 40
Using SmartTags 41
Working with the Planning Wizard 42
Introducing the Gantt Chart View 43
The Active Split Bar 46
The Split Bar and the Split Box 47
The Divider Bar 47
Changing Views 47
Scrolling and Selecting Data Fields 48
Using the Scrollbars 49
Scrolling the Timescale with the Keyboard 49
Locating a Taskbar on the Timescale 50
Finding Tasks or Resources by Name 50
Selecting Data Fields in Tables 50
Scrolling and Selecting Fields in Forms 51
Troubleshooting 52

3 Setting Up a Project Document 55

Supplying Information for a New Project 56
Using the Project Information Dialog Box 57
Using the Properties Dialog Box 62
Selecting the Environment Options 65
Reviewing Critical Options 68
Setting Other Useful Options 73
Defining a Calendar of Working Time 76
Scheduling with Calendars 77
Editing the Standard Calendar 78
Creating a New Calendar 82
Saving or Canceling Calendar Changes 84

Working with Calendars .84
Copying Calendars to the Global Template .89
Copying a Calendar from One Project to Another .90
Troubleshooting .93

4 **Managing Project Files** .95

Saving and Protecting Files .96
Designating a Default Save Location and File Format .96
Version Compatibility .97
Activating Auto Save .98
Saving a File .99
Providing Security for Saved Files .100
Saving Files in HTML Format .102
Saving the Workspace .102
Program Integrity .103
Creating and Using Templates .103
Opening Template Files .104
The Global Template: GLOBAL.MPT .104
Using the Microsoft Project Sample Templates .104
Creating a New Template .106
Modifying Template Files .107
Working with the Organizer and the Global File .107
Using the Organizer to Modify GLOBAL.MPT .109
Copying Objects by Using the Organizer .109
Renaming an Object by Using the Organizer .111
Deleting an Object by Using the Organizer .111
Troubleshooting .112

II Scheduling Tasks

5 **Creating a Task List** .115

Approaching the Planning Process .116
Entering Tasks in a Gantt Chart .118
Understanding the Fields in the Task Table .119
The ID Field .119
The Indicators Field .120
The Task Name Field .120
The Duration Field .120
The Start and Finish Fields .120
The Predecessors Field .123
The Resource Names Field .123
Entering Task Names .123
Typing Task Names .124
Copying Task Names from Another Application .125

Displaying Long Task Names 126
Adjusting the Height of Task Rows 126

Editing the Task List 127
Undoing Changes in the Task List 127
Inserting, Deleting, and Clearing 128
Moving and Copying Tasks 129
Using the Fill Command 130

Using the Task Information Dialog Box to Edit Tasks 131
Working with the Task Information Dialog Box 131
Using the Multiple Task Information Dialog Box 131

Entering Task Duration 132
Using Tentative Duration Estimates 133
Understanding the Duration Time Units 134
Using Time Unit Abbreviations 134
Defining Elapsed Duration 135

Defining Milestones 136

Using Recurring Tasks 137
Creating Recurring Tasks 138
Editing Recurring Tasks 142

Attaching Notes to Tasks 142
Typing and Formatting Notes 142
Inserting Hyperlinks in Notes 144
Inserting Objects in Notes 144
Attaching Notes to the Overall Project 146

Attaching Hyperlinks to Tasks 147
Attaching Hyperlinks to Existing Files or Web Pages 148
Attaching Hyperlinks to New Files 149
Attaching Hyperlinks to Tasks or Resources in the Same Project 150
Using Hyperlinks to Create Email Messages 150
Editing and Deleting Hyperlinks 150
Placing Hyperlinks in the Custom Text Fields 150

Using Other Views to Create Tasks 151
Using a Network Diagram to Create Tasks 151
Using the Task Entry View 152
Using the Task Sheet View 154

Outlining the Task List 154
Understanding Summary Tasks and Subtasks 154
Understanding Duration for Summary Tasks 156
Indenting and Outdenting Tasks 156
Collapsing and Expanding the Outline 157
Editing Outlined Projects 159
Selecting the Display Options for Outlining 160
Using Rollup Taskbars 161

Using Custom WBS Codes 163
Creating Custom WBS Codes 164
Inserting, Deleting, and Moving Tasks with Custom WBS Codes 167
Editing Custom WBS Codes 167
Renumbering the Custom WBS Codes 168
Using Custom Outline Numbers 169
Printing the Project Task List 170
Troubleshooting 170
Project Extras: Letting Project Calculate Duration 171

6 Entering Scheduling Requirements 175

An Overview of Scheduling 176
Understanding Dependency Links 177
Defining Dependency Links 177
Choosing the Dependent Task 179
Allowing for Delays and Overlaps 180
Defining the Types of Dependency Link Relationships 181
Linking Summary Tasks 184
Entering Dependency Links 185
Creating Links by Using the Menu or Toolbar 187
Creating Links by Using the Task Information Dialog Box 188
Entering Leads and Lags 189
Creating Links by Using the Task Form View 190
Creating Links Using the Entry Table 193
Creating Links by Using the Mouse 194
Working with the Automatic Linking Option 196
Modifying, Reviewing, and Removing Dependency Links 198
Auditing the Task Links 199
Working with Task Constraints 201
Understanding the Types of Constraints 202
Entering Task Constraints 206
Deciding to Honor Links or Honor Constraints 212
Finding and Reviewing Tasks That Have Constraints 214
Removing Task Constraints 216
Resolving Conflicts Caused by Constraints 216
Entering Deadline Dates 217
Splitting Tasks 220
Creating and Using Task Calendars 223
Troubleshooting 226
Project Extras 228
Creating a Modified Constraint Dates Table 228
Filtering for Missed Deadline Dates 229

7 Viewing Your Schedule .231

Working with the Gantt Chart View .232
Components of the Task Table .232
Moving Around in the Task Table .233
Altering the Task Table Display .236
Components of the Timescale .240
Moving Around in the Timescale .242
Altering the Timescale Display .244
Viewing More Task Details .245

Adding Graphics and Text to Gantt Charts .247
Introducing the Drawing Toolbar .247
Descriptions of the Drawing Buttons .248
Working with Drawing Objects in the Gantt Chart View .250
Placing Independent Text on the Gantt Chart .256

Working with the Calendar View .258
Understanding the Calendar View .258
Moving Around in the Calendar View .260
Editing a Project in the Calendar View .262

Working with the Network Diagram View .265
Understanding the Network Diagram View .266
Zooming the Network Diagram View .267
Outlining in the Network Diagram View .269
Scrolling and Selecting in the Network Diagram View .269
Editing a Project in the Network Diagram View .270

Troubleshooting .274

III Assigning Resources and Costs

8 Defining Resources and Costs .277

Understanding How Project Uses Resources and Costs .278

Understanding Resources and Costs .279
Defining Resources .279
Defining Costs .281

Defining the Resource Pool .286
Using the Resource Sheet View .287
Using the Resource Information Dialog Box .288
Using the Assign Resources Dialog Box .289
Using the Task Form View .291

Using the Resource Fields .292
ID .293
Indicators .293
Name .294
Type .294

Material Label .295
Initials .295
Group .295
The Resource Availability Fields .297
The Resource Cost Fields .302
Code Field .307
Workgroup Fields .308

Setting the Automatically Add New Resources and Tasks Option .308

Sorting Resources .310

Grouping Resources .314

Filtering Resources .315

Troubleshooting .318

9 Understanding Resource Scheduling .321

Learning About Resource Scheduling .322

Reviewing the Essential Components of Work Resource Assignments .322

Understanding the Resource Assignment Fields .324
Assigning a Resource Name .324
Understanding the Assignment Units Field .325
Assigning the Work .329

Understanding the Work Formula .330
Applying the Work Formula in New Assignments .331
Applying the Work Formula to Changes in Existing Assignments .335

Choosing the Task Type .335

Understanding Effort-Driven Tasks .338

Modifying Resource Assignments .341
Scheduling a Late Start for an Assignment .342
Splitting a Task Assignment .345
Using Overtime to Shorten Duration .346
Contouring Resource Usage .348
Scheduling with Task Calendars .353

Understanding the Driver Resource Concept .355

Calculating Task Duration with Multiple Resources Assigned .357

Troubleshooting .358

10 Assigning Resources and Costs to Tasks .359

An Overview of Assigning Resources .360

Selecting the Appropriate Task Settings .361
Setting the Task Type .361
Choosing a Task's Effort-Driven Status .364

Assigning Resources to Tasks .365
Using the Assign Resources Dialog Box .366
Assigning Resources with the Task Entry View .379

Assigning Resources with the Task Usage View 387
Assigning Resources with the Task Information Dialog Box 393
Assigning Resources with the Task Table 395

Assigning Fixed Costs and Fixed Contract Fees 396

Troubleshooting 399

11 Resolving Resource Assignment Problems 401

Understanding How Resource Overallocations Occur 402

Identifying Resource Overallocations 405
Viewing Resource Overallocations 409
Filtering Overallocated Resources 409
Working with the Resource Usage View 410

Strategies for Eliminating Resource Overallocations 417
Increasing Availability of Overallocated Resources 418
Reducing the Workload for an Overallocated Resource 419

Eliminating Resource Overallocations Yourself 421
Increasing the Availability of the Overallocated Resource 421
Reducing the Workload of the Overallocated Resource 432

Letting Project Level Overallocated Resources for You 454
Configuring Settings in the Resource Leveling Dialog Box 455
Using the Level Now Command 459
Clearing the Effects of Leveling 462
Understanding the Pitfalls of Automatic Leveling 462

Troubleshooting 463

IV Reviewing and Distributing the Project

12 Reviewing the Project Plan 467

Looking at the Big Picture 468
Reviewing Project-Level Statistics 468
Compressing the Timescale 469
Collapsing the Task List Outline 470
Using Custom WBS Code Formats 471
Using Custom Outline Codes 471
Filtering the Task or Resource List 472
Sorting and Grouping Project Data 474

Realigning the Plan 479
Shortening the Critical Path 480
Strategies for Crashing the Schedule 480
Reducing Costs 481
Strategies for Reducing Costs 482
Comparing Project Versions 483

Finalizing the Plan .486
Checking for Spelling Errors .486
Distributing Copies of a Project via Email .486
Troubleshooting .487

13 **Printing Views and Reports** .489

Using the Print Commands .490
Changing the Printer Setup .490
Using the Project Guide Toolbar .492
Printing Views .493
Preparing a View for Printing .493
Changing the Page Setup .496
Using Print Preview .509
Using the Print Command .512
Printing Project's Predesigned Reports .514
Troubleshooting .515

V Tracking and Analyzing Progress

14 **Tracking Work on a Project** .519

An Overview of Tracking .520
Using Project Guide for Tracking .521
Working with Project Baselines .522
Saving a Baseline .522
Clearing Baselines .526
Viewing Baselines .527
Tracking a Project's Performance and Costs .528
Understanding the Fields Used in Updating the Project Schedule .529
Entering Tracking Information at the Task Level .531
Entering Tracking Information at the Assignment Level .536
Understanding the Calculation Options That Affect Tracking .539
Choosing a Tracking Method .546
Using Project's Facilities for Updating Tasks .549

15 **Analyzing Progress and Revising the Schedule** .555

Project Management Overview .556
Reviewing the Current Status of a Project .557
Reviewing Status vis-à-vis the Current Schedule .557
Reviewing Status vis-à-vis the Project Plan .563
Analyzing Performance with Earned Value Analysis .575
Understanding Earned Value Measurements .576
Controlling the Calculation of Earned Value .587

Using Earned Value Analysis in Project 2003 589
Creating Earned Value Graphs with Microsoft Excel 590

Revising a Schedule to Complete on Time and on Budget 595
Reducing Scope 596
Reducing Cost 596
Reducing Scheduled Duration 597

Troubleshooting 599

VI Coordinating Projects and Sharing Data

16 Working with Multiple Projects 603

Using the Window Commands 604
Viewing All the File Windows at the Same Time 605
Hiding and Unhiding Open Windows 606
Using the Save Workspace Command 607

Displaying Tasks from Different Files in the Same Window 607
Using the New Window Command 608
Filtering and Sorting Combined Tasks 610

Creating Subprojects and Master Projects 612
Combining Projects into One File 612
Working with Inserted Projects 613
Breaking a Large Project Apart by Using Inserted Projects 615
Maintaining Inserted Projects 616
Identifying Tasks That Are Inserted Projects 617
Deleting Inserted Projects 617

Creating Links Between Tasks in Separate Projects 618

Sharing Resources Among Projects 621
Creating the Resource Pool 621
Using the Resource Pool 621
Saving Multiple Files in a Workspace 625
Discontinuing Resource Sharing 625
Identifying Resource Pool Links 626
Viewing Resource Loads Without Sharing a Pool 627

Troubleshooting 629

17 Exporting and Importing Project Data with Other File Formats 631

Exchanging Project Data with Other Applications 632

File Formats Supported by Microsoft Project 2003 632

Importing Project 2003 Data from Other Project Management Applications 636

Exporting Project 2003 Data to Older Versions of Microsoft Project 636

Using the Import/Export Wizard 637

Saving an Entire Project in a Database 640
Using the Microsoft Project Database Format 640
Using the Microsoft Access Format 645
Saving and Opening Projects Using an ODBC Data Source 647
Exchanging Selected Parts of a Project with Other Formats 649
Working with Import/Export Maps 649
Reviewing the Predefined Import/Export Maps 651
Creating Import/Export Maps for Access and ODBC Sources 656
Working with Microsoft Excel Formats 665
Saving Project Data as an Excel Worksheet 665
Working with Web-Enabled Project Data 681
Working with Text File Formats 682
Importing a Task List from Outlook 684
Using Microsoft Project 2003 As an OLE DB Provider 687
Troubleshooting 689

18 Copying, Pasting, and Inserting Data with Other Applications 691

Copying Selected Data Between Applications 692
Copying Data from Other Applications into Project 694
Copying Microsoft Project Data into Other Applications 695
Linking Selected Data Between Applications 697
Linking Microsoft Project Data Fields to External Sources 697
Refreshing Linked Data in Microsoft Project 699
Deleting Links to External Sources 701
Identifying Tasks or Resources with Links Attached 702
Pasting Links to Microsoft Project Data into Other Applications 702
Working with Objects 703
Pasting Objects 703
Inserting Objects 706
Placing Objects into Microsoft Project 706
Pasting Objects in the Gantt Chart View 706
Inserting Objects in the Gantt Chart View 708
Placing Objects in the Notes Field 712
Placing Objects in the Task or Resource Objects Box 715
Placing Objects in Headers, Footers, and Legends 717
Placing Project Objects into Other Applications 719
Using the Copy Picture Command to Copy a View 720
NEW Using the Copy Picture to Office Wizard 724
Using the Copy Command to Copy a View 727
Troubleshooting 729

VII Using and Customizing the Display

19 Using the Standard Views, Tables, Filters, and Groups 735

Exploring the Standard Views 736
The Calendar View 737
The Gantt Chart View 737
The Rollup Views 738
The Specialized Gantt Chart Views 741
PERT Analysis Views 744
The Task Relationship Diagram Views 745
Sheet Views for Tasks Lists 747
Form Views for Tasks 748
Sheet Views for Resources 751
Form Views for Resources 753
The Resource Graph View 754
Combination Views 754

Exploring the Standard Tables 757
The Task Tables 757
The Resource Tables 760

Exploring the Standard Filters 761
Applying a Filter to the Current View 762
Using the Standard Filters 764
Describing the Standard Filters 765
Using the AutoFilter Feature 769

Exploring the Standard Groups 770
Applying the Standard Groups 770
Describing the Standard Groups 772

Troubleshooting 773

20 Formatting Views 775

Using the Common Format Options in the Standard Views 776
Sorting the Tasks or Resources in a View 776
Formatting Text Displays for Categories of Tasks and Resources 778
Formatting Selected Text 781
Formatting Gridlines 781
Using the Outline Options 783
Formatting Timescales 785
Using Page Breaks 789

Formatting the Gantt Chart View 790
Formatting the Gantt Chart View Manually 790
Using the Gantt Chart Wizard 801

Formatting the Calendar View 802
Formatting the Timescale for the Calendar 803
Selecting Calendar Bar Styles Options 804
Setting the Layout Options for the Calendar View 806

Formatting the Network Diagram View .807
Using the Box Styles Options .807
Using Data Templates for Network Diagram Nodes .809
Controlling the Network Diagram Layout .811
Using the Zoom Command .817
Formatting the Task and Resource Form Views .817
Reviewing the Format Options for the Form Views .817
Using the Entry Field Options .817
Formatting the Resource Graph View .819
Reviewing the Format Options for the Resource Graph View .821
Selecting the Values to Display .822
Using the Bar Styles Dialog Box .824
Formatting the Resource Usage View .826
Choosing the Details for the Resource Usage View .827
Formatting the Detail Styles in the Resource Usage View .828
Formatting the Task Usage View .829
Formatting the Sheet Views .830
Troubleshooting .830

21 Customizing Views, Tables, Fields, Filters, and Groups .833

Creating New Views .834
Entering the Name of the View .836
Selecting the Starting Format .836
Selecting the Table for the View .837
Selecting the Group for the View .837
Selecting the Filter for the View .837
Displaying the View Name in the Menu .838
Saving the View Definition .838
Creating a Combination View .838
Using and Creating Tables .840
Entering a Table Name .841
Adding and Changing the Columns in the Table .841
Completing the Definition of the Table .843
Changing Table Features from the View Screen .845
Customizing Fields .847
Accessing the Custom Fields .848
Naming Custom Fields .849
Creating Calculated Fields .850
Controlling Field Behaviors .852
Creating Indicator Fields .853
Creating and Using WBS Code Formats .854
Creating and Using Custom Outline Fields .854
Managing Custom Fields .859

Creating Custom Filters 859
Naming a Filter 860
Defining Filter Criteria 861
Using More Filter Criterion Tests 862
Using Interactive Filters 864
Creating Calculated Filters 866
Creating Multiple Criteria Filters 866
Creating Custom Filters with AutoFilter 867
Creating Custom Groups 868
Accessing Custom Groups 868
Selecting Grouping Fields 869
Defining Group Intervals 870
Formatting Group Displays 871
Saving Custom Groups 872
Organizing Views and Other Custom Elements in Project Files 873
Troubleshooting 875

22 Using and Customizing the Standard Reports 877

Understanding the Standard Reports 878
Accessing the Standard Reports 878
Common Report Elements 880
The Overview Reports Category 880
The Current Activities Reports Category 884
The Cost Reports Category 886
The Assignment Reports Category 889
The Workload Reports Category 890
Customizing Reports 891
Customizing an Existing Report 892
Using the Custom Category of Reports 893
Creating Reports 894
Creating a New Report Based on an Existing Report 894
Designing a New Report 895
Using the Common Customization Controls 896
Controlling Page Breaks in a Report 896
Choosing the Page Setup Options for a Report 896
Formatting Text in a Report 897
Changing the Sort Order for a Report 898
Collapsing Task Detail in a Report 899
Customizing Specific Report Types 899
Customizing the Project Summary Report 899
Customizing the Calendar Reports 901
Customizing Task and Resource Reports 901
Customizing Crosstab Reports 910
Customizing the Monthly Calendar Type Report 915

Saving and Sharing Custom Reports .918
Troubleshooting .918

23 Customizing Toolbars, Menus, and Forms .921

Altering the Behavior of Personalized Menus and Toolbars .922
Adjusting the Behavior of Menus .922
Adjusting the Behavior of Toolbars .923
Quickly Customizing Personalized Toolbars .924

Customizing Toolbars .925
Reviewing the Built-in Toolbars .926
Displaying Toolbars .927
Positioning Toolbars on the Screen .928
Using the Customize Dialog Box .929
Organizing Toolbar Buttons .930
Creating New Toolbars .934
Restoring the Built-in Toolbars .936
Customizing Command Buttons .936

Customizing Menu Bars .941
Adding New Menus to a Menu Bar .943
Renaming Menus and Commands .944
Adding Items to a Menu .945
Removing and Restoring Menus and Commands .946
Moving Menus and Commands .946
Changing the Attributes of a Menu or Command .946
Managing Toolbars with the Organizer .947

Customizing Forms .949
Reviewing the Forms Supplied with Microsoft Project .950
Using Custom Forms .950
Creating a New Custom Form .953
Placing Items on a Form .956
Renaming, Editing, and Copying Custom Forms .959

Troubleshooting .960

VIII Using Project Server and Project Professional

24 Introduction to Microsoft Office Project Server 2003 .965

Enterprise Project Management Using Microsoft Office Project Server 2003 .966
What Is Enterprise Thinking? .966
Reading Part VIII .967

System Architecture and Requirements .968
System Architecture .968
Microsoft Office Project Server 2003 Software Product and Version Requirements .969

Planning for Enterprise Information Sharing 970
Planning Enterprise Roles and Group Responsibilities 971
Planning Enterprise Project Management Processes 973
Reporting 974
Planning for Global Settings 975
Planning Project Attributes 975
Planning Resource Attributes 975
Other Planning Considerations 976
Using Enterprise Global Settings 978
Using Enterprise Project Outline Codes to Create Project Attributes 979
Using Enterprise Resource Outline Codes to Create Resource Attributes 980
Creating Consistent Project Schedules 981
Creating Consistent Views in Project Professional 982
Configuring Time Reporting 983
Using Collaboration and Document Management 983
Managing Roles, Security, and Views 984

25 Enterprise Project Administration 985

System Administration 986
Project Web Access Administration 986
Users, Groups, and Permissions 987
Managing Views 987
Creating and Modifying a Project Center View 987
Creating or Modifying a Resource Center View 991
NEW Modifying a Timesheet View 993
Building OLAP Cubes and Updating Resource Tables 994
Managing Project Versions 999
Adding the Version Field to Views 1000
Database Administration and Management 1001
Checking in Enterprise Projects 1001
Checking in Enterprise Resources 1002
Cleaning Up the Project Server Database 1003
Project Professional Administration 1004
Logging in to Project Server from Project Professional 1004
Managing the Enterprise Global Template 1007
Understanding GLOBAL.MPT, the Enterprise Global Template, and the Enterprise Cache 1008
Modifying the Enterprise Global Template 1009
Working Offline with Enterprise Global Template Data 1010
Using Enterprise Outline Codes and Custom Fields 1010
Creating Enterprise Outline Codes 1011
Creating Enterprise Custom Fields 1016

Managing Enterprise Project and Resource Calendars 1018
Managing Enterprise Project Calendars 1018
Performing Enterprise Global Backup and Restore 1019
Backing Up Enterprise Global Template Data 1020
Importing Resources 1021
Using the Import Resources Wizard 1022
Importing Projects 1024
Using the Import Projects Wizard 1025

26 Enterprise Project Management 1029

Using the Project Center Views 1031
Viewing Project Summary Information 1032
Editing Enterprise Project Information 1034
Viewing Project Detailed Information 1035
NEW Using Project Center Build Team 1036
Build Team from List 1037
Filtering Enterprise Resources 1038
Change Booking Type 1039
Viewing Resource Availability 1040
NEW Opening and Using Multiple Enterprise Projects 1040
Open Multiple Projects from Project Center 1040
Open or Delete Projects from Microsoft Project 2003 Professional 1042
Link Tasks Across Multiple Projects 1043
NEW Check-in Projects from Project Center 1046
NEW Using Administrative Projects 1047
Analyzing Enterprise Projects 1048
Analyzing Projects in the Portfolio Analyzer 1049
Modeling Projects with the Portfolio Modeler 1054
Using Enterprise Templates 1065
Working with Enterprise Versions 1066
Working with Enterprise Project Codes 1067
Applying Outline Codes and Custom Fields to Projects 1067

27 Enterprise Resource Management 1069

An Overview of Enterprise Resource Management 1070
Managing Enterprise Resources in Resource Center 1072
Using the Resource Center's View Options 1073
Analyzing Resources in Portfolio Analyzer 1077
Viewing Resource Assignments 1078
Creating Custom Enterprise Resource Outline Code 1081
Enabling Proficiency Levels per Skill 1086
Enabling Multiple Skills per Resource 1087
Enterprise Resource Multi-Value Fields 1088
Matching Skill-sets 1088

Working with Enterprise Resources 1090
Working with the Enterprise Resource Pool 1091
Using Generic and Actual Resources 1092
Creating a New Enterprise Resource 1094
Applying Outline Codes and Custom Fields to Resources 1096
Working with the Resource Pool in Microsoft Project Web Access 1097
Working with the Resource Pool in Microsoft Project Professional 1102
Adding Resources to a Project Schedule 1103
Using the Resource Substitution Wizard 1110

28 Enterprise Collaboration 1119

Introduction to Enterprise Collaboration 1120
Understanding Enterprise Collaboration Flow 1121

Using Project Web Access Tasks for Timesheets 1122
Understanding Timesheets 1123
Notifying Team Members of Task Assignments 1123
Submitting Timesheets for Approval and Update 1126

NEW Updating and Revising Timesheets 1128
Approving Timesheets Prior to Updating Schedules 1128
Timesheet Lockdown Periods 1128
Revising Timesheet Data 1129

Using Project Status Reports 1129
Requesting Status Reports 1130
Submitting Status Reports 1131
Compiling and Using Status Reports 1132

Storing Project Artifact Documents 1133
Understanding Document Libraries 1134
Using Document Libraries 1134
Linking Documents to Tasks 1135

NEW Managing Risks 1135
Creating and Assigning Risk Items 1136
Linking Risks to Tasks 1137
Updating and Closing Risks 1137

Managing Issues 1137
Creating and Assigning Issues 1138
Updating and Closing Issues 1138
Linking Issues to Tasks 1138

Using Microsoft Outlook with Project Server 2003 1139
Setting Up Outlook to Work with Project Server 1139
Setting the URL for Outlook to Connect to Project Server 1140
Importing Reviewing Project Tasks in Calendar Views 1140
Submitting Time with Outlook 1140

Index 1143

Extra Chapters on the CD-ROM

CD1 Publishing Projects on the Web 1

An Overview of Project 2003's Internet Features 2

Exporting Project Data to Web Pages 3
- Saving a Project as an HTML Document 3
- Viewing a Project as an HTML Document 9

Defining Import/Export Map HTML Options 10

Modifying Project's HTML Templates 13
- Changing the Background Color of a Web Page 14
- Defining a Background Graphic for a Template 16
- Displaying a Graphic Image in a Project Template 17
- Changing the Title Bar Text 18
- Adding Hyperlinks to a Project HTML Template 19
- Displaying a Gantt Chart Image in a Project Web Page 22

Publishing Web Documents 24

Troubleshooting 24

CD2 Using Visual Basic with Project 2003 27

Why Use Visual Basic Macros? 28

Getting Started with Visual Basic Macros 29

Creating a Macro That Works in Different Situations 30

Fixing a Macro 33
- Fine-tuning the Macro and Giving User Feedback with Message Boxes 33

The VBE 35
- The Project Explorer 35
- The Properties Window 36
- The Object Browser 36

Working with Tasks 36
- Initializing Variables 39
- Testing and Nesting 41
- Working with the Object Properties 42
- Reporting to the User 42

Debugging Code 42
- Syntax Checking 43
- Breakpoints, Watches, and the Immediate Window 43

The TraceDependencies Macro 46
- Public Versus Private Variables 50
- The Main Subroutine 51
- Requesting User Input by Using the Input Box 51
- Requesting User Input by Using the Message Box 52
- Calling a Subroutine Without Parameters 52
- Using a Case Statement 53

Calling a Subroutine with Arguments 54
Recursion 55
Controlling Filtering and Views 56

Working with Other Applications 58
Exporting to a Text File 61
Opening a File for Writing 61

Working with Events 62

Working with Application-Level Events 63

Getting Help 64

CD3 Customizing and Administering Project Server Access 65

Creating and Deleting Users from Project Server 66
Creating a New User Account 66

Managing User Groups 68

Project Server User Security 69
Creating Accounts from Workgroup Messages and/or Status Reports 69
Creating Accounts Through Workgroup Updates and/or Status Reports 69
Creating Accounts When Delegating Tasks 69

Using Categories to Control Access to Project Information 70

Using Security Templates 70
Modifying Existing Security Templates 70
Adding Security Templates 71
Deleting Security Templates 71

Authentication Options 72
Using Project Server and/or Windows Authentication 72
Changing the Authentication Method 73
The Authentication Options Screen 73

Creating Custom Views 74
Table Selection 75
Available Fields 75
Splitter-bar 75
Gantt Chart Format 75
Grouping Format 76
Default Group, Sort 76
Filter 76
Available Categories 77
Creating a Portfolio Analyzer View 77

Setting Features Available on a Project Server 84

Adding New Menu Choices 84
Adding a Custom Top-Level Menu Choice 85
Adding a Custom Sublevel Menu Choice 85

Windows SharePoint Services 86
Creating a Subweb 86
Using SharePoint Document Libraries 86
Managing Documents 87
Using Issues Tracking 89
Using Risk Tracking 90

Customize Microsoft Project Web Access 92
Gantt Chart Formats 92
Grouping Formats 93
Reporting Nonworking Time 93
The Default Home Page Appearance 94
Notifications and Reminders 94

About the Authors

Lead Author

Timothy W. Pyron, Ph.D., is an independent consultant and trainer for Microsoft Project users. His first book was Que's *Using Microsoft Project 3.0* (1991), and he has revised and expanded the book for each release of Project since then. He also authored *Sams Teach Yourself Microsoft Project 98 in 24 Hours* and *Sams Teach Yourself Microsoft Project 2000 in 24 Hours*. His books have sold more than a quarter-million copies—not including all the European and Asian translations. Earlier in his career, Tim was an economics professor and a professional classical musician. Tim is the lead author for this book, and in addition to his own assignments, he also collaborated with the other authors on the chapters they wrote or revised.

Contributing Authors

Jonathan Brandon is an engagement manager at Project Assistants, Inc., a Premier Microsoft Project Partner and Solution Provider specializing in implementation services, integration, training, and custom software development for Microsoft Project. He has extensive project management experience and is a Rational Certified Consultant trained in requirements management, project management, and object-oriented analysis and design. Jonathan can be reached at `jbrandon@projectassistants.com`. Jonathan revised chapter CD 3.

Kelvin Kirby has more than 24 years experience as a project management consultant and trainer. His career affiliations include several blue-chip companies, such as Land Rover Ltd., BL Technology Ltd., The Rover Group, Jaguar Cars PLC, Amazon Computers Ltd. (now Computacenter PLC), and ECS. An M.B.A. graduate, Kelvin also has an M.Sc. in information systems and a B.Sc. in engineering. Kelvin has won the PM Times award for Project Management Excellence for the fourth year running (2000, 2001, 2002, 2003) and was recently awarded the PM Foundation's highest honor as Consultant of the Year and the PM Foundation's Fellowship Award. In 1990, Kelvin founded his own Microsoft Project consultancy company, Technology Associates International, which is now a global organization with offices around the world and clients in more than 38 countries. Technology Associates is a Microsoft Gold Certified Partner and one of only nine Microsoft Project Enterprise Premier Solution Providers worldwide. Kelvin was the world's first ever Microsoft Project MVP (Most Valued Professional). He is also the principal author of the recently launched (Dec 2003) ITC2 qualification in Project Management (ECPMP). Once described as the "Red Adair" of Microsoft Project, you can contact Kelvin on +44 (0)1789 292150 or via email at `kkirby@techassoc.com`. Kelvin revised chapters 3, 7, 11, 14, 15, 16, 17, 19, 20, 21, and 22.

Milestone Consulting Group provides best of breed enterprise project management (EPM) solutions based solely on the Microsoft solution for EPM. Milestone focuses on developing a complete EPM package by implementing project management best practices, defining a solution architecture, configuring and customizing the EPM environment, educating on the custom EPM environment, and integrating with other enterprise applications. Milestone's solutions help companies reduce project lifecycle time, project cost, and reuse project team best practices. Milestone is actively involved in PMI and MPUG, and pioneered the Microsoft Project Lunch and Learn series. Milestone's clients include Fortune 500 and Fortune 100 clients as well as progressive small and medium-sized businesses. More information may be obtained about Milestone by email at `Sales@MilestoneConsultingGroup.com`. Milestone has five contributing authors who helped in the revision of Que's *Special Edition Using Microsoft Office Project 2003*:

> **Genea Mallow-Jensen**, PMP, senior consultant (`geneam@MilestoneConsultingGroup.com`)
>
> **David P. Fischer**, co-founder, president, and CEO (`davef@MilestoneConsultingGroup.com`)
>
> **Brandon Thornton**, co-founder and principal consultant (`brandont@MilestonConsultingGroup.com`)
>
> **Richard Courtney**, principal consultant and director of medium enterprise consulting (`richardc@MilestoneConsultingGroup.com`)
>
> **Daniel T. Renier**, principal consultant and director of education (`drenier@MilestoneConsultingGroup.com`)

Milestone Consulting revised chapters 4, 8, 9, 12, 13, and 23.

Fred Oettle, Ph.D., is the director of project management training for Project Assistants, Inc. Fred is well known for consulting and software development in project management, providing project management infrastructures built around Microsoft Project and Project Central. Fred has also worked as a radio/TV announcer and as a newspaper editor. Fred founded his own general management consulting and training company, and has conducted hundreds of seminars for government and private-sector organizations. Fred can be contacted at `foettle@projectassistants.com`. Fred revised chapter CD 1.

QuantumPM, LLC is a Colorado-based consulting firm specializing in high-quality project management services to the business and information technology sectors of project-oriented firms. The company's focus is improvement of organizational bottom lines through effective project and portfolio management. QPM effects change in the field through alliances with strategic partners such as the Project Management Institute and Microsoft, targeting a balance of philosophy and tools. QuantumPM is a Microsoft Premier Project Partner and a Registered Education Provider for the Project Management Institute. These partnerships allow QuantumPM to provide state-of-the-art products and services to its customers. Additionally, QuantumPM's classes provide students with PMI professional development units (PDUs), which are required to obtain/maintain PMI's Project Management Professional (PMP) certification. For more information visit `www.QuantumPM.com`. QuantumPM has four contributing authors who helped in the revision of Que's *Special Edition Using Microsoft Office Project 2003*:

> **Rose Blackburn**, PMP, founding partner of QuantumPM, LLC (`rmblackburn@quantumpm.com`)
>
> **Cristian Filip**, PMP, senior project manager (`cfilip@quantumpm.com`)

Patty Jansen, PMP, project manager
(pjansen@quantumpm.com)

Russ Young, senior project manager
(russ.young@quantumpm.com)

QuantumPM revised chapters 24, 25, 26, 27, and 28.

Joël Séguin, PMP, is a project management information systems (PMIS) consultant. Joël started his own consulting firm, GO Project Management, Inc. (go-project.com), a Microsoft Partner, and works as a senior system integrator and business analyst for many customers from a wide variety of industries, from fashion to bulk transportation and construction and pharmaceuticals. He has more than six years of experience teaching Microsoft Office Project and project management, and is currently providing training for a few project management schools both in English and French: International Institute for Learning and Institut de Formation en Gestion de Projets. He provides free advice on newsgroups and received a Microsoft MVP award for his efforts in making Microsoft Office Project an easy system to use. Joël collaborates with the Microsoft Office Project product development team on beta testing and customer requirements for the next versions and the documentation. Joël revised chapters 1, 2, 5, 6, 10, 18, and CD 2.

About the Technical Editor

Brian Kennemer has worked in the Microsoft Project world for more than six years. He currently works for QuantumPM (www.quantumpm.com), a provider of enterprise portfolio management products and service solutions as well as installation and integration services for Project 2002 and Project Server. Before working at QuantumPM, Brian was a program manager for Pacific Edge Software, where he helped design and support Pacific Edge's project portfolio management system, Project Office. He has also worked for The Boeing Company, where he developed a Project 98-based work management system for tracking work done in the manufacturing of the 767 and 747 jetliners. Microsoft has recognized his knowledge of Project by making him a member of the MVP program for the past three years. He is also active in the MPUG as a charter officer in the Puget Sound chapter of the group and as a columnist for the MPUG newsletter. Brian lives near Seattle, Washington, with his wife, Alicia, his daughter, Alivia, and his two sons, Riley and Jesse.

Dedication

As with all the previous editions, this book is dedicated to Gerlinde K. Pyron. The dedication is only partly in appreciation for her support during the long process of bringing the book to completion. It's also in recognition of her contributions to the content, for she has taught me more valuable lessons about business and management than I was ever taught in my MBA program. Wise manager, cutting-edge ecommerce consultant, unstinting social volunteer, gifted artist, and adored grandmother—Gerlinde is a remarkable Renaissance woman.

—Tim Pyron

Acknowledgments

When I wrote the first edition of this book 13 years ago, I learned just how inadequate the Acknowledgements page of a book really is. Even though I was the sole author, the familiar phrases "couldn't have done it without…" and "…made it all possible" took on a deeply personal meaning. I must acknowledge that publishing a book is entirely a team project, and the author is just one of many links in the chain that stretches from supportive families through the publishing house to the bookstores and the readers who provide their valuable feedback.

Nowadays, it takes a team of writers to explore the depth and breadth of a new version of a complex software product such as Microsoft Project and to capture that understanding in revised or new chapters, all in time to get to press as the software is released. A number of consultants and writers contributed their expertise and insight to this revision. I encourage you to read about each of them in the section "About the Authors" in the preceding pages, as well as "About the Technical Editor." I'm sure you will be hearing more good things about these capable folks in the future. My thanks to each of them for their hard work.

I also want to thank **Stephanie McComb** at Que, who as acquisitions editor was responsible for corralling all of us unruly writers and trying to keep us on course. **Mark Cierzniak**, as development editor, was responsible for seeing that the content met Que's high standards. I would also like to thank **Ben Berg** for his diligent copy editing of this book, and **Tonya Simpson**, and all the other Que folks who made this book actually happen.

Our technical editor for this book is **Brian Kennemer**. He examined closely and tested every list of instructional steps, every screen capture, and every other assertion, to be sure that what is presented as fact is, in fact, fact. You owe him a debt of gratitude, for he rescued the truth more often than I, for one, would prefer to admit.

Finally, my special thanks go to **Adrian Jenkins** at Microsoft, who served as the Microsoft Project beta coordinator. Adrian researched questions and provided answers to a wide range of questions about this new release for all of us. Congratulations to Adrian and the project team at Microsoft for a job very well done.

Tim Pyron

We Want to Hear from You!

As the reader of this book, *you* are our most important critic and commentator. We value your opinion and want to know what we're doing right, what we could do better, what areas you'd like to see us publish in, and any other words of wisdom you're willing to pass our way.

As an associate publisher for Que Publishing, I welcome your comments. You can email or write me directly to let me know what you did or didn't like about this book—as well as what we can do to make our books better.

Please note that I cannot help you with technical problems related to the topic of this book. We do have a User Services group, however, where I will forward specific technical questions related to the book.

When you write, please be sure to include this book's title and author as well as your name, email address, and phone number. I will carefully review your comments and share them with the author and editors who worked on the book.

Email: `feedback@quepublishing.com`

Mail: Greg Wiegand
Associate Publisher
Que Publishing
800 East 96th Street
Indianapolis, IN 46240 USA

For more information about this book or another Que Publishing title, visit our Web site at `www.quepublishing.com`. Type the ISBN (excluding hyphens) or the title of a book in the Search field to find the page you're looking for.

INTRODUCTION

Microsoft Office Project 2003 and Microsoft Office Project Server 2003 are the newest releases of the best-selling project management software in the world. While most of the new features added to the product line have been added to the Project Server product, there are still things to learn about the desktop product for this release as well.

Why You Should Use This Book

Almost anyone in the workplace can make good use of Microsoft Project at one time or another, but for project managers in particular, it's a life-support system. Microsoft Project is adaptable to both large and small projects. Managers of large, decade-long projects rely heavily on project management software to keep track of all the interrelated tasks and phases of projects.

This book provides direct answers about how to put a project schedule together by using Microsoft Project 2003. It's organized to follow the project cycle of initializing and developing a plan, implementing the plan, tracking progress and adjusting to changes and unforeseen events, and preparing the final reports. You'll find step-by-step procedures for using Project's features, plus you'll get help with common problems (such as avoiding unintended constraints on tasks, adjusting task duration when resources are added, maintaining resource information among multiple projects, and many more). *Special Edition Using* books from Que offer comprehensive coverage of software. You can be sure you will find what you need in this book to make Project work for you.

Why You Should Use Microsoft Project

Managing projects is a specialized field within management—and it's a rapidly growing field at that. There are professional associations, journals, professional certifications, and university courses and degrees for project managers. A project manager oversees all stages of a project, from concept and planning through the completion and drafting of final summary reports.

NOTE

> One of the best Web sites for project management information is maintained by the Project Management Institute (PMI), at `www.pmi.org`. At this site you can find valuable references to publications, discussion forums on the Internet, other relevant Web sites, project management special interest groups (SIGs) in your area, educational opportunities, employment opportunities, PMI chapters in your area, and membership information. You can also download a copy of the Institute's *Guide to the Project Management Body of Knowledge,* which documents the most up-to-date best practices in project management.

Microsoft Project is, at its core, a scheduling and planning tool for project managers, providing easy-to-use tools for putting together a project schedule and assigning responsibilities. Project also gives you powerful tools to carry you through to the end of the project.

After you have defined the scope and goals for a project, you can start putting Microsoft Project 2003 to use. Project is an invaluable planning tool for helping you do the following:

- Organize the project plan and think through the details of what must be done
- Schedule deadlines that must be met
- Schedule the tasks in the appropriate sequence
- Assign resources and costs to tasks and schedule tasks around the availability of resources
- Fine-tune the plan to satisfy time and budget constraints or to accommodate changes
- Provide links between elements of the project (tasks, resources, and assignments) and related project management documents in other applications
- Collaborate with other project stakeholders by reviewing the schedule and by notifying resources of their assignments
- Initiate and track discussions and resolutions of issues related to the project
- Prepare professional-looking reports to explain the project to stakeholders such as owners, top management, supervisors, workers, subcontractors, and the public
- Review the portfolio of all projects in the enterprise to analyze the impact of adding the new project on resource usage and cash flow
- Use portfolio modeling to optimize resource assignments across all enterprise projects
- Publish the project on a server for other project managers to access and for stakeholders to review, via Internet browsers

When work begins on the project, you can use Microsoft Project to do the following:

- Track progress and analyze the evolving real schedule to see if it looks like you will finish on time and within budget
- Notify resources of changes in their assignments and get progress reports on work that has been accomplished and that is yet to be done

- Revise the schedule to accommodate changes and unforeseen circumstances
- Try out different versions of proposed changes in a project, using "what-if" analysis, before making actual modifications to the plan
- Communicate with team members about changes in the schedule (even automatically notify those who are affected by changes) and solicit feedback about their progress
- Post automatically updated progress reports on the Project Server, or on an Internet Web site or a company intranet
- Produce final reports on the success of the project and evaluate problem areas for consideration in future projects

What's New in Microsoft Project 2003

NEW Project 2003 extends the dramatic changes that were introduced in Project 2002. If you are new to project management and its terminology, you might not fully appreciate some of the items listed in this review of new features. But if you are a seasoned user of Microsoft Project, you will be very excited by these enhancements.

Two Editions of Microsoft Project 2003

Microsoft Project 2003 is still available in two editions: Microsoft Project 2003 Standard edition and Microsoft Project 2003 Professional edition. The only real difference between these two versions for this release is that Project Standard is no longer able to connect to Project Server. In order to save and publish projects to Project Server 2003, you must have Project Professional.

Project Standard is best for project managers who are managing single projects or projects that do not share information about resources, while Project Professional and Project Server are the best choice for organizations that manage many projects that share resources, or for organizations that need to gather status information from their resources and share it via the Web with other members of the organization.

Using Project Server and Project Professional, a project manager or others on the project team can publish relevant documents and issues for discussion to Windows SharePoint Services, linking the documents and issues or risks to specific projects, tasks, or resources. The documents and discussion issues might relate to the goals of the project, specifications for completing tasks, change orders, budgets, and so forth. Furthermore, resources and others can also post issues and documents for review by the project team.

File Compatibility

Project 2003 can read Project 98, Project 2000, and Project 2002 files, and it can save to these formats as well. However, you don't have to save in the Project 2002 format for a Project 2002 user to be able to open the file, because Project 2002 can open, work with, and save Project 2003 files. Of course, the Project 2002 user will not see features or field data that Project 2002 doesn't support, but in general those features and fields are simply hidden and remain unchanged when you open the file in Project 2003 again to work with it.

Ease-of-Use Features

When creating filters that use fields that have value lists assigned, the value list choices now appear in the filter dialog box so that you can pick from the value list when creating the filter.

The Project Guide now has a new wizard to assist users with formatting views to optimize them for printing. This set of guide pages ensures that the view you see will be printed in a way that makes it easy to read.

There is also a new feature called Copy Picture to Office. This wizard helps you optimize the creation of an image file that is a snapshot of what you see on the screen. But this wizard goes further than just asking what format the image should be. It helps you pick which fields should be visible, which rows should be shown, and more.

Project 2003 also uses the new Assistance Center help features that, when connected to the Internet, will search an online database of help topics and articles on the Microsoft Web site before it searches the local help information. In this way, the Office 2003 family of applications gives its users access to updated and current content via the Web.

The Template Gallery on the Microsoft Office Web site now contains Project templates. The gallery is available as a sidepane in Project 2003 and makes the searching for and downloading of templates fast and easy.

The Watson error reporting tool has been improved to provide Microsoft with more helpful information about system or application crashes. This tool, when the user chooses to send the report to Microsoft, will send information directly to the product team about how the application crashed. During the beta testing of Project 2003, huge numbers of bugs were fixed based on information sent to the product team from the new Watson technology.

Project Server 2003

Project Server 2002 introduced a new wave of features to Microsoft Project users to allow for Enterprise Project Management (EPM). Project Server 2003 has built on that wave by improving and stabilizing the features introduced with Project Server 2002, as well as adding some important new abilities of its own. There are many changes and new features in Project Server 2003. Below we will cover the major changes, but this by no means covers all the changes. On the installation CD for Project is a document called WhatsNew.doc. It contains a complete listing of all the changes. Review this document for more detailed information about the new features of Project Server and Project Standard/Professional.

One of the most obvious changes in Project Server 2003 is the integration with Windows SharePoint Services. This replaces the SharePoint Team Services integration in Project Server 2002. Windows SharePoint Services (WSS) provides a much more robust and complete solution for document, issue, and risk management. Risks have been added in a way similar to issues, which allows users to capture information about risks to the projects in

Project Server. The document management features are a big change in WSS. WSS allows for document check-in and check-out, as well as versioning of documents. While it may not compete with full featured document management systems, it does provide the features that most organizations will need for managing their Project-related documents.

Project Server 2003 also adds the capability for administrators to more tightly control the reporting periods used to collect status from resources. These time periods can be defined and then locked down so that resources can be stopped from editing status for past time periods. This is an important feature for organizations that integrate Project Server with accounting for timesheet systems.

Project Server now has integration with Active Directory that allows administrators to let a user's membership in Active Directory groups control their membership in the Project Server Enterprise Resource Pool or in Project Server User Groups. Once the integration is set up, when a user's Windows account is made a member of a specified Active Directory group, Project Server will automatically add them to the Project Server group that is linked to that Active Directory group. The same works for the Enterprise Pool. This can help streamline the administration of users and resources in Project Server.

Resource managers no longer need to have a copy of Project Professional in order to add resources to specific projects. Project Server 2003 adds a browser-based version of the Build Team dialog box. It allows resource managers to assign resources to projects directly from the Project Web Access interface. In some cases, this can reduce the number of Project Professional seats an organization needs to purchase.

There have been huge improvements in the programmability of Project Server. There is now a full timesheet API that allows for full programmatic access to the timesheet submission and approval process. This will allow developers to create customized timesheet applications that work directly with Project Server's own methods but that are customized to the needs of the customer. Likewise, there is also a full Enterprise Custom Field API that allows developers to programmatically create and edit enterprise custom fields and outline codes. The PDS now also allows for the programmatic creation and editing of Enterprise Resources and Enterprise Projects.

HOW THIS BOOK IS ORGANIZED

This book is divided into eight parts. Although the first seven parts are written for those who use the Standard edition, all of the features and procedures documented in those chapters also apply to those who use the Professional edition. Part VIII contains chapters that show how to use the additional features that you get with the Professional edition. Following is a brief review of these parts and the chapters you'll find in each part.

PART I, "GETTING STARTED WITH MICROSOFT PROJECT 2003"

Part I introduces you to Microsoft Project 2003 and shows you how to set up and manage project documents.

Chapter 1, "The Power of Microsoft Project 2003," introduces you to project management concepts and the major phases of managing a project.

Chapter 2, "Learning the Basics of Microsoft Project," introduces you to the Microsoft Project workspace. With few exceptions, this workspace is the same for both Standard and Professional editions. In this chapter, you'll learn to navigate the screen display, scroll and select data, and select different views of a project.

Chapter 3, "Setting Up a Project Document," reviews the preliminary steps you take when creating a project. You'll learn how to specify the calendar of working days and hours, how to enter basic information about the project, and how to specify the planned date for starting or finishing the project. You'll also learn how to adjust the most critical of the default values that govern how Microsoft Project displays and calculates a project.

Chapter 4, "Managing Project Files," presents the information you need to work with project files. Included is a comprehensive discussion of the Global template file and how you use it.

Part II, "Scheduling Tasks"

Part II shows how to build and organize the list of tasks that make up the project plan.

Chapter 5, "Creating a Task List," explains how you define and enter the tasks, milestones, and recurring tasks that must be completed to successfully finish a project. You'll also learn how to organize the task list in outline form, in accordance with top-down planning principles. You'll learn how to edit the data in a project and how to use different forms for editing the task data.

Chapter 6, "Entering Scheduling Requirements," shows how to define the special conditions that govern the scheduling of tasks in a project, including specific deadlines and sequencing requirements for the tasks.

Chapter 7, "Viewing Your Schedule," explains and compares the most popular views you can use in Microsoft Project to display the task list: the Gantt Chart view, the Calendar view, and the Network Diagram view.

Part III, "Assigning Resources and Costs"

Part III describes how to define and assign resources and costs to the tasks in a project.

Chapter 8, "Defining Resources and Costs," shows how to define the resource pool that you plan to use in a project and how to define the working and nonworking times for those resources. You'll learn how to sort, group, and filter the resource list and how to save the resource pool as a template for use in other project documents.

Chapter 9, "Understanding Resource Scheduling," explains how Project calculates a schedule when resources are assigned to tasks—both when you first assign resources and when you change resource assignments. The detailed instructions for actually assigning the resources are covered in Chapter 10.

Chapter 10, "Assigning Resources and Costs to Tasks," shows how to assign resources and costs to specific tasks. You'll learn how to create assignments and then to modify the default schedule that Project creates by scheduling overtime, delaying or splitting assignments, and contouring the assignments. You'll also learn how to assign fixed costs to parts of a project. Finally, you'll learn how to view the resources, costs, and task assignments in useful ways for auditing the project plan.

Chapter 11, "Resolving Resource Assignment Problems," is a guide for troubleshooting problems in the schedule for assigned resources. Typically, some resources are scheduled for more work than they can possibly do in the time allowed; this is where you learn ways to resolve the conflicts.

Part IV, "Reviewing and Distributing the Project"

Part IV covers the part of the project cycle when you have completed the initial planning and need to review the schedule and refine it to ensure that it meets the objectives of the project. At that point, you generally want to publish the final plan in printed reports or on an intranet or on the Internet.

Chapter 12, "Reviewing the Project Plan," introduces features that help you review the task schedule for completeness and accuracy. You'll learn how to get an overview of the project to see if you can complete the project plan in a timely fashion and at an acceptable cost. You'll also learn how to view the task list through filters that focus on important aspects of the project and to sort and print the task list. You'll learn how to spell check the schedule and how to view the summary statistics for the project.

In Chapter 13, "Printing Views and Reports," you'll learn how to use the standard views and reports to publish a plan for a project.

Part V, "Tracking and Analyzing Progress"

Part V shows you how to keep track of actual work on a project and how to understand what is going on, with special emphasis on catching problems early so that corrective measures can be taken.

Chapter 14, "Tracking Work on a Project," deals with your role as project manager after work on the project begins. You'll learn how to save a copy of the finalized project plan to use as a baseline for comparison with what actually happens. This chapter teaches you how to track the actual beginning and ending dates for tasks, the actual work amounts, and the actual costs.

Chapter 15, "Analyzing Progress and Revising the Schedule," is an important presentation of ways to look at tracking information to see how well a project is meeting its objectives. Project offers many techniques and reports that you will learn to use in this chapter. This chapter emphasizes the use of earned-value reports.

PART VI, "COORDINATING PROJECTS AND SHARING DATA"

The chapters in Part VI discuss advanced topics that the beginning user will usually not encounter initially. Therefore, they are separated from the earlier parts, which cover the basic steps of developing and tracking a project schedule.

Chapter 16, "Working with Multiple Projects," explains how to link one or more subprojects to a master or summary project and how to link an individual task in one project to a task in another project. You'll also learn how to consolidate multiple projects and how to manage multiple projects that share a common resource pool.

Chapter 17, "Exporting and Importing Project Data with Other File Formats," describes how to export and import task, resource, and cost data with other applications and file formats, including the database formats. You'll also learn how to save entire projects in database formats.

Chapter 18, "Copying, Pasting, and Inserting Data with Other Applications," shows how to copy and paste selected data and objects between Project and other applications. You'll learn how to copy Project's timephased data into other applications and how to manage embedded and linked objects in Project and in other applications.

PART VII, "USING AND CUSTOMIZING THE DISPLAY"

The chapters in Part VII describe how to take advantage of the extensive options that Microsoft Project provides for displaying the data in a project. Some of the views and reports described in Part VII are mentioned in earlier chapters as well. This section provides a comprehensive reference to all the major views and reports.

Chapter 19, "Using the Standard Views, Tables, Filters, and Groups," explains the many options for using tables, forms, graphic images, groups, and filters to display your project in a view.

Chapter 20, "Formatting Views," describes the formatting options for all the major views and how to create custom views. You'll also learn procedures, including tips and techniques, for changing the appearance of graphic elements and text display for categories of items and individual items.

Chapter 21, "Customizing Views, Tables, Fields, Filters, and Groups," shows how to modify and customize the components of views. You will learn how to create custom tables and filters, how to define custom fields to calculate values for special data needs, and how to create custom grouping of the data.

Chapter 22, "Using and Customizing the Standard Reports," explains how to use the standard reports to supplement the printed views, how to modify the elements in the reports, and how to create new reports.

Chapter 23, "Customizing Toolbars, Menus, and Forms," explains the options for customizing the display of the Microsoft Project interface. You'll learn how to change the standard toolbar buttons and how to attach commands and macros to a button. You'll learn also how to customize menus and how to create your own forms for data entry and review.

Part VIII, "Using Project Server and Project Professional"

Chapter 24, "Introduction to Microsoft Office Project Server 2003," focuses on enterprise thinking and an overall view of Microsoft Office Project Server 2003. This will help you see how all the pieces of Project Server 2003 fit together from a portfolio manager's perspective.

Chapter 25, "Enterprise Project Administration," describes functional system administration of Project Server 2003 for the PMO system administrator and others who need to know what settings are required to create the enterprise views your organization needs.

Chapter 26, "Enterprise Project Management," describes Project Web Access and Project Professional from a PMO and project manager's perspective.

Chapter 27, "Enterprise Resource Management," describes how executives, resource managers, and project managers view and use the resource information that is available via Project Web Access and Project Professional.

Chapter 28, "Enterprise Collaboration," describes how team members will use the document management and collaboration features of Project Web Access, including time tracking, status reporting, managing to-do lists, issues, risks, and document management.

Web Elements

Three chapters can be found on this book's companion CD.

Web 1, "Publishing Projects on the Web," describes how to save views of a project for HTML display on Web sites and intranets.

Web 2, "Using Visual Basic with Project 2003," is a basic guide for nonprogrammers who want to record and use simple macros in Microsoft Project.

Web 3, "Customizing and Administering Project Server Access," covers what you need to know about administering Project Server and customizing the Web pages it uses to represent the project data.

Special Features in This Book

This book contains a variety of special features to help you find the information you need—fast. Formatting conventions are used to make important keywords or special text obvious. Specific language is used to make keyboard and mouse actions clear. And a variety of visual elements are used to make important and useful information stand out. The following sections describe the special features used in this book.

Visual Aids

Notes, tips, cautions, and other visual aids give you useful information. The following are descriptions of these elements.

New features that are introduced in Microsoft Project 2003 are flagged with an icon in the margin.

NOTE

Notes provide useful information that isn't essential to the discussion. They usually contain technical information, but they can also contain interesting but less critical information.

TIP

Tips enhance your experience with Project 2003 by providing hints and tricks you won't find elsewhere.

CAUTION

Cautions warn you that a particular action can cause unintended results, some of which may be difficult or impossible to undo. Given the many not-so-obvious calculations that Project processes at every turn, you shouldn't skip the cautions in this book.

Cross-references point you to specific sections within other chapters so that you can get more information that's related to the topic you're reading about. Here is what a cross-reference looks like:

➔ To learn more about working with project plans, **see** Chapter 2, "Learning the Basics of Microsoft Project," **p. 29**.

Best Practice tips will help you learn the ins and outs of effective project management. These tips are related to the project management process recommended by the Project Management Institute. These tips will help you along with the responsibilities of managing projects both with and without software.

At the end of many of the chapters, a "Troubleshooting" section highlights anticipated problems you might have and provides possible solutions. The problem is stated in *italic* type, and the answer or solution follows.

Keyboard Conventions

In addition to the special features that help you find the information you need, this book uses some special conventions to make it easier to read:

Feature	Convention
Key combinations	Key combinations are joined with the plus sign (+). For example, Alt+F means hold down the Alt key, press the F key, and then release both keys.
Menu commands	A comma is used to separate the parts of a pull-down menu command. For example, "choose File, New" means to open the File menu and select the New option.
Special-purpose keys	These keys are referred to by the text that actually appears on them on a standard 101-key keyboard (for example, press Esc, press F1, press Enter).

FORMATTING CONVENTIONS

This book uses some special typeface conventions to help you understand what you're reading:

Convention	Description
Italics	Italics indicates new terms. It also indicates placeholders in commands and addresses.
`Monospace`	This typeface is used for onscreen messages and commands. It also indicates addresses on the Internet and filenames.
`Bold monospace`	Bold monospace indicates text that you type.

PART I

Getting Started with Microsoft Project 2003

1 The Power of Microsoft Project 2003 15

2 Learning the Basics of Microsoft Project 29

3 Setting Up a Project Document 55

4 Managing Project Files 95

CHAPTER 1

THE POWER OF MICROSOFT PROJECT 2003

In this chapter

Exploring Project Management 16

What Microsoft Project 2003 Can Do for You 18

Some General, Common-Sense Guidelines for Project Managers 19

A Checklist for Using Microsoft Project 22

Project Management Scheduling Techniques 24

Troubleshooting 27

1

EXPLORING PROJECT MANAGEMENT

You might have been anxious to try out the new Microsoft Project software—to get your hands on the keyboard and mouse and to see how it all works. So, you dove right in…and now you're looking for additional help. That's perfectly understandable, because becoming a confident user of Microsoft Project is not easy, especially if you don't have a project management background. There are many special terms to learn (such as *critical path*, *task dependencies*, and *leveling resources*), and most of the screens in Project are unlike any you've seen in Word or Excel. You will learn faster if you start with some understanding of the special requirements of project management. So, unless you're an old hand at project management, take the time to browse through this chapter.

Project management differs from conventional management in that managing a *project* is more limited and narrowly focused than managing an enterprise or even managing a small department within an organization. Traditional management functions are concerned with managing the ongoing operations of an organization, to ensure its long-term success and survival. In contrast, project management is concerned with goals that can be said to be *temporary*. They have a definite end point and do not continue for the life of the organization.

Take time to supplement your professional development by attending training to learn effective tools and techniques of project management. Keep in mind that Microsoft Project will not make you a better project manager any more than Microsoft Word will make you a better writer.

PROJECTS ARE TEMPORARY

A project is a temporary assignment relative to the life of the organization—lasting only until the project's stated objectives are achieved. A project involves a one-time goal, produces a unique product or outcome, and has defined start and finish dates. Defining projects and project management by using the term *temporary* is relative. A sales project might have a life of two weeks and a project to build a nuclear power plant might have a life of 20 years. But both are shorter than the life span of the organization; both are temporary in that sense.

PROJECT OBJECTIVES ARE SPECIFIC AND MEASURABLE

Project goals are stated in terms of specific performance objectives. Vague generalities that call for unspecified improvements won't provide the focus needed for a project. You can measure the success or failure of a project by the degree to which the measured performance satisfies the objectives set out in the goal.

It is often said that what gets measured gets managed. Project management offers the opportunity to improve ongoing operations, fulfill the strategic mission of the organization, and rise above crisis management, a mode of "fire fighting" many of us constantly employ. Project management concentrates on organized task management by recognizing the details while still maintaining the big picture.

PROJECTS ARE CONSTRAINED BY TIME, COST, AND SCOPE AND QUALITY

Scholarly project management studies usually define a *project* as a collection of activities or tasks designed to achieve a unique short-term goal of the organization, with specific performance requirements, and subject to time and cost constraints. In other words, a project exists to deliver a specific performance objective, and the quality of the performance must be satisfactory while staying within the time allowed and without going over the budget.

These constraints are first apparent when you're planning a project. Usually, either the project start or finish date (or both) must meet some time requirement. Individual tasks of the project might also be subject to time constraints. Projects are subject to resource or cost constraints because there is always a limit to how much money you can spend to achieve a project's objectives. The minimal acceptable quality and scope of the deliverables are also constraints. These three constraints—scope and quality (performance expectations), time, and cost—are also interrelated when changes are requested in the project plan:

- If you are asked to improve the quality of the deliverable, the project will generally cost more and/or take longer to complete.
- If you are asked to finish a project more quickly, the project may cost more or require that you reduce the quality of the deliverable. That's the meaning of the old adage "haste makes waste."
- If you are told to reduce the cost of a project, you either have to reduce the quality of the deliverable or switch to less costly resources (who often require more time to finish the work).

The constraints imposed by scope and quality, time, and cost are often illustrated by the *triple constraint* diagram, also called the constraint triangle. See Figure 1.1.

For an authoritative survey of the full scope of project management get a copy of *A Guide to the Project Management Body of Knowledge.* This manual (which is the standard reference in the project management industry), affectionately called the *PMBOK Guide*, is available from the Web site of the Project Management Institute (`www.pmi.org`). PMI is the premier professional organization for project managers in general, and the PMI Web site is the single most important site for project management information. PMI is also the organization that administers the Project Management Professional (PMP) certification exam.

1

Figure 1.1
The project manager must work within the constraints of time, cost, and scope and quality.

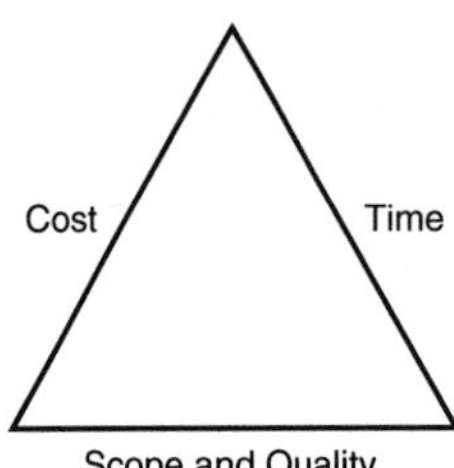

The type of organization greatly affects how resources are deployed. The organization's structure can run the spectrum from functional to projectized, with various matrix structures in between. Details of key project-related characteristics of the major types of enterprise organizational structures are well-documented in PMI's *PMBOK Guide*.

What Microsoft Project 2003 Can Do for You

Microsoft Project 2003 helps you achieve project goals on time and within budget. Computer software can aid significantly in project management, as a tool for recording, calculating, analyzing, and preparing presentations to help communicate the details of the project. However, Microsoft Project cannot produce or even guarantee a successful project plan. Still, in a number of ways, Microsoft Project can be invaluable in planning and managing projects:

- **Microsoft Project helps you develop a better plan**—Because the software requires you to specify precisely the tasks necessary for meeting the project goal, you must think carefully about the details of the project. The discipline imposed by entering these details helps you organize a solid plan.

  The screen views provide an organized presentation of the details of the plan, which makes it easier for you to visualize, organize, and refine the plan.
- **Microsoft Project makes calculated projections easy and more reliable**—Based on the data you enter, Project calculates a schedule that shows when each task should begin and end and when specific resources (which includes people, equipment, facilities, and so on) are scheduled to perform specific tasks. If you have provided the necessary data, this schedule also shows the probable costs of the project.
- **Microsoft Project makes it easy to test various what-if scenarios, to search for the optimum project plan**—Project lets you experiment with different elements of a plan, to arrive at the best plan for your organization. This is a particularly strong feature of Microsoft Project 2003 Professional.
- **Microsoft Project helps you detect inconsistencies and problems in the plan**—Project detects when resources are scheduled for more hours than they are available or when deadlines are impossible to meet, given the constraints you've entered. It helps you find and resolve resource overallocations and problems with deadlines.

- **Microsoft Project helps you communicate the plan to others**—Project provides printed reports and Internet HTML displays that make it easier to get the customer's or upper-level management's approval for the plan. Similarly, Project makes it easy to communicate the plan to supervisors and workers, and that simplifies getting their approval and cooperation. The ease with which you can produce useful reports has been one of the main selling points of Microsoft Project over the years.
- **Microsoft Project helps you track progress and detect potential difficulties**—After the project is underway, as work on the tasks is begun and completed, you replace the projected dates for the tasks in the schedule with actual dates. The software revises the schedule to incorporate these actual dates, and it projects new completion dates and costs. This new projection provides you with valuable advance warning of potential delays or cost overruns, so you can take corrective measures if necessary.
- **If external circumstances change after the project is under way, Project helps you adjust the plan and see the consequences**—For example, when new pay rates go into effect or the organization is subject to new regulations.

It cannot be stressed too much, however, that project management software, like any software, is only as useful as the reliability and completeness of the data you supply. And that, my friends, takes lots and lots of time. So plan on it—or hire someone to take care of it for you.

"Buy-in" from the project stakeholders greatly ensures the success or failure of a project. The stakeholders include not only the project manager and performing organization, but also the customer who ends up using the product of the project and the sponsor who is the individual or group within the performing organization who provides the financial resources for the project. All these people make up a successful project team.

SOME GENERAL, COMMON-SENSE GUIDELINES FOR PROJECT MANAGERS

These guidelines are offered to help promote your success with projects. Most of them are common-sense management techniques, but reviewing them from time to time can be a useful exercise:

- Remember that your success as a project manager depends largely on your ability to motivate people to cooperate in the project. No software program or well-designed plan can compensate for ineffective people skills. Computers might respond to logic, but people respond to human emotions.
- Establish your authority as project manager and your role as coordinator of project planning at the outset. If you are appointed, ask the officer who makes the appointment to distribute a statement that validates your authority. Don't post it outside your door unless you provide cork backing as protection against sharp-pointed projectiles.

1

- Make the planning stage a group effort as much as possible. You're sure to find that you can't think of everything, and a wider base of experience and expertise is immensely helpful. You will also find it much easier to secure approval of the plan and to get people committed to the plan if they help in its formulation.
- Set a clear project goal, including the following:
  - State the goal of the project precisely and simply in a manner that everyone associated with the project can understand. This includes your supervisors who approve the project, managers who work with the project, and those who actually do the work. Prepare a concise summary statement of the project goal. State your goal in realistic and attainable terms that can be measured. It will then be possible to measure success.

If you want to use Project as a starting point to your project's documentation repository, see "Providing Access to Related Documents" in the "Troubleshooting" section at the end of this chapter.

  - Secure agreement on the goal by all who must approve the project or who must provide supervision during the execution of the project.
  - State a definite time frame in the goal—it should be part of the commitment to the project. The goal "Install a new word processor throughout the company," for example, is ill defined. "Select and install a new word processor throughout the company and train all personnel in its use by June 1," is measurable.
  - Define the performance requirements and specifications carefully.
  - Discover and record all fixed deadlines or time constraints.
  - Determine the budgetary limitations of the project.
  - State the performance or quality specifications of the project with great care. Write and then distribute these specifications, in a statement of work, to the creators of the specifications and to the supervisors and workers when they are assigned to tasks. Make sure no misunderstanding exists about what you expect. Misunderstood specifications can jeopardize a project's success.
- Organize the work of the project into major phases or components and establish *milestones*, or interim goals, to mark the completion of each of these phases. Milestones serve as checkpoints by which everyone can gauge how well the project is on target after the work begins. This is a *top-down* approach, and it provides organization for the project plan from the outset.

If you have trouble finding when to stop decomposing the tasks into smaller activities, see "Determining the Level of Detail to Include in the Task List" in the "Troubleshooting" section at the end of this chapter.

  For example, the conversion to a new word processing product might involve the following phases and milestones (the milestones are italicized):

  - Select the software

    Determine the features required

    Review available products

Select the product

Software selection complete

- Acquire and install the software

  Buy the software

  Set up a help desk

  Install the software

  Software installed

- Convert to the new software

  Convert old documents

  Train users

  Conversion complete

- Define the work that must be completed to reach each milestone as distinct tasks, and estimate how long each task will take. If a task takes too long (some say any more than 10 working days!), you will probably be better off breaking it down into more components.
- Diagram the flow of activity to show the instances where tasks must be performed in a specific sequence.
- Distribute the project plan to all who are responsible for supervising or doing the work. Secure their agreement that the assumptions of the plan are sound and that all involved are willing to do their part. Revise the plan as needed to secure agreement.
- Distribute printed copies of the revised schedule with charts and tables, to clearly identify the scope of the project and the responsibilities of all who must contribute to making the project a success.
- Secure from resources their firm commitment to do the work assignments that are outlined in the plan.
- After work on the project is underway, monitor progress by tracking actual performance and entering the results in the project plan. This is the best way to discover problems early so you can take corrective actions before disaster strikes.

  Tracking these performance details also helps document the history of the project so you can learn from the experience. It's especially helpful if you have problems meeting the goals, and it will be valuable to you if you have to explain why the project goals are not met.

  If problems arise that jeopardize finishing the project on time or within budget, you can give superiors ample warning so they can adjust their expectations.
- After the project is completed, document the whole process, not only to sum up what was accomplished but also with an eye to what lessons can be learned for the future.

1

A CHECKLIST FOR USING MICROSOFT PROJECT

Microsoft Project is so rich with options that you can easily lose sight of the forest as you explore all the interesting new trees. The following sections give you an overview of planning a project with Microsoft Project.

PRELIMINARIES

Before you start entering tasks in Project, it's a good idea to define some basic parameters that govern how Microsoft Project treats your data. (These topics are covered in detail in Chapter 3, "Setting Up a Project Document.") To get started, follow these steps:

1. Customize Microsoft Project's calendar of working time to define when Project can schedule work on the project. This includes defining your organization's working days, nonworking days, and regular working hours. While you're at it, be sure that you use the terms *day* and *week* to mean the same number of hours that Microsoft Project does.

> **TIP**
>
> When you enter a task that you estimate will take a day or a week, Project translates those terms into hours (actually minutes, but hours will do for this explanation). Project's default "day" is 8 hours, and its "week" is 40 hours. If your day and week differ from Project's, you must define those terms for Project, or it will interpret your estimate incorrectly.

2. Enter some basic descriptions for the project: a project title, the name of the organization, the project manager, and the expected start or finish date. These descriptions will appear on reports.
3. Prepare a list of the resources you will use in the project. This includes defining resource costs and recognizing working days and hours when a resource is not available. You can add names to the list later, but most users like to have the list ready when they start entering the tasks in the planning phase.

PLANNING

Planning is the phase in which you outline the project plan, refine it, and distribute it to all who are involved in the project. (These topics are explored in detail in Chapters 5 through 13.) To plan the schedule, you need to follow these steps:

1. List the major phases of the project in outline form and then fill in the detailed tasks and milestones in the project. Estimate how long each task will take or how much work is involved. This is the topic of Chapter 5, "Creating a Task List."
2. If the start or finish date of a task is constrained to a fixed date, enter the date at this point. Also define the required sequencing of tasks—that is, specify where tasks must be scheduled in a certain order. These topics are covered in Chapter 6, "Entering Scheduling Requirements." You can view the schedule in several different ways. See Chapter 7, "Viewing Your Schedule," for a quick overview of the different views and how to use them.

3. Define the resources that you will use. Defining resources is covered in Chapter 8, "Defining Resources and Costs," Chapter 9, "Understanding Resource Scheduling," and Chapter 10, "Assigning Resources and Costs to Tasks."
4. Review the schedule that Microsoft Project has calculated so far, and correct all problems by taking the actions discussed in the following list:
   - Identify and resolve scheduling problems where deadlines can't be met or where resources are assigned to do more work than they have the time to do. These problems are discussed in Chapter 11, "Resolving Resource Assignment Problems."
   - Identify costs that are over budget and find ways to lower the costs, as described in Chapter 12, "Reviewing the Project Plan."
   - If the time constraint for the overall project is not met by the schedule, you must find ways to revise the schedule to meet the requirements of the project goal. Auditing and refining the schedule are covered in Chapter 12.
5. Distribute the project schedule for review by the managers who must approve the plan and by project supervisors and workers who must agree to do the work. Printing the project schedule and assignments is covered in Chapter 13, "Printing Views and Reports."

   If you install Microsoft Project 2003 Server along with Microsoft Project Standard or Professional, the project stakeholders can view the project details by logging on to Project Server with an Internet browser. See Chapter 24, "Introduction to Project Server," for details about using Project Server for collaboration.

→ If you want to publish the schedule on an Internet or intranet Web site, **see** the chapter "Publishing Projects on the Web" that is available on the CD accompanying this book.

6. Revise the plan, if necessary, to accommodate suggestions or changes that are submitted in the review (see Chapter 12).
7. Publish the final schedule for final approval by all parties, and secure from each party a firm commitment to the plan.

Managing the Project

In the management phase, you monitor progress on the project, record actual work done on the project, and calculate a new schedule when actual dates fail to match the planned dates. These topics are covered in Chapter 14, "Tracking Work on a Project," and Chapter 15, "Analyzing Progress and Revising the Schedule." In this phase you do the following:

1. Make a baseline (original) copy of the final schedule plan to use later for comparing actual start and finish dates with the planned dates.
2. Track actual start dates, finish dates, percentage of work completed, and costs incurred, and enter these details into Project. Project incorporates these changes in the schedule and calculates a revised schedule with revised cost figures.

1

3. Review the recalculated schedule for problems and, if possible, take corrective measures. Notify all participants about changes in the schedule that concern them.
4. After the project is completed, prepare final reports as documentation to show the actual work and costs and to compare those with the baseline copy of the plan you saved earlier.

Tracking progress moves the project manager into the Controlling phase of the iterative process model of project management, whose components are Initiating, Planning, Executing, Controlling, and Closing. It ensures that the project objectives are being met, via monitoring and measuring progress by comparing actual progress against the baseline and taking corrective action, if necessary.

PROJECT MANAGEMENT SCHEDULING TECHNIQUES

The methods used by project management software to schedule dates and times for tasks (and the resources assigned to them) are ingenious. You will need to understand the general concepts if you are to use Microsoft Project effectively. However, you don't need to master the details of how calculations are made. Although the applications of these methods are reviewed as needed in upcoming chapters, gaining an overview can be useful before you get into the details of planning and coordinating a project.

YOU MUST PROVIDE THE RAW DATA

You must provide accurate task information in order for Microsoft Project to calculate a schedule for a project. This usually requires a lot of guesswork, but without it, Project won't be as helpful to you. The less time you take in putting together reasonable task information, the less likely the computer projections will be reasonable. Start entering the data by following these steps:

- Enter a list of all the tasks that must be scheduled in order to complete the project. You must include either the duration of each task (how long it should take to do the work) or the total hours of work that the task requires. When this is combined with the resources you assign to the task, Project can calculate the work (if you estimate duration) or the duration (if you estimate the work).
- Include as milestones any major turning points in the project, such as the end of a major phase or a point where new decision making is called for.
- You must include any sequencing requirements (that is, dependencies) that will govern when the task can be scheduled. A *sequencing requirement* is a requirement that the scheduled date for a task has to be tied to the scheduled date for some other task. When you build a house, for example, you schedule the carpenters to start erecting the walls after the foundation has been finished. You link the date for starting the walls to the date when the foundation is scheduled to be finished.

- If a task must start or finish by a specific date, enter this requirement as a constraint on the scheduling of the task. For example, you might stipulate that a certain task can't start until the third fiscal quarter, due to cash-flow problems. Or, you might have a contract that requires that a task be finished by a specific date. When calculating a schedule of dates for tasks, Microsoft Project normally schedules each task to begin as soon as possible, considering the task's position in the sequence of tasks. However, Project takes note of your constraints and warns you if the schedule doesn't allow constraints to be met.

The Calendar Used for Scheduling

Microsoft Project uses its internal standard calendar to calculate a schedule for the tasks you enter. The default standard calendar has no holidays and assumes that work can be scheduled eight hours a day, from 8:00 a.m. to 5:00 p.m., Monday through Friday, with one hour for lunch. You must customize the standard calendar to make it represent the workdays and shifts of your organization. This standard calendar is used to schedule all tasks that do not have resources assigned to them.

How Project Calculates the Schedule

Project starts calculating a schedule when you enter the first task. With each added detail, the schedule is updated. The primary method used in project management software for scheduling is called the Critical Path Method (CPM). CPM calculates the overall duration of a project by chaining tasks together in their required sequences and then summing up the combined duration of all tasks in the chain.

Figure 1.2 illustrates a simple project that contains six tasks and a Project Finish milestone task. Tasks A, B, and C must be performed in sequence; Tasks X, Y, and Z must also be performed in sequence. Both sequences can occur at the same time; however, both sequences must finish in order for the project to be complete.

If parallel task sequences are in progress at the same time, the overall duration of the project is the duration of the longest of these task sequences. In Figure 1.2, the sequence A-B-C takes 11 days, and the sequence X-Y-Z takes 9 days. Therefore, it takes 11 days to complete the project because this is the duration of the longest sequence.

You cannot complete the project on schedule unless the tasks on the longest sequence are finished on schedule. These tasks, known as *critical tasks*, are vital to keeping the overall project on schedule. A sequence of critical tasks is called a *critical path*. All tasks on the critical path must be finished on time as scheduled, or the finish date for the project will slip.

In Figure 1.2, Tasks A, B, and C are critical tasks, and the sequence A-B-C is the critical path. Tasks X, Y, and Z are not critical to finishing the project on time. You could delay the completion of any one of these tasks for up to two days without causing a delay of the overall project. The X, Y, and Z noncritical tasks are therefore said to have *slack*.

Critical tasks do not have slack. These tasks cannot be delayed if the project is to finish on schedule. So, having zero slack is one way to identify or define a critical task.

1

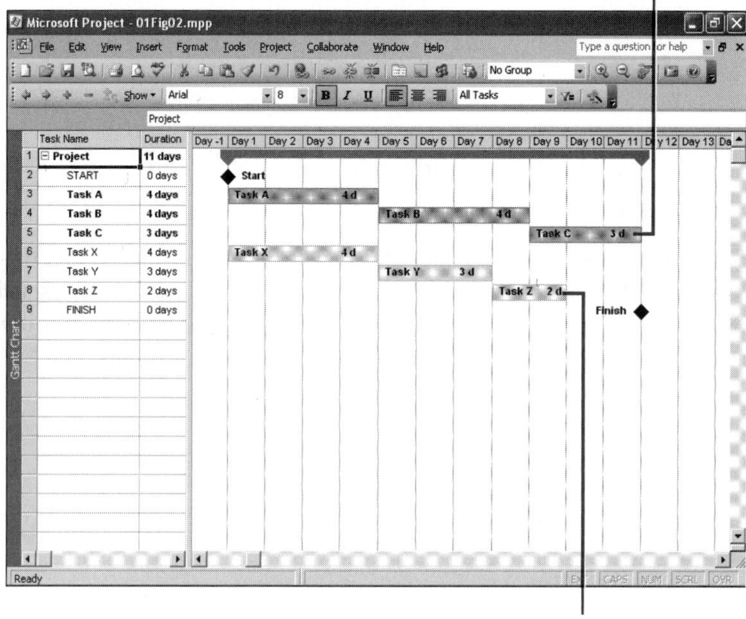

Figure 1.2
The longest sequence of tasks (the critical path) determines the finish date for the project.

Why Should You Care About the Critical Path?
Identifying the critical tasks is an important time saver in managing a project. Suppose you need to shorten the duration of the overall project (sometimes called *crashing the schedule*), and you're looking at the list of tasks to find some that you can finish more quickly than planned. (For example, you might add more resources to a task to finish its work sooner, or you might reduce the scope of a task or the quality of the work so that it takes less time to complete.) You don't have to look at each and every task in the project to find potential time savings; you can safely limit your analysis to ways to shorten the critical tasks and not worry about shortening the noncritical tasks. That's because reducing the duration of noncritical tasks would have no effect on the finish date. This knowledge can save you a great deal of time in trying to find ways to shorten a project's schedule.

How Resource Assignments Affect the Schedule

When you assign resources to tasks, the calculated schedule can change dramatically. Every resource has its own scheduling calendar, which shows when the resource is not available (such as maintenance downtime or vacations) or when the resource is available in addition to the standard nonworking times for the organization. The project's base calendar is used to calculate schedules for tasks that have no resources assigned to them. When a resource is assigned, the task schedule changes to reflect the availability of the resource.

Changing the number of resources assigned to a task also affects its schedule. Some tasks have a *fixed duration*: No matter how many workers or resources you assign to the task, the duration remains unchanged. If you scheduled a task to deliver a small package to a customer in an outlying suburb, for example, you would assign a driver and a truck. You probably couldn't shorten the duration of the task by placing two drivers in the truck. In that case, the task would have a fixed duration. If, however, the task were to deliver a truckload of packages, a second driver could reduce the time it takes to load and unload the packages and thus reduce the duration of the task. If changing the number of resources assigned to a task leads to a change in the duration of the task, the task's duration is said to be *resource driven* (also called *effort driven*). The schedule for the task is driven or determined by the number of resources assigned to the task.

Microsoft Project assumes that tasks are effort driven—that is, that they are *not* fixed-duration tasks. If a task has a fixed duration, you must define the task explicitly as fixed duration because Project assumes that you can shorten the duration of a task if you increase the resources assigned to do the work.

TROUBLESHOOTING

PROVIDING ACCESS TO RELATED DOCUMENTS

I have a lot of documents about the overall project, specifications for individual tasks, contracts for resources, and so forth. How can I link those documents to the tasks, resources, or assignments they refer to?

As you'll see in Chapter 5 and Chapter 10, you can provide links to other documents in the notes for individual tasks, resources, or assignments. If you have Project Server installed, you can also place documents in the SharePoint Document Library and provide links to the project there.

DETERMINING THE LEVEL OF DETAIL TO INCLUDE IN THE TASK LIST

I've been told that my project needs more detail. Are there any guidelines about how finely you should subdivide the work into distinct tasks?

You will want individual tasks to be long enough to manage easily. A good general rule of thumb is to subdivide the work into tasks that are at least a day long and no more than two weeks long. If you have weekly status meetings for the project, you might want to create tasks that are no more than a week long. That makes it much easier to keep track of progress and to know very early when things are falling behind.

These are general guidelines. If a project is extremely time critical—for instance, a project which involves upgrading equipment that would necessarily disrupt other operations—you might want to subdivide the work into tasks that are as short as an hour.

CHAPTER 2

Learning the Basics of Microsoft Project

In this chapter

Starting and Exiting Microsoft Project 30

Exploring the Microsoft Project Window 32

Using Learning Aids 39

Introducing the Gantt Chart View 43

Changing Views 47

Scrolling and Selecting Data Fields 48

Troubleshooting 52

2

STARTING AND EXITING MICROSOFT PROJECT

When Microsoft Project is installed, the Setup program places the executable on the Start menu. So, to start Project choose Start, All Programs, Microsoft Office, Microsoft Office Project 2003.

When Project starts, a new project document file named `Project1` opens. The default features in this file are based on Project's template for new files, the `GLOBAL.MPT`. If you plan to use this blank file to start a project, then you can enter pertinent data like the start date at this time.

Project displays the Task pane (see Figure 2.1), which lets you choose the file you will work with. The Task pane also appears any time you select File, New to create a new document.

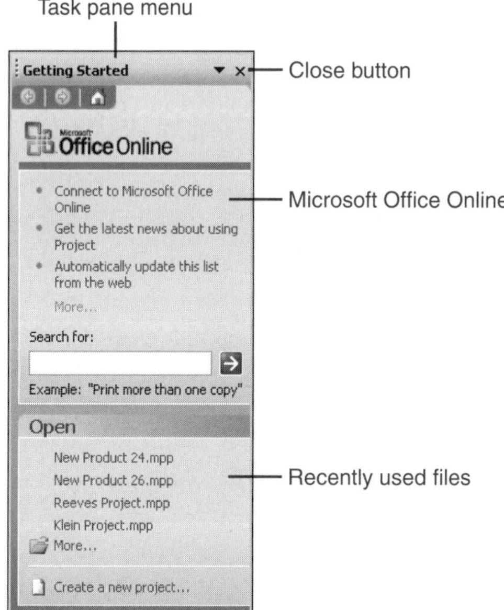

Figure 2.1
The Task pane presents all the options for selecting a file to work with.

The Task pane gives you options for starting a new file or for opening an existing file to work with:

- Click the Close button to close the Task pane if you want to use the blank document that has just been started.
- If you want to resume working on a recently used file, look for its name in the list under Open. If you find the name, simply click it. If the name is not there, click More to display the Open dialog box, where you can browse for the file.
- If you want to start working on a new project, you can use the Create a New Project option. There are three ways to create your new project (see Figure 2.2).

Figure 2.2
The Task pane presents all the options for creating a new project.

- You can use the Blank Project option when you have been working on other files and want to start a new project file. When you start Project, you already have a blank document to work with.
- If you want to make a copy of an existing project to use for a new project, you can use the From Existing Project option. Browse for the file on which you want to base the copy. Select the file you want to copy and click the Create New button. The file initially has the same name as the original, but when you attempt to save the new file, Project displays the Save As dialog box, where you need to provide a unique name so that you don't overwrite the original version of the file, behaving like it was a template.
- If you want to base a new file on a template other than the Global template, check the list of options under the Templates section, which lets you browse for the template on Office Online, on your computer, or on your own Web sites. Choose Office Online to select a template from the Microsoft Office Online Templates. You can also search Office Online directly from Project by using the Search invite. Choose On My Computer to open the Templates dialog box, where you find the templates that Project provides and the templates you previously saved. Choose On My Websites if you have identified favorite network places in Microsoft Explorer.

NOTE

> The typical installation of Project doesn't install any templates. You might need the Project CD if you want to install those templates later.

TIP

> If you need to search for a file based on text contained within it, select File, Open, click the Tools button, and choose Search. By default, the Basic Search pane appears, but you can click the Advanced Search tab.
>
> In the Basic Search tab, you can type the text you want to find in the Search Text box. You must also select a location for the search in the Search In box. You can specify the file types to accept in the Results Should Be box.
>
> In the Advanced Search tab, you can select the file property you are looking for in the Property box. To search for text, choose Text or Property. The file properties are Windows file properties such as size and date modified and Outlook item properties. Microsoft Project file properties such as Manager, project Title, and custom properties are included in the list of properties to be searched.

EXPLORING THE MICROSOFT PROJECT WINDOW

After you select a file to work on, you see the Microsoft Project title bar at the top of the screen, along with the menu bar, toolbars, and the Entry bar. In the center of the screen are the View bar, the Project Guide sidepane, and the *view* area itself—where Project displays a view of the project data. Figure 2.3 shows a project displayed in the Gantt Chart view.

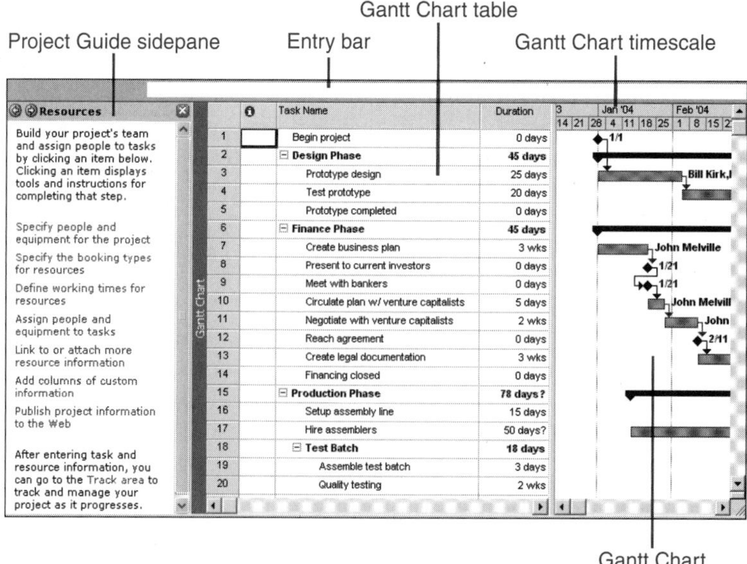

Figure 2.3
The Gantt Chart view is the most commonly used view in Microsoft Project.

The Gantt Chart view, Project's default view, is divided into two parts: a table on the left that shows a list of task names and a timescale on the right where taskbars show the beginning and end of each task.

Some views include graphic representations of project data. For example, Figure 2.4 shows the Network Diagram view. This is the same project data shown in Figure 2.3, but this view illustrates the sequencing of tasks in the project, similarly to a flow chart.

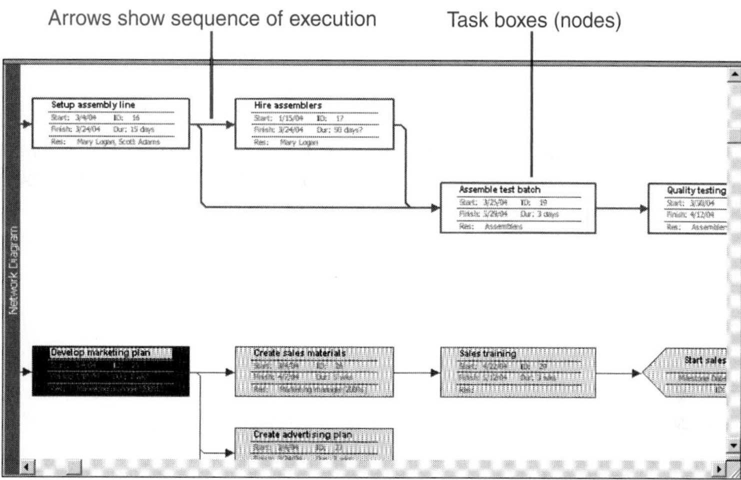

Figure 2.4
The Network Diagram view is a graphic view that shows the sequencing of tasks in a project.

Other views are like spreadsheets or database tables, where the data is arranged in columns and rows. An example of a spreadsheet-like view is the Resource Sheet view, which displays information about the resources in a project (see Figure 2.5).

Figure 2.5
The Resource Sheet view lists the people, equipment, materials, supplies, and facilities that constitute the resources for the project.

	ⓘ	Resource Name	Type	Material Label	Initials	Group	Max. Units	Std. Rate	Ovt. Rate	Cost/Use	Accrue At
1		Bill Kirk	Work		BK	Design	100%	$41,600.00/yr	$20.00/hr	$0.00	Prorated
2		Howard Thompson	Work		HT	Sales	100%	$22.50/hr	$22.50/hr	$0.00	Prorated
3		Jenny Benson	Work		JB	Personnel	100%	$35.00/hr	$35.00/hr	$0.00	Prorated
4		John Melville	Work		JM	Finance	100%	$62,400.00/yr	$30.00/hr	$0.00	Prorated
5		Linda Elliot	Work		LE	Marketing	100%	$83,200.00/yr	$40.00/hr	$0.00	Prorated
6	◊	Mary Logan	Work		MaL	Production	100%	$10.00/hr	$15.00/hr	$0.00	Prorated
7		Mel Lloyd	Work		ML	Shipping	100%	$15.00/hr	$15.00/hr	$0.00	Prorated
8		Scott Adams	Work		SA	Production	100%	$41,600.00/yr	$20.00/hr	$0.00	Prorated
9		Assemblers	Work		Asm	Production	300%	$9.00/hr	$13.50/hr	$0.00	Prorated
10		Draftspersons	Work		D	Design	500%	$0.00/hr	$0.00/hr	$0.00	Prorated
11		Engineers	Work		ENG	Design	300%	$56,160.00/yr	$27.00/hr	$0.00	Prorated
12	◊	Marketing manager	Work		MMGR	Marketing	200%	$56,160.00/yr	$27.00/hr	$0.00	Prorated
13		Warehouse workers	Work		WW	Distribution	600%	$17.00/hr	$34.00/hr	$0.00	Prorated
14		Warehouse Manager	Work		WMGR	Distribution	100%	$72,800.00/yr	$35.00/hr	$0.00	Prorated
15		Delivery truck	Work		TRUCK	Shipping	200%	$25.00/hr	$25.00/hr	$1,000.00	Prorated
16		Salespersons	Work		SALES	Sales	200%	$18.00/hr	$18.00/hr	$0.00	Prorated
17		Drafting Paper	Material	Rolls	dp			$100.00		$0.00	Prorated
18		Lab kits	Material	Kits	lk			$10.00		$0.00	Prorated

Some views are forms that show more details about one task or resource than you can see in a table like the one in Figure 2.1. The Task Form view in Figure 2.6 shows details for the Test Prototype task, including a list of all the resources assigned to the task and the predecessor tasks that must be finished before the task can begin.

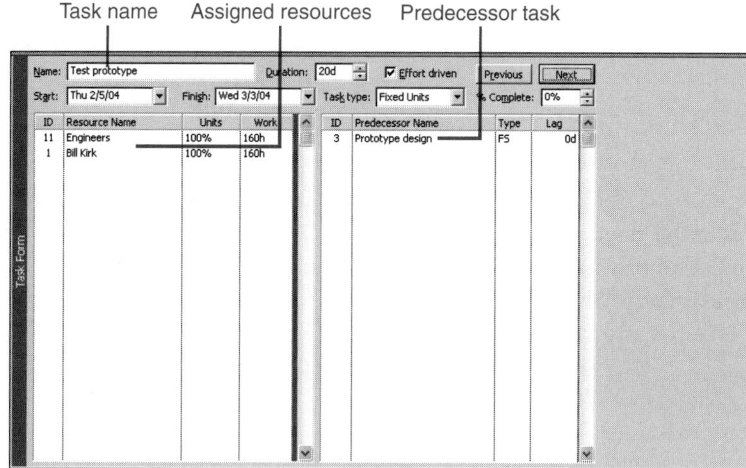

Figure 2.6
Among other things, the Task Form view identifies the resources that will be assigned to a task and the other tasks that must finish before this one can start.

Still other views are combinations of these basic types. The Task Entry view shows the Gantt Chart view in the top half of the screen and the Task Form view in the bottom half (see Figure 2.7). We'll examine this combination in greater detail later in this chapter.

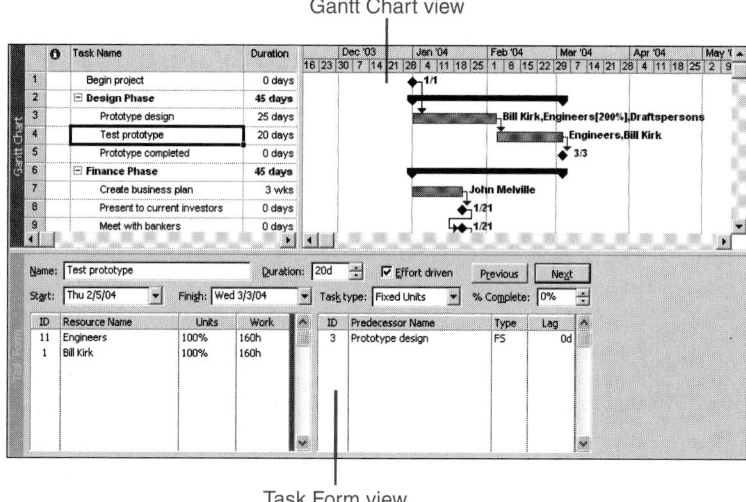

Figure 2.7
The Task Entry combination view contains the Gantt Chart view in the top pane and the Task Form view in the bottom pane.

Each of these views draws on the same set of data but presents it differently. Learning to make effective use of the different views is a key to successfully managing projects in Microsoft Project. Later in this chapter, you'll learn how to display other views in Project.

→ For detailed explanations of the most popular views, **see** Chapter 7, "Viewing Your Schedule," **p. 231**. For a list of all the standard views, see "Exploring the Standard Views," **p. 736**.

THE MENU BAR

The menus in Microsoft Project are very similar to the menus in the other Microsoft Office products (Word, Excel, PowerPoint, and Access). The menu commands are defined and described in detail in later chapters, as the functions they perform are discussed.

In Project 2003 (as in Office 2003), the menus are by default personalized—showing only the most basic commands at first. The full (nonpersonalized) menus are displayed in the figures in this book. To display the full menus, choose Tools, Customize, Toolbars to display the Customize dialog box (see Figure 2.8). Click the Options tab, and select the check box labeled Always Show Full Menus.

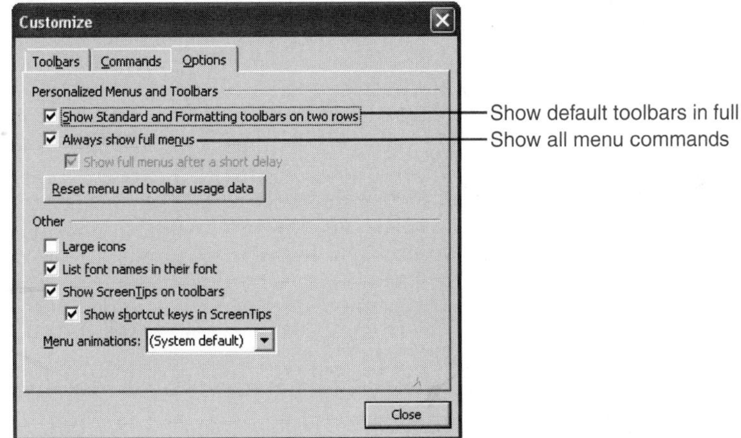

Figure 2.8
You can use the Customize dialog box to control how Project displays menus and toolbars.

THE TOOLBARS

Appearing below the menu bar are the Microsoft Project toolbars. By default, the Standard and Formatting toolbars share one row below the menu bar, with the full Standard toolbar and a small portion of the Formatting toolbar displayed. You use the drop-down arrow at the end of a toolbar to see additional buttons. When you use one of the hidden buttons, the toolbar adjusts by hiding a button you haven't used. Thus the toolbars become "personalized" to fit your use. To see the entire group of buttons on each toolbar, you must have them on separate rows. You can manually move a toolbar by dragging its move handle, or you can change the setting that controls this behavior in the Options tab of the Customize dialog box (which is described in the previous section). To show the full Standard and Formatting toolbars, select the check box labeled Show Standard and Formatting Toolbars on Two Rows. In the figures in this book, the toolbars are displayed on separate rows.

If you are looking for a toolbar but can't see it displayed, see "Missing Toolbars" in the "Troubleshooting" section at the end of this chapter.

The individual buttons on the toolbar are described as you encounter them in the following chapters. When you slide the mouse pointer over the button for a second or two, a *ScreenTip* appears to explain the button's function.

TIP

For more complete descriptions of the toolbar buttons, use the What's This? Feature on the Microsoft Project Help menu. When you choose Help, What's This? (or simply press Shift+F1), your mouse pointer gets a question mark attached to it. Click the toolbar button you are interested in learning more about, and a mini help screen provides you with additional information on that button.

2

There are 16 toolbars provided with Microsoft Project 2003 Standard Version. The 2 toolbars displayed by default are the Standard toolbar and the Formatting toolbar. You can add toolbars to the display (or remove them), and you can create your own custom toolbars.

→ To alter the toolbar and menu settings, **see** "Customizing Toolbars, Menus, and Forms," **p. 921**.

→ To create a custom toolbar that displays only the buttons you use regularly, **see** "Creating New Toolbars," **p. 934**.

The quickest way to show additional toolbars (or to hide ones that are currently displayed) is to use the shortcut menu. Position the mouse pointer over any visible toolbar and right-click to display the shortcut menu (see Figure 2.9). Toolbars that are checked are currently displayed. Choose a checked toolbar to hide it; choose an unchecked toolbar to display it.

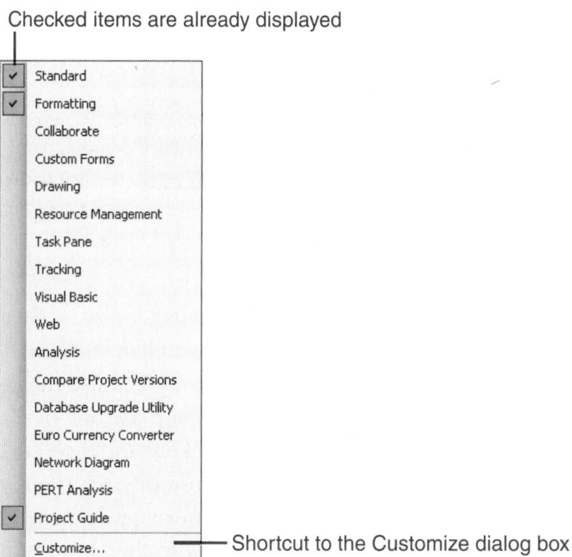

Figure 2.9
You can use the shortcut menu to show or hide toolbars: Simply click the toolbar name to change its display status.

NOTE

You can display and hide toolbars by selecting either View, Toolbars or Tools, Customize, Toolbars.

THE ENTRY BAR

The Entry bar, which is on the line below the toolbars (see Figure 2.10), performs several functions:

- The left end of the Entry bar displays progress messages that let you know when Microsoft Project is engaged in calculating, opening and saving files, leveling resources, and so on.
- The center and right portions of the Entry bar contain an entry area where data entry and editing take place. When you are entering or editing data, Cancel and Enter buttons also appear.

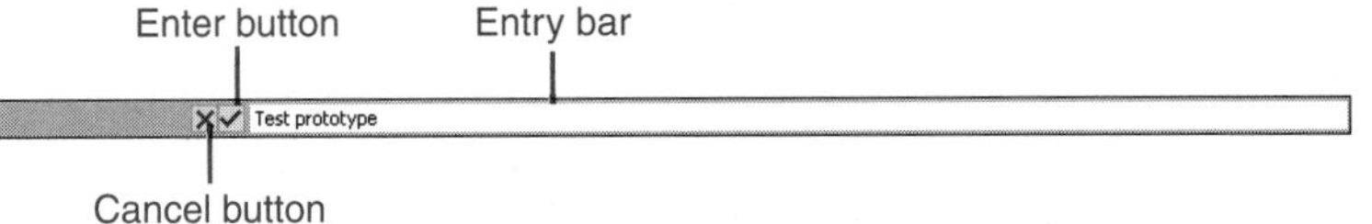

Figure 2.10
The Entry bar is typically used to edit data in a project.

You can use the entry area to type data into a field or to edit data that was previously placed in a field. You use the entry area primarily when you change data in cells in tables, or when you enter task data in the Network Diagram view.

NOTE

When the Entry bar is active, many features of Microsoft Project are unavailable. Most menu commands, toolbar buttons, and shortcut keys are also unavailable. Make sure you close the Entry bar by pressing Enter to accept the text in the Entry bar. You can also click the green check mark (Enter button) to accept the changes. To cancel changes, press Esc or click the red X mark (Cancel button) on the Entry bar.

THE VIEW BAR

The View bar provides quick access to the most commonly used views. For each of the views listed in the View menu, the View bar has an icon you can click to display that view. You can click the scroll arrow at the bottom of the View bar to see additional views (refer to Figure 2.10). When you scroll to the bottom of the View bar list, you see the More Views option, which takes you to a dialog box that lists all the views that are available in Microsoft Project.

To show or hide the View bar, choose View, View Bar. Similarly to the way you can select that views and toolbars be shown, you can select the View bar to show it and deselect it to hide it.

NOTE

You also can use the shortcut menu to show or hide the View bar. Right-click the View bar to display the shortcut menu and simply click in front of the name View Bar to change its display status.

Whenever the View bar is not being displayed, Project still indicates which view you are in on the active split bar (the thin vertical blue bar between the Project Guide sidepane and the project data). There are initially 24 standard views you can work with in Project, and the View bar helps you quickly switch between the views and keep track of which view is being displayed. Some menu commands add special views to the list the first time they are used; so, you may eventually have more views on your list.

In order for a view to appear on the View bar, the view has to be defined to display in the menu (and in turn, the view is also displayed in the View bar). Chapter 23, "Customizing Toolbars, Menus, and Forms," describes how to customize the definition of views.

→ If you want to list a view you use regularly on the View menu, **see** "Creating New Views," **p. 834**.

The Project Guide Toolbar and Sidepane

Microsoft Project 2003 includes step-by-step guidelines for building and working with a project file. These guidelines, which appear in the Project Guide sidepane, are divided into four categories: Tasks, Resources, Track, and Report. You use the buttons on the Project Guide toolbar to select the category you want to display.

→ **See** "Using Learning Aids," **p. 39**, for more information about Project Guide.

The Status Bar

The status bar is located at the bottom of the window. It shows the status of special keys and displays advisory messages (refer to Figure 2.10). At the left end of the status bar is the *mode indicator*. This indicator says Ready when Microsoft Project is waiting for you to begin an operation. The mode indicator says Enter when you initially enter data, and it says Edit when you edit a field where you have already entered data. It is also used to provide information for the action that is currently taking place, including seeing messages when you have a dialog box displayed, opening or saving a file, and previewing a document before printing.

The middle of the status bar displays warning messages when you need to recalculate and when you've created circular relationships while linking tasks. The far right end of the status bar indicates the status of keys on the keyboard—the Extend (EXT), Add (ADD), Caps Lock (CAPS), Num Lock (NUM), Scroll Lock (SCRL), and Insert (OVR) keys. When you turn on one of these keys, the key name appears in the status bar. You can use the Office Assistant to find more information on these keys.

ScreenTips

When you rest the mouse pointer on certain items on the screen, a *ScreenTip* provides additional information about that item. ScreenTips appear primarily in views that contain tables (such as the Gantt Chart and Resource Sheet views), and in graphic views such as the timescale side of the Gantt Chart view or the Network Diagram view. For example, when you position the mouse pointer on the Select All button in the upper-left corner of the Gantt Chart view (see Figure 2.11), a ScreenTip appears; it provides information about the table and view displayed, and it indicates that you can right-click to select a different table.

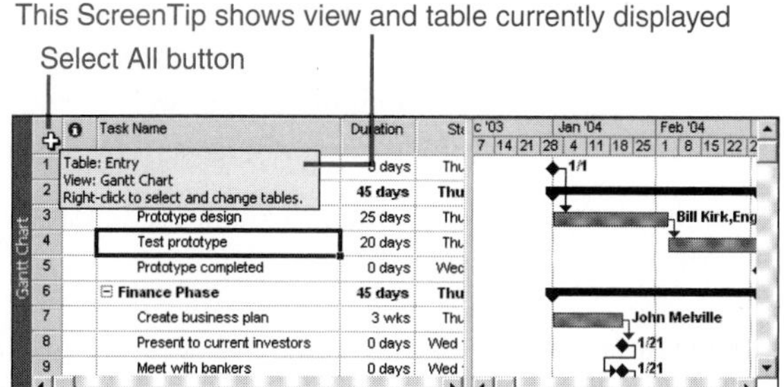

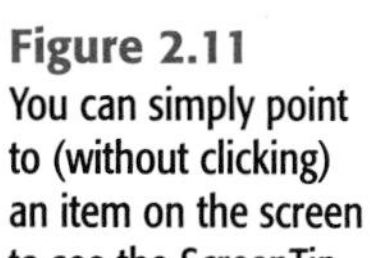

Figure 2.11
You can simply point to (without clicking) an item on the screen to see the ScreenTip.

Although it is not an all-inclusive list, here are several other places you will notice ScreenTips:

- When a field in the table side of the Gantt Chart view is not completely visible, you can point to the field to display the contents. This occurs when the column is not wide enough to display the data—such as when a task name is particularly lengthy or when a date or cost figure displays a series of pound symbols (#) instead of the data.
- When you point to a taskbar or milestone diamond in the timescale side of the Gantt Chart view, a ScreenTip appears, providing information such as start date, finish date, and duration.
- Pointing to the date unit tiers at the top of the Gantt Chart timescale displays the date range associated with the segment of the tier on which the mouse pointer is resting. So if the tier units are months and you point to the month February, the ScreenTip displays the dates for that month (including February 29, if it is a leap year).
- If you have zoomed out in the Network Diagram view, when you point to a node, the node is magnified so that you can read its fields.

USING LEARNING AIDS

Microsoft Project has extensive help, both about using Microsoft Project and about managing projects effectively. There are many special features to help you learn how to use Project and the wizards that you can call on to guide you through processes, or that pop up voluntarily to intercept your actions when they may potentially cause problems.

NEW Like the rest of the Microsoft Office 2003 suite, Project offers a new approach to how help is delivered by taking advantage of your connectivity to the Internet. This approach is called Microsoft Office Online (refer to Figure 2.1). When searching the help contents, Project will also search the online contents on the Microsoft Office Project Web site to find relevant items, if you are already connected. The help contents will then vary over time to include better subjects on how to solve your problem or teach you a feature with instant, online training.

Microsoft Office 2003 also introduces the Customer Experience Improvement Program, which you are free to anonymously participate in, and then automatically provide the product team with your hardware and software configuration, as well as issues you encounter, to ultimately make the product better by fixing common bugs and by enhancing features.

Help service options can be changed or confirmed through Help, Customer Feedback Options. This includes the Online Contents options.

WORKING WITH PROJECT GUIDE

Project Guide is a sequence of tasks or activities (see Figure 2.12) that guides you through the process of creating a project plan, tracking actual work, and generating reports. You can click the sequenced links in the Project Guide sidepane to go through the steps of managing a project file. When you click one of the steps, the sidepane changes to display detailed instructions and wizards to help you complete that task.

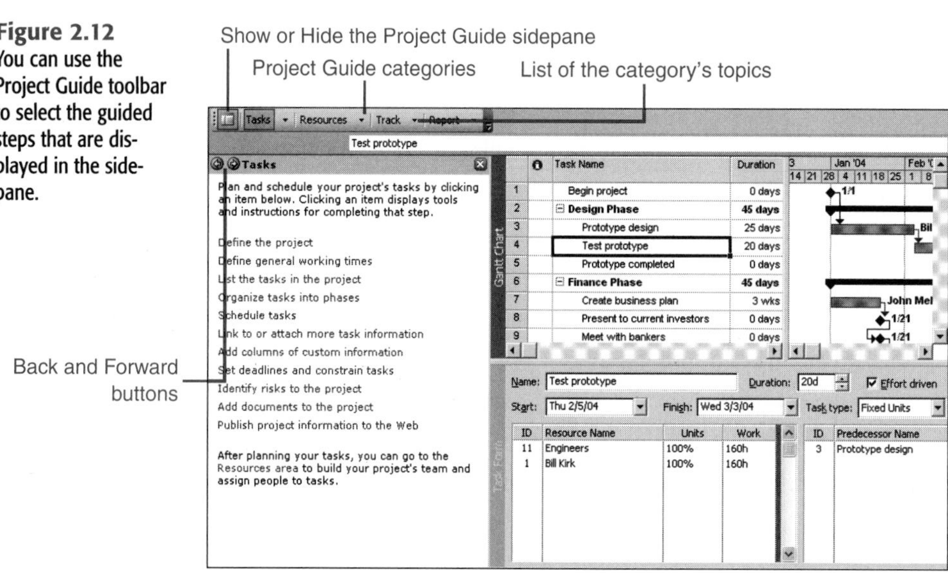

Figure 2.12
You can use the Project Guide toolbar to select the guided steps that are displayed in the sidepane.

By default, Project Guide is enabled, but you can hide it if you prefer. To disable Project Guide, choose Tools, Options, and choose the Interface tab. Clear the check box labeled Display Project Guide.

When Project Guide is enabled, you might also find it convenient to use the Project Guide toolbar. To display the toolbar, right-click over the toolbar area and click Project Guide. Four of the buttons on this toolbar display the four Project Guide sidepanes:

- **Tasks**—You can click the Tasks button to display the Tasks sidepane, which provides sequenced activities, advice, and wizards to help you build a task list and create a schedule.

- **Resources**—You can click the Resources button to display the Resources sidepane, which guides you through creating the resource pool, assigning resources to tasks, and publishing a project in Project Central.

- **Track**—You can click the Track button to display the options that guide you through saving the baseline, setting up the tracking method, entering tracking information, and reporting on progress.

- **Report**—You can click the Report button to display a sidepane that gives you various options for reporting on the project and customizing the look of the reports.

If you want to hide the Project Guide sidepane, click the Toggle Taskbar tool on the Project Guide toolbar. Click the button again to display the Project Guide sidepane.

You can use the drop-down lists to see a list of all the category's topics included in the Project Guide steps and select one to jump to immediately.

NOTE

> **You can display the Project Guide toolbar even when you have Project Guide disabled. In that case, the buttons simply don't function.**

→ You can write your own Project Guide pages to be displayed in the sidepane. See the bonus chapter, "Using Visual Basic with Project 2003," on the CD that came with this book.

USING SMARTTAGS

Several procedures in Microsoft Project consistently cause problems for novice users. Project 2003 displays a SmartTag (see Figure 2.13) to alert the user about the possible problem and to offer a choice of actions that Project can take. SmartTags appear for the following actions:

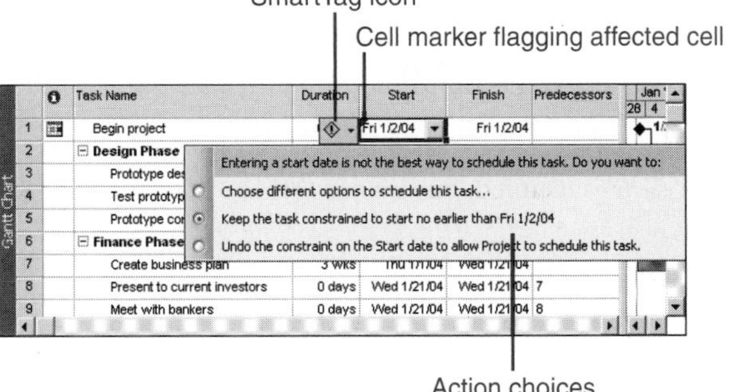

Figure 2.13
SmartTags intercept commonly troublesome actions and offer choices for how Project should proceed.

- Pressing the Delete key clears the cell that is selected. If the selected cell is the Name field, a SmartTag appears to offer the option to delete the entire record.

  However, if you select the entire row (by clicking the ID number or pressing Shift+spacebar), the Delete key deletes the row. The only key combination that deletes a row when you have just a cell selected is the Ctrl key plus the minus sign on the number keypad.
- When you edit the start or finish date for a task, a SmartTag alerts you that this action sets a constraint on the task and offers guidance about avoiding the constraint.
- When you add to or subtract from the number of resource names assigned to a task, a SmartTag offers to let you choose whether you want Project to change duration, work, or units for the other resources.
- When you change the duration, units, or work for an assignment, a SmartTag lets you choose how Project should calculate the change in the assignment.

Immediately after you take one of these actions, Project executes a default response but then displays the SmartTag to let you choose a different action if you prefer. It also displays a small green triangle in the upper-left corner of the cell to flag where the change was recorded and displays the SmartTag icon to the left of that cell. You can click the SmartTag to see the action choices.

NOTE

> SmartTags remain displayed only as long as the action is reversible. Because Project has only a one-step Undo capacity, the SmartTag disappears as soon as another action has begun.

You can disable any of the four SmartTag responses by choosing Tools, Options and clicking the Interface tab. Then, you clear the check box next to the SmartTag that you don't want generated.

WORKING WITH THE PLANNING WIZARD

The Planning Wizard is a feature that continuously monitors your use of Microsoft Project and displays alerts that range in urgency from simple tips for easier ways to do things to warnings telling you that you might create a problem if you proceed. For example, the message in Figure 2.14 appears when the Planning Wizard detects that a task is being moved to a nonworking day; it suggests appropriate ways to complete the procedure.

NOTE

> If the Office Assistant is active, the suggestions and warnings offered by the Planning Wizard are displayed through the Office Assistant. If the Office Assistant is not active, the Planning Wizard uses its own standard dialog boxes, such as the one shown in Figure 2.14, to display messages.

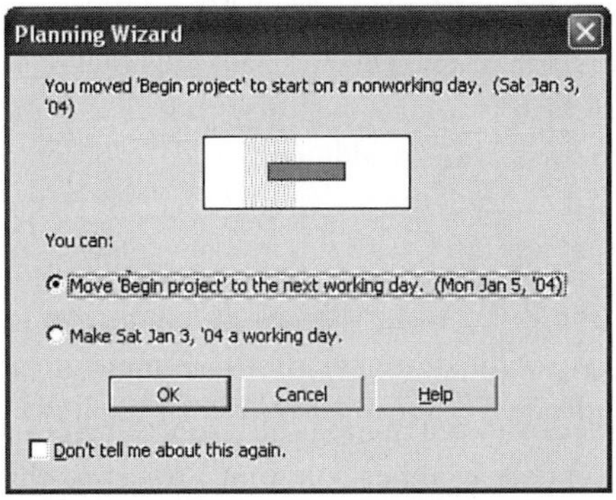

Figure 2.14
The Planning Wizard monitors your work and offers suggestions to improve your use of Microsoft Project.

2

The Planning Wizard is enabled by default and its alerts are controlled on the General tab of the Options dialog box. There are three categories of alerts: general usage problems, scheduling problems, and errors. To disable alerts from any of the categories, choose Tools, Options, select the General tab, and clear the check box next to the category you want to disable.

Many Planning Wizard dialog boxes also include a disabling check box labeled Don't Tell Me About This Again. If you have disabled a Planning Wizard alert, the Planning Wizard group it belongs to displays a gray mark in its check box on the General tab of the Options dialog box. If you want to turn the alert back on, choose Tools, Options, and select the General tab. Then click the check box once to clear the gray mark or click twice to enable the group of alerts.

INTRODUCING THE GANTT CHART VIEW

The default view for a new project is the Gantt Chart view (shown in Figure 2.15). This is the most often used view for listing project tasks.

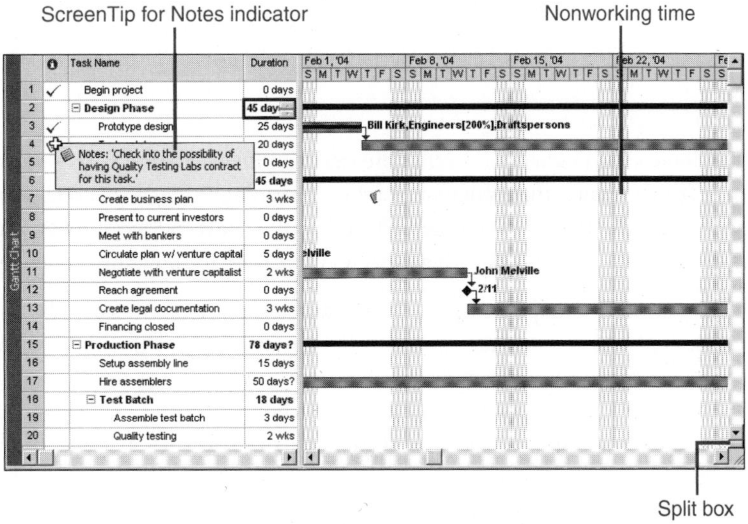

Figure 2.15
The Gantt Chart view is the most often used view in Microsoft Project because it shows both the outlined structure of the task list and the timescale for tasks.

The Gantt Chart view is a graphical view that contains a *table* on the left side and a bar chart (known as the *timescale*) on the right side. The table displays the task list, which includes, by default, the name and duration of each task. The table also contains additional columns that are hidden behind the bar chart. You can scroll the additional fields into view with the arrow keys or by using the horizontal scrollbar beneath the table. A task list can be created in an outline format to show the major phases of a project, with subordinate details indented to the right.

The default Gantt Chart table (the Entry table) displays an interactive Indicators column. The indicator symbols provide you with additional information about each task. When you use the mouse to point to the indicator, a ScreenTip appears, explaining the indicator. For example, if you have attached a note to a task, when you point to the symbol, the note appears. There are symbols for notes, and there are also symbols that show when a task has a constraint date, when a task is 100% complete, and when one project is inserted into another.

Notes can be an effective way to communicate project rationale, including a scope statement, statement of work (SOW), constraints, limitations, and assumptions regarding the project or the scheduling of tasks within it. Many project managers include this information in the notes field of the start milestone, so that they can effectively communicate this information right from the start.

The timescale on the right side of the Gantt Chart view displays the start and finish dates for tasks as a bar chart. A horizontal bar begins at each task start date and ends at that task's finish date. The current date is displayed on the timescale as a vertical dashed line. The vertical stripes of shading represent nonworking time. For example, if the unit of time is a day, the shading represents nonworking days. The taskbar is normally solid from the start to the end of the task, thus possibly stretching over days that are nonworking time.

TIP

If you want taskbars to show only working time, choose Format, Timescale from the menu and click the Nonworking Time tab. Change the Draw option from Behind Taskbars to In Front of Taskbars and click OK. This displays the nonworking-time shading in front of the taskbar so that the solid parts of the bar reflect only actual working time.

The longer the taskbar connecting the start and finish dates, the longer it takes to complete the task. By comparing the taskbars for tasks, you can quickly see which tasks start or finish first and which take longer to complete. Text displayed next to each bar shows the resources assigned to the task. Lines with arrows connect tasks to show the sequence links between them.

The bars vary in shape and color, depending on the type of task. The bars representing the project's phases (known as *summary tasks*) are displayed as thick black bars with triangular points on either end of each bar. The bars representing the detail tasks (known as *normal tasks*) are typically displayed as light blue rectangular bars. The names of the resources assigned to the task are displayed at the ends of these bars. If a task has been started, it has an interior *progress bar*, indicating how much of that task is complete. The Prototype Design task shows a progress bar across the entire taskbar and a check mark indicator, both of which indicate that the task is 100% complete. Finally, *milestones* in a project are commonly represented by black diamonds. Each milestone bar displays the date of the milestone. In Figure 2.15, the Begin Project and Prototype Completed tasks are milestones.

You use the horizontal scrollbar below the bar chart to scroll through the timescale. The vertical scrollbar at the right of the Gantt Chart view enables you to scroll up and down the task list without affecting the selected task.

NOTE

> If you drag the horizontal scroll button on the timescale, an information box identifies the date to which you are scrolling. If you drag the vertical scroll button, an information box tells you the task that will appear on the top visible row when you release the button.

You can split the Gantt Chart view into a combination view by choosing Window, Split (or by double-clicking the split box; refer to Figure 2.15). This places a form in the bottom pane (see Figure 2.16). If the view in the top pane is a task view, such as the Gantt Chart view, the Task Form view is displayed in the bottom pane. If the view in the top pane is a resource view, the Resource Form view appears in the bottom pane. The particular combination of the Gantt Chart view over the Task Form view is called the Task Entry view, and it is useful for working with resource assignments or reviewing the linking relationships between tasks.

TIP

> Many long-term users of Project prefer to use the Task Entry view instead of the Gantt Chart view. You can make it the default view by choosing Tools, Options, and selecting Task Entry in the Default View box on the View tab.

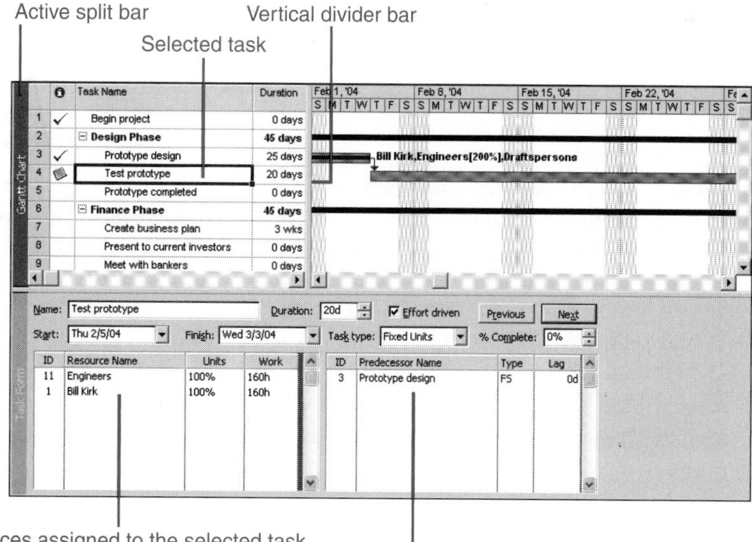

Figure 2.16
The bottom pane (the Task Form view) shows additional detail about the task that is selected in the top pane.

The bottom pane of a combination view always displays details about the row you select in the top view pane. For instance, the rows in the top pane of the Task Entry view are tasks. Your selection of a cell in the top pane determines the task whose details are displayed in the bottom pane. If the view in the top pane displays resources, the bottom view shows details for the resource that is selected in the top view.

NOTE

> You can use the F6 key to switch between panes in a combination view, or you can click the mouse pointer anywhere in the pane you want to activate.

THE ACTIVE SPLIT BAR

The active split bar is a thin vertical bar just to the left of view. When you are using a combination view, each pane has its own active split bar, but the colors are different for each one. The color for the active pane is the same color as the window title bar (which is normally blue, unless you've changed the default Windows colors). When the pane is inactive, the active split bar displays the same color as an inactive window title bar (which is normally gray).

TIP

> It's important to distinguish which pane is active in a split window. Many of the menu commands and tools on the toolbar are not active or available to be used if the bottom pane is active.

When the View bar is not displayed, Project uses the active split bar to display the name of the view that is in that pane (see Figure 2.17).

Inactive split bar with view name

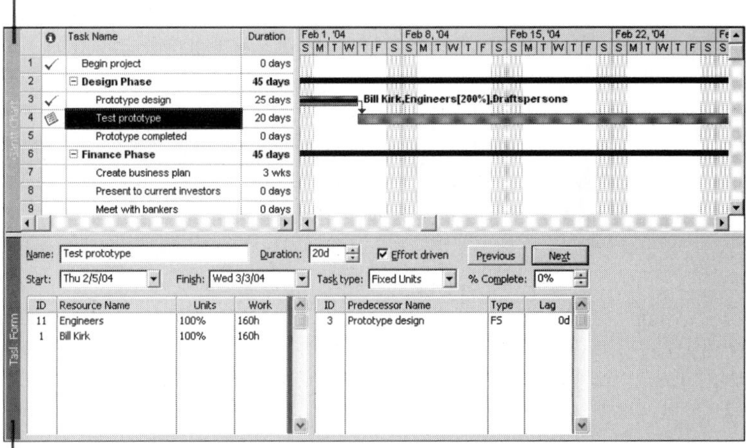

Active split bar with view name

Figure 2.17
The active split bar displays the name of the view you are in when the View bar is hidden.

THE SPLIT BAR AND THE SPLIT BOX

With combination views, a split bar separates the top and bottom panes. You can use the mouse to drag the split bar up or down, to change how much of each pane appears. To move the split bar, position the tip of the mouse pointer over the split bar until the pointer changes into the shape illustrated in Figure 2.17. Drag the split bar with the mouse to its new position.

TIP

> You also can use Shift+F6 to move the split bar with the keyboard, and then you can use the arrow keys or the mouse to resize the panes. You must press Enter or click the left mouse button to finish moving the split bar after you use Shift+F6.

If you double-click the split bar, a combination view becomes a single-pane view that displays only what was formerly in the top pane.

TIP

> If there is a form in the bottom pane, you can use a shortcut menu to remove the bottom pane. Right-click in the bottom pane and choose Hide Form View.
>
> Right-clicking the timescale (in a single pane or the upper pane of a split screen view) also activates a shortcut menu. You can choose Split or Remove Split as desired.

THE DIVIDER BAR

Some panes have a vertical divider bar. The Gantt Chart view, for example, has a vertical divider bar between the table area and the timescale. You can relocate the vertical divider bar just as you do the horizontal split bar, by dragging with the mouse or by using Shift+F6 and the left and right arrow keys. This action enables you to display more of the table or the timescale area.

CHANGING VIEWS

You can use many views to display project data. To display other views, you can use the View bar or the View menu, which displays the same list of views. Using the View bar, as described earlier in this chapter, is the quickest way to switch between the most commonly used views. The View bar lists the task views first (in alphabetical order), followed by resource views (also in alphabetical order). If the view you are seeking is not on the View bar, you can scroll to the bottom of the list and choose More Views to display the More Views dialog box. You can also access the project views through the View menu. The View menu lists the most frequently used views—the same set of views that's displayed on the View bar. If you choose View, More Views, the More Views dialog box appears, showing the entire list of views that are available in Microsoft Project. Figure 2.18 shows the More Views dialog box. After you select the view you want, you click the Apply button to display the view.

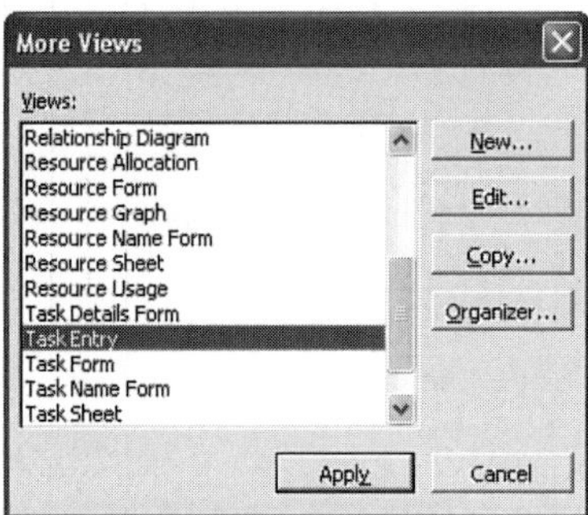

Figure 2.18
You can use the More Views dialog box to select from all the available views in Microsoft Project.

2

Most views listed in the menu display single-pane views that you can choose to place in the top pane or the bottom pane. When you choose a view from the menu, the view appears in the pane that was active when you accessed the menu. However, when you choose a combination view, such as the Task Entry view, the views in both panes are replaced.

If your current view is a combination view and you want to change the display in the top pane to the Task Sheet view, follow these steps:

1. Activate the top pane by clicking anywhere in the top pane.
2. Choose View, More Views.
3. Scroll through the list of views and choose Task Sheet.
4. Click the Apply button.

If your current view is a combination view and you want to replace it with a full-screen display of one of the views listed in the View menu, you can press the Shift key as you click the new view in the View bar. The view you select becomes a full-screen view. If you prefer to use the View menu to select a view, you can press the Shift key as you select the View menu and then select the new view.

For example, suppose that you're viewing the Task Entry view (with the Gantt Chart view in the top pane and the Task Form view in the bottom pane) and you want to view the Network Diagram view as a full-screen view. Hold down the Shift key as you click Network Diagram on the View bar (or use Shift as you choose the View menu and then select Network Diagram).

Similarly, if your current view is a full-screen view, and you want to split the screen and add another view from the menu in the bottom pane, you simply use Shift as you select the new view. Project splits the window and adds the new view in the bottom pane.

SCROLLING AND SELECTING DATA FIELDS

Unless a project is very small, you probably can't see more than a small portion of all the data onscreen at any one time. There are several ways to scroll through the data fields in a project.

Scrolling through the data fields differs from moving through the data fields. Scrolling changes the screen display to show new data fields without changing the field selected for data entry or editing. Moving changes the selected data field. Scrollbars are provided on all views except the forms. Forms typically fill the screen, and there isn't a need to scroll. With forms you use buttons to view the next screen's data.

The most widely used scrolling and moving methods are described in the following sections. More specific methods are presented in the chapters that introduce the different views.

USING THE SCROLLBARS

You use the vertical scrollbar on the right side of a view to scroll through the rows of tasks or resources displayed in the view. If you drag the scroll box, you see a small information box next to the top of the scrollbar that identifies the task or resource that will be at the top of the screen when you release the mouse button. You can drag the scroll box all the way to bottom of the scrollbar to see the last row in the view.

When a view displays data in a table (as rows and columns), you can use a horizontal scrollbar along the bottom of the view to scroll through the columns of data. When a view displays data in a timescale, you can use the horizontal scrollbar beneath the timescale to scroll to different dates. If you drag the scroll box, you see a small box next to the scrollbar that shows the date that will appear at the left of the timescale when you release the mouse button. You can drag the scroll box all the way to the left to go to the beginning date for the project, and you can drag it all the way to the right to go to the ending date for the project.

SCROLLING THE TIMESCALE WITH THE KEYBOARD

You can change the date that is displayed on the timescale by using the Alt key and the cursor movement keys on the keyboard. These key combinations and their functions are described in Table 2.1.

TABLE 2.1 KEYBOARD SHORTCUTS FOR NAVIGATING THE TIMESCALE

Key Combination	Result
Alt+Home	Beginning of project
Alt+End	End of project
Alt+left-arrow key	Left one unit of time
Alt+right-arrow key	Right one unit of timescale
Alt+Page Up	Left one screen
Alt+Page Down	Right one screen
Ctrl+Shift+F5	Beginning of selected taskbar

Locating a Taskbar on the Timescale

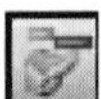

In large projects, it is often time-consuming to scroll the timescale to hunt for the taskbar that corresponds to a particular task. To quickly find the taskbar for a specific task, select the task name in the table on the left of the Gantt Chart view and click the Go to Selected Task button on the Standard toolbar. The timescale scrolls to the beginning date for the selected task.

Finding Tasks or Resources by Name

2

If you're looking for a task by name, choose Edit, Find (or press Ctrl+F) to display the Find dialog box. The Find dialog box is by default set up to search for names (task names or resource names, depending on the view you are using) that contain the keyword you supply. In the Find What box, enter a keyword or string of characters that is part of the task name (see Figure 2.19). This search is not case sensitive; you don't need to be concerned about uppercase letters.

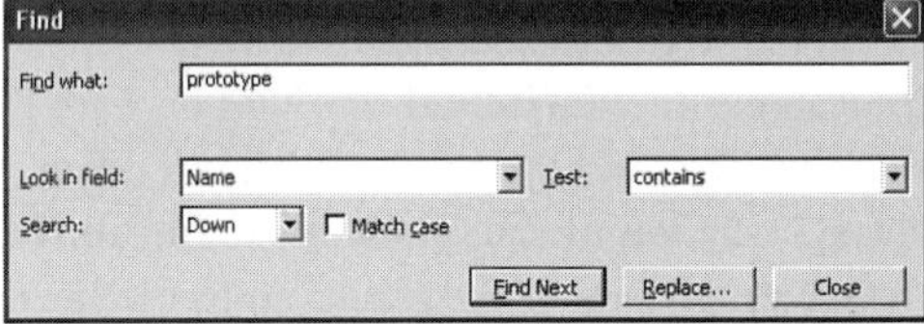

Figure 2.19
You can use the Find dialog box to search for tasks or resources by name.

You can click the Find Next button to initiate the search down the task list for the next task name that contains the values you entered. By default, the search always starts with the currently selected task (not with Task 1) and searches down the list of tasks. You can change the Search option to Up to search up the task list.

If a task is found that matches your search criteria but is not the task you were looking for, you can click the Find Next button again to locate the next match.

If you close the Find dialog box and then want to search for the next occurrence of keyword or characters, you can press Shift+F4 to continue the search in the same direction.

If you want to search other fields or other tests for finding values, see "Using the Find Command Options" in the "Troubleshooting" section at the end of this chapter.

Selecting Data Fields in Tables

You must select a data field if you want to enter data; edit the existing data in the field; or copy, move, or delete the data in the field. You can select data fields in any view or dialog box by clicking the mouse on a field. In tables, you can also use the arrow keys to move the selection.

You can use the keyboard to move through the project data and select new data fields. The keys in Table 2.2 function in the same way in all views that contain tables.

TABLE 2.2 KEYBOARD METHODS FOR MOVING TO DIFFERENT FIELDS/ROWS

Key or Key Combination	Result
Up-arrow key	Up one row
Down-arrow key	Down one row
Left-arrow key	Left one field
Right-arrow key	Right one field
Home	Left end of a row
End	Right end of a row
Page Up	Up one screen
Page Down	Down one screen
Ctrl+Page Up	Left one screen
Ctrl+Page Down	Right one screen
Ctrl+Home	First field in first row
Ctrl+End	Last field in last row

When you're in a table view, you can extend the selection to include multiple data fields by dragging the mouse pointer through all fields you want to select. You can also hold down the Shift key as you use the arrow keys to extend the selection. Pressing the Extend key (F8) allows you to extend the selection without holding down the Shift key. When you press F8, EXT appears in the status bar. You can use the arrow keys to extend the selected data fields. Then you can carry out the action you want to apply to all the selected data fields.

If you want to add fields that are not adjacent to the current selection, you can use the Ctrl key as you select the additional fields with the mouse. You can also use the Add key (or press Shift+F8) to extend the selection. Pressing the Add key keeps the current selection from going away while you move to the next fields. For example, after selecting the first group of fields, press the Add key. Then move to the next field you want to add. The status bar displays ADD in place of EXT. Then press the Extend key again and extend the selection, use the Shift key with arrow keys to extend the selection, or drag with the mouse to extend the selection.

SCROLLING AND SELECTING FIELDS IN FORMS

Form views display details about one task or resource at a time. You can move through the project's tasks or resources with the Previous and Next buttons that appear in most forms. You can use the Tab and Shift+Tab keys in forms and dialog boxes to move to and select successive fields. The text next to each field in a form has an underlined character (that is, a hotkey). Hold the Alt key and press the underlined letter to move the selection directly to that field. You cannot extend the selection in forms.

TROUBLESHOOTING

MISSING TOOLBARS

I seem to be missing a toolbar; only one is displayed on the screen. How can I see which one is displayed and add the one I'm missing?

The simplest way is to right-click on the toolbar or menu bar. A shortcut menu appears, listing all the toolbars. Each one that is currently displayed has a check mark beside it. The two toolbars that are displayed normally are the Standard and Formatting toolbars. If one of these does not have a check mark beside it, simply click on the toolbar name, and the toolbar will appear. If both of these have check marks by their names, then they are sharing one row on the screen. To have each one appear on its own row, click Customize on the shortcut menu. Select the Options tab in the Customize dialog box and remove the check by the option Standard and Formatting Toolbars Share One Row.

USING THE FIND COMMAND OPTIONS

The Find command is set up to search for names, but how can I use it for more complicated searches?

Several options are available in the Find dialog box for conducting much more sophisticated searches:

- **Find What**—Although the most common use of the Find command is to search for a specific value, you can also use wildcards in the search string. The asterisk (`*`) stands for any number of unspecified characters, and the question mark (`?`) stands for a single unspecified character. For example, the search string `*code 4??3*` would select any record with a text entry that contains the characters code 4, followed by two characters that can be anything, followed by the character 3. The beginning and ending asterisks indicate that the word *code* may not be the first word in the field and the number 3 may not be the last.

  To use wildcards in a Find operation, you must choose either the *equals* or *does not equal* test (see below), and beginning and ending asterisks are necessary, unless your search string is intended to specify the starting and ending text in the field.

  If you want to search for the asterisk or question mark character itself, precede the character with a caret (^). Thus, you could use the search string `*^?*` if you want to search the Notes field for questions that have been entered in a note.
- **Look in Field**—By default, Project searches the Name field (the task name in a task view, the resource name in a resource view). But in the Look in Field box, you can change the field that is to be searched.
- **Search**—By default, Project searches down the list of tasks or resources. You can change the direction to Up in the Search box.
- **Match Case**—When you want the search to be case sensitive, check the Match Case option.

- **Test**—The Test setting tells Project the conditions under which it can accept a match with your entry in the Find What box. By default the condition is *contains*, which means the field contains your search text somewhere within it. Other tests are as follows:
  - The default test *contains* (and its opposite *does not contain*) are only for fields that contain text (which includes the Duration field because of the time units that are attached to the duration number).
  - The *equals* and *does not equal* tests can be used in almost all fields, whether the data type is text, numbers, or dates. Project requires an exact match for the *equals* test; anything else qualifies for the *does not equal* test.
  - The relative-comparison tests (*is greater than*, *is greater than or equal to*, *is less than*, and *is less than or equal to*) are primarily for numbers and dates, but you can also use them for duration fields. For example, to find tasks that have duration greater than one week, you would enter **`1 week`** in the Find What box, and **`is greater than or equal to`** in the Test box.
  - The value range tests (*is within*, *is not within*) look for numbers, dates, and duration values that fall within a range that you enter into the Find What box. You enter the smallest and largest values for the range, separated by a comma. For instance, to find all start dates that fall on or between Christmas Day, 2003, and New Year's Day, 2004, you would enter **`12/25/03,1/1/04`**.
  - The test *contains exactly* is designed for fields that allow comma-separated entries. For example, the Predecessors and Resource Names task fields use comma-separated lists of predecessors and resource assignments. This test selects a task if one of the items in the comma-separated list matches the search text exactly.

CHAPTER 3

Setting Up a Project Document

In this chapter

Supplying Information for a New Project 56

Selecting the Environment Options 65

Defining a Calendar of Working Time 76

Troubleshooting 93

SUPPLYING INFORMATION FOR A NEW PROJECT

Setting up a new Project document correctly from the beginning will help make your use of Microsoft Project 2003 much easier. Before you enter the first task in a new project, it's a good idea to examine several settings and make any required changes to them. Although there are no defined rules for doing this, by following the steps outlined in this chapter, you will be able to create a more accurately calculated schedule.

You generally use most of the default settings in Microsoft Project 2003 to schedule tasks. Microsoft Project 2003 also allows flexibility and adaptability to accurately reflect the actual workings of each individual project. You can change many of these settings after tasks and resources have already been entered into the project. However, by addressing these issues up front, you are guaranteed to create a schedule that is based on logic and calculated reason.

NOTE

> Although you can address the preliminaries of a project in any order, the order in which the topics are presented in this chapter is the order recommended when you begin developing your first project.

You should understand the working conditions in a project, including the working calendar and holidays, before attempting to set up the project. Microsoft Project 2003 calculates the schedule for activities based on this information, so you should outline this information before you begin using Microsoft Project 2003 to schedule tasks.

When you begin working with Microsoft Project 2003, you typically start by setting up the environmental working options. Next, you define the working time calendar, considering working hours and nonworking time. After you set up a calendar, you might want to print it for review at a later time. You might also want to use the same calendar for other projects; to do this, you need to use the Organizer, which is described later in this chapter (see the section titled "Working with the Organizer," or you could also use a template upon which to base new projects.

Microsoft Project 2003 includes two wizards to assist in the process of setting up your project: the New Project Wizard and the Calendar Wizard. Using wizards in Microsoft products makes the setup process easy and complete. You are strongly encouraged to take advantage of these new wizards to expedite your setup time and allow you to focus on defining the scope of work for the project.

When you start a new project, you must consider whether you want the project to be scheduled from a specific start date or scheduled backward from a predetermined finish date. It is not possible to do both. When Microsoft Project 2003 calculates the forward-scheduling of tasks, it considers many factors, including the duration of the tasks, the base calendar selected, the settings set by the user, dependencies defined between activities, the calendar of the resource assigned, and, if one is created, a specific task calendar that is assigned to the activity. When Microsoft Project 2003 calculates the backward-scheduling of tasks, it does essentially the same thing it does when forward-scheduling, except that it calculates backward from the project's fixed end date.

In addition to calendar information, you need to provide summary information; Microsoft Project 2003 inserts this information into many of the reports it can generate, and this information enables Microsoft Project 2003 users to search for specific contents of files saved on your computer. You enter this summary information into the Properties dialog box, which you access by selecting File, Properties. The following sections describe how you input data into the Project Information and Properties dialog boxes.

Using the Project Information Dialog Box

To start a new file, choose File, New or click the New button on the Standard toolbar. Microsoft Project 2003 now displays the options available to you in a sidepane called "New Project." You then need to select whether you want to create a new project from a template or start a blank project. Selecting Blank Project automatically initiates the Project Guide to guide you through the process of creating a new project. The pane now displayed is the Tasks Pane, which is part of the default Project Guide. Each option is designed for you to select each option in turn and be "guided" through the process of creating your new project.

Selecting Define the Project, for example, allows you to enter the start date of your project without ever having to manually select commands from the menu.

→ After each option has been invoked in the Tasks Pane, the Project Guide will allow you to move on to other aspects of project creation. After you have worked your way through each section of the guide, you will have created your project plan. The Project Guide makes the whole process intuitive and easy for novice users to get up and running quickly with Microsoft Project 2003. For more information on the Project Guide, **see** the section titled "Using the New Project Wizard" on **p. 85**.

Of course, if you are a more experienced user you may prefer to simply access the Project Information dialog box.

You use the Project Information dialog box to record basic information about a project, such as the project start date and the base calendar to use for scheduling. To access the Project Information dialog box at any time, you choose Project, Project Information.

Figure 3.1 shows the Project Information dialog box that appears in the Standard edition of Microsoft Project 2003. Figure 3.2 shows the Project Information dialog box that appears in the Professional edition of Microsoft Project 2003.

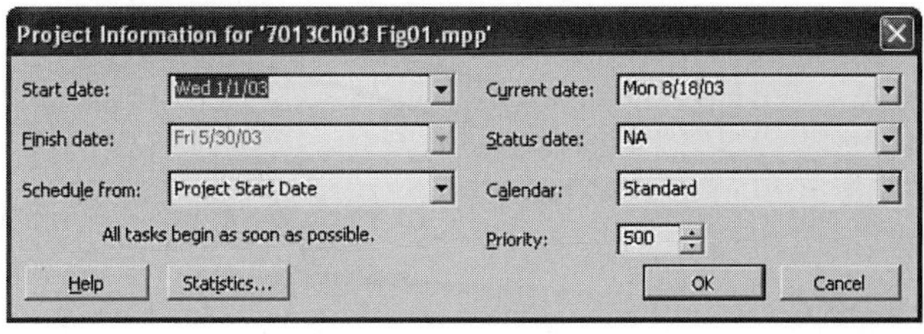

Figure 3.1 The Project Information dialog box defines the start date for a project.

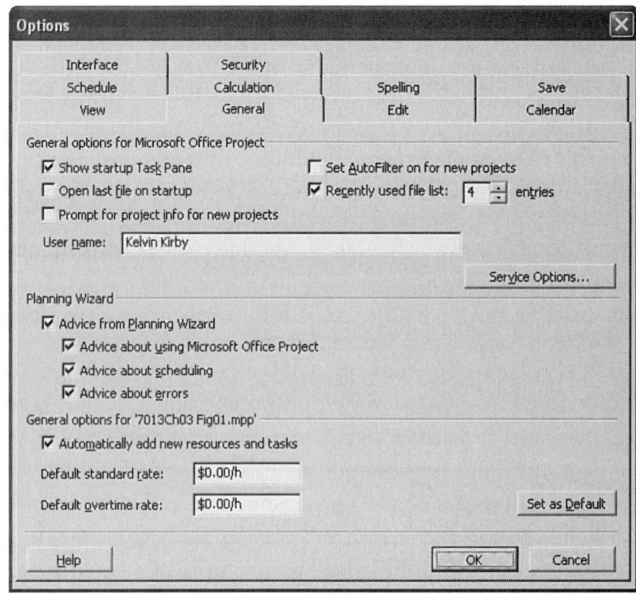

Figure 3.2
The option to have the Project Information dialog box appear when you open a new project is available under the General tab of the Options dialog box.

3

TIP

If the Project Information dialog box does not display when you open a new project, choose Tools, Options. On the General tab, mark the Prompt for Project Info for New Projects check box. Then start a new file; the Project Information dialog box should now appear (see Figure 3.3).

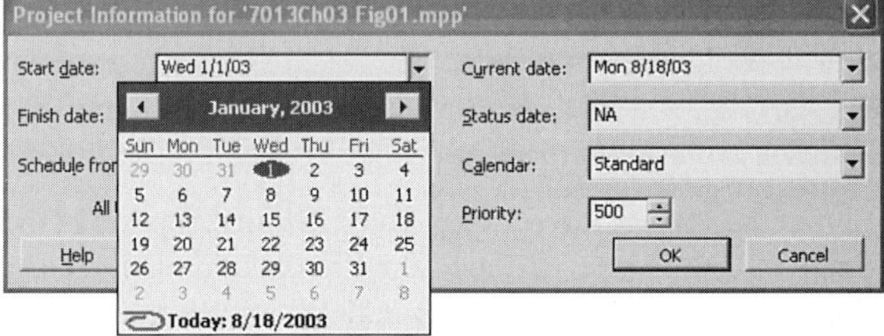

Figure 3.3
The start date of the project should be defined from within the Project Information dialog box, not the start field of the first task of the project.

The fields in the Project Information dialog box are as follows:

- **Start Date, Finish Date, and Schedule From**—The Schedule From drop-down selects whether the project forward-schedules from a start date or backward-schedules from a finish date. To define a specific date for a project to start, you can type the date in the Start Date text box or click the Start Date drop-down button to choose a date on a calendar. If you must schedule a project to finish on a specific date, select the Schedule From list box and choose Project Finish Date. You can then type a specific date in the Finish Date text box. This will move the project to schedule backward from this date.

- **Current Date and Status Date**—Microsoft Project 2003 uses the information in these fields to perform several date-related calculations. If you leave the Status Date field set to NA (for example, if you want to see the values in the Earned Value fields calculated up through and including the current date or a date you specify), Project uses the date in the Current Date field as the status date. This date is also used in the Complete Through field in the Update Project dialog box, as well as in the placement of progress lines in the Gantt Chart view. See the section "Changing the Current Date and Status Date Text Boxes," later in this chapter, for more information about when and how you might want to use this field.

➔ For information on telling Microsoft Project 2003 that work on the current project is complete through a specific date, **see** "Analyzing Progress and Revising the Schedule," **p. 555**.

- **Calendar**—You can use the Calendar list box to select a different base calendar for scheduling the project. The section "Scheduling with Calendars," later in this chapter, explains when you should use the default base calendar (Standard) and when you should consider using a different calendar.

NOTE

If the base calendar you want to use is defined in a different project file from the one you're currently using, you must use the Organizer to copy that calendar into the current project file before you can select it (see the section "Working with Calendars," later in this chapter).

- **Priority**—When you are sharing a pool of resources across multiple projects, you can identify which project has the highest priority by changing the Priority field in the Project Information dialog box. You can set this project level priority between 0 and 1000 (1000 being the highest priority).

➔ When you have a resource that is assigned too much work, and they don't have enough time in which to do the work, then the resource is said to be *overallocated*, and you can have Microsoft Project 2003 attempt to resolve the problem. For more information, **see** "Resolving Resource Assignment Problems," **p. 401**.

UNDERSTANDING THE START AND FINISH DATE TEXT BOXES

When you're starting a new project document, you enter either a start date or a finish date into the Project Information dialog box to function as an anchor point for scheduling the tasks in the project. Microsoft Project 2003 computes the other date. You cannot specify both a start date and a finish date.

If you enter the start date, Microsoft Project 2003 schedules the first task in the project to begin at that time and calculates the project's finish date based on that starting date and the sequence of tasks that come after the first task. New tasks that are added begin as soon as possible when you schedule from a start date.

If you enter the finish date, Microsoft Project 2003 schedules the tasks from the end of the project first and works backward. The final task is scheduled to end by the finish date; the task that precedes the final task is scheduled to end in time for the final task to begin, and so on. By the time Project schedules all tasks to end in time to meet the finish date requirement, the program has calculated a start date (that is, the date by which the first task must begin for the project to be completed by the specified finish time). New tasks that are added begin as late as possible when you schedule from a finish date.

You can use the Schedule From list box to change a project's schedule as often as you like. If you want to see when a project must start in order to finish by a deadline date, you can change the Schedule From option to Project Finish Date and enter the deadline date. When you choose OK, Project recalculates the schedule, including a new start date. You can then view the Project Information dialog box again to see what the required start date is, given the new finish date deadline. While in the Project Information dialog box, you can switch back to scheduling from a fixed start date.

To select a start date or finish date, you can either type the date or click the drop-down button to select a date from a calendar (see Figure 3.4). To select a date in the current month, you simply click that date. To select a date in a different month, you use the left and right arrows to select a different month and then click the date.

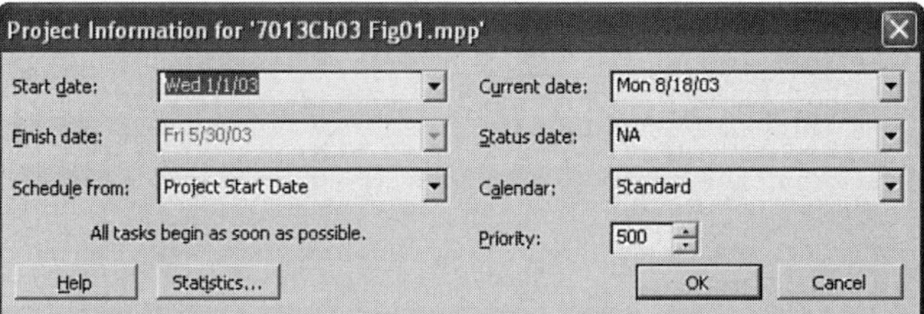

Figure 3.4
The Project Information dialog box allows the selection of dates via the pop-up calendar.

When you're managing a project, it's best to schedule forward based on a start date. If you schedule the project based on a fixed finish date, all activities must flow backward based on durations, linkages, and the calendars assigned; this is fine until you begin tracking the project. When you schedule from a fixed finish date, the start date is based on the actual time needed to complete each phase. What's wrong with this picture? Because both the start and finish dates are fixed, the schedule cannot expand or contract.

Also, scheduling from the finish date assumes that there is no project buffer, or extra time added to the end of the project, to allow for delays in completion of the project, unless you take that into consideration in selecting the finish date from which to schedule backward.

When you encounter a date field, you can use the built-in pop-up calendar to select a date.

NOTE

If you change your mind about the date you selected, you can click the area designated Today at the bottom of the calendar to immediately return to today's date. This closes the calendar pop-up. Of course, pressing Esc closes the window entirely, without saving the changes you've made.

CHANGING THE CURRENT DATE AND STATUS DATE TEXT BOXES

The computer's internal clock initially determines the date listed in the Current Date text box. Changing this text box has several implications:

- The date determines the location of the dashed (current) date line on the Gantt Chart view time line.
- The current date appears in the header of the Project Summary standard report as an As Of date. You also can display the Current Date text box in headers or footers on other reports by typing the appropriate code in the header or footer definition.
- You can customize Project to start new tasks based on the current date instead of on the project's start date. You do so by selecting Tools, Options, selecting the Schedule tab, and changing a setting next to New Tasks: Start on Project Start Date or Start on Current Date.

The Current Date can be used for benchmarking the progress of tasks, but you can use an alternative date for this as well. If you specify a date in the Status Date field in the Project Information dialog box, this is the date Project uses for placing the progress lines in the Gantt Chart view. In addition, if there is a date in the Status Date field, Project uses this date when calculating the Earned Value fields and for tracking purposes in the Update Project dialog box.

To change the Current Date field or enter a date in the Status Date field, select the field and type the date or click the drop-down arrow to select a date from a calendar pop-up.

DISPLAYING THE PROJECT STATISTICS DIALOG BOX

You use the Statistics button at the bottom of the Project Information dialog box to display the Project Statistics dialog box (see Figure 3.5). You can also display this dialog box by clicking the Project Statistics button on the Tracking toolbar.

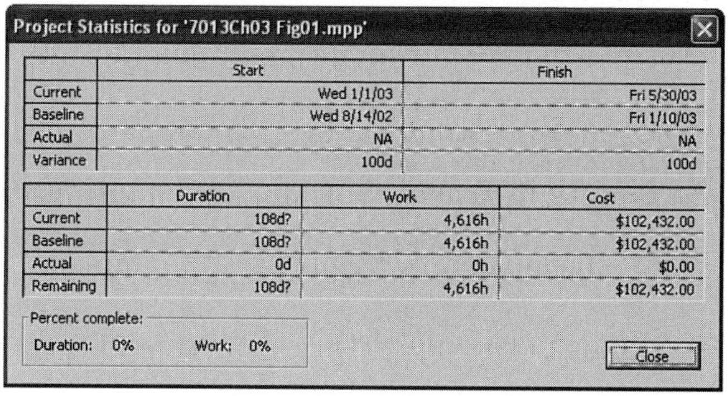

Figure 3.5
The Project Statistics dialog box gives a quick summary of the status of a project.

Project Statistics for '7013Ch03 Fig01.mpp'

	Start	Finish
Current	Wed 1/1/03	Fri 5/30/03
Baseline	Wed 8/14/02	Fri 1/10/03
Actual	NA	NA
Variance	100d	100d

	Duration	Work	Cost
Current	108d?	4,616h	$102,432.00
Baseline	108d?	4,616h	$102,432.00
Actual	0d	0h	$0.00
Remaining	108d?	4,616h	$102,432.00

Percent complete:
Duration: 0% Work: 0%

Close

The Project Statistics dialog box displays summary information about a project. You cannot manually change the data in this dialog box; you can only view and print it.

NOTE

You can use the Project Summary report (in the Overview category) to print out the project statistics. Reports are accessed from the View menu.

The Project Statistics dialog box shows the current, or currently scheduled, values for five project parameters: the start date, finish date, total duration, work, and cost. If you have saved the baseline copy of the schedule, the baseline values also are displayed, for comparison.

When work is actually performed on the project and progress on tasks is recorded, the information in the Actual row is updated. The percentage complete of the duration and work of the project are shown at the bottom of the dialog box, in the Percent Complete section.

To close the Project Statistics dialog box, click the Close button.

USING THE PROPERTIES DIALOG BOX

In the Properties dialog box, you can view and edit a number of options that describe a project. To open the Properties dialog box, choose File, Properties. The Properties dialog box has five tabs; the Summary tab is the default.

NOTE

You can display information from the fields in the Properties dialog box—especially fields from the Summary tab—in the header or footer area of printed views or reports for a project. See Chapter 13, "Printing Views and Reports," for more information.

THE SUMMARY TAB

In the Summary tab of the Properties dialog box (see Figure 3.6), you can supply descriptive information about a project and the people associated with it. You can include the options at the top of the tab (Title, Subject, Author, Manager, and Company) in reports as header or footer text. The options Category, Keywords, and Comments are useful when you're searching through previously created project files on your hard disk. You can use the Hyperlink Base option to indicate the main address to the hyperlinks you have in your project. This can be a link to another file on your computer or server or a link to a location on the Web.

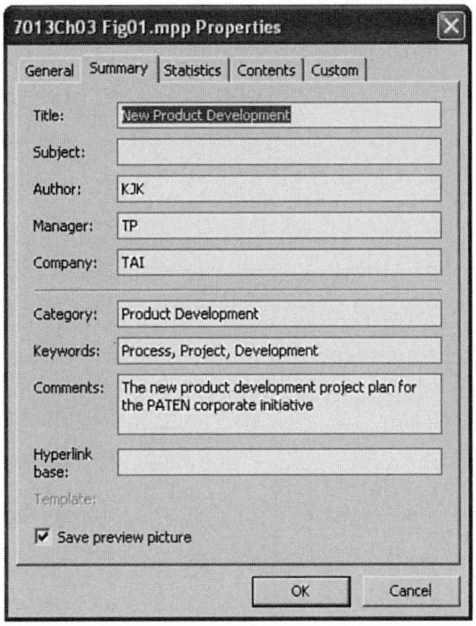

Figure 3.6
The Summary tab of the Properties dialog box presents descriptive options that are useful in reports and for searching for files to open.

To change any of the options on the Summary tab, select its text box and type an entry. Press the Tab key after you have finished typing the entry to move to the next option. Except in the Comments list box, pressing the Enter key on this tab selects the OK button and closes the dialog box.

If the newly created project originated from a template, the template name appears at the bottom of the dialog box.

You can select the Save Preview Picture check box to have Project save a thumbnail sketch of the current view when you save the file. You can browse these preview pictures when you search for files by using the File, Open command. The Save Preview Picture check box is not selected by default.

If you have trouble locating files in the future, you can use the Open dialog box to search for words entered in the fields of the Summary tab to find the needed file.

THE GENERAL TAB

The General tab of the Properties dialog box describes the file that stores the project document. It provides statistics about the project file: the name, type, location, and size of the file, as well as the dates when the file was created, last modified, and last opened. This tab is blank until the document is saved as a file.

THE STATISTICS TAB

The Statistics tab of the Properties dialog box provides useful statistics about your work with the project document, including when it was created, last modified, last accessed, and last printed. It also shows who last saved the file, which is useful for shared files in a workgroup. The Statistics tab also shows how many times the document has been revised and the total amount of computer time spent editing the file.

THE CONTENTS TAB

The Contents tab of the Properties dialog box displays the most commonly reviewed statistics about the current project schedule: the start and finish dates; the scheduled duration, work, and cost; and the percentage completed for both duration and work. The Contents tab displays summary statistics about the project schedule.

THE CUSTOM TAB

With the Custom tab of the Properties dialog box you can add additional properties to a file. Then, you can search for files by the values of these properties. Based on the information in Figure 3.7, for example, you could search for all projects that have Marketing in the Department Value field. The bottom row in the Properties list box shows that a property named Department has been created for this document, with the text value Marketing.

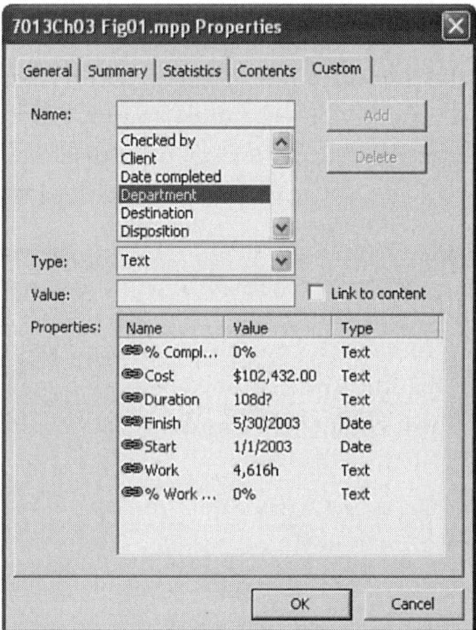

Figure 3.7
The Custom tab of the Properties dialog box allows you to set up custom search parameters.

To create a custom property for a project, follow these steps:

1. Choose File, Properties.
2. Choose the Custom tab.
3. Type a property name in the Name list box. The drop-down list below the Name list box lists commonly used properties. If you want to use one of these, select it.
4. Use the Type drop-down list to define the type of data to place in the field. You should use this option only when you will type the value of the property instead of linking it to a field in the project file. When you link the property value to a project field, the Type

drop-down list is unavailable. The allowable data types are Text, Date, Number, and Yes or No (logical).

5. If you chose Text, Date, or Number previously, type a value in the Value text box. If you chose the Yes or No option in the Type list box, you see Yes and No buttons in the Value box. Select the one you want to use.
6. Click the Add button to add the property to the list in the Properties dialog box.

If you want to link a property value to a project field, follow these steps:

1. Choose File, Properties.
2. Choose the Custom tab.
3. Type a property name in the Name list box.
4. Select the Link to Content check box (refer to Figure 3.7). The Type list box is grayed out, and the Value text box becomes a drop-down list. The name of the text box changes to Source.
5. In the Source drop-down list box, choose the field that has the value you want the property to reflect.
6. Click the Add button to add the property to the list in the Properties dialog box.

If you want to delete a custom property, select it in the Properties list and click the Delete button.

If you want to modify the value for a property, select the property name in the Properties list. This places the current name and value in the text boxes at the top of the dialog box. Change the Type or Value fields as needed, and the Add button automatically changes to Modify. If you change the Name field, you have to use the Add button to include it as a new property. You can then use the Delete button to remove the original, leaving the newly named version. Then you can click the Modify button to complete the change.

When you finish the custom properties list, click the OK button unless you want to make additional changes on one of the other tabs.

SELECTING THE ENVIRONMENT OPTIONS

Microsoft Project makes many assumptions regarding projects. You can review these default settings, which control the behavior of the application, in the Options dialog box. The options are divided into two types: global and file-specific options. To display the Options dialog box (see Figure 3.8), choose Tools, Options. The options in this dialog box are conveniently organized into categories on a number of tabs.

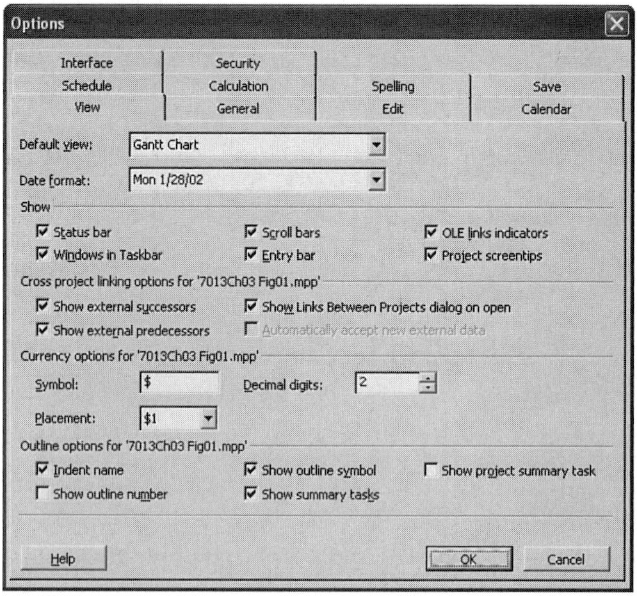

Figure 3.8
The View tab is the default tab in the Options dialog box.

Most of the settings in the Options dialog box affect the way you view all projects, and are referred to as *global options.* Changes you make to global options affect projects that have already been created, the current project you are working on, and any future projects you create. For example, changing the date format (which might include hours and minutes instead of just rounding to the day) affects all projects, including those that you originally created with a different date format. The new format remains in effect for all projects until you change the setting again.

Some of the options in the Options dialog box are specific to the file you are currently working with. These options include the filename in the section title. For example, the dialog box in Figure 3.8 shows three sections that contain file-specific options: Cross Project Linking Options for 'New Product,' Currency Options for 'New Product,' and Outline Options for 'New Product.' Changes made to these settings affect only the current project you are working on—in this case `New Product.mpp`. Any options that are not part of a section or for which the section title does not include the filename in the title (such as the Show section in Figure 3.8) are global options.

The Cross Project Linking Options For section of the View tab controls links between projects. For example, the setting in this section in Figure 3.8 is set for the active file only—the default is to display all external links. In addition, when you attempt to open a file that contains links to other projects, a dialog box alerts you that the file has external links.

Selecting the Show Outline Number option in the View tab of the Options dialog box displays the task list of the project in a traditional Work Breakdown Structure (WBS) outline format, tying the schedule of the project to a previously defined scope of work. This is useful to ensure that all the necessary work of the project has been captured.

Also, when you select the option to display a project summary task, a roll-up summary task (numbered 0) appears at the top of the Gantt Chart view and spans the entire duration of the project you have created. Many times, Project users create this manually by indenting, or demoting, all subsequent tasks to the first one, simply because they are not aware of this feature.

NOTE

If the Office Assistant is active, the external link message appears in an Office Assistant pop-up.

In some cases, file-specific options can be changed for the current file and new files if the section containing the file-specific settings has a Set as Default button (see Figure 3.9). If you click the Set as Default button, Project updates the Global template to reflect the option settings. The Global template controls the settings for all new project files. The current document, as well as all new project documents, incorporates these options, but previously created documents do not change.

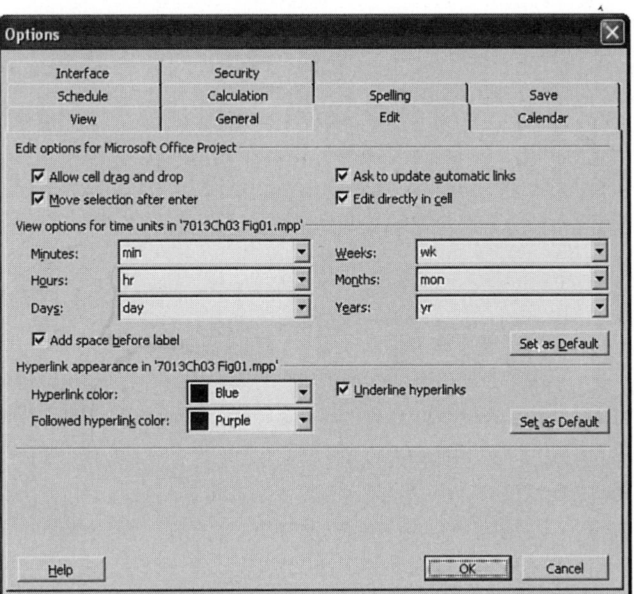

Figure 3.9
The Edit tab of the Options dialog box has two sections that include Set as Default buttons.

The following sections focus on a few choices in the Options dialog box that are critical in defining any new project and a few options of general interest.

NOTE

All changes you make in the Options dialog box are saved in the Windows Registry.

Reviewing Critical Options

There are several important settings on the Calendar tab that you should confirm are appropriate for your organization. These options determine how the calendar is used on printed reports, how your fiscal year is designated, and, most importantly, how your use of the terms *day*, *week*, and *month* are interpreted by Microsoft Project 2003. Figure 3.10 shows the settings on the Calendar tab.

3

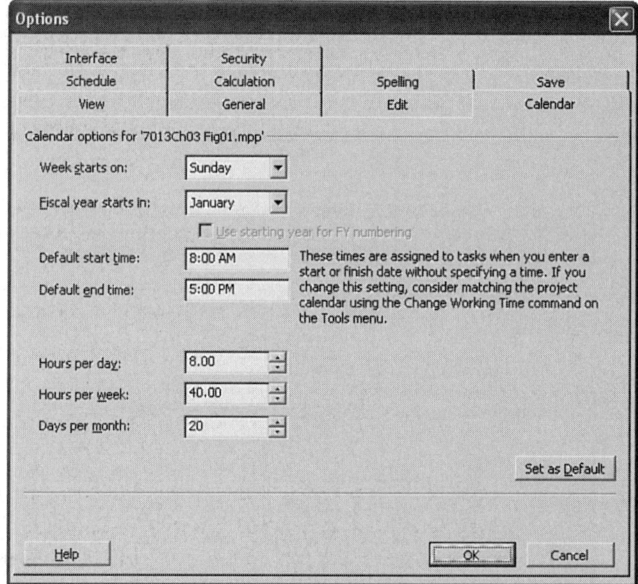

Figure 3.10
The Calendar tab of the Options dialog box enables you to customize project plan settings to your organization's working hours.

Defining Days, Weeks, and Months

The three most critical settings are those that define the meaning of the basic task duration units—days, weeks, and months. The fundamental unit of time in Microsoft Project 2003 is the minute. When you enter any other unit for a task duration, Project internally converts these terms into minutes, based on the definitions in the Options dialog box. All calculations dealing with duration are carried out in minutes. When you ask Microsoft Project 2003 to display a task duration in days, weeks, or months, Project uses these settings to convert the display. Therefore, the options Hours per Day, Hours per Week, and Days per Month are crucial to the interpretation and display of your estimates of task duration (refer to Figure 3.10).

Thus, for example, if you estimate a task duration to be 2 days, Project uses the entry in the Hours per Day text box to internally set the duration to minutes. If the Hours per Day entry is 8.00, the duration is recorded as 960 minutes (that is, 2 days×8 hours/day×60 minutes/hour). If the Hours per Day entry is 10.00 and you estimate the duration to be 2 days, then the task duration is recorded as 1,200 minutes, which is much more work than if the Hours per Day entry is 8.00.

You need to make sure these settings are appropriate for your organization. For example, if you work for an organization that has a 4-day work week (that is, each employee works 10 hours per day for 4 days each week), you should change the Hours per Day field to 10 and leave the Hours per Week field at 40. If your organization normally works 8 hours per day Monday through Friday and ½ day Saturday, you might prefer to change the Hours per Week to 44 so that when you estimate a task to take a week, the duration means the same thing to Microsoft Project 2003 as it does to you.

Note that the definition of the task duration is set at the time you estimate it, according to the definition of the terms you use (day, week, or month). If you later change the definition of a day, for example, to be 10 instead of 8 hours, Project does not change the minutes defined for each task duration. However, the display of those minutes in days or weeks is affected.

The Project Management Institute (PMI) suggests that no task be longer than 80 hours (or 2 weeks' duration, based on a 40-hours-per-week calendar). In other words, the work should be broken down to increments that are no longer than this span of time.

Also, defining months can be difficult because it is typically an inconsistent measure of time, so it's better to use hour or week duration units.

CAUTION

If you change the definitions for a day, week, or month after you enter the project data, Microsoft Project 2003 doesn't redefine the minute duration of tasks; it merely displays these minutes as a different number of days or weeks. For example, if you originally entered the duration of a task to be 1 week (at 40 hours per week) and later changed the number of hours in a week on the Calendar tab from 40 to 44 hours, the duration for the task would read .91w. The task would still be 40 hours, but 1 week would now be equal to 44 hours, not 40. This is one reason for establishing option settings before entering task and duration information.

→ To learn how Microsoft Project 2003 interprets duration, **see** "Creating a Task List," **p. 115**.

DEFINING THE DEFAULT START AND END TIME OF DAY

When you define the working days, hours, and months for the Standard calendar (see "Defining a Calendar of Working Time," later in this chapter), you define the hour when work normally begins and ends. It's important that you also record those standards in the Default Start Time and Default End Time text boxes on the Calendar tab of the Options dialog box. Microsoft Project 2003 uses these settings in several places:

- When you specify the date but not the time for the start or finish date of the project in the Project Information dialog box.
- When you put a constraint on a task, such as Finish No Later Than.
- When you begin tracking the actual work on the project.

For example, say that the normal work hours for an organization are 7:00 a.m. to 4:00 p.m. If you define these hours in your Standard calendar but leave the setting for Default Start Time at 8:00 a.m., Microsoft Project 2003 schedules the first task in the project to start 1 hour later than the actual start of work.

In addition, when you use the Tracking toolbar buttons to designate the percentage completed for a task, the time a task started is assumed to be the default start time from the Calendar tab in the Options dialog box. Even though time might not be displayed as part of the Start Date field format, it is stored with the date. So if the Standard calendar hours are from 7:00 a.m. to 4:00 p.m. and you mark a task as 100% complete, the actual start date shows the task starting at 8:00 a.m. and the actual finish date shows the task ending the next day at 8:00 a.m. If only the dates and not the time are displayed in the Start and Finish Date fields in the Gantt Chart view, it appears that there is an error—a task with a duration of 1 day (8 hours) starts on one day but ends on the next day. The culprit is typically an inconsistency between the time used on the Standard calendar and the time designated on the Calendar tab of the Options dialog box.

TIP

It's a good idea to display a date format that also displays time. The Date Format setting is on the View tab of the Options dialog box.

If you change the default start and end times, be careful to coordinate these time settings with the Standard calendar you create for your organization.

If you are having problems changing the default start times, see "Start Times Don't Match" and "Making Start and End Time Changes Permanent" in the "Troubleshooting" section near the end of this chapter.

DEFINING THE START OF THE FISCAL YEAR

The name of the month that begins the fiscal year is a critical option. This choice affects displays and reports that show annual and quarterly amounts. If the fiscal year begins in October, for example, you might want all reports to include October through December figures in first-quarter totals and the annual figures to be calculated by using the October through September figures. The Fiscal Year setting is on the Calendar tab of the Options dialog box.

By default, the fiscal year is assumed to be numbered by the year in which the fiscal year ends. Therefore, the year in which the fiscal year ends will be used with all months in that fiscal year. For instance, if the fiscal year begins October 2003 and ends September 2004, then the actual calendar month November 2003 would belong in the fiscal year that ends in 2004.

On the Calendar tab, you have the option to have the fiscal year numbering use the starting year instead of the ending year (see Figure 3.11). If you select the Use Starting Year for FY Numbering check box, a fiscal year running from October 2003 to September 2004 would have the calendar month of February 2004 belong in fiscal year 2003; the second quarter of fiscal year 2003 would be the calendar months January, February, and March 2004.

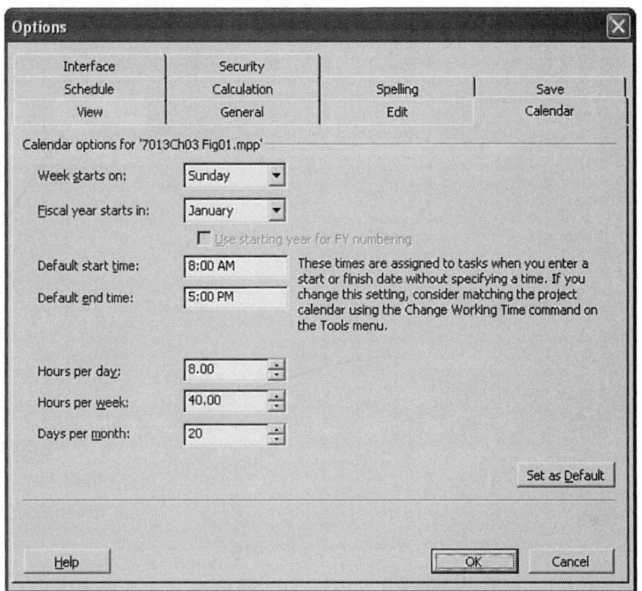

Figure 3.11
You can change the Fiscal Year Starts In option if you want to set some month other than January as the beginning of the fiscal year.

TIP

> The Fiscal Year Starts In and Use Starting Year for FY Numbering settings are file-specific settings. If you want to change these settings for all future project files as well as the active file, click the Set as Default button near the bottom of the dialog box.

In some previous versions of Microsoft Project 2003, changing the Fiscal Year Starts In setting in the Options dialog changed the display of the calendar in the timescale of the Gantt Chart view; since Project 2000, this has not been the case. You can either retain the calendar year or show the fiscal year. To choose whether to retain the calendar year or show the fiscal year, you must access the Timescale dialog box by either choosing Format, Timescale or right-clicking the timescale headings in the Gantt Chart view and choosing Timescale from the shortcut menu. The Timescale dialog box appears. To display the fiscal year instead of the calendar year, click the Use Fiscal Year check box (see Figure 3.12).

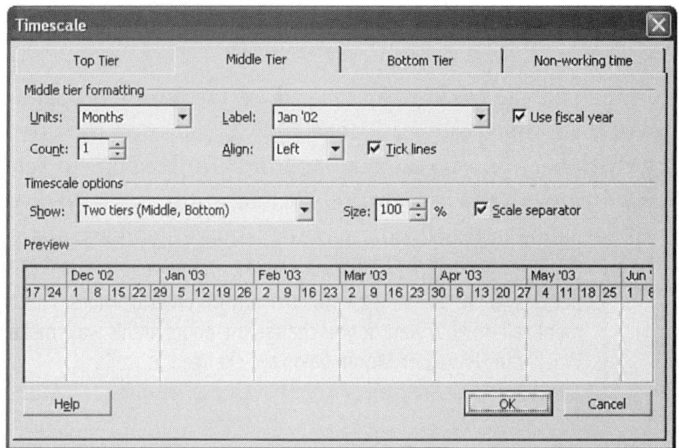

Figure 3.12
The timescale headings can display fiscal years instead of calendar years.

You can display the fiscal year on either the major or minor scale of the timescale, which is the first or second calendar displayed. A useful display would be to have the fiscal year on one scale and the calendar year on the other scale, using the same unit for both scales.

NOTE

> You can only change settings in the timescale of the current view. To update the timescale in another view, such as the Task Usage or Resource Usage view, you have to display that view and change the Timescale settings there.

The timescale display in the Gantt Chart view uses fiscal year numbers instead of calendar year numbers only when the timescale is formatted to display the year, not when displaying months or days.

SETTING OPTIONS IN THE CALENDAR TAB

To set critical calendar preferences, follow these steps:

1. Choose Tools, Options. The Options dialog box appears.
2. Click the Calendar tab.
3. If your fiscal year does not start in January, select the correct month from the Fiscal Year Starts In drop-down list. The default is for the next calendar year to be the fiscal year.
4. If your work day doesn't start at 8:00 a.m., enter the appropriate time in the Default Start Time text box. You can enter time in 12-hour or 24-hour format. If you use the 12-hour format, be sure to add p.m. to hours past noon (and remember that noon itself is 12:00 p.m.).
5. Change the Hours per Day, Hours per Week, or Days per Month fields, if necessary, to accurately represent your organization.

6. Click the Set as Default button to make the values you entered for Fiscal Year Starts In, Default Start Time, Default End Time, Hours per Day, Hours per Week, and Days per Month the default values for all new project documents.
7. When you are finished, click the OK button.

TIP

> Some organizations change the hours to reflect the hours they expect to work on the project minus the hours needed for other activities (for example, to account for meetings that normally happen in the course of a 40-hour work week). You might change Hours per Day to 6h, allowing 2 hours per day for other activities. This type of change is a judgment call on your part. If you change the hours in this way, make sure the Hours per Week and Hours per Month fields are changed as well.

Companies typically split the day as 75% (for example, 6 hours/day, 30 hours/wk) productive time, or time worked on project-related tasks, and 25% (for example, 2 hours/day, 10 hours/wk) administrative time, or time for office-related tasks. Some companies expect a 45-hour work week in which 8 hours per day are billable and 1 hour is set aside for administrative matters.

When you're planning your project, it's best to consider the specifics of how your organization operates–or how your particular project will work.

SETTING OTHER USEFUL OPTIONS

You can change other settings to make data entry easier. It is a good idea to review the current settings in the Options dialog box for each of the following items:

- Click the General tab to confirm that your name is in the User Name text box. Project uses this name for the Author and Last Saved By properties of the document.
- Click the Schedule tab to select the time unit you plan to use most often when estimating task duration (see Figure 3.13). Choose the Duration Is Entered In drop-down list to select Minutes, Hours, Days, Weeks, or Months. The Duration setting provides Microsoft Project 2003 with instructions about the unit of time to use if you enter a task duration without specifying the unit of time. For example, suppose most of your tasks will have the duration listed in days, and you have selected Days as the time unit in the Duration Is Entered In list box. In the Gantt Chart view, if you enter a 2 in the Duration column, Project records the task duration as 2d (that is, 2 days). Any other duration type has to be entered manually. For example, you would enter a task with a duration of 3 weeks as 3w.
- Click the View tab to change the default view for new projects. If you prefer to work in a view such as the Network Diagram view or the Task Sheet view—rather than the Gantt Chart view—when starting a new project, change the Default View setting (see Figure 3.14).

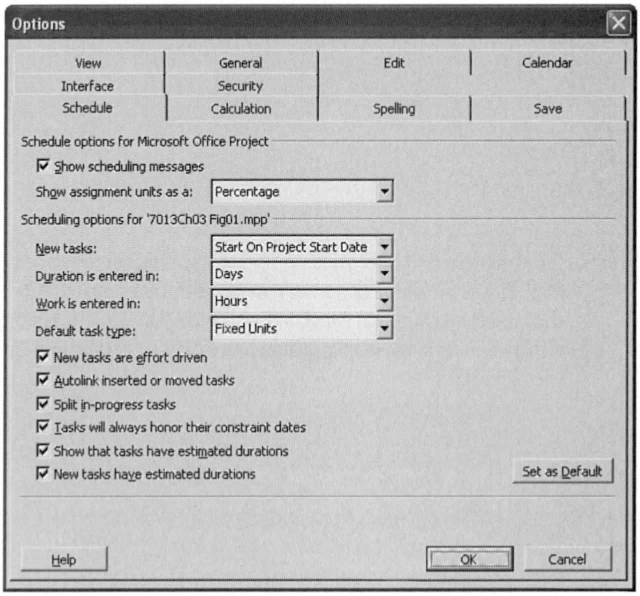

Figure 3.13
You can set the default time unit you want used for displaying task duration.

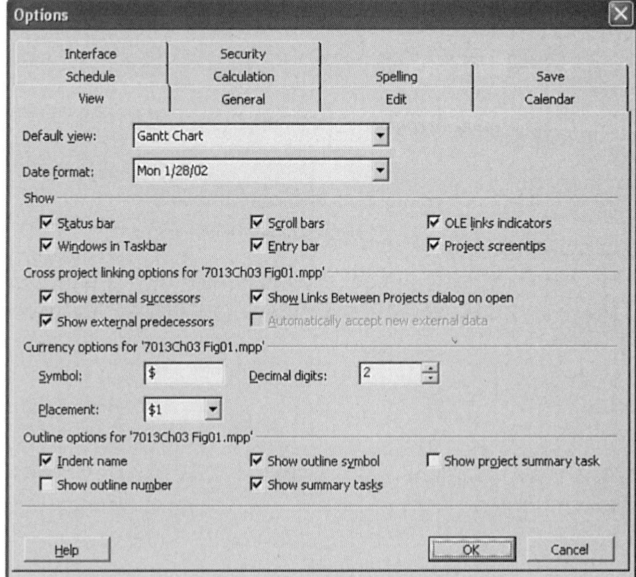

Figure 3.14
You can set the default view on the View tab.

NEW You can set the security settings for your project.

- Click the Security tab to determine whether you want to save any existing file properties with the saved file. You can choose to remove this information (for example if you are using an older file or a template) when you save the file. This tab also allows you to choose the macro security settings for how Microsoft Project 2003 should deal with macros and add-ins.

- On the View tab, choose Date Format to specify how to display dates. The default format displays the date, with the day of the week. The Date Format list box provides alternative format options (such as the date and time together or just the date).

TIP

> You can use the Control Panel to set the international regional style for entering date and time. To change the regional date and time formats, open the Windows Start menu and choose Settings, Control Panel. In the Control Panel folder, choose Regional Settings to display the Regional Settings dialog box. Choose the Date and Time tabs, and then make your selections.

- On the View tab, choose the Decimal Digits text box in the Currency Options Format section to specify the number of decimal points to use in displaying money amounts. The preset value is two decimal points, but you can change that to zero to suppress decimal-point display. As mentioned previously, you can use the Regional Settings dialog box in the Control Panel to select currency units and decimal display.
- In Microsoft Project 2003 views that contain tables (such as the Gantt Chart view), the Enter key causes the selection to advance automatically to the cell below—for example, when you type data in a sheet column, such as the left side of the Gantt Chart view or the Resource Sheet view. You can turn off this feature by deselecting the Move Selection After Enter check box on the Edit tab.

TIP

> Many users enter tasks by typing the activity name, tabbing to the right to enter the duration, and then returning to the left to enter the next task name. Because Project won't automatically return to the next line and requires you to select the next task name field with the mouse or arrow keys, you might find it helpful to select the range of cells that you are entering tasks into. When you do so, the Tab key advances the selection to the right and then back to the left after the duration has been typed.

- Click the Save tab to change the default save format and path (see Figure 3.15). For example, if you want to save all your Project files as Microsoft Project 2003 templates or in a previous version of Microsoft Project 2003, click the Save Microsoft Office Project 2003 Files As drop-down and choose one of the listed options. You can also designate the default path where your Project files should be stored. The original default is `C:\My Documents`. From the File Locations list box, select the file type you want to change, and then click Modify to identify another path. However, if you are using Project Professional in a Project Server configuration, then your projects are saved to the Project Server database by default.

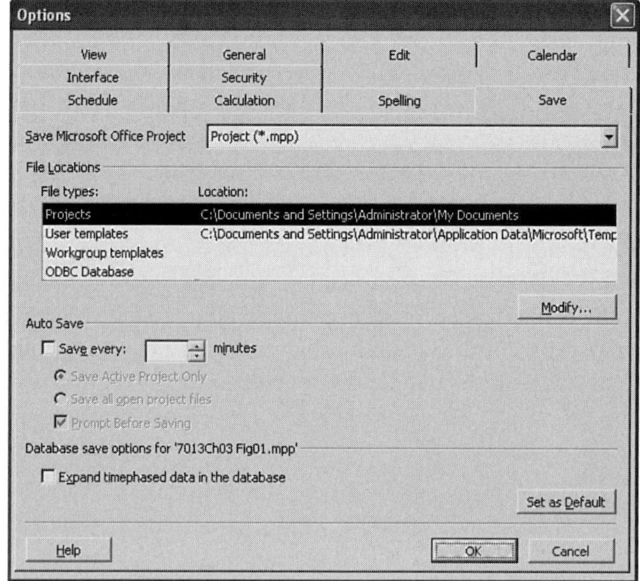

Figure 3.15
You use the Save tab to set save options, including the default save location, where to store templates, and autosave and database save features.

DEFINING A CALENDAR OF WORKING TIME

Microsoft Project uses a calendar, called the *base calendar*, to define the default working and nonworking days used for scheduling tasks in projects. Three base calendars are built in to Microsoft Project 2003:

- **Standard**—The 5-day, 40-hour week, with work from 8:00 a.m. to 5:00 p.m. that's standard in the United States.
- **24 Hour**—A round-the-clock operation from 12:00 a.m. to 12:00 a.m.
- **Night Shift**—An example of a calendar for those whose work shift starts toward the end of one day and ends in the morning of the next day.

All projects are assigned to a base calendar, and the default assignment is to the Standard base calendar. You can edit the Standard calendar, use one of the other built-in calendars, or create additional base calendars and assign a project to one of them if you want.

The Standard calendar assumes 5 working days per week, Monday through Friday, with 8 hours of work per day (including an hour off for lunch). The default schedule is 8:00 a.m. to 12:00 p.m. and 1:00 p.m. to 5:00 p.m. No designated holidays are set in the original Standard calendar.

You can edit the Standard calendar to reflect your organization's regular working and nonworking days and hours. You can also designate the exceptions to the normal workdays, such as holidays, or time periods when the organization will be closed for remodeling, a companywide meeting time when no work should be scheduled, and so on.

Base calendars are also used as the basis for resource calendars. Each resource has its own calendar, and the resource calendar is linked to a designated base calendar (by default the Standard calendar). The resource calendar inherits all the working days and hours of its base calendar, as well as all the holidays and other exceptions in its base calendar. The resource calendar can be edited to record the days and hours when the availability of the resource differs from the normal working times found in the base calendar. Examples of resource exceptions are vacation days, sick leave, and unusual hours on particular days.

→ To learn more about adjusting calendars to reflect the available resources, **see** "Understanding Resource Scheduling," **p. 321**.

For example, the base calendar for an organization in the United States might show that Thanksgiving Day, the third Thursday in November, is a company holiday. Suppose a security guard is scheduled to work on Thanksgiving Day and to have the following Friday off. The resource calendar for this worker would initially show the company holiday, Thanksgiving Day, as a nonworking day and the next Friday as a working day. For this security guard only, the resource calendar needs to be edited to reverse the status of both days.

3

If a resource has only a few exceptions to the Standard calendar, it's easy to edit the resource calendar. If the resource has working times that are radically different from the standard working times, the editing job can require a lot of work. If there are several resources with the same unique set of working times, it's easier to create an additional base calendar that has those unique working times and link each unique resource to that custom base calendar. For example, night and weekend security guards have unique days and hours. Instead of greatly altering a number of individual resource calendars, it's easier to create a Security Guard base calendar to reflect the special working times for security guards. Then, you can link each security guard to that base calendar.

Many organizations allow people to have flex-time schedules. This gives you a business reason to create several variations of a base calendar. For example, you could configure base calendars for working hours of 6 a.m.–3 p.m., 7–4, 8–5, and so on. After you complete the calendars, you can assign them to the different resources that use those working hours. To keep this straight in your mind, think of the Standard calendar as the hours of operation for the business and think of the defined flex-time calendars as applying only to your resources, each with unique hours that they work.

On the other hand, some companies schedule all tasks based on the Standard calendar, suggesting that the task be scheduled to the day of the working calendar and not the hour of the working resource. In this case, the company is not interested in specifically which hour the task is worked—only that it is completed on the day that it is scheduled for completion.

It's important to keep your organization's work environment in mind when you are configuring base calendars for projects.

→ To adjust the resource calendars, **see** Chapter 9, "Understanding Resource Scheduling," **p. 321**.

SCHEDULING WITH CALENDARS

Project uses the base calendar for an overall project and the resource calendars to schedule the start dates for tasks. When Project schedules a task, it notes the earliest possible starting date, based on when the predecessors to the task will be completed. If no resources are assigned to work on a task, the project's base calendar is used to schedule the start and finish of the task. Otherwise, Microsoft Project 2003 checks to see what resources are assigned to work on the task and when the resource calendars for these resources show them being available for work. The task is then scheduled to start on the next available working hour for the assigned resources.

NOTE

> The resource calendars take precedence over the project's base calendar. In the absence of a resource calendar, the task is scheduled using the project base calendar.

To select a base calendar, choose Project, Project Information. Click the Calendar drop-down list and choose one of the calendars—Standard, 24 Hour, and Night Shift—from the list.

EDITING THE STANDARD CALENDAR

Changing the working days and hours on the Standard calendar affects the scheduled work time for all tasks that have no resources assigned to them and for all tasks whose resources are linked to the Standard base calendar.

CHANGING WORKING AND NONWORKING DAYS

The original Standard calendar shows all weekdays, Monday through Friday, as working days and all Saturdays and Sundays as nonworking days. You can change the status of any day to make the day working or nonworking, and you can specify the number of hours available for work on any day by defining the starting and ending times for work shifts on that day.

To edit the Standard calendar, choose Tools, Change Working Time. The Change Working Time dialog box appears (see Figure 3.16). The Change Working Time dialog box can display a calendar of working and nonworking times for any of the base calendars and resource calendars defined for the project.

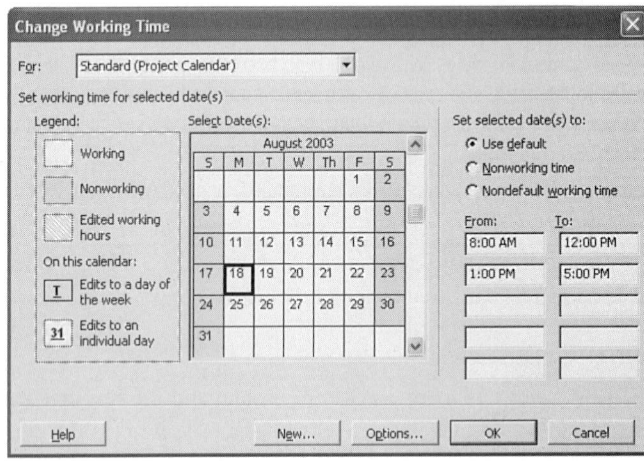

Figure 3.16
You can use the Change Working Time dialog box to define the days and hours when work can be scheduled by Microsoft Project 2003.

The dialog box contains a monthly calendar form, daily working times, buttons to change the calendar, and a legend. The legend indicates how working and nonworking days will be displayed, along with days that have different hours from the default hours. Each date that is modified from the default has the date underlined. If you modify a day of the week for the entire project—for example, you make the working time on every Monday from 1 p.m. to 5 p.m.—the letter M in the Working Time calendar is underlined and in bold. You can use the calendar scrollbar to change months and years. The calendar spans the period from January, 1984, to December, 2049.

To change the status of a single day or a consecutive period of days from working to nonworking or vice versa, you click the day with the mouse. You can select consecutive days by clicking and dragging. You can select multiple days that are not consecutive by pressing the Ctrl key as you click the extra dates. On the right side of the dialog box, there are several options in the Set Selected Date(s) To area; you can use these options to change the working or nonworking status of a day.

3

In the Set Selected Date(s) To area of the dialog box, you select the Nonworking Time option button to make the selected day(s) nonworking. To make the selected day(s) working days, you select the Nondefault Working Time option button.

TIP

> To select days by using the keyboard, use the arrow keys to move to the first day you want selected. Hold down the Shift key and use the arrow keys to select additional consecutive days.

You can also change the working status of any day of the week for all weeks throughout the year. If your organization works on Saturdays, for example, you will want to make all Saturdays working days.

To change the working status of a day for all weeks, you select the day of the week by clicking the day letter at the top of the calendar (for example, S for Saturday). Then, you select the Nondefault Working Time or Nonworking Time option button in the Set Selected Date(s) To area of the dialog box.

After the working status of a day of the week is set, that becomes the default status for that day of the week. For example, suppose you have made every Friday, with the hours 8:00 a.m. to 12:00 p.m. (noon), a working day. If you changed a particular Friday to either a full working day or a nonworking day and then wanted to change it back to the default hours for Fridays, you would need to select the Use Default option button to reset the hours from 8 a.m. to 12 p.m. Selecting any specific date and the Use Default option button sets that date's working hours to the default for its day of the week.

Figure 3.17 shows the Change Working Time dialog box for the month of December 2003. The company is having a holiday party on Friday, December 19. No work is likely to be accomplished on this project in the afternoon, so this day has been marked as a partial working day. Because the company gives all its employees the afternoon of December 24 as well as all of December 25 and 26 to celebrate Christmas, these days are marked as nonworking days. Partial working days are marked with slash marks; full nonworking days are marked in gray.

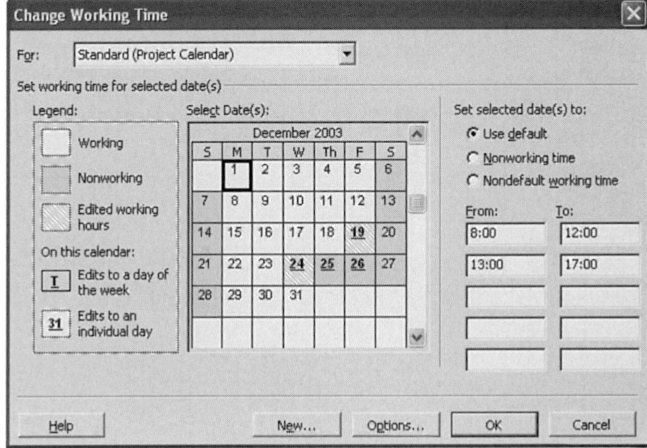

Figure 3.17
You use the Change Working Time dialog box to define the days and hours when work can be scheduled by Microsoft Project 2003.

CHANGING THE STANDARD WORKING HOURS

You can define the work periods for each day by supplying up to five work periods in the From and To text boxes of the Change Working Time dialog box. The default 8-hour work time periods each day are 8:00 a.m. to 12:00 p.m. and 1:00 p.m. to 5:00 p.m.

Most of the time only the first four boxes (under From: and To:) are used. The remaining six boxes are typically filled in when the working times go across midnight, to account for several breaks or meal times, or for some other unusual work schedule. The section "Creating a New Calendar," later in this chapter provides a good example of using the six time boxes.

To change the working hours in the Change Working Times dialog box, follow these steps:

1. Select the From text box for the first time period you want to change.

TIP

> You can use Alt+F to select the first From text box, and then use the Tab key to advance to the other time boxes. You can use Shift+Tab to return to previous boxes.

2. Enter a time. For acceptable time formats, see the next section, "Entering Time Formats."
3. Select the To text box and enter a time.
4. Repeat this process, by clicking (or using the Tab key) on each subsequent From and To text box, to change the time in that box.

5. To stay in the Change Working Time dialog box, simply click any day in the calendar. Otherwise, click OK.

NOTE

> Project checks all time entries for consistency. Each successive time must be later in the day than the time in the preceding time text box.
>
> You cannot leave a work period blank and put data in a work period beneath it. Therefore, you must use the top pair of From and To text boxes first; then you can fill in the next pair.

ENTERING TIME FORMATS

You can use several formats for entering times in the text boxes of the Change Working Time dialog box. You can use either the 12-hour clock or the 24-hour clock to enter times. If you enter times based on the 12-hour clock, make sure that you use the a.m. and p.m. suffixes to ensure that the program understands your intent. If you enter a time without using an a.m. or p.m. suffix, Project uses the first instance of the time following 8:00 a.m. (or whatever time you designate as the Default Start Time on the Calendar tab of the Options dialog box).

For example, if you enter **`3:30`** without a suffix, Project assumes that you want to use 3:30 in the afternoon and attaches the p.m. suffix. If you wanted to set a work shift to start at 5:00 in the morning, you would need to enter **`5 am`** instead of **`5:00`** because the program interprets 5:00 to mean 5:00 p.m. (If the time you want to enter is on the hour, you can simply enter the hour number.)

NOTE

> You enter noon as `12:00 pm` and midnight as `12:00 am`.

CLEARING THE WORKING HOURS TEXT BOXES

To remove a work period from the working hours text boxes in the Change Working Time dialog box, you need to delete both the From time and the To time for that period. To do so, follow these steps:

1. Select the From text box for the work period you want to remove.
2. Press the Delete key to clear the text box.
3. Move to the To text box and select the time entry. Press Delete to remove that time period.

RESETTING A CALENDAR

You can select the Use Default option button in the Set Selected Date(s) To area of the Change Working Time dialog box to cancel changes you have made for calendar days. Selecting individual days and choosing Use Default returns those days to the original working hours for those days of the week (as defined in the base calendar). Selecting the day of the week letters at the top of the calendar and choosing Use Default returns all days in the selected column to the standard 8-hour day, 8 a.m. to 5 p.m. (or whatever timeframes you have designated for the calendar). Selecting all the weekday letters at the top of the calendar and choosing Use Default returns the working hours—as well as any other exceptions—back to the default of the currently selected calendar. A warning message appears, indicating that the calendar will be reset to the original settings.

CREATING A NEW CALENDAR

Suppose you have a processing crew that works from 5:00 p.m. to 2:00 a.m., Monday through Friday. You can create a Processing Crew calendar to use as a base calendar for the resources in that group. On this calendar, the regular shift begins at 5:00 p.m. and continues to 2:00 a.m. the following day. An hour break is scheduled from 9:00 p.m. to 10:00 p.m.

Say that on Monday the crew starts at 5 p.m., breaks for dinner at 9 p.m., comes back to work at 10 p.m., and finishes the day at 12 a.m. (midnight). The work from midnight to 2 a.m. is entered on Tuesday. Tuesday through Friday the working times would show 12 a.m. to 2 a.m., then 5 p.m. to 9 p.m., and 10 p.m. to 12 a.m. Saturday would reflect the last hours (12 a.m. to 2 a.m.) of Friday night's shift. (Figure 3.21, later in this chapter, illustrates this example.)

You can create a new base calendar for this group by following these steps:

1. Click the New button at the bottom of the Change Working Time dialog box to create a new base calendar. The Create New Base Calendar dialog box appears (see Figure 3.18).

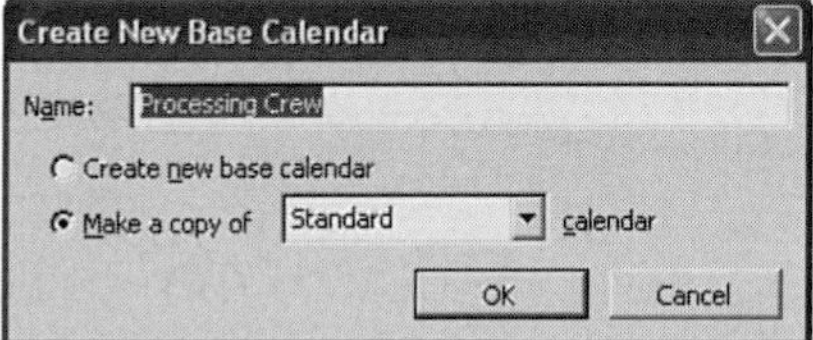

Figure 3.18
You can start a new calendar from scratch or you can use a copy of any existing base calendar.

2. In the Name text box, type a distinctive name, such as **`Processing Crew`**, for the new calendar.
3. Select the Create New Base Calendar option button if you want to start with no holidays and the standard 40-hour week. Or Choose the Make a Copy of...Calendar option button to start with a copy of an existing base calendar and all its holidays and exceptions. Then select an existing base calendar from the drop-down list. If you have already defined all regular company holidays on the Standard calendar, you should start with a copy of it so you don't have to enter those holidays again.
4. Click OK to start defining the new calendar. If you made changes in another calendar that you haven't saved, you see the warning shown in Figure 3.19 before you can proceed to make changes in the new calendar. Click the Yes button to save the changes you made in the other calendar. The new calendar name then appears in the For list box in the Change Working Time dialog box.

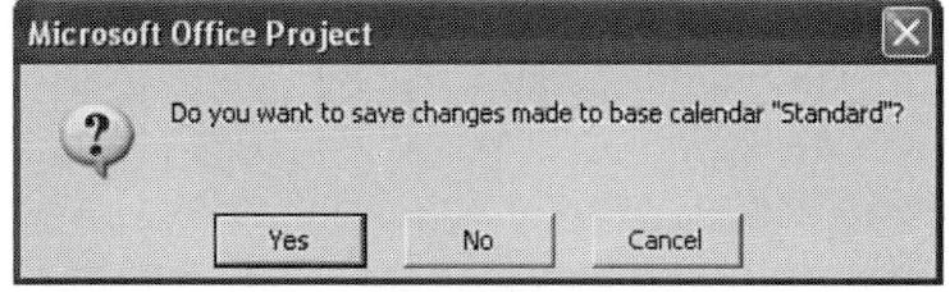

Figure 3.19
You must save or discard earlier, unsaved changes in another calendar before you can start working on a new calendar.

5. To change the hours for a weekday such as Monday, select the letter at the top of the day column and enter the shift hours for that day in the From and To text boxes (see Figure 3.20). The hours for Mondays are 5:00 p.m. to 9:00 p.m. and 10:00 p.m. to 12:00 a.m. The remainder of the shift appears in the From and To boxes for Tuesdays.

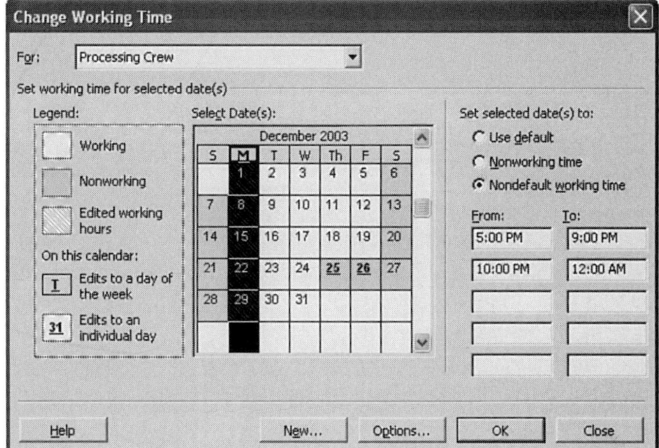

Figure 3.20
You can select the day letter at the top of a day column to change the hours for that day for every week.

6. To change the hours for several days that have identical hours, drag from the letter for the first day to the last day in the group and enter the common hours in the text fields on the right side of the dialog box. The Tuesday through Friday schedules require three shifts, as shown in Figure 3.21. The first shift is the continuation of the previous evening's shift. The second and third shifts show the periods for the beginnings of the next evenings' shifts.

7. To set hours for a day that is currently a nonworking day, you must first make the day a working day. Then you can enter the hours in the From and To text boxes. The Saturday hours in the Processing Crew calendar are just from midnight to 2:00 a.m. (see Figure 3.22). Select the S at the top of the Saturday column and choose the Nondefault Working Time option to make it a working day. Then you can enter the hours in the From and To text boxes.

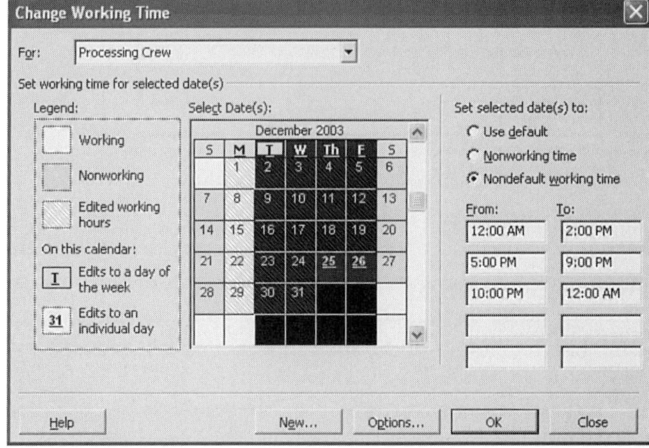

Figure 3.21
You can select several days by highlighting the letters for the days at the top of calendar display.

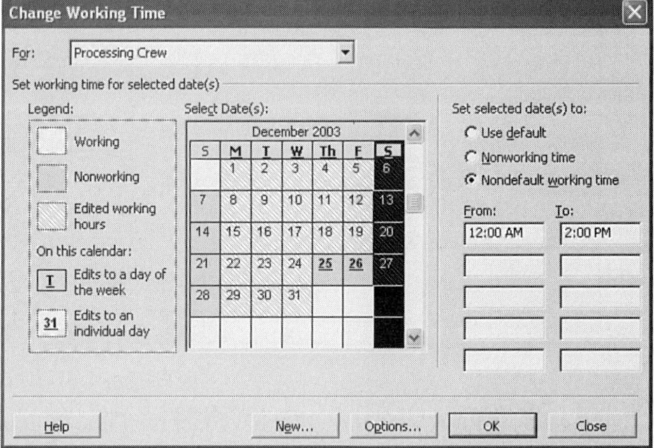

Figure 3.22
You must make a day a working day before you can define working times for it.

SAVING OR CANCELING CALENDAR CHANGES

To finish editing base calendars and save the changes you have made, click the OK button at the bottom of the Change Working Time dialog box. When you save the calendar, all the calendar information is saved along with the task and resource information in the project document. Clicking the Cancel button causes Project to ignore all the changes you have made.

WORKING WITH CALENDARS

If you create a base calendar in one project and want to use the same base calendar in future projects, you can use the Organizer to copy the calendar to the Global template (`GLOBAL.MPT`). The calendars in the `GLOBAL.MPT` file are automatically included in any new project file. You can also use the Organizer to copy a calendar to another existing project file, to delete a calendar from the active file, and to rename a calendar in the active file. The following section describes how to access the New Project Wizard and how to use it.

NOTE

The `GLOBAL.MPT` file is stored in the directory with the Microsoft Project 2003 program files, which is usually `C:\Program Files\Microsoft Office\Office11\1033`.

→ In an environment where Project Server is being used, all the default calendars are held in the Enterprise Global and are automatically applied whenever a new project is created. We are really only considering Project Standard in this chapter, but for details of the Enterprise Project Management Solution (referred to as EPM), please refer to "Using Enterprise Global Settings," **p. 978**.

Using the New Project Wizard

A great feature of Microsoft Project 2003 is the New Project Wizard, which steps you through the process of creating a new project plan. It also enforces the correct use of Enterprise custom fields, encourages collaboration, and provides opportunities to attach supporting documentation to a project.

There are two ways to access the wizard:

- By selecting Define a Project from the Goal-Based User Interface
- By selecting File, New and then selecting New Blank Project from the wizard dialog box

NOTE

If the Goal Based User Interface is not on, the New from Wizard option does not appear in the sidepane.

The following steps describe the dialog boxes that take you through the wizard:

1. **General information**—You are asked to enter a start date for the project you are creating, unless the project is set to be scheduled backward from a finish date, in which case you are asked if you are sure that you want to schedule the project from a finish date, since the default is to schedule from the start. If there is required project information, a link to the Project Information dialog will appear, and in it you can populate the Enterprise Custom fields needed by your organization. No other information in this dialog box can be edited.
2. **Collaborate on your project**—This step is only displayed if you are using Project Professional and Project Server. This step offers the opportunity to connect to the Microsoft Project 2003 Server for collaboration with project resources. If you have already accessed the Microsoft Project 2003 Server, the Yes radio button is selected by default, and connection information to the Microsoft Project 2003 Server is populated; otherwise, the No radio button is selected. If you select Yes but have not used the server before, a link to the Set Connection dialog box will be displayed. If you select to change the server connection, the link Change Connection Information is displayed. If you select No, information on how to set up Microsoft Project 2003 Server later is displayed.

3. **Save your project**—Your project must be saved at this point before you proceed. If you are using Project Server, a dialog box appears, advising that your file will automatically register with the Project Server anytime you save information.
4. **Add documents that relate to your project**—This step in the wizard takes you to the SharePoint document library, where you can upload documents that are pertinent to your project plan, such as a project charter, a scope statement, feasibility analysis documents, budgeting documents, and change management requirements information.
5. **Enter additional information**—At this point in the wizard, you are directed to the link Save and Finish, which causes you to exit the wizard and allows you to continue to follow the steps within the sidepane to start entering tasks in the project.

You can programmatically modify the New Project Wizard to enforce the best practices in attaching required documents, which might include many of the ones described in step 4.

USING THE NEW CALENDAR WIZARD

The New Calendar Wizard gives you a single, convenient place to set up calendars and options that affect a project (see Figure 3.23).

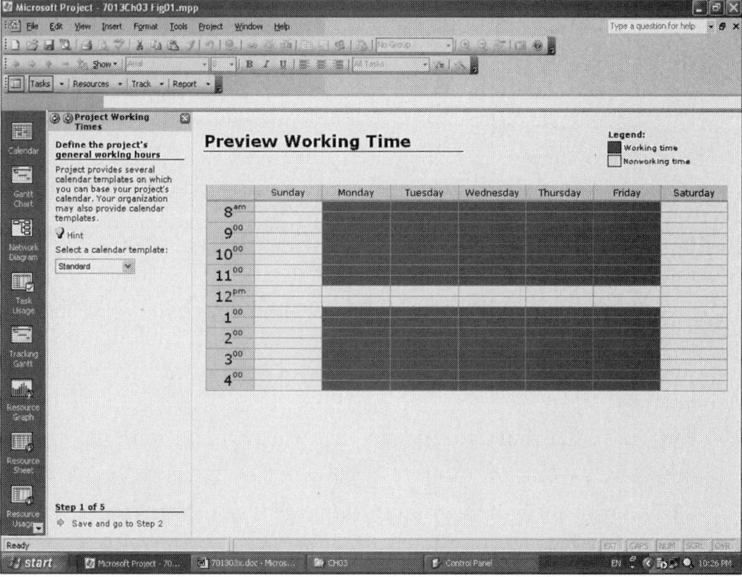

Figure 3.23
The New Calendar Wizard steps you through the process of defining the working times for a project.

You access this wizard via the Goal-Based User Interface by selecting Tasks and then selecting Define Project's General Working Hours. When you run the wizard, you work a series of steps. The following steps describe the dialog boxes that appear in sequence:

1. **Define the project's general working hours**—This step draws a graphical representation for the working time to the right, defined by the template that you've selected.

The drop-down list for templates includes all base calendars defined within the global file. If no template is selected, a standard working calendar of 8 a.m. to 5 p.m. Monday through Friday is displayed.

2. **Define the work week**—You need to define the working days of the project. You have the option to accept the current default working hours or to define new working hours. If you select the radio button to adjust the working hours, the sidepane displays a drop-down list from which you can select the day you want to change. There are two sets of fields for editing the working time, known as shifts. If you want to show and edit more shift times, click the link Specify Additional Shifts. You can then select to apply the new working time to all working days or select a new day from the drop-down list. You can also select to make the new hours a default in all project files by selecting Set as Default. Your changes are saved before you proceed.
3. **Define exceptions**—If you want to define exceptions to the calendar, such as company holidays (and have Project schedule over these nonworking times), click the link Change Working Time, and the Change Working Time dialog appears. The sidepane provides detailed descriptions on how to make exceptions. Again, your changes are saved before you proceed to the next step.
4. **Define time units**—In this step, you define how many hours will equal a day, along with how many days will equal a week and a month. These units are synchronized with those that are defined on the Calendar tab of the Options dialog box, which you access via the Tools menu. Your settings are again saved before you proceed.
5. **Set the project calendar**—This step informs you that you have just set the calendar that affects all the resources utilized within the project. If you need to set up additional calendars for resource groups, you can click the – link. Otherwise, you can save and exit the wizard. If you select the Define Working Times for Resources link, you are taken through the following steps as well.
6. **Define additional calendars**—You are asked whether you would like to create a new calendar or edit an existing one. If you select New, you need to name the new calendar you are creating. You can also choose Edit and then click Next to choose from a list of available base calendars.
7. **Define general working hours**—This process is very similar to the process in step 1, where you define the project's general working hours. However, in this case, you are setting the working hours for a new calendar or for one you have chosen to edit.
8. **Define the work week**—This is the same process as outlined in step 2, where you define the work week.
9. **Define exceptions for specific dates**—This step is the same process as outlined in step 3, where you define exceptions to the calendar.
10. **The additional calendar is set**—The calendar is now set. Click Finish to save and exit the wizard.

3

USING THE DEFINE WORKING TIMES FOR RESOURCES WIZARD

Project provides the Define Working Times for Resources Wizard for setting resource calendars. You access this wizard by clicking Resources from the Project Guide toolbar and then selecting Resource Calendars. You are then walked through how to set resource calendars by proceeding through a series of steps. The following steps describe the dialog boxes in the wizard:

1. **Specify working hours for individual resources**—A Resource Sheet view is displayed, with the Calendar field displayed so you can review what calendar your resources are already set up to use. You can then click the link Define Additional Calendars if you need to define a calendar for a group of resources who have working times that are different from the project base calendar. If you want to change working time for one resource at a time instead of for a group of resources, select one resource name at a time and continue through the steps of the wizard.
2. **Define general working hours**—Follow the same process as defined in step 1.
3. **Define the work week**—Follow the same process as defined in step 1.
4. **Define exceptions for specific dates**—Follow the same process as defined in step 1.
5. **The resource calendar is set**—You can choose to save and exit the wizard or to loop back through to work with additional resources that need calendar changes.

WORKING WITH THE ORGANIZER

You can use the Organizer to copy items (such as calendars) from one project or template to another. You can also use the Organizer to delete or rename a calendar. If you copy a calendar to the `GLOBAL.MPT` file, the calendar becomes part of all newly created project documents. For example, to customize the Standard calendar for all new projects, you follow these basic steps:

1. Choose Tools, Change Working Times to edit the Standard calendar in an active project document. Define special working times, holidays, and hours in the Standard calendar, as described in the section "Editing the Standard Calendar," earlier in this chapter.
2. Use the Organizer to copy the customized Standard calendar to the `GLOBAL.MPT` file, replacing the existing Standard calendar in the `GLOBAL.MPT` file. The Standard calendar for all new projects will then have the customized features. See the section "Copying Calendars to the Global Template," later in this chapter.

You can use the Organizer to manage not only calendars but also other customized items (such as views, reports, macros, forms, tables, filters, toolbars, and menu bars). Therefore, you can activate the Organizer from several points in Project. Probably the most convenient way to access the Organizer is by choosing Tools, Organizer.

NOTE

> You can also access the Organizer through several other dialog boxes, such as those you access by choosing the following options:
>
> - View, More Views, Organizer
> - View, Table, More Tables, Organizer
> - Project, Filter For, More Filters, Organizer
> - Project, Group By, More Groups, Organizer

COPYING CALENDARS TO THE GLOBAL TEMPLATE

You can access the Organizer through the Tools menu. The active file—that is, the file that contains the calendar—is referred to as the *source file*. The file in which you would like to place a copy of the calendar is referred to as the *target file*.

Follow these steps to copy a calendar to the `GLOBAL.MPT` file:

1. Choose Tools, Organizer to display the Organizer.
2. Choose the Calendars tab (see Figure 3.24). The calendars in the active file are listed on the right side of this tab. The calendars in the `GLOBAL.MPT` file are listed on the left.

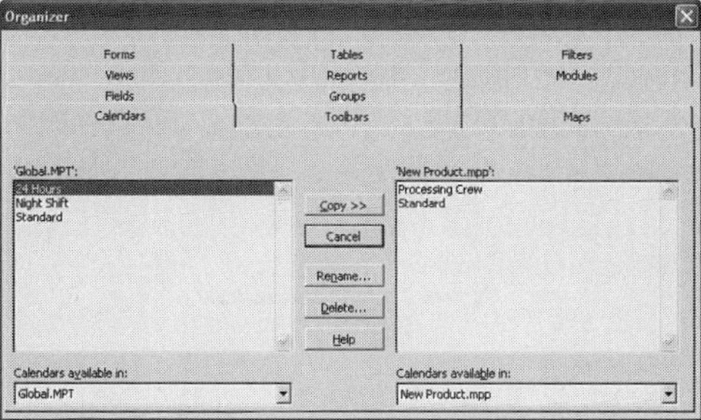

Figure 3.24
You can use the Organizer to make customized calendars available for use in other projects you are working on.

3. Choose the calendar you want to copy from the list of calendars in the source file on the right side of the dialog box.
4. Click the Copy button. If there is a calendar in the target file that has the same name as the source file you've selected (for example, the Standard calendar), Project asks for confirmation to override the former calendar (see Figure 3.25).

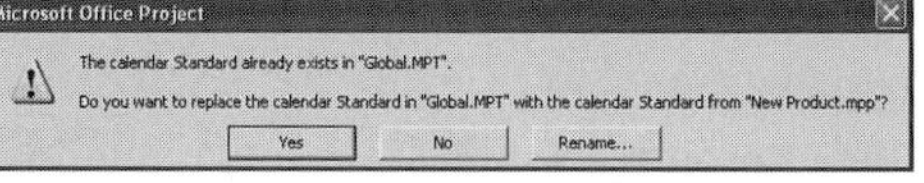

Figure 3.25
You must confirm that you want to replace the Standard calendar in the `GLOBAL.MPT` file with the Standard calendar from the source file.

5. Click the Yes button to replace the calendar in the target file with the new calendar from your active file. Or click the Rename button to copy the calendar to the target file by using a name that is not being used by another calendar.
6. Click the Close button to exit the Organizer.

NOTE

> **You cannot directly edit the calendars in the `GLOBAL.MPT` file. To edit a calendar in the `GLOBAL.MPT` file, copy it to a project file by using the Organizer. Edit the calendar in the project file, and then use the Organizer to copy it back to the `GLOBAL.MPT` file.**

COPYING A CALENDAR FROM ONE PROJECT TO ANOTHER

You also use the Organizer to copy a calendar from one project document to another. For example, if you want to place a copy of the Processing Crew calendar from the Building Construction file in the Business Case Construction file, follow these steps:

1. Open both the source and target files.
2. Choose Tools, Organizer to display the Organizer dialog box.
3. Choose the Calendars tab. The calendars in the active file (for example, Building Construction in Figure 3.26), are listed on the right. The calendars in the `GLOBAL.MPT` file are listed on the left.

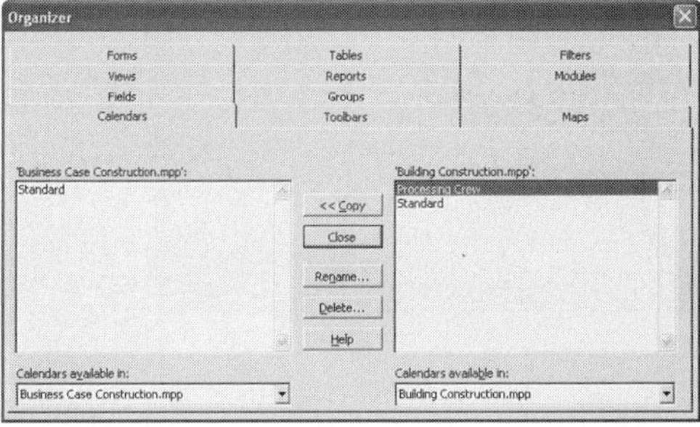

Figure 3.26
You can display the target and the source files in the Organizer dialog box.

NOTE

> **The source file does not always have to appear on the right. You can copy from right to left or left to right. When you select the item you want to use as the source, the Copy button's arrow changes direction accordingly.**

4. Use the Calendars Available In drop-down list box on the bottom-left side to choose the target file. Figure 3.26 shows the Business Case Construction project as the target.
5. Choose the calendar you want to copy from the list of calendars in the source file.

6. Click the Copy button. If there is a calendar with the same name in the target file, such as the Standard calendar, Project asks you for confirmation to override the former calendar.
7. Click the Yes button to replace the calendar in the target file with the new calendar from your active file. Or click the Rename button to copy the calendar to the target file by using a name that is not already being used by a calendar in the target file.
8. Click the Close button to exit the Organizer.

→ You can also use the Organizer to share items you customize with other project files (such as views, reports, and tables). For more information, **see** Chapter 21, "Customizing Views, Tables, Fields, Filters, and Groups," **p. 833**.

Printing the Base Calendars

You can print a report to show the details of each of the base calendars in the active project file. Printing reports is covered in detail in Chapter 13 and Chapter 22, "Using and Customizing the Standard Reports." This section is a quick reference on how to print the Working Days report, a report that provides information about the working and nonworking days in all your base calendars.

To print the Working Days report, follow these steps:

1. Choose View, Reports. The Reports dialog box appears, as shown in Figure 3.27.

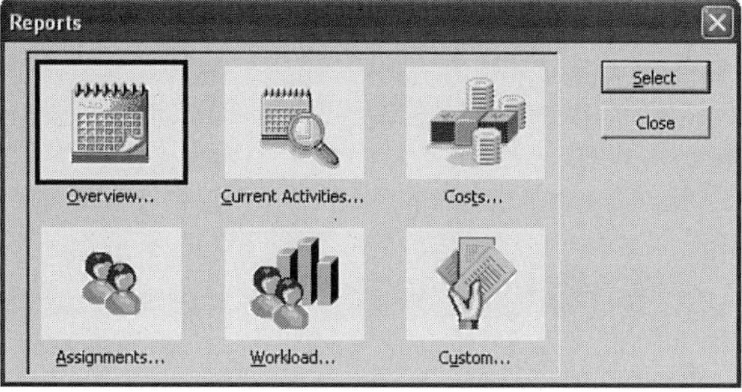

Figure 3.27
The Reports dialog box organizes reports into five standard categories plus a Custom option for customizing reports.

2. Choose the Overview category by double-clicking the Overview icon or by selecting the icon and then clicking the Select button. The Overview Reports dialog box appears (see Figure 3.28).
3. Click the Working Days report. Click the Select button to preview the report or simply double-click the Working Days report (see Figure 3.29).
4. Click the Print button to access the Print dialog box and send the report to your printer.
5. Click Close to return to the project workspace.

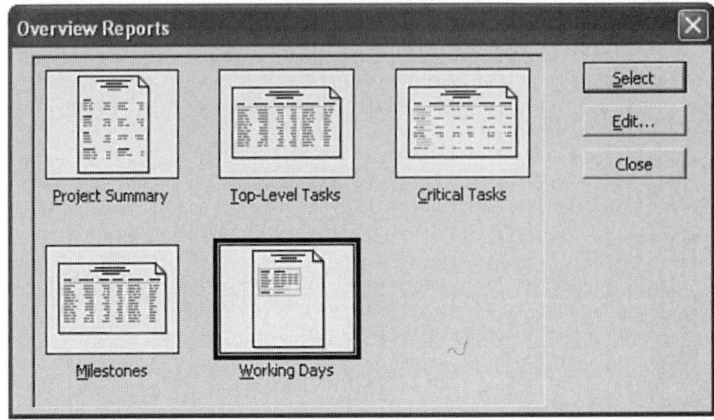

Figure 3.28
The Working Days report prints all calendars for the active project.

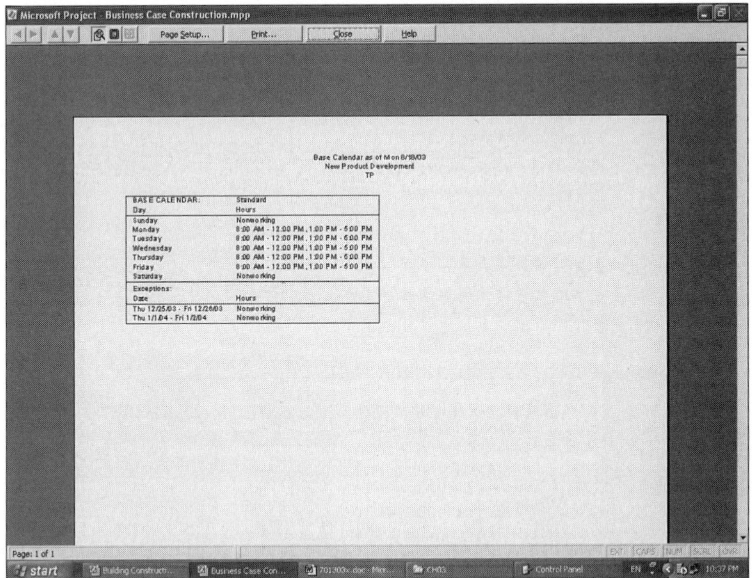

Figure 3.29
The Print Preview screen shows the layout of the Working Days report.

The report shows the standard working hours for each day of the week, followed by a list of the exceptions for individual days. Each base calendar prints on a separate page. Figure 3.30 is an illustration of the report for the Processing Crew base calendar. Holidays are listed as exceptions below the standard days and hours.

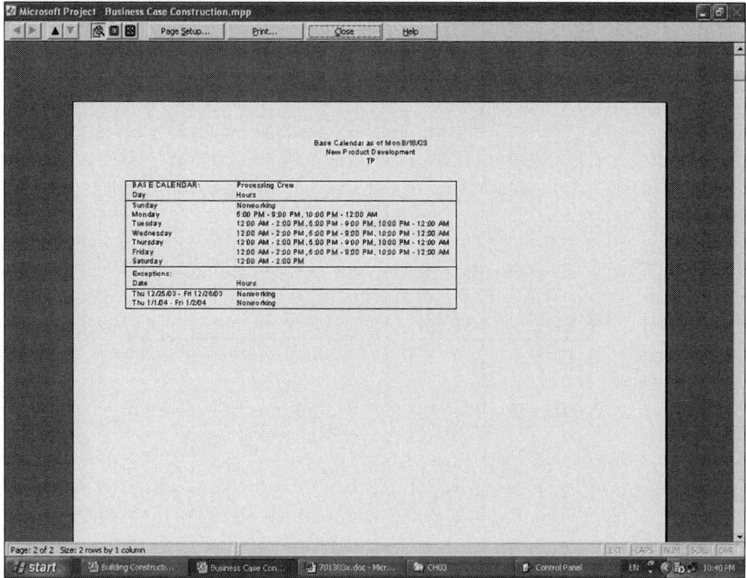

Figure 3.30 The Working Days report for the Processing Crew base calendar shows the standard working times plus the exceptions (such as holidays).

TROUBLESHOOTING

START TIMES DON'T MATCH

I've changed my default start time to be 7:00 a.m. and coordinated this change with my Standard calendar, but my first task is still starting at 8:00 a.m. What's wrong?

If you choose Project, Project Information, you'll notice that the project starts at 8:00 a.m. This start time occurs because when you initially entered the project start date (in the Project Information dialog box) or accepted the default time, Project also assumed that this was the start time. The work time for the project was set to the hours of 8:00 a.m. to 5:00 p.m. You later made changes to the Calendar tab of the Options dialog box, but changes in this dialog box are not retroactive; you also have to change the start time for the project in the Project Information dialog box. This is one reason you should format all dates to display the time (through the Options dialog box). You can enter a date and time in the Start Date field of the Project Information dialog box, even though time is not set to display in that field. Choose Project, Project Information to recalculate the project start time.

MAKING START AND END TIME CHANGES PERMANENT

I've changed my default start and end times, but when I create a new project, the times revert to the default (8:00 a.m. to 5:00 p.m.). How can I make this change permanent?

There are two types of environmental options in the Options dialog box: file-specific options and global options. Start and end times are file-specific options. However, if you click the Set as Default button on the Calendar tab of the Options dialog box (where you set the start and end times), your custom start and end times become the default for any new files you create. The setting is changed for the current project file as well as any new files you create. Any existing project files are not changed, however, and need to be adjusted as explained previously.

CHAPTER 4

Managing Project Files

In this chapter

Saving and Protecting Files 96

Creating and Using Templates 103

Working with the Organizer and the Global File 107

Troubleshooting 112

Saving and Protecting Files

Understanding how to effectively work with project files is important for project managers. This chapter discusses how to manipulate project files, save and protect your work, use project templates, and use the Organizer.

You can save files as project documents, HTML files, or workspace files. In addition, if you are working with a group of people who need access to a project file, you might want to protect files against accidental changes.

Designating a Default Save Location and File Format

When you save a project, the file is saved as a project file type (with the extension `.mpp`) in the `My Documents` folder. These are the default settings for file type and location. However, Project allows you to designate a different default location and file type for project files. Not only can you specify the default settings for project files, but you can designate default locations for your own templates (user templates) and templates you share with others (workgroup templates).

To change these default settings, choose Tools, Options and click the Save tab (see Figure 4.1).

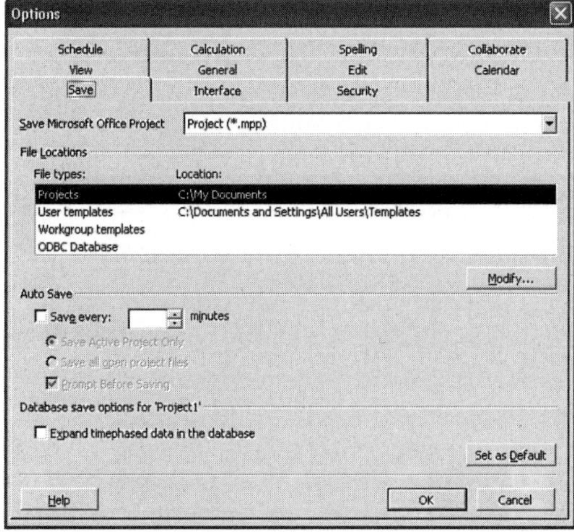

Figure 4.1
Workgroup templates are standardized project templates that you can create for a team or an organization to share.

→ If you need to share a Project 2003 file with people who are using versions of Project older than 98, **see** "Exporting Project 2003 Data to Older Versions of Microsoft Project," **p. 636**.

To change the default file type, click the Save Microsoft Project drop-down list and choose one of the types listed in Table 4.1.

TABLE 4.1 MICROSOFT PROJECT FILE TYPES

File Type	Description
Project (*.mpp)	This is the standard file type used for individual project files.
Template (*.mpt)	This is a special type of project file that contains either a standard set of tasks or group of resources used as a starting point for creating similar new project files.
Project Database (*.mpd)	This file type is used when you want to be able to export project data to other programs, including Microsoft Access. This format replaces the .mpx format from versions prior to 2000.
Project 98 (*.mpp)	You use this format when you have Project 2000, 2002, or 2003 but are sharing project files with others who have Project 98.
Microsoft Access Database (*.mdb)	This file format is convenient when you need to routinely use project data in Microsoft Access.
ODBC Database	This file format is used to export project data in a compliant database format for a SQL server or an Oracle server.

➔ To learn about using Project with Microsoft Access, **see** "Using the Microsoft Access Format," **p. 645**.

To change the location in which project files are stored, select the file type from the File Locations box. For example, in Figure 4.1 the Projects file type is selected. Then click the Modify button. The Modify Location dialog box, which is similar to the Open and Save As dialog boxes, appears; in this dialog box, you can identify a different location. After you navigate to the folder that you want to be the new default location, click OK, and you should see the location change in the File Locations box.

VERSION COMPATIBILITY

Project 2003, 2002, and 2000 share the same file types, so if you are using Project 2003, it is not necessary to change file types in order to share your projects with someone who is using Project 2000 or 2002. When a 2003 project is opened in 2000 or 2002, references to features that are unique to 2003 are kept in hidden fields that cannot be recognized by the older versions. However, when the file is again opened in 2003, changes made in 2003 will take precedence.

Project 98 files can be read in the more recent versions, but files created in 2000, 2002, or 2003 must be saved in the 98 format before they can be read in Project 98.

You can save an existing project in other formats by using the Save as type drop-down list in the Save As dialog box (see Figure 4.2).

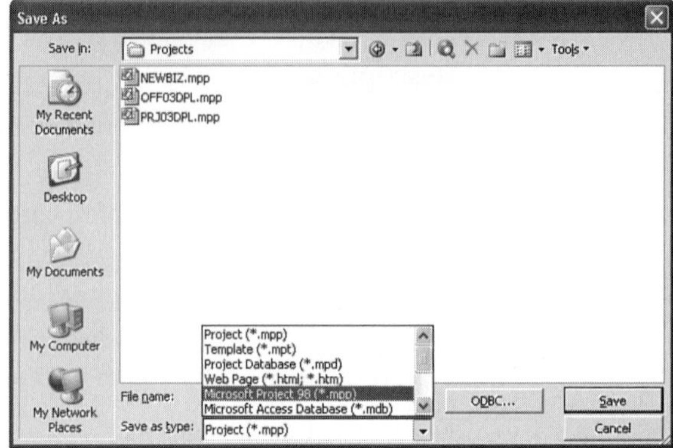

Figure 4.2
Saving project files in the Project 98 format allows you to share documents created in 2003 with people who are using Project 98.

NOTE

> Project 2003 is designed to handle future version compatibility by including "unknown data" fields that allow Project to store but not use data and represent it as unavailable rather than hide the unknown data.

ACTIVATING AUTO SAVE

The Auto Save feature in Project enables you to select a time interval at which Microsoft Project will automatically save your project files. You can choose to have the Auto Save feature save just your active project or all open project files.

To enable this feature, choose Tools, Options and click the Save tab in the Options dialog box (see Figure 4.3). Mark the Save Every check box and type the time interval or use the spinner arrows to select a unit of time. Then choose either Save Active Project Only or Save All Open Project Files.

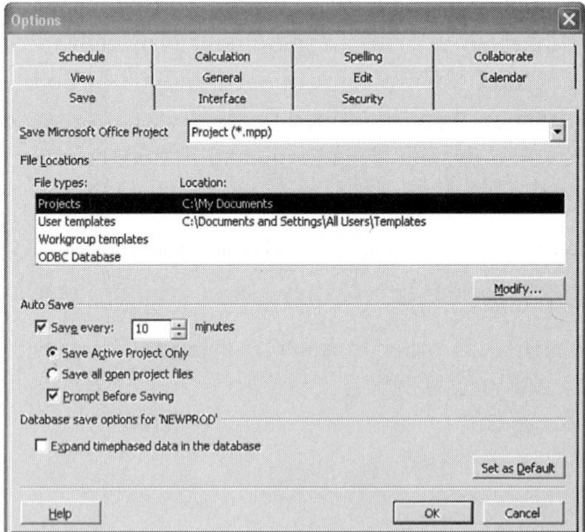

Figure 4.3
You must check the Save Every check box to activate the Auto Save choices.

As a precaution, Project can prompt you each time it is preparing to Auto Save files, as shown in Figure 4.4. However, Auto Save only prompts you to save the file if you have made changes to it since the last time the file was saved. If no changes have been made, you do not receive this prompt.

If you do not want to be notified before saving, you can deactivate this feature by removing the check from the Prompt Before Saving check box (refer to Figure 4.3).

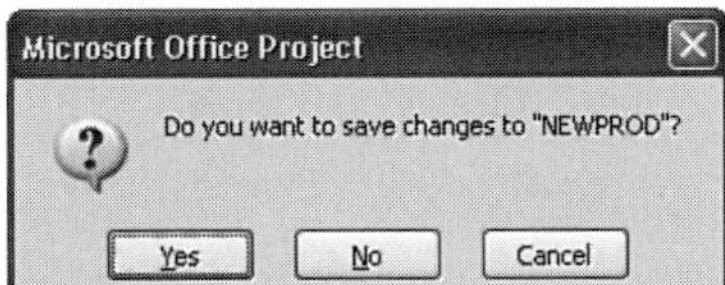

Figure 4.4
The Auto Save prompt appears only if you have not saved your changes.

Project is not only a scheduling tool; it is also an analysis tool for what-if scenarios. Users can make changes to task or resource information and then see what impact the changes have on the project. Typically, you would not want to have these changes saved automatically. However, because you can be prompted as to whether you want to save (if the Prompt Before Saving option is selected), you can avoid saving changes until you are certain you want them. Don't hesitate to use Project to help you play out various scenarios for your projects.

4

SAVING A FILE

The first time you save a file, the Save As dialog box—which is very similar to the Open dialog box—appears and lets you specify the name and location you want to use to save the file (see Figure 4.5). Choose File, Save to save the file.

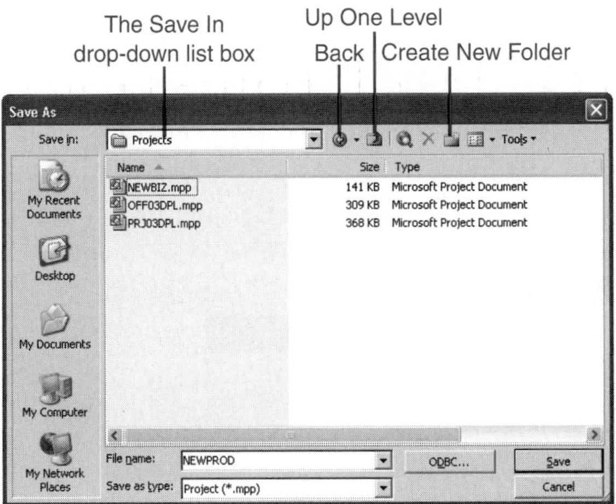

Figure 4.5
You can also use the Save As dialog box to change any aspect of the way in which you save a file.

Select the location in which you want to save the file. Then give the file a more descriptive name than the default, `Project1`, `Project2`, and so on.

NOTE

> Project filenames can be up to 200 characters long, including spaces. Certain characters are not permitted, including /, ?, \, :, *, ", <, >, and ¦.

You can choose File, Save As if you later want to change any aspect of the way you save a file. This includes changing the file's name, the location where the file is saved, the file's password security, or the file format.

CAUTION

> When you are working with programs that support only filenames of eight or fewer characters (for example, in MS-DOS or Windows 3.1), a longer filename used in Newer versions of Windows is truncated. The first six characters of the filename are then followed by a tilde (~), and then by a number, usually a one (1). For example, the filename `Office Move.mpp` would be displayed as `Office~1.mpp`.

PROVIDING SECURITY FOR SAVED FILES

In the Save As dialog box, you can choose the Tools drop-down and select General Options to set the following security features for a file (see Figure 4.6):

- You can make a backup copy of the previous version of a file every time you save the file.
- You can password-protect the file. If you do this, a user cannot access the file without knowing a password.
- You can write-protect the file so others can open and view the file under the original name but cannot save any changes to the original file. Changes can be saved under a different name. This feature protects the data you placed in the file, yet allows others to view the data.
- You can save the file with a warning message that says that you prefer users to open the file as a read-only file.

Figure 4.6
You can protect a file from being changed by others or even from being read by others in the Save Options dialog box.

PASSWORD-PROTECTING A FILE

To password-protect a file, you can type up to 17 characters as a password in the Protection Password text box. The password text box is case sensitive and accepts any character, including spaces, numbers, and keyboard symbols. When you choose OK, you are prompted to confirm the password by typing it again. You are notified if you fail to type it exactly the same and have to reenter the password and confirmation. Choose OK to close the warning box and try again.

After you specify the security options, if any, choose OK to save the file. The password remains with the file each time you save the file.

When you attempt to reopen the file, you must enter the password exactly as typed when you saved the password. If you do not enter the password correctly, including the upper- and lowercase of individual characters, you are warned and given another chance to type it correctly. There is no limit to the number of attempts you can make to type in the password.

CAUTION

> **It is important to use passwords you can easily remember. If you forget a password, there is absolutely no way to open the file. Not even the people at Microsoft can help you open a file whose password is lost!**

4

To remove a password, open the file, and choose File, Save As. In the Save As dialog box, choose Tools, General Options. The Save Options dialog box appears. Delete all characters from the password field, and choose OK.

SAVING A READ-ONLY FILE

To write-protect a file with a write-reservation password, type a password with up to 17 characters in the Write Reservation Password text box. A write-reservation password enables all users to open the file, but a warning appears, stating that the file is write-reserved (see Figure 4.7). If the user supplies the correct password in the Password text box, the file opens and the user has the right to make changes and save the original file. If the user doesn't supply the correct password, they can only open the file as read-only; they must save changes under a different filename. Saving a file with a write-reservation password ensures that only users who have the password can replace the data in the file.

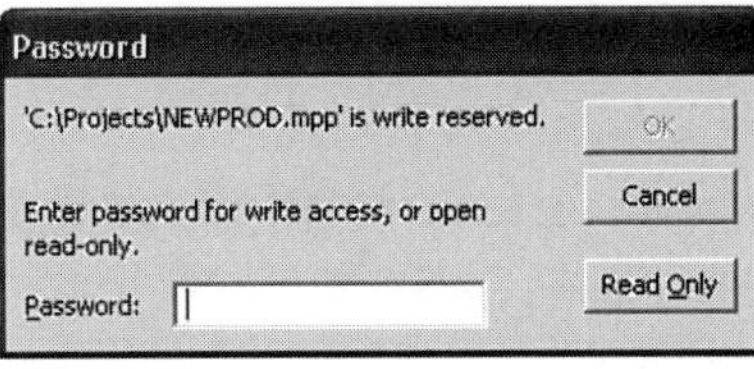

Figure 4.7
Unless you know the password, you cannot open a write-reserved file with read/write privileges; you can only open it as read-only.

Saving a File as Read-Only Recommended

If you select the Read-Only Recommended check box in the Save Options dialog box (refer to Figure 4.6), users who try to open the file are warned that you want them to open the file as a read-only file. Users can choose to accept the Read-Only default or bypass the warning and open the file with read/write privileges. This option doesn't effectively prevent users from replacing the data in the file, but it does warn the users that the file is shared with others.

Using the Create Backup File Option

If you select the Always Create Backup check box in the Save Options dialog box (refer to Figure 4.6), the original file is saved under the original name with a `.bak` extension. The revised version of the active file is then saved under the original name, with the `.mpp` extension. This procedure retains a copy of the previous version of the file on disk. For example, suppose you created a project file named `MOVE.mpp` in April. In July you open the file to make several changes. If Always Create Backup is active when the revised file is saved, the April version is saved as `MOVE.bak`, and the revised file is saved as `MOVE.mpp`. If you make additional changes to the file in September, the July version *replaces* the April version and is saved with the `.bak` extension; the September version then has the `.mpp` extension and the April version is no longer available.

4

Saving Files in HTML Format

In order to publish a document on the World Wide Web, you can save portions of a project's files in the Hypertext Markup Language (HTML) format that is required by the Web. To save a file in HTML format, choose File, Save As Web Page.

→ For more information on Web capabilities, see the bonus chapter, "Publishing Projects on the Web," on the CD accompanying this book.

Saving the Workspace

The File, Save Workspace command saves a small file that contains a list of the names of all the project files currently open in memory. When you open a workspace file, all the files contained in the list are opened. A workspace file acts as a *pointer* to the files; it does not contain a *copy* of the files.

Suppose you're working on three project files when you go to lunch. If you use the Save Workspace command before you save and close the individual files, you can restore all the files to the screen just by opening the one workspace file. A workspace file can also be used to list files you work with routinely, so that each morning when you open the workspace, all the files you need are opened.

The Open dialog box does not allow you to select multiple files to open; each file has to be opened separately. Creating a workspace file is a great way to open several project files at the same time and is a nice feature for people who are managing multiple project files.

When you choose File, Save Workspace, the program displays the Save Workspace As dialog box. Workspace filenames have the extension `.mpw`. Microsoft Project suggests the default workspace filename `resume.mpw`, but you can change the name in the File Name text box. Unless you choose another drive or directory, the workspace file is saved in the current directory. Microsoft Project prompts you to save all open files that have changed since the last save. You might also see the Planning Wizard message about saving a baseline if tasks have been added that were not added to the baseline.

NOTE

If you have created a file but have not saved it, you are prompted to make a decision about including that project file in the workspace file. New project files that are empty are not added to the workspace file.

When you open a workspace file, all active files are closed before the workspace file is opened. You are prompted to save any active file in which changes have been made but not yet saved. You choose File, Open to open a workspace file, which opens all the files contained in its list of filenames.

PROGRAM INTEGRITY

Project 2003 provides special protection against system instability with the Safe Mode feature. If your system experiences file or registry corruption or an unexpected crash, Safe Mode allows Project 2003 to start, with certain parts disabled, to allow you to continue working with your project files.

CAUTION

Continuing to work in an unstable environment can be risky. It is strongly recommended that you save and close all open files, close open applications, and restart Windows or reboot your computer to regain stability.

Project 2003 also offers the ability to notify the Microsoft Project Development Team if Project 2003 fails to respond or experiences a fatal error. The Office Watson feature displays a dialog box that allows you to restart Project and view details of the error report, and then provides you the opportunity to send a report to Microsoft.

CREATING AND USING TEMPLATES

A *template* is a project file that contains a typical or standard set of tasks or resources that can be used as a blueprint or starting point for creating similar new project files. Microsoft Project provides 20 sample templates, but you can create your own templates as well. For example, you might create a template that lists a standard set of tasks that are common to the type of projects you perform. Likewise, if the same group of people is always involved in your projects, you can create a template that contains the resource information so you won't have to enter it for each new project file. Each template file has an `.mpt` extension.

Opening Template Files

When you open a template, you are opening a copy of the file, not the original template. You use this copy as a starting point for a new project.

To open a template file that you or another user has created, choose File, New. From the task pane, choose Templates On My Computer. In the Templates dialog box, select the template you want to open, and then choose Open or double-click the filename. (The sample templates included with Microsoft Project are discussed later in this chapter.)

When you save such a file, the Save As dialog box opens. The project name defaults to the name of the template, but the file type is changed to `.mpp`, with the exception of `GLOBAL.MPT`. You can use the default name or supply a different name.

The Global Template: `GLOBAL.MPT`

When you open a new, blank project document, the new file is based on a default project template, `GLOBAL.MPT`. The new file inherits all the features of `GLOBAL.MPT`. All new projects begin with generic document titles (`Project1`, `Project2`, and so on). `GLOBAL.MPT` is typically stored in the `\Program Files\Microsoft Office\Office11\1033` directory or the `Windows\Application Data\Microsoft\MS Project\1033` directory, depending on the operating system.

4

NOTE

> To designate the language in which Windows and Office are installed, Microsoft uses folders with numerical names. `1033`, mentioned above, designates English. If you have a different language version of Windows or Office installed, the folder name is a different number.

→ The `GLOBAL.MPT` can be used as a vehicle for sharing custom objects with other users that have similar needs. **See** the "Working with the Organizer and Global Files" and "Troubleshooting" sections later in this chapter for more information about sharing custom objects in the `GLOBAL.MPT`.

→ When using Microsoft Project 2003 Professional in an enterprise environment, there is also an enterprise global template for companywide standardization. To learn more about the enterprise global template, **see** Chapter 27, "Enterprise Resource Management," **p. 1069**.

Using the Microsoft Project Sample Templates

Microsoft Project includes a wide range of sample files you can use as starting points for your own projects. Each template contains a detailed list of tasks, organized into phases that are appropriate for the type of project for which the template is designed. Each phase includes the typical activities with logical relationships (links) to other activities in that phase or another phase.

For example, the Project 2003 Commercial Construction template specifies the common tasks required to construct a multiple-story commercial space and shows the relationships between those tasks. This template can be used as the foundation for a variety of commercial construction projects, ranging from supermarkets and fast food restaurants to hotels and airports. The Commercial Construction Project template is organized into a number of phases: general conditions, long-lead procurement, mobilize on site, and so on.

Microsoft Project Help contains a detailed description of each template. From the Help menu, choose Microsoft Project Help or press the F1 key on your keyboard. In the Search For box, type **`available templates`**, and then click the Start Searching green arrow. Select Available Templates from the list of Search results, and then click on one of the template choices to see its description.

The easiest way to access a sample template file is to choose File, New, to display the New Project sidepane, which lists recently used custom templates and a link to the Templates On My Computer (see Figure 4.8). Note that you *cannot* use the New button on the Standard toolbar to access the templates. The sample templates can be set up to install when you first attempt to use them. However, these template files are on the Project 2003 installation CD-ROM and are not automatically included with the installation of Microsoft Project 2003 unless a full custom installation is done. Therefore, you may need to access Project installation files to install these templates. Some organizations copy the installation files to a network server so that users can access the installation files without the CD-ROM.

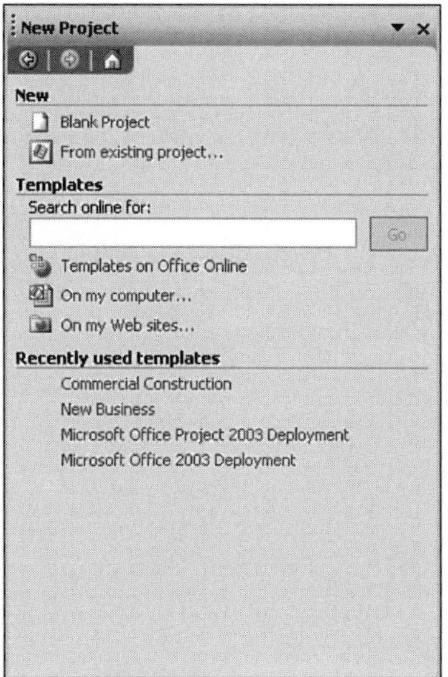

Figure 4.8
You can use the Project sidepane to access the predefined Project template files.

4

After you select On My Computer, select the template you want to use, and then click OK (or double-click the filename). When you create a new file based on one of Microsoft Project's templates, you are creating a copy of the file, not accessing the original template. You can then use this copy as a starting point for your own project.

NOTE

> When you use a template to begin a file, the name of the template appears at the bottom of the Summary tab in the Properties dialog box (which you open by selecting File, Properties).

CREATING A NEW TEMPLATE

An existing project file can be saved as a template for projects with similar content and structure.

TIP

> You can open an old project file, make changes, and use the File, Save As command to save the file as a new template. Thus you can avoid accidentally saving the new file over the old project file.

To save an active file as a template, choose File, Save As. Enter the filename you want to use, and choose Template from the Save as Type drop-down list at the bottom of the Save As dialog box. The filename extension changes to `.mpt` automatically. Microsoft Project stores templates in a default folder that is designated for User templates. The path to this folder is `C:\Windows\Application Data\Microsoft\Templates\` or `C:\Documents and Settings\all users\Templates`, depending on the operating system.

NOTE

> You can designate a default location for your personal templates (user templates) and for templates you share with other people (workgroup templates) through the Tools, Options dialog box. Refer to the section "Designating a Default Save Location and File Format" earlier in this chapter for the specific steps.

When you save a project file as a template, the window shown in Figure 4.9 appears, enabling you to strip data such as baseline values and actual values from the template, if necessary. This is a valuable feature that enables you to use completed or active projects as the basis for new projects, removing data that is unique to each project.

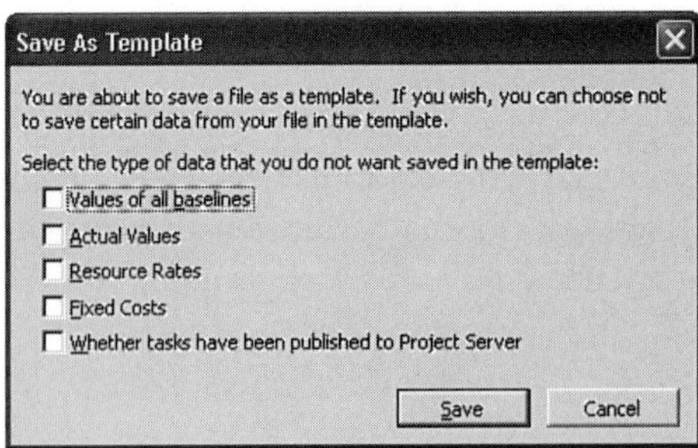

Figure 4.9
You can keep project-specific values from being saved with the template through the Save As Template dialog box.

When you use a template file as the basis for a new project, a copy of the file is displayed with the extension automatically changed to `.mpp` so you can save the new working copy as a regular project file.

MODIFYING TEMPLATE FILES

There is no way to directly open the `.mpt` file. Therefore, when you want to make modifications to a template, you must open a copy of the template, make the desired changes, and save the file under the default name, with the `.mpt` extension. You must make certain to choose Template from the Save as Type drop-down list to change the file type. The filename extension changes automatically, and the corrected template saves over the original template.

WORKING WITH THE ORGANIZER AND THE GLOBAL FILE

When you modify an existing object—such as the Standard Base Calendar—or create a new customized view or report, the modified or custom object is available to only the project you are currently working with. The Organizer lets you share objects in one project or template with another project or template. This is accomplished by copying the objects from one file to the other (see Figure 4.10).

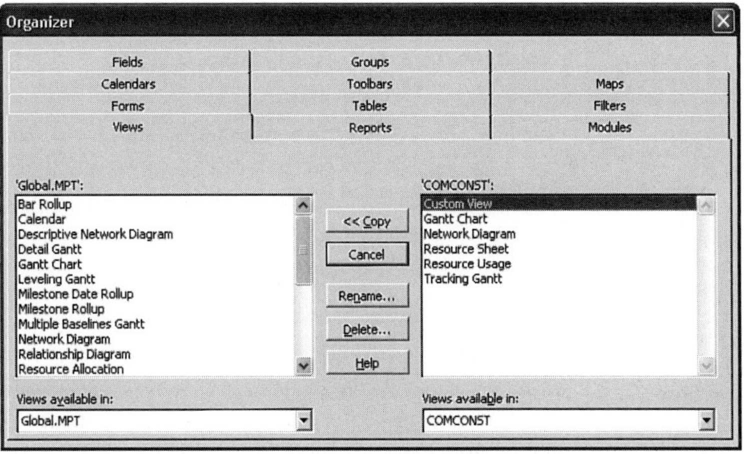

Figure 4.10
The Organizer dialog box provides access to items that can be customized and shared in Project.

The Organizer is most often used to copy modified or custom objects to other project files or to the Global template. You can also use the Organizer to delete an object that is no longer needed or to rename an object. The Organizer is set up as a series of tabs, each tab focusing on a different type of object.

Table 4.2 lists the types of objects contained in the Organizer.

TABLE 4.2 OBJECTS IN THE ORGANIZER

Type	Description
Views	Views are screen displays that are used to enter, organize, and examine project information. Some views are designed to look at primarily task information, and some are for examining resource-oriented information. There are three types of views in Microsoft Project: charts or graphs, sheets, and forms. Custom views can be created to meet your specific needs.
Reports	A report is a predefined, printable representation of project information. You can create custom reports to meet your specific needs.
Modules	When you design a macro, the macro is stored in a module. Microsoft Project uses Visual Basic to create macros.
Forms	A form is a specific type of view that provides detailed information about a selected task or resource. You can design custom forms to meet your specific needs.
Tables	A table is a collection of fields organized into columns and rows, much like a spreadsheet. Tables are used with views such as Gantt Chart, Task Sheet, and Resource Sheet. You can create custom tables to meet your specific needs.
Filters	A filter is used to highlight specific information in a view. There are two types of filters: task filters and resource filters. You can create custom filters to meet your specific needs.
Calendars	Project uses task, resource, and project calendars to create the project schedule. You can also create custom calendars to meet your needs.
Toolbars	A toolbar provides shortcut buttons to Project features and/or functionality. You can customize these toolbars or create your own custom toolbars.
Maps	The Maps tab is used to track data that is exported to other programs. Export maps are sets of instructions that track exactly what types of data are to be exported, relating field to field.
Fields	A field is a column or box with a specific type of information about a task, resource, or assignment. You can customize fields to meet your specific needs.
Groups	A group is a tool used to organize and summarize the display of project information. There are two types of groups: task groups and resource groups. You can create custom groups to meet your specific needs.

The easiest way to access the Organizer is through the Tools menu, by choosing Tools, Organizer. You can also access the Organizer through several other dialog boxes, by choosing one of the following:

- **More Views dialog box**—Choose View, More Views, Organizer.
- **More Tables dialog box**—Choose View, Table, More Tables, Organizer.
- **More Filters dialog box**—Choose Project, Filter for, More Filters, Organizer.
- **More Groups dialog box**—Choose Project, Group by, More Groups, Organizer.

USING THE ORGANIZER TO MODIFY GLOBAL.MPT

NOTE

> The first time you open Project, a copy of the original GLOBAL.MPT file (GLOBAL.MPT) is created and becomes the active GLOBAL.MPT file, on which all new documents are based from that point forward. The original GLOBAL.MPT file is then preserved, safe from customization, as a backup copy.

New blank project documents are based on a copy of the Global template—the active GLOBAL.MPT file. Changes you make to the active GLOBAL.MPT affect all new project files. Changes to the active GLOBAL.MPT file must be made from the Organizer or by selecting Tools, Options. If you want to customize the original, backup GLOBAL.MPT file, you can open it directly, and you can also open earlier Global templates (from Project versions 2002, 2000, 98, 4.1, or 4.0), and transfer objects from your former Global templates into your original Project 2003 Global template. When you open the file, the Organizer is displayed. If you upgrade to Microsoft Project 2003 from an older version of Microsoft Project (2002, 2000, 98, 4.1, or 4.0), customized items in the old Global template are automatically included in the new GLOBAL.MPT file.

Customized views allow the organization to fully exploit the capabilities of the tool, not only in regard to formatting, but also in regard to incorporating company logos, methodologies, and so on. This is a very effective way of standardizing the formatting of project information for both internal and external communications.

4

TIP

> If you make a copy of your GLOBAL.MPT file from an earlier version of Project (that is, 4.0, 4.1, 98, 2000, 2002), name it something like GLOBAL98.MPT, and then open the file in Project 2003, you can distinguish the two Global template files from one another in the Organizer. Otherwise, because the Global files in each version have the same name, it can be confusing which GLOBAL.MPT you are looking at.

The following subsections describe how to access the Organizer through the Tools menu. The steps given here are generic, and they are useful when copying any object managed by the Organizer. The active file—that is, the file that contains the object—is referred to as the *source file*. The file in which you would like to place a copy is referred to as the *target file*.

COPYING OBJECTS BY USING THE ORGANIZER

To copy an object using the Organizer, follow these steps:

1. If you are copying an object to a file other than GLOBAL.MPT, make sure that both the source and target files are open.
2. Choose Tools, Organizer to display the Organizer.

3. Choose the tab that contains the object you want to copy. In Figure 4.11, the Tables tab is selected. The tables in the active file that have been used, altered, or newly created are listed on the right. The tables in the `GLOBAL.MPT` file are listed on the left.

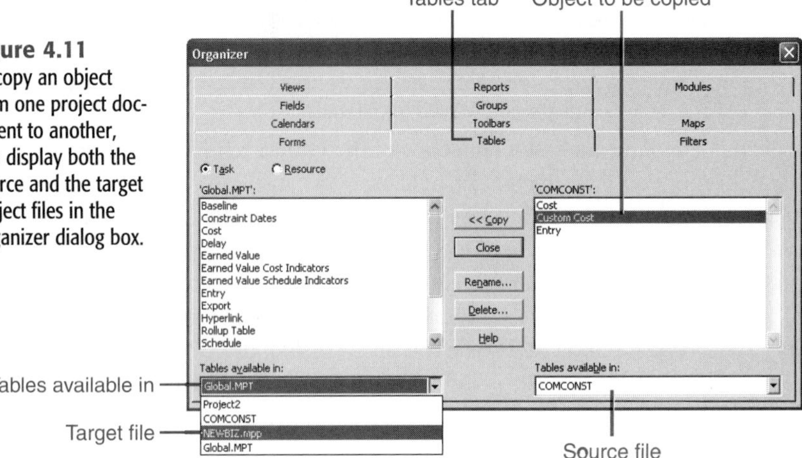

Figure 4.11
To copy an object from one project document to another, you display both the source and the target project files in the Organizer dialog box.

4

If you are copying an object to a file other than `GLOBAL.MPT`, use the Tables available in the drop-down list box on the bottom-left side to choose the target file. On the right side of the dialog box in Figure 4.11, the Custom Cost table is highlighted in the source file (`COMCONST.mpp`), and on the left side of the dialog box, the target file (`NEWBIZ.mpp`) is being selected.

NOTE

You must have the intended Target file open. The Tables available in the drop-down list box lists only files that are currently open.

4. Select the Task option for tables containing task type fields or the Resource option for resource tables containing resource type fields.
5. Choose the table you want to copy from the list of tables in your source file on the right side of the dialog box.
6. Click the Copy button. If there is a table with the same name in the target file, Project asks you for confirmation to override the former table (see Figure 4.12).

Figure 4.12
The Organizer allows you to share objects with other projects or the `GLOBAL.MPT`.

7. Click the Yes button to replace the table in the target file with the new table from the active file.

   Or, you can use the Rename button to copy the table to the target file by using a name that is not already being used.

TIP

> You can also restore an object to its original default state by copying the object from the GLOBAL.MPT file over a customized object in the target file, as long as the object in GLOBAL.MPT has not previously been customized.

8. Click the Close button to close the Organizer dialog box.

Renaming an Object by Using the Organizer

You must use the Organizer if you want to rename an object you created in a project document. To rename an object, follow these steps:

1. Open the Organizer and choose the tab for the object you want to rename.
2. In the project or GLOBAL.MPT file that you want to reflect the change, select the object to be renamed.
3. Click the Rename button. The Rename dialog box appears.
4. Type the new name for the object.
5. Click the OK button to complete the name change.
6. Click the Close button to close the Organizer.

4

NOTE

> GLOBAL.MPT does not automatically update when an object is revised. Changes to a custom object must be recopied to the GLOBAL.MPT file in order to be reflected in new project files. Any existing projects using that object must be updated manually as well.

Deleting an Object by Using the Organizer

Customized objects, such as tables, that you create in a project document cannot be deleted with the same menu or dialog box that you used to create them. You must delete them with the Organizer. To delete an object, follow these steps:

1. Activate the Organizer by choosing Tools, Organizer.
2. Choose the tab for the object you want to delete.
3. In the project or GLOBAL.MPT file that contains the object, select the object you want to delete.
4. Choose the Delete button. A confirmation dialog box appears.

5. Click the Yes button to confirm the deletion.
6. Click the Close button to close the Organizer.

TROUBLESHOOTING

USING THE GLOBAL.MPT FILE

How do I copy my GLOBAL.MPT *file to a disk so that I can share it with someone else?*

GLOBAL.MPT might be located in several locations on your hard drive, depending on which operating system your computer is using. You can easily locate both the original GLOBAL.MPT backup file and the active GLOBAL.MPT file, along with any custom objects that have been copied to it, by using the Microsoft Windows Search feature, which you access by selecting Start, Search, For Files or Folders. It is important that you check the date on which each file was last modified to ensure that you copy the correct one (the original, backup copy is the oldest GLOBAL.MPT file).

PART II

SCHEDULING TASKS

5 Creating a Task List 115

6 Entering Scheduling Requirements 175

7 Viewing Your Schedule 231

CHAPTER 5

CREATING A TASK LIST

In this chapter

Approaching the Planning Process 116

Entering Tasks in a Gantt Chart 118

Understanding the Fields in the Task Table 119

Entering Task Names 123

Editing the Task List 127

Using the Task Information Dialog Box to Edit Tasks 131

Entering Task Duration 132

Defining Milestones 136

Using Recurring Tasks 137

Attaching Notes to Tasks 142

Attaching Hyperlinks to Tasks 147

Using Other Views to Create Tasks 151

Outlining the Task List 154

Using Custom WBS Codes 163

Using Custom Outline Numbers 169

Printing the Project Task List 170

Troubleshooting 170

Project Extras: Letting Project Calculate Duration 171

APPROACHING THE PLANNING PROCESS

After securing approval for a concise but comprehensive goal statement that defines the scope of a project, your next major planning function is to draw up a list of activities, or *tasks*, that must be completed to achieve the project goal.

Microsoft Office Project is a scheduling tool, which addresses only one aspect of the project planning. That planning phase is typically preceded by a project initiation where the scope of the project and its product is defined and refined. Some early stages of the planning process also come before the scheduling itself, such as establishing a project charter, which empowers the project manager to spend some time and budget on achieving the defined scope. As a project manager, you should make sure to have the proper information before creating your schedule, or even your work breakdown structure (WBS).

There are two basic approaches to creating a task list: the top-down approach and the bottom-up approach. In the top-down approach, you start by listing the major *phases* of the project. Then you indent under each major phase the detail tasks that make it possible to complete the phase. The phase then becomes what is called a *summary task*, and the indented detail tasks are called *subtasks*. This method is probably the most common approach to project planning, and it provides an outlined organizational structure that helps people comprehend the scope of the project.

In the bottom-up approach, you begin by listing all the task details. Although it is not required, many people prefer to have the list in a somewhat chronological order. If your project is not too complex, the list might be adequate for understanding the scope of the project. However, for more complex projects, you might need to organize the task list into an outline, so that the end result is similar to the result produced by the top-down approach.

5

Outlining produces an organizational form that is functionally identical to the organizational chart format that is traditionally used by project managers and that is called the *Work Breakdown Structure* (WBS). As shown in Figure 5.1, the WBS identifies major components of a project and shows multiple levels of detail under each major component. WBS codes are traditionally used to number each task in such a way that the code identifies where the task fits into the project's hierarchical structure. In Microsoft Project these codes are by default identical to the outline numbers that are automatically provided for each task. The outline numbers (the default WBS codes) are shown before each task name in Figure 5.2.

The WBS can appear in several formats, the most common of which are the chart format and the outline format. It doesn't matter which format is used; it is simply important to capture the entire scope of work for the project within the WBS. The chart format tends to be favored over the outline format simply because it is easy to add to the list under each element. However, Project doesn't support this type of charting function. Instead, you must do it manually or with some other software package. Using the more prevalent outline format requires pushing tasks down in order to insert additional tasks, regardless of whether the top-down or bottom-up approach is used.

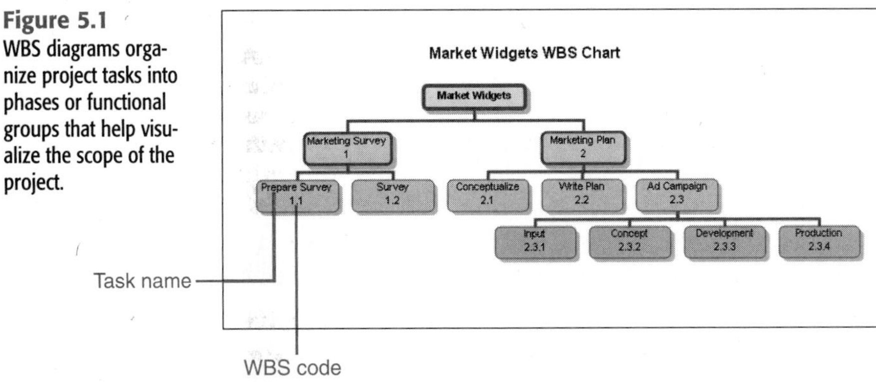

Figure 5.1
WBS diagrams organize project tasks into phases or functional groups that help visualize the scope of the project.

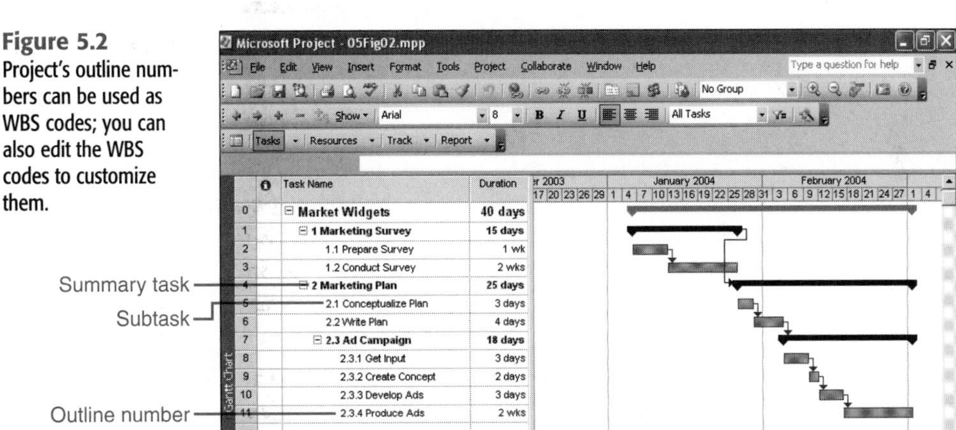

Figure 5.2
Project's outline numbers can be used as WBS codes; you can also edit the WBS codes to customize them.

An outline is not necessary for a complete project plan. However, outlining has many advantages and can significantly enhance a plan's flexibility and usefulness as a planning and reporting tool:

- Outlining encourages an orderly planning process, with less likelihood of leaving out crucial steps.
- You can display outlined projects with different levels of detail, both on the screen and in printed reports. You can collapse the outline to major phases only or to any level of detail, depending on the intended audience.
- Summary tasks in outlined projects automatically provide summary calculations for the subtasks under them. The duration, cost, and work for all the tasks indented beneath them are summed (that is, *rolled up*) into the summary task.

A task list contains three main types of tasks:

- **Normal tasks**—These are tasks that represent the activities that produce the actual work on the project.
- **Milestones**—These are tasks that represent a point in time in the project where a major goal is achieved, a deliverable is completed, or a significant decision point is reached.

- **Summary tasks**—These tasks group together and summarize other tasks that are related in some way. The tasks indented under a summary task are called *subtasks*.

ENTERING TASKS IN A GANTT CHART

You can type a task list directly into a view such as the Gantt Chart view. Alternatively, if the list already exists in another application (such as Excel, Outlook, or Word), you can import or paste a copy of the list into Project. This chapter focuses on typing the list directly into Project.

NOTE

> Project 2003 includes a task list template for Excel called Microsoft Project Task List Import Template, which you can use to create a task list in Excel that you can then import into Project. There is also a new Import Outlook Tasks command on the Tools menu to expedite importing tasks from Outlook. See Chapter 17, "Exporting and Importing Data with Other File Formats," for detailed instructions on importing from other applications.

The Gantt Chart view (see Figure 5.3) is the best view for creating a task list. However, you can use other views, and several are discussed later in this chapter, in the section "Using Other Views to Create Tasks."

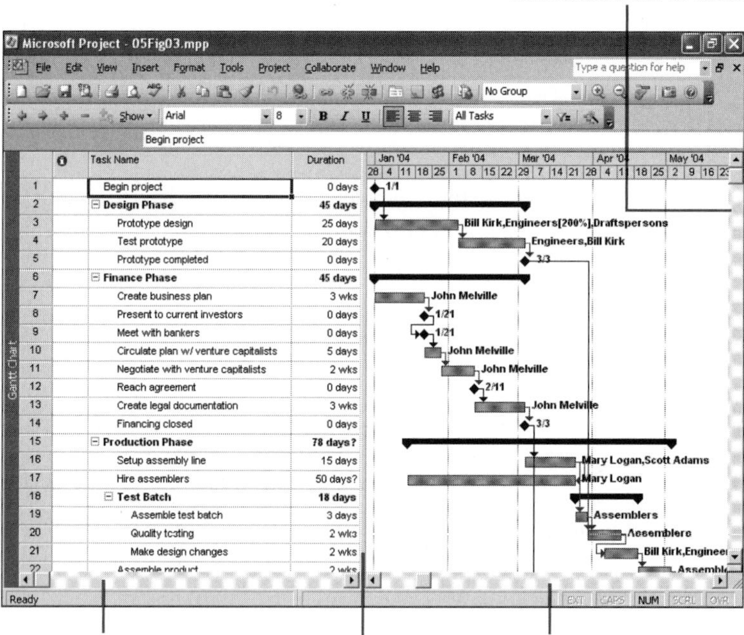

Figure 5.3
The Gantt Chart view is one of the most versatile views in Microsoft Project for managing the task list.

The task table on the left in the Gantt Chart view is ideal for creating and editing the task list. You can edit the list of tasks, easily rearrange their order, and change the outline by indenting and outdenting tasks. You can enter a maximum of 1 million tasks in a single project, so the task table can be expanded to a million rows. You can include up to 65,535 levels of outlining indentation to organize the project into major phases or processes. Pop-up forms are easily accessible for any task to add or view more details than are provided in the table.

→ Microsoft Project provides drag-and-drop features in the Gantt Chart view for moving, copying, outlining, linking, and assigning resources, all of which make editing the task list easier. See "Working with the Gantt Chart View," **p. 232**.

→ There are many options for customizing the Gantt Chart display. If you want to learn more about using those options, **see** "Using the Common Format Options in the Standard Views," **p. 776**, and "Formatting the Gantt Chart View," **p. 790**.

UNDERSTANDING THE FIELDS IN THE TASK TABLE

Before you start creating a list of tasks, you should understand what the columns in the task table on the left of the Gantt Chart view mean because Project supplies default values in most of them as you create task names. You usually have to scroll to the right to see all the columns. Alternatively, you can use the mouse to drag to the right the vertical divider bar that divides the table and the timescale. When you do this, you can see more of the task table and less of the timescale.

By default Project displays the predefined Entry table, which contains columns for the several task fields that provide information like the task name, the start and finish dates, and so forth. The fields shown in the Entry table are briefly described in the following subsections, and full information about using them is presented later in this chapter.

THE ID FIELD

The column of row numbers at the left of the table is known as the ID field. The task ID shows the task's position in the task table and is also used to reference a task. References to a task use the ID number instead of the task name because duplicate task names are permitted. You can't edit the task's ID field directly, but it is automatically recalculated when a task moves to a different row.

NOTE

In addition to the ID number displayed on the screen, there is also a permanent ID number stored in a task field named Unique ID. Project assigns that number when the task is first created, and that number does not change unless you cut and paste the task into a new row, in which case it gets a new unique ID. If a task is deleted, its unique ID is not reassigned. Internally, Project uses the unique ID to identify and link tasks.

5

THE INDICATORS FIELD

The Indicators field is the column headed by an icon that shows a small white letter "i" on a blue circle. This column displays icons that reveal additional information about a task that is not shown in the other columns. For example, a check mark will appear in this column when a task has been completed. Pause the mouse pointer over an indicator to read what the indicator reveals about the task.

THE TASK NAME FIELD

The column headed Task Name contains the text you choose to describe the task. A task name can contain up to 255 characters and, as mentioned previously, does not have to be unique.

➔ For information about showing all the text in long task names, **see** "Displaying Long Task Names," **p. 126**.

In creating a list of task names, you have to exercise judgment about how finely detailed you want the list to be. You should list only tasks that you think it worthwhile to monitor, and only to a level to which you want to manage. Also, you should not include more detail than necessary for activities that are already understood by those who must do the work.

As a rule, tasks should be broken down (decomposed) to no more than 80 hours of effort to complete and no less than 8 hours. This provides the opportunity to take corrective action should the activity take 10%–20% longer (that is, 8–16 hours) than it was originally estimated to take.

THE DURATION FIELD

5

The Duration field is one of the most important fields for scheduling tasks. This field is where you enter an estimate of how long it takes to complete a task. When you first enter a task name, Project supplies the default value 1 day? in the Duration field. The question mark flags this entry as a tentative, estimated duration.

THE START AND FINISH FIELDS

The Start and Finish fields show the date and time when work on a task is scheduled to start or finish. The initial display format for the date fields shows only the date portion of the field, but the field can display the time of day also.

Generally, you should let Project calculate the schedule of task dates for you—after all, that is one of the chief benefits of using project management software. However, you can also enter dates in these fields yourself, although doing so limits Project's capability to calculate a revised schedule if circumstances change. Generally, you should not enter dates in the Start or Finish fields but should instead give Project the information it needs to schedule the dates for you. Until you provide that information (which is the subject of Chapter 6, "Entering Scheduling Requirements"), Project arbitrarily sets the task at either the start or finish of the project.

When you enter a date in the Start or Finish field, the task becomes constrained to the specified date. If you find yourself constantly entering a specific date for the tasks within the project, you are not realizing the benefits of using a project management tool to build a schedule based on estimated durations, logical dependencies, resource assignments, and calendars. In that case, a scheduling tool, such as Microsoft Outlook, might work best for you. Specifying dates in the schedule defeats the purpose of working through the planning process.

THE DEFAULT START AND FINISH DATES

If you have chosen to schedule a project from a fixed start date (called a *forward-scheduled* project), Project normally sets the start for new tasks to be the same as the date and time when the project starts. It then adds the task duration to derive the task finish date and time. If you have chosen to schedule the project from a fixed finish date (that is, a *backward-scheduled* project), Project sets the finish for new tasks to be the date and time when the project finishes, and it subtracts the task duration to derive the task start.

If the project start date is not the current date, the taskbar might not be visible until you scroll to the date for the start of the project.

TIP

You can use the Go To Selected Task button on the Standard toolbar to go to the beginning date for the task that is currently selected. You move the button in the horizontal scrollbar beneath the timescale to the far left or right to go to the start or end of the project.

Instead of scheduling new tasks at the project start or finish, you can optionally tell Project to start new tasks on the current date (that is, the date when you are adding the new task to the project file). For instance, after a project is under way, you might have to add new tasks as circumstances change. In this case, you probably want to have new tasks start on the current date because the project start date is behind you at that point. But for creating a plan for a future project, you want to have new tasks initially set to the project start or finish date.

To set the default start date for new tasks, choose Tools, Options, and select the Schedule tab. Using the drop-down list for New Tasks, choose either Start on Project Start Date or Start on Current Date as the default schedule for new tasks. For projects with fixed finish dates, the choices are either Finish on Project Finish Date or Start on Current Date. (You wouldn't want Project to set the finish of the task on the current date because that would put the start in the past!)

NOTE

Recall from Chapter 3, "Setting Up a Project Document," that the project current date and either the start date or finish date are defined in the Project Information dialog box.

THE DEFAULT TIME OF DAY

Each date field in Project contains both date and time of day components, even when the display of the date is not formatted to show the time of day. The default start date for a task also includes the default start time of day for scheduling the task.

When you don't enter a time of day with a start date, Project appends the default start time (initially 8:00 a.m.). Similarly, if you enter a finish date for a task and don't include the time of day, Project appends the default end time (initially 5:00 p.m.).

You can change the default start time and end time in the Options dialog box (see Figure 5.4).

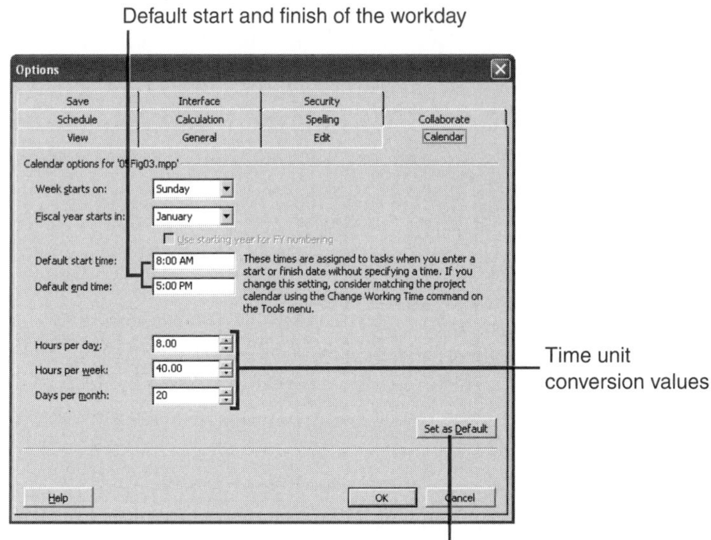

Figure 5.4
You set the default start and end of the workday to determine when Project starts and ends new tasks.

TIP

Even if date fields do not display the time of day, you can enter a time along with the date in any date field. For example, to stipulate that a task should not start before 2:00 p.m. on January 5, 2003, you would enter `1/5/2003 2:00 PM`.

To set the default time of day for starting or finishing new tasks, follow these steps:

1. Choose Tools, Options to display the Options dialog box. Select the Calendar tab.
2. In the Default Start Time field, enter the time of day you want Project to use when you don't include the time of day with a start date.
3. In the Default End Time field, enter the time of day you want Project to use when you don't include the time of day with a finish date.

4. To make these the default values for all new project files that you create, click the Set as Default button. Note that this does not change any existing project files; it only ensures that new project files contain these values.

➔ The default start time for tasks must also be a working hour on the calendar, or else tasks can't actually be scheduled to start at that time. **See** "Defining a Calendar of Working Time," **p. 76**, for help in defining the calendar.

Displaying the Time of Day with Dates

If you want to display the time component of dates, use the Tools, Options command to display the Options dialog box. The Date Format list box on the View tab has a drop-down list of date formats, the first of which contains both date and time.

TIP

If you switch to a longer date format, the Start and Finish fields might display pound signs as an indication that they are not wide enough to display the longer format. You can widen the column by double-clicking the column heading for each field and clicking the Best Fit button.

You can enter time in the 24-hour format, no matter which setting you have chosen in the Control Panel. For example, you can enter January 5, 2003, 3:30 p.m. by typing either **`1/5/2003 3:30 PM`** or **`1/5/2003 15:30`**. If you want to display time in the 24-hour clock format, however, you must select that format in the Windows Control Panel for all applications to use. In the Regional Settings applet, select the Time tab and choose the HH:mm:ss style in the Time Style box.

The Predecessors Field

The Predecessors field shows the ID numbers for any other tasks whose scheduled start or finish must be taken into account before calculating a task's start or finish. For example, if a task must be scheduled to start only after task number 5 is finished, the ID number 5 would appear in that task's Predecessor field. Chapter 6 contains much more information on predecessors.

The Resource Names Field

The Resource Names field shows the names of the resources assigned to work on the task. Part III, "Assigning Resources and Costs," covers resource assignments in more detail.

Entering Task Names

You can create task names by typing into the Task Name field of the Gantt Chart view or by pasting names that you have copied from elsewhere. The most common method is undoubtedly the old-fashioned method—typing—but both methods are described in the following sections.

TYPING TASK NAMES

When you type text into the Task Name field on a blank row, you create a new task. You can use any combination of keyboard characters and spaces, and the name can contain up to 255 characters. You complete the cell entry by pressing Enter, by clicking the green check mark in the Entry bar, or by selecting another cell. You can cancel the cell entry before entering it by pressing the Esc key or by clicking the red X in the Entry bar. In that case, the field reverts to its former contents.

TIP

If you make an entry in *any* field on a blank row of the task table, you create a task, even if it has no task name yet. If you accidentally create a task this way, you can remove it by selecting the ID number and pressing the Delete key.

It is a good practice in building projects to name activities in a verb-noun format, such as Install Computers, Write Design Specifications, or Move Warehouse. By using this concise call-to-action naming convention, it is easy to define the tasks and clearly communicate what work needs to be done in the project. It also makes it easy to estimate task durations by simply asking, "How long does it take to…?"

NOTE

By default Microsoft Office's AutoCorrect feature is enabled in Project. Common errors are corrected as soon as you press the spacebar or type a punctuation mark. Note also that the list of spelling corrections is shared with all Office applications. You can manage the AutoCorrect feature (including disabling it altogether) by choosing Tools, AutoCorrect.

As soon as you press Enter or move to another cell, Project supplies the default duration 1 day? for the new task, and it supplies a default start and finish date for the task. It also displays a taskbar that starts at the project start date under the timescale in the Gantt Chart view, to the right. Then it moves the selection to the next row so that you can enter the next task.

TIP

If you don't want the selection to change when you press Enter, you can disable that feature. Choose Tools, Options and select the Edit tab. Clear the check box for Move Selection After Enter and click OK.

CAUTION

One more time: You should usually avoid changing the start or finish dates in the date columns. They are intended to be calculated by Project, based on the links between tasks that you'll create in Chapter 6. If you enter dates here, a constraint is created that might limit Project's ability to reschedule the task as needed.

→ If you really want to create a constraint for a task, **see** "Entering Task Constraints," **p. 206**.

→ If you have created a task constraint that you want to remove, **see** "Removing Task Constraints," **p. 216**.

NOTE

> You can also use the mouse to create tasks by drawing bars on the Gantt Chart view where there is no task in the table on the left. Although this feature is easy to use, it has drawbacks. You still must go to the table to name the task, and you usually need to adjust the duration of tasks when they are created this way. Also, the task automatically has either a constrained start or finish. If you drag from the start to the finish when creating the bar, the task is constrained to start no earlier than the date where the taskbar starts. If you drag from the finish to the start, the task is constrained to finish no earlier than the finish date. You should rarely create a task by using the mouse.

COPYING TASK NAMES FROM ANOTHER APPLICATION

If task names have already been entered into another application such as a word processor, spreadsheet, or database, you can copy the list to the Windows Clipboard and paste it into Project.

NOTE

> If there is additional information for each task that you want to copy into Project, the process is rather complicated because special data types such as dates and duration must be pasted into the correct columns. **See** "Exchanging Selected Parts of a Project with Other Formats," **p. 649.**

To copy a list of task names from another application into Project, follow these steps:

1. Open both Project and the other application.
2. In the other application, select the list of names you want to copy. Note these requirements for the source list:
   - If the source is a word processing document or presentation document (such as Microsoft Word or Microsoft PowerPoint), each task name must be on a separate row of text.
   - If the source is a spreadsheet (such as Microsoft Excel), each task name must be in a separate cell in a column of entries, and all the names you want to copy must be adjacent to each other.
   - If the source is a database (such as Microsoft Access), the task names must be in a single field of the database. Select the cells in that field only; do not select the records because that would select other fields also, and Project wouldn't know what to do with the other fields.
3. Use the Copy command to copy the list to the Clipboard.
4. Select the cell in the Task Name field in Project where you want to place the first name in the list, and then use the Paste command.

DISPLAYING LONG TASK NAMES

If a task name is too long to see in the Task Name column, you can adjust the width of the column by using the mouse. Drag the right border of the cell that contains the column title to the right or left to change the column width. The pointer changes into a double-headed right and left arrow when it's in position to change the column width. If you double-click instead of drag, Project adjusts the column's width automatically to the longest entry it finds in the column.

If you don't place the mouse pointer directly on the title cell's borderline, the pointer does not change into a double-headed arrow, and double-clicking the mouse opens the Column Definition dialog box (shown in Figure 5.5). If that happens, you can still adjust the column width to the widest entry by clicking the Best Fit button.

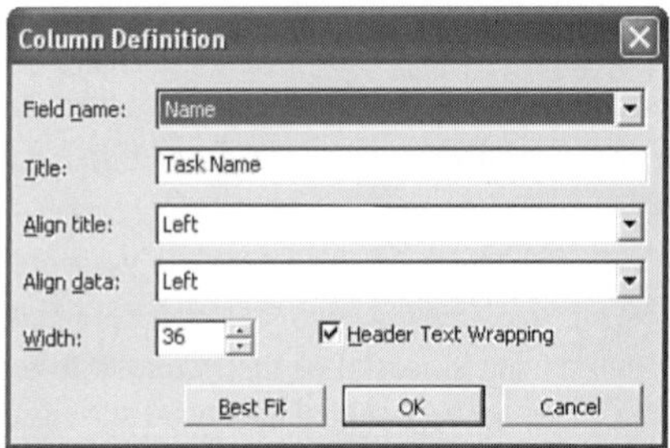

Figure 5.5
You use the Column Definition dialog box for, among other things, adjusting the column width.

ADJUSTING THE HEIGHT OF TASK ROWS

Initially, each row in a table displays a single line of text. In this case, the row height is said to be 1. But you can adjust any or all rows to display variable numbers of text lines. The maximum row height is 20 (that is, 20 lines of text). Project automatically wraps text if extra lines are available and if the text entry is longer than the column width can display. Figure 5.6 shows wrapped task names.

To adjust the height of a row, you drag the bottom (not the top) of the cell that contains the row number down to display more lines or up to display fewer lines. Note that row height is not infinitely variable. It can only be changed in increments of lines of text from 1 to 20.

NOTE

> Unlike with adjusting column widths, you cannot double-click the line dividing row numbers to automatically set the best fit.

You can also change the heights of multiple rows at once. Select the row numbers that you want to change. Use Ctrl+click to select nonadjacent rows. To select all rows, click the Select All button—the blank column header above the row numbers. Drag the bottom of any row number cell to adjust all selected rows to the same height.

→ For information about setting specific row heights for a table, **see** "Using and Creating Tables," **p. 840**.

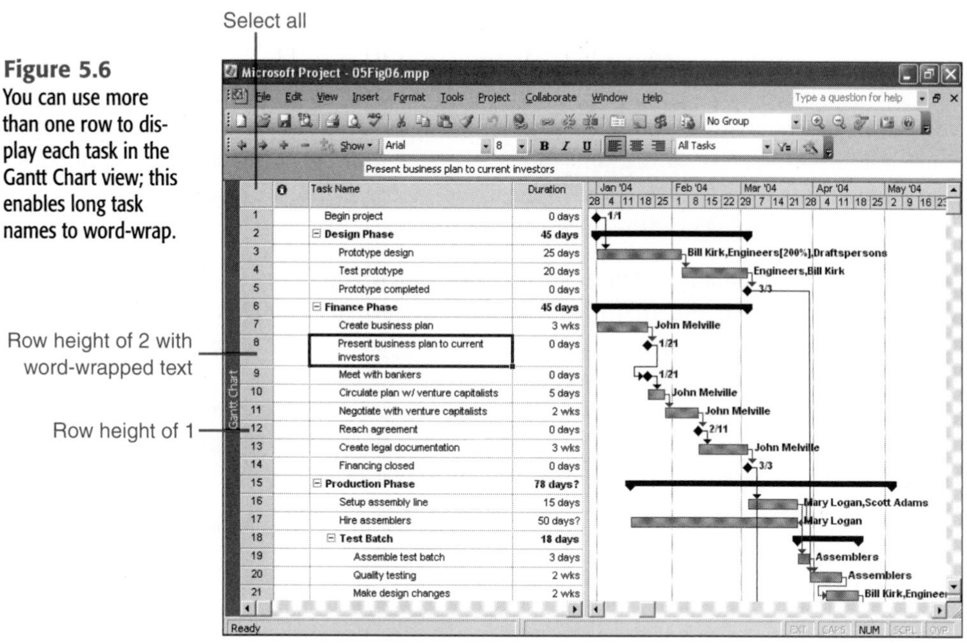

Figure 5.6
You can use more than one row to display each task in the Gantt Chart view; this enables long task names to word-wrap.

EDITING THE TASK LIST

After you start creating a task list, you inevitably need to edit list entries. This section describes a collection of commands and techniques that can be used for editing. These commands and techniques apply to all views, not just the Gantt Chart view.

You can edit cell contents in the Edit bar above the table or directly in the cell. The simplest way to edit the entry directly in the cell is to select the cell and then press the F2 function key. The insertion point appears at the end of the text in the cell, and you can reposition it by clicking elsewhere.

You can also initiate in-cell editing by using a mouse. Select the cell by clicking it once. The mouse pointer should change into an I-beam when it is over the right side of the cell entry or when it is to the left of the beginning of the entry. When the pointer is an I-beam, click; the insertion point appears at the point in the entry where you clicked.

UNDOING CHANGES IN THE TASK LIST

You can undo nearly any change made in the task list by using the Edit, Undo command. However, you can only undo the most recent change. You can also usually reverse the last undo; when you use the Undo command a second time, Project calls the undo a redo. You can also activate Undo by using the Undo tool on the Standard toolbar or by pressing Ctrl+Z.

INSERTING, DELETING, AND CLEARING

As you revise a project, you often need to insert new tasks or remove tasks from the task list. To insert a task between other tasks in Gantt Chart view, first select a cell in the row where you want the new task to appear. New rows are always inserted above the selected one. If you want to insert several tasks at the same location, extend the selection to include the number of rows that you want to add. Choose Insert, New Task (or press the Insert key), and all the details of the tasks included in the selection shift down to make room for new blank rows.

In some previous versions of Project, pressing the Delete key automatically deleted a task if any of its cells were selected. Many unhappy users accidentally deleted tasks when they thought they would simply clear the contents of the selected cell. Pressing the Delete key in Project 2003 only clears the selected cell(s)—unless the Task Name cell is selected. If the Task Name cell is selected, a SmartTag appears to let you choose to clear the cell or delete the task. You can also delete a task by clicking the task ID number and pressing the Delete key. Or, with any cell in the task selected, you can choose Edit, Delete Task, or press Ctrl+–.

You can undo the deletion if you choose Edit, Undo before making another change.

As mentioned previously, you can clear a selected cell by pressing the Delete key. You can also use the Edit, Clear command. The Clear command can remove selected content or features of tasks. The Clear command displays a menu that has the following choices:

- **Formats**—You use Formats to clear only the formatting of the selected cells, leaving their content unchanged.
- **Contents**—You use Contents to clear only the content of the selected field(s). If you have one or more individual cells selected, the command affects only the selected cells. If you have clicked the task ID to select the task row, the command is applied to all task fields—even those that are not displayed in the current view. The shortcut key for clearing contents only is Ctrl+Delete. The Clear Contents command also appears on the shortcut menu when you right-click a cell.
- **Notes**—You use Notes to clear just the Notes field for the task, no matter which cell (or field) you have selected. This option is provided because the Notes field is not usually visible.
- **Hyperlinks**—You use Hyperlinks to clear any hyperlinks that have been attached to the task. The Hyperlinks fields are not readily available, and this option provides an easy way to clear an unwanted hyperlink.
- **All**—You use the All command to execute all the preceding options at once, clearing the formatting, contents, notes, and hyperlinks. If you had the task row selected, this choice would cause Project to clear the contents of all fields but leave the row as a task. It would then immediately reapply the default duration and start and finish dates, even though the task now has no name.
- **Entire Task**—You use Entire Task to clear all cells and fields for the task and leave a blank row that is no longer a task.

NOTE

> You can undo all the Clear commands except for Formats. You can't restore formats that have been cleared.

Moving and Copying Tasks

You can copy or move cells or whole tasks to another location in the task list or to another project file. Whether you are moving or copying, your selection must contain only adjacent cells or tasks.

CAUTION

> If you want to cut or copy an entire task or group of tasks, you must select the entire task by clicking the task ID number or by selecting a cell in the task and pressing Shift+spacebar. This selects all fields for the task (even those not displayed in the current view). If you select a limited number of cells in a task or group of tasks, the cut and copy commands copy to the Clipboard only the data in these cells.

To move or copy a task or group of tasks, follow these steps:

1. Select the original task by clicking its ID number or by selecting any of its cells and pressing Shift+spacebar. To select a group of adjacent tasks, you can click the first task, press and hold the Shift key, and click the last task to be included. All tasks between those two points are included in the selection. You can also use the Shift key with the arrow keys to select adjacent task ID numbers.
2. To move the selection, choose Edit, Cut Task (or press Ctrl+X) or use the Cut Task tool on the Standard toolbar. To copy the selection, choose Edit, Copy Task (or press Ctrl+C) or use the Copy Task tool.
3. Select the task row where you want to relocate the data. Even if you are moving or copying more than one task, select only the first row at the new location. If a task already resides on the row you selected, this task and all tasks below it automatically shift down to make room for the task or tasks you're inserting there.
4. Choose Edit, Paste (or press Ctrl+V) or use the Paste button on the Standard toolbar to paste the task(s) at the selected row. The Paste command inserts a new row or rows at the target selection point and copies the tasks to the inserted rows.

After you copy data to the Clipboard by using the Copy command, you can paste the data multiple times.

If you select just one or more fields for a task instead of selecting the entire task (for example, if you select just the Task Name field), and then you use the Cut or Copy command, the Paste command doesn't insert a new row to create a new task at the target location. Instead, Paste copies the text to the new cell you have selected. If no task exists on the target row, the new entry resulting from the Paste command creates a new task with a default duration.

In addition to the cut-and-copy method for moving and copying, Project also includes drag-and-drop to perform the same commands. To *move* a task or group of tasks by using drag-and-drop, follow these steps:

1. Select the original task entries by clicking the ID number(s) for the tasks. Remember that they must be adjacent rows.
2. Position the mouse pointer over the ID number for any one of the tasks selected; it changes into a four-headed arrow.
3. Hold down the mouse button and drag the pointer in the direction of the new location. A shadowed I-beam appears as you drag the pointer to its destination. Release the mouse when the I-beam is located where you want to insert the selected tasks. The selected tasks are inserted where the I-beam was located.

To *copy* a task or group of tasks by using drag-and-drop, follow the same steps just given, but in step 3, press and hold the Ctrl key as you drag the tasks to the new location.

TIP

> If you move a task by using the cut-and-paste method, the task is really cut from the task list and then a new task is created. Therefore, the new task gets its own unique ID number. However, the unique ID doesn't change if you sort the task list, insert or delete other tasks above it, or use the mouse to drag the task to a new row. This might be important when you're comparing versions of a project file.

Using the Fill Command

5

If you want several cells in a column to have the same value (for example, many tasks with the same duration), you can place that value in one cell and have Project copy it to other selected cells, either below it or above it. You first select the cell with the value to be copied and then, while holding your mouse click, select cells above it or select cells below it that are to receive a copy of the value. You use Ctrl+click to add nonadjacent cells to the selection. When you do so, one of the following happens:

- If the selected cells are all adjacent, the cell with the value to be copied can be the top cell or the bottom cell in the selection. Choose Edit, Fill, Down to copy the value in the top cell of the selection down to the rest of the selection. Use Edit, Fill, Up to copy the value in the bottom cell up to the rest of the selection. Fill Down has a shortcut key combination—Ctrl+D.
- If the selected cells are not all adjacent, the cell with the value to be copied must be the top cell in the selection. Choose Edit, Fill, Down to copy the value in the top cell down to the rest of the selection.

You can also drag a cell's *fill handle* (that is, the small black square in the lower-right corner of the cell) to copy the cell's value to adjacent cells above or below the cell. When the mouse points to the fill handle, it turns into a plus sign (+). You can click the fill handle and drag the mouse to adjacent cells.

USING THE TASK INFORMATION DIALOG BOX TO EDIT TASKS

You can quickly see more fields of information about a task in any task view by selecting the task and then displaying the Task Information dialog box (see Figure 5.7). The Task Information dialog box provides a fast way to modify task details when the current view doesn't display the field(s) you want to edit.

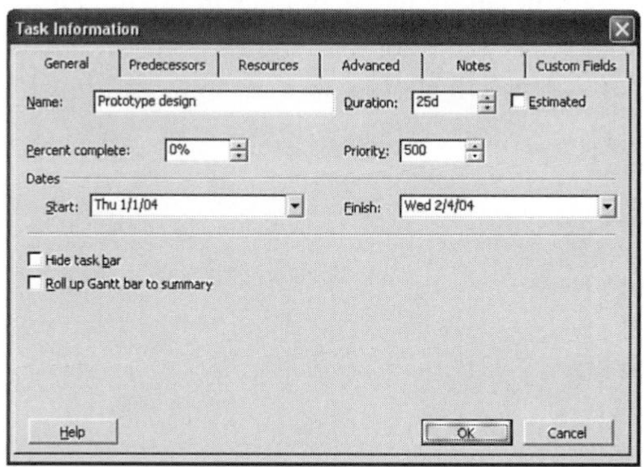

Figure 5.7
You use the Task Information dialog box for quick access to commonly used task fields that are not available in the view you are currently using.

WORKING WITH THE TASK INFORMATION DIALOG BOX

To display the Task Information dialog box, click the Task Information tool on the Standard toolbar, or choose Project, Task Information from the menu. You can also simply double-click the task name.

Six tabs organize the task fields in the Task Information dialog box: General, Predecessors, Resources, Advanced, Notes, and Custom Fields. These tabs contain additional details about the task that is selected, and most of these fields are not immediately available on the Gantt Chart view. In fact, no one predefined view contains all the fields you find in the Task Information dialog box. (All the fields found on the various tabs are explained in this and later chapters.)

You can click the tab that contains the field you want to edit, or you can use Ctrl+Tab or Ctrl+Shift+Tab to cycle through the tabs and select the tab you want to use. You can then move from field to field with the Tab and Shift+Tab keys, or you can move directly to a field by clicking it. You can also move directly to a field by pressing the Alt key plus the underlined letter in the field label. You press Alt+D, for example, to move directly to the Duration text box.

When you are finished, click OK to accept the changes or click Cancel (or press Esc) to close the dialog box without changing anything.

USING THE MULTIPLE TASK INFORMATION DIALOG BOX

An important feature of the Task Information dialog box is its ability to make an identical change in several tasks at once. If you select multiple tasks before activating the dialog box, the Multiple Task Information dialog box appears (see Figure 5.8). Any entry you make is copied to all the tasks you selected. For example, to assign a duration estimate of 2 weeks to several tasks at once, select the tasks and then choose the Task Information button on the Standard toolbar. (The double-click method does not work when multiple tasks are selected.) Enter the duration on the General tab and click OK to close the dialog box. The duration for each of the selected tasks changes to 2 weeks.

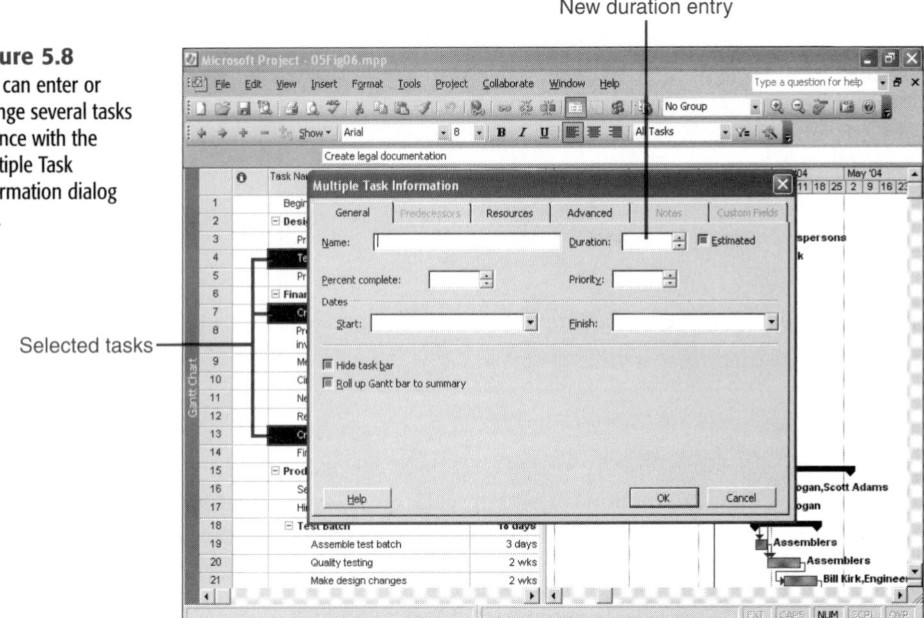

Figure 5.8
You can enter or change several tasks at once with the Multiple Task Information dialog box.

ENTERING TASK DURATION

The project calendar defines the hours and days when work can be scheduled on a project (see the section "Defining a Calendar of Working Time" in Chapter 3). The *duration* of a task refers to the amount of time that is scheduled on the project calendar for work on the task. A task with an estimated duration of 8 hours is scheduled for work during 8 hours of time on the project calendar. There might be one person or many people assigned during those 8 hours, but the duration is still 8 hours.

When you estimate the duration of a task to be, say, 8 hours, you should keep these points in mind:

- The working hours do not have to be continuous, although Project initially assumes that they are the first available hours for work on the calendar following the start of the task. You can later modify the schedule so that the task could be worked on for 1 hour per day for 8 days. The duration (that is, the amount of time spent working on the task) would still be the same.

- A task that is completed by one person working on it full-time for 8 hours has a duration of 8 hours. But so does a task that is completed by five people working on it full-time for 8 hours. Duration doesn't measure the total amount of work or effort needed to complete the task; it measures the number of units of time on the calendar that are scheduled for work on the task.
- When estimating durations, you should consider past experience with similar tasks, the experience and skill level of the resources you plan to use, and the number of resources you plan to use. You need to remember these assumptions when you later assign the resources to the task, so you can assign the same number you were thinking about when you estimated the duration. If you are not assigning resources as you estimate the task duration, you might want to use the Notes field to remind yourself of the resource configuration you assumed for the duration estimate. For more information, see the section "Attaching Notes to Tasks," later in this chapter.

NOTE

> If you already have predetermined dates for starting and finishing all your tasks, you can enter those dates in the Task Form view and let Project calculate the duration implied by the dates; see "Project Extras: Letting Project Calculate Duration," at the end of this chapter.

USING TENTATIVE DURATION ESTIMATES

When you create a task, Project tentatively assigns the task a default duration of 1 day and displays the duration as 1 day?, with the question mark to indicate that it is a tentative, *estimated duration*. When you overwrite the default value with your own (hopefully) informed estimate of duration, the question mark goes away.

TIP

> You can use the question mark with your own duration estimates. If you want to enter a tentative duration value that you want to reconsider at a later time, you can add a question mark to your entry as a reminder. You can use the Tasks with Estimated Durations filter to display all the duration estimates that are tentative.

→ If you want to use the Tasks with Estimated Durations filter or other filters for tasks, **see** "Working with the Gantt Chart View," **p. 232**.

NOTE

> If you have reliable duration estimates from past experience, you can improve the reliability of your duration estimates by using Project's PERT Analysis toolbar. PERT analysis is discussed in detail in the article "Using PERT Analysis," which is available at `www.quehelp.com`.

UNDERSTANDING THE DURATION TIME UNITS

Project offers considerable flexibility in the time units you can use to express duration. The default time unit is days, but you can also use minutes, hours, weeks, or months. When you type a duration value and attach one of these time units, Project displays the duration, using the time unit you type in. However, if you enter a value in the duration column without appending a time unit, Project appends the *default duration time unit* to your entry and displays the value with that time unit. Project also uses the default time unit for duration when it creates the default duration value for a new task. Initially, the default time unit is days.

If you want to change the default time unit for the Duration field, open the Options dialog box by selecting Tools, Options, and select the Schedule tab. The Duration Is Entered In textbox has a drop-down list of the possible time units that you can use (Minutes, Hours, Days, Weeks, or Months).

When you enter a duration estimate using day, week, or month units, Project internally converts these units to minutes because it does its calculations in minutes. Project bases its conversion to minutes on the assumption that an hour is always 60 minutes and on the definitions for the other time units found in the Options dialog box, Calendar tab (refer to Figure 5.4). The default conversion rates are as follows:

- 1 day = 8 hours
- 1 week = 40 hours (or five 8-hour days)
- 1 month = 20 days (or 160 hours)

If an organization works six 8-hour days a week, you would want to adjust the definition of a week to be 48 hours. Then, when you enter a duration of 1 week, Project knows your frame of reference, and it stores 48 hours for the duration. Similarly, if your organization works four 10-hour days a week, you would want to change the definition of a day to 10 hours but leave the definition of a week at 40 hours.

5

To redefine the conversion rates for duration time units, follow these steps:

1. Choose Tools, Options to display the Options dialog box.
2. Select the Calendar tab.
3. Enter the number of work hours in a day in the Hours per Day field.
4. Calculate the number of work hours in a week and enter that number in the Hours per Week field.
5. Decide on the number of days you want Project to use when you enter the month time unit, and enter that number in the Days per Month field.
6. Click OK to save your definitions.

USING TIME UNIT ABBREVIATIONS

When entering duration units, you can use the complete word or either of two abbreviations. For example, to enter 1 day you can type **1 d**, **1 dy**, or **1 day**. Project also supports plural versions of the time units. The following is the full list of spellings Project supports for the time units:

- m, min or mins, minute or minutes
- h, hr or hrs, hour or hours
- d, dy or dys, day or days
- w, wk or wks, week or weeks
- mo, mon or mons, month or months

Although you can use any of the spellings when you enter duration values, Project uses a default spelling for displaying each of the time units. For example, if you set the default display for weeks to wk, no matter whether you enter **w**, **wk**, or **week**, Project displays the result as wk (or its plural, wks).

You can select the default spelling for the time units by choosing Tools, Options to display the Options dialog box. Select the Edit tab, and use the drop-down lists in the View Options for the Time Units section to select the default spellings.

NOTE

> The Years field setting has nothing to do with duration time units. It is used exclusively to enter pay rates for resources who are paid on an annual basis.

DEFINING ELAPSED DURATION

The duration values discussed thus far in this chapter have referred to an amount of time to be scheduled on the project calendar. The project calendar has nonworking time (night, weekends, and holidays) around which the regular duration must be scheduled.

5

You can also schedule a task that has *continuous*, or uninterrupted, activity around the clock. For example, if a chemical process takes 5 hours, that usually means 5 continuous hours. If you schedule the process to start at 3:00 p.m., it needs to continue until 8:00 p.m. the same day. However, if the Working Time calendar in Project has been set up to show that work stops at 5:00 p.m., Project would schedule the task to stop at 5:00 p.m. and resume the following workday at 8:00 a.m.

To schedule a task that should not be restricted by the working time calendar, enter the duration as *elapsed duration*. To do this, insert the letter *e* before the time unit abbreviation (for example, **5eh**). Project would then schedule the chemical process described previously to continue until 8:00 p.m., as needed.

NOTE

> The elapsed day is defined as 24 hours, the elapsed week is 168 hours (that is, seven 24-hour days). The elapsed month is arbitrarily 720 hours (thirty 24-hour days).

CAUTION

> You should be cautious in your use of elapsed duration for tasks with resources assigned to them. The resource calendar (which governs when Project can assign work to the resource) may not allow the resource to be scheduled outside the normal workday. You may have to assign overtime to the resource or modify the resource calendar in order to staff the task. Instead of using elapsed duration, you might consider assigning a *task calendar* to the task–one that has been defined with extended working time. Using a task calendar gives you the option to tell Project that it should ignore the resource calendar in scheduling work. See Chapter 9, "Understanding Resource Scheduling," for more information on resource scheduling. See Chapter 6 for more information on task calendars.

Figure 5.9 illustrates the differences between normal and elapsed duration. Task ID number 1 is a task with normal 5-day duration. Work begins on a Thursday but is interrupted by the weekend. Work is continued on the following Monday and continues through Wednesday, for a total of 5 workdays. The taskbar looks longer (7 calendar days) than the 5 workdays because it spans the shaded nonworkdays defined in the calendar. Total work during the period is 40 hours (that is, five 8-hour workdays).

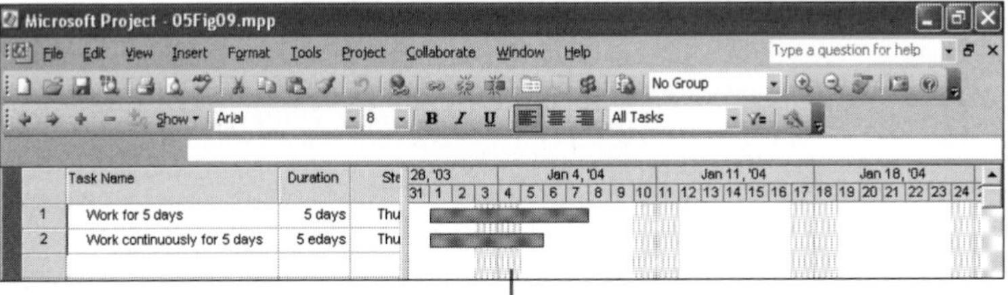

Figure 5.9
Work on elapsed duration tasks proceeds through nonworking times and continues for 24 hours per day until complete.

Task ID number 2 is a task with an elapsed duration of 5 days. Project schedules work on the task around the clock for five 24-hour time periods. Work continues through weekend days and holidays. Total work during the period is 120 hours (that is, five 24-hour workdays).

DEFINING MILESTONES

A *milestone* represents a significant landmark, decision point, or turning point in the life of the project. You commonly use milestones to mark the completion of major phases, dates for deliverables, or other major events in the project. The great advantage of defining milestones is that you can filter the task list to show only the milestones, thereby seeing instantly the important dates that they represent.

You should create milestone tasks at points you want to monitor closely in a project. In a project to construct a building, for example, one milestone might be the completion of all the tasks involved in laying the foundation. The milestone could be named Foundation Completed and have a duration of zero.

To create a milestone, you enter the number `0 (zero)` in the Duration field for the task. That causes Project to classify the task as a milestone.

You can also use the Project Guide to mark a task as a milestone. Choose Tasks from the Project Guide toolbar and select List the Tasks in the Project in the sidepane. Select the task to be marked as a milestone and fill the Milestone check box, or clear the check box to remove the milestone status of a task.

You can use the Task Information dialog box to change the milestone status of a task. Click the Task Information button on the Standard toolbar, or double-click the task name. Choose the Advanced tab and click the Mark Task as Milestone check box to change its milestone status. Choose OK to close the dialog box.

The default Gantt Chart view displays a milestone as a diamond shape, without a duration bar (see Figure 5.10). You can modify the symbol for a milestone and for all other taskbars by using the Format, Bar Styles command in the Gantt Chart view.

→ To learn how to change the display for milestones, **see** "Formatting the Gantt Chart View," **p. 790**.

Figure 5.10 illustrates the power of using milestones. This view of the project displays the entire project on one screen, and it has been filtered to show only the milestones. In one glance you can see all the important dates for the project.

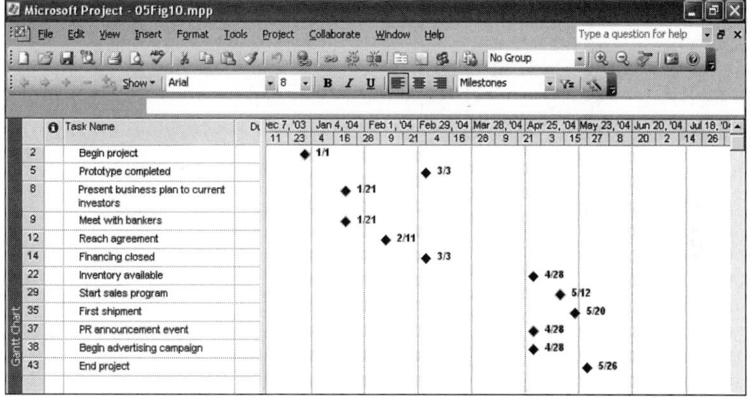

Figure 5.10
Using milestones highlights the major events in a project.

→ For instructions on creating a view like that shown in Figure 5.10, **see** "Working with the Gantt Chart View," **p. 232**.

Although you can mark a task that has nonzero duration as a milestone, it's not a good practice because doing so causes you to lose the normal taskbar for the task and is very misleading.

USING RECURRING TASKS

If you have one or more tasks that need to be repeated regularly during the life of a project, you can enter them as *recurring tasks*. For example, you might want to schedule weekly project status meetings every Monday from 4:00 p.m. to 5:00 p.m. Other examples could be monthly inspections or biweekly equipment maintenance.

Recurring tasks are a great way to capture time and effort on a project and do not have to be specifically tied to work-related tasks. Status meetings are the most common use of this feature of the software, but other uses include quality reviews, risk assessment, and change review meetings.

CREATING RECURRING TASKS

To insert a recurring task in a task list, follow these steps:

1. Select the Task Name field on the row where you want to insert the recurring task. You don't have to create a blank row for each recurring task; each row is inserted automatically, and the row you have selected is pushed down to make room for it.
2. Choose Insert, Recurring Task. The Recurring Task Information dialog box appears (see Figure 5.11).
3. Type the task name in the Task Name text box and the duration of each occurrence of the task in the Duration box.
4. From the Recurrence Pattern group of controls, choose a general frequency: Daily, Weekly, Monthly, or Yearly. In Figure 5.11, the Weekly option has been selected.

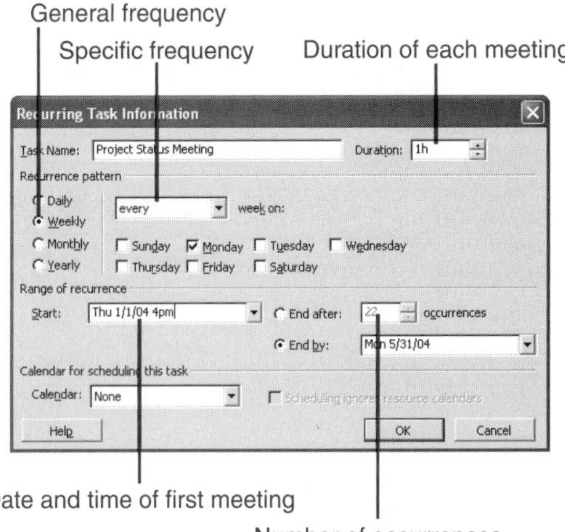

Figure 5.11
You use the Recurring Task Information dialog box to add tasks that repeat regularly.

5. Define the specific frequency in the group of options to the right of the general frequency selection. This group varies, depending on the general frequency you choose. If you choose Weekly, you can use the Week On drop-down list to specify a frequency ranging from every week to every 12th week. Then, select the day of the week on which you want to schedule the tasks. The specific frequency choices for Daily, Monthly, and Yearly are discussed later in this section.
6. Next, define how often the task is repeated by defining the date range within which the tasks should be scheduled or by specifying the number of times you want the task scheduled. Project shows the projected number of occurrences in the Occurrences box.

NOTE

Initially, the Start and End By text boxes show the start and finish dates for the project, and the End After <*nn*> Occurrences box shows the calculated number of occurrences that can be scheduled in that date range.

If you want the first occurrence of the recurring task to start some time after the project starts, change the Start date. Specify a start date in the Start box. If you want the tasks to be scheduled at a specific time of day, enter the time as well as the date in the Start text box. To select a date from a calendar, click the drop-down arrow.

Change the End By date if you want to specify when the last occurrence of the recurring task should be scheduled. Alternatively, select the End After <*nn*> Occurrences option and enter a number to specify how many occurrences are to be scheduled.

CAUTION

If you enter a number larger than the calculated default, Project schedules the number of occurrences you enter, but the later occurrences are beyond the original finish date of the project, which extends the duration of your project.

7. If you have a special task calendar you have created for scheduling the recurring task, select its name in the Calendar box. Task calendars are covered in Chapter 6.

→ If you want to create and assign a special calendar for a task, **see** "Creating and Using Task Calendars," **p. 223**.

8. Each resource you assign to a task has its own calendar of available working times. If you assign a calendar to the task, you can select Scheduling Ignores Resource Calendars if you want Project to ignore the availability of assigned resources when scheduling the recurring task. This is useful when you expect resources to work on the task some but not all the time (for example, to attend some but not all the meetings).

→ To learn how to define resources and their working times, **see** "Understanding Resources and Costs," **p. 279**.

9. Click OK or press Enter to complete the recurring task definition.

Sometimes, your definition of a recurring task might lead Project to place a task on a non-workday. If this occurs, Project warns you (see Figure 5.12) and asks you how to proceed:

- Click Yes to let Project reschedule the affected tasks at the earliest available working time.
- Click No to skip those dates and leave those tasks out of the series of recurring tasks.
- Click Cancel to stop the creation of the recurring tasks altogether.

When you have entered the recurring task, it is placed in the task list as a specially formatted *summary task* (see Figure 5.13). Like all summary tasks, this one spans multiple subtasks; in this case, it extends from the beginning of the first meeting to the end of the last meeting. The formatting for this summary task is the special *rollup* formatting: instead of being one solid bar, it shows short segments that represent the scheduled times for the subtasks.

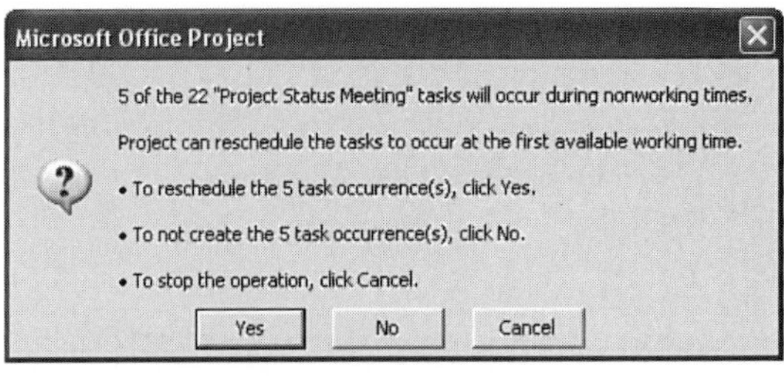

Figure 5.12
Microsoft Project adjusts recurring tasks to the working calendar.

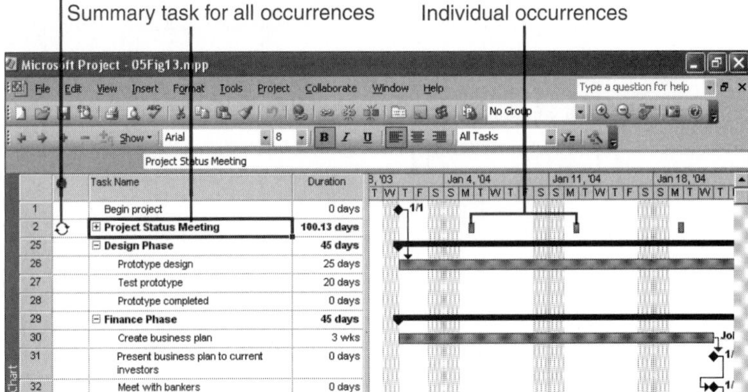

Figure 5.13
The summary task for a recurring task displays the rolled-up schedule for all the subtasks on a single row of the Gantt Chart.

TIP

> An icon representing recurring tasks is displayed in the Indicators column to the left of the task name (refer to Figure 5.13). If you point to the indicator with the mouse, Project displays a ScreenTip showing the number of occurrences and the overall date range for the group of tasks.

Unlike the duration of normal tasks, the duration of a summary task is the amount of working time on the project calendar from the start of the first subtask (in this case, the first occurrence) to the end of the last subtask (that is, the last occurrence). In Figure 5.13, the Duration column for the recurring task shows 100.13 days, but this doesn't mean that those who attend the meetings log a total of 100.13 days of meeting time. Rather, the last meeting ends 100.13 workdays after the first meeting begins. Remember, there were 21 meetings in this example (see the Occurrences box in Figure 5.11). That's one meeting per week (every 5 days). The start of the last meeting is exactly 20 weeks after the start of the first meeting (100 days). The finish of the last meeting is another hour later, which is 1/8, or .125, day (which Project rounds to .13).

In Figure 5.13, the task ID numbers 3 through 23 do not appear. That's because the summary task for the recurring task has hidden subtasks (the individual meetings that are currently hidden from view). Each of the subtasks is *rolled up* to the summary taskbar.

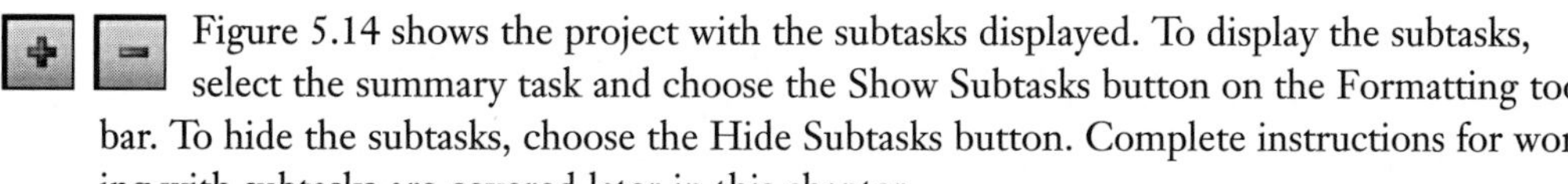

Figure 5.14 shows the project with the subtasks displayed. To display the subtasks, select the summary task and choose the Show Subtasks button on the Formatting toolbar. To hide the subtasks, choose the Hide Subtasks button. Complete instructions for working with subtasks are covered later in this chapter.

Hide/Show subtasks

Constraint indicator

Figure 5.14
You can display and hide the subtasks (that is, recurring tasks) by clicking the outline symbol to the left of the summary task or by double-clicking the task ID number.

NOTE

You can link individual occurrences of the recurring task to other activities in the project. To create the link, you must show the subtasks as described previously. See the section "Entering Dependency Links," in Chapter 6 for more information.

CAUTION

Each of the subtasks in a recurring task is constrained to start no earlier than its scheduled date. Constraints can create problems in a schedule if you make major changes in the project schedule. To learn more about working with task constraints, see the section "Entering Task Constraints," in Chapter 6.

The steps outlined previously describe how to create weekly recurring tasks. The process for creating daily, monthly, and yearly recurring tasks is equally flexible and very similar. The Recurring Task Information dialog box changes based on the general frequency you select.

EDITING RECURRING TASKS

If you select the summary task for a recurring task and choose the Information button, the Recurring Task Information dialog box appears, as though you were beginning to create the recurring task. After you make changes, click OK. A Microsoft Project warning message warns you that Project will change the frequency of the recurring task (see Figure 5.15). Click OK if you do not mind losing the existing subtasks that need to be deleted to change the frequency of the recurring task.

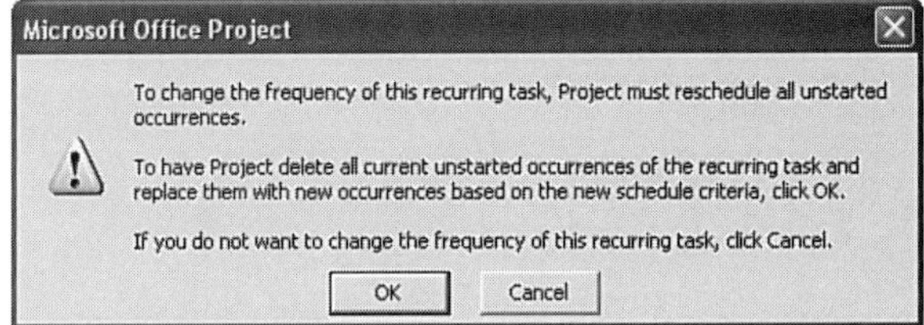

Figure 5.15
Project must delete the existing tasks if you change the frequency of a recurring task.

ATTACHING NOTES TO TASKS

Providing good documentation about the details of a project is a hallmark of good project management. These notes are invaluable in a complex project because without them you can easily forget details about why you made specific decisions. They also provide essential information to other users of the project file or to your successor, should you move on to other duties.

5

Include in your notes any assumptions that you make about the tasks and any reminders you need to document. Figure 5.16 shows a note for the Prototype Design task. You can also include the notes in printed reports by choosing File, Page Setup and selecting the Print Notes check box on the View tab.

In addition to providing background information on a task, notes can be inserted regarding changes made to scope and the impact on the estimated durations. Scope creep is a significant cause of project overruns in both time and costs and should be well documented within a project, especially when examining variance (that is, the difference between the current schedule and baseline). For this reason, notes can also be printed as an addendum page to the project plan.

Tasks with notes attached display the Task Notes icon in the Indicators column to the right of the ID number in table views. The ScreenTip for the icon displays the beginning of the note's text.

TYPING AND FORMATTING NOTES

To enter notes for tasks, choose Tasks on the Project Guide toolbar and select Link To or Attach More Task Information in the sidepane. Select the task and choose Add a Note. This takes you directly to the Notes tab of the Task Information dialog box.

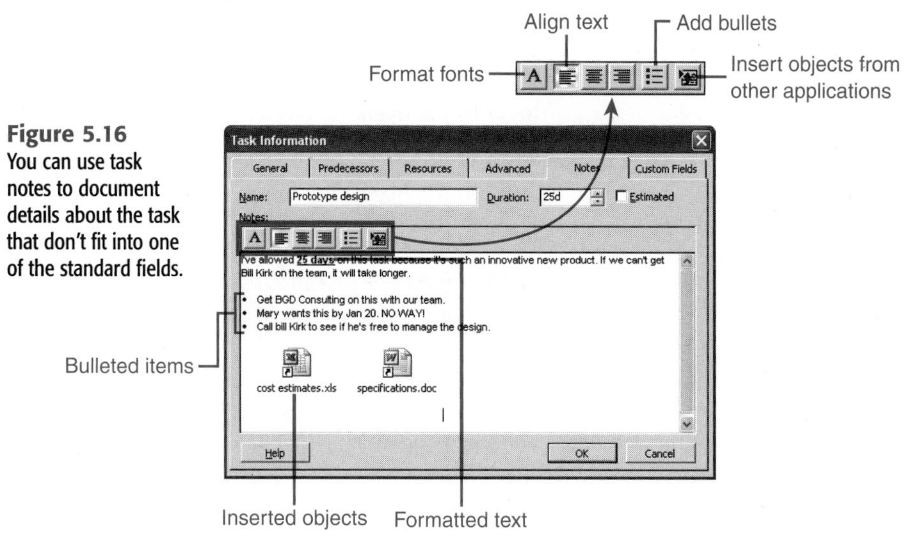

Figure 5.16
You can use task notes to document details about the task that don't fit into one of the standard fields.

You can click the Task Notes button on the Standard toolbar to go directly to the Notes tab and type a note in the Notes text box. Project automatically wraps text as you type. Notes can contain hundreds of thousands of characters; but if you have that much to record, you should probably insert a link to an external document, as described in the next section.

A toolbar at the top of the Notes text box provides formatting options for the notes (refer to Figure 5.16). You can change the font and alignment for the notes, create a bulleted list, and even insert images or documents from other applications. You can also use the conventional Microsoft shortcut keys for bold (Ctrl+B), italics (Ctrl+I), and underline (Ctrl+U).

CAUTION

> Although you can type thousands of characters in a note, Project's ability to search the Notes field to find specific text is limited. For one thing, Project searches only the first 255 characters in each note. Project also stops the search as soon as it encounters most non-printable characters. It is really best to keep most extensive text in linked documents that reside outside Project. See the section "Inserting Objects in Notes" later in this chapter.

TIP

> To avoid the problem where the Find command stops searching a note when it encounters the Enter key, use Shift+Enter when you want to start a new line or paragraph.

You can use the following keys to move through the Notes text box:

Key	Effect
Home	Moves to the beginning of the current line
End	Moves to the end of the current line
Ctrl+Home	Moves to the beginning of the note
Ctrl+End	Moves to the end of the note
Ctrl+left arrow	Moves one word to the left
Ctrl+right arrow	Moves one word to the right

You can use drag-and-drop to edit notes. After selecting a word or group of words, you can drag the selection to a new location within the note. If you want to copy the selection, hold down the Ctrl key as you drag the note to the new location.

The notes editor that Project uses has multiple levels of Undo and Redo (although Project itself has only one level). However, the Undo/Redo stack of actions is lost as soon as you click OK after editing a note.

INSERTING HYPERLINKS IN NOTES

You can store hyperlinks to Internet sites in a note. However, Project does not help you create the hyperlink by displaying a browser history list or list of Favorites. You must type the text of the hyperlink into the note in the usual format (for example, `http://www.`*`sitename`* or `ftp://ftp.`*`sitename`*). Project displays the hyperlink with the underline and color the machine uses for displaying hyperlinks, and when you click the hyperlink, the browser goes to the indicated Web page. For information on more flexible hyperlink capabilities, see "Attaching Hyperlinks to Tasks," later in this chapter.

5

INSERTING OBJECTS IN NOTES

You can insert data objects from other applications into a note. An *object* is a data file in the file format that another application maintains (pictures, spreadsheets, word processing documents, presentations, sound files, video clips, and so on). For instance, you could insert an Excel worksheet within a note and edit the worksheet from within the note to show calculations you need to keep handy.

Examples of objects that can be inserted include reference documents required at the start of a task and work products, which can be deliverables of task completion. Including these items assists with the knowledge transfer processes that are often lacking within organizations. It also helps prevent people from reinventing the wheel with each new project.

You can create a new object or insert one that already exists as a file. If the object already exists, you have the option to insert the object file itself or to insert only a *link* to the object. If you insert the object itself (called *embedding* the object), you increase the size of the project file by the size of the object file. Embedding many such objects can quickly bloat a project file and affect performance.

If you merely insert a link to an object, the object resides outside the project file, and the size of the project file is affected only minimally. Project opens the object when you click the link so that you can view or edit the object's contents. Any changes you make are saved outside Project. This is clearly the best option if the object is a document that others need to be able to see and edit. Clicking the link always opens the current version of the document; on the other hand, if you embed the document, you cannot see changes made by other people.

The Task Information form does not expand to provide an adequate display area for viewing large objects. Consequently, with large objects, you probably only want to display an icon for the object in the note instead of the object itself. You can double-click the icon, and Project opens the application and lets you read or edit the data as needed.

➔ For more information on working with objects, **see** "Working with Objects," **p. 703**.

To insert a data object in a note, follow these steps:

1. Select the location where you want to insert the object and open the Insert Object dialog box by clicking the Insert Object tool or by right-clicking and choosing Object in the shortcut menu.

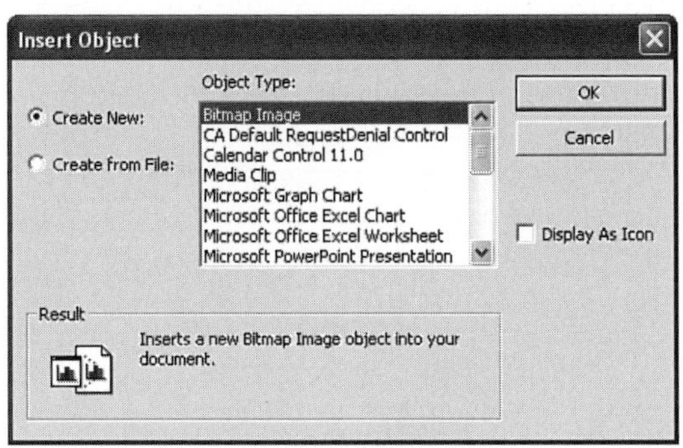

Figure 5.17
You select the object to display and how it's displayed in the Insert Object dialog box.

2. Choose Create New to insert a blank object that you can design and edit only from within Project. Then use the Object Type list to select the application to create the object.
3. Choose Create from File to insert an object that is already saved as a file (see Figure 5.18). Type the path and filename for the object in the File box, or click the Browse button to select the file from the directory structure.

   You can also use this step to create a new file on-the-fly and insert it as an object. After browsing to the folder where the file is to be stored, right-click over a blank space in the file list, select New from the shortcut menu, and select the application that will create the file. Replace the default name for the new file with the name you want to use and click Insert. After you finish step 6, you can double-click the object to create the data it should contain.

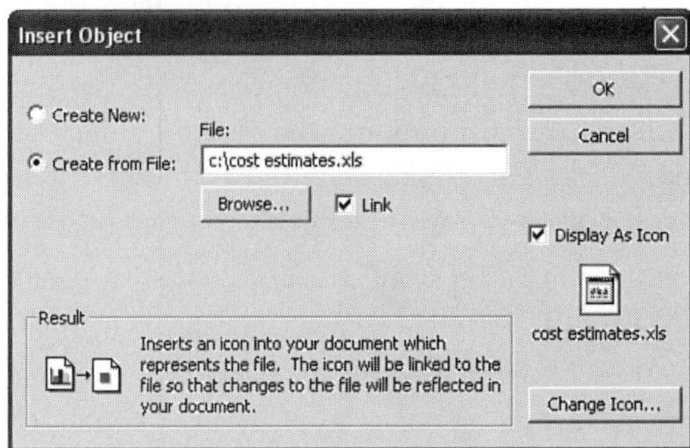

Figure 5.18
You can insert in a note copies of files or links to the most current versions of files.

4. Select the Link check box if you want to insert only a link to the object. When you click the object or its icon, Project opens the current version of the file for you. Deselect the Link check box if you want to store a permanent copy of the object as it now exists in the project file.
5. Check Display as Icon to display an icon for the object in the Notes text box instead of displaying the contents of the object. For most objects, it is better to simply display the icon and double-click it when you want to see the contents of the object.
6. Click OK to store the object in the note.

CAUTION

If you insert the Notes field as a column in a table, be aware that editing the note in the table causes you to lose any objects that have been inserted. Fortunately, a warning message appears to remind you of the danger.

Attaching Notes to the Overall Project

You can attach a note to an entire project instead of to a particular task. For a very short or simple note, you can use the File, Properties command to display the Properties dialog box. The Comments text box on the Summary tab displays the note that is attached to the project. However, you can't work with objects in this dialog box.

For more substantial notes, it's best to display the project summary task and use the Task Information dialog box to display the Notes tab. To display the project summary task, choose Tools, Options and select the Show Project Summary Task check box on the View tab. You can then select that task and display its Task Information dialog box to enter the notes.

CAUTION

If you insert objects in the project summary task note, they will be lost if you later edit the note in the Comments text box on the File, Properties dialog box. When you click OK after editing the Comments box, you should receive a warning that objects will be lost if you change the note. You can then choose No to cancel the changes. For this reason, some users create a milestone task at the top or bottom of the task list to hold a note that contains links to important documents.

NOTE

If you are using Project Server for collaboration, you should store objects that other team members should be able to see in SharePoint Team Services. For more information, see Chapter 24, "Introduction to Microsoft Office Project Server 2003."

Attaching Hyperlinks to Tasks

In addition to storing hyperlinks to Web sites in the Notes field, you can use the Hyperlink field for storing a hyperlink with each task. These hyperlinks are more versatile than those you can store in Notes, for three reasons:

- To click a hyperlink that is inserted in the Notes field, you must display the Notes field in the Task form or in the Task Information dialog box. If there is a link in the Hyperlink field, it appears as an icon in the Indicator column and you can click it there.
- The hyperlinks in the Notes field only jump to Internet or intranet sites. With the link in the Hyperlink field, you can do the following:
    - You can jump to other files on your computer, network, and even specific locations within those files (for instance, to a specific task in another project file, a specific cell in an Excel file, a word or section in a Word document, or a slide in a PowerPoint presentation).
    - You can open a file folder (presumably one that contains documents related to the task) and select a file to open.
    - You can jump to another task or resource within the current project and display it in a specific view.
    - You can initiate an email message to a specific addressee.
- When you define the Hyperlink field, you can browse to find the location of the targeted file or Web site. In the Notes field, you must know the URL for the site.

5

Unfortunately, there is only one Hyperlink field per task, whereas you can store many hyperlinks in a note.

When you attach a hyperlink to a task, the Hyperlink indicator appears in the Indicators column. Simply click the indicator to jump to the target defined by the link.

To attach a hyperlink to a task, click Tasks on the Project Guide toolbar and choose Link To or Attach More Task Information. You can then select a task and click Add a Hyperlink in the sidepane. Or, you can simply select the task and click the Insert Hyperlink tool on the Standard toolbar, choose the Hyperlink command on the Insert menu, choose the Hyperlink command on the shortcut menu when you right-click over the task, or press Ctrl+K.

If you want to link to a specific location in another file, you can take a more direct route. Open the file, select the location you want to link to, and copy it to the Clipboard by using the Copy command. Then, select the task and choose Edit, Paste as Hyperlink.

ATTACHING HYPERLINKS TO EXISTING FILES OR WEB PAGES

To attach a hyperlink to a Web site or an existing file by using the Insert, Hyperlink command, follow these steps:

1. Select the task you want to attach the link to.

2. Click the Insert Hyperlink tool or choose Insert, Hyperlink from the menu (or press Ctrl+K) to display the Insert Hyperlink dialog box (see Figure 5.19).

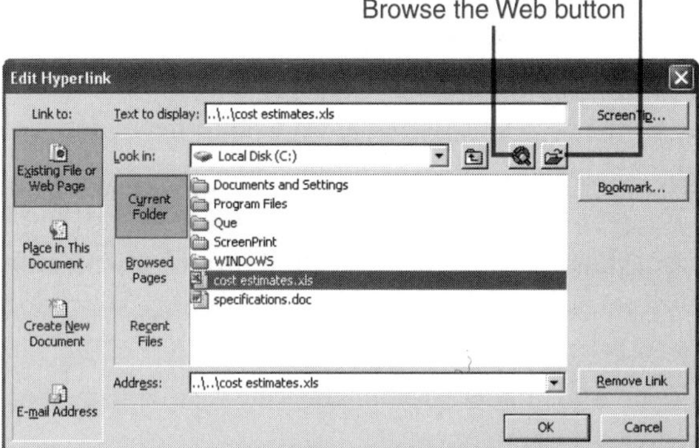

Figure 5.19
The Insert Hyperlink dialog box helps you locate Web sites or files that you want to insert as hyperlinks.

3. Click Existing File or Web Page to link to a Web site or an existing file.
4. You can enter the full path and filename in the Address box or browse for the address. The Insert Hyperlink dialog box offers the following aids to help you locate the address of the filename or Web site you want to link to:
   - Click the drop-down arrow in the Address box to choose from the list of recently accessed folders and Web sites.
   - Click Current Folder to use this dialog box to browse the folders on your PC, starting in the folder listed in the Look In box.
   - Click the Browse for File button to use Windows Explorer to browse for the file you want to link to, again starting in the folder listed in Look In.

- Click Browsed Pages to choose from the list of recently viewed Web pages.
- Click Recent Files to choose from the list of recently opened files.
- Click the Browse the Web button to open your Internet Browser to search for a Web site.
- If you have chosen a file that supports bookmarks, you can click Bookmark to see a list of bookmarks that are defined in that file. Choosing a bookmark causes the hyperlink to go directly to that part of the document.

5. Change the entry in the Text to Display field if you want to display the link by using custom text.
6. Click the ScreenTip button if you want to customize the ScreenTip that appears when the mouse points to the Hyperlink indicator.
7. Click OK to save the link.

To create a hyperlink by using the Paste as Hyperlink command, follow these steps:

1. Open the document and find the specific location you want to link to.
2. Select some part of the document at that location and choose the Copy command. Different applications require different selections:
    - In Excel, select a cell or group of cells.
    - In Word, select a word or section title.
    - In Project, select a cell in a task row.
    - In PowerPoint, select a word or title in a slide or in the outline.
3. Return to Project and select a cell in the row for the task you want to contain the link.
4. Choose Edit, Paste as Hyperlink, and the link is established.

When you click the Hyperlink icon in the Indicators column, Project opens the necessary application, opens the target document, and then locates the exact word or cell you copied to paste the link (if it still exists).

ATTACHING HYPERLINKS TO NEW FILES

To insert a hyperlink to a document that doesn't already exist, click the Create New Document button in the Insert Hyperlink dialog box. Enter a name in the Name of New Document box. Be sure to include the file extension so that Project knows what application to open to create the file. The default path that Project shows is the path for the active project file, but you can click Change to select a different folder. Finally, select either Edit the New Document Later or Edit the New Document Now.

ATTACHING HYPERLINKS TO TASKS OR RESOURCES IN THE SAME PROJECT

You can use the hyperlink to jump to another task or resource in the same project, and you can specify the view to use for that task or resource. To create this type of hyperlink, follow these steps:

1. Find the task or resource you want the hyperlink to jump to and note its ID number. You can't browse for this information while attaching the link.

2. Select the task you want to attach the hyperlink to and open the Insert Hyperlink dialog box (by pressing Ctrl+K).
3. Choose Place in This Document.
4. Enter the ID number for the task or resource in the Enter the Task or Resource ID box.
5. Select the view to be displayed for the task or resource in the Select a View in This Project box. Selecting a resource view is the clue that tells Project that the ID number is for a resource. If you don't select a view, Project assumes that you want to keep the current task view.

USING HYPERLINKS TO CREATE EMAIL MESSAGES

You can use a hyperlink to jump to an email program such as Outlook to compose a message. When you click the hyperlink, the email program opens, with a new message already addressed and waiting for you to supply the message content.

To create an email hyperlink for the selected task, open the Insert Hyperlink dialog box and click E-mail Address. Type the address for the recipient in the E-mail Address box. Although the address is required, there is, unfortunately, no link to the address book or contacts folder to help you select an existing address. However, addresses you have used recently in this dialog box are listed in the Recently Used E-mail Addresses box for you to reuse. If you provide text in the Subject box, the message will have the subject field filled in when the message opens for you to edit it.

EDITING AND DELETING HYPERLINKS

To edit or delete a hyperlink, select a cell in the task and click the Insert Hyperlink tool or press Ctrl+K. The Edit Hyperlink dialog box appears, and you can make the changes you want. Click Remove Link to delete the hyperlink.

PLACING HYPERLINKS IN THE CUSTOM TEXT FIELDS

There is only one Hyperlink field for each task. However, you can use any of the 30 custom text fields to store additional hyperlinks and then use the hyperlinks to jump to the targeted site. To use the hyperlink, you have to display the text field as a column in the task table.

To use the Project Guide to insert a text field, follow these steps:

1. On the Tasks sidepane, choose Add Columns of Custom Information.
2. Select Show Me Custom Fields.

3. Choose Text as the field type.
4. Choose one of Text1 through Text30 and click Insert.

Scroll to the far right column in the task table to see the inserted field.

You can also just click on an existing column heading and choose Insert, Column. In the Column Definition dialog box, use the list control in the Field Name box to select one of the text fields, and then click OK.

There are some limitations on the use of text fields for storing hyperlinks:

- The hyperlink must be the only thing typed in the text field.
- As with task notes, there is no browse facility to help you define the hyperlink. However, if you find the site with your browser and copy the URL to the Clipboard, you can paste it into the text field.
- You must supply the complete URL. For example, `www.woodyswatch.com/project/` does not work as a hyperlink in a text field, but `http://www.woodyswatch.com/project/` does take you to Woody's Project Watch, and `ftp://ftp.microsoft.com/deskapps/project/` takes you to the Project area of Microsoft's FTP server.

  For links to files stored on your local computer or network, precede the path with `File:\\` and supply the complete path for local files or complete UNC for network files. For example, `File:C:\My Documents\Projects\Cost Estimates.xls` opens Excel and loads `Cost Estimates.xls`. If the file is on a local network, use a link such as `File:\\servername\sharename\folder\filename.ext`.

5

USING OTHER VIEWS TO CREATE TASKS

Although the table in the Gantt Chart view is the most efficient place to create a task list, some people prefer other views. Many project managers were trained to create a project plan by drawing a network diagram. Others like to split the screen and add the task form or Task Details form to the Gantt Chart view to facilitate adding resources and task linking as they enter the tasks. Instructions for using the other fields in these views are given in later chapters.

NOTE

> If you enter or change task data in any view, all other views that display tasks show changed values. The views are just alternative ways of displaying the information in the task table of the project database.

USING A NETWORK DIAGRAM TO CREATE TASKS

The network diagram is a time-honored way of displaying the tasks in a project and can also be used to create the task list (see Figure 5.20). A network diagram provides a road map of the sequencing of tasks in a project. However, it does not show the time relationships of tasks as clearly as a Gantt Chart does.

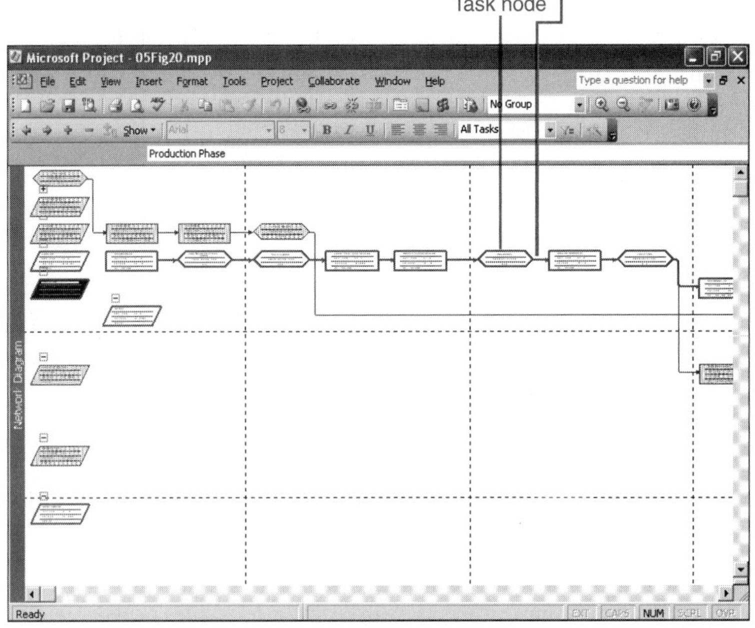

Figure 5.20
A network diagram shows clearly how one task follows another in sequence.

Each task is represented on a network diagram by a box (called a *node*), and a line is drawn to link one task node to another to show that they are to be scheduled in sequence. If you print a network diagram, it generally takes many pages, but if you assemble the pages in order, you have a large diagram that enables you to see the progression of tasks from the start to the finish of the project. A network diagram is less useful onscreen than in printed form because you can't see very much of the project at once. Most people find it difficult to keep the overall structure in mind when using the screen version.

5

→ To find information about using the Network Diagram view, **see** "Working with the Network Diagram View," **p. 265**, and "Exploring the Standard Views," **p. 736**.

In project management terms, a network diagram is synonymous with the precedence diagramming method (PDM), which uses nodes to represent the activities and connect them with arrows. Keep in mind that PDM notation does not allow for loops–nonsequential activities, such as a task that must be repeated more than once–or conditional activities, such as a task(s) that might not be necessary (but the Gantt Chart view doesn't allow for conditional activities, either).

USING THE TASK ENTRY VIEW

The Task Entry view is a combination view that displays a Gantt Chart in the top pane and a task form in the bottom pane. The Task form in the bottom pane shows details for the task that is selected in the top pane (see Figure 5.21).

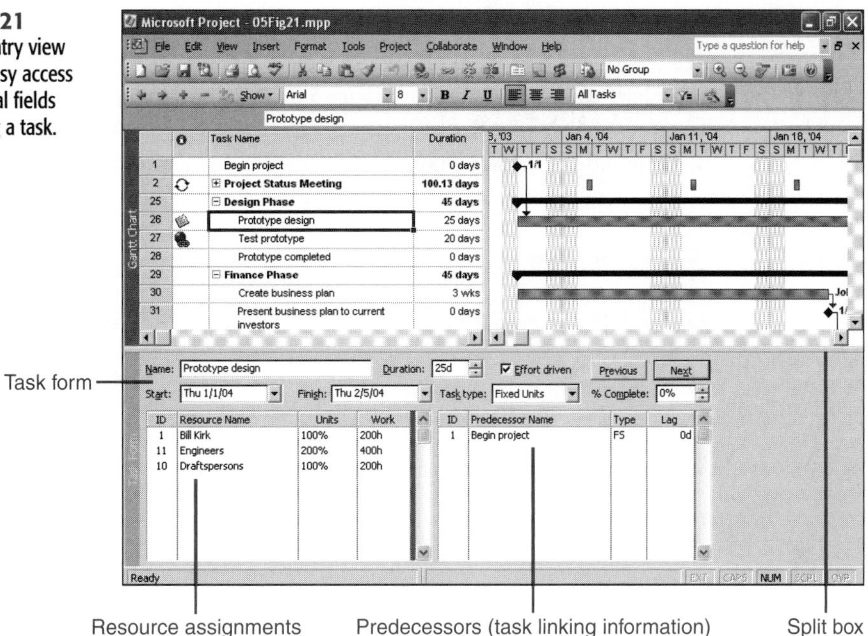

Figure 5.21
The Task Entry view provides easy access to additional fields for defining a task.

The task form in the bottom pane is not particularly useful if you are just typing task names and durations. But it's very efficient if you want to assign resources and link tasks while you are creating a task list. Extensive use of the Task Entry view is covered in Chapter 10, "Assigning Resources and Costs to Tasks." The section "Project Extras: Letting Project Calculate Duration" at the end of this chapter gives an example of using the Task Entry view.

You can easily change the Gantt Chart view to the Task Entry view by choosing Window, Split. Project initially displays the task form in the bottom pane whenever you split the screen with a task view onscreen.

NOTE

> You can double-click the split box located just below the vertical scrollbar to the right of the timeline. The Split command also appears on the shortcut menu that is displayed if you right-click over the timeline area.

Initially, the Task Form view displays tables for resource assignments and for predecessor relationships. The predecessor tasks are tasks whose scheduled dates must be taken into account when scheduling the selected task. You use the Format, Details command to display alternative task information at the bottom of the task form. To remove the bottom pane from the view, click Window, Remove Split.

USING THE TASK SHEET VIEW

The Task Sheet view displays the same task table that the Gantt Chart view displays, but without the Gantt Chart view's timeline (see Figure 5.22). The Task Sheet view is a great tool for reviewing the major details of a task list because you can see several columns for many tasks at the same time. It's also a good view to print if you just want to see the task outline without the timeline graphics.

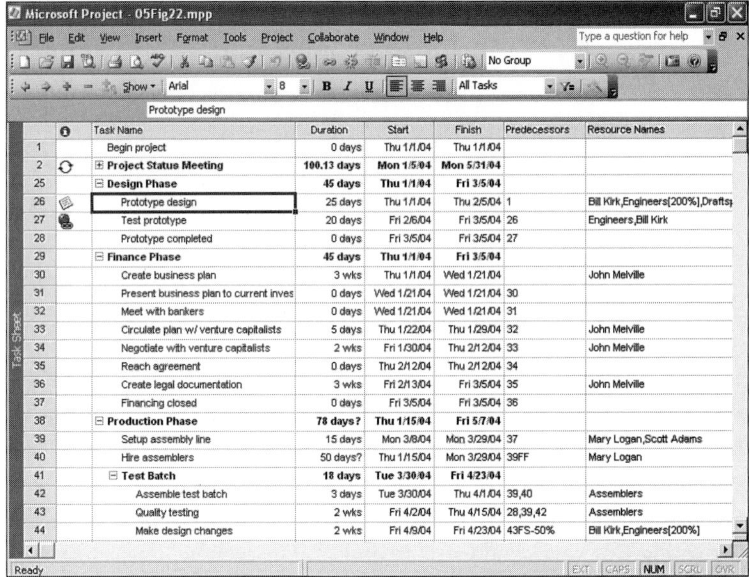

Figure 5.22
The Task Sheet view displays the essential task fields without the timeline graphics of the Gantt Chart view.

5

To display the Task Sheet view, choose View, More Views, and select Task Sheet from the Views list. Then click the Apply button to display the view.

OUTLINING THE TASK LIST

Outlining is Microsoft Project's method of organizing the details of a project into groups of activities that correspond to the major phases of a project, and it is the equivalent of the traditional WBS (refer to Figures 5.1 and 5.2). Each task has an outline number, which Project calculates by using the legal numbering system. For example, if a task has an outline number of 2, the subtasks that are indented under it would be 2.1, 2.2, and so on. The outline number serves to identify the group containing the task in the overall structure of the project.

UNDERSTANDING SUMMARY TASKS AND SUBTASKS

Like WBS, outlining organizes tasks into functional groups. Outlining is usually thought of in terms of its visual effect: You indent detail topics under major topics, creating *subtasks*. Figure 5.23 shows an expanded task list. The major topics, called *summary tasks*, control and summarize the subordinate detail tasks, called *subtasks*. In project scheduling, indenting a task is called *demoting* the task, and the task you demote becomes a subtask. The task under which the task is indented automatically becomes a summary task that both controls and summarizes the subtasks.

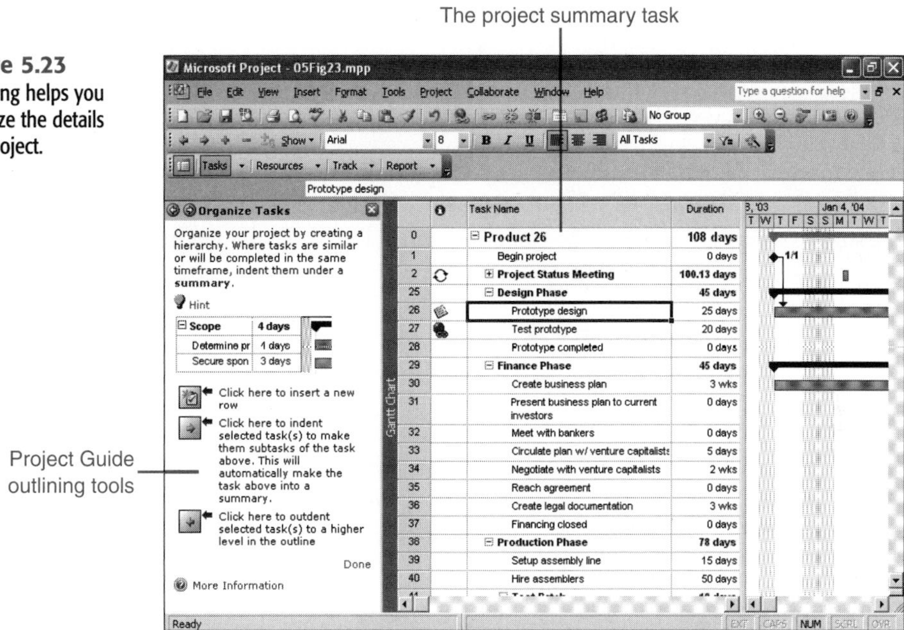

Figure 5.23
Outlining helps you organize the details of a project.

NOTE

What appears to be the first task in Figure 5.23 is actually a project summary task (notice that its ID number is 0). It is useful to summarize the entire project with one task. The section "Selecting the Display Options for Outlining," later in this chapter, lists instructions for displaying a project summary.

A summary task serves both to identify major groups of tasks and to summarize the duration, cost, and amount of work expended on its subtasks. When a task is transformed into a summary task, the task's start date is determined by the earliest start date of any of its subtasks, and the finish date is determined by the latest finish date of any of its subtasks. You cannot type a start date or finish date for a summary task. These dates can be calculated only from the related subtasks. The costs and amount of work associated with the subtasks are rolled up and summarized in the cost and work fields of the summary task.

Be careful when communicating task assignments based on task ID numbering. Any additions or deletions of tasks renumber the tasks that have been inserted below the new task. In other words, if the project manager comments on Task 9 and since that time another single task has been inserted before it, the ID changes to Task 10. You can easily overcome this problem by using custom WBS codes, described later in this chapter, along with renumbering the project after making significant changes.

UNDERSTANDING DURATION FOR SUMMARY TASKS

Project calculates the duration for a summary task and does not let you modify it. The summary task start date is the earliest start date of any of its subtasks, and the summary task finish date is the latest finish date of any of its subtasks. The duration of the summary task is the amount of work time that is defined on the base calendar, between the earliest start date and the latest finish date. A summary task whose first subtask starts at 8:00 a.m. one day and whose last subtask finishes at noon the next day would have a duration of 1.5 days (that is, 12 working hours).

The duration for summary tasks is always displayed with the default setting for the Duration Is Entered In option on the Schedule tab of the Options dialog box. This is true even when the subtasks are expressed in other duration units. To change the duration units for summary tasks, you must change the Duration Is Entered In setting.

INDENTING AND OUTDENTING TASKS

There are several methods you can use to indent (that is, demote) or outdent (that is, promote) a task or group of selected tasks. They all produce equivalent results.

If you're new to outlining in Project, you should use the Project Guide (refer to Figure 5.23). Choose Tasks on the Project Guide toolbar, and choose Organize Tasks into Phases. Select one or more tasks to be indented or outdented and click the Indent tool or the Outdent tool in the sidepane.

If you're not using the Project Guide, you can use the Formatting toolbar, the mouse, the menu, or keyboard shortcuts to indent or outdent tasks. First, select the task or tasks you want to indent or outdent. Then do one of the following:

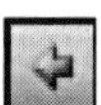 

- Use the Indent or Outdent buttons on the Formatting toolbar to change the outline level of the selected tasks. The Indent button points to the right, and the Outdent button points to the left.
- Use the mouse to drag the task name to the right or left. Place the mouse pointer over the first letters of the Task Name field until it becomes a double arrow, pointing left and right. Drag the pointer to the left or right to change the indent or outdent level of the task. If you select multiple tasks first, all of them are indented or outdented together.
- Choose Project, Outline, and then choose Indent or Outdent.
- Use the task shortcut menu to indent and outdent. Select the ID number for a task or group of tasks. Right-click the ID numbers and choose Indent or Outdent from the shortcut menu.
- Use the shortcut key combination Alt+Shift+right arrow to indent and the combination Alt+Shift+left arrow to outdent a task or group of tasks.

CAUTION

> If you demote a summary task, its subtasks are demoted even further. In fact, all actions you apply to a summary task also apply to its subtasks. If you delete, copy, move, promote, or demote a summary task, all the subtasks–including subordinate summary tasks and their subtasks–are deleted, copied, moved, promoted, or demoted along with the summary task.

You can promote tasks that are already indented by *outdenting* them—that is, shifting them to the left. When you promote an indented task, the tasks immediately beneath the promoted task are affected in one of the following ways:

- If the tasks below are at the same level of indentation as the new promoted task, the tasks become subordinate to the new summary task. To keep them at the same level as the task you are promoting, select all the tasks and promote them together.
- If the tasks below are subordinates of the promoted task, these tasks remain subordinates but shift to the left, to follow the summary task.
- If the tasks below are at a higher outline level (that is, already further to the left than the promoted task), these tasks are unaffected by the promotion.

If you want to introduce a new task into the task list and make the new task a summary task, you must insert the task just above the task(s) you plan to have it summarize. You can then indent the subtasks. Or, if the new summary task is not at the first outline level, you can outdent the summary task rather than indent its subordinates.

COLLAPSING AND EXPANDING THE OUTLINE

A major advantage of outlining is that you can collapse the outline by hiding subtasks to view only the major components of the project (see Figure 5.24). Collapsing an outline merely suppresses the display of the subtasks; it does not delete the subtasks.

5

Figure 5.24
You can look at the ID numbers to see which tasks are hidden; they are missing row numbers.

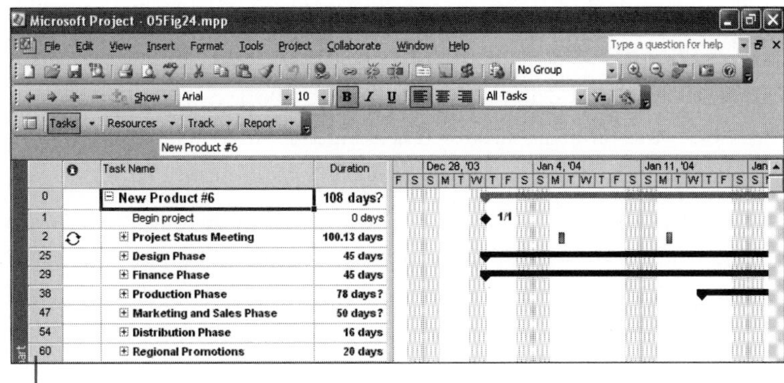

You can also collapse an entire outline and then expand just one part to focus on the details of that part and see how they fit into the overall picture (see Figure 5.25).

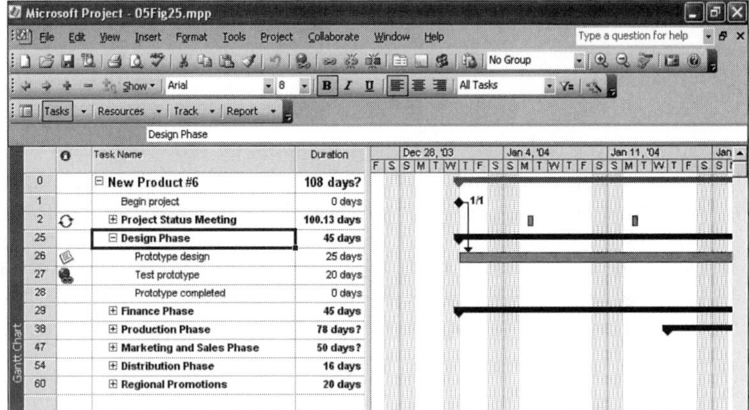

Figure 5.25
You can show the subtasks in one section of the plan but hide all other subtasks to highlight how those tasks fit into the overall project.

You can display all tasks or only selected levels of the outline by using the Show command. Click the Show button on the Formatting toolbar, or choose Project, Outline, Show to display the Show submenu. Select the outline level you want to be exposed: Select All Subtasks to display all levels; select Outline Level 1 to display only the top-level tasks (whether they have subtasks or not); select Outline Level 2 to display the top-level tasks plus the first level of subtasks; and so forth. The maximum number of levels you can control with this tool is nine.

You can hide or display subtasks for a selected summary task in a variety of ways. The simplest technique is to double-click the task ID to toggle between hidden and displayed subtasks.

If you select a summary task, you can hide its subtasks by clicking the Hide Subtasks tool, or (if the subtasks are already hidden) you can click the Show Subtasks tool to display them again. You can also use the menu to hide and show subtasks for individual tasks, by following these steps:

1. Select the summary task or tasks whose subtasks you want to hide.
2. Choose Project, Outline to display the Outlining submenu.
3. Choose Hide Subtasks to collapse that part of the outline or choose Show Subtasks to expand that part of the outline.

TIP

If outline symbols are displayed (see "Selecting the Display Options for Outlining," later in this chapter), you see a small plus or minus to the left of each summary task. These outline symbols are miniature Hide Subtask and Show Subtask buttons that you can click to hide or display the subtasks. If the subtasks are currently displayed, a minus sign appears to the left of the summary task name, and clicking it hides the subtasks. If the subtasks are currently hidden, a plus sign appears to the left of the summary task name, and clicking it displays the subtasks.

In general, it is a good practice to have a minimum of three levels within a project: project level (that is, a summary task over the entire project), phase level (that is, summary tasks outlining the required project components), and work level (that is, where the work package, or lowest level of the WBS, is located). Of course, it is possible to have more than three levels in a complex project. No matter how many levels you have, the lowest indented level is always where the work package is located. It is at this level that the tasks should be linked and the resources assigned to do the work.

EDITING OUTLINED PROJECTS

If you select a summary task and click the Task Information tool, Project displays the Summary Task Information dialog box (see Figure 5.26). Some fields (such as Duration) are grayed out because they can't be edited for summary tasks, but you can edit all the other fields. Summary tasks have their own Notes field, and you should make free use of notes to document important assumptions and background for summary tasks, just as you do for other tasks.

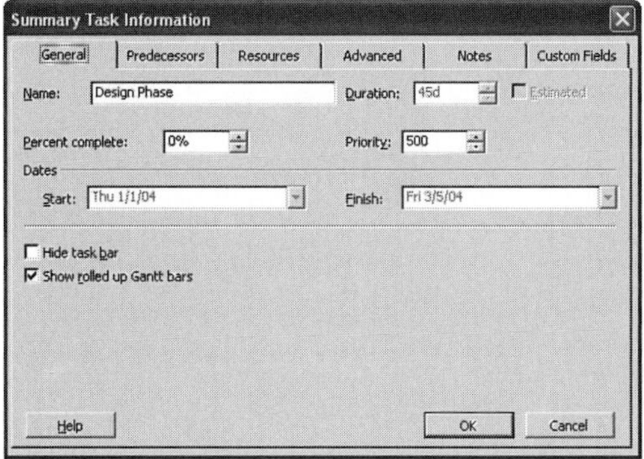

Figure 5.26
You can control some features of summary tasks in the Summary Task Information dialog box.

When you delete, copy, cut, paste, promote, or demote a summary task, all its subtasks are included in the same operation. For example, if you delete a summary task, you also delete all its subtasks. If you demote a summary task, you further demote its subtasks.

To learn how to delete, copy, cut, paste, promote, or demote a summary task without also affecting its subtasks, see "Moving Summary Tasks" in the Troubleshooting section near the end of this chapter.

5

SELECTING THE DISPLAY OPTIONS FOR OUTLINING

Project provides several display options for emphasizing the outline organization of a task list. Some of these are turned on by default. For example, by default Project displays summary tasks along with normal tasks and milestones, and it indents subtasks under their summary tasks.

The formatting options for displaying the outline structure of your project are as follows:

- Normally subtasks are indented to emphasize the organization of the outline. You can choose to display all tasks left-justified, just like the top-level tasks. This might be useful to avoid taking up a lot of room on the screen or in a printed report.
- If you disable indenting, you should probably display the task outline number next to the task name as a substitute for the visual reminder of the structure. Outline numbers are stored in the Outline Number field and cannot be edited. See the section "Using Custom Outline Numbers," later in this chapter, for other outlining options.
- Normally Project displays outline symbols to the left of the summary tasks. These symbols are the minus sign (such as the Hide Subtask tool) and the plus sign (such as the Show Subtask tool). If the symbols are present, you can click them to hide and show subtasks for the summary task. They also serve as an indicator that a task is a summary task and, if a plus is showing, as a reminder that there are hidden subtasks. You can choose to hide these outline symbols.
- You can hide the summary tasks themselves, leaving only the milestones and normal (working) tasks in the display. This option is especially useful when you want to sort normal tasks and milestones by start date, duration, or alphabetically by task name for a special report. You would probably also disable indenting subtasks in that case.
- Project can display an overall summary task for the entire project. Project displays it with the ID number 0 at the top of the task list. Note that all tasks are indented one level when the Project Summary task is displayed. The task name for the Project Summary task is taken from the project title that is entered on the Summary tab of the File Properties dialog box. Editing the Project Summary task name also changes the entry in the Properties dialog box. You enter notes for the project summary task note in the Comments field in the Properties dialog box.

If you want to change the outline formatting features, the active view must be a task view that must be the only pane or the top pane in the window. Follow these steps to select the outline options:

1. Choose Tools, Options to display the Options dialog box, and select the View tab (see Figure 5.27).
2. Uncheck the Indent Name check box if you prefer to left-justify all task names.
3. Check the Show Outline Number check box to display outline numbers to the left of task names.

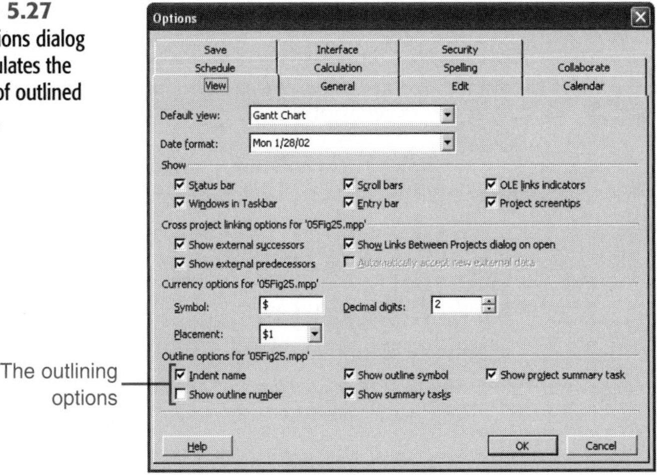

Figure 5.27
The Options dialog box regulates the display of outlined projects.

4. Uncheck the Show Outline Symbol check box if you want to hide the plus and minus symbols next to summary task names.
5. Uncheck the Show Summary Tasks check box if you want to hide the display of summary tasks. Unchecking this check box makes the Show Project Summary Tasks check box unavailable.
6. If the Show Summary Tasks check box is checked, you can check the Show Project Summary Task check box to display a summary task for the overall project.
7. Click OK to display the new settings.

5

USING ROLLUP TASKBARS

The taskbar for the summary task spans the bars for all its subtasks and is usually a solid bar. However, you can choose to roll up the subtask taskbars to the summary taskbar. When you choose this option, each subtask's taskbar start and finish are marked on the summary taskbar. Together, the rolled-up bars produce a segmented bar that shows how long each of the subtasks lasts (see Figure 5.28).

To roll up *all* taskbars to their summary taskbars, choose Format, Layout to display the Layout dialog box, and fill the Always Roll Up Gantt Bars check box (see Figure 5.29). The rollup bars appear in front of the standard summary taskbar. You can choose to display the rollup bars only when their subtasks are hidden. Fill the Hide Rollup Bars When Summary Expanded check box to suppress their display when the outline is expanded.

TIP

> You can display the Layout dialog box by right-clicking in the bar chart area to display the shortcut menu and selecting Layout.

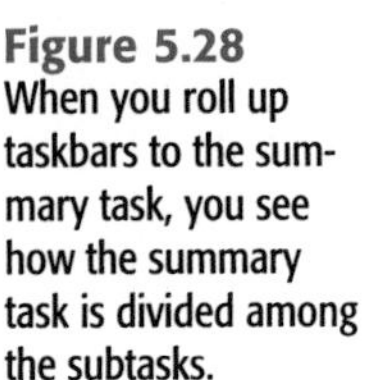

Figure 5.28
When you roll up taskbars to the summary task, you see how the summary task is divided among the subtasks.

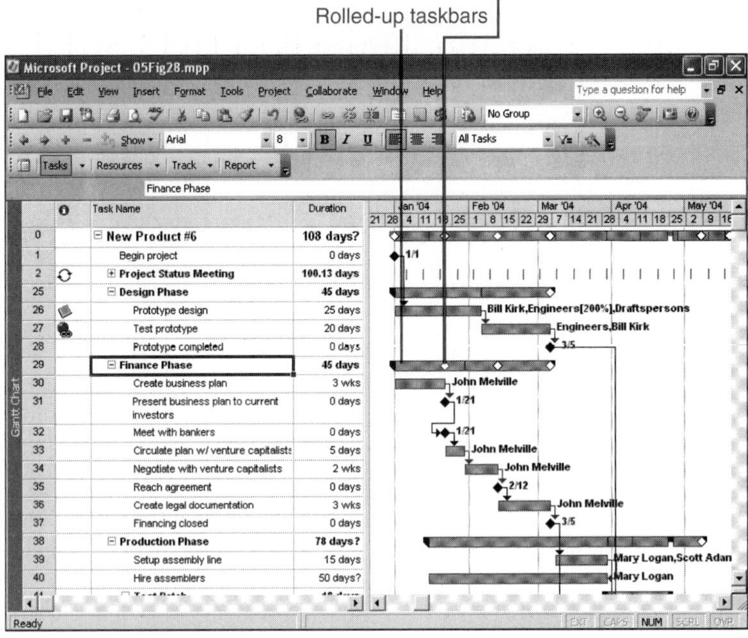

Figure 5.29
The Layout command controls aspects of how the Gantt Chart view is displayed.

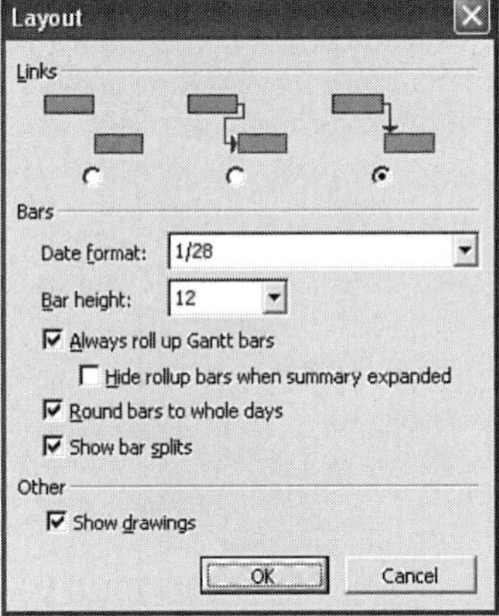

If you just want to roll up particular taskbars and leave others alone, you have to mark each subtask you want to be rolled up and you have to mark its summary task to display the rollup. Also, you must clear the Always Roll Up Gantt Bars check box.

To mark a subtask for rollup, follow these steps:

1. Select the subtask you want to roll up and click the Task Information tool.
2. On the General tab, select Roll Up Gantt Bar to Summary and click OK.

3. Select the summary task you want to show the rollup. If the subtask's summary task is itself a subtask, the higher-level summary task can display the rollup also (even if the lower-level summary task is not marked to display it). Each has to be selected separately to control the display of rollup bars.
4. Click the Task Information tool to display the Summary Task Information dialog box.
5. Fill the check box next to Show Rolled Up Gantt Bars if you want the summary task to display rolled-up taskbars.
6. Click OK to save the settings.
7. Repeat this process for each summary task above the subtask that you want to display the rollup bar.

TIP

You can change the display of rolled-up bars to show milestone markers at their finish date instead of showing the whole bar. If you want this format, choose Tools, Macro, Macros, select Rollup_Formatting, and click Run. Run the macro again to reverse the changes. Be warned, however, that this macro discards any custom bar styles you have created. If you have custom bar styles, you should edit the bar styles directly to change the display of rolled-up tasks. See "Formatting the Gantt Chart," in Chapter 20.

USING CUSTOM WBS CODES

Project automatically creates a default WBS code in the WBS field for each task. (See the beginning of this chapter for a description of WBS and the WBS codes.) The default WBS codes are identical to the outline numbers that Project generates (and that are stored in the Outline Number field).

You can display the WBS field in a table by inserting the WBS column. You can also view the WBS field on the Advanced tab of the Task Information dialog box. If your organization, or a client, requires a specific format for WBS codes, you can edit the codes in either of these places, replacing the Project outline number with your own WBS codes.

NOTE

Editing the WBS field does not change the entry in the Outline Number field.

You can define a customized format that matches a particular WBS code scheme. Project uses the custom format to generate default codes for the WBS field (instead of using the value in the Outline Number field). The custom format can include numbers, letters, and symbols (including ASCII characters). An added advantage of using the custom format is that it enforces consistency and uniformity.

TIP

> Don't take the time to re-create a custom WBS format if you've already defined one in another Project file. Use the Fields tab of the Organizer to copy a custom WBS format from one project file to another. Also, if you have a standard format you want to use in all projects, copy the definition to the Global template. See "Working with the Organizer," in Chapter 3.

CREATING CUSTOM WBS CODES

To customize the WBS code format, you create a *WBS code mask* that Project can use to generate the custom codes. The mask contains numbers or characters for each outline level, starting with level one, with separator characters in between each level. You can define code segments for as many levels as you want, but the total length of the WBS code can't be greater than 255 characters.

For example, if you created the code mask `AAA-111.aa.**` for the first four levels of the outline, it would mean the following:

- **AAA-**—Use three uppercase letters for top-level tasks (that is, those with no summary task above them). Also use these codes as a prefix for all subtasks under the top-level task and follow them with a hyphen as a separator. You can edit and replace the letters Project initially supplies, but the mask requires that you use three uppercase letters. If you edit these characters in the top-level task, the edited version is used as a prefix for all the task's subtasks.
- **111.**—Use three numbers for second-level subtasks, followed by a period separator if there are subtasks. Project automatically numbers subtasks at this level 001, 002, and so forth, but you can edit those numbers at will.
- **aa.**—Use two lowercase letters for third-level subtasks, followed by a period separator if needed.
- ******—Use any mixture of characters on the keyboard for fourth-level subtasks. Project places the default characters ** in the code it generates, but you can change them to any characters you choose.

You can also include a project-level code to be used as a prefix for all tasks. This would be especially helpful to distinguish tasks that are from different subprojects in a consolidated (master) project.

You should display the WBS field as a column in the task table before creating the WBS mask. (Choose Insert, Column and select WBS in the Field Name box.) That way, you can see the effects of creating a WBS code mask immediately.

To create the custom WBS code mask, follow these steps:

1. Choose Project, WBS, Define Code to display the WBS Code Definition dialog box (see Figure 5.30).

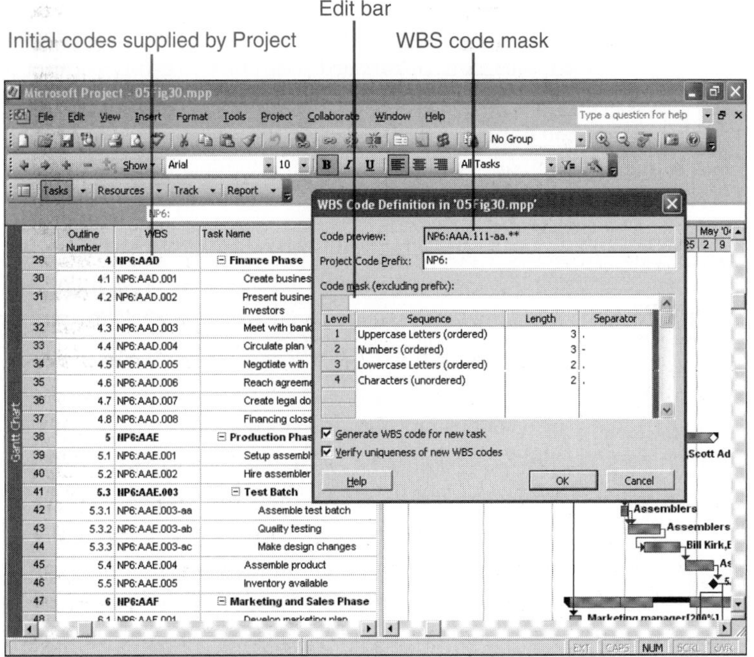

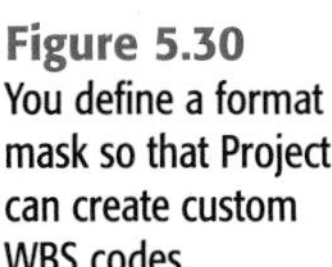

Figure 5.30
You define a format mask so that Project can create custom WBS codes.

2. Enter a code prefix for the project, if you like, in the Project Code Prefix box. It's best to include a colon or another separator to show where the project prefix ends and the task code starts. The prefix appears in the sample display in the Code Preview box at the top of the dialog box.
3. In the Code Mask table, click the first blank row under the Sequence column to define the code format for top-level tasks. Use the pull-down arrow to display the options, which are as follows:
    - Choose Numbers (Ordered) to have Project insert sequential numbers in this part of the code. Remember that you can edit the numbers.
    - Choose Uppercase Letters (Ordered) to use sequential uppercase letters.
    - Choose Lowercase Letters (Ordered) to use sequential lowercase letters.
    - Choose Characters (Unordered) to have Project insert the * character, which you can then change to any character on the keyboard.
4. In the Length column, use the pull-down arrow to display the options for the number of characters to be used for this part of the format:
    - Choose Any if you want to be able to edit this part of the code and use a varying number of characters.
    - Choose 1 through 10 to set a fixed number of characters for this section of the format.

5

5. In the Separator column, enter the symbol to use following the sequence code for subtasks. You can use the pull-down arrow to display the most common separators (the period, hyphen, plus sign, or forward slash) or you can type other symbols from the keyboard. You can use up to three symbols as the separator (for example, three asterisks). If you don't want a separator, click the Edit bar just above the Sequence column and delete the default symbol. Note that you must have a separator if you have chosen Any as the code length.
6. Repeat steps 3, 4, and 5 for all outline levels that you want to define in the mask.
7. Check the check box Generate WBS Code for New Task if you want Project to calculate the WBS code for new tasks. If you leave it unchecked, you must type in WBS codes for new tasks, but you must honor the format of the mask.
8. Check the check box Verify Uniqueness of New WBS Codes if you want Project to warn you if a new code is not unique. This happens only when you edit the codes; you then need to modify the code to achieve uniqueness. If you leave this check box unchecked, Project does not detect duplication of codes. You should generally check this check box.
9. Click OK to save the mask. Project automatically replaces the outline number codes that are displayed by default in the WBS field with sequential codes that match the new mask.
10. You might need to widen the WBS column to see the new codes. To do so, double-click the WBS column heading and choose Best Fit in the Column Definition dialog box.

NOTE

> If a project has more outline levels than you have provided for in the mask, Project uses the conventional outline numbering system for the lower-level tasks that the mask doesn't define.

Checking the check box to verify the uniqueness of new codes only makes Project check the code when it is created or edited. If you have a project file with custom WBS codes that have this feature disabled and then you decide to enable unique codes, Project does not check all the existing codes for uniqueness. You can force Project to renumber all the codes (that is, generate new codes from the mask) to correct nonunique codes. This also causes you to lose any codes you manually retyped. (See the section "Renumbering the Custom WBS Codes," later in this chapter.)

TIP

> You can edit every task's code to force Project to check for each task's uniqueness. The simplest way to do this is to select the WBS column (so that all cells are selected), press F2 to edit the first cell, and then press Enter to force the uniqueness check. If the code is unique, Project moves to the next cell in the selection, and you press F2 and Enter again. You can move down the column quite rapidly this way, as long as the codes are unique. If a code is not unique, you are forced to change the code before continuing.

NOTE

> You can delete only the bottom-most level in the Sequence table. If you want to reduce the number of defined levels in the mask, click the bottom-most level and use the Delete key; then work your way up the list, deleting from the bottom.

Inserting, Deleting, and Moving Tasks with Custom WBS Codes

When you insert a new task into a project, it is automatically given the next highest code for its level in the outline. If you delete a task, tasks below it at the same level are renumbered automatically, unless you tell Project to renumber the project (see the section "Renumbering the Custom WBS Codes," later in this chapter).

If you move a task to another row within its current summary task, it keeps its custom WBS code, even if it's not now in sequence. If you move a task from under one summary task to a different summary task, it automatically acquires the correct prefix codes for its new summary task. If the final part of its code would create a duplicate in its new subtask group, it is changed to one number or letter higher than the highest existing number or letter in that subtask group. If no duplicate would be created, the final part of the code remains the same as it was before the move.

Editing Custom WBS Codes

After the custom code mask is defined and Project has provided default codes based on the mask, you can edit the last segment of any default code. Everything prior to the last segment is derived from higher-level summary tasks and can't be changed except by editing the code for the summary task itself. If you edit the final segment for a summary task, its subtasks automatically acquire the new segment as the prefix for their code. For example, in Figure 5.31 the major phases have been edited to be abbreviations or acronyms for the name of the phase. The default WBS code for the Finance phase had been AAD, but it has been changed to FIN for easier identification. This makes recognizing a task's place in the WBS much easier and is much closer to conventional practice.

5

TIP

> To display tasks in WBS code order, choose Project, Sort, Sort By and select the WBS field in the Sort By box.

CAUTION

> If you edit custom codes for summary tasks and then tell Project to renumber the tasks, your edited codes will be lost. Read the troubleshooting note "Preserving Edited Custom WBS Codes" at the end of this chapter for a workaround.

If the WBS column is not displayed in the table, you can edit the code in the Summary Task Information dialog box. Project 2003 displays custom fields on the Custom Fields tab (see Figure 5.32). Select the Value cell for the field you want to change and enter the change in the Entry bar, above the list of fields.

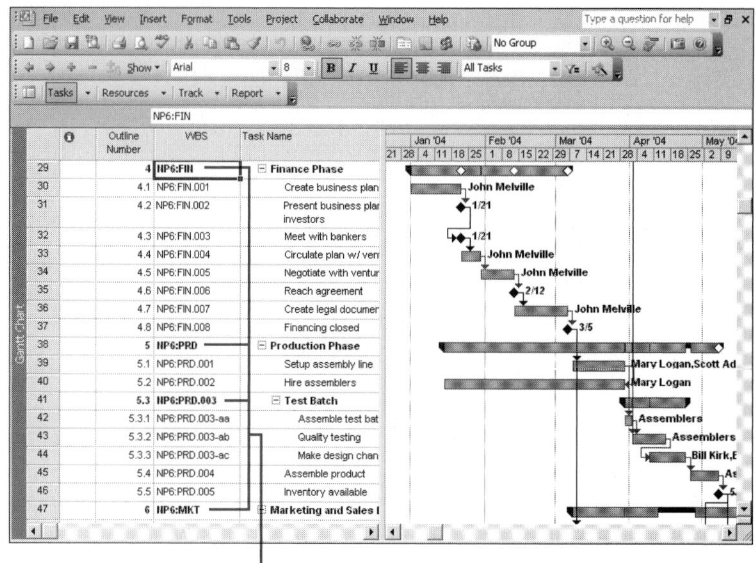

Figure 5.31
You can edit the default letters assigned by Project in the custom WBS codes to describe the task's place in the structure.

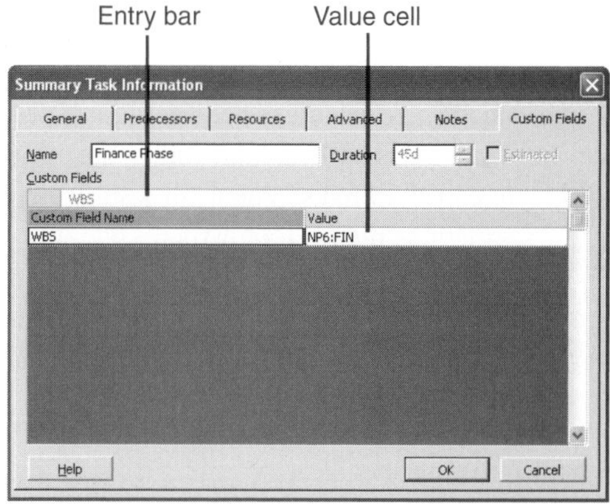

Figure 5.32
You can edit the custom WBS code on the Custom Fields tab of the Summary Task Information dialog box.

RENUMBERING THE CUSTOM WBS CODES

When you are designing a project, you usually have to revise the task list. If you defined custom WBS codes, they might not be in sequence after all the editing. You can have Project recalculate the WBS codes for the whole project, to put them in sequence. If you've only rearranged a small segment of the project, you can select those tasks and have Project recalculate the codes just for the selected tasks. To renumber the WBS codes, follow these steps:

1. If you want to renumber just a selected set of tasks, select those tasks first. The tasks must be adjacent to one another. The first of the selected tasks is not renumbered, but it serves as the starting point for renumbering the rest of the selection.
2. Choose Project, WBS, Renumber from the menu to display the WBS Renumber dialog box (see Figure 5.33).

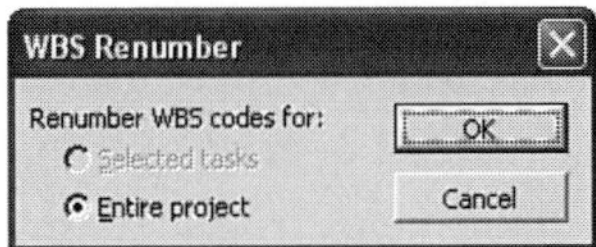

Figure 5.33
You can have Project recalculate the WBS codes for the entire project or for just a set of selected tasks.

3. Choose Selected Tasks or Entire Project, according to your needs.
4. Click OK to start renumbering.
5. If you chose to renumber the entire project, Microsoft Project asks you to confirm your intent. Click Yes, and the renumbering takes place.

TIP

Renumbering an entire project can change a lot of codes, and you can use Undo to restore the original codes. As always, however, you must use Undo before you make any other changes.

If you edit customized WBS codes and then ask Project to renumber all tasks, Project overwrites your editing and reverts to sequential numbers and letters. See "Preserving Edited Custom WBS Codes" in the "Troubleshooting" section at the end of this chapter.

5

Using Custom Outline Numbers

The custom WBS codes discussed in the preceding section are always tied to the outline structure. Each segment of the WBS code mask is linked to a specific outline level. Sorting the task list according to the WBS code produces the same order as sorting according to ID numbers. If you want complete control over a coding system for tasks that is independent of the outline structure you have created, you can use any of 10 custom outline fields (Outline Code 1 through Outline Code 10) to create alternative labeling systems that you can use to sort and group tasks in different orders. Creating and using custom outline codes is described in detail in Chapter 21, "Customizing Views, Tables, Fields, Filters, and Groups."

→ For more information on creating and using custom outline codes, **see** "Customizing Fields," **p. 847**.

Printing the Project Task List

You can print a task list in a number of ways. You can print views such as the Gantt Chart view, the Network Diagram view, or the Task Sheet view, all of which appear on paper much as they appear onscreen. You can also choose from a number of standard reports. Note that you cannot print the form views, and you cannot print combination views (views with two panes).

→ For full instructions on printing views of a task list, **see** Chapter 13, "Printing Views and Reports," **p. 489**.

→ If you want to enhance the display before printing a view, see Chapter 20, "Formatting Views," **p. 775**, for ways to customize a view.

There are six report categories for printing standardized and custom reports in Microsoft Project. Chapter 22, "Using and Customizing the Standard Reports," explains how to work with these reports. At this stage of developing your project, only the reports in the Overview category are of much use. The reports in this category are as follows:

- The Top-Level Tasks report displays the task list but includes only the tasks that are in the first level of the outline.
- The Milestones report lists all milestone tasks.
- The Working Days report summarizes the calendar information, showing the normal workdays and hours plus all exceptions to those normal working times.

Troubleshooting

Moving Summary Tasks

I don't understand how to move summary tasks without moving their subtasks. What do I need to do?

First, outdent the subtasks so that the summary task becomes a regular task. Then you can move, copy, cut, delete, promote, or demote the task without affecting its former subtasks.

Preserving Edited Custom WBS Codes

After I customize my summary task WBS codes, they seem to disappear when I have Project renumber tasks. What am I doing wrong?

If you have edited custom WBS codes for summary tasks and then want Project to renumber the tasks, your edited changes are lost unless you take the following steps:

1. Choose Tools, Options to display the Options dialog box and select the View tab.
2. Clear the Show Summary Tasks check box and click OK to close the dialog box. Only normal and milestone tasks are then displayed.
3. Select one of the column headings to select all displayed tasks.
4. Select Project, WBS, Renumber to display the WBS Renumber dialog box.

5. Click the Selected Tasks button (instead of Entire Project).
6. Click OK to start the renumbering process.
7. Restore the display of summary tasks by choosing Tools, Options and filling the Show Summary Tasks check box on the View tab. Then click OK to close the dialog box. You can click any cell to deselect all tasks.

The entire task list is displayed again. The summary tasks have not lost their edited codes, but all other tasks are renumbered based on their current order in the outline.

PROJECT EXTRAS: LETTING PROJECT CALCULATE DURATION

If you have start and finish dates already estimated for tasks, and therefore you have implied durations, you can manually enter those dates and let Project calculate the Duration field for you. Even better, if the task names and dates are already in a file (such as an Excel or a Word file), you can paste the task values directly into Project to create the tasks and durations.

It's generally not a good idea to enter the dates for tasks; you should let Project schedule the task dates for you. However, in this case, you can more quickly calculate and transfer duration estimates into Project by entering dates. This produces constraints on the tasks, but you can remove the constraints after the duration estimates are in place and give Project the flexibility to create a new schedule of dates.

To manually enter predetermined task start and finish dates for tasks, follow these steps:

1. Display the Task Entry view by first displaying the Gantt Chart view and then selecting Window, Split to display the task form in the bottom pane (see Figure 5.34).
2. Select the first row in the top pane, and then click in the bottom pane to activate its fields. From this point on, you can use the Previous and Next buttons in the task form to move up and down the rows of the top pane without having to leave the bottom pane.
3. If this is a new task, select the Name field and enter the first task name. Notice that the Previous and Next buttons have become OK and Cancel buttons. Don't click OK yet.
4. Select the Start field and enter the start date.
5. Select the Finish field and enter the finish date.
6. Either press Enter or click OK to complete the task. Project posts your three entries in the Gantt Chart view at the top of the pane and calculates the duration as the difference between the dates you entered (see Figure 5.35). The OK and Cancel buttons revert to Previous and Next.

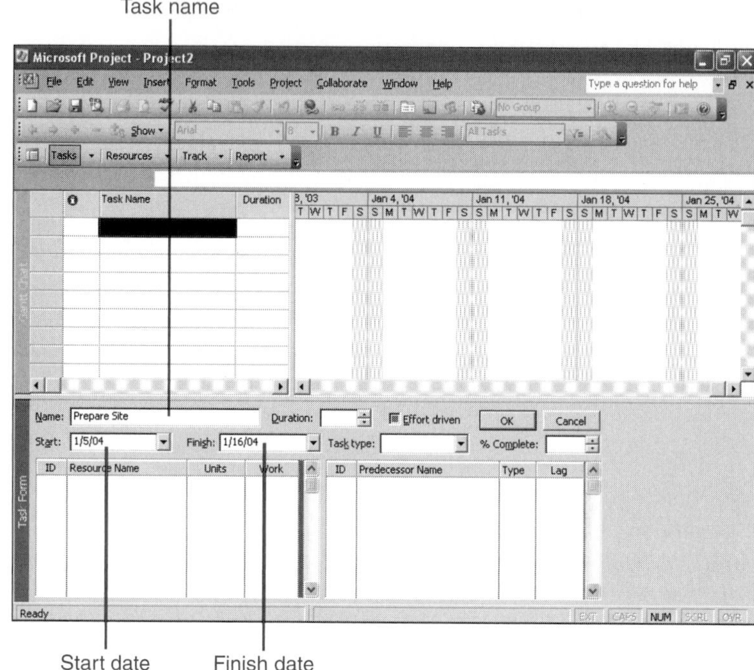

Figure 5.34
The Task Entry view consists of the Gantt Chart view in the top pane and the task form in the bottom pane. You can define tasks in the bottom pane as well as in the top pane.

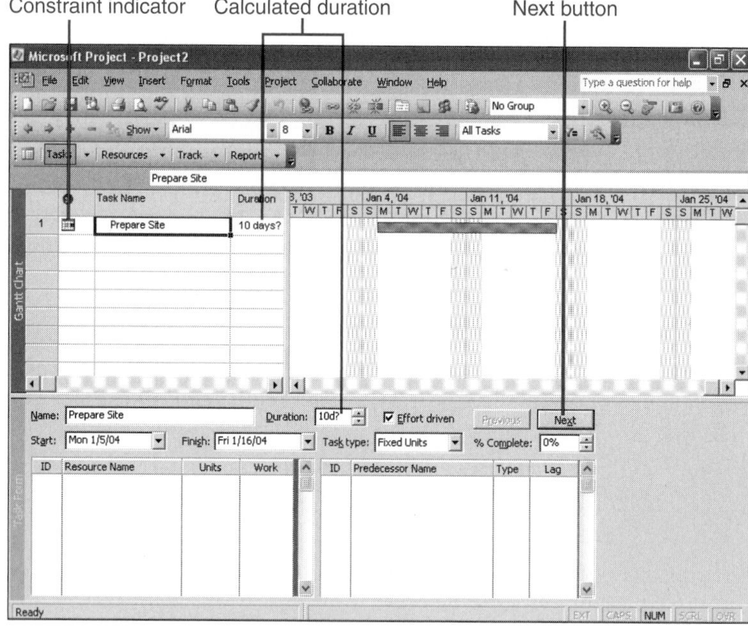

Figure 5.35
After you enter both start and finish dates in the task form, the task has a calculated duration that is the difference between these dates.

7. Press Enter again, or click the Next button to start the next task. Repeat steps 3 through 6 for all tasks.

Notice an indicator next to the task in the Gantt Chart view that reminds you that the task has a constraint. If you slide the mouse pointer over the indicator, you see that it is a Start No Earlier Than constraint, so Project does not schedule the task any earlier than the start date.

After all the tasks are entered, the schedule should match the schedule from which you copied the tasks. Chapter 6 describes how to give Project the instructions it needs to schedule tasks for you. At that point, you might want to remove the constraints from the list and start the more sophisticated and flexible scheduling process that Project makes possible.

You can remove all the constraints by clicking one of the column headings (such as Task Name) to select all tasks. Then click on the Task Information tool to display the Multiple Task Information dialog box and go to the Advanced tab. In the Constraint Task group of fields, select the constraint type As Soon As Possible (or, if the project is scheduled from a fixed finish date, select As Late As Possible).

If the task names and dates are already stored in another document, you can copy the data into Project instead of manually typing all the data. The source task list can be in Excel, Word, Access, or PowerPoint, and your first step is to modify the source data (if necessary) to meet the following requirements:

- Each task must be on its own row.
- If the source is Excel or Access, the task names and dates must be in separate columns or fields. If the list is in Word or PowerPoint, tabs must separate the entries in each row. You can use outlined text from Word or PowerPoint as the source, but if you do, the tasks are not indented in Project and you have to manually outline the task list after it's pasted.
- The dates must be in one of the formats that Project recognizes (for example, 1/19/2004 or Mon 1/19/2004 4:00 PM). You can see the list of recognized formats by choosing Tools, Options and displaying the pull-down list of options in the Date Format box at the top of the View tab.
- The task names and dates must be arranged in columns that are in the same order as the columns in the view you will be using when you paste them into Project. You can either adjust the source data or adjust the column order in Project. If you start with the standard Gantt Chart view and hide the Duration column, the order for those columns in Project is Task Name, Start, and Finish. Therefore, the order of the columns in the source document should be the same: Task Name, Start, and Finish. If the source data includes a fourth column for deadlines, you must insert the Deadline column to the right of the Finish field in Project.

Next, you must prepare the Project document to receive the list:

- Using the standard Gantt Chart view as an example, hide the Duration column by right-clicking the Duration column heading and choosing Hide Column, and insert any additional fields being imported to the right of the Finish field. The Task Name, Start, and Finish columns should now be next to each other and in just that order. After copying in the tasks, you can insert the Duration column again.
- If this is a new project document, you should establish the project start or finish date before you paste in the task list. This is especially important if the project has a fixed finish date. Choose Project, Project Information and set the start date; or choose Schedule from the Project Finish Date and set the finish date.

To copy data, select the data in the rows and columns to be copied in the data source and use the Copy command to place the selection in the Clipboard. Do not include column titles in the selection. In Project, select the single cell in the Task Name column on the row where you want the first imported task to appear, and choose the Paste command. You might receive an error message saying that the date for the first task can't be pasted. You can usually just ignore this message and select the No option in the error dialog box to continue pasting without displaying the error messages for each task. As long as your dates were properly formatted in the source list, they should paste correctly. If you did not include the time of day in the source dates, Project applies its default start time for all the start dates and the default end time for all the finish dates.

To display the Duration column again, you can right-click the Start column heading and choose Insert Column. In the Field Name box, display the drop-down list and scroll to Duration. Click Best Fit to display the Duration column with a width sufficient to show the title and all values.

After linking the tasks, you can remove the constraints as described earlier in this section for the manually entered tasks with dates.

→ To learn about more sophisticated importing of data from other applications, **see** Chapter 17, "Exporting and Importing Project Data with Other File Formats," **p. 631**.

CHAPTER 6

Entering Scheduling Requirements

In this chapter

An Overview of Scheduling 176

Understanding Dependency Links 177

Entering Dependency Links 185

Working with Task Constraints 201

Entering Deadline Dates 217

Splitting Tasks 220

Creating and Using Task Calendars 223

Troubleshooting 226

Project Extras 228

An Overview of Scheduling

After you enter project tasks and estimate durations, you must focus on developing the schedule of start and finish dates. Up to this point in the book, you've used Microsoft Project as a basic word processor or spreadsheet program—entering tasks and durations in a task view. This chapter explores how to link these tasks to define the logical sequence of activity, thus giving Project specific information for calculating a schedule. It also examines how to record constraints and deadlines, assign task calendars, and split tasks.

The project schedule depends on a number of factors, including the following:

- The project schedule either begins on a fixed start date or is calculated to end on a fixed finish date. You control this factor in the Project Information dialog box.

  → For more information on defining the start or finish of a project, **see** "Using the Project Information Dialog Box," **p. 57**.

- Project normally schedules tasks only during the working times defined by the base calendar that you select for the project. Exceptions can occur when you assign resources or attach task calendars to tasks. Both exceptions are described in this list.

  → For guidelines on defining the project base calendar, **see** "Defining a Calendar of Working Time," **p. 76**.

- The schedule depends heavily on the duration estimates for the individual tasks. The duration of the tasks is one of the driving forces of the schedule. The longer the task duration for any given start date, the later the scheduled finish date for that task. Chapter 5, "Creating a Task List," covers estimating durations.
- The schedule also depends on the logical order, or scheduling sequence, for the tasks. Typically, most tasks have start or finish dates that depend on the start or finish date of some other task. This chapter is largely devoted to defining these *dependency links*.
- The schedule accommodates any arbitrary limits, or *constraints*, that you might impose on the start or finish dates for individual tasks. Imposing date constraints is covered later in this chapter.
- You can modify the schedule for an individual task by assigning a *task calendar*. Assigning calendars to tasks is covered in the section "Creating and Using Task Calendars," later in this chapter.
- By default, a task is scheduled without interruption for the duration of the task. You can insert one or more interruptions in the work on a task by splitting the task schedule. See the section "Splitting Tasks," later in this chapter.
- The task schedule also depends on the availability of resources that are assigned to work on the tasks. Chapter 9, "Understanding Resource Scheduling," explains the effects on the schedule of resource availability.
- The schedule is affected if you delay a resource assignment to start after other resources have started or if you contour the daily work assignment for a resource. Chapter 9 discusses both contouring and delaying resource assignments and the effects they have on the task schedule.

In practice, after you learn to use Microsoft Project, you will probably outline, link, and impose constraints on the task list as you enter the tasks. The process is divided into separate chapters in this book to focus on all the options and techniques possible for each activity.

By far the most important topic in this chapter for you to understand is linking tasks. The sequencing or linking of tasks makes it possible for Project to calculate a schedule—and that's one of the main reasons for using Microsoft Project. It is also what makes it possible for Project to identify for you the critical tasks—those that must finish on time or may be worthwhile attempting to finish faster when you need to compress the overall duration of the project.

➔ For a quick review of the terms *critical task* and *critical path,* **see** the overview topic "How Project Calculates the Schedule," **p. 25**.

UNDERSTANDING DEPENDENCY LINKS

Usually some tasks in a project cannot start until one or more other tasks have finished. One common reason for this requirement is that a task might need to use the output generated by another task. For example, in building a house, the foundation must be laid before you can frame the walls. Therefore, the start of the task Frame the Walls is determined by, and should be linked to, the finish of the task Lay the Foundation. The link expresses the dependency of the framing schedule on the schedule for the foundation.

An inexperienced scheduler in this building project might just list the tasks in Excel and type in start and finish dates for all the tasks. But what if the scheduler later finds out that for some reason the Lay the Foundation task will be delayed? The scheduler would then have to go through the entire project, typing in later start and finish dates for all the tasks that will be affected by the delay. However, if the tasks are typed into Microsoft Project and dependency links are defined, the scheduler can simply enter a delayed start date for Lay the Foundation, and Project will calculate new start and finish dates for all the tasks that are dependent, directly or indirectly, on that task. The reason you take the time to define links between tasks is so that Project can recalculate the schedule for you quickly when there is a change in the schedule that affects the scheduling of other tasks.

DEFINING DEPENDENCY LINKS

When tasks are linked to show a dependency relationship, the dependent task is called the *successor* task and the task on which its schedule depends is called its *predecessor*. These names were adopted a long time ago, when the only scheduling links envisioned had dependent tasks coming after the tasks they depend on, and they serve well for describing the vast majority of linked tasks. You will soon see that more sophisticated linking can create a situation where they simply aren't appropriate.

To illustrate the usage of the terms *predecessor* and *successor*, suppose you need to schedule the application of two coats of paint to the exterior walls of a small structure. There will be four tasks involved: Prepare Surfaces, Apply First Coat, Apply Final Coat, and Clean Up. The start of Apply First Coat depends on the finish of Prepare Surfaces; therefore, Prepare Surfaces is the predecessor to Apply First Coat. Similarly, Apply First Coat is the predecessor to Apply Final Coat, and Apply Final Coat is the predecessor to Clean Up. The start date for the successor task should be linked to the finish date for the predecessor. As illustrated in Figure 6.1, Project draws a small arrow from the finish of each predecessor task to the start of its successor task.

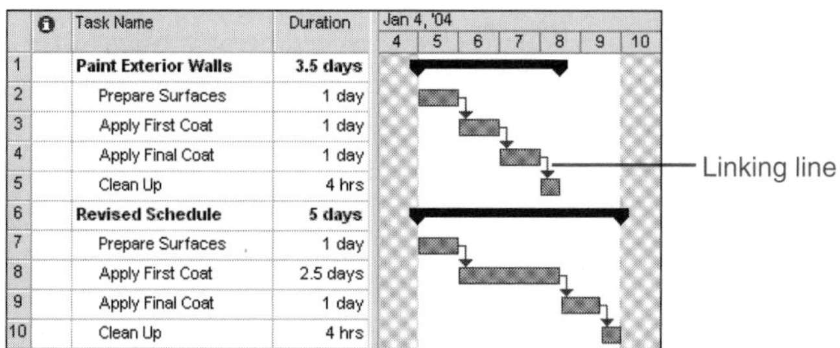

Figure 6.1
When you link a dependent task, its schedule depends on the schedule of its predecessor.

When you refer to a dependency link, the linked date of the predecessor task (either its start or its finish) is named first, and the linked date of the successor task is named last. In the painting example in Figure 6.1, the dependency relationships are called *Finish-to-Start links* because the predecessor's finish determines the successor's start. Finish-to-Start is the most common type of link, but there are also three other types you can use: Finish-to-Finish, Start-to-Start, and Start-to-Finish. The section "Defining the Types of Dependency Link Relationships," later in this chapter, describes the use of all types of links.

By establishing the link in the painting example, you instruct Project to set the start date for Apply Final Coat based on the scheduled finish date for Apply First Coat. Any change that alters the calculated finish date for the predecessor causes Project to also reschedule the start date for the dependent or successor task. In Figure 6.1 the Apply First Coat task in the revised schedule on row 8 has been given a longer duration than it had in the original schedule, on row 3. Accordingly, the Apply Final Coat task on row 9 is scheduled to start and finish later than it was on row 4, reflecting the longer duration of its predecessor. If you define task links, Project automatically reschedules dependent tasks when the schedule for the predecessor changes.

CAUTION

Do not link two unrelated tasks just to level out the workload for a resource who is assigned to work on both tasks. It is true that the link forces Project to schedule the tasks one after the other, thus allowing the worker to complete one task before starting the next. But what if the worker is later removed from working on one of the tasks? There is no way to tell that the link no longer serves a purpose and can be removed (unless you just happen to remember it), and you will be left with an unnecessary delay that could delay the finish of your project. The preferred way to deal with this problem is to *delay* one of the tasks by using the Leveling Delay field.

→ For the steps to follow in using leveling delays, **see** "Resolving Overallocations by Delaying Assignments," **p. 440**.

CHOOSING THE DEPENDENT TASK

Deciding which of two tasks is the dependent task and which is the predecessor is often self-evident. In many cases, as with the building example used earlier, the dependent task requires the output of another task; in such a case, you make that other task its predecessor. Other times, however, it's not so simple.

Consider the following case, in which a person, not a computer, is doing the scheduling:

> Elaine is an on-the-job trainee for a residential construction project, and she is responsible for making sure that lumber and materials are on hand when the foundation is finished and it's time to frame the walls of the new house. Elaine is to watch the progress on finishing the foundation and call the lumberyard four days before the foundation is finished to schedule the materials' delivery. Elaine's instructions are to avoid ordering the materials any earlier than necessary because that would mean paying interest on borrowed money for a longer period of time. Although the term *just-in-time scheduling* wasn't used in Elaine's instructions, this is, in fact, an example of that management principle.
>
> When it's just about time to call the lumberyard, Elaine learns that the carpenters are being diverted to another project that has a higher priority, and the framing phase of the project has been put on hold for a week. Elaine's common sense tells her that the materials' order is really linked to the start of the framing, not to the finish of the foundation, and she delays placing the delivery order until two days before the new start date for framing.

If you were scheduling this example in Microsoft Project, you would want to give Project enough information to be able to do what Elaine did—delay the start of the delivery task if the framing task is delayed. To do that, you need to treat the delivery of materials as a task that is dependent on the start of the framing task.

This type of linking was not envisioned when the terms *predecessor* and *successor* became popular. Recall that the term *successor* was coined to refer to the dependent task. In this example, where the delivery task's schedule depends on the framing task's schedule, we have to call the delivery task the successor and the framing task the predecessor, even though the successor in this case is to take place a day or so before its predecessor. This usage flies in the face of our everyday use of the terms *predecessor* and *successor*. (We really should call them something like *driver task* and *dependent task* instead of predecessor and successor.) However, it's just the result of keeping old labels for more modern methods.

The decision about which task should be the predecessor and which the dependent, or successor, task might hinge on which task you have more control over. If you have equal scheduling control over both tasks, make the task that must come first the predecessor and let the later task be the dependent successor. In cases in which the schedule for one task is out of your control, you might want to arbitrarily make the more flexibly scheduled task the dependent task—regardless of which task actually must come first in time.

For example, suppose an office building project will have a world-famous artist paint a mural in the entrance to the building. The artist is available only at certain times, and a change in the artist's availability would mean a change in the schedule. The artist's task will probably be defined as the driver (the predecessor) for other tasks that are more flexible—tasks such as having scaffolding erected for the artist to use and maybe even when to start construction. On the other hand, if the mural were to be painted by a talented local artist who is anxious to get the work, you would probably let earlier steps in construction drive the schedule for painting the mural.

When one of two linked tasks is a support function that merely facilitates the other task (such as ordering lumber and materials for framing, erecting scaffolding for painting a mural), you will usually want to make the main task the predecessor and the support function the dependent task.

ALLOWING FOR DELAYS AND OVERLAPS

Sometimes you might need to schedule a delay as part of the linkage between the predecessor and the successor tasks. For instance, in the painting example, you need to allow time for the first coat of paint to dry before you apply the final coat. This kind of delay is known as a *lag* or as *lag time* in task scheduling, and you could add a one-day lag to the Finish-to-Start link between the Apply First Coat and Apply Final Coat tasks. The successor task's start would lag behind the predecessor's finish.

Other times you might want to allow the dependent task to overlap or start before the predecessor task is finished. You add *lead time* to a link when you want the linked date for the successor task to anticipate the linked date of its predecessor. For example, the cleanup crew can begin the Clean Up task when the painters are close to finishing the Apply Final Coat task. The successor task's start would lead to the predecessor's finish.

Figure 6.2 shows the painting example again. The first set of tasks has no lead or lag defined; the revised schedule has lead and lag time added to the links. There is a lag added to the link between the first and final coats of paint, and there is lead time between the Apply Final Coat and the Clean Up task. The lag adds to the overall duration of the painting project, but the lead allows the project to finish faster than it would otherwise.

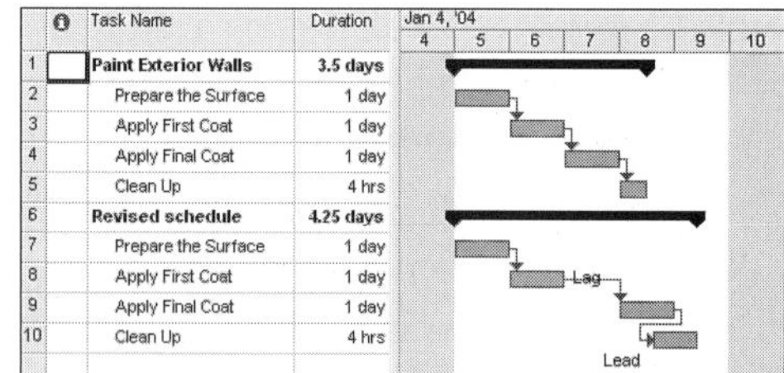

Figure 6.2
You can use lag time to delay the successor task. Lead time allows tasks to overlap, meaning that the project can finish earlier than would be possible otherwise.

TIP

Identifying task relationships where overlaps such as lead time are possible is one of the best ways to shorten the overall time it takes to finish a project.

→ For more information on compressing, or crashing, a schedule, **see** "Shortening the Critical Path," **p. 480**.

Lags and leads can be defined in ordinary duration units or in elapsed duration units. If you want Project to schedule the lag during working time on the calendar, you use ordinary duration units. If Project can use nonworking time also for scheduling the lag, you use elapsed duration units. For example, what if the Apply First Coat task were to finish on a Friday, the last working day of the week? If the one-day lag for the Apply Final Coat task were defined as one ordinary day (typically 8 hours of working time, on a standard calendar), Project would let one day of working time pass before scheduling the start of the Apply Final Coat task. The next working day after Friday is Monday; therefore, the successor task would be scheduled for Tuesday. But if the lag were defined as one elapsed day (that is, 24 hours of continuous time), Project would use the weekend days for the lag and the final coat could begin on Monday.

→ For more information about using elapsed duration, **see** "Defining Elapsed Duration," **p. 135**.

Although you usually define lags and leads in fixed time units (such as 4 hours or two elapsed days), Project also allows you to define lags and leads as a percentage of the duration of the predecessor. With the percentage format, Project makes the length of the lag or lead a multiple of the length of the predecessor task. Using the different methods of entering leads and lags is discussed in the section "Entering Leads and Lags," later in this chapter.

DEFINING THE TYPES OF DEPENDENCY LINK RELATIONSHIPS

You can create four types of dependency relationships, depending on whether you use the start dates or finish dates when linking tasks. The name for each dependency type includes a reference to the linked date for the predecessor (either its start date or its finish date), followed by a reference to the linked date for the dependent task (either its start or finish date). Therefore, a Finish-to-Start relationship signifies that the finish date of the predecessor task is used to schedule the start date of the dependent task. The predecessor is referenced first, and then the dependent or successor task is referenced.

Project usually uses two-letter code abbreviations for the four dependency types, as shown in Table 6.1. The first letter in the code refers to the predecessor's start or finish, and the second letter refers to the dependent task. Thus, the code for Finish-to-Start is FS. The following subsections describe the different dependency types.

TABLE 6.1 THE LINKING RELATIONSHIPS IN MICROSOFT PROJECT

Code	Dependency Type	Meaning
FS	Finish-to-Start	Predecessor's finish determines successor's start.
SS	Start-to-Start	Predecessor's start determines successor's start.
FF	Finish-to-Finish	Predecessor's finish determines successor's finish.
SF	Start-to-Finish	Predecessor's start determines successor's finish.

USING THE FINISH-TO-START RELATIONSHIP

In the Finish-to-Start relationship, the finish date of the predecessor determines the start date of the successor task. For example, framing the walls of a new house should be scheduled to start after the foundation is prepared. The links in the painting example in Figures 6.1 and 6.2 are all Finish-to-Start links. The linking arrow in the Gantt Chart is drawn from the finish of the predecessor task to the start of the dependent task. This is the most common dependency type and is the default relationship created via the Edit, Link Tasks command.

USING THE START-TO-START RELATIONSHIP

In the Start-to-Start relationship, the start date of the predecessor task determines the start date of the successor task. You can schedule the two tasks to start at or near the same time by using this type of relationship. The two tasks are scheduled to run in parallel.

NOTE

> A lag often is associated with Start-to-Start links. The start of the dependent task is delayed until some time after the predecessor task is underway.

For example, suppose an organization leases new office space and plans to move to the new space when remodeling is completed. As part of the move from one office to another, several tasks need to be accomplished—packing boxes, disconnecting desktop computers, disassembling furniture, and loading the boxes and furniture into the moving van. Because the movers can start loading the vans almost immediately after the packing task starts, the start of the Load Vans task can be linked to the start of the Pack Boxes & Disassemble Furniture task, with a small amount of delay or lag time (see the tasks in Scenario A in Figure 6.3). Pack Boxes & Disassemble Furniture is the predecessor task; Load Vans is the successor task. The arrow is drawn from the start of the predecessor to the start of the dependent task.

If the availability of the loading vans drives this operation, you could make the Pack Boxes & Disassemble Furniture task dependent on Load Vans, with a small amount of lead time. The linking shown in the Scenario B taskbars in Figure 6.3 illustrates this alternative. The start of the Pack & Disassemble Furniture task is linked to the start of the Load Vans task, with a two-hour lead, to ensure that packing starts shortly before the loaders are ready to start.

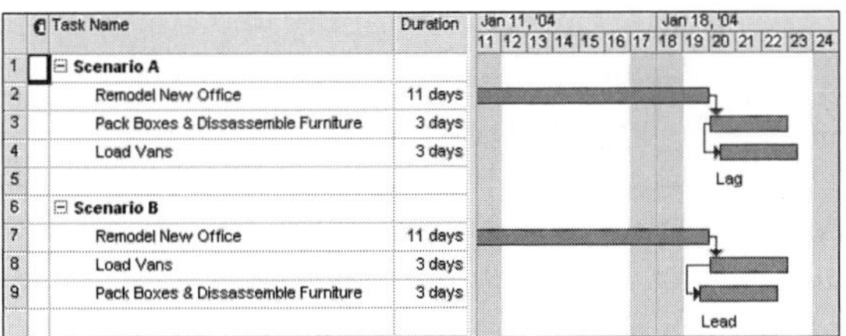

Figure 6.3
You can link the start of the Load Vans task to the start of the Pack Boxes & Disassemble Furniture task, with a two-hour lag. Alternatively, you can link the Pack Boxes & Disassemble Furniture task to the Load Vans task, with a two-hour lead.

Using the Finish-to-Finish Relationship

In the Start-to-Start relationship, the start date of the predecessor to the Finish-to-Finish relationship, the finish date of the predecessor determines the scheduled finish date of the successor task; you schedule two tasks to finish at or about the same time. For example, in remodeling a kitchen, the acquisition of the kitchen appliances should be completed by the time the cabinetmakers finish installing the kitchen cabinets, so the cabinetmakers can install the appliances in and around the new cabinets (see Figure 6.4).

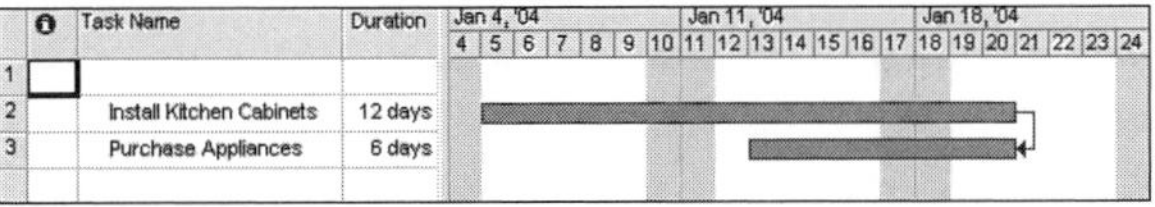

Figure 6.4
The kitchen appliances should all be purchased by the time the kitchen cabinets are completed; this is a Finish-to-Finish relationship.

NOTE

> The link types Start-to-Start and Finish-to-Finish with leads and lags can be used to schedule tasks to overlap and are standard techniques for *fast-tracking* a project–that is, compressing the overall duration of the project by overlapping tasks.

Using the Start-to-Finish Relationship

In the Start-to-Finish relationship, the start date of the predecessor task determines the scheduled finish date of the successor. With this type of relationship you schedule a task to finish just in time to start a more important task that it supports. This is the link type you would use in the example about helping Elaine schedule the delivery of framing materials. Here are some more examples that illustrate the Start-to-Finish relationship:

- When scheduling the delivery of merchandise to a new store, the grand opening date determines when the deliveries must be scheduled. A delay in construction that pushes back the grand opening leads to calls to the merchandise suppliers to delay their deliveries.

- *Just-in-time scheduling* in manufacturing is a policy that strives to stock raw materials just in time for the manufacturing process to begin. This policy saves money by not tying up cash in materials' inventories any longer than necessary.

Figure 6.5 illustrates Elaine's project, where the framing materials are to be purchased just in time for framing the walls. In the first set of tasks (the original schedule), the Purchase Materials task is scheduled to finish just as the Frame Walls task begins. Purchase Materials is dependent on Frame Walls, making Frame Walls its predecessor. If the framing is delayed, the purchase of materials will be delayed, too. The link is a Start-to-Finish link, and the arrow is drawn from the start of the predecessor to the finish of the dependent task.

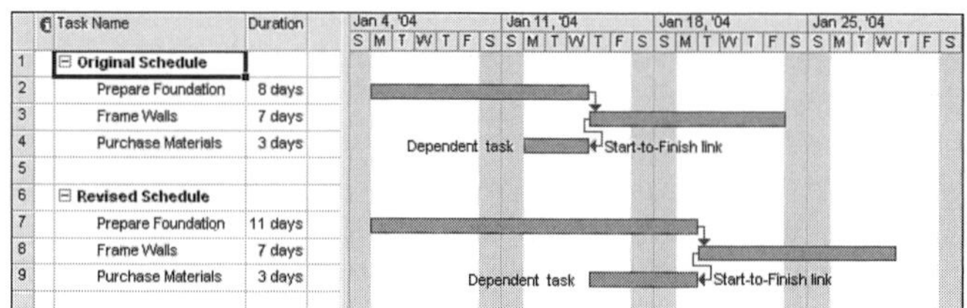

Figure 6.5
The Purchase Materials task must be completed in time for the Frame Walls task to begin, making its schedule dependent on the schedule for Frame Walls.

In the revised schedule in Figure 6.5, the Prepare Foundation task has a longer duration than in the original schedule, and that delays the scheduled start for Frame Walls. Automatically, Project delays the dependent task Purchase Materials just enough so that it will still be finished just in time for the new start date of Frame Walls.

Linking Summary Tasks

Standard practice is to link subtasks—the working tasks in the project—and not to link summary tasks. However, summary tasks can be linked to each other or to subtasks under other summary tasks. A summary task is already implicitly linked to its own subtasks; therefore, Project won't let you establish an explicit link between a subtask and its summary task.

If the summary task is linked to a predecessor, the predecessor relationship dictates when the summary task (and therefore its subtasks) can begin. Likewise, as you will see later in this chapter, if the summary task has a date constraint, its subtasks are effectively constrained to that date also. If the summary task has no links or date constraints, its start and finish dates are derived from the earliest start and the latest finish of any of its subtasks.

Linking summary tasks is generally not considered to be good practice. Summary tasks do not define the activities where work gets done—and links should generally reflect the scheduling requirements of the tasks where work is done.

If a summary task represents a discrete, self-contained group of tasks, and no subtask of the would-be dependent summary task needs to be linked to the predecessor summary task, it may be useful. In that case, linking the phases has the advantage that you can change the subtasks within each of the two phases without worrying about redefining the link between the phases.

NOTE

> If you select all tasks and let Microsoft Project link the tasks in an outlined project, Project links all tasks at the first outline level to each other, whether they are summary tasks or not. It then links the next level of subtasks within any summary tasks to each other, and so forth, until all outline levels in all summary tasks are linked at their own levels. All links are the default Finish-to-Start link type.

If you create a task link that involves a summary task as the dependent or successor task, you can use only the link types Finish-to-Start and Start-to-Start. Project does not let you establish the other link types (those where the summary task's finish date is linked). However, if the link involves a summary task as the predecessor to a nonsummary task, you can use any of the four possible link types. These rules apply the same in both fixed start-date and fixed finish-date projects.

CAUTION

> Be sure you establish no links between subtasks under the same summary task that try to schedule one of the subtasks to start before the first subtask in the summary group. For example, suppose Subtask A starts when the summary task starts. If you link another subtask in the same group to Subtask A with a Start-to-Start link and add lead time to the link, you would be telling Project to start the second subtask before the summary task begins. Project would ignore the lead time and schedule both tasks to start at the same time.

ENTERING DEPENDENCY LINKS

You can create task links in Project in a number of ways, depending on the active view. The Project Guide provides a quick way to create the most common link types (all but the Start-to-Finish type). Choose Task on the Project Guide toolbar and select Schedule Tasks to display the Schedule Tasks sidepane (see Figure 6.6). Select the tasks you want to link and choose the appropriate link buttons in the Project Guide.

You can also use the Project Guide to break a link. Select a single task and click the Unlink Tasks button to remove all links to other tasks. Select a pair of tasks and click the button to remove just the link between those two tasks.

You can link tasks in a number of other ways. Each of the methods described here is discussed in detail in the following sections. Some can be used only in very restrictive circumstances, so read about all the methods instead of adopting just one.

To create a default Finish-to-Start link with no lead or lag, you can do one of the following:

- Select the tasks to be linked in a table view and use the Link Tasks tool on the Standard toolbar.
- Link the selected tasks in a table view by selecting Edit, Link Tasks.
- Link the selected tasks in a table view by using the keyboard shortcut Ctrl+F2.
- Drag the mouse pointer from the graphic for a predecessor task to the graphic for its successor task in a view such as Gantt Chart, Network Diagram, or Calendar.

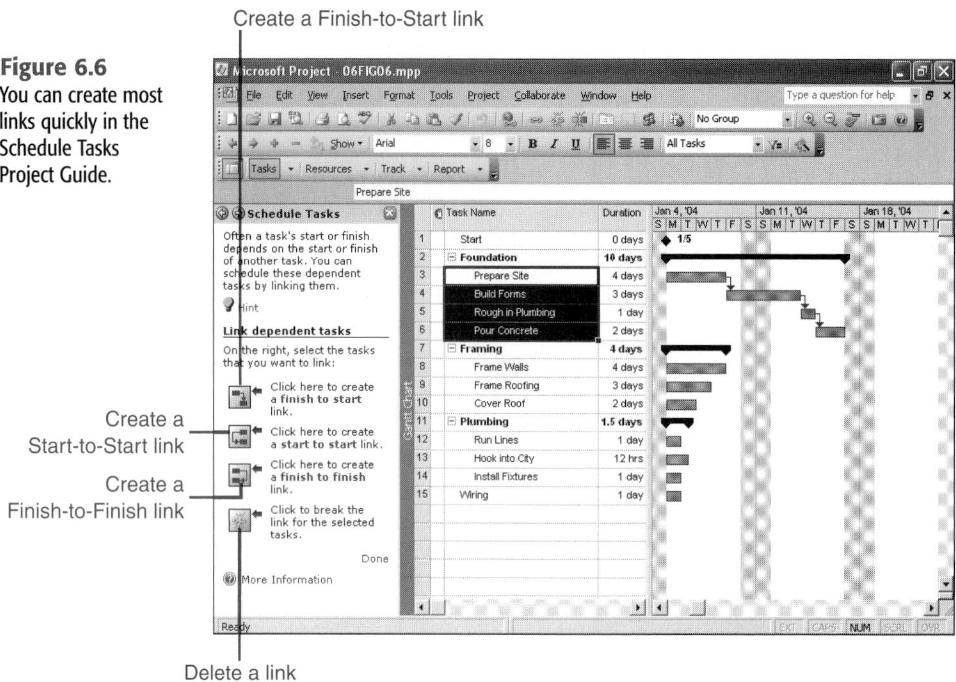

Figure 6.6
You can create most links quickly in the Schedule Tasks Project Guide.

To create any of the link types (with or without lead or lag time) or to edit one of the links created using a technique in the preceding list, you can do any of the following:

- Select the successor task and define its predecessors in the Predecessors tab of the Task Information dialog box.
- Define predecessors or successors for a selected task in the Task Form view.
- Define predecessors for a task in the Predecessors column of a task table. For example, the default table for the Gantt Chart view is the Entry table, and it includes the Predecessors field. You could also display the Successors field in a column and use it to define a task's successors.

TIP

> As you will see in later discussions in this chapter, using these last three methods requires you to know or look up the name or ID number for the task you want to link to. In a large project, that can be cumbersome. I almost always use one of the quick methods in the first list to create a standard link (because it's easier to select the tasks in the view than in a dialog box); then I edit the links that require it, by using one of the methods described next.

To edit a link—for example, to include lag time or lead time or to change the type of link—Microsoft Project provides these equivalent methods:

- Select the successor task and use the Predecessors tab in the Task Information dialog box.
- Use the Predecessors and Successors tables in the Task Form view to modify a task's links to other tasks.
- Use the Predecessors (or Successors) field in the Entry table of a task view such as the Gantt Chart view.
- Double-click the linking line for a dependency relationship in the Gantt Chart view or the Network Diagram view to display the Task Dependency dialog box.

NOTE

You can't change the order of the link (that is, make the successor the predecessor) by using any of these methods. You always have to break the link and start over if you want to designate a different dependent task.

To learn how to create links between tasks that are not part of the same project, see "Linking Tasks from Different Projects" in the "Troubleshooting" section near the end of this chapter.

CREATING LINKS BY USING THE MENU OR TOOLBAR

The simplest and easiest way to link tasks is to select the tasks and then click the Link Tasks tool on the Standard toolbar, or choose Edit, Link Tasks from the menu, or press Ctrl+F2. These links are always default Finish-to-Start links, without lag or lead. You have to edit the links if you want a different link type or you want to add lag or lead. In Figure 6.7, four tasks are selected and have been linked in series with the Link Tasks tool.

There is no limit to the number of tasks you can select for linking with the menu or Link Tasks tool. You can link just one predecessor and one successor at a time, or you can link all the tasks in the project in the same operation.

If you select adjacent tasks by dragging the mouse pointer or by using the Shift+down arrow or Shift+up arrow key combinations, Project links the selected tasks from the top down—that is, tasks higher in the list (those with lower ID numbers) are predecessors for the tasks below them (those with higher ID numbers). The same thing applies if you select all tasks by clicking one of the column headings, such as Task Name.

If you build the selection by using Ctrl+click to add tasks, Project links the tasks in the order in which they are added to the selection. The first selected task is the predecessor to the second, and so forth.

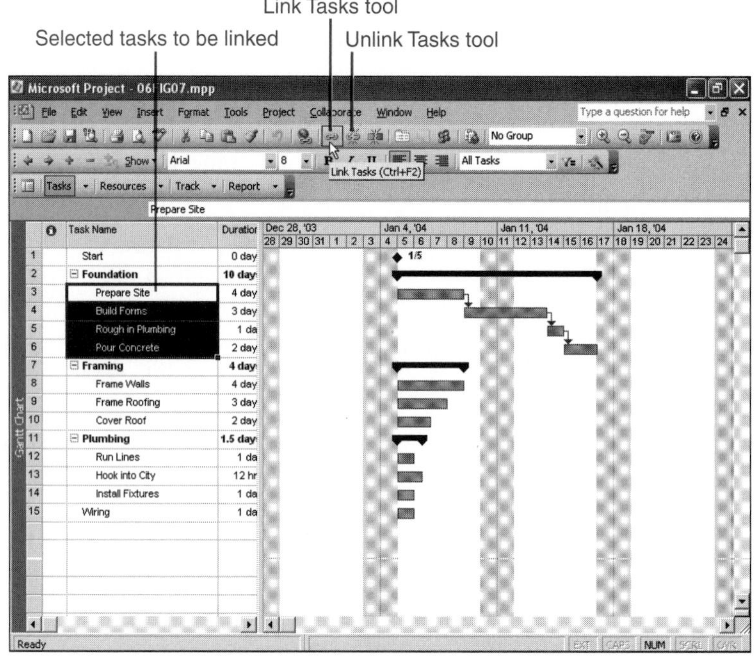

Figure 6.7
You can quickly link selected tasks by using the Link Tasks button. This links the tasks in a Finish-to-Start relationship.

TIP

> To select a task for linking, click any field in the task row or click the taskbar in the Gantt Bar graphic. You do not need to select the entire task row.

To remove a task link, select the linked tasks and either click the Unlink Tasks tool, use the Edit, Unlink Tasks command, or press Ctrl+Shift+F2. To remove all links to a task, including all of the task's predecessors and successors, select just the task itself and use the Unlink Tasks toolbar button or command.

CREATING LINKS BY USING THE TASK INFORMATION DIALOG BOX

No matter what view is active, you can use the Predecessors tab of the Task Information dialog box to define and edit a selected task's predecessor links (see Figure 6.8). Unlike the Edit, Link Tasks command, the Task Information dialog box enables you to choose the type of link and to enter lag or lead time.

To create a dependency relationship by using the Task Information dialog box, follow these steps:

1. Select the dependent (that is, successor) task.

2. Click the Task Information tool on the Standard toolbar, or double-click the task to open the Task Information dialog box.

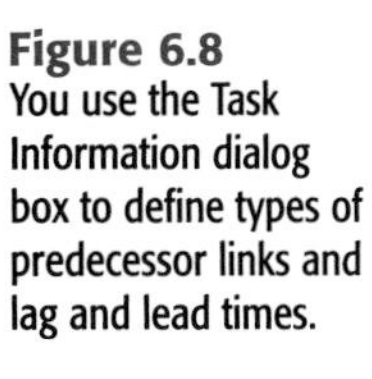

Figure 6.8
You use the Task Information dialog box to define types of predecessor links and lag and lead times.

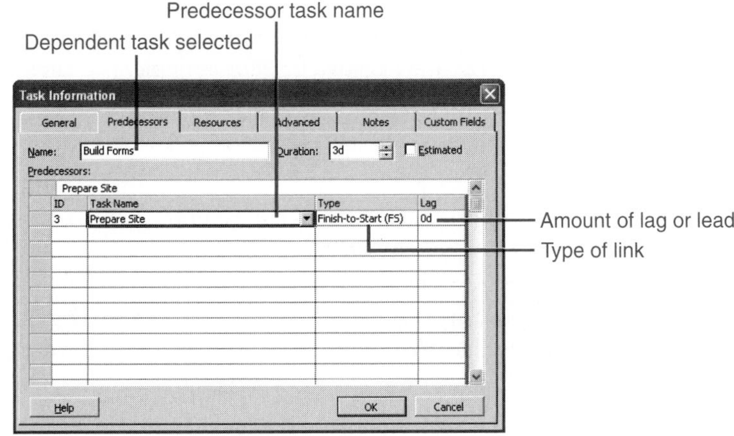

3. Click the Predecessors tab. The Predecessors tab features a table in which you can define predecessors, including the type of link and any lead or lag time (refer to Figure 6.8).
4. Activate the first blank cell under the Task Name field. Choose the name of the task to be the predecessor task from the drop-down list in the field. Project automatically supplies the ID number and the default Finish-to-Start link type, with no lag, unless you choose otherwise.

   Alternatively, if you remember the ID number for the predecessor task, you can enter it in the cell in the ID column. Press Enter to finish the cell entry or select the green check button on the Entry bar. Project automatically supplies the Task Name for that ID number and supplies the default Finish-to-Start link type, with no lag.
5. Use the drop-down list in the Type column to change the dependency type, if needed.
6. To create lag or lead time, click in the Lag field and type the amount of lag or lead time, followed by a time unit (unless you want to use the default time unit). See the following section for more details about entering leads and lags.
7. If additional predecessors exist for the task, repeat steps 4 through 6 as needed for each predecessor.
8. To delete a predecessor, select any cell in its row and press the Delete key.
9. Click OK or press Enter to accept the changes.

ENTERING LEADS AND LAGS

Entering leads and lags is done the same way whether you use the Task Information dialog box mentioned previously or other forms or dialog boxes. When entering lags and leads, bear in mind that both are entered in the same Lag box on Microsoft Project forms. You use positive numbers to represent lag time and negative numbers to represent lead time.

You can enter lag or lead as a number followed by one of the regular or elapsed time code letters you use for entering duration time (that is, m or em, h or eh, d or ed, w or ew, or mo or emo). Lead time is entered as a negative lag. For example, you enter **2d** to define a two-day lag and **-4h** to define a four-hour lead. You type **2ed** to schedule a lag of two elapsed days. If you type a number without a time unit, Project appends the default duration unit (which is initially days).

You can also express lag or lead time as a percentage of the predecessor's duration. Therefore, if you want a task to start when its predecessor is within 10% of being finished, you can enter a Finish-to-Start link with a 10% lead (entered as **-10%**). Project schedules the task to start so that it overlaps the last 10% of the predecessor task duration. Using percentage lags and leads enables the amount of lag or lead to vary with changes in the duration of the predecessor. Thus, the longer the duration of the predecessor, the more time a percentage lag or lead would entail.

When you use percentage lags and leads, Project uses the start or finish of the predecessor (as specified in the link type) for the starting point and offsets the start or finish of the successor from that point by the lag percentage multiplied by the duration of the predecessor. For example, if the predecessor has a duration of four days, a Start-to-Start lag of 25% causes the successor's start to be scheduled one day after the predecessor's start. A Finish-to-Start lead of 75% produces the same start date for the successor—as long as the duration of the predecessor remains unchanged. Subsequent changes in the duration of the predecessor, however, cause these two links to result in a different start date for the successor.

Entering a percentage lag time ensures that the scheduling of the successor task always starts relative to its predecessor, regardless of the duration. Creating this relationship works well in outlining company methods and templates in which the scaling of the project is dependent on the relationship delay or overlap, not a specified duration.

CREATING LINKS BY USING THE TASK FORM VIEW

6

With a task view such as the Gantt Chart view in the top pane, you can split the window and use the Task Form view in the bottom pane to define the predecessor and successor relationships (see Figure 6.9). This is an easy way to define or edit complex dependency relationships. You select a task in the top pane and define its predecessor or successor link in the predecessor or successor details in the bottom pane.

The default display of task details in the Task Form view is to show resources and predecessors. If you want to display both predecessor and successor details, right-click over the Task Form and choose Predecessors and Successors. Or you can activate the Task Form view and choose Format, Details, Predecessors and Successors.

If you display the predecessor details, you can define a predecessor for the dependent task by following these steps:

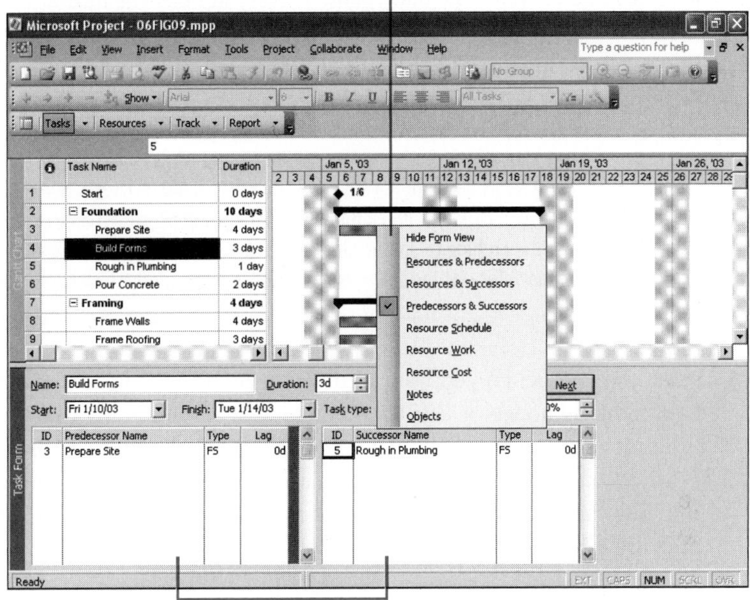

Figure 6.9
The shortcut menu for the Task Form view offers several choices for displaying task link details in the bottom of the form.

1. Select the dependent task in the top pane or use the Previous and Next buttons in the lower pane to move to the desired task.

NOTE

> If you want to enter the successor details in the Task Form view, select the predecessor task in the top pane and use the successor detail fields in the steps that follow instead of the predecessor detail fields. The link is defined exactly the same in either detail area.

2. In the bottom pane, activate the first cell in either the ID or Predecessor Name column.
3. If you selected the Predecessor Name field, use the drop-down list of task names to select the name of the task to be the predecessor. The Task Form view still shows the OK button because selecting the task name completes only the cell entry.

   You can also type the predecessor's ID number in the ID field and press Enter to complete the cell entry. Project automatically fills in the predecessor name when you click the OK button to complete the linking definition.

   If you do not know the ID number of the predecessor, you can use the vertical scrollbar in the top pane to view the predecessor task. The ID field remains selected while you scroll the task list. Do not select the predecessor; just view its ID number. Type this number into the ID field. You can then press Enter or click the green check button on the Entry bar to complete the cell entry for the ID number.

6

4. Select the predecessor's Type field if you want to define a link type other than Finish-to-Start. If you leave the Type field blank, Project supplies the default Finish-to-Start type when you choose the OK button. Type in the two-letter code (FF, FS, SF, or SS) or use the drop-down list to select the code. Press Enter to complete the cell entry in the Type field.

NOTE

> The Type field only accepts the two-letter abbreviations for link types. If you have an AutoCorrect entry for the link type you want to use, Project converts it to the AutoCorrect text when you click OK—and it then rejects the result because it only accepts the abbreviations. There is nothing to do but click Cancel at this point, and then either delete the AutoCorrect definition or edit the link elsewhere (for example, in the Task Information dialog box).

5. Select the Lag field if you want to define a lag or lead time. The default of 0d (zero days, meaning no lag or lead time) is supplied automatically when you click the OK button if you leave this field blank. You can move the spinner control up to display lags (positive values) or down to display leads (negative values) in the default duration time unit. You can also type in a value by using any of the duration or elapsed duration time units or by using a percentage amount.
6. You can add more predecessors on the following rows in the Predecessors table by repeating steps 2–5.
7. To delete a predecessor, click any cell in its row and press the Delete key.
8. Click the OK button to execute the changes you entered in the Task Form view. Figure 6.10 shows the completed details for Task 5's link with Task 4 as a Start-to-Start predecessor with a two-day lag.

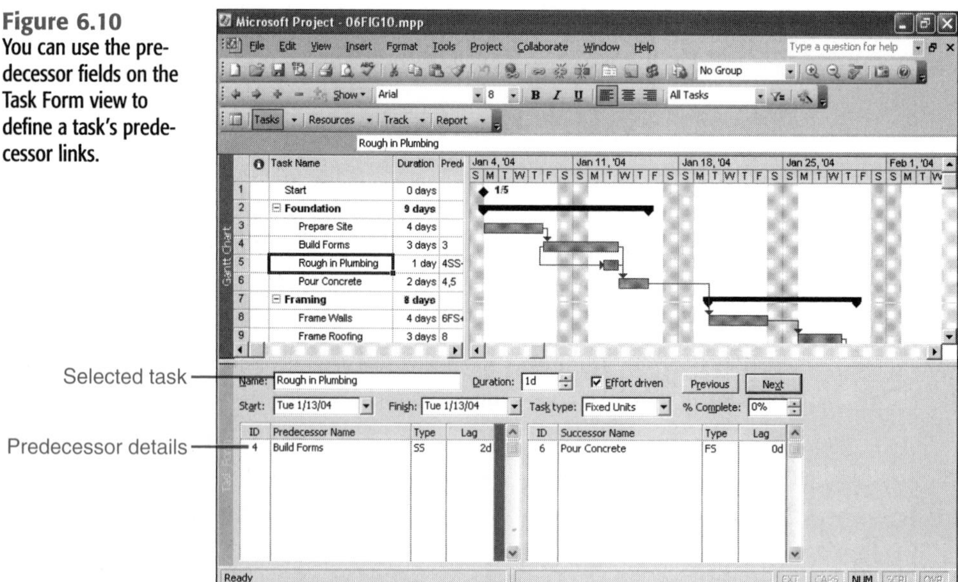

Figure 6.10
You can use the predecessor fields on the Task Form view to define a task's predecessor links.

CREATING LINKS USING THE ENTRY TABLE

You can create or edit dependency relationships in the Predecessors field on the Entry table (see Figure 6.11). The Entry table is the default table displayed in the Gantt Chart view. To see the Predecessors field on the table, either move the vertical split bar to the right or click the right arrow on the horizontal scrollbar at the bottom-left side of the Gantt Chart view.

NOTE

You can add the Successors field to the table and edit both predecessors and successors for tasks in the table.

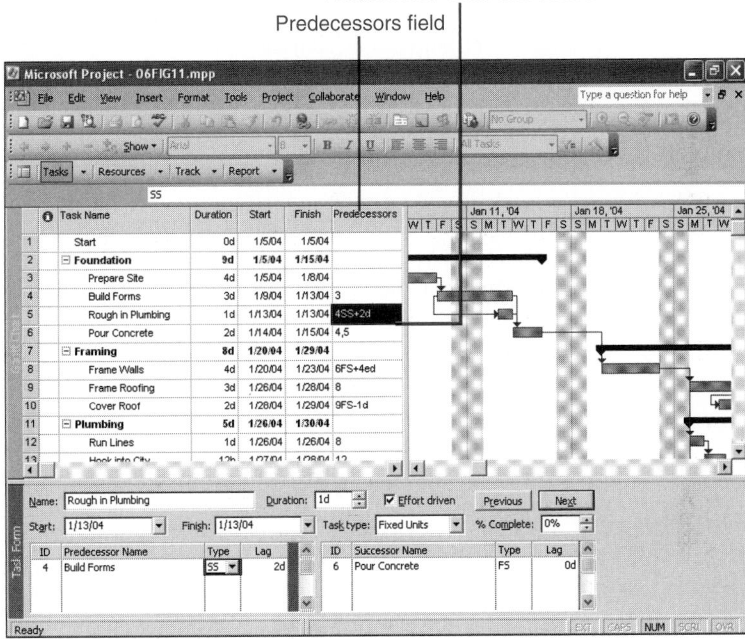

Figure 6.11
The codes entered in the Predecessors field define links just as do entries in the predecessor Details area of the Task Form view.

You can enter the simplest relationship, Finish-to-Start, by just entering the task ID number for the predecessor task in the Predecessors field (or the ID for the successor in the Successors field). The other dependency relationships require a very specific pattern of coding.

Assume that you want to make Task 5 a predecessor with a Start-to-Start link and a two-day lead. The code in the Predecessors column would be **5SS-2d**. The explanation for the code is as follows:

- You enter the ID number for the predecessor first (in this case, **5**).
- You follow the ID number (without any spaces) by the abbreviation for the type of link (in this case, **SS**). If the link is the default FS (for which you usually don't have to include the abbreviation), you must add the abbreviation in order to add a lag or lead.

- Optionally, you can follow the link type by a plus sign (+) for a lag or a minus sign (–) for a lead. You cannot omit the plus sign with a lag.
- You follow the plus or minus sign with the length of the lag or lead, using duration units (that is, m, h, d, w, mo), elapsed duration units (that is, em, eh, ed, ew, emo), or a percentage (such as 10% or –5%). If this example had a two-day lag, the code would be **5SS+2d**. If the lag were two elapsed days, the code would be **5SS+2ed**. If a lead were 10%, the code would be **5SS-10%**.

If a task has more than one predecessor, you separate the predecessor definitions with commas (without any spaces). For example, the code **5SS-2d,6,3FS+1d** would link the task to tasks 5, 6, and 3.

TIP

If you do not remember the ID number of the predecessor, leave the cell you are editing selected while you scroll through the task list to find the predecessor task. Do not select the predecessor; just view its ID number. As you start typing, the row for the cell you are editing returns to the screen, and you can finish the link definition.

NOTE

You form codes for the Successors field identically to the way you form the codes for the Predecessors field. The only difference is that you begin with the ID number for the successor instead of the predecessor.

Creating Links by Using the Mouse

You can use the mouse to link taskbars on the timescale side of the Gantt Chart view or in the Network Diagram view or Calendar view. You can also use the mouse to edit the linking relationship in the Gantt Chart view or the Network Diagram view.

To link tasks with the mouse in the Gantt Chart view, center the mouse over the predecessor task until the pointer changes into a four-arrow icon. Then click and drag the pointer (which should then turn into a linked-chain icon) over the center of the successor task. Hold the mouse button until Project interprets your action as creating a link, changes the pointer into a linked-chain icon, and displays the Finish-to-Start Link information box (see Figure 6.12).

6

Using the mouse for linking is most convenient when you can see both tasks you are trying to link onscreen at the same time. If only one taskbar is visible, you have to drag offscreen, and Project begins scrolling the task list at a furious pace. You can probably do better with one of the other methods of linking the tasks, such as selecting the two tasks (select the predecessor first) and using the Link Tasks tool.

If you made mistakes while linking your tasks, and have problems repairing your links, see "Task Linking Mistakes" in the "Troubleshooting" section near the end of this chapter.

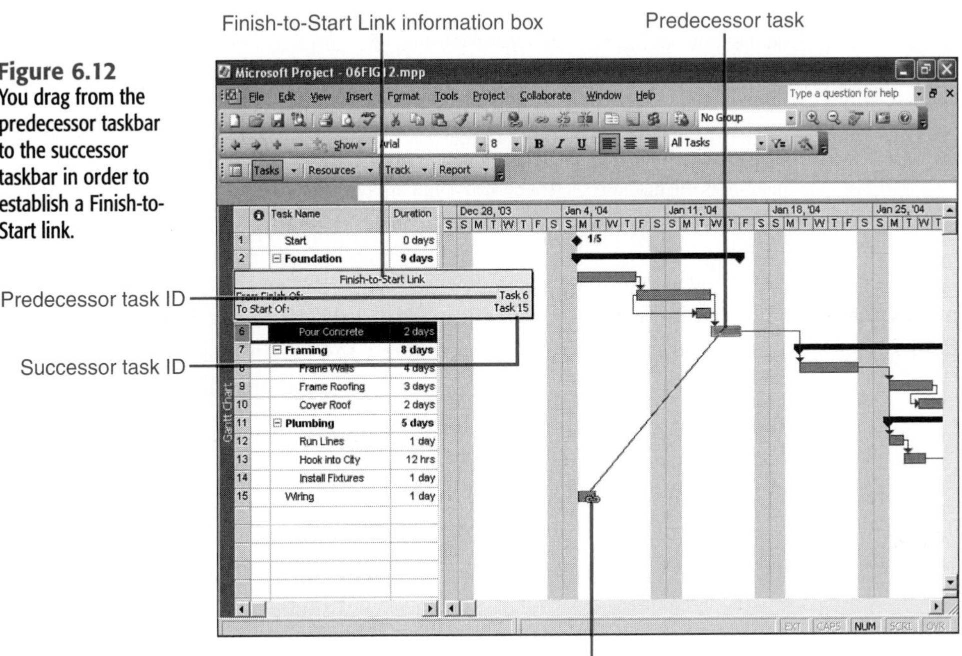

Figure 6.12 You drag from the predecessor taskbar to the successor taskbar in order to establish a Finish-to-Start link.

CAUTION

Be careful when creating links with the mouse. The mouse pointer is designed to perform a number of actions on tasks. It is easy to accidentally move the task or mark the task as being partially complete. You must watch the shape of the mouse pointer carefully, to ensure that you're doing exactly what you intend to do.

TIP

If you start using the mouse to link tasks and then want to cancel the linking procedure, simply drag the mouse up to the menu or toolbar area of the Gantt Chart view or the Calendar view and release the button. In the Network Diagram view, you must return the mouse to the task you started with before releasing the mouse button, or you will create a new successor task.

6

If Project scrolls too fast for you to see the taskbar you are looking for, see "The Mouse and Task Links" in the "Troubleshooting" section at the end of this chapter.

NOTE

In the Network Diagram and Calendar views, you must drag from the *center* of the predecessor task's box or taskbar, and the pointer is the plain white cross, not the four-arrow shape you look for in the Gantt Chart view. In those views, the four-arrow shape appears when the pointer is over the border of the task box or taskbar and means that you will move the task if you drag the border. In all cases, make sure that the mouse pointer is the linked-chain shape when you are over the successor task before you release the mouse button.

The dependency type created with the mouse is always a Finish-to-Start relationship. You can change the link type, add a lag or lead, or even delete the link by displaying the Task Dependency dialog box with the mouse in the Gantt Chart or Network Diagram views.

To display the Task Dependency dialog box, scroll to display any portion of the linking line between the predecessor and successor tasks. Position the tip of the mouse pointer on the line connecting the tasks whose links you want to edit. A ScreenTip should appear, with the details of the link. Double-click the linking line, and the Task Dependency dialog box appears, as shown in Figure 6.13. The From task in the dialog box is the predecessor, and the To task is the successor. You can change the dependency type with the drop-down list in the Type field. Choosing None removes the link, as does clicking the Delete button. You can redefine the lag or lead in the Lag field. Click the OK button to complete the change.

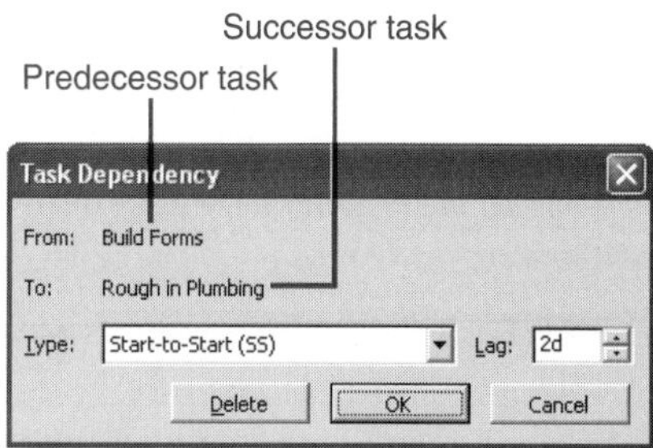

Figure 6.13
You can double-click a task's linking line to display the Task Dependency dialog box for editing task links.

6

NOTE

You can't change the names of the linked tasks in the Task Dependency dialog box, nor can you change which task is the predecessor and which is the successor.

If you double-click a linking line but the wrong tasks are listed in the Task Dependency dialog box, see "The Mouse and Task Links" in the "Troubleshooting" section at the end of this chapter.

WORKING WITH THE AUTOMATIC LINKING OPTION

If you use only simple Finish-to-Start links in a project, Project's Autolink feature (which is enabled by default) can help you maintain the dependency link sequences when you move, delete, or insert tasks within a linked sequence of tasks. However, Autolink works only if the affected links are Finish-to-Start links.

When you change the order of tasks, and thus their ID numbers, in a task table (such as the one in the Gantt Chart view), Autolink acts as follows:

- If you cut or delete a task from within a chain of Finish-to-Start linked tasks, Autolink repairs the break in the chain by linking together the former predecessor and successor of the deleted task.
- If you insert a task in a chain of Finish-to-Start linked tasks, Autolink breaks the former link between the tasks. The new task is inserted between the existing tasks, and then the newly inserted task is linked to the task above and below it to keep the linked sequence intact.
- If you move a task from one Finish-to-Start sequence to another, Autolink repairs the chain at the task's old site and inserts the new task into the chain at the new site.

In the Network Diagram and Calendar views, Autolink behaves this way only when you delete a task or insert a new task (because you can't cut, copy, or move tasks to a different ID order in those views).

NOTE

If you add a task to or remove a task from the beginning or end of a linked chain, instead of in the middle of the chain, Autolink does not include the new task in the chain. Thus, inserting a task at the beginning of a series of linked tasks or after the last task in a linked sequence does not cause Autolink to extend the chain to include the new task.

To include a task in a sequence, when the task has been added either to the beginning or end of the sequence, you must link the tasks yourself, using one of the previously discussed methods.

By default, Autolink is enabled, but you can disable it by changing the status of the Autolink option. Choose Tools, Options, and display the Schedule tab in the Options dialog box. Deselect the Autolink Inserted or Moved Tasks check box. To set the option status as a global default for all new projects, choose the Set as Default button. Otherwise, the change you make affects only the active project document.

TIP

If you have disabled Autolink and need to insert or paste tasks into a Finish-to-Start sequence, you can quickly reestablish the sequence to include the new tasks. Select the tasks, starting with the row above the insertion and including the row below the insertion, and use the Unlink Tasks tool to break the original link. Then, with the tasks still selected, use the Link Tasks tool to include the new tasks in the sequence. If there was a lead or lag included in the old link, you need to decide which of the new links should include it.

If you delete or cut tasks from a Finish-to-Start sequence, select the rows above and below the deleted rows and click the Link Tasks tool.

6

CAUTION

> As convenient as Autolink can be when editing a simple task list, it can cause problems in large or complex projects by creating unintended task links when tasks are inserted. You should double-check the links to ensure that they are as intended for the project. Unintended task links can become a vexing problem in a project schedule.
>
> If automatic linking is enabled and you rearrange an outline, you should carefully review the links that result each time you move a task or group of tasks in the outline. You might have to edit the links to reflect exactly the relationship you want defined.

TIP

> I leave Autolink disabled because it makes changes without asking for my approval, and I have found that I sometimes don't notice an unintended change in the linking for my task lists.

MODIFYING, REVIEWING, AND REMOVING DEPENDENCY LINKS

As you develop a project plan, you will inevitably make changes in the task list, and you will then have to adjust the sequence of links you have established. You might want to modify the type of link between tasks, insert lag or lead time, or remove a link entirely. You can modify existing links in the following locations, all of which are described in detail in previous sections of this chapter:

- Select the successor task and modify its predecessor links in the Predecessors tab of the Task Information dialog box.
- Split the window and display the Task Form view in the bottom pane, beneath a task view. With the predecessor and successor details displayed in the Task Form view, select a linked task and modify its links in either the Predecessors or Successors table.
- Double-click a linking line in the Gantt Chart or Network Diagram views to display the Task Dependency dialog box, where you can modify the link.

If two tasks are linked in the wrong direction—in other words, the predecessor should be the successor—see "Reversing a Dependency Link" in the "Troubleshooting" section at the end of this chapter.

6

If you find that a link between tasks is no longer necessary, or if you prefer to change a link to another task, you have to remove the existing link. Just as you can use several ways to create links, you can use many different methods to remove links. You can use the following techniques to remove links:

- You can easily unlink tasks in any of the task views by using the menu or toolbar. Select the tasks you want to unlink and click the Unlink Tasks button on the Standard toolbar, choose Edit, Unlink Tasks, or press Shift+Ctrl+F2. The result depends on the task(s) selected:
    - If you select a single task and then choose Unlink Tasks, Project removes all predecessors and successors for that task.

- If you select multiple tasks, Project removes all links between any pair of the selected tasks.
- To remove all links from the project, display any view with a task table and select all tasks by clicking a field name, such as a Task Name, before using Unlink Tasks.

- You can select a successor task and remove its predecessor links by using the Task Information dialog box. For each predecessor listed on the Predecessors tab that you want to remove, click the row for the predecessor and press the Delete key. Clicking OK closes the dialog box and removes those links.
- With a task view in the top pane and the Task Form in the bottom pane, you can display the resource and predecessor—or predecessor and successor—details in the bottom pane. Select the successor task in the top pane. For each predecessor link you want to remove, click its row in the details area and press the Delete key. Click OK to finish the deletion. If you display one of the detail's choices that includes successors, you can select the predecessor task in the top pane and delete the link in the Successors table in the bottom pane.
- In a view that includes a task table, such as the Gantt Chart view, click on the row for the successor task and clear the entry in its Predecessors field by pressing Ctrl+Delete. Remember not to press the Delete key alone, for that deletes the entire task.
- You can double-click a linking line in the Gantt Chart or Network Diagram views to display the Task Dependency dialog box and choose Delete to remove the link.

AUDITING THE TASK LINKS

The project schedule is heavily influenced by the linking relationships you establish among tasks. It is very easy to accidentally link tasks or break task links, and if you work with Autolink enabled, some changes you haven't noticed might have been made. Therefore, you should review the link relationships carefully before committing to the project schedule. Accidental links can easily skew the finish date of the project.

The Network Diagram view concentrates on the linking relationships by representing each task as a box or node with arrows from predecessor to successor tasks. Because you see so few tasks on the screen in these views, you might want to print the views when using them to review all task links.

6

→ For information about using the Network Diagram view, **see** Chapter 7, "Viewing Your Schedule," **p. 231**.

The Gantt Chart view shows the task links as arrows connecting the taskbars, with the arrow always pointing to the successor task. The Gantt Chart view shown earlier in this chapter, with the predecessor and successor details in the Task Form view in the bottom pane, provides a good review of the task links. For the task you have active, the predecessor and successor tasks are listed in the bottom pane, along with any lag or lead associated with the link. You use the Previous and Next buttons in the bottom pane to review the links.

Perhaps the most useful view for auditing task links is the Relationship Diagram view (see Figure 6.14). It shows the predecessors and successors for just the selected task as task nodes, like the Network Diagram view, and it is useful for confirming that you have defined the task relationships as intended. You can display the Relationship Diagram view by itself, but it is most useful when displayed in the bottom pane, beneath another task view in the top pane, such as the Gantt Chart or Network Diagram views.

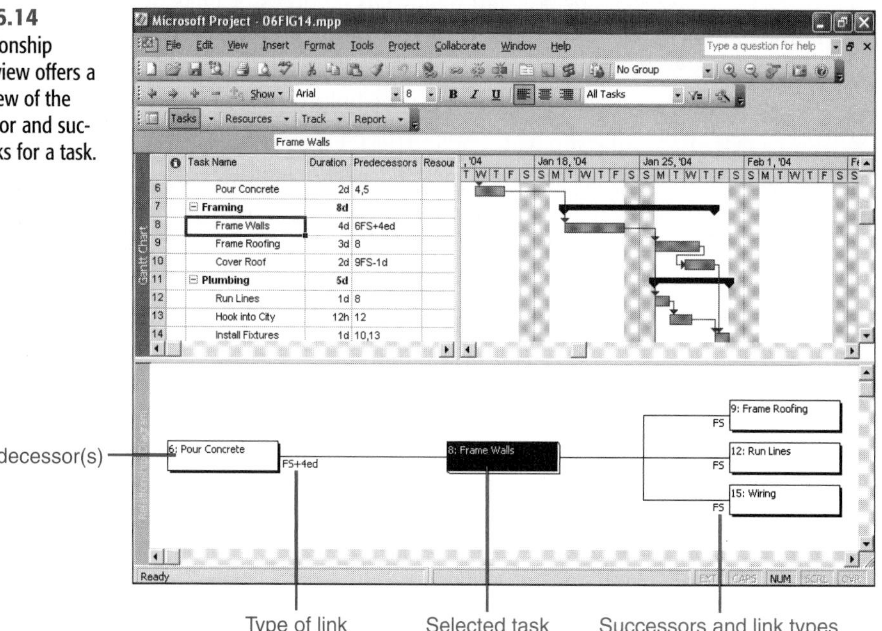

Figure 6.14
The Relationship Diagram view offers a good review of the predecessor and successor links for a task.

The task you have selected in the top pane is represented by a box or node in the center of the relationship diagram in the bottom pane, with links to nodes for its predecessors and successors on the left and right. The type of relationship and any lag or lead is shown next to the linked task nodes. In Figure 6.14, the relationship diagram in the bottom pane makes it clear that there are three successors to the Frame Walls task, something that is not easy to see in the Gantt Chart in the top pane.

NOTE

> The Relationship Diagram view is a display-only view. You can't make changes in this view, nor can you print it. You can, however, display the Task Information dialog box for the selected task and make changes there.

To display the Relationship Diagram view below the Gantt Chart view, split the window and activate the bottom pane. Choose View, More Views, and select Relationship Diagram in the More Views dialog box. Then click the Apply button to display the view.

You can select tasks in the top pane to see their predecessors and successors displayed graphically in the bottom pane.

TIP

> If you select multiple tasks in the top pane, you will see only one of the selected tasks in the center of the bottom pane at a time. You can use the horizontal scrollbar in the Relationship Diagram pane to scroll through all the selected tasks. Pressing the Home key displays the view for the first of the selected tasks, and pressing the End key displays the view for the last of the selected tasks. You can use these same techniques to scroll through the tasks if you display the Relationship Diagram view as a full-screen view.

WORKING WITH TASK CONSTRAINTS

In a project with a fixed start date, you probably want Microsoft Project to schedule tasks as soon as possible after the start of the project in order to minimize the overall duration of the project. For the same reason, if the project is scheduled from a fixed finish date, you want Project to schedule tasks as late as possible so that they are close to the fixed finish date and keep the duration of the project as short as possible. However, there are many circumstances in which a task must be scheduled to start or finish by a specific date. These fixed-date requirements are called *task constraints* in Microsoft Project. They might be due to requirements from outside the project, or they might be the result of interim deadlines imposed by the project manager. External constraints might be deadlines imposed by customers, contractors, the government, or policies within the organization that are external to the project. Constraints that are internal to the project might be such things as progress reviews and reevaluations of the schedule as each major phase of the project nears completion. The following are some specific examples of task constraints:

- A manufacturing project contract might call for delivery of the product no later than a specific date; thus, the delivery task must finish on or before that date.
- A contract with a vendor might stipulate the earliest delivery date for some parts or the finish date for a service; therefore, the finish of this task should be scheduled on or after that date.
- A government agency might require an environmental impact test at a specific point in time after the project starts, with the test results delivered by a specific date; therefore, the task to conduct the test must start on a specific date and the task to submit the results must be finished on or before another specific date.
- Senior management might require project progress reports to be delivered on specific dates.

In all these cases, either the start or finish of a task is to be linked to a specific date in the schedule, and you want Project to take this constraint into consideration when scheduling the task.

If you change your project start or finish date and want to change all the constraints in your project at once, see "Using the Adjust Dates Macro" in the "Troubleshooting" section near the end of this chapter.

UNDERSTANDING THE TYPES OF CONSTRAINTS

Constraints are defined by entries in the Constraint Type and Constraint Date task fields (see Figure 6.15). By default, a new task you create has no constraint date. When you add a task to a project that is scheduled from a fixed start date, Project supplies As Soon As Possible in the Constraint Type field as a default entry. This entry means that there is no fixed date requirement—in other words, no constraint—and the task will be scheduled as soon as possible after its predecessor requirements are met. The Constraint Date field for the task is given the default entry NA.

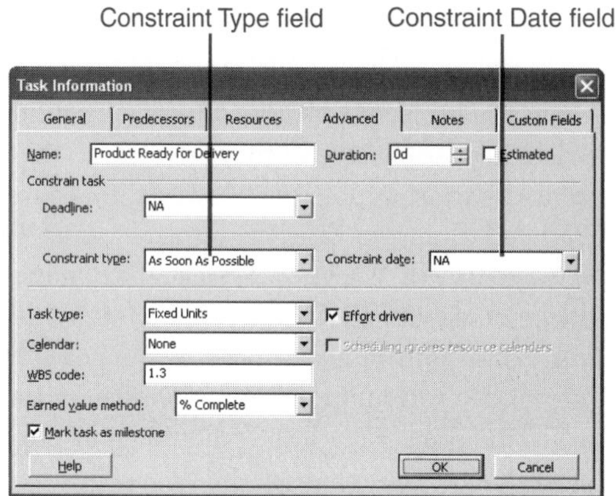

Figure 6.15
The default constraint type is As Soon As Possible and the default constraint date is NA on the Advanced tab of the Task Information dialog box.

If the project is scheduled from a fixed finish date, Project supplies new tasks with the default entry As Late As Possible in the Constraint Type field. This entry also means that there is no constraint and the task will be scheduled as close to the finish date of the project as possible (considering the schedule for successor tasks, which must also finish before the project's finish date). Again, the Constraint Date field has the default entry NA.

The Constraint Type and Constraint Date fields are available on the Advanced tab of the Task Information dialog box. They can also be inserted as columns in a task table. The Constraint Type field provides a drop-down list of the eight possible constraint types that you can use to define any possible date constraint. These types are described in Table 6.2. Constraint types are usually referred to by the acronym shown in the first column of the table.

TABLE 6.2 THE CONSTRAINT TYPES

Acronym	Constraint Type	Description
ASAP	As Soon As Possible	Marks a task as not constrained and not requiring a constraint date. The task will be scheduled as soon as its predecessor requirements are met.
ALAP	As Late As Possible	Delays the task as long as possible, considering the scheduling requirements of its successor tasks, all of which must finish before the project finish date. This constraint type does not require a constraint date.

Acronym	Constraint Type	Description
SNET	Start No Earlier Than	Means the task must start on or after the defined constraint date.
SNLT	Start No Later Than	Means the task must start on or before the defined constraint date.
FNET	Finish No Earlier Than	Means the task must finish on or after the defined constraint date.
FNLT	Finish No Later Than	Means the task must finish on or before the defined constraint date.
MSO	Must Start On	Means the task must start exactly on the defined constraint date.
MFO	Must Finish On	Means the task must finish exactly on the defined constraint date.

The first two constraint types in Table 6.2, ASAP and ALAP, have no associated constraint date—in fact, they are really nonconstraints.

The duration of a sequence of tasks can expand for a variety of reasons; for instance, new tasks might be inserted in the sequence or existing tasks might experience *duration inflation* (that is, increases in duration values). In a forward-scheduled project (that is, one with a fixed start date), the expansion of duration pushes tasks to later dates. If the tasks in the sequence have the constraint type ASAP, they can be rescheduled to later dates without limit as the sequence expands. In a project with a fixed finish date, the expansion pushes tasks back to earlier dates. If the tasks in the sequence have the constraint type ALAP, they can be rescheduled to earlier dates without limit as the sequence expands.

The constraint types are classified as *flexible* and *inflexible*, based on whether they present a barrier to an expanding project schedule. The ASAP and ALAP constraints present no barriers in any situation and are always classified as flexible.

The last two constraints in Table 6.2, MSO and MFO, are considered inflexible in all circumstances because they can block the expansion of a task sequence. If the linked sequence expands so much that it requires a task with one of these constraints to move beyond an MSO or MFO constraint date, Project can't honor the defined links and at the same time honor the defined constraints. By default Project honors the constraint and ignores the dependency link, forcing the constrained task to overlap its linked task in a way that is contrary to the intent of the link. (See the section "Deciding to Honor Links or Honor Constraints," later in this chapter, for information about changing this default.)

Figure 6.16 illustrates the conflict between a task link and an inflexible constraint. The milestone Product Ready for Delivery must be completed by March 11, 2004. It has a Finish-to-Start link to its predecessor, Prepare for Shipping. The predecessor finishes in time for the milestone to meet its deadline in Scenario A. In Scenario B, however, the predecessor has been delayed because of duration inflation in an earlier task, and now it is impossible to honor both the link and the constraint. By default Project honors the constraint and schedules the milestone on its constraint date, which requires that it ignore the intent of the link. The predecessor finishes after the milestone's date, causing the linking line to wrap back around as though the link were defined with lead time.

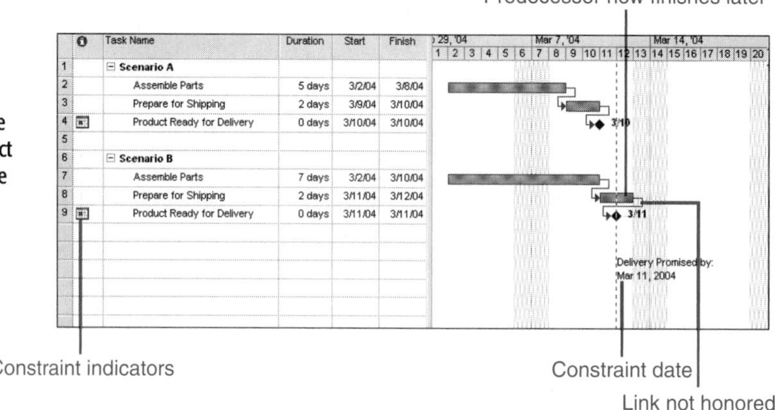

Figure 6.16
When a task's link definition and constraint definition are incompatible, Project normally honors the constraint.

In a fixed start-date project, duration inflation in predecessor tasks tends to push successor tasks to later dates. Constraints that prohibit successor tasks from being rescheduled to later dates are therefore inflexible constraints. The SNLT and FNLT constraint types are therefore called inflexible in fixed start-date projects. But the SNET and FNET constraints are flexible in fixed start-date projects.

In a fixed finish-date project, duration inflation in successor tasks tends to push predecessor tasks to earlier dates. Constraints that prohibit predecessor tasks from being rescheduled to earlier dates are therefore called inflexible constraints. Consequently, the SNET and FNET constraint types are called inflexible in fixed finish-date projects. But the SNLT and FNLT constraints are flexible in fixed finish-date projects.

NOTE

> Although the SNET and FNET constraints are flexible for the expansion of the fixed start-date schedule, they nevertheless create a barrier if you are attempting to compress the project's duration. To shorten the overall project, you must shorten the critical path, and if a task with one of these constraints is on the critical path, it can block your efforts. Although you might shorten the duration of its predecessors, an SNET or FNET task will not move to an earlier date, and the critical path will not be shortened.
>
> Similarly, in fixed finish-date projects, the SNLT and FNLT constraints are called flexible because they don't inhibit the natural expansion of the project; however, they can block compression of the project duration.

CAUTION

> If you change a project from fixed start date to fixed finish date, the ASAP constraint type for existing tasks is replaced with ALAP constraints; however, all new tasks are given the new default ALAP constraint type. Likewise, changing a fixed finish-date project to a fixed start-date project leaves the ALAP constraints unchanged, but new tasks are set to ASAP. Neither of these results affects the duration of the project, but some tasks are scheduled earlier or later than they could possibly be without affecting the start or finish of the project.

If you change a fixed start-date project to a fixed finish-date project, what were flexible SNET and FNET constraints become inflexible. Similarly, the flexible SNLT and FNLT constraints in a fixed finish-date project become inflexible if you switch to fixed start-date scheduling. If you change the project scheduling type, you should look for constraints that switched from flexible to inflexible and consider modifying them to avoid potential conflicts as the schedule changes.

TIP

> If you decide to permanently change a project from fixed start date to fixed finish date (or vice versa) and want to change all the old default constraints to the new default (for example, to replace ASAP with ALAP), you can use Project's Replace command. For example, type `As Soon As Possible` in the Find What box, type `As Late As Possible` in the Replace With box, select the field Constraint Type in the Look in Field box, and select Equals in the Test box.

Unwittingly creating constraints is one of the most common mistakes made by novice users of Microsoft Project. Any time you type a date into the Start or Finish fields for a task, or drag the taskbar to a new date in the Gantt Chart view, Microsoft Project creates a constraint to honor that date. When you create a recurring task, Project also creates a constraint for each occurrence.

Fortunately, Project always makes these flexible constraints. Thus, if you type in the start date for a task in a fixed start-date project, Project changes the constraint type to SNET and places the date in the Constraint Date field. The task is then scheduled to start on the date you typed (even if its predecessors would allow it to be scheduled earlier), but it can be freely moved to later dates if its predecessors experience duration inflation. Similarly, in a fixed finish-date project, the flexible constraints SNLT and FNLT are supplied when you specify start or finish dates for tasks.

NOTE

> Some constraints also affect the critical path:
>
> - If you apply a Must Start On or Must Finish On constraint, Project automatically makes the task a critical task.
> - If you are scheduling from a fixed start date, an ALAP constraint makes the task critical.
> - If you are scheduling from a fixed finish date, an ASAP constraint makes the task critical.

When a task has a constraint type other than ASAP or ALAP, Project displays an icon in the Indicators field of the Gantt Chart view. The icon looks like a calendar with either a blue or a red dot in the middle. A blue dot signifies a flexible constraint, and a red dot signifies an inflexible constraint. Table 6.3 summarizes the flexible/inflexible status for the eight constraint types in both fixed start-date and fixed finish-date projects and describes the indicators you see for them.

TABLE 6.3 FLEXIBLE AND INFLEXIBLE CONSTRAINTS AND THEIR INDICATORS

Constraint Type	Fixed Start Date	Fixed Finish Date
ASAP	Flexible (no indicator)	Flexible (no indicator)
ALAP	Flexible (no indicator)	Flexible (no indicator)
SNET	Flexible (blue dot)	Inflexible (red dot)
FNET	Flexible (blue dot)	Inflexible (red dot)
SNLT	Inflexible (red dot)	Flexible (blue dot)
FNLT	Inflexible (red dot)	Flexible (blue dot)
MFO	Inflexible (red dot)	Inflexible (red dot)
MSO	Inflexible (red dot)	Inflexible (red dot)

ENTERING TASK CONSTRAINTS

As mentioned previously, if you enter a date in a task's Start or Finish field or drag the taskbar in the Gantt Chart view, you create a flexible constraint for the task. You can also create task constraints by using the Schedule Tasks Project Guide or by filling in the Constraint Type and Constraint Date fields in the Task Information dialog box. If you want to create or modify many task constraints, you might want to add the constraint fields to the Entry table or display the Task Details Form view, which makes the constraint fields available for editing.

6

TIP

> Because creating inflexible constraints can affect a schedule so significantly, it's very important that you document why a constraint has been defined. You should always add an explanation to the Notes field to explain the purpose of the constraint. This is especially important information if you are sharing the project file with colleagues or if someone else takes over the project. It's also a valuable reminder if there is later a conflict that you must resolve.

If you change your project start or finish date and want to change all the constraints in your project at once, see "Using the Adjust Dates Macro" in the "Troubleshooting" section near the end of this chapter.

TIP

> When you type a constraint date, you can also include the time of day with the date. If you don't append the time of day, Project supplies one for you. Using the default values from the Calendar tab of the Options dialog box, Project appends the default start time for all constraint types that restrict the start of a task and the default end time for all constraints that restrict the finish of a task.

NOTE

> No matter which method you use for creating constraints, if you create an inflexible constraint, the Planning Wizard displays a warning. How to deal with that warning is covered at the end of this section.

CREATING CONSTRAINTS WITH THE SCHEDULE TASKS PROJECT GUIDE

To add a constraint to a single task by using the Project Guide, click Task on the Project Guide toolbar and choose Set Deadlines and Constrain Tasks to display the deadline and constraint definition controls (see Figure 6.17). Select the task to be constrained, and then select the constraint type and enter the constraint date under the Constrain a Task section.

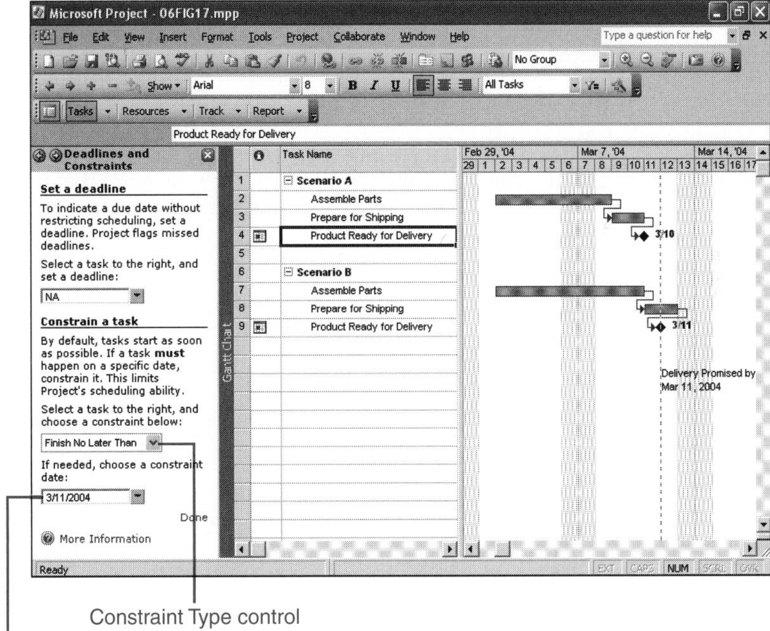

Figure 6.17
The quickest way to create constraints is to use the Schedule Tasks Project Guide.

Remember to click the Task Notes tool on the Standard toolbar to document the purpose for the constraint in the Notes field.

CREATING CONSTRAINTS IN THE TASK INFORMATION DIALOG BOX

To enter task constraints in the Task Information dialog box, follow these steps:

1. Select the task you want to modify and click the Task Information tool to display the Task Information dialog box (see Figure 6.18).

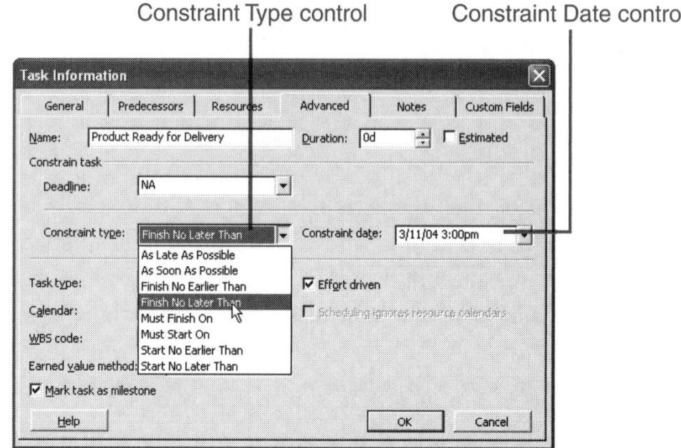

Figure 6.18 You use the Task Information dialog box to create constraints and document their purpose.

2. Select the Advanced tab.
3. In the Constraint Type field, select the constraint type from the drop-down list.
4. For constraints that require a date (that is, all the constraints except ASAP and ALAP), enter the constraint date in the Constraint Date box. Append the time of day if you want a time other than the default start time or default end time.

   If you do not enter a date, Project uses the task's current start or finish date as the constraint date—the start date and time for start date constraints and the finish date and time for finish date constraints.
5. Select the Notes tab and add a note explaining the reason for the constraint.
6. Click OK to complete the constraint definition.

CREATING CONSTRAINTS IN A TASK TABLE

If you need to create or edit a number of constraints, you can display the Constraint Dates table in the Gantt Chart view (see Figure 6.19). This is also a good view to use when reviewing the constraints in a project. To display the Constraint Dates table and create a constraint, follow these steps:

1. Display a task view that includes a table, such as a Gantt Chart.

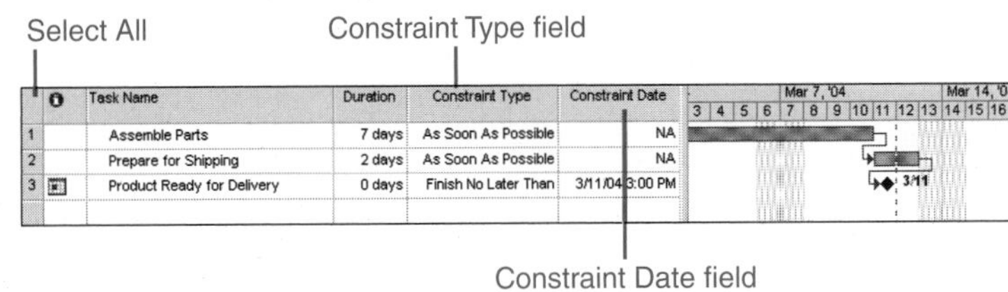

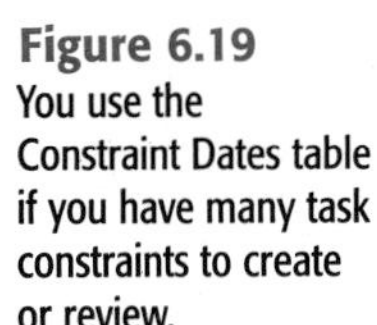
Figure 6.19
You use the Constraint Dates table if you have many task constraints to create or review.

2. Right-click the Select All button and choose More Tables. In the More Tables dialog box, select Constraint Dates and click Apply.
3. On the row for a task you want to constrain, use the drop-down list in the Constraint Type column to choose the type. Press Enter to assign the constraint. (As mentioned previously, if you have defined an inflexible constraint, the Planning Wizard makes you confirm that you want to keep the constraint.) Unless the constraint type is ASAP or ALAP, Project supplies a default date in the Constraint Date column; to do so, Project uses the task's start date and time if the task's start is constrained and the finish date and time if its finish is constrained.
4. If appropriate, type a different date or use the drop-down calendar to select one. Append the time of day if you don't want Project to supply the default time.

NOTE

> To return to the Entry table with its task fields, repeat step 2, but select Entry Table in the More Tables dialog box.

NOTE

> You can add the constraint fields to any task table. See "Creating a Modified Constraint Dates Table" in the "Project Extras" section at the end of this chapter.

CREATING CONSTRAINTS IN THE TASK DETAILS FORM

The Task Details form provides easy access to the constraint fields. It is best used in the bottom pane with the Gantt Chart view or another task view in the top pane (see Figure 6.20). To enter task constraints in the Task Details form, first display the Gantt Chart view or other task view in the top pane and split the window. When the window is split, activate the bottom pane and choose View, More Views to display the More Views dialog box. Select Task Details Form from the Views list and click Apply. Right-click over the Task Details form and choose the Notes details for display so that you can document the reasons for the constraint.

You can select the task to be constrained in the top pane, or use the Previous and Next buttons in the bottom pane to scroll to the task. Then in the bottom pane, select the constraint type from the drop-down list in the Constraint box, and enter the constraint date and time in the Date field.

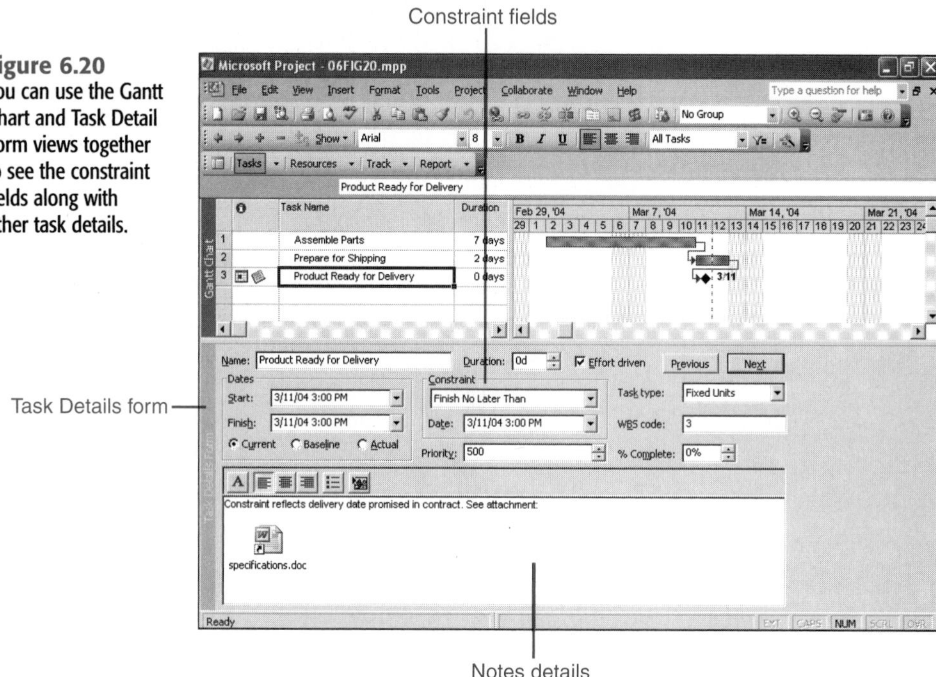

Figure 6.20
You can use the Gantt Chart and Task Detail Form views together to see the constraint fields along with other task details.

RESPONDING TO WARNINGS FROM THE PLANNING WIZARD

As mentioned previously, if you define an inflexible constraint for a task that has dependency links, you create a potential conflict between the requirements of the constraint and the requirements of the links. When you create an inflexible constraint, the Planning Wizard warns you that your action could create a problem either now or in the future and makes you confirm the action. The Planning Wizard displays the dialog box in Figure 6.21 to warn you and give you three options. You must select the third option to create an inflexible constraint.

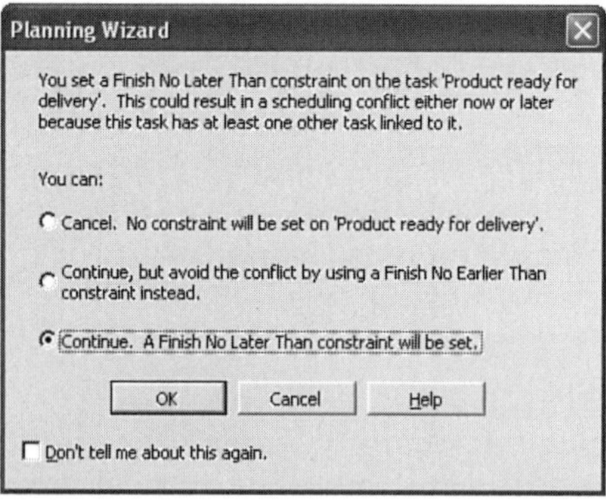

Figure 6.21
The Planning Wizard alerts you when a constraint might cause a problem. This can prevent you from accidentally placing constraints you didn't intend.

- You can select Cancel (which is the default). If you leave the default option selected, you can click either the OK button or the Cancel button to cancel the action, and no constraint will be set.
- You can select the second option: Continue But Avoid the Conflict By Using a Finish No Earlier Than Constraint Instead. If you select this option and click OK, Project substitutes the flexible version of the same constraint. For example, if you define an FNLT constraint in a project that is scheduled from a fixed start date, Project offers to change it to an FNET constraint.
- You can select the third option: Continue. A Finish No Later Than Constraint Will Be Set. You must both select this option and click the OK button to actually create the constraint you specified.

If you confirm the creation of the inflexible constraint and the constraint creates an immediate conflict with the task's dependency links, the Planning Wizard displays another warning that requests you to confirm that you want to go ahead and create the conflict (see Figure 6.22).

Figure 6.22
If a constraint creates an immediate conflict, you are usually warned by this second Planning Wizard dialog box.

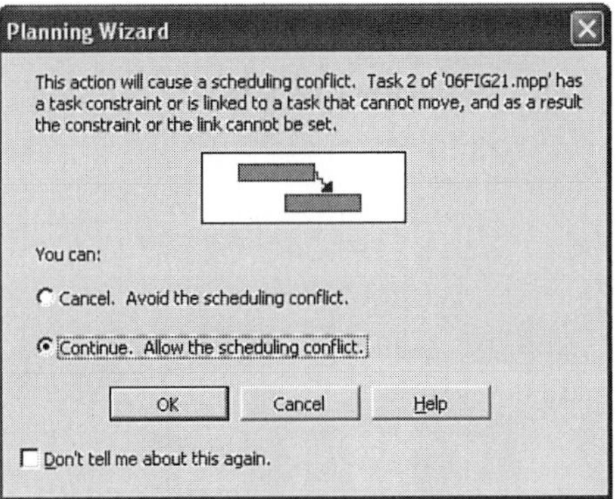

Your choices are to cancel (in which case the constraint will not be created) or to continue (in which case the constraint will be created and the scheduling conflict will exist). Again, you must choose the Continue option before you click OK to actually create the constraint.

6

NOTE

> Project does not display the second warning if you have deselected the Tasks Will Always Honor Their Constraint Dates check box on the Schedule tab of the Options dialog box (which is explained in the next section, "Deciding to Honor Links or Honor Constraints").

The Planning Wizard warning in Figure 6.22 is also displayed by any other action that causes a constraint date to be in conflict with a dependency link. You see it, for example, if you create new links or increase the duration of a predecessor task so much that the constraint date becomes a barrier.

The Planning Wizard warning that a constraint conflict has been identified includes a task ID number to help you troubleshoot the conflict (refer to Figure 6.22). The ID number is usually the ID for the predecessor to the task that has an inflexible constraint. (In a fixed finish-date project, it would be the successor task's ID.) However, in some instances the ID number is for the constrained task itself. Thus, in Figure 6.22 the message identifies Task 2, and that is the predecessor to the task that is being given an inflexible constraint.

If you see this warning from the Planning Wizard and choose to continue and allow the conflict to be created, you should make a note of the task ID number because you will not see this message again and you need to do something to resolve the conflict. (For ways to find and resolve constraint conflicts, see the sections "Finding and Reviewing Tasks That Have Constraints" and "Resolving Conflicts Caused by Constraints," later in this chapter.)

DECIDING TO HONOR LINKS OR HONOR CONSTRAINTS

As mentioned earlier in the chapter, in the section "Understanding the Types of Constraints," when you define an inflexible constraint for a task, it might be impossible for Project to honor both the constraint and one or more links that you have defined for the task. When this type of conflict arises, Project's default scheduling method is to honor the constraint definition and ignore the link definition, as shown in Scenario B in Figure 6.16. When Project honors inflexible constraint dates, the inflexible constraints are called *hard constraints*. You can change Project's default behavior and force it to honor a task's links instead of its constraint by choosing Tools, Options, and then clicking the Schedule tab and clearing the check box labeled Tasks Will Always Honor Their Constraint Dates (see Figure 6.23). With this change, the inflexible constraints are *soft constraints*.

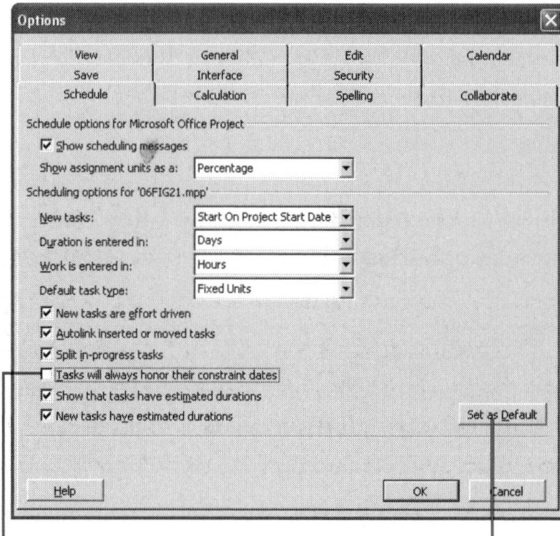

Figure 6.23
You can choose to make inflexible constraints soft constraints by clearing the Tasks Will Always Honor Their Constraint Dates check box.

In Figure 6.24 another set of tasks, Scenario C, is added to those from Figure 6.16 to show how Project schedules soft constraints to honor their links instead of their constraint dates.

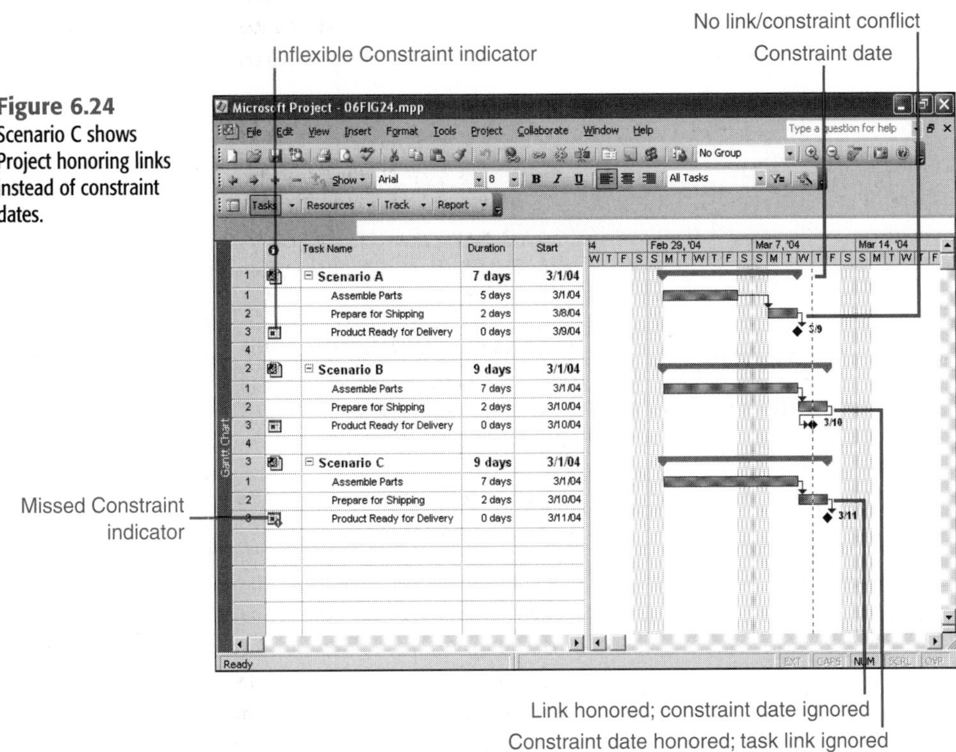

Figure 6.24
Scenario C shows Project honoring links instead of constraint dates.

In Scenario A, there is no constraint conflict. In Scenario B, the Product Ready for Delivery milestone is a hard constraint and is scheduled to honor its constraint date (as indicated by the dashed line on March 10, 2004). In Scenario C, a soft constraint is scheduled to honor its link; therefore, it falls on the day after the constraint date.

Notice the Missed Constraint icon in the Indicator column in Scenario C. This indicator tells you that a task's schedule violates its constraint date. The constrained tasks in Scenarios A and B have the standard Inflexible Constraint indicator. There is nothing special to flag the conflict between the constraint and the link in Scenario B. The Missed Constraint indicator is the only flag that Project provides to identify constraint conflicts, and it appears only if you have deselected Tasks Will Always Honor Their Constraint Dates.

If you go back into the Options dialog box and select the Tasks Will Always Honor Their Constraint Dates check box again (in other words, turn soft constraints into hard constraints again), the existence of any existing constraint conflicts in the project causes Project to display the warning shown in Figure 6.25. You should make a note of the task identified at the start of this message so that you can find the tasks involved in the conflict and resolve the issue.

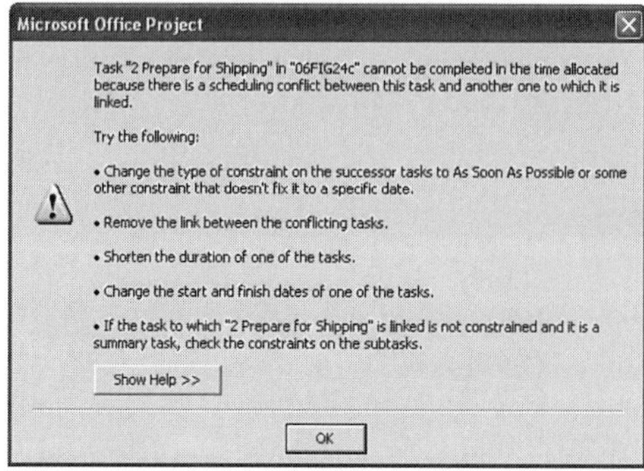

Figure 6.25
Forcing Project to honor constraint dates when there are already constraint conflicts produces this warning.

If all the links and constraint definitions are both appropriate and necessary to the project, it is best to use soft constraints (that is, to have tasks honor their links), for the following reasons:

- **Honoring links is usually most realistic.** The project manager needs to revise the schedule so that the constraint can be met while honoring the links. This requires shortening the duration of the linked sequence of predecessors (or successors, in a fixed finish-date project) that have caused the conflict.
- **Honoring links causes the Missed Constraint indicator to appear in the Indicators column.** This is the only reliable way to find constraint conflicts in a schedule. You can scan the Indicators column to see if you find tasks that have the indicator and then do something to the schedule to remove the indicator. Honoring constraints, on the other hand, merely causes the linking line to curve around the task that has a conflict, which is visually no different from a link with lead time. These missed links are very difficult to find in the schedule; you have to carefully scan all linking lines in the entire timeline, and therefore the need for remedial action is often overlooked until too late.

TIP

> Based on these two points, I recommend that you clear the Tasks Will Always Honor Their Constraint Dates check box as described previously and make it the default for all your new projects by clicking the Set as Default button, as shown in Figure 6.23. However, be aware that doing this means that you no longer get the warning shown in Figure 6.22 when you create a conflict between links and constraints. In this case, you have to diligently search for them, as described in the next section.

FINDING AND REVIEWING TASKS THAT HAVE CONSTRAINTS

Just as it is important to double-check the task sequencing links before committing to a project schedule, you should also review all the task constraints to be sure they are warranted and correctly defined. At the very least, you should attempt to identify any constraint conflicts and resolve them, or your project schedule will be unrealistic.

To review the constraint conflicts, disable Tasks Will Always Honor Their Constraint Dates on the Schedule tab of the Options dialog box, as described in the previous section. Then scroll down the list of tasks in the Gantt Chart view while you watch for the Missed Constraint indicator in the Indicators column. If your project is large, it will be easier if you also filter the task list for constrained tasks, as described next. When you find a task with the Missed Constraint indicator, follow the guidelines outlined in the section "Resolving Conflicts Caused by Constraints," later in this chapter.

If your project is scheduled from a fixed start date, you can use the Tasks with Fixed Dates filter to display the tasks that have a constraint other than ASAP, for both flexible and inflexible constraints. This filter also selects tasks that have an actual start date entered; so, if you apply this filter after you start tracking work on the project, it also selects tasks that have started. However, if you use it during the planning stage of a fixed start-date project, it selects just the tasks that have a nondefault constraint.

To apply the Tasks with Fixed Dates filter, choose Project, Filtered For, More Filters, and select Tasks with Fixed Dates from the list of filters. Click Highlight to highlight the selected tasks, or click Apply to hide all but the selected tasks. You can also click the drop-down list arrow in the Filter tool on the Formatting toolbar and choose the Tasks with Fixed Dates filter, but you can't apply a highlight filter if you use that tool.

Project selects all tasks that do not have the constraint type ASAP (as well as those that have a start date entered). Project also displays the summary tasks for the selected tasks, which is helpful for remembering where the task falls in the outline in a large project. You can scroll through the filtered task list to easily review the constrained tasks.

TIP

A convenient view for reviewing constraints is the Gantt Chart view, with the Task Details Form view and the Notes field in the bottom pane, as described in the section "Entering Task Constraints," earlier in this chapter.

When you are finished using the filter, press the function key F3 to clear the filter or select All Tasks from the drop-down list on the Filter tool.

→ For help working with filters, **see** "Filtering the Task or Resource List," **p. 472**.

TIP

A handy way to review tasks that have constraints is to display the Constraint Dates table in the Gantt Chart view, as described in the earlier section "Entering Task Constraints." Even better, you can create a customized version of this table that is more useful (see "Creating a Modified Constraint Dates Table" in the "Project Extras" section at the end of this chapter). Click the AutoFilter tool on the Formatting toolbar. In the title cell of the Constraint Type column, click the AutoFilter drop-down list arrow. The drop-down list includes the names of all constraint type names that appear at least once in that column. Click one of the constraint type names in the list, and Project displays all tasks that have that constraint type, along with their summary tasks.

You can create much more useful filters for finding inflexible constraints, for both fixed start-date and fixed finish-date projects. If you often work with fixed finish-date projects or want to be able to isolate constrained tasks after tracking has begun, or if you want to find scheduling conflicts, these filters are well worth adding to your Global template. You can find files with these filters already defined on the companion Web site for this book, at `www.quehelp.com`. Use the `Inflexible Constraint Filters.MPP` file. Follow the instructions in the note attached to the project summary task to copy the filters to your `GLOBAL.MPT` file.

Removing Task Constraints

To remove a task constraint, simply change the constraint type to ASAP (or ALAP in a fixed finish date project), using one of the methods discussed earlier for creating constraints.

If you want to return several tasks to an unconstrained status, select all the tasks you want to change. Click the Task Information tool to display the Multiple Task Information dialog box. Choose the Advanced tab and select As Soon As Possible or As Late As Possible from the Constraint Type drop-down list. When you click OK, the changes are made in all the selected tasks. To remove all constraints in the project, select a column heading in the task list table and choose the As Soon As Possible or As Late As Possible constraint type in the Task Information dialog box.

Resolving Conflicts Caused by Constraints

When you add an inflexible constraint to a linked task or link to a task that has an inflexible constraint, the Planning Wizard displays the potential conflict warning shown in Figure 6.21. If Project is honoring task constraints (the default) and the potential conflict becomes a reality, the Planning Wizard gives you the warning shown in Figure 6.22. This can happen when you complete the constraint definition, or the link definition, or it can happen later, as a result of changes in the schedule that push the linked task past its constraint. If Project is not honoring task constraints, you do not get the warning shown in Figure 6.22, but you see the Missed Constraint indicator that's displayed in Figure 6.24.

6

CAUTION

> You can discontinue the display of Planning Wizard warnings by marking the Don't Tell Me About This Again check box. However, you might then be unaware of the conflict. You should leave the Planning Wizard active to warn you about scheduling conflicts.

As mentioned previously, if you see the Planning Wizard warning and choose to create the constraint conflict, you should make a note of the task ID number in the message because you'll not see this warning again. You need to examine that task and the task to which it is linked to find a way to resolve the conflict.

TIP

> When you first open a project document, you can press F9 (the Calculate key) to force Project to display its most recent scheduling error message. The message you see should be similar to the one displayed in Figure 6.25. However, you see only one warning message like Figure 6.25, even if there are several constraint conflicts.

The three fundamental ways to resolve a constraint date scheduling conflict are as follows:

- Reassess the need for the constraint and the conditions that make the constraint necessary. Substitute a flexible constraint if possible.
- Reevaluate the dependency relationships in the sequence of tasks that are linked to the constrained task. Be certain that all links are necessary and defined in order to allow maximum overlapping of tasks (using Start-to-Start, Finish-to-Finish, and lead time, where reasonable).
- Change the duration of individual tasks that are in the linked sequence by using techniques such as those described in Chapter 12, "Reviewing the Project Plan."

→ To learn how to change the duration of individual tasks, **see** "Shortening the Critical Path," **p. 480**.

You must choose the course of action that makes the most sense in your project. Frequently, a careful review of the tasks, constraints, and task relationships reveals that new definitions are called for; conditions might have changed since the original definitions were entered and the definitions might now be more restrictive than they need to be.

TIP

> Check to see whether a task note exists that might explain the need for the constraint. This might give you some guidance about how to resolve the conflict.

Entering Deadline Dates

You saw in the previous section that you can define a constraint date for a task when the task must be finished by a certain date. You can also use the Deadline Date field to record a task's finish deadline. The Gantt Chart view shows a deadline marker next to the taskbar, and if the task finish is scheduled after the deadline date, a special icon appears in the Indicators column to alert you that the task finish is scheduled after the deadline date (see Figure 6.26).

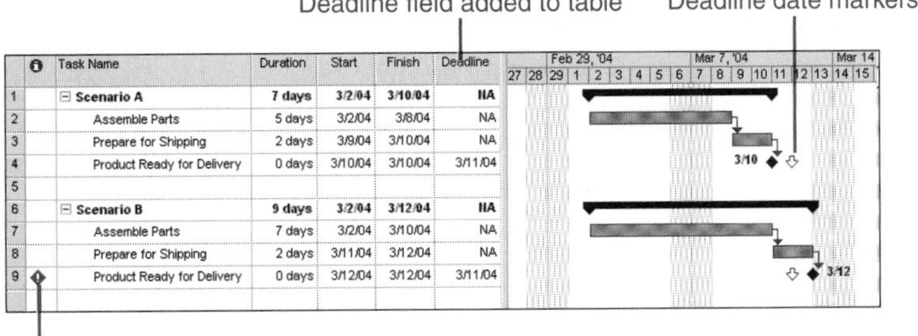

	Task Name	Duration	Start	Finish	Deadline
1	Scenario A	7 days	3/2/04	3/10/04	NA
2	Assemble Parts	5 days	3/2/04	3/8/04	NA
3	Prepare for Shipping	2 days	3/9/04	3/10/04	NA
4	Product Ready for Delivery	0 days	3/10/04	3/10/04	3/11/04
5					
6	Scenario B	9 days	3/2/04	3/12/04	NA
7	Assemble Parts	7 days	3/2/04	3/10/04	NA
8	Prepare for Shipping	2 days	3/11/04	3/12/04	NA
9	Product Ready for Delivery	0 days	3/12/04	3/12/04	3/11/04

Figure 6.26
The Missed Deadline icon is in the Indicators column and the taskbar is past the deadline date marker.

NOTE

> If you are highlighting critical tasks, a missed deadline also turns the task into a critical task.

Unlike an inflexible constraint date, there are no conflict error messages or warnings when a deadline date is missed. However, you can apply the Tasks with Deadlines filter to select all the tasks that have deadlines defined, and you can check the Indicators column for the Missed Deadline icon. To create a custom filter to select missed deadlines, see "Filtering for Missed Deadline Dates" in the "Project Extras" section at the end of this chapter.

An especially useful application of the Deadline Date field is for tasks that have a constraint date defined for the task start and also a deadline for the task finish. Because you can have only one constraint date per task, the deadline date allows you to define requirements for both the start and finish of a task.

Figure 6.26 shows the same sets of tasks shown in Figure 6.16, except that the milestone in both scenarios has a deadline date instead of a constraint date set on 3/11/04. In Scenario A, the milestone is scheduled for 3/10, which falls to the left of the deadline, as represented by the downward-pointing arrow. In Scenario B, the milestone is scheduled on 3/12, which is after the deadline; consequently, the Missed Deadline indicator appears in the Indicators column. If you pause the mouse over the Missed Deadline indicator, the ScreenTip message is "This task finishes on 3/12/04 which is later than its Deadline on 3/11/04."

You can define deadline dates in the Project Guide, in the Task Information dialog box, or in the Deadline column if you add the field to a table. When you enter a deadline date, you can also append the time of day. If you fail to enter the time of day, Project supplies the default End Time, as defined on the Calendar tab of the Options dialog box (normally 5:00 p.m.).

To create a deadline with the Project Guide, choose Task on the Project Guide toolbar, and select Set Deadlines and Constrain Tasks. Select the task to receive the deadline, and then type in a date or use the deadline date control in the Project Guide to select the date (see Figure 6.27). You can append the time of day after the date is entered. To remove a deadline, enter **NA** in the Deadline field.

6

To define a deadline date in the Task Information dialog box, follow these steps:

1. Select the task and activate the Task Information dialog box by either double-clicking the task or using the Task Information tool.
2. Select the Advanced Tab (see Figure 6.28).
3. Type a date, including the time of day if appropriate, in the Deadline field, or activate the drop-down box and choose the date in the Calendar control. To remove a deadline, type **NA** instead of a date. You can append a time of day after the date is entered.
4. Click OK to complete the definition.

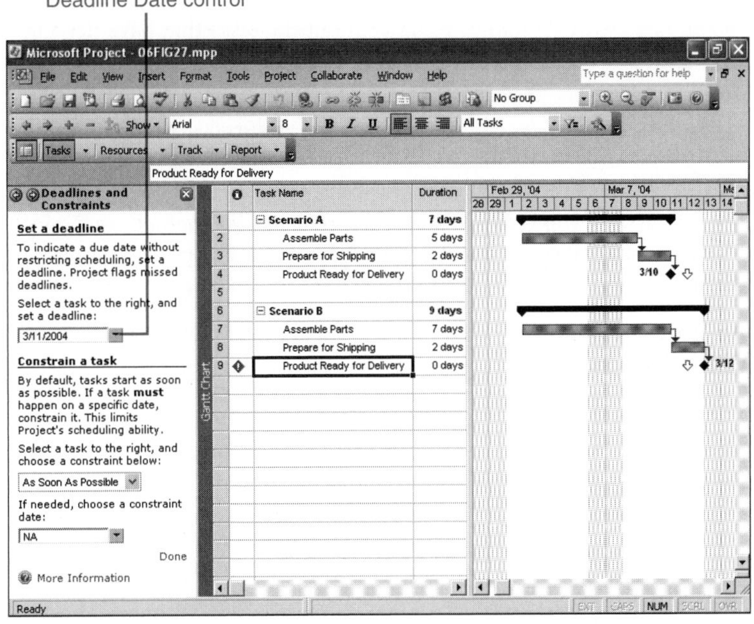

Figure 6.27
You can use the Schedule Tasks Project Guide panel to quickly enter deadline dates for one or more selected tasks.

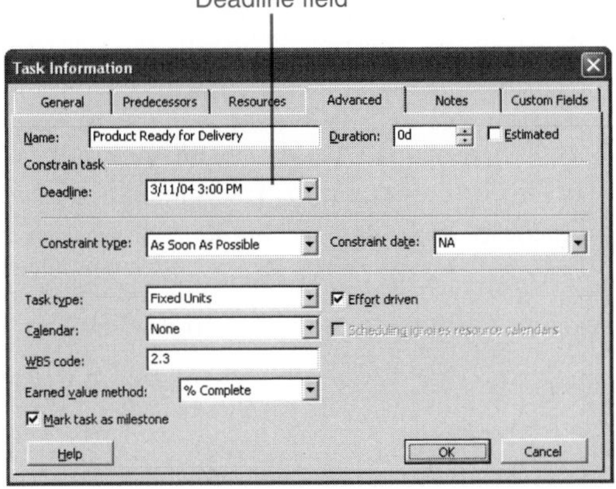

Figure 6.28
You can enter the Deadline date on the Advanced tab of the Task Information dialog box.

6

If you want to enter many deadlines, or if you want to review all the deadlines, you might want to add the Deadline field to a task table (refer to Figure 6.26). Click the column heading where you want to insert the field and press the Insert key. Select Deadline in the Field Name box on the Column Definition dialog box and choose Best Fit to display the column. You can then enter deadline dates in this column for any task.

Project includes a built-in filter that lets you select the tasks for which deadlines are defined. You might want to insert the Deadline field in a table to review the deadlines. Otherwise, you have to use the Task Information form for each selected task to see the deadline date.

To apply the filter, click the Filter tool on the Formatting toolbar and choose the filter named Tasks with Deadlines to hide all but the tasks that have deadlines in the display. If you want to merely highlight the tasks that have deadlines, choose Project, Filtered For, More Filters, select Tasks with Deadlines in the More filters dialog box, and click the Highlight button to display the full task list with tasks that have deadlines highlighted.

NOTE

> Project doesn't provide a filter for *missed deadlines*. See "Filtering for Missed Deadline Dates" in the "Project Extras" section at the end of this chapter.

SPLITTING TASKS

Normally Project schedules work on a task to continue uninterrupted until the task is complete. If you know that there will be interruptions or periods of inactivity on a task or if, having started work on the task, you find that you must interrupt the work and resume at a later date, you can split the task into two or more scheduled segments.

Several examples of tasks that would be good candidates for task splitting include the following:

- Suppose someone is scheduled to work on a task, but a weeklong business trip is planned during the time she is scheduled to work on this task. The work on the task is going to stop during the week she is gone and will resume when she returns. You can incorporate the interruption in the planning stage of the project by splitting the task around the business trip.
- Suppose that a specialized employee is working on a low-priority task when a task with a higher priority requires his or her attention. You can split the low-priority task and reschedule the remainder of its work after the higher-priority task is completed.
- Suppose work on a task has already begun but nothing has recently been done on the task. The remaining work needs to be rescheduled to start now or in the future. You can split the task at the point where work is completed and reschedule the remaining work to a later date.

6

NOTE

> A task can have an unlimited number of splits. When you link to a task that is split, the link is to the task; you cannot create a link to a split segment of a task.

The easiest way to split a task is in the Gantt Chart view, where you use the mouse to split a taskbar and drag the right-hand segment to the right to resume at a later date. To split a task in the Gantt Chart view, follow these steps:

1. Activate the Gantt Chart view.

2. Click the Split Task tool on the Standard toolbar or right-click the taskbar and select Split Task from the shortcut menu. You can also choose Edit, Split Task from the menu. The Split Task information box appears (see Figure 6.29).

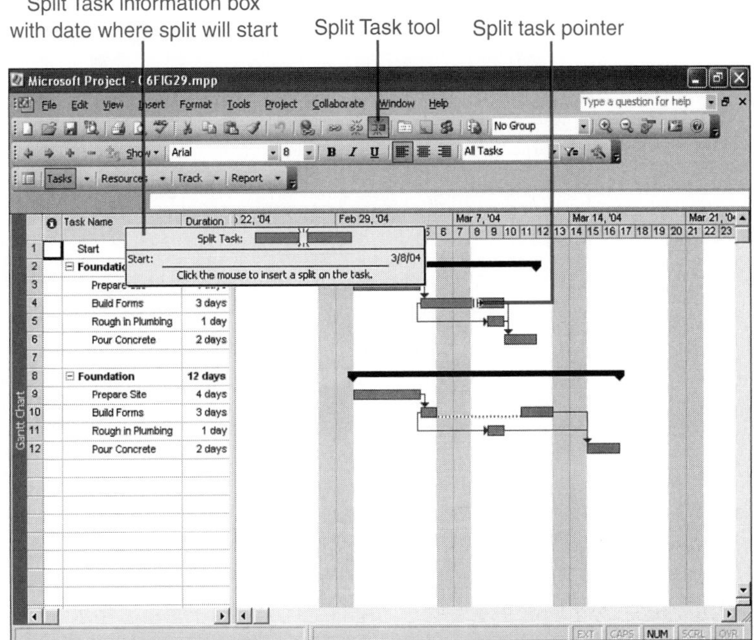

Figure 6.29
The Split Task information box guides you in selecting the date where you will split a task.

3. Position the mouse pointer over the taskbar you want to split; do not click yet. As you slide the pointer right and left over the taskbar, the Start date in the Split Task information box tells you the date where the split will occur when you click the mouse.
4. When you locate the correct Start date, you can either click the taskbar or click and drag. The different results are as follows:
   - If you click the taskbar, Project inserts a split in the schedule, starting on the date in the Split Task information box, at the default start time of day (normally 8:00 a.m.). The length of the split or interruption is one unit of the time unit used in the minor scale of the timescale. If the minor scale is days, even if it displays every third day, the split is one day.
   - If you click and drag, you insert the split as you would by clicking the taskbar, but you also drag the remainder of the task on the right to begin on another date (thus modifying the length of the split). As soon as you start dragging, the Split Task information box is replaced by the Task information box (see Figure 6.30), which tells you the start date for the new segment (that is, the date when the task will resume) and the finish date for the task. Release the mouse when you reach the date on which you want the new segment to start.

6

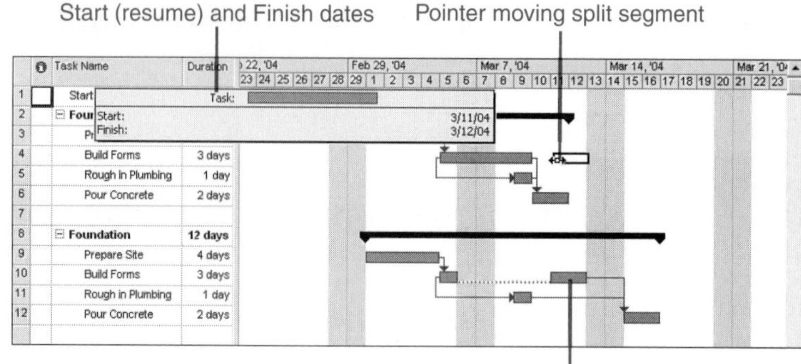

Figure 6.30
When you split a task, the Task information box tells you when the task will resume and finish.

CAUTION

If calculation is set on manual, a task split does not appear graphically on the Gantt Chart until you press F9 to recalculate and refresh the screen. To check the calculation settings, go to Tools, Options, Calculation, Calculation Options for Microsoft Project. The default setting is Automatic.

TIP

Watch the start and finish dates in the Split Task information box carefully to determine when this segment of the split task resumes.

If your timescale units are minutes or hours, or if you want to control the exact time of day when a split begins, see "Splitting Tasks with Precision" in the "Troubleshooting" section at the end of this chapter.

NOTE

You can also split tasks in the Task Usage view, and if resources are assigned to a task, you can split the resource assignments to the task in the Resource Usage view. If all assignments are split at the same point, the task itself is effectively split.

→ For instructions on creating splits in tasks and assignments with the Task and Resource Usage views, **see** "Resolving Overallocations by Delaying Assignments," **p. 440**.

After you have split a task, resting the pointer over a split segment displays the Task information box for just that segment, telling you the start date, finish date, and duration for that segment.

Dragging the first segment of a split task moves all segments of the task together. Holding down the Shift key as you drag a later segment also moves all segments together.

You can drag any but the first segment to the right or left to change the start and finish of that segment of the task (as long as you don't touch another segment of the task).

You can remove a split (that is, rejoin segments of a split task) by dragging the segment on the right toward the left until it touches the next segment.

CAUTION

> Do not drag a middle segment to the right to touch a later segment. Project often loses track of part of the task duration.

To change the duration of a segment (and thus the duration of the task), drag the right end of the segment to the right or left. The Task information box appears and shows the effect of the current position of the cursor on the finish and duration. If you are adjusting the final segment of the split task, the finish and duration are those for the entire task. If you are adjusting any other segment, the finish and duration are those for that segment.

CREATING AND USING TASK CALENDARS

Typically, tasks without resource assignments are scheduled according to the working time on the project calendar (as specified in the Project Information dialog box). Tasks with resource assignments are scheduled according to the working time on the resource calendars. You can also assign a custom base calendar to a task to replace the project calendar for scheduling that task. The process involves creating a custom base calendar that reflects the schedule you want to use for the task and then assigning that calendar to the task.

A task calendar provides specific control over the dates and hours when a task can be scheduled, and it affects only the task or tasks to which it is assigned. Task calendars are ideally suited to tasks that involve equipment resources that must be scheduled outside the normal working hours of the project calendar.

TIP

> A task calendar might be a viable alternative to task splits when there are many interruptions in the planned schedule for a task.

For example, suppose that as part of deploying Microsoft Project 2003, an organization plans to upgrade its servers. The Upgrade Servers task is to be scheduled over a weekend, while most users are normally offline. You could create a task calendar named Upgrade Servers that defines Saturdays and Sundays as working days and Mondays through Fridays as nonworking days.

If a resource is assigned to a task that also has a task calendar, Project normally schedules the assignment only during periods when working times on both the task calendar and the resource calendar intersect. Project gives you the option, however, of ignoring the resource calendar and using only the task calendar for scheduling the resource assignment.

In addition to using task calendars for normal tasks, you can also assign task calendars to recurring tasks and to summary tasks. Assigning a task calendar to a recurring task also assigns it to each occurrence (that is, subtask) and therefore affects the scheduling of the individual instances of the recurring task. Thus, you could use a task calendar to schedule regular maintenance on equipment during the off-hours of a project. Assigning a calendar to a summary task, however, does not affect the schedule for any subtasks and therefore doesn't automatically change the schedule for the summary task.

→ For more information about resources and task calendars, **see** "Scheduling with Task Calendars," **p. 353**.

To assign a calendar to a task, follow these steps:

1. Create a base calendar that contains the working days and hours when you want the task to be scheduled. Refer to the section "Defining a Calendar of Working Time" in Chapter 3, "Setting Up a Project Document," for details on creating new base calendars.

TIP

> It's a good idea to distinguish base calendars you create to be used as task calendars from the other base calendars by starting the calendar name with an identifier such as an asterisk or a prefix such as `TC:` You can also include some wording in the name to identify the task or set of tasks for which it is designed. This makes it easier to find the calendar you want when assigning calendars.

2. Select the task and display its Task Information dialog box by double-clicking the task or by clicking the Task Information tool. Figure 6.31 shows the Task Information dialog box for a normal task.

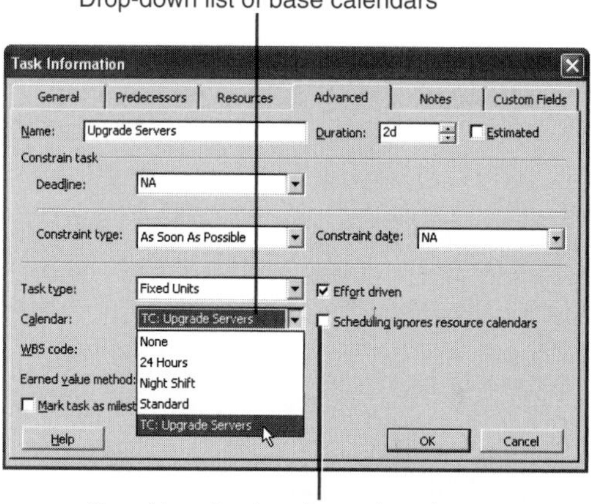

Figure 6.31
You can assign task calendars in the Task Information dialog box.

6

3. For normal tasks and summary tasks, activate the Advanced Tab. For recurring tasks, all fields are on the same tab.

4. Change the selection in the drop-down list in the Calendar field from None (the default) to the base calendar you created for the task. In Figure 6.31, the selected calendar is TC: Upgrade Servers.
5. Fill the check box labeled Scheduling Ignores Resource Calendars if you want Project to ignore the working and nonworking time on the resource calendars and schedule the task by the task calendar alone.
6. Click OK to finish assigning the calendar.

Figure 6.32 shows the Upgrade Servers task scheduled for Saturday and Sunday (even though its predecessor finished two days earlier) because the TC: Upgrade Servers calendar has been assigned to the task.

TIP

> Notice the Task Calendar indicator in Figure 6.32. If you pause the mouse over the indicator, the ScreenTip tells you the name of the calendar that is assigned to the task.

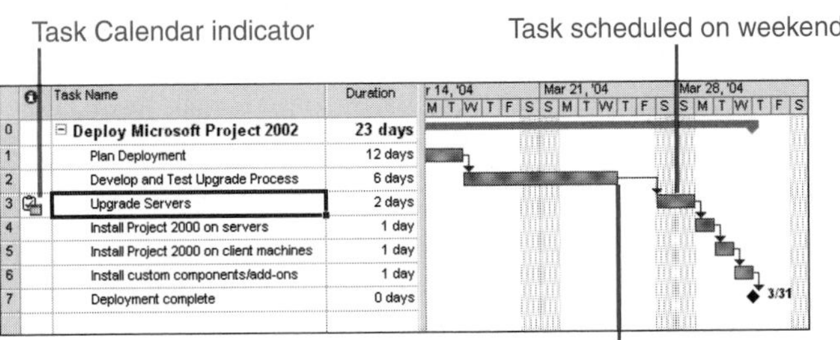

Figure 6.32
The Upgrade Servers task is scheduled on the weekend because its task calendar has only weekend working days.

If you assign a calendar to a task that has resources assigned or if you assign a resource when there is already a task calendar assigned and Project discovers that there are no intersecting working time periods for the task calendar and the resource calendar, an error message displays (see Figure 6.33). The message tells you that the resource calendars will be ignored and the task will be scheduled during the working times on the task calendar, and an indicator (see Figure 6.34) flags the task as having inconsistent calendars assigned to it.

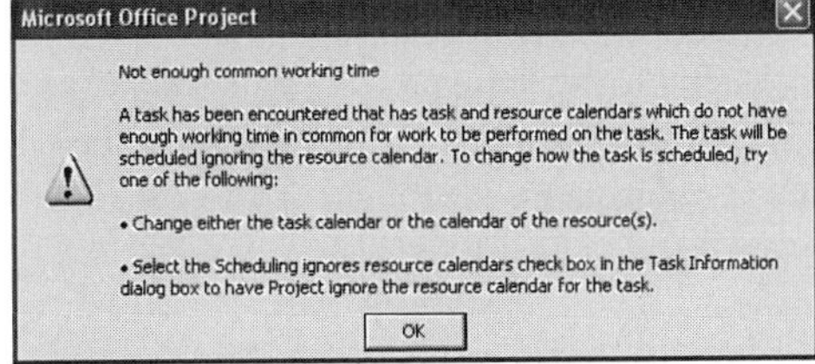

Figure 6.33
If a task calendar and the calendars for assigned resources have no intersecting working times, Project uses the task calendar and ignores the resource calendars.

6

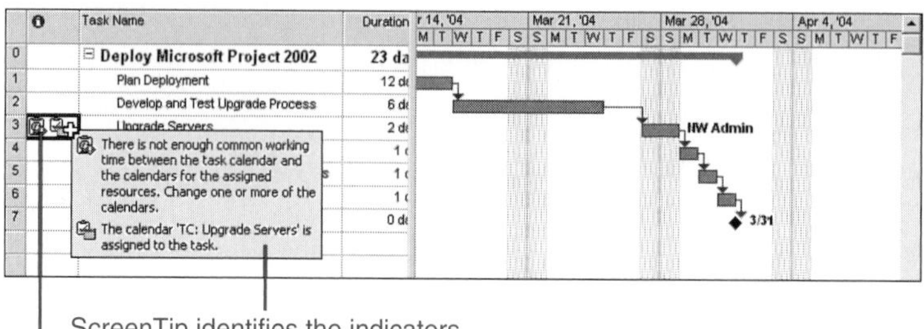

Figure 6.34
A special indicator flags tasks that have inconsistent task calendars and resource calendars.

Project provides a filter to identify tasks that have task calendars assigned. To apply the filter, click the Filter tool on the Formatting toolbar and select Tasks with a Task Calendar Assigned. To clear the filter, press the F3 key.

TROUBLESHOOTING

THE MOUSE AND TASK LINKS

When I try to link tasks with the mouse, the screen scrolls too fast for me to find the successor task. What can I do?

When tasks you want to link aren't close enough for both to be visible onscreen at once, you can try to make them both visible at the same time by using the Zoom Out tool to compress the timescale or by hiding subtasks under summary tasks that lie between the two tasks in the task list to place both taskbars onscreen.

If that doesn't work or is too much trouble, you can simply select the tasks and use the Link Tasks tool. You can select both tasks by clicking the predecessor task (or its taskbar) first to select that task, using the scrollbars to bring the dependent task into view, and then holding down the Ctrl key as you click the dependent task or taskbar. Then click the Link Tasks tool.

No matter where I double-click on the dependency linking line, the Task Dependency box doesn't display the task names of the two tasks whose link I want to modify. What am I doing wrong?

There must be more than one linking line where you are clicking. Project frequently draws linking lines to them on top of each other to simplify the display. Find a point where the two lines separate, usually near one of the linked tasks. Otherwise, use another method to change the link. For example, click on the dependent task's taskbar (or node in the Network Diagram view) and click the Task Information tool to display the Task Information dialog box and change the link on the Predecessors tab.

TASK LINKING MISTAKES

What can I do if I make a mistake in linking tasks by using drag-and-drop?

The answer is almost always to undo the action immediately. Because Project supports only one level of Undo, you should verify the results of a drag-and-drop operation immediately, while you can still take advantage of Undo. The shape of the pointer always advertises the type of action you will perform when you release the mouse button. Learn the various shapes, so you can more easily avoid making mistakes. In the Gantt Chart and Calendar views, you can drag the pointer to the menu or toolbar area, and the action is voided when you release the mouse button. In the Network Diagram view, however, you must return to the point of origin before releasing the button if you want to void the action.

REVERSING A DEPENDENCY LINK

I linked two tasks and accidentally got the wrong task as the predecessor. How do I reassign the predecessor to be the successor and vice versa?

You can't reverse the direction of the dependency relationship after it's created. You must delete the link and create it again.

LINKING TASKS FROM DIFFERENT PROJECTS

I want to link a task in one project to a task that is in another project. How do I do that?

To link tasks that are in different projects, you need to put both projects in a consolidated file. Open a blank project document and use Insert, Project for each of the projects that contain tasks you want to link. Expand the outlines for each project so that you can select the individual tasks to be linked. Click on a predecessor task and use the Ctrl key as you click on its successor. Then click the Link Tasks tool. Alternatively, you can drag from the predecessor taskbar to the successor taskbar to create the link. These are the only simple methods for creating external links; all the other methods involve special codes that can easily be typed incorrectly.

→ For more information about linking tasks between projects, **see** Chapter 16, "Working with Multiple Projects," **p. 603**.

USING THE ADJUST DATES MACRO

I have a project that has constraints, and now I need to change the start date for the project. I want all the constraints to change by the same number of days as the change in the project's start date. How do I accomplish this?

Use the Adjust Dates tool to reschedule the start or finish of the project. This also changes all constraint dates by the same number of days.

To use the Adjust Dates tool, follow these steps:

1. Open the project document whose dates you want to adjust. Don't adjust the project start or finish date yet; let the tool do that for you.
2. Display the Analysis toolbar by right-clicking over the toolbars and choosing Analysis from the shortcut menu.

3. Select the Adjust Dates tool to display the Adjust Dates dialog box.
4. Enter the new start date or finish date in the input box.
5. Click the OK button. Project enters the new date in the Start Date (or Finish Date) field of the Project Information dialog box and adjusts all task constraint dates by the same number of days.

SPLITTING TASKS WITH PRECISION

I want to specify the exact time of day when a split begins. How do I do that?

Project lets you choose the date when a split begins. If you want to control the hour when the split starts, you must adjust the timescale to show individual hours on the bottom tier. Double-click the timescale or choose Format, Timescale, and change the Bottom Tier Units to Hours with a Count of 1. If you have displayed hours in the timescale, start the split under the hour when you want the split to begin. If the bottom tier scale is less than a day, the split starts at the beginning of the unit over the point where you clicked. Note that the Split Task information box that appears while you are selecting the point of the split doesn't show the hour unless you have chosen a date format on the View tab of the Options dialog box that includes the time of day.

PROJECT EXTRAS

CREATING A MODIFIED CONSTRAINT DATES TABLE

It is easier to analyze constraint conflicts if you modify the standard Constraint Dates table to include the Indicators, Predecessors, and Successors fields. The Indicators field allows you to see the Constraint conflict indicators (if Project is honoring task links instead of constraint dates). The Predecessors field allows you to identify the link(s) that conflict with the constraints in a fixed start-date project, and the Successors field serves the same function in a fixed finish-date project.

To customize the table, follow these steps:

1. In a task view such as the Gantt Chart view, right-click over the Select All cell (the table's upper-left cell over the ID number column) and choose More Tables from the shortcut menu.
2. In the Tables list in the More Tables dialog box, select Constraint Dates and click the Copy button.
3. In the Name box, change the name for the new table if desired.
4. To insert the Indicators field, click on the row below ID in the Field Name column and click the Insert Row tool to insert a blank row.
5. Select Indicators in the Name column. Press Enter to add the field.

6. Repeat step 5 in the blank rows at the bottom of the list of field names to add the fields Predecessors and Successors. You should change the Align Data entry to Left for both of these fields.
7. Fill the Show in Menu check box if you want this table to appear on the menu of table names.
8. Click OK to create the table and click Apply to display it.

FILTERING FOR MISSED DEADLINE DATES

The standard Tasks with Deadlines filter selects all tasks with deadline dates, whether the deadlines are missed or not. The deadline is missed when the task's Finish date is later than the date in the task's Deadline field.

To create a filter that selects only missed deadline dates, follow these steps:

1. Choose Project, Filtered For and select More Filters.
2. Select the Tasks with Deadlines filter name and choose the Copy button.
3. Type **`Missed Deadline Dates`** or another suitable name in the Name text box.
4. In the table of criteria, select the first blank cell on the second row (under the column named And/Or) and type **`and`**.
5. In the Field Name column, type **`Finish`**.
6. In the Test column, type **`is greater than`**.
7. In the Value(s) column, type **`[Deadline]`**.
8. Fill the Show in Menu check box if you want this filter on the Filtered For menu.
9. Click OK to complete the filter and click Apply if you want to apply it immediately.

CHAPTER 7

Viewing Your Schedule

In this chapter

Working with the Gantt Chart View 232

Adding Graphics and Text to Gantt Charts 247

Working with the Calendar View 258

Working with the Network Diagram View 265

Troubleshooting 274

WORKING WITH THE GANTT CHART VIEW

The previous chapters in this book discuss creating projects and establishing a task list. Most of these discussions are centered on the Gantt Chart view, which is probably the most widely used view in Microsoft Office Project. This chapter is devoted to expanding your knowledge of the Gantt Chart view (and several other views) to effectively work with a project schedule. You'll find a number of cross-references in this chapter, pointing you to other sections of the book that provide more detailed information on scheduling and customizing the views.

One of the reasons the Gantt Chart view is so widely used is the array of information that is readily available in this view. The Gantt Chart view is divided into two components: the task table and the timescale. The task table is similar to a spreadsheet. It displays task data in columns and rows. The default table is the Entry table, although other tables are available for you to view.

➔ For a complete discussion of the task tables, **see** "The Task Tables," **p. 757**.

COMPONENTS OF THE TASK TABLE

As you can see in Figure 7.1, each row in the task table represents a separate task. Each column in the table displays some information about that task. The columns are *fields* in the project database. Typically you enter new tasks and their durations. Then, based on the project start date and the links between the various tasks, Project calculates the start and finish dates for that task.

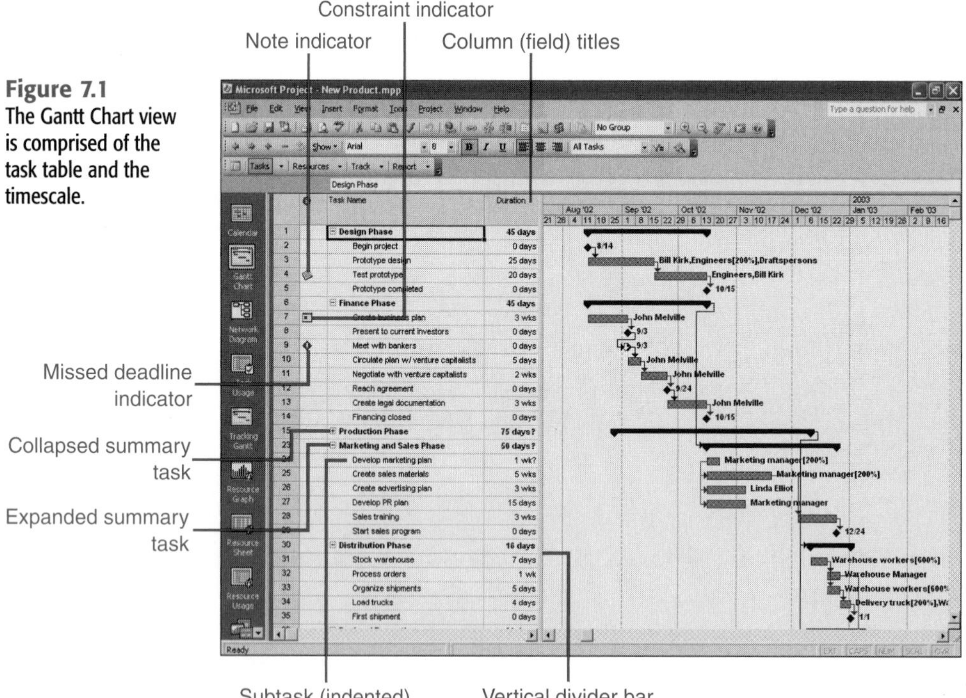

Figure 7.1
The Gantt Chart view is comprised of the task table and the timescale.

OUTLINED TASK LISTS

As you build a project schedule, you typically have phases and specific tasks underneath each phase. These phases, or main tasks, are called *summary tasks* and are displayed in bold in the task table. Project indents the specific tasks, called *subtasks*, under the summary tasks. Any task that has subtasks displays an outline symbol in front of the task name. Collapsed summary tasks display a plus (+) sign; expanded summary tasks display a minus (–) sign (refer to Figure 7.1).

Phases of a project are often dependent on the product, service, or system being developed. The breakdown of the project life cycle can be created based on deliverables, life cycle phases, product components, functional areas, geographical locations, cost accounting, or time phases. Because all projects are unique, the composition of projects varies from industry to industry.

→ To learn more about working with task lists, **see** "Outlining the Task List," **p. 154**, and "Collapsing and Expanding the Outline," **p. 157**.

TASK INDICATORS

Other visual cues you might see in the Indicators column of the Gantt Chart view include task note and constraint icons (refer to Figure 7.1). The note indicators look like yellow sticky notes and appear in the Indicators column. These notes are task-specific notes. You enter notes through the Task Information dialog box, which you can access via the Task Notes button on the Standard toolbar.

Constraint indicators are symbols that alert you when a task has a date constraint associated with it. Constraints are either something you intentionally add for a particular purpose (such as a Finish No Later Than constraint to indicate a scheduling restriction) or appear as a result of some action you have taken (such as entering the start and/or finish date for a task). You set and modify task constraints through the Task Information dialog box, which you access by clicking the Task Information button on the Standard toolbar.

→ For more information on using the Task Information dialog box, **see** "Using the Task Information Dialog Box to Edit Tasks," **p. 131**.

→ To learn more about task constraints and how to work with them, **see** "Working with Task Constraints," **p. 201**.

In addition, there are other types of indicators that you might encounter. For instance, some indicators alert you when a task is complete, when the task has slipped past its assigned deadline, or when the task has been assigned to a resource but the resource has not yet confirmed the assignment.

MOVING AROUND IN THE TASK TABLE

As you enter tasks and work with a task list, it is useful to understand how to move from row to row and column to column. Likewise, in a large project, it is helpful to be able to locate tasks quickly. You can move around the task table by using some of the keyboard movement keys:

- **Arrow keys**—Pressing the arrow keys moves the active cell (indicated by the heavy, dark border) in the direction of the arrow you press: up, down, left, or right.
- **Page Up and Page Down keys**—These keys move you up or down one screen's worth of tasks. If you are viewing tasks 1–18, for example, Project displays tasks 18–35 when you press the Page Down key. The last visible task (18, in this example) is displayed as the first task when you press Page Down.
- **Home and End keys**—Home moves the active cell to the first column in the current row, and End moves the active cell to the last column in the active row.

Other techniques for moving around include scrolling and using the Edit, Find command. These techniques are described in the next two sections.

Scrolling in the Task Table

The Gantt Chart view has three scrollbars: A vertical scrollbar on the far right of the view changes which tasks are shown onscreen, a horizontal scrollbar at the bottom of the task table changes which table columns are visible, and a second horizontal scrollbar at the bottom of the timescale moves the bar display along in time. When you drag the vertical scrollbar box, a pop-up appears to indicate what task will be listed at the top of the view when you release the mouse (see Figure 7.2).

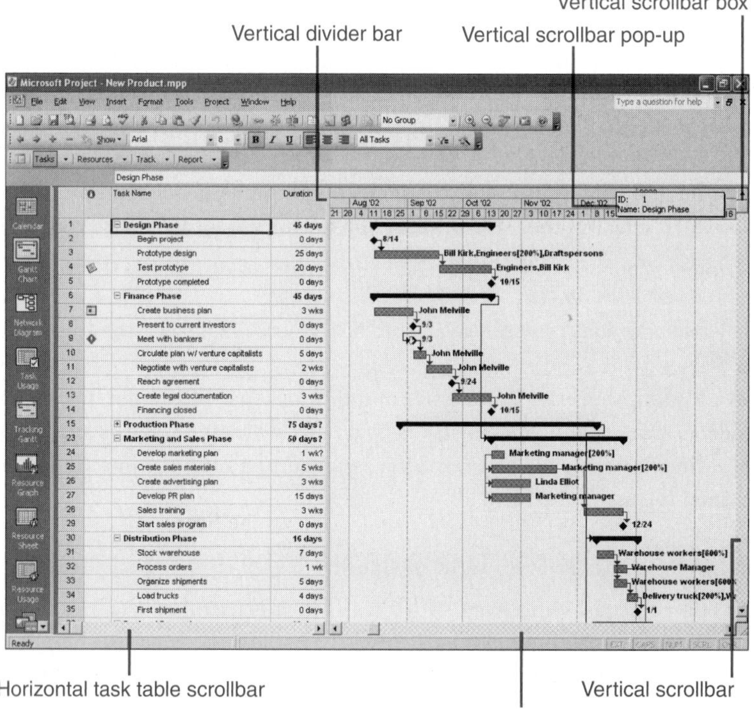

Figure 7.2
You can drag the scrollbar box to quickly move down or up the task list.

The task table is composed of a series of columns, or *fields*. Initially, just a few columns are visible when you display the Gantt Chart view: ID, Indicators, Task Name, and Duration. However, several other columns are hidden underneath the timescale. There are three ways to see the data in these columns: You can use the horizontal task table scrollbar, move the vertical divider bar out of the way, or use the Home, End command and arrow keys to scroll in the table columns.

When you drag the horizontal scrollbar in the task table, it does not display a pop-up or even move the display. You have to guess when to release the mouse. As a result, it can be a little tricky to figure out just how far to scroll to see additional columns. Clicking the arrows on the scrollbar gives you more control.

USING FIND TO LOCATE TASKS

When you have a long list of tasks and you want to search for all the tasks that contain a specific word or numbers in a task field, you can use the Find command. To find a task by searching for one or more words in the task name, follow these steps:

1. Select any task. If you want to search from the beginning of the task list, press Ctrl+Home to scroll to the beginning of the project.
2. Choose Edit, Find (or press Ctrl+F). The Find dialog box appears, as shown in Figure 7.3.

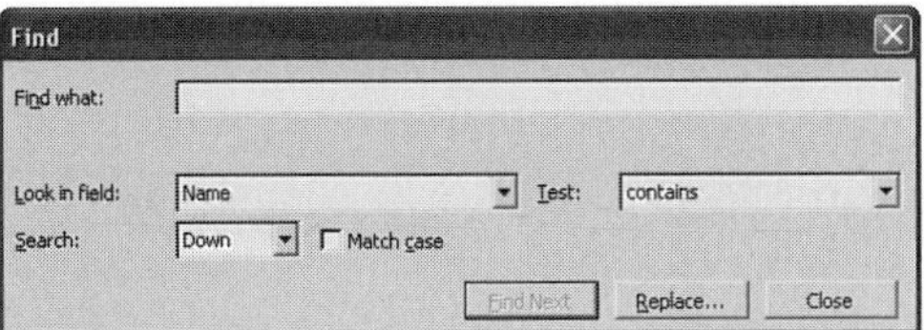

Figure 7.3
You can use the Find command to search for a task by name or for any other field value.

3. In the Find What text box, type the characters you want to search for. You can enter whole words or phrases, or just parts of words. In Figure 7.3, the word `Phase` is being located.
4. By default, the Name field is searched. However, you can select any task field to search. Select the Look in Field drop-down list box to choose the task field you want to search. Figure 7.3 has the Name field selected.
5. The Test box provides the criteria for the search. The default is Contains. Other options include Equals, Is Greater Than, and Is Greater Than or Equal to.
6. Choose the direction to be searched from the Search drop-down list box. The choices are Down and Up from the selected task.
7. You can further tailor the search by making it case sensitive. Marking the Match Case option requires the results to match the text typed in the Find What text box.
8. Click Find Next to locate the first task that matches your criteria. Each time you click Find Next, it will advance to the next task that matches your criteria.

You might have to move the dialog box to see the selected task. After you have located the task(s) you are looking for, click the Close button to close the Find dialog box.

TIP

> If you've closed the dialog box, you can use your last Find criteria again by pressing Shift+F4 to continue searching through the task list in the same direction, or you can press Ctrl+Shift+F4 to search the task list in the opposite direction.

ALTERING THE TASK TABLE DISPLAY

As you work with projects in the Gantt Chart view, there will be times when you want to change the display of the task table to show more data or change the appearance of the data. One of the changes you might want to make is to the font and font attributes of the tasks. For example, although the default settings have summary tasks in bold, you can customize the appearance to display in other colors, in italic, or in a different font.

If you want to apply an entirely different table, you can choose a table by using the View, Table command.

Other display changes you might want to make include showing more of the built-in columns in the task table, adjusting the height of individual rows, using the rollup task feature, altering the date format, and inserting new columns in the task table. These display options are illustrated in the next few sections.

VIEWING MORE COLUMNS IN THE TABLE

When you want to see more of the task table columns that are hidden beneath the timescale, you have to move the vertical divider bar. When positioned over the vertical divider bar, the mouse pointer changes to the shape of two vertical parallel lines with arrows pointing left and right. Hold the mouse button down and drag it to the desired position. A thick gray line appears, indicating the bar's position (as shown in Figure 7.4).

NOTE

> If you position the vertical divider bar in the middle of a column, double-click to move it to the closest border of the column.

NOTE

> You can adjust the widths of columns displayed in the task table. Position the mouse pointer on the right-column border, up next to the column name. The mouse pointer changes to a single vertical line with arrows pointing left and right. Click and drag it to make the column width wider or more narrow, or double-click to cause the column to adjust to the longest entry.

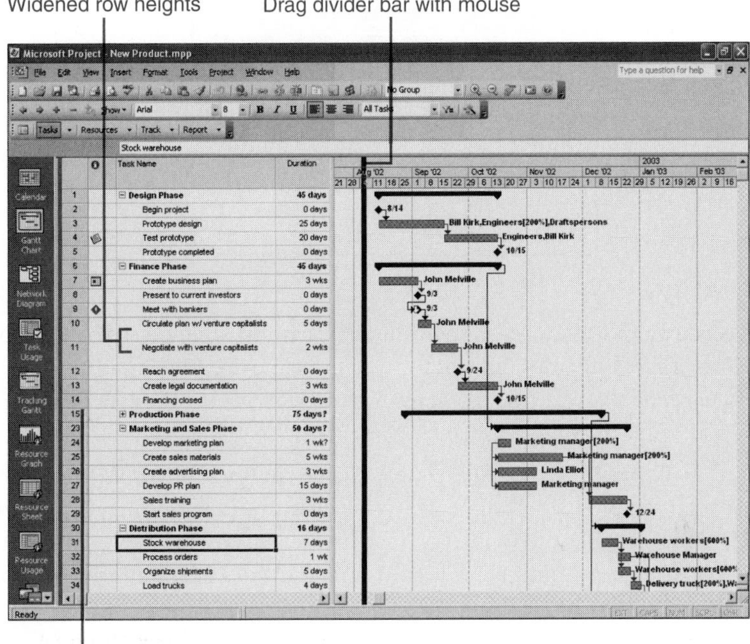

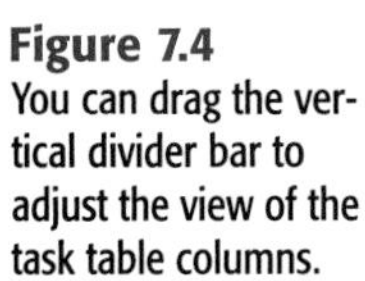
Figure 7.4
You can drag the vertical divider bar to adjust the view of the task table columns.

You can adjust the positions of individual columns displayed in the task table by simply highlighting and clicking and dragging the column to a new position.

ADJUSTING ROW HEIGHT

You can adjust the height of each row independently. Position the mouse pointer on the bottom row border, beneath the row number. The mouse pointer changes to a plus sign with arrows pointing up and down. Click and drag to make the row height deeper or more shallow. Figure 7.4 shows a few rows that have been adjusted; the text automatically word-wraps in the cell to fit the new height.

➔ To learn how to work with row size, **see** "Adjusting the Height of Task Rows," **p. 126**.

INSERTING AND CHANGING COLUMNS IN THE TASK TABLE

Sometimes, you might want to change the column titles to match some more common names used within your organization, or you might want to change which field is displayed in a column. For example, you could change the title of the Task Name column to What Has to Be Done. To modify a column, simply double-click its column title, and Project displays the Column Definition dialog box (see Figure 7.5). The following list describes the options in the Column Definition dialog box:

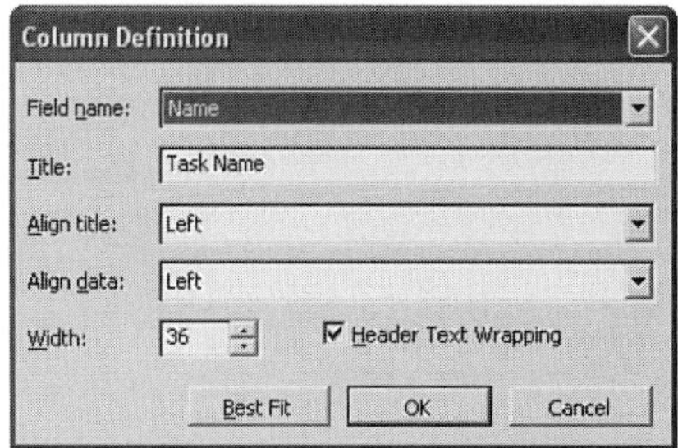

Figure 7.5
You access the Column Definition dialog box by double-clicking the column title in the task table.

- If you want to replace one column with the contents of another Project database field, select a different field from the Field Name drop-down box.
- Change the entry in the Title box to modify the column title. If you don't supply an entry in the Title box, Project displays the field name as the column name. Note in Figure 7.5 that the field name is Name and the title displayed onscreen is Task Name. Please note that changing the entry in the Title box only changes the title in the current table. If you want to permanently change the title (sometimes called the *alias*) for a custom field so that the title automatically appears in every view where that column appears, you must use the Tools, Customize, Fields option. Or you can right-click on the column title and choose Customize Fields. The Customize Fields option only works for custom type fields.
- You can select the alignment (left, center, right) for the title by using the Align Title drop-down box and for the data by using the Align Data drop-down box.
- The Width box reflects the current width, which can be changed in this dialog box.
- If the column title is long, you can check the Header Text Wrapping option to allow header text to display on more than one line, which allows a more narrow column width.
- Clicking the OK button implements the changes you have selected.
- Clicking the Best Fit button applies the changes like the OK button does, but it also adjusts the column width to the longest cell entry.

Instead of changing the contents and layout of a displayed column, you might want to add or remove table columns. There are two methods for showing and hiding columns:

- **Using the Hide and Insert commands**—To remove a column from a displayed table, right-click the column title and choose Hide Column from the shortcut menu. To add this or any other column to the table, select the title of the column that is in the position where you want the new column to be, right-click the mouse, and choose Insert Column from the shortcut menu. The Column Definition dialog box appears, and in it you can select the column options as described previously.

  You can also select a column title and press the Delete key to remove a column from view, or you can press the Insert key to add a column onscreen.

- **Using the mouse**—This method is similar to procedures you may already know from Microsoft Excel. To close a column onscreen, position the mouse on the right divider of the column title and drag it back to the left. For example, to close the Start column, drag the line that is between the words Start and Finish to the left until the Start column is hidden. To reopen the Start column, approach the divider by moving the mouse slowly from right to left. When the pointer changes shape, click and drag the column open.

NOTE

Double-clicking on a column title edge applies best-fit width formatting to the column.

NOTE

It's important to note that hiding or deleting a column from view does not delete the data stored in the cells of that column. The contents are still stored in the database and will be visible when the hidden column is reinserted into any table.

You cannot mix and match the two techniques for adding and hiding columns. Columns hidden by choosing Hide Column can't be reopened via the mouse dragging method. If you use the methods described here to delete (or hide) and insert columns in the task table, you are in fact *customizing* the table for the active project. When a modified table is applied to any other view, the revised layout, not the original table, is displayed.

➔ For specific information about customizing tables and sharing those custom settings with other project files, **see** "Using and Creating Tables," **p. 840**.

CHANGING THE DATE FORMAT

The default date display format uses the mm/dd/yy pattern. This is the format that you see in the Start and Finish columns of the task table. You can add the time of day to the display, or you can switch to any one of a number of data format options. Be aware, however, that changes you make to the date format affect the date display in all your project files—not just the active project. You can change the date display at any time.

To change the date display format, follow these steps:

1. Choose Tools, Options, and the Options dialog box appears. (see Figure 7.6).
2. On the View tab, select the format that you want in the Date Format drop-down box.
3. Click the OK button to make the change effective.

Depending on the date format you select, you might see a series of # symbols displayed in the cells in the Start and Finish columns. This indicates that you need to widen the column to display the date in the new format.

Figure 7.6
You can change the date format in the Options dialog box.

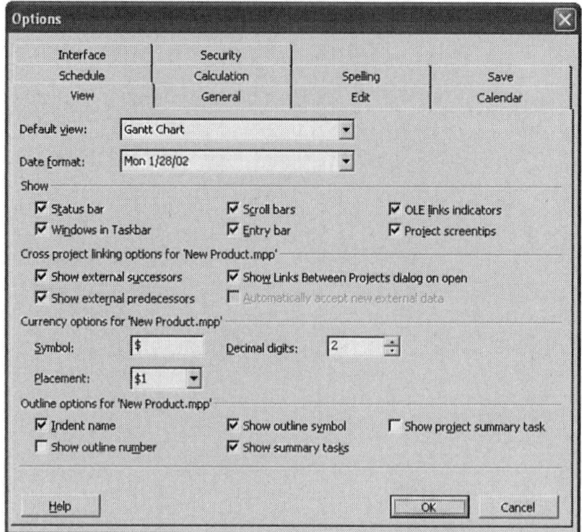

NOTE

> If you want to use an international date or time format, you must set this through the Regional Settings applet in the Microsoft Windows Control Panel.

COMPONENTS OF THE TIMESCALE

The timescale is the graphic portion on the right side of the Gantt Chart view. The timescale displays several items: a time line, taskbars, bar text, and linking lines. These items are identified in Figure 7.7.

In addition, you can add graphic drawing objects to the timescale, such as text boxes and arrows. Placing graphic objects on the timescale is discussed later in this chapter.

TASKBARS

There are three types of taskbars in Project: Summary, Normal, and Milestone. The default display of these bars is shown in Figure 7.7. However, by using the Gantt Chart Wizard, you can significantly alter the display of the taskbars, as shown in Figure 7.8.

You access the Gantt Chart Wizard by clicking the button on the Formatting toolbar, by choosing Format, Gantt Chart Wizard, or by right-clicking in the display area of the timescale and choosing Gantt Chart Wizard.

→ To learn more about using the Gantt Chart Wizard and other options for formatting the timescale, **see** "Using the Gantt Chart Wizard," **p. 801**.

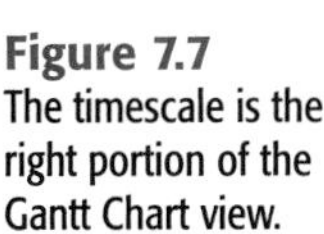

Figure 7.7
The timescale is the right portion of the Gantt Chart view.

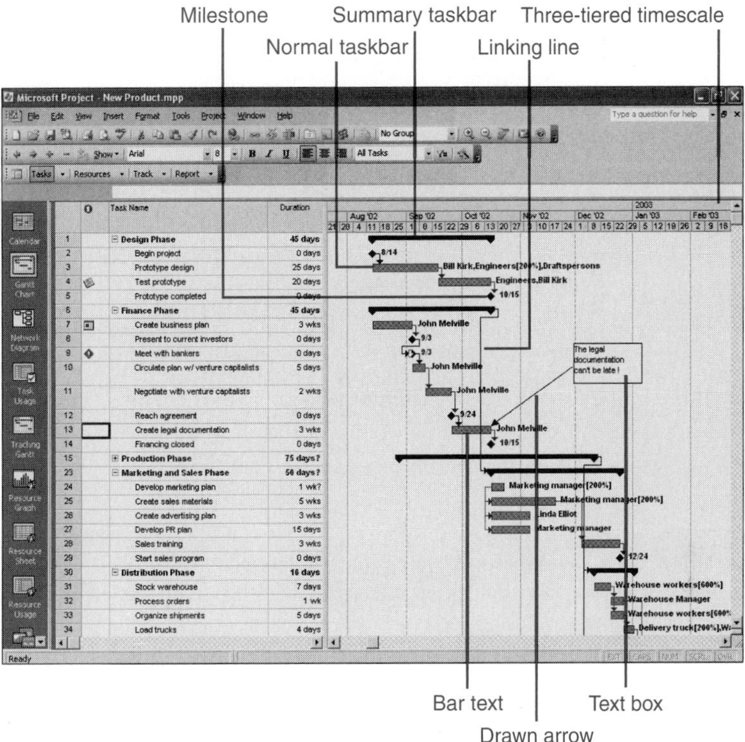

Figure 7.8
You can significantly alter the display of the timescale by using a number of tools, the easiest of which is the Gantt Chart Wizard.

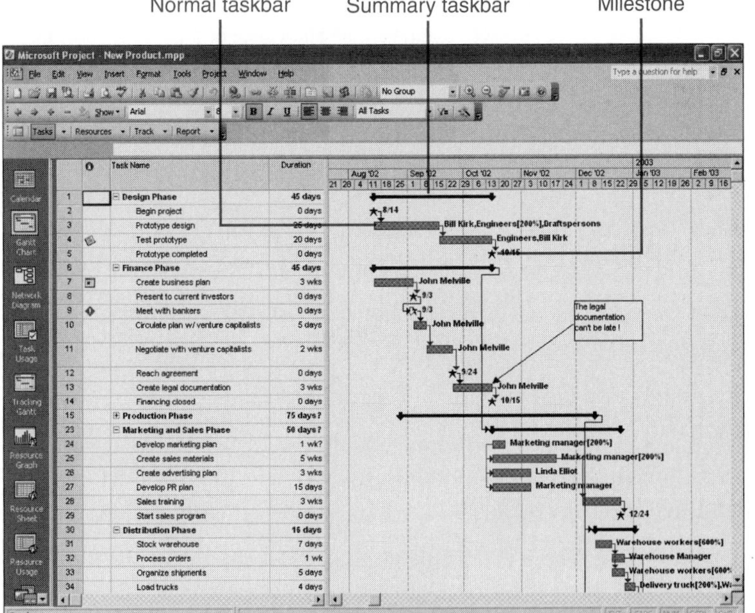

BAR TEXT

The default settings for the taskbars display the name of the resource at the end of Normal tasks and the start date next to Milestones. You can designate the data and placement that appear with a taskbar in the Bar Styles dialog box. Choose Format, Bar Styles, and select the bar type at the top of the dialog box. Two tabs at the bottom of the dialog box display the Text and Bars settings for the selected bar type.

→ For more information on working with timescale taskbars, **see** "Using the Bar Styles Dialog Box," **p. 824**.

LINKING LINES

The lines that connect the taskbars represent links between tasks, and they define the order in which the tasks must be done. The position of a linking line indicates the type of link. If the linking line extends from the end of one task to the beginning of another, there is a Finish-to-Start link between the tasks. There are four different link types. In addition, you can build in lead time and lag time between linked tasks.

Historically, a Gantt chart did not display linking lines. Instead, the positioning of the tasks on the bar chart indicated when things were scheduled to occur, not which tasks were dependent on one another. Regardless, it's fair to say that the popularity of Microsoft Project has redefined the expected appearance of a Gantt chart. In large projects, however, it's often necessary to remove the linking lines from the view to reduce the cluttered appearance. You can turn off the linking lines in the Layout dialog box.

CAUTION

Linking lines may sometimes be drawn on top of each other, making it difficult to tell which tasks they are connecting. Also, two similar, but different, relationships can result in identical linking lines being drawn. You can verify the link types by reviewing the Predecessors column on the Entry table or the Predecessors tab in the Task Information dialog box.

→ For more information about the link types, as well as lead and lag time, **see** "Understanding Dependency Links," **p. 177**.

MOVING AROUND IN THE TIMESCALE

After you have created a project schedule, it is useful to understand how to quickly move around the timescale. This is especially true when you have a large, extensive project. With a few keystrokes or mouse clicks, you can move from the beginning to the end of the timescale, move incrementally through the timescale, or scroll to a specific task. The following are some of the techniques you can use:

- **Alt+right-arrow key or Alt+left-arrow key**—Holding down the Alt key and pressing the right-arrow key scrolls the timescale to the right one unit of the smallest timescale tier displayed. No matter how many of the three timescale tiers are displayed, Project uses the bottom, smallest time increment for moving the timescale with the arrow keys. Using the left-arrow key with the Alt key scrolls the timescale one unit back in time.

- **Alt+Page Up key or Alt+Page Down key**—Using Alt+Page Down scrolls you to the right one screen's worth on the timescale. So, if you are viewing the weeks of January 7 through January 21, using Alt+Page Down displays the weeks of January 28 through February 10. Using Alt+Page Up scrolls you to the left one screen's worth on the timescale.
- **Alt+Home key or Alt+End key**—Using Alt+Home scrolls the timescale to the beginning of the project, the time frame that shows the first project tasks. Using Alt+End scrolls the timescale to the end of the project.

CAUTION

> Pressing Alt+up-arrow key or Alt+down-arrow key might appear to have no effect. These combinations do not scroll the timescale horizontally, but they do have effects on the table. If the active cell is in a date column, pressing Alt+up-arrow key or Alt+down-arrow key displays a calendar object in the cell and scrolls through the calendar, selecting a different date for the cell unless you press Esc to turn off the object. Similarly, if the active cell is in the Duration column, pressing Alt+up-arrow key or Alt+down-arrow key activates the spinner in the cell, and a new duration value is chosen unless you press Esc to leave the cell-edit mode.

SCROLLING IN THE TIMESCALE

The timescale uses two scrollbars: the vertical scrollbar on the far right of the view and a horizontal scrollbar at the bottom of the timescale portion of the Gantt Chart view. The vertical scrollbar is used primarily to scroll through the task list.

As discussed earlier in the chapter, the horizontal scrollbar at the bottom of the table changes which columns are visible. However, when you drag the horizontal scrollbar in the timescale, it displays a pop-up to indicate the date you will be scrolling to when you release the mouse button (see Figure 7.9).

LOCATING A TASKBAR OR SPECIFIC DATE IN THE GANTT CHART

Often when you are working in the Gantt Chart view, you have a task selected but the corresponding taskbar is not visible on the screen. This is especially true when you zoom in to see minutes, hours, or days in the timescale.

To have the timescale scroll to show the taskbar associated with a specific task, select the task in the table and click the Go To Selected Task button on the Standard toolbar. Project scrolls to show the beginning of the taskbar.

You can also use the Edit, Go To command (or press Ctrl+G) to display the Go To dialog box (see Figure 7.10) if you want to jump to a specific date in the timescale. You can enter a date in the Date box or click the drop-down calendar object to select a date.

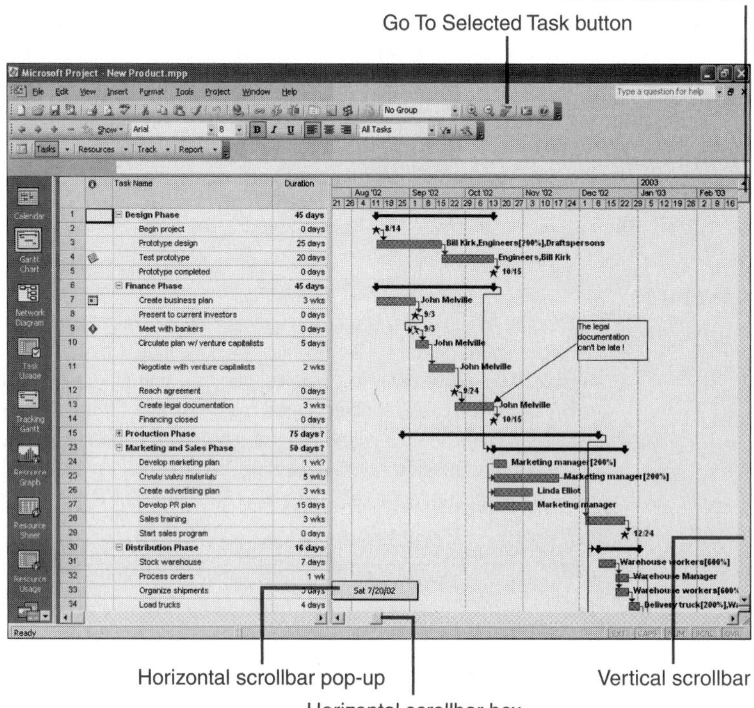

Figure 7.9
You can drag the horizontal scrollbar box on the timescale to quickly move to a specific date.

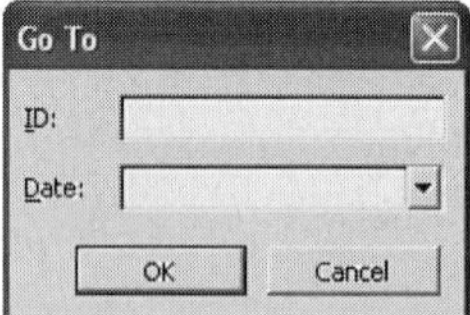

Figure 7.10
You can type in a task ID to go to a specific task.

NOTE

You can use `today` or `tomorrow` in the Date box to jump to the corresponding dates.

ALTERING THE TIMESCALE DISPLAY

The timescale in the right side of the Gantt Chart view is made up of the rows at the top of the view. A maximum of three rows, or *tiers*, can be displayed: a top tier, middle tier, and bottom tier. At least one tier must be visible onscreen at any time. Gray dotted lines extend down the screen to mark the division between units on the middle tier only, if the tier is turned on. You can customize the amount of time encompassed by the units on each of the scales and you can change the labels that appear in the units.

The quickest way to adjust the timescale units is to zoom in or zoom out, using the appropriate buttons on the Standard toolbar. You can also control the chart scaling by using the Format, Zoom dialog box.

Another way to adjust the timescale is to choose Format, Timescale to access the Timescale dialog box (shown in Figure 7.11). You use the Timescale tab to establish the settings for each of the three tiers. You use the Non-working Time tab to set the display options for non-working days, such as weekends.

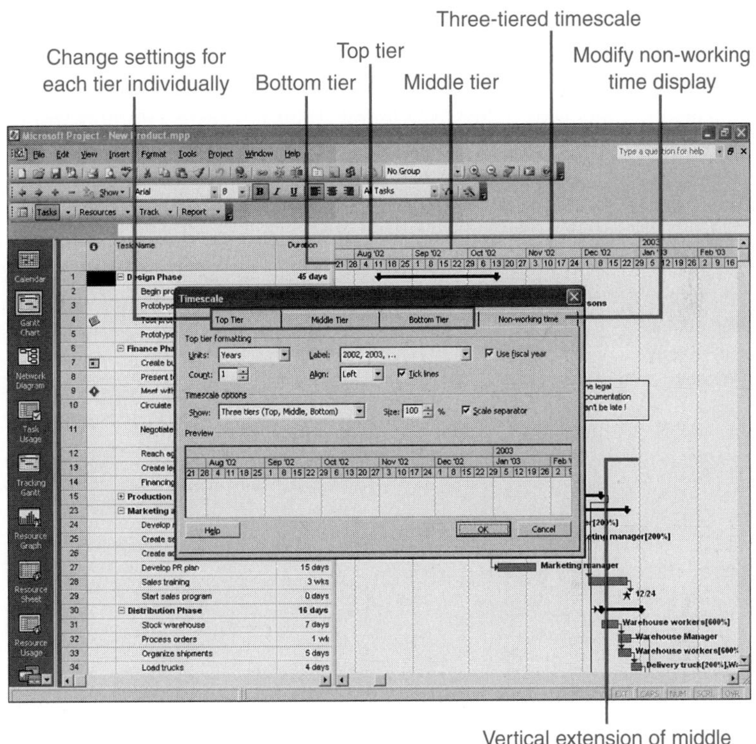

Figure 7.11 Individual adjustments to the timescale can be set by using the Timescale dialog box.

➔ To learn how to effectively use the settings in the Timescale dialog box, **see** "Formatting Timescales," **p. 785**.

VIEWING MORE TASK DETAILS

Although the Gantt Chart view contains a lot of information, you can see even more details about individual tasks either with the Task Information dialog box or by splitting the screen and viewing the Task Form view.

USING THE TASK INFORMATION DIALOG BOX

You can click the Task Information button on the Standard toolbar to display a pop-up dialog box that displays many details about the selected task. The six tabs in the dialog box provide access to many additional fields. If you have a summary task selected, the Summary Task dialog box appears. Similarly, if you have more than one task selected, the dialog box becomes the Multiple Task Information box. Some fields are unavailable on the Summary Task and Multiple Task dialog boxes, usually because those fields are calculated by Project.

USING COMBINATION VIEWS

One of the most useful and powerful display techniques that Microsoft Project provides is the capability to split the screen in half (top and bottom) to see two different views of the project simultaneously. Choose Window, Split to create a combination view screen (see Figure 7.12).

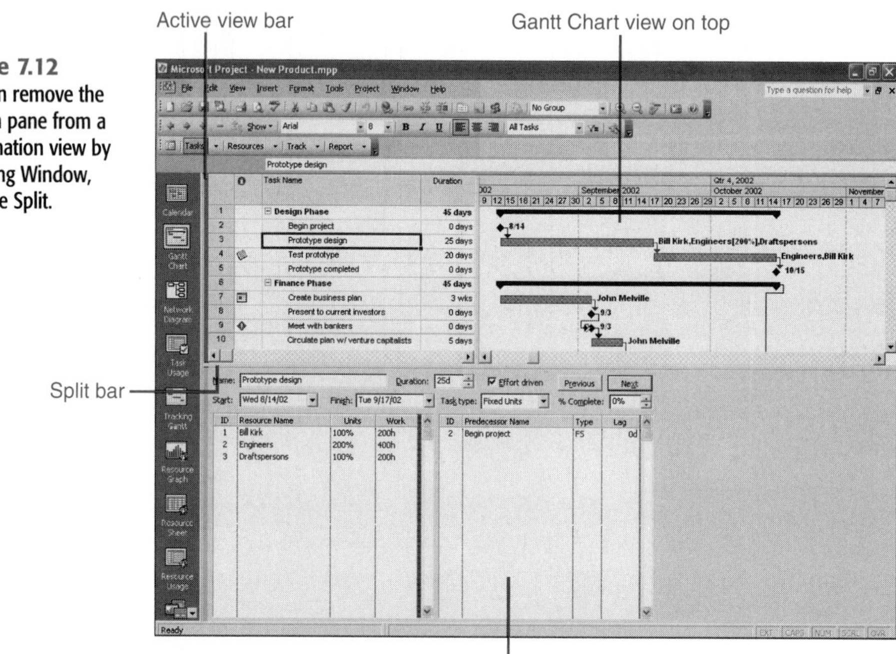

Figure 7.12
You can remove the bottom pane from a combination view by choosing Window, Remove Split.

The window splits into two panes: The top pane shows the view you were working in before splitting the screen, and the bottom pane shows either the Task Form view (if you started with a task view) or the Resource Form view (if you started with a resource view). Figure 7.12 shows the Gantt Chart view in the top pane and the Task Form view in the bottom pane.

Task 3, "Prototype Design," is selected in the top pane in Figure 7.12. The bottom pane shows detailed information about Task 3. The bottom pane displays all the fields that are in the columns in the Gantt Chart view, including the ones that are hidden beneath the standard timescale. This screen arrangement enables you to see the values in those fields, eliminating the need to display a large number of columns in the task table. With a split screen, you can see how the task fits into the overall scheme of things in the top pane, and view many significant details in the bottom pane.

You can enter task information in either pane, but you must activate the pane before you can use it. To activate the bottom pane, simply click anywhere in the bottom pane. You can also use the F6 function key to toggle back and forth between panes. The pane that is active displays a dark blue color on its half of the Active View bar (refer to Figure 7.12).

The two minitables at the bottom of the Task Form view initially display resource and predecessor details. You can select different details to display in these areas. First, activate the bottom pane. Then choose Format, Details. A submenu appears, with alternative data you can display.

ADDING GRAPHICS AND TEXT TO GANTT CHARTS

You can significantly enhance the Gantt Chart view by adding graphic and text objects to draw attention to or explain particular events within the project. Microsoft Project provides a set of drawing tools to help you enhance the appearance of Gantt charts. The drawing tools produce graphic objects that can be moved, resized, and placed in front of, alongside of, or behind the taskbars.

Included among the drawing tools is a Text Box tool that lets you place free text anywhere in the Gantt Chart display. This section shows you how to create and modify graphics and text in the Gantt Chart view.

NOTE

> Graphic objects can be placed only in the timescale side of the Gantt Chart view. Graphic objects you place on the Gantt Chart view are not displayed when the Gantt Chart view is in the bottom pane of a combination view.

INTRODUCING THE DRAWING TOOLBAR

You create text and graphic objects on the Gantt Chart view by using buttons on the Drawing toolbar. When the toolbar is displayed, you can create objects by selecting an object button and creating an example of the object on the Gantt Chart area. After the objects are created, you can modify them to create the effect you desire. Figure 7.13 shows an example of a text message overlaid on the Gantt Chart and an arrow directing your attention to the circled tasks that the message describes.

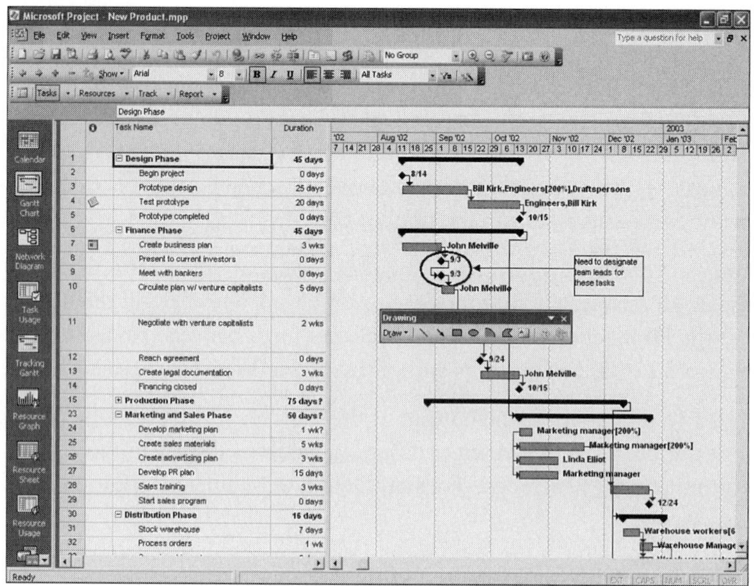

Figure 7.13
Text and graphics elements can be used to annotate a Gantt Chart or to emphasize one of its aspects.

To display the Drawing toolbar, choose Insert, Drawing or choose View, Toolbars, Drawing. You can also display the Drawing toolbar by right-clicking any toolbar and choosing Drawing from the shortcut menu.

DESCRIPTIONS OF THE DRAWING BUTTONS

The first button on the Drawing toolbar is a drop-down menu that provides options for arranging and editing the objects you draw. The next seven buttons on the toolbar are used to create objects on the Gantt Chart view. These buttons create lines, arrows, rectangles, ovals, arcs, polygons, and text boxes. The remaining two buttons provide access to various editing possibilities.

THE DRAW DROP-DOWN MENU

You use the Draw button when you want to arrange and edit the objects you draw. From its drop-down menu, it includes the following options:

- **Bring to Front**—Bring a selected object to the forefront, placing it before all other objects that originally overlaid it.
- **Send to Back**—Send an object to the back, placing it behind all other objects in the same area.
- **Bring Forward**—Move an object in front of other objects, one at a time, toward the viewer. Objects in front hide objects that are behind them.
- **Send Backward**—Move an object behind other objects, one at a time, away from the viewer.
- **Edit Points**—Change the shape of a polygon.

THE DRAWING OBJECTS BUTTONS

The buttons that draw objects are described in the following sections. Table 7.1 shows each of the seven drawing buttons and describes its use.

TIP

With some objects, you can use the Shift key to create a perfectly symmetrical object—for example, a perfect square, a perfect circle, or a perfect arc. To draw a square or circle, select the appropriate drawing button and then hold down the Shift key as you begin to drag the mouse to create the object.

TABLE 7.1 DRAWING BUTTONS ON THE DRAWING TOOLBAR

Icon	Name	Click and Drag to Draw...	Shift+Click and Drag to Draw...
	Line	A line without arrowheads	(N/A)
	Arrow	A line with arrowheads	(N/A)
	Rectangle	A rectangle	A perfect square
	Oval	An elliptical figure	A perfect circle
	Arc	An elliptical arc	A symmetrical arc from circles
	Polygon	A many-sided figure of any configuration	(N/A)
	Text Box	A rectangular box for typing text	A perfect square for typing text

To add a drawing object to the Gantt Chart view timescale, follow these steps:

1. Display the Gantt Chart view, if it is not already displayed.
2. Choose Insert, Drawing to display the Drawing toolbar.
3. Click the button for the object you want to draw.
4. Move the mouse to the place you want to draw the object; the mouse pointer should be a crosshairs.
5. Hold the mouse button down and drag to create the object.
6. When you release the mouse button, the object is drawn.

7

The last two buttons on the toolbar are the Cycle Fill Color button and the Attach to Task button. The Cycle Fill Color button allows you to change the inside color of the selected object, cycling through the palette of color choices each time you click the button. With the Attach to Task button, you open the Format Drawing dialog box to change how an object is anchored to the Gantt Chart view or to modify the attributes of the object.

TIP

> You can double-click the Polygon button to have the computer draw the final line that connects the last point to the starting point, producing a closed figure.

WORKING WITH DRAWING OBJECTS IN THE GANTT CHART VIEW

You can hide, move, resize, copy, or delete objects you have drawn. Objects can be attached to a specific task or date so that when you zoom out, the object stays with the task or date it is attached to. The color of the border surrounding the object and the inside of the object can be changed to enhance the object's appearance.

Before you can make any changes to an object, you must first select the object you want to modify.

SELECTING OBJECTS

You can use the mouse to select objects in the timescale. Move the tip of the mouse pointer to an object's line or border. When a small cross appears below and to the right of the pointer arrow, click to select the object. When the object is selected, small black resizing handles appear around it. Only one object can be selected at a time.

TIP

> For solid figures (rectangles, ellipses, arcs, or polygons with a fill pattern), you can point to the interior of an object to select it. This is easier than pointing to the border.

You can also use the keyboard to select objects. The F6 function key toggles back and forth between selecting the task table and a graphic object in the timescale. (If a combination view is displayed, the bottom view is also selected in turn if you press the F6 key.)

TIP

> If you have created multiple drawing objects, when one of them is selected, you can use the Tab key to cycle the selection to the other drawing objects, one at a time. You can press Shift+Tab to cycle backward through the drawn objects.

ATTACHING OBJECTS TO A TASKBAR OR A DATE

When you create an object, it has both horizontal and vertical attachment points. Horizontally, it is automatically attached to the date on the timescale where you created it. Vertically, an offset value dictates how far down from the Timescale tiers the object should be displayed. The vertical offset is more visible when you zoom in on the timescale. A drawn object stays with the date it is associated with as you scroll or zoom the timescale.

CAUTION

Be aware that if you zoom out in the Gantt Chart view, your objects might be placed on top of each other because the timescale is compressed.

If an object is attached to a date in the timescale, when you move the object, it remains attached to the timescale but at the new date and vertical position where you move it. You can see the attachment by examining the Size & Position tab of the Format Drawing dialog box for the object (see Figure 7.14).

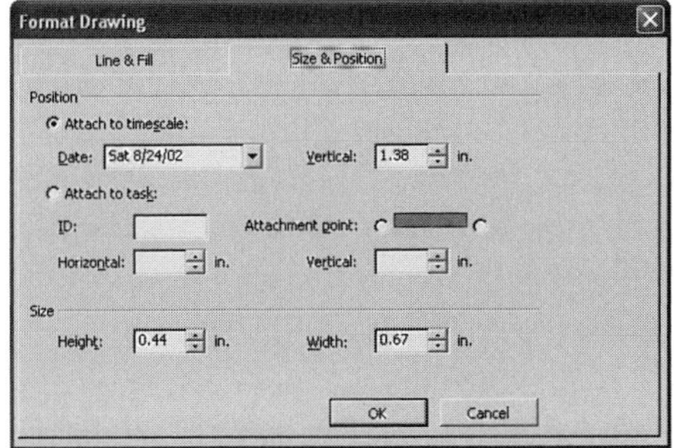

Figure 7.14
You use the Format Drawing dialog box to attach an object to a task or to the timescale.

To view the Format Drawing dialog box, you can simply double-click most objects. Text box behavior is a bit different. If a text box is already selected, double-clicking it turns on text edit mode. If the text box isn't selected, double-clicking it opens the Format Drawing dialog box just like other drawing shapes does.

There are several other ways to display the Format Drawing dialog box. You can select the object and use the Attach to Task button on the Drawing toolbar. If you prefer to use the menu bar, you can choose Format, Drawing and choose Properties from the submenu. Or, to use the shortcut menu (see Figure 7.15), position the mouse pointer over the object so that the pointer displays a small cross to its right. Right-click to see the shortcut menu, and then select Properties to open the Format Drawing dialog box shown previously in Figure 7.14.

Rather than have a drawn object attached to a date, you can attach it to a task in the table portion of the Gantt Chart view. To attach an object to a task, follow these steps:

1. Make a note of the ID number of the task to which you want to attach the object. You need to enter the ID number on the dialog box, and there is no way to browse or search for the ID number after the dialog box is active.
2. Activate the Format Drawing dialog box and choose the Size & Position tab.
3. Choose the Attach to Task option button.

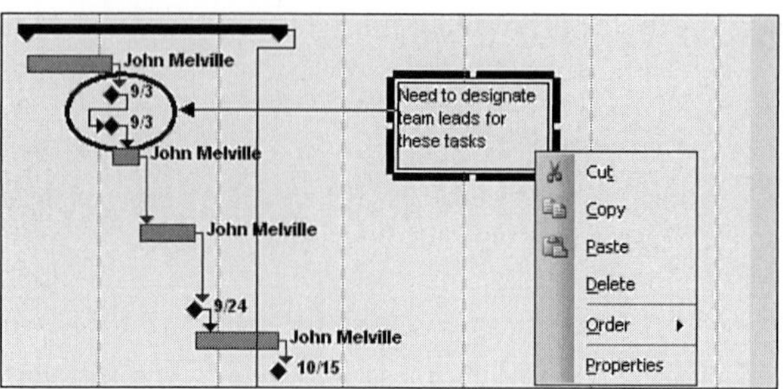

Figure 7.15
The drawing objects shortcut menu is a quick way to work with drawn objects.

4. Enter the task number in the ID text box. If you do not remember the ID number, you have to close the dialog box, find the number, and then come back to the dialog box.
5. Attach the object to the beginning or the end of the taskbar by choosing the Attachment Point on the sample taskbar.
6. The Horizontal and Vertical fields show the offset from the attachment point where the object's top-left corner will be placed. Positive offset values are to the right horizontally and down vertically. Negative offset values are to the left horizontally and up vertically. You should enter `0` in both these text boxes unless you are absolutely certain that you know the values that will look best. The zero values ensure that the drawing object is displayed next to the taskbar. You then can use the mouse to reposition the object as desired.

   After the object is attached to the task, you can move it with the mouse, and the horizontal and vertical offset values are recorded automatically. The object remains attached to the task as you move the task.
7. Click OK to return to the workspace.

If you later decide to unlink the object from the task to fix it at a particular date, return to the Size & Position tab and choose the Attach to Timescale button. Then move the task with the mouse to the preferred position.

Hiding Objects on the Gantt Chart View

The drawn objects you place on the Gantt Chart view remain visible and print with the Gantt Chart view unless you elect to hide them. You can hide them for a printing, for example, and then display them again later.

To hide the drawing objects, use these steps:

1. Choose Format, Layout. The Layout dialog box is displayed (see Figure 7.16).
2. Clear the Show Drawings check box at the bottom.
3. Click OK to implement the change.

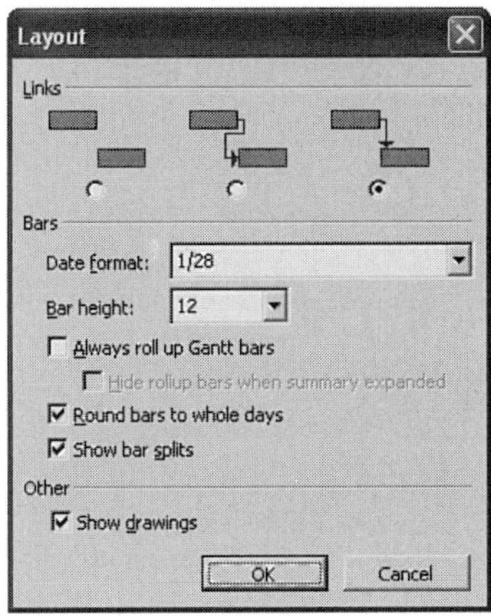

Figure 7.16
Graphic objects are hidden from view if you clear the Show Drawings check box on the Layout dialog box.

Moving Objects

You can move an object by moving the mouse pointer over the object, away from the selection handles. Watch for the small cross to appear to the right of the pointer arrow, and then click and drag the object to a new position.

CAUTION

> It is very easy to accidentally move a taskbar or create a new taskbar when your intention is to move or resize a graphic object. If the mouse pointer does not have the cross beside it, you are not moving the object. Do not click the mouse until the cross appears.

Resizing Objects

Although you can size an object by using the Height and Width fields at the bottom of the Size & Position tab in the Format Drawing dialog box (refer to Figure 7.14), it is much easier to use the mouse to achieve the same end.

Selection handles appear at each end of line and arrow objects. When a two-dimensional object is selected, its selection handles are evident in a rectangular array around the object. You can change the size of the object by moving the mouse pointer over one of the selection handles until the pointer changes into a pair of opposing arrows. Drag the handle to the position you desire (see Figure 7.17).

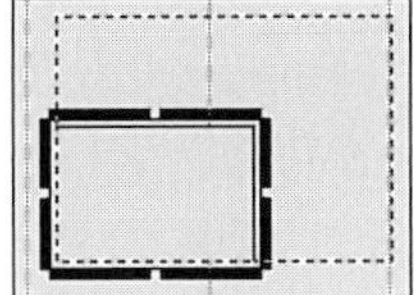

Figure 7.17
You can use the selection handles to resize an object.

The corner handles resize both of the sides that meet at the corner. For instance, if you use the selection handle in the lower-right corner, you can resize the right and bottom sides of the object at the same time. The handles along the top and bottom midpoints resize vertically, and the handles along the sides resize horizontally.

TIP

> Use the Shift key while dragging one of the corner handles to resize the object proportionally along both horizontal and vertical dimensions.

Polygons are a special case when it comes to reshaping. Because a polygon has multiple sides, you can reshape it by adjusting its points. The *points* on a polygon are the locations where the shape changes direction. Sometimes points are called *nodes*.

To reshape a polygon, you must first select it. Then click the Draw button on the Drawing toolbar and choose Edit Points. The selection handles of a polygon disappear when you click the Edit Points option on the Draw drop-down list on the Drawing toolbar (see Figure 7.18). Instead, you see reshaping handles at the points. Use these handles to reposition the points and thus change the shape of the drawing. To move a connecting point, position the mouse pointer directly over the handle; when it turns into a large plus sign, click and drag to the desired shape. When you are finished reshaping the figure, click the Edit Points tool again to display the selection handles again.

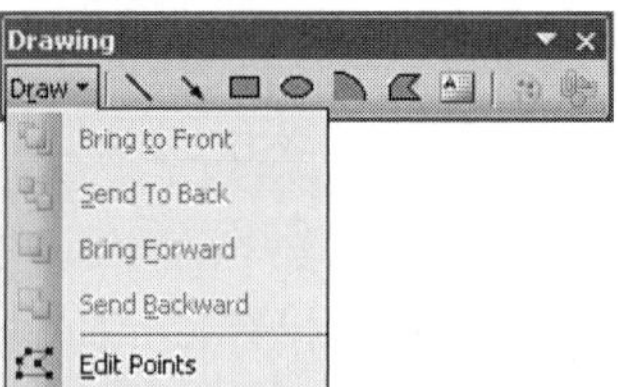

Figure 7.18
The Edit Points option on the Drawing toolbar allows you to edit the points on a polygon.

If you want to increase or decrease the size of a polygon without changing its shape, you can make proportional changes to its Size fields on the Format Drawing dialog box. For example, to double the size of a selected polygon, double-click the polygon and double the values in the Height and Width fields in the Format Drawing dialog box.

COPYING OBJECTS

Sometimes when you draw an object in the Gantt Chart view, you might want to copy the object to another area of the chart or to another Project document. If the place to which you want to copy the object is visible onscreen, you can easily use the mouse to drag a copy of the object to the new location. However, if the place to which you want to copy the object is not visible, or you want to copy the object to another file, you're better off using the traditional methods for copying and pasting.

Follow these steps to copy an object with the mouse:

1. Select the original object.
2. Hold down the Ctrl key as you drag away from the original object. You will be dragging a copy of the original.
3. Continue dragging the copy until it is in its new position. The copy appears as an outline until you release the mouse button.
4. Release the mouse button when the copy is in position.

The traditional copy and paste techniques use the Clipboard to copy an object. You must use copy and paste to copy the object to another file.

CHANGING THE LINE AND FILL STYLE OF AN OBJECT

To enhance the appearance of a drawn object, you can change the thickness and color of the object's lines and borders. You can also apply a background pattern or color that fills the interior of the drawn object. You select both the outline and color options from the Line & Fill tab of the Format Drawing dialog box (see Figure 7.19).

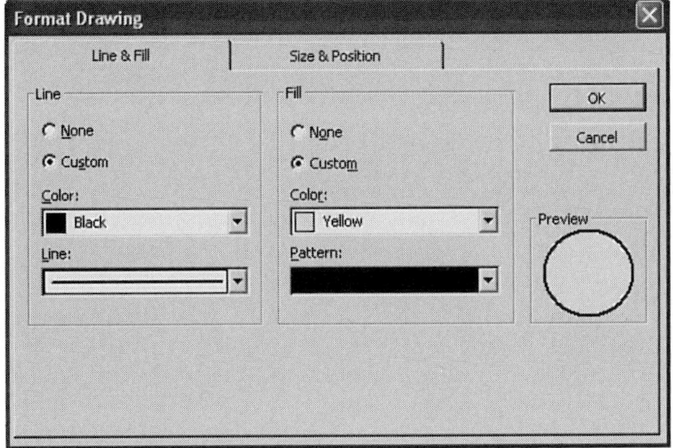

Figure 7.19
You can customize the attributes of a line and the interior fill of an object.

To change an object's line and fill attributes, use these steps:

1. Select the object and display the Format Drawing dialog box by double-clicking the object or by choosing Format, Drawing, and selecting Properties.
2. Select the Line & Fill tab.
3. If you want the line or border to be invisible, choose the None button in the Line section. If you select a line color or line style, the Custom button is activated automatically.
4. To select the color for a line, choose a sample color band from the drop-down list below the Color label.
5. To select the thickness of a line, choose a sample line from the drop-down list below the Line label.

6. If you want the background of the object to be transparent so that you can see taskbars or other objects behind the object, choose the None button in the Fill section. If you choose a color or a pattern, the Custom button is activated automatically.
7. The default fill pattern is solid; the default color is white. If you want to display a different color in the interior of the object, simply select a different color from the drop-down list below the Color label. Selecting the object and using the Cycle Fill Color button on the Drawing toolbar can also change the color of an object.
8. Whatever is black in the pattern is displayed in the color you select. Whatever is white in the pattern remains white. If you leave the default white color selected and select a pattern, you get a white pattern color on a white background. Select a color for the pattern in order to see the pattern on the object.
9. Choose a pattern by selecting a sample from the drop-down list below the Pattern label. The first pattern in the entry list appears white. It is a clear pattern, equivalent to choosing the None button in the Fill section. The second pattern in the entry list is solid black. Choose the solid band to display a solid background in the color you selected from the Color field. The remaining patterns are displayed against a white background, with the pattern appearing in the foreground in the color you selected from the Color field.
10. Use the Preview box at the lower-right corner of the tab to assess the choices you have made. Change the choices until the Preview box looks the way you want the object to look.
11. Click OK to implement the changes. Choose Cancel to leave the object unchanged.

DELETING OBJECTS

You can delete any object by simply selecting it and then pressing the Delete key.

PLACING INDEPENDENT TEXT ON THE GANTT CHART

You use the Text Box drawing button to place text on the Gantt Chart time line. Text added with this method is not stored in a database field associated with any particular task; it is considered to be *independent*. After you draw the text box on the screen, enter the text into the box. You can change the line and fill attributes, as well as the position of the text box, as described in the preceding sections. You can also edit the text and select the fonts for the text display.

CREATING A TEXT BOX

To display a text message in the Gantt Chart view, you need to bring into view the area of the time line where the message is to appear and then follow these steps:

1. Click the Text Box button on the Drawing toolbar.
2. Drag the mouse in the Gantt Chart view to create a box at the approximate location and of the approximate dimension you need. You can later adjust the box to fit the text. An insertion point cursor then blinks in the text box.

3. Type the text that you want to appear in the box. The text automatically word-wraps within the current size of the text box. It also word-wraps automatically when you resize the text box later. Press Enter when you want to start a paragraph on a new line in the text box.
4. When you finish entering text, click outside the text box.

EDITING THE TEXT IN A TEXT BOX

To modify the text in a text box, click to select the text box, and then click again to activate the edit mode. Make sure you don't double-click the text box, as this displays the Format Drawing dialog box. When the edit mode is active, the mouse pointer appears as a capital I (sometimes referred to as the *I-beam*) within the text box. The flashing cursor indicates the keyboard position within the text; if you begin typing, the text is entered at the point of the flashing cursor (see Figure 7.20).

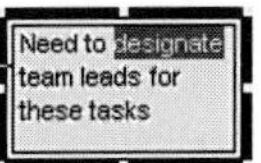

Figure 7.20
You can use normal editing techniques in a text box.

To edit text inside a text box, you can use many of the text-editing techniques with which you are already familiar: For example, you can double-click a word to select it, press the Delete key to remove characters to the right of the flashing cursor, and press the Backspace key to remove characters to the left of the flashing cursor.

After you edit the text, click outside the text box.

> **NOTE**
>
> **Unlike with the other drawn objects, selecting the interior of the text box does not allow you to move it. Instead, you are allowed to select formatting options for the entire text box or edit the text.**

CHANGING THE TEXT FONT

The only method for changing the font or font attributes of text in a text box is through the menu; the formatting options on the Formatting toolbar are deactivated when the text box is selected. You choose the font or font attributes for the text by selecting the text box and choosing Format, Font. Then you can choose the font type, color, style, or size desired.

Your selections are applied to all text within the text box. You cannot apply different fonts or font attributes to individual words or phrases within a text box. Text within a text box is left aligned, and it cannot be centered or right aligned.

CHANGING THE PROPERTIES OF A TEXT BOX

When you create a text box, it is automatically given a lined border and white background fill. If you want the text to float freely without lines so that the Gantt chart shows through the text box, you must choose the None button in both the Line & Fill sections of the Format Drawing dialog box.

WORKING WITH THE CALENDAR VIEW

You will often find it useful to display a project in the familiar monthly calendar format. After creating a project file by using the other views provided by Microsoft Project, it can be very helpful to distribute reports showing tasks in the calendar format. Although it isn't the most efficient view for designing and creating lengthy or complex projects, you can use the Calendar view to create simple, short-duration projects.

UNDERSTANDING THE CALENDAR VIEW

You display the Calendar view by clicking the Calendar button on the View Bar or by choosing View, Calendar. The standard Calendar view appears (see Figure 7.21). The Calendar view cannot be displayed in the bottom pane of a split-screen view.

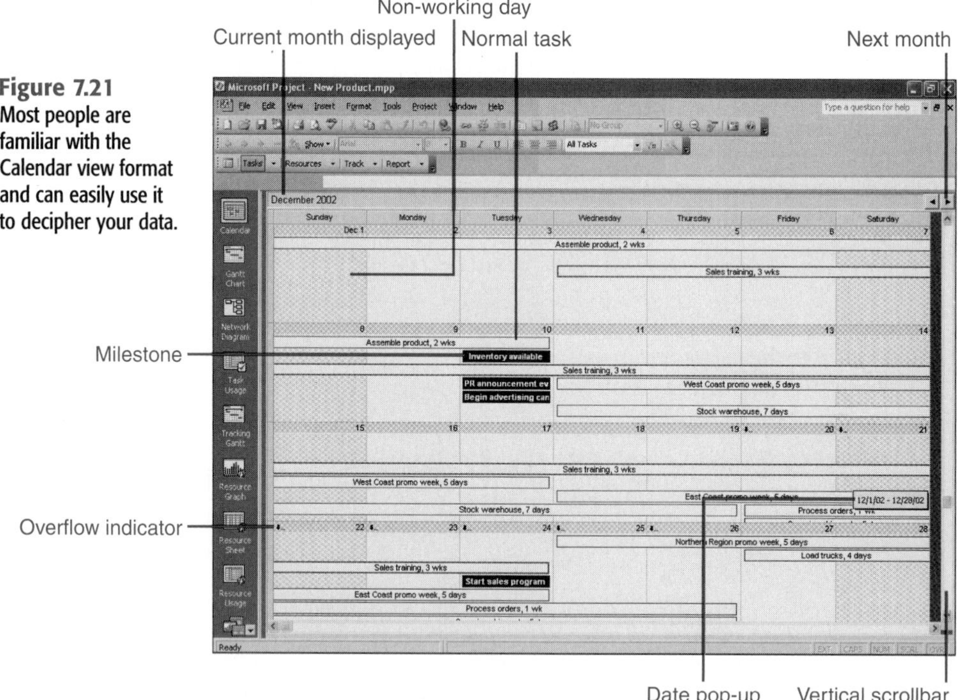

Figure 7.21
Most people are familiar with the Calendar view format and can easily use it to decipher your data.

The Calendar view features a month and year title, and it shows one or more weeks of dates, with taskbars stretching from their start dates to their finish dates. The default display shows four weeks at a time and includes bars or lines for all tasks except summary tasks. You can include summary tasks and you can change many other features of the display by customizing the Calendar view. Milestone tasks are represented by black taskbars with white text. In some cases, there isn't enough room in the calendar to display all the tasks whose schedules fall on a particular date. When this happens, you see an overflow indicator—a black arrow with an ellipsis—in the left corner of the date box (refer to Figure 7.21). The overflow indicator indicates that there is more data to see.

You can see all the tasks scheduled for a given date by displaying the Tasks Occurring On dialog box for that date (see Figure 7.22).

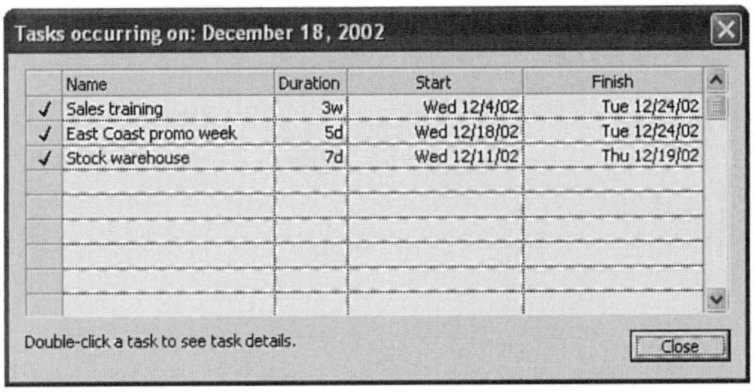

Figure 7.22
All tasks that occur on a specific date are shown in a list; you can double-click any of the tasks to see details for that task.

Tasks occurring on: December 18, 2002

	Name	Duration	Start	Finish
✓	Sales training	3w	Wed 12/4/02	Tue 12/24/02
✓	East Coast promo week	5d	Wed 12/18/02	Tue 12/24/02
✓	Stock warehouse	7d	Wed 12/11/02	Thu 12/19/02

Double-click a task to see task details. Close

To display the Tasks Occurring On dialog box, double-click the gray band at the top of the date box or follow these steps:

1. Position the mouse pointer over any portion of the gray band at the top of the date box. (The day number appears at the right of this gray band in the default calendar layout.)
2. Right-click to display the shortcut menu for dates.
3. Choose Task List from the shortcut menu. The Tasks Occurring On dialog box appears for the specific date you pointed to.
4. When the Tasks Occurring On dialog box is displayed, you can double-click a task to see details for that task on the Task Information dialog box. Click the Cancel button to close the Task Information dialog box without saving any changes and return to the Task Occurring On dialog box.
5. After reviewing the list of tasks, click Close to close the Tasks Occurring On dialog box.

The Tasks Occurring On dialog box lists all tasks whose schedule dates encompass the date you selected. The tasks whose bars appear in the calendar have a check mark to the left of the listing. To increase the number of tasks that appear on the calendar, you can use the Zoom command (see "Using Zoom," later in this chapter) or you can make changes in the calendar format.

The Calendar view, like other views, has a number of shortcut menus and navigation options such as Go To and Zoom. One approach to learning about this view is to just start right-clicking different spots on the view. Shortcut menus offer access to the Task Information dialog box, a list of tasks occurring on specific dates, and formatting options for virtually every element of the calendar.

MOVING AROUND IN THE CALENDAR VIEW

As with other views, your effective use of the Calendar view depends on your ability to move around and find the information you want to focus on. It's helpful to know how to change the display of the calendar to show only selected information.

SCROLLING THE CALENDAR

You can use the scrollbars to move forward and backward in time on the calendar. When you drag the scroll box on the vertical scrollbar, a date indicator pop-up box helps you locate a specific date (refer to Figure 7.21). The beginning and end points on the scrollbar are approximately the start and end dates of the project.

You can press Alt+Home and Alt+End to jump to the beginning and ending dates of the project, respectively. You can also use the Page Up and Page Down keys to scroll through the display, showing successive weeks in the life of the project.

You scroll through the months of the year with the left- and right-arrow buttons that are to the right of the month and year title. As you scroll through the months, the beginning of each successive month appears in the first row of the calendar, no matter how many weeks are displayed in the view. You can use Alt+up-arrow key and Alt+down-arrow key to scroll, by months, through the project calendar.

LOCATING A SPECIFIC TASK OR DATE

As on the Gantt Chart view, you can use the Go To command in the Calendar view to move directly to a specific task ID or date. You can right-click the month and year title or a date in the calendar and choose Go To from the shortcut menu that appears. You can also choose Edit, Go To to access this dialog box.

CAUTION

> On the default Calendar view, the summary taskbars are not displayed. The Go To command cannot select tasks that don't display taskbars in the Calendar view. Therefore, you can't go to a summary task. You can use the Format, Bar Styles command to change the default and have the Calendar view display summary taskbars.

→ To learn more about working with project calendars, **see** "Formatting the Calendar View," **p. 802**.

When a given date has more tasks than can be shown in a Calendar view date box, the calendar shows the first few tasks and indicates that there are more by placing an arrow next to the date. If you enter an ID in the Go To dialog box for a task whose taskbar is not visible on that date, Project selects the task, and its beginning date scrolls into view—but you can't see the task or a selection marker to indicate which date is the beginning date.

However, because the task is selected, you can choose the Information button on the toolbar to view the Task Information dialog box. The task start date is on the General tab. Close the Task Information dialog box by choosing the Cancel button, and double-click the start date for the task to see the other tasks scheduled on that date.

Another way to locate tasks is by using the Find command. You can use Find to locate tasks by their field values, usually by the value in the Name field. As with the Go To command, if the task you find is not currently displayed in the calendar, you cannot see it, even though it is selected. A detailed discussion of this feature appears in the section "Using Find to Locate Tasks," earlier in this chapter.

NOTE

> You must select a taskbar in the Calendar view before you can use the Find command.

USING ZOOM

You might want to look at a calendar from different perspectives, backing away at times to see the big picture (although this has practical size limitations) or zooming in on the details for a specific week. To change the perspective, you can use choose View, Zoom or use the Zoom In and Zoom Out buttons on the Standard toolbar. Each click on one of these buttons displays one, two, four, or six weeks, in ascending or descending order, depending on the button you use.

The calendar in Figure 7.23, for example, is zoomed in to a two-week view to get a good understanding of the tasks that have activity during that time.

Choose View, Zoom to display the Zoom dialog box (refer to Figure 7.23). You can also right-click an empty spot on the calendar and choose Zoom from the shortcut menu that appears. You have more options in the Zoom dialog box than the toolbar options allow. You can zoom to a custom level, specified in weeks, or you can designate a from date and a to date.

Using the Zoom command on the Calendar view has no effect on the printed Calendar view; only the screen display is affected.

→ For more information about using the Page Setup dialog box to control the printing of calendars, **see** Chapter 13, "Printing Views and Reports," **p. 489**.

USING FILTERS TO CLARIFY THE CALENDAR VIEW

When a project has many overlapping tasks, the Calendar view can quickly become very cluttered and difficult to read. As previously discussed, you can zoom in to see more detail, but you can also use *filters* to narrow the list of tasks that display at one time. A filter limits the display of tasks to just those that match the criteria defined in the filter. For example, you can have Project display only the critical tasks in the project by applying the Critical filter.

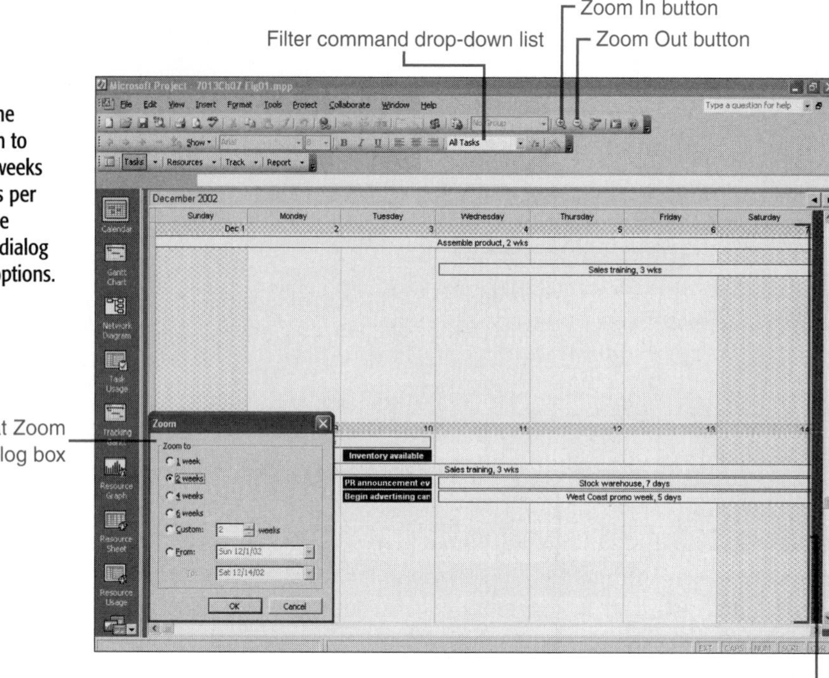

Figure 7.23
You can click the Zoom In button to display fewer weeks and more tasks per day or open the Format, Zoom dialog box for more options.

To apply a filter to a Calendar view, do one of the following:

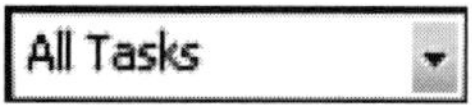

- Click the Filter button on the Formatting toolbar, and then select from the available filters on the drop-down list.
- Choose Project, Filtered For and choose from the predefined filters.
- If you want to highlight a particular category of tasks, choose Project, Filtered For, More Filters. Select the filter you want to apply and then choose the Highlight button.

→ To learn more detailed information about filters, **see** "Filtering the Task or Resource List," **p. 472**.

Editing a Project in the Calendar View

As mentioned in the section "Working with the Calendar View" earlier in this chapter, it isn't recommended to use the Calendar view to create a complex project. After the project is created, this view is most useful for reviewing and printing tasks and the time frames in which they occur. However, you can use this view to edit task data. This section describes techniques for viewing and modifying task information.

7

Viewing Task Details in the Calendar View

The display of individual task information is minimized in the Calendar view. You can view and edit details about a task by selecting the task and opening the Task Information dialog box. Alternatively, you can use the Calendar view as the top part of a dual-pane view.

You can open the Task Information dialog box for a task in the Calendar view in several ways. Use either of the methods listed here for tasks that display taskbars:

- Double-click the taskbar to both select the task and display the Task Information dialog box.
- Right-click the taskbar. This selects the task and displays the shortcut menu. Choose Task Information or choose Task Notes to go directly to the Notes tab of the Task Information dialog box.

If the taskbar is not displayed, you must first select the task by using the Go To command or the Find command, as described in the earlier section "Locating a Specific Task or Date." After you select the task, you can use one of the following methods to display the Task Information dialog box:

- Choose Project, Task Information. (Choose Project, Task Notes if you want to go directly to the Notes tab of the Task Information dialog box.)

- Choose the Information button on the Standard toolbar to view the General tab of the Task Information dialog box. (Choose the Task Notes button if you want to go directly to the Notes tab.)
- Press Shift+F2.

Another way to view task details is to use a combination view in which you display the Calendar view in the top pane with another view in the bottom pane. You can split the view window into two panes, either by choosing Window, Split or by right-clicking anywhere in the calendar except on a task to open the shortcut menu and then choosing Split. When you choose the Split command, Project puts the Task Form view in the bottom pane by default. With the Task Form view active, choose Format, Details, Notes to see any notes entered for the selected task.

You can replace the Task Form view with any view you want, although displaying the Network Diagram view in the bottom pane is not particularly useful. When a specific task is selected in the Calendar view, only the node for the selected task appears in the bottom pane. If you display the Relationship Diagram view in the bottom pane, it illustrates task dependencies for the task that is selected in the Calendar view in the top pane. The best view choices for the bottom pane are Task Form, Task Details Form, and Task Usage.

INSERTING TASKS IN CALENDAR VIEW

Although it's easy to create tasks in the Calendar view, you might not want to use the Calendar view in this manner for two reasons:

- With the Gantt Chart view, as well as other views, you can insert a new task in the middle of the project and near other tasks to which the new task is related; the task is given an ID number where it is inserted. When creating a task in Calendar view, however, it is always given the next highest ID number in the project, regardless of where the task is inserted. If you view the new task in Gantt Chart view (or any view that has a table), the task is at the bottom of the list—even if its dates fall in the middle of the project or you link it to tasks in the middle of the task list.

- The task you create in Calendar view is often automatically given a date constraint. You would want to remove the constraint as soon as you create a task in the Calendar view. To remove the constraint, set the constraint type to As Soon As Possible in the Advanced tab of the Task Information dialog box.

CAUTION

> Adding tasks to a project in Calendar view can result in task constraints that, unless removed, needlessly produce scheduling conflicts.

Whether tasks created in the Calendar view are constrained depends on whether you selected a task or a date when you created the new task:

- If you select a task and then insert the new task by using the Insert menu or the Insert key, the new task is not constrained (its constraint type is As Soon As Possible).
- If you select a date when you create the new task, or if you create the task by dragging with the mouse (which automatically selects the date where you start dragging), the new task is constrained.

If the task is constrained when you create it, the constraint type depends on whether you schedule the project from a fixed start date or a fixed finish date. If you create the task by dragging with the mouse, the constraint type also depends on the direction you drag the mouse: from start to finish or from finish to start. Remember to check the constraint type of any task you create in the Calendar view (following the steps that are outlined below) and change it appropriately.

To insert a task in the Calendar view, follow these steps:

1. Select the date for the start of the task if you want the start date constrained. Another option is to select any task, if you do not want the new task to be constrained; the task will be added to the end of the project.
2. Choose Insert, New Task. You can also simply press the Insert key. Project inserts a new, untitled task in the project, with a default duration of one day (estimated). Because the task has no name yet, its taskbar displays only the task's duration. If there is no room to display the bar for the new task, it seems to disappear, but the new task is in fact selected.
3. Choose Project, Task Information (or choose the Information button on the Standard toolbar) to open the Task Information dialog box.
4. Provide a name and any other information for the task. For example, you probably need to enter the duration. You might also want to choose the Notes tab and type comments about the task.

5. Because most tasks created in Calendar view are automatically given a date constraint, you should choose the Advanced tab and change the entry in the Constrain Task Type field as appropriate.
6. Click OK to close the dialog box.

As an alternative, you can insert a task with the mouse. First, scroll the calendar until you see the start date (or finish date) for the task. Drag the mouse from the start date to the finish date for the task (or from the finish date to the start date). Click the Information button on the Standard toolbar to display the Task Information dialog box, and then supply the task name and any other information you want to specify. Then choose the Advanced tab and correct the Constrain Task Type as appropriate.

Deleting Tasks in the Calendar View

The Delete key behaves differently in the Calendar view than it does in the Gantt Chart view. In Project 2003, pressing Delete on the Gantt Chart view merely clears the contents of the selected cell. But in the Calendar view, pressing Delete removes the entire task. To delete a task, you simply select it and choose Edit, Delete Task or press the Delete key. If the taskbar is not displayed, you must use the Go To command or the Find command to select it. (See the section "Locating a Specific Task or Date," earlier in this chapter.)

Note

If you accidentally delete a task when you didn't mean to, you can use the Undo feature to get it back. Click the Undo button; choose Edit, Undo; or press Ctrl+Z. You must do this right away, though, because Undo can undo only your last action.

Creating Links Between Tasks in the Calendar View

There are several ways to create task dependency links in Calendar view. One method is to select the tasks you want to link, using the Ctrl key to add tasks to the selection. Then choose the Link Tasks button on the Standard toolbar. You can also use the mouse. Simply click the *center* of the taskbar for the task that will be the predecessor task, hold down the mouse button, and drag down to the intended successor task. The mouse pointer changes into a chain-links symbol and a pop-up box indicates the creation of a Finish-to-Start relationship between the two tasks.

To change to a different kind of relationship or to add lag or lead time, display the Task Information dialog box for the dependent (successor) task and choose the Predecessors tab.

→ To learn more about linking tasks, **see** "Understanding Dependency Links," **p. 177**.

Working with the Network Diagram View

Another view that is useful for examining a project is the Network Diagram view. The diagram is a graphic display of tasks in a project, in which each task is represented by a small box, or *node* (see Figure 7.24). Lines connect the nodes to show task dependencies. Instead of developing a plan in a Gantt Chart view, you can use the Network Diagram view to enter a task list and create a project schedule.

The Network Diagram view is most useful for an overall view of how the process or flow of task details fit together. Some project managers print the diagram on a plotter and post the printout for team members to view. Project progress is easy to see because diagram boxes are marked as being in progress or complete.

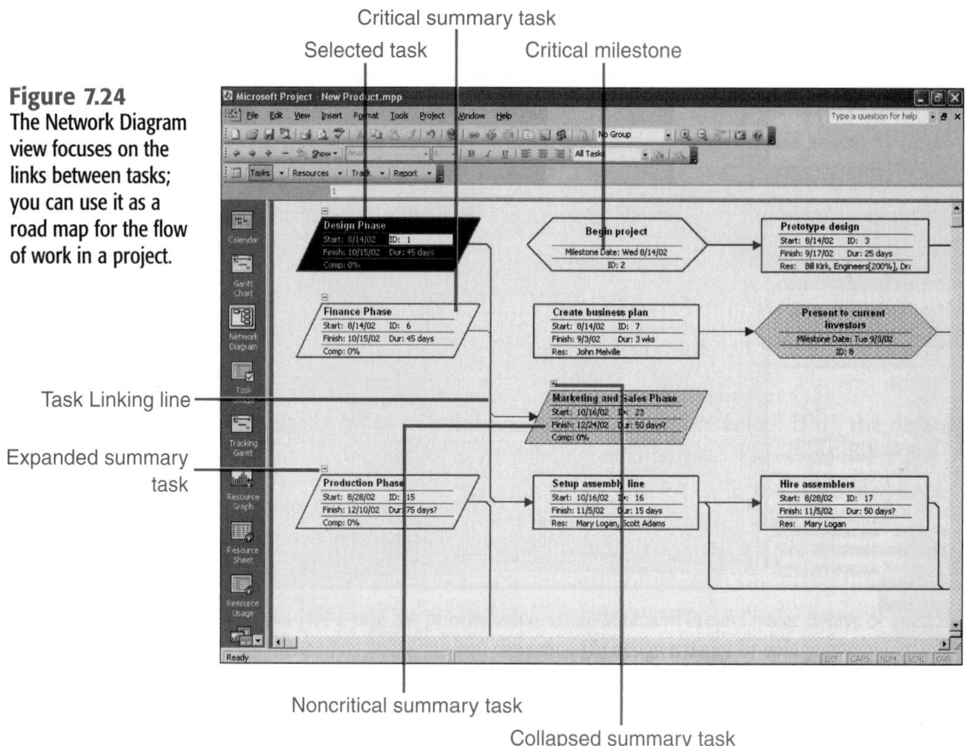

Figure 7.24
The Network Diagram view focuses on the links between tasks; you can use it as a road map for the flow of work in a project.

Understanding the Network Diagram View

The Network Diagram view shows a flowchart view of a project. The view reveals information about an individual task, as well as information about the task's place in the flow of activity. Figure 7.24 shows the default Network Diagram view of the New Product project. In this figure, Design Phase is the currently selected task. The default format for most nodes displays six fields: the task name, task ID, duration, start, finish, and either % complete or the resources assigned to the task.

NOTE

You can select other fields to display in the node; in fact, there is a great deal of flexibility in the customization you can perform on these nodes. You can remove one of the default fields, add fields, or substitute a field that is more useful to you. You can even design your own node templates that display primarily cost or work information in the nodes, thus designing your own custom network diagrams, which display the information in which you are most interested.

➔ To learn more about customizing the Network Diagram nodes, **see** "Formatting the Network Diagram View," **p. 807**.

Each node represents a task, which is connected to predecessors and successors by linking lines. In the default layout of the diagram, dependent (successor) tasks are always placed to the right of or beneath predecessors. Different border styles or colors distinguish summary tasks, critical tasks, and milestones. Summary tasks are above and to the left of subordinate tasks.

Table 7.2 describes a few of the most common task types and the node borders that are displayed in Figure 7.24.

TABLE 7.2 TASK TYPES AND NETWORK DIAGRAM NODE DESCRIPTIONS

Type of Tasks	Node Shape and Color
Noncritical Summary Tasks	Parallelogram with a thin blue border and aqua background.
Critical Summary Tasks	Parallelogram with a thick red border and white background.
Noncritical Milestones	Hexagon with a thin blue border and aqua background.
Critical Milestones	Hexagon with a thick red border and white background.
Noncritical Normal Tasks	Rectangle with a thin blue border and aqua background.
Critical Normal Tasks	Rectangle with thick red border and white background.

To view the network diagram, click the Network Diagram button in the View bar or choose View, Network Diagram. You cannot display the Network Diagram view in the bottom pane in a split screen.

ZOOMING THE NETWORK DIAGRAM VIEW

In the network diagram in Figure 7.24, each node is large enough to read the field data easily. If you want to get an overview of the links among more tasks, you can zoom out on the view to show more tasks. Figure 7.25 shows the same task, Design Phase, that is selected in Figure 7.24. When the view is zoomed out, you get a better feel for how that task fits into the overall project, but the individual node contents might be hard to read.

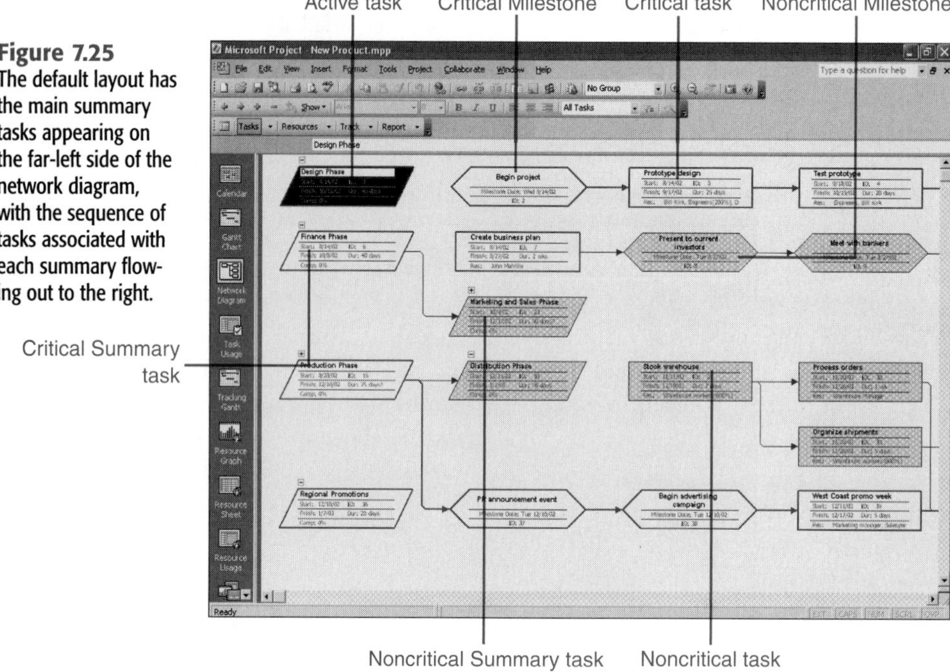

Figure 7.25
The default layout has the main summary tasks appearing on the far-left side of the network diagram, with the sequence of tasks associated with each summary flowing out to the right.

TIP

> To view the contents of a node on a compressed network diagram, hover over the node with the mouse. The field contents expand temporarily for easier viewing.

You can zoom out to view more tasks by using the Zoom Out button on the Standard toolbar. You can zoom in to see the task details by using the Zoom In button. The Zoom In and Zoom Out buttons increment and decrement the zoom percentage by using the preset percentages 25%, 50%, 75%, 100%, and 200%. Each time you click one of the Zoom buttons, the percentage increases or decreases according to the preset percentages. The normal magnification is set to 100%. The supported zoom range, however, is from 25% to a maximum of 400%. You get more options for zooming when you open the View, Zoom dialog box. This is the same dialog box used to rescale other views. To change the zoom percentage, select one of the percentage buttons or fill in the Custom text box with a value between 25% and 400%. Select the Entire Project button to select the percentage (between 25% and 400%) that fits the entire project in the window. If the entire project cannot be displayed in one screen at the lowest zoom number, 25%, the Zoom command displays a warning. Click OK to close the alert, then enter a valid zoom percentage.

NOTE

> Using the Zoom command affects only the screen view in the Network Diagram view. It does not affect how much of the chart is printed.

OUTLINING IN THE NETWORK DIAGRAM VIEW

In the Network Diagram view, you can collapse and expand the summary task nodes as you would in the Gantt Chart view. The summary task boxes are parallelogram shapes. The outline buttons, which are initially minus signs, appear just above these boxes (refer to Figure 7.24). Clicking an outline button collapses or hides the tasks under a summary task. The outline button then becomes a plus sign.

SCROLLING AND SELECTING IN THE NETWORK DIAGRAM VIEW

You can use the horizontal and vertical scrollbars or the movement keys (the arrow keys, Page Up, Page Down, Home, and End) to scan through the Network Diagram view. However, the rules for moving through the diagram are quite different from the rules for navigating in other views.

Scrolling does not change the currently selected node. After you scroll, you probably cannot see the selected node, although the selected field in that node still displays in the Entry bar. To put the selected node back in the screen where you can see it, press the Edit key (F2) as though you plan to change the selected node. To cancel the editing, press the Esc key. To select one of the visible nodes after scrolling, just click the node.

You use the selection keys to move around the Network Diagram, selecting different nodes as you go. The rules that the selection keys follow in selecting the next node are not apparent. Here's what these keys do:

- **Right-arrow key**—Selects nodes to the right, until there are no more nodes directly to the right; then selects the next node down and to the right and continues to the right.
- **Down-arrow key**—Selects nodes directly below, until there are no more nodes; then select the next node that is down and to the right and continues down.
- **Left-arrow key**—Selects nodes to the left, until no more nodes lie directly to the left; then selects the next node up and to the left and continues to the left.
- **Up-arrow key**—Selects nodes directly above, until there are no more nodes; then selects the next node above and to the left and continues up.

The rest of the selection keys behave as they do in other applications, such as Excel; here's what the other selection keys do:

- **Page Down**—Displays a screen's worth of data down from the group of tasks you are viewing.
- **End**—Selects and displays the last task in the project.
- **Page Up**—Displays a screen's worth of data up from the group of tasks you are viewing.

- **Home**—Selects and displays the first task in the project.
- **Ctrl+Page Down**—Scrolls a screen's worth of data to the right.
- **Ctrl+Page Up**—Scrolls a screen's worth of data to the left.
- **Ctrl+End**—Makes the first box in the last horizontal row of boxes the active task.
- **Ctrl+Home**—Makes the first task in the Network Diagram view the active task—that is, the first box in the first horizontal row of boxes.

EDITING A PROJECT IN THE NETWORK DIAGRAM VIEW

Some people prefer to use the Network Diagram view to create and edit project tasks. You can use the Network Diagram view to change task data, add and delete tasks, and create and modify task links.

CHANGING TASK DATA IN THE NETWORK DIAGRAM VIEW

To change the field data displayed in a node, you must first select the task and cell to edit by clicking the mouse pointer on the node or by using the selection keys. When you click to select a task, you also select the field at which the mouse was pointing. If necessary, you can select another field by using the Tab and Shift+Tab keys or by clicking the field.

If you want to change data in fields that don't appear in the node (such as constraints or fixed duration), you must use the Task Information dialog box. Select the node you want to edit and click the Task Information button on the Standard toolbar, or choose Project, Task Information to display the Task Information dialog box. Then select the tab in the Task Information dialog box where you want to make changes. Click the OK button to apply the changes.

TIP

> You can also double-click inside the node to display the Task Information dialog box. Double-clicking the border of a node takes you to a formatting dialog box.

ADDING TASKS IN THE NETWORK DIAGRAM VIEW

You can add tasks directly to a project in the Network Diagram view. Project inserts a task you add in the Network Diagram view just after the currently selected task. Three methods for adding new tasks in this view are discussed in this section.

When you insert a task in the Network Diagram view, the ID number assigned to that task is the number that immediately follows the task that was selected when you inserted the new task. In other words, if there are 20 tasks in the project and Task 4 was selected, the newly inserted task would be Task 5 and the subsequent tasks would automatically be renumbered. This behavior is different from behavior in the Gantt Chart view, where the selected task is also renumbered. Using the Gantt Chart view, if Task 4 were selected when a task was inserted, the newly inserted task would become Task 4.

In Figure 7.26, Task 7 (Create Business Plan) was selected before the new task was inserted. The new task is numbered Task 8 (notice that it does not have a task name) and the task that was formerly Task 8 (Present to Current Investors) is now Task 9.

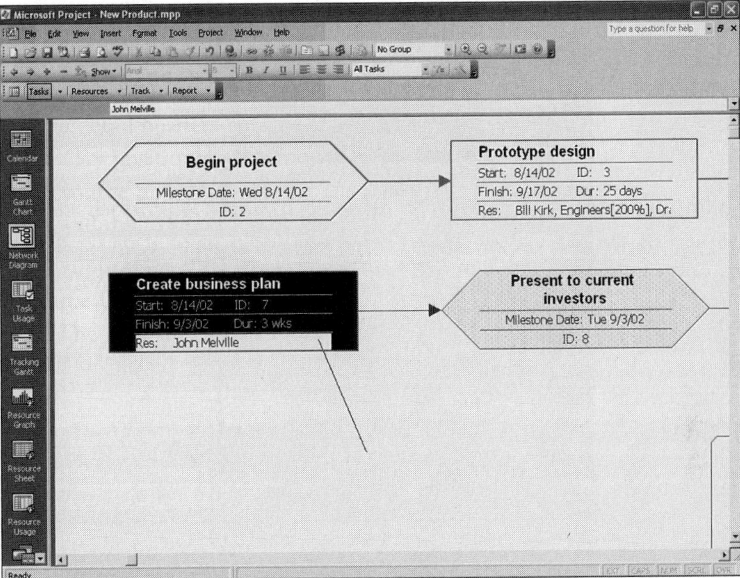

Figure 7.26
You insert a new task by selecting the task that is to precede it and pressing the Insert key.

One method for adding a new task is to simply select the task you want the new task to follow, and then choose Insert, New Task (or press the Insert key) to insert a blank node to the right of the selected task. After you have inserted the new task, enter a new name for the new task. Tab to the Duration field and estimate the duration. Do not enter the start or finish date unless you want the task constrained to one of those dates.

A second method for adding tasks in the Network Diagram view is to simply drag the mouse from a task box out into an open space on the diagram. When you release the mouse, a new task is created, and it is automatically linked in the default Finish-to-Start relationship to the task you dragged from.

There is a third method for creating a new task node. You can drag the mouse pointer in an empty area of the diagram to form a rectangle (see Figure 7.27). The ID number of the new task is still one greater than the currently selected task. In Figure 7.27, Task 3 (Prototype Design) is selected; therefore, the new task will be Task 4. It's important for you to note that the default layout settings for the Network Diagram view are set to automatically position boxes when they are added to the view. In other words, where you draw the node might not be exactly where it will end up. If you want Microsoft Project to keep the boxes in the exact position in which you draw them, you need to open the Layout dialog box (by selecting Format, Layout) and change the Layout Mode setting to Allow Manual Box Positioning.

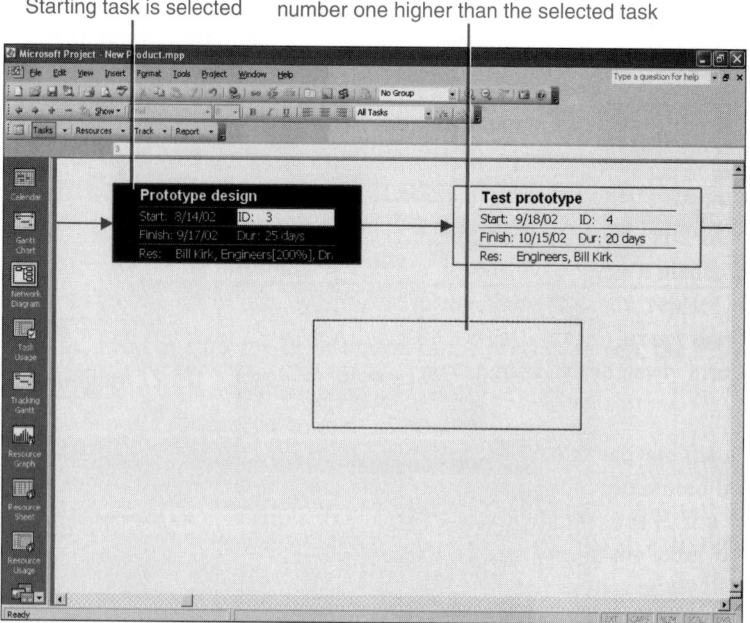

Figure 7.27
You can drag the mouse to create a rectangle in the position you want the new task to occupy.

NOTE

> Automatic linking of tasks is not enabled while you add a task in the Network Diagram view by drawing a rectangle in an open space.

Deleting Tasks in the Network Diagram View

To delete a task while displaying the Network Diagram view, select any cell in the task node and choose Edit, Delete Task or press the Delete key. This is not the same Delete key behavior as on the Gantt Chart view in Project 2003. Pressing Delete in the Network Diagram view still removes the entire task from the project.

If you delete a task in the middle of a linked chain of tasks, Project automatically extends the link to maintain an unbroken sequence of tasks.

Linking Tasks in the Network Diagram View

You can create task links in the Network Diagram view by dragging the mouse from the predecessor task to the successor task. Make sure you start in the middle of the predecessor task node. Dragging the border of a task node merely repositions the node. The task relationship is Finish-to-Start, with no lead or lag. Just as in the Gantt Chart view, if you want to delete or modify the task link, you can double-click the line that links the two tasks to activate the Task Dependency dialog box, where you can redefine the task relationship.

You can also modify the task-linking relationships in the successor's Task Information dialog box. Double-click the successor task's node to open the dialog box. Then, make changes or deletions on the Predecessors tab.

REARRANGING TASK NODES IN THE NETWORK DIAGRAM VIEW

You can change the layout of the Network Diagram view nodes by accessing the Layout dialog box, in which you can customize the layout of the task nodes. To display the Layout dialog box (see Figure 7.28), choose Format, Layout.

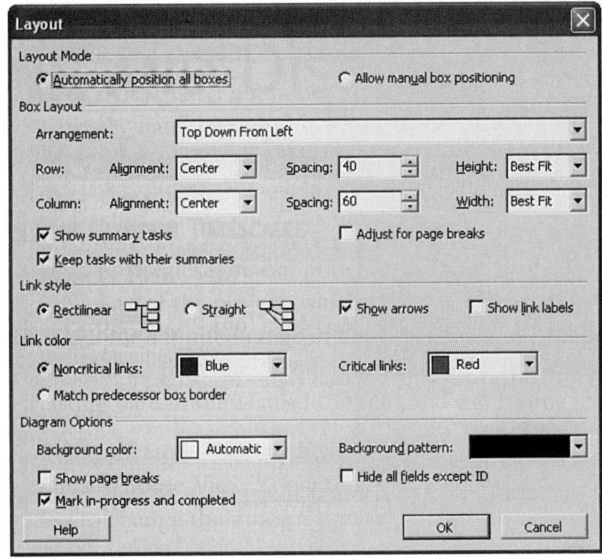

Figure 7.28
The Layout dialog box contains all the formatting options for the task boxes in the Network Diagram view.

TIP

You might find it useful to zoom out so you can see an overview as you redesign the layout of the Network Diagram view.

To drag nodes on the Network Diagram view and have Project maintain the new positions, the automatic layout feature must be turned off. At the top of the Layout dialog box, change the Layout Mode setting to Allow Manual Box Positioning.

You can select and move multiple task nodes by drawing a selection box around them. This is sometimes called *lassoing* the items to be selected. Say you have a rectangle that encloses only the nodes you want to select. Move the mouse pointer to one of the corners of this imaginary rectangle. Hold down the mouse button and drag the mouse pointer diagonally to the opposite corner of the imaginary rectangle, creating the rectangle. All task nodes that fall even partly in the area of the rectangle are selected.

TIP

> There is a quick way to select all the subtasks under a summary task. Press the Shift key as you select a task, and Project selects that task plus all its dependent (successor) tasks.

The Layout dialog box contains an extensive set of options for formatting the Network Diagram view.

➔ For a detailed discussion of the options for displaying the Network Diagram view, **see** "Controlling the Network Diagram Layout," **p. 811**.

Troubleshooting

Attaching to a Taskbar

My drawing won't stay with the taskbar I want it associated with. What should I do?

Choose Format, Drawing, Properties to attach the drawing to the task instead of to a date on the timeline.

Missing Taskbar

The taskbars are hidden by the drawing and I can't see them. What should I do?

You need to select the drawing and use the shortcut menu to move the drawing back to a lower drawing layer. This will draw the object behind the taskbars.

If an object seems to disappear after you attach it to a taskbar, open the Format Drawing dialog box again and change the horizontal and vertical offset values to zero. Then the object appears right next to the taskbar, and you can reposition it with the mouse.

Linking Lines and the Task Dependency Box

If I double-click a linking line in the Network Diagram view, the Task Dependency dialog box doesn't display the relationship between the two tasks I'm interested in. What should I do?

Linking lines in the Network Diagram view (and also the Gantt Chart view) are sometimes drawn on top of other linking connections, which makes it hard to pinpoint the pair of tasks you want. Your best bet is to open the Task Information dialog box for the successor task in the pair. Then you can make changes to the linking relationship on the Predecessors tab of the dialog box.

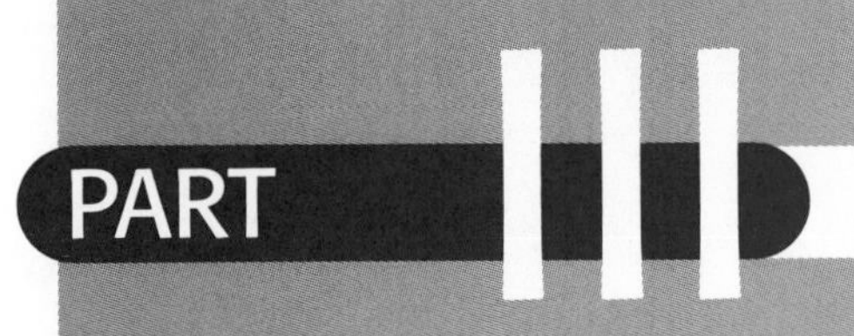

Assigning Resources and Costs

8 Defining Resources and Costs 277

9 Understanding Resource Scheduling 321

10 Assigning Resources and Costs to Tasks 359

11 Resolving Resource Assignment Problems 401

CHAPTER 8

DEFINING RESOURCES AND COSTS

In this chapter

Understanding How Project Uses Resources and Costs 278

Understanding Resources and Costs 279

Defining the Resource Pool 286

Using the Resource Fields 292

Setting the Automatically Add New Resources and Tasks Option 308

Sorting Resources 310

Grouping Resources 314

Filtering Resources 315

Troubleshooting 318

8

UNDERSTANDING HOW PROJECT USES RESOURCES AND COSTS

This chapter focuses on resources and costs—understanding what resources are, how to create a resource pool, and how resource costs are calculated in Microsoft Project. You will learn how to define resources and their costs and how to define costs that are not associated with a particular resource. With this foundation, you will then be ready in ensuing chapters to assign resources and costs to tasks, modify those assignments, and resolve conflicts that arise with overallocated resources.

Although you can create a schedule in Microsoft Project without assigning resources to the tasks, such a schedule is based on the assumption that you will have all the necessary resources on hand whenever you need them—and that assumption is rarely realistic. People take vacations, have sick leave, or have unique work schedules. Machinery and equipment need downtime for maintenance. Employees leave the organization and new ones arrive. New facilities are not ready for occupancy until midway through a project. All these are examples of situations in which a resource that is necessary to complete a task might not be available when Project schedules the task. You can make a project schedule more realistic by defining and assigning resources to tasks. At the very least, you should assign to each task the name of the person who is responsible for seeing it through to completion.

There are several major benefits of including resources in a project file:

- If you provide the working time information for each resource, Project automatically schedules tasks only during those times.
- After you assign resources to all the tasks, Project can help you see how many units of each resource you will need to complete the project.
- Every project manager needs to know how much the project will cost. If you include the cost information for each resource, Project automatically calculates the cost of each resource assignment to individual tasks, and sums those costs to show the total cost of each task and the overall cost of the project. You can use these cost calculations in estimating the budget for the project.

You can define a comprehensive list of resources at the outset, including resource cost rates and availability information. Later, you will assign these resources to tasks. Alternatively, you can define the resources as you create the tasks, while you are thinking about how the work will be done. When you assign new resource names to a task, Project adds these names to the list of resources (see Figure 8.1). If you create resources on-the-fly, you must remember to go back later and enter the resource cost rates and availability information.

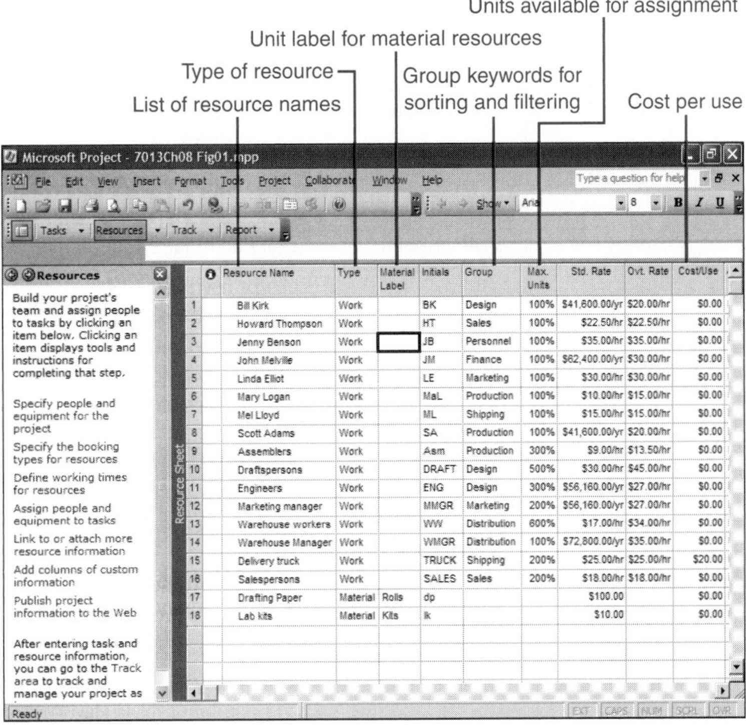

	Resource Name	Type	Material Label	Initials	Group	Max. Units	Std. Rate	Ovt. Rate	Cost/Use
1	Bill Kirk	Work		BK	Design	100%	$41,600.00/yr	$20.00/hr	$0.00
2	Howard Thompson	Work		HT	Sales	100%	$22.50/hr	$22.50/hr	$0.00
3	Jenny Benson	Work		JB	Personnel	100%	$35.00/hr	$35.00/hr	$0.00
4	John Melville	Work		JM	Finance	100%	$62,400.00/yr	$30.00/hr	$0.00
5	Linda Elliot	Work		LE	Marketing	100%	$30.00/hr	$30.00/hr	$0.00
6	Mary Logan	Work		MaL	Production	100%	$10.00/hr	$15.00/hr	$0.00
7	Mel Lloyd	Work		ML	Shipping	100%	$15.00/hr	$15.00/hr	$0.00
8	Scott Adams	Work		SA	Production	100%	$41,600.00/yr	$20.00/hr	$0.00
9	Assemblers	Work		Asm	Production	300%	$9.00/hr	$13.50/hr	$0.00
10	Draftspersons	Work		DRAFT	Design	500%	$30.00/hr	$45.00/hr	$0.00
11	Engineers	Work		ENG	Design	300%	$56,160.00/yr	$27.00/hr	$0.00
12	Marketing manager	Work		MMGR	Marketing	200%	$56,160.00/yr	$27.00/hr	$0.00
13	Warehouse workers	Work		WW	Distribution	600%	$17.00/hr	$34.00/hr	$0.00
14	Warehouse Manager	Work		WMGR	Distribution	100%	$72,800.00/yr	$35.00/hr	$0.00
15	Delivery truck	Work		TRUCK	Shipping	200%	$25.00/hr	$25.00/hr	$20.00
16	Salespersons	Work		SALES	Sales	200%	$18.00/hr	$18.00/hr	$0.00
17	Drafting Paper	Material	Rolls	dp			$100.00		$0.00
18	Lab kits	Material	Kits	lk			$10.00		$0.00

Figure 8.1
The list of resources includes information about the availability and cost of using the resources.

NOTE

The Automatically Add New Resources and Tasks option (which is available on the General tab of the Options dialog box) determines how Project treats undefined resources that you assign to tasks. See the section "Setting the Automatically Add New Resources and Tasks Option," later in this chapter, to learn about the hazards of using this option.

UNDERSTANDING RESOURCES AND COSTS

The most important resources for a project are the people who do the work, but you also have to provide those people with the facilities in which to do the work and the equipment and materials they need to do their jobs. The cost of a project is usually based on the sum cost of all the resources needed to complete each task.

DEFINING RESOURCES

The term *resource* refers to the people and assets that must be assigned to work on a task until it is completed. Resources include workers, supervisors, managers, the plant and equipment, facilities, supplies, and materials. You might also choose to assign as resources people who don't actually work on the task or whose work you do not need to measure (such as outside contractors or vendors), but whose name you want associated with the task. The list of resources available for work on a project is known as the *resource pool*.

8

Resources that are necessary to complete activities within a project typically fall into three categories.

People are the most common resource category tracked and are usually listed one of three ways. The first way is by name; the second way is by type, which can be listed in the pool as a skill set; and the third way is by outsourced vendor, providing an indication of accountability or responsibility for the task.

The next most common category of resources tracked is equipment. Sometimes use of a truck, crane, or computer might be necessary to complete work within a project. Often, use of a facility, such as a training room or testing lab, falls into this category of resource.

Finally, materials and supplies comprise the third category of resources that is often closely monitored.

DEFINING THE WORK AND MATERIAL RESOURCE TYPES

Microsoft Project distinguishes two resource *types*: work resources and material resources. *Work resources* contribute their time and effort (that is, their work) to a task during the time they're scheduled to work on a task, but when the task is completed, they have not been consumed by the task and they have future time that they can devote to other tasks. People, facilities, and equipment are examples of work resources. *Material resources*, on the other hand, are consumed or used up when they are assigned to a task and are no longer available to be assigned to other tasks. Lumber, concrete, and camera film are examples of material resources. Chapter 9, "Understanding Resource Scheduling," explains the way Project handles resource availability and costs for both of these resource types.

DEFINING SINGLE AND GROUPED RESOURCES

Some resources that you add to a resource list represent *individual* people or assets. You can use a person's name, for example, as a resource name, and you can name a single piece of equipment, a facility, or a raw material as a resource. If you outsource a task to a vendor who is totally responsible for the task, you could name the vendor as a resource name (even though there might be many individuals on the team who actually work on the task).

You can also define a *group resource* (what Microsoft Project sometimes calls *consolidated resources*) to represent multiple identical or interchangeable resources. These could be individual people with identical skills or multiple pieces of identical equipment. For example, you might define a group of five electricians as the Electricians resource and a set of four forklifts as the Forklifts resource. With a consolidated resource, you are not concerned (in your project plan) with which individual resource is assigned to a given task. You let the manager in charge choose the individuals to do the work.

CAUTION

All the individuals in a consolidated resource must share a common cost rate and must be scheduled by a single resource calendar that is defined for the group. You cannot assign unique cost rates to individual members of a consolidated resource, and you cannot recognize individual vacation days or other nonworking times for the individuals.

DEFINING GENERIC AND PLACEHOLDER RESOURCES

When multiple individual resources share a certain skill set or capacity, and you haven't decided which specific individual to assign to a specific task, it's useful to create a *generic* resource to represent that specific pool of talent. For instance, if you have a staff of 20 engineers and are planning a new project, you could create a resource called Engineers as a generic resource and assign the Engineers resource to the individual tasks. Later you can substitute the names of specific engineers in the task assignments. This method has the advantage of letting you calculate how many engineers you will need on the project without committing individuals to specific tasks. You will see in the section "Grouping Resources," later in this chapter, how you can aggregate the assignments for a generic resource such as Engineers with the assignments for individual engineers to calculate the total usage of engineers in the project.

NOTE

> **Using generic resources to forecast resource needs is especially important when many project managers share a common resource pool. When contemplating a new project, you should add a draft of the project to see exactly what impact it will have on resource needs.**

→ If you use the Professional edition of Project 2003, you can automatically optimize the substitution of resources with similar skill-sets. Identifying generic resources is key to that process. **See** "Using the Resource Substitution Wizard," **p. 1110**.

DEFINING COSTS

Project stores and calculates a number of measures of cost. It is important that you understand what the different terms mean so that you can provide the required information that will enable accurate cost calculations.

RESOURCE COSTS, FIXED COSTS, AND TOTAL COSTS

Most of the costs of a project are due to the cost of using resources to complete the project, and these costs are called *resource costs*. The cost of each work resource assigned to a task is generally based on the hours of work or effort associated with the assignment and the hourly cost of using the resource. If a task's duration changes, then its hours of assigned work and the cost of the resource assignment will change as well. Therefore, Project adjusts costs as you revise a project schedule. For material resources, the cost is based on the cost of each unit of the material and the number of units assigned to the task.

If there are costs that are not specifically related to any one named resource, you can attach the amounts of those costs directly to the task. These costs are called *fixed costs*.

The sum of the resource costs and fixed costs is called *total cost*.

8

Resource Cost Calculations

When you assign a work resource to a task, Project calculates the cost of the task by multiplying the cost rate per unit time for the resource by the amount of time the resource spends on the task. Thus, if a work resource costs $10 per hour and it spends two hours on a task assignment, Project calculates $20 as the cost of that assignment. If you assign multiple resource names to a task, the sum of all the individual resource assignment costs is totaled as the resource cost of the task.

Material resource costs, on the other hand, are based solely on the number of units consumed or used up by the task, and are only indirectly, if at all, based on the duration of the task. If the material resource goes directly into the output of the task, like lumber goes into framing a house, then the duration of the task has no effect on the number of units of material required for the task. The material cost is simply the number of units of the resource (the board feet of lumber) multiplied by the per-unit cost of the resource (the cost per board foot of lumber).

If the material resource is consumed by a work resource, like diesel fuel is consumed by a bulldozer, the number of units consumed can be affected by the duration of the task. The longer the task, the more hours of work required from the work resource (the bulldozers) and therefore the more material resource (the fuel) that is needed. Using the bulldozer as an example, the material cost is calculated by multiplying the number of units consumed per unit of time (that is, the gallons of fuel per hour) by the cost per unit (that is, the cost per gallon).

Fixed Costs

If there are costs that are incurred in completing a task but you don't want to define a resource to associate the cost with, you can treat the cost as what Project calls a *fixed cost*. The legal fees associated with a contract or construction permit fees could be treated as fixed costs. But if you want to keep track of the legal fees or permit fees, you should create an appropriately named resource and assign it to the task. A fixed cost is entered in the task table as a lump-sum amount.

TIP

> You should always document the reasons for the fixed cost and how the amount is determined in the task Notes field. This is especially important in the event that you hand the project over to someone else to manage.

→ To learn the steps you take to actually assign fixed costs to tasks, **see** "Assigning Fixed Costs and Fixed Contract Fees," **p. 396**.

Total Cost

Together, the resource costs and the fixed costs add up to the total cost. The field name is just Cost, but it is titled Total Cost in many views. Figure 8.2 shows how assignment costs, fixed cost, and total cost are related. The Gantt Chart view with the Cost table is displayed in the top pane and the Task Form with the details for Resource Cost is shown in the bottom pane. Note that the column titled Total Cost in the top pane is the total cost for the task, whereas the column titled Cost in the bottom pane is the cost of the individual resources assigned to the task.

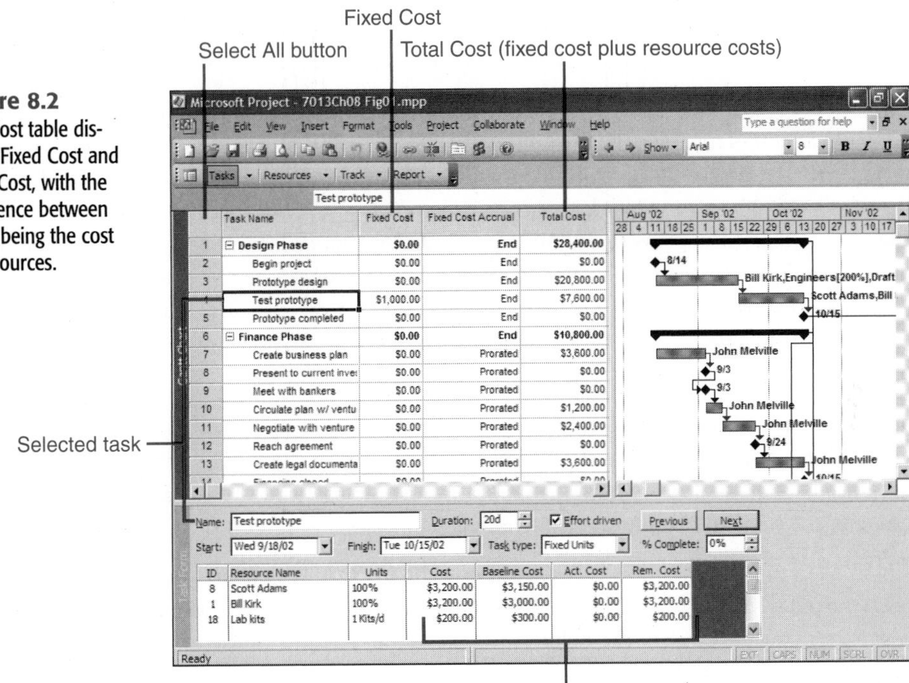

Figure 8.2
The Cost table displays Fixed Cost and Total Cost, with the difference between them being the cost of resources.

To display the Cost table, right-click the Select All button and click Cost on the shortcut menu.

In Figure 8.2, the Test Prototype task is selected in the top pane. Its fixed cost and total cost appear in the top pane, and the details for the assigned resources are shown in the bottom pane.

The cost of the work by Bill Kirk and Scott Adams plus the cost of the lab kits brings the resource cost to $6,600.00 for the task. There is also a $1,000.00 fixed cost for the task, which brings the task's total cost to $7,600.00.

SCHEDULED COSTS, BASELINE COSTS, ACTUAL COSTS, AND COST VARIANCES

The total cost described in the preceding section (that is, the sum of resource and fixed costs that is displayed in the Cost field) is calculated as part of the current schedule and is sometimes also called the *scheduled cost* or the *current cost*. At the end of the planning stage, just before you start the actual work on the project, the project schedule contains the final projections or estimates of what the project should cost (which your budget should reflect). You must remember to use the Save Baseline command to make a copy of these final cost estimates in the Baseline Cost field (also called the *budgeted costs*). You will use the baseline cost later for benchmark comparisons with actual costs.

The scheduled costs will probably change because of revisions in the schedule after work gets under way. For example, if you find that a task is going to take longer to finish than originally estimated and you change the duration of the task in the schedule, Project calculates new scheduled costs because of the additional work that the resources must then complete. But the baseline costs that you have set aside remain unchanged, as a record of the planned cost.

As work is completed on the project, you should track the progress on a regular basis, marking tasks as completed or partially complete, and recording the actual duration and actual work. If the task takes longer than originally scheduled, Project calculates the added costs of the resources. The cost of work that is completed on a task is accumulated in the Actual Cost field. (See the next section, "Accrued Costs," for more information about calculating actual costs.) Project also automatically copies actual costs to the Cost field. The Baseline Cost field retains the original planned costs throughout this process. With actual cost updates added to the Cost field, the scheduled costs now provide a more accurate estimate of the cost of the completed project.

The difference between the Cost field (scheduled cost) and the Baseline Cost field (planned or budgeted cost) is called the *cost variance* and is stored in the Cost Variance field. The Cost Variance is calculated as Cost minus Baseline Cost. Thus when the variance is a positive number, the schedule is running over budget.

These additional cost fields are displayed in Figure 8.3, in which the vertical divider bar has been moved to the right to display more of the Cost table. In the lower pane, the scheduled cost for the selected task is the column titled Cost and the actual cost is the column titled Act. Cost.

To illustrate the baseline and actual costs, some actual work has been recorded in Figure 8.3. Although you don't see a column in the table for the percentage complete, the Prototype Design task has been marked as 100% complete, and its actual cost is now the same as its scheduled and baseline costs, with zero variance. The selected task is Test Prototype and you can see its details in the bottom pane. Before the initial work on Test Prototype was started, its estimated duration was increased from 20 days to 22 days—a change that has increased the scheduled cost of the resources that are assigned to the task. Also, the work on the Test Prototype task has now been marked as 50% complete.

The increase in the duration of the Test Prototype task in Figure 8.3 has increased the work, and therefore the Cost entries for the assigned resources in the bottom pane. The total of the resource costs has risen from $6,600 (the sum of the entries in Figure 8.2) to $7,260 (the sum in Figure 8.3). Project calculated the Actual Cost entries by taking 50% of each of the Cost entries. The sum of the Actual Cost amounts for the resources is $3,630. Notice that this is the same value that is in the Actual column in the top pane. In other words, the Actual amount includes only resource costs from the bottom pane. Project did not calculate any part of the Fixed Cost as having been incurred (that is, *accrued*) at the halfway point in finishing the task. The following section explains why.

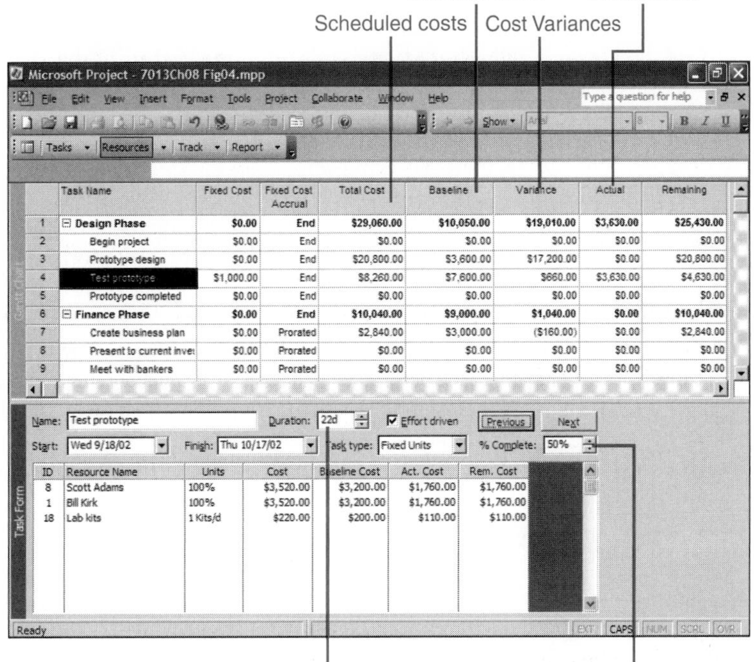

Figure 8.3
The Cost table displays the baseline cost, actual cost, and cost variance (the difference between the scheduled and baseline costs).

ACCRUED COSTS

When you mark a task as partially complete, Project must calculate what part of the scheduled cost will be shown as Actual Cost. Until the task is complete, these costs are *accrued costs* and the way Project calculates them is governed by the *accrual method* selected for the resources and for the task's fixed cost. By default, if you mark a task as partially complete, Project prorates the scheduled resource costs. In Figure 8.3, for example, the selected task is marked 50% complete and Project has applied 50% of the scheduled resource costs to actual cost. In Figure 8.3, the Fixed Cost Accrual setting for this task is End; Project will therefore apply all $1,000 of the fixed cost to actual cost only when the task is marked 100% complete.

You specify the accrual method for determining when resource cost will be recognized as actual cost when you define the resource. (See the Accrue At column in Figure 8.1.) You can use one of the following three methods for accruing costs:

- **Prorated**—The default accrual method for both material and work resources is the Prorated method. With this method, Project recognizes a prorated portion of the scheduled cost as actual cost based on the percentage complete of the duration for the task.
- **Start**—This method recognizes the resource cost at the moment work on the task is scheduled to start. For example, if the resource must be paid in full up front before it

starts an assignment, you could recognize the full cost as being expended at the start of the task.

- **End**—This method withholds recognition of the cost until the task is completed. For example, if the resource will be paid only if the finished work is satisfactory, you might withhold recognition of the cost until the task is finished.

Note that the choice of the accrual method is significant only when a task has started but is not yet complete. All three accrual methods yield the same result after a task is completed. Thus, only interim cost reports are affected by the accrual method.

NOTE

If you are using timephased cost reporting, the choice of accrual method is important from a reporting perspective. For example, if you report on a daily basis for the task cost using the start method, all task cost is reported on the first day of the task. The total cost for the task is, however, the same with any method when the task is complete.

DEFINING THE RESOURCE POOL

When you first begin working with Microsoft Project, you will probably define a separate resource pool in each project file. If you have multiple projects that use the same resources, however, you will soon want to define a resource pool that can be shared by all your projects. When you use a shared resource pool, Project can show you the total demands being made on the shared resources from all projects sharing that pool.

➔ To learn more about working with resources across multiple overlapping projects, **see** "Sharing Resources Among Projects," **p. 621**.

Some users create a project template that contains no tasks but that defines a standard set of resources. When a new project file is started, the project is created from a copy of this template, which then provides an established resource list for their projects.

You can create a resource pool at any time, before or after you define the tasks. You can also add resources to the pool on-the-fly, by assigning new resources to tasks. By default, Project automatically adds new names to the resource pool.

NOTE

See the section "Setting the Automatically Add New Resources and Tasks Option," later in this chapter, for information about using or not using Project's default resource creation setting.

You can type the resource pool information into Project, or you can import resource names from another application. You can include resources from a spreadsheet, database, Project Server, company address book, or even from the company directory.

If you try to copy a list of resources from another application and paste it into Project, you might encounter some unexpected results. See "Pasting a Resource List from Another Application" in the "Troubleshooting" section near the end of this chapter for instructions on doing it successfully.

➔ If you use Microsoft Office Project 2003 Professional, you can use the Build Team tool to select the resources for a project. For more information, **see** "Using the Project Center Build Team," **p. 1036**.

You can use several different views and view combinations to create a resource list. The following sections briefly introduce the views and tools you are most likely to use, without pausing to provide a full explanation of the many fields that are available. The following sections use those views to show you how to best use the individual fields.

USING THE RESOURCE SHEET VIEW

The Resource Sheet view is perhaps the most effective view you can use for manually entering basic resource information. The Resource Sheet enables you to see many resources on the screen at once, and it also shows you a number of important fields for each resource (see Figure 8.4). Indicators notify when there is critical information in other fields. To display the Resource Sheet view, choose View, Resource Sheet.

Although it might not be obvious, the resources defined within the Resource Sheet view create the resource pool. This pool details what resources are available to the specific project you are working on or to all the projects in the case of a shared-resource pool solution. The resource pool does not specifically define which resources are assigned to tasks, but rather which ones are available to be assigned.

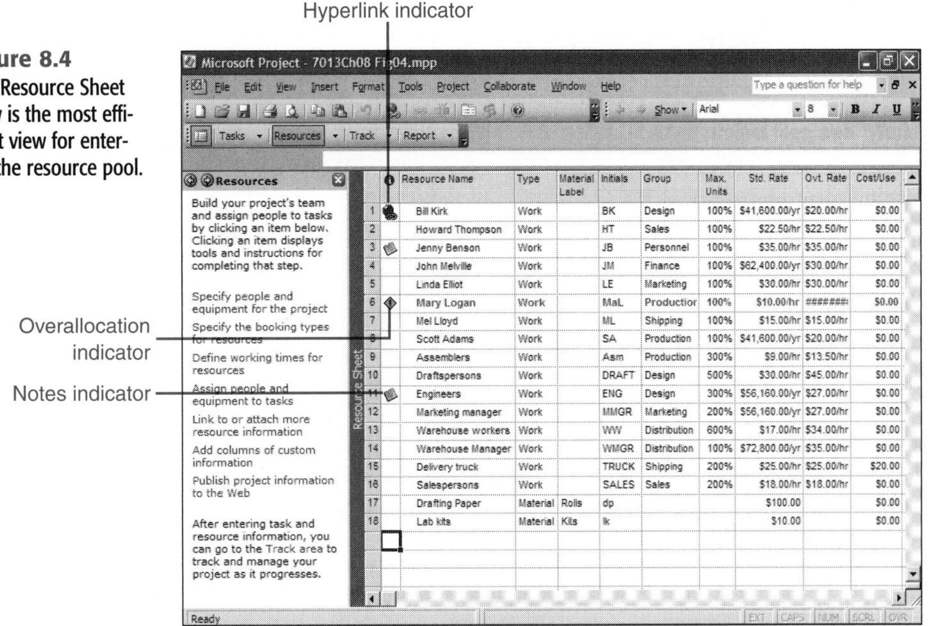

Figure 8.4
The Resource Sheet view is the most efficient view for entering the resource pool.

If your video resolution is 800×600 pixels or less, you will not be able to see all the columns of the Resource Sheet without scrolling to the right. Use the Window, Split command to display the Resource Form view in the bottom pane (see Figure 8.5), and you see all the fields for the resource that is selected in the top pane.

You can also use the Resource Form view to display and edit the Notes field. To display the notes in the form, activate the Resource Form view, choose Format, Details, and select Notes. Figure 8.5 shows the Notes field in the details section of the Resource Form view.

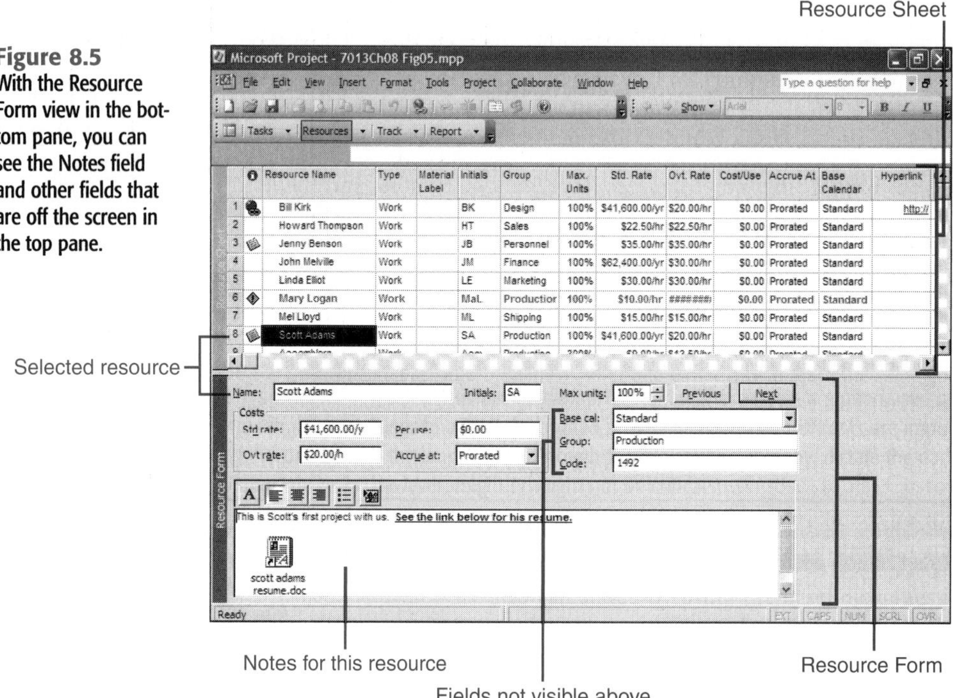

Figure 8.5
With the Resource Form view in the bottom pane, you can see the Notes field and other fields that are off the screen in the top pane.

To add a resource in the Resource Sheet view, select an empty cell in the Resource Name column and type in a descriptive name for the resource. Project automatically supplies default values for a number of fields to the right. Replace the default values or fill in the blanks for the rest of the fields, using the definitions and instructions in the "Using the Resource Fields" section, later in this chapter.

USING THE RESOURCE INFORMATION DIALOG BOX

Several important resource fields are not available on the Resource Sheet view or the Resource Form view. The Resource Information dialog box, on the other hand, contains almost all the important resource definition fields (see Figure 8.6). The additional fields on the Resource Information dialog box supply information such as the following:

- When the resource is normally available for work (General tab)
- When the normal working times are changed for vacations or other exceptions (Working Time tab)
- Alternative cost rates to use for different types of work (Costs tab)
- When different cost rates for the resource will become effective (Costs tab)
- How to provide electronic communication with the resource (General tab and Details button)
- Notes about the resource (Notes tab)
- Custom fields defined for the resource such as department, division, skills, and so on

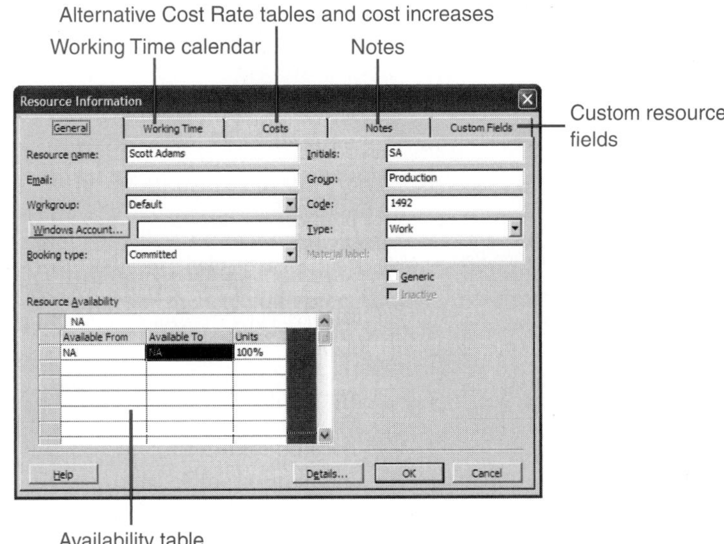

Figure 8.6
The Resource Information dialog box contains all the important resource definition fields on five tabs.

You can use the Resource Information dialog box with the Resource Sheet to complete the definition of the resource. Enter at least the resource name on the Resource Sheet. Then use the Resource Information button on the Standard toolbar (or double-click the resource name) to display the Resource Information dialog box for that resource. Fill in the rest of the fields, and then click OK to return to the Resource Sheet view.

Using the Assign Resources Dialog Box

If you are using a task view such as the Gantt Chart view, you can add names to the resource list by using the Assign Resources dialog box (see Figure 8.7), without switching to the Resource Sheet view. You can also open the Resource Information dialog box from within the Assign Resources dialog box to modify the rest of the resource fields. To display the dialog box, click the Assign Resources tool on the Standard toolbar. There are additional options on the dialog box that you can see if you click the Resource List Options button.

8

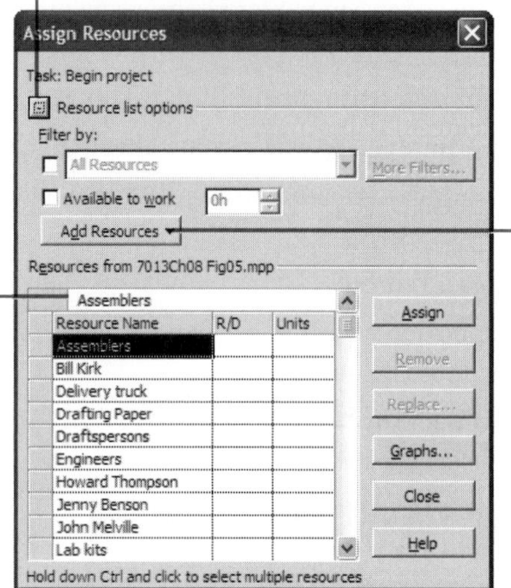

Figure 8.7
The Assign Resources dialog box lets you view and modify the list of resources and can also be used to jump to the Resource Information dialog box.

TIP

The Assign Resources dialog box can be left open on the workspace as you switch between it and an underlying view. You can open the Assign Resources dialog box only when the active underlying view is a task view. After it is open, however, you can use it to create resource names, no matter what the underlying view.

To add resource names with the Assign Resources dialog box, select a blank cell in the Name column and type the name. The name then appears in the cell and also in the entry box at the top of the dialog box as you type. Press Enter once, or click the green check mark next to the entry box to add that name to the resource pool.

CAUTION

Be careful if you are creating the resource name and don't intend to assign it to the task that is selected in the underlying view. When you press Enter after typing the name, the Assign button becomes activated, and pressing Enter again would assign the resource to the currently selected task.

Alternatively, if you click the Resource List Options button to display more options, you can use the Add Resources button to copy existing names from various sources. Click Add Resources and choose the following:

- Choose From Active Directory to select names from Microsoft Active Directory.
- Choose From Address Book to select names from your Outlook address book or from Exchange Server.

- If you are using Microsoft Project Professional, choose From Microsoft Project Server to open the Build Team dialog box to select resources from the Global resource pool.

→ **See** "Enterprise Resource Management," **p. 1069**, for details about the Global resource pool.

If you draw names from an address book or from Project Server, Project automatically knows how to contact the resource to communicate details about assignments and to request updates on progress. For example, Figure 8.8 shows the user's email address book being used to select contact names to add to the resource list.

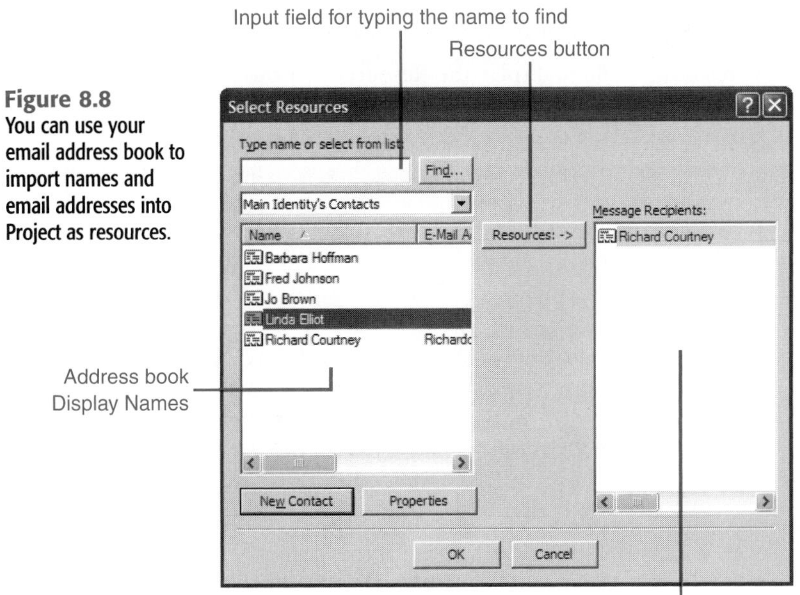

Figure 8.8
You can use your email address book to import names and email addresses into Project as resources.

However you add names to the resource list, you can double-click the name in the Assign Resources dialog box to view the Resource Information dialog box for that resource and fill in additional resource definition fields.

USING THE TASK FORM VIEW

The Gantt Chart view with the Task Form view in the bottom pane is one of the popular views for assigning resources. You can also add resources to the resource pool in that view, by using the resource details in the lower pane. To add resources in the Task Form view, follow these steps:

1. Display the Gantt Chart view and then choose Window, Split to display the Task Form view in the lower pane.

2. If the resource details are not displayed in the Task Form view, click anywhere in the lower pane to activate it and then choose Format, Details from the menu and select Resources and Predecessors (see Figure 8.9).
3. Select a task in the top pane.
4. Click in the Resource Name column in the Task Form view, where you can select an existing resource to assign to the task or you can type in the name of a new resource to assign. In Figure 8.9, `Jenny Benson` is being typed in as an addition to the resource pool. If you type in a new name and click the OK button, Project adds the resource to the resource pool and supplies default values for the assignment Units and Work if you didn't. Chapter 10, "Assigning Resources and Costs to Tasks," discusses how to use the Units and Work fields.
5. Double-click the resource name to display the Resource Information dialog box, where you can fill in the rest of the fields that define the resource.

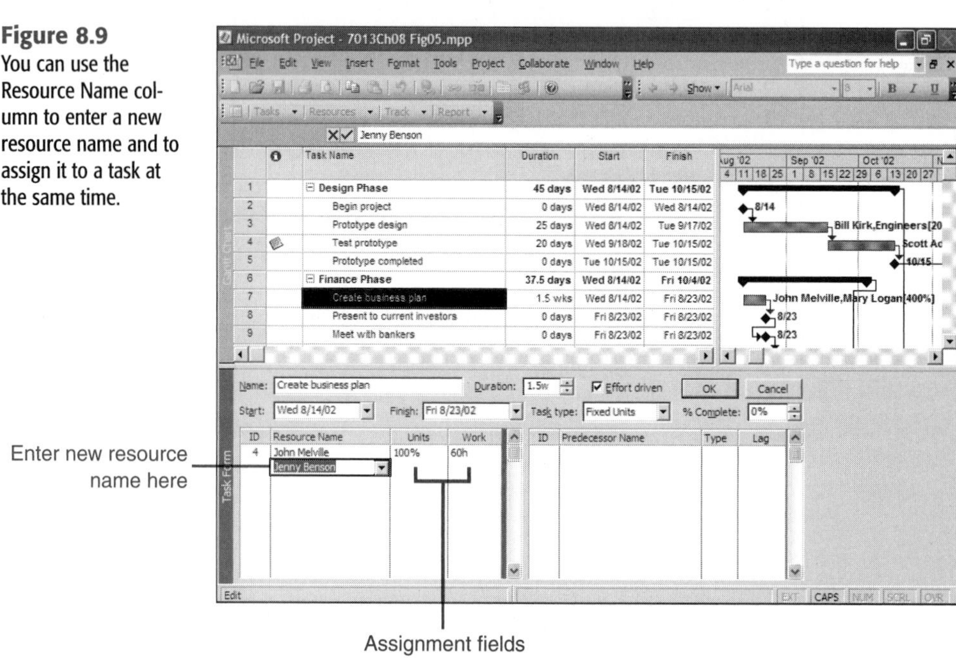

Figure 8.9
You can use the Resource Name column to enter a new resource name and to assign it to a task at the same time.

→ For a full discussion of the assignment fields, **see** "Understanding the Resource Assignment Fields," **p. 324**.

USING THE RESOURCE FIELDS

As stated earlier in this chapter, the best view for typing and reviewing the list of resources is the Resource Sheet view. You can use it in combination with the Resource Information dialog box to enter all the important fields of information that define a resource. The Resource Sheet view and Resource Information dialog box are shown in Figure 8.10.

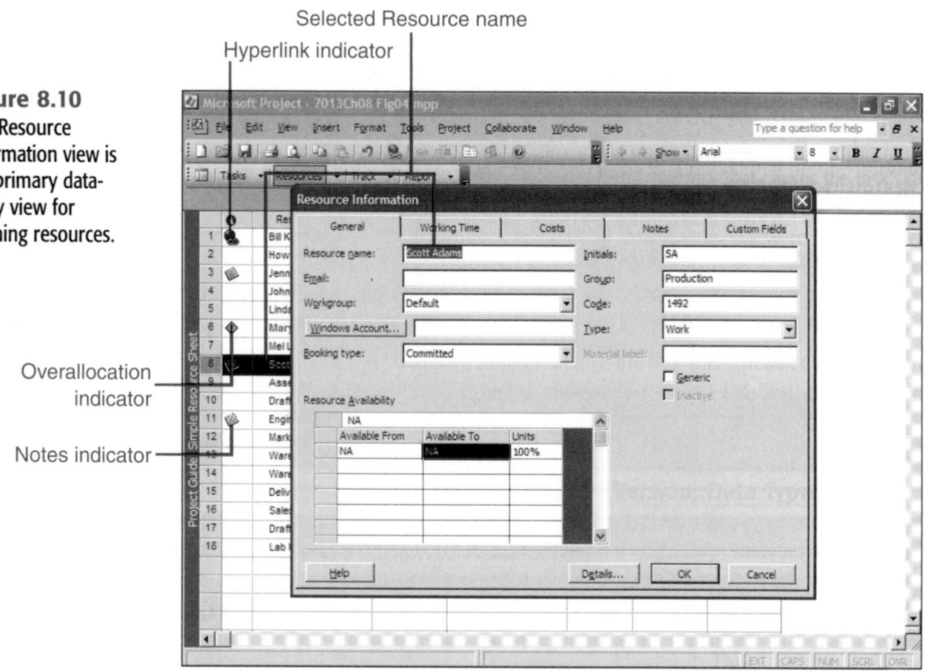

Figure 8.10
The Resource Information view is the primary data-entry view for defining resources.

When you define a resource, you should provide a resource name and information about the availability and cost of the resource. The fields that are commonly used in defining resources are listed in the following sections. The order of these sections is based mainly on the order of the columns in the Resource Sheet view and on the related fields in the Resource Information dialog box.

ID

The row numbers on the Resource Sheet view are the ID numbers for the resources. As with task ID numbers, you cannot edit this field, but if you move a resource on the list, it automatically acquires the ID number for the row number you move it to. The ID number does not appear in the Resource Information dialog box.

INDICATORS

The Indicator field displays icons that show the status of critical fields that might not normally be displayed. For example, the Overallocation indicators in Figure 8.10 mean that those resources have been overallocated at some point in the project (that is, they have been assigned to work on two different tasks at the same time). The Note indicators show that there is text in the Notes field for those resources. The Hyperlink indicator indicates a hyperlink associating the resource with a Web site or a document file. Indicators only appear on resource table views such as the Resource Sheet view.

8

Name

You use the Resource Name field to provide a descriptive name for a resource. The name can contain any characters except the Windows separator character (which is, by default, the comma in the United States) and the square brackets ([]). Resource names can be up to 255 characters long. The resource name can be a specific name, such as Anita Salinas, or it can describe a group of resources, such as Electricians.

CAUTION

If you add a resource name that is a duplicate of another name in the list, Project accepts it and does not warn you that you have duplicate names. However, if you assign a non-unique resource name to a task, Project uses the first resource it finds with that name in the resource list. You must take care to avoid duplicate resource names.

In any organization, it is wise to come up with a standard naming convention for resources. Whether you are using Project Professional with Project Server or Project Standard standalone, reporting and sharing will be easier with a standard convention for naming resources. Two approaches are commonly used: full first name space full last name, and full last name space full first name. The format last comma first is not allowed in many language versions because Project uses the comma list separator in the resource names field when assigning multiple resources to a task.

Type

As stated previously, Project distinguishes between *work resources*—resources that contribute their work to tasks but are not consumed in the process—and *material resources*—resources that are consumed by their assignments. The cost of the work resources is based on the number of hours they work on a task and the hourly cost for the resource. The cost of the material resources is based on the cost of a unit of the resource and how many units are consumed. The default resource type is Work, but you can use the drop-down arrow in the Type field to select either Work or Material.

Work resources units can be formatted as percentage (the default) or decimal values. Material resources are formatted only as decimal values.

CAUTION

When you assign a resource to a task, its type determines how the assignment affects the schedule for the task. If it is a work resource, the resource calendar determines when work can take place; if it is a material resource, there is no resource calendar to consider. Thus, if you try to change the type of a resource after it has been assigned, Project warns you with a dialog box that the schedule will be affected and that the changes cannot be undone. Be cautious about changing resource types after they are assigned to tasks.

If the amount of the material resource that is consumed doesn't depend on the duration of the task, it is said to have a *fixed consumption rate*. For example, the amount of concrete used in pouring a foundation does not depend on the duration of the task.

If the amount of the material resource consumed varies with the duration of the task, it is said to have a *variable consumption rate*. For example, the amount of diesel fuel consumed by construction equipment depends on the number of hours in operation. In calculating the cost of using a variable-consumption-rate material resource, Project factors the duration of the task into the calculation. In order to tell Project that it should factor duration into the calculated cost for a material resource, you have to append a time unit abbreviation when you enter the assignment units. For example, to assign 5 gallons of diesel fuel per hour to a task, you would enter the units as **`5/h`**.

→ For details on assigning material resources to tasks, **see** "Assigning Material Resource Units," **p. 328**.

MATERIAL LABEL

You use the Material Label field to define the unit of measure for material resources (for example, gallons, bushels, tons, liters). You use that unit to define the unit cost of the resource. This field is unavailable for work resources.

INITIALS

The Initials field provides a place for a shortened form of the resource name that can be used in views such as the Gantt Chart or Network Diagram views to save space and reduce the clutter that using the full names sometimes creates. When you first enter the resource name in a new row, Project supplies the first character of the name as the default initial and makes no attempt to keep it unique. You should edit the initial to make it uniquely identify the resource.

GROUP

In the Group field, you can enter an identifying label or keyword that you can use for sorting, grouping, or filtering resources. For example, you could identify all management personnel by entering **`Management`**, all equipment resources by entering **`Equipment`**, and all vendors and contractors by entering **`Vendors`**. Some users put the name of the department that manages a resource in the Group field. With these values entered, you can then use the Resource Group filter to view only the resources that have one of those values in this field.

If a resource belongs to multiple groups, or if you want to be able to group the resources in several different ways, you can enter multiple labels in the Group field, as long as they are separated by a comma. You can enter any combination of letters, numbers, spaces, or other characters, up to a total of 255 characters. However, sorting on the field might not be as meaningful if you use a comma-separated list of entries for each resource.

For example, suppose you want to identify resources by the department that is managing them (Production, Marketing, Finance, and so on), their job title (Manager, Foreman, Carpenter, Driver, and so forth), and the skill level they bring to their task assignments (for example, Trainee, Semi-Skilled, Skilled, Expert). For a trainee electrician in the production department, you could enter this text string in the Group field:
`Production,Electrician,Trainee`.

NOTE

> When applying a filter to locate one keyword in a list in the Group field, you should use the logical test `contains` rather than `equals`. See the section "Filtering Resources," later in this chapter, for an example of using filters.

Many users put skills in a custom text field so they can filter the resource list for resources who have comparable skills. It's also useful to identify the skill level. The most effective method is to combine the skill category with the skill level. For example, if you adopt the scale 1=Trainee, 2=Semi-Skilled, 3=Skilled, and 4=Expert, then an expert electrician could be identified with `electrician4`. Use commas to separate the entries for people who have multiple skills.

TIP

> If you use a generic resource as a placeholder for individuals who have the same skill-set, be sure to use the same keyword in the field for skills that you use for the individuals. That way, the total assignments to the placeholder and the individual resources can be summed to evaluate the total requirements for resources in that skill category.

TIP

> In Project Server, skills are defined using enterprise outline codes and enterprise resource multi-value codes (ERMVs). Even when you are not using Project Server, you can use resource custom outline codes to define skill-sets. Figure 8.11 illustrates a skill implemented in a custom outline code. Note that each level of the outline gets more specific about the skill of the resource. This allows you to find an engineer, a mechanical engineer, or specifically an advanced mechanical engineer based on the level of specificity you request when searching the skill field.

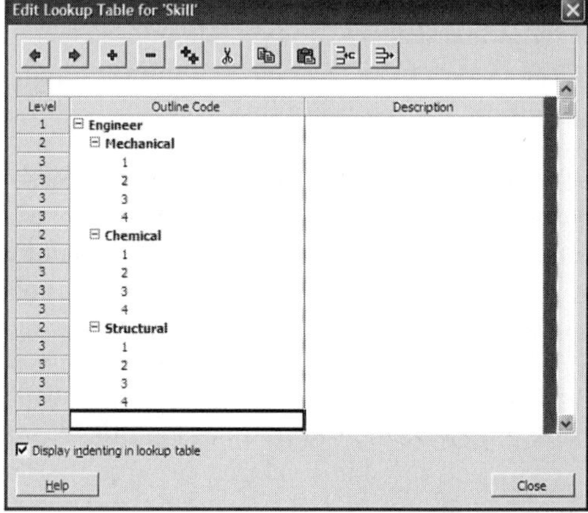

Figure 8.11 When working with either Project Standard or Project Professional with Project Server, outline codes provide a great way to define a hierarchical set of skills.

→ **See** "Customizing Fields," **p. 847**, for information on creating and using custom fields.

If you have put multiple group labels in the Group field and want to filter the resource pool for one of the labels, see "Filtering for Labels Contained in the Group Field" in the "Troubleshooting" section at the end of this chapter.

CAUTION

Don't confuse the Group field with the concept of a group resource. A *group resource* is a resource which represents a set of resource units that all serve the same function and are identified with one ID and name.

Also don't confuse the Group field with the Group By command on the Project menu. That command can sort and group records based on the entries in any field (including the Group field). See the section "Grouping Resources," later in this chapter.

The Resource Availability Fields

There are several fields that together define the *availability* of a resource—that is, exactly how many units of the resource are available for work and how many hours of work can be assigned to the resource on any given date:

- The Max Units field specifies the number of units of the resource that are available on the current date.
- If that number will be changing over time during the project, the changes are listed in the Resource Availability table in the Resource Information dialog box.
- One of the project's base calendars is designated to define the normal working days and hours for the resource.
- Working and nonworking times for individual days are defined on the Working Time tab of the Resource Information dialog box.

You can enter the max units and the base calendar to which the resource is linked on the Resource Sheet view, but you must use the Resource Information dialog box to enter the rest of the availability information.

Max Units

You use the Max Units field to enter the maximum number of units that can currently be assigned to tasks at any one time. Project uses the Max Units field to determine when more units of the resource have been assigned than are available—in other words, when the resource is overallocated.

The Max Units field can be formatted as a percentage or as a decimal, with the default being the percentage format. Chapter 9—in the section "Understanding the Assignment Units Field"—explains why the percentage format is used as the default.

Suppose that Sam's Max Units field shows 75%. That means that Sam is available to spend up to 75% of his working time on tasks in your project. If you assign Sam to spend 40% of his time on one task and 50% of his time on another task, and if the scheduled dates for those two tasks happen to overlap, you will have assigned 90% of Sam's time during the period of the overlap. Since this is more than the Max Units of 75%, Project calculates that the resource is overallocated and displays a symbol in the Indicator field to flag the overallocated resource for you.

NOTE

> You can change the format for the Max Units field in the Options dialog box. Choose Tools, Options, and then select the Schedule tab. Use the drop-down list in the box Show Assignment Units as A, and select either Percentage or Decimal.

By default the resource is assumed to be available 100% of the available time on its calendar, for the duration of the project. Resources that work half-time would be available for only 50% of the hours on the calendar. Group resources could work a multiple of the hours on the calendar in any one day. For example, five electricians could work 500% of the hours on the calendar in one day.

Project supplies a default Max Units value of 100% (or 1, in decimal format) when you create a resource. However, you can enter any value between 0% and 6,000,000,000% (between 0 and 60,000,000 in decimal format). For a single-unit resource, the default value of 100% means that this resource is available to work 100% of the hours on its calendar on this project. If you are grouping resources into a set, you enter a value greater than 100%. Thus, if you have five full-time electricians in an Electricians resource, you enter 500% (or 5, in decimal format).

NOTE

> There is no Max Units value for material resources. Project assumes that you will acquire as many units as you have assigned.

RESOURCE AVAILABILITY

Sometimes a resource isn't hired until after the project starts, so up until that date its Max Units is 0%. Or a resource might leave the organization before the project is completed, so after its last day with the organization, the Max Units field is 0%.

You might also intend to add more units of the resource over the duration of the project. In this case, you need to record the dates when the additional units would come on board.

You use the Resource Availability table on the General tab of the Resource Information dialog box to define the time periods and the units (Max Units) for each time period (see Figure 8.13). The default values in the Resource Availability table are NA for both the Available From and Available To columns and 100% in the Units (Max Units) field. The NA value means that a value is not applicable because there is no From or To date associated with the units on that row. Figure 8.12 shows that Scott Adams will not start work until 8/1/2003, even though the project starts earlier, but he is expected to be with the organization from then on.

Figure 8.13 shows the Resource Availability table for the Assemblers resource. The table shows that this resource will not start work until 8/1/2003, with 300% units, even though the project starts 8/14/2002. The assemblers will be ramped up to 500% units on 11/1/2003 and to 800% units on 3/1/2004.

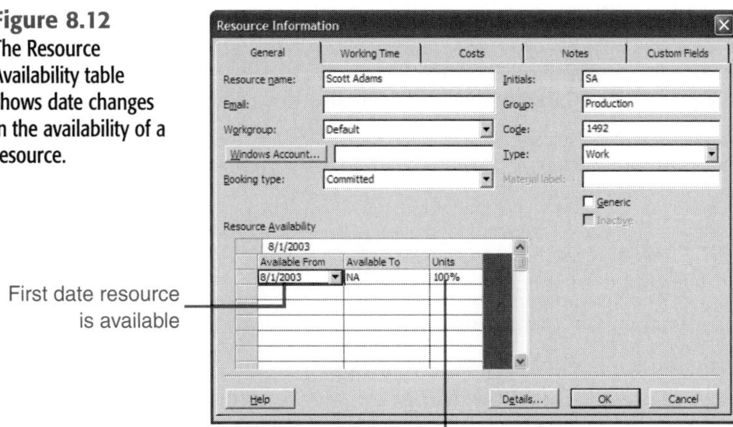

Figure 8.12
The Resource Availability table shows date changes in the availability of a resource.

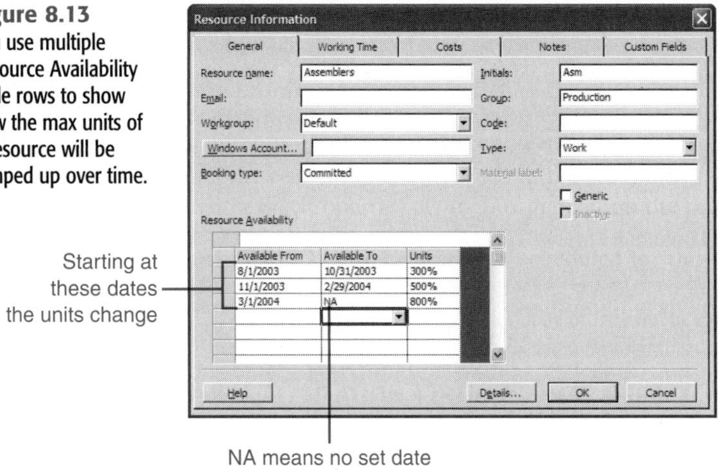

Figure 8.13
You use multiple Resource Availability table rows to show how the max units of a resource will be ramped up over time.

Starting at these dates the units change

NA means no set date

The Max Units field on the Resource Sheet view and on the Resource Form view displays the Units value from the Resource Availability table for the *current date*. The current date is normally the computer's current date, but it can be any date you choose to enter into the Current Date field in the Project Information dialog box. If you look at the Max Units field for Assemblers on the Resource Sheet view on any date prior to 8/1/2003, the value will be 0%; after that date, it will be 300%, 500%, or 800%, depending on the current date when you look at the Resource Sheet view.

When Project examines this schedule to see if the Assembler resource is overallocated, it shows the overallocated indicator if the total assignments for the Assembler resource exceed 300% on any date up to 10/31/2003, exceed 500% on any date between 10/31/2003 and 2/29/2004, or are more than 800% on 3/1/2004 or later.

To change the Resource Availability table for a resource, follow these steps:

1. In a view that shows resource names, select the resource and click the Resource Information button on the Standard toolbar. You can also just double-click the resource name.
2. Click the General tab if it is not displayed.
3. Click the cell for the date you want to change under the Available From or Available To column. You can either type in the date or use the drop-down arrow to display the date-picker and select the date.
4. Enter the max units for that row's date range in the Units column.
5. After all entries are completed, click OK to save the changes. Or you can click Cancel to close the dialog box without saving any changes.

TIP

Be sure that the dates in the Resource Availability table are in sequential order and that you leave no gaps in the dates from one row to the next. If you have an Available From date that is more than one day later than the Available To date on the previous row, Project uses 0% as the Max Units value for the dates in the gap.

If you have more than one row in the Resource Availability table, you shouldn't have an NA entry in the Available From column, except possibly on the first row, and you shouldn't have an NA entry in the Available To column, except in the last row.

NOTE

The Resource Availability table is disabled for material resources, which are assumed to be always available to the project.

BASE CALENDAR

You use the Base Calendar field to name the project calendar on which the working time in the resource's calendar is based. The Base Calendar field is available both in the Resource Sheet view and on the Working Time tab of the Resource Information dialog box.

NOTE

Material resources do not have a calendar because they are assumed to be always available. The Working Time tab in the Resource Information dialog box is unavailable for material resources.

You use the drop-down arrows to show a list of all the base calendars that have been defined and select the one that most closely fits this resource. The resource calendar inherits all the working days and hours as well as the individually marked nonworking days and hours that are defined in its base calendar. The default base calendar is Standard.

TIP

If you have more than one named resource with the same set of exceptions to one of the standard base calendars, you might want to create a special base calendar for those resources. Otherwise, you will have to mark the same exceptions in each of the resource calendars. For example, if a number of resources will be assigned to work on a project on a night shift and they all have the same basic schedule of night work hours, creating a base calendar for night-shift work and then using that base calendar for all workers with those hours saves you time. With this method, you define the hours only once, instead of customizing each night-shift worker's resource calendar.

TIP

If you create additional base calendars in your project that resources or tasks are linked to, remember to make organizationwide changes in working days and hours to all base calendars. If your company decides to make December 24 a holiday, for example, you need to edit each base calendar used by resources or tasks in order to apply the holiday to all schedules.

→ For instructions on creating base calendars, **see** Chapter 3, "Setting Up a Project Document," **p. 55**.

Working Time

As mentioned earlier in the chapter, the resource calendar is based on one of the base calendars, and it inherits the base calendar's normal working times per week, as well as all the holidays or other exceptions to the normal working times. You use the resource calendar to enter exceptions for the resource to the working time on the base calendar. You use the date and time fields on the Working Time tab of the Resource Information dialog box to enter the resource's exceptions. For instance, in Figure 8.14 the resource calendar for Scott Adams shows that he will not be working August 25–29. This is a week of vacation he has scheduled.

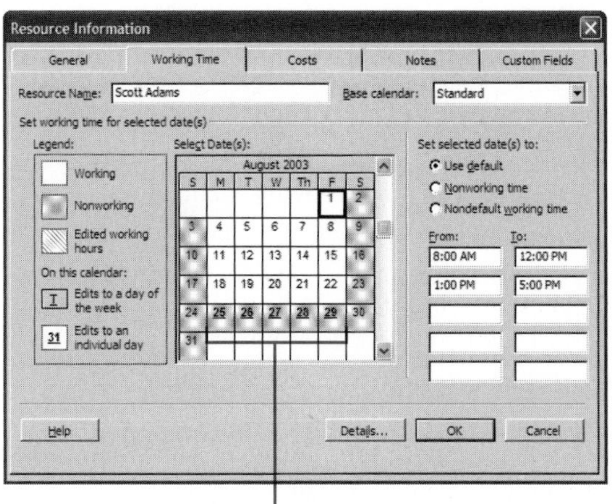

Figure 8.14
You use the resource calendar on the Working Time tab to define exceptions to the working and nonworking days on the base calendar.

8

NOTE

> You can edit a resource calendar from the Change Working Time dialog box, although you can't change the name of the base calendar it's linked to there. Choose Tools, Change Working Time to display the Change Working Time dialog box, and then use the drop-down list in the For box to select the resource name.

To edit the calendar days and hours, use the techniques described in Chapter 3, in the section "Defining a Calendar of Working Time." Follow these additional steps to edit a resource calendar:

1. Select the resource in a resource view or on the Assign Resources dialog box and double-click the resource name to display the Resource Information dialog box. Select the Working Time tab to display the resource calendar and time fields.
2. Use the Base Calendar drop-down list to select the base calendar for the resource.
3. To give the resource time off on dates that are normal working dates on the base calendar, select the dates and click the Nonworking Time button. For example, in Figure 8.15 the date November 7 is a standard working day, but Scott Adams has chosen to take the day off.
4. To schedule a resource for work on dates that are normally nonworking dates, select the dates (they are shaded before you select them) and click the Nondefault Working Time button. The dates are no longer shaded, but the underlined date numerals indicate that they are an exception. For example, Scott Adams has agreed to work on a date that is normally a holiday (November 28) to make up for the nonworking day on November 7. To show this on his calendar, you would select November 28 and click the Nondefault Working Time button.
5. Modify the hours of work on any date as needed. The date appears with a diagonal shading pattern to indicate that the hours are nonstandard for that day of the week, and the date is underlined to show that it is an exception to the base calendar.
6. If a date is marked as an exception on the resource calendar, but you want to remove the exception and return it to the default for the base calendar, select the date and click the Use Default option button.
7. Click the OK button to save your changes in the resource calendar, or click the Cancel button to abandon the changes without saving them.

THE RESOURCE COST FIELDS

You can associate three cost measures with a resource: its standard rate (for work during normal working hours), its overtime rate (for work during overtime hours), and its cost per use (a special one-time cost per assignment that is independent of the number of hours worked). Each of these cost measures has a default rate that you can define in the Resource Sheet view or in the Resource Information dialog box.

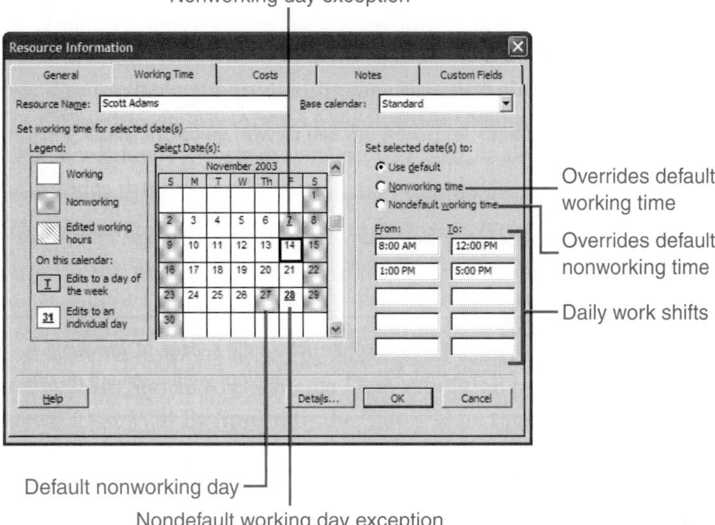

Figure 8.15
You use the Working Time tab to record exceptions to the base calendar on which the resource calendar is based.

If you want to charge different rates for different kinds of work, you can create four additional sets of the three rates in the Resource Information dialog box. You can also define time periods when the rates will change. These features are covered in the section "The Cost Rate Tables," later in this chapter.

STANDARD RATE

You use the Standard Rate field to show the current default cost of each unit of the resource assigned to a task:

- For work resources, the standard rate is the amount to charge per unit of normal working time. You enter the rate as a number, followed by a forward slash and one of the following time units or its abbreviation: minute (m), hour (h), day (d), week (w), month (mo), or year (y). If you type just a number (without a time unit), Project assumes it's an hourly rate. For example, you can type **`600/w`** for $600 per week, **`35000/y`** for $35,000 per year, or just **`15.5`** for $15.50 per hour. For example, suppose that you were to rent a bulldozer for $1,200 per week. You could create a resource named Bulldozer and enter the standard rate **`1200/week`**.
- For material resources, the standard rate is the amount to charge tasks per unit of the resource consumed. There is no time unit appended to the dollar amount. You enter the standard rate as an amount, with no time unit, and it is understood to be the amount per unit of the resource, where the unit to use is defined in the Material Label field. For example, if you include diesel fuel as a material resource for the bulldozer, its material label might be gallons and the standard rate might be 1.50 (which means $1.50 per gallon).

If the standard rate is entered with a time unit, the rate is converted to an hourly rate and is applied to the number of hours of work it takes to complete the task. For annual rates, the hourly rate is calculated by assuming 52 weeks in a year, and the number of hours per week is that which is defined on the Calendar tab of the Options dialog box. For the standard workweek of 40 hours, for example, the annual rate is divided by 2,080 (52×40) to get an hourly rate. For monthly rates, the hourly rate is calculated using the Calendar tab's definitions for days in a month and hours in a day.

In addition to the default standard rate, you can define four additional rates that can be used for assignments when you want to charge more or less than the default rate. See the section "The Cost Rate Tables," later in this chapter, for details.

Although the standard rate is frequently the salaried rate for a resource, organizations often define the standard rate as the billed-at rate. When the standard rate is defined in this manner, a project plan serves as a budget estimate for the work to be performed under contract.

Many times, a defined project plan demonstrates to a client early in the proposal stage that client requirements are understood and acknowledged. Expectations are then "level-set" for the project in the early stages of planning, as opposed to being "discovered" during project execution. Estimates of costs and work are based on defined work rather than ballpark estimates, which mitigates some of the risks in contracting for work.

OVERTIME RATE

Project uses the entry in the Overtime Rate field when calculating the cost of overtime hours that you schedule for a work resource. There is no overtime rate for material resources. The default overtime rate is zero (0.00), so for salaried employees you can leave the zero value if these resources are not paid for their overtime hours. If the rate for overtime work is the same as the regular rate, you must enter that amount again in the Overtime Rate field, or overtime hours will be charged at the zero default rate.

NOTE

You can use the overtime rate to reflect the opportunity cost of using a resource in overtime. For example, if a salaried employee with an overtime rate of zero were to be assigned to do all the work on a task in overtime, the cost of the task would be zero and the task would add nothing to the cost of the project! This seems like a great way to lower costs.

Though the time spent working overtime on a task might not add to payroll costs, that time could be used on completing other tasks or projects, and the failure to complete those other tasks is an opportunity cost to the organization.

By this logic, the overtime rate should never be zero; it should be at least as much as the standard rate, to reflect the opportunity cost to the organization of using the resource to complete the task.

As with the standard rate, you can define four additional overtime rates for each resource and use them for special tasks. See the section "The Cost Rate Tables," later in this chapter, for more information.

NOTE

> You can set default values for the standard and overtime rates for all new resources in the Options dialog box. Choose Tools, Options, and then click the General tab. Enter an amount per time unit in both the Default Standard Rate and the Default Overtime Rate fields. All resources added from that point on initially show these default rates.

Cost Per Use

The Cost Per Use field (which is titled Cost/Use in the Resource Sheet view and Per Use Cost on the Resource Information dialog box) contains any cost that is to be charged once for each 100% of a unit of the resource that is assigned to a task, regardless of the duration of the assignment. It was designed to be used for material resources before there was a Type field to distinguish material and work resources from one another. Because Project has the resource type designation for material resources, you should use the Standard Rate field to show the cost of each unit of a material resource.

You should always be careful about using the Cost Per Use field with work resources. The amount entered in that field will be charged once for each 100% of the resource that is assigned to any task. For example, if you rent a piece of equipment by the hour but also have to pay a flat charge of $200 for having it delivered to the work site, you could treat the delivery charge as a Cost Per Use cost. If you assigned the equipment to more than one task, however, the delivery charge would be charged multiple times (once for each assignment), which would overstate the true costs. It would be better in this example to record the delivery charge as a fixed cost attached to one of the tasks that use the resource or to a summary task that includes all the tasks that are affected.

Be sure to take advantage of the Cost Per Use field when you're laying out your project plans. One example of this would be a required trip charge for deploying that resource. Perhaps a refrigerator repair man charges $50 to examine a problem with your refrigerator, regardless of the number of hours spent and the materials necessary to fix the problem. The Cost Per Use field allows you to assign flat-rate costs to various tasks.

The Cost Rate Tables

The Costs tab of the Resource Information dialog box contains five Cost Rate tables (A through E), which show the default cost rates (Table A) plus four other levels of cost that you can define for different types of assignments. For example, an Electrician resource's Table A would contain its default rates, which might be for new commercial wiring assignments. Table B might contain the rates for new residential wiring assignments, Table C might show rates for modifying commercial wiring, and Table D might contain the rates for modifying residential wiring. You can select the rate to apply to an assignment in the Assignment Information dialog box.

→ For use of the Cost Rate tables in assignments, **see** "Assigning Resources and Costs to Tasks," **p. 359**.

TIP

Because you can't change the labels on the five cost tabs to something more descriptive than A–E, you should document what each rate is to be used for in the resource Notes field.

Figure 8.16 shows Cost Rate Table A for Scott Adams. This table defines the default cost rates to use for Scott's assignments.

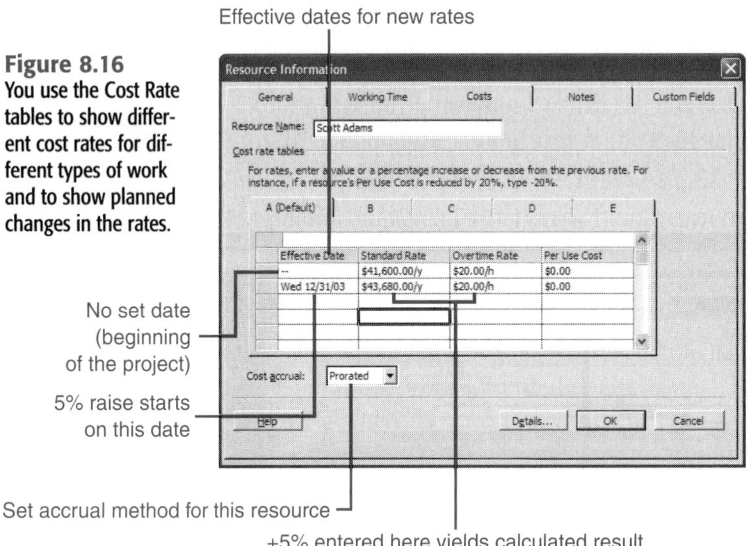

Figure 8.16
You use the Cost Rate tables to show different cost rates for different types of work and to show planned changes in the rates.

You can also allow for changes over time in these rates. For example, if you assume that inflation will cause your costs to rise by 5% per year, you could show different rates for each of the years during which the project lasts. In Figure 8.16, you can see that Scott Adams will get a raise on 12/31/2003, which is the end of his probationary period.

The entry in the first cell of the Effective Date column is always two dashes, signifying that there is no set start date for that level of rates. To enter additional levels for subsequent dates, enter the change date in the Effective Date column and then enter the values for the Standard Rate, Overtime Rate, and Per Use Cost columns. You can enter up to 25 dated rate changes in each of the five tabs.

If you want Project to calculate a percentage increase or decrease in one of the rates, enter the plus or minus percentage (with a percent sign), and when you leave the cell, Project applies that increase to the value in the cell just above it, displaying the result instead of the percentage you entered.

Often, the various cost tables allow for the use of a resource that might serve various functions within the project and be billed at different rates for various services. Say, for example, that your resource pool has a programmer who is billed at one rate for programming in Visual Basic but charges a different rate for programming in C#. By factoring in the resource's competency in using each programming language, a different rate can be charged for utilizing the same resource with various skill sets within the same project.

Cost Accrual

The Cost Accrual field determines when costs are recognized for standard and overtime costs. You can choose one of the three options: Start, End, or Prorated.

The default accrual method is Prorated, which means that if you mark a task as 25% completed, the actual costs for all assigned resources would be estimated to be 25% of the scheduled or estimated cost of those assignments.

If you choose Start as the accrual method, then as soon as you indicate that any of the task work has been done, Project considers the entire standard and overtime costs of the assignment as actual cost. Any report generated after the task has started shows the entire cost of the assignment as already having been incurred.

If you choose End, Project defers recognition of the actual cost until you enter a finish date and the assignment is 100% complete.

The Cost Accrual setting only matters when you're printing interim reports and when work on a task assignment has started but is not finished. The Cost Per Use value is always added to actual cost the moment work starts on a task, no matter what the Cost Accrual setting happens to be.

NOTE

The Cost Per Use value is always accrued at the Start of an assignment, no matter which accrual method you choose for the resource. Only the standard and overtime rates are affected by the accrual method you choose.

Code Field

The Code field can be used to enter any arbitrary code that you want to associate with a resource. It was used in earlier versions of Project to show cost accounting codes so that you could relate assignment costs to the organization's accounting system. The outline codes discussed in Chapter 5, "Creating a Task List," provide better functionality for that purpose because they allow you to create lookup lists to use when filling in the codes. You can enter any kind of information and can use any combination of up to 255 symbols and characters in this field.

8

TIP

> You can use the Code field to help keep track of miscellaneous information about specific resources. For example, you can use this field to include the Employee ID number, Social Security number, or phone number for the resource.

Workgroup Fields

Project can help you communicate with project team members by posting project information to Microsoft Project Server, where Microsoft Project Web Access makes it available as a Web page that the resource can view with a browser. With the advent of the Project 2003 edition, only Project Professional can work with Project Server. The email collaboration features have been removed in Project 2003.

➔ For information on using Project Server for collaboration, **see** Chapter 24, "Introduction to Microsoft Office Project Server 2003," **p. 965**.

NOTE

> If you have created the resource from the Assign Resources dialog box by choosing Add Resources from Address Book (see the section "Using the Assign Resources Dialog Box," earlier in this chapter), Project automatically puts the display name you chose from the address book into the Name field and the Email field. The email address enables reminder and notification emails to be sent by Project Server.

Using the Details Button

The Details button on the Resource Information dialog box helps you verify that Project can find an email address or helps you determine the display name or address to place in the Email field. When you click the Details button, Project attempts to find a matching display name for the Email field entry or, if that's blank, for the resource name.

If Project finds a single match, it shows the display name and email address for that entry in the address book.

Windows Account

If you are using Project Server, you can use the Windows Account button to find the resource's account name among the registered user accounts on the server and Project will place the account name in the box (refer to Figure 8.13).

Setting the Automatically Add New Resources and Tasks Option

The setting of the Automatically Add New Resources and Tasks option determines how Project reacts when you assign a resource to a task, but the resource is not currently in your pool of resources.

When you assign a resource name to a task, Project checks the resource pool for the name you have entered. By default, if Project doesn't find the resource in the resource pool, it adds it to the pool without asking your permission. All resource fields for the new name receive default values, and you must remember to update those fields later. You can end up with miscalculations in your costs if you neglect to go back and fill in the data for the new resource, because the default cost rates are usually zero.

This feature can be dangerous because it can allow you to accidentally create multiple resource names for the same resource. For example, suppose you have created a pool of resources that includes Peter, Maria, and Ivan. As you are assigning resources to tasks, you type in **Pete** instead of Peter. A new resource, Pete, is added to the list of resources, and you then have Peter, Maria, Ivan, and Pete. You end up not having a comprehensive list of the assignments for Peter, because they are split between the Peter and Pete resources.

If the Automatically Add New Resources and Tasks option is disabled, Project prompts you to choose whether it should add the resource to the resource pool. In Figure 8.17, the resource name Bill Kirkk was accidentally typed in an assignment, and Project prompts you to decide whether this is a new resource you want added to the pool. If you confirm that you want to add the resource, the resource is added, and you must remember to define the rest of the resource fields. In this example, you would choose the No button to avoid adding a misspelled version of Bill Kirk's name to the pool.

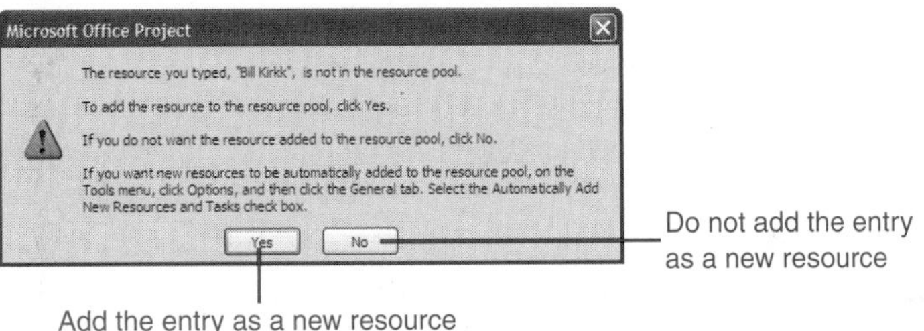

Figure 8.17
You should disable the Automatically Add New Resources and Tasks option so that you will be prompted if you attempt to assign a nonexistent resource.

➔ To see how resource assignments work, **see** "Assigning Resources and Costs to Tasks," **p. 359**.

TIP

It's a good idea to disable the Automatically Add New Resources and Tasks option to avoid the possibility of creating new resources if you make a typing error. If you are going to leave the option enabled, you should avoid typographical errors by always using the pick list of resource names that is available when you assign a resource to a task.

To disable or enable the Automatically Add New Resources and Tasks option, choose Tools, Options, and then click the General tab. Clear the check box Automatically Add New Resources and Tasks to disable the feature; check it to enable the feature.

8

SORTING RESOURCES

Normally, the resource names in the Resource Sheet view are listed according to ID number, which initially reflects the order in which you enter the resources. You can temporarily sort the resource list for a special report or for purposes of analysis. You can also sort the list and have Project permanently change the row ID numbers to match the new order.

NOTE

Permanently changing the ID numbers does not change the unique ID that is assigned when you add a resource.

CAUTION

Never change the order of resource rows by cutting and pasting if you have already assigned resources to tasks. Because cutting deletes the original resource, its assignments are deleted also, and the new resource you paste in will have a new unique ID and will have no assignments.

For example, after entering all the resources, you could permanently sort the list so that all the work resources are listed first—in alphabetical order by name—and then the material resources are listed in order by name (see Figure 8.18). Or, if you have used generic resource names, you might sort the list to show the generic names first and then the actual names. Another useful application of sorting would be if you want to see which resources add the most cost to the project; in this case, you could apply the Cost table to the Resource Sheet view, to show the cost of all the task assignments for each resource, and then you could sort the resource list by the Total Cost field, in descending order (see Figure 8.19).

You can sort a table by up to three fields at a time, and each of those fields can be sorted in ascending or descending order. For example, to produce the sort order in Figure 8.18, you would sort first on the resource Type field, in descending order (to put work resources before material resources). Then you would sort by the Resource Name field in ascending order (to list the names in alphabetical order).

NOTE

If you sort the resource table by the Standard Rate field, Project sorts the work resources that have been defined with annual cost rates using the hourly equivalent of the annual amount (based on 52 weeks of 40 hours each).

You can sort resources by choosing Project, Sort to display the Sort submenu. Sorting by cost, name, or ID is done so often that these options appear on the submenu. If you choose Cost, the sort order is in descending order, but both Name and ID sort in ascending order by default. These three choices use the current settings at the bottom of the Sort dialog box.

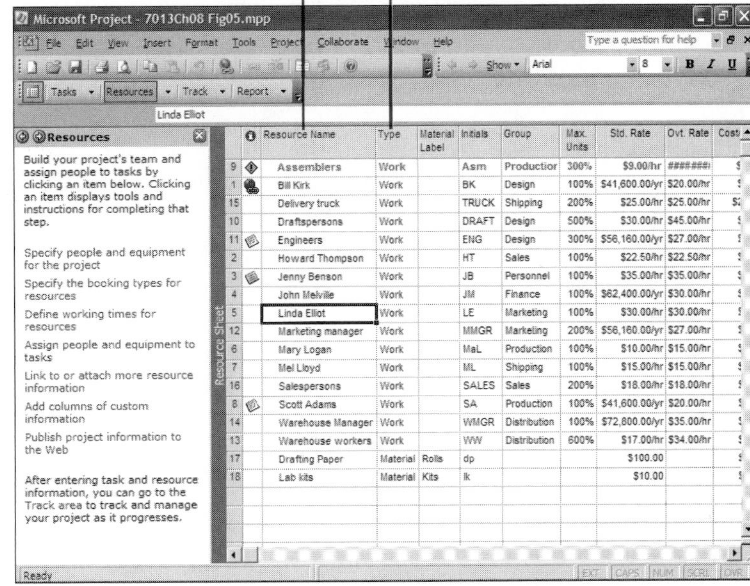

Figure 8.18
You can sort the resource pool by type and by name for special reports or as a permanent order with new ID numbers.

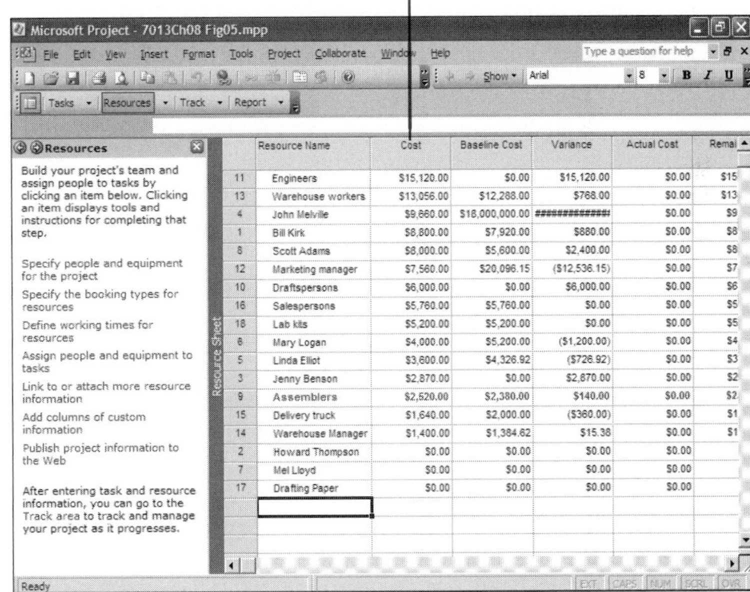

Figure 8.19
Sorting the resource list by total cost identifies the resources that add the most cost to the project.

8

If you choose Sort By at the bottom of the Sort submenu, Project displays the Sort dialog box, where you can define up to three fields to use for sorting, and each can be sorted in either ascending or descending order (see Figure 8.20).

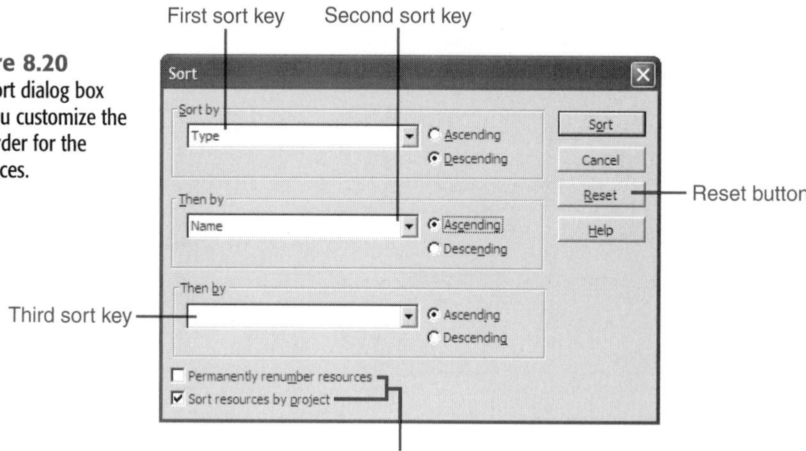

Figure 8.20
The Sort dialog box lets you customize the sort order for the resources.

To produce the sort order by Type and then by Name, as illustrated in Figure 8.18, follow these steps:

1. Display the Resource Sheet view, by choosing View, Resource Sheet.
2. Choose Project, Sort, Sort By to display the Sort dialog box.
3. You can sort on a maximum of three fields, using the Sort By, Then By, and Then By fields. Enter the first sort field in the Sort By box. In the example shown in Figure 8.20, the field is the resource Type field. Use the drop-down arrow to display the list of fields. Type the first letter of the field name (in this case, **t**), and Project highlights the first field that begins with that letter. Scroll down to select the Type field.
4. Click the Ascending button if you want the field sorted in normal order. In this example, you click the Descending button to list work before material resources.
5. In the first Then By box, select the Name field.
6. Select Ascending to sort the names in normal order.
7. Select the Permanently Renumber Resources check box if you want Project to change all ID numbers to match the new sort order. See the following caution if you elect to fill this check box.

CAUTION

If you fill the Permanently Renumber Resources check box in a sort operation, then as soon as the sort is completed, you should immediately open the Sort dialog box again, click the Reset button, and then click Sort. The Reset button disables the Permanently Renumber Resources option and sets the sort key to ID. If you don't take this extra step, the Permanently Renumber check box remains filled, and any future sorting with the Sort submenu also permanently renumbers your resources. And future sorting of tasks also permanently renumbers the tasks.

If you decide to cancel a sort operation and you have already filled the Permanently Renumber Resources check box, be sure to clear the check box (or click the Reset button, which also clears it) before clicking the Cancel button.

8. If you have combined several project files into a consolidated display, you can select the Sort Resources By Project to keep the resources for each project together and sort them within that grouping.
9. When all settings are ready, click the Sort button to close the dialog box and execute the sort, or click the Cancel button to close the dialog box without sorting the resources.

TIP

If you have done a custom sort previously in the same session and used three sort keys, the previous settings will be in place when you open the Sort dialog box. If you no longer need the extra sort keys, click the Reset button to clear the second and third sort keys.

NOTE

You can undo a sort operation, even after you permanently renumber the resources. Of course, you have to do it before you make any other changes. Just as a precaution, it might be wise to save a copy of the file before permanently renumbering the resources, just in case you want to undo it later.

You can put the rows back into the order in which they were originally entered by sorting on the Unique ID field.

When you are ready to return the list to the ID order, you can either press Shift+F3 (which cancels the current sort order) or choose Project, Sort, ID from the menu.

TIP

If you have sorted the resource list in a special order and have made changes that might make the order of the resources no longer fit the sort order you defined, you can press Ctrl+Shift+F3 to reapply the last sort instructions. For example, if you sorted by resource type and cost and then you make task assignments or change some resource cost rates, the list might no longer be in descending cost order within each type. You can press Ctrl+Shift+F3 to sort by type and cost again.

NOTE

> If you frequently use a custom sort order and would like to place it on the Sort submenu, you can create a macro and customize the Sort menu to include that sort order.

→ To learn the steps needed to create the macro **see** the chapter "Using Visual Basic with Project 2003," located on the CD accompanying this book.

→ **See** "Customizing Toolbars, Menus, and Forms," **p. 921**, for information about customizing the menu.

GROUPING RESOURCES

You can use the Group By command to sort tasks or resources into groups, based on the entries in one or more of the fields. For example, you could group resources by resource types (see Figure 8.21) or by the entries in the Group field. You can find a full explanation of the Group By command in Chapter 21, "Customizing Views, Tables, Fields, Filters, and Groups."

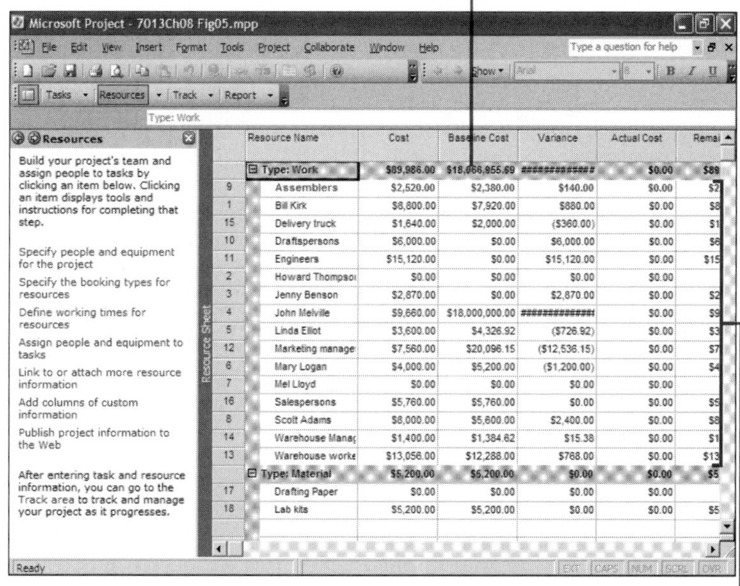

Figure 8.21
You can use the Group By command to sort resources and show summary totals for all resources in each group.

NOTE

> If you define a custom outline code for resources and use that field for the Group By order, Project displays the resource list in outline format by outline code number.

→ For a full discussion of using the Group By command, **see** "Creating Custom Groups," **p. 868**.

→ For instructions on creating custom outline codes, see "Customizing Fields," **p. 847**.

The difference between sorting and grouping is that in grouping, a Group By record is inserted at the start of each group as a pseudo-summary task. Project calculates totals for any numeric fields in this record for the records grouped beneath it. In Figure 8.21, the cost table has been applied and the fields show various measurements of the cost of assignments for the resources. You can see that the total cost of assignments for work resources is $89,986, whereas the total cost of assignments for material resources is only $5,200. The inserted grouping rows have no resource ID or row number, and they disappear when you remove the grouping.

TIP

If you create a custom outline code for resources–perhaps outlining them geographically by divisions, cities, departments, and job codes–you will find that grouping on that outline field produces a hierarchical outline with rolled-up costs that can be very useful.

If you use a custom text field to identify resource skills, you can insert the Work column in the table, and then group by the skills and by start dates to see the total amount of work needed for each skill per week or month. If you insert the Peak column (which shows the maximum number of units assigned for a resource at any moment during a given time period), you could forecast the number of units of a skill that are needed per time period.

To group resource records on the resource type as in Figure 8.22, choose Project, Group By, Work vs. Material Resources. To remove the grouping, choose Project, Group By, No Group (or press Shift+F3).

You can change the sort order while the resources are grouped. The sort settings are applied within each group—in other words, resources do not move to a different group as a result of the new sort order. (The resource list in Figure 8.22 is sorted by cost, in descending order.) You can also apply filters while the resources are grouped. The next section provides a discussion of filters.

FILTERING RESOURCES

You can use filters to select all the resources that meet some condition that you specify. For example, you might want to select all your material resources. The condition in this instance—that the resource Type must be Material—is called the filter *criterion*. Project has a built-in filter named the Resources - Material filter that imposes this criterion for you (see Figure 8.22).

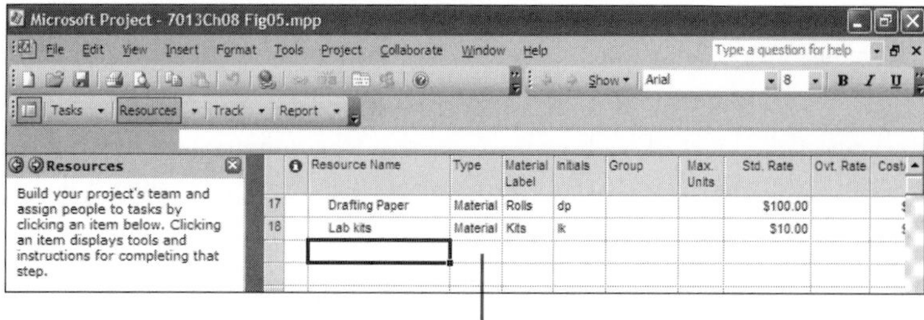

Figure 8.22
The resource pool is filtered to show only the material resources.

> **TIP**
>
> Filtering for specific resources is a great way to isolate only the resources that meet specific criteria that you've defined and to temporarily omit the other ones. By doing so, you can apply a change that affects an entire group of resources instead of having to find each one independently in order to make the change.

After Project selects the resources that meet the criteria, it normally changes the display to show only the selected resources, temporarily hiding all those that don't meet the criteria. However, you can also choose to use the filter as a *highlight filter*, and Project merely highlights the selected resources, without hiding all the others. In Figure 8.23, the Resources - Material filter is applied as a highlight filter. (The highlight in this figure is formatted with bold and a larger font size, to make it stand out more.)

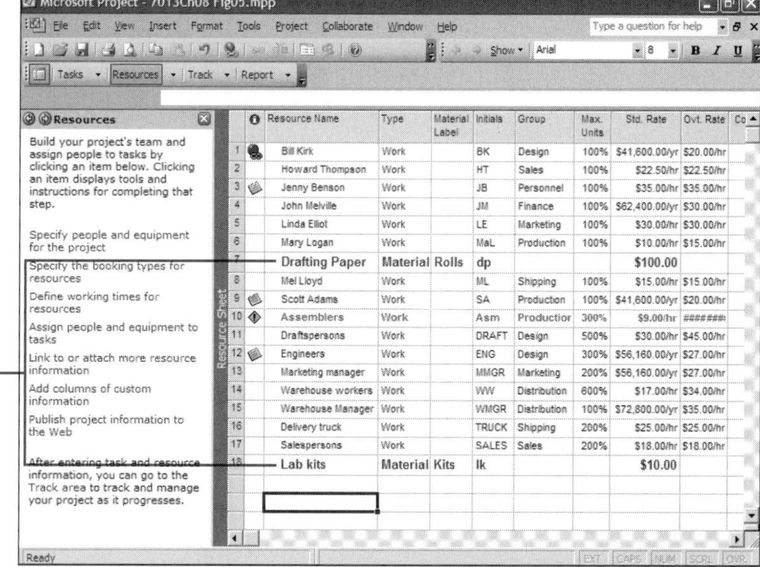

Figure 8.23
The filter has highlighted all the material resources, without hiding the resources that don't match the filter criterion.

→ If you want to customize the highlight that is used for filters, **see** "Formatting Text Displays for Categories of Tasks and Resources," **p. 778**.

When you finish using the filtered display, you must apply the All Resources filter to return to the normal display, or simply press the F3 key.

Another useful filter for reviewing how you categorized your resources is the Group filter. If you have entered keywords in the Group field, you can quickly filter the list to show all the resources that have a specific keyword. For example, if you entered department names in the Group field, you could filter the list for Production to identify all the resources that are managed by the Production department. If you used job titles, you could use the filter to isolate resources who might qualify for a certain resource assignment.

Project 2003 lets you filter the list of resources to be displayed in the Assign Resources dialog box. This dialog box is especially useful for substituting one resource for another. Usually, you want to substitute resources that have the same skill set. So, if you use a custom text field to enter skill keywords, you can filter the resource list to see all resources that might be suitable substitutes. If you include a comma-separated list of multiple skills, you need to define a special filter for this purpose.

TIP

Project 2003 also lets you use the Assign Resources dialog box to do availability based scheduling. When you highlight a task and check the Available to Work check box, Project will only show you resources that have a specified amount of availability during the time a task is scheduled. This technique is extremely valuable when trying to find the right people to work on a schedule that has inflexible dates.

If you have multiple group labels in the Group field and want to filter resources for one of the group labels, see the instructions in "Filtering for Labels Contained in the Group Field" in the "Troubleshooting" section near the end of this chapter.

After work on the project has begun, you can use filters to quickly check the status of resources, to see at a glance where problems might lie. The following partial listing illustrates how useful filters can be in managing a project. The following built-in filters allow you to identify specific categories of resources:

- You can use the Overallocated Resources filter to focus on resources that are assigned to more work than they can possibly finish in the scheduled time period.
- You can use the Cost Overbudget filter to find resources whose scheduled costs are more than you had budgeted.
- You can use the Work Complete filter to find resources who have finished all their work.
- You can use the Slipping Assignments filter to see which resources are taking longer than planned to finish their assignments.
- You can use the Resource/Assignments with Overtime filter to see which resources have been assigned overtime work.

→ For a complete list of the built-in filters and how to use them, **see** "Exploring the Standard Filters," **p. 761**.

→ For instructions on creating your own filters, **see** "Creating Custom Filters," **p. 859**.

NOTE

> You can apply filters only to full-screen views or views that are in the top pane of a combination view. You cannot apply filters to views in the bottom pane because those views are already filtered for the task or resource that is selected in the top pane.

You can apply a filter with the menu or by using the Filter button on the Formatting toolbar. If you want to apply the filter as a highlight filter, you must use the menu. For example, if you want to display only material resources in a resource view, you would follow these steps:

1. Display one of the resource views that has a table of resources in the top pane.
2. Click the Filter tool to display the drop-down list of resource filters, and then click Resources - Material.

   Or, choose Project, Filtered For to display the Filter menu, and then click Resources - Material.

   Whichever method you use, Project hides all but the resources that have Material in the resource Type field.

TIP

> To use a filter that is on the menu as a highlight filter, simply hold down the Shift key as you select the menu choices, and Project highlights the filtered (selected) records without hiding the other records.

TIP

> If you have applied a filter and then made changes that might alter which resources are selected by the filter, use Ctrl+F3 to reapply the filter.

TROUBLESHOOTING

PASTING A RESOURCE LIST FROM ANOTHER APPLICATION

How do I copy and paste a list of resources into Project from an Excel file or a Word file?

You can easily copy and paste a list of resources into Project from another application, but you might have to prepare the list correctly and prepare Project to receive the data or you will not get the results you intended.

→ For a more comprehensive discussion of importing data into Project, **see** Chapter 17, "Exporting and Importing Project Data with Other File Formats," **p. 631**.

If you have a list of resource names in another application that you would like to copy into Project and the list contains nothing but a column of resource names, then the process is very simple. You just follow these steps:

1. Select the list in the other application and use the Edit, Copy command (or press Ctrl+C) to copy the list to the Clipboard. It's important to note that the source list must be in separate rows in the other application—it must be in separate cells in the same column of a spreadsheet or on separate lines in a text document.
2. Select a cell in the Resource Name column of the Resource Sheet view in Project 2003. The pasted list begins in this cell.
3. Choose Edit, Paste, and Project copies the list into the Project document. All the new resources are given default values for the other resource fields.

If your list contains more columns than just the names, copying the list into Project is a little more complicated. For example, if the source list also contains a column with a money amount that you want to use as the standard rate for the resources, you must prepare the source list and also prepare the Resource Sheet view to accept the list when it is copied.

To prepare the source list, you must do these things:

- In a spreadsheet, you must arrange the data so that each resource is in a separate row and the data you want to copy is in adjacent columns. For example, the money amount column should be just to the right of the resource names column.
- In a text document, the resource name and the money amount must be on the same line, separated by a tab character or in adjacent cells of a table.
- If the money amounts are all hourly rates, they do not have to have a time period appended to them. But if they are rates for any other time period, you must append a slash and the word or abbreviation for the time period. For instance, if they are annual salaries, you must append **y** or **/year** to each of them. Without the appended time period, Project treats them as hourly rates.

To prepare the Project file to receive the resources, you must set up a table that has columns that are in the same order as the data you are pasting. To prepare the resource table, follow these steps:

1. Display the Resource Sheet view. Add temporary columns to receive the pasted data.
2. Click the column title for the column immediately to the right of the Resource Name column (by default, it is the Type column).
3. Select Insert, Column to display the Column Definition dialog box.
4. Select the Standard Rate field in the Field Name box.
5. Click OK to insert the column.
6. Repeat steps 2 through 5 for each column of data you are pasting in, being careful that the order of the columns matches the order of the data you are pasting.

After the source and the target location are prepared, select the source data and copy it to the Clipboard. Then select the blank Resource Name cell below any existing resource names and choose Edit, Paste.

After you have copied the data in, you should remove the columns you added to the display by selecting the column titles and choosing Edit, Hide Column.

FILTERING FOR LABELS CONTAINED IN THE GROUP FIELD

How do I filter the Group field when individual cells contain multiple keywords?

If you put multiple group labels in the Group field and want to filter the resource pool for one of those labels, you need to modify the standard Group filter to use the `contains` test. The same type of filter would also be used in a custom text field that lists multiple skills for some resources.

The standard Group filter uses the `equals` test when it searches for the label you ask it to filter for. The `equals` test requires that the entire entry in the Group field contains exactly the label you tell it to search for—no more and no less. If you create a copy of the Group filter that uses the `contains` test, it selects all resources whose Group fields *contain* the label you are searching for.

If you choose Project, Filter For, the Filters menu displays. Notice that the Group... filter is on the menu and that its first letter is underlined. The underlining signals that the user can simply type the underlined letter (that is, the hotkey) to select the item. The three periods at the end of the filter name are a convention that signals the user that the filter asks for input before executing; in this case, the filter asks the user to type in the group label that the user wants the filter to find.

The steps that follow add the Group Contains... filter to this menu and underline the first *n* as the hotkey. They start with a copy of the Group filter and merely change the name and the logical test from `equals` to `contains`.

To create a copy of the Group filter named the Group Contains filter, follow these steps:

1. Choose Project, Filter For, More Filters to display the More Filters dialog box.
2. Click the Resource button to display the list of defined resource filters.
3. Select the Group... filter in the Filters list.
4. Click the Copy button to display the Filter Definition dialog box for a new filter. The default name for the new filter is Copy of &Group, and you need to change that.
5. Change the entry in the Name field to **`Group Co&ntains...`**, with the ampersand before the first *n* and three periods at the end. The ampersand causes the following character to be the hotkey.
6. Leave the Show in Menu check box selected so that this filter appears on the Filter menu.
7. Click the equals entry in the Test column, and either type in **`contains`** or use the drop-down list to select it.

CHAPTER 9

Understanding Resource Scheduling

In this chapter

Learning About Resource Scheduling 322

Reviewing the Essential Components of Resource Assignments 322

Understanding the Resource Assignment Fields 324

Understanding the Work Formula 330

Choosing the Task Type 335

Understanding Effort-Driven Tasks 338

Modifying Resource Assignments 341

Understanding the Driver Resource Concept 355

Calculating Task Duration with Multiple Resources Assigned 357

LEARNING ABOUT RESOURCE SCHEDULING

This chapter prepares you for the next several chapters, in which you will be assigning resources to tasks and dealing with the changes in the schedule and the scheduling conflicts that occur when you assign resources to tasks in your project. This chapter gives you the background and understanding you need to use resource scheduling effectively. The details of using different views both to enter assignment information and to deal with changes and conflicts in the schedule are covered in the next two chapters.

This chapter explains how Microsoft Project calculates resource assignments, and schedules and reviews the controls you can exercise over those calculations. Project performs numerous calculations in the background as you edit the data for resource assignments, and many of them are not obvious—especially if you're not trained in project management or in using software such as Microsoft Project. It can be very frustrating to make a change that you assume will have only a small effect on a resource's schedule and then find that Project has amplified that small change into a chain reaction that affects many other resources and costs. This chapter helps you understand how Project proceeds with its calculations and helps you understand and predict the consequences of data entries, and therefore it helps you achieve the scheduling results you're looking for.

In Chapter 8, "Defining Resources and Costs," you learned about the data fields that you use to define resources and costs. This chapter shows you how the values in those fields influence the way Project schedules work when you assign a resource to a task.

With the topics in this chapter under your belt, you will be better able to focus on the many views, tools, and features of Project that you will see in the next two chapters, as you go through step-by-step instructions for actually entering the details of resource assignments and correcting problems in a schedule.

REVIEWING THE ESSENTIAL COMPONENTS OF WORK RESOURCE ASSIGNMENTS

When a work resource is assigned to work on a task (in other words, to spend time or effort on the task), Microsoft Project initially schedules work for the resource in specific time periods, based on several controlling factors that are outlined in the discussion that follows. Note that material resources do not "work," and therefore this discussion is about scheduling work resources. We will deal with material resources in the section "Assigning Material Resource Units."

Before you assign resources to it, a task already has scheduled dates that are derived from the factors discussed in Chapter 6, "Entering Scheduling Requirements." These include the defined project start date (or finish date), the task's duration, its links to other tasks, and any date constraint that might be imposed on it. There can also be task splits and/or a task calendar attached to the task. Figure 9.1 shows a project schedule before resources are assigned to the tasks and it incorporates the scheduling factors listed previously.

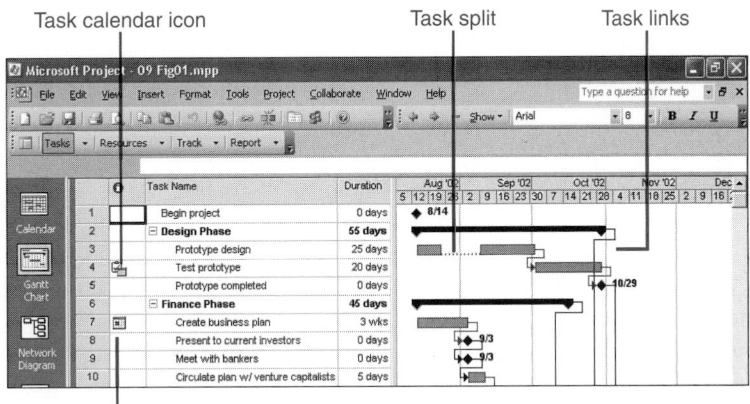

Figure 9.1
The start and finish dates in the task schedule are the basis for scheduling a resource when it is assigned to a task.

The schedule of work for an assigned resource is initially built around the task schedule based on the following factors:

- When you assign a resource to a task, Project schedules the resource's work to start at the time that the task is scheduled to start, and schedules the work to continue uninterrupted and at a constant rate during the times the task is scheduled until all the work assigned to the resource is completed.
- Normally, Project schedules work only during the dates and times that are defined as working time on the resource's calendar. Thus, Project does not schedule work for a resource during weekends, vacations, or other times that have been marked as nonworking on the resource calendar. Therefore, the task schedule changes to reflect the available working times on the resource calendar.
- If there is also a task calendar attached to the task, Project by default schedules work only during times that are working times on both the task calendar and the resource calendar. However, Project also allows you to disregard the resource calendar and schedule work for the resource whenever the task is scheduled.
- The amount of work scheduled on any given day is the number of working time hours defined for that day in the relevant calendar, multiplied by the number of resource units that are assigned to the task.

Project runs through all the calculations mentioned previously when you assign a resource to a task, and it calculates the dates and hours of work that constitute the initial assignment schedule. You can then modify the initial schedule to suit specific requirements or the needs of the resources. You can make a variety of adjustments to the assignment schedule, including the following:

- You can introduce a scheduled delay in the start of the work for one resource, leaving other resources to start the task as originally scheduled. For example, if a resource performs a specialized function on the task that is not needed until the task is almost finished, the work schedule for that resource can be delayed until toward the end of the task.

- You can interrupt the flow of assigned work by splitting the assignment, setting periods of no work for this resource in the middle of the schedule while other resources continue to work. For example, you can temporarily pull a resource off a long task to work on something more pressing by splitting that resource's assignment to the long task, to allow for the interruption.
- You can override the even distribution of the work that Project normally schedules by manually adjusting the amount of work assigned in each period, thus creating periods of high and low activity on the task for the resource. For example, if you know that a resource is needed only part time on a task during the second week but full time otherwise, you can edit the assignment for the resource during that week to be fewer hours per day than Project assigned.
- You can instruct Project to apply one of its predefined work contours, which vary the amount of effort scheduled during the assignment. For example, the *front-loaded* contour schedules the resource to put its full effort into the early periods of the assignment but to taper off to part-time involvement as the task nears completion.
- If the schedule has *overallocated* a resource (that is, assigned more units of the resource than the maximum units available of the resource), you can add a *leveling delay* to one of the assignments. This delay is similar to the scheduled delay mentioned previously, but it serves a different purpose. The scheduled delay likely remains in place permanently because that's the way the task should normally be scheduled. The leveling delay might become unnecessary if other ways are found to eliminate the resource's overallocation. For instance, you could substitute a different resource for the one that is overallocated, to reduce its workload during the time of the overallocation.

Before tackling these more advanced topics of customizing a resource assignment, you must first understand the basic assignment fields and how the initial schedule is calculated.

UNDERSTANDING THE RESOURCE ASSIGNMENT FIELDS

When you assign a resource to a task, you must at least identify the resource that is being assigned (in which case Project provides default values for the other essential assignment fields). You can optionally also specify the number of resource units to dedicate to the task and the amount of work that the assignment entails. The fields in which you enter this information are described in the following list and are shown in the task form illustrated in Figure 9.2.

ASSIGNING A RESOURCE NAME

You must identify the resource by its name (or its ID number, if you know it). In most views, the Resource Name field offers a drop-down list of the names that are already defined in the resource pool. You can select one of those names or you can type a new resource name, and Project adds that name to the pool as it assigns the name to the task.

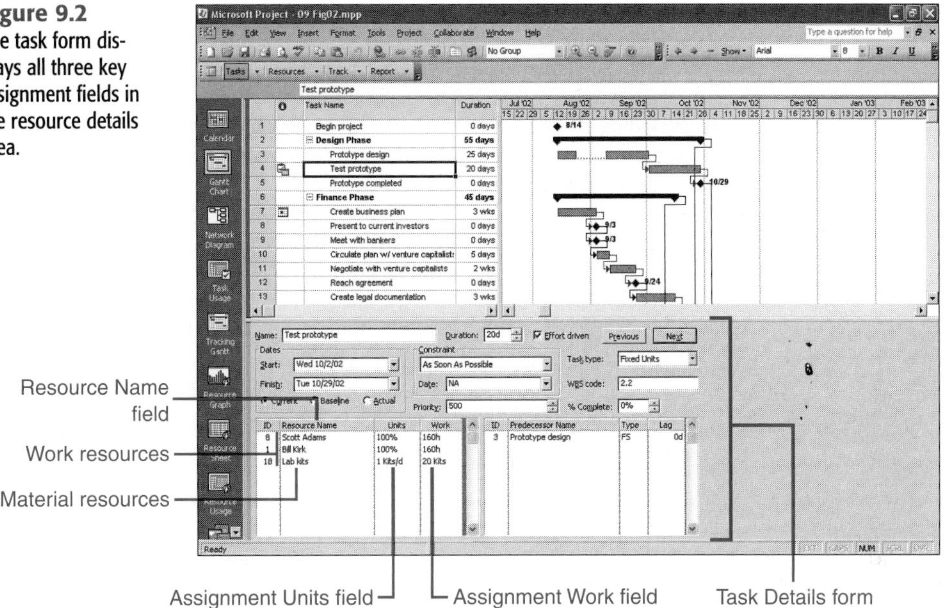

Figure 9.2
The task form displays all three key assignment fields in the resource details area.

9

CAUTION

> As described in Chapter 8, you should require that Project alert you before a new name is added to the resource pool, because it is possible to accidentally mistype the name of an existing resource. If you don't have the chance to intervene, Project creates a new variation of the same resource in the pool, with a slightly different spelling. Furthermore, the workload of the correctly spelled resource is misrepresented because it does not include the assignments that have been given to its typographically challenged alter-egos.

➔ To learn more about when and why Project adds to your resource pool, **see** "Setting the Automatically Add New Resources and Tasks Option," **p. 308**.

UNDERSTANDING THE ASSIGNMENT UNITS FIELD

Chapter 8 introduced the resource field named Max Units, which defines the maximum amount of a specific resource that can be assigned to tasks at any one time. Now we'll examine the assignment field named Assignment Units (which is usually labeled just Units). Assignment Units defines how much of a resource is assigned to an individual task.

NOTE

Project does not enforce the maximum number of available units when you make resource assignments. Project enables you to assign more units than the Max Units value when you are planning a project, but if you exceed the maximum for any resources, you get a special indicator by those resource names in the Resource Sheet or the Resource Usage view. If this happens, you might consider increasing the maximum units (by acquiring more resource units) or reducing the number of units assigned to various tasks.

Defining the Format for the Units Fields

By default, both the Max Units and Assignment Units fields show units for work resources in percentage format, but you can change these fields to decimal format. The percentage format has advantages, especially when you're assigning individual people resources, but it is inherently confusing when you're assigning consolidated or group resources. The following section explains the meaning of the percentage format.

In practice, many organizations define the decimal format of assigning resources "FTEs" or Full Time Equivalents. When not rounded to a whole number, the assignment is considered to be a part-time resource necessary to complete the effort, and works well in estimating the total number of "bodies" needed on a single task assignment.

To choose the format for the resource units fields, choose Tools, Options and select the Schedule tab. In the Show Assignment Units as A field, select Decimal or Percentage. This setting affects the display for all work resources.

Material resources are always shown in decimal format, no matter which format you choose for work resources. For both work and material resource types, the Assignment Units field defines the number of resource units to be assigned to a particular task.

Assigning Work Resource Units

When the Assignment Units field for a programmer who is named Juanita is 100%, the assignment is a full-time assignment, and Project schedules 100% of Juanita's time on the task. If the Assignment Units value is 25%, Juanita is not working full time on this task; instead, she is probably assigned to several different tasks each day and spends no more than 25% of her time on this task. The percentage format is easy to understand for individual named resources.

However, when you assign a team of five programmers to a task, it's more intuitive to say that the units should be the decimal number 5 instead of the percentage 500%. It's even more difficult to understand the percentage format when you assign 25000% assembly-line workers (which is clearer as 250, in decimal format) or 1600% delivery trucks (that is, 16 delivery trucks). On the other hand, if you use decimal format for an individual resource, assigning Juanita to a task at .25 units is not very intuitive either.

The percentage format emphasizes the way Project uses the Assignment Units field. Project uses this field to calculate how many hours of work it will schedule for the resource per hour of working time on the calendar. For example, suppose you have a task that a team of two carpenters can finish in 4 hours. If you assign the two carpenters to the task, you expect 1 hour of work from each of them during every hour of time they spend on the task. And that's what Project does if you assign units of 200%: It assigns 2 hours of work for every hour of working time on the calendar until the task is complete.

Thus, for work resources, Project uses the Units field as a *multiplier*, to calculate how many hours of work to schedule per hour of working time on the calendar:

- If the Assignment Units value is 100%, Project schedules 1 hour of work for every hour of working time on the calendar until the task is complete.
- If the Assignment Units value is 200%, Project schedules 2 hours of work for every working hour on the calendar.
- If the Assignment Units value is 25%, Project schedules work equal to 25% of the available time during each period on the calendar until the task is complete.

NOTE

Note that when you assign 25% units of a resource to work on an 8-hour task (which is 2 hours of work during the 8 hours), Project schedules 15 minutes of work each hour. This would accurately portray the schedule for a chemist who needs to monitor an experiment for 15 minutes each hour. But in many other cases, the resource would probably do the 2 hours of work at one or two sittings. In this case, if you're not concerned about the exact amount of time the resource will actually spend during each hour, but you are content with the overall total (2 hours), then you can safely ignore the difference between Project's schedule and the way the work would actually be done. If you want the resource to work full time for 2 hours and then be idle for the rest of the task duration, enter the units as 100% and specify that the work will be only 2 hours.

For work resources, the default Units value for an assignment is generally 100% (or 1, in decimal format). However, if the Max Units value for the resource is less than 100%, the default assignment value is the same as the Max Units value. You can assign any number of units between 0% and 6,000,000,000% (between 0 and 60,000,000 units, in decimal format).

You can also assign a resource to a task with 0% units. In that case, Project calculates the work as zero and consequently calculates the cost of the work as zero also. For instance, you could assign zero units when you assign a contractor to a task and the contractor agrees to complete the task for a fixed fee. The amount of work is the responsibility of the contractor—all you need to record is the fee, which you would enter in a cost field.

NOTE

> Note that if the only resource assigned to a task is assigned at 0%, Project makes the task a milestone. It is generally better to handle fixed-cost tasks like this example as described in "Assigning Fixed Costs and Fixed Contract Fees," **p. 396.**

NOTE

> You can enter fractions of a percentage in the Assignment Units field, but they display as rounded whole percentage numbers. If you want to specify that a worker spends 1 hour per 8-hour day on a task (that is, one-eighth, or 12.5%, of a day), you see 13% displayed after you enter 12.5%. Project uses fractional percents in its calculations (down to tenths of a percent); it just doesn't display them.

ASSIGNING MATERIAL RESOURCE UNITS

For material resources, the Units value is always formatted as a decimal. If you fail to enter the assigned units, Project supplies the default value, which is 1 followed by the material label you defined for the resource. For example, if you defined the material resource Concrete with the label `Yd` (for cubic yard), the default units supplied by Project would be 1 Yd. This means that the task consumes exactly 1 cubic yard of concrete.

ASSIGNING FIXED CONSUMPTION RATES

If you enter just a numeral (or a numeral with the material label) in the Units column for a material resource assignment, it is called a *fixed consumption rate* for the resource. The amount consumed is fixed and independent of the task duration. For example, to assign 4 yards of concrete to a task, you could type `4` or `4 yd`; either way, Project would respond with the value 4 Yd. If the task duration changes, this consumption rate does not change.

Note that if you type something Project doesn't understand, such as `4 yards` when the material label is Yd, Project displays a warning that it is not a valid Units value (see Figure 9.3). The simplest method is to enter just the numeral and let Project provide the label.

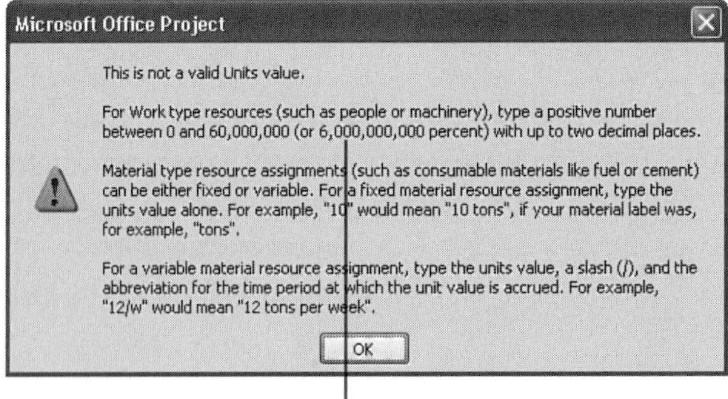

Figure 9.3
Entering an unrecognized Units value causes Project to display this warning.

ASSIGNING VARIABLE CONSUMPTION RATES

You can assign material resource units that have a *variable consumption rate*, where the total amount consumed depends on the duration of the task. To create a variable consumption rate, simply enter the units, followed by a forward slash (/) and the abbreviation for the time period during which that many units would be consumed. For example **4/d** or **4 Yd/d** means 4 yards per day.

For example, suppose you are using a bulldozer on a task that consumes about 6 gallons of fuel per hour. You can define a material resource Diesel Fuel with the label Gal (for gallons). Then, you can assign the fuel to the task by entering **6/h** or **6 gal/h** in the Units field. For either entry, Project displays the equivalent, 6 Gal/hour, in the Units field. Project then calculates the total number of units consumed by multiplying this rate by the task duration.

ASSIGNING THE WORK

A work resource spends hours of time or effort attending to the task, and you measure its contribution in hours (or days, or some other time unit). It is this effort of the work resources that causes a task to have duration in the first place: It takes time to complete the necessary work on a task. In fact, if you estimate the duration for a task, you are really thinking about how long it will take the work resources to complete the work associated with the task. A material resource, on the other hand, doesn't expend effort: It is passively consumed by the task. You measure its contribution in physical units consumed.

Both the hours of work for work resources and the units consumed for material resource are displayed in the Work field. However, in calculating the total work for a task, Project ignores values for material resources and sums just the hours for the work resources.

ASSIGNING WORK WITH WORK RESOURCES

For work resources, the term *work* (which is also called *effort*) measures the time actually expended by a resource on the task during the assignment. By default, Project displays work in hours, but you can change the default to any of the standard time units (minutes, hours, days, weeks, or months). To change the time unit used for displaying work, choose Tools, Options and click the Schedule tab. Select the time unit in the Work Is Entered In list box.

Work can be entered by the user, but if it is not, Project calculates it automatically. No matter what time unit you use to display work, you can enter work by using any time unit, as long as you follow the number with the time unit label.

If a work resource is scheduled full time (100%) on a task that has a duration of 1 week (40 hours), the resource is assigned to 40 hours of work (100% of 40 hours). However, if the resource is assigned to the task only half time (that is, Units is 50%), the resource is assigned only 20 hours of work. If two resource units work full-time (200%) all week, there are 80 hours of work. Other things being equal, the following hold true:

The longer the duration of the task, the more work is scheduled.

The larger the resource units assigned, the more work is scheduled.

The amount of work that Project schedules for the resource is tied to the duration of the task and the number of units assigned to the task. This relationship is defined more precisely in the section "Understanding the Work Formula," later in this chapter.

Assigning Work with Material Resources

For material resources, the Work field shows the total number of physical units of the resource that are consumed in completing the task. If you enter the units, Project calculates the work units for you.

For fixed-rate consumption assignments, the Work field is the same as the Units field. If you assign **`48 Gal`** of fuel, the Work field shows 48 Gal. If, however, you assign **`48 Gal/d`** to a 10-day task, Project calculates the value 480 Gal for the Work field.

Understanding the Work Formula

As described previously in this chapter, Project uses assignment units as a multiplier to calculate how much work it must schedule. When you assign two carpenters (200%) to work on a task with a duration of 4 hours, Project schedules 2 hours of work for each of the 4 hours of duration. The total work is therefore 8 hours.

The formula for calculating work is as follows:

Duration × Units = Work

In symbols, it is represented as follows:

$$D \times U = W$$

That is, you multiply the task duration by the assigned units to calculate work.

NOTE

> These formulas do not apply to assignments for material resources that have a fixed consumption rate. For those assignments, the value in the Work field is identical to the value in the Units field. The formulas do apply to material resources that have variable consumption rates. However, these formulas were developed and implemented before the material resource type was introduced, and the following discussion makes more sense if you think in terms of work resources.

Simple algebra can be used to reformulate this equation to calculate values for Duration when Work and Units are given:

Duration = Work / Units

In symbols, it looks like this:

$$D = W / U$$

Also, when Duration and Work are given, Project can calculate Units with this variation of the formula:

Units = Work / Duration

In symbols, it looks like this:

$U = W / D$

Although the duration can be displayed in minutes, hours, days, weeks, or months, Project converts the duration to minutes when calculating work and then displays it in the default unit for work, which is normally the hour. Thus, if a 1-day task has 100% units assigned to it (that is, one full-time unit of the resource), the work is calculated as follows:

$D \times U = W$

8 hrs × 100% = 8 hrs

APPLYING THE WORK FORMULA IN NEW ASSIGNMENTS

Before you assign resources to a task, it has duration but usually does not have a work value associated with it. When you create the resource assignments, Project calculates the work for the assignments and sums that value in the task's Work field. As you will see, in some cases the work called for in an assignment can't be completed within the initial duration estimate for the task, and Project might have to change the task duration to accommodate the needs of the assignments. If the task has multiple resources assigned and some of those assignments take longer to complete than others, the task duration is calculated to be at least as long as the longest assignment. However, if the task is a fixed-duration task, Project can't recalculate duration. See the section "Choosing the Task Type," later in this chapter, for more information.

To ingrain your understanding of how Project calculates the changes brought about by assigning resources, we will examine the simplest case first—where you assign a single resource in an initial assignment. Then we will examine the case where you assign multiple resources in an initial assignment. After that, we will examine how Project responds when you change existing assignments.

You should experiment with each of these cases to solidify your understanding. Display the Gantt Chart view and use the Window, Split command to display the Task Form view in the bottom pane. Right-click over the Task Form view and choose Resources and Predecessors from the Detail list. The Assignment Units and Work fields appear next to the resource name in the resource details (refer to Figure 9.2). Try different values for units and work until you feel you can predict the outcome when you create an assignment.

ASSIGNING A SINGLE RESOURCE IN AN INITIAL ASSIGNMENT

The duration for a task is already defined before you assign the first resource to the task. Therefore, one of the values in the work formula—task duration—is already established. Project handles your entries when assigning the initial resource slightly differently for work and material resources, so we will consider them separately.

ENTERING A NEW ASSIGNMENT FOR WORK RESOURCES

The following cases show what happens for the initial assignment of a work resource. The distinctions are based on which fields you fill in: Units only, Work only, or both Units and Work. All the cases assume that the task has a duration of 1 day, and that days and weeks are defined to be 8 hours and 40 hours, respectively. They also assume that the task type is Fixed Units (see "Choosing the Task Type," later in this chapter, for more information).

Project's responses to your entries when creating a work resource assignment are as follows:

- If you enter the resource name when creating the assignment and you don't provide the values for units or work, Project assumes that you want the default units (usually 100%) and calculates the work from the duration and units. For example, if you assign a work resource to a 1-day task without specifying the units, Project supplies 100% to the Units field and calculates 8 hours for the Work field, as follows:

  $D \times U = W$

  $8 \text{ hrs} \times 100\% = 8 \text{ hrs}$

- If you enter the Units value, Project uses that value with the duration to calculate the work. For example, if you assign a resource to the 1-day task and enter 50% in the Units field, Project calculates the work as follows:

  $D \times U = W$

  $8 \text{ hrs} \times 50\% = 4 \text{ hrs}$

  The task duration is still 1 day.

- If you enter the Work value but do not supply the units, Project assumes that you want the default units (usually 100%) and calculates a new value for the duration, based on the specified work and the assumed value for units. For example, if you assign a resource to the 1-day task and enter 16 hours in the Work field but leave the Units field blank, Project calculates a new Duration value as follows, because it takes more than 1 day for a single resource unit to complete 16 hours of work:

  $D \times U = W$

  $D \times 100\% = 16h$

  $D = 16h / 100\% = 16$ hours (that is, 2 days)

- If you enter both the Units and Work values, Project recalculates the existing task duration, using the new entries. For example, if you assign Units the value 200% and Work the value 32 hours, Project calculates a new task Duration by using this variation of the work formula:

  $D \times U = W$

  $D \times 200\% = 32h$

  $D = 32h / 200\% = 16$ hours (that is, 2 days)

ENTERING A NEW ASSIGNMENT FOR MATERIAL RESOURCES

When the resource is a material resource, there are fewer alternatives to consider than with work resources. Again, assume that the task is a 1-day task. This time, the resource is the material resource Concrete, and its label is Yd. Recall that for material resources, the Units field is always displayed in decimal format. Project's responses to your entries when creating a material resource assignment are as follows:

- If you just enter the material resource name but don't provide either the Units value or the Work value of the assignment, Project assumes that the Units value is 1 and calculates the work to be 1 Yd. For example, if you assign the Concrete resource to a 1-day task without specifying the units, Project supplies 1 Yd to both the Units and Work fields.
- If you enter the Units value as a numeral (in other words, as a fixed consumption rate), Project enters that value into both the Units and the Work fields. For example, if you assign the Concrete resource to the 1-day task and enter **2** in the Units field, Project supplies 2 Yd to both the Units and Work fields.
- If you enter the units value as a variable consumption rate, Project uses that rate with the task duration to calculate the Work field. For example, if you enter **2/d** in the Units field, Project converts that to 2 Yd/day and multiplies that value by the duration (1 day) to calculate the Work field entry 2 Yd.
- If you enter the Work value but do not supply the units, Project assumes that the amount you entered has a fixed consumption rate and puts that amount in both the Units and Work fields.
- If you enter a number in the Units field (a fixed consumption rate) and also enter a number in the Work field, Project ignores the entry in the Units field and places the Work field entry in both the Units and Work fields.
- If you enter a variable consumption rate in the Units field and also enter a number in the Work field, Project recalculates the duration so that the consumption rate yields the total units in the Work field.

USING MULTIPLE RESOURCES IN AN INITIAL ASSIGNMENT

One of the advantages of using the Task Form view to create assignments is that the initial assignment can include all resources that are to be assigned to the task, and you can specify units and/or work for each assignment. Other methods of assigning resources require you to complete each assignment individually or don't let you regulate both units and work. As you will see in later sections of this chapter, individually assigning multiple resources to a task creates additional variations in how Project calculates the task work and duration. Therefore, listing all the resources in the initial assignment sometimes saves you time and annoying hassles.

CAUTION

> You must be very careful when including variable-consumption-rate material resources along with work resources in an initial assignment. Project often calculates unexpected results for this combination. In fact, you should include in the initial assignment only the work resources and any fixed-consumption-rate material resources; you can add the variable-consumption-rate material resources later.

To create multiple assignments with the initial assignment, you simply enter multiple rows in the resource details table before you click the OK button. Project then calculates each of the assignments individually, using the principles outlined previously and using the existing task duration in each calculation.

For example, Figure 9.4 shows two task forms. The top form shows the initial assignment being created, and the bottom form shows the result after the OK button is clicked. The task is a 4-day task; four cement workers are being assigned, along with a supervisor who will spend only 50% of her time on the task. The task will also consume 10 cubic yards of concrete.

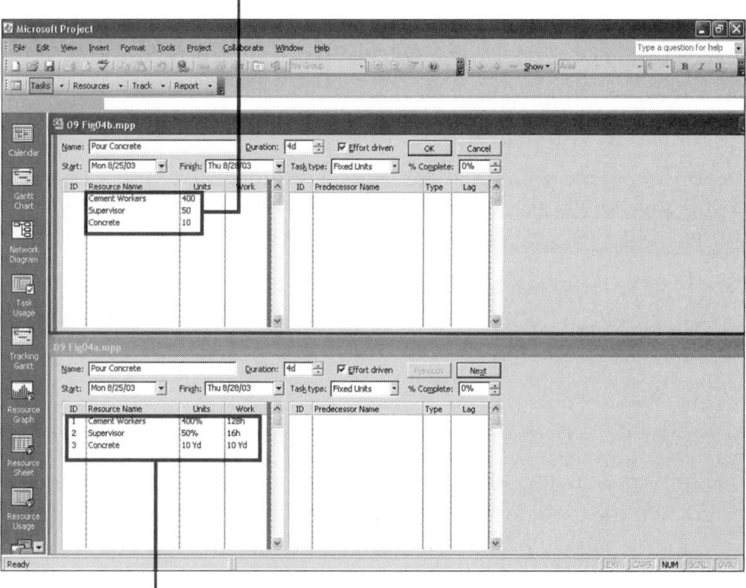

Figure 9.4
You can initially assign multiple resources by listing them all before clicking OK.

APPLYING THE WORK FORMULA TO CHANGES IN EXISTING ASSIGNMENTS

In the examples so far in this chapter, it has seemed that Project is free to recalculate any of the three variables in the work formula. However, in the next section you will see that one of the three variables in the equation is always fixed for a task, and therefore it is fixed for any assignments to that task. Project is not allowed to change the fixed value when it has to recalculate the work equation for an assignment.

For example, by default, tasks are created as Fixed Units tasks, as indicated by the underline in the following formula:

$$D \times \underline{U} = W$$

Thus, if you change the duration, Project has to leave the units unchanged and must recalculate the work, or if you change the work, Project has to change the duration. You can define which variable is fixed for a task and is therefore fixed for all that task's assignment calculations. In this way you can control how Project responds when you make changes in assignments.

CHOOSING THE TASK TYPE

All tasks are one of three types, as defined in the Task Type field: Fixed Units (the default), Fixed Work, or Fixed Duration. Sometimes the task by its very nature falls easily into one of the three categories. Perhaps the task duration is set by a client, by the government, or by another organization, and you must work within that time frame. You could define that task as a fixed-duration task to keep Project from changing the duration. On the other hand, you might contract to provide a fixed amount of work for a client. In that case, you could define that task as a Fixed Work task so Project can't change the amount of work that is scheduled.

You can also use temporary changes in the Task Type field to control how Project responds to an assignment change. For instance, if you want to increase the duration for a task but keep the total amount of work constant, you can make it a Fixed Work task and then change the duration.

Table 9.1 summarizes which variable Project recalculates when you change a value in an existing assignment. The table assumes that your initial change is an increase in the respective variables (as indicated by the plus signs in that column). If your initial change is a decrease, you can simply reverse the plus and minus signs in the columns to the right.

The first column lists the variable that you might change. The three columns to the right show which variable Project recalculates as a result; the plus or minus sign indicates the direction of the resulting change. The formulas in Table 9.1 use an underline for the fixed variable, to help you follow the logic of the changes. Thus, in the first row, an increase in Duration for a Fixed Units task leads to an increase in Work, but for a Fixed Work task it leads to a decrease in Units.

TABLE 9.1 TASK TYPES AND WORK FORMULA CALCULATIONS

Initial Change	Fixed Units Result	Fixed Work Result	Fixed Duration Result
+ Duration	+ Work	- Units	*- Units*
+ Units	*- Duration*	- Duration	+ Work
+ Work	+ Duration	*+ Duration*	+ Units
Formulas:	$D \times \underline{U} = W$	$D \times U = \underline{W}$	$\underline{D} \times U = W$

When an initial change is the fixed variable itself, the rule is a little more complicated. Those results are underlined in the table. Remember that duration is a task variable and that units and work are assignment variables. When you change one of the assignment variables (Units or Work), and it is the fixed variable, Project leaves the other assignment variable alone and changes task duration. When Duration is fixed and you change it, Project leaves the assignment work unchanged and adjusts the units.

As an example of how you can use this powerful tool, even in initial assignments, suppose you want to force Project to calculate the number of resource units you need to assign when you know the duration of the task and the amount of work you want done. You can make the task a Fixed Duration task and enter the amount of work. Project has to calculate the necessary units in order to keep the work formula in balance.

You can define a task's type in the Task Information dialog box and in the Task Form view (or you can add the Task Type field to any task table). Figure 9.5 shows the Task Type field in the Task Information dialog box and on the Task Form view.

As mentioned previously, the default task type for Project is Fixed Units, which means that new tasks are automatically assigned the Fixed Units task type. You can change the default type for new tasks in a project by selecting Tools, Options. In the Options dialog box, select the Schedule tab and the type you want as the default in the Default Task Type field (see Figure 9.6).

It might be helpful now to add recognition of task types to the rules about how the work formula is calculated. Project responds in the following ways when you create a new assignment for a task:

- If you enter a value in Units and leave the Work field blank, Project calculates the unknown Work (because both Units and Duration have been given values). This is true no matter what the task type.
- If you enter a value in Work and leave the Units blank, Project's calculation depends on the task type:
    - If the task is not a Fixed Duration task (that is, if it's Fixed Units or Fixed Work), Project adjusts the Duration value. It assumes that the Units value is the default (100%, or less if the Max Units value is less) and calculates the Duration value that is necessary for the resource to complete the amount of work you assigned.

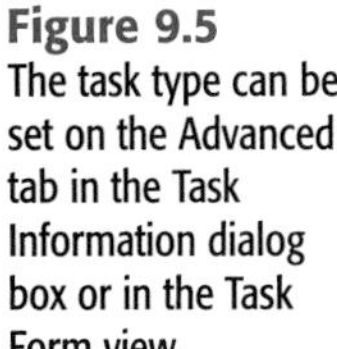

Figure 9.5
The task type can be set on the Advanced tab in the Task Information dialog box or in the Task Form view.

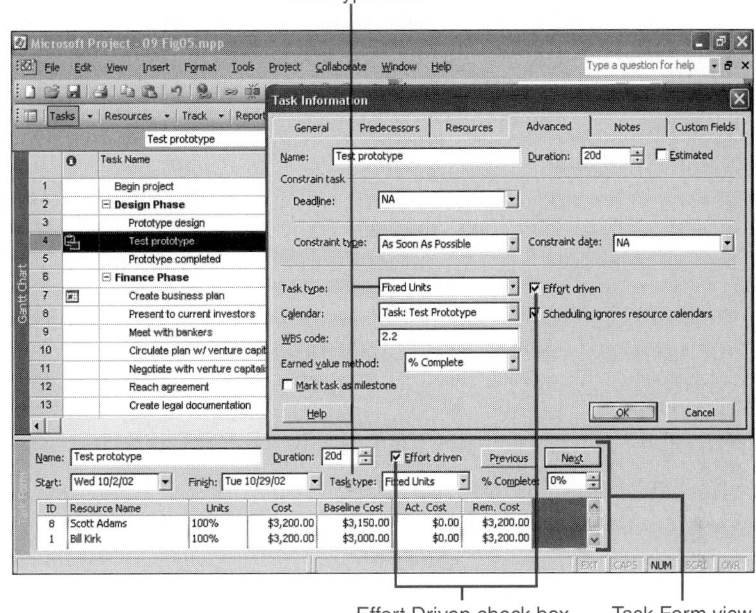

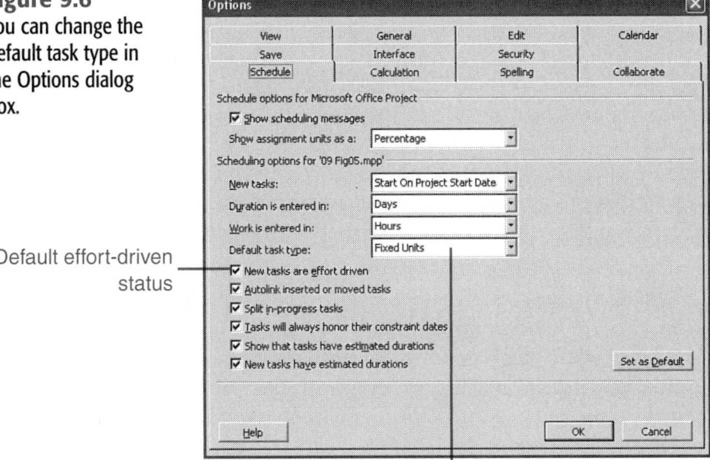

Figure 9.6
You can change the default task type in the Options dialog box.

    - However, if the task is a Fixed Duration task, Project cannot change the Duration entry, and it calculates the Units needed to complete the Work value you entered and places that value in the Units field.

- If you entered values in both Units and Work, Project again bases its calculations on the task type:
    - If the task is not a Fixed Duration task, Project adjusts the Duration to accommodate the Work and Units values you entered.
    - If the task is a Fixed Duration task, Project keeps the Work amount you entered and calculates a new Units value that can do the specified work in the given (fixed) duration.

9

Understanding Effort-Driven Tasks

You saw in the previous sections that if a task is marked as Fixed Work and you increase the number of units in an assignment, Project leaves the Work amount the same and reduces the duration of the task. For example, suppose a Dock Workers resource has been assigned to load 100 boxes onto a delivery truck. The original assignment is 200% units (2 people), but then you change it to 400% units (4 people). Because the work is presumed to be fixed, you would expect Project to cut the duration in half.

The same concept can apply when you increase the number of named resources assigned to a task, for that constitutes adding units also. If two individual resources, named Sam and Bob, are originally assigned to load the boxes, but then you add Juan and Bill to help with the task, you would want Project to cut the duration in half.

For every activity within a project, you will arrive at an effort estimate and cost estimate for each resource assigned. Often, in an attempt to decrease the amount of time a task takes, additional resources are added to the activity. While most project management software calculates the effort to be divided equally among both resources (1 person taking 1 week, 2 people taking 1/2 week, and so on), most experts believe that the most you can expect in decreasing the duration of a task in this manner is 40% because of an expected "learning curve," or "ramp-up time" for the newly acquired resource.

As you continue to add people to an effort, the time is decreased, but the cost/labor hours may also go up, depending on the cost rates associated with the assigned resources. At some point, this goes vertical and is called the "crash point," which suggests that no additional efficiencies can be realized by adding resources and that the task is going to take a fixed amount of time regardless of the number of resources involved. This is referred to as the "law of diminishing returns."

Project managers need to account for this fact of life, that is that adding resources will not automatically reduce the duration of a task, regardless of what the project management software calculates.

The latter case is an example of an *effort-driven* task calculation: You want the total amount of work for the task to be fixed so that when you add resources to the assignment list, Project reduces the workload for the resources who are already assigned to the task. By the same token, if you have to remove a resource from the assignment, it means more work for the resources that remain assigned to the task, and Project calculates increased amounts of work for them. When you add resources to an effort-driven task, Project reduces the duration; when you remove resources, Project lengthens the duration.

NOTE

> When we use the phrases *add resources* and *remove resources*, we mean that you add or delete names on the list of assignments. Changing the number of resources assigned is not the same as changing the number of units assigned for one resource.

However, a task might not need to be treated as an effort-driven task for all increases or decreases in resources. Suppose that you decide to add Andy to the box-loading task, to monitor the work and make sure inventory records are accurate. This is not the same work; it is an additional aspect of the task, and you want Project to add Andy's work to the total of the work done by the people who are moving the boxes. This is an example of a calculation that is not effort driven: You do not want the work to remain the same after you add the new resource name to the task.

By default, Project makes all new tasks effort driven, but you should consider the effort-driven status of a task before you increase or decrease resources, in order to be sure that Project calculates the change correctly. The Effort Driven field is a check box on the Task Information dialog box and on the Task Form view (refer to Figure 9.5).

NOTE

> Adding or removing material resource names to the list does not affect effort-driven calculations because the work for material resources is not hours of effort but units consumed.

NOTE

> When you make a task a Fixed Work task, it automatically becomes an effort-driven task because effort-driven means "fixed work." Project automatically fills the Effort Driven check box and dims it so that you can't clear it.

The effort-driven status of a task is not a factor in the calculations when you first assign resources to a task because there is no work defined for the task until after the first work assignment. Thus, if you are using the Task Form view and you create a list of resource names with assignments before clicking the OK button, Project calculates the hours of work for each of the work resources and sets the sum as the total work amount for the task.

You can change the default effort-driven status for new tasks in the Options dialog box, right next to where you change the default task type (refer to Figure 9.6). Choose Tools, Options from the menu and select the Schedule tab on the Options dialog box. Deselect the New Tasks Are Effort Driven check box to change the default setting.

If, after the initial assignment of resources to a task, you add more work resources or remove some of the work resources, Project must consider the effort-driven status of the task in its calculations. If Effort Driven is on, as it is by default, Project redistributes the total work for the task across the revised work resource list, prorating the work for each resource according to its share of the total number of work resource units assigned to the task.

When you increase resources for an effort-driven task, Project reapportions the work among the existing resources, and it does so in proportion to the resources' share of the total work units assigned. Suppose that Mary and Scott are initially assigned to a 5-day (40-hour) effort-driven task, as shown in Figure 9.7. Figure 9.7 is the table portion of a Task Usage view, showing three numbered tasks and their resource assignments indented beneath them.

Task 1 (Task A) shows the original assignment of Mary and Scott. The total work is 60 hours, and because it is an effort-driven task, the work will remain fixed if you assign more or fewer resources.

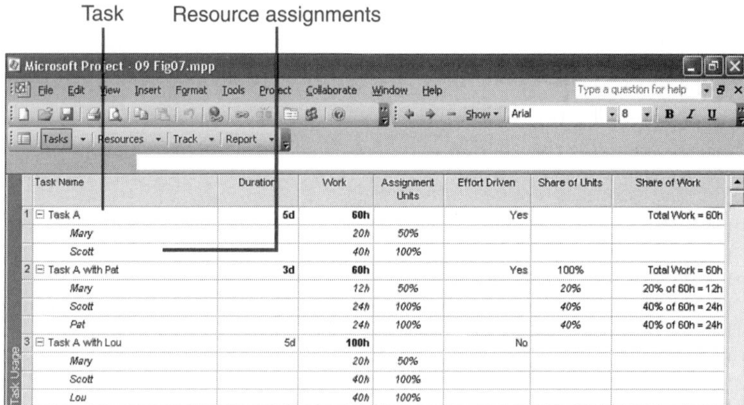

	Task Name	Duration	Work	Assignment Units	Effort Driven	Share of Units	Share of Work
1	Task A	5d	60h		Yes		Total Work = 60h
	Mary		20h	50%			
	Scott		40h	100%			
2	Task A with Pat	3d	60h		Yes	100%	Total Work = 60h
	Mary		12h	50%		20%	20% of 60h = 12h
	Scott		24h	100%		40%	40% of 60h = 24h
	Pat		24h	100%		40%	40% of 60h = 24h
3	Task A with Lou	5d	100h		No		
	Mary		20h	50%			
	Scott		40h	100%			
	Lou		40h	100%			

Figure 9.7
Resource assignments are displayed slightly indented beneath each task in the Task Usage view.

Task 2 (Task A with Pat) shows what happens when you assign Pat to the task at 100% units. Because Task A is effort driven, the total work remains unchanged, at 60 hours. You can see in the Assignment Units column that the sum of the units assigned is 250%. The custom column Share of Units shows that Mary contributes 20% of the total units (50%/250%), and Scott and Pat each contribute 40% of the total (100%/250%). This column shows how Project calculates the work assignment for each resource. Project assigns Mary 20% of the total work for the task, which is 12 hours. Scott and Pat are each 24 hours. Each of these new work assignments can be completed in 3 days; therefore, the duration of the task is changed from 5 days to 3 days.

If Pat were removed from the assignment, the changes would be reversed. Without Pat's assignment, Mary would contribute 1/3 of the units and Scott would contribute 2/3. Mary would be assigned 1/3 of the total 60 hours (20h), and Scott would be assigned 2/3 (40h).

If you disable the Effort Driven field (by clearing the check box in the Options dialog box), Project assumes that the work of a newly assigned resource is to be added to the existing work of all other named resources. The assignments of the existing resources are not changed. Task 3 (Task A with Lou) illustrates the result when Lou is assigned to the original Task A but with the Effort Driven field disabled. Lou is assigned at 100% for the 5-day duration of the task, and the 40 hours of new work is added to the task total.

Similarly, if you remove a named resource from a task, with the Effort Driven check box unchecked, Project reduces the total work for the task by the amount of that resource's work assignment and does not recalculate other resource assignments.

If you are having issues adding resources to a fixed duration effort driven task, see "Understanding Effort Driven Fixed Duration Tasks" in the "Troubleshooting" section at the end of this chapter.

NOTE

The Effort Driven setting regulates calculations only when you add to or subtract from the list of assigned resources. For example, if you change the duration of an effort-driven task, Project does not keep the work of the assigned resources the same, but it does change their work to fit the new duration.

When you change the number of assigned resources, you must think about whether you want total work to be changed and then change the Effort Driven status for the task as appropriate. You will do this most often when you build a list of assigned resources one at a time. For example, suppose that you created a task for 20 hours of work moving stock in a warehouse, and you have already assigned warehouse workers to the task. Now you want to assign the forklifts they will be using. If the duration, work, and units for the workers' assignment is based on the assumption that they will have forklifts to work with, you need to clear the Effort Driven check box before adding the forklifts. After the forklifts are added, you can turn Effort Driven back on for future calculations.

Modifying Resource Assignments

You have seen that you can define a resource assignment by specifying the task duration, the assignment units, and the work for the assignment. You have seen that your choice of the task type and its effort-driven status also affect resource assignments. In this section, we will examine other options for fine-tuning resource assignments. The choices include the following:

- Adding a delay to a resource's start date so that it starts after other resources have started on the task
- Splitting a resource's schedule on a task to accommodate time when the resource is needed elsewhere
- Assigning overtime work to a resource
- Applying one of the predefined work contours to an assignment

- Manually adjusting the work contour for an assignment
- Scheduling the resource based on a task calendar in conjunction with, or instead of, the resource calendar

SCHEDULING A LATE START FOR AN ASSIGNMENT

Sometimes one of the resources assigned to a task is expected to perform a function that is needed not at the beginning of the task, but only after some work on the task has been completed by others. For example, suppose that a team assigned to design a new accessory to its main product needs the opinion of an expert consultant on the feasibility of its initial design. The expert's assignment to the design task can be delayed so that it starts only after the task has been under way long enough for the team to decide the questions they need to ask. Suppose that one member of the team is a draftsman whose sole contribution will be to prepare a drawing of the design on the next-to-last day so the team can review and confirm their recommendations on the last day. The draftsman's assignment should be delayed to near the end of the task.

In Figure 9.8, Mary and Scott are assigned full time to the 5-day Design Accessory task, but the Consultant and Draftsman each have only 4 hours of work assigned. As explained later on, Task 1 represents the way Project initially assigns the work, and Task 2 shows how individual assignments can be delayed.

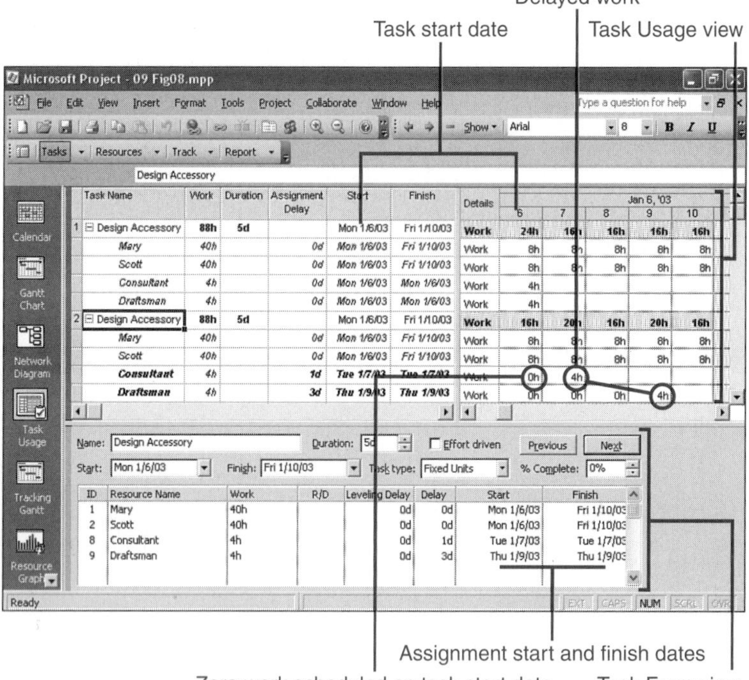

Figure 9.8
You can create a delay in an assignment to recognize the fact that the resource is not necessary at the start of the task.

Figure 9.8 displays the Task Usage view, which, like the Resource Usage view, shows timephased assignment details in the grid on the right. The names of assigned resources are indented under the task names, and the assignment values are rolled up or summed on the row for the task. The Work column in the table on the left shows, for each row, the total of the timephased work details in the grid.

Task 1 shows how Project, by default, schedules the hours for all assignments at the start of the task (January 6). Task 2 shows the delayed hours for the Consultant (January 7) and the Draftsman (January 9).

The bottom pane shows the Task Form view, with the Resource Schedule details table at the bottom. The column titled Delay shows the amount of any assignment delay (as does the Assignment Delay column in the table in the top pane). The Start and Finish fields show the scheduled dates for the assignment. (The Leveling Delay column is a different kind of delay, and it is explained in Chapter 11, "Resolving Resource Assignment Problems.")

You can create an assignment delay in one of several different ways:

- You can enter the amount of the delay in the Delay column in the resource schedule details of the Task Form view (refer to Figure 9.8). (The Delay field is also available in the schedule details on the Resource Form view.) If you enter a value in the Delay field, Project automatically calculates the delayed dates for the Start and Finish date fields.

NOTE

> The default entry in the Delay field is 0d, which means no delay. The Delay field is never blank. You can remove a delay by entering zero in the Delay field; however, you cannot erase an entry and try to leave the field blank.

- You can enter a delayed start date in the Start field to the right of the Delay field. Project automatically calculates the value for the Delay field as well as a new finish date.

NOTE

> If you enter a date in the Finish field to the right of the Delay field in the Task Form view, Project does not calculate a delay for the start date. Instead, it recalculates the amount of work that is completed between the (unchanged) start of the assignment and the new finish date you just entered.

- If you add the Assignment Delay column to the Task Usage view, as has been done in Figure 9.8, you can enter the delay or the start date for the assignment on the row for the assignment.
- You can also create a delay for an assignment by editing the timephased work details in the grid in the Task Usage view or the Resource Usage view. You can simply select the cells that contain the hours of work you want to delay and drag them to a later date. In Figure 9.8, I used the mouse to drag the Consultant's 4 hours of work from January 6

to January 7. Project then calculated the values for the Assignment Delay, Start, and Finish fields.

- If you double-click anywhere in an assignment row in either the Task Usage or Resource Usage view, or if you select a cell on that row and click the Assignment Information tool on the Standard toolbar, Project displays the Assignment Information dialog box for that assignment (see Figure 9.9). You can enter a delayed start date in the Start box or use the calendar control to the right of the field to select a start date. Although the Delay field does not appear on the Assignment Information dialog box, its value is recalculated if you enter a new date in the Start field.

→ For a complete description of the Assignment Information Dialog Box, see "Using the Assignment Information Dialog Box," **p. 390**.

Figure 9.9
You can use the Assignment Information dialog box to change the start date for an assignment.

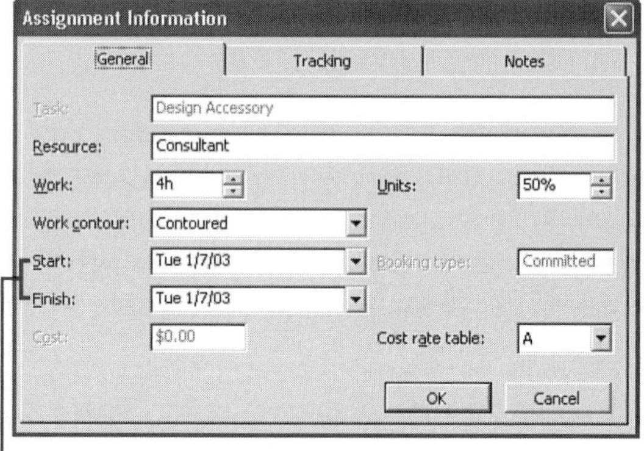

To change an assignment start date from the Task Form, see "Adjusting Assignment Start Dates from the Task Form" in the "Troubleshooting" section at the end of this chapter.

This discussion about delaying assignments has been presented in terms of projects that are scheduled from a fixed start date. In those projects, Microsoft Project schedules tasks and assignments as soon as possible, calculates the start date for both tasks and assignments first, and then calculates the finish dates. A delay in an assignment is tantamount to a late start, and it offsets that assignment schedule from other resource assignment schedules on the same task.

If your project is scheduled from a fixed finish date, Microsoft Project first schedules the last tasks in each chain of linked tasks to end on the project's fixed finish date. Task and assignment finish dates are calculated first, and then their start dates are calculated. Project then works backward along the chain of linked tasks, scheduling later tasks before earlier tasks until the start of the project is reached and a project start date is calculated.

You cannot introduce delays (late starts) for assignments in fixed-finish-date projects because that would delay the project finish date, which is by definition fixed. You can, however, modify assignments to schedule some assignments to finish earlier than others—in other words, you schedule an early finish instead of a late start.

You can enter an early finish for an assignment in a fixed-finish-date project in the same Delay field used for late starts, but you enter it as a negative number. Alternatively, you can enter an early finish date in the assignment's Finish field, and Project calculates the (negative) Delay value as well as a new date for the Start field.

If you enter a date in the assignment Start field, Project does not adjust the Delay value but calculates a new amount of work for the assignment, based on the (unchanged) finish date and the start date you enter.

NOTE

> You can enter negative amounts in the assignment Delay field only if the project is scheduled from a fixed finish date. You can enter positive amounts only if the project is scheduled from a fixed start date.

SPLITTING A TASK ASSIGNMENT

Splitting an assignment means that you schedule an interruption in the work, usually extending the duration of the assignment to make up for the time lost to the interruption. There are two basic methods for splitting a work assignment:

- You can split the task, and Project automatically splits each resource assignment for the task, with zero work scheduled during the period of the split.
- You can split an individual resource assignment by inserting one or more periods of zero work in the middle of the assignment.

If you introduce a split in an individual resource assignment, Project does not show a split in the task unless it is the only resource assignment for the task or unless you introduce the same split in all assigned resources.

Figure 9.10 shows three tasks to which both Mary and Pat are assigned. The view has the Gantt Chart view in the top pane and the Task Usage view in the bottom pane. The work detail in the bottom pane for their assignments to the Prepare for Conference task shows a split in the assignment on Wednesday. This split was the result of splitting the task; thus, the schedules of all assigned resources are split.

Pat also has a 1-day split on the following Wednesday, in his assignment to the Write Up Proceedings task. However, the Gantt bar for the task in the top pane of Figure 9.10 is not split because Mary, who is also assigned to the task, continues to work on those days, while Pat is diverted to another task.

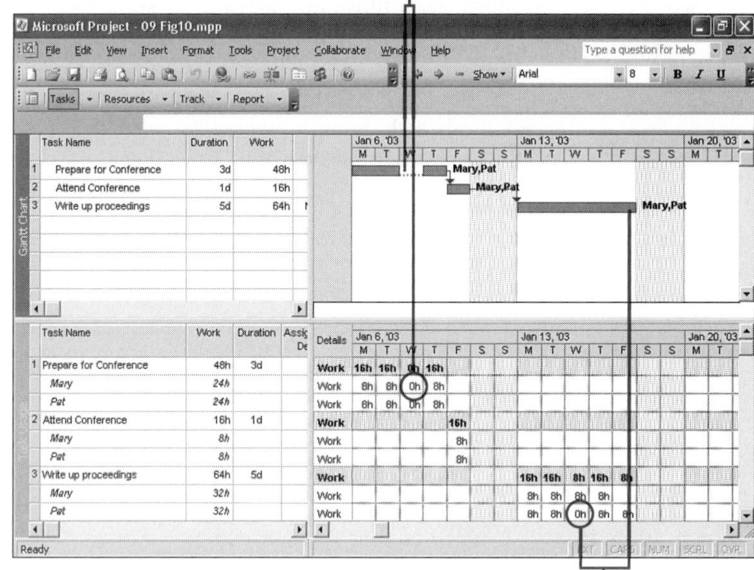

Figure 9.10
You can introduce a split in a task assignment when the resource needs to work on another task temporarily.

Using Overtime to Shorten Duration

You can reduce the duration for a task by scheduling some of a resource's work as overtime. *Overtime work* means work that is scheduled outside the resource's normal working hours. In Project that means work that is scheduled during nonworking time on the resource calendar. Assigning overtime doesn't reduce the total amount of work for an assignment, but the amount that is scheduled during regular working time is reduced by the amount of the overtime. Also, Project charges the resource's overtime rate for overtime work; cost might therefore go up, depending on your entry in the Overtime Rate field.

Planned overtime is a common pitfall of scheduling and should be avoided. It leaves no time for corrective action should an activity slip and often impacts productivity and performance. Also, since efficiency of a resource often goes down, quality is impacted as well.

Additionally, scheduling weekend activities may cause a task to slip an entire week if the predecessor activity slips one day.

For example, suppose that Bill has been assigned full time (100% units) to write a report that is scheduled to take 60 hours of work and requires a duration of 7.5 days to complete (see Task 1 in Figure 9.11). Bill is scheduled to start on a Monday and finish at midday on Wednesday the following week. The cost of the task is $1,200 (based on Bill's standard rate of $20/hour). This task is illustrated as Task 1, Write Report (No Overtime), at the top of Figure 9.11.

The assignment details on the right have been augmented to show not only work (which is total work per time period), but also the regular work and overtime work components of total work, as well as the cost of the assignment. The Regular Work, Overtime Work, and Cost columns have been added to the table on the left. They and the Work column show the task totals for the corresponding timephased details in the grid.

→ For information about adding fields to the timephased data, **see** "Formatting the Resource Usage View," **p. 826**.

For Task 1 (No Overtime), the total work is 60 hours, which is the sum of the work hours in the grid. You can see that the total work for each day is made up of regular work only. The duration of Task 1 is 7.5 days, and that is due to the fact that there are 7 full days of work and 1 half day of 4 hours. The total cost of the task is $1,200, which is the sum of the daily Cost values in the grid.

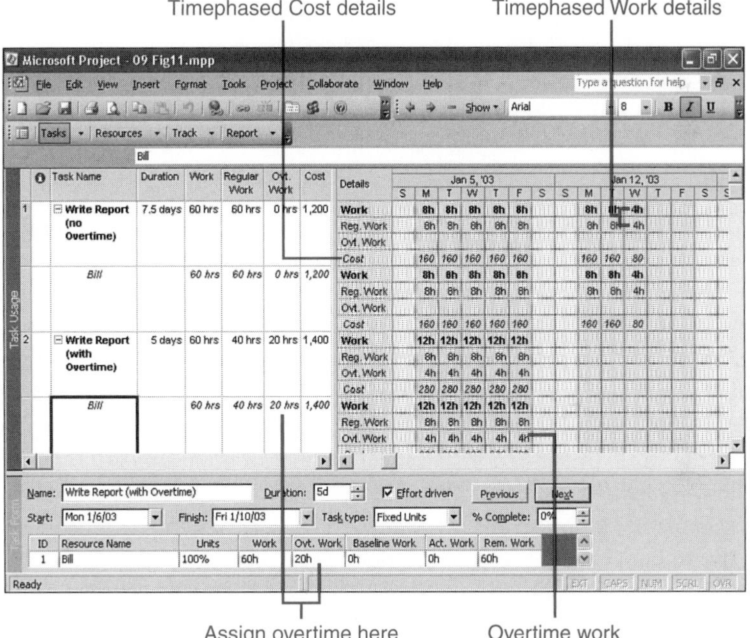

Figure 9.11 Scheduling overtime work shortens task duration but can lead to increased cost.

Task 2, Write Report (with Overtime), shows what would happen if Bill's manager decided that she needs the report in no more than 5 days and authorizes 20 hours of overtime work for Bill. Bill still spends a total of 60 hours on the report, but 20 hours are overtime hours and only 40 hours are regular working time. Bill now does 12 hours of work per day—8 hours of regular work plus 4 hours of overtime. All 60 hours of work are completed in just 5 days; thus, the task duration is 5 days. The cost for each day is $280. This is made up of $160 standard-rate hours (8 hours at $20/hour) plus $120 of overtime-rate hours (4 hours at $30/hour). Note that had Bill's Overtime rate been left as the default zero, the cost for the task would actually have fallen to $160 (the cost of the regular work hours).

NOTE

> Overtime work that is scheduled by Project cannot be adjusted manually. That is, you can't edit the cells in the grid to change the number of overtime hours scheduled on a particular day. However, when you are tracking progress on a task, you can add Actual Overtime Work to the details in the grid and enter the amount of actual overtime work in each time period to show exactly when the overtime work was performed.

The bottom pane in Figure 9.11 shows the Task Form view with the resource work details displayed at the bottom. Because Task 2 is selected in the top pane, the details show the values with overtime assigned. Note that the Ovt. Work field displays 20 hours. The Work field shows the total work, 60 hours, which includes overtime.

The easiest way to assign overtime hours for a resource is to display the Task Form in the bottom pane of a task view (or the Resource Form view, if the top pane is a resource view) and to display the resource work details (or work details, in the Resource Form view) at the bottom of the form. You could also add the Overtime Work column to the table in a usage view and enter the amount of overtime on the row for the assignment. To remove overtime work, you must reset the Overtime Work field to zero (it can't be "cleared").

CONTOURING RESOURCE USAGE

The traditional resource work pattern is the so-called *flat pattern*. In the flat pattern, Project schedules a resource's work to begin when the task begins, using the same units assignment every day until the assigned work is completed. Sometimes, you might want a resource to put greater effort into a task at the outset and then to taper off the daily effort until the task is finished. In that case, you want to assign more units and hours for the days at the beginning of the task and then use a reduced number of units and hours each day to complete the task. This is called *front loading* the work on the task. Other times, you might want to *back load* the work, by starting with a small number of hours and assignment units up front and then increasing the work as the task nears completion. Varied scheduling patterns like these are available in Project as *work contours*. The default resource schedule is the Flat contour pattern, but you can have Project modify an assignment schedule by applying one of seven predefined work contours. You can also create your own contour by editing the timephased values in the usage view grid.

To change the scheduling pattern, you display either the Task Usage view or the Resource Usage view. The Resource Usage view is similar to the Task Usage view in that it displays all the resources with their assignments indented beneath them and provides assignment details for each period in the timescale in a grid of cells. Both these views enable you to apply contoured assignments, either by applying one of the built-in contours or by editing the work assigned in any given time period in the grid.

To illustrate contouring, suppose that Bill is assigned to write a report that's estimated to take 40 hours to complete. At the beginning, he needs to concentrate completely on the report, but he can start spending more time on other tasks once it's underway. You could schedule his assignment like the "before and after" example in the Task Usage view in

Figure 9.12. Task 1 is named Write Report (Flat), and it shows the standard assignment schedule.

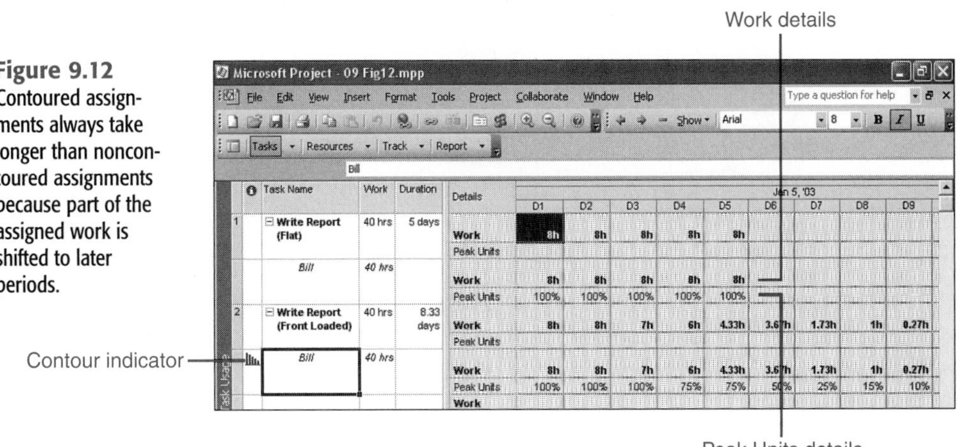

Figure 9.12
Contoured assignments always take longer than noncontoured assignments because part of the assigned work is shifted to later periods.

Note that the grid in Figure 9.12 shows an added detail field, Peak Units. The Peak Units field shows the maximum units that are assigned to the task at any moment in time during the time period covered by the cell. You can see from the Units field in the bottom pane that Bill's initial assignment to the task was at 100%. In the standard schedule, that means his Peak Units is 100% in all 5 days and he is assigned 8 hours of work each day.

Task 2 shows Bill's assignment schedule after the front-loaded contour is applied. Note the icon in the Indicator column that flags this assignment as having a front-loaded contour. Bill's assignment units start at 100% but soon drop to lower and lower levels, until all the work is completed. Consequently, the value for the hours of work scheduled for each day becomes less and less; Bill still does 40 hours of work, but now it takes more days to complete the work. Note that the duration for Task 2 is 8.33 days instead of 5 days.

Figure 9.13 shows the Resource Usage view of Bill's front-loaded task. The main record is now the resource Bill instead of the task, but indented under it is the same assignment record, now labeled with the associated task name, Write Report (Front Loaded). The details in the grid are the same as those for Task 2 in Figure 9.12.

The bottom pane of Figure 9.13 contains the Resource Graph view. This view displays a histogram (a vertical bar chart) to give a graphical image of the resource assignment detail that you select. In this case, the peak units detail is graphed and illustrates very nicely the declining nature of the front-loaded work contour. In fact, this graph is the source of the image that is used in the indicator for front-loaded contours.

→ For more information about the Resource Graph, **see** "The Resource Graph View," **p. 754**.

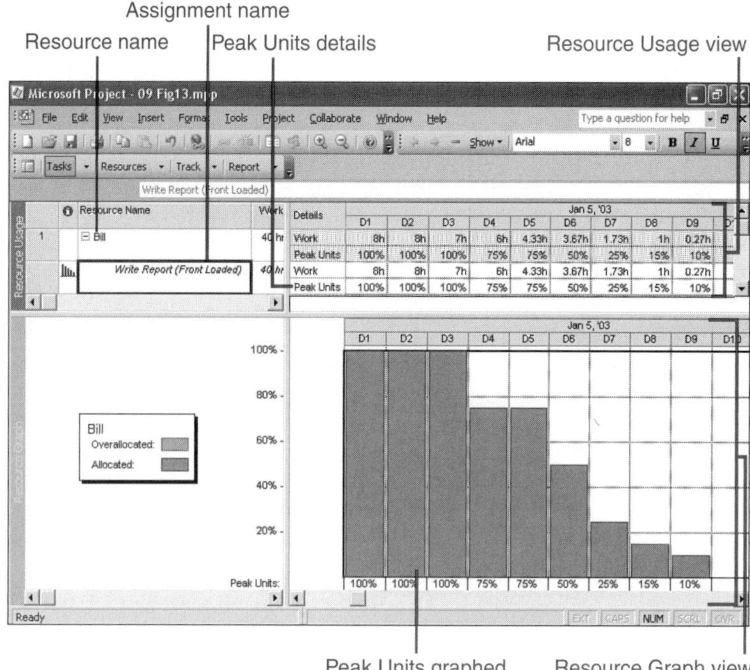

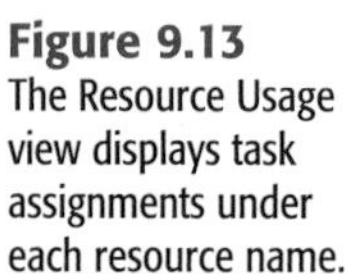

Figure 9.13
The Resource Usage view displays task assignments under each resource name.

Project provides eight predefined work contour patterns that you can apply to a resource assignment. These are in addition to the default assignment pattern, the flat pattern, that is used when Project initially calculates an assignment. The contour patterns are illustrated in Figure 9.14 and are described as follows:

- **Flat**—This is the pattern that Project uses in the initial assignment calculation. All work is assigned as soon as the task starts, and it continues until the assignment is completed. There is no indicator icon for this pattern.
- **Back Loaded**—The daily workload starts light and builds until the end of the task.
- **Front Loaded**—The heaviest daily load is at the beginning of the task and tapers off continuously until the end of the task.
- **Double Peak**—The daily workload starts low, builds to an early peak, drops off, builds to another peak, and then tapers off to the end of the task.
- **Early Peak**—The daily workload starts light, builds rapidly to a peak, and then tapers off until the end of the task.
- **Late Peak**—The daily workload starts light, builds slowly to a peak near the end of the task, and then drops off somewhat at the end.
- **Bell**—The daily workload starts light, builds to a peak in the middle of the assignment, and then tapers off until the end of the assignment.

- **Turtle**—The daily workload starts somewhat light, builds rapidly to a plateau, remains there for most of the rest of the assignment, and drops back to a somewhat light level at the end.

- **Contoured**—This pattern does not illustrate a predefined contour; rather, it illustrates the fact that you can edit the work assignments to produce your own work pattern. The indicator, with a pencil on the bar chart, shows that the work assignment has been manually edited. Note that you can only edit the Work cells. You cannot edit the Peak Units values directly.

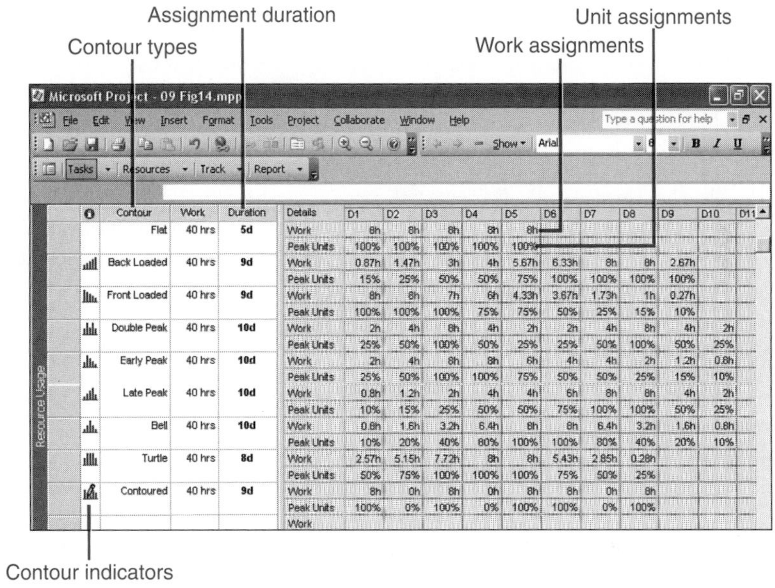

Figure 9.14
Work contours redistribute assigned work over a longer duration.

Figure 9.14 illustrates the contour types in an actual calculation by Microsoft Project. The first row, labeled Flat, shows how the default assignment of 40 hours of work to a 5-day task was scheduled for a resource with a unit assignment of 100%.

In the timephased details on the right, you can see the work and peak units for each day. The resource is assigned 100% to the task, and for all 5 days, 100% of its time is allocated to the task.

Rows 2 through 8 show how Project would schedule the work if one of the predefined contours were applied. The total work remains 40 hours in all cases, as shown in the Total Work column. The work assignment for each day varies, depending on the contour pattern, as do the peak units.

Each of the contours reduces the unit assignment during selected days in the assignment; the choice of which days determines the pattern that is the source of the different contour names. Because less work is scheduled on some days, the total assignment necessarily takes longer to complete. Note that the duration of the task is extended when the contours are applied. Instead of the task being completed the first week, work must continue into the following week.

The last row in Figure 9.14 is labeled Contoured and is not a predefined contour pattern. That's the name Project applies when the user edits the work details for an assignment. In this case, the work is scheduled on Mondays, Wednesdays, and Fridays. In either the Task Usage or Resource Usage view, you can edit the assigned hours in the work details cells.

To apply a contour to an assignment, you display either the Task Usage or Resource Usage view and then select the indented assignment that you want to change. Double-click the assignment row or use the Assignment Information tool on the Standard toolbar to display the Assignment Information dialog box (see Figure 9.15). Display the pull-down list of contours in the Work Contour box and select the one you want to apply. Note that the first contour is the Flat contour. You select Flat to reset an assignment back to a standard schedule with no contour.

Scheduling back loaded work effort on a task is not a good practice. This idea promotes the "student syndrome" of procrastination and consumes the available float during the scheduled duration of the task, forcing the work to be performed at the very end of the duration. Slippage of this work effort could impact the scheduling of the successor activity and, possibly, the end date of the project.

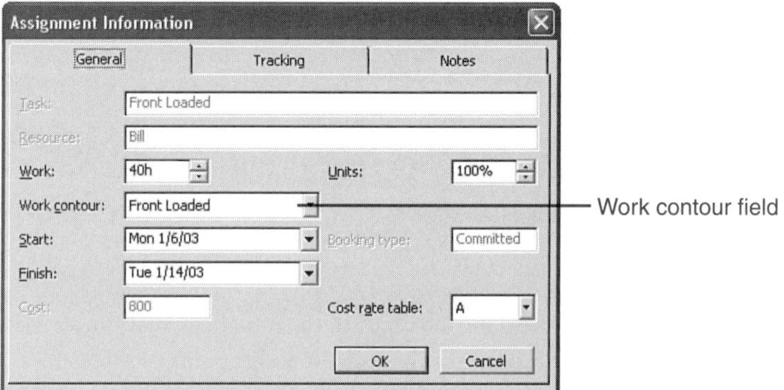

Figure 9.15
The Assignment Information dialog box displays settings that affect the scheduling of the assignment.

TIP

If you change the work contour, it's a good idea to document why you made the choices you made in the assignment Notes field. Click the Notes tab in the Assignment Information dialog box (refer to Figure 9.15) and enter supporting documentation about an assignment, including links to external documents such as job specifications or standards.

NOTE

If overtime hours are assigned to a task when you apply a contour, Project spreads out the overtime evenly, over the duration of the assignment, no matter which contour is applied.

TIP

> If you want to add a resource with a contoured assignment to an existing task that has other resources already assigned and if you don't want the task duration or the other resource schedules to change when you apply the contour to the new resource's assignment, you can make the task a Fixed Duration task and disable Effort Driven before assigning the contour. You can later return the task to its previous task type and effort-driven status. Project applies the contour but has to stop scheduling hours when it reaches the end of the task duration. As a result, the new resource has a lower total amount of work than it initially did. You will undoubtedly have to manually edit the work assignment values to get the results you want.

SCHEDULING WITH TASK CALENDARS

If a task has its own special calendar assigned to it, by default, Project schedules work for the resources only in the times when the working times for both the task calendar and the resource calendar intersect. Project displays the Assigned Calendar indicator (see Figure 9.16) for the task.

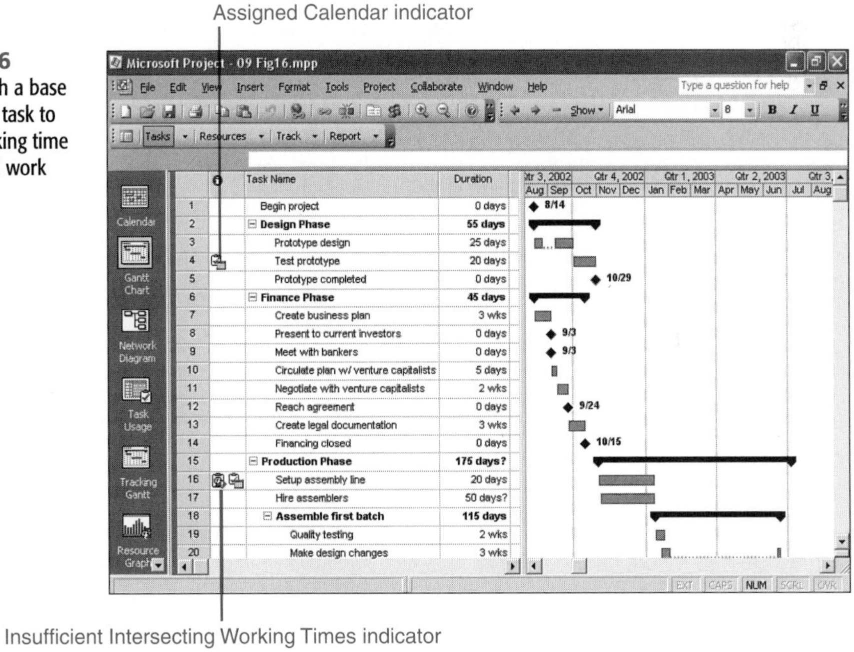

Assigned Calendar indicator

Insufficient Intersecting Working Times indicator

Figure 9.16
You can attach a base calendar to a task to limit the working time for scheduled work on a task.

This facility is useful when there are special nonworking times associated with the task but you don't want to enter those nonworking times on the resource calendars because they would interfere with scheduling other task assignments for the resources.

One application for a task calendar is when a key resource for a task has unique nonworking times, and no other resources can work when that key resource is unavailable. For example, equipment maintenance might take an assembly line offline for 4 hours every week. You could create an Assembly Line Maintenance base calendar to define these nonworking hours and assign it to the task. The alternative would be to add the nonworking times for this key resource to the calendars for all the other resources assigned to the task. Again, that could interfere with scheduling the other resources for other tasks.

Another good use of task calendars is when you need to schedule a task during normally nonworking times. If, for example, you wanted to schedule the upgrade for a network server on a weekend to minimize user inconvenience, you could create a task calendar and assign it to the task that has working time only on the days and hours when you want the task scheduled.

To assign a calendar to a task, you have to create the special base calendar first, using the Tools, Change Working Times command. Then select the task and display the Task Information dialog box. On the Advanced tab, you display the drop-down list of base calendars in the Calendar box and select the appropriate calendar (see Figure 9.17).

→ For instructions on creating base calendars, **see** "Defining a Calendar of Working Time," **p. 76**.

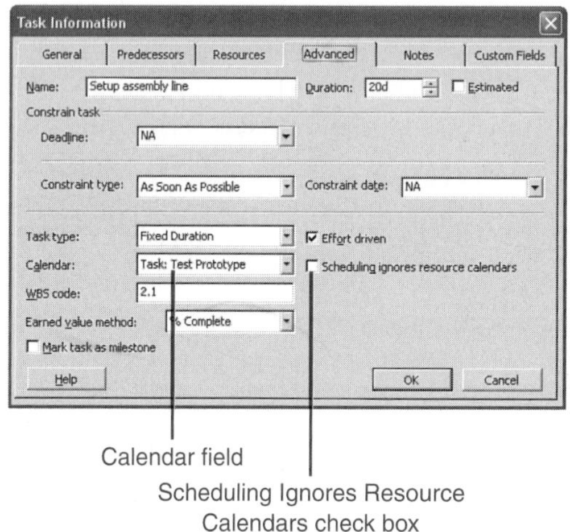

Figure 9.17
You can assign task calendars in the Task Information dialog box.

If you want Project to ignore the resource calendar working times, check the Scheduling Ignores Resource Calendars check box. When you do, the number of hours of work scheduled for a resource on any given day depends on the units assigned and the work hours defined on the task calendar, not the resource calendar. It is up to you to verify that the resources can, in fact, meet this schedule.

For example, Bill gets assigned to the network server task scheduled for a Saturday using a task calendar that specifies only weekend days as working times. Bill's resource calendar is based on the standard calendar that specifies that weekend days are nonworking time. In this case, there is insufficient intersecting working time for both the task calendar and the resource calendar to be honored.

If the task and resource calendars do not intersect for enough hours to complete the task, Project displays a warning to alert you that there are insufficient intersecting working times (see Figure 9.18). You then need to modify one of the calendars or tell Project to ignore the resource calendar.

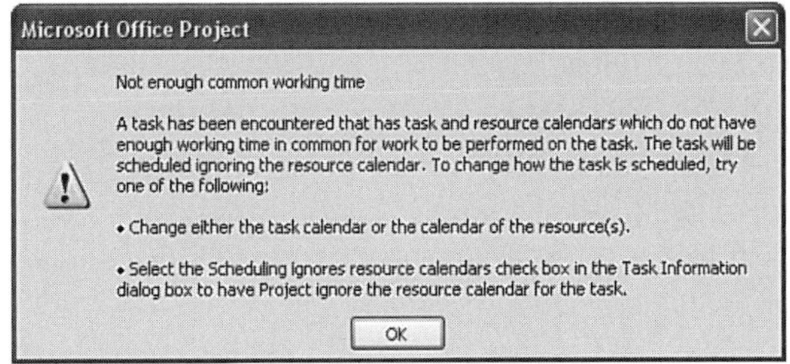

Figure 9.18 Project warns you when a task's resources and task calendar have insufficient overlapping working times.

UNDERSTANDING THE DRIVER RESOURCE CONCEPT

The various changes in assignments described so far in this chapter produce changes in assignments and in the task duration. It helps to understand the changes in assignments if you understand the concept of the driver resource.

The term *driver resource* is used to identify resources whose assignments determine the duration or finish date for the task. Recall that when there are multiple resources assigned to a task, the task duration is at least as long as the longest assignment. The resources with the longest assignments are the *driver resources*. Other resources whose assignments finish earlier are *nondriver resources*. Anything that causes a driver resource's assignment to finish later causes the task to finish later. Thus, increasing the workload for a driver resource typically increases the task duration; but increasing the workload for a nondriver resource (at least up to a point) does not affect task duration.

NOTE

> The discussion here is based on a project that is scheduled from a fixed start date. In fixed-finish-date projects, the driver resources determine the *start* date for the task, and anything that moves the start of the assignment to an earlier date moves the task start to an earlier date and increases the duration of the task.

It's not unusual to have one resource that only adds some finishing touches to a task and whose smaller amount of work is scheduled right at the end of the task. Unfortunately, Project doesn't allow you to schedule one assignment to start "as late as possible" while the others start when the task starts. You saw in the section "Modifying Resource Assignments," earlier in this chapter, that you can edit an assignment to delay its start past the start of the task. If you delay an assignment so that it finishes at the same time that the task finishes, that resource would become a driver resource also. Any increase in the amount of time scheduled for the resource delays the finish of the task (unless you offset the increase by reducing the amount of delay).

As stated previously, the significance of the driver resource concept is that increasing the duration of a driver resource assignment affects the task duration, but modest increases in the duration of a nondriver resource have no effect. There is an important corollary: Increasing or decreasing the duration of the task changes the work assigned to driver resources, but it does not affect the work assigned to nondriver resources (unless duration is reduced so much that the nondriver resources become drivers also).

Figure 9.19 illustrates the driver resource concept. Mary, Pat, and Scott are assigned to Task A-1 with differing work amounts, as shown in the Work column. The custom column Assignment Duration shows how long it will take each of them to complete the assigned work, given the assignment units. Mary and Pat will both require 4 days, but Scott can finish in 1 day. The task duration is 4 days, and Mary and Pat are both driver resources.

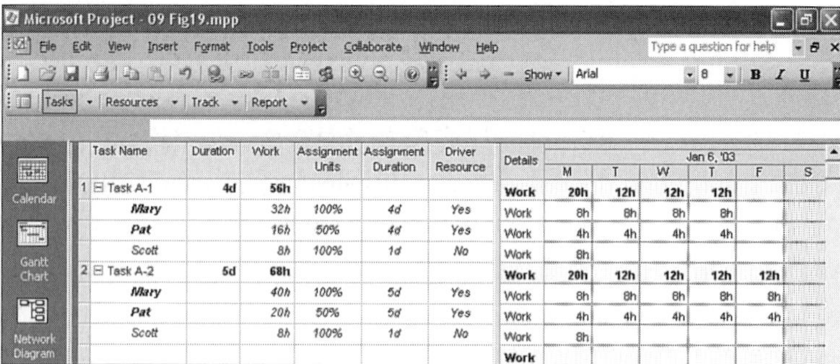

Figure 9.19
Driver resources are resources that are working on the task when it finishes.

NOTE

> Note that Scott is assigned full time for 1 day, but because he has only 8 hours of work, he finishes before the task finishes. If he were assigned 8 hours at 25% units, it would take him all 4 days to complete his work, putting in 2 hours each day. In that case, he would also be a driver resource.

If you were to change the assigned work or units for Mary and/or Pat, it could affect the duration of the task. For example, if you increased Mary's workload to 50 hours, she would need a longer time to finish, and the task duration would have to increase. However, an increase in Scott's workload (up to a point) would not affect the duration of the task:

- You could increase the work assigned to Scott from 8 hours to 32 hours, without needing to increase the task's duration.
- You could also change Scott's units from 100% down to as low as 25% before it would affect his ability to complete his assignment in the current duration.
- Similarly, you could reduce the task duration from 4 days down to 1 day without affecting Scott's assignment (8 hours at 100% effort).

If you change the task duration, only the *driver resources* are affected. However, if you shorten the task duration so much that nondriver resources cannot complete their work, they are affected also. Task A-2 in Figure 9.19 shows what happens when the duration is increased to 5 days. Both Mary and Pat are assigned more hours of work, but Scott is unaffected.

The following are some important points about driver resources:

- When you change the duration for a task, only the assignments for driver resources (those who need the full duration to complete their assignments) are affected. Project applies the work formula to calculate changes in the assignments. Nondriver resources are not affected, as long as the change in duration still leaves them enough time to complete their assignments.
- When you change the assigned units or the work for driver resources, task duration is affected, and Project recalculates the assignment values for all driver resources but not those for nondriver resources.
- When you change the assigned units or the work for a nondriver resource without making it a driver resource, Project does not recalculate the assignment for that resource or for any other resources assigned to that task.

CALCULATING TASK DURATION WITH MULTIPLE RESOURCES ASSIGNED

Task duration is defined by Microsoft Project as the number of active working time periods on the calendar required to complete a task. When multiple resources are assigned to a task, some might not be scheduled during the entire task duration. Individual schedules for some resources can be modified to delay an assignment or to split the assignment with a period of inactivity.

NOTE

The consumption of material resources is not considered in calculating duration.

As an example, suppose Bill and Mary are both assigned 5 days of work preparing for a conference. The task duration is 5 days if Bill and Mary do their work during the same time periods. Suppose that Bill is taking 2 vacation days when the task starts, so Mary starts working on the task alone. Bill also has 1 more vacation day at the beginning of the following week. Bill starts working on the task 2 days later than Mary does. Then, they work together for 3 days, at which time Mary has completed her part of the task. Bill still has 2 days of work to do, but he doesn't do those days until after his second vacation.

Bill's work schedule does not match Mary's. Mary's earlier start date and Bill's later finish date define the task's start and finish dates. The task duration is the number of time periods during which anyone is working on the task. In this case, the task duration is 7 days—2 days when Mary worked alone, 3 days when they were both working on the task, and 2 days when Bill worked alone after Mary finished her part and after he got back from vacation.

Figure 9.20 illustrates this example. The top pane displays the Task Usage view, and the timephased work details show the precise work schedule for both Mary and Bill. Bill's work doesn't start until 2 days after Mary's begins. Mary completes her assignment on Friday. Bill has the day off on the following Monday and then completes the last 2 days of his assignment. The taskbar in the Gantt Chart view in the bottom pane shows a continuous bar over 8 working days. However, the task duration is only 7 days because there are 7 days when at least 8 hours of work is done by someone.

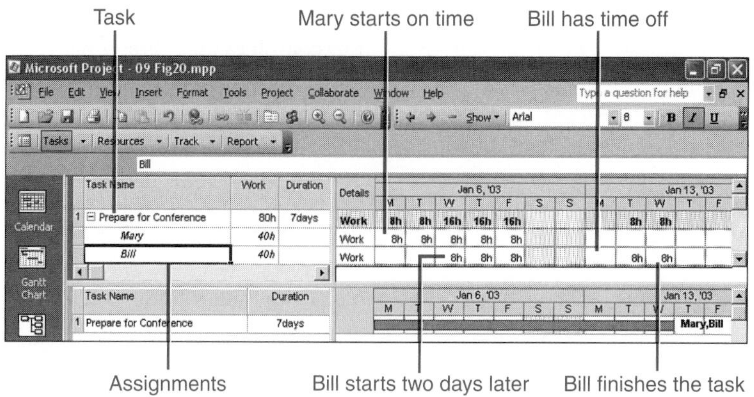

Figure 9.20
Task duration is the number of time units when at least one resource is working.

You can see in Figure 9.20 that Bill and Mary work independently some days and together some days. If you count the number of days in the task row where total work is a full day or more (8 hours or more), you see that there are 7 such days, and that is what determines the task duration of 7.

TROUBLESHOOTING

UNDERSTANDING EFFORT-DRIVEN, FIXED-DURATION TASKS

When I try to set the units value for an additional resource assignment on an effort-driven, fixed duration task, Project gives me an error message and won't allow it. What am I doing wrong?

By definition, fixed-duration tasks that are effort driven have both Work and Duration values fixed. Project will always calculate the Units value in this case and hence will present you with an error dialog if you try to set the Units value yourself. You need only pick a resource name in this situation and Project will reassign the remaining work across all assigned resources on the task by using the Max Units value for the new resource(s) plus the existing Units values for previously assigned resources and applying the same work formula of resource units divided by total units, as shown in Figure 9.7. If you need to set the Units values directly, you can do so after Project has created the assignment.

ADJUSTING ASSIGNMENT START DATES FROM THE TASK FORM

How can I adjust the start date for an additional resource assignment on a task to be different than the start date for the task?

Right-click on the task form and pick Resource Schedule. From this view, you can directly edit the start date of each assignment on a task. To return the Task Form to its previous format, right-click on the task form and select Resources & Successors.

CHAPTER 10

Assigning Resources and Costs to Tasks

In this chapter

An Overview of Assigning Resources 360

Selecting the Appropriate Task Settings 361

Assigning Resources to Tasks 365

Assigning Fixed Costs and Fixed Contract Fees 396

Troubleshooting 399

AN OVERVIEW OF ASSIGNING RESOURCES

This chapter describes how to use Microsoft Project's views and tools to assign resources and to modify resource assignments. To benefit the most from this chapter, you should understand the contents of Chapter 8, "Defining Resources and Costs," and Chapter 9, "Understanding Resource Scheduling." The intricate relationships among task and resource fields are covered in those chapters.

When you are assigning resources to tasks, there are a number of data fields you can use to give Microsoft Project the information it needs to calculate schedules and costs as you intend:

- You can choose the task type and effort-driven settings at the task level to control how Project calculates changes in the schedule due to resource assignments.
- You *must* identify the resource by using its ID or its name when you assign it to a task.
- You can define the number of assigned units, or otherwise let Project assign the default number of units or calculate the number of units based on the amount of work to be done and the duration of the task.
- You can define the amount of work the resource performs or let Project calculate that from the task duration and number of units.
- You can let Project use the default cost rates for the resource or select a special Cost Rate table you have defined if the task is to be charged rates different from those normally used for this resource.
- To speed up progress on the task, you can assign the resource overtime work or modify the resource calendar to provide additional available hours on specific days.
- You can accept the default work pattern for the assignment, which is an even amount of work each day until the task is complete, or you can modify the work contour to schedule more work at different times in the assignment. You can also delay the start of the assignment beyond the start of the task and split the assignment to work around interruptions in the availability of the resource.

As you can see, Project gives you the opportunity to fine-tune resource assignments so that schedule and cost calculations can be very precise. On the other hand, you can also get by with just the minimum amount of definition if you don't need all that sophistication.

This chapter shows how to enter all the information needed to assign resources to tasks. It also describes how to use tools that record the minimum amount of information needed to get the job done. There are a number of different views and tools you can use to assign resources, and you will see how to use all of them. Each has advantages, depending on your objective.

Selecting the Appropriate Task Settings

If you don't assign resources to tasks or if you assign only material resources, you do not have to be concerned with selecting the task type or whether the task is effort driven. However, most assignments are for work resources, and for those you need to consider the task type and the effort-driven setting for a task each time you make or change resource assignments for the task.

NOTE

> The effort-driven setting and the task types are defined and explained in detail in Chapter 9. Only a summary of the distinctions among the task types is given here. Similarly, the data fields that define a resource are covered in detail in Chapter 8 and are not explained again in detail here.

→ For detailed explanations of the use of the resource fields, **see** "Using the Resource Fields," **p. 292**.

Setting the Task Type

The work formula is defined in terms of the values for duration, units, and work. When one of these values is changed, Project automatically recalculates the values for either one or both of the other values in order to keep the formula valid. The task type tells Project how you want it to calculate changes in the formula, and therefore changes in task assignments and the task schedule, when you assign resources or change resource assignments.

→ For more information about task types and the work formula, **see** "Choosing the Task Type," **p. 335**.

The three task types are named Fixed Units, Fixed Work, and Fixed Duration. The default type for new tasks in Microsoft Project is Fixed Units. You can make any one of the three task types the default for new tasks by choosing Tools, Options and selecting the type in the Default Task Type field on the Schedule tab.

To verify or change the task type setting for a task, follow these steps:

1. Select the task.

2. Click the Task Information tool to display the Task Information dialog box.
3. Select the Advanced tab.
4. Set the task type by choosing the list arrow and selecting Fixed Duration, Fixed Units, or Fixed Work (see Figure 10.1).
5. Click OK.

You can also select the task's type on the Task Form view (see Figure 10.2), which is the view displayed in the bottom pane when you split a full-screen task view. To change the task type settings using the Task Form view, follow these steps:

To display the Task Form view, follow these steps:

1. If it is not already displayed, choose a task view such as the Gantt Chart view, the Task Sheet view, or the Task Usage view.

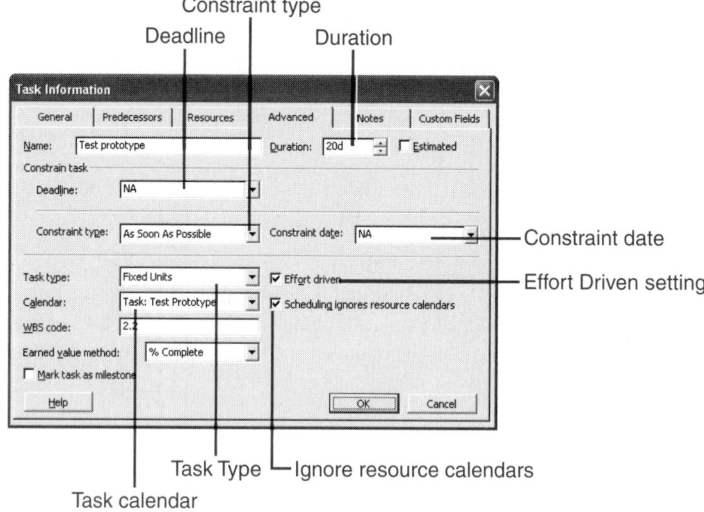

Figure 10.1
You can use the Task Information dialog box to access additional fields of information about each task.

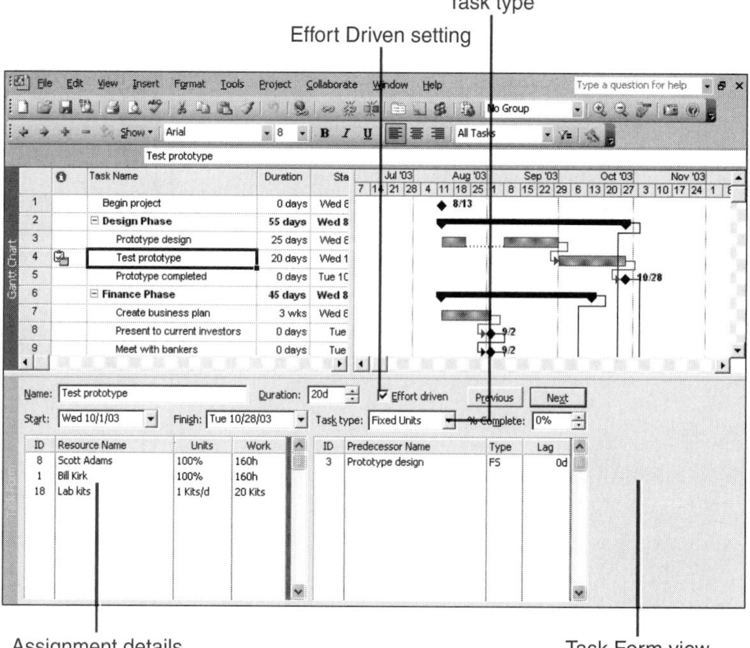

Figure 10.2
You can access the Task Type field in the Task Form view.

2. Split the view by choosing Window, Split. The bottom pane displays the Task Form view.
3. Activate the bottom pane. If resource details are not visible, choose Format, Details, and select one of the options that includes resources, such as Resources & Predecessors.
4. Use the Task Type list box to choose a new task type.

If you know the duration you want, you should replace the default duration before you start assigning resources. Also, you must consider what you want Project to calculate for you and choose the appropriate task type. For example, if you have defined the duration and work that you want for the assignment and you want Project to calculate the units, you have to choose the appropriate task type before assigning the resource.

Table 10.1 provides the guidelines you need to determine which task type is appropriate for each pair of values you might want to define.

TABLE 10.1 TASK TYPES FOR INITIAL ASSIGNMENT

You Define This:	You Want Project to Calculate This:	Use This Task Type:
Duration and units	Work	Any task type
Duration and work	Units	Fixed Duration
Units and work	Duration	Fixed Units or Fixed Work

If you want Project to just calculate the work, any task type will do. If you want Project to calculate the units that you need to assign, you need to use Fixed Duration. Finally, if you want Project to calculate duration, you can use either Fixed Units or Fixed Work.

If you want to change one of the variables in an existing assignment, you can use the task type to control which variable Project changes. Table 10.2 shows which task type to choose when you want Project to change a specific variable as a result of a change that you make.

TABLE 10.2 TASK TYPES FOR ASSIGNMENT CHANGES

You Change This:	You Want Project to Change This:	Use This Task Type:
Units	Duration	Fixed Work
Units	Work	Fixed Duration
Work	Duration	Fixed Units
Work	Units	Fixed Duration
Duration	Work	Fixed Units
Duration	Units	Fixed Work

Choosing a Task's Effort-Driven Status

Closely allied to the choice of a task type is the choice of whether a task is *effort driven*. This choice has importance only when you change the number of work resources assigned to a task. It does not have any effect if you merely change the number of assigned units for an already assigned resource or if you change the material resources assigned to the task.

→ For more information about effort-driven tasks, **see** "Understanding Effort-Driven Tasks," **p. 338**.

If a task is effort driven, when you add new work resource names to the assignment list, Project reapportions the existing work among all the resources, which results in less work for the preexisting resources and a shorter duration for the task. Conversely, if you remove a named work resource from a task, Project assigns its work to the remaining resources, and the task duration increases.

If a task is not effort driven, Project does not change the workloads of existing resources when you add a new work resource, and the task duration does not change. Total work for the task increases due to the addition of a new work resource.

To verify or change the Effort Driven setting for a task, follow these steps:

1. Select the task.

2. Click the Task Information tool to display the Task Information dialog box. The Effort Driven field also appears on the Task Form (refer to Figure 10.2).
3. Select the Advanced tab.
4. Look at the Effort Driven check box (refer to Figure 10.1). If the check box is filled, the task is effort driven; if it is empty, the task is not effort driven. Click the check box if you want to change the status.
5. Click OK.

The default status for new tasks in Project is effort driven, but you can change that default on the Options dialog box. Choose Tools, Options and select the Schedule tab on the Options dialog box. Deselect the New Tasks Are Effort Driven check box to change the default setting.

Before you make any change in resource assignments, you should ask yourself these two questions:

- What do I want Project to leave unchanged when I enter this new information: duration, units, or work? Be sure to select the appropriate task type to force Project to do what you want.
- Am I changing the number of named work resources that are already assigned to this task, and if so, do I want the total work for the task to remain the same or to be changed? If you want the total work to change, be sure you uncheck the Effort Driven field for the task.

You need to make sure that the task type and the effort-driven status are appropriate for the result you want to see.

ASSIGNING RESOURCES TO TASKS

As discussed in the previous section, the initial assignment schedule is influenced by task settings such as Task Type and Effort Driven, as well as by the choice of assignment units and work. As shown in Chapter 9, you can then customize the initial assignment by delaying its start, splitting the work, assigning overtime, choosing a work contour, and so forth. You can use a variety of views and dialog boxes to assign resources to tasks. They are listed here, with those that give you the most control over the assignment details listed last:

- You can use the Task table in either the Gantt Chart view or the Task Sheet view to enter assignments in the Resource Names column, but the syntax is strict, and you can specify only the assignment units, not the assignment work.
- You can display the Task Information dialog box in any task view, and you can assign resources on its Resources tab. However, you don't have as much control when you assign multiple resources to a task as you do when you use a combination view with a task view in the top pane and the Task Form view (or Task Details Form view) in the bottom view. That combination is described shortly.
- Using the Assign Resources dialog box is the easiest and quickest way to assign resources. You can display this pop-up dialog box in any task view, and it stays on top of the workspace as you select different tasks.

  The Assign Resources dialog box offers powerful features that aid in choosing the resource that is appropriate for an assignment. You can filter the list of resource names to find qualified resources, and you can view a graph of resource availability.

  However, if a task is effort driven (which is the default), the Assign Resources dialog box doesn't let you enter work and have Project calculate units; and in any case, you can't enter both work and units.

  Furthermore, unless you use the default assignment units for each resource, you can't assign multiple resources to a task all at once as you can with the combination views described later.
- The Task Form view is the most versatile single view for assigning resources, especially when it appears in the bottom pane of a task view such as the Gantt Chart view (which is a combination called the Task Entry view), the Task Usage view, or the Network Diagram view. The Task Form view enables you to define the duration, task type, and effort-driven status of the task, and to define the units, work, or both units and work for the assignment. You can assign multiple resources at once, and you can also assign overtime and a delayed start for an assignment.
- You get the most control over the assignment process when you use the Task Usage view in the top pane with the Task Form view in the bottom pane. The Task Usage view replaces the taskbars of the Gantt Chart view with a grid of cells that show details about the assignment during each period in the timescale. You can edit the cells to modify scheduled work in specific time periods after making the assignment.

  In the Task Usage view you can double-click a task to access the Task Information dialog box, where you can quickly review or modify more details about the task. You can also double-click an assignment in the Task Usage view to access the Assignment Information dialog box, where you can specify work contours, select a different cost rate for the assignment, and document the assignment with notes and links to documents stored elsewhere. In the Task Form view, you can double-click a resource name to access the Resource Information dialog box to review or modify details about the resource.

Finally, you can also display the Assign Resources dialog box on top of the combination view, to help identify the most appropriate resources for tasks.

In the following sections, we will first discuss how to use the Assign Resources dialog box for less complex assignments and to help choose which resource to assign. We will then use the Gantt Chart view with the Task Form view to see how to handle more complex assignments. Then, we will put the Task Usage view in the top pane and work on fine-tuning the timephased work schedule. Finally, we will briefly explore how to use the other views and dialog boxes mentioned previously, in case you want to use them too.

Using the Assign Resources Dialog Box

The Assign Resources dialog box is a versatile tool for choosing which resource to assign to a task and for creating the most common assignments. A task view (other than one of the task forms) must be active in order to initiate the display of the Resource Assignment dialog box. To display the dialog box, click the Assign Resources tool, choose Tools, Assign Resources, or press Alt+F10.

Figure 10.3 shows the Assign Resources dialog box over the Gantt Chart and Task Form views. This figure shows the resource list options expanded to display the options to apply filters and to add resources. Click the little plus-sign button to the left of Resource List Options to expand the dialog box.

The selected task in Figure 10.3 is Test Prototype. You can see in the Assign Resources dialog box which resources are assigned to the task because they appear first in the Resource Name list and have check marks next to their names when that task is selected. The underlying view shows more detail about the assignments in the Resources area of the Task Form view in the bottom pane.

TIP

> Because you might need to change the task type or effort-driven status of a task before making or changing a resource assignment, you usually want the Task Form view in the bottom pane of the underlying view. Remember to consider the settings for those parameters before making any changes in assignments.

CAUTION

> The Undo command is not available for resource assignment actions you take with the Assign Resources dialog box.

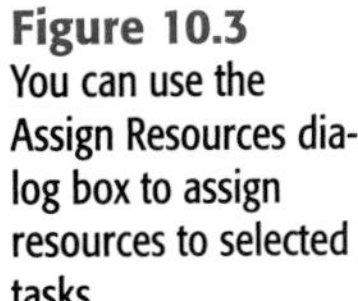

Figure 10.3
You can use the Assign Resources dialog box to assign resources to selected tasks.

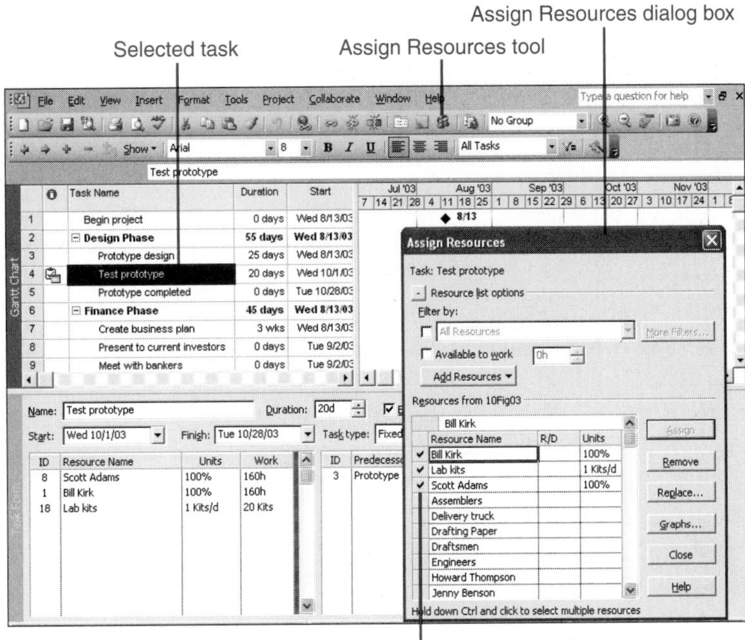

The Assign Resources dialog box is the only pop-up dialog box that you can leave on the workspace while switching back and forth between the dialog box and the underlying views while selecting different tasks. When displayed, the dialog box remains accessible even if the underlying active view is not a task view—and even in different projects. However, it has reduced functionality if the active view is a form or is not a task view.

The following list and Figure 10.4 highlight the powerful features of the Assign Resources dialog box:

The Assign Resources dialog box offers the following features:

- You can select a blank cell in the Resource Names list to add a resource name to the list, then type the name in the Edit bar.
- You can click the Add Resources button to look up names in a server directory or email address book and add them to the resource list.
- You can double-click a resource name to view and edit the Resource Information dialog box for that resource, no matter what underlying view is active.
- You can apply a named filter (or create one on-the-fly with the More Filters button) to identify resources with specific characteristics. For example, you can filter for material or work resources, or for resources that have a particular skill.
- You can filter the resource list to select resources that have enough working time for the task that is selected in the underlying view.

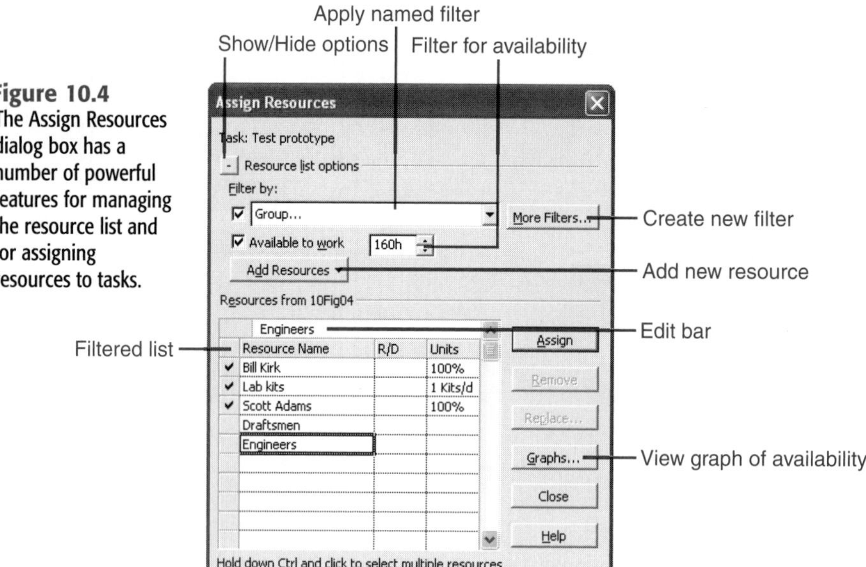

Figure 10.4
The Assign Resources dialog box has a number of powerful features for managing the resource list and for assigning resources to tasks.

10

- If the underlying active view is a task view (other than one of the forms), you can use the dialog box to assign one or more resources to one or more selected task(s) at the same time.
- If the underlying active view is a task view, you can use the dialog box to remove one or more resources from one or more selected tasks.
- If the underlying active view is a task view, you can use the dialog box to replace one resource with another resource for selected tasks.
- If you have already selected a task in the active view, all the resources assigned to that task are shown at the top of the resource list. The rest of the list is automatically alphabetized.
- You can view a graph that shows the work or available work time for the selected resource.
- If you assign the resource to the selected task, you can view a graph that shows the impact that assignment has on the resource's workload, easily identifying whether the assignment leads to an overallocation for the resource.

NOTE

> If you are using Microsoft Project 2003 Professional, you see an additional column titled R/D in the Assign Resources dialog box. This topic is addressed in the "Assigning Resource Units" section later in this chapter, on page **374**.

Filtering the Resource List

If you have a large number of resources, the list of resource names in the Assign Resources dialog box can be quite long. At the top of the list are the resources, if any, who are assigned to the selected task. The rest of the list is alphabetized, with resources of different types intermingled. Applying a filter can shorten the display to just the resources that meet the filter criteria.

NOTE

> Note that resources that are already assigned to the selected task (those that are checked at the top of the list) are listed whether they meet the filter criteria or not.

You can apply two types of filters:

- **Named resource filters**—You can apply any of the named resource filters, or you can create a new one on-the-fly and apply it immediately. For example, you could apply the Resources - Material filter to get a short list of just the material resources.
- **The Available to Work filter**—You can apply the Available to Work filter that is accessible only from the Assign Resources dialog box. If it is used correctly, this filter shows you a list of the resources who have enough calendar working time to do the work required for a specific task during the time the task is currently scheduled.

These two filter types can be used alone or in combination for greater precision in finding the right resource for a task.

Using the Named Resource Filters

Several predefined resource filters come with Project 2003 and can be helpful in finding the resource you want to use:

- The Resources - Work filter shows only the work resources, thus making it easier to find them in a long resource list.
- The Resources - Material filter shows just the material resources.
- The Group filter prompts you to type a keyword that you expect to find in the Group column of the Resource sheet. It then shows only the resources that have that exact entry in the Group field. For example, if you have entered job titles in the Group column, you can use this filter to select the resources that have a job title that qualifies them to work on a particular task.

TIP

> The Group filter selects only the resources whose Group field value matches exactly what you enter in response to the prompt. You might find it more useful if you change the filter test from *equals* to *contains* (or *contains exactly* if you put multiple comma-separated values in the field).

→ **See** "Creating Custom Filters," **p. 859**, for help with customizing filters.

To make the most effective use of resource filters, you should use custom fields, in which you enter special keyword values that you can use when filtering the resource list. For example, you might use a custom text field to list resource skills. Then you would create an interactive filter that prompts you to specify the skill you want so it can display a short list of resources with that skill.

→ For instructions on how to use custom fields **see** "Customizing Fields," **p. 847**.

> **NOTE**
> If some resources have multiple skills, you can use comma-separated entries in the field. The filter needs to test that the field `contains` or `contains exactly` the specified skill. Note that you must not include a space after the comma separator if you use the `contains exactly` test.

Another useful custom field that you could use for filtering is one that contains the city where a resource is located so that you can select resources that are near the facility where work will take place. Other examples include fields that contain department or organization codes, job codes, or cost accounting codes.

To apply a filter to the list of resource names in the Assign Resources dialog box, follow these steps:

1. Display the Assign Resources dialog box by clicking the Assign Resources tool on the Standard toolbar.
2. Fill the check box under Filter By.
3. Select the filter in the list box to the right or click the More Filters button to display the More Filters dialog box, where you can create a new filter or customize an existing filter.

> **NOTE**
> If you create a new filter from the Assign Resources dialog box, be sure to click the Apply button to close the More Filters dialog box. The new filter does not appear in the Assign Resources list of filters until you close and reopen that dialog box.

To remove the filter after you finish using it, choose All Resources in the filter list.

USING THE AVAILABLE TO WORK FILTER

Suppose you select a two-day task that is scheduled for Monday and Tuesday and that you want to assign a resource to do the 16 hours of work on the task. If you enable the Available to Work filter and enter **16h** in the criterion box, Project displays only the resources that have at least 16 hours of working time available during the Monday and Tuesday when the task is scheduled. To select the resources that the filter will display, Project does the following calculation (see Table 10.3):

1. Project looks at each resource's calendar of working time and notes the number of hours available on that particular Monday and Tuesday. For example, say that Resource A has 8 hours available each day, as shown in the Calendar Working Time row of Table 10.3.
2. Project looks at the Resource Availability table on the General tab of the Resource Information dialog box, for the maximum units available on that Monday and Tuesday. For example, say that Resource A is a consolidated resource and that there are 200% maximum units both days, as shown on the Max Units row in Table 10.3.
3. Project multiplies each day's available hours by the number of units available. For Resource A that would be 8 times 200% for each day, or 32 hours of working time for the 2 days (see the Total Working Time row in Table 10.3).
4. Project looks at other assignments during the same period for the resources. Say that Resource A is already assigned to do 8 hours of work on another task on Monday but has no other assignments during Tuesday (see the Other Assignments row in Table 10.3).
5. Finally, Project subtracts the hours already assigned (8, in this example) from the total working time available (32, in this example) and calculates the total hours available to work. For Resource A, that is 24 hours, as shown in the last row of Table 10.3. Because in this case the filter is looking for resources with at least 16 hours available, Resource A would be one of the resources that is displayed by the filter.

Table 10.3 Calculating the Available to Work Value for Resource A

Calculation Steps	Monday	Tuesday	Total
Calendar Working Time	8h	8h	16h
Max Units	200%	200%	200%
Total Working Time	16h	16h	32h
Other Assignments	8h	0h	8h
Available to Work	8h	16h	24h

To use this filter, you need to fill the Available to Work check box and then enter the amount of work you require for the task. For the example illustrated in Table 10.3, you could enter **16h**. You can enter the work by using any time units (for example, **2d** would work in this case), but Project converts the entry to hours. When the filter is turned on, you can select different tasks in the underlying task view, and the list of names is adjusted for the duration of each selected task.

Graphing Resource Availability

Suppose that you want a specific resource to work on a task, but the resource doesn't have available work hours during the time the task is currently scheduled. One of the possible solutions could be to reschedule the task to a time when the resource has enough work time available. You can select the resource in the Assign Resources dialog box and click the Graphs button to display timeline graphs and accompanying data tables that show information about the selected resource's availability and currently assigned work. You can choose among three graphs:

- **The Remaining Availability graph**—You can choose the Remaining Availability graph to see the remaining available working time along a timeline (see Figure 10.5). You can zoom in or out on the timeline to view the data by hours, days, weeks, months, and so forth. If you have selected multiple resources, the data for each is color coded, and check boxes in the graph legend let you temporarily remove and restore individual resources in the display.

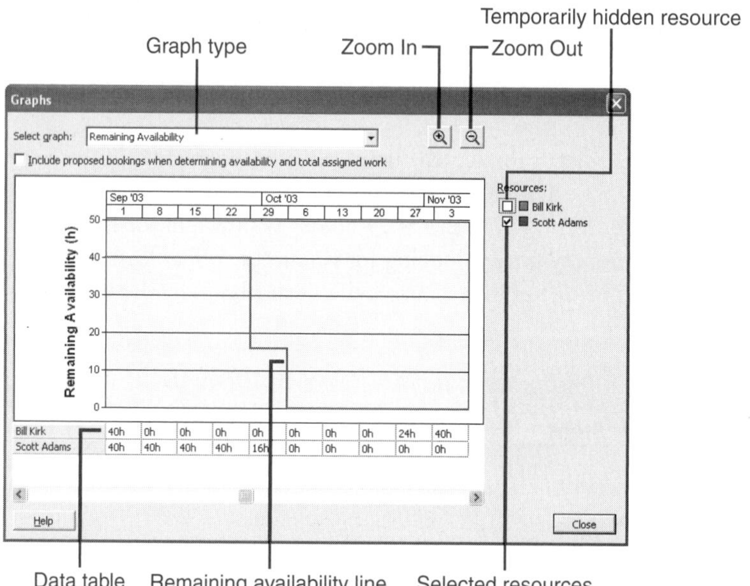

Figure 10.5
The Remaining Availability graph shows the number of hours available for assignments.

- **The Work graph**—The Work graph looks similar to the Remaining Availability graph, but it shows already assigned work. You can zoom the time line, and multiple resources are color coded and can be removed and restored from the graph.
- **The Assignment Work graph**—You can choose the Assignment Work graph (see Figure 10.6) to see both the work already assigned and the total availability. If you select a task in the underlying view to which the resource is assigned, this graph also distinguishes the work assignment on the selected task from assigned work on all other tasks. For example, if you select a task and assign the resource to it, this graph shows you the total available work for the resource, the amount of work assigned to the selected task, and the total work assigned to other tasks. You can easily see if the total of all the assignments exceeds the availability for the resource. If it does, you know you have overallocated the resource.

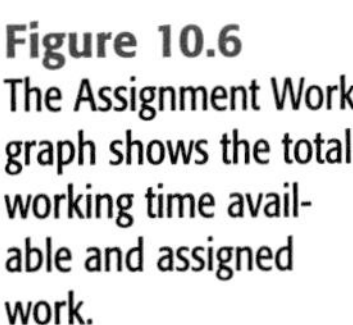

Figure 10.6
The Assignment Work graph shows the total working time available and assigned work.

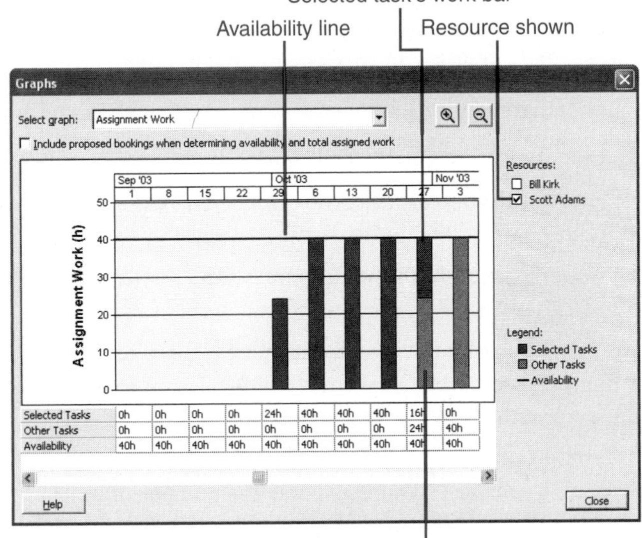

To view a graph, follow these steps:

1. Display a task view as the active view; it cannot be one of the task forms.

2. Display the Assign Resources dialog box by clicking the Assign Resources tool on the Standard toolbar.
3. Select one or more resources whose data you want included in the graph. Use Ctrl+click to add nonadjacent resources to the selection.
4. If you are going to view the Assignment Work graph and want currently assigned tasks to be included, select the tasks now. After the graph window opens, you can't change the selection. The quickest way to include all tasks assigned to the selected resource(s) is to select all tasks by using the Select All button (the blank space above the ID column).
5. Click the Graphs button to display the Microsoft Graph window.
6. Choose the graph type in the Select Graph box.
7. If you selected multiple resources, remove and restore individual resources by using the check boxes next to their names in the legend.
8. Use the Zoom In and Zoom Out buttons to compress or expand the time line.
9. When you are finished, click the Close button.

NOTE

> You can't modify the formatting of the graph. Your only controls are those listed here.

10

Assigning Resource Units

The preceding sections show how to use the Assign Resources dialog box to select a resource for an assignment. You can also use this dialog box to create assignments.

To add a resource assignment to a selected task or group of tasks, follow these steps:

1. Select the task or tasks to which you want the resource assigned.

2. Display the Assign Resources dialog box by clicking the Assign Resources tool on the Standard toolbar.
3. Select the resource name from the Resource Name list or type the name for a new resource.
4. If the resource is a work resource, the default for the Units field is 100% (or the max units for the resource, if that is less than 100%). If you want to assign a different number of units, select the Units cell to the right of the resource name and enter the new value.

   If the resource is a material resource, enter the number of units to be consumed by the task in the Units cell. If you enter just a numeral, Project schedules that total number of units to be consumed by the task, no matter what the task duration. If you enter a number with a time period appended (for example, **2/d**), Project schedules that number to be consumed per time period for the duration of the task.

10

TIP

> For work resources, the units should be no greater than the maximum units available for the resource at the time the task is scheduled. If you do not know the maximum units available, double-click the resource name to see the Resource Information dialog box. The Resource Availability table in that dialog box shows the maximum units for different time periods.

5. Click the Assign button or press Enter to assign the resource and unit information to the selected tasks.
6. If you are using Project Professional, select either Request or Demand in the R/D field. A *requested* resource is equivalent to a soft-booked resource that will eventually work on something else. A *demanded* resource will not be automatically replaced by the Resource Substitution Wizard. Note that this field, if left blank, will consider the assignment as a *request* only. This field is useless if Project Professional is used without Project Server or if the Resource Substitution Wizard is not to be used.
7. If you are adding more resources to the same tasks, select the next resource name to be assigned, type the number of units in the Units field, and select Assign to assign this resource to the selected tasks.

When you use the Assign Resources dialog box to change resource assignments, Project displays a SmartTag to let you choose how it should calculate changes in the schedule (see Figure 10.7). The SmartTag feature compensates for the limited control you have over the variables when you modify an assignment in the Assign Resources dialog box. For example, if you change the units assigned, Project immediately changes the task duration (unless it's a fixed-duration task). But you can use the SmartTag to have Project put duration back where it was and change the work instead.

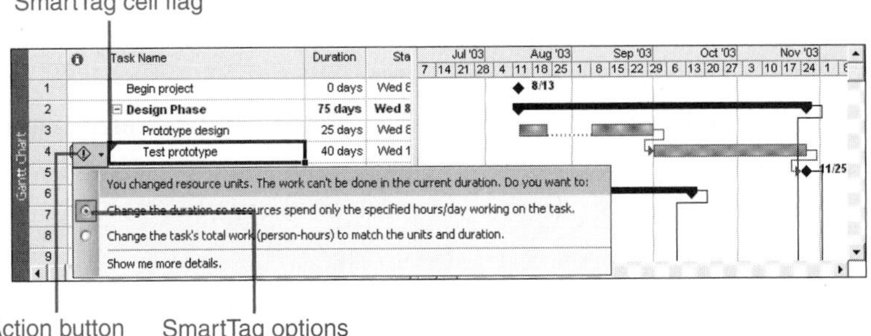

Figure 10.7
SmartTags present options for how schedule changes will be calculated.

As soon as you change the assignment, a small green triangle appears in the top-left corner of the task name cell. If you select the cell or merely move the mouse over the cell, an Action button appears, and you can click it to display the calculation options. SmartTags stay visible only as long as you can undo an action.

For example, if you change the units for an assignment, the SmartTag lets you choose to have either work or duration change as a result. If you assign an additional resource to a task or remove an existing resource, the SmartTag lets you choose to change duration (keeping work and units unchanged), change work (keeping duration and units constant), or change units (keeping work and duration constant).

NOTE

> SmartTags are triggered by assignment changes that are made in the Assign Resources dialog box and in cells in tables. They are not triggered when you make changes by using the Task Form view or the Task Information dialog box, because in those venues, you can control all the scheduling variables before you click OK.

SCHEDULING RESOURCES FOR A SPECIFIC AMOUNT OF WORK

For work resources, you can also use the Assign Resources dialog box to calculate the number of units needed to complete a specified amount of work within the task's current duration. Normally, you enter a simple percentage in the Units column of the Assign Resources dialog box. If you enter a work amount in the Units column (a number followed by a time unit, such as `40h` for 40 hours), Project calculates the number of units of that resource that are needed to do that much work within the current duration for the task. This procedure does not work if the task is effort driven and this is the initial assignment of the resource to the task. You can use the technique to recalculate an existing working resource assignment, even if the task is effort driven.

To assign resources by using a work amount, follow these steps:

1. Select the task or tasks to which you want the resource assigned.
2.  Display the Assign Resources dialog box by clicking the Assign Resources tool on the Standard toolbar.
3. Select the resource name from the Name list.
4. Select the Units field and type the work amount followed by the unit it's measured in: `m` (min), `h` (hour), `d` (day), `w` (week), or `mo` (month).
5. Select a different cell, click the Assign button, or press Enter to have Project calculate the units and assign the resource to the selected tasks.

ADDING RESOURCES BY USING DRAG-AND-DROP

With the Assign Resources dialog box, you can create an assignment by dragging a resource name to a task. An advantage to using this drag-and-drop assignment method is that you do not have to preselect the task for which a resource should be assigned. However, Project automatically assigns the default units (usually 100%).

To assign resources to a task by using the drag-and-drop method, perform the following steps:

1.  Display the Assign Resources dialog box by clicking the Assign Resources tool on the Standard toolbar.
2. Select the resource by clicking the Name field.
3. Position the mouse pointer over the gray button just to the left of the resource name. The Assign Resources graphic appears below the mouse pointer. You can see the pointer and graphic in Figure 10.8, where Jenny Benson is being assigned to a task.
4. Hold down the mouse button (a plus sign appears next to the pointer graphic) and drag the mouse pointer to the task for which the resource should be assigned.
5. When the task is highlighted, release the mouse button to assign the resource.

TIP

> To assign multiple resources to a task by using the drag-and-drop feature, hold down the Ctrl key while selecting the resource names in the Assign Resources dialog box. When you click on one of the gray buttons and drag the mouse pointer to the task, all selected resources are assigned at once.

REMOVING RESOURCE ASSIGNMENTS FROM ONE OR MORE TASKS

To remove a resource assignment from one or more selected tasks, follow these steps:

1. Select the task (or tasks) in the view that has resource assignments you want to remove.
2.  Display the Assign Resources dialog box by clicking the Assign Resources tool on the Standard toolbar.

Figure 10.8
When you point to the gray button beside a selected resource, the mouse pointer appears as a selection arrow that carries a resource.

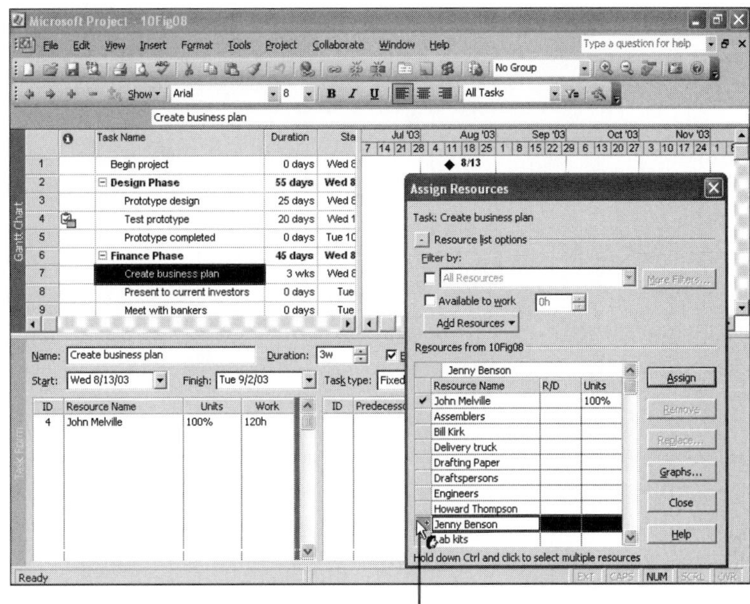

3. Select the resource you want to remove from the assignment by clicking the row for the resource. Use Ctrl+click to select multiple resources for removal.

NOTE

> Resources assigned to the selected task are identified by check marks to the left of the resource name. If a check mark is gray instead of black, your task selection in the view includes some tasks that have that resource assigned and some that do not.

4. Choose the Remove button. The resources that are selected in the Assign Resources dialog box are removed from any assignments they might have with the tasks that are selected in the underlying view.

Modifying an Assignment

You can use the Assign Resources dialog box to replace one resource with another, to change the assigned units for a resource, or to change the amount of work assigned to a resource. Each assignment should be modified individually, and different techniques can be used, depending on what you want to modify.

To replace an assigned resource with another resource name, follow these steps:

1. Select the task. You can select multiple tasks by using the Ctrl key if you want to make an identical assignment change in all of them. In Figure 10.9, the Prototype Design task is selected, and Mary Logan will replace Bill Kirk in the resource assignments.

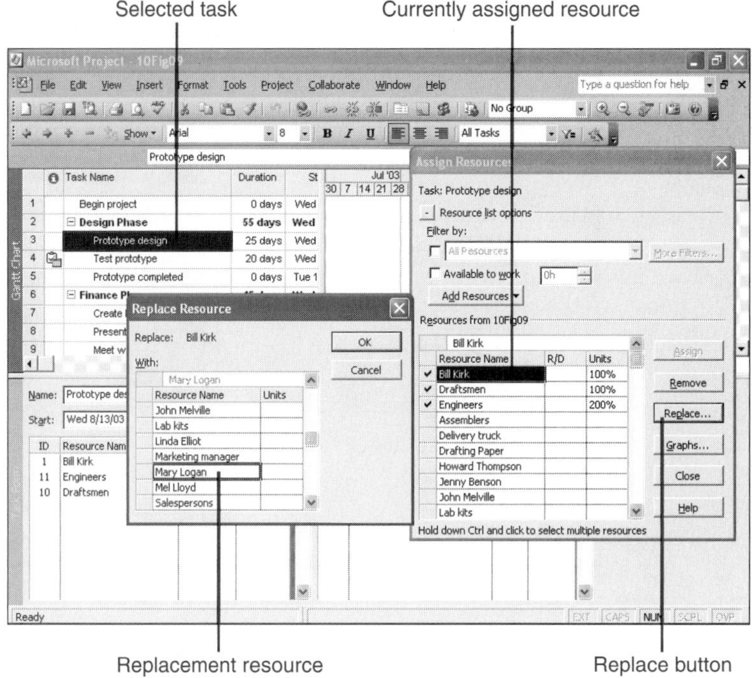

Figure 10.9
The Replace Resource dialog box provides a list of replacement resources to choose from.

2. Display the Assign Resources dialog box by clicking the Assign Resources tool on the Standard toolbar.
3. Select the resource name to be replaced.
4. Click the Replace button. Project displays the Replace Resource dialog box over the Assign Resources dialog box. In Figure 10.9, the Replace Resource dialog box has been moved so that you can see both dialog boxes.
5. Select the new resource name.
6. Select the Units field for the selected resource and a new value if you don't want to use the same units value.
7. Click OK or press Enter.

NOTE

> If you have filtered the list of resource names, the list in the Replace Resource dialog box is filtered also.

To replace the number of units in a resource assignment, you simply edit the entry in the Units field. You select a different cell or press Enter to complete the change. You can then use the SmartTag to override Project's default calculation.

To replace the amount of work assigned to a resource, select the cell for the units and type a work amount (a number followed by a time unit abbreviation). Project divides the task duration by the work amount you entered and assigns the resulting units. You can use the SmartTag to override Project's default calculation.

ASSIGNING RESOURCES WITH THE TASK ENTRY VIEW

The Task Entry view, with the Gantt Chart view in the top pane and the Task Form view in the bottom pane, is one of the best combination views for assigning resources. You have access to the important fields that govern the task, and the form can display resource assignment details in a table at the bottom of the form. The most commonly displayed details are ID resource, name, units, and work for each assigned resource, but you can also display the overtime work fields and the scheduled delay fields for fine-tuning individual assignments. This is a convenient place for assigning resources because it enables you to enter resource units, work, or both for each resource assignment.

TIP

If you use the Task Form view to create and modify assignments, you might still want to use the Assign Resources dialog box to filter the resource list to help determine the best resource to assign.

The Task Entry view is the view you get when you display the Gantt Chart view and use the Window, Split command. The Task Form view is displayed in the bottom pane, with one of eight possible sets of details. You can right-click over the form and select the details you want to use (see Figure 10.10). For assigning resources, you should use either the default details, Resources and Predecessors, or you should use Resource Work.

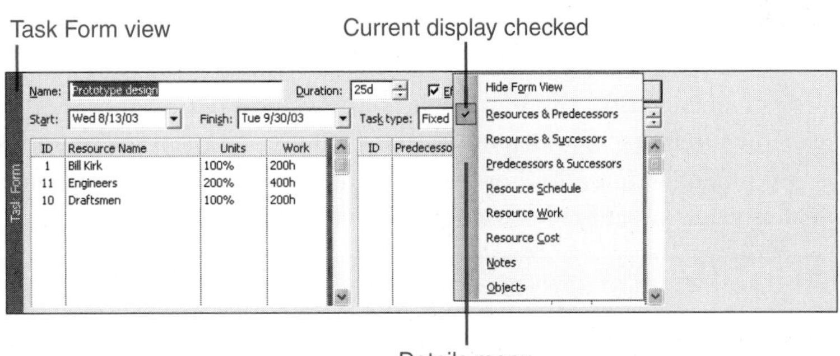

Figure 10.10 The Details menu for the Task Form view shows the current display with a check mark and enables you to select a new display.

ENTERING THE ASSIGNMENT VALUES

To assign resources by using the Task Form view, follow these steps:

1. Select the task in the top pane.
2. Check the Task Type field to be sure that it is set appropriately to manage the calculations for the assignments you are about to enter. For instance, if you are adding work

resources and you want to be sure the duration doesn't change, make the task a fixed-duration task for this assignment and then return it to its prior setting after completing the assignment.

3. If you are adding new work resource names to (or deleting existing resource names from) an existing list of resource name assignments, check the Effort Driven field for its appropriateness. If the changes you are about to enter change the total work associated with the task, clear the Effort Driven check box. However, if the changes simply redistribute the existing total work among the resources assigned to the task, you should leave the field checked.
4. Select the Resource Name field and identify the resource by selecting the resource name from the drop-down list. You can also type the name, but if you misspell it, Project might create a new resource for the misspelled name.
5. If you leave the Units field blank, Project assigns the default (the lesser of 100% or Max Units for the resource). If you want to specify the units for the assignment, select the Units field and enter the units you want to assign, as follows:
    - For work resources, type a units value as a percentage (for example, **200%**) unless you have chosen to use a decimal format for units (for example, **2**).
    - For material resources that have a fixed consumption rate, type a decimal number that represents the total units to be consumed by the task. For example, if 20 gallons of fuel are to be assigned, enter **20**. Project replaces this entry with 20 plus the material label.
    - For material resources that have a variable consumption rate, type the number of units as a decimal, followed by a slash and a time unit, to indicate a rate of consumption. For example, to assign 20 gallons of fuel per week, enter **20/wk**. Project replaces this entry with 20 gal/wk.
6. If you leave the Work field blank, Project calculates the work based on the task duration and the assigned (or default) units. If you want to specify the amount of work for the assignment, select the Work field and type the work amount. For work resources, work must be entered with a number plus the unit of measure: **m** (min), **h** (hour), **d** (day), **w** (week), or **mo** (month). For material resources, enter a decimal value, and Project uses this value as the fixed consumption rate for the task.

PMI recommends that no activity be estimated to take more than 80 hours of effort and no fewer than 8. This is for purposes of managing the activity. With 80 hours, a 10% slippage (that is, 8 hours) would typically require overtime to make up. This is why most project status meetings should occur on a weekly or biweekly basis. For activities that take less than 8 hours, most project managers would not be interested in micromanaging the work.

NOTE

Recall that if you enter both units and work when you assign the first resource, Project recalculates the duration. However, with fixed-duration tasks, Project keeps the duration and work and recalculates units.

7. If you are assigning multiple resources, you can enter additional resources in the next rows of the Resource Name column before you click the OK button. For instance, Figure 10.11 shows the resources to be assigned to the Prototype Design task.
8. After all resource assignments are made for the task, click the OK button, and Project calculates the fields that were left blank.

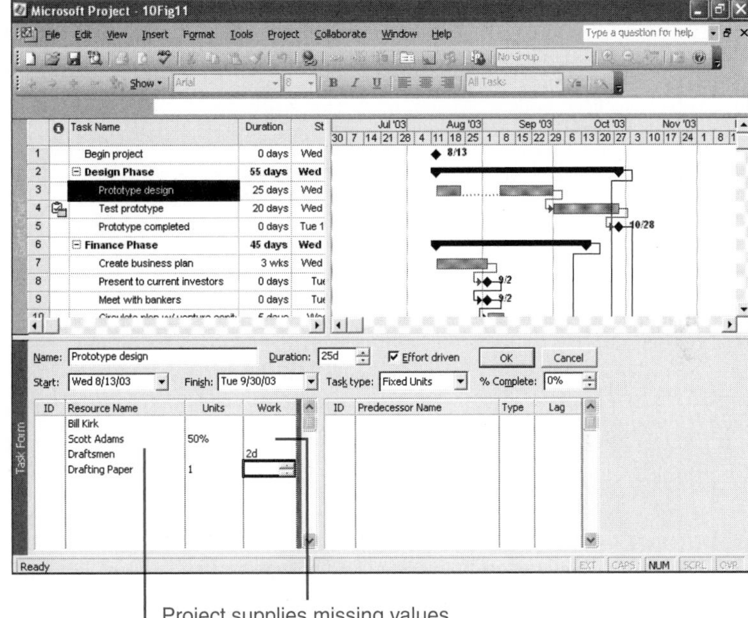

Figure 10.11
Initially entering all the resources that are to be assigned to a task at once makes the calculations easier to manage.

When you click OK, Project calculates the values for the fields that you did not fill in, in accordance with the principles discussed in Chapter 9 (see Figure 10.12).

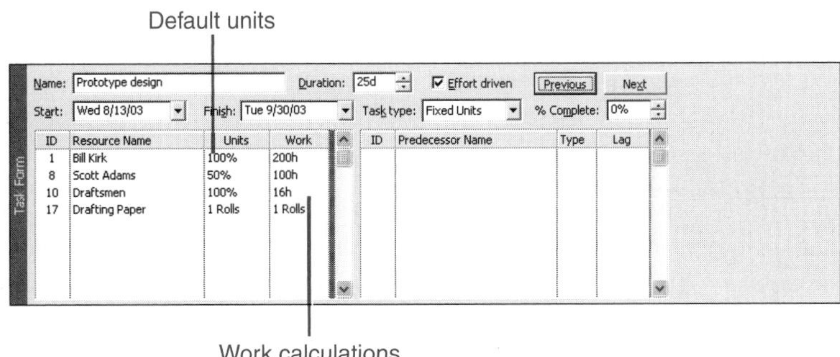

Figure 10.12
Project calculates all the initial assignments at once, filling in the fields you don't supply.

ADDING DELAY TO AN ASSIGNMENT IN FIXED-START-DATE PROJECTS

When you assign a resource to a task in a project that has a fixed start date, Project schedules the work to start when the task starts. Sometimes, however, one or more of the resources assigned to a task might be allowed to delay starting until after the task is partly completed by other resources.

NOTE

> This discussion is presented in terms of *forward-scheduled* projects–projects with fixed start dates. The case of the project with a fixed finish date is explained later in the section "Adding Delay in Fixed Finish Date Projects."

For example, if you assign a marketing manager, an engineer, and a draftsman to draw up a preliminary design for a product, the draftsman's work on the task doesn't really start until some design details have already been proposed. To accurately schedule the draftsman's work, Project needs to delay the start of the draftsman's scheduled work to some time after the task starts.

Microsoft Project provides an Assignment Delay field, which you can use to force a delay in the scheduled work for a resource beyond the start of the task. If you want to enter a value in the Delay field on the Task Form, you need to display the resource schedule details, where the Delay field is available for editing.

NOTE

> You can get to the Delay field by replacing the Task Form view with the Resource Form view and displaying the schedule details (which is just like the resource schedule details on the Task Form view).
>
> You can also enter delays on the Task Usage and Resource Usage views. The Task Usage view is discussed in the section "Assigning Resources with the Task Usage View" later in this chapter. The Resource Usage view is explored in greater detail in Chapter 11, "Resolving Resource Assignment Problems."

Figure 10.13 shows the Task Form view with the resource schedule details displayed. The Prototype Design task is selected, and the assigned resources are listed in the assignment details. The Draftsmen resource is scheduled to work only 16 hours, which is much less than the hours for the other work resources.

You can also see in Figure 10.13 that Project has scheduled all resources except the draftsman to start at the start of the task, which is 8/13/03, and to finish on 9/30/03. (Because of the task split, the difference between the start and finish dates is more than the task duration.) In reality, the draftsman is expected to execute his assignment in the last 2 days of the task (9/29/03 and 9/30/03), after the other resources have completed most of their work.

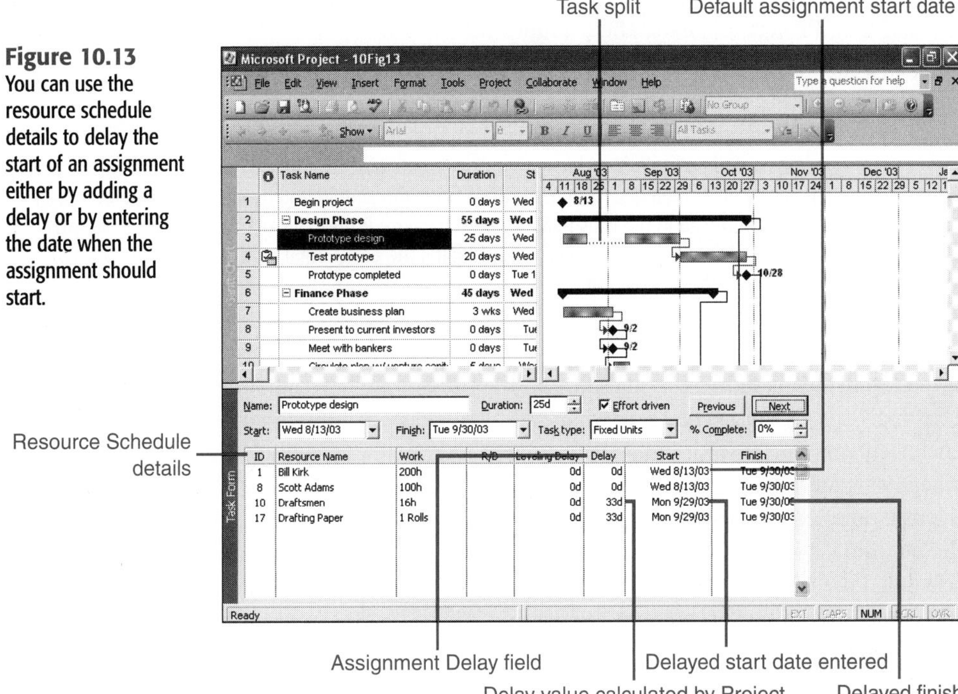

Figure 10.13
You can use the resource schedule details to delay the start of an assignment either by adding a delay or by entering the date when the assignment should start.

You can create a delay in the Task Form view by entering the amount of the delay in the Delay field or by entering the start date for the assignment. Because of the task split, it is easier to create this particular delay by entering the start date for the draftsmen assignment (9/29/03) than to try to calculate the amount of the delay.

In Figure 10.13, the date 9/29/03 was entered in the Assignment Start field for the Draftsmen resource, and Project has calculated the delay to be 33d and the assignment finish to be 09/30/03. Note that all resources finish their assignments on the same date (which is also the finish of the task). Of course, if the delay causes the draftsman's assignment to finish after all the other assignments are finished, it also delays the finish of the task and increases the task's duration.

To enter a delay in an assignment, follow these steps:

1. Display the Task Form view or Task Details Form view in the bottom pane of a task view.
2. Activate the form in the bottom pane and display the schedule details by right-clicking and choosing Resource Schedule.
3. Select the task for the assignment in the top pane.
4. Select the cell in the Delay field for the resource name you want to delay, and then enter a delay value. Use a number followed by the measurement units for the delay (minutes, hours, days, weeks, or months).

Alternatively, you can enter a delayed start date for the assignment in the Start field, and then Project calculates the amount of the delay.

5. Click the OK button to complete the entry.

CAUTION

> As noted earlier in the chapter, you can create a delay either by entering the Delay value or by entering a new date in the Start field. You should not, however, attempt to enter a delayed date in the Finish date column because Project doesn't treat that as a delaying tactic. Instead, Project treats it as extending the assignment, and it recalculates the Work value of the assignment.

10

If the Draftsmen resource doesn't start work until 9/29/03, then the material resource Drafting Paper is not needed until that date also. Delaying a material resource can be done effectively only in the Task Usage or Resource Usage views because of the way Project schedules material resources. The units of a material resource are distributed evenly over the task duration. In this case, the 1 roll of paper would be distributed over the 25 days of the task duration, with .04 roll scheduled each day. If you were to delay that assignment, the scheduled use of paper would be pushed out past the current finish date for the task. We will come back to this problem in the section "Assigning Resources with the Task Usage View," later in this chapter.

To remove a delay for an assignment, you enter **0** in the Delay field and click the OK button. Project reschedules the assignment at the start of the task.

If you have delayed an assignment in a fixed-duration task, even though the assignment appears to be shorter than the task duration, Project increases the task duration! See "Scheduling Short Assignments in Fixed-Duration Tasks" in the "Troubleshooting" section at the end of this chapter.

Adding Delay in Fixed-Finish-Date Projects

As noted earlier, the discussion in the previous section is based on a project with a fixed start date, and the delay is used to offset the start of an assignment from the start of the task. If a project has a fixed finish date, Project schedules the finish dates for tasks first and then works backward to calculate the start date. Thus, in fixed-finish-date projects, Microsoft Project already delays tasks and assignments to As Late As Possible. So, in a case such as the draftsman who should start later than the others, Project automatically does that.

Suppose, however, that you have a task for which one resource has a small amount of work that needs to be done toward the beginning of the task and other resources who continue on the task after that one is finished. In a project with a fixed finish date, Project would schedule that one resource's work at the end of the task. You need to force Project to schedule an early finish for that one resource. Thus, the concept of the delayed start becomes an early finish. Instead of adding the value in the Assignment Delay field to the task start to calculate the assignment start, in fixed-finish-date projects, the Assignment Delay value is *subtracted* from the task finish to calculate an early assignment finish. That in turn leads to an earlier start for the assignment.

For fixed-finish-date projects, the Assignment Delay field accepts only negative numbers, and the delay amount is subtracted from the task finish date, to calculate an early finish for the assignment; then the start is calculated. You can also enter an earlier date in the Finish date field, and Project calculates the negative delay and new start date for you. If you enter a new date in the Start Date column, Project recalculates the Work value of the assignment instead of calculating a delay. As before, to remove a delay, you set the entry in the Assignment Delay field to **0**.

ASSIGNING OVERTIME WORK

Recall that Project schedules work during the working times that are defined in the resource calendar (or in the task calendar, if one is assigned and you have elected to ignore the resource calendars). Work that is scheduled during calendar working times is called *regular work* in Microsoft Project. If you want a resource to complete more work than can be done in regular time for a given period, you can assign part of the work as *overtime*. Project reduces the amount of the assignment's work that is scheduled during the regular hours, but the total work, regular plus overtime, remains the same.

Note that when you enter overtime work hours, you do not designate the exact days and hours when the overtime work takes place; you just tell Project that a certain number of hours on the task are overtime hours. Project schedules the overtime work by spreading it out evenly over the duration of the assignment. Later, when you enter actual work completed, you can specify exactly how many hours of overtime were completed in any given time period.

The cost of the overtime hours is calculated by using the overtime rate that you defined in the Resource Information dialog box for the period in which the work took place.

Another way to schedule more work during a specific time period is to change the resource calendar and increase the working time hours for that time period. You can edit the resource calendar and change nonworking days or hours into working times. Be aware, however, that Microsoft Project charges the standard rate for work scheduled during the regular working time hours. If the overtime rate for the resource is not zero, changing nonworking days or hours into working times is not a good solution because the cost is misrepresented. However, if you don't pay for overtime, editing the calendar is satisfactory. Indeed, editing the calendar gives you the ability to state explicitly when the extra work time takes place. The drawback in this situation is that if you are to reassign the resource to different tasks, or if the task gets rescheduled to a different date range, you no longer need the extra working time. Project uses the time for other assignments unless you remember to remove the extra working time from the calendar.

You can view scheduled overtime in the Task Usage and Resource Usage views, but you cannot enter overtime in those views unless you add a column to the table for the Overtime Work field. The Overtime Work field appears in three views for you to view and edit:

- The Task Form view, with the resource work details table displayed at the bottom of the form

- The Task Details Form view, with the resource work details table displayed at the bottom of the form
- The Resource Form view, with the work details table displayed at the bottom of the form

NOTE

If you assign all the work to be done in overtime, Project reduces the duration of the task to zero and automatically flags the task as a milestone. You can remove the Milestone flag by opening the Task Information dialog box and clearing the Mark Task as Milestone check box on the Advanced tab. The milestone symbol no longer appears in the Gantt Chart view for the task, although its duration is still zero.

To enter overtime in the Task Form view, follow these steps:

1. Choose a task view such as the Gantt Chart view from the View menu for the top pane.
2. Select the task for which you want to schedule overtime.
3. Display the Task Form view in the bottom pane by choosing Window, Split.
4. Press F6 to activate the Task Form view in the bottom pane.
5. In the bottom pane, right-click the form and select Resource Work from the shortcut menu, to display the Resource Work fields in the entry table (see Figure 10.14).
6. Select the Ovt. Work field and enter the amount of work that you are scheduling in overtime. Enter a number followed by a time unit abbreviation (m, h, d, w, or mo), and then press Enter. (Do not reduce the entry in the Work field. That field's entry must show the *total* amount of work to be done, including both the regular work and the overtime work.)
7. Click OK to complete the overtime assignment.

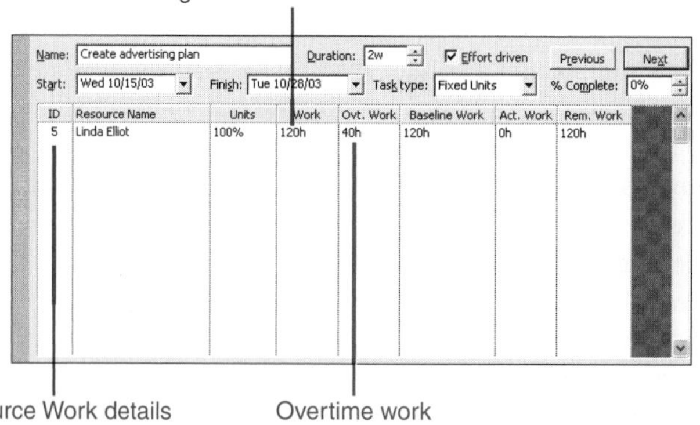

Figure 10.14
You can enter overtime hours and reduce task duration with the Task Form view.

NOTE

If you want to eliminate overtime, you must enter **0** in the Overtime field. You cannot leave the field empty because this field must contain a value.

In Figure 10.14, overtime has been entered for Linda Elliot's assignment to the Create Advertising Plan task. The total workload for this assignment is 120 hours, which was originally scheduled to take 3 weeks, but after recording 40 hours of overtime, the regular hours are only 80 and the task duration is reduced to 2 weeks. Usually, overtime is scheduled for just this reason—to reduce the calendar time required to complete a task.

Assigning Resources with the Task Usage View

Everything you accomplished in the previous section with the Gantt Chart view in the top pane can also be done with the Task Usage view in the top pane. In fact, you can do much more:

- You can display the Assignment Information dialog box, where you can apply work contours and different Cost Rate tables to an assignment and where you can write documentary notes about the assignment.
- You can view the *timephased* work schedule. The timephased view shows work broken down into specific time periods.
- You can display a number of timephased work and cost measures.
- You can edit many of the timephased values directly in the grid cells. For example, you can reapportion work among the time periods or create and fine-tune splits or delays in an individual assignment.

Figure 10.15 shows the Task Usage view in the top pane and the Task Form view in the bottom pane.

To display the Task Usage view, click the icon for the view on the View bar or choose View, Task Usage.

The table area of the Task Usage view displays all the tasks in the project, using (by default) the Usage table. Indented under each task are rows for that task's assignments. You can hide or show the assignments by using the outline icon to the left of the task name. The Work field for the task is the sum of the Work field values for the assigned resources.

The right side of the view is a timescale grid of cells that show timephased assignment details. In Figure 10.15, the work details are displayed in the grid. This is the default assignment detail, but you can display other details if desired. However, for creating and editing assignments, the Work detail is the most important. The value in the Work field for each resource in the table on the left is the sum of the timephased values displayed in the cells on that row in the timescale.

➔ For detailed instructions on changing the details displayed in a usage view, **see** "Changing the Timephased Details," **p. 412**.

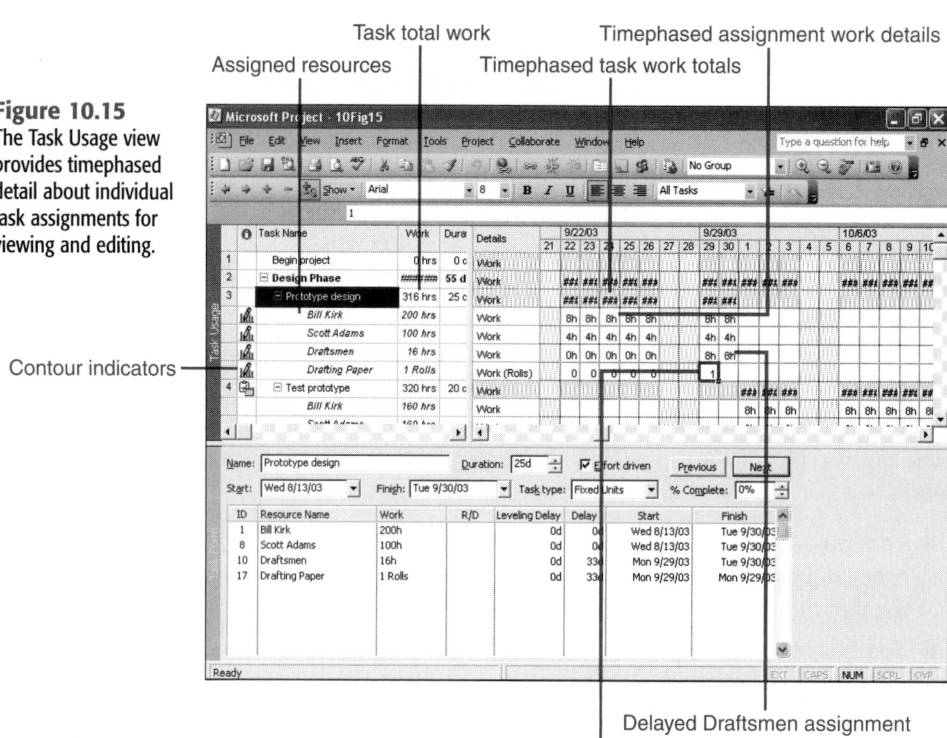

Figure 10.15
The Task Usage view provides timephased detail about individual task assignments for viewing and editing.

Figure 10.15 shows the delay in the Draftsmen resource's assignment: The timephased work values are all zero until the last two days of the task duration. You can also see that the Drafting Paper material resource usage has been delayed to the date when the Draftsmen resource starts. The following section explains how this was done.

Modifying Work Schedules with the Task Usage View

As mentioned previously, you can use the Task Usage view to customize the amount of work scheduled for each time period and to split and delay task assignments.

To change the amount of work scheduled for any given time period in the Task Usage view, simply select the timephased cell, type a new value, and either press Enter or select another cell. When you type a value for a work resource, Project assumes that the unit is hours unless you provide a different measurement unit.

NOTE

> If you type a value with a time unit that is not hours, Project converts the value to hours in the display. For example, if the timescale unit is days (that is, each cell is one day) and you type `1 week`, Project displays 40h (40 hours) in that cell. If the assignment units is 100%, this is too many hours for that one day. This example also serves to warn you that you should not enter a work value that represents more hours than are available for that time period.

You can use several techniques for editing the cells in the timephased grid:

- If you select a cell or group of consecutive cells in a row, you can use Ctrl+C to copy those values or Ctrl+X to cut those values from the grid. You can then select a cell at a new location and use Ctrl+V to paste the values into the cell at that location. If you chose to cut cells, the cells then display 0h.
- If you select a cell or group of consecutive cells in a row, you can drag the border around the selection to a new location and drop the cells into that new location. The original location cells display 0h.
- If you select a cell or group of consecutive cells in a row, you can drag a copy to a new location by holding down the Ctrl key as you drag the selection border to the new location. The caution about dropping cells on nonworking days applies here also.
- The bottom-right corner of the cell selection border displays a small black square, which is called the *fill handle*. You can drag this handle to bordering cells in the same row to copy the value in the selection into those cells.
- If you select a cell or group of consecutive cells in a row, you can press the Insert key to insert nonworking time (`0h`) in place of the selection, pushing the selected values to the right. Thus, you effectively introduce a split.
- If you select a cell or group of consecutive cells in a row, you can press the Delete key to remove that work from the assignment. After clearing the cells you had selected, Project shifts to the left any cells on the right that contain work, to fill in the space you deleted.

10

For example, if you want to increase the work and duration of an assignment, you can select the last cell in the assignment and drag its fill handle to the right to fill as many additional work periods as you choose. Also, if you want to introduce a split in an assignment, you select the cells where the split is to occur and press the Insert key. To remove the split, you can select the cells that display 0h and press the Delete key.

If you modify a timephased cell on the task Work row, the new value is apportioned among all the work resource assignments that had work scheduled for that time period. The relative proportions of the total work for each resource are kept the same. If you modified a timephased cell on an assignment row, the new values change the sum in the row for the task.

When you complete a cell modification, Project immediately recalculates the task and assignments as follows:

- If you modified a cell on the task row, the changes are applied to all assignments that were scheduled during that time period.
- If you modified a cell on a row for a work resource, Project updates the summary value for that time period on the task row.
- The Work column entries for assignments in the table on the left are updated. These are the totals for all time periods for each assignment.

- The Work column entry for the task in the table on the left is updated. This is the total for all assignments for all time periods.
- The duration for the task is updated. If you have not changed the number of time periods in which work is scheduled, there is no change in the duration.

CAUTION

> **Be very careful when using these editing techniques when you have a project with a fixed finish date. The results are not the same as for a fixed-start-date project and therefore are likely to cause you to lose a lot of time trying to correct the changes.**

To introduce a split in a task or in an individual assignment using the Task Usage view, follow these steps:

1. Display the Task Usage view in the top pane. You can type changes into timephased cells in the bottom pane, but you can't use drag-and-drop techniques in that pane.
2. Select the cell or cells that currently have work in them where you want to insert the split. If you select cells on the task row, the split is applied to all the resource assignments for the task. If you select cells on an assignment row, only that assignment is affected.
3. Press the Insert key. Project shifts the work values to the right, leaving the selected cells with no scheduled work during that period.

To delay an assignment, you could select the cell for the beginning of the assignment and press the Insert key repeatedly until the work is moved to the date when you want the work to start. Alternatively, you could select all the work cells for the assignment and drag the selection to the period where you want the work to be scheduled.

In Figure 10.15, the usage of the material resource Drafting Paper is shown to be delayed until 9/29/03. Originally, Project had distributed the 1 roll of paper evenly over the 25 days of the task duration (0.04 rolls per day). To create a delayed usage as in Figure 10.15, you would have to delete all the fractional units and type in the new usage, as shown in the figure. The quick way to remove all the fractional units is to type `0` in the Work column on the left. Then select the timephased cell for the date where you want to schedule the usage (9/29/03) and type in the value.

TIP

> **Drag-and-drop can be difficult to use if the destination is offscreen, because when you drag past the last visible cells, the screen scrolls quite rapidly. In those instances, it is easier to cut the selection, scroll to the destination, and paste.**

Using the Assignment Information Dialog Box

You can display the Assignment Information dialog box by selecting an assignment row in either the Task Usage view or the Resource Usage view and then clicking the Assignment

Information tool (or by double-clicking the assignment row). You can also display the dialog box by choosing Project, Assignment Information.

Figure 10.16 shows the Assignment Information dialog box for the draftsmen's delayed assignment from the previous example. As you can see, the dialog box provides several fields that you have already worked with on forms and tables, including Assignment Work, Assignment Units, and Start and Finish. The Cost field is a read-only total cost for the assignment. You can also change the name of the assigned resource here, but there is no drop-down list to choose the resource, so you must know how to spell the name—or you might end up creating a new resource out of a typographical error.

Figure 10.16
You can use the Assignment Information dialog box to enter assignment notes, to choose the Cost Rate table for the assignment, or to apply predefined work contours.

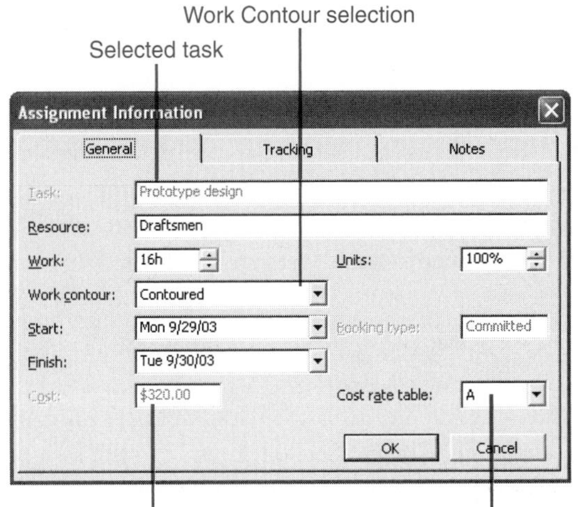

There are three fields in the Assignment Information dialog box that you won't find on any other standard view or dialog box in Project:

- The Work Contour field, on the General tab, enables you to choose from a set of predefined work contours. A *contour* is a planned pattern of scheduled work that is spread over the duration of an assignment. For example, the Front Loaded contour schedules a lot of work per day at the start of the assignment, and the daily work tapers off toward the end of the assignment.

  The default contour is Flat, which means the resource is scheduled to work the same number of hours each day, as called for by the assigned units and the hours available on the resource calendar. Thus, the workload is the same every day unless the calendar has varying amounts of working time. If you have edited the assignment or applied one of the other contours, you can return the assignment to the standard schedule by applying the Flat contour.

  The only other way to access and select the predefined contours is to display the Work Contour field as a column in the table in the Task Usage view or Resource Usage view.

- The Cost Rate Table field on the General tab enables you to select one of the five different Cost Rate tables as the standard and overtime rates for the assignment. The default assignment is Table A. The Cost Rate Table field can also be displayed as a column in the table.
- The Notes field on the Notes tab enables you to record notes about an assignment. For instance, you should record why you have delayed an assignment or chose a different Cost Rate table. You could also embed links to other documents such as job specifications, cost worksheets, or Web sites.

The Tracking tab has fields you can use to monitor work progress and record when work starts, how much work has been done so far and when work is completed. See Chapter 14, "Tracking Work on a Project," for information about using those fields.

SELECTING A PREDEFINED CONTOUR

By default, the work that Project schedules for an assignment is evenly distributed across the available time periods of the assignment (that is, the Flat contour). As you have already seen, you can edit the assignments in individual time periods to customize the schedule. You can also choose one of eight predefined contour patterns for Project to apply to an individual assignment.

→ For a more extensive discussion of the use of predefined contours, **see** "Contouring Resource Usage," **p. 348**.

For example, if a resource schedule needs to show lots of hours up front, with a tapering off toward the end, you can assign the Front Loaded contour to the assignment, and Project changes the work in the individual periods to reflect that pattern.

To select a contour for an assignment, follow these steps:

1. Select the assignment in the Task Usage view or the Resource Usage view.
2. Display the Assignment Information dialog box by clicking the Assignment Information tool or by double-clicking the assignment row.
3. On the General tab, use the drop-down list in the Work Contour field to select one of the predefined contours.
4. Click OK to have Project calculate the new assignment pattern.

SELECTING A COST RATE TABLE FOR AN ASSIGNMENT

One of the important features in Project is the ability to define a graduated scale of standard and overtime cost rates for a resource so that work on assignments can be charged at different rates for different types of work. For example, a consulting firm might assign a seasoned consultant to highly technical cases at higher rates than it would use for other more mundane tasks.

The only way to change the Cost Rate table for an assignment is to display the assignment by using either the Task Usage view or the Resource Usage view. The most convenient method in those views is to use the Assignment Information dialog box (but you can also display the Cost Rate Table field in the table on the left of the view). Choose one of the lettered cost tables in the drop-down list in the Cost Rate Table field to assign that cost table's standard, overtime, and per-use rates to the assignment. If there are dated changes in the rates, Project applies the rates that are defined in the table for the dates in which the task is scheduled.

NOTE

You can edit the Cost Rate tables only in the Resource Information dialog box. First, display a view with fields for resources, and then either double-click a resource name or click the Information tool on the standard toolbar to display the Resource Information dialog box. Click the Costs tab to display the five Cost Rate tables, A through E.

10

Creating Assignment Notes

You use the Notes tab of the Resource Information dialog box to document an assignment. You can type and format the note text just as you do the text of task notes and resource notes. You can insert documents into the note or insert links to documents that are stored outside the Project file. You can also insert hyperlinks to Web sites.

→ To learn more about using the Notes field, **see** "Attaching Notes to Tasks," **p. 142**.

Assigning Resources with the Task Information Dialog Box

You can use the Resources tab on the Task Information dialog box to add, change, or delete the resource assignment information for a selected task. As with the Assign Resources dialog box, you can use the Units field of the Task Information dialog box to enter either units or work; you are prevented from creating a new assignment on an effort-driven task by defining the work. If you enter work (by using a numeral followed by a time unit), Project calculates the units that would produce that much work, given the task's duration.

To change assignments by using the Task Information dialog box, follow these steps:

1. Select the task for which you want to add or change a resource assignment.

2. Display the Task Information dialog box by clicking the Task Information tool on the Standard toolbar. You can also access the Task Information dialog box by selecting the task, clicking the secondary mouse button, and choosing Task Information from the pop-up shortcut menu. Still another method is to use the shortcut key Shift+F2. The fields in the dialog box show the current data for the task (see Figure 10.17).
3. Select the Advanced tab and review the selections for the Task Type and Effort Driven fields. Be sure these are appropriate for the change you intend to implement.
4. Select the Resources tab to assign or view the resource information for the selected task.

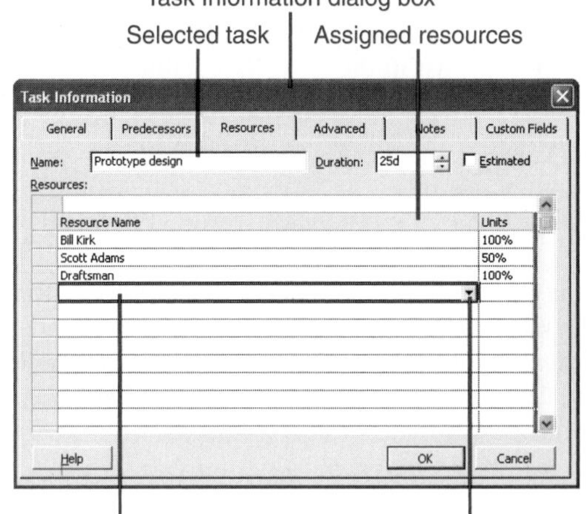

Figure 10.17
The Task Information dialog box contains a Resources tab that you can use to assign or edit resource assignments.

5. In the Resource Name box, edit an existing entry or choose a blank row to add a new resource. To add or change the resource, select a resource from the drop-down list in the field.
6. Type the unit assignment for the resource in the Units field. If you leave the Units field blank, Project supplies the default value (the lesser of 100% or the Max Units value for the resource).

   You can modify an existing assignment by entering a work amount followed by a time unit in the Units field. If you enter a work amount, Project adjusts the assigned units, not the duration of the task.
7. To add additional resources to the selected task, click the next Resource Name field and repeat the preceding steps.
8. After you complete all resource assignments for the task, click OK.

If you use the Ctrl key to select more than one task before opening the Task Information dialog box, Project displays the Multiple Task Information dialog box so that any resource you select is automatically assigned to all selected tasks. The resource assignment entries you make in the Multiple Task Information dialog box are added to existing resource assignments for the selected tasks.

NOTE

> You cannot change existing resource assignments for multiple tasks by using the Multiple Task Information dialog box.

Assigning Resources with the Task Table

You can use the Resource Name field on the Task table to assign resources to a task. However, entering the resource assignment data in the Resource Name field requires a text entry that has very specific syntax, and you will not likely assign resources here often. The entry must have the following syntax:

```
ResourceName1[Units],ResourceName2[Units],ResourceName3[Units] ...
```

When entering data using this format, note that the Units value follows immediately after the resource name, without an intervening space, and it is placed in square brackets. Units values of 100% do not need to be included. Notice, too, that multiple resource assignments are separated by commas. For example, the Resource Name field entry for the Prototype Design task might be

```
Bill Kirk,Scott Adams[50%],Draftsmen,Drafting Paper[1 Rolls]
```

Figure 10.18 shows this assignment. Because of the width of the Resource Names column, other columns and the Gantt Chart view are hidden in the figure.

10

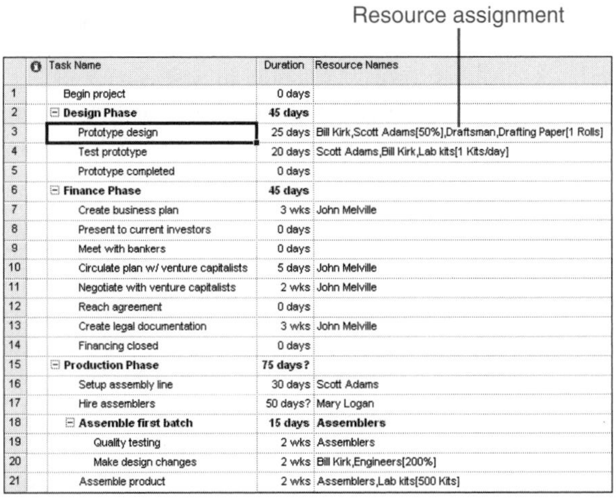

Resource assignment

		Task Name	Duration	Resource Names
1		Begin project	0 days	
2		⊟ **Design Phase**	**45 days**	
3		Prototype design	25 days	Bill Kirk,Scott Adams[50%],Draftsman,Drafting Paper[1 Rolls]
4		Test prototype	20 days	Scott Adams,Bill Kirk,Lab kits[1 Kits/day]
5		Prototype completed	0 days	
6		⊟ **Finance Phase**	**45 days**	
7		Create business plan	3 wks	John Melville
8		Present to current investors	0 days	
9		Meet with bankers	0 days	
10		Circulate plan w/ venture capitalists	5 days	John Melville
11		Negotiate with venture capitalists	2 wks	John Melville
12		Reach agreement	0 days	
13		Create legal documentation	3 wks	John Melville
14		Financing closed	0 days	
15		⊟ **Production Phase**	**75 days?**	
16		Setup assembly line	30 days	Scott Adams
17		Hire assemblers	50 days?	Mary Logan
18		⊟ **Assemble first batch**	**15 days**	**Assemblers**
19		Quality testing	2 wks	Assemblers
20		Make design changes	2 wks	Bill Kirk,Engineers[200%]
21		Assemble product	2 wks	Assemblers,Lab kits[500 Kits]

Figure 10.18
You can use the Resource Names field to review or enter resource assignments.

TIP

If you want to import a list of tasks with resource assignments, you must have used the Resource Name field format in the source data to identify the resource assignments. For information about importing data, see Chapter 17, "Exporting and Importing Data with Other File Formats."

To assign resources to tasks in the Resource Names field, follow these steps:

1. View a Task table like the one in the Gantt Chart view.

2. If the Resource Names column is not displayed (after you scroll through the columns), choose View, Table and apply any table that includes a Resource Name column, such as the Entry table.
3. Select the Resource Names column of the Task table for the task to which you want to assign resources.
4. Enter the resource name. You can select the name from the drop-down resource list, which appears in the cell when the Resource Names column is active.
5. If the number of units is something other than 100%, type the units, enclosed in square brackets, immediately after the name in the edit bar.
6. If you want to assign more resources to the same task, use the list separator (which is a comma in North America) to separate the resources, and then repeat steps 4 and 5 until all resources are complete.
7. Press Enter or select any other cell to complete the resource assignment.

ASSIGNING FIXED COSTS AND FIXED CONTRACT FEES

Some tasks might have costs that aren't linked to a particular resource that you have named and aren't affected by the task duration. This type of cost is treated as a *fixed cost* in Project, and it is entered in the Fixed Cost column of the Cost table on a task view such as the Gantt Chart view. Project adds the fixed cost amount to the total of the resource costs and displays the sum in the Cost (Total Cost) columns of various views.

NOTE

> You can associate fixed costs with summary tasks as well as with normal tasks. Because the field might be used for summary task fixed costs, Project doesn't roll up the Fixed Cost field to summary tasks. In other words, although the fixed cost is included in the Total Cost column, you cannot see a total for all fixed costs.

You can also have a cost that is associated with a resource but that is not affected by the task duration or any variations in work for the resource. For instance, the resource might be a contractor or vendor who is to deliver the completed task at a fixed cost. In these cases, the contractor or vendor should be listed as a resource, and the cost should be entered as part of the assignment information on the Task Form view. If you were to simply add this cost to the task fixed cost, you would lose the identification with the resource.

To display the Fixed Cost field, display a task view such as the Gantt Chart view in the top pane. To display the Cost table, right-click over the Select All button (the blank area just above the row numbers) and choose Cost (see Figure 10.19).

TIP

You should document any fixed cost amounts in the task Notes field so that you and others will always know what the cost represents.

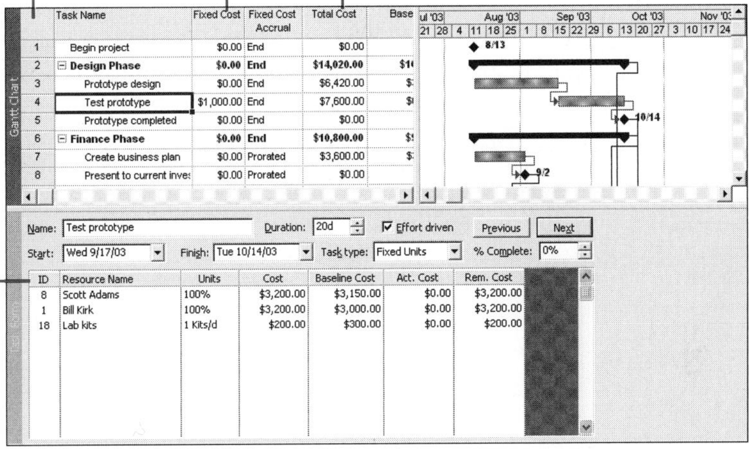

Figure 10.19
You can enter costs that are not associated with a particular resource and that do not change with the task duration in the Fixed Cost column of the task Cost table.

In Figure 10.19, the resource cost details for the Test Prototype task are displayed in the Task Form view in the bottom pane. The sum of those costs is $6,600. In the top pane, the $1,000 entry in the Fixed Cost column is added to the resource costs, to create the value in the Total Cost column.

TIP

If you enter an amount in the Total Cost (Cost) field to overwrite the calculated value that is displayed there, Project treats this as the sum of the calculated resource costs and a new fixed cost amount. It then changes the entry in the Fixed Cost column to support this interpretation.

If a resource that is assigned to a task is working for a fixed fee (for example, a contractor or vendor on an outsourced task), you want that cost to remain fixed no matter what happens to the task duration. In this case, you do not need Project to track the hours of work for the resource because those hours are important to the contractor or vendor but not to you. Your cost isn't affected if the job takes more work or money than estimated, as long as it is completed on time.

To record fixed resource costs for an outsourced task, make the task a fixed-duration task and assign the contractor or vendor as a resource to the task; however, enter **0** in the Units field for the assignment. The work amount is calculated as zero; therefore, the hourly resource cost value for this resource is also zero. After you click OK to complete the assignment, Project allows you to enter the contract amount in the resource Cost field, and that entry is not overwritten by Project's calculations.

Suppose that we decide to outsource the Test Prototype task and that Quality Testing Labs has offered to do the work in 20 days as scheduled for a fixed cost of $5,000. That's less than the $7,600 we estimated for doing it in our own testing lab (see Figure 10.19). To record this in Project, follow these steps:

1. Display a task view such as the Gantt Chart view and split the window to display the Task Form view in the bottom pane (see Figure 10.20).

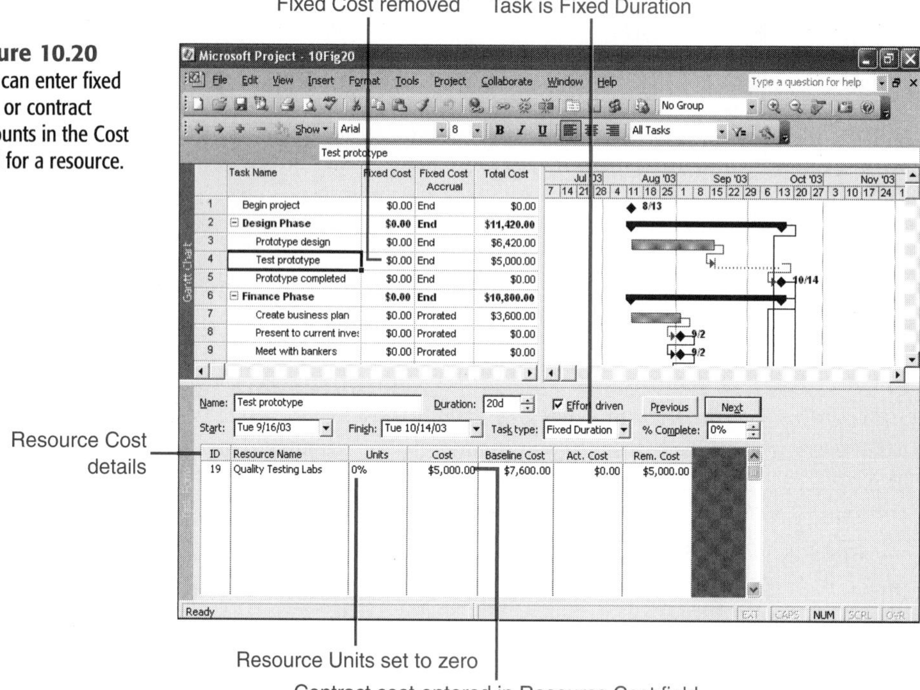

Figure 10.20
You can enter fixed fees or contract amounts in the Cost field for a resource.

2. Display the cost details in the Task Form view by right-clicking and selecting Resource Cost from the shortcut menu.
3. If Fixed Costs were associated with the task but are no longer needed, enter `0` in the Fixed Cost field in the top pane.
4. If there are resources already assigned that will no longer be used, delete them in the Task Form view and click OK.
5. If there are no other resources working on the task, change the task type to fixed duration so that assigning 0% units won't make the task a milestone. If other resources will also work on the task, you do not necessarily need to change the task type.

6. Add the contractor or vendor name in the Resource Name column, assign 0% units, and then click OK. With zero units, Project does not calculate work for the assignment and does not calculate costs for the resource. (Note that you must click OK before you can complete the last step.)
7. Enter the fixed cost of the task in the assignment Cost field (in the bottom pane) and click OK again.

TROUBLESHOOTING

SCHEDULING SHORT ASSIGNMENTS IN FIXED-DURATION TASKS

How can I schedule a short assignment in a fixed-duration task without extending the duration of the task?

When you add a short assignment (one that could be finished before the other assigned resources finish) to a fixed-units or fixed-work task, Project schedules all the work at the beginning of the task, and the assignment finishes before the task finishes. But when you add a short assignment to a fixed-duration task, Project spreads out the work evenly over the duration of the assignment and reduces the units to reflect the reduced workload during each period.

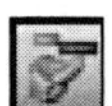

If you want to concentrate the short assignment's work to the start, finish, or other point in the task duration, you have to edit the assigned work in the Task Usage view or the Resource Usage view. With one of the usage views displayed, select the short assignment and note the total work for the assignment in the Work column of the table on the left. Click the Go to Selected Task tool to scroll the timephased data for the assignment into view. You need to replace the distributed work in the grid with work concentrated in the periods you choose. The fastest method is to clear all the current work entries by typing **0** into the Work column for the assignment in the table. Then, type the work amounts you want to schedule into the time periods of your choice, until the total in the Work column is back to the original amount.

CHAPTER 11

Resolving Resource Assignment Problems

In this chapter

Understanding How Resource Overallocations Occur 402

Identifying Resource Overallocations 405

Strategies for Eliminating Resource Overallocations 417

Eliminating Resource Overallocations Yourself 421

Letting Project Level Overallocated Resources for You 454

Troubleshooting 463

Understanding How Resource Overallocations Occur

A resource is *overallocated* when it is assigned to work more hours during a given time period than it has available for work on the project. The number of hours the resource has available for the project during any given time period is determined by two values that you define:

- **The units of the resource that are available during the time period**—You can define time periods and units by double-clicking on a resource name in either the Assign Resources dialog box or the Resource Sheet table to display the Resource Information dialog box. You can then change both the units and availability (over time) of the resources in the Resource Availability table on the General tab of the Resource Information dialog box. *Units* refers to the number of resources available to work (for example, you might have 10 programmers, but you would only ever have 1 unit of Scott Adams).
- **The number of working hours the resource has for the time period in the resource calendar**—You define working time on the Working Time tab of the Resource Information dialog box.

Multiplying the units available for the resource by the calendar working hours in a given time period determines the hours of work the resource has available for that time period. Table 11.1 shows several examples of the work availability calculation. A single work resource typically has 8 hours available per day and has maximum available units of 100% (that is, one full-time unit). Remember that a resources calendar simply defines availability to work and not necessarily what the actual work output will be.

Case A shows that this resource can be assigned up to 8 hours of work each day. But, if the employee has only 4 hours of working time per day defined on his calendar, Case B shows that you are limited to assigning no more than 4 hours per day to that resource. Case C shows a consolidated or group resource with 300% units available and 8 hours of working time per day defined on its calendar. This resource can deliver up to 24 hours of work in the time period.

Table 11.1 Determining the Working Hours Available for a Resource

Case	A	B	C
Maximum resource units available	100%	100%	300%
Calendar working hours for the period	8 hrs	4 hrs	8 hrs
Maximum working hours available for the period	8 hrs	4 hrs	24 hrs

Overallocations generally occur for two reasons:

- A resource is overallocated if you assign more units of that resource to a single task than the maximum units available for that resource during the period the task is scheduled. For example, if you assign a group or team resource that has five units available (500%) to a task by entering six units (600%), you would automatically overallocate that resource.
- A resource is overallocated if you assign the resource to multiple tasks that are scheduled to take place during the same time period and the sum of the assigned units is greater than the maximum units available. This second case is the most common cause of overallocated resources.

When Microsoft Project calculates a task schedule for you, it can easily create an overallocation by scheduling multiple-task assignments for a resource during the same time period. Before resource assignments are made, Project schedules tasks in forward-scheduled projects to start as soon as possible, based on three factors: the first possible date (as determined by the start of the project and any predecessors for the task), the earliest date that leaves constraints satisfied, and the next available working time on the project base calendar (or task calendar, if one is assigned).

NOTE

Forward-scheduled projects are those that are scheduled from a *fixed start date*. Project calculates the finish date of the project. This explanation and most others in this chapter are worded in terms of forward-scheduled projects. Microsoft Project automatically makes tasks in such projects As Soon As Possible tasks, to minimize the project duration and achieve the earliest finish date for the project.

If a project is scheduled from a *fixed finish date*, Project automatically makes the project's tasks As Late As Possible tasks, in order to minimize the overall duration for the project and achieve the latest possible project start date.

When you assign a resource to work on a task, Project substitutes the resource calendar for the project base calendar and schedules the task assignment on the first available date on the resource calendar that meets the conditions described in the preceding section. However, Project does not normally look to see whether the resource is already assigned to other tasks during the times it schedules for the new assignment. Because Project ignores existing assignments when scheduling new assignments, it is very possible for a resource to be overallocated.

NOTE

If there is an assigned task calendar, the dates that are scheduled must normally be working dates on both the task calendar and the resource calendar. If the task field labeled Scheduling Ignores Resource Calendars is checked, the resource calendar is ignored and the task calendar is the only calendar considered. If this results in work being scheduled during periods that are nonworking times on the resource calendar, Project does not consider this to be an overallocation of the resource.

TIP

> The default behavior for Project is to ignore other assignments. However, you can change the default behavior and have Project check for other assignments each time it schedules a resource and, if necessary, delay the new assignment until the resource is free to work on it. Before you decide to change this default, however, you should read the rest of this chapter, especially the section "Understanding the Pitfalls of Automatic Leveling."

If there is more than one assignment for a resource during a given time period, the combined work and units for that period might exceed the resource availability, as illustrated in Table 11.2 for Scott Adams. The first two rows in the table spell out the resource availability: Scott has 100% units available for assignments and 8 hours of working time on each day; thus, his available work is 8 hours each day.

Scott has three assignments during this week, and on Thursday two of them overlap. Task C starts before Task B is completed. The total assigned units on Thursday is 150% (which exceeds Scott's max units), and the total assigned work on that day is 12 hours (which exceeds the 8 available hours on the calendar). Therefore, Scott is overallocated on Thursday.

TABLE 11.2 SCOTT ADAMS'S ASSIGNMENTS FOR ONE WEEK

	Mon	Tue	Wed	Thu	Fri	Weekly Total
Max Units	100%	100%	100%	100%	100%	
Working Time	*8h*	*8h*	*8h*	*8h*	*8h*	*40h*
Task A Units	**100%**	**100%**				
Task A Work	***8h***	***8h***				
Task B Units			**100%**	**100%**		
Task B Work			***8h***	***8h***		
Task C Units				**50%**		
Task C Work				***4h***		
Combined Units	100%	100%	100%	150%	0%	
Combined Work	*8h*	*8h*	*8h*	*12h*	*0h*	*36h*
Overallocated	No	No	No	Yes	No	(No)

Note that this example involves only 36 hours of work for the week, which is less than the 40 hours of work available for the week; therefore, averaged out over the week, Scott Adams is not overallocated. In fact, if you could just reschedule the 4 hours of work assigned for Thursday to take place on Friday, there would be no overallocation.

IDENTIFYING RESOURCE OVERALLOCATIONS

Project alerts you when resources are overallocated by highlighting them in any view that displays a resource table. For example, the Resource Sheet, Resource Usage, and Resource Allocation views all highlight overallocated resource names by using red text. In the Resource Sheet view in Figure 11.1, three resource rows are highlighted: those for Scott Adams, Mel Lloyd, and Howard Thompson.

NOTE

> By default Project uses red text to highlight overallocated resources. Because that color doesn't show up well in this book's black-and-white figures, we've used a bold black font as the highlight in the figures. Where we mention highlighted overallocations, look for red text on your screen and for bold text in these figures.

NOTE

> You can modify the format for overallocated resources in any resource table by choosing Format, Text Styles to display the Text Styles dialog box. In the Item to Change box, select Overallocated Resources from the drop-down list. Use the other controls in the dialog box to create the style you want. When you're finished, click OK to implement the change.

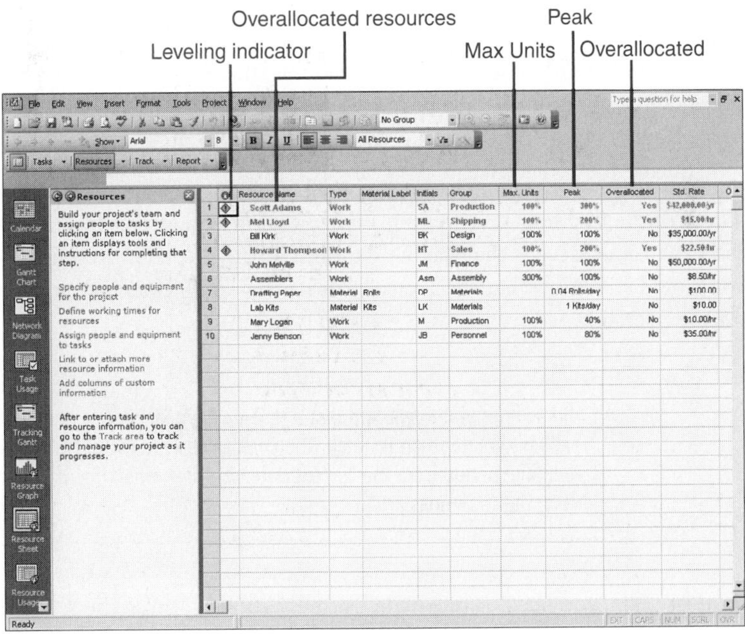

Figure 11.1 Views that display resource tables highlight the names of overallocated resources in red (shown here in bold).

Recall from Table 11.2 that in this example, the overallocation is due to more work being scheduled in a given time period than the resource is allowed to work (based on the availability defined by the maximum available units for the given time period and the working hours on the resource calendar). The cause of the overallocation is that the sum of the assigned units exceeds the max units for that period. Project maintains a calculated field named Peak, which shows for any designated time period the largest number of simultaneously assigned units during that time period. Project also maintains a calculated resource field named Overallocated that contains Yes if Peak is greater than Max Units for *any* time period and No if otherwise. If the Overallocated field contains Yes, the resource is highlighted in red onscreen.

Figure 11.1 shows the Resource Sheet view with both the Peak and Overallocated fields displayed to the right of the Max Units field. The Max Units field displays the maximum units for the *current date* and is taken from the Units column of the Resource Availability table in the Resource Information dialog box.

TIP

> The current date is normally determined by the computer's internal clock, but you can set the current date to any date. To do so, open the Project Information dialog box (by choosing Project, Project Information) and change the Current Date field.

The column for Peak in Figure 11.1 shows the peak units for the life of the project; the value displayed is the largest amount of simultaneously assigned units (the peak resource requirement) at any time in the project. Thus, the peak of 300% for Scott Adams means that at some point during the project, Scott's simultaneous assignments total 300% units. Mary Logan, on the other hand, is never required to provide more than 40% units at any time during the project.

Three of the first four resources in Figure 11.1 are flagged as being overallocated because the Peak value exceeds the Max Units value. If the Overallocated field were not displayed, you would still know that these resources were overallocated because of the highlight used for the overallocated resources.

NOTE

> Sometimes you might find that a resource appears in red even though its max units value is greater than its peak. The peak value (and the overallocation) occurs at a different time period from the current date, at a time when the maximum units value is lower than the peak units.

In most cases, you need to reconcile overallocations because the schedule indicates that the resource can't possibly do what he or she is scheduled to do. You reconcile overallocations by leveling the workload for the resource by reassigning tasks to other resources, delaying tasks until the resource is available, or making other adjustments to the schedule (as discussed later in this chapter, in the section "Strategies for Eliminating Resource Overallocations").

Sometimes you can regard overallocation as a mere technicality that's simply a product of the way Project calculates schedules. For example, suppose a regular full-time employee is scheduled to work 100% on two tasks on a given day, and each task will only take an hour to complete. That's only 2 hours of work for the day and is hardly an overallocation for an 8-hour day. But if both tasks have been scheduled by Project to begin first thing in the morning, at 8:00 a.m., Project flags the resource as overallocated because the schedule calls for peak units of 200% at that time. In reality, the resource could easily finish both tasks in the day by delaying one task until the other is finished. You might prefer not to be bothered by dealing with overallocations like this when the conflict is small enough that the resource can adjust the schedule and finish its assigned work for the day.

To help you focus only on overallocation cases that you think really warrant your rescheduling efforts, Project lets you choose a leveling *sensitivity* that it uses to flag the overallocations that are considered too severe to ignore. In the example just given, you would need to do something about the schedule if it is important that the project be on schedule on an hour-by-hour basis. But you might be content to let resources manage the conflicts as long as they can be on schedule on a day-by-day basis.

You can choose the sensitivity setting for Project to use when evaluating overallocations in the Resource Leveling dialog box. Choose Tools, Level Resources, and select the setting in the box labeled Look for Overallocations on a … Basis. The choices are Minute by Minute, Hour by Hour, Day by Day, Week by Week, and Month by Month.

11

If you choose the Hour by Hour sensitivity setting (which means assigned work must be completed within the assigned hour), Project displays the Leveling indicator that you see in Figure 11.1. But if you choose the Day by Day setting, there is no indicator because the work will be completed within the assigned day.

Table 11.2 shows an example where Scott Adams is overallocated for the day on a Thursday, but his workload for the week is fine. If you are content to let Scott manage the conflict by pushing back his Task C work until Friday, after he has finished Task B, the sensitivity setting can be defined as Week by Week, and there would be no Leveling indicator.

All resources with any overallocation appear highlighted in resource tables, but if you don't see the Leveling indicator, the overallocation is acceptable within the boundaries of the leveling sensitivity setting.

TIP

You can rest the mouse pointer over the Leveling indicator to see the time period covered by the current sensitivity setting. This is quicker than opening the Resource Leveling dialog box, where the leveling sensitivity is defined.

NOTE

If a worker reschedules a *critical task* (that is, a task whose delay will delay the completion of the project), there are consequences to the finish date of the project. For this reason, you do not want to select an overly long sensitivity setting.

In Figure 11.1 the resource names Scott Adams, Mel Lloyd, and Howard Thompson are highlighted, to indicate that there is at least one time period in which these resources' workloads exceed their availability. Both Scott and Howard have the Leveling indicator, so you need to look at the overallocations for those resources.

Figure 11.2 shows the same resources in the Resource Usage view. In Figure 11.2 you can see the ScreenTip for the Leveling indicator next to Howard Thompson. The ScreenTip says "This resource should be leveled based on a Week by Week setting."

11

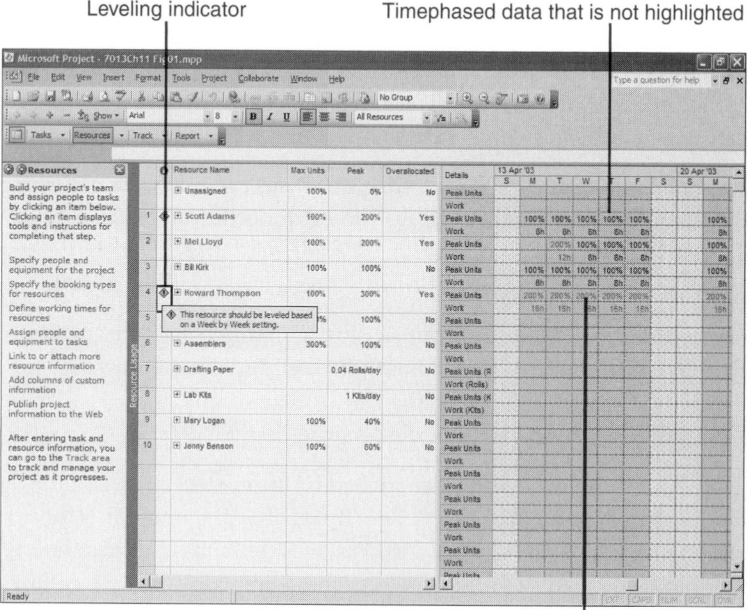

Figure 11.2
The Leveling indicator appears in the Indicators column in resource views that have tables, such as the Resource Usage view shown here.

Instead of emphasizing the resource definition fields, the Resource Usage view emphasizes a timescale that has the scheduled activity for each resource broken down into discrete time periods—what Project calls *timephased* assignment data. In Figure 11.2, the Work and Peak Units fields are displayed for each day in the timescale.

Mel Lloyd is overallocated because his max units value for the period shown is 100% and he is assigned for 200% units on Tuesday. He does not have a Leveling indicator because the leveling sensitivity setting is Week by Week, and Mel has fewer than 40 hours of assigned work for the week. Although Mel is overallocated on Tuesday, his assignment does not need leveling because he can do the weekly work he has been assigned. Howard Thompson, on the other hand, has far more than 40 hours of work assigned during the week; therefore, on a Week by Week basis, his assignments need to be leveled.

VIEWING RESOURCE OVERALLOCATIONS

To identify all the overallocated resources by name, you need to use one of the three resource views that display a table: the Resource Sheet view, the Resource Usage view, or the Resource Allocation view. Figure 11.1 shows the Resource Sheet view, and Figure 11.2 shows the Resource Usage view. The Resource Allocation view includes the Resource Usage view and is discussed more in later sections of this chapter. If a resource is overallocated during any period in the life of the project, the resource name is highlighted in any of these views.

FILTERING OVERALLOCATED RESOURCES

If a resource list is extensive, you can filter it, to display only the resources that are overallocated. You can display all overallocated resources, not just those with the Leveling indicator. In Figure 11.3, the Resource Sheet view is filtered for overallocated resources; in this case, only three resource names appear.

NOTE

There is no way to filter for just resources that have the Leveling indicator displayed. Project calculates this indicator on the fly, and there is no field that shows the result of the calculation other than the Indicators field—and you can't apply a filter to the Indicators field.

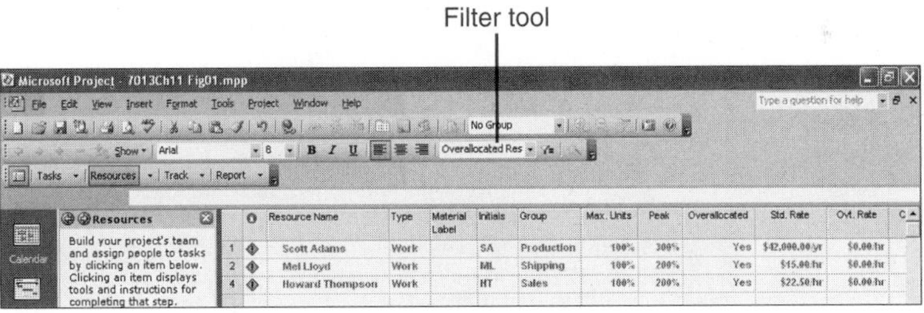

Figure 11.3
Applying the Overallocated Resources filter reduces the display to just the resources that are overallocated.

To apply the Overallocated filter, select the top pane view if you are in a combination view, and choose Overallocated Resources from the Filter tool drop-down list. Or, you can choose Project, Filtered For, Overallocated Resources. Filters can be applied only in the top pane because the bottom pane is already filtered to show details for the selection in the top pane.

NOTE

In a combination view, the bottom pane always displays a subset of the selected tasks or resources that are highlighted in the upper view.

TIP

> If you correct the overallocation problem for a resource that is displayed by a filter, the resource remains in the display until the filter is applied again. This is because the display of filters is not automatically refreshed. You can press Ctrl+F3 to refresh the filtered list.

To remove a filter, choose Project, Filtered For, All Resources, or press the F3 function key.

WORKING WITH THE RESOURCE USAGE VIEW

You must use a resource view with a timescale if you want to see assignment data for each time period or to see exactly when a resource overallocation occurs. The Resource Usage view is a standard view that can display a wealth of assignment information, including timephased details for each time period displayed in the timescale. In addition to listing all the resources and highlighting those that are overallocated, you can display rows indented under each resource for all the resource's assignments (see Figure 11.4). Furthermore, you can display multiple timephased assignment field values for each of the assignments, and you can edit some of the fields directly in the cells of the timescale grid. In Figure 11.4, both the Peak Units and the Work values are displayed for each assignment and summarized for each resource. The cells in the timescale grid break down the assignment values into discrete time periods. Because you can choose the time unit displayed in the timescale, you can zoom in to view the assignment details minute by minute or zoom out to see summaries for months, quarters, or years.

If you experience problems identifying the specific fields that are displayed in the Resource Usage View, please see "Displaying Detail Headers" in the "Troubleshooting" section at the end of this chapter.

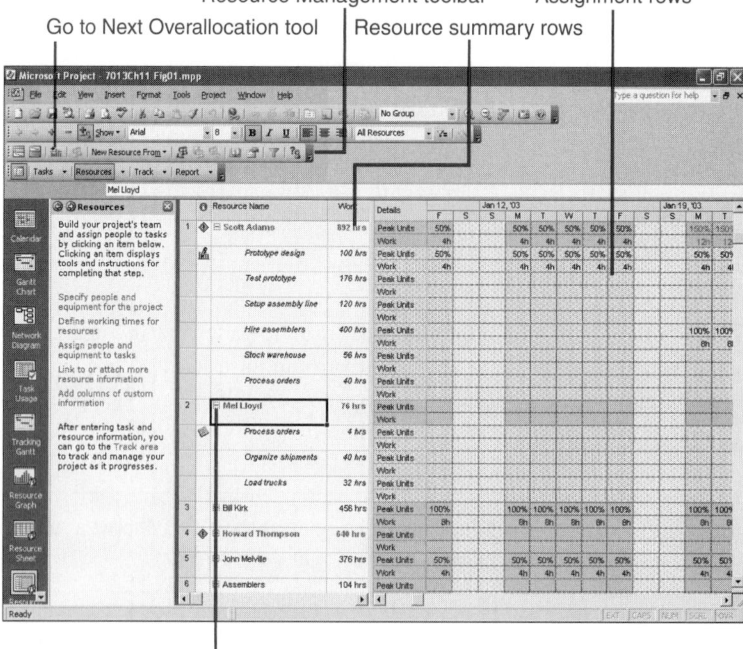

Figure 11.4
The Resource Usage view allows you to view all the assignments under each resource.

The Resource Usage view in Figure 11.4 shows the individual assignments for Mel Lloyd and Scott Adams. You can click the outline symbol that appears to the left of a resource name to hide or display the assignments for that resource. If some assignments are not displayed, the outline symbol is a plus sign (for example, Howard Thompson and Bill Kirk in Figure 11.4). If the assignments are displayed, the outline symbol is a minus sign (for example, Mel Lloyd and Scott Adams in Figure 11.4). If a resource has no assignments, an outline symbol does not appear next to the resource's name.

You can also use the Hide Assignments tool on the Formatting toolbar to hide or display the assignments for one or more resources that you have selected. To hide or display all assignments, select one of the column headings (such as Resource Name) to select all the resources and then click the Hide Assignments tool.

TIP

> If you apply a filter (for example, the Overallocated Resources filter) in the Resource Usage view, you can see the assignments for other resources by clicking on the plus symbol that appears to the left of the resource name, in the Resource Name column. If the symbol is a minus symbol, try clicking on it anyway. If it changes to a plus symbol with the first click, you need to click the symbol again to display the assignments for that resource.

For each assignment row in the Resource Usage view, the default display in the cells in the timescale grid is the timephased work for the time period spanned by that cell. You can add additional rows to display other timephased values, such as overtime work, cost, available units, peak units, baseline work, and actual work. In Figure 11.4, for example, there are six assignments listed under Scott Adams on the left side of the table. Each assignment has two timephased rows in the timescale—one for peak units and one for work. Timephased Peak Units and Work rows for Scott Adams also serve to display the totals of the Peak Units and Work cells for his assignments.

If any assignment value in a cell in the grid is itself greater than the resource availability for the time period, the assignment value is highlighted (typically in red). For example, if you assigned 200% units of a resource with only 100% max units for that time period, the values in the assignment timephased cells for that assignment would all appear highlighted.

The cells in the rows for the resource name contain the sums of the values in the assignment rows beneath them. If a resource is overallocated during any time period, the resource name is highlighted, as are the summary values in the timephased cells for the periods in which the overallocations occur. This allows you to locate the exact time periods when overallocations occur.

TIP

If you see a highlighted value in a cell and want to know exactly when during the period spanned by the cell the overallocation occurred, you can drill down by using the Zoom In tool to view shorter and shorter time periods, until you find the exact time when the overallocation occurred. If there is an overallocation at any time during the period spanned by a cell, Project highlights text in that time period's cells in red, no matter how far you may zoom out to compress the timescale.

USING THE GO TO NEXT OVERALLOCATION TOOL

If you are in the Resource Usage view and have displayed the Resource Management toolbar (choose View, Toolbars, Resource Management), you can use the Go to Next Overallocation tool to find the next time period in which a resource has an overallocation (refer to Figure 11.4). The timescale automatically scrolls to the beginning of the next overallocation and selects the resource that is associated with that overallocation. You can click the Go to Next Overallocation tool again to find the next overallocation. Project then selects the next resource that is involved in the current overallocation or moves on to the next date where an overallocation occurs.

11

If you use the Go to Next Overallocation tool in a view that has a task list, such as the Gantt Chart view or the Task Sheet view, the task list scrolls to the first task associated with an overallocation and selects that task. Successive use of the Go to Next Overallocation tool selects other tasks assigned to overallocated resources during the same time period. When all tasks associated with overallocations for that time period have been identified, the Go to Next Overallocation tool identifies the next time period that has an overallocated resource and selects the first associated task for that time period.

If you want to be able to view the overload graphically, you can split the screen and display a combination view with the Resource Graph view in the bottom pane. You do this by going to the Window menu and selecting Split. By default, this displays the Resource Form view in the lower view. To change this, select the lower view to make it the active view and then go to the View menu and select Resource Graph (or select it from the View bar). This allows you to see (by default) peak units for the selected resource highlighted in the upper view (see Figure 11.5). To view other values such as work, right-click over the Resource Graph view and choose an option from the pop-up menu that appears.

CHANGING THE TIMEPHASED DETAILS

The Resource Usage view displays rows for all resources, with their assignments indented beneath them. You can choose different timephased field values to display in the timescale grid. Each timephased field you choose to display has its own rows in the display—one for each resource and one for each resource assignment. For example, if you choose to display four timephased field values, each resource has four summary rows and each assignment has four detail rows. The default timephased value displayed is the Work field, which shows the total hours of assigned work per unit of time.

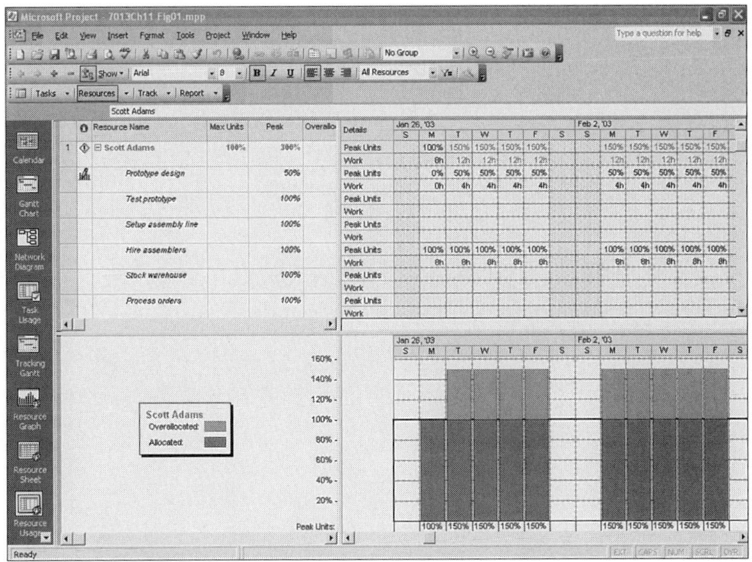

Figure 11.5
The Resource Usage view with the Resource Graph view in the bottom pane allows a quick view of overallocations. Note that the upper and lower views are exactly synchronized to the same timescale.

The display of the timephased details is governed by the Detail Styles and the Details commands on the Format menu. The Details command is a short selection menu of timephased fields to display or remove from the display. All fields that are currently displayed are listed on the Details menu, with a check mark next to each field name. You can click the field to remove it from the display. The Details menu also contains a standard list of fields that you can add to the display by clicking. The list of fields to be included in this standard list is governed by the Detail Styles dialog box.

To remove a timephased field from the display, or to display one of the fields on the standard selection menu, choose Format, Details and click the field you want to add to or remove from the display. Or, you can just right-click over the timescale grid to display the Details shortcut menu, which includes the selection list as well as the command to open the Detail Styles dialog box (see Figure 11.6).

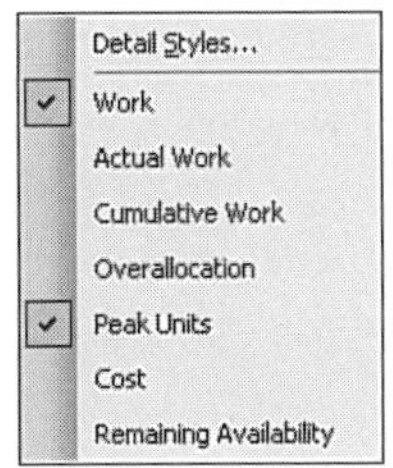

Figure 11.6
The Details shortcut menu displays a check mark for each field that is currently displayed and lets you change the display by clicking a field name.

➔ If you need to manage the timescale units, **see** "Formatting Timescales," **p. 785**.

Microsoft Project 2003 includes SmartTags to explain project scheduling engine calculations and advise you of alternative actions that might provide more effective or efficient schedules. This feature is similar to the scheduling messages included in previous versions of Microsoft Project; the difference is that SmartTags are less intrusive to the workspace than the old messages. A red or green triangle in the edited cell indicates that the edit just performed has made a change to the task or assignment that has some scheduling implications. The indicator appears only in the Gantt Chart view, Sheet view, and Usage type views. Hovering over the indicator displays a SmartTag that notifies you of a scheduling change (see Figure 11.7). Clicking on the indicator displays an alternative choice. The indicator in most cases displays as long as the edit is undoable; then, after another edit is made, the indicator disappears. SmartTags display for the following edits:

- Resource assignment
- Edits to start and finish dates
- Edits to work, units, or duration
- Deletions in the Name column

You can turn off SmartTags by selecting Tools, Options and then selecting the Edit tab from the Options dialog box.

When you are editing fields in the Resource Usage grid, the scheduling behavior is largely dictated by whether the task type is Fixed Units, Fixed Work, or Fixed Duration and also whether the task is effort-driven and whether there are multiple resources or a single resource assigned to a task.

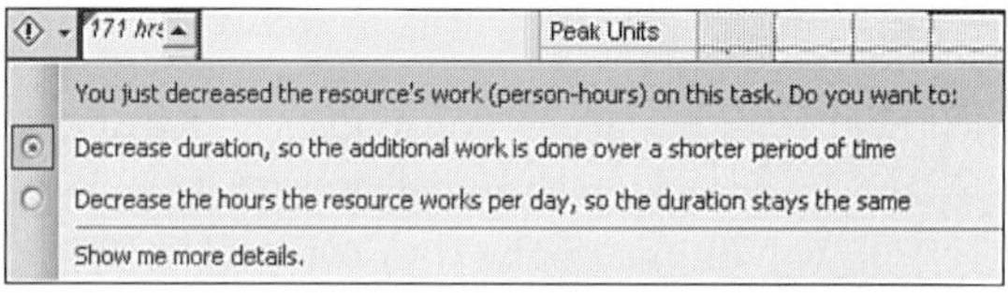

Figure 11.7 This SmartTag shows the possible implications of editing a task or an assignment on the schedule and prompts the user to make an appropriate selection.

→ For a more detailed explanation of task types and effort-driven scheduling, **see** Chapter 9, "Understanding Resource Scheduling," **p. 321**.

To display the Detail Styles dialog box, you choose Format, Detail Styles (see Figure 11.8). You can also right-click over the timephased grid and choose Detail Styles from the shortcut menu.

Figure 11.8
The Usage Details tab of the Detail Styles dialog box governs which timephased details are displayed in the Resource Usage view and how they are formatted, as well as which ones appear on the Details menu.

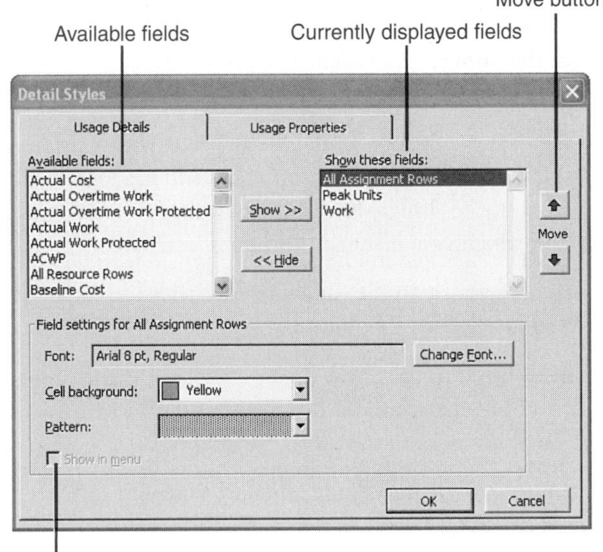

The Usage Details tab of the Detail Styles dialog box contains a full list of all the timephased assignment fields that can be displayed in the view. If the fields are already displayed in the view, they are listed in the Show These Fields list on the right; otherwise, they appear in the Available Fields list on the left. You can select a field from either list to define its formatting or to assign it a place on the Details menu.

The list of timephased fields includes a wide range of actual, baseline, and scheduled values for work and for cost, as well as availability and assigned values for units and work. Here is a list of the different fields:

- The cost fields include Actual Cost, Baseline Cost, (scheduled) Cost, Cumulative (scheduled) Cost, and the earned value fields (ACWP, BCWP, BCWS, CV, SV, CPI, SPI, SVP, CVP), plus the Custom Baseline Cost fields 1 through 10.
- The work fields include Actual Work, Actual Overtime Work, Baseline Work, (scheduled) Work, (scheduled) Regular Work, (scheduled) Overtime Work, Cumulative (scheduled) Work, Work Availability, Remaining Availability, Overallocation, and Percent Allocation (that is, the percentage of available work that is assigned already), plus all the Custom Baseline Work fields 1 through to 10.
- Units fields include Peak Units and Unit Availability.
- Other fields include Percent Complete and Cumulative Percent Complete.

The list of fields also includes the entries All Resource Rows and All Assignment Rows. These are not fields, but they are included so that you can define separate formatting for the resource rows and assignment rows in the grid.

To add a timephased field to the standard selection list displayed by the Format Details command, select the field (whether it's in the Available Fields list or in the Show These Fields list) and click the Show in Menu check box. Note that this does not display the field; it just adds the field to the standard list in the Details menu.

To display a field that is not currently in the Show These Fields list, select the field in the Available Fields list and click the Show button. The field is added to the Details selection menu until you choose not to display it in the timescale grid (unless its Show in Menu check box has been filled, in which case it remains on the Details menu).

To move a field that is currently in the Show These Fields list back to the Available Fields list, select the field and click the Hide button.

The order of the fields listed in the Show These Fields list is the order in which their rows appear in the grid. You can change the order by using the Move arrows: You select a field name and move it up or down in the list with the arrows.

You can define distinguishing formats for individual timephased fields in the resource summary rows, but the format you choose is not applied to a field's rows for assignments. To change the display characteristics of a resource field row, click the field (in whichever list it appears) and click the Change Font button to select a different font. Select the Cell Background drop-down list to change the color of the row of cells or the Pattern drop-down box to change the fill pattern for the cells in that row. The selected format remains defined for the field, no matter which list it appears in.

TIP

> If you design special formats for the Resource Usage view and want to use those format settings for all projects, you can use the Organizer to copy the view into other projects and into the Global template for all new projects.

You can assign distinct formats to all resource rows or to all assignment rows. Assignment rows can have a different background to distinguish them from the resource rows in the grid. To define a general font or background for the assignment rows or for the resource rows, select the All Assignment Rows entry or the All Resource Rows entry (in whichever list it appears) and use the Change Font button, the Cell Background drop-down list, or the Pattern drop-down list to define the format. To apply the format, you move the All Assignment Rows or the All Resource Rows entry to the Show These Fields list. If you apply a special format to All Resource Rows, it overrides any special formats you may have defined for individual timephased fields.

If you want individual fields to retain their own formatting, you need to remove the All Assignment Rows entry from the right-hand list in the dialog box. Using the same mechanism, you can have all resource rows adopt the same formatting by adding the All Resource Rows option to the list on the right-hand side of the dialog box.

The Usage Properties tab of the Detail Styles dialog box controls the display of row titles in the grid and the alignment of data within the cells (see Figure 11.9). In this tab you can do the following:

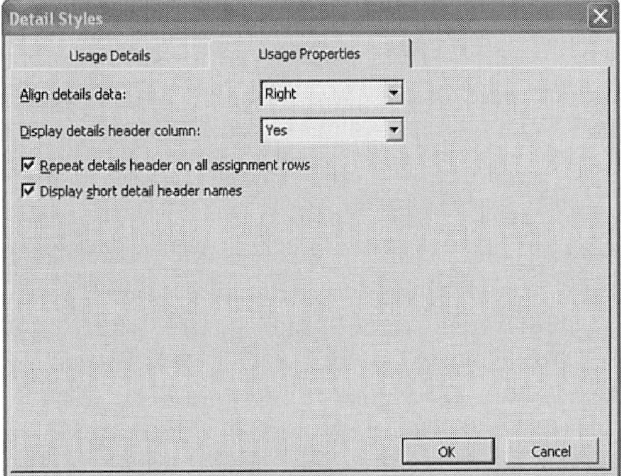

Figure 11.9
The Usage Properties tab of the Detail Styles dialog box governs how the details are displayed.

- Use the Align Details Data drop-down list to select Right, Left, or Center alignment of timephased data within the grid cells.
- Select Yes or No in the Display Details Header Column list box to display row headers for each assignment field row. Without these headers, you cannot tell what the value display represents.

If the headers don't appear on your screen for the detail rows in the timephased data, see "Displaying Detail Headers" in the "Troubleshooting" section at the end of this chapter.

- Select the Repeat Details Header on All Assignment Rows check box to display the headers on every row in the display, for resource and assignment rows alike. Leave the check box empty if you want the row headers to appear next to the resource rows but not for each assignment row.
- Select the Display Short Detail Header Names check box to use shorter names for the detail headers. Leave the check box empty to use the long names.

STRATEGIES FOR ELIMINATING RESOURCE OVERALLOCATIONS

If overallocated resources exist in a project plan, the resources will not be able to complete all their assignments in the scheduled time period. Some of the assigned work will not be completed within that time period—either the work will not be done, it will not be done thoroughly, or it will have to be done at a later time. If the work is never done or is not done well, the full scope of the project delivery will not be realized. If the work is done later, the project finish date might be delayed and cause you to miss the final deadline.

11

You can resolve an overallocation by looking for ways to do either or both of the following:

- Increase the availability of the resource during the time period in question.
- Reduce the total work assigned to the resource in that time period.

INCREASING AVAILABILITY OF OVERALLOCATED RESOURCES

Remember that the availability of a resource during any time period depends on the settings in both the Resource Availability table in the Resource Information dialog box and the Resource Calendar (the Working Time tab). If you want to try to increase the availability of an overallocated resource, you can try the following:

- The Resource Availability table in the Resource Information dialog box lets you define when the resource is available and how many units are available during each time period. The resource is overallocated if the assigned units exceed the available units for any time period. You might be able to change the available units for the period to encompass the overallocated assignment. The units available are typically 100% (or 1 unit) for individual resources and a larger number than that for group or team resources. If an individual resource has less than 100%, you can see if the resource can work full-time. If a group resource is overallocated, you can increase the number of units available by adding more units to the group.

TIP

> Although part-time workers can be given a Max Units Available setting of less than 100% to show that they are part time, it is generally best to enter the units as 100% and modify their available working hours on the calendar to reflect exactly *when* they are available each day. That way, they are available 100% during the hours when they are scheduled to work. If a part-time resource uses flexible working hours, however, and works at different times as needed, you could give that resource a regular 8-hour calendar setting and enter 50% in the Max Units field.

If additional workers have to be hired to increase the number of units, you must consider the substantial added costs of searching, hiring, increased payroll, fringe benefits, and all the other factors associated with permanent employment. This solution is generally not feasible unless there is a demonstrated need for a permanent increase in the employment roster. If additional workers can be added as temporary employees, the added cost is probably less than the cost of a permanent hire, but it still must be figured into the decision. If the group resource is already made up of nonemployees—for example, contract workers or workers supplied by a vendor for an outsourced task—requesting additional units to work during the peak demand time is not necessarily an added cost to the project. If those workers were going to be paid for completing this task anyway, although over a longer duration, you could just as easily pay them for a shorter duration to meet the demand.

- If the overallocation is not substantial, you can see whether the resource is willing to work more hours during the period of overallocation. One way to show this in Project is to schedule overtime hours for the overallocated resource. Overtime hours are charged to the task at the overtime rate defined for the resource and, therefore, potentially increase the cost of the task because Project substitutes these hours for hours during the regular calendar hours.
- Alternatively, you can temporarily increase the working time by changing the working hours on the resource calendar during the overallocation time period. You should use this alternative instead of assigning overtime when the resource is not paid a premium-wage rate for working overtime. You can control exactly when the additional hours are available by using this solution, but you cannot specify when overtime hours will be worked in the schedule.

CAUTION

> As in earlier releases of Project, in Microsoft Project 2003 you cannot schedule overtime hours for specific dates or time periods. You assign the resource to work overtime on a specific task, and Project schedules the overtime work. Project spreads the overtime evenly over the duration of the task. When tracking actual work, you can, however, record the actual overtime work in the time period when the work was done.

TIP

> A quick way to view overallocations and to establish their impact on your project is to use the Resource Usage view in the top pane and the Gantt Chart view in the bottom pane. If the Gantt Chart view is formatted to show critical and noncritical tasks, you can easily see which tasks will affect the project (critical tasks) and which tasks could be delayed, moved, or extended without necessarily affecting the project. If, as a result of a change, a task becomes critical, you know that you need to undo this and find an alternative solution.
>
> Using this combination view also helps when you're considering replacing or substituting resources because adding a resource to a critical task can reduce a task's duration and thereby reduce the project's duration. In addition, removing resources from a noncritical task might enable you to extend that task without affecting the project. But this reduction could remove an overallocation. Extending this logically, you might conclude that it is possible to remove a resource from one task–say, a noncritical task–and add it to a critical task. This has the effect of more efficiently utilizing the resources that are available in the project.

→ For the steps to display critical tasks, **see** "Formatting the Gantt Chart View," **p. 790**.

REDUCING THE WORKLOAD FOR AN OVERALLOCATED RESOURCE

If a resource has peaks of activity that result in overallocations, you can remove the overallocations by *leveling*—that is, by reducing the workload during the peaks to level out the amount of work expected from the resource. To reduce the workload for a resource in an overallocated period, you can do the following:

- Reduce the total work defined for one or more task assignments during the period.
- Reduce the number of tasks assigned to the resource during the period.
- Shift the workload for one or more assignments to other periods by delaying assignments or by changing the contour of assignments to move work to later time periods.

Reducing the total work defined for a task can help ease the overallocation for the resources assigned to the task. This reduction might result from lowering the performance requirements for completing the task, removing unnecessary work from the task definition, or reassessing the work estimate for completing the task. But you must consider the effect of this downscaling of the project on the scope and goal expectations of the project.

You can reduce the number of tasks assigned to the resource during the overallocated period in several ways:

- You can cancel one or more tasks. This option may reduce the scope of the project's delivered outcome. But, depending on the extent to which the task list includes unnecessary elements, you have some latitude in removing tasks without seriously affecting the project scope.
- You can substitute other resources for the overallocated resource in the assignments for the task. This is frequently the most satisfactory solution for resolving resource overallocations. However, this solution requires you to do more investigative work.
- You can keep the resource assigned to all the tasks if you can postpone or delay the assigned work for some of the tasks to a later period, when the resource has more availability to perform that work. Delaying any assigned work in the project schedule naturally extends the duration for the task and may compromise finishing the overall project on time.

To delay some or all work on an assignment, you can try one of the following strategies:

- You can delay one or more tasks to start at a later date in order to free the overallocated resource to work on higher-priority tasks. This may not be a viable option when deadlines are important because delaying tasks can extend the project finish date. If critical tasks are delayed, the project finish date is delayed. See the section "Delaying a Task," later in this chapter.
- Instead of delaying the entire task, and therefore delaying the assignments for all resources assigned to that task, you can delay just the overallocated resource's assignment on a task. Other resources can continue to work as scheduled, and the overallocated resource will do his or her part later in the project. See the section "Delaying Individual Assignments," later in this chapter.
- If work on the task has already begun, you can split the task to stop work temporarily, thus freeing the resource for other tasks during the overallocation period. Splitting the task stops work for all resources assigned to the split task. This does not change the task duration or the total work for the task. See the section "Splitting a Task," later in this chapter.

- Instead of splitting the task, and therefore interrupting all resource assignments for the task, you can split just the assignment for the overallocated resource, thus leaving other resources to continue their work as originally planned. This increases the duration of the task, but it does not increase the total work for the task. See the section "Splitting Individual Assignments," later in this chapter.
- You can change the contour of the overallocated assignment, to move more of the work to later time periods. The default assignment contour is the Flat contour, which means work is evenly distributed throughout the duration of the task. You can choose one of several other predefined contours that set higher workloads at later points in a task's schedule. You can also edit the resource's work assignment on each task yourself, to reduce the workload during the overallocated time period. See "Extending the Available Hours on the Resource Calendar," later in this chapter, for more information.

ELIMINATING RESOURCE OVERALLOCATIONS YOURSELF

The first two sections of this chapter provide an overview of the possible ways to resolve resource overallocations. The preceding section shows how Microsoft Project's Leveling command can eliminate overallocations, using the sole strategy of delaying assignments. This section shows you how to use Microsoft Project's views to analyze the facts and use your own judgment to implement the strategy you think best fits the situation.

INCREASING THE AVAILABILITY OF THE OVERALLOCATED RESOURCE

One way to eliminate resource overallocations is to increase the availability of the resource that is overallocated. After negotiating with the resource, you can use the tools in this section to implement the changes.

The best place to change the availability of a resource is in the Resource Information dialog box because many of the fields that govern availability are accessible there. To display the dialog box, you must be in a view that contains resource data fields or you must have the Assign Resources dialog box open on the workspace. The best overall view for dealing with overallocations is the Resource Allocation view, which places the Resource Usage view in the top pane and the Leveling Gantt Chart view in the bottom pane. After selecting a resource name, click the Resource Information tool on the Standard toolbar to display the Resource Information dialog box.

If the order of task information in the lower view does not appear to be correct or you want to change it, please see "Sorting Assignments in the Resource Allocation View" in the "Troubleshooting" section at the end of this chapter.

NOTE

> Although resource names seem to appear in the Task Usage view, the records are really *assignment* records, not *resource* records, and the Information ScreenTip on the toolbar changes, depending on whether you have a task or an assignment selected. If you double-click on an assignment, the Assignment Information dialog box appears.

TIP

> You can access the Resource Information dialog box by double-clicking the resource name in most views where the resource name is displayed and in the Assign Resources dialog box. This doesn't work in the Resource Form and Resource Name Form views. Double-clicking the task name in task views displays the Task Information dialog box, and double-clicking an assignment displays the Assignment Information dialog box.

Increasing the Resource Availability Settings

To change the dates when a resource is available (assuming that it is not available for the entire project), you need to modify the Resource Availability table on the Resource Information dialog box for the resource.

→ For a thorough explanation of working with the Resource Availability table, **see** "The Resource Availability Fields," **p. 297**.

To change the units available for a resource, follow these steps:

1. Select the resource name in a view onscreen.
2. Click the Resource Information tool (or double-click the resource name) to display the Resource Information dialog box. Choose the General tab (see Figure 11.10).

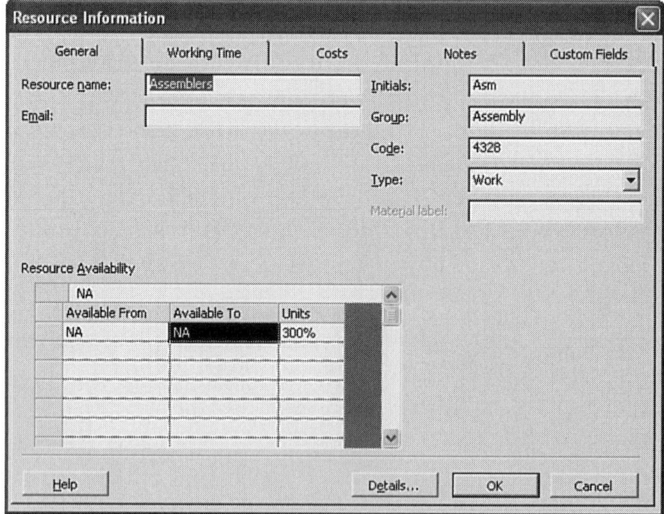

Figure 11.10
You can use the Resource Information dialog box if you want to increase either the time periods when the resource is available or the units available during those time periods.

3. Select the row for the appropriate time period in the Resource Availability table and enter a new value in the Units column.
4. Click OK to accept the changes.

To check a resource's availability or current workload in the Gantt Chart view, display the Assign Resources dialog box, select the resource name, and click the Graphs button. A graphical view of that resource's workload appears. You can change the display of work by selecting Remaining Availability or Assignment Work from the drop-down list (see Figure 11.11).

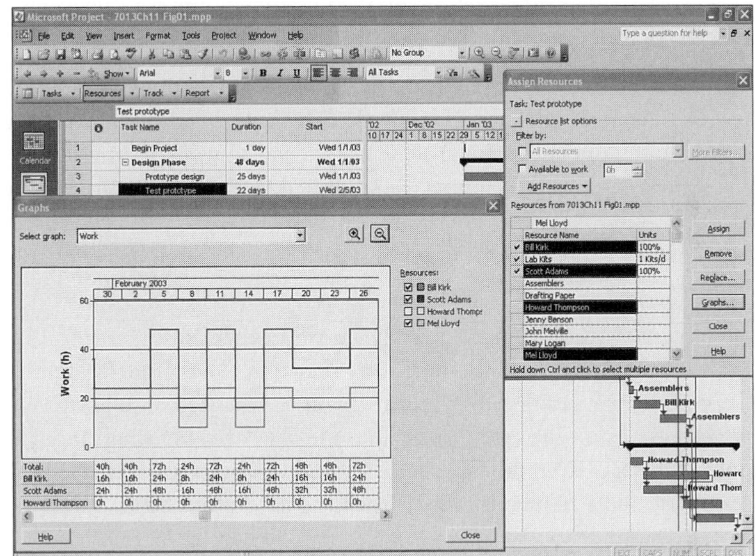

Figure 11.11
You can use the Graph option in the Assign Resources dialog box to assess workload for one or more resources.

SCHEDULING OVERTIME FOR A RESOURCE

You can schedule overtime hours for a resource to supplement the regular calendar working hours. If you enter overtime hours, Microsoft Project subtracts this number of hours from the total amount of work that was to have been scheduled during the regular working hours. The regular working hours are those that are defined as working time on the resource calendar. The total work remains the same as in the original schedule, so you should not change the total amount of work for the task when adding overtime hours; you simply enter the number of hours that should be assigned as overtime. Of course, overtime hours are frequently paid for at premium hourly rates. Using overtime to solve overallocation problems may be a costly method of solving the problem, but it's not usually as costly as hiring new resources.

Before you enter overtime hours for an assignment, all the work is scheduled as regular work. When you enter overtime hours for an assignment, Microsoft Project performs these calculations:

- It first calculates a new value for regular working hours by subtracting the overtime hours from the total hours for the assignment.
- It schedules the new regular working hours in the available working time on the calendar, reducing the duration of the assignment.
- It spreads the overtime hours equally over the new time period for the assignment.

If the work assignment is contoured, the overtime hours are still evenly distributed over the duration of the regular hours, no matter which contour is applied.

Note that you cannot directly enter the number of overtime hours to be scheduled during specific time periods in the timephased grid. You can, however, manually contour the regular working hours in individual cells. In fact, as you will see, Microsoft Project's calculations almost always leave the resource overallocated, even after you apply overtime, because of the way Microsoft Project distributes the work. You need to manually contour the assignment to show Microsoft Project how to remove the Overallocation indicator when you apply overtime.

You can enter overtime in the Task Form view or the Resource Form view. In either case, you need to display the work details in order to see overtime. If you use the Task Form view, you see only one task listed at a time. If you use the Resource Form view, all tasks to which the resource is assigned are displayed in the Work field's listing, and you can assign overtime to multiple tasks from the same screen. You can also enter overtime in the Resource Usage view if you add a column to display the Overtime Work field.

Let's look at two examples of using overtime to solve a scheduling problem:

- You need to shorten the duration of a task without reducing the work.
- You use overtime to deal with overlapping assignments.

Figure 11.12 shows a before-and-after version of an assignment for Mel Lloyd to load trucks. The original task is represented by the first resource "Mel Lloyd (no overtime)" and is scheduled to take four days. If the task needs to be finished in two days instead of four, and if other resources are not available to help, the scheduler could ask Mel to work a lot of extra hours to complete the task earlier.

Figure 11.12 displays the Resource Usage view in the top pane and the Resource Form view in the bottom pane. In the Resource Form view, the Work Details table is displayed at the bottom, to make the Ovt. Work field available for entering overtime.

The timephased data in the top pane displays details for work (which is total work for the task), regular work (which is work during working times on the calendar), and overtime work. The Overtime Work field has also been added to the table, on the left, as an alternative way to schedule overtime for assignments.

The second resource, "Mel Lloyd (with overtime)," has 16 hours of overtime scheduled, and Microsoft Project has shortened the duration of the task to two days. The overtime could have been entered either in the Overtime Work column in the top pane or in the Ovt. Work column in the Resource Form view in the bottom pane.

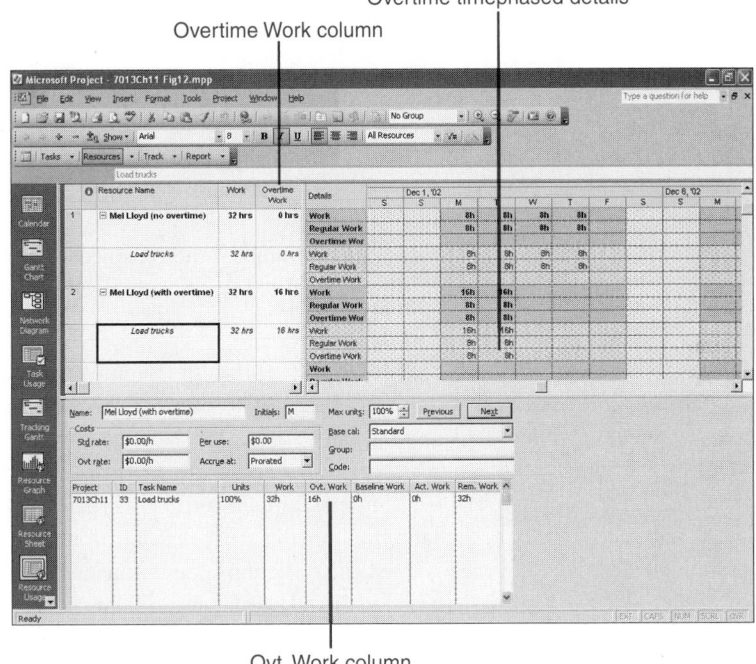

Figure 11.12 You can use the Resource Usage view to apply and fine-tune scheduled overtime.

To enter overtime hours for a task by using the Resource Form view, follow these steps:

1. Select the pane in which to place the Resource Form view. In Figure 11.12, the bottom pane is used. With the Resource Usage view in the top pane, you can just double-click the split box to display the Resource Form view; this always works when a resource view is in the top pane.
2. Make the Resource Form view the active pane.
3. Choose Format, Details, Work. Or right-click in the Resource Form and choose Work from the shortcut menu. In either case, the Resource Work fields are displayed at the bottom of the form (refer to Figure 11.12).
4. If the Resource Form was placed in the bottom pane, as it is in Figure 11.12, you can select the resource in the top pane or use the Next and Previous buttons on the Resource Form view until you find the resource. If the Resource Form view is in the top pane, you can use the Next and Previous buttons to select the resource name.
5. Select the task for which you want overtime hours scheduled.

11

6. In the Ovt. Work column, type the amount of overtime work. You must use a number, followed by a time unit. If you don't specify a time unit, Microsoft Project assumes that the time unit is hours.

   If you want to remove the overtime, you must type **0** into the Ovt. Work field.

7. Click OK to complete the entry.

NOTE

> If the resource is paid for overtime work, be sure that the resource doesn't have a zero overtime rate in the cost fields of the Resource Form view. Some Microsoft Project users mistakenly leave the overtime rate zero if overtime is paid at the same rate as regular hours.

If you have displayed the Overtime Work column in the Resource Usage view, you can enter overtime on the rows for assignments (the rows for resources do not allow data entry) just as you do in the Ovt. Work column of the Resource Form view.

In cases in which an overallocation has resulted from overlapping assignments, you can assign overtime work to one or more of the tasks to remove the overallocation. If you have two or more tasks that are assigned to one resource and that are scheduled at the same time, the simplest method is to assign all the work of one or more of the assignments (usually the shorter assignments) to overtime. This leaves the assignments that have overtime work with zero (0) hours of regular work, and it eliminates the overallocation. However, if the resource is the only resource assigned to any of those tasks, the zero (0) hours of regular work causes Microsoft Project to treat the task as having no duration and to display it as a milestone. Although you can choose Format, Bar to give the milestone a distinctive appearance, it is nevertheless confusing to see a milestone graphic on the Gantt Chart view when the task will really be ongoing until the overtime work is completed.

A better solution is to assign some overtime to both (or all) the tasks that are competing for the resource's work. For example, suppose that Mel Lloyd has two task assignments, Process Orders and Organize Shipments, which are competing for his time. Figure 11.13 shows two versions of the assignments, without and with overtime. The top resource, "Mel Lloyd (no overtime)," shows the original situation. The Process Orders task will take 1 week or 40 hours and the Organize Shipments task will take 3 days or 24 hours. The total work for the week is 64 hours, which is 24 hours more than Mel has available per week. During the time that Organize Shipments is scheduled to occur, Mel is overallocated by 8 hours per day for 3 days (that is, a total of 24 hours of overallocation).

The second resource listing in Figure 11.13, "Mel Lloyd (with overtime)," shows how Microsoft Project calculates the assignments if you assign 12 hours of overtime to both tasks. With 24 hours of overtime assigned, the regular work for the week is just 40 hours for the week, but the regular work for Monday and Tuesday is still excessive, at 16 and 12 hours, respectively, because Microsoft Project still schedules 8 hours of regular work for both tasks until the task is completed. The Leveling indicator is still displayed because the sensitivity setting is Day by Day.

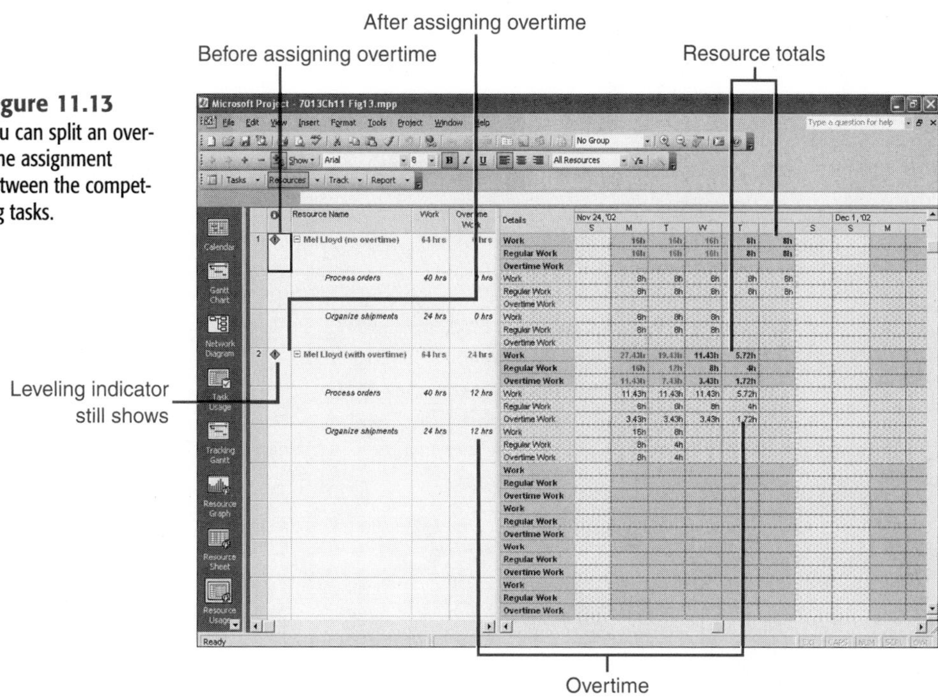

Figure 11.13
You can split an overtime assignment between the competing tasks.

To get Microsoft Project to remove the Leveling indicator, you must reduce the units assigned to each task to 50% so that the total units value is 100% (the units available) and no more than 4 hours of regular work is scheduled per day for each task. Figure 11.14 shows this change. The top resource repeats the bottom resource in Figure 11.14. The bottom resource shows what happens when the units assigned are reduced to 50% for each task. The Leveling indicator is gone, but the duration of the longer task, Process Orders, has been increased and work is scheduled for Monday and Tuesday of the following week. With the 50% units assignment, the scheduling calculations keep the regular hours down to 4 hours per day, even on Thursday and Friday, when the Organize Shipments task is completed and Mel could work 8 hours a day instead of just 4. That lost time is scheduled the following week.

The final adjustment that is needed is to compact the regular work for the Process Orders task at the end of the task, where the reduced units have resulted in unused available hours. On both Thursday and Friday, the 50% units assignment causes only 4 hours to be scheduled, but 8 hours are available when the Organize Shipments task is finished. The reduced hours make it necessary to schedule work on Monday and Tuesday of the following week. Figure 11.15 shows the effect of manually adjusting the regular work schedule for those days. The top resource is a copy of the bottom resource in Figure 11.14, and the bottom resource shows the edited schedule. The regular work cells for Thursday and Friday for the Process Orders assignment were selected and **8h** was typed in to replace the 4h that Microsoft Project scheduled. Then the regular work cells for the following Monday and Tuesday were selected and the Delete key was pressed to remove work for those days. Because of the editing, the Contour indicator is displayed for the Process Orders task. The final result shows the two tasks with the same duration and total work as in the original schedule, but the Leveling indicator is gone.

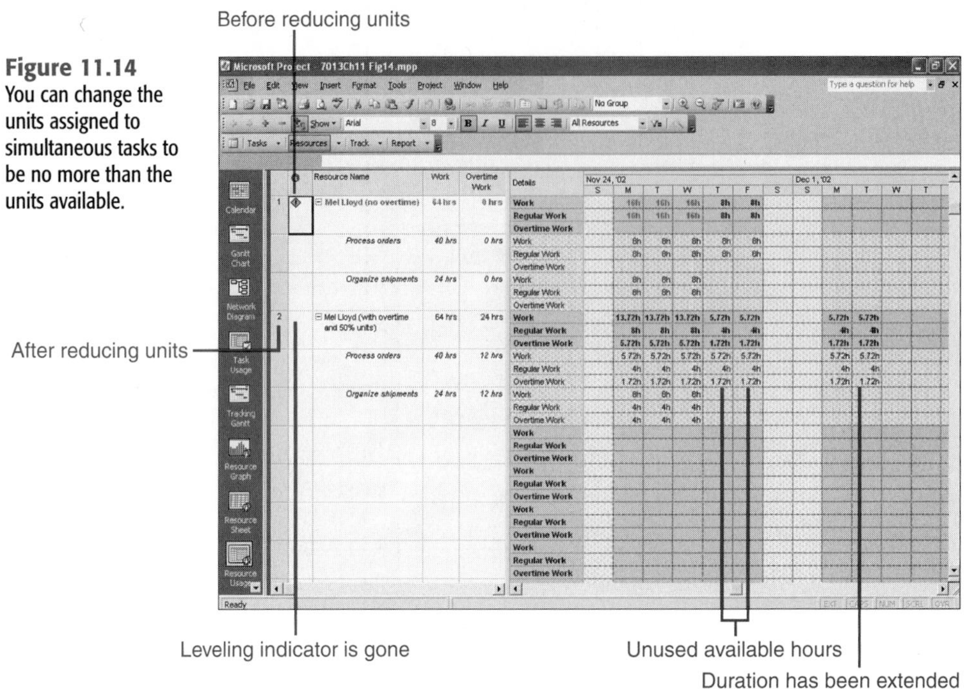

Figure 11.14
You can change the units assigned to simultaneous tasks to be no more than the units available.

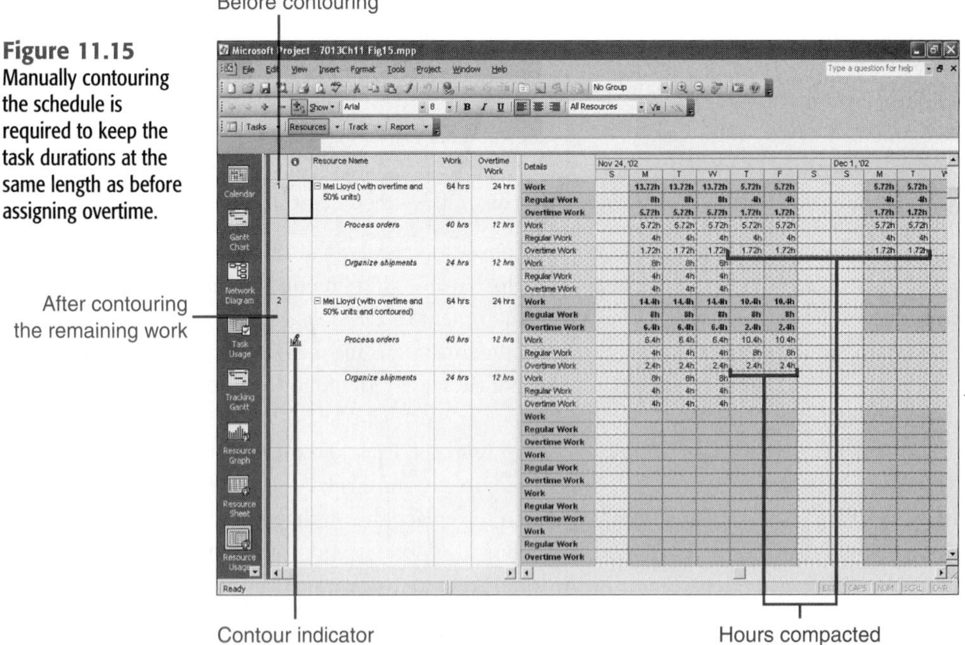

Figure 11.15
Manually contouring the schedule is required to keep the task durations at the same length as before assigning overtime.

EXTENDING THE AVAILABLE HOURS ON THE RESOURCE CALENDAR

If you want resources to work extra hours, you can adjust the calendar for the resource to add extra hours on specific days instead of assigning overtime. Unlike with assigning overtime, you can specify precisely when the extra work will take place. However, you cannot specify which task assignments will be scheduled during the extra time unless you manually contour the assignments. Microsoft Project uses the extra hours for any assignment that has started at that point in time, and you may have to edit the assigned work for tasks it has scheduled but that you don't want scheduled during those extra hours.

NOTE

> Remember that all working hours on the calendar are charged at the standard rate for the resource. Therefore, if these hours are really overtime hours and there is a premium rate for overtime, you should assign overtime rather than add hours to the calendar.

If only certain resources work the added hours, you need to make the changes on the individual resource calendars. If the added hours are to be worked by all resources, you can make the changes on the base calendar (or calendars) for resources in the project.

To extend the normal working hours for one or all resources, follow these steps:

1. From the Gantt Chart View choose Tools, Change Working Time to display the Change Working Time dialog box (see Figure 11.16).

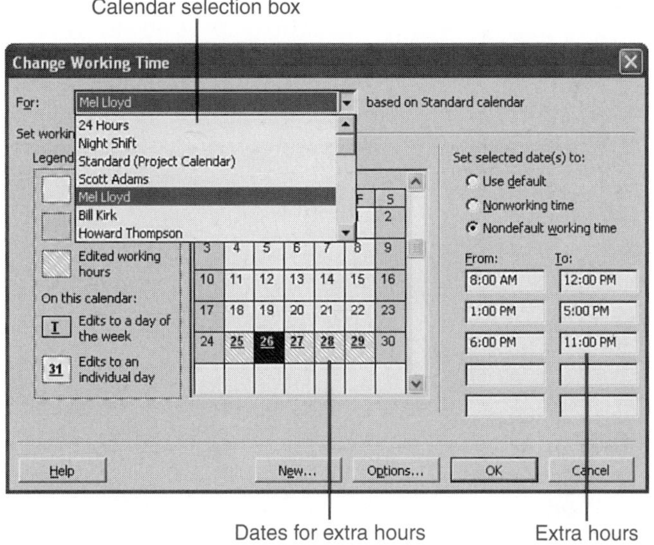

Figure 11.16 You can increase the working hours on the calendar to extend a resource's availability.

2. Select the resource calendar or the base calendar whose hours you want to extend in the For drop-down list.
3. Select the date or dates on which you want the extra hours worked. Use click-and-drag to select adjacent dates. Use the Ctrl key to add nonadjacent dates to the selection.
4. Enter the extra time in the From and To text boxes.
5. Click OK to close the dialog box and execute the changed hours.

TIP

> If the Change Working Time command on the Tools menu is grayed out (unavailable), you probably have the bottom pane of a combination view active. Activate the top pane, and this command should be available. As an alternative, you can click in any resource field that is visible, in either the top or bottom pane, and click the Resource Information tool on the Standard toolbar to view the Resource Information dialog box for that resource. Then, click the Working Time tab to modify that resource's calendar.

In Figure 11.16, Mel Lloyd's resource calendar is being modified to extend his hours during the week of November 25, 2002, by adding 5 hours of work for each of those days, from 18:00 to 23:00. Figure 11.17 shows the before-and-after effects of extending Mel's regular hours in the same situation that is used to illustrate overtime in Figure 11.13. Resource 1, labeled "Mel Lloyd," has 8 available hours per day (that is, 40 hours per week), as shown in the Work Availability detail row. The total work required for the two tasks is 64 hours, which is 24 hours more than the hours available. Mel is overallocated, and the Leveling indicator is displayed next to his name.

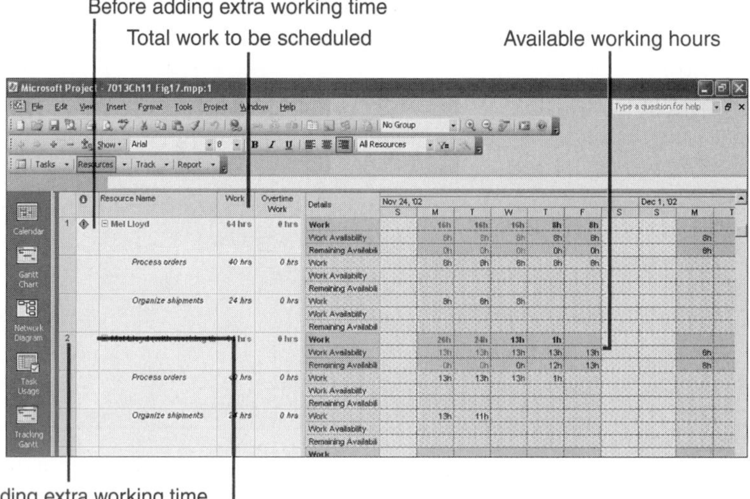

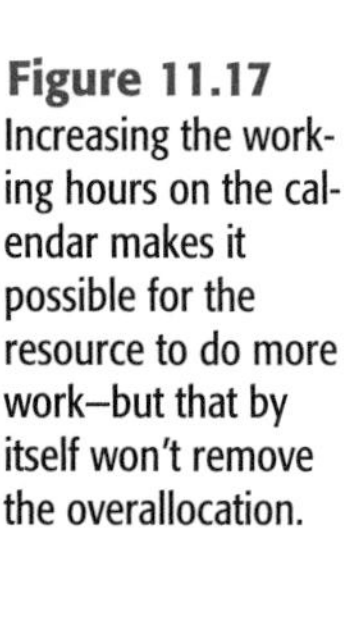

Figure 11.17
Increasing the working hours on the calendar makes it possible for the resource to do more work—but that by itself won't remove the overallocation.

Resource 2, labeled "Mel Lloyd (more working time hours)," shows that Mel's availability after adding the extra hours has risen to 13 hours per day (or 65 hours for the week). With the extended hours, Microsoft Project is able to schedule all 64 hours of the work during regular hours. And because the Leveling indicator sensitivity setting is Week by Week, the Leveling indicator is not displayed. However, the schedule is totally unrealistic, for Mel is assigned to both tasks at 100% and is scheduled for 26 hours of work on Monday and 24 hours on Tuesday. To make the schedule realistic, and to remove the overallocation highlight, the units must be reduced so that they total no more than 100%.

Figure 11.18 shows the before-and-after effect of reducing the units assigned to 50% for each task. Resource 1, labeled "Mel Lloyd (more working time hours)," is the same resource schedule shown in Figure 11.17. Resource 2, labeled "Mel Lloyd (adjusted units)," shows the schedule that Microsoft Project calculates when the unit assignments are changed to 50%. The resource name is no longer highlighted as an overallocated resource because the daily work is no greater than the work availability.

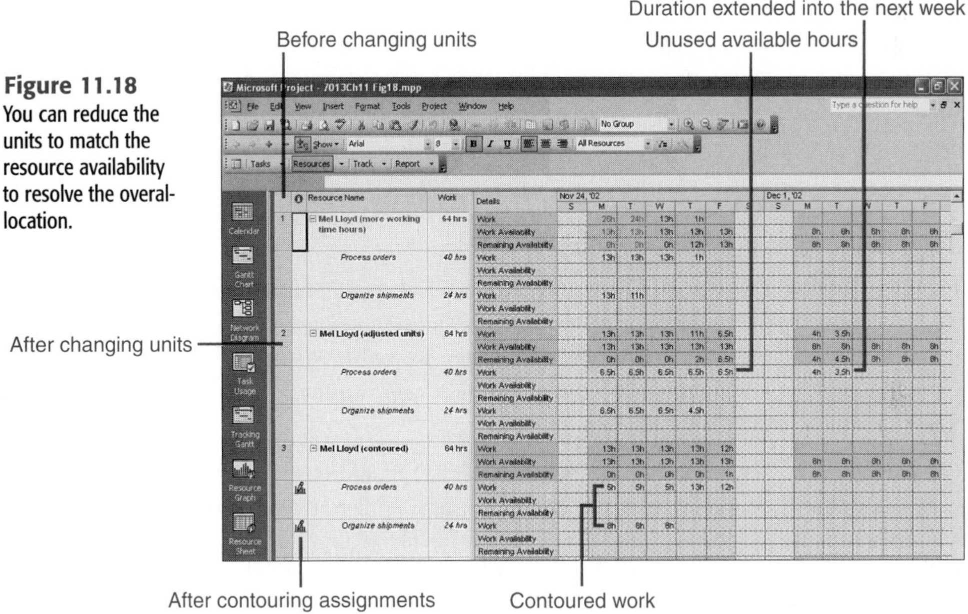

Figure 11.18 You can reduce the units to match the resource availability to resolve the overallocation.

However, due to the reduced units, Microsoft Project's new schedule has increased the duration of the Organize Shipments task (assigning only 6.5 hours per day instead of 13 hours as before), and Microsoft Project doesn't use all the available hours for the Process Orders task when it is the only task that needs work. The Remaining Availability detail row shows that 2 hours are not used on Thursday and 6.5 hours go unused on Friday. Because the Process Orders task is not finished, the remaining work has been pushed back to the following week. As with scheduling overtime, the final step to make the schedule reflect your real intentions is to manually edit the assignment contour to take advantage of all the available hours at the end of the longer task.

Resource 3 in Figure 11.18, labeled "Mel Lloyd (contoured)," shows the results of editing the timephased work assignments to take advantage of all available hours. The Work cells for the Organize Shipments task have been restored to 8 hours per day, and that task still finishes in three days, as it did in the original schedule. During those three days, the remaining 5 available hours are assigned to the Process Orders task. The Remaining Availability details calculate how many hours can be assigned to the Process Orders task on Thursday and Friday, and those cells are edited to finish the task by Friday. Editing the work values on the Process Orders task for Monday, Tuesday, and Wednesday as 5 hours each day reduces the total work value for the assignment to 30 hours. But you originally wanted Mel to work 40 hours on this task. So now you can adjust the working hours on Friday to compensate because Mel appears to have 13 hours of work availability. Increasing the working hours on Friday to 12h (instead of 2h) brings the total work for this assignment back up to 40 hours.

Reducing the Workload of the Overallocated Resource

Instead of increasing the availability of the resource that is overallocated, you can look for ways to reduce the demands on the resource during the overallocated period. You can cancel nonessential tasks, reassign tasks to other resources, or delay one or more assignments until the resource has time to work on them. The Resource Allocation view is an efficient view to use for these strategies.

Using the Resource Allocation View

The Resource Allocation view (see Figure 11.19) provides a good starting point for tackling the problem of reducing the demand for an overallocated resource. To access this view, you can click the Resource Allocation View tool on the Resource Management toolbar or choose View, More Views and then select Resource Allocation from the Views list. Then, click the Apply button to display the view.

The combination view in Figure 11.19 shows the names and task assignments of all resources in the Resource Usage view in the top pane. This view highlights overallocated resources and displays the Leveling indicator for resources that need your attention. Timephased assignment details in the grid on the right let you edit assignment schedules down to the hour or the minute. The bottom pane displays the Leveling Gantt Chart view, which shows, for the resource name you have selected in the top pane, all the tasks to which the resource is assigned. The Leveling Gantt Chart view has special formatting that is especially helpful in leveling resource assignments.

You can use the Go to Next Overallocation tool in either pane to pinpoint overallocated resource assignments. In the top pane, which is a resource view, the Go to Next Overallocation tool scrolls the timescale to the next date when an overallocation begins and selects the resource that is associated with the overallocation. Clicking the tool again finds the next overallocation in the timescale and selects its associated resource.

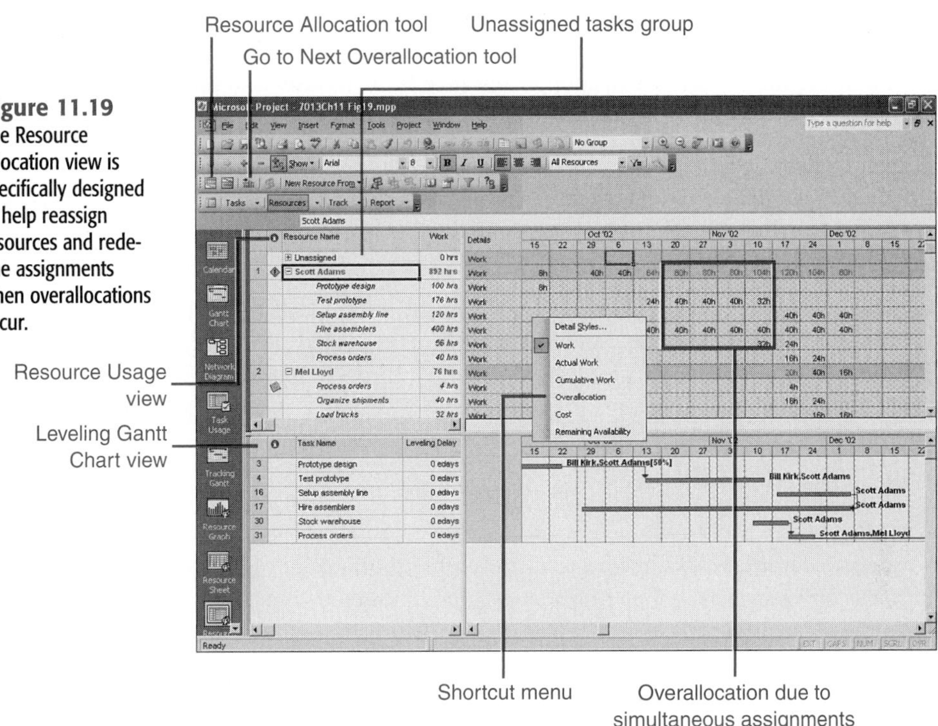

Figure 11.19 The Resource Allocation view is specifically designed to help reassign resources and redefine assignments when overallocations occur.

11

The bottom pane is a task view that shows only the set of tasks that are assigned to the resource that is selected in the top pane. When the bottom pane is active, the Go to Next Overallocation tool finds the next overallocation associated with one of the tasks in the restricted set. Clicking the tool again causes Microsoft Project to select the next task associated with that same overallocation or to find the next overallocation in the timescale that is associated with one of the tasks in the restricted set.

NOTE

If you are trying to locate the overallocations for a particular resource, you will find that using the Go to Next Overallocation tool in the top pane can be pretty tedious because it finds overallocations for all resources. Selecting the resource in the top pane, activating the bottom pane, and using the tool there narrows the search considerably. However, the overallocation that Microsoft Project finds may be for a different resource that is also assigned to one of the tasks in the restricted set. To confirm that the overallocation is for the selected resource, check the grid in the top pane to see if there is highlighting in the timephased data for that resource.

You can use the top pane to remove a task assignment from an overallocated resource, either by reassigning the task to another resource or by leaving the task unassigned for the time being. If you want to remove an assignment from a resource without designating another resource to take its place, you can simply select the assignment and choose Edit,

Delete Assignment (or press the Delete key). The assignment disappears from under the resource and reappears in the Unassigned category at the top of the Resource Usage view. You can move the assignment to another resource later. You can also select the row for the assignment and drag the assignment to the Unassigned group.

If you want to redefine a task—for example, by reducing its duration to help deal with an overallocation—you can select the overallocated resource in the top pane and then select the task in the bottom pane. You can either double-click the task or use the Task Information tool to display the Task Information dialog box, where you can modify the task definition.

By using the Assign Resources dialog box, you can quickly and graphically get an idea of the workload of a single resource or a group of resources by selecting the resource names and selecting Graphs. This enables you to view work, remaining availability, or assignment work in a graph-type view. If you're viewing a group of resources, any one of the resources can be removed from the graph by clicking the check mark to the left of the resource name listed on the right side of the dialog box.

When dealing with a large number of resources and using the Assign Resources dialog box to assign resources to tasks in a project, it is useful to be able to filter resources so that you can focus on a particular group of resources. You can use the new Filter By option in the Assign Resources dialog box to filter the resources displayed in the resource list.

SUBSTITUTING UNDERUSED RESOURCES FOR OVERALLOCATED RESOURCES

Probably the most conventional method of dealing with the problem of overallocated resources is to find substitute resources to take some of the load off the overallocated resources. To use this approach in a cost-effective manner, you need to consider a number of things, including the following:

- **The list of overallocated resources and their current workloads per time period**—This tells you when overallocations occur. The overallocated resources are identified in the Resource Usage view, the top pane of the Resource Allocation view. You can use the Go to Next Overallocation tool to identify overallocations.
- **The tasks that each overallocated resource is currently assigned to work on during the periods of overallocation**—This identifies the tasks for which you might want to seek substitutes. These tasks are identified in the top pane by the timephased data in the grid and in the bottom pane by the taskbars.
- **The total work commitment for each of the tasks for which resources may be substituted**—This helps you decide which of two tasks to give to a substitute and which to keep for the overallocated resource. You can give the task that involves the most total work to the lower-cost resource to keep costs low. The total work for each assignment is displayed by default in the Usage table's Work column, which displays on the left of the top pane.
- **The availability of other resources during the overallocated time periods**—This helps you find resources that can be used as substitutes. Although not displayed by default in the Resource Usage view, the Remaining Availability detail is one of the details you can choose to display in the timescale grid (see Figure 11.21).

- **The standard-rate cost for using each of the resources**—This tells you the cost of resources for those that are currently assigned to the tasks. Although it is not in the default display of the table in the Resource Usage view, the Standard Rate field can be added as a column in the table. In Figure 11.20, later in this section, it is being added to the right of the Work field. By comparing the cost rates of resources you can identify whether a cheaper resource has suitable availability and could be reassigned to another task for which a more expensive resource is already assigned. This allows you to reduce overall resource costs on a project by utilizing cheaper resources where it is practical to do so.
- **The skill level of other resources available to do the work and the time it may take them to learn the tasks that need to be done**—The comparative skill levels of resource substitutes can be used to estimate how many units of the substitute resource should be assigned and to reassess how long the assignment will take. This is not a standard field in Microsoft Office Project, but you can use one of the custom resource text or number fields to hold this data and then display it in the table on the Resource Usage view for reference when reassigning tasks.

It is certainly not required that you add the information suggested in this list, but the additional information promotes more cost-effective assignments.

Because the default table for the Resource Usage view is the Usage table, you can add the Standard Rate field to that table. The following steps show the quickest method of adding this column:

➔ For more options about customizing tables, **see** "Using and Creating Tables," **p. 840**.

1. Click the column heading for the Work column. For example, you can insert a column to the left for the Standard Rate field.
2. Choose Insert, Column to display the Column Definition dialog box (see Figure 11.20).

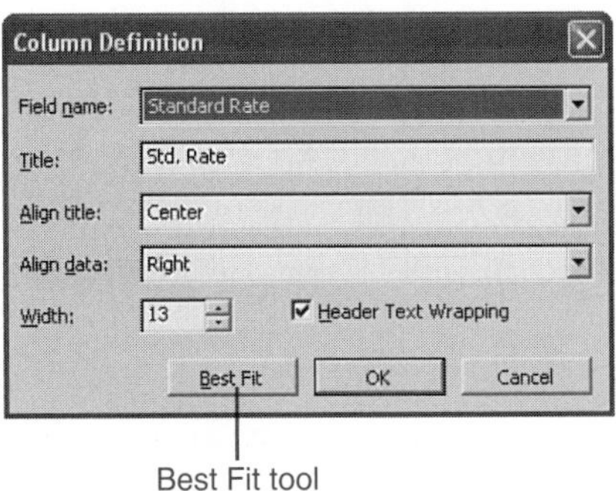

Figure 11.20 You can insert columns in your tables to show field values that help you make decisions.

3. Type **s** in the Field Name field to jump to the field names in the list that start with *s*. Standard Rate appears because it is the first *s* field in the list. Click Standard Rate or press Enter.
4. Select the Title text box and type a shorter name, such as **Std.Rate**.
5. Click the Best Fit button to insert the column with the width adjusted to the widest entry.

11

6. If necessary, adjust the column widths and the vertical divider bar so that you can see both the Std. Rate and Work columns.

Displaying details in the Resource Usage timescale is described earlier in this chapter, in the section "Working with the Resource Usage View." See that section for instructions on displaying and formatting the Remaining Availability field in the timescale. The resulting view should be similar to the one shown in Figure 11.21.

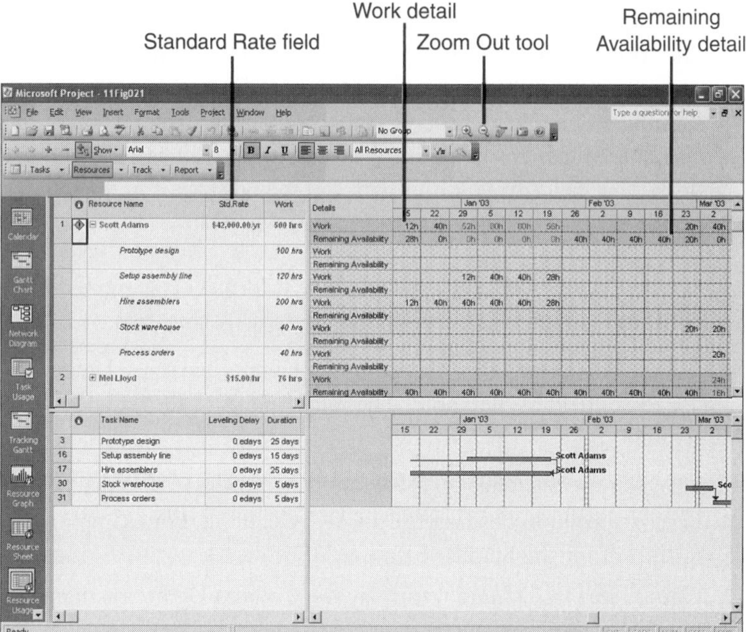

Figure 11.21 This modified Resource Allocation view displays the cost and availability of potential substitute resources.

TIP

In substituting resources, you might consider using a strategy whereby you assign only generic resources to tasks that are scheduled more than three months ahead. This provides valuable information regarding resource-loading requirements for the future and therefore an indication of what possible human resources, recruitment, or retraining implications there might be in the future. Replacing any generic resources with real named resources within a rolling three-month window (and on an ongoing basis) can form a useful strategy for dealing with resources. In the Standard version of Microsoft Project you can use a text or flag field to indicate which of your resources are generic or nongeneric. However, for more detailed requirements or automated replacement of generic resources based on required skills, you may want to consider using the Professional version of Microsoft Project in which generic resources are fully supported. Details on these features are covered in Chapter 26, "Enterprise Project Management."

To substitute another resource for one of the assignments of an overallocated resource, select the overallocated resource in the top pane and scroll the timescale to the start of the project. (In Figure 11.21 Scott Adams is selected in the top pane.) Then activate the bottom pane and use the Go to Next Overallocation tool to find the next time period when the selected resource is overallocated. In Figure 11.21, the first overallocation for Scott is in the week of January 12, 2003, when he is scheduled to work on the Setup Assembly Line task and the Hire Assemblers task at the same time. The Zoom Out tool was used to compress the minor timescale in Figure 11.21 to weeks in order to get a better perspective on the length of the tasks. You need to decide which task will be reassigned to another resource. The task that requires the least work and takes the least time in this example is Setup Assembly Line; therefore, you can look for a suitable substitute resource for that task.

By double-clicking the Setup Assembly Line task in the bottom pane to display the Task Information Form view, you can tell that the task is scheduled from January 2, 2003, to January 23, 2003. To see what other resources might have available hours during that period, you can scroll down the list of resources and look at the Remaining Availability values for other resources. You need to find a resource with at least as many hours available during each week as the work that the task requires: 12 hours the first week, 40 hours in each of the next two weeks, and 28 hours the final week.

TIP

If the list of resources in the top pane is long, you can highlight the time periods when the substitute must have available hours. Then, click and drag across the time units in the minor scale of the timescale to highlight those weeks for all resources (see Figure 11.22). Finally, scroll down the list, looking for available hours in the highlighted range.

You might find it helpful to hide the assignments in the top pane so that you only see the rows for resources (see Figure 11.22). To hide all assignments, click one of the column headings to select all rows and then click the Hide Subtasks button. If you want to continue to view the working hours for the assignment for which you're looking for a substitute, click the plus-sign outline symbol next to the resource that is currently assigned to the task.

TIP

If you have placed in the Group field, or in any text field, labels that identify resources that are qualified substitutes for Scott, you can filter the resource list in the top pane to focus on those resources. For example, the Setup Assembly Line task might require a Manager resource. If managers are identified in the Group field, you could filter the list for managers, to shorten the list of potential substitutes.

Both Mel Lloyd and Mary Logan have enough available time during the period shown, and Mary's standard rate is greater than Mel's. However, we will assume that the task is better suited to Mary's abilities and assign her to the task. Mary's standard rate is also higher than Scott's; therefore, the substitution is going to increase the cost of the task.

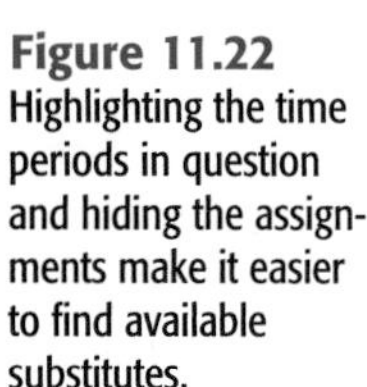

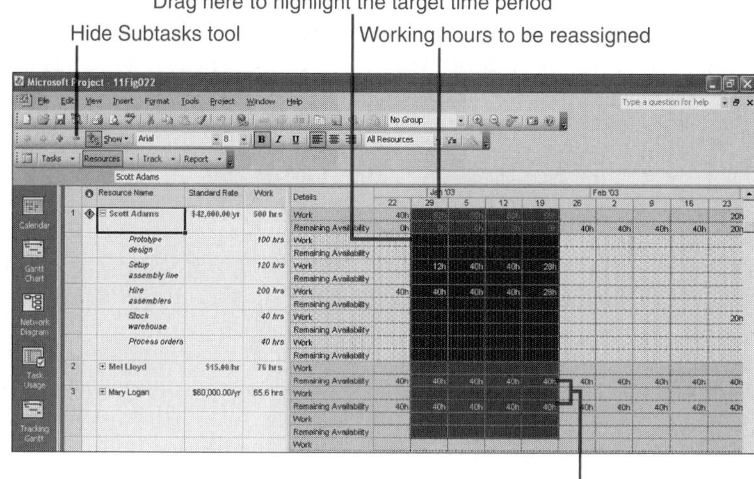

Figure 11.22
Highlighting the time periods in question and hiding the assignments make it easier to find available substitutes.

After a task and resource combination is selected, you can use the Resource Assignment dialog box to replace one resource with another:

1. Select the task for the substitution in the bottom pane. As shown in Figure 11.23, the task is Setup Assembly Line.

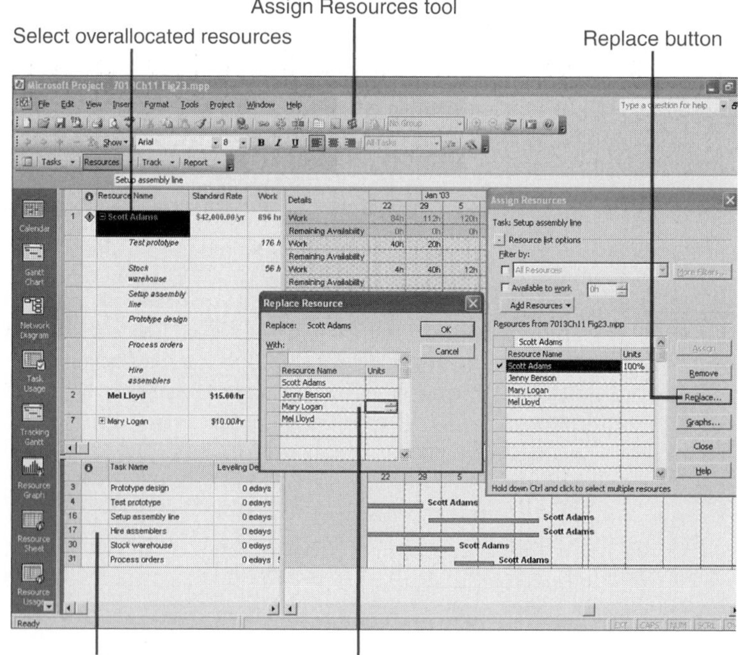

Figure 11.23
You can substitute Mary Logan for Scott Adams on the Setup Assembly Line task to relieve Scott's overallocation during this period.

2. Click the Assign Resources tool (or press Alt+F8) to display the Assign Resources dialog box.
3. Select the resource you want to replace (Scott Adams) and click the Replace button to display the Replace Resource dialog box.
4. Select the name of the resource that you want to assign as a substitute in the With list box.
5. Change the units assigned if necessary. By default, Microsoft Project assigns the same number of units for the new resource as were assigned for the original resource.
6. Click OK to complete the substitution.

TIP

> If the new resource is more or less efficient or skilled at the task than the original resource, you should manually adjust the assignment after the replacement to show how many hours it will take the new resource to complete the task.

Figure 11.24 shows the schedule after you substitute Mary Logan for Scott Adams. Scott's workload is reduced, and he is no longer overallocated in this period.

11

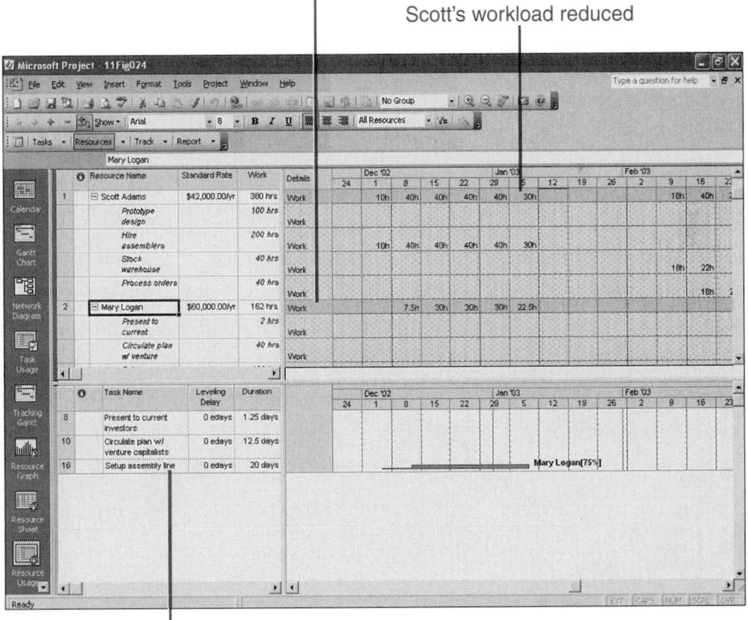

Figure 11.24
The schedule after substituting Mary Logan for Scott Adams shows that Scott's overallocation has been fixed.

After the new assignment has been added to the replacement resource, you can modify the assignment in the Assignment Information dialog box. To do so, you select the assignment row in the top pane and click the Assignment Information tool or simply double-click the assignment.

Resolving Overallocations by Delaying Assignments

If resource overallocation is the result of scheduling multiple tasks at the same time, you can delay one or more task assignments to a later date to spread out the demands on the resource over a longer period of time and thereby reduce the demand in the overallocated period. You can delay assignments yourself by examining the schedule and selecting the assignments to delay, or you can have Microsoft Office Project choose the assignments to delay—either on your command or automatically as task assignments are added to the schedule. This section shows you how to level assignments yourself, on a case-by-case basis.

NOTE

> This discussion is built around the case of forward-scheduled projects. Delaying overallocations means offsetting one or more tasks that would otherwise be scheduled at the same time. In forward-scheduled projects, you add a delay to a task's start date to push it back to a later date. In projects that are scheduled from a fixed finish date, however, you insert an offset at the finish of the task to cause it to be scheduled for earlier dates. Delay values are entered as positive numbers in forward-scheduled projects and as negative numbers in projects that are scheduled from a fixed finish date.

There are several ways to delay assignments yourself:

- You can use the Delay field of the task database to enter a delay in the start date for a task, thus delaying all assignments to that task.
- You can use the Assignment Delay field to delay the start of the assignment for just the resource that is overallocated, leaving other resources' assignments for the task unchanged.
- If work on a task is scheduled to have started already when the overallocation begins, you can split the task at that point and resume the task when the overallocated resource is available again. Of course, other resources assigned to the task will have their assignments split also.
- Instead of splitting the task, and all assignments, you can split just the assignment for the overallocated resource, leaving other resource assignments unchanged.
- Instead of delaying all the work on the overallocated resource's assignment, you can merely reduce the hours assigned during the period of overallocation and increase the hours later. This is called *contouring* the assignment and can be done by manually editing the assigned work in each period or by choosing one of the predefined contour patterns to apply to the assignment.

DELAYING A TASK You use the Resource Allocation view when leveling resource work loads manually. With the Resource Usage view in the top pane to help you select the overallocated resources, the bottom pane displays the Leveling Gantt Chart view, with the Leveling Delay field in the table next to the task name (see Figure 11.25). The Leveling Delay field is zero by default, but if you enter an amount of time in the field, Microsoft Project delays the start of the task—and therefore all assignments to the task—by the amount of that delay value.

For forward-scheduled projects, the delay value is a positive number that, when added to the task's original start date, makes it a later start date. For projects with fixed finish dates, the delay value is a negative number that makes Microsoft Project push the task finish date back to an earlier date.

Delay amounts are shown in elapsed time. Elapsed time ignores the distinction between working time and nonworking time on calendars. Using elapsed time makes it easier for you to estimate the amount of time you should enter in the Leveling Delay field. You can count the time units in the timescale of the Gantt Chart view and enter that number without having to check to see if any of those units fall on nonworking days.

→ For more information about using elapsed duration, **see** "Entering Task Duration," **p. 132**.

The Delay table also includes the Successors field, to give you information about what tasks are directly affected if you delay the selected task. You must scroll the columns in the table to see the Successors field. The taskbars display the names of assigned resources to the right of the bar.

The Leveling Gantt Chart view shows the amount of any *free slack* (that is, the amount of time between the end of a task and the start of a successor task) as a thin teal-colored Slack bar that extends to the right, beyond the bottom edge of the taskbar. You can delay a task by as much as the free slack without affecting the scheduling of other tasks. Of course, if you delay tasks beyond the free slack, the start and finish of successor tasks will also be delayed; if you delay a task beyond the total slack (not shown in the Leveling Gantt Chart view), the finish of the whole project is delayed.

NOTE

Free slack is the amount of time that a task can be delayed without delaying successor tasks. *Total slack* is the amount of time that a task can be delayed without delaying the project.

The term *slack* is synonymous with the accepted project management term *float*. Microsoft Project uses the term *slack* to illustrate float time within a project.

NOTE

ScreenTips identify any taskbars that appear in the view. In Figure 11.25, the pointer rests over the Slack bar, and the ScreenTip shows the name of the bar and gives information about the task

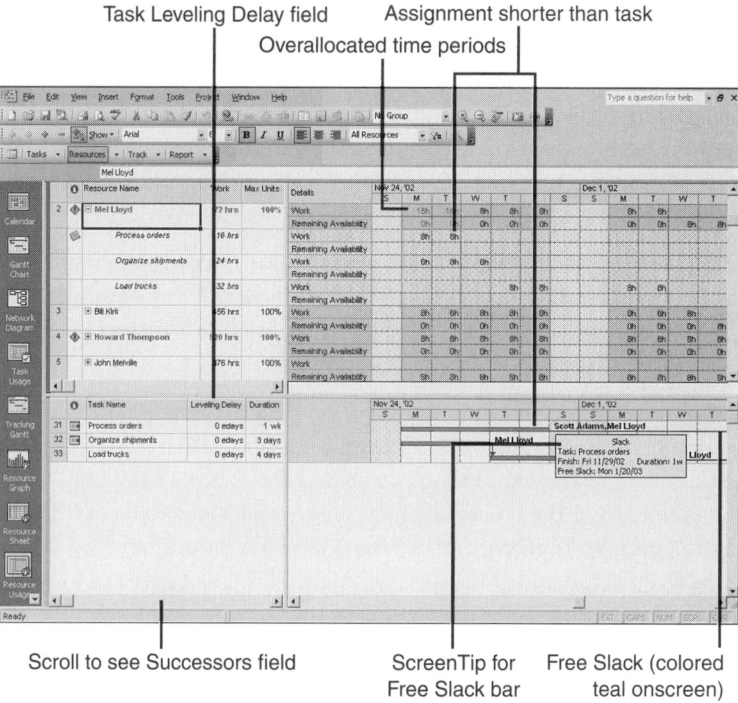

Figure 11.25
The Leveling Gantt Chart view is especially helpful for delaying tasks to level resource assignments.

As shown in Figure 11.25, Mel Lloyd is an overallocated resource in the week of November 24, 2002. Selecting his name in the top pane causes the tasks to which he is assigned to appear in the bottom pane. After using the horizontal scrollbar in the timescale to move to the beginning of the project, you can click the Go to Next Overallocation tool to locate the first time period during which Mel is overallocated. The overallocation is due to the overlapping assignments for the Process Orders and Organize Shipments tasks. You could delay either of these tasks to remove the overallocation for Mel.

Scott Adams is also assigned to the Process Orders task, and if you delayed the task, both Mel's and Scott's assignments would be delayed. However, the existence of the Slack bar to the right of the Process Orders task shows that delaying the task will not delay any other tasks or the project as a whole. If you were to delay the Organize Shipments task to resolve Mel's overallocation, the absence of a Slack bar for the task would show that other tasks and the overall project would be delayed as a result. You can safely delay the Process Orders task.

To delay the task, select the Leveling Delay field for the task and estimate the amount of delay. You can see from the Duration field in the bottom pane that Organize Shipments is a three-day task, so entering **`3 days`** for the Process Orders task should remove the overallocation.

Figure 11.26 shows the results of entering the delay. The Leveling Gantt Chart view displays the amount of the delay in the Leveling Delay field on the left, and it displays the Delay bar to the left of the taskbar to show the amount of the delay graphically. The tasks no longer overlap, and Mel's initial overallocation period is now free of overallocation. However, Mel now has a three-day conflict with his Load Trucks assignment. If that conflict is resolved by delaying the Load Trucks assignment, it will mean a three-day delay in the completion of the project. Also, because the entire task was delayed, the assignment for Scott Adams had to be delayed also, and that could possibly create an overallocation for Scott.

Figure 11.26
The Leveling Gantt Chart view shows the amount of the delay as a thin bar to the left of the main taskbar.

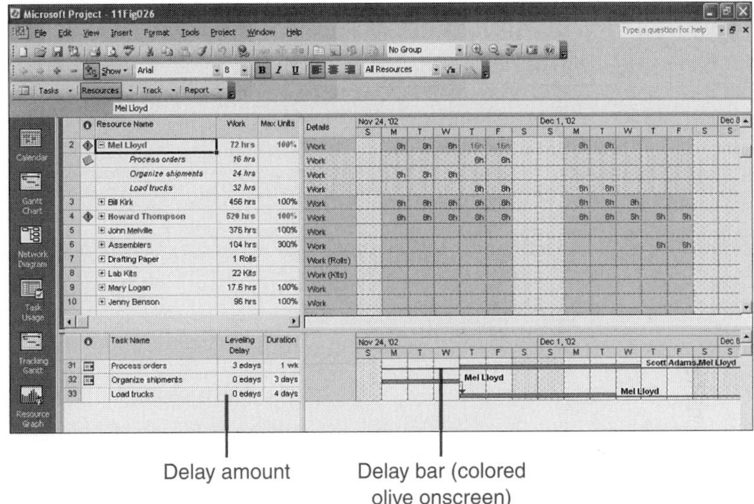

You can use Undo (Ctrl+Z) immediately after entering a delay amount to restore the previous values to the Delay field entries. You also can remove a delay by entering `0` in the Delay field. Note that you can't leave the Leveling Delay field blank. If there are many delay values to be cleared, you might want to use the Clear Leveling command. To use the menu to return the delay values to zero for a single task or group of tasks, follow these steps:

1. Select the tasks for which you want to reset the delay to zero. Click and drag to select adjacent tasks. Press Ctrl while clicking to select nonadjacent tasks.
2. Choose Tools, Resource Leveling. The Resource Leveling dialog box appears.
3. At the bottom of the Resource Leveling dialog box, click the Clear Leveling tool to display the Clear Leveling dialog box.
4. Choose the Selected Tasks option to change the values for only the tasks that you selected. If you want to remove all delay values for all tasks, use the Entire Project option.
5. Click OK. All tasks with nonzero delay values are reset to zero delay.

DELAYING INDIVIDUAL ASSIGNMENTS When tasks have multiple resources assigned to them, it can be better to resolve an overallocation for just one of the resources by delaying the assignment for just that resource, leaving the other resources unaffected. Of course, if the delayed assignment then has a finish date that is later than the task finish date before the delay, the task duration is increased. This section shows how to delay individual assignments for tasks.

Returning to the previous example, you can delay Mel Lloyd's assignment on the Process Orders task instead of delaying the task and Scott's assignment with it. In the Resource Allocation view, you can delay an assignment in one of four ways:

- You can add the Leveling Delay field to the Usage table in the top pane and enter the amount of the delay in that column.
- You can manually edit the timephased work data in the top pane to shift working hours to the right to later dates and times.
- You can change the assignment's start date in the Assignment Information dialog box.
- You can add the Assignment Delay field to the Usage table in the top pane and enter the amount of the delay in that column.

If the purpose for delaying an assignment is to avoid an overallocation, you should use the Leveling Delay field, which is specifically designed to show delays due to overallocations. If you later want to remove all the leveling delays that you or Microsoft Project have inserted, you can use the Clear Leveling command to remove the delay if it's in this field.

The Leveling Delay field is not included in the standard Usage table, but you can easily add it to the table by clicking the column heading where you want the field to go and choosing Insert, Column. In the Column Definition dialog box, choose Leveling Delay in the Field Name box and click the Best Fit button to adjust the column width to the widest entry. You might need to adjust the vertical divider bar so that you can see the new column.

NOTE

> Unlike task delay values, which are *elapsed* time periods, leveling delay values are regular, nonelapsed, time periods.

Figure 11.27 shows the Leveling Delay field added to the table in the top pane. Note the delay in Mel's Process Orders assignment.

To remove the delay, type **0** or use the spinner control to select zero.

NOTE

> The Leveling Delay field only accepts zero or positive numbers for projects that are scheduled from a start date. It only accepts zero or negative numbers for projects that are scheduled from a finish date.

To edit the timephased data, select the cells that contain work that is to be delayed and press the Insert key. The cells you selected shift to the right, also pushing to the right all later work cells for the assignment. The Contoured indicator then appears in the Indicators column for the assignment.

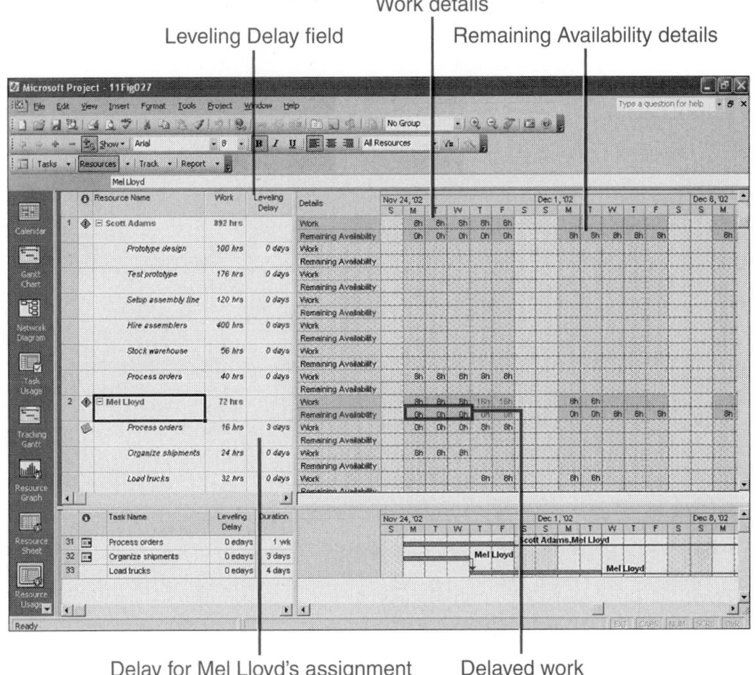

Figure 11.27 You can use the Leveling Delay field in a Usage table to enter and remove assignment-leveling delays.

TIP

You might need to zoom in to see smaller time units, to detect exactly how many days and hours the assignment needs to be delayed. To do this, zoom in until you can clearly see exactly when the task that is not being delayed finishes. Then shift the work for the delayed task one cell further to the right.

To remove the delay, select the assignment cells that have 0h in them and press the Delete key. All work cells to the right of the selection then shift to the left.

If you want to delay the assignment by modifying the start date and time for the assignment until just after a conflicting assignment is completed, you need to be able to determine exactly when the conflicting assignment finishes. To determine the finish time, you must first instruct Microsoft Project to display time along with dates. To display dates with the time of day appended, choose Tools, Options and display the View tab. In the Date Format box, select from the drop-down list one of the formats that includes the date and time of day.

In this example, we will delay Mel's Process Orders assignment so that it starts immediately after the conflicting assignment Organize Shipments finishes. You can find out when the Organize Shipments assignment finishes by double-clicking that assignment to display its Assignment Information dialog box. In Figure 11.28, the Assignment Information dialog box for Organize Shipments shows that the task finishes on November 27, 2002, at 5:00 p.m. The Process Orders task would be delayed to start on November 28, 2002, at 8:00 a.m. to resolve the conflict.

Figure 11.28
You can use the Assignment Information dialog box to find out when an assignment finishes.

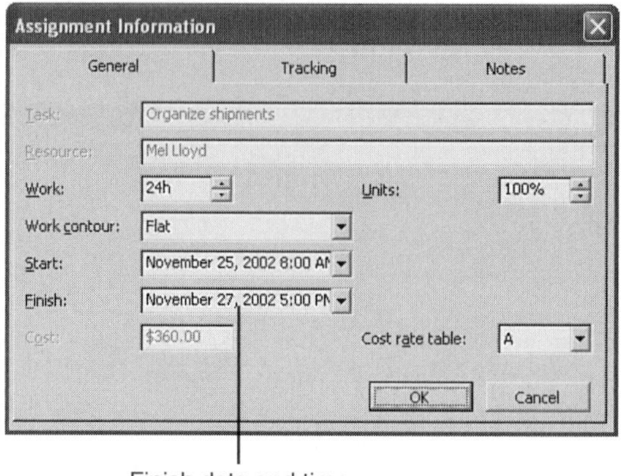

To delay the start of an assignment, follow these steps:

1. Double-click the assignment you want to delay in order to display its Assignment Information dialog box.
2. Enter the delayed start date and time in the Start field or click the date control and select the date from the calendar and then append the time.
3. Click OK to complete the entry.

Figure 11.29 shows the effect of delaying Mel's assignment on the Process Orders task from Monday to Thursday. The original cells for his assignment now have 0h in them, and Mel is no longer overallocated during that period. You can also see that Scott Adams' assignment on that same task continues to start on Monday.

When you delay an assignment by editing the Start field of the Assignment Information dialog box or by editing the timephased data in the grid, Microsoft Project translates the difference between the previous start date and the new one as an *assignment delay* and stores that value in the Assignment Delay field. You can also delay an assignment by entering the amount of the delay directly into the Assignment Delay field. However, as pointed out earlier, if the purpose of the delay is to level resource usage, the Leveling Delay field is a better field to use.

NOTE

The Assignment Delay and Leveling Delay fields produce the same result—they delay the start of the assignment—but there are some differences between them. Microsoft Project uses the Leveling Delay field to enter a delay when you use the Level Now command to resolve resource overallocations. There is also a Clear Leveling command that resets all Leveling Delay values to zero.

Microsoft Project does not make entries in the Assignment Delay field, nor is there a command to clear those entries. The Assignment Delay field is intended to be used to delay one resource's assignment when there is a valid operational reason for the delay (for example, if one resource contributes finishing touches on a task and should be scheduled at the end of the task).

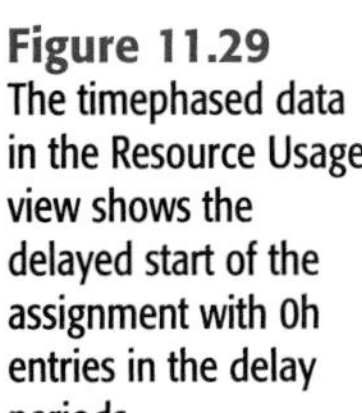

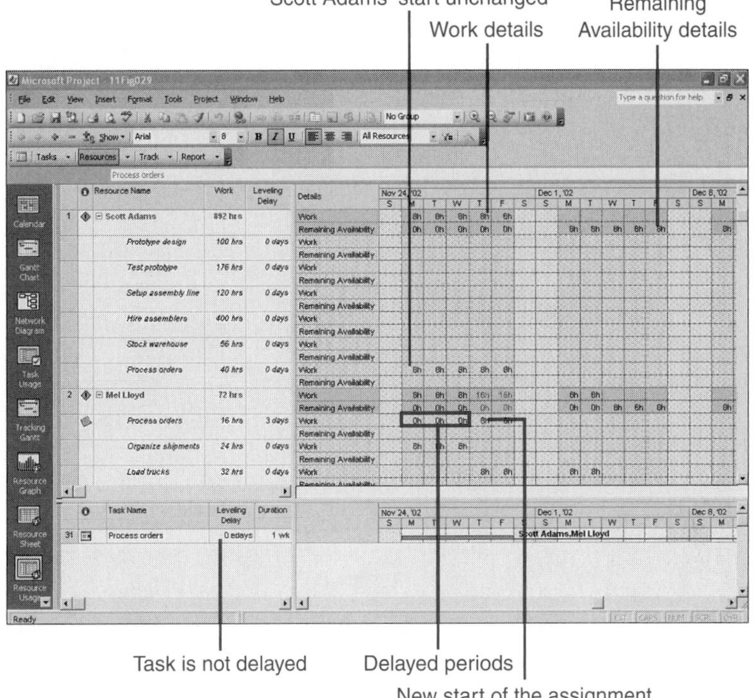

Figure 11.29
The timephased data in the Resource Usage view shows the delayed start of the assignment with 0h entries in the delay periods.

11

If Leveling does not appear to be working, please refer to "Level Now Seems Not to Be Working" in the "Troubleshooting" section at the end of this chapter.

The Assignment Delay field is not included in the standard Usage table, but you can easily add it to the table by clicking the column heading where you want the field to go and choosing Insert, Column. In the Column Definition dialog box, choose Assignment Delay in the Field Name box and click the Best Fit button to adjust the column width to the width of the widest entry.

The Clear Leveling command does not reset assignment delays to zero. The easiest method to use if you want to remove an assignment delay is to display the Assignment Delay field in the Resource Usage view or the Task Usage view and change delay values to zero. You can also find inserted nonworking time periods in the grid and delete them, but it's easier to identify nonzero values in the Assignment Delay field.

TIP

If you want to review all the assignment delays or leveling delays in a project, you can design a filter to display only tasks where the Assignment Delay field is not equal to zero or the Leveling Delay field is not equal to zero. Using the criterion Not Equal to Zero instead of Greater Than Zero allows the filter to find both projects with positive delay values (those scheduled from a fixed start date) and projects with negative delay values (those scheduled from a fixed finish date).

→ For detailed help in creating a filter, **see** "Creating Custom Filters," **p. 859**.

SPLITTING A TASK Suppose that an overallocation occurs because an assignment starts while another assignment, which has already started, is still in process. You could, as in the preceding examples, delay all work on the new assignment until the already started assignment is finished. Or you could interrupt the work on the already started assignment (that is, *split* the assignment) until the new assignment is completed. If you introduce the split at the task level, all assignments to the task are split at the same point. If you just split the assignment itself, other resource assignments to the task are not split.

In Figure 11.30, the Create Advertising Plan task is assigned to both Howard Thompson and Mary Logan. It is scheduled to be already started when the Sales Training task starts. Howard Thompson is assigned to both tasks, and he is overallocated during the period when the tasks overlap.

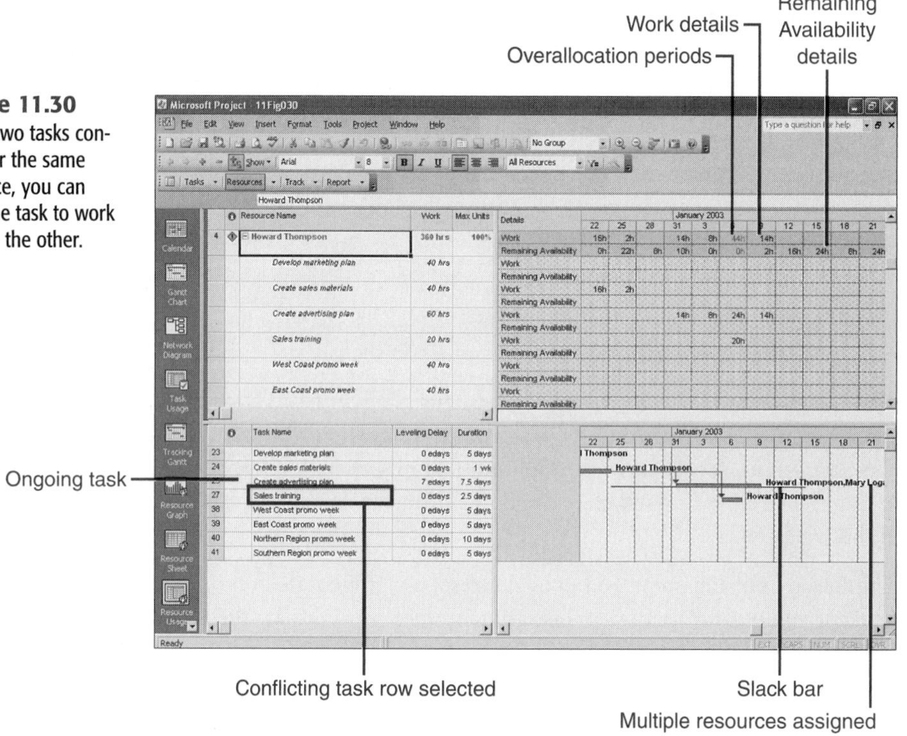

Figure 11.30 When two tasks contend for the same resource, you can split one task to work around the other.

The ongoing task, Create Advertising Plan, has slack (as evidenced by the Slack bar in the bottom pane) and its finish can be delayed without affecting the project finish date. However, the new task, Sales Training, does not have a Slack bar and should not be delayed if you want to avoid delaying the finish of the project. You could split Howard's assignment to the Create Advertising Plan task and avoid delaying the project. Splitting the task would split both Howard's and Mary's assignments. If you split just Howard's assignment, Mary would continue her work as scheduled and Howard would complete his after the Sales Training is finished. The duration for the Create Advertising Plan task would be increased to incorporate Howard's delayed work.

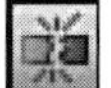

If you are using the Resource Allocation view, you must split tasks in the Leveling Gantt Chart view in the bottom pane because only resources and assignments (not tasks) are displayed in the top pane. You use the Split Task tool to split a taskbar in the Leveling Gantt Chart view, thus splitting the task and all its assignments.

TIP

> If you were to display the Task Usage view in the top pane, you could split a task by inserting nonworking cells in the timephased data for the task. To do so, select the cell or cells for the time period when the split should occur and press the Insert key.

You first need to determine exactly when the split should start and when it should end. You want the split to start when the new task starts and to end when the new task finishes. You can determine the start and finish of the new task by double-clicking it in the bottom pane to view the Task Information Form view. The start and finish dates are on the General tab. You could also scroll the table in the bottom pane to the right to see the Start and Finish fields for the task. In the table in Figure 11.31 you can see the start and finish dates for the Sales Training task. The task starts January 6, 2003, at 10:00 a.m. and finishes on January 10, 2003, at 3:00 p.m.

TIP

> When you scroll a table horizontally and the Name field will scroll out of view, you can select the row ID to highlight the entire row (as was done previously, in Figure 11.30). Then you can easily identify the row when you get to the column you want to examine (as in Figure 11.31).

TIP

> It's a good idea to have the time of day included in the date format so that you can coordinate the timing of the tasks.

If you want to split a task down to the hour, you must format the timescale to show hours. In Figure 11.31, the Zoom In tool has been used to display quarter-days, which is a format that includes hours on the minor scale.

To split a task in the Leveling Gantt Chart view, follow these steps:

1. Activate the pane with a task view—in this case, the Leveling Gantt Chart view—in the bottom pane.
2. Determine the exact date and time when the split should start and end. In Figure 11.31, the dates are shown in the selected task row in the bottom pane.

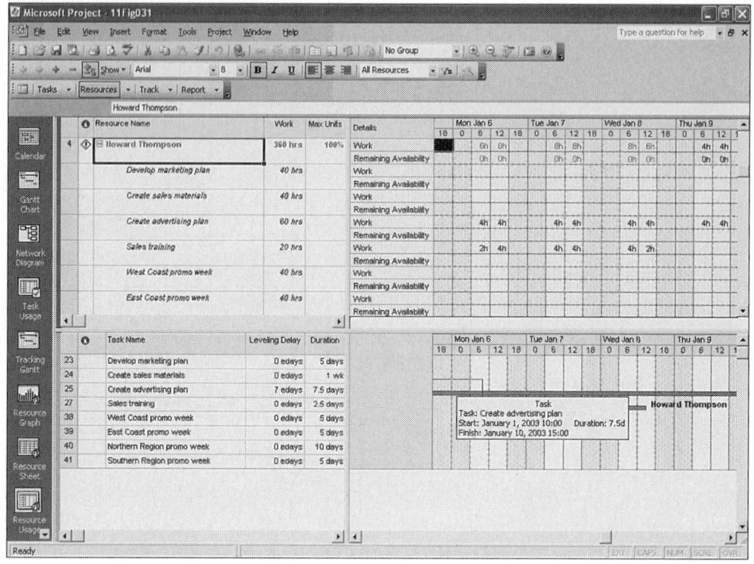

Figure 11.31
You can use the Split Task tool to split taskbars in the bottom pane of the Resource Allocation view.

3. Click the Split Task tool to activate the Split Task ScreenTip. As you move the pointer over the taskbars, the ScreenTip shows the date and time for the pointer's position on the screen. When you click over a taskbar, you see the date and time when the split will start. Do not click anywhere until you are in position over the taskbar you want to split and the ScreenTip shows the date and time when you want the split to start.

TIP

> If at this point you decide to abandon the split operation, simply press the Esc key to cancel the split command. If you decide to cancel the command after you have started dragging the split in the following steps, drag the pointer to an area where it is not over the taskbar and release the mouse button.

4. When you are over the correct taskbar and the ScreenTip shows the date and hour when you want the split to start, click and hold down the mouse button to start dragging the remainder of the task to the right, to locate the date and time when work should resume.

   The Split Task ScreenTip disappears and a Task ScreenTip appears. The Start field in this ScreenTip shows the date and time where the pointer is currently located. This is the date and time when work on the task will be scheduled to resume.

5. Drag the remainder of the task to the correct date and time (as shown in the Split Task ScreenTip) to resume work on the task. Figure 11.32 shows the pointer in position to resume work after 3:00 p.m. on January 8, 2003.

TIP

> When you are dragging part of the task to a new date, if the destination date is off the screen, you can drag the pointer just beyond the edge of the screen slowly; the timescale scrolls until you reach the destination.

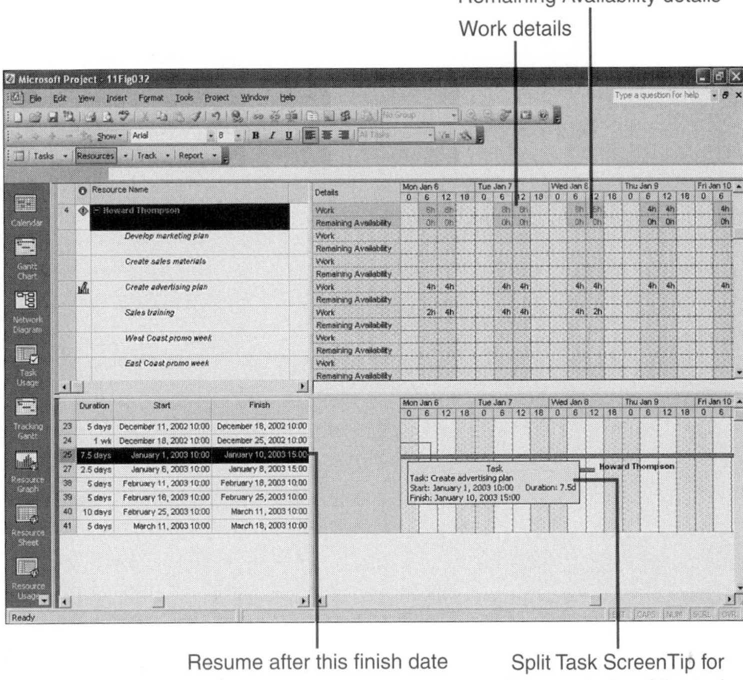

Figure 11.32
You can drag the remaining portion of a split task to the date and time when you want work to resume.

Figure 11.33 shows the task after the split has been created, with the timescale formatted the same as in Figure 11.31. In Figure 11.33, you can see both assignments to the task that was split. Mary Logan and Howard Thompson both have a 0h cell in the middle of their assignments, during the period for which the taskbar shows the split.

To remove a split in a task, you use the mouse to drag the part of the task that's on the right toward the part on the left. When they touch, Project removes the split and rejoins the taskbar.

SPLITTING INDIVIDUAL ASSIGNMENTS In Figure 11.32, the task was split to resolve an overallocation problem, and that split all resource assignments for the task, whether they were overallocated or not. You can also split just the assignment for the resource that is overallocated (Howard Thompson), thus leaving other assigned resources (Mary Logan, in this case) on their existing schedules. To split an assignment, you must open either the Resource Usage view or the Task Usage view and edit the timephased work cells for the assignment. Select the cells where the interruption will take place and press the Insert key to shift those work amounts to later dates.

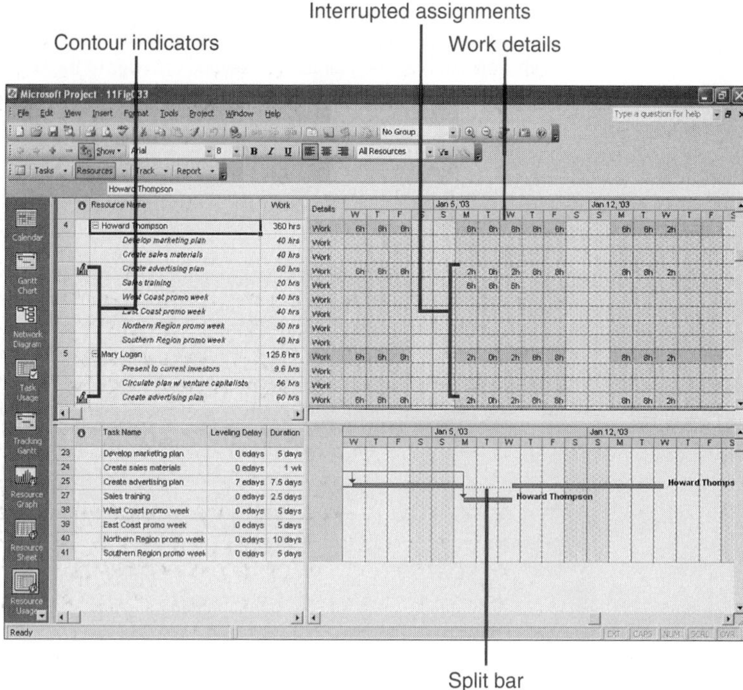

Figure 11.33
Splitting a task also splits all assignments to the task.

In Figure 11.34, the Zoom In tool has been used to view quarter-days because we need to reschedule the assignment to stop at 10:00 a.m. and resume at 3:00 p.m. If those particular hours were not shown on the timescale, you would need to zoom in further until the time periods you needed to schedule appeared in the timescale.

In the table on the left of the bottom pane in Figure 11.34, the columns have been rearranged so that you can see the task's duration and finish date. Before the assignment is split, the task duration is 7.5 days and the finish date is January 10, at 3:00 p.m.

The timephased work cells where the split will occur are selected in the figure. With the cells selected, you can create the split by pressing the Insert key or by choosing Insert, Cell from the menu. The contents of the selected cells are then shifted to the right, and all cells to the right of the insertion cells are shifted also.

CAUTION

> If you type `0` in an assignment work cell instead of pressing the Insert key, you create a split in the assignment, but the work scheduled for that day is lost.

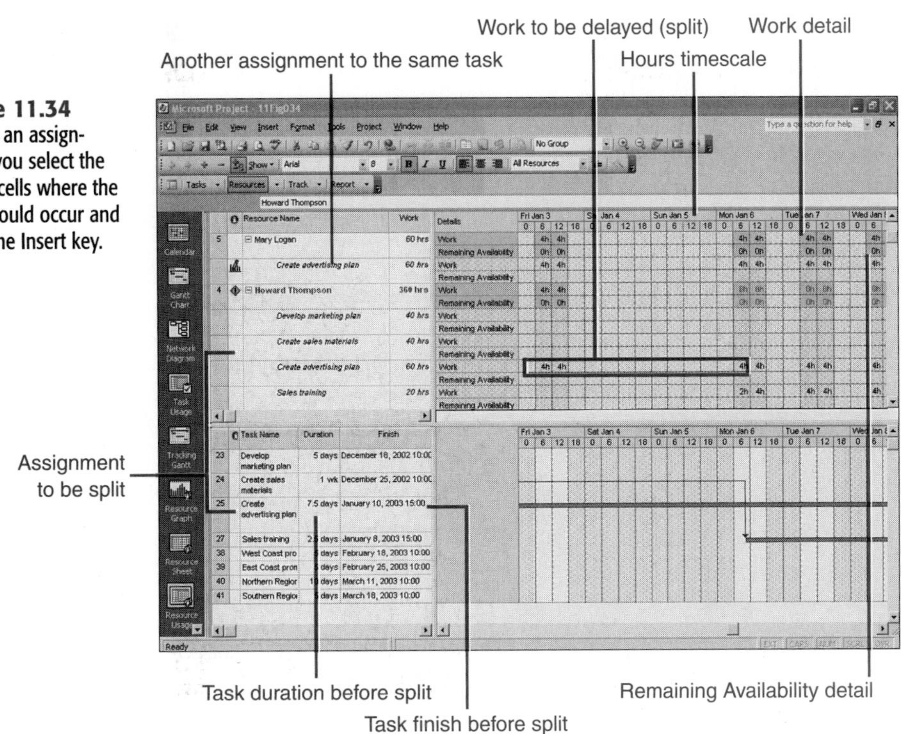

Figure 11.34
To split an assignment, you select the cell or cells where the split should occur and press the Insert key.

Figure 11.35 shows the assignment schedule after the split has been inserted. The cells that were selected now have zero hours of work for Howard Thompson, but Mary Logan still has work scheduled in those same time periods. The taskbar in the Gantt Chart view does not show a split because Mary Logan is continuing to work during the period of the split. The total work for the assignment has not changed, but the duration of the task has increased from 7.5 days to 10.5 days, and the finish date is pushed back from January 10, 2003, to January 15, 2003. Notice the contour indicator on the assignment row, which shows that the timephased values for the assignment have been edited.

TIP

> To select a series of assignment cells, drag the mouse across them or, after selecting the first cell, hold down the Shift key as you click the last cell to select. You can then press the Insert key to shift work assignments past the last selected cell.

To remove the splits in an assignment, select the cell or cells that have 0h in them and press the Delete key. Unfortunately, there is no easy way to identify the assignments that have been edited, other than to look for the existence of the Contour indicator on those assignment rows. In order to find the edited cells, you have to scroll the timescale for the contoured assignment to find cells that contain 0h.

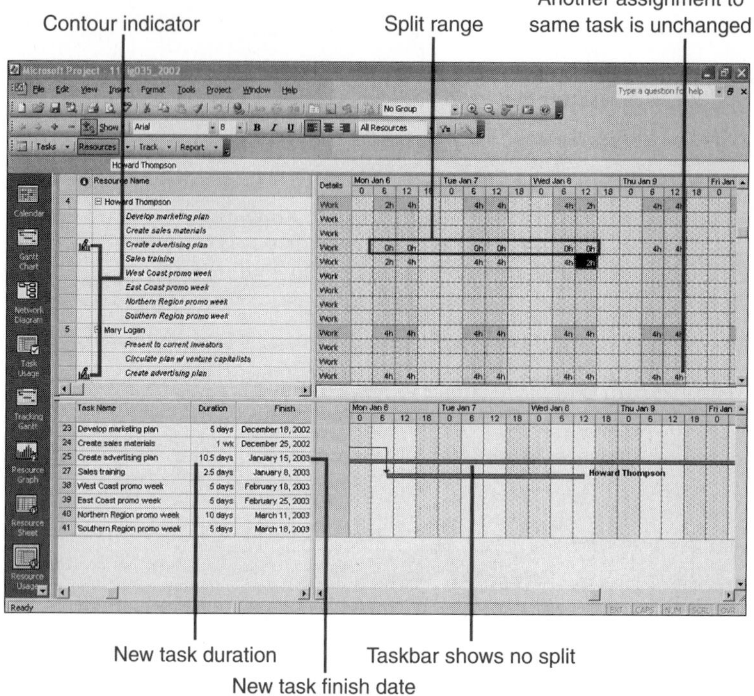

Figure 11.35 The split appears as cells with zero work in the assignment row.

11

TIP

> If you select and remove 0h cells by pressing Delete, the contour indicator is still displayed. If you have deleted a delay or split and you're sure there are no other edited changes you want to preserve, you can remove the Contour indicator by double-clicking the assignment to display the Assignment Information dialog box and selecting Flat on the drop-down list in the Work Contour box.

LETTING PROJECT LEVEL OVERALLOCATED RESOURCES FOR YOU

Instead of leveling individual tasks and assignments on your own, you can have Microsoft Project calculate task or assignment delays to remove resource overallocations. Microsoft Project searches through the project, looking for resources that display the Leveling indicator. Using the settings in the Resource Leveling dialog box, which is described later in this chapter in the section "Configuring Settings in the Resource Leveling Dialog Box," Microsoft Project selects tasks to be delayed in order to resolve overallocations for resources that display the Leveling indicator.

NOTE

Microsoft Project doesn't delay material resource assignments. However, if the leveling operation changes the duration of a task, the material assignments might be contoured also.

If the project is scheduled from a start date, Microsoft Project adds *positive* delays to tasks to remove overallocations. If a critical task is delayed, the leveling procedure causes the project to finish later. If the project is scheduled from a finish date, Microsoft Project adds *negative* delays to tasks to remove overallocations. A negative delay causes a task to finish *earlier* and therefore to be scheduled to start earlier. If the task is a critical task, the effect of leveling on a fixed-finish-date project is to schedule an earlier start date for the project.

TIP

Do not attempt to use the Leveling command until after you enter all the tasks and all the information about each task and resource. If you use leveling prior to entering all information, you need to repeat the leveling operation after adding more tasks or redefining resources and resource assignments to accurately reflect the changes.

CONFIGURING SETTINGS IN THE RESOURCE LEVELING DIALOG BOX

There are a number of settings you should confirm or change before using Microsoft Project's Leveling command. The Resource Leveling dialog box contains the controls for the leveling operation (see Figure 11.36). You should generally open this dialog box when a task view is active because then you will have access to all the buttons and fields.

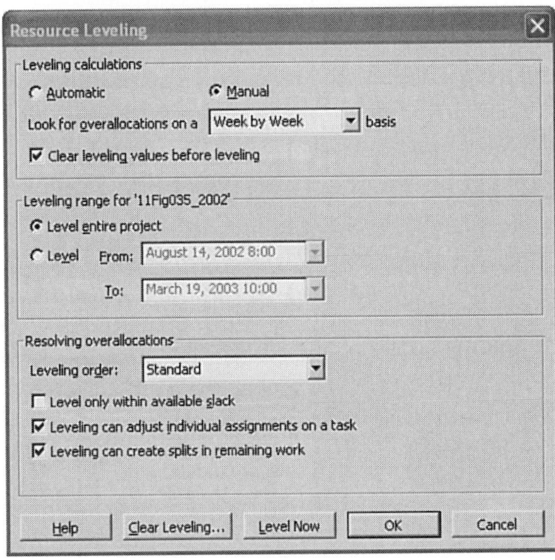

Figure 11.36
The Resource Leveling dialog box has many settings that determine how Microsoft Project calculates the schedule when it does leveling calculations for you.

Whether a Leveling indicator is displayed in a resource table depends on your selection in the Look for Overallocations in a list box. As you change this selection, the highlight for overallocated resources is not affected, but the Leveling indicator appears less often if you select larger time units. Thus, if you increase the time basis from Day by Day to Week by Week, some Leveling indicators may disappear.

Table 11.3 outlines the choices and tools in the Resource Leveling dialog box and provides a brief description of each choice.

TABLE 11.3 THE LEVELING OPTIONS IN THE RESOURCE LEVELING DIALOG BOX

Option	Description
Automatic	Instructs Microsoft Project to level tasks the moment one or more overallocated resources is detected. Automatic leveling takes place as you enter the tasks into the project or change the schedule in other ways.
Manual	Causes leveling to be executed only when you choose Tools, Resource Leveling, Level Now. Manual is the default status for leveling.
Look for Overallocations on an *x* by *x* Basis	Determines the timescale sensitivity of leveling calculations. The choices in this drop-down list box are Minute by Minute, Hour by Hour, Day by Day, Week by Week, and Month by Month.
Clear Leveling Values Before Leveling	Tells Microsoft Project to remove all leveling delays from tasks before calculating new ones. If this box is not checked, Microsoft Project leaves all leveling delays in place and adds to them.
Level Entire Project	Tells Microsoft Project to search for overallocations that need leveling from the beginning to the end of the project. This choice does not keep you from choosing to level just selected resources or all resources.
Level From, To	Limits the date range that Microsoft Project scans for overallocations that need to be corrected. Overallocations outside this date range are allowed to remain.
Leveling Order	Provides three choices—ID Only, Standard, and Priority, Standard—for establishing how Microsoft Project decides which of several tasks to delay when the tasks cause a resource overallocation conflict.
Level Only Within Available Slack	Causes tasks to be delayed only within the amount of total slack; the finish date of the project is not delayed. With this setting constraining the amount of leveling delay that Microsoft Project can add, the leveling operation may not resolve the overallocation problem. If you clear this box, and no task constraints exist to serve as impediments, Microsoft Project can resolve the resource overallocation through leveling, although often with a delay in the finish date of the project.

Option	Description
Leveling Can Adjust Individual Assignments on a Task	Causes Microsoft Project to delay just the assignments for resources that are overallocated on a task instead of delaying the task and consequently all assignments. The task duration is increased if this box is selected because the total work effort is more spread out. This setting affects all tasks unless the task's Level Assignments field is set to No.
Leveling Can Create Splits in Remaining Work	Causes Microsoft Project to split the remaining work into pieces that can fit into available time slots for the resource, thus working around later task assignments that have constraints. This choice affects all tasks unless a task's Leveling Can Split field is set to No.

The following are the three possible values for the Leveling Order drop-down list box:

- **ID Only**—If the ID number is the only basis for selecting which of several tasks will be delayed, tasks with higher ID numbers (those that are further down on the task list) are always delayed before tasks with lower ID numbers (those that are higher up on the task list). If the task list is created in chronological order—with earlier tasks listed at the top of the list and with one sequence of tasks leading to the finish date—the ID Only scheme essentially delays tasks with the later start dates. Delaying the tasks with later start dates minimizes the number of successor tasks affected by imposing leveling delays.
- **Standard**—The Standard order, which is the default leveling order for Microsoft Project, uses seven factors (described later in this section) to determine which of several conflicting tasks is to be leveled first. One of those factors is the Priority rating that you can assign to tasks. In the Standard order, the Priority rating has relatively less weight than most of the other factors.
- **Priority, Standard**—The same factors considered in the Standard order are used for the Priority, Standard order. Primary weight is given to the Priority assignment of each task (a factor that you can control).

In deciding which of two tasks should be delayed and which should be left unchanged, the Standard order and the Priority, Standard order use the same set of factors, the difference being only in the greater weight assigned to the tasks' Priority value in the Priority, Standard order. These are the factors, listed in descending order of importance:

- **Predecessor**—Tasks that do not have successor dependencies are picked before those that have successor dependencies.
- **Amount of total slack**—Tasks with more total slack are chosen before those with less slack.
- **Start date**—Tasks that start later are delayed before those that start earlier.
- **Priority**—You can raise or lower each task's priority value to affect the selection of those to delay. The lower-priority tasks are chosen for delay before the higher-priority tasks. In the Leveling Order choice Priority, Standard, this factor is moved to the top of the list.

- **Constraints**—Tasks with constraints are less likely to be delayed than those without constraints.

Other fields influence how Microsoft Project treats tasks and resources when leveling is applied. These fields determine how likely it is that a task or an assignment will be delayed or split. With these fields, you can instruct Microsoft Project to exempt a specific resource or task from being delayed or split by leveling:

- **Can Level**—This resource field contains a Yes or No value. If the value is the default Yes, Microsoft Project can delay assignments for that resource if it needs to in its leveling calculation. If the value is No, Microsoft Project does not delay the resource's assignments. The field does not appear on any prepared views or information forms. You can add the field to any resource table and enter No for those resources whose assignments you want to keep from being delayed.
- **Level Assignments**—This task field contains a Yes or No value. If the value is the default Yes, Microsoft Project can delay assignments to the task if it needs to in its leveling calculation. If the value is No, Microsoft Project does not delay the task's assignments. This field overrides the Leveling Can Adjust Individual Assignments on a Task check box in the Resource Leveling dialog box. You must add this field to a task view because it doesn't appear in any standard tables.
- **Leveling Can Split**—This task field contains a Yes or No value. If it's the default Yes, Microsoft Project can split tasks in its leveling calculations. This field overrides the Leveling Can Create Splits in Remaining Work check box in the Resource Leveling dialog box. You can add this field to a task view that contains a table.

11

TIP

If you give a task the priority value 1,000, Microsoft Project never delays or splits the task when leveling (although you can manually assign a delay or split yourself). Microsoft Project also leaves unchanged any leveling delay or split for such a task when you apply the Clear Leveling command.

You can assign priority values to projects as well as to tasks. When you level resources that are assigned to multiple projects, tasks in those projects with lower priority values are chosen for delay before tasks in projects with higher priority values. The priority value 1,000 ensures that no task in that project will be given a leveling delay when leveling the plan.

The priority value for the project overrides the relative priority values for tasks. For example, if one project has a higher priority value than the other, all tasks in the higher-priority project (even those with priority values close to zero) have higher priority than any task in the lower-priority project (except for those that have a priority value of 1,000, which are never delayed).

To assign a priority value to a task, follow these steps:

1. Select the task in a view that displays one or more task fields. You can select multiple tasks if you want to set them all to the same priority value with one step.

2. Click the Task Information tool on the Standard toolbar to display the Task Information dialog box (see Figure 11.37) or the Multiple Task Form dialog box (if more than one task has been selected).

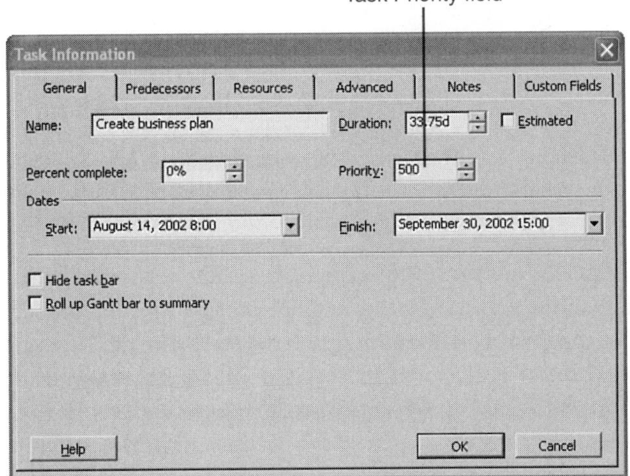

Figure 11.37
Setting priorities for a task controls how likely it is to be delayed because of leveling.

3. Select the General tab and type the priority value into the Priority box, using values between 1,000 (highest priority—least likely to be delayed) and 0 (most likely to be delayed). Or use the spin control to raise or lower the default priority value, which is 500. Remember that the higher the number, the less likely it is that the task will be delayed because of leveling operations; tasks with the priority value of 1,000 are never delayed.
4. Click OK to close the dialog box.

To change the priority level for a project, follow these steps:

1. Open the project.
2. Choose Project, Project Information to display the Project Information dialog box.
3. In the Priority box, enter the priority level, using values between 1,000 (highest priority—least likely to be delayed) and 0 (most likely to be delayed). Or use the spin control to raise or lower the default value of 500.
4. Click OK to close the dialog box.

USING THE LEVEL NOW COMMAND

After establishing your choices in the Resource Leveling dialog box, you can instruct Microsoft Project to level the project by using the Level Now command. If you select this command from a task view, the leveling occurs immediately, without prompts. If you select the command from a resource view, you see the Level Now dialog box (see Figure 11.38), which prompts you to choose between leveling all resources and leveling only the resources that you have selected.

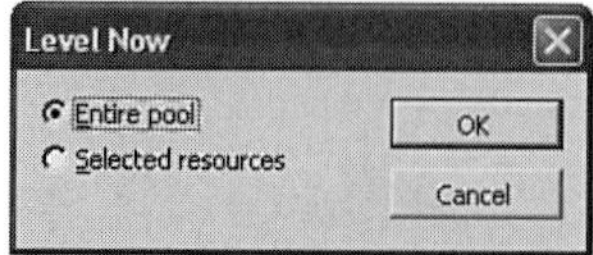

Figure 11.38
You can level assignments for all overallocated resources or for just those that you have selected.

If you choose Selected Resources, only the overallocations for the resources in the selection are reviewed for leveling operations. If you select Entire Pool, all resources and all tasks are reviewed.

When you click OK, Microsoft Project tries to resolve the resource overallocations by adding leveling delays to tasks—within the bounds you specify in the Resource Leveling dialog box. For the first overallocation problem it encounters, Microsoft Project identifies the tasks causing the overallocation and notes the tasks that *cannot* be delayed. These include tasks that have hard constraints, tasks that have higher-priority assignments, and tasks that are already started. Note that task deadline dates do not keep Microsoft Project from delaying a task. If more than one task that can be delayed exists, Microsoft Project uses the set of seven factors previously discussed to select one or more of the tasks to delay.

NOTE

> You can undo the changes made via the Level Now command if you choose Edit, Undo Level before changing anything else in the project.

Figure 11.39 shows the result of the leveling operation for the resource Howard Thompson. A deadline date has been added to the Create Advertising Plan task to illustrate how Microsoft Project respects deadlines when leveling (it doesn't).

Only one delayed task is shown in Figure 11.39—Sales Training is delayed by six elapsed days. However, Howard's assignment to the Create Advertising Plan task was also delayed (see the highlighted timephased work data in Figure 11.39), but Mary Logan's assignment was not delayed. This combination of assignments extended the task's duration past the deadline date for the task (note the deadline date marker in the figure) and the Missed Deadline indicator appears in the Indicators column, to alert you that the task deadline will be missed in the current schedule.

Note the new taskbars in the Gantt Chart view. When the Level Now command is executed, Microsoft Project saves the current (before leveling) start and finish dates of all tasks into fields called Preleveled Start and Preleveled Finish. The Leveling Gantt Chart view displays these dates as preleveled taskbars above the scheduled bars for tasks so that you can easily see the scheduled dates before and after the leveling operation. Notice in Figure 11.39 that the lower bar for Sales Training is shifted to the right of the preleveled bar just above it, thus reflecting the leveling delay.

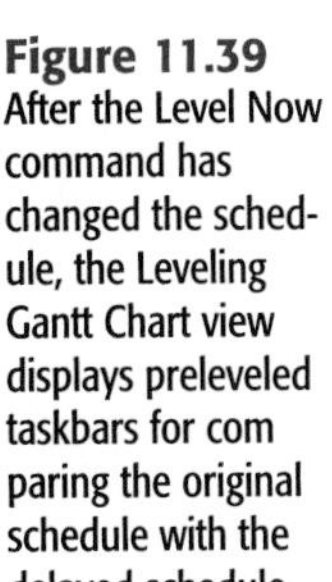

Figure 11.39
After the Level Now command has changed the schedule, the Leveling Gantt Chart view displays preleveled taskbars for comparing the original schedule with the delayed schedule.

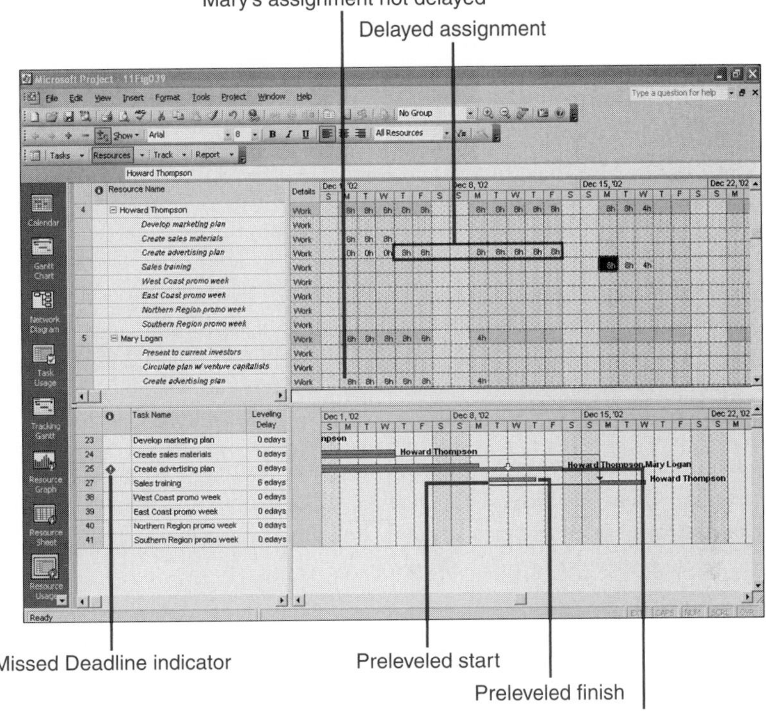

If one or more assignments are found where overallocations can't be resolved, you see a message similar to the message in Figure 11.40.

If you entered a delay for a task in your project and this does not appear in your preleveled Gantt view, please refer to "Managing Preleveled Taskbars" in the "Troubleshooting" section at the end of this chapter.

Figure 11.40
Sometimes the Level Now command can't resolve all the overallocation problems and Microsoft Project prompts you for directions.

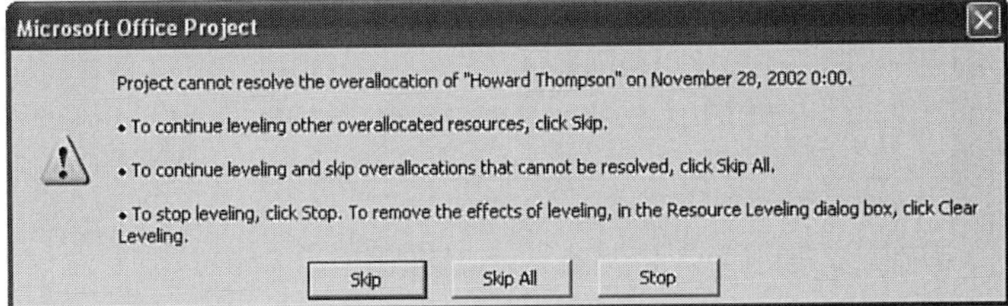

11

To respond to the unresolved overallocations message, you can do one of the following:

- Click Skip to have Microsoft Project skip this resource and continue looking for other overallocations.
- Click Skip All to have Project skip this resource and all others that cannot be resolved without pausing to alert you to those that cannot be resolved.
- Click Stop to stop the leveling process and erase all the delays that have been entered so far.

Clearing the Effects of Leveling

You can use the Clear Leveling tool in the Resource Leveling dialog box to have Project reset leveling delays to zero for all tasks or for just the selected tasks. As mentioned previously, Project does not clear the leveling delay for tasks that have a priority setting of 1,000.

To use the Clear Leveling command, you must be in a task view. Choose Tools, Resource Leveling, Clear Leveling. The Clear Leveling dialog box appears (see Figure 11.41). Select Entire Project or Selected Tasks and click OK. All Leveling Delay fields are reset to 0 for the entire project or for the selected tasks.

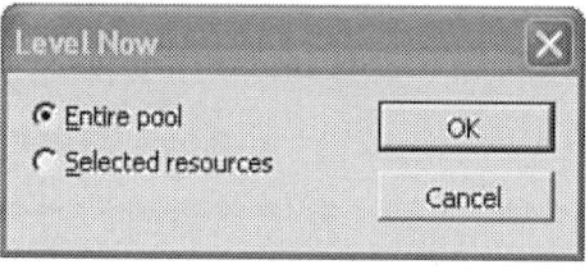

Figure 11.41 You can quickly remove all leveling delays from the entire project or from selected tasks with the Clear Leveling command.

Understanding the Pitfalls of Automatic Leveling

The first option on the Resource Leveling dialog box is Automatic Leveling. If you select this option, Microsoft Project watches for resource overallocations as you assign resources and as the project schedule changes. The moment Project detects an overallocation, it quietly attempts to resolve it by delaying tasks in the background as you go on building the schedule. This seems like a powerful and useful option, but it has some drawbacks.

Most importantly, you are a far better judge than Microsoft Project of the best choices for your schedule. You can't provide Microsoft Project with all the information you bring to the decision-making process as you make scheduling choices. If you select Automatic Leveling, you will not be aware of the leveling decisions going on in the background. In some cases, if you saw a Leveling indicator, you might be able to think of an alternative that doesn't require delaying tasks or the project finish. It's not uncommon to wind up with a bloated schedule that has lots of unproductive time because of all the leveling delays.

You also should note that Microsoft Project doesn't optimize the leveling strategy. Microsoft Project doesn't examine all possible combinations of task delays in order to choose the best solution in terms of lowest cost, earliest project finish date, or any other consideration.

TROUBLESHOOTING

DISPLAYING DETAIL HEADERS

I can't tell what data field is displayed in the timephased data of the Resource Usage view because there are no headers for the rows. How can I tell which rows contain which fields?

There are two reasons why you might not see the detail headers:

- The width of the detail headers column might have been accidentally or deliberately reduced to zero. Try positioning the mouse just slightly to the right of the border that separates the Resource Sheet view and the Timescale grid in the timescale header at the top of the view, and drag the mouse to the right to expand the Details column again.
- You might have suppressed the display of the headers in the Detail Styles dialog box. With the Resource Usage view active, choose Format, Detail Styles and click the Usage Properties tab. The Display Details Header Column box must contain Yes in order for the headers to be displayed.

SORTING ASSIGNMENTS IN THE RESOURCE ALLOCATION VIEW

In the Resource Allocation view, the list of assignments in the top pane under a resource name is not in the same order as the list in the bottom pane, and this makes it hard to find the task in the bottom pane. How can I get them in the same order?

Activate the top pane and choose Project, Sort, By ID to have Project sort the top pane by ID number. The lists should then be in sync. If not, activate the bottom pane and sort it by ID also.

LEVEL NOW SEEMS NOT TO BE WORKING

I used the Level Now command, but there are still overallocated resources, even though Project didn't give me any alerts saying it was unable to resolve an overallocation. What did I do wrong?

The Level Now command tackles only overallocations that trigger the Leveling indicator. So if your project has the leveling sensitivity set to Week by Week, for example, there might still be resources that are overallocated on an hour-by-hour or day-by-day basis.

Another reason is that resources may have been assigned to both summary tasks and the detail tasks. In this instance, the overallocation cannot possibly be resolved because it is impossible to delay a summary task without also delaying the detail tasks that make up that summary task. As a general rule, you should try to avoid assigning resources to summary tasks and detail tasks. You should assign resources either at summary level only or at detail task level only. The only exception to this is when you want to assign someone as being responsible for the task, but that person may or may not be doing any work on the detail tasks. In this instance, you can assign a resource to a summary task but assign the resource with 0h work.

MANAGING PRELEVELED TASKBARS

I entered a leveling delay for a task in the Leveling Gantt Chart view, but Microsoft Project doesn't show the preleveled taskbar for the task.

The preleveled taskbar is based on the dates in the Preleveled Start and Preleveled Finish fields. These fields contain NA until you use the Level Now command for the first time; therefore, you don't see these bars until you use the Level Now command. You can't edit the dates in these fields because they can only be calculated by Microsoft Project. You can hide the Preleveled bar if you choose Format, Bar Styles and delete the bar from the display or choose a clear bar style that will not show onscreen.

PART IV

Reviewing and Distributing the Project

12 Reviewing the Project Plan 467

13 Printing Views and Reports 489

CHAPTER 12

Reviewing the Project Plan

In this chapter

Looking at the Big Picture 468

Realigning the Plan 479

Finalizing the Plan 486

Troubleshooting 487

LOOKING AT THE BIG PICTURE

After you create a first draft of a project, it is a good idea to carefully review all project, task, resource, and assignment information. After Project calculates the schedule and costs of the project, you need to step back from the details and look at the big picture. Does it make sense? How successfully has the project plan met the overall objectives? Is the project going to finish on time? Are costs within budget?

Often, the first draft of a project includes missed deadlines, costs that have exceeded the project budget, and other inconsistencies. After Project has calculated the schedule, a task's finish date might now be scheduled five business days after an internally imposed deadline, and the total cost for the project might be in excess of $5,000 over the contractually approved budget.

This chapter describes tools for evaluating the overall project against the objectives laid forth in the project initiation and planning processes. Microsoft Project offers many tools to make this evaluation easy. The following are some of the things you can do to review a project plan:

- Review the overall picture of the project by viewing the project in a variety of ways.
- Review tasks, resources, and assignments through the use of tables, filters, groups, and sorting to focus on those that need special attention.
- Review the critical path to pinpoint tasks where duration might be able to be reduced to meet internal and contractual schedule deadlines.
- Review project costs and strategies for reducing costs where current estimates have exceeded budgetary limitations.
- Ensure accuracy by spell-checking the plan, and then distribute the plan via email or printed reports.

You might feel overwhelmed by the multitude of details in a large project. From time to time, you might need to step back and look at the overall project to keep a global perspective. You can begin by reviewing Project statistics to compare values against project objectives. You can then compress the timescale to review the project from a macro perspective, and collapse the task outline to view major phases of the project.

To learn how to generate a report based on information displayed in the Project Statistics dialog box, see "Printing Project Statistics" in the "Troubleshooting" section near the end of this chapter.

REVIEWING PROJECT-LEVEL STATISTICS

After you have defined project, task, resource, and assignment information, you can use the Project Statistics dialog box, shown in Figure 12.1, to view currently estimated start and finish dates, as well as duration, work, and cost values. To display the Project Statistics dialog box, click the Project Statistics button on the Tracking toolbar or in the Project Information dialog box.

Figure 12.1
You can use the Project Statistics dialog box to review project summary information.

Project Statistics for 'New Product.mpp'

	Start	Finish
Current	Thu 8/14/03	Thu 5/13/04
Baseline	NA	NA
Actual	NA	NA
Variance	0d	0d

	Duration	Work	Cost
Current	191d?	4,707.15h	$125,584.08
Baseline	0d?	0h	$0.00
Actual	0d	0h	$0.00
Remaining	191d?	4,707.15h	$125,584.08

Percent complete:
Duration: 0% Work: 0%

Close

You can use the Project Statistics dialog box to review project summary information. After you start work on the project and enter tracking information, the Actual Start, Start and Finish Date Variance, Actual and Remaining Duration, Work, and Cost values are also displayed.

NOTE

Notice that all baseline information in Figure 12.1 appears as NA. Chapter 14, "Tracking Work on a Project," describes how to capture and update the project baseline, which causes these fields to be populated.

➔ To establish a baseline for a project, **see** "Working with Project Baselines," **p. 522.**

COMPRESSING THE TIMESCALE

You can usually gain an overview of the flow of activity in a project by viewing the Gantt Chart view with the timescale compressed. In Figure 12.2, for example, a project is displayed with the timescale compressed to show years in the top tier, months in the middle tier, and weeks in the bottom tier. (For clarity, a custom Gantt Chart view is displayed in which resource names and dependency arrows have been removed from the Gantt Chart).

12

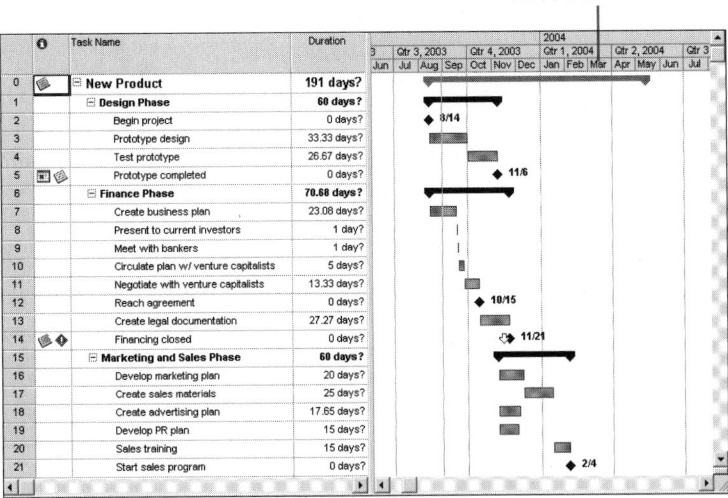

	Task Name	Duration
0	New Product	191 days?
1	Design Phase	60 days?
2	Begin project	0 days?
3	Prototype design	33.33 days?
4	Test prototype	26.67 days?
5	Prototype completed	0 days?
6	Finance Phase	70.68 days?
7	Create business plan	23.08 days?
8	Present to current investors	1 day?
9	Meet with bankers	1 day?
10	Circulate plan w/ venture capitalists	5 days?
11	Negotiate with venture capitalists	13.33 days?
12	Reach agreement	0 days?
13	Create legal documentation	27.27 days?
14	Financing closed	0 days?
15	Marketing and Sales Phase	60 days?
16	Develop marketing plan	20 days?
17	Create sales materials	25 days?
18	Create advertising plan	17.65 days?
19	Develop PR plan	15 days?
20	Sales training	15 days?
21	Start sales program	0 days?

Figure 12.2
You can compress the timescale to get an overall view of the time dimension of a project.

To compress the timescale, click the Zoom Out button on the Standard toolbar. Larger time units are then visible in each unit of the timescale. You can use the Zoom In button on the Standard toolbar to subdivide time into smaller units. You can also choose View, Zoom, Entire project to change the zoom on the timescale so that you can view the entire project.

→ To learn more about ways you can alter the appearance of views, **see** "Customizing Views, Tables, Fields, Filters, and Groups," **p. 833.**

TIP

> **You can double-click any part of the timescale tiers to access the Timescale dialog box, where you can customize the appearance and values of each tier. To display all three tiers of the timescale, click the Top Tier tab, and in the Timescale options section, open the Show drop-down list and choose Three Tiers (Top, Middle, Bottom).**

COLLAPSING THE TASK LIST OUTLINE

The compressed timescale might be more meaningful if you also collapse the task outline. In Figure 12.3, the task list is collapsed to show Outline Level 1 of the Work Breakdown Structure (WBS). This view provides an overview of the major phases of the project. You can collapse or expand the outline to any of the first nine levels by clicking Show on the Formatting toolbar.

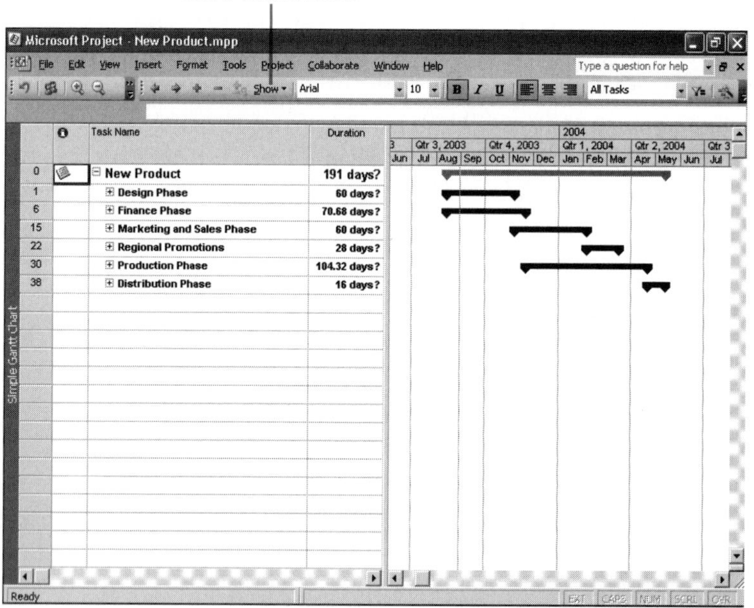

Figure 12.3 You can hide the subtasks in an outlined project to focus on the major phases of the project.

12

To collapse the outline to the first level, activate a pane that displays a task list table (for example, the Gantt Chart view), and then Click the Show button on the Formatting toolbar and choose Outline Level 1 from the list that appears.

You can also collapse and expand the outline by using the Hide Subtasks button (minus sign) and Show Subtasks (plus sign) button on the Formatting toolbar. These buttons hide or show subtasks for the selected task.

Summary tasks within the Gantt Chart view should correspond to the WBS that was previously created. Remember that the WBS is not a time-driven schedule, like the Gantt Chart; rather, it is a method to ensure that all the necessary work to complete the project is included and has been properly captured. The *Project Management Body Of Knowledge Guide,* issued by the Project Management Institute, defines a WBS as "a deliverable-oriented grouping of project elements which organizes and defines the total scope of the project with each descending level representing an increasingly detailed definition of a project component."

USING CUSTOM WBS CODE FORMATS

It is also important to analyze the Work Breakdown Structure to ensure that the project contains the proper level of detail. WBS codes in Project are calculated for each task, or may be manually entered if corporate methodologies call for custom WBS codes. The WBS format allows numbers, letters, and characters, which can be very useful when reviewing tasks based on custom corporate codes.

To see the WBS codes that are currently being used in a project, you may temporarily insert the WBS field in a task table that's part of a task view, such as the Entry table in the Gantt Chart view. You can create custom WBS codes by selecting Project, WBS, Define Code to designate the WBS format.

➔ To learn how to create and use custom WBS code formats, **see** "Creating Custom WBS Codes," **p. 164.**

12

USING CUSTOM OUTLINE CODES

There might also be internal codes that would help you to ensure that the structure of your plan is correct. When you need to apply a custom code to a task or resource, such as an internal accounting code or a predesignated organizational code, you can use Outline Code fields instead of Project's WBS field. Ten Outline Code fields are available for use. These fields enable you to apply your own codes to tasks or resources.

The Outline Code fields provide a drop-down list from which users can look up and select authorized codes. By limiting codes to a predefined list, you prevent errors that inadvertently arise when codes are manually typed in.

You can also change the displayed field name to reflect the actual name you want to use for a custom code.

➔ To learn how to alter properties of Outline Code fields, **see** "Customizing Fields," **p. 847.**

FILTERING THE TASK OR RESOURCE LIST

When reviewing the content and structure of a plan, you might want to filter for specific task and/or resource information. When you filter the task list, you impose conditions that must be met in order to display a task. All tasks that meet the conditions are displayed and are known as *filtered tasks*, and all tasks that fail to meet the conditions are not displayed. You can apply filters, for example, to display critical tasks or milestones as shown in Figure 12.4.

Figure 12.4
A filtered task list that shows only milestones lets you focus solely on important completion dates.

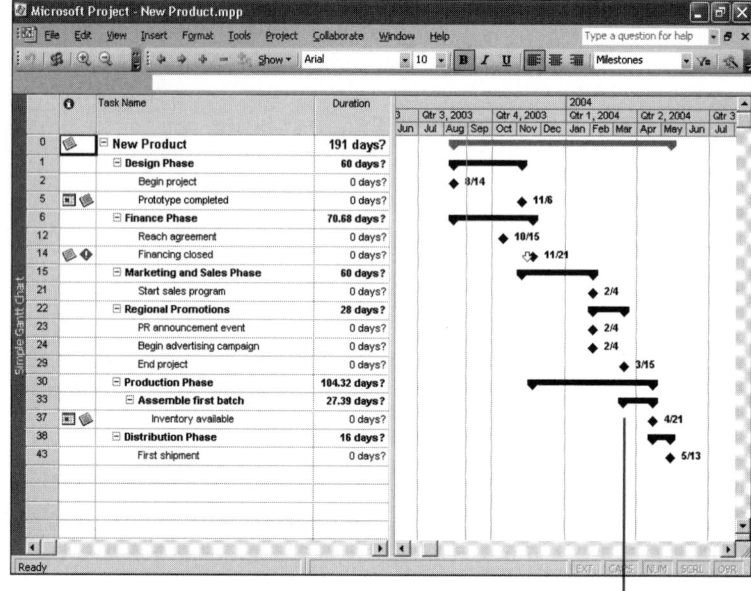

Filtered list contains only the milestone tasks and their summary tasks

You can also use a highlight filter, which displays all tasks, whether they meet filter conditions or not. The names of the tasks that meet the conditions are shown in blue, and the names of the tasks that do not meet the filter conditions are shown in black (see Figure 12.5). To apply a highlight filter, select Project, Filtered For, More Filters; select the name of the filter you wish to apply; and then click Highlight in the More Filters dialog box. You can use the Text Styles dialog box (which you open by selecting Format, Text Styles) to alter the color of highlighted tasks. You can also use filters in resource views to display specific resources.

NOTE

> The summary tasks for filtered tasks are displayed based on a setting in the Filter Definition dialog box. If you don't want to display summary tasks for a particular filter, select Project, Filtered For, More Filters; select the appropriate filter; click the Edit button; and then clear the Show Related Summary Rows check box.

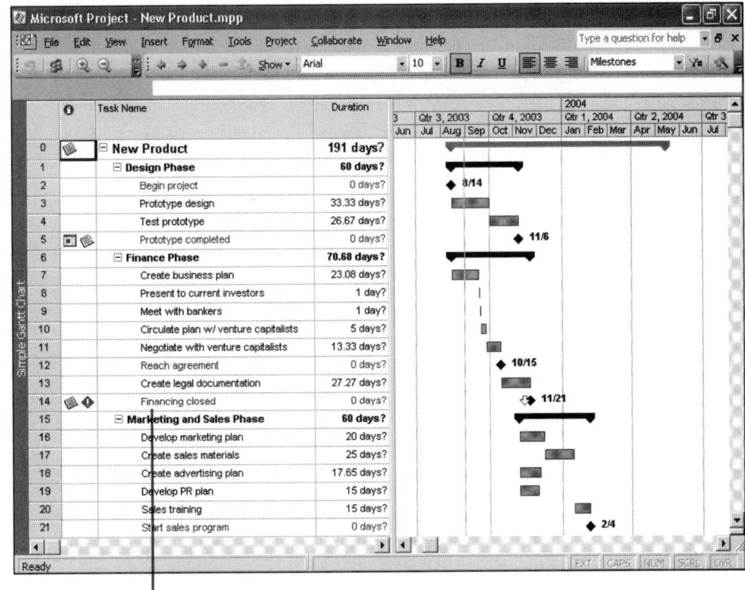

Filtered tasks highlighted in blue

Figure 12.5
Having filtered tasks appear highlighted makes them stand out in the display.

Microsoft Project provides many predefined filters, a few of which are interactive. A standard filter displays values that meet filter conditions immediately, while interactive filters prompt the user for values against which to apply conditions. The Date Range filter, for example, prompts you for two date values: the beginning and ending dates for the date range. Project then displays all tasks whose schedule includes dates that fall within the user-defined dates.

Table 12.1 lists recommended predefined Project filters for reviewing a project.

TABLE 12.1 PREDEFINED TASK FILTERS FOR REVIEWING A PROJECT

Filter	Description
Critical	Displays only critical tasks.
Milestones	Displays only milestone tasks.
Summary Tasks	Displays only summary tasks.
Tasks with Deadlines	Displays tasks for which you have set a deadline date.
Tasks with Fixed Dates	Displays all tasks with a constraint type other than As Soon As Possible.

TIP

> The Summary Tasks filter is not usually a good substitute for collapsing the task outline, as the filter only displays summary tasks. If you are attempting to view the highest level summary tasks in your project, you may be better served by selecting Outline Level 1 from the Show button on the Formatting toolbar. Furthermore, if any first-level task in the outline is not a summary task, the task is not included in the filtered list of tasks. If you want to focus only on the tasks up to a certain level in the outline, collapsing the entire outline to that level of tasks is a preferred method.

When your review of filtered tasks is complete, you may return to viewing all tasks by pressing F3 or by applying the All Tasks filter.

CAUTION

> If you edit tasks or resources while a filter is applied, you might change an element of a task or resource that affects whether the task continues to meet current filter conditions. If you make changes, you must reapply the filter to make the filtered display accurate. For example, suppose you apply the Tasks with Deadlines filter to display only tasks with deadlines. If you then remove a deadline from one task, the filter does not automatically refresh and remove that edited task from the filtered list. You can use Ctrl+F3 to reapply (refresh) the current filter.

One of the most useful filters is the Tasks with Fixed Dates filter. You use this filter to identify all tasks that have constrained dates. Users often inadvertently place constraints on tasks and then don't understand why Project doesn't recalculate start and finish dates as expected. The Tasks with Fixed Dates filter allows you to review constrained tasks and be certain that the constraints are in fact necessary.

→ To better understand how Project defines constraints, **see** "Working with Task Constraints," **p. 201**.

→ To learn more about Project's built-in filters, **see** "Exploring the Standard Filters," **p. 761.**

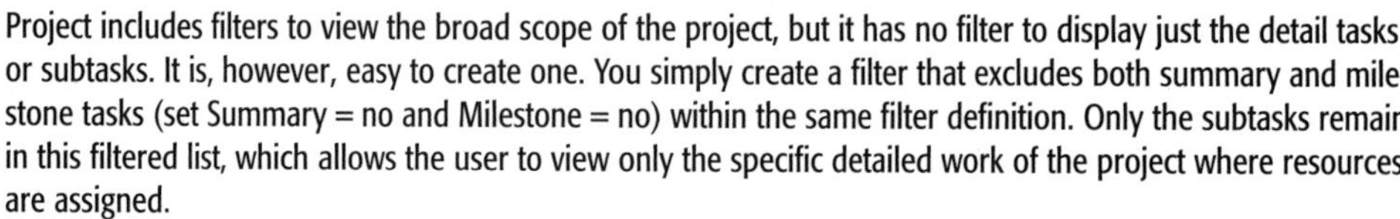

BEST PRACTICE TIP

Project includes filters to view the broad scope of the project, but it has no filter to display just the detail tasks or subtasks. It is, however, easy to create one. You simply create a filter that excludes both summary and milestone tasks (set Summary = no and Milestone = no) within the same filter definition. Only the subtasks remain in this filtered list, which allows the user to view only the specific detailed work of the project where resources are assigned.

SORTING AND GROUPING PROJECT DATA

You can reorganize a list of tasks or resources in a project to better visualize certain aspects by sorting or grouping data. *Sorting* involves reorganizing rows of information. You can design a sort that uses up to three fields to sort by. For example, by using a single-field sort, you could order the resource list by resource name (the Name field) to come up with an alphabetical list of resources. Or, you could use a multi-field sort to order the resource list first by group, to display everyone from a particular department together, and then by name.

Grouping, on the other hand, can both sort and summarize a list of tasks or resources. With this powerful feature, you can designate the groups you want to create. For example, you can group a task list by critical and noncritical tasks and then group the list by resource group as shown in Figure 12.6. The critical tasks are listed first, grouped by resource group. You simply scroll to see the noncritical tasks and the resource groups associated with those tasks.

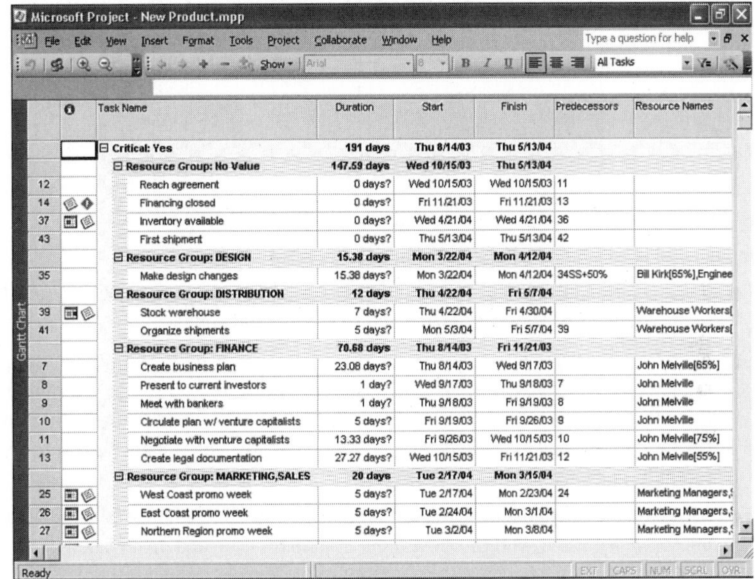

Figure 12.6
The grouping feature allows you to select from several formatting options to alter the appearance of grouped data.

SORTING TASK AND RESOURCE LISTS

When you sort an outlined project, you can retain or ignore the outline structure. If you retain the outline structure, all tasks at Outline Level 1 are sorted (carrying their subtasks with them); then, within each summary task, all subtasks at the next outline level are sorted (carrying their subtasks with them), and so forth. If you choose not to keep the outline structure, subtask groups are broken up and dispersed throughout the task list independently of their summary tasks. If you do not keep the outline structure, you might consider suppressing the display of summary tasks and the indentation of subtasks.

To sort tasks or resources, choose Project, Sort, Sort By to access the Sort dialog box (see Figure 12.7).

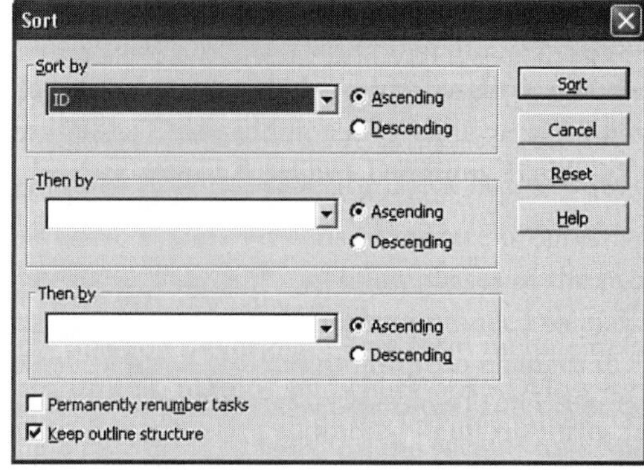

Figure 12.7 You can change the default settings in the Sort dialog box.

You need to keep in mind a number of issues related to sorting:

- If you choose to ignore the outline structure during sorting, you cannot permanently renumber the tasks to match the new sort order–that would restructure the outline.
- If the Permanently Renumber Tasks (or Resources) option in the Sort dialog box option was selected the last time the Sort command was used, it will be used when you sort by selecting from the short list of fields (Project, Sort submenu). This will cause the most recent renumbering of ID numbers to be changed once again. Unless you immediately undo renumbering, you will not be able to return the list to its most recent ID numbers.
- You can undo renumbering if you act immediately. To do so, choose Edit, Undo Sort. If you don't undo the sort immediately, you can close the file without saving and then open it again. However, any changes you made to the file that have not been saved are then lost.
- If the task list is filtered when you sort, or if some tasks are hidden because the outline is collapsed, the hidden tasks remain hidden and are not displayed after sorting.
- Some of the most commonly used fields for sorting appear in a short list when you choose Project, Sort. The limitation with the short list is that you may only sort on one field.
- Some fields in Project have been given a custom field label for display purposes. For example, what appears to be the Task Name field displayed in a task table is really the Name field in the Sort drop-down list. The rationale for using slightly different names is to provide the user with more descriptive names when entering and viewing data. In a resource table, the Name field has a custom field label of Resource Name.

→ To learn more about sorting resources, **see** "Sorting Resources," **p. 310**.

If you are sorting a list of tasks, you might want to hide the display of summary tasks and remove the indentation from the display of subtasks. To do so, complete the following steps:

1. Choose Tools, Options to open the Options dialog box.
2. Click the View tab.
3. Uncheck Show Summary Tasks and Indent Name, and then click OK to close the Options dialog box.

If you edit a list that has been sorted, the list doesn't automatically re-sort based on recent changes. To sort the list again using the current sort keys, press Ctrl+Shift+F3 or activate the Sort dialog box. The sort keys are still defined as you last set them so you can simply click the Sort button to reapply the sort.

To reset the list to normal order (by ID number), press Shift+F3, or access the Sort dialog box and click the Reset button and then click the Sort button.

GROUPING THE TASK AND RESOURCE LISTS

Grouping lets you reorder and summarize a task or resource list to better assess your project. When you organize the list into groups, the individual data for each item in that group is rolled up into totals for the entire group. Grouping project data is an excellent way to generate summary information that would otherwise be difficult to ascertain.

No Group

Microsoft Project contains several predefined groups. To apply a predefined group to a task sheet or resource sheet, click the Group By tool on the Standard toolbar and select a group. Some of the most useful groups for reviewing a project are shown in Tables 12.2 and 12.3.

TABLE 12.2 PREDEFINED TASK GROUPS FOR REVIEWING A PROJECT

Group Name	Description
Constraint Type	Groups tasks by type of constraint, such as Start No Earlier Than or Must Finish On.
Critical	Groups tasks based on whether they are critical (0 days of total slack) or noncritical (greater than 0 days of total slack).
Duration	Groups together tasks that have the same duration.
Milestones	Groups tasks that are milestones and groups tasks that are not milestones.
Priority	Groups tasks based on their numerical priority of 0–1,000, lowest to highest.

12

TABLE 12.3 PREDEFINED RESOURCE GROUPS FOR REVIEWING A PROJECT

Group Name	Description
Resource Group	Groups resources based on respective groups designated in the Group field.
Standard Rate	Groups resources based on standard rate of pay.
Work versus Material Resources	Groups resources based on Resource Type.

CUSTOMIZING GROUPS

In addition to using predefined groups, you can customize existing groups or create new groups. There are two ways to customize existing groups:

- **Use the Customize Group By Option**—If you have applied a group to data and then want to customize the active group, you can use the Project, Group By, Customize Group By option. This displays the Customize Group By dialog box, which shows the specific settings for the active group (see Figure 12.8). In this dialog box you can specify Field Name, Sort Order, Text Font and Color, Background Color and Pattern, and (where applicable) Group Intervals.

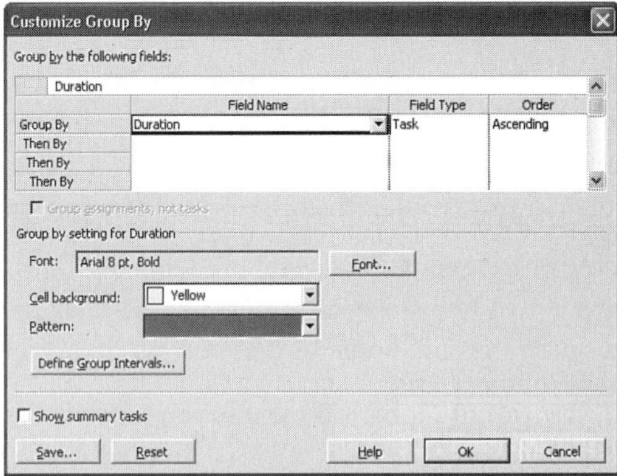

Figure 12.8
You use the Customize Group By dialog box to change an active grouping temporarily.

If you alter a predefined group, the changes you make are temporary. To retain changes, you must save the revised group under a different name. Click the Save button in the Customize Group By dialog box to save the group.

12

CAUTION

Clicking the Reset button in the Customize Group By dialog box removes all settings in the dialog box; it does not restore the original settings to the group.

- **Edit an Existing Predefined Group**—If you have not applied a group to the data (or you want to alter a group other than the active group), you can select Project, Group By, More Groups. This displays the More Groups dialog box, from which you can select a group and click Edit. A dialog box that is virtually identical to the one shown in Figure 12.8 appears, and in it you can permanently edit the settings for a predefined group. It is highly recommended, however, that you create a new group as opposed to editing predefined groups.

  Some fields that you can group on allow you to designate *intervals*, or ranges, for the group. For example, the Duration group may be more useful if tasks are grouped based on intervals of 10 days of duration beginning at 1, as opposed to each duration value. If you want to group based on intervals, click the Define Group Intervals button (refer to Figure 12.8) to display the Define Group Interval dialog box, shown in Figure 12.9.

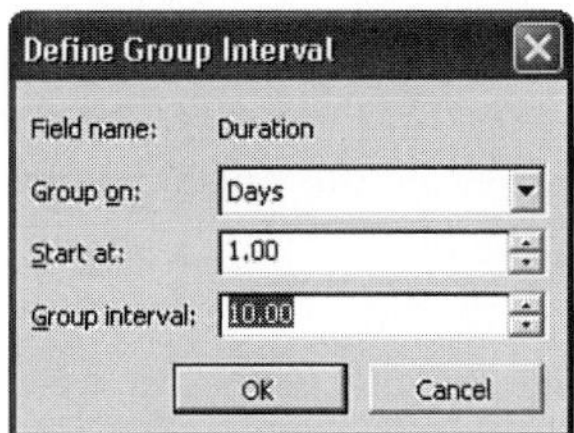

Figure 12.9
You use the Define Group Interval dialog to group lists based on intervals rather than each value.

Other fields that allow you to designate intervals are Cost fields, Integer fields, Percentage fields, Work fields, Date fields, and Text fields.

- **Creating New Groups**—You can also create your own custom groups to sort and summarize project information, leaving the predefined groups available for future use. To create a group to meet your specific needs, select Project, Group By, More Groups, New.

NOTE

> Like other new items you create, such as tables and filters, new groups you create are a part of the active project only. If you want to use a new group in another project file, you can copy the new group to the other project through the Organizer. If you want to make it available to all project files, you can use the Organizer to copy the new group in to the Global template file. Refer to Chapter 4, "Managing Project Files," for more information on using the Organizer and the Global template.
>
> To delete a custom group, you must use the Organizer.

→ To learn more about custom groups, **see** "Creating Custom Groups," **p. 868.**

→ For information on copying custom groups to other project files, or to all project files, **see** "Working with the Organizer and the Global File," **p. 107.** (ch 4)

You can print a view to which a group has been applied just as you would print any view. Start by selecting File, Print Preview (or by clicking the Print Preview button on the Standard toolbar).

→ To learn about the printing options you have access to, **see** "Printing the Project Task List," **p. 170.**

REALIGNING THE PLAN

After you review the big picture, it might become clear that the plan must be realigned to meet the strategic objectives of the project. The following sections suggest strategies for reviewing the plan in more detail in order to realign the plan with the initial project objectives.

SHORTENING THE CRITICAL PATH

Your review might indicate that the project is now finishing late. It is therefore necessary to reduce the overall duration of the project, to schedule the finish date sooner (or the start date later, for a project that is scheduled from the finish date). The popular phrase for this process is *crashing the schedule*. In order to affect the finish date, it is necessary to first identify the tasks that are directly affecting the project finish date—the *critical path*—and second, to make necessary revisions to those tasks.

IDENTIFYING THE CRITICAL PATH

You can use any task view to identify critical tasks. One powerful view for identifying and crashing tasks on the critical path is the Task Entry view. This combination view consists of the Gantt Chart view over the Task Form view. The Gantt Chart view will allow you to pinpoint critical tasks, and the Task Form view will allow you full control over Project's primary scheduling engine components necessary to crash critical tasks. In addition, you can use the Network Diagram view to identify critical tasks. This view, however, is not very effective for crashing critical tasks.

Probably the most dramatic way to identify critical tasks is to use the Gantt Chart Wizard, which you activate by selecting Format, Gantt Chart Wizard.

It is important to distinguish between *critical* activities and *important* ones. These terms are often used interchangeably, but they mean different things to a formally trained project manager. *Critical tasks* are important to a project because they contribute to the longest path through the project and, thereby, dictate the earliest possible finish date. *Important tasks,* however, might or might not be critical.

→ To learn how to format the Gantt Chart view to display the critical path by using the Gantt Chart Wizard, **see** "Formatting the Gantt Chart View," **p. 790.**

12

Another alternative is to filter the task list to show only critical tasks. However, as you redefine the project, some tasks might change from noncritical to critical (and vice versa). When relying on the Critical filter while editing, remember to reapply the filter following each edit by pressing Ctrl+F3.

After critical tasks are identified, it may be necessary to make revisions to realign the project. Reducing the duration of individual tasks might be no more complicated than reassessing the estimated duration and entering a more optimistic figure. Often, however, reducing the overall duration of the project requires much more effort.

STRATEGIES FOR CRASHING THE SCHEDULE

No matter which view you use, you can move through the project from one critical task to the next, looking for opportunities such as the following to crash the schedule:

- **Re-estimating duration estimates or changing the scope**—You can remove critical activities or re-estimate the duration of critical tasks, which means changing the scope of the project or removing any padding from duration estimates. By removing activities, you often cut from the specifications of the project. Cutting the estimate may require that you need to do the same amount of work in less time. Assuming that your duration estimates are not padded, changing scope in a well-defined, closely assessed project typically means compromising content or quality. Basically, you need to remove tasks from the project or compromise quality (perform the work in less time) to get work done.

- **Assigning additional resources**—Assigning additional resources to an effort-driven task means that the same amount of work gets done in less time. With an effort-driven task, if one resource can perform the work of a task in one week, two resources may be able to perform the same amount of work in half a week. However, the law of diminishing returns can actually limit the effectiveness and create an unrealistic schedule. Adding additional resources may increase the total work and cost of a task due to greater communications needs.
- **Making changes in task relationships**—You can examine the predecessor and successor relationships and try to identify discretionary dependencies that you can change from Finish-to-Start to one of the overlapping relationships (Start-to-Start or Finish-to-Finish) with lag time applied. This strategy is usually most beneficial because many users hastily define most relationships as Finish-to-Start, even though more lenient definitions could be applied. Ask whether the predecessor to the task really needs to be 100% complete before the successor can start, or whether almost finished or partially finished would suffice.
- **Scheduling overtime**—One additional strategy to crash the critical path is to schedule overtime work for resources on critical tasks, therefore reducing regular work hours each day.

You might find it easiest to concentrate on each of these strategies if you go through the project task list once for each of the strategies listed. Remembering what you are looking for is sometimes easier if you look for the same thing as you examine task after task.

After you make changes, remember that some formerly noncritical tasks may now be critical; therefore, a new set of tasks may be able to be crashed. A useful combination view at this point to study activity relationships is the Gantt Chart view in the top pane and the Relationship Diagram view in the bottom pane. This combination view allows you to analyze predecessor and successor relationships for the selected task in the bottom pane in a network diagram type format (see Figure 12.10).

→ To learn more about the Relationship Diagram view, **see** "Exploring the Standard Views," **p. 736.**

→ For information on creating custom views that consist of one view in the top pane and another view in the bottom pane, **see** "Creating New Views," **p. 834.**

REDUCING COSTS

To reduce project costs, you can examine the project schedule to look for possible cost savings. There are two types of costs associated with each task: variable costs and fixed costs. Because variable costs all derive from resource assignments, you might want to focus on ways to reduce the cost of the resources that are assigned to individual tasks.

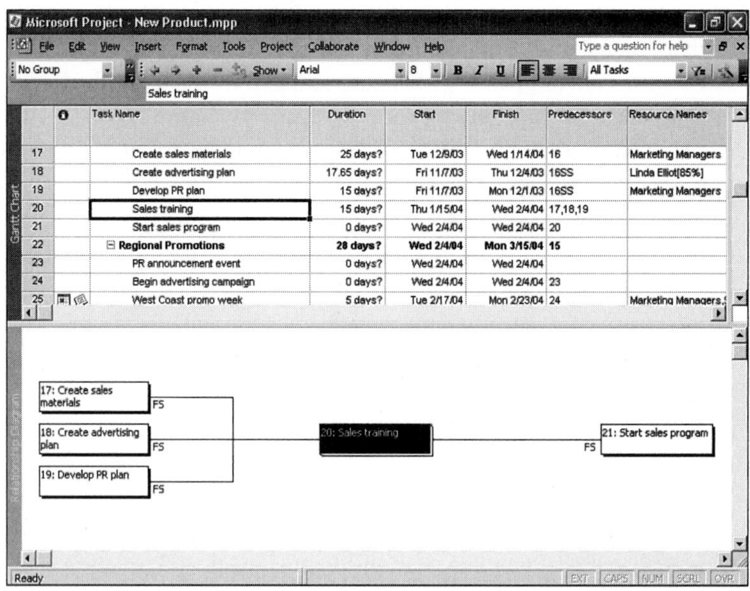

Figure 12.10
The Relationship Diagram view in the bottom pane provides visual verification of task predecessors and successors.

➔ To learn more about how Microsoft Project determines cost, **see** "Understanding Resources and Costs," **p. 279**, and "Assigning Fixed Costs and Fixed Contract Fees," **p. 396**.

REVIEWING THE COST SCHEDULE

You can see the total for each task if you apply the Cost table to the task sheet in the Gantt Chart view or the Task Sheet view. If you choose Window, Split to display the Task Form view in the bottom pane, and then choose Format, Details, Resource Cost, you can view resource assignments, including cost for each assignment in detail.

If you want to focus on only tasks with costs in excess of some predetermined amount, you can create a filter to display only these tasks.

➔ To build your own filters, **see** "Creating Custom Filters," **p. 859**.

➔ To learn more about using views, tables, and filters, **see** Chapter 19, "Using the Standard Views, Tables, Filters, and Groups," **p. 735**.

STRATEGIES FOR REDUCING COSTS

Using less expensive resources that perform the same quality of work as more expensive resources in the same amount of time will obviously lower your costs.

You may also be able to reduce costs if you can substitute with more expensive but more efficient resources. You can justify the extra cost if the number of hours of work to complete the task is reduced more than proportionally. For example, if you can reduce work hours 25% by substituting with a resource with a standard rate 20% higher than the old resource, the substitution would result in a cost savings. For example, an eight-hour task with a $10/hr resource assigned would cost $80. If a $12/hr resource could accomplish the same task in six hours, the task would cost $72, providing a savings of $8.

You might also be able to assign tools or equipment to the task, and thereby increase the efficiency of the labor so that reduced hours of work result in reduced total labor costs.

COMPARING PROJECT VERSIONS

A useful feature in Project 2003 allows you to compare the differences between your first draft of the project and a revised version. Analyzing the differences between duration, date, cost, and other values allows you to pinpoint and report the net effect of such changes. After completing a first version, you can use File, Save As to set the stage for the comparison process.

To compare versions, follow these steps:

1. After completing and saving your first version (Version 1), create a second version (Version 2) by selecting the File, Save As command.
2. Make necessary revisions and Save Version 2.
3. Open Version 1, which should have closed when you created Version 2, and then reactivate Version 2 through the Window menu.

NOTE

It is recommended that you run Compare Project Versions from Version 2 as this will automatically position Version 2 as the *later version* in the Compare Project Versions dialog box.

4. Apply the Compare Project Versions toolbar by selecting View, Toolbars, Compare Project Versions. The toolbar is shown in Figure 12.11.

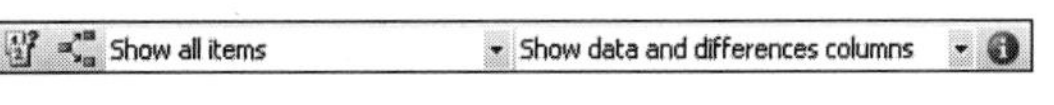

Figure 12.11 The Compare Project Versions toolbar allows you to navigate to tasks and resources and apply filters and tables.

CAUTION

When you choose File, Save As for a project that shares resources from a resource pool, you end up with Version 1 and Version 2 linked to the pool causing duplication of assignment information and falsifying availability information. After you have compared versions, you should select the version you plan to discard and break its link to the resource pool.

→ To learn more about breaking a link to a resource pool, **see** "Sharing Resources Among Projects," **p. 621.**

12

5. Click the Compare Project Versions button to open the Compare Project Versions dialog box as shown in Figure 12.12.

Figure 12.12
You can compare versions and select tables from the Compare Project Versions dialog box.

6. Select an appropriate task table and resource table in the (Choose the tables to be used in the comparison) section, and then click OK.
7. In the Compare Project Versions – Done dialog box, click Yes to view the Compare Project Versions legend or No to immediately begin viewing differences between versions in the Comparison Report project plan as shown in Figure 12.13.

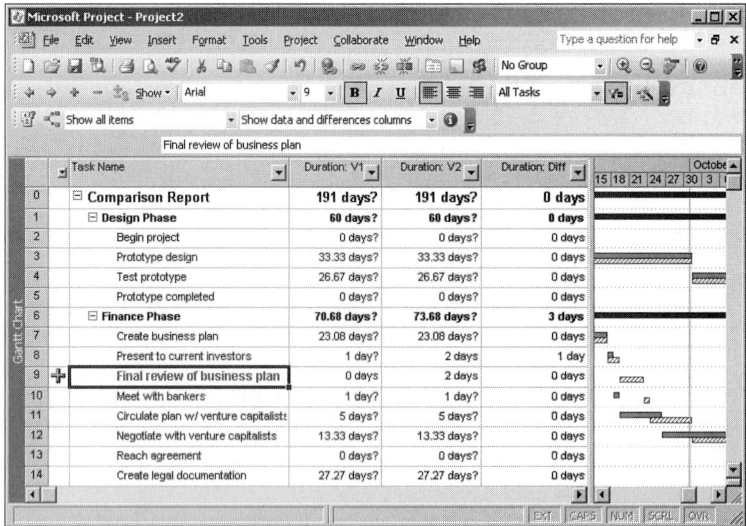

Figure 12.13
A custom table and Gantt bars represent Version 1 and Version 2 in the Comparison Report project.

If you try to compare cost information by using compare versions, but not all the information shows up in the comparison project, see "Compare Version's Use of User-Defined Fields" in the "Troubleshooting" section near the end of this chapter.

In the Comparison Report project, a custom table is applied to the task sheet. The Comparison Report table includes three custom fields for each field from the table selected in Version 2. For example, there are three Duration fields in the comparison plan task table, based on the Duration field being present in the Entry table in Version 2.

In the preceding steps, the Entry table is selected for both tasks and resources. Table 12.4 includes custom field labels, actual field names, and respective version and data type based on the Task Entry table from Version 2.

Table 12.4 The Comparison Report: Task All Columns Table Utilizes Several User-Defined Fields

Field Label	(Actual Field Name)	Version: Data Type
Duration: V1	(Duration1)	Version 1: Duration
Duration: V2	(Duration2)	Version 2: Duration
Duration: Diff	(Duration3)	Comparison version: Duration
Start: V1	(Start1)	Version 1: Date
Start: V2	(Start2)	Version 2: Date
Start: Diff	(Duration4)	Comparison version: Duration
Finish: V1	(Finish1)	Version 1: Date
Finish: V2	(Finish2)	Version 2: Date
Finish: Diff	(Duration5)	Comparison version: Duration
Predecessors: V1	(Text1)	Version 1: Text
Predecessors: V2	(Text2)	Version 2: Text
Predecessors: Diff	(Text3)	Comparison version: Text
Resource Names: V1	(Text4)	Version 1: Text
Resource Names: V2	(Text5)	Version 2: Text
Resource Names: Diff	(Text6)	Comparison version: Text

Click the More Information button on the Compare Project Versions toolbar to review the legend for the schedule, task and resource list, and filter and table definitions.

There are a couple issues to be aware of in regard to the Compare Project Versions feature:

- Compare Project might not have enough custom fields available to display all the data. The Compare Project Versions tool warns you when you have too many user-defined fields, as shown in Figure 12.14.

12

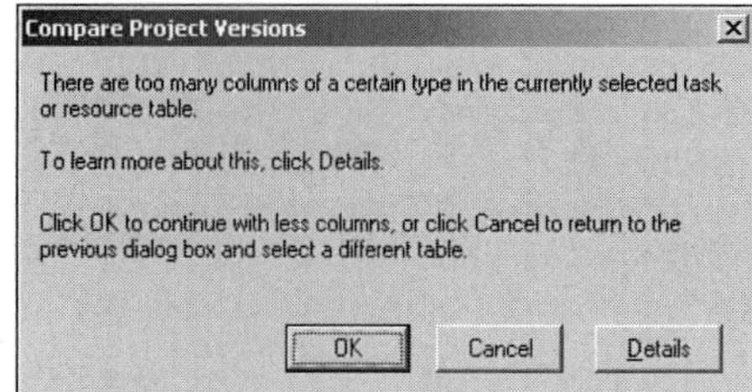

Figure 12.14
A currently selected table includes too many fields for comparison purposes.

- User-defined fields will remain intact. The Comparison Report project utilizes its own set of custom fields. The Comparison Report project does not change your custom fields. If your custom fields are listed in the table that the comparison report is run against, version values and differences are listed the same way as for the Duration and Cost fields.

Finalizing the Plan

Once the project is realigned within the stated strategic objectives, it is a good idea to check spelling, and then create and distribute reports.

Checking for Spelling Errors

Before you distribute any project information to colleagues or clients, it is a good idea to run a spell check on the file. Microsoft Project has a spelling checker that you can use to verify spelling in all name, note, and special text fields for tasks, resources, and assignments. To check spelling, click the Spelling button on the standard toolbar.

Distributing Copies of a Project via Email

As part of the review process, you might want to let others review the project schedule. One way to accomplish this is to electronically distribute a copy of the project file. You can send it directly to each person who needs to review it, or you can route a single copy of the file sequentially from one person to another.

To send a copy of the file to one person or a group of people, choose File, Send To, Mail Recipient (As Attachment). You then complete the addressing information just as you would with any other email. To route a copy of the file through a series of people, choose File, Send To, Routing Recipient. A routing slip appears, on which you identify the order in which the recipients review the file.

NOTE

> This chapter introduces a variety of ways to modify the display of the project plan to explain it to others, to identify potential problems, and to improve its efficiency. Chapter 13, "Printing Views and Reports," shows how to transfer a project plan onto paper.

TROUBLESHOOTING

PRINTING PROJECT STATISTICS

I need to generate a report, but I don't seem to be able to print out the information in Project Statistics dialog box. Am I doing something wrong?

In the Overview Report category, choose the Project Summary report. It provides a one-page snapshot view of a project, and it shows the same information that is displayed in the Project Statistics dialog box.

COMPARE VERSION'S USE OF USER-DEFINED FIELDS

When I try to compare cost information by using Compare Versions, not all the information shows up in the comparison project. How can I get all the cost information I need?

Because there are a limited number of user-defined fields available and Compare Project uses several of these fields for each type of information in its comparison, some of the information may not be included. For instance, if you select the Task Cost table for comparison purposes, Project takes advantage of user-defined Cost fields for the comparison report. The Cost table includes 6 fields with cost values, but Project only allows use of the first 3 Cost fields in the table. The reason for this limitation is that 18 user-defined cost fields would be needed, but only 10 are available. In the Cost table, Project applies Cost1—Cost9 to the Fixed Cost, Total Cost, and Baseline Cost fields, for comparison purposes. Project uses Text1—Text3 for Fixed Cost Accrual. Therefore, you should create a custom table for comparing the Cost Variance, Actual Cost, and Remaining Cost fields if a comparison is necessary. This is the case for any table where the number of fields outnumbers available user-defined fields.

CHAPTER 13

Printing Views and Reports

In this chapter

Using the Print Commands 490

Changing the Printer Setup 490

Using the Project Guide Toolbar 492

Printing Views 493

Printing Project's Predesigned Reports 514

Troubleshooting 515

USING THE PRINT COMMANDS

One of the main functions of project management software is to print project data that will communicate your project plan to others in a clear and informative format.

There are two formats in which Project will print data:

- Many times you just want to print the view of the data that appears onscreen. The printed version is nearly identical to the display format onscreen. A few views cannot be printed: combination views (that is, a split screen with one view in the upper pane and another in the lower pane), the Relationship Diagram view, and the forms views (such as the Task Form, Resource Form, and Tracking Form views).
- Microsoft Project provides 29 predesigned reports for printing. The report formats include a monthly calendar with tasks shown on the scheduled dates, comprehensive lists of tasks and resources, and a summary page that resembles the Project Statistics dialog box.

Selecting the Print button sends a copy of the current view to the printer immediately; you cannot control the way the report looks. Through the commands introduced in this chapter, you will learn how to make changes to the page setup before using the Print button.

Choosing the Print Preview button allows you to see what the printed copy will look like and also gives you access to the Page Setup and Print commands. You should almost always start a print job with the Print Preview button instead of the Print button, if only to see how many pages will be printed.

As in all Windows applications, the printer commands are located on the File menu. The Page Setup command defines headers, footers, page orientation, and so on for printed views. You can also use Page Setup to select the printer and change any printer-specific options available for the printer. The Print Preview and Print commands are used to print views. In addition, there are 29 predesigned reports in Microsoft Project that you access by choosing View, Reports. The Page Setup and Print buttons that are displayed when you're viewing a report work the same way the commands on the File menu work.

CHANGING THE PRINTER SETUP

Before you start a print job, make sure that you select the correct printer, because Print Preview uses the selected printer driver settings. You can select the default printer for any Windows application by selecting the Start button on the taskbar and choosing Settings, Printers. Then, you select the printer you want to set as the default printer by right-clicking on its icon, and then selecting Set as Default Printer in the context menu that appears.

The default printer is selected when you initially print in Microsoft Project. If you want to use a printer other than the default printer, you can select the printer by choosing File, Print. The Print dialog box appears (see Figure 13.1). From this dialog box, choose the Name drop-down list to select a different printer.

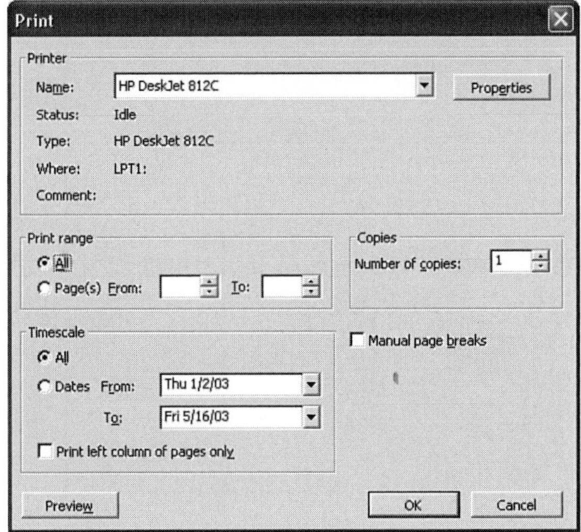

Figure 13.1
From the Print dialog box, you choose the printer you want to use.

The list of installed printers appears in the Name drop-down list. If you want to change just the printer you are printing to, simply click the printer you want to use. If you want to change the way the printer is set up, choose the printer you want and then click the Properties button. The Properties dialog box for the selected printer appears.

The options listed in the Properties dialog box depend on the printer that is selected. For example, Figure 13.2 shows the options for a Hewlett Packard DeskJet 812C printer that is set up for normal color output. Some of the settings include selecting the paper size, selecting a paper feeder source, and changing the resolution of graphic objects. You also can change the orientation of the report on the paper from portrait (upright) to landscape (sideways). Your printer might have different options. Select the options you want and click OK when you're finished. Until you change the printer or the options, Microsoft Project uses the default printer and its settings.

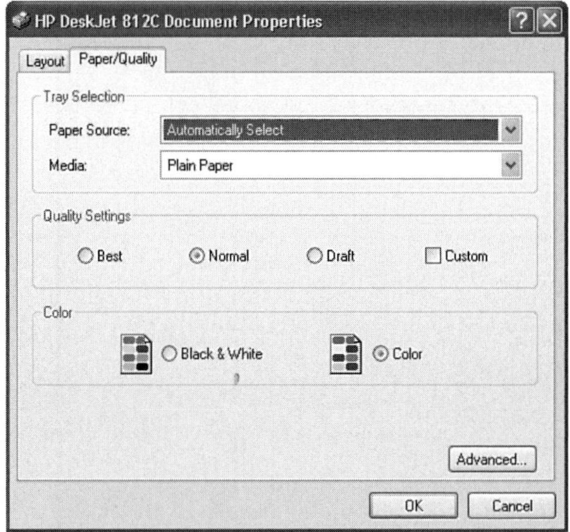

Figure 13.2
The Properties dialog box contains some basic printer options, based on the printer that is selected.

Using the Project Guide Toolbar

Report If the Project Guide toolbar is not visible, right-click on any toolbar and select Project Guide Toolbar. When you click the Project Guide toolbar's Report button, you see a selection of options in a new sidepane that is titled Report, as shown in Figure 13.3.

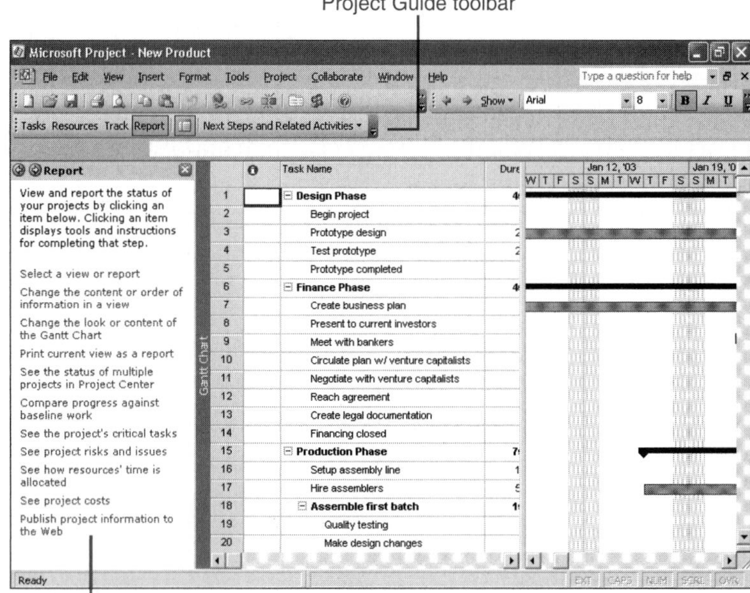

Figure 13.3
You can click the Report button on the Project Guide toolbar to reveal the Report sidepane.

13

If you chose the hyperlink Select a View or Report, you are taken to the Select View or Report sidepane, shown in Figure 13.4, where you can choose the type of report or view that you want. The default Select a View radio button allows you to choose a view from a pick list, and it also gives a brief statement of what that view can be used for.

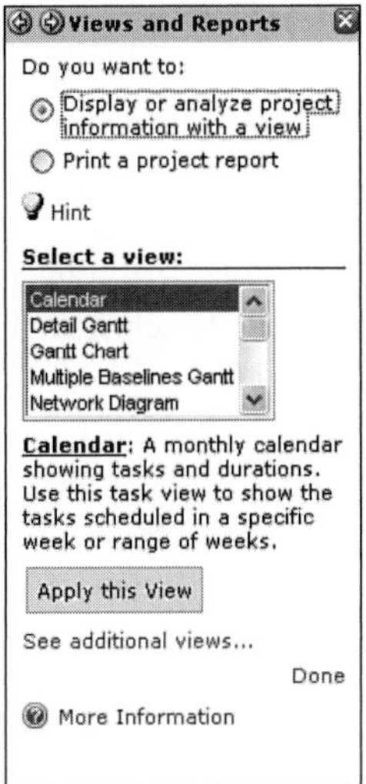

Figure 13.4
You can choose what to print from the sidepane Select View or Report.

The various selections that you can make are described in the rest of this chapter.

PRINTING VIEWS

You will often want to print specific views, such as the Gantt Chart view or the Resource Sheet view. This section provides a few pointers about preparing the screen views for printing. Chapter 7, "Viewing Your Schedule," Chapter 20, "Formatting Views," and Chapter 21, "Customizing Views, Tables, Fields, Filters, and Groups" contain detailed instructions for refining the display with special formatting and graphics features. This chapter focuses on the use of the print commands after the screen presentation is established.

→ To add text boxes and arrows to the Gantt Chart view, **see** "Introducing the Drawing Toolbar," **p. 247.**

→ To format views before you print, **see** "Using the Common Format Options in the Standard Views," **p. 776.**

→ To print the Gantt Chart view, using any of the built-in tables, **see** "Using and Creating Tables," **p. 840.**

PREPARING A VIEW FOR PRINTING

The first step in printing a view is to set up the screen to display the project data just as you want the information to appear on the printed report. You use the View, Tools, Format, and Project menus to get the combination of data and display features that present your data in the desired way.

Choosing the View Fundamentals

You must choose the appropriate view to print. You can view tasks or resources in either a worksheet table layout or a graphic layout. In views that contain timescales, the timescale that is displayed is printed. For instance, in the Gantt Chart view, the timescale can be displayed with

Minutes	Weeks	Quarters
Hours	Thirds of months	Half-years
Days	Months	Years

You can use the Zoom In or Zoom Out buttons on the Standard toolbar to adjust the timescale to show most of these time measurement units. To select a specific time unit, choose Format, Timescale. The Thirds of Months setting is available only through the Timescale dialog box.

Many organizations want to review project-related information on a quarterly basis instead of a weekly or monthly basis. By setting the view to quarters over weeks, project managers can easily review their projects in this manner.

If you filter tasks or resources, only the data that is displayed is printed. Moreover, if the screen is split into panes, you must choose the pane to print. If the top pane is active, all tasks or all resources are printed, unless you filter the data. If the bottom pane is active, only the tasks or resources associated with the selection in the top pane are printed. You might decide to print from the bottom pane, for example, if you want to isolate all the resources assigned to a selected task, or you might want to print a list of all the tasks to which a selected resource is assigned.

→ To learn about which tables are useful for viewing baseline data and tracking work on a project, **see** "Tracking Work on a Project," **p. 519.**

→ If you want to learn more about Project's built-in tables, **see** Chapter 19, "Using the Standard Views, Tables, Filters, and Groups," **p. 735.**

→ To create your own custom tables, **see** "Using and Creating Tables," **p. 840.**

13

NOTE

In a view that shows a table to the left of a timescale, you should check the columns of the table that are visible onscreen. By default, the rightmost column that is *completely* visible is the last column of the table that appears on the printed report. For example, in the initial Gantt Chart view (where ID, Task Name, and Duration are the only columns that are visible), the printed report doesn't show the other columns in the table. You must move the dividing line between the table and the timescale if you want to display more columns, or you can choose the Print All Sheet Columns option on the View tab of the Page Setup dialog box to print all the table columns. If you want to change the order in which the columns are displayed, you can delete a column and insert it in its new place, or simply highlight the column and drag it to the desired location.

Finally, if you want the printed view to focus on just part of the project, you can use a filter to display only a subset of the tasks or resources. Filters are useful tools in building and managing a project, allowing you to work with a subset of the overall project data. To apply a predefined filter, choose Project, Filtered For, and choose the appropriate filter.

➔ For information on using filters, including how to use the AutoFilter capability, **see** "Filtering the Task or Resource List," **p. 472.**

➔ To learn about Project's built-in filters and their uses, **see** "Exploring the Standard Filters," **p. 761.**

➔ To create custom filters, **see** "Creating Custom Filters," **p. 859**, and "Creating Custom Filters with AutoFilter," **p. 867.**

A quick way to apply a filter is to use the Filter drop-down list box or the AutoFilter button on the Formatting toolbar.

SORTING AND GROUPING THE DISPLAY

After displaying the data you want to print, you might want to rearrange the order of the tasks or resources by sorting or grouping the data. Grouping sorts and summarizes a list of task or resource information. If you have not used the Sort or Group By commands before, see Chapter 12, "Reviewing the Project Plan," for a comprehensive discussion of sorting and grouping.

➔ To reorganize and summarize project data, **see** "Sorting and Grouping Your Project Data," **p. 474.**

ENHANCING THE DISPLAY OF TEXT DATA

You can format text data to emphasize or highlight selected categories of tasks or resources. For example, you might want to display summary tasks in bold, milestones in italic, or overallocated resources (in a resource view) as underlined. You can customize the display of the gridlines and the column and row separator lines as well. In a view that has a timescale, you can customize the time units and labels used to represent the time units. In graphic views, you might select special graphical features from a palette. All these customizing features are covered in Chapter 21. You can use these display enhancements selectively to improve the presentation quality of your reports.

SETTING AND CLEARING PAGE BREAKS

You can force a page break when you're printing task and resource lists so that a new page starts at a specific task or resource—even if the automatic page break doesn't occur until further down the list. Page breaks are tied to the task or resource you select when you set the page break. Even if you sort the list or hide a task by collapsing the outline, a new page starts at the task or resource where the page break was set.

Page breaks also affect the printing of the built-in reports. The final dialog box you see just before printing offers an option to use or ignore the page breaks you set manually. This feature prevents you from having to remove all page breaks for one special printout and later having to replace the breaks. You can remove one page break or all page breaks with relative ease.

NOTE

The Manual Page Breaks setting in the Print dialog box is retained when you save a project file.

To set a page break, select the row just below the intended page break. This row becomes the first row on a new page. Choose Insert, Page Break. A dashed line appears above the selected row to indicate the presence of a manually inserted page break.

To remove a page break, reselect the row just below the page break. Choose Insert, Remove Page Break. (Notice that when a page break row is selected, the menu choice changes from Page Break to Remove Page Break.) The selected page break is removed.

To remove all page breaks, select all the rows in the active view by clicking the first column heading on the far left of the view. Typically, this is an empty gray rectangle above the task or resource ID number. Choose Insert, Remove All Page Breaks. (The wording of the Page Break command changes to Remove All Page Breaks when all rows are selected.)

Page breaks are a great way to create several separate projects within one master project. By properly placing page breaks, you can effectively print different parts of a project–perhaps assigned to different resources on a team that are responsible for different phases of the project–and still manage the project within a single file. This makes it much easier to distribute hard copies of the project without having to cut and paste into different files.

In the Network Diagram view, page breaks are automatically displayed, but you might have to zoom out to see them. To do so, choose View, Zoom or click the Zoom Out button. You cannot set page breaks in the Network Diagram view. However, you can move task boxes to either side of the automatic page breaks. To do this, select Format, Layout, and then choose Allow Manual Box Positioning and click OK. When you choose this setting, Project allows task boxes to be placed on page breaks. The option Adjust for Page Breaks in the Layout dialog box corrects where the page breaks fall, but only after you redraw the Network Diagram view by choosing the Format, Layout Now command.

NOTE

Page breaks are automatically displayed in the Network Diagram view. If page breaks have been turned off, you can display them by selecting Format, Layout and marking the Show Page Breaks check box.

CHANGING THE PAGE SETUP

You can change the appearance of the printed pages for any view by using the Page Setup command. For example, you can modify the margins, orientation, headers and footers, and legend for graphic views. A separate page setup configuration is available for each of the views and reports. This means that changing the header and footer you design for Gantt charts does not change the header and footer you design for task sheets.

To change the page settings for the active view, choose File, Page Setup or choose the Page Setup button in Print Preview. (If the active view cannot be printed, the File, Page Setup command is not available.) The Page Setup dialog box is displayed for the active view.

Figure 13.5 shows the Page tab of the Page Setup dialog box for Gantt charts. You use this tab to set the page orientation for printing and to designate the starting page number.

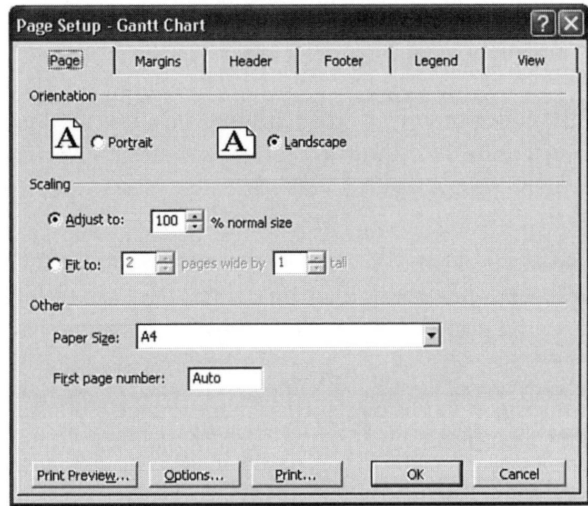

Figure 13.5
The name of the active view appears in the title bar of the Page Setup dialog box.

NOTE

A number of the print settings you select in the Page Setup and Print dialog boxes are saved with the project, including the setting for manual page breaks, the range for views that contain timescales, and the Print Left Column of Pages Only setting.

The following sections describe the print settings in the Page Setup dialog box.

USING THE PAGE SETUP DIALOG BOX

The current settings on the Page Setup dialog box for any view are saved with the project file; they are available when you print the same view, using another project file. To use those custom settings in another project file, the custom item (in this case, the view) has to be copied to the other file. You do this in the Organizer.

→ To copy custom views from one project file to another, **see** "Working with the Organizer and the Global File," **p. 107.**

Like other dialog boxes, the Page Setup dialog box has multiple tabs (refer to Figure 13.5) that access different settings. To see the settings for a particular topic, choose the appropriate tab.

Selecting the Orientation

The Page tab, shown in Figure 13.5, contains options that are used to set the page orientation to Portrait or Landscape. This setting overrides the default orientation set in the Print Setup dialog box. If you intend to add the printout to another document or if you have a number of tasks and a short timescale, the portrait orientation would be best. If, on the other hand, you have a longer timescale, you might want to use the landscape orientation, which would display more of the timescale per printed page.

Scaling the Printout

Scaling can be used to reduce or enlarge your printout by a specified percentage or by a given number of pages. Figure 13.6 shows a project previewed for printing. As shown in the preview, four pages will be printed, two pages wide by two pages tall. The final task is printed on the bottom two pages. Instead of printing the bottom pages for just one task, you can adjust the printout to compress the pages so that the last task is included in the top two pages. Select the Fit To option in the scaling area of the Page tab (refer to Figure 13.5). In this case, you would set the printout to fit to two pages wide by one page tall.

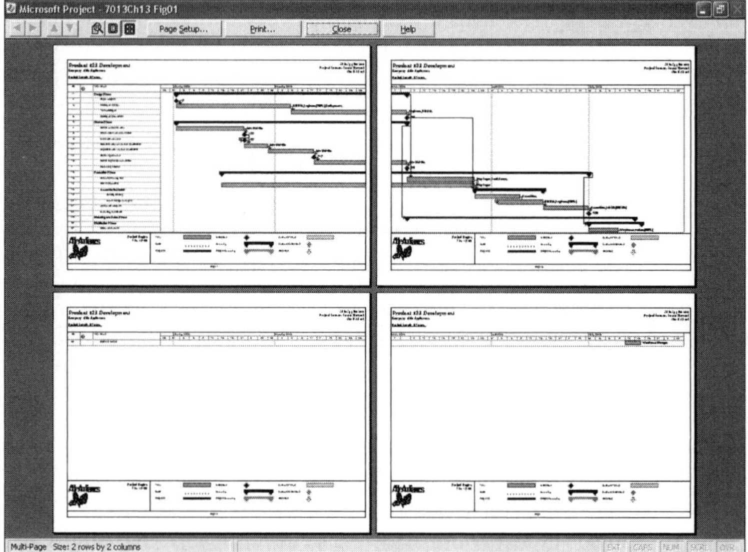

Figure 13.6
Four pages will be printed unless you use the Fit To option on the Page tab to compress the printout.

Designating the Paper Size

You can set the paper size in the Page Setup dialog box instead of having to go into the printer Properties dialog box. The Paper Size option is located at the bottom of the Page tab in the Page Setup dialog box (refer to Figure 13.5).

NOTE

> You can choose the paper size in the printer Properties dialog box, which is accessed several ways: via the Options button in the Page Setup dialog box (refer to Figure 13.5) or via the Properties button in the Print dialog box (refer to Figure 13.1).

SETTING THE PAGE NUMBERING

You can designate the first page number for the printed pages. For example, suppose two pages printed from a project will be the fifth and sixth pages in a document. You can set First Page Number to start at 5 for the printed pages (refer to Figure 13.5).

SPECIFYING THE MARGINS

You use the Margins tab in the Page Setup dialog box to set the margins (see Figure 13.7). The default margin is one-half inch for the top, bottom, left, and right margins. Microsoft Project prints with a quarter-inch margin, even if you reduce the margin to zero. If a header or footer is added or if borders are displayed on every page, the margin automatically expands to fit the text, but no change is displayed in the Page Setup dialog box.

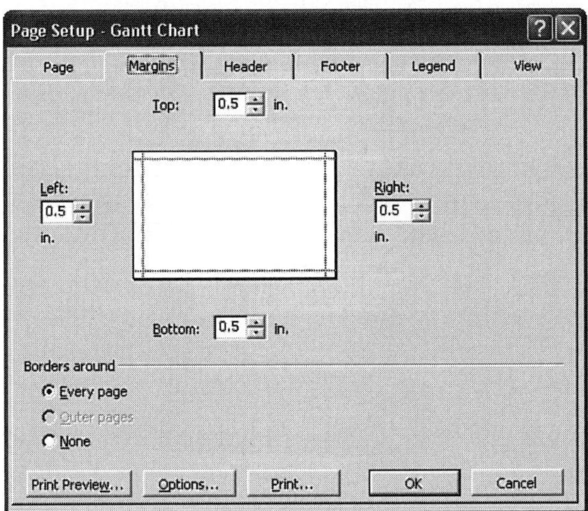

Figure 13.7
The Margins page is used to change the width of the margins of a printout.

PLACING BORDERS

The Margins tab of the Page Setup dialog box has options for placing borders on the printed page. You can use borders to surround the page and separate the body of the report from the header, footer, and legend. By default, borders are printed with every page. For multiple-page network diagrams that you want to tape together, this capability makes cutting and pasting easier if you place borders around the outer pages only.

To enclose each page in a lined border, choose Every Page in the Borders Around section on the Margins tab. To place borders on the outside pages only, choose Outer Pages (for the Network Diagrams view only). To suppress all borders, choose None.

Using the Header and Footer Buttons

The Header and Footer tabs of the Page Setup dialog box include seven buttons that can be used to format, insert system codes, or insert pictures into the header or footer (see Figure 13.8).

When you point with the mouse to any of the buttons in the Header or Footer tab, a ScreenTip appears to identify the action the button performs.

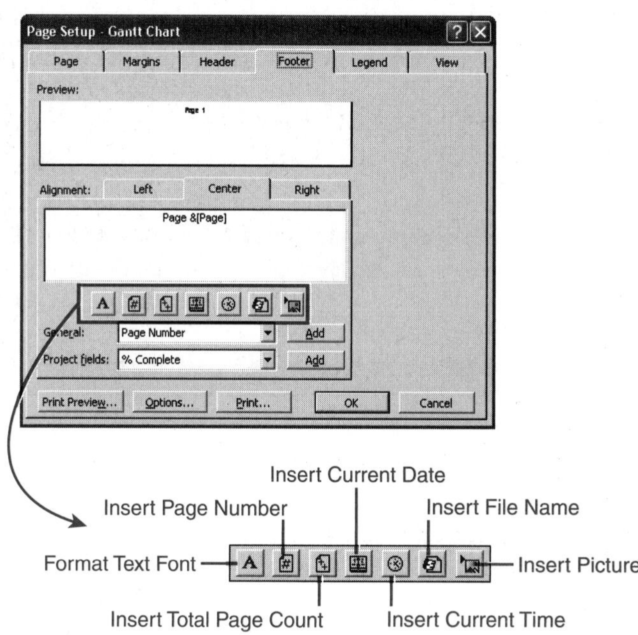

Figure 13.8
Most views do not have a default header, but most views have the printed page number as the default footer.

From left to right, the buttons shown in Figure 13.8 are as follows:

- **Format Text Font**—Clicking this button displays the Font dialog box, where options for formatting font, font style, size, and color are available. You can format text that you type, system codes that have been inserted, and any of the project information items added from the General or Project Fields list boxes by using the Format Text Font button. You must first highlight the text or code to be formatted before choosing the Format Text Font button.
- **Insert Page Number**—Clicking this button inserts the code `&[Page]` for the current page number. Only the page number is printed. If you want the header or footer to display "Page 2," where 2 represents the number of the page, you must type the word **Page** followed by the code. The header or footer would show `Page &[Page]`.
- **Insert Total Page Count**—Clicking this button inserts the code `&[Pages]` for the total number of pages. Only the number representing the total number of pages is printed. If you want the header or footer to display "Page 2 of 10," where 2 represents the current page and 10 the total number of pages, you must type the word **Page** followed by the

Page Number code; then type the word **of** followed by the Total Page Count code. The header or footer would show Page &[Page] of &[Pages].

- **Insert Current Date**—Clicking this button inserts the code &[Date], which is based on the date in your computer system. You use this to indicate the date on which the view or report was printed.
- **Insert Current Time**—Clicking this button inserts the code &[Time], which is based on the time in your computer system. You use this to indicate the time when the view or report was printed.

NOTE

It is very useful to print the date and time on your view and reports, especially if you are producing several revisions in a single day or over several days.

- **Insert File Name**—Clicking this button inserts the code &[File], which reflects the name of the project file. The file extension (that is, .mpp) is not displayed with the filename, unless you have Windows set to display file extensions.
- **Insert Picture**—Clicking this button inserts any type of picture file, including WMF, PCS, CGM, TIF, BMP, and GIF. This is particularly useful for inserting a company logo.

Many times, a project plan is used during the initial proposal stage of a project as part of the scope statement, to outline the work that is going to be performed on behalf of a client. Including the client's company logo, downloaded from a Web site or scanned to create a file, can easily customize and spruce up a proposal.

ENTERING HEADERS AND FOOTERS BY USING THE DROP-DOWN LIST BOXES

In addition to the header and footer buttons, you can also use the General or Project Fields drop-down list boxes to enter project data in the printed header and footer (refer to Figure 13.9).

The General drop-down list box contains the same data as provided by the Header and Footer insert buttons (for example, Page Number), as well as data that comes from the Project Properties dialog box (for example, Company Name). (To access the Properties dialog box, choose File, Properties. The Properties dialog box is discussed in detail in Chapter 3, "Setting Up a Project Document.")

13

TIP

If you want to insert the name of the project file and the path to its location, use the Filename and Path option in the General drop-down list. This option inserts the &[Filename and Path] code in the header or footer.

→ To learn how to effectively use properties, **see** "Using the Properties Dialog Box," **p. 62**.

You can use the Project Fields drop-down list box to insert information that is specific to the project. It lists fields from the project that contain information about cost, duration, work, and dates, as well as custom text and number fields. The next section describes how to insert data from these lists into the header and footer.

ENTERING HEADERS AND FOOTERS

You can enter up to five lines of header text and three lines of footer text to repeat on each page of a printed document. You can type in the text you want to appear in the header and footer, or you can place codes that are replaced with system variables, such as the `&[File]` code, which is replaced by the actual filename when the pages are printed.

You can align headers and footers to the left, center, or right, by adding the text or code to the desired alignment tab (see Figure 13.9). In either the Header or Footer tab of the Page Setup dialog box, the Preview text box at the top of the tab shows what your header or footer will look like.

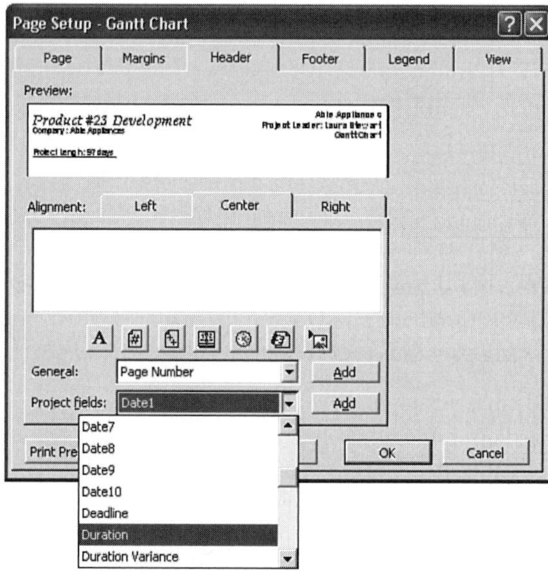

Figure 13.9
You format header or footer text by clicking the Format Text Font button.

13

To enter a header or footer, follow these steps:

1. Select either the Header or Footer tab of the Page Setup dialog box.
2. Choose the desired Alignment tab (Left, Center, or Right).
3. Use the box below the Alignment tabs to type the text that you want to appear on the header or footer.

   Or, choose one of the buttons to insert a system code—for example, page number, total page count, date, time, or filename.

Or, select either the General or Project Fields drop-down box below the buttons to insert information from the project—for example, project name, project manager, project start date, or the name of a filter applied to the view. Scroll through the list, which has many options to choose from. If you want to use one of the items in a drop-down box, select it and then click the Add button associated with that list box to insert the information into the header or footer.

4. If you want to format any of the text or codes in the header or footer, highlight the text or code and use the Format Text Font button. Figure 13.9 shows a sample header.

TIP

There are keyboard shortcuts for applying formats. Select the text or code and use Ctrl+B to apply bold formatting, Ctrl+I to apply italics, and Ctrl+U to underline the selection.

The header in Figure 13.9 contains the project title, from the General drop-down list box, in the first line. In the second line, the word `Company:` was typed, followed by the Company Name code, inserted from the General drop-down list box. The third line is blank, to create some space in the header text area. In the fourth line, `Project Length:` was typed, followed by the Duration field code from the Project Fields drop-down list. After all the text was entered into the header, each line was selected and formatted, using the Format Text Font button. Note that you are not restricted to applying the same format for the entire line. Line two in the header has the label Company: formatted with bold italic and the actual company name just bold.

USING LEGENDS

If the view you are printing has graphic elements (as do the Network Diagram, the Gantt Chart, and the Resource Graph views), you can place a legend in the printout to explain the graphic elements used. Choose the Legend tab to display choices for configuring the display of the legend (see Figure 13.10).

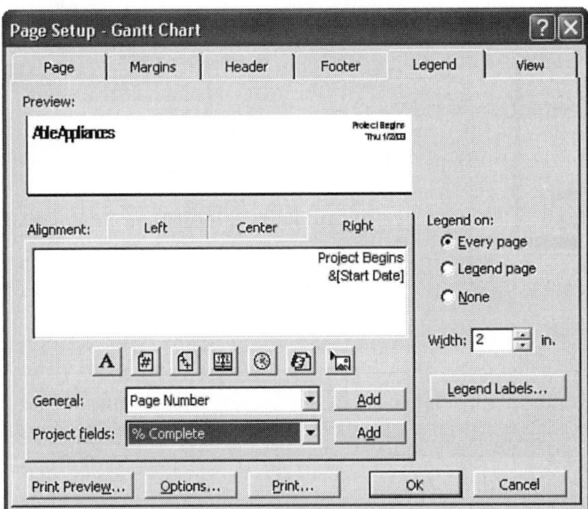

Figure 13.10
The Legend tab of the Page Setup dialog box provides options for customizing the legend in a printout.

13

You can enter up to three lines of legend text in each of the three alignment areas to repeat on each page of the printed document. As on the Header and Footer tabs, you can use the same seven buttons on the Legend tab to format, insert system codes, or insert pictures into the legend. In addition, the two drop-down list boxes enable you to insert information that is specific to the project. The default legend displays the project title and the date the view or report was printed in the Left alignment tab.

The text area can occupy up to half the legend area. You regulate the width of the legend text area by typing a number from 0 to 5 in the Width box; the number represents how many inches of the legend area are devoted to the text. If you type **0**, the entire legend area is devoted to the graphical legends. If you type **5**, 5 inches of the area is reserved for text. The default is 2 inches.

The formatting of the legend text is controlled via the Format Text Font button on the Legend tab, in the same manner as for header and footer text.

The Legend On option enables you to select where to display the legend. You can choose from the following:

- **Every Page**—Prints the legend at the bottom of each page.
- **Legend Page**—Prints the legend once, on an extra page at the end of the report.
- **None**—Suppresses the display of a legend entirely.

Figure 13.10 shows coding for a sample legend, which will be placed at the bottom of every page. The start and finish dates for the project, as well as the project filename, will be printed in the legend text area. The text area occupies 2 inches of the legend area width.

TIP

> You can disable unused bar styles by clicking Format, Bar Styles in the Gantt Chart view and inserting an asterisk in front of the name of each style you don't want to display.

13

FORMATTING HEADER, FOOTER, AND LEGEND TEXT

The Format Text Font button is available for changing the text formatting of header, footer, and/or legend. You need to select the Alignment tab that has the text you want to format. Project gives you the options of formatting all the text on that tab the same, applying a different format to each line of text, or formatting individual words or codes.

First, select the text you want to format, and then click the Format Text Font button. Use the Font dialog box (see Figure 13.11) to apply formatting to the text in the header, footer, or legend.

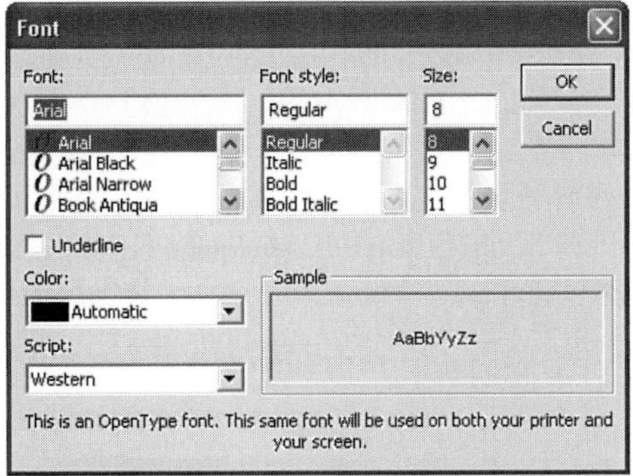

Figure 13.11
The Font dialog box enables you to format all the text or apply different formats to individual lines or words.

You can choose a font by selecting the entry list arrow to the right of the Font box. You can choose the font style attributes you want (bold, italic, or a combination) by selecting from the Font Style list box, and you can turn on underline by checking the Underline check box. You can choose the font point size (if multiple sizes are available) by selecting from the Size list box. If you are using a color printer or plotter, you can also choose the color of the text. After all items are formatted, click OK to return to the Page Setup dialog box.

TIP

> If the point size you want doesn't appear to be available, highlight the current font size and type the size in the box directly below the Size heading to get a custom font size.

Figure 13.11 shows the Font as Book Antigua, with the font style Bold Italic. The size is 14-point font with a blue color. Figure 13.12 shows these settings in Print Preview applied to the top line of a header.

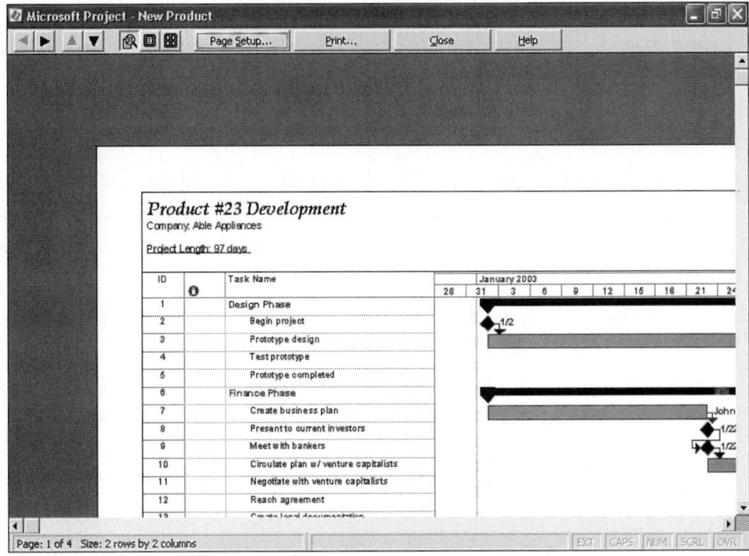

Figure 13.12
A preview of the header, zoomed in. Each line or part of a line can be formatted differently.

After you configure all page setup options, click OK to close the Page Setup dialog box. Alternatively, you might choose to preview your changes (as shown in Figure 13.12) or print directly from the Page Setup dialog box by clicking the Print Preview or Print buttons.

SELECTING SPECIAL OPTIONS FOR VIEWS

You use the View tab in the Page Setup dialog box, shown in Figure 13.13, to see options that are specific to the view being printed. These settings are for all views except the Calendar view. Some options on the View tab do not apply to all views and are dimmed to indicate that they are inactive for these views.

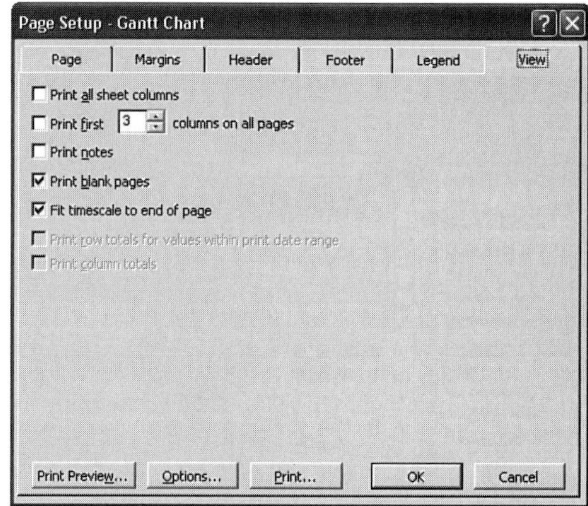

Figure 13.13
This version of the Page Setup dialog box View tab appears for all views except the Calendar view.

The View tab displays some of the most valuable print settings:

> **NOTE**
> When you're printing the Calendar view, the options on the View tab will be different from those listed here.

13

- For views with sheets—such as the Gantt Chart, Delay Gantt, Detail Gantt, Task Sheet, and Resource Sheet views—click the Print All Sheet Columns check box to print all columns of the sheet, regardless of whether they are completely visible on the screen.
- Select the check box Print First *x* Columns on All Pages to override the default of printing only the ID numbers, indicators, and task names on the first column of pages (refer to Figure 13.13). This option allows you to print a specified number of columns on all pages.

The feature that allows you to print a specified number of columns on all pages is especially useful if you don't have access to a plotter or if you don't intend to tape a multiple-page project together to make one large sheet. Also, the option for printing blank pages as described later in this chapter might also be unchecked for the same reason.

- Select the Print Notes check box to print notes that have been entered for tasks or resources.

Printing the notes for a project plan creates a separate addendum page along with the chart that is being printed. This is particularly useful to communicate the scope, constraints, assumptions, and limitations of the project if they have been included in the Notes field of the Start milestone. It is a good practice to include these important pieces of information along with your Start milestone.

- Uncheck the Print Blank Pages option to suppress the printing of blank pages. The default is for all pages to print.
- Check the check box for Fit Timescale to End of Page to ensure that a timescale unit (a week, for example) does not break across pages.

The View tab includes some new options for views that contain time-phased and sheet data, such as the Task Usage and Resource Usage views:

- Check Print Column Totals if you want to add a row to the bottom of the printout. Project calculates totals for the data that is selected to be printed and inserts them into the Total row.
- Check Print Row Totals for Values Within Print Date Range if you want to add a column to the end of the printout. Totals for time-phased data will be for the date range specified in the Print dialog box. Row totals always print on a separate page, after the timescale is complete and before any notes pages.

The following options are available for the Calendar view on the View tab of the Page Setup dialog box (see Figure 13.14):

- Months Per Page enables you to choose to print either 1 or 2 months on a page.
- Marking the Only Show Days in Month check box displays a blank box indicating a day from another month, like a placeholder. However, the calendar does not display the dates or tasks in boxes for days in other months. For example, if September is the current month and September 1 is a Tuesday, then the dates and tasks for Sunday (assuming that you've set in the Options dialog box Calendar tab that the week starts on Sunday) and Monday of that week (August 30 and 31, respectively) do not display on the printout.
- If you mark the Only Show Weeks in Month check box, only those weeks from the month are displayed. Weeks from other months are not printed. If the Calendar view is displaying six weeks—all five weeks in September and a week in October—only the

weeks in September will print. The printout will not reflect the sixth week (which is in October).

- Weeks Per Page is very useful if you have many tasks and want to print one or two weeks on a page. If you have more than eight weeks per page, however, the information becomes unreadable.

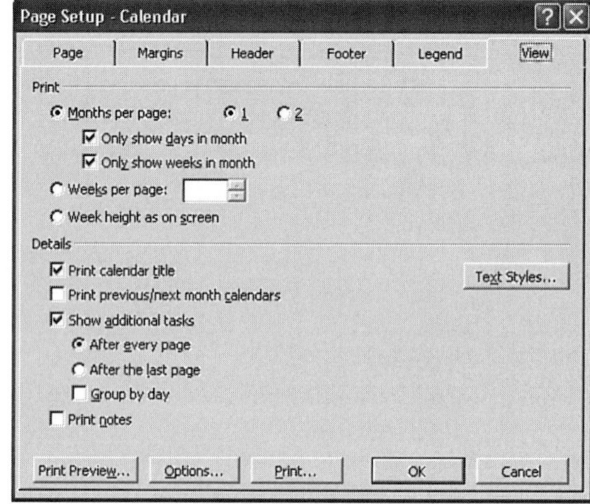

Figure 13.14
This version of the Page Setup dialog box View tab appears only for the Calendar view.

- The Week Height as on Screen option makes the printed calendar match the week height on the screen display of the Calendar view.
- The Print Calendar Title check box can be use to print the calendar title at the top of each page.
- The Print Previous/Next Month Calendars option causes miniature calendars of the previous and next months to appear in the upper-left and upper-right corners of the printed calendar. Only the dates are printed for the miniatures; no project information is displayed.
- The Show Additional Tasks option is used when more tasks exist than can be displayed on the calendar. You have the choice of printing these overflow tasks after every page or after the last page. The default for displaying additional tasks is After Every Page.

  The Group by Day check box displays the overflow page, with each day listed. If a task occurs across several days, it is listed beneath every date the task is being worked on. By default, this check box is not selected, and the additional tasks are listed once, based on the day the task starts.
- The Print Notes option can be used to print the notes for the tasks. The notes are printed on a separate page after the calendar or overflow page. The task ID and name appear with the note.
- The Text Styles button allows you to format the font type; font style, size, and color for all printed text; monthly titles; previous/next month miniature calendars; or additional (overflow) tasks (see Figure 13.15).

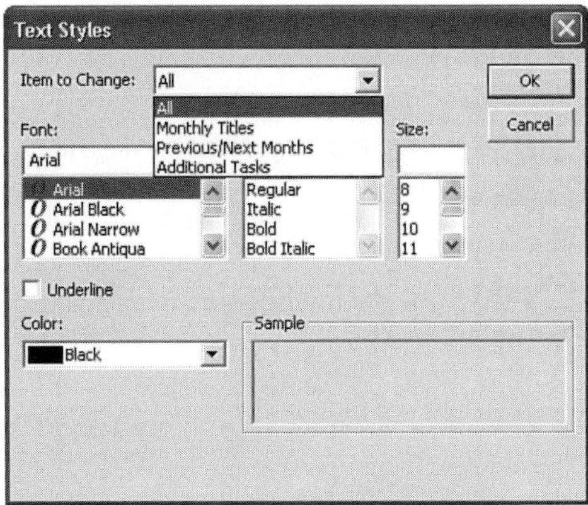

Figure 13.15
In the Calendar view, you have the option to format the way certain text appears when printed.

Using Print Preview

You can choose File, Print Preview (or the Print Preview button from the toolbar) to preview onscreen the look of the printed document. You can also choose the Print Preview button in the Page Setup dialog box. Figure 13.16 shows the Print Preview screen for the settings illustrated to this point in this chapter.

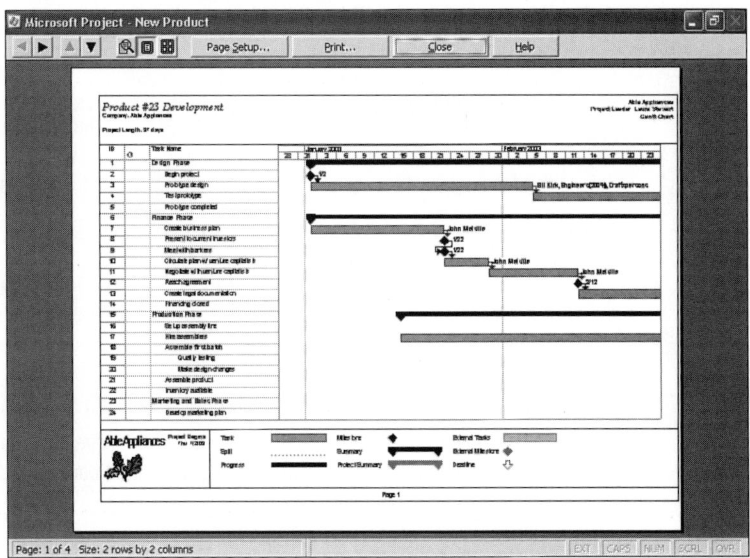

Figure 13.16
You should always preview before you print.

The initial preview screen shows the entire first page of the view that is being printed. If multiple pages exist, you can use the buttons at the top left of the preview screen to scroll left, right, up, and down one page at a time (see Table 13.1). You can zoom in on the details of a page by choosing the Zoom button or by using the mouse pointer, which changes to a magnifying glass when it is positioned over a page. Simply click the part of the page you want to see in greater detail. The magnifying glass appears only while the pointer is over the page; otherwise, the pointer is an arrow.

Using the Print Preview facility is particularly important on large projects. Within the status bar in the lower-left corner of the screen, the total number of pages to be printed is displayed. It is important to ensure that what is being printed is precisely what is required by the project manager in order to avoid wasting paper or tying up a network printer.

TABLE 13.1 THE PRINT PREVIEW BUTTONS

Button	Effect	Keyboard Shortcut
◄	Move left one page	Alt+left-arrow key
►	Move right one page	Alt+right-arrow key
▲	Move up one page	Alt+up-arrow key
▼	Move down one page	Alt+down-arrow key
	Zoom in on one page	Alt+1 (one) (Click area of page to zoom in to.)
	View one full page	Alt+2 (Click specific page to view.)
	View multiple pages	Alt+3 (Click area outside page.)

You use Alt+Z to switch between the Zoom, One Page, and Multiple Page views. The Alt+1, Alt+2, and Alt+3 shortcuts work only with the numbers above the alphanumeric keys, not those on the number pad.

13

NOTE

If the Print Blank Pages option on the View tab of the Page Setup dialog box is not checked, blank pages are displayed with a gray shaded background and are not printed.

Figure 13.17 shows the zoomed-in view of the title area of page 1 of a Gantt Chart view. Figure 13.18 illustrates the multiple-page preview of the same report. Note that Figure 13.18 shows eight pages and that the status line indicates that the size of the printout will be two rows by four columns. Pages are numbered down the columns, starting from the left. Therefore, page 2 of the report is the bottom page in the left column onscreen.

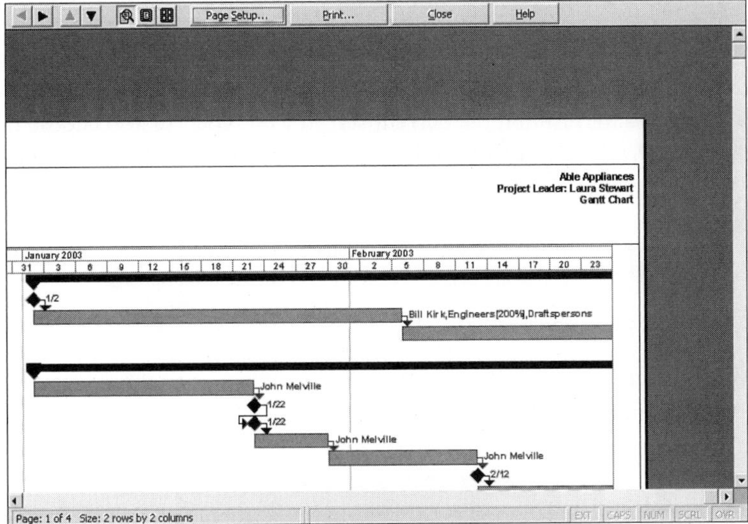

Figure 13.17
This is a preview of a Gantt Chart zoomed in to show the title area.

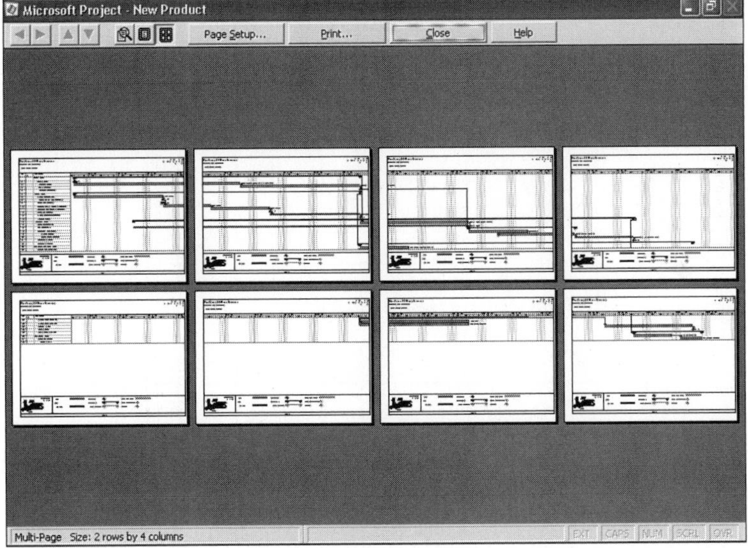

Figure 13.18
Here you can see a multipage view of a Gantt Chart, in the preview screen.

You can open the Page Setup dialog box from the Print Preview screen by choosing the Page Setup button at the top of the preview screen. If you have a question about one of the available options, click the Help button for context-sensitive online help. When you are ready to print, choose the Print button (see the following section). To make modifications, or if you decide against printing at this time, click the Close button to return to the project view.

After you have established the print options, these settings become a permanent part of the project file. You can change the settings at any time.

USING THE PRINT COMMAND

When the view is refined onscreen and the page setup and printer options are selected, the final step in printing is to choose File, Print. The Print dialog box appears and presents you with choices for printing the current screen view. You can also choose the Print button from the Print Preview screen or the Print button from the toolbar, or you can press Ctrl+P.

CAUTION

The Print button on the toolbar sends the view directly to the printer, without first presenting the dialog box where you choose print options.

When you choose File, Print or click the Print button in the preview screen, the Print dialog box appears (see Figure 13.19).

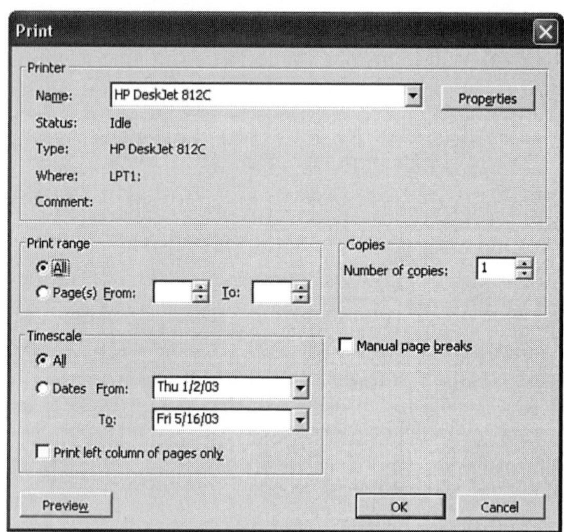

Figure 13.19
You can choose what to print, the quality of the printout, and the number of copies in the Print dialog box.

Some options on the Print dialog box do not apply to all views and might be dimmed to indicate that they are inactive for the view you are printing.

SELECTING THE PAGES TO PRINT

In the Preview screen, you can see the number of pages that will print. When you display the Print dialog box, the default is to print all pages, as indicated in the All option of the Print Range area. If you want to print only some of the pages, enter the starting page number in the Page(s) From box and the ending page number in the To box. To reprint just page five of a view, for example, type **5** in both the Page(s) From and To boxes. On views that include timescales, the default is to print from the start date of the project through the finish date. You can limit the printed output to a specific time span. See the upcoming section, "Printing Views That Contain Timescales," for details.

If you embedded manual page breaks in a task list or a resource list, these page breaks are not used in printing unless the Manual Page Breaks check box is marked. Unmark the check box if you want to ignore the manual page breaks.

NOTE

> Printing with manual page breaks is inappropriate if you previously sorted the list for a particular report, because the manual page breaks may make no sense in a different sorted order. See the sections "Sorting and Grouping the Display" and "Setting and Clearing Page Breaks," earlier in this chapter, for more information.

SELECTING THE NUMBER OF COPIES

For multiple copies of a view, enter a number in the Number of Copies box. You must collate the multiple copies by hand because Microsoft Project instructs the printer to print all copies of the first page, then all copies of the second page, and so on.

PRINTING VIEWS THAT CONTAIN TIMESCALES

For views that contain timescales, you can print the full date range of the project, from the start date to the finish date of the project, which is the default setting. Alternatively, you can print the timescale data for a limited range of dates. Choose the All option button to print the entire project, or choose the Dates From option button to specify a limited range of dates. Enter the starting date in the Dates From box and the ending date in the To box.

The screen display dictates whether the information is printed showing, for example, weeks or quarters. Choose View, Zoom or click the Zoom In or Zoom Out buttons on the Standard toolbar to change the timescale on the screen.

Choose the Print Left Column of Pages Only check box to print only the pages on the far left in print preview, with a multipage layout. In Figure 13.18, for example, the two pages that contain the task names are the two pages in the left column.

SENDING THE VIEW TO THE PRINTER

Before you print the document, you should preview it, especially if you have made changes in the Print dialog box. You can choose the Preview button in the Print dialog box or the Print Preview button in the Page Setup dialog box to review the effects of the choices you made. If you are not currently viewing the Print or Page Setup dialog boxes, you can also access Print Preview by using the Print Preview button on the Standard toolbar. If you selected a limited number of pages to print, the Print Preview screen still shows the entire report. Nevertheless, when you are actually printing, only the selected pages are printed.

To start the print job, click OK in the Print dialog box. Or you can use the Print button on the Standard toolbar.

NOTE

The Print button causes data to be sent to the printer immediately; if you use it, you do not get a chance to make selections in the Print dialog box.

PRINTING PROJECT'S PREDESIGNED REPORTS

Project has designed reports for you to use; you can customize these reports or create your own reports. Of the 29 total predesigned reports, 22 have been divided into five standard categories of reports and are available by choosing View, Reports.

Report From the Project Guide toolbar, click the Report tool, and in the sidepane click the radio button Select a Report to Print Project Information. Then click the Display Reports hyperlink. This displays the Reports dialog box shown in Figure 13.20.

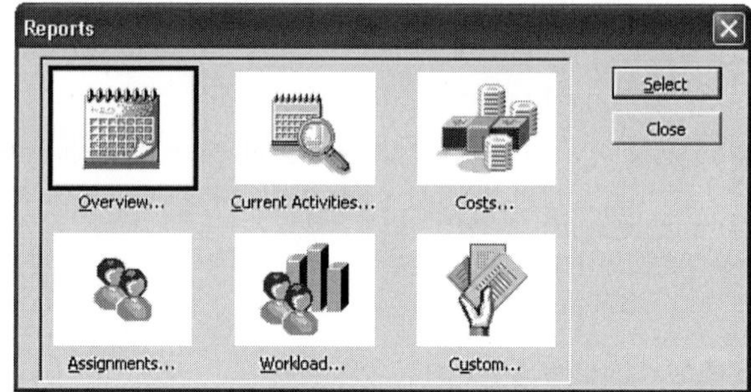

Figure 13.20 You can select one of the categories in the Reports dialog box to choose from several impressive built-in reports.

You can double-click the category of reports that you want to view, or you can click a category and choose Select. A subsequent dialog box lists the individual reports available for each category (see Table 13.2).

TABLE 13.2 PROJECT'S PREDEFINED REPORTS

Category	Report Name
Overview	Project Summary Top-Level Tasks Critical Tasks Milestones Working Days (Base Calendar)
Current Activities	Unstarted Tasks Tasks Starting Soon Tasks in Progress Completed Tasks Should Have Started Tasks Slipping Tasks

Category	Report Name
Costs	Cash Flow Budget Overbudget Tasks Overbudget Resources Earned Value
Assignments	Who Does What Who Does What When To-Do List Overallocated Resources
Workload	Task Usage Resource Usage

A final category, Custom, includes all the reports that fall into the five categories as well as the remaining reports: Cross Tab, Resource, Resource (Material), Resource (Work), Resource Usage (Material), Resource Usage (Work), and Task.

After you select a report, you are taken into the Print Preview screen. From there, you can access the Page Setup and Print dialog boxes. To print a report, simply choose the Print button in the preview screen.

You use the Page Setup dialog box, the Print Preview screen, and the Print dialog box options the same way for reports as for views, as discussed in earlier sections of this chapter. Due to the nature of the reports, some of the page setup and print options might not be available. See the earlier sections "Changing the Page Setup" and "Using the Print Commands" for more information on these options.

➔ To learn more about the built-in reports in Microsoft Project, **see** Chapter 22, "Using and Customizing the Standard Reports," **p. 877**.

TROUBLESHOOTING

THE VIEW APPEARANCE AND PRINTOUT DON'T MATCH

I've changed the display in the Gantt Chart view to view only the task ID, by moving the partition to the far left. Yet both the ID and the Indicator columns continue to be printed. What should I do?

By default, the ID and Indicator columns are both printed on the Gantt Chart view, even if you change the screen display to show only the ID column. To change this, first, make sure that only the ID column is being displayed on the screen. Then edit the table that is currently being used in the view by choosing View, Table, More Tables. Click the Edit button to display the Table Definition dialog box. You need to uncheck the Lock First Column check box. When this box is not checked, only the first column, ID, prints.

➔ For more information about customizing views, **see** Chapter 21, "Customizing Views, Tables, Fields, Filters, and Groups," **p. 833**.

Using Manual Page Breaks

Project is ignoring the manual page breaks I have set. What should I do?

Check the Print dialog box and make sure that the Manual Page Breaks check box is selected.

→ For more information about the Print dialog, **see** "Changing the Printer Setup," **p. 490**.

Avoiding Gantt Chart Timescale Truncation

When I print Gantt Chart view, the timescale begins flush to the Task Names column. It also chops off the resource names on the last few tasks of the printout because they extend beyond the finish date. How do I avoid this?

By default, the start and end dates of the project are displayed in the Timescale section of the Print dialog box. This causes the printout to display the beginning of the Gantt chart bars flush against the task names on the left side of the printed view. It also has the printout stop when the last task is completed, regardless of whether the resource names that are printed to the right of the last few taskbars are visible.

You need to display a gap between the table side of the Gantt chart and the beginning of the taskbars and leave a few extra days at the end of the printed project view. You can accomplish this by changing the Dates From entry to a date slightly earlier (two or three days) than the beginning of the project. This starts the Gantt chart timescale at that date, which pushes all taskbars slightly to the right for better display on paper. If you can't see the resource names on the last few tasks, extend the Dates To entry slightly (by two or three days). Use the Preview button to see how this will look before you begin printing the pages.

→ For more information about customizing views, **see** "Preparing a View for Printing" **p. 493**.

PART V

TRACKING AND ANALYZING PROGRESS

14 Tracking Work on the Project 519

15 Analyzing Progress and Revising the Schedule 555

CHAPTER 14

Tracking Work on a Project

In this chapter

An Overview of Tracking 520

Using Project Guide for Tracking 521

Working with Project Baselines 522

Tracking a Project's Performance and Costs 528

AN OVERVIEW OF TRACKING

Far too many project managers use only half of the power of Microsoft Project. They use Microsoft Project to plan the schedule, estimate the budget, and generate reports that will help the project sponsor make a decision about whether to go ahead with the project. After the final plan is approved and instructions are given to the project team, these project managers put the Project file away and begin managing the project without taking advantage of Microsoft Project's powerful support for the execution phase of the project.

Microsoft Project offers many features that help manage a project after the initial planning is finished. The following are some of these features:

- Microsoft Project can save a "snapshot" copy of the final plan for future reference. This copy is called the *baseline*, and it can be useful if you have to revise the plan during the execution phase because it lets you compare the original plan with the revised plan. The baseline is especially important if you are going to use Microsoft Project to keep track of what actually happens during the execution phase. As you will learn in this chapter, when you track performance, you actually revise the plan, replacing the estimated dates, work, and cost with actual dates, work, and cost. If you have a baseline, you can compare the actual performance with the original plan.
- Microsoft Project provides a number of tools that help you record what actually happens during the execution phase of a project. This is called *tracking*, and it provides a valuable record of actual performance.
- When Microsoft Project incorporates actual performance into a schedule, replacing planned dates and cost with actual dates and cost, it automatically recalculates the schedule for the remaining tasks. If actual finish dates are earlier or later than originally planned, Microsoft Project reschedules the remaining successor tasks accordingly. This might require some adjustments to ensure that key resources are available, and it might even lead to changes in the scope of the project.
- Microsoft Project provides powerful analysis tools that help you predict the impact that actual performance will have on the project's overall budget and completion date, at any point in the project.
- When the project is complete, Microsoft Project helps you prepare reports to document what actually happened and to compare performance with the original plan. These reports not only justify your claims to success (or failure) in managing the project, but they also provide useful information for future project plans.

This chapter describes how to save and use baselines and how to record actual performance by using Microsoft Project. Chapter 15, "Analyzing Progress and Revising the Schedule," shows you how to assess actual performance and adapt a plan in response to changes in the schedule.

USING PROJECT GUIDE FOR TRACKING

If you're new to tracking, you might find it helpful to begin by using Project Guide's Track sidepane (see Figure 14.1). This sidepane enables you to do the following:

- Save a baseline
- Select a tracking method and prepare a custom view for tracking
- Incorporate actual progress information into the project
- Check the status of tasks
- Modify the project in light of tracking information
- Track issues related to the project
- Request periodic text-based assessments of general status from key resources
- Publish new and changed assignments to Project Server

Most of these topics are discussed in greater detail in the sections that follow. (See the section "Choosing a Tracking Method," later in this chapter.) The Project Guide toolbar steps for tracking were designed with users of Microsoft Project Server in mind; therefore, the last three topics in the list are covered in Chapter 24, "Introduction to Project Server."

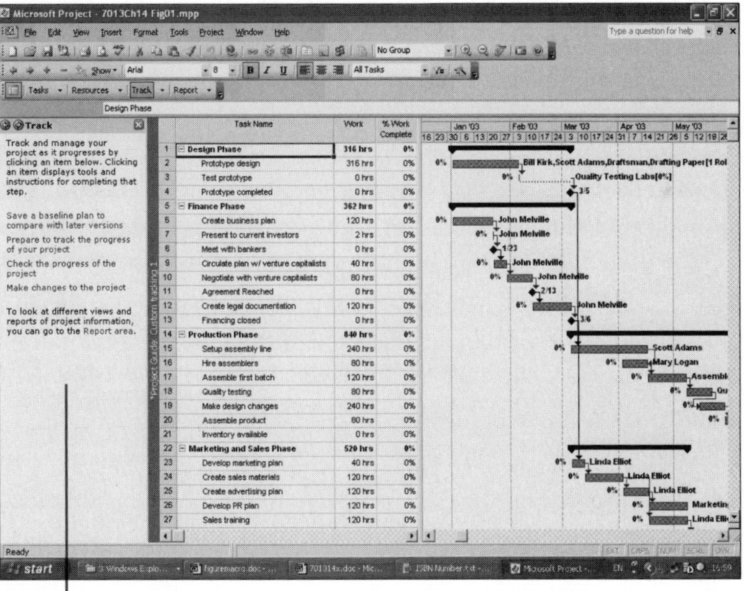

Figure 14.1
The Project Guide toolbar is a good place to begin learning about tracking.

WORKING WITH PROJECT BASELINES

As work progresses on a project, circumstances almost always arise that require the originally scheduled activities to be modified. For example, there might be a revision in the list of activities needed to complete the project, especially if the project scope changes. Or resources might not be available, meaning that substitutes have to be assigned. There might be a change in the estimates of the duration of tasks or the amount of work required to finish tasks. Furthermore, as you begin to record actual start and finish dates for tasks, unless you are able to perform project planning miracles, some of these dates will differ from the originally planned dates. As you enter the actual dates, Microsoft Project reschedules successor activities and milestones to reflect the changed circumstances. Therefore, unless you have saved a baseline, you will have no record of the plan as it existed when project execution began.

A Zen Buddhist philosophy says, "no matter where you go, there you are." This saying is reminiscent of the ever-changing project schedule. If you never set a baseline, you have nothing to measure performance against, and you never have a sense of how well you are progressing.

The PMBOK Guide (that is, the Project Management Institute's Guide to the Project Management Body of Knowledge) defines the baseline as the original plan plus or minus approved changes, and it usually has a modifier along with it (for example, cost baseline, schedule baseline, performance measurement baseline). When you set a baseline, all schedule elements (start date, finish date, duration, cost, and work) are captured so that you can use variance and earned value analysis to determine how well the work is being performed and whether the project is proceeding according to plan.

SAVING A BASELINE

If you click Track on the Project Guide toolbar, the first step in the Track sidepane is Save a Baseline Plan to Compare with Later Versions. If you select this option, the Save Baseline sidepane appears, as shown in Figure 14.2. Clicking the Save Baseline button in this sidepane has the same effect as choosing Tools, Tracking, Save Baseline, as described later in this section, but it does not give you an opportunity to select any of its options. However, you do not need to use those options the first time you use the command. In order to understand the baseline options, you must first understand what the baseline is.

A *baseline* is a snapshot of the current schedule for all tasks (including milestones and summary tasks), all resources, and all assignments. Project copies the schedule information (including duration, start and finish dates, assigned work, and costs) into baseline fields that are static, or unchanging, because they are not recalculated as the schedule changes. Thus, it copies the Start field values for all tasks into the task Baseline Start field, and it copies the task Cost field into the task Baseline Cost field. The default baseline fields are listed in Table 14.1.

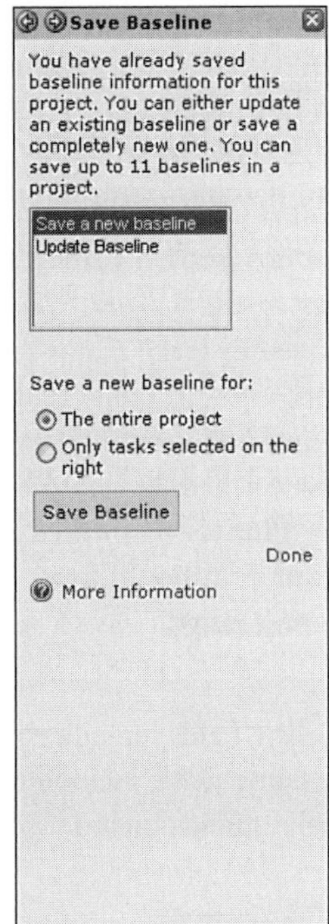

Figure 14.2
Saving a baseline with Project Guide is quick and easy, as long as you want all the default options.

Table 14.1 The Default Baseline Fields

Tasks	Assignments	Resources
Regular Fields		
Baseline Duration		
Baseline Start	Baseline Start	
Baseline Finish	Baseline Finish	
Baseline Work	Baseline Work	Baseline Work
Baseline Cost	Baseline Cost	Baseline Cost
Timephased Fields		
Baseline Work	Baseline Work	Baseline Work
Baseline Cost	Baseline Cost	Baseline Cost

14

NOTE

Project stores task splits in the baseline, but there is no field that you can display to show splits. However, the baseline splits show up in a Gantt Chart similar to the tracking Gantt Chart that shows baseline taskbars, and splits also show up as time periods with zero hours of work in the timephased data of the Usage views.

The field names in Table 14.1 are the fields that contain values for the *default*, or primary, baseline, and that baseline is named simply Baseline. Microsoft Project 2003 allows you to save up to 10 additional versions of a project's baseline, and these are named Baseline 1, Baseline 2, and so forth. These additional baseline versions have all the same fields listed in Table 14.1, but they are named Baseline1 Duration, Baseline1 Start, and so forth.

You can use these extra baseline versions to capture progressive snapshots at important junctures during either the planning or execution phases of the project. You might also occasionally find that even after execution has begun, you need to make major revisions in the project plan because of scope changes, unforeseen changes in the availability of key resources, and so forth. You, the project sponsors, and other decision makers might then decide that saving a new baseline based on the revised schedule would be more relevant for reports and comparisons than the original baseline. This is often called *rebaselining* the plan. In the event that you decide to rebaseline the project, you should first copy the original primary baseline to one of the other baseline versions so that you have a record of the original plan.

For all baseline versions, the task and resource baseline fields include rolled-up summaries of the assignment baseline fields. Thus, the task baseline fields include the sum of the work and the cost of each assignment. The resource baseline fields include the sum of all assignment baseline values for each resource.

To save baseline data, or to copy baseline data from one version to another, choose Tools, Tracking, Save Baseline to display the Save Baseline dialog box (see Figure 14.3).

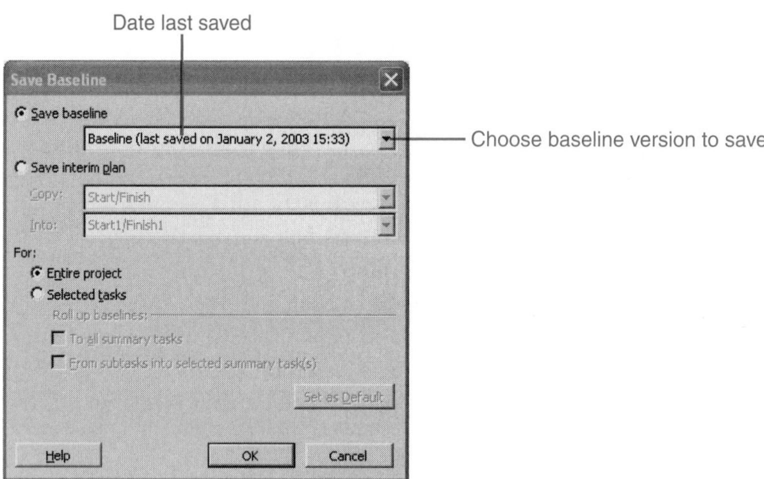

Figure 14.3
Use the Save Baseline dialog to keep track of your progress.

The Save Baseline dialog box has the following options:

- **Save Baseline**—This is the default option, and it saves data from the current schedule into the fields of one of the baseline versions. The default version is Baseline, but you can click the down arrow in the text box to select a different version.
- **Save Interim Plan**—This option is used mainly to copy data from one version into another version. For example, you might decide to back up the default baseline by making a copy of it and saving it as Baseline 10. To do this, you select Baseline in the Copy text box and Baseline 10 in the Into text box.

NOTE

> In Microsoft Project 2000 and earlier versions, before the introduction of the 11 extra fully timescaled baselines, the Save Interim Plan option allows you to save "interim plans," which are mini-baselines that contain only the start and finish dates. Those interim plan sets are still available in Microsoft Project 2002 and 2003, for backward compatibility. They use the custom Start and Finish date fields, which are named Start1 through Start10 and Finish1 through Finish10.

- **For**—This option lets you choose to copy baseline data for the entire project or for just selected tasks. You should use the Selected Tasks option when you have added or changed one or more tasks after execution begins and have decided to rebaseline the task(s). The baseline data for other tasks will not be affected.
- **Roll Up Baselines**—This option appears only when you choose the For Selected Tasks option. By default, after a baseline is initially saved, Microsoft Project does not update the baseline for a summary task when a subtask is added, modified, or deleted. This set of two options lets you choose to roll up baseline changes for subtasks to their parent summary tasks. You choose To All Summary Tasks to update all summary tasks that include the rebaselined subtask. To update only selected summary tasks that include the subtask, select those summary tasks along with the subtask(s) that are to be rebaselined (by using Ctrl+click to add them to the selection) and choose From Subtasks into Selected Summary Task(s). If you want to make your selection for either or both of these options the default for all new projects, you should click the Set as Default button.

NOTE

> You can undo changes to the baseline if you execute Undo immediately after using the Save Baseline command.

If the baseline version that you are saving into already has data in it, you will see a "last saved" date next to the baseline version name, as shown in Figure 14.3. If you choose to save to a baseline that has been saved before, a warning message appears, to remind you that all data in that version will be replaced by the data for the current schedule (see Figure 14.4).

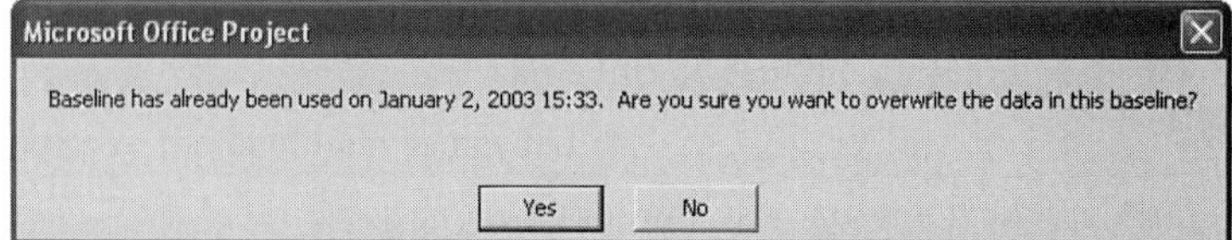

Figure 14.4
Project warns you about accidentally overwriting an existing baseline.

If you are still in the planning stage of a project, you can safely click Yes to overwrite the old baseline data. However, if you are in the execution stage of a project, you would only click Yes if it has been necessary to make major revisions to the project plan. In that case, you should first copy the existing Baseline to one of the other 10 baselines so that you have a record of the original plan.

Remember that a good practice in project management is to save the baseline after the final plan is adopted and before project execution begins. You should leave the baseline unchanged thereafter. However, in the case of significant scope creep of a project (or feature creep, in the case of product development), it is sometimes necessary to create another baseline, but if you do so, you should still retain the ability to review previous baseline commitments by making a copy of the original baseline in one of the other baseline versions.

CLEARING BASELINES

You can remove the saved data from any of the baseline versions—for all tasks or for just the tasks that you have selected—by choosing Tools, Tracking, Clear Baseline. The Clear Baseline dialog box appears (see Figure 14.5). You can select the baseline version to clear in the Clear Baseline Plan text box. To clear one of the mini-baseline date sets, select it in the Clear Interim Plan text box. The default is Entire Project, but if you have selected specific tasks that are the only ones to be cleared, you should choose Selected Tasks. Click OK to clear the data. You can restore the cleared data if you execute Edit, Undo immediately after using the Clear Baseline command.

Select the full baseline version to clear

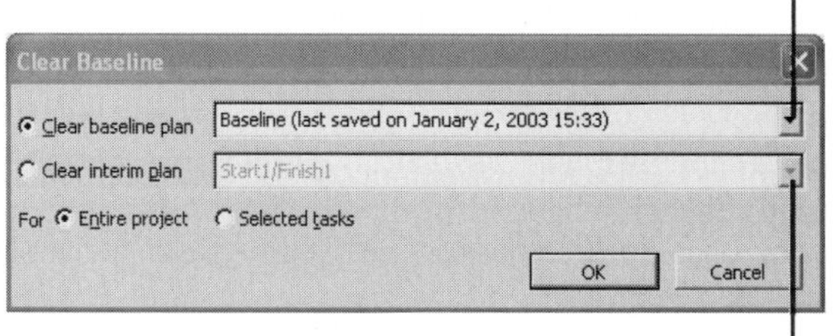

Select the interim baseline to clear

Figure 14.5
You can remove data from a baseline by using the Clear Baseline command.

14

CAUTION

Be *really* careful that you don't accidentally clear the primary baseline after you are past the planning stage. If you choose to clear it on purpose, be sure that it's backed up in one of the other baseline versions.

VIEWING BASELINES

You can display the regular baseline fields that are listed in Table 14.1 as columns in task and resource tables. For example, the task Baseline table displays all the task Baseline fields for the default (primary) baseline. To display the Baseline table in a task view such as the Gantt Chart view or the Task Usage view, right-click the Select All button (the blank cell above the row numbers), choose More Tables, select Baseline, and click Apply. If you apply the table in the Task Usage view (see Figure 14.6), assignment baseline values appear on assignment rows, and task baseline values appear on task rows.

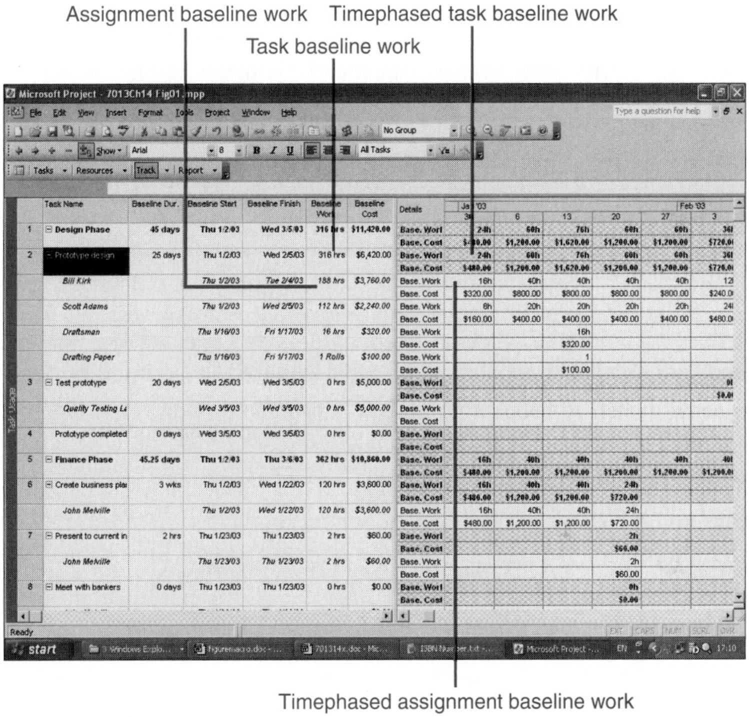

Figure 14.6
The task Baseline table applied to the Task Usage view shows all task and assignment baseline values.

NOTE

> Although you can edit the baseline data when it's displayed in a table or in the timephased grid, you should generally avoid changing baseline data. When you do need to make changes (such as adding a new task), you should use the Save Baseline command to be sure all the relevant data is saved.

14

Because there are only two regular resource fields, Baseline Cost and Baseline Work, there is no Baseline table defined for resources. The Baseline Cost field is included in the resource Cost table, and the Baseline Work field is included in the resource Work table. To display these tables in a resource view such as the Resource Usage view, you right-click the Select All button and choose Cost or Work.

You can display the timephased baseline fields only in the Usage views. Figure 14.6 shows task and assignment timephased baseline work and baseline cost details. To display the baseline details, you can right-click over the timephased data grid and choose Detail Styles (or choose Format, Detail Styles). You can double-click Baseline Cost and Baseline Work in the list on the left to move them to the Show These Fields list on the right. You can double-click any other fields in the list on the right that you don't want to include; then, click OK.

All the baseline fields in the standard views, tables, and forms are fields from the primary baseline. If you want to view fields from one of the other baseline versions, such as Baseline 5, you could create a custom table or form to display Baseline5 Start, Baseline5 Finish, and so forth. However, you could also copy Baseline 5 into the primary baseline, and then the standard views would display data from that version. Before you copy the primary baseline, however, you should be sure to back it up by copying Baseline to one of the other versions.

As discussed in Chapter 15, all of Microsoft Project's variance calculations are also based on the primary baseline. Copying another baseline version, such as Baseline 5, into the primary baseline, as just described, is the only way to have variances that are based on Baseline 5.

TIP

Before you copy another baseline version such as Baseline 5 into Baseline, you need to copy Baseline into an unused version (such as Baseline 10). You then have to remember to copy Baseline 10 back into Baseline. A safer and easier way to reach the same goal is to make a temporary copy of the project file and in that file copy the baseline version you want to use into the primary baseline for viewing or reporting. The main copy of the file would still retain the correct data in the baseline fields.

Earned value fields provide valuable information about performance when you enter the execution phase of a project, and they are also calculated by using the baseline values in the primary baseline. However, Project 2003 also allows you to designate any of the other 10 baseline versions to be used for calculating the earned value fields.

→ For information about selecting the baseline to use for earned value calculations, **see** "Controlling the Calculation of Earned Value," **p. 587**.

Tracking a Project's Performance and Costs

To track progress on tasks in a project, you need to get periodic feedback from resources about their progress and then enter that information into the project plan. Microsoft Project can help you get feedback from resources by automatically requesting that they send you progress updates, using either Project Server or regular email. With both of these options, the resource receives a timesheet-like form that he or she fills out and submits to you. Then you review the entries and, if they are satisfactory, you update the project plan automatically with the resource's responses. If you don't use Project Server or email to gather progress information, you need to determine progress manually and manually enter the progress information into the plan.

Before choosing the method you will use for tracking, you should understand what tracking information can be gathered and how Project uses that information. You will then be in a better position to decide which method to use.

UNDERSTANDING THE FIELDS USED IN UPDATING THE PROJECT SCHEDULE

The scheduled start, finish, and duration for a project's tasks are determined by the values in the task Start, Finish, and Duration fields. If resources are assigned to a task, the scheduled amounts of work, overtime work, cost, and overtime cost for each assignment are stored in the assignment Work, Overtime Work, Cost, and Overtime Cost fields, and the totals for the task are stored in the task fields with the same names. During the planning stage, Microsoft Project recalculates these fields in response to a number of changes, such as a change in the estimated duration of a predecessor or a change in the estimated project start date.

These fields are all hypothetical values until a task is actually completed. At that point you find out when the task actually started and how long it took, when each assignment actually started and how much work and overtime work was actually done, when the task and assignments actually finished, and what the cost and overtime cost of each actually was. These *actuals* are stored in the assignment fields for Actual Start, Actual Finish, Actual Work, Actual Overtime Work, Actual Cost, and Actual Overtime Cost. The task actuals are stored in similarly named task fields. In addition, there is an Actual Duration field for tasks.

When you track actual performance, you enter—or cause Project to calculate entries for—one or more of those actual fields. For example, when work on a task actually starts, you should record the actual start date for the task, replacing the hypothetical start with the actual start. If that date is earlier or later than the previously scheduled start, successor tasks might be able to start sooner or might have to start later than previously scheduled. Consequently, when you enter an actual start date, Microsoft Project does two things:

- It copies the entry you made in the Actual Start field into the (scheduled) Start field and recalculates the schedule for any successor tasks. This gives you information about the implications of early or late starts and allows you to adapt the remaining schedule if you need to.
- It marks the Start field for the task as fixed (that is, not subject to recalculation). After an actual start is recorded, Project is not allowed to recalculate that value. Of course *you* can change the actual start, but Project can no longer calculate it on its own.

In a similar fashion, after you enter (or cause Project to enter) an actual finish date for a task, Project marks all the schedule fields for the task as fixed and copies the actual values into the schedule fields. The baseline is now the only record of the originally estimated schedule, but your schedule is now more accurate than it was when it held hypothetical values only.

Many methods are available for getting the actual values into a project plan. Some involve more time and effort than others. The following are just some of the possibilities:

- You can simply mark tasks as completed when the work is finished, without replacing the estimated schedule dates, work, and cost with what really happened. This is the fastest, least onerous method of tracking, but it gives you no information about how well you estimated what it would take to complete the project, and it gives you no guidance when planning future projects.

- You can record when tasks actually finish but not concern yourself with how much actual work or cost was really involved. This method at least gives you the ability to compare planned and actual completion dates.
- You can record when tasks actually start and, at regular intervals, how far along each task is toward completion. This gives you the added ability to spot tasks that are not progressing as planned (tasks that might finish late or run over budget), and with this information you might be able to intervene and put the project back on course.
- You can manually collect timesheets from resources and record how much work they actually did during each time period. This method provides the most information about performance, especially for individual resources. However, it requires a great deal of time if you have to do all that data entry manually.
- You can use Project Server or workgroup email to request timesheet reports from resources and have Project automatically update the project's actual fields from the data submitted. This method requires little of your time and is the best way to track progress.

Reporting of percentage complete is often preferred at an executive level, where there's little room for analysis and interpretation into the whys and hows of performance. In the strictest sense, this information is for the benefit of the project manager, so he or she can take corrective action when necessary. At a higher level, it becomes more of a bottom-line interpretation of project performance. In other words, the project is either done or not done, and there is no in-between.

Which tracking method you choose depends on how much detailed information you need about actual performance and on how much time and cost you can devote to the tracking process. Whether you record actual information manually or let Project update actuals from timesheet reports, you need to understand how the various tracking fields interact. The following sections explain the way Project responds to entries that you make in the task tracking fields and the assignment tracking fields.

NOTE

The descriptions of Project's behavior that are given in the following two sections, "Entering Tracking Information at the Task Level" and "Entering Tracking Information at the Assignment Level," assume that the options on the Calculation tab of the Options dialog box are set to the original default values. This means that updating the status of a task automatically updates the status of its assignments. For example, if you mark a task as being 50% complete, Project not only records actual work for the task but also records actual work for the task's assignments. It also means that you can't enter actual costs manually until after a task is marked as being complete. Until that time, Project calculates costs and overwrites any edits you make to the task Cost field. The use of those and other options is discussed later in this chapter, in the section "Understanding the Calculation Options That Affect Tracking."

ENTERING TRACKING INFORMATION AT THE TASK LEVEL

This section describes how you can use tracking fields at the task level to update the status of a task. This is what most managers who enter progress manually do. The next section describes how you use the tracking fields at the assignment level to update task status. That's what you do if you use Project Server or workgroup email to have resources enter progress and then let Project update the project automatically.

This section examines the following task-tracking fields:

- Actual Start
- Actual Finish
- % Complete
- Actual Duration
- Remaining Duration
- Actual Work
- % Work Complete
- Remaining Work
- Timephased Work

You can view and edit most of these fields on the task Tracking table. Figure 14.7 shows the Gantt Chart view with the Tracking table applied. To display the table in a task view, right-click the Select All button and select Tracking. The % Work Complete and Remaining Work fields can be edited on the Work table, and timephased work can be entered in the timephased grid on the Task Usage view. There are also forms that make these fields available. The views you use for tracking are described later in this chapter, in the section "Using Project's Facilities for Updating Tasks."

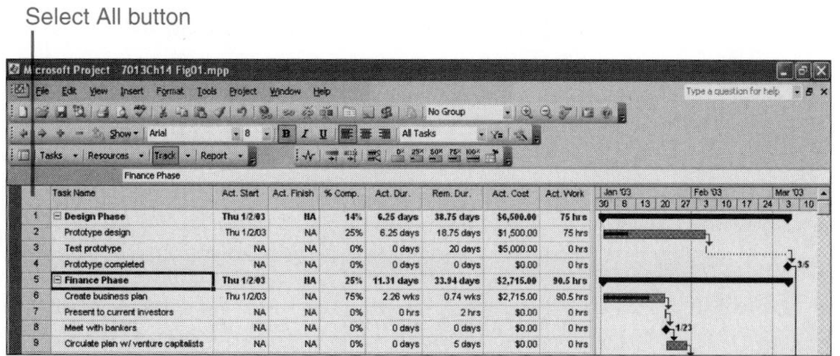

Figure 14.7
The task Tracking table provides most of the fields you might use for tracking progress at the task level.

It is good practice to record actual work performed at the activity or task level, not at the summary level. By definition, the summary displays the overall work progress for that component of the project, but only by managing at the activity level where the work package is located can a project manager truly monitor what is happening within the project. As the saying goes: The devil is in the details.

EDITING THE TASK ACTUAL START DATE

Before an actual date is entered, the Actual Start field's value is NA. When you enter an actual start date for a task, Project replaces NA with your entry. As discussed at the beginning of the section "Understanding the Fields Used in Updating the Project Schedule," earlier in this chapter, Project also copies the actual start date into the scheduled start date for the task. Any assignments to the task that had the same scheduled start date as the task are also given an actual start equal to the task actual start. Project then recalculates all assignments to the task as well as all successor tasks and their assignments.

If the Actual Start field contains NA and you make an entry into any other actual field that implies that the task must have started, Project assumes that the task started when it was scheduled to start, and it copies the date in the (scheduled) Start field into the Actual Start field. For example, if you record that the task is 50% complete and have not previously entered an actual start date, Project copies the Start field date into the Actual Start field.

TIP

> If a task does not start on schedule, you should enter the actual start date before you use any of the other fields described in the following sections for tracking progress. Otherwise, you will not have an accurate record of the actual start of the task.

EDITING THE TASK ACTUAL FINISH DATE

The Actual Finish Date field also displays NA until the task finish date is entered or calculated. As with the Actual Start field, the Actual Finish field is calculated by Project from the scheduled Finish field if you make an entry into any other tracking field that implies that the task is finished. For example, if you enter 0 in the Remaining Duration field, Project assumes that the task finished as scheduled.

When you enter an actual finish date, Project makes the following changes:

- It replaces the current entry in the Actual Finish field with your entry.
- It replaces the task scheduled finish with the actual finish.
- If the actual start for the task or for any assignments are NA, it replaces NA with the scheduled start for the task or assignment. Therefore, entering an actual finish that is later than the scheduled finish lengthens the duration of the task.
- It places 100% in both the % Complete and % Work Complete fields for the task and all assignments.
- It calculates actual duration (based on actual start and actual finish), and it changes the scheduled duration to the same value.
- It changes the remaining duration to zero.
- It calculates the actual work and actual cost for the task and assignments.
- It changes the remaining work and remaining cost to zero for the task and assignments.
- If the task was a critical task, Project changes it to noncritical because this task is no longer one you might consider rescheduling in order to shorten the critical path.

As you can see, entering an actual finish date causes Project to calculate all actual values for the task and its assignments (other than actual starts that had already been recorded). However, Project uses the scheduled values if you haven't provided actuals yourself.

NOTE

> For all the tracking task fields being discussed here, an entry that causes the task's actual finish date to be later than the scheduled finish causes Project to copy the task actual finish to the assignment actual finish. This is for all assignments that were scheduled to finish at the same time that the task was scheduled to finish. Thus, scheduled and actual work and cost for those assignments increase by an amount that is commensurate with the extended working time.
>
> If an assignment was scheduled to finish before the task was scheduled to finish, however, Project assumes that the assignment finished as scheduled. The scheduled finish, work, and cost are copied into the Actual Finish, Actual Work, and Actual Cost fields for the assignment.

EDITING TASK % COMPLETE (PERCENTAGE COMPLETE)

The % Complete field is based on the amount of task duration that has been completed. Its value is 0% until actual duration is greater than zero. Its formal definition and its related fields are as follows:

% Complete = 100 × (Actual Duration / Duration)

Duration = Actual Duration + Remaining Duration

You can enter the percentage complete for the task directly, or you can let Project calculate the value by entering the actual duration or its complementary value, the remaining duration (or any other tracking field that causes Project to calculate Actual Duration as greater than 0).

When you edit the % Complete field, Project does the following:

- If the Actual Start field is NA, it is replaced by the scheduled start.
- If you enter 100% complete, the actual finish date is set equal to the scheduled finish date.
- Actual duration is set equal to % Complete × Duration.
- Remaining duration is set equal to Duration – Actual Duration.
- Actual Work and Actual Cost are set to match the scheduled timephased work and cost for the period of time given by the actual duration.
- % Work Complete is set equal to 100 × Actual Work / Work.
- Remaining Work is set equal to Work – Actual Work.

NOTE

> The Tracking table also includes the new Physical % Complete field. This field is only used for an alternative calculation for earned value and has no effect on any of the actual fields, such as Actual Duration and % Complete. Entering a nonzero value does not even cause Project to change the Actual Start field from NA. You can learn about using this field in Chapter 15, in the section "Controlling the Calculation of Earned Value."

EDITING TASK ACTUAL DURATION

The Actual Duration field displays the amount of working time on the calendar that has been used thus far for completing the task.

If you enter a value that is less than the scheduled duration, Microsoft Project assumes that progress is proceeding as planned. Consequently, it performs the following calculations:

- If the Actual Start field is NA, it is replaced by the scheduled start.
- % Complete is calculated as 100 × Actual Duration / Duration.
- Remaining Duration is replaced by Duration – Actual Duration.
- Actual Work and Actual Cost are calculated as the sum of the timephased work and cost that was scheduled for that duration.

If you enter a value for Actual Duration that is longer than the scheduled duration, Project assumes that the task is finished and that it took longer than scheduled. Project then carries out these calculations:

- Actual Finish is calculated to match the longer duration.
- Scheduled Duration and scheduled Finish are changed to match the Actual Duration and new Actual Finish.
- % Complete is set to 100%, and Remaining Duration is set to 0.
- If the task type is Fixed Units or Fixed Duration, assignments that were scheduled to finish when the task finished have their Actual Finish fields moved to match the task Actual Finish field. The Work, Actual Work, Cost, and Actual Cost fields for these assignments are increased proportionally. Assignments that were scheduled to finish before the task finished are assumed to have finished on time, with the scheduled amount of work and cost copied into Actual Work and Actual Cost fields.
- If the task type is fixed work, then assignment Actual Work and Actual Cost are set equal to the scheduled work and cost. Assignments that were scheduled to finish when the task finished get the same actual finish as the task. Their assignment units are adjusted to a lower level, commensurate with the longer duration, but the work is unchanged. The assignments' Actual Work and Actual Cost are the same as their scheduled Work and Cost fields. Assignments that were scheduled to finish before the task finished are assumed to have finished on time, with the scheduled Work and Cost fields copied into the Actual Work and Actual Cost fields.

EDITING TASK REMAINING DURATION

Editing the Remaining Duration field when the Actual Start field still contains NA has no effect on the other tracking fields—it merely changes the scheduled duration. However, if Actual Start is not NA, the new value in Remaining Duration is treated as follows:

- If you reduce the value in Remaining Duration, Project increases Actual Duration and recalculates % Complete, Actual Work, and Actual Cost. If you reduce the value to zero, Project changes Actual Finish to the scheduled finish and marks the task 100% complete. All task and assignment values are calculated as described for entering Actual Duration.
- If you increase the value in Remaining Duration when the task has already started, Project assumes that the scheduled duration is being increased and calculates new values for % Complete (Actual Duration / a longer Duration), scheduled Finish, Work, Cost, Remaining Work, Remaining Cost, and % Work Complete.

EDITING TASK ACTUAL WORK

The Actual Work field displays the amount of work that has been completed by the resource(s) assigned to the task. The Actual Work field is zero until tracking of the task begins. If you enter an amount in the task Actual Work field, the work is distributed among the assignments in proportion to their scheduled Work entries. For example, if Mary and Pat are scheduled to work 40 hours and 20 hours, respectively, on a task, the proportion of scheduled work is 2 to 1. If you enter 30 hours in the task Actual Work field, Project records 20 hours of actual work for Mary and 10 hours of actual work for Pat.

As with entering Actual Duration, if the Actual Work value you enter is greater than the scheduled Work value, Project assumes that the task is finished and calculates Actual Start as scheduled if it is NA, calculates Actual Duration and Actual Finish commensurate with the added work, sets % Complete and % Work Complete to 100%, and sets Remaining Duration to zero.

EDITING TASK % WORK COMPLETE

If you edit the % Work Complete field and the Actual Start field contains NA, Project assumes that the task has started and sets Actual Work accordingly. Project next calculates Actual Work by multiplying % Work Complete times Work (for the task). It then assumes that the work that was scheduled was completed up through the amount of Actual Work, and that determines the Actual Duration. Then % Complete is calculated by dividing Actual Duration by Duration. Actual Cost is updated with the amount of cost scheduled for Actual Work.

EDITING TASK REMAINING WORK

As with entering Remaining Duration, if the Actual Start contains NA, your edits do not affect any of the other tracking fields. The new value is used to change the scheduled work. If the task has started, however, decreasing Remaining Work implies that more actual work has been completed. Consequently, Project recalculates Actual Work, % Work Completed, Actual Duration, % Complete, Remaining Duration, and Actual Cost.

Increasing Remaining Work, on the other hand, implies that the total work requirements for the task have increased, and Project recalculates scheduled Work, Duration, Finish, % Complete, % Work Complete, and Remaining Duration.

EDITING TASK TIMEPHASED ACTUAL WORK

If you display the Task Usage view, you can edit Actual Work and Actual Overtime Work for the specific time periods in which they were performed. To display the timephased Actual Work field, right-click in the grid on the right and choose Actual Work. If you want to record actual overtime work, right-click again and choose Detail Styles. Double-click Actual Overtime Work in the list on the left to place it in the list on the right. Then click OK.

Each cell in the grid covers a time period, and edits to the cell are distributed evenly between the beginning and ending dates for the cell. Therefore, if the bottom tier in the timescale displays weeks and you enter 8 hours in a week that contains a 1-day holiday, Project distributes 2 hours of work in each of the remaining 4 days of the week. If you want to place all 8 hours in one day, you must zoom in to display 1-day intervals in the timescale.

Edits to task timephased Actual Work roll down to the assignment level and are distributed among assignments in proportion to the scheduled work for each assignment for that time period. Note that any existing actual work for assignments for that time period is overwritten.

If the edited cell is the first actual work recorded (that is, the task Actual Start was NA), the Actual Start for the task is set to the begin date for the cell that you edited. If there is no remaining work after the edit, the task Actual Finish is set to the end date for the cell.

If the entered Actual Work is less than the scheduled Work for that cell, the remaining work for the cell is rescheduled after the end date for the task. If the entered Actual Work is greater than the scheduled Work for that cell, then the extra work is evenly deducted from the remaining cells in the task.

If any periods are skipped when entering Actual Work, the skipped periods get zero timephased task actual work, and the zeros roll down to timephased assignment actual work. The work originally scheduled for those zeroed days is rescheduled at the end of the task.

ENTERING TRACKING INFORMATION AT THE ASSIGNMENT LEVEL

When you use Project Server or workgroup email to solicit progress reports from resources and update the project with that data, the update data produces edits to the assignment tracking fields. These edits can cause recalculations for the assignment and for the task (because assignments roll up to the task level).

If you are using Project Server, the server administrator for your organization might have restricted the tracking fields that you can use; therefore, you might not have available all the fields listed in the following sections. However, these fields will still be available to you to edit manually.

EDITING ASSIGNMENT ACTUAL START

As with tasks, when you edit the Actual Start for an assignment, Project changes the assignment's scheduled Start to match the assignment Actual Start. Then Project recalculates the assignment scheduled Finish date.

If the task Actual Start was still NA when you edited the assignment, Project also sets the task Actual Start. If there is only one assignment, then the task Actual Start matches the assignment Actual Start. If there are multiple assignments, then there are three possible scenarios:

- If the assignment started as scheduled (that is, Actual Start was equal to scheduled Start), the task Actual Start is set to the task scheduled Start. This occurs even if the assignment's scheduled Start is later than the task's scheduled Start (which is the case when you schedule a delayed start for the assignment).
- If the assignment Actual Start is the same as the task scheduled Start, the task Actual Start is set to the task scheduled Start (and coincidentally equal to the assignment Actual Start). This occurs even if the assignment's scheduled Start was later than the task's scheduled Start. If the assignment starts earlier than it was scheduled to start, but on the task scheduled Start date, then the task is given the same Actual Start as the task scheduled Start.
- If the assignment started earlier or later than its scheduled Start (but not on the task's scheduled Start), Project sets the task's Actual Start equal to the assignment's Actual Start. Project then needs to reschedule any other assignments to that task, as well as the schedules for all successor tasks and their assignments.

EDITING ASSIGNMENT ACTUAL FINISH

If the assignment Actual Start displays NA when you edit Actual Finish, Project assumes that the assignment started as scheduled and ended on the edited finish date. If the edited Actual Finish is different from the scheduled Finish date, Project adjusts the work and cost accordingly. If the assignment is the only assignment for the task, after recalculations the task and assignment tracking fields are identical (except for Actual Cost, which might include some task fixed cost).

If there are multiple assignments to the task, editing Actual Finish for one assignment causes Project to recalculate the task Actual Work and Actual Cost, Actual Duration, % Complete, % Work Complete, Remaining Duration, Remaining Work, and Remaining Cost. As discussed in the section "Editing Task Actual Duration," the task type determines how work and duration are recalculated.

EDITING ASSIGNMENT ACTUAL WORK

If the assignment (or task) Actual Start displays NA, edits to the assignment Actual Work field cause Project to set the assignment Actual Start to the assignment scheduled Start (and the task Actual Start to the task scheduled Start). They also cause Project to recalculate both assignment and task % Work Complete, Remaining Work, Actual Cost, and Remaining Cost. Project also recalculates task Actual Duration, % Complete, and Remaining Duration.

NOTE

Task Actual Duration is calculated by taking the task Actual Work (the sum of all assignments' actual work) and calculating how long it would have taken to complete that amount of work if *all* assignments (not just the ones that show work completed) had completed work as scheduled. Then % Complete and Remaining Duration are calculated by using that value for Actual Duration.

EDITING ASSIGNMENT % WORK COMPLETE

You can edit the assignment % Work Complete field if you display the Task Usage view with the Work table.

If the assignment has not previously started, edits to this field cause Project to make the assignment Actual Start date equal to the scheduled Start date. Project also sets the task Actual Start equal to the task scheduled Start date if that was also NA. If the edited value of % Work Complete is 100%, the assignment Actual Finish date is set to the scheduled Finish date.

Project also recalculates the assignment and task Actual Work, Remaining Work, % Work Complete, Actual Cost, and Remaining Cost fields. The task Actual Duration, % Complete, and Remaining Duration fields are also updated. If % Complete is 100%, the task Actual Finish date is set equal to the scheduled Finish date.

EDITING ASSIGNMENT REMAINING WORK

The Remaining Work field for assignments is also available on the Task Usage view with the Work table. Edits to this field behave like edits to Remaining Work for tasks. If the assignment is not started, edits to Remaining Work change the scheduled Work for the assignment, and that leads to a change in the scheduled Finish for the assignment (unless the task is Fixed Duration, in which case it might lead to a change in the assigned units).

If the assignment has already started, edits that *decrease* Remaining Work lead to increases in Actual Work and % Work Completed (which then lead to the changes described earlier for edits to Actual Work).

Edits to already started assignments that *increase* Remaining Work redefine the total scheduled Work for the assignment and therefore lead to recalculated values for the assignment's scheduled Finish date, scheduled Cost, and % Work Complete. These in turn lead to recalculated values for the related task fields as well.

Remaining Work is one of the fields made available by default on the timesheet that resources can fill out in Web Access on Project Server and in the email form that you can send to resources for progress reports. Updating the project with this feedback from resources produces edits to assignment Remaining Work, as described in the section "Editing Task Remaining Work," earlier in this chapter.

EDITING ASSIGNMENT TIMEPHASED WORK

If you provide resources with a timecard that allows them to fill in for each day or week the amount of actual work completed (and optionally the amount of actual overtime work as well), updating the project with these timecards produces edits to the assignment timephased fields Actual Work and Actual Overtime Work. These edits lead to recalculated values for assignment Actual Work, Remaining Work, % Work Complete, Actual Cost, and Remaining Cost. Those in turn lead to recalculations of task tracking fields, as described earlier in this chapter, in the section "Editing Assignment Actual Work."

Recall that each cell in the grid covers a time period and that edits to the cell are distributed evenly between the beginning and ending dates for the cell.

If the edited cell is the first actual work recorded (that is, the assignment Actual Start was NA), Actual Start for the assignment is set to the begin date for the cell that you edited. If there is no remaining work after the edit, the assignment Actual Finish is set to the end date for the cell.

If the task type is Fixed Work or Fixed Units and the entered Actual Work is less than the scheduled Work for that cell, the remaining work for the cell is rescheduled after the end date for the assignment. If the entered Actual Work is greater than the scheduled Work for that cell, the excess work is deducted from the end of the assignment. If the task type is Fixed Duration, differences between the scheduled and actual work for the period are evenly distributed among the remaining time periods in the assignment.

If any periods are skipped when entering Actual Work, then the skipped periods get zero timephased Actual Work. The work originally scheduled for those zeroed days is rescheduled at the end of the assignment (unless the task is fixed duration, in which case the work for the assignment is reduced).

UNDERSTANDING THE CALCULATION OPTIONS THAT AFFECT TRACKING

In the previous sections, "Entering Tracking Information at the Task Level" and "Entering Tracking Information at the Assignment Level," the descriptions of edits to task and assignment tracking fields assume that the default calculation options are enabled—specifically, that edits to task status are also applied to assignments and that actual costs are calculated by Microsoft Project. This section examines the impact of those options on tracking calculations and the implications of still other options that are by default disabled.

You can enable or disable each of these options by choosing Tools, Options and clicking the Calculation tab. These are what Project calls "local" settings, which means that the setting of the option (enabled or disabled) is saved in the project file. You can change the default setting for each of the options by clicking the Set As Default button on the Calculation tab.

USING THE UPDATING TASK STATUS UPDATES RESOURCE STATUS OPTION

When Updating Task Status Updates Resource Status is enabled (its default setting), edits to task % Complete cause Project to calculate Actual Work and % Work Complete at both the task and the assignment levels. The link is reciprocal; that is, edits to assignment Actual Work cause Project to recalculate task Actual Duration, % Complete, and Remaining Duration.

When Updating Task Status Updates Resource Status is disabled, note these calculation features:

- Edits to task % Complete affect only task Actual Duration and Remaining Duration. Actual Work, % Work Complete, and Remaining Work remain unaffected at both the task and assignment levels.
- Task Actual Work continues to be the rolled-up sum of assignment Actual Work. Edits at the task level to Actual Work, % Work Complete, and Remaining Work still roll down to assignments. Edits to those fields at the assignment level still roll up to the task.
- Edits to Actual Work (or % Work Complete or Remaining Work) do not affect task % Complete, Actual Duration, or Remaining Duration.

CAUTION

There is one exception to the last point in this list. If you reset each assignment's Actual Work to zero, Project resets task % Complete to 0%–thus causing you to lose any manual edit to the % Complete field. This does not happen if you reset the task Actual Work to zero. This might be an unintended calculation; you would expect it to be consistent whether entered at the task or assignment level.

If you work with Updating Task Status Updates Resource Status disabled and then decide to return the setting to enabled, Project does not immediately recalculate the work and duration tracking fields to align their values—it waits for you to edit either a task duration tracking field (% Complete, Actual Duration, or Remaining Duration) or a work tracking field at either the task or assignment level (Actual Work, % Work Complete, or Remaining Work). If your first edit is to a duration tracking field, Project recalculates the rest of the duration tracking fields and then recalculates all the work tracking fields, using the new Actual Duration. If your first edit is to a work tracking field, Project recalculates all the rest of the task and assignment work tracking fields and then recalculates the duration tracking fields based on your edits to actual work.

TIP

One handy use you can make of disabling the Updating Task Status Updates Resource Status option is to coerce Project into calculating earned value fields by using % Work Complete values instead of % Complete. First, save the file and perform the following steps with a copy of the file that you can delete when you are finished using it:

1. With the Updating Task Status Updates Resource Status option disabled, and with both % Complete and % Work Complete displayed as columns in a task table, select the column for % Work Complete and use the Copy command.
2. Select the column for % Complete and use the Paste command.

TIP

You can then conduct your analysis of earned value, knowing that the earned value calculations are much closer, though still not exactly identical, to those you would get by using the traditional method of calculating earned value. See the section "Analyzing Performance with Earned Value Analysis" in Chapter 15 for more information.

USING THE ACTUAL COSTS ARE ALWAYS CALCULATED BY MICROSOFT PROJECT OPTION

When the Actual Costs Are Always Calculated by Microsoft Project option is enabled (which it is by default), Project calculates Actual Cost as you track progress on the task by adding accrued Fixed Cost to the sum of the Actual Costs for all assignments.

Assignment Actual Cost is calculated as follows:

$$\text{Assignment Actual Cost} = (\text{Actual Work} \times \text{Cost Rate}) + (\text{Actual Overtime Work} \times \text{Overtime Cost Rate}) + \text{Cost Per Use}$$

where the cost rate and overtime cost rates are taken from the cost rate table defined for the assignment.

While Actual Costs Are Always Calculated by Microsoft Project is enabled, you cannot edit Actual Cost at the task or assignment level until the task is 100% complete. When the task is complete, however, you can edit the task Actual Cost field, the assignment's Actual Cost field, and the task or assignment timephased Actual Cost field. (The Remaining Cost field is always a calculated field and can't be edited under any circumstances.)

The following list describes the effects of editing the actual cost fields after the task is complete, when Actual Cost has been calculated by Microsoft Project:

- Edits to assignment Actual Costs roll up to the task Actual Cost. As with other actual fields, the value in Actual Cost is copied to the scheduled Cost field.
- Edits to the assignment timephased Actual Costs also roll up to the task timephased Actual Cost and then to task Actual Cost.
- The task Actual Cost field sums the rolled-up assignment Actual Cost field entries; therefore, edits directly into the task Actual Cost field are *not* rolled down to the assignments. Instead, they are assumed to be actual fixed cost adjustments, and the difference between the edited value and sum for the assignments is added to Fixed Cost (which is then added to the total in the Cost field). The net result is that the Cost field is equal to the Actual Cost field.

Thus, if you increase task Actual Cost by $10, the Fixed Cost field rises by $10 and so does the Cost field. If you decrease task Actual Cost by $10, the Fixed Cost field falls by $10 (and may become a negative amount).

Interestingly, you can enter negative amounts in the Actual Cost field, and these values then also appear in the Cost field. This might be useful if a task has been outsourced to a contractor who incurred such horrific performance penalties that the net cost was negative (that is, penalties outweighed payments).

- Edits to the task timephased Actual Cost field are distributed among assignments for that same time period (in proportion to their share of existing task Actual Cost for that time period). Project then recalculates assignment Actual Cost for each assignment and rolls up the total to the task Actual Cost field. Therefore, edits to task timephased Actual Cost do not lead to a change in Fixed Cost (as direct edits to task Actual Cost do).

You can view Actual Fixed Cost in the timephased Actual Fixed Cost field. The timephased Actual Fixed Cost field is a calculated field only, so you can't edit actual fixed cost here.

If you disable Actual Costs Are Always Calculated by Microsoft Project, you are able to enter your own actual costs—indeed you *have to* enter them because Project no longer calculates the field based on work completed.

The Cost field initially shows the estimated cost of completing a task or an assignment. It is actually calculated as the estimated cost of work that remains to be done plus the actual cost already recorded. Before the task starts, the Cost field shows the same value as the Remaining Cost field (which you can see if you display the Cost table).

Normally, as you record work that is completed, the remaining cost portion of cost falls and is replaced by the actual cost of the completed work. However, if Project is not calculating Actual Cost, the effect on the Cost field when you record actual work is that Cost falls until you enter the Actual Cost field information yourself. If you were to mark a task as 100%, without entering Actual Cost, you would see its Cost field fall to zero.

When you edit the Actual Cost field, the Cost field rises by the same amount as the Actual Cost field. Note that, unlike when Project is calculating actual cost, edits to the Actual Cost field do not change the Fixed Cost field.

You are still unable to overwrite Project's *scheduled* costs for assignments; they continue to be calculated based on resource work and cost rates plus cost per use.

The following list describes the effects of editing the Actual Cost fields when Actual Cost is not calculated by Microsoft Project:

- Edits to assignment Actual Cost or assignment timephased Actual Cost roll up to the task Actual Cost and task timephased Actual Cost and are also added to the assignment Cost.
- Edits to task Actual Cost roll down to the assignments and are distributed among the assignments in proportion to Remaining Cost for the assignments (not counting any Remaining Overtime Cost).

- Edits to task timephased Actual Cost roll down to the assignments in the same time period, also in proportion to Remaining Cost (as evidenced in the timephased Cost field).

Although disabling Actual Costs Are Always Calculated by Microsoft Project might give you more ability to match accounting costs in your project plan, it also means a great deal more work for you and it hides the cost implications of the schedule.

Re-enabling Actual Costs Are Always Calculated by Microsoft Project causes Project to immediately overwrite any manually entered Actual Cost values with the calculated Actual Cost, based on work and % Complete.

When Actual Costs Are Always Calculated by Microsoft Project is disabled, the Edits to Total Actual Cost Will Be Spread to the Status Date suboption becomes available. The Edits to Total Actual Cost Will Be Spread to the Status Date option governs how Project distributes the timephased values when you manually edit the task or assignment Actual Cost field. Normally Actual Cost edits are distributed from the start of the task or assignment as planned in the scheduled cost distribution. If you enable Edits to Total Actual Cost Will Be Spread to the Status Date and then edit task Actual Cost, the increase (or decrease) in task Actual Cost is distributed evenly over the empty timephased cells, starting after the last period in which timephased Actual Cost was recorded up through the Status Date (or the Current Date, if the Status Date has not been defined). Enabling Edits to Total Actual Cost Will Be Spread to the Status Date has the effect of smoothing out the timephased Actual Cost fields.

NOTE

To define Status Date, choose Project, Project Information, and fill in the Status Date field.

Using the Edits to Total Task % Complete Will Be Spread to the Status Date Option

By default, Edits to Total Task % Complete Will Be Spread to the Status Date is disabled. Edits to Total Task % Complete Will Be Spread to the Status Date only affects how timephased % Complete is distributed when you edit the task % Complete field. The distribution of the timephased % Complete field affects earned value calculations and the display of progress lines. It has no impact on how timephased actual work is actually distributed among the time periods.

→ For more information on progress lines, **see** "Using Progress Lines," **p. 559**.

When Edits to Total Task % Complete Will Be Spread to the Status Date is disabled, your edits to the task % Complete field cause the amount of task Actual Work to be calculated and the timephased Actual Work to be distributed from the start of the task as scheduled for all assignments until all the actual work is accounted for. The timephased % Complete field shows the percentage of total work completed in each time period, with the entries adding up to the edited amount for % Complete.

When Edits to Total Task % Complete Will Be Spread to the Status Date is enabled, the timephased Actual Work is distributed exactly the same, but the timephased % Complete field is evenly distributed among the time periods from the last recorded timephased % Complete value to the Status Date (or to the Current Date, if the Status Date has not been defined). This has the effect of smoothing out the increments in earned value over time instead of causing discrete jumps. This option must also be enabled if you want progress lines to connect to tasks that have actual work completed ahead of schedule.

Options to Reschedule Parts of Partially Completed Tasks

Because tasks are rarely completed exactly as scheduled, you often have tasks that should have been completed at the time that you enter tracking information but that still have incomplete work.

In Figure 14.8 the Status Date is the end of Day 5. Task A was not scheduled to begin until Day 6, yet Project shows that Task A already has 2 days of actual duration. Project assumed that the task started as scheduled; therefore, the progress bar falls in the future. The completed portion of the task should be moved back to the left of the status date, to more accurately reflect what actually happened. Furthermore, you don't want resources to be scheduled for work they have already done.

Task D was scheduled to be completed by the status date, but only 2 days of actual duration were reported for the status update. The remaining work still needs to be completed, but it remains scheduled for days that are in the past.

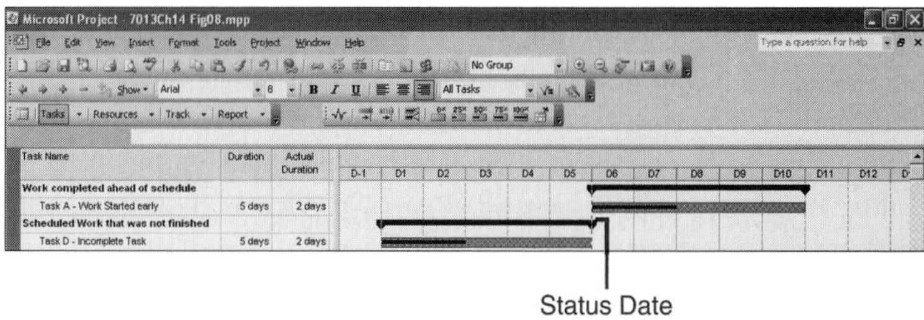

Figure 14.8 Unfinished work that is overdue should be rescheduled to a reasonable start date.

The options that are described in the following sections automatically reschedule parts of tasks like those in this example as you track actual progress. It is important to note that each of these four options functions only at the moment that you enter a change in the amount of the task that is completed. If you enter the tracking information and then turn on the option, Project does not reschedule the work of the task.

NOTE

> The Split In-Progress Tasks check box, which is found on the Schedule tab of the Options dialog box, must be enabled (which it is by default) in order for the following rescheduling options to work.

USING THE MOVE END OF COMPLETED PARTS AFTER STATUS DATE BACK TO STATUS DATE OPTION

As described in the preceding section, Task A in Figure 14.8 was scheduled in the future, but 2 days of work have already been completed. If Move End of Completed Parts After Status Date Back to Status Date is enabled when you record the Actual Work (and by default it is disabled), Project moves the completed part of the task to an earlier date so that the task finishes on the status date. The rescheduled part of the task is illustrated by Task B in Figure 14.9. Using the Move End of Completed Parts After Status Date Back to Status Date option saves you the trouble of remembering to enter the actual start date for tasks that start early.

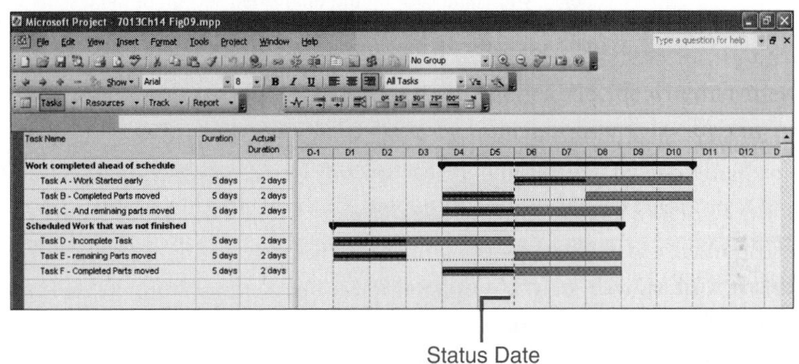

Figure 14.9 Project can automatically reschedule parts of partially completed tasks to correct the schedule.

TIP

> The Move End of Completed Parts After Status Date Back to Status Date feature actually produces a task split; you can drag the right-hand section to the left and right in order to reschedule it.

The And Move Start of Remaining Parts Back to Status Date suboption is by default disabled, and it becomes available only when the Move End of Completed Parts After Status Date Back to Status Date option is enabled.

In Figure 14.9, Task B shows a split in the task, with the remaining work still scheduled to take place when it was originally scheduled. If work is actually going to continue now that the task has started, you would want to move the remaining work to start on the status date. When And Move Start of Remaining Parts Back to Status Date is enabled and you record the actual work on a "future" task, Project not only moves the completed portion before the status date, but it also moves the remaining part to the status date so that work is scheduled to continue uninterrupted. Task C in Figure 14.9 shows the end result.

USING THE MOVE START OF REMAINING PARTS BEFORE STATUS DATE FORWARD TO STATUS DATE OPTION

The Move Start of Remaining Parts Before Status Date Forward to Status Date option, which is disabled by default, can be enabled to automatically reschedule any unfinished work that was scheduled before the status date to start on the status date. You can then move the rescheduled part to even later dates if you choose.

In Figure 14.9, Task D started on schedule but still has unfinished work as of the status date. If this option had been enabled when the actual duration was entered, Project would have entered the scheduled Start in the Actual Start field and automatically rescheduled the remaining duration to start on the status date (as illustrated by Task E). If work will not resume right away, you can drag the remaining duration further to the right, to the date when you want to schedule work to resume.

TIP

> Even if the option to automatically reschedule the unfinished work had not been enabled, you could click on the unfinished section of the taskbar in Task D and drag it to the right to reschedule it. Project would automatically split the task at the end of the actual duration.

When you enable Move Start of Remaining Parts Before Status Date Forward to Status Date, the And Move End of Completed Parts Forward to Status Date suboption becomes available.

When And Move End of Completed Parts Forward to Status Date is enabled, Project also moves the completed section of the task to join the unfinished section at the status date (as illustrated by Task F in Figure 14.9). Thus, if a task started late and is still in progress when you enter the tracking information, And Move End of Completed Parts Forward to Status Date changes the Actual Start of the task to make the completed work finish on the status date and to make the unfinished work start on the status date. This option saves you the trouble of remembering to enter the actual start date for tasks that start late.

CHOOSING A TRACKING METHOD

By far the most convenient tracking method for you to use is to install Project Server and Web Access and let the human resources or their managers record progress on individual assignments. You, as project manager, can then simply elect to update the project with the progress reports that are submitted (or you can reject a report and ask for clarification or changes).

→ For guidelines and instructions about using Project Server to communicate with resources, **see** Chapter 24, "Introduction to Microsoft Office Project Server," **p. 965**.

Each resource has a timesheet view in Web Access that shows just his or her personal assignments, and you can choose which assignment fields to make available to the resource for updating from among the following: % Work Complete, Actual Work, Timephased Actual Work, Remaining Work, Actual Overtime Work, Timephased Actual Overtime Work, and Remaining Overtime Work. You can also have the resource enter Actual Start. When you update the project with this timesheet data, you are editing the assignment fields, and the calculations described in the previous sections govern how Project modifies the project.

You can also use workgroup email to send requests to resources, asking them to fill out a timecard-like form with assignment fields like those described for Project Server. Although this method is not as convenient as using Project Server, it saves you a great deal of time over using manual data entry.

→ For more information on using workgroup email, see "Managing Collaboration with Email Only" on the CD accompanying this book.

If the number of tasks and/or resources is small, you might choose to simply poll resources for information about their progress and manually enter it into the project plan.

The Project Guide toolbar provides a Tracking Setup Wizard to help you choose a tracking method and prepare a customized tracking view. To use the wizard, select Track from the Project Guide toolbar and click Prepare to Track the Progress of Your Project

In the first step of the wizard, Entering Progress, you select Yes if you will be using Project Server, or you select No if you will be entering tracking information manually (see Figure 14.10).

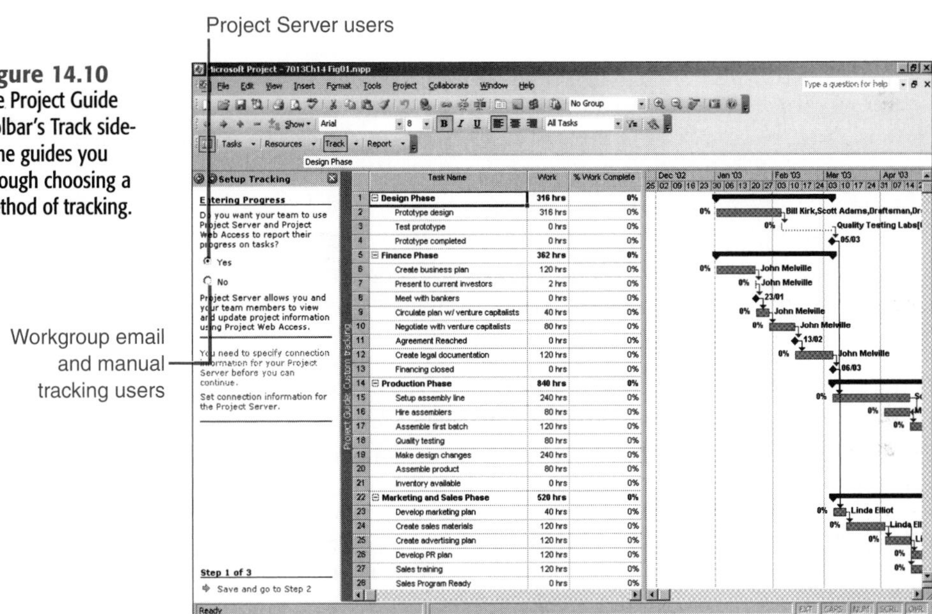

Figure 14.10
The Project Guide toolbar's Track side-pane guides you through choosing a method of tracking.

TIP

> Manual entry is not actually the only alternative to using Project Server to enter tracking information. Even if you don't use Project Server, you still have the option to use regular email to communicate with resources, and (if your email system is 32-bit MAPI compliant) you can update project progress from the email responses almost as easily as you can from the responses of resources through Project Server. Project Server is by far the most robust and rewarding tracking solution; however, it might not be as cost-effective as the email solution in a really small environment.

In the second step of the wizard, Tracking Method, you choose the type of information you normally plan to enter for tracking purposes (see Figure 14.11). This choice does not keep you from entering other tracking information, but it does help Project provide you with a custom view for entering or reviewing tracking information.

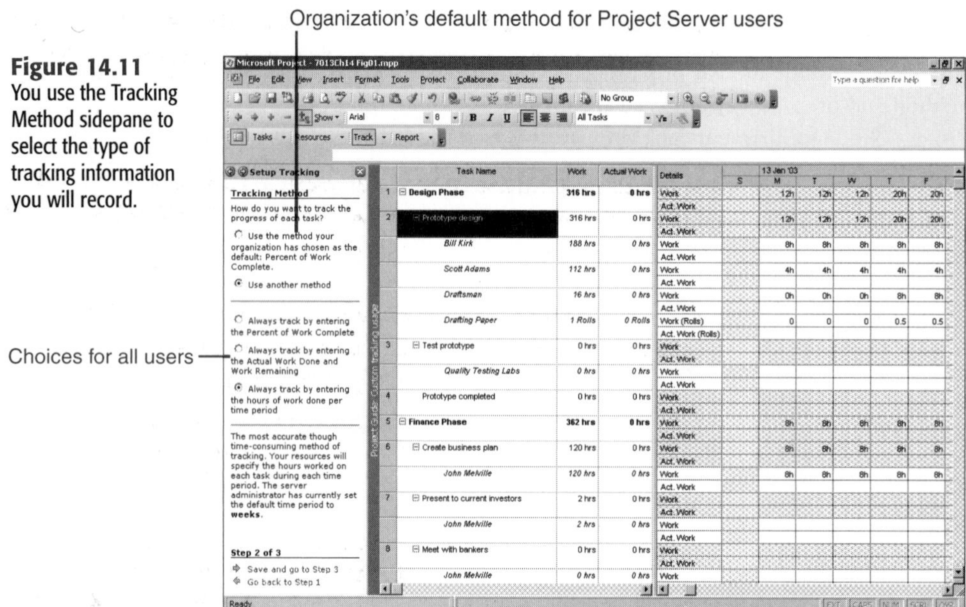

Figure 14.11
You use the Tracking Method sidepane to select the type of tracking information you will record.

If you are using Project Server, you will see a choice to use the tracking method that the Project Server administrator has chosen as a default, which is one of the three choices outlined in the following list, or you can choose your own method from the following list. If you are not using Project Server, you will simply see the following list of choices:

- **Always Track by Entering the Percent of Work Complete**—As the descriptive text in the sidepane indicates, this is the easiest but least precise method of tracking progress. If you choose this method, Project generates a custom view named Project Guide: Custom Tracking that includes the % Work Complete column in a custom task table named Project Guide: Custom Tracking Table.

  Because this view is not based on the Task Usage view, % Work Complete is applied at the task level—not to each resource assignment. In most cases, this produces the same results as when you enter that same value in the % Complete field. However, you might want to replace the % Work Complete field with the % Complete field by double-clicking the column title and changing the Field to % Complete.

- **Always Track by Entering the Actual Work Done and Remaining Work**—By having resources not only record the work completed but also change the remaining work if they think it's not accurate, you get them to alert you to changes in the estimated task duration. The wizard generates a custom view named Project Guide: Custom Tracking that displays a custom table named Project Guide: Custom Tracking Table that includes the Actual Work and Remaining Work fields.

- **Always Track by Entering the Hours of Work Done per Time Period**—This is the most time-consuming of the three methods—especially if you're not using Project Server or workgroup email. However, it provides the most accurate tracking of when work was actually done. The view generated for this choice is named Project Guide: Custom Tracking Usage because it is the Task Usage view with Work and Actual Work details already displayed in the timephased grid. The table has the Work, Actual Work, and Duration fields (among others) for your use. However, it is expected that you will do most of your data entry in the timephased grid.

When you have made a choice, you can click Save and Go To Step 3 if you are connected to Project Server, or you can click Save and Finish if you are not using Project Server. If you go on to Step 3, you can click Customize Information to choose which fields of information are made available for resources to update on the timesheet that is displayed when they log in to Project Server. You can also click Publish Assignments to send all the task assignments to Project Server so that resources can begin filling out their timesheets.

USING PROJECT'S FACILITIES FOR UPDATING TASKS

Microsoft Project provides a number of views and forms for recording tracking information. The following sections describe the ones that are used most frequently.

THE TRACKING TOOLBAR

The Tracking toolbar (refer to Figure 14.11) provides several shortcuts to frequently used menu commands. The ones that are most often used in tracking are the following:

- **Quartile Percentage**—Use these buttons to set % Complete for the selected task(s).

- **Update as Scheduled**—Use this button to set the selected task's Actual Start to its scheduled Start and to record Actual Duration complete through the Status Date (or the Current Date, if Status Date is not defined).

- **Reschedule Work**—Use this button to reschedule incomplete work to start on the status date (or the current date) for the selected task.

- **Add Progress Line**—Use this button to add a line that highlights tasks that have unfinished work as of the date you select for placing the progress line. When you click this button, Project waits for you to click a date on the time line. You can slide the mouse over the current date or the status date and click to display the progress line there. Peaks are drawn from the line to the left for tasks that should be but are not finished as of the progress line date. You can use this device to find tasks that might be missing their tracking information or that need to be rescheduled.

➔ For more information on progress lines, **see** "Using Progress Lines" **p. 559**.

- **Update Tasks**—Use this button to display the Update Tasks form for the selected task(s). See the section "The Update Tasks Form," later in this chapter, for details on how to use this form.

Using these buttons affects only the selected task or tasks.

THE GANTT CHART VIEW

You can use the Gantt Chart view with the Tracking table to edit most of the tracking fields described in this chapter. You can apply the Work table to edit % Work Complete and Remaining Work. If you used the Project Guide toolbar to set up tracking at the task level (as opposed to recording actual hours of work for each resource for each time period), you can display the custom view that was created by clicking on Incorporate Progress Information into the Project in the Track sidepane. Using the Gantt Chart view with those tables allows you to enter task-level tracking data directly into those fields. It also allows you to use the mouse to perform the following tracking functions:

- You can drag the pointer from the start of a task to the right to draw a progress bar and to record actual duration. The pointer turns into a percent sign, and an information box displays the Complete Through date. Complete Through is a tracking field that is not exposed for direct editing except if you drag the mouse. Complete Through marks the end of Actual Duration. When the mouse rests over a progress bar a ScreenTip displays the Complete Through date plus the Actual Start date and the % Complete for the task. You can also edit Actual Duration by dragging the right end of the taskbar.
- You can click on the unfinished part of a partially complete task (the part to the right of the progress bar) and drag to the right to reschedule the remaining work. Project automatically splits the task at the end of the progress bar. After you create the split, you can drag the remaining work to the right or left to reschedule the unfinished work.

To focus on tasks that are not yet complete, you can apply the Incomplete Tasks filter (by choosing Project, Filter For, Incomplete Tasks). To focus on tasks that have started but are not yet complete, you can apply the In Progress Tasks filter.

THE TASK USAGE VIEW AND RESOURCE USAGE VIEW

The Task Usage view and Resource Usage view allow you to enter tracking data at either the task level or the assignment level, and they allow you to enter totals or timephased values.

You should use the Resource Usage view when you have a paper timesheet from an individual resource to be incorporated into the plan. All the assignments for that resource are grouped under the resource name, making it convenient to manually enter all the information for that one resource. Otherwise, you should use the Task Usage view because with it you can edit actual progress at either the task level or the resource level.

You should display the Tracking table with the Task Usage view for maximum flexibility in recording task and assignment progress. If you used Project Guide to set up a tracking view and chose to enter timephased data, the custom view is a Task Usage view with a custom table that includes the Actual Work field. However, the regular Task Usage view with the Tracking table affords more flexibility for tracking.

You can display the timephased tracking fields by choosing Format, Details or Detail Styles. You can use Zoom In or Zoom Out to set the time period intervals you want to use for tracking (hours, days, or weeks). Remember that when Project processes edits to timephased Actual Work cells, it takes the start date of the first cell containing Actual Work hours as the Actual Start for the assignment. Also, the data within each cell is distributed evenly across all the working time spanned by that cell. Therefore, if you enter 8 hours in an Actual Work cell that spans a week (5 working days), Project distributes 1.6 hours of actual work to each day. You need to change the timescale to Days if all 8 hours occur in 1 day.

THE UPDATE TASKS FORM

Even if you do not have a "tracking friendly" view displayed, you can enter task-level tracking information for one or more selected tasks by using the Update Tasks form, which is shown in Figure 14.12. To open this form, choose Tools, Tracking, Update Tasks.

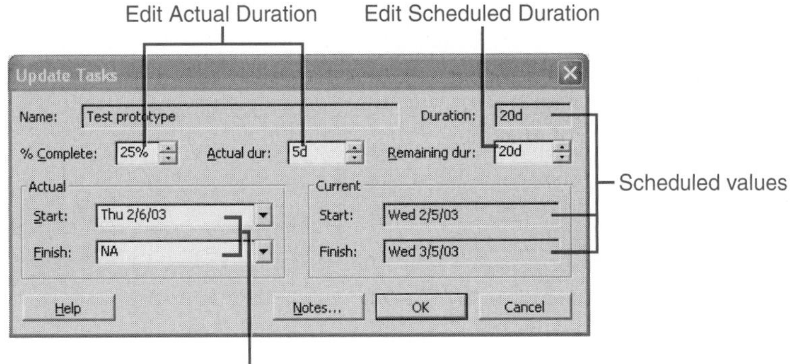

Figure 14.12
You can use the Update Tasks form from any task view to record actuals for selected tasks.

Using the Update Tasks form is sometimes even preferable to using the Tracking table. For example, suppose that a task that is scheduled for 10 days is reported as 60% complete after only 4 days of actual duration. Obviously, the estimated duration of 10 days was too long. If you record 60% complete in the Tracking table, Project changes Actual Duration to 6 days. Changing Actual Duration back to 4 days changes % Complete to 40%. The only way to accurately record this status using the Tracking table is to figure out what the Remaining Duration will be (given the faster performance) and update that field also. It's easier to reset the task to 0% complete, and then open the Update Tasks form and enter **60** in the % Complete field and **4d** in the Actual Duration (Actual Dur.) field. When you click OK, Project calculates the Remaining Duration to be 2.67 days and the new Duration to be 6.67 days (4 days + 2.67 days).

THE UPDATE PROJECT FORM

If your tracking method is not very detailed, you can use the Update Project form to enter tracking information for all tasks that are scheduled to start before the Current Date (or the Status Date). To display the form choose Tools, Tracking, Update Project. Figure 14.13 shows the Update Project form.

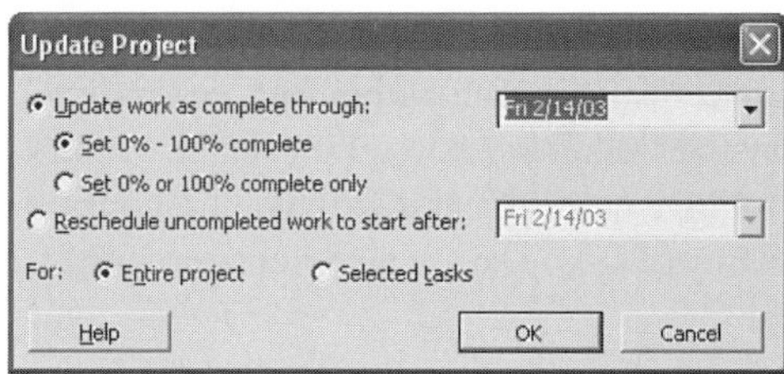

Figure 14.13
You use the Update Project form for very general tracking with little detail.

You can quickly perform two tracking functions with this form, and by default they both apply to all tasks in the project (or just those you have selected) that are scheduled to start before the status date: You can update work as complete through the status date, or you can reschedule uncompleted work to start on a date that you choose.

USING THE UPDATE WORK AS COMPLETE THROUGH OPTION

You can use the Update Work as Complete Through option to mark all scheduled work as completed up through the status date. If you have defined a status date, this date appears by default in the date box. Otherwise, the current date appears.

NOTE

> If you edit the Date box, the new date becomes the project status date.

When you use this option, Project sets the actual start date equal to the scheduled start date for all tasks that were scheduled to start before the status date, and it also sets the actual finish date to the scheduled finish date for tasks that were scheduled to finish before the status date.

If you use the default suboption Set 0% - 100% Complete, Project also sets actual duration as complete through the status date and calculates % Complete. If you select the suboption Set 0% or 100% Complete Only, tasks that were scheduled to finish on or before the Status Date are also marked 100% complete. Those that are not marked complete are left with 0% in the % Complete field.

By default the option Entire Project is selected, and changes are applied to all tasks in the project. If you want to apply the update to only selected tasks, you need to select them before displaying the form and click the Selected Tasks option on the form.

USING THE RESCHEDULE UNCOMPLETED WORK TO START OPTION

Instead of marking work that was scheduled before the status date as completed, the Reschedule Uncompleted Work to Start option assumes that the work was not completed and needs to be rescheduled. If you use this option, you need to be sure that the date in the top date box is the date by which work should have been completed. Then you need to enter the date when work is to resume in the second date box (next to this option). By default the second date box shows the current date (or status date, if defined). You can change it to any date. Editing this date does not reset the project status date.

Also, you should click Selected Tasks only if you have already selected a subset of tasks to be updated.

When you click OK, Project reschedules any uncompleted work for tasks that have started to the date entered in the second date box.

NOTE

The Split In-Progress Tasks check box, which is found on the Schedule tab of the Options dialog box, must be enabled (which it is by default) in order for this rescheduling option to work.

You can think of the Reschedule Uncompleted Work to Start feature as "the bulldozer of time." In other words, whatever work is not completed is automatically moved (or rescheduled) to the current date entered. This procedure ensures that the work is constantly moved forward and accounted for within the project.

For a task that has not started but should have, Project reschedules the entire task by giving it a Start No Earlier Than constraint for the date shown in the second date box. In earlier versions of Project this happened to all tasks—even those that had hard constraints defined for them. Project 2003 does not reschedule a task if it has any type of constraint other than As Soon As Possible or As Late As Possible. A Planning Wizard dialog box alerts you if one or more tasks had constraints (see Figure 14.14) and suggests that you examine the tasks individually for possible rescheduling.

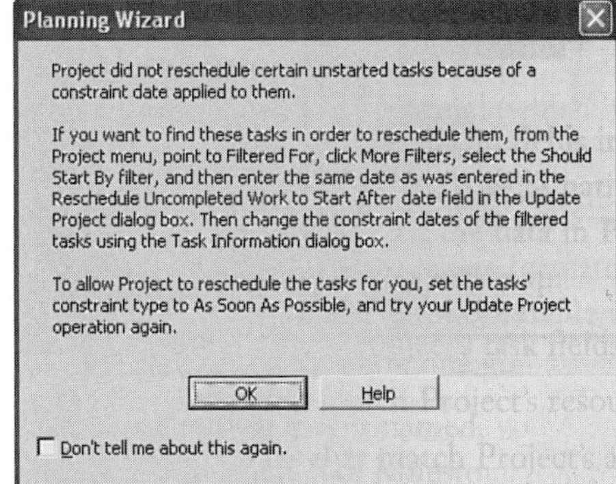

Figure 14.14
Tasks with constraints are not rescheduled, as explained by the Planning Wizard dialog box that appears.

If you see this Planning Wizard dialog box, you have to deal with rescheduling the constrained tasks manually. As the dialog box suggests, you can identify the tasks that were not rescheduled by applying the Should Start By task filter. To do this, choose Project, Filtered For, More Filters, and then select Should Start By and click Apply. This is an interactive filter, and it asks you to supply the start by date (the date by which tasks should have started). Enter the current date (or the status date, if it is defined) because that is the date that was used in the Update Project command. The filter then selects all tasks that have not started but that have scheduled start dates that are before the date you entered.

You can reschedule a constrained task manually by selecting it and displaying its Task Information dialog box. Then, change the Constraint Type on the Advanced tab to Start No Earlier Than, and enter the rescheduled date in the Constraint Date box. If you want to remove all the constraints and run the Update Project reschedule command again, select all the constrained tasks, click the Task Information button to display the Multiple Task Information dialog box, change the Constraint Type to As Soon As Possible, and click OK.

CHAPTER 15

Analyzing Progress and Revising the Schedule

In this chapter

Project Management Overview 556

Reviewing the Current Status of a Project 557

Analyzing Performance with Earned Value Analysis 575

Revising a Schedule to Complete on Time and on Budget 595

Troubleshooting 599

PROJECT MANAGEMENT OVERVIEW

Chapter 14, "Tracking Work on a Project," examines the important process of recording actual work and cost for a project. This chapter looks at using the information you get as a result of that effort. Microsoft Project 2003 offers a number of techniques for evaluating the status of a project and for comparing actual performance with the scheduled performance and with the planned performance, as captured in the baseline.

The iterative process model of project management supported by Project Management Institute (PMI) involves steps for initiating, planning, executing, controlling, and closing. The controlling aspect of the model requires the project manager to step back from the project and ask, "How are we doing?" After evaluation, it is often necessary to implement a change control, which requires a return to planning before re-executing work. This then completes the feedback loop of the process model.

Projects invariably deviate from their original plans. They take more or less time to complete, involve more or less work, or cost more or less than budgeted in the plan that was adopted and captured in the baseline. If you track actual performance from the start of a project and compare those results with the original plan, you will be in a position to correct, or at least mitigate, any unfavorable deviations from the plan.

The process of adjusting the project schedule to align it again with the baseline, which is evaluated through variance analysis, is called *corrective action*.

As a project manager, you should expect to make changes to control the schedule because changes are an inevitable part of managing a project. In other words, you will always have variance because projects rarely proceed exactly as planned. In the project manager role, you are most interested in what the tolerance is for making changes to the schedule to ensure conformity to the baseline, and what the impact is to the project in terms of dates, durations, costs, and work estimates.

The project plan, as captured in the baseline, represents the *best estimate* of how the project will proceed, as envisioned by the project manager, the project team, and all other project stakeholders. The baseline is also the benchmark against which progress is measured. If actual progress is not keeping up with the performance assumed in the baseline, then corrective actions should be put in place to get back on track, or the project will likely not finish when planned or within the budget. This chapter explains the tools that Microsoft Project provides to review the status of a project and to assess the implications of past performance on the remainder of a project. This chapter also discusses what you must do to bring an errant project back on track.

The techniques introduced in this chapter are discussed in increasing level of sophistication. We begin by showing simply how to spot tasks that are behind (or ahead of) schedule. We then look at how Project uses variance calculations to show the impact that actual performance and changes in the schedule have had on the estimated final finish date and cost of the project. Finally, we use earned value analysis to assess whether the effort and cost incurred to date have produced the output that was expected and to estimate what the final finish date and cost of the project will be if the current rate of progress continues.

We conclude with a general discussion of the adjustments to the schedule that might be necessary to get a project back on track and within budget.

REVIEWING THE CURRENT STATUS OF A PROJECT

The first level of analysis is to simply review progress vis-à-vis the current schedule and to assess the effects of actual performance on Project's estimated finish date and cost for the project. To do this you can use the Status and Status Indicator fields, or you can use the graphical progress lines to quickly distinguish between the tasks that are on schedule and the tasks that are behind schedule. You can also use reports and views that show how the actual performance has modified the scheduled finish date and cost of the project that was captured in the baseline.

REVIEWING STATUS VIS-À-VIS THE CURRENT SCHEDULE

The first line of defense against having a project finish late is to watch for tasks that are behind schedule. Project 2003 provides two fields that you can add to a table to see instantly whether there are unfinished tasks that are behind schedule. Or you use *progress lines* in the Gantt Chart view if you prefer to see this information in a graphical display. You can also apply special filters that allow you to focus on just the tasks and assignments that are slipping.

USING THE STATUS AND STATUS INDICATOR FIELDS

The current schedule tells you when tasks are supposed to finish, and it also contains timephased data that shows how much work should be completed during each day of the project. If tracking information has been accurately recorded, then you can look at the schedule for any given date to see if the tasks that should be finished by that date are finished and if the tasks that should be partially completed are progressing as scheduled. The Status field does this comparison for you and labels each task as completed, in progress and on schedule, in progress and behind schedule, or as a future task (not yet due to be started). It uses the status date that you enter in the Project Information dialog box for this comparison, or, if you haven't entered a status date, it uses the current date. To set a status date, choose Project, Project Information, enter the date in the Status Date field, and click OK. To clear the Status Date enter **NA** in the Status Date field.

The Status Indicator field does exactly the same thing as the Status field, but it displays an indicator instead of a text label. Figure 15.1 shows the Status and Status Indicator fields, showing which tasks are complete, which are on schedule, which are late (behind schedule), and which are future tasks.

The four status labels and their indicators are listed in Table 15.1.

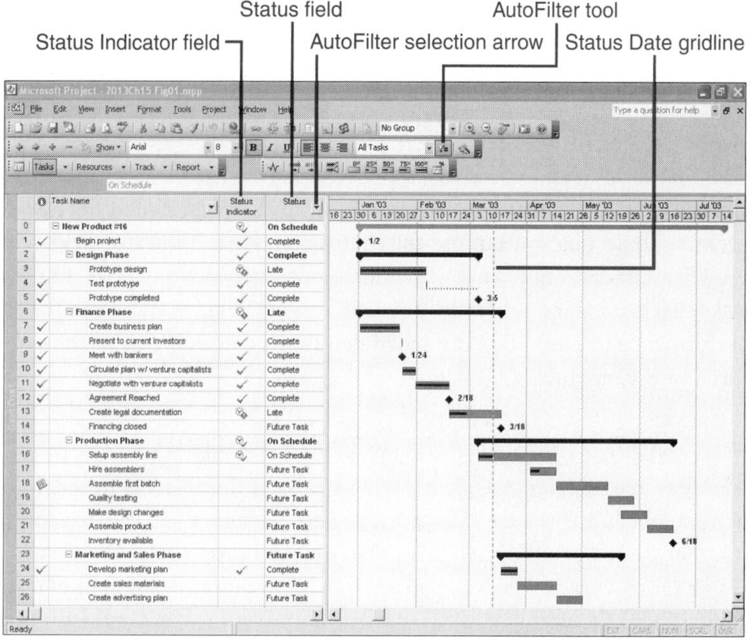

Figure 15.1
The Status and Status Indicator fields quickly reveal the tasks that are behind schedule.

TABLE 15.1 STATUS LABELS AND INDICATORS

Status	Indicator	Explanation
Complete		This status indicates that the task is 100% complete.
On Schedule		This status indicates that the task is not yet complete, but all work that is scheduled for completion by the status date has been completed.
Late		This status indicates that there is work that is scheduled to be completed by the status date which has not been completed.
Future	(no indicator)	This status indicates that the task is not scheduled to start until after the status date. There is no indicator for future tasks.

You can click the AutoFilter tool on the Formatting toolbar if you want to filter the task list for just the tasks marked Late. Then you can click the drop-down selection arrow in the title cell of the Status field and choose Late. Project then hides all but the late tasks and their summary tasks. You can Press F3 to clear the filter.

USING PROGRESS LINES

A *progress line* is a line that is drawn vertically down the Gantt Chart view on a particular date of interest. The date is usually the current date or the status date when tracking information was last updated. The progress line is intended to lead your eye quickly to tasks that are either behind or ahead of schedule. Figure 15.2 shows a progress line at the status date (3/13/03), and the spikes to the left draw your attention to tasks that have not been completed as scheduled as of the progress line date. The spikes to the right point to tasks for which work has been done ahead of schedule.

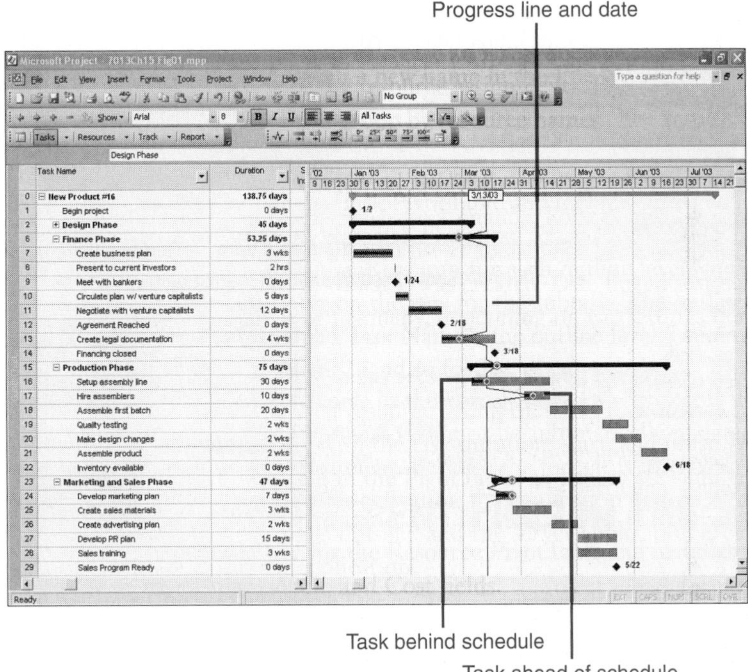

Figure 15.2
The progress line indicates whether you are running behind schedule or have completed work ahead of schedule.

The progress line is centered over the date that you select. The date can be the current date, the status date, or another specific date of interest to you. If a future or past task has started but not finished, the progress line connects to the point in its taskbar that represents the percentage complete for the task's duration. In the default Gantt Chart view, there is a black progress bar already drawn up to that point in the middle of the taskbar. If a task is scheduled for the past and has not started, its percentage complete is zero and the progress line connects to the task's start date. If the task is scheduled for the future and is complete, the progress line connects to the task's finish date (the end of its progress bar). The progress line ignores past tasks that are already completed and future tasks that have not started. Thus, the progress line peaks to the left to show tasks that are behind schedule as of the progress line date and peaks to the right to show tasks that are ahead of schedule.

NOTE

In order for progress lines to be drawn to future tasks that already have actual work, the option labeled Edits to Total Task % Complete Will Be Spread to the Status Date (which is found on the Calculation tab of the Options dialog box) must be enabled when you record the actual work for those tasks.

Perhaps the most common progress bar is one that is drawn for the project's status date, as shown in Figure 15.2. To draw this progress line, you choose Tools, Tracking, Progress Lines to display the Progress Lines dialog box (see Figure 15.3). You can also right-click over the graphic area of the Gantt Chart view and choose Progress Lines from the shortcut menu. Select the check box labeled Always Display Current Progress Line, and then check the option At Project Status Date. By default, this special progress line displays in red on the Gantt Chart view. You can choose instead to display the current progress line at the current date. If you haven't defined the status date in the Project Information dialog box, Project uses the current date.

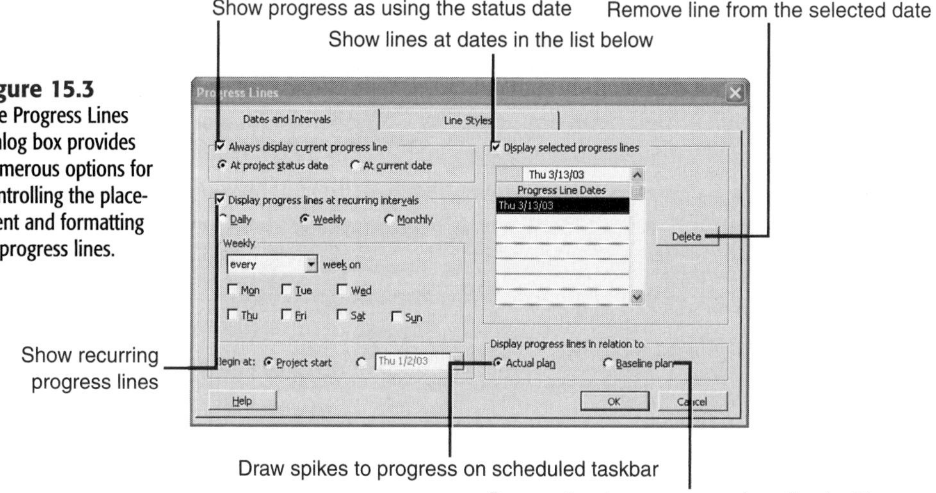

Figure 15.3
The Progress Lines dialog box provides numerous options for controlling the placement and formatting of progress lines.

To display a progress line on a specific date, select the Display Selected Progress Lines check box, enter the date in the Progress Line Dates list box, and click OK. You can display multiple progress lines by adding more dates to the list. To remove a date from the list, select it and press the Delete key or click the Delete button. To temporarily hide these progress lines, clear the Display Select Progress Lines check box. The date list remains, and you can redeploy those progress lines later by selecting the check box.

You can also have Project display progress lines at regular intervals. To do this, you can use the options in the Display Progress Lines group to define how often the lines will occur (daily, weekly, or monthly) and exactly when, within each time unit, they will be drawn. By default, the recurring progress lines begin at the start of the project, but you can also define a different start date for the series of progress lines.

Progress lines are usually drawn using dates in the current schedule. In the bottom-right corner of the Progress Lines dialog box, you can choose to use dates in the baseline schedule instead. The default is Actual Plan, which means you want to use the current schedule, including actual start and finish dates. If you choose Baseline Plan, Project draws the progress line to the date that represents the percentage complete, as applied to the baseline schedule. If the Gantt Chart view displays baseline bars, the progress line is drawn to the baseline bars. If it does not, the progress line is drawn to the calculated date anyway, even if that doesn't fall on a scheduled taskbar.

TIP

After you display a progress line, you can double-click anywhere on the progress line to display the Progress Lines dialog box to modify the display.

The Line Styles tab on the Progress Lines dialog box provides numerous options for displaying progress lines. These display options give you a great degree of control over the types, colors, shapes, and date interval of progress lines. Figure 15.4 shows the Progress Lines dialog box with the Line Styles tab selected.

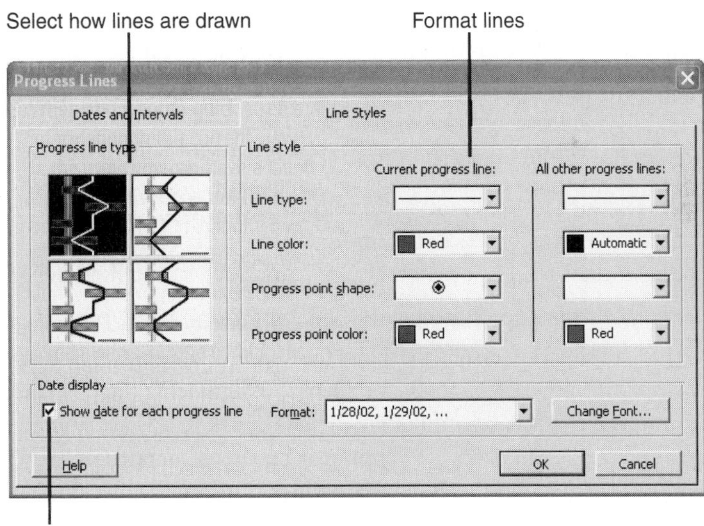

Figure 15.4
The Line Styles tab in the Progress Lines dialog box allows you to format the look of progress lines.

You can also display a progress line at a selected date by using the Add Progress Line tool on the Tracking toolbar. When you click the tool, the mouse pointer changes shape to look like a progress line, and a Progress Line information box pops up as you move the pointer over the timeline in the Gantt Chart view. The information box displays the date that

Project will use to display the progress line if you click where the pointer is currently located. Figure 15.5 shows the information box.

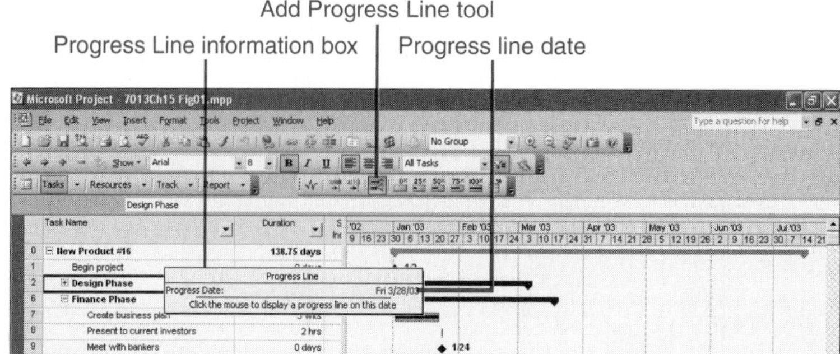

Figure 15.5
The Progress Line information box displays the date on which the progress line will be placed.

FILTERING FOR SLIPPING TASKS

Another quick way to identify tasks that are not on schedule is to apply a filter to a task or resource table, to display only tasks and/or resource assignments that are not on schedule. Project's Slipping Tasks and Slipping Assignments filters show you tasks and assignments that are not on schedule. A task or an assignment is said to be *slipping* when it's not yet finished and its scheduled finish date is after its baseline finish date.

To apply the Slipping Tasks filter, choose Project, Filtered For, More Filters. Select the Slipping Tasks filter from the list and click Apply (or click Highlight to show all tasks but apply highlighting to those that are slipping). You can also select the filter from the Filter drop-down list on the Formatting toolbar.

In a task view such as the Gantt Chart view, the Slipping Tasks filter shows which unfinished tasks are currently scheduled to finish after their baseline finish dates. If the baseline has not been captured for a task, that task will not be selected by the filter.

If you apply the Slipping Tasks filter to the Task Usage view, Project selects resource assignments that are slipping, displaying both the slipping assignment and its task. This affords you the opportunity to zero in on the specific assignments that are causing a task to slip. Note, however, that the selection may include a task that is *not* slipping but has one or more resources whose assignments are slipping. That would happen only if the slipping assignments were scheduled to finish before the task finishes.

You can apply a similar filter for resources, the Slipping Assignments filter, to the Resource Usage view to see slipping assignments grouped by resource. This view affords the opportunity to see whether some resources have a significantly larger number of slipping assignments than others. Armed with this information, you can investigate the causes and perhaps correct the problem.

When you analyze slipping tasks, you should pay special attention to tasks that are critical. Critical tasks contribute to the longest path in the project and push out the expected finish date. Identifying these tasks allows a project manager to concentrate on shortening those tasks (called *crashing the schedule*) in order to ensure that the project finishes on time. Of course, the critical path might change to another "longer" path following crashing, so you then need to consider crashing tasks on the new critical path.

Reviewing Status vis-à-vis the Project Plan

The previous section describes ways to identify problems with tasks that have not or are not scheduled to finish on time. The Status and Status Indicator fields tell you only whether work is progressing as currently scheduled—they do not tell you if a project is progressing as defined in the baseline. This is also true for progress lines that are drawn to the scheduled dates.

When you record actual progress, Microsoft Project recalculates the estimated final finish date, the total work, and the cost of the task and the project. The features described in the previous section do not help you identify changes in the total effect on tasks or the project. The following sections look at ways to examine the impact of schedule changes and actual performance on those estimates of final results.

Defining Variances

You can use a variety of tables, filters, views, and reports to quickly identify how a project's schedule is deviating from the baseline. Before we get into the analysis of progress, we need to take a look at how Project calculates and stores the information that we will use.

For certain key measures (duration, work, cost, start date, and finish date) Project automatically calculates a *variance* when a difference occurs between the value in the current schedule and the value in the baseline. The *variance* fields are Duration Variance, Work Variance, Cost Variance, Start Variance, and Finish Variance. To the extent that values in the current schedule match those in the baseline, the variances will be zero. Changes in the schedule produce nonzero variances.

To calculate a variance, Project takes the value in the current schedule and subtracts the baseline value, as follows:

Duration Variance	=	Duration	–	Baseline Duration
Work Variance	=	Work	–	Baseline Work
Cost Variance	=	Cost	–	Baseline Cost
Start Variance	=	Start	–	Baseline Start
Finish Variance	=	Finish	–	Baseline Finish

15

NOTE

> If you fail to capture the baseline, the variances will be equal to the scheduled values.

When the current schedule's value is greater than the baseline value—in other words, when the current schedule value is greater than planned—the resulting variance will be a positive number. Positive variances are considered unfavorable; they mean that the current schedule calls for a longer duration, more work, more cost, and a later start or a later finish than the original plan, as recorded in the baseline. Conversely, negative variances are considered favorable because they mean that the current schedule calls for a shorter duration, less work, less cost, an earlier start, or an earlier finish than the baseline.

Until you enter actual values to track progress on a task, the variances show the differences between the current estimated values of the schedule and the estimated values in the baseline. When you update the project by tracking actual progress, Project automatically replaces the estimated values of the current schedule with the actual values. Therefore, when actual values are entered, the variance fields show the difference between what actually happened and the original plan. Thus, if Task A actually starts on Monday, May 13, but it was originally scheduled to start on Monday, May 6, Project replaces the current estimated start date with the actual start date, and it calculates the start variance to be 5 working days. If Project didn't update the scheduled start date, it couldn't calculate the ripple effect that the delayed start will have on the start of other tasks that are successors to Task A.

In addition to the variances, Project also calculates two fields that show the percentage complete for tasks: % Complete (which is the percentage of the duration that is complete) and % Work Complete (which is the percentage of work that is complete). Note that unlike the variance fields, these two fields compare actual and scheduled values, not scheduled and baseline values.

It is important to understand the differences between these two fields because they give you two different perspectives on progress:

- **% Complete**—This field is based on duration and is calculated as actual duration divided by scheduled duration. It shows what percentage of the working time that was scheduled for finishing the task has been used up.
- **% Work Complete**—This field is based on work and is calculated as actual work divided by scheduled work. It shows the percentage of scheduled work that has been completed.

You might expect that these two percentages would always be equal, reasoning that if you've worked 40% of the time allotted to a task, then you should have completed 40% of the work. But the two measures can differ for a number of reasons. For example, a resource might actually work overtime while working 40% of the duration, thus doing more than 40% of the work. Or, one or more resources assigned to the task might have been scheduled with delayed start dates for their part of the task's work, thus scheduling more work per day in the final days of the task duration than in the beginning days.

REVIEWING STATUS AT THE PROJECT LEVEL

There are several easy ways to get a quick overview of how an entire project is performing against the schedule and against the original plan. The Project Statistics dialog box and the Project Summary Report both display summary statistics for the overall project in one compact image. You can also display the project summary task in a view and use several predefined tables to see the same information.

DISPLAYING PROJECT STATISTICS

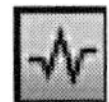

The quickest way to see a project's overall progress in a single view is to display the Project Statistics dialog box (see Figure 15.6). You can open this dialog box by clicking the Project Statistics tool from the Tracking toolbar, or you can choose Project, Project Information, and click the Statistics button. The Project Statistics dialog box shows the project's current (scheduled), baseline, and actual start and finish dates, as well as the start and finish variances. For duration, work, and cost, the dialog box shows the current, baseline, actual, and remaining values (but no variances for these three aspects of the project). The bottom of the dialog box shows the percentage complete for duration (% Complete) and work (% Work Complete). Figure 15.6 shows the project statistics for the example we've been using.

Project Statistics for '7013Ch15 Fig06.mpp'

	Start	Finish
Current	Thu 1/2/03	Tue 7/15/03
Baseline	Thu 1/2/03	Tue 7/8/03
Actual	Thu 1/2/03	NA
Variance	0d	5d

	Duration	Work	Cost
Current	138.75d	3,502h	$86,306.00
Baseline	133.75d	3,390h	$83,946.00
Actual	48.37d	762h	$23,280.00
Remaining	90.38d	2,740h	$63,026.00

Percent complete:
Duration: 35% Work: 22%

Close

Figure 15.6
The Project Statistics dialog box shows a snapshot of the current plan versus the baseline plan.

THE PROJECT SUMMARY REPORT

Similar to the Project Statistics dialog box, the Project Summary report displays an analysis of the current versus baseline plans for the entire project. In addition, it also includes the variances for duration, work, and cost. To preview the report choose View, Reports, and then double-click Overview and double-click Project Summary. Project shows a preview screen of the one-page report (see Figure 15.7), which you can review onscreen or send to a printer.

USING THE PROJECT SUMMARY TASK

You can see most of the same summary data that is shown in the Project Statistics dialog box and Project Summary report by displaying the project summary task in views that include tables. To display a project summary task, choose Tools, Options, and then select the View tab and select the check box next to Show Project Summary Task. The information in the first row of the summary summarizes the entire project. However, you have to apply different tables to see the full range of data that is displayed in the Project Statistics dialog box or the Project Summary report, and even then not all the statistics are included

15

on the standard tables that are included in Project. For example, Duration Variance is not on any of the standard task tables, and to see that you would have to add the field to a table.

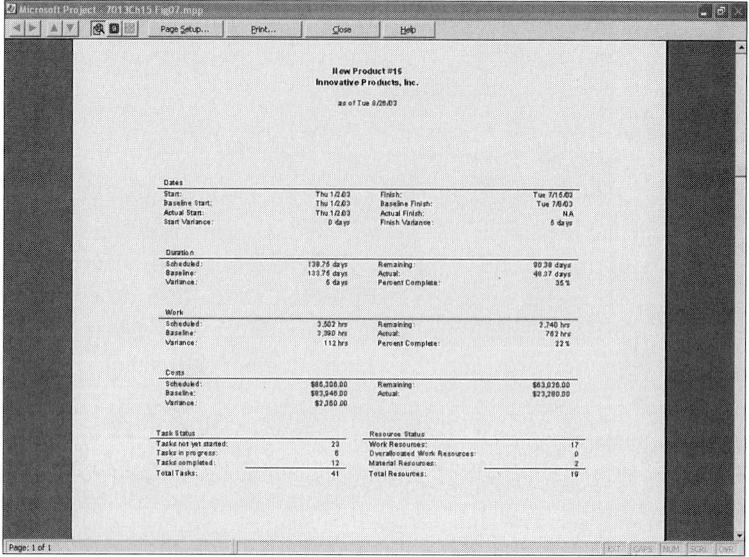

Figure 15.7
Part of the Print Preview screen for the Project Summary report.

As a rule, it is a good practice to have a project summary task on all of your projects. You can create it by turning on the option outlined previously. Or you can create a project summary task by defining the first task as a project summary and then indenting, or "demoting," all subsequent tasks underneath it.

You can also create your own project summary task by inserting a task at the top of the project and indenting all other tasks beneath it. However, this method has drawbacks. The built-in project summary task does not alter the Work Breakdown Structure (WBS); Project assigns it the ID 0 while maintaining the numbering of the other tasks. In contrast, when you demote all other tasks to create a project summary task, the project summary is assigned the task ID 1. Not only would the WBS coding be burdened with an unnecessary level, but the filters and special analysis views that are discussed later in this chapter could give misleading results (as noted in the following sections). Furthermore, you lose the advantage of easily toggling the display of the summary task for printing and customization purposes.

NOTE

There is one very useful application for creating a project summary task. If you consolidate multiple projects in Project Standard in order to get an overview of progress for a project portfolio, the project summary task you create provides baseline information at the project level that Microsoft Project does not provide in the consolidated file. Without that project-level baseline information, you can't display the baseline schedule for the projects in the portfolio.

If you are using Project 2003 Standard and want to consolidate your projects into one file in order to get an overview of progress on your project portfolio, see "Displaying Variances in a Consolidated File" in the "Troubleshooting" section at the end of this chapter. If you are using Project 2003 Professional, you automatically get an analysis of your portfolio when you use Microsoft Project Web Access and display the Projects view.

You can apply the Work table to review total project work, including the scheduled, baseline, variance, actual, remaining, and percentage of work complete values. To apply this table, you can right-click on the Select All button to display the Tables shortcut menu and then choose Work (see Figure 15.8).

Figure 15.8 shows that the total work variance is 112 hours (which is unfavorable) and that 22% of the work is complete.

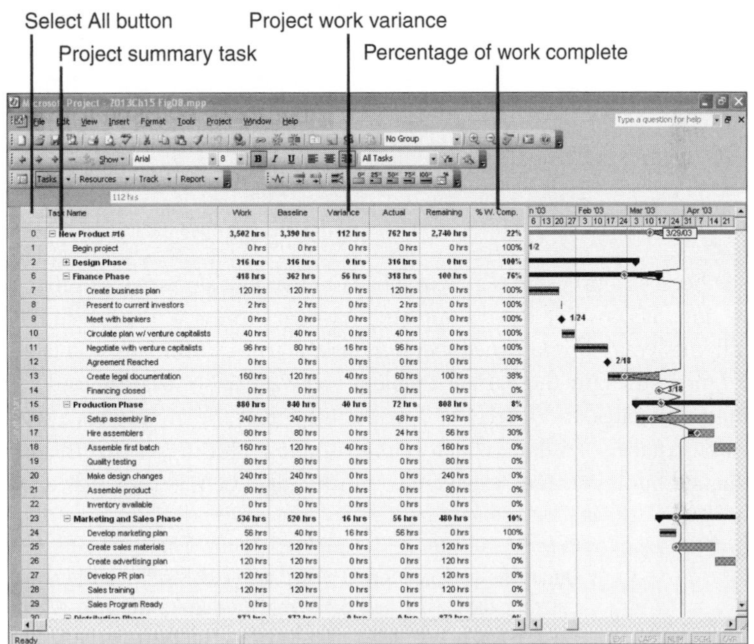

Figure 15.8
Work table values roll up to the project summary task.

You can use the Tables shortcut menu to apply the Cost table if you want to review a project's overall costs. Figure 15.9 shows the Cost Variance field for the project. The project summary task shows a total cost variance of $2,360.00 (which is unfavorable). The original estimated cost (baseline) was $83,946, but based on current progress, the project is expected to go over budget, with a total cost of $86,306.

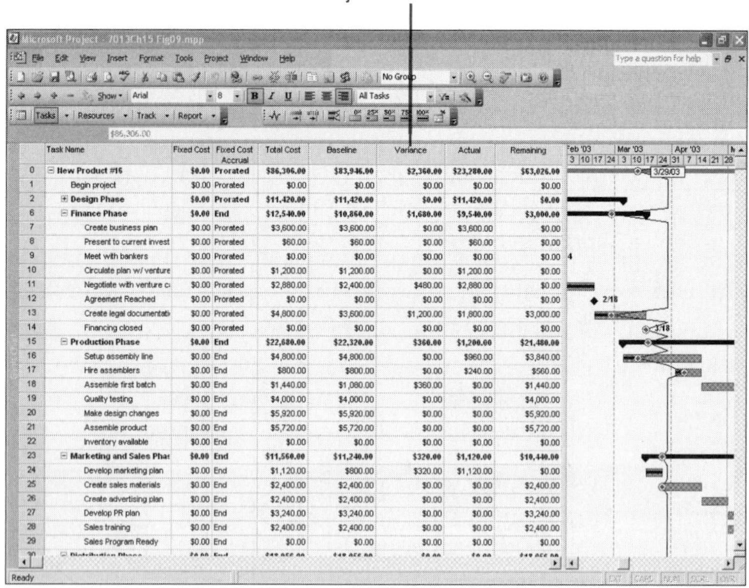

Figure 15.9
The project summary task shows total cost data for the project when the Cost table is applied.

Just because a project has a favorable work variance doesn't mean that the project will finish on time. It's possible to be completing tasks according to the baseline work estimates but to still miss your targeted finish because tasks start or finish late. You can use the Tables shortcut menu to apply the Variance table if you want to see baseline and variance values for start and finish dates. In Figure 15.10, you can see that the project has a start variance of 0 but a finish variance of 5 days (which is unfavorable). This means that the project started as planned but is currently expected to finish 5 days behind the original schedule.

TIP

During the tracking process, you should consistently update actual start and actual finish dates for each task if they differ from the current schedule. When you enter an actual finish date that is later than originally estimated, there can be two important effects to note. First, if the total duration from actual start to actual finish is longer than the projected duration, Project will not only increase the total actual duration for the task but will also increase the actual work and actual cost (if you have not turned off the default calculation option Updating Task Status Updates Resource Status). Second, successor tasks will also be delayed. If the task that is being delayed is on the critical path, your project's overall finish date will likely be pushed to a later date.

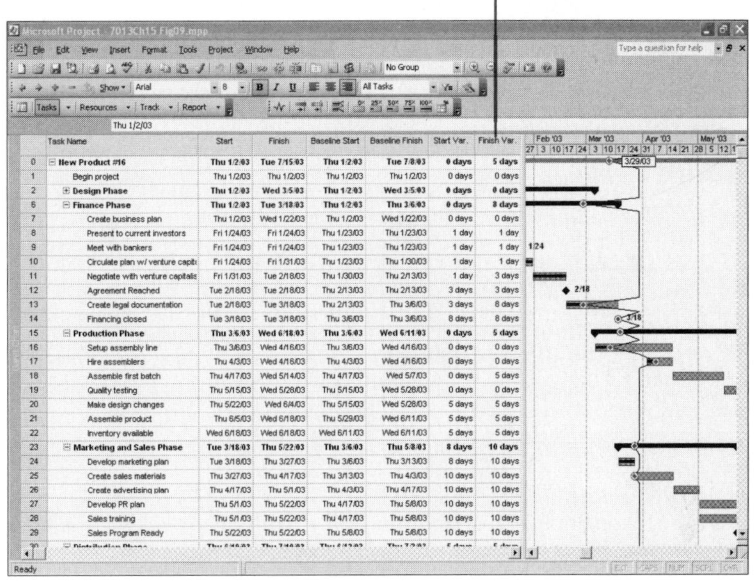

Figure 15.10 Project variances are shown on the project summary task with the Variance table applied.

Show ▾

After you review the values for the overall project, you can go to the next level of detailed analysis and examine the highest-level summary tasks in your project. These high-level summary tasks are often called *phases*. To review progress statistics by phase, you can hide all but the top-level tasks (those at Outline Level 1). The simplest way to do this is to choose Outline Level 1 on the drop-down list of the Show tool on the Formatting toolbar. These tasks are usually summary tasks, but there might also be individual tasks at high outline levels.

It is good practice to have a minimum of three levels within a project. These levels are typically identified as project level, phase level, and work (or activity) level.

The project-level summary task would be at Level 1, as described earlier in this chapter.

Level 2 defines the phases of work to be completed and typically corresponds to a WBS, which is the skeletal structure of the project, each defining a unique deliverable for that component of the project. Examples include the design phase, production phase, and financing phase.

Finally, the work level is the lowest level, where the activity is identified, the resource is assigned, and dependencies are established.

15

CAUTION

In most cases, you can also apply the Top Level Tasks filter to hide all tasks below Outline Level 1. However, if you have created a Summary task by inserting a task on Row 1 and demoted all other tasks beneath it, the "top level" tasks that you want to display will be at Outline Level 2. In that case, you should use the Show tool and select Outline Level 2. This is another reason to use the Show Project Summary Task option in the Options dialog box instead of manually demoting all tasks under a Summary task that you create.

To apply the Top Level Tasks filter to hide Top Level Tasks filter, click the arrow in the Filter button on the Formatting toolbar and select Top Level Tasks. You can apply the Cost, Work, or Variance tables, combined with the Top Level Tasks filter, to analyze the variances for the phases in the project.

Reviewing Status at the Task Level

It's a good idea to plan to analyze variances in your schedule at least as often as you track progress. If you apply actual and remaining work on a weekly basis, you should plan to analyze variances on a weekly basis. It doesn't do much good to key in actuals every week and then not pay attention to what these numbers are telling you. Subtle increases of work and costs over the original baseline can add up quickly. The sooner you spot trouble and revise the plan, the more likely you are to achieve the project's objectives of on-time, on-budget completion.

BEST PRACTICE TIP

Remember that a "revised" plan includes not only scheduled dates but also changes in estimates of durations, work, and costs.

Costs can be adjusted one of two ways: changes made to resource assignments and/or additions or deletions of fixed costs. Also, changes to calendars can modify the schedule as to when work is performed on the project. These changes can be made to the overall project calendar or to specific resource calendars. Either one can affect the scheduling of the remaining tasks within the project.

Project provides a number of views, filters, and reports to assist you in spotting trouble at the task level of detail. Let's take a look at how you can analyze variances that are occurring on individual tasks in a plan.

To quickly isolate unfavorable values for a variance field, you can use AutoFilter to find positive (that is, unfavorable) variances. First apply the Cost, Work, or Variance table. Then enable AutoFilter by clicking the AutoFilter button on the Formatting toolbar or by choosing Project, Filtered For, AutoFilter.

If you have the Cost table displayed, you can click the AutoFilter drop-down list in the Variance column and choose > 0 (that is, greater than zero) from the list. If you are in the Work table or the Variance table, you have to create a custom filter to display only positive variances. To do this, select Custom from the AutoFilter drop-down list in the Variance column. Set the test to Is Greater Than, and set the value to 0 (that is, zero). Click OK to apply the filter.

NOTE

> Note the test for positive values using AutoFilter assumes that the baseline was captured for all tasks. If the baseline was not captured, all the variances are positive, and the test is meaningless.

REVIEWING TASK START AND FINISH DATE VARIANCES

Date variances such as those shown for tasks in Figure 15.10 are created whenever the current start and finish estimates are different from the baseline dates. This can happen in a variety of ways:

- A predecessor task is delayed or completed early, forcing a successor task to be rescheduled.
- You set an actual start or finish date that's different from the baseline date because the task began or finished at a different time than originally planned.
- You record more, or less, actual work than originally planned, causing the task's duration and dates to change.
- You adjust a task relationship to alter the start or finish date of the task.

If you record progress on a task by entering the percentage complete, Project automatically copies the scheduled (estimated) Start date to the Actual Start date. Project also inserts an Actual Start date if any Actual Work is entered for the task or for a resource assigned to the task. If you don't explicitly enter an actual start date, Project assumes that work started on the estimated start date. Thus, you might not see start date variances for a large number of the tasks in your project if you use these tracking methods.

Applying similar logic to actual finish dates, Project automatically copies the estimated task finish date to the actual finish date when either the task percentage complete or the percentage work complete is set to 100%. Project also inserts an actual finish date when the remaining work or the remaining duration is set to zero. If you don't explicitly tell Project when the task actually finished, Project assumes that the task finished on the estimated finish date.

When you determine that you have unfavorable date variances, it is important to trace their causes. Annotations to Notes or Comments fields can prove invaluable if the problem isn't fresh enough to recall. It's very important to devise corrective action to get the project back on schedule. The section "Revising a Schedule to Complete on Time and on Budget," later in this chapter, addresses that issue.

REVIEWING TASK COST VARIANCES

Unfavorable cost variances are created whenever the current cost estimates are higher than the baseline cost estimates. Tasks can start and finish on time and complete within their original estimates and still have cost variances. For example, if you estimated that the programming would be completed with a Visual Basic for Applications (VBA) programmer at $50 per hour but you're forced to reassign the task to a programmer whose rate is $60 per hour, your costs will be overbudget, even if the hours remain constant. Hopefully, the programmer with the higher rate can complete the task in fewer hours than originally scheduled, but this will not always be the case.

TIP

> Project does not take into account the competencies of resources available to the project, so assigning a different resource will not automatically shorten the duration of a task. Factoring this element into revising the duration for the task is often necessary for skill-based assignments.

To spot problems with unfavorable costs, you can apply the Cost Overbudget filter. This filter looks for tasks that were baselined and that have a current estimated cost greater than the baseline cost (that is, the original estimate). To actually see the costs, you must apply the filter with the Cost table applied (as in Figure 15.9).

TIP

> Because you likely will often use the Cost Overbudget filter with the Cost table, you might find it convenient to create a new view that always displays the Cost table with the Cost Overbudget filter. For information on designing views, see Chapter 21, "Customizing Views, Tables, Fields, Filters, and Groups."

REVIEWING TASK WORK VARIANCES

Work variances are calculated for each task by subtracting the task's baseline work from the currently scheduled work. A negative work variance is favorable because it means that the currently scheduled work is less than originally planned. In contrast, a positive work variance is unfavorable because it means that to complete the task, resources must expend more work than originally estimated. The fastest way to see the work variances for each task in a plan is to apply the Work table (as in Figure 15.8). The Variance column displays the work variances for each task in the plan.

To focus on trouble spots, you should look at tasks that have unfavorable work variances. Project provides a filter called Work Overbudget that should behave like the Cost Overbudget filter discussed earlier—it should select tasks with work estimates that are larger in the current schedule than in the baseline. However, the Work Overbudget filter uses the field Actual Work instead of Work in its comparison with the Baseline Work field. Therefore, it doesn't include tasks that have yet to start but have unfavorable work variances. You can redefine the filter by using the following steps:

1. Chose Project, Filtered For, More Filters and select the Work Overbudget filter.
2. Click the Edit button.
3. If you want to preserve the original Work Overbudget filter, change the name to something like "Work Overbudget (revised)".
4. In the first row under Field Name, change Actual Work to Work.

5. Click OK to finish editing the filter definition.
6. If you want the new version of the filter to be available in all new project files, click the Organizer button. The filters defined in the Global template are listed on the left of the Organizer dialog box. Select the filter you just edited in the list on the right and then click the Copy button. If you did not modify the name of the filter, you are asked to confirm that you want to replace the existing filter in the template. Click Yes, and then click the Close button.
7. In the More Filters dialog box, click Apply to apply the filter or Close to close the dialog box.

→ For more information on customizing filters, **see** "Creating Custom Filters," **p. 859**.

REVIEWING STATUS AT THE RESOURCE LEVEL

In addition to analyzing progress and variances for tasks, you can analyze progress and variances for resources. The concept is very similar to many of the analyses performed on tasks in the preceding section.

Project saves baseline date, work, and cost values for each assignment. The baseline assignment values for work and cost are rolled up to the task level and to the resource level. Thus, the baseline work and cost for a resource are the total baseline values for all that resource's assignments, just as the resource's scheduled work and cost and actual work and cost are the totals for all its assignments. A resource's work and cost variances compare these rolled-up scheduled and baseline totals.

By analyzing resource variances, you might determine that the reasons for task variances are related to specific resources, as in the following examples:

- Resources arrived late onto the project.
- Tasks were assigned to resources who have the wrong skills to perform the task.
- The amount of work on tasks for one resource was consistently underestimated.
- Resources have not been able to apply the percentage of time to the project that was originally anticipated.
- Tasks that are slipping seem to be assigned to the same resource or combination of resources.
- The original cost of a resource was under- or overestimated.
- Customer or user resources are not applying the appropriate effort to the project.

Rather than repeat the steps that you performed on tasks for work, date, and cost variances in the preceding section, Table 15.2 shows the tables and filters you can select to show useful resource variances. You can apply these to the Resource Sheet view to simply identify resource names that are selected by the filters. However, to see which assignments contribute to resource variances, you need to display the Resource Usage view.

TABLE 15.2 SUGGESTED VARIANCE ANALYSES FROM TABLES APPLIED TO THE RESOURCE USAGE VIEW

Table	Filter	Shows You
Cost	Cost Overbudget	Resources whose current estimated cost is higher than the originally estimated baseline cost.
Entry	Slipping Assignments	Resource assignments that are estimated to finish later than originally planned.
Entry	Should Start/Finish By	Resource assignments that should have started or finished by dates that you specify (an interactive filter).
Entry	Should Start By	Resource assignments that should have started by a date that you specify (an interactive filter).
Work	Work Overbudget	Resources whose current estimated work is higher than originally estimated baseline work; note that the Work Overbudget filter is defined correctly—it uses work instead of actual work.

REVIEWING STATUS AT THE ASSIGNMENT LEVEL

As discussed in the preceding section, the baseline assignment values for work and cost are rolled up to the resource and task levels. To see the assignment details, you must display either the Task Usage view or the Resource Usage view. You can see work and cost variances at the assignment level in either the Task Usage view or the Resource Usage view (see the preceding section). However, resources do not have baseline start or finish fields, so there are no start and finish variances for resources, either. You must display the Task Usage view to see start and finish variances at the assignment level.

To display tasks and assignments, you can select View, Task Usage. Then, you can display the Work, Cost, or Variance tables to see assignment variances in the table on the left. To see timephased baseline work values for each assignment, you can right-click on the grid, under the timescale, and choose Baseline Work from the shortcut menu. (You might need to widen the column of row labels in the grid by dragging the right boundary of the Detail cell in the timescale.)

Figure 15.11 shows the Task Usage view with the Cost table on the left and the Work and Baseline Work details displayed in the grid on the right. Both Bill Kirk and Scott Adams were assigned to the Prototype Design task. Bill finished his assignment with 12 fewer hours of work than planned, and he had a favorable cost variance of –$240. Scott, on the other hand, was not finished with his assignment as the end of the task neared, so he worked on the assignment 8 hours instead of the planned 4 hours for each of the last 3 days. Scott has an unfavorable cost variance of $240. The two assignment variances offset each other in this case, and the task variance is 0.

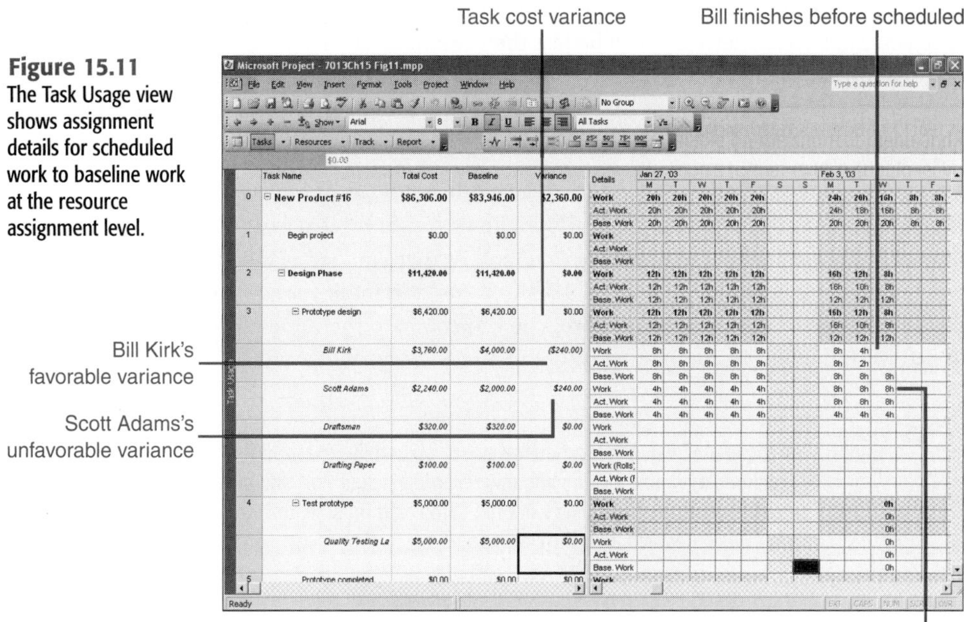

Figure 15.11
The Task Usage view shows assignment details for scheduled work to baseline work at the resource assignment level.

If you display the Cost table, you can see cost variances by assignment. To display cost details in the grid, you can right-click over the grid and choose Cost from the shortcut menu. To display timephased baseline cost, you can right-click over the grid and choose Detail Styles from the shortcut menu. In the Detail Styles dialog box, select Baseline Cost in the list on the left and click the Show button. If you want Baseline Cost to always be available on the shortcut menu, select the Show in Menu check box at the bottom. Then click OK to return to the Task Usage view.

ANALYZING PERFORMANCE WITH EARNED VALUE ANALYSIS

As discussed in the preceding sections, one way to analyze the status of a project is to look at the cost, work, and finish variances. These measures tell you the impact of experience to date on the total work, total cost, and finish date of the project and its component tasks. One problem with using these variances for analysis is that when one is favorable and another is unfavorable, it's difficult to tell which value is more critical to the project's success. They are measured in different units: the cost variance is measured in dollars, the work variance is measured in hours, and the date variances are measured in time units.

Another problem with using the simple variances is that you can't tell if the costs you have incurred to date have produced as much work and output as you had assumed in the baseline plan. In other words, they don't tell you whether productivity (output per dollar cost) is at the levels you planned. If there is a problem with productivity, then an unfavorable cost variance you might have detected may be just the beginning of an ever-expanding cost variance as work continues on the project and actual values replace estimated values. You can't tell from the simple variances if there is enough left in the budget to finish the project as planned.

Earned value analysis measures performance (productivity) as of a specific date in the life of the project—usually the current date. This allows you to receive early warning signals if a project is not producing the output per dollar cost that you had planned. Earned value analysis makes it possible to compare work and cost variances because work is converted to the dollar value of the work. Therefore, you can compare the value of the work completed to date with the cost of completing it.

NOTE

> If the earned value measurements are to accurately reflect performance, your tracking methodology must include not only recording actual start and finish dates, work, and costs, but also rescheduling work not completed on time and work that is completed but that was scheduled after the status date.

UNDERSTANDING EARNED VALUE MEASUREMENTS

Projects *must* generate value for their sponsors, or the projects would not be undertaken and funded. Furthermore, that value must be at least as great as the project's estimated cost (its baseline cost) or the sponsors would not approve the project. If the project produces output that is to be sold at a profit, then the buyer must have an even higher value for the project's output. Therefore, you take the baseline cost of the project as a measure of the value of the output of the project. It is at least a *minimum* measure of the planned value of the project.

When resources perform work on the tasks in a project, they generate the value that the project delivers. Cost accountants like to say that the resources "earn" for the employer the value that will be sold to the buyer. Consequently, the "earned value" of an assignment, a task, or a project at any moment in time is the portion of the planned value that is associated with the work that has been completed.

For example, if you have a project with a baseline cost of $1 million, then you say that the planned value of the project is $1 million. The planned value of each summary task, task, and task assignment in this project will also be its baseline cost. If on a specific date—say, the end of September—you find that 60% of all the work that is scheduled for the project has been completed, you say that the *earned value* as of that date is 60% of the value of the project, or $600,000. If the baseline schedule called for the project to be 50% complete as of the end of September, then you say that the *planned value* for that date is $500,000. Thus, the project appears to be earning value at a faster rate than planned. Finally, suppose that the *actual cost* as of the end of September is $550,000. You have spent more than you budgeted to spend by that date! Do you have enough left in the budget to finish the project? There's a high probability that the answer is yes because the value of what has been produced is not only greater than you had planned, but it's also greater than the actual cost.

The productivity is greater than you anticipated, and the project will likely come in at least on time, if not early, and under budget.

The comparison of planned value, earned value, and actual cost helps you assess performance better than simple variances do. Earned value analysis uses these core measurements (planned value, earned value, and actual cost) to create earned value variances and productivity indexes that you can use to predict, based on experience thus far, when the project will finish and what the total cost will be when the project finishes.

Whereas the cost, work, and time variances are based on estimated values at the end of the project, the preceding example makes it clear that earned value analysis compares planned work and cost with actual work and cost as of a given *status date*. By default, Project uses the current date (which is taken from the computer's system date) as the status date. If you last updated tracking information three days ago but use today's date for the earned value calculations, Project would not have any actual work and cost to offset the planned work and cost for the past three days. Therefore, you generally want to define the status date as the last time you brought actual values up-to-date.

The meanings of the three core earned value measures (planned value, earned value, and actual cost) are summarized as follows:

- **Planned value**—The planned value is the amount of baseline cost that was scheduled to be spent on work up through the status date. PMI formerly called this measure *budgeted cost of work scheduled (BCWS)*, but it now calls it simply planned value. Microsoft Project 2003 still uses the older term, and the actual field name in Project is BCWS. BCWS is calculated as soon as the baseline is saved, and it is the cumulative sum of baseline costs for each period up to and including the status date.
- **Earned value**—The earned value is that part of planned value that has already been earned by the amount of actual work performed as of the status date. PMI formerly called this the *budgeted cost of work performed (BCWP)*, but now calls it simply earned value. Project uses both terms, but the actual field name in Project is BCWP.

  To calculate earned value, you must determine what portion of a task or assignment has been completed. For tasks, Microsoft Project bases its calculation on the percentage of *duration* completed (that is, the % Complete field). For assignments, the calculation is based on the percentage of *work* completed (that is, the % Work Complete field).

  Note that the percentage complete (however it is measured) is based on the current schedule, not on the baseline amount of duration or work. Suppose a task has a baseline cost of $1,000 and its baseline work is 100 hours. If actual work as of the status date is 60 hours, but the scheduled work has changed to 120 hours, the task is really only half completed, and only half of its value has been generated thus far. The percentage complete is 50% (60hrs/120hrs), and the earned value is $500.

If work on a task has been completed as scheduled up to the status date, the earned value and planned value are the same. Differences, however, can arise for several reasons. For example, as just shown, if the scheduled duration and/or work for the task has increased since the baseline was captured, the actual work generates a smaller portion of the total value than was planned. Also, if overtime was used but not scheduled, more work is completed than was scheduled, and earned value is greater than planned value. If a resource has been diverted to another, higher-priority, task or project, the earned valued is less than the planned value.

- **Actual cost**—Actual cost, also called *actual cost of work performed (ACWP)*, is the actual cost of work that was completed as of the status date. The actual costs of the completed work might differ from the planned costs due to a number of circumstances. For example, you might have actually used overtime that is paid at a premium when none was included in the baseline schedule, resource cost rates might have risen since the baseline was captured, or more expensive resources might have been substituted for those assumed in the original estimates.

NOTE

Cost accrual methods determine when costs are scheduled and when they are recognized as actual costs. Microsoft Project spreads most costs over the duration of the task. The hourly costs of work resources (both standard and overtime costs) and the unit costs of material resources are incurred as work is scheduled for the assignment. By default, fixed cost for a task is also prorated over the duration of the task; but you can change the fixed cost accrual method to Start or End if you want to accrue the total fixed cost at the start or finish of the task. Resource cost per use is always accrued at the start of an assignment. These accrual methods determine when costs show up in the timephased data that is used for variance calculations (and for earned value calculations, as you will see later in this chapter). If the accrual method stipulated for a task's fixed cost is changed after the baseline is captured, that change alone creates a cost variance for status dates between the start and the finish of the task. However, after a task is complete, all costs are counted and the accrual method is no longer an issue.

Microsoft Project calculates the three core earned value measures at the assignment level, the task level, and the summary task level. At the summary task level they are simply the rolled-up sums for subtasks. At the task level, planned value (BCWS) and actual cost (ACWP) are rolled-up sums for the assignments. However, earned value (BCWP) is calculated using a unique formula that only Microsoft Project uses and the result is sometimes different from the rolled-up earned values of the assignments. This formula uses the task % Complete (which is a measure of completed duration), whereas the assignment level calculations use % Work Complete.

The fact that earned value at the task level is not equal to the rolled-up earned values of assignments may not invalidate the use of Microsoft Project's implementation of earned value analysis. The method used is, after all, a weighted average, and it does provide valuable information about performance, even if it's not theoretically accurate. As you will see later, it's often more useful to examine the *trend* in earned value over time than to calculate a specific number at a moment in time. Because the calculation method is consistent over time, an analysis of the trend is valuable even if you question the precision of an individual calculation.

To illustrate the three core measures and to help you understand what they mean, let's use several variations on a simple example. Assume that Task 1 is scheduled with a duration of 4 days and the resource named Abe is assigned 100% to the task. To keep the math simple, duration is shown in hours (32 hours), and Abe's standard rate is simply $1. Figure 15.12 illustrates the task and Abe's assignment before any actual work is recorded.

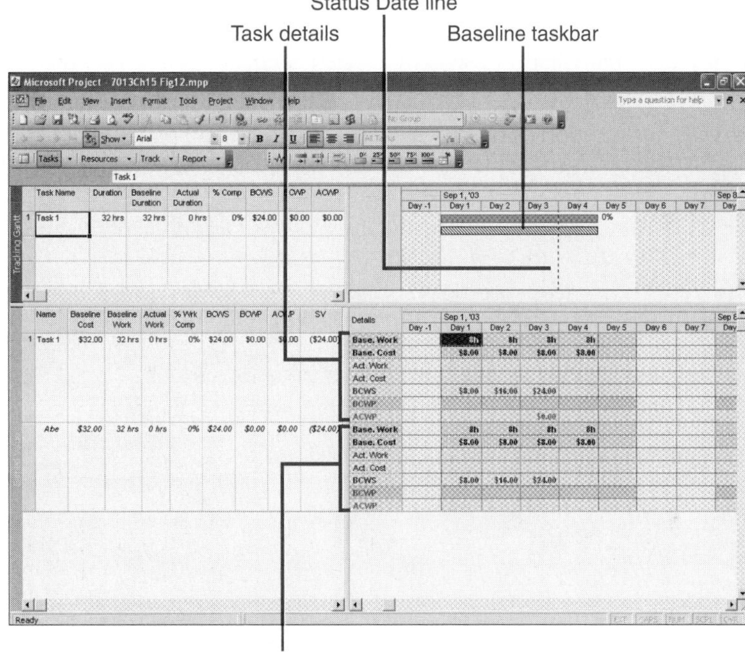

Figure 15.12
Project calculates planned value (BCWS) up to the status date as soon as the baseline is captured, but earned value (BCWP) and actual cost (ACWP) require some actual work in order to be calculated.

Note these features in Figure 15.12:

- The Gantt Chart view in the top pane shows the scheduled taskbar above the baseline taskbar. The dashed vertical line dropping down between Day 3 and Day 4 is the Status Date line; therefore, the status date is Day 3 (September 3), which we will assume is the current date for the project manager.
- The table in the top pane shows the scheduled and baseline duration to be 32 hours, with actual duration and % Complete both 0. The table also shows the task's values for BCWS, BCWP, and ACWP. Because no actual work has been recorded, both BCWP and ACWP are 0.
- The Task Usage view in the bottom pane shows timephased details for Task 1 and for Abe's assignment. The timephased data in the grid shows that baseline work and cost

are 8h and $8 per day. The total baseline cost and work are shown in the table on the left.

- Note that BCWS (planned value) is calculated for each day up through the status date. This happens as soon as the baseline is captured. However, BCWP (earned value) and ACWP (actual value) aren't calculated until actual work is recorded.
- Note that BCWS is a cumulative calculation. Each day's value is that day's baseline cost added to the previous day's BCWS. The BCWS on the status date is the value you see in the table on the left. Earned value (BCWP) and actual cost (ACWP) are also cumulative when calculated, and the value shown on the status date in the grid is the value you see in table's columns on the left.

Now let's assume that it's Day 3 (the status date), and the project manager finds out that Abe has worked only 2 of the 3 days and the task is 50% complete. Figure 15.13 shows what happens to the calculations when the project manager enters 50% in the % Complete field. Project makes actual work equal to scheduled work for each day in the timephased grid until it reaches the 50% point in the task duration. The BCWP and ACWP values for Day 3 are the same as for Day 2 because no additional work was done on Day 3.

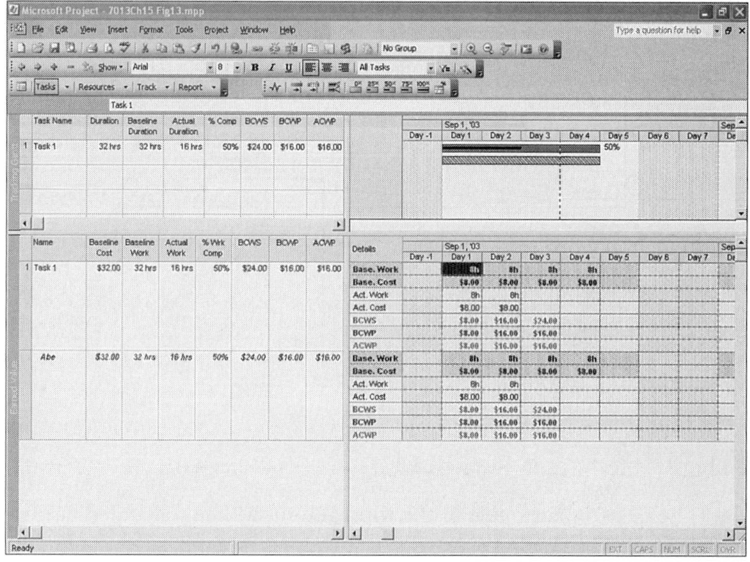

Figure 15.13
When actual work is recorded, Project calculates the BCWP and ACWP fields up to the status date.

Because Abe's assignment is 50% complete, he has earned 50% of the planned value of $32 (that is, $16), and the BCWP (earned value) field shows $16. By comparing earned value with planned value, you see that Abe earned $8 less value than you had planned, and the reason was because he didn't stay on schedule.

Microsoft Project calculates three earned value schedule indicators that compare earned value with planned value to show you the impact on your project. Figure 15.14 shows the three earned value schedule indicators. They tell you at a glance whether your project is earning value at the rate that was planned. To save space in the figure, all the timephased detail rows except for the earned value fields have been hidden.

The table on the left in both panes in Figure 15.14 is called the Earned Value Schedule Indicators table. This table has all three of the following schedule indicators:

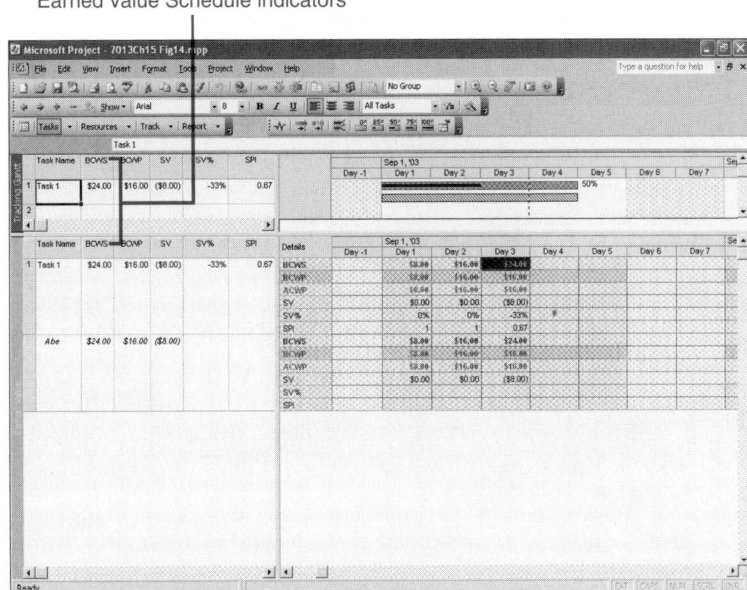

Figure 15.14
The schedule variance fields SV, SV%, and SPI express the differences between earned value and planned value as a number, a percentage, and a ratio.

- **SV (schedule variance)**—This field shows the difference between planned value and earned value and is calculated as earned value minus planned value (BCWP–BCWS). If SV is negative, as in Figure 15.14, where it's –$8.00, it is unfavorable because it means that the project has earned that much less than it was planned to earn as of the status date. You can think of a negative SV as a shortfall, or deficit, in earned value relative to planned value.

  If SV is positive, it is favorable because it means that the project earned more than it had planned to earn as of the status date—the resources did more work than was planned, and the work rate is ahead of the planned work rate. The implication is that the project will likely finish ahead of schedule. You can think of a positive SV as a surplus in earned value relative to planned value.

  Because both BCWP and BCWS apply the same budgeted cost to different amounts of work, the difference between them represents a difference between the amount of scheduled work and the amount of actual work. When SV is negative, it means that less work was done on the project than was planned. That's why it's called the *schedule* variance. Negative values for SV imply that the rate of work is not keeping up with the planned work rate. The implication is that it will be difficult to finish the project on time unless productivity increases or project scope is reduced.

15

- **SV% (schedule variance percentage)**—This field in Project 2003 expresses SV as a percentage of planned value. Generally, expressing values in percentages is most useful when you're comparing those measurements for tasks or projects that differ substantially in size.

  SV% is calculated by dividing SV by BCWS (SV/BCWS). It expresses the earned value deficit or surplus as a percentage of planned value. In this case, where SV% is –33%, it means that the shortfall in earned value was 33% of the planned value. When SV% is positive, it means that there's a surplus in earned value of that percentage. A negative value for SV% implies that something is keeping work from being completed on time, and the project manager should determine what factors are at play in order to avoid missing the finish goals. It might suggest that additional resources should be assigned to the task or project. A positive value implies that work is running ahead of schedule, and it might be possible to reallocate some resources to other tasks or projects and still meet the project's deadline.

  Note that SV% is not calculated at the assignment level.

- **SPI (schedule performance index)**—This is the ratio of earned value to planned value (BCWP/BCWS). In our example it is $0.67 ($16/$24), and it means that the project earned only $0.67 of every $1 of value that we planned for it to earn. In terms of productivity, it means that the project was only 0.67 as productive as we planned for it to be. Values lower than 1.0 are unfavorable, with the same implications as negative values for SV%. Values over 1.0 are favorable and imply the same things that positive SV% values imply.

  The SPI can be used to estimate the project completion date by dividing the remaining duration by the SPI. In our example, half of the task's duration (16 hours) remains to be completed after the status date. If productivity continues at the same rate, it will take approximately 24 more hours (Remaining Duration/SPI, or 16h/0.67) to finish the project. That's 3 more days from the status date (Day 3), and it would put the finish date on Day 6 of the project instead of on Day 4, as scheduled.

  Note that SPI is not calculated at the assignment level.

In the preceding example, earned value (BCWP) and actual cost (ACWP) are the same. To illustrate how they might differ, and what that would mean, let's modify the example and assume that although Abe was scheduled to perform the work, he was unavailable at the last minute, and the project manager assigned Sam to replace Abe. Thus, Sam worked only 2 days. However, Sam's standard rate is 25% higher than Abe's, $1.25 per hour. Obviously, actual costs will be higher than planned.

When the resource substitution is recorded and 50% actual % Complete is recorded, the calculations look like those in Figure 15.15.

Figure 15.15
You can compare the BCWP and ACWP fields to see whether you spent more than the planned value of the work that was produced.

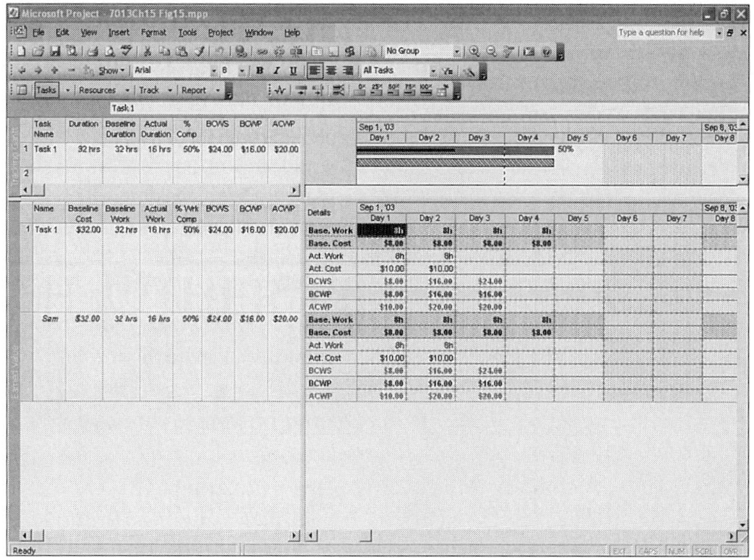

The timephased and total values for planned value (BCWS, $24) and earned value (BCWP, $16) in Figure 15.15 are the same as those for Abe in Figure 15.13. Consequently, you would have the same SV (schedule variance, –$8). In this example, though, the timephased actual cost is $10 per day instead of the budgeted (that is, baseline) $8 per day, and the actual cost (ACWP) as of the status date is $20. The earned value up through the status date is $16 (that was the planned value of the actual work), but the actual cost was $20. Therefore, it cost $20 to generate the earned value of $16. The "overrun" of $4 clearly has negative implications for the final cost of the project if it is a pattern that is repeated.

Many organizations consider favorable variances to be poor project management. Increased scope encourages *gold-plating*, a practice of delivering more than expected with little added value to the customer. Underbudget expenses and finishing early imply excessive padding to both time and cost estimates, and are usually scrutinized by a project's sponsor in future projects. In addition, the early release of resources means underutilization because people can rarely start right away on their next assignment. It's like a plane arriving early at an airport: It typically means waiting on the tarmac for the assigned gate to become available or an extended wait for passengers making connections. Experience shows that customers are most appreciative of delivery of what is expected–no more, no less.

A comparison of BCWP and ACWP produces cost indicators similar to the schedule indicators shown in Figure 15.14. Figure 15.16 shows the same example, with the earned value cost variance fields displayed. The table on the left of each view is named the Earned Value Cost Indicators table.

15

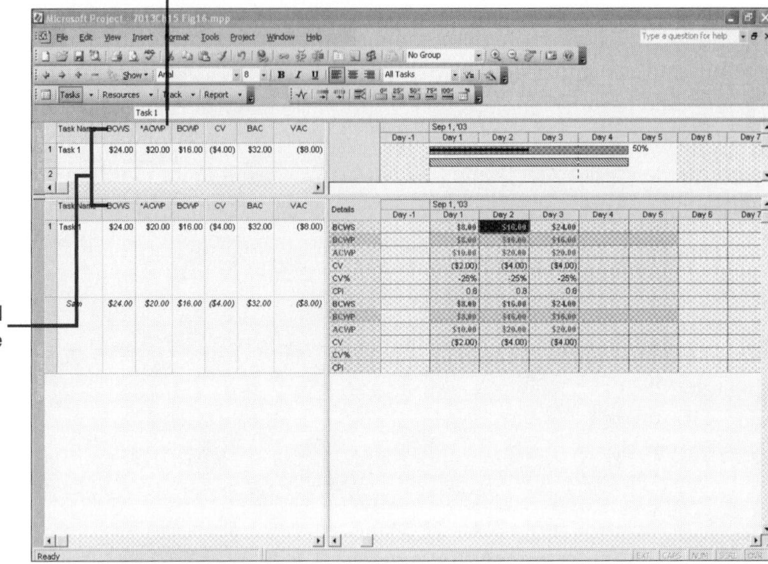

Figure 15.16
The Earned Value Cost Indicators table summarizes the effectiveness of cost thus far in generating the planned value.

NOTE

Note that the Earned Value Cost Indicators table contains the BCWS field but does not, by default, include the ACWP field. Because ACWP is used in calculating the indicators, and BCWS is not, the table in Figure 15.16 has been modified to include the ACWP field. For this illustration it's titled *ACWP, to remind you that it's not by default included in the table.

You should redefine the table and store the redefined table in your Global template. To redefine the table, choose View, Table, More Tables, Earned Value Cost Indicators, and click Edit. Select BCWS in the Field Name column and change it to ACWP. Click OK to save the definition in the active project. Click the Organizer button to display the Organizer dialog box. Select the Earned Value Cost Indicators table in the list on the right (the list of table definitions in the active project). Click the Copy button to copy that definition to the Global template. Click Yes to replace the current definition in the template. Then click Close to close the Organizer and click Close to close the More Tables dialog box.

→ For more information about managing the template, **see** "Working with the Organizer and the Global File," **p. 107**.

The cost indicators in Figure 15.16 have the following meanings:

- **CV (cost variance)**—This indicator shows the difference between earned value and actual cost, and is calculated as earned value minus actual cost (BCWP–ACWP). In this example the CV is –$4, and it means that the actual cost of production was $4 more than the earned value of the output. Because BCWP and ACWP both apply cost to the same amount of work, the difference between them represents a difference between the budgeted and actual cost rates. If CV is positive, it is favorable because it means the earned value of the work was greater than the cost to produce it. If CV is negative, it is unfavorable because it means the value of the work was lower than the cost to produce it—you spent the amount of CV over and above the value earned.

- **CV% (cost variance percentage)**—This is a field that expresses CV as a percentage of earned value (BCWP). It's calculated by dividing CV by BCWP (CV/BCWP). In this example, where it is –25%, it means that you spent 25% more of the budget than was planned for the value that was earned. If this continues, you will not be able to finish the task (and perhaps the project) within budget. Or, to put it another way, you will not have enough left in the budget to complete the remaining work.

  Note that CV% is not calculated at the assignment level.

- **CPI (cost performance index)**—This is defined as the ratio of earned value to actual cost (BCWP/ACWP) up through the status date. It is the ratio of budgeted to actual costs for the actual work completed as of the status date. It tells how much value you earn for every dollar of actual cost.

  In our example the CPI is 0.80 ($16/$20), which means that every dollar of actual cost earned only $0.80 of planned value.

  The CPI is often used to predict whether a project will go over budget and by how much. In fact, Project 2003 includes a field for that calculation—the EAC (estimate at completion) field, which is discussed later in this section.

  Note that CPI is not calculated at the assignment level.

There are still more fields to the right of CPI in the Earned Value Cost Indicators table. Figure 15.17 shows those additional fields in the top pane:

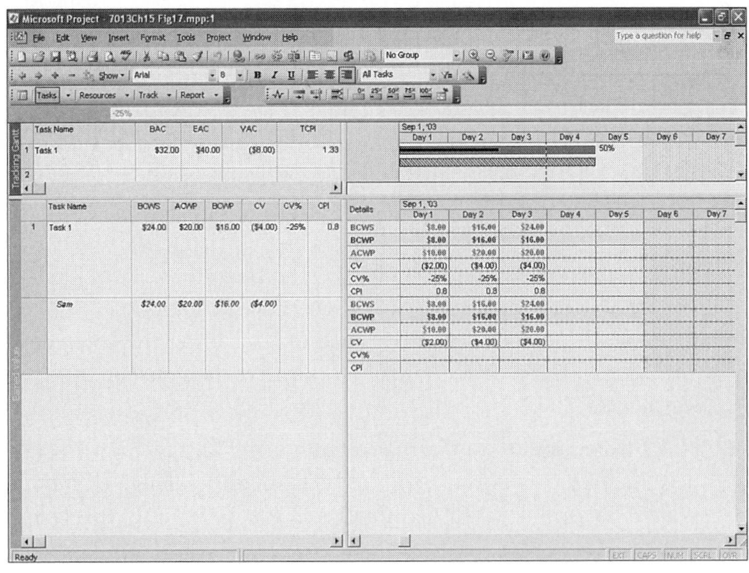

Figure 15.17
The cost indicators can be used to estimate the total cost of finishing the project, given the current cost performance index.

- **BAC (budget at completion)**—This is actually the Baseline Cost field, shown with the title BAC. BAC is the term that traditional earned value analysis usually gives to baseline cost. This field shows the total budgeted cost of the task ($32, in this case). It therefore represents the total planned value of the completed task.
- **EAC (estimate at completion)**—In Project 2000 and earlier versions, this field was equivalent to the Cost field (the total estimated or scheduled cost). In Project 2002 and 2003, EAC calculates an estimate of what the total cost will be when the task is completed if the CPI rate of performance, as of the status date, prevails for the remainder of the project. (To the amount of actual cost already incurred, it adds an estimate for completing the task based on the CPI.)

  The formula for the EAC is ACWP+(BAC–BCWP)/CPI.

  The following is an explanation of this formula:

  1. First, the actual cost thus far—ACWP—is included ($20, in this case).
  2. Next, you estimate the amount of planned value that has yet to be earned: (BAC–BCWP).

     If the BAC is the planned value for the completed task, then BAC minus earned value thus far (BCWP) is the remaining value to be earned or produced. In this example the BAC is $32 and the earned value (BCWP) is $16. Therefore, you still have $16 of value yet to be earned or generated.
  3. Divide the value that's yet to be earned by the CPI, to estimate what it will cost to generate that amount of remaining value at the current performance rate for costs.

     The CPI tells you what you are currently earning for each dollar of actual cost you spend. Dividing the remaining value to be earned by the amount you earn for each dollar of actual cost tells you the number of actual cost dollars it will take to generate the remaining value. In this example, the remaining value to be earned is $16, and you only earn $0.80 for each dollar of actual cost. Dividing $16 by 0.8 yields $20 as the number of dollars it will cost to generate $16 of value.
  4. Adding the $20 that's already spent to the $20 that's needed to finish the task gives you $40 for the EAC.

- **VAC (variance at completion)**—VAC is calculated as BAC–EAC and is the difference between the total baseline cost (BAC) and the estimated total cost (EAC), given the current rate of performance. In this case, that's $32 minus $40, or –$8. If VAC is positive, the cost estimate based on experience so far is lower than budgeted cost. If VAC is negative, the current cost run rate is greater than budgeted and the project will likely run over budget.
- **TCPI (to complete performance index)**—TCPI is the ratio (as of the status date) of the value of the work remaining to be done to the budgeted funds remaining to be spent. The formula is (BAC–BCWP)/(BAC–ACWP). In this formula, (BAC–BCWP) is the value of the work remaining to be done and (BAC–ACWP) is the budgeted funds remaining to be spent.

The ratio measures the amount of value each remaining dollar in the budget must earn in order to stay within the budget. If TCPI is greater than 1.0, each remaining dollar in the budget must earn more than $1 in value—there is more work to be done than there is budget to cover it, and you either need to increase productivity or reduce the work to be done. A value less than 1.0 means you should be able to complete the project without using all the remaining budget—you have opportunities to increase scope, quality, or profit, or you can choose to save the money in the budget.

CONTROLLING THE CALCULATION OF EARNED VALUE

Project 2003 provides for an alternative method of calculating earned value (BCWP) at the task level. Sometimes an assignment or a task involves the production of physical units of output or the processing of physical units of input, and you might want to base earned value on the number of units produced (or processed) as of the status date instead of on the default method, which uses the % Complete field (the percentage of actual duration completed). The Earned Value Method field lets you choose to use Physical % Complete in the calculation instead of % Complete. This field is available at the bottom of the Advanced tab of the Task Information dialog box, where it is labeled Earned Value. It has two possible values: % Complete (which is normally the default) and Physical % Complete. You could also add the field to a table. If you choose to use the Physical % Complete method, you enter that percentage complete to be used in the calculation in the Physical % Complete field, which is now included on the standard Tracking table.

Figure 15.18 shows the Earned Value table with the Earned Value Method and Physical % Complete fields inserted. Tasks 17 and 18 are duplicates of the same task, Assemble First Batch, which is a trial run of a new assembly process. Each version is scheduled for 20 days and is expected to produce 4 fully assembled units. Work has proceeded as scheduled on both versions of the task, and the status date is April 28, which is the 40% complete mark for the task. However, as of the status date, only 1 unit has been assembled. (You assume that the remaining units will go together faster now that the team has worked out the kinks in the process.) The task Assemble First Batch 1 uses the conventional % Complete method of calculating earned value. The task Assemble First Batch 2 uses the Physical % Complete method. Because only 1 of the 4 units is completed, the Physical % Complete is 25%. The baseline cost for each task is $1,080 (not shown in the figure). The earned value (BCWP) for Assemble First Batch 1 is 40% of $1,080—that is, $432. The earned value for Assemble First Batch 2 is 25% of $1,080—that is, $270.

Normally the default method of calculation uses % Complete. You can change the default by choosing Tools, Options, to display the Options dialog box. Click the Calculation tab and then click the Earned Value button. The Earned Value dialog box lets you choose the default calculation method (see Figure 15.19). Note that changing the setting affects only tasks that are inserted after the default is changed. If there are existing tasks already in the project, they have the old default value unless you have manually changed them. If you want this to be the default for all your new projects, you can click the Set As Default button. Of course, existing projects are not affected by this—their default setting will not have been changed, and their tasks will not use the new method. You have to open those projects, change the default calculation method, and change the method for any task that you want to use the new method.

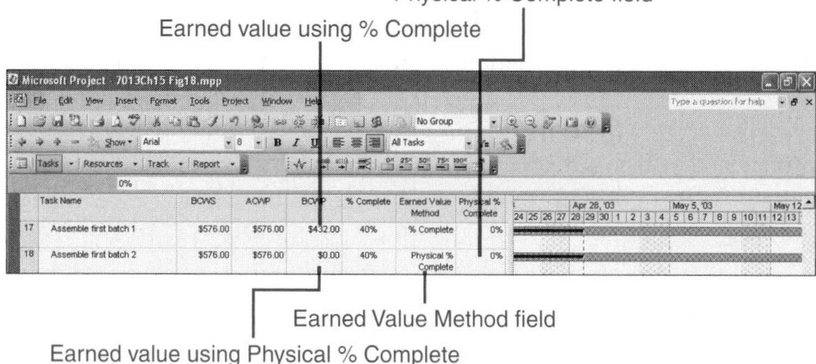

Figure 15.18
You can use the Physical % Complete method of calculating earned value for selected tasks.

Baseline for Earned Value
Default Task Earned Value Method
Earned Value button
Set as Default button

Figure 15.19
You can control the calculation of earned value for individual tasks by selecting the method of calculation.

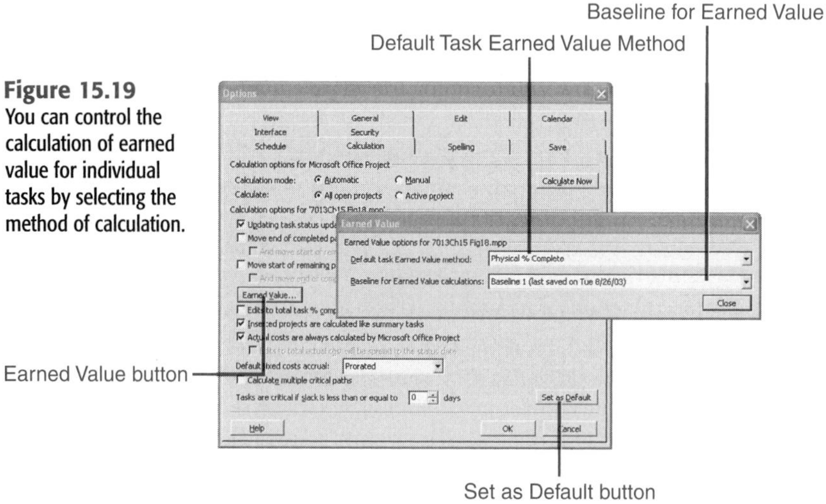

Figure 15.19 also reveals another earned value feature in Project 2003. As you learned in Chapter 14, Microsoft Project 2003 allows you to save a total of 11 baselines—the default baseline plus 10 baselines named Baseline 1 through Baseline 10. In the Earned Value dialog box, the field labeled Baseline for Earned Value lets you choose which of the 11 baselines will be used to calculate earned value. Note that this choice has no effect on the duration, work, cost, start, and finish variances—they continue to use the standard baseline fields.

For example, if a project schedule had to be revised dramatically after work actually started, you might have decided to capture the revised schedule as Baseline 1. That way you could show progress reports against the original baseline but also show reports against the revised baseline (which might be more meaningful).

USING EARNED VALUE ANALYSIS IN PROJECT 2003

If you want to view earned value measurements and indicators for a project, you must take three necessary preliminary steps:

1. You must capture the baseline for the project.
2. You must update the project with the latest tracking information. The more thorough your tracking methodology, the more meaningful the earned value indicators will be.
3. You must set the status date to the latest date you entered tracking information.

You can use any of the major task views, but the Gantt Chart view is probably the view that is used most often. There are three tables you can apply to the view to see earned value calculations:

- **The Earned Value table**—This table displays the three core calculations, planned value, earned value, and actual cost (BCWS, BCWP, and ACWP), as well as the earned value schedule and cost variances (SV and CV). It also includes the estimated final cost (EAC), the budgeted cost (BAC), and the variance at completion (VAC). (See Figure 15.20.)

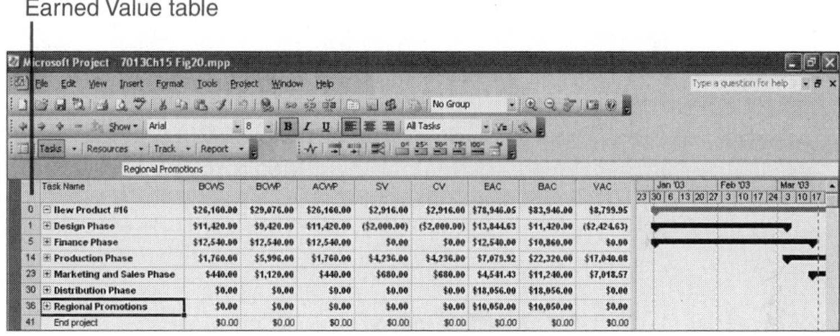

Figure 15.20
The Earned Value table shows highlights of the earned value calculations.

- **The Earned Value Schedule Indicators table**—This table focuses on the schedule variance and indicator calculations (refer to Figure 15.14). It includes fields for BCWS, BCWP, SV, SV%, and SPI.
- **The Earned Value Cost Indicators table**—This table focuses on the cost variance and indicator calculations (refer to Figure 15.16). It includes planned value and actual cost, and it includes the earned value cost variance, as CV, CV%, and CPI. It also includes the estimated final cost fields (BAC, EAC, and VAC) and the TCPI field. Recall from the discussion earlier in this chapter that you should permanently modify the table and insert the earned value field (BCWP).

You can display the table you want to use by choosing View, More Views, and then selecting the table you want in the More Views dialog box. Figure 15.20 shows the Earned Value table displayed for the New Product example used for the simple variances earlier in this chapter.

Project also provides a custom form that contains the same fields as the Earned Value table (see Figure 15.21). You can display this form to show earned value calculations for a single task or summary task that you have selected. To display the form, display the Custom Forms toolbar (right-click in the toolbar area and choose Custom Forms) and then click Task Earned Value. You can also display the form by choosing Tools, Customize, Forms, and then selecting Task Earned Value in the Customize Forms dialog box.

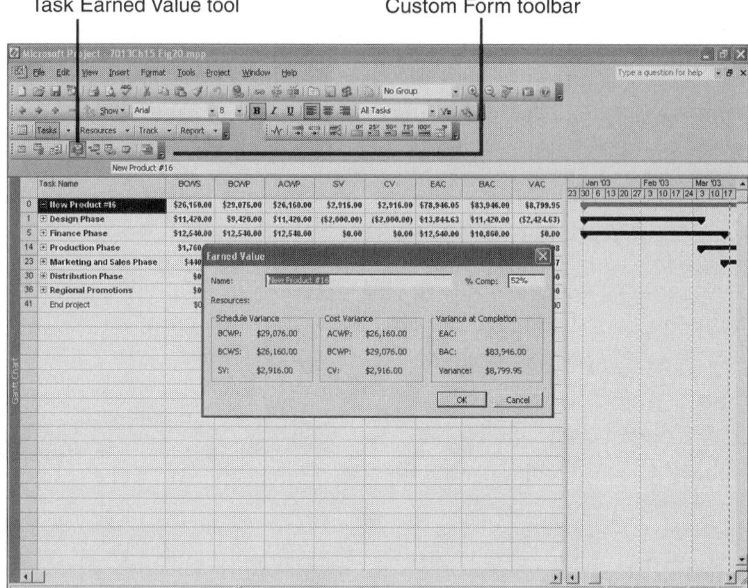

Figure 15.21
The Task Earned Value custom form shows the same fields as the Earned Value table, but for a single task.

CREATING EARNED VALUE GRAPHS WITH MICROSOFT EXCEL

As discussed earlier in this chapter, one of the most meaningful ways to analyze earned value data is by examining trends and tendencies. Although hard numbers are informative, they do not provide the whole picture that will best help you manage projects and make informed decisions. Tracking the earned value data graphically over time allows you to see and assess trends in earned value over the life of the project.

Microsoft Project does not generate a graph for earned value, but it can export the timephased data you need to Excel, which can then create the graph for you. The Analyze Timescaled Data in Excel command on the Analysis toolbar exports timephased information into Excel for any of the tasks and fields that you choose. This command lets you export timescaled data for any of the detail rows that you can view in the Task or Resource Usage views—including BCWS, BCWP, and ACWP.

To display the Analysis toolbar, you right-click over a toolbar and choose Analysis from the list of toolbars. When the project you want to analyze is active on the workspace, click the tool named Analyze Timescaled Data in Excel… to start the Analyze Timescaled Data Wizard. There are five pages in the wizard. Follow these steps to export the data to Excel:

1. In Step 1 of the Analyze Timescaled Data Wizard (see Figure 15.22), you select the default Entire Project and then click Next. Although you can select specific tasks before starting the wizard and then choose Currently Selected Tasks in this step, to get the totals for the project, you must select Entire Project.

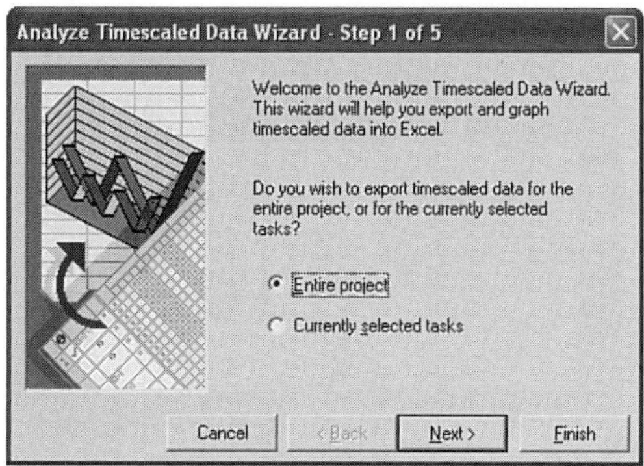

Figure 15.22
Choose Entire Project unless you want to graph the data for only a selected set of tasks.

2. In Step 2 of the wizard, you select the timephased fields you want to export. For an earned value graph, you can just select BCWS, BCWP, and ACWP. Click each of those fields in the list on the left, and then click the Add button (or you can simply double-click each of the fields). Also, remove the default Work field from the list on the right by clicking it and then clicking Remove (or by simply double-clicking it). Click Next when the list on the right contains BCWS, BCWP, and ACWP (see Figure 15.23).

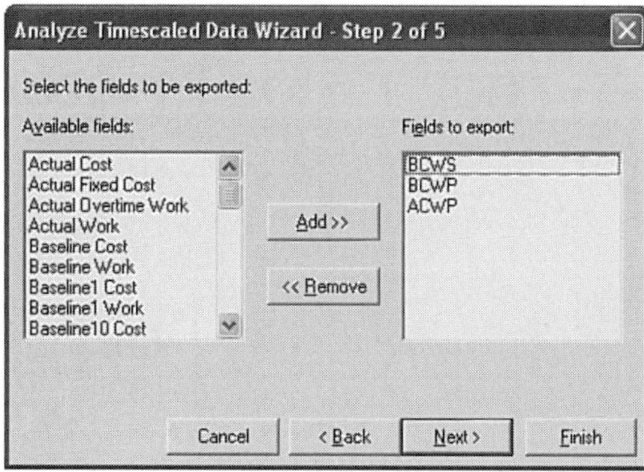

Figure 15.23
In Step 2, you choose the timephased detail fields to be included in the graph.

3. In Step 3 of the wizard (see Figure 15.24), you define the range of dates you want to include. The project start and finish dates are supplied by default. If you want to concentrate on progress up to the current status date, enter the status date in the To field. Or, if you want to prepare these graphs periodically for comparison purposes, leave the

default dates in place. In this example, the default dates for the start and finish of the project have been accepted.

In the Units field, select the time period to be plotted in the graph. You can choose Hours, Days, Weeks, Months, Quarters, or Years. This example was created with Weeks as the Units selection.

Click Next after you have chosen the date range and the units.

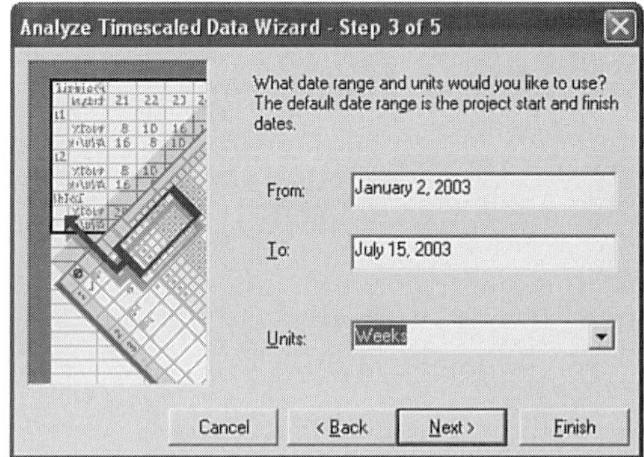

Figure 15.24 You should use the date range for the entire project unless you want to focus on a narrower date range.

4. In Step 4 of the wizard (see Figure 15.25), you elect to have Excel generate a graph of the data (by selecting the default Yes, Please) or to export the data only, without creating a graph (by selecting No, Thanks). Click Next after you make a choice. In this example, Yes, Please is selected.

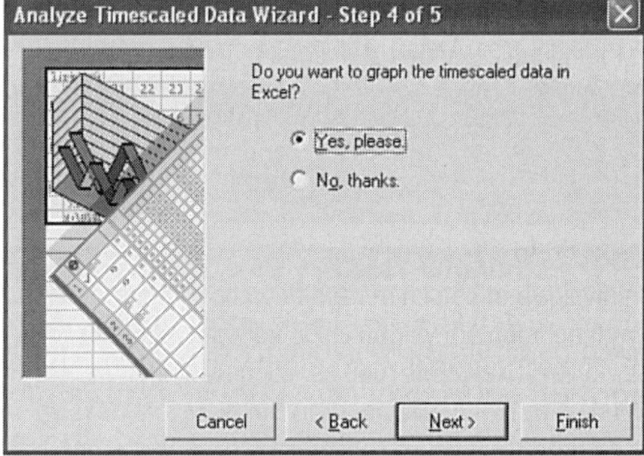

Figure 15.25 You can save yourself the time of defining a graph by letting the wizard create one for you.

5. In Step 5 of the wizard, you click Export Data if you're ready to export the data, you click Back if you want to change the parameters, or you click Cancel if you want to abort the wizard (see Figure 15.26). Click Export Data to finish the wizard.

Figure 15.26
The final step of the wizard gives you the option to back up, continue, or cancel.

When Project exports the data, Microsoft Excel automatically opens, and the exported data is displayed in a graph if you elected to create one; otherwise, the data is displayed in a worksheet. The default graph that's created by Excel is three-dimensional (see Figure 15.27). If you chose the default date range, the graph has many zero-valued points plotted for values after the status date.

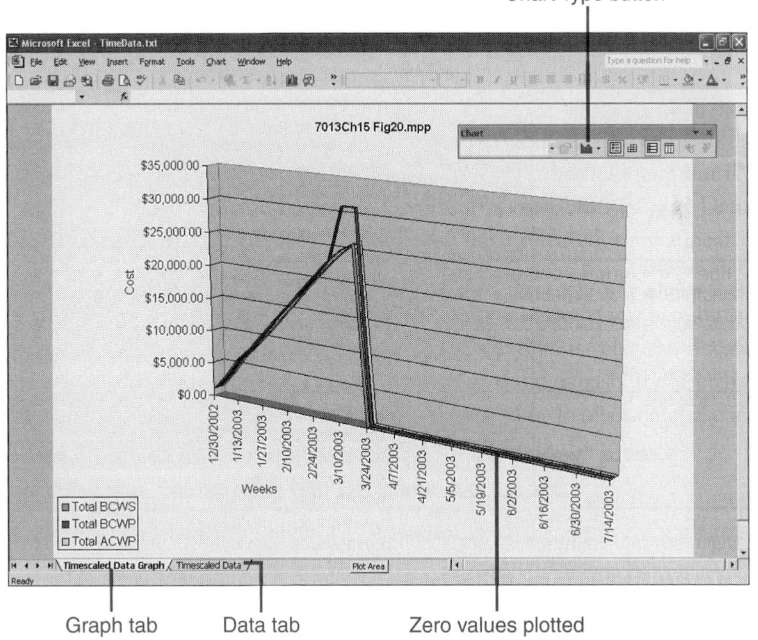

Figure 15.27
The initial graph is three-dimensional, and it also includes many zero-valued data points.

6. Change the chart to a line chart by clicking the Chart Type button on the Chart toolbar and selecting Line Chart.
7. Edit the data on the Timescaled Data tab to remove the points that were plotted for zeros.

   Click the Timescaled Data tab. The data that's actually plotted in the graph is at the bottom of this worksheet, where Excel has calculated the sums of the timescaled values for all tasks. Press Ctrl+End to jump to the last time period in the last row, and then press Home to jump to Column A for that row.

   The labels that are used in the graph legend are in Column B, but those labels are also used in the `SUMIF()` formulas in the cells to the right. You should not edit the labels unless you first paste the formula values over the formulas. To replace the formulas with values, select all the formulas in the last three rows and press Ctrl+C (or choose Edit, Copy). Then choose Edit, Paste Special, choose Paste Values, and click OK. You can then change the labels to Planned Value, Earned Value, and Actual Costs.

   While you have the values selected, change the display to zero decimal places, to reduce some of the clutter in your graph. Choose Format, Cells, click the Number tab, and change Decimal Places to 0.

   Finally, delete the zero-valued cells in the last three rows that occur after the status date. Deleting them keeps Excel from plotting those cells in the graph.

   Figure 15.28 shows the graph after it is changed to a line graph, after the zero values are removed and the other numbers are rounded to whole numbers, and after the legend text is changed as described earlier.

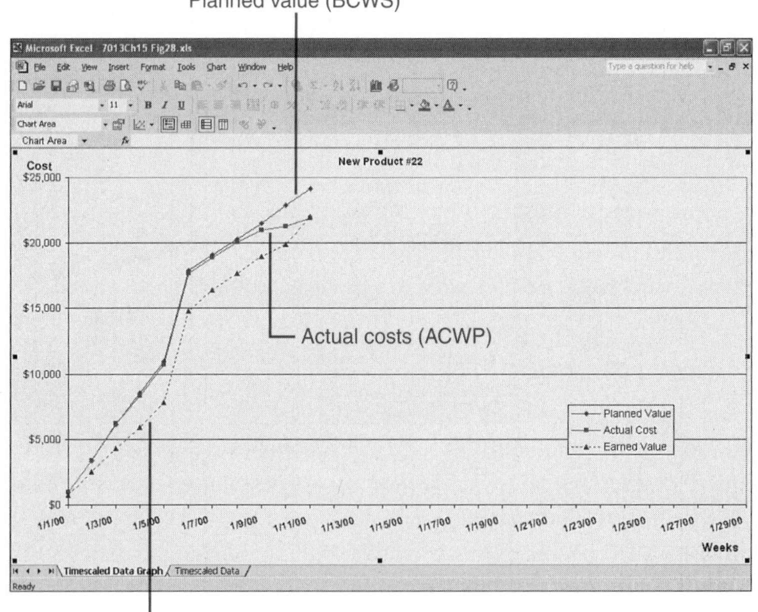

Figure 15.28
The graph of the core earned value calculations illustrates changes over time in the performance of the earned value and the actual costs relative to the planned value.

8. Excel always gives the file it creates for the exported data the name `TimeData.txt`. Save the file as an Excel file with a new name, in order to preserve the graph.

What can you tell from a graph of earned value measurements such as Figure 15.28? First, for any status date along the X-axis, the vertical distance between the Earned Value curve and the Planned Value curve measures the Schedule Variance (SV). In this example, Planned Value is above Earned Value, which means that SV is negative at the current status date (the last plotted points). That's unfavorable because it means that at the present performance level, the project won't be completed on time. The vertical distance between the Earned Value curve and the Actual Costs curve at any date measures the Cost Variance (CV) as of that date. In this case, that is close to zero as of the current status date, although it's been negative for most of the project because Actual Cost has been higher than Earned Value. When CV is negative, it means that you are paying more than you budgeted for the amount of value you're actually generating. If the project continues until all work is completed (which the unfavorable SV predicts will be past the scheduled finish date), that work will have cost more than budgeted.

An earned value table can tell you just as much as the graph (or maybe more) for any chosen status date. The graph adds the ability to see the trend in the variances—to see whether things have been getting better or worse. In this example, the SV continues to be unfavorable, which means that you have not resolved the problem(s) that cause you to be behind schedule. But the CV has recently been reduced to zero, and that means that you have begun to bring costs down to the level they were scheduled for the amount of work that is actually being done.

If the purpose of earned value analysis is to tell you the type of corrective measures you need to take to meet your project goals, the graph helps you assess whether your corrective measures are working.

REVISING A SCHEDULE TO COMPLETE ON TIME AND ON BUDGET

If you have determined that a plan is encountering unfavorable variances, you have to do something about it. If the project is in trouble, it's important to remember one thing: You should use the plan to manage the project. Don't deviate from the plan; change it! Depending on the type of problem you are having, you can employ different strategies to get the plan back on track. The bottom line is that something needs to change if you still plan to deliver on time and on budget with high quality and all expectations met.

Project provides many tools to help you revise a schedule, but first you have to know what will work for you on this project and in your particular situation. Remember that when it comes to revising a project plan there are limits: scope, time (the schedule), and costs (resources). Project managers must choose a combination of changes to stay within those limits.

15

Making trade-offs to maintain a schedule is known as the "good, fast, or cheap argument." Balancing competing demands requires careful assessment of which element the customer is willing to compromise on. In other words, you need to pick two of three qualities: good, fast, and cheap.

Good encompasses both scope and quality, which means that what is good to one person in terms of features and benefits might not be good to someone else. *Fast* means time in regard to schedule. Perhaps more work can be done in less time. Usually, it requires an increase in the third consideration, which is cost (*cheap*). Money might not be a first factor, but it always remains in the formula.

The answer is often a compromise on all three to arrive at an acceptable project plan.

Before you even begin to modify a plan in Project, chances are that there are users, customers, sponsors, and managers that you'll need to talk to before you can reflect your strategy in Project. Whatever you decide, you are likely to be forced to make trade-offs. If you use a less expensive resource to stay within budget, the work estimates might increase due to a lack of experience of the less expensive resource. If you reduce scope, you are probably sacrificing some of your objectives to stay within schedule and budget. If you overlap tasks to meet deadlines, you increase the risk of failing to meet other objectives. The harsh reality is that, if there were serious oversights when the plan was developed, the chances of completing the plan according to all its original expectations will take quite a bit of creativity on your part.

The following sections describe what these options mean in Project.

Reducing Scope

When you cut scope, you're reducing function, taking something out of your project objectives, or delivering less than originally committed. You might also be compromising on the quality of the project goal. Reducing scope in Project can be deployed in limited ways:

- Deleting tasks
- Reducing work

Negotiating a reduction in scope or a redefinition of project quality can be among the most difficult tasks you'll face as a project manager. After you define your initial project objectives, removing functions from the deliverables is often technically complicated, requiring advice from many different members of the team. It's hard to decide what you can take out and still have everything function smoothly. Add to this dilemma a group of sponsors who have had high expectations, and you'll find yourself in a pretty difficult situation.

Reducing Cost

A project might be on target for the completion date and meeting scope and quality requirements but running over budget to achieve those goals. Typically, if you "throw money" at a project, anything is possible. But if staying within the project budget is an important consideration, you need to find ways to conserve expenditures. Possible options include the following:

- Substitute less expensive workers for more expensive ones. The less expensive resource also might be less experienced than the more expensive one, however, causing a reworking of hours required on the tasks. A bonus here is that the more expensive resource might now be available to work on another task and actually reduce that task's duration.
- Reduce allowable overtime for resources that can be billed against the project at an increased overtime rate.
- Schedule resources that have a per-use fee to work on their assigned tasks simultaneously. For example, if a delivery fee is associated with a resource, schedule all deliveries together, to avoid being charged multiple delivery fees.
- Negotiate with suppliers, if possible, to reduce fixed costs and materials costs.
- Reducing project scope might be the only option for reducing overall cost of the project.

REDUCING SCHEDULED DURATION

If your targeted project finish date is in jeopardy, reducing the project scheduled duration means you first have to find out which tasks are extending the schedule, and then you have to figure out some way to make those tasks finish sooner. In Project, you can reduce the schedule by trying the following:

- Add more resources to the project, so that some tasks can be completed sooner.
- Break links between tasks and allowing them to occur simultaneously, which is usually a risky proposition.
- Overlap dependent tasks by introducing lead (the opposite of lag).
- Reduce duration by increasing a resource's percentage of commitment to tasks or allowing overtime.
- Replace inexperienced resources with more experienced resources. You might be able to reduce work estimates, thereby completing tasks in less time.

Schedule reductions can be accomplished in a variety of ways, but the decision should be made with caution. Many elements of risk are introduced to a project plan when you agree to reduce work, overlap tasks, add resources, and maintain scope. Reducing the schedule might lower your confidence in completing on time while increasing your risk of delivering quality. Despite these concerns, project managers are sometimes forced to revise a plan and bring it in early. Here are some ways to reduce the schedule:

- Overlap dependent tasks. If two tasks are linked, Project sets the default relationship to Finish-to-Start and the lag to 0d. You can overlap tasks by setting the lag to a negative number. A negative lag is usually referred to as *lead*. If you introduce lead for tasks that are on the critical path, the project finish date is recalculated to an earlier date.
- Increase a resource's percentage of commitment to a task. For tasks with fixed work, increasing the resource units on a task reduces the task's duration.

15

- If a resource is already assigned 100% to a task, consider using the Overtime Work field to reduce duration.
- Look for underallocated resources. The Resource Usage view can be used to look for resource overallocations. You can also use this view to look for underallocated resources, by selecting View, Resource Usage, Format, Details, Remaining Availability, and then setting the display to Remaining Availability. Keep resources assigned up to their maximum availability, to ensure that the schedule is as efficient as possible.

- Add more experienced resources to tasks. If you decide to replace a resource with a different, more experienced, resource, the trade-off is usually higher cost versus lower work estimates. To replace a resource, you use the Resource Assignment dialog box.

TIP

> When you reduce a schedule, Project does not automatically remove unneeded occurrences of a recurring task. Don't forget to get rid of unneeded tasks, such as weekly status meetings, by modifying the number of occurrences of recurring tasks (on the Task Information dialog box) or by deleting individual occurrences.

Adding resources is sometimes an effective way to recover a schedule that is falling behind, but it usually comes at a price—the budget. Adding resources is easy in Project. Finding the right resource at the right time for the right price can be challenging.

If you add resources, there are some things you might need to do:

- Reassign work to the new resource.
- Modify task duration to reflect redistribution of work on the task.
- Split complex tasks into smaller, more manageable tasks, with less work and less complex resource assignments on each.
- Modify work estimates so that they are realistic for the new resource.

When you're done revising the schedule, your resources might have become overloaded. Load leveling is the final step to ensuring that a revised schedule remains realistic.

Many of these strategies are easy to implement in Project. The hard part is likely to be convincing your project team and sponsors that your strategies for adjusting the plan are viable and acceptable to all involved.

TIP

> Before you adjust a project plan, it's a good idea to make frequent backups of your project's `.mpp` file. You might at some point decide that the changes you are making to the schedule are not working out. Rebuilding the plan without a good backup can be painful if you're not careful.

TROUBLESHOOTING

EARNED VALUE FIELDS ALL SHOW ZEROS

I've displayed each of the earned value tables described in this chapter, and all my tasks show zero values in the earned value fields. What am I doing wrong?

The earned value fields are calculated only up to the status date (or the current date, if you haven't defined a status date). Even then, these fields are zero if you haven't captured data into the baseline that's being used for earned value calculations. Therefore, you should first check the status date by choosing Project, Project Information. You should also check to see which baseline is being used for earned value by choosing Tools, Options, and then selecting the Calculation tab and clicking the Earned Value button. The baseline that appears in the Baseline for Earned Value field should have the date when it was saved next to its name. If there is no date, you haven't captured that baseline.

DISPLAYING VARIANCES IN A CONSOLIDATED FILE

I'm using Project Standard, and I've combined all my projects into a consolidated file in order to get an overview of my project portfolio. However, the project-level variances for each inserted project display as zero. How do I get the project-level variances and earned value indicators to calculate in a consolidated file?

Project automatically rolls up the baseline values for all tasks to the built-in project summary task (ID number 0). But when that project is inserted into a consolidated file, the project summary task you see in the consolidated file is a surrogate for the project summary in the source file—it's really a task defined in the consolidated file. Project does not copy the baseline field values to the surrogate summary task in the consolidated file. Therefore, you do not automatically get any of the variances at the project level for the inserted projects.

The quickest resolution of this problem is to follow these steps:

1. Insert all the projects into the consolidated file. Leave each project collapsed (with subtasks hidden).
2. Apply the Baseline table to the view in the consolidated file. Choose View, Table, Baseline. Columns for all the task baseline fields then appear.
3. If you call the first inserted project file by the name Project A for now, open Project A in its own window and display the Baseline table in that file, also. Also display the project summary task (by choosing Tools, Options, selecting the View tab, and selecting Show Project Summary Task).
4. Select the cells in the baseline columns in the first row of the Project A file. Copy those cells to the Clipboard by pressing Ctrl+C.
5. Select those same cells values in the consolidated file on the row for the surrogate task for Project A. Choose Edit, Paste Special, Paste Link.
6. Repeat this procedure for each inserted file.

When you've done this for all the subprojects, you will be able to display and compare variances and earned value indicators for the projects in your portfolio.

PART VI

Coordinating Projects and Sharing Data

16 Working with Multiple Projects 603

17 Exporting and Importing Data with Other File Formats 631

18 Copying, Pasting, and Inserting Data with Other Applications 691

CHAPTER 16

Working with Multiple Projects

In this chapter

Using the Window Commands 604

Displaying Tasks from Different Files in the Same Window 607

Creating Subprojects and Master Projects 612

Creating Links Between Tasks in Separate Projects 618

Sharing Resources Among Projects 621

Troubleshooting 629

USING THE WINDOW COMMANDS

Sometimes, working with just one project file does not allow you to accomplish your objectives. Working in a Windows environment typically offers the capability to work with more than one file at a time, and this is certainly true with Microsoft Project.

Consider the following situations when it would be beneficial to work with more than one file at a time:

- A task in one project might depend on a task in another project. For example, the start date for one task might need to be linked to the start or finish date for a task in another project.
- Several projects, managed by different people, might be placed under the supervision of a manager who coordinates dates and resources between the various projects.
- A project might be so large that it is easier to organize and manage if it is broken into several smaller, more manageable units. These separate files can then be linked back together so that you can see the whole project. The benefit of doing this is similar to that gained by outlining a project—but on a larger scale.
- Several projects might use the same set of resources and need to be coordinated so that the right resources are available to each project at the right time.
- A project might be too large to fit into the computer's memory at one time. Breaking it into smaller projects can overcome the memory limitations.

In Microsoft Project 2003, you can have 50 files open in separate windows at the same time. If you are using inserted projects, you can have up to 1,000 files open in any one file, assuming that your system resources and memory allow it. (For all practical purposes, though, 1,000 is far more than anyone is ever likely to need.) When multiple files are open at the same time, you use the Window menu to control and move between the various open windows. You can also use the Ctrl+F6 key combination to move between active project windows. As shown in Figure 16.1, a list of open project files appears at the bottom of the Window menu. A check mark appears in front of the name of the active window. When more than nine files are open at the same time, there is an additional option, More Windows, at the bottom of the Window menu. When you choose More Windows, Project displays a list of all the project files that are open. You can then choose the project file that you want to make active, and files that are not closed are simply moved to the background.

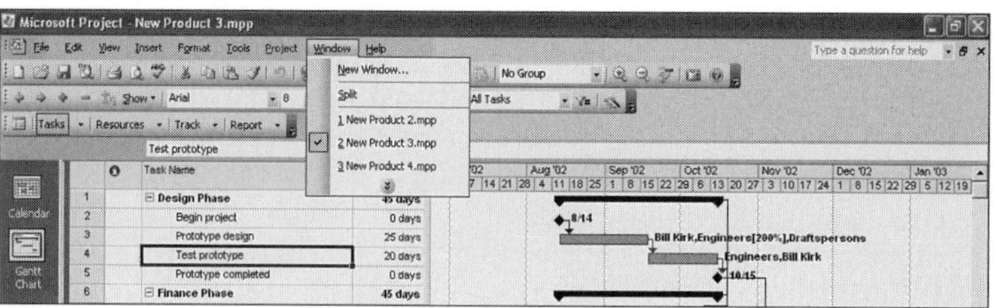

Figure 16.1
The Window menu includes a list at the bottom that you can use to locate other open project files.

NOTE

> The More Windows list of files is different from the one displayed at the bottom of the File menu, which is simply a list of the last few files that were opened, but which are not necessarily open now. The user can control the number of files listed in the File menu by selecting Tools, Options.

In addition to switching between screens, you can use the Window, Split command when dividing the screen for a combination view. Combination views can be very helpful during many different stages of a project's life. For example, you can display the Resource Sheet view in the upper half of the screen and the Gantt Chart view in the lower half of the screen. When a resource is selected in the upper screen, a "mini" Gantt Chart, showing just the tasks to which that resource is assigned, is shown in the lower half of the combination view. By selecting more than one resource, it's possible to show all the tasks to which all selected resources have been assigned, thereby making it easier to decide whether a resource can be replaced on a task with an alternative resource.

→ For more information on the views supplied with Project, **see** Chapter 19, "Using the Standard Views, Tables, Filters, and Groups," **p. 735**.

→ To learn about creating custom views, **see** "Creating New Views" **p. 834**

Viewing All the File Windows at the Same Time

To view more than one project file in its own distinct window at the same time, you can open the projects that you want to see onscreen at the same time and then use the Window, Arrange All command. Depending on how many project files are open, each window is sized and moved so that each file can be seen onscreen simultaneously (that is, the screens are *tiled*). As you can see in Figure 16.2, the name of each file is displayed in its title bar, and the active window has a brighter color title bar as well as the active pane indicator. This method is obviously practical only when a few project files are open at one time or when some of the project files are hidden (see the section, "Hiding and Unhiding Open Windows").

TIP

> If you saved a version of a project at the end of last month and you now want to compare the current project and last month's project side-by-side, you can use the Window, Arrange All command. You can then compare specific tasks by using the AutoFilter function in the Gantt Chart view to pick out a specific task. In this way, you can get a side-by-side comparison of how a project has changed over time. You can extend this idea and use it with more than one project. In Project 2003, you can save up to 11 full baselines, negating the need for saving versions of the project plan as independent files. Nevertheless, some users prefer to adopt the approach of saving several versions of the same files (for example at the end of each month), as it allows others to review, compare, and analyze historical project data independently of the current project file.

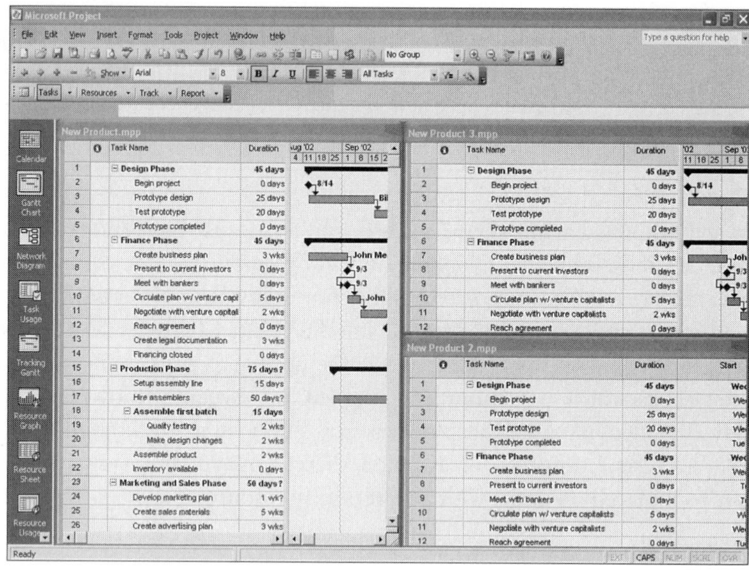

Figure 16.2
Displaying several windows at the same time can be very convenient when you're coordinating several project files.

NOTE

> The window that is active when you choose Window, Arrange All appears at the top-left corner of the screen and remains active.

TIP

> When a project file is not maximized, a handy shortcut menu appears when you right-click the title bar of the file. Useful commands on this shortcut menu include Save, Print, Spelling, and Project Information.

When you maximize any one window, all other windows become maximized as well. You can't see them because the active file covers the full screen, but when you move to any other file, it is already maximized.

HIDING AND UNHIDING OPEN WINDOWS

In some cases, you might have some project files open but you don't want them included in the Arrange All display (obtained by using Window, Arrange All). Instead of closing them, you can temporarily hide them by using the Hide command. To redisplay a hidden window, you choose the Window menu again, and if any files have been hidden, an Unhide command is available on the menu. If you choose the Unhide command, the Unhide dialog box opens and displays a list of files that have been hidden. You can choose the file you want to unhide and click OK. If you exit Project with windows hidden, you are prompted to save them if necessary.

USING THE SAVE WORKSPACE COMMAND

If you have been working on several files at the same time and you want to be able to resume your work by opening the same files together later, you can save the workspace in addition to saving the individual files. To save the workspace, follow these steps:

1. Choose File, Save Workspace.
2. If any files have unsaved changes, you are prompted to save the individual files. In the File Save dialog box, click the Yes button.
3. The Save Workspace As dialog box is displayed. Select the directory for the workspace if you want to store it somewhere other than the default directory. The name of the workspace file is initially `resume.mpw` (indicating that you can resume later with the same files), but you can change it by typing a new name in the File Name text box.
4. Click the Save button to complete the operation.

To open all the files in a workspace, choose File, Open. Select the workspace file and click OK.

16

NOTE

> Workspace files are automatically saved with the extension `.mpw`.

→ You should not confuse workspace files (described in this section) with Shared Workspaces, which require Windows SharePoint Services to work. For more information on Shared Workspaces, **see** "Using Windows SharePoint Services and Shared Workspaces," **p. 628**.

DISPLAYING TASKS FROM DIFFERENT FILES IN THE SAME WINDOW

The Window, New Window command deserves special attention. When you combine it with the Insert, Project command, you can merge multiple project files into one window to edit, view, print, or even link their tasks in one view. Each task retains its native ID number, so you see more than one task with ID 1. You can modify the display to add a column that identifies the project file that each task came from (for example, you could include the Project field; this way you can tell which task exists in which project). You can sort the task list as if it were one file; you can filter the merged list in the same way you use filters in one file. You can apply any table or view, including the Network Diagram view, to see the merged view. You can print views or reports from the merged window as though it were a single project file. You can even insert and delete tasks.

There are two basic approaches to combining projects into one window. One is by using the Window, New Window command. This approach assumes that all the files to be combined are already open. The second method is to use the Insert, Project command, which allows access to files that are not currently open. This second approach is described in the section "Combining Projects into One File," later in this chapter.

Using the New Window Command

To combine the tasks from multiple projects that are currently open into the same view, follow these steps:

1. Choose Window, New Window to display the New Window dialog box (see Figure 16.3).

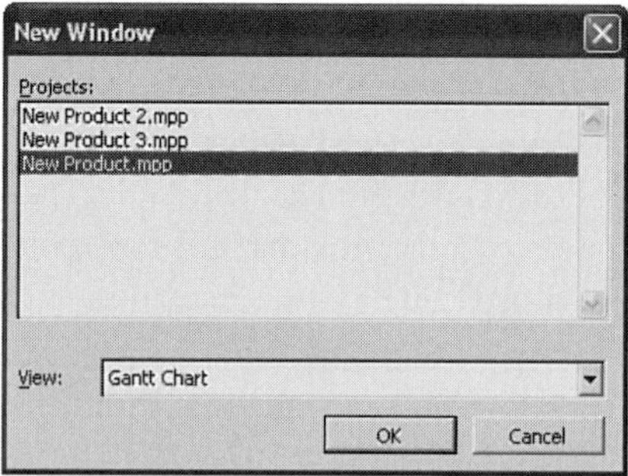

Figure 16.3
In the New Window dialog box, you can choose the projects that you want to combine into one window.

2. From the Projects list, select all the files you want to include in the new window. Use the Ctrl key to add nonadjacent filenames to the selection.
3. Choose the View list box located at the bottom of the dialog box and change the view if you want. You can also change the view later, after the new window is displayed.
4. Click OK to display the new window.

The merged window has the title `Project#`, where `#` is the consecutively assigned number that is given each time you create a new project file. When you open the Window menu, you see that the `Project#` choice is a separate entry on the open projects list, and the individual project files have been left open. You can save the merged window for further use by selecting File, Save.

As you can see in Figure 16.4, when any of the task sheet views are active (including any of the Gantt Chart views), the Indicators column displays an icon for an inserted project. If you hover the mouse pointer over this icon, a message with the name of the source file is displayed. This icon simply tells you that the inserted project is just pointing to the source file that contains some tasks. In the Gantt Chart view for each inserted file, the corresponding project summary task name is shown, and the task ID for this project summary task indicates the order in which the selected files were merged. You can use the Outline symbol in front of the project summary task name to hide the details of the task, just like working with the tasks in an outline. On the timescale side of the Gantt Chart view is a gray taskbar that represents the Project Summary task, and it appears in much the same way as a summary taskbar.

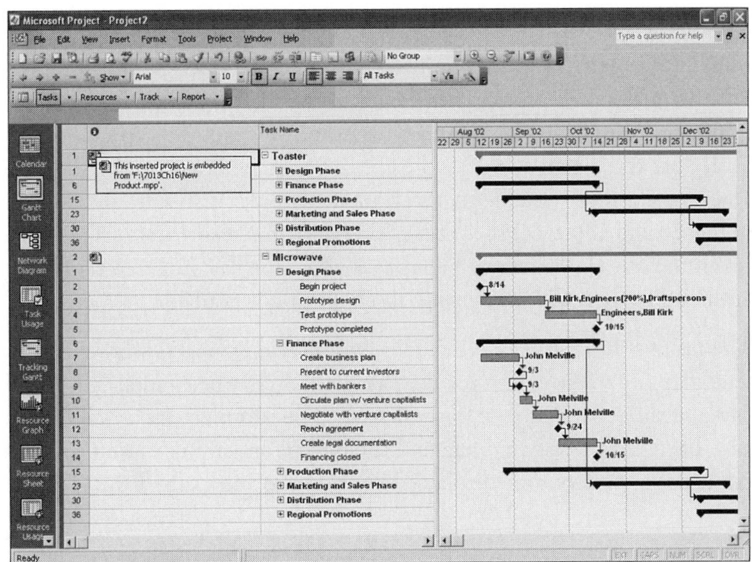

Figure 16.4
Hovering over the icon in the indicator column displays information about the inserted project.

16

NOTE

The Show command on the Formatting toolbar lets you easily choose the level of outline detail to be displayed.

TIP

When you want to quickly see a different view of a project without losing all the layout information in the current view, you can simply create a new window for the new view. In this way, you can have a Gantt Chart view with a split screen showing the Task Usage view in the lower half of the screen in one window and a Resource Sheet view with various filters active in a another window.

You can select Window, New Window when you want to see two different window views of the same project. In essence, this allows you to see more than a standard combination view. By using this method, you could see two separate combination views, two full-screen views, or one combination view and one full screen view—all of the same project. To do this, choose Window, New Window, but select only one project file. The title bar of the new window has the project name followed by a colon and a number, indicating the second instance of this project file. You can use either the Window menu or Ctrl+F6 to move between them. Any changes that you make and save to one instance of the project file are saved in the other window as well. There is only one file open here: It's simply displayed in two separate windows, much like the combination views you have already seen.

FILTERING AND SORTING COMBINED TASKS

Initially, all the tasks in a combined project are grouped by the file from which they came. For the most part, you can sort the list using the Sort command, or you can filter tasks by using the Filter drop-down list or the AutoFilter method. To sort the list, choose Project, Sort, Sort By to gain access to the check box that allows you to keep the outline structure. You might want to be able to sort by start date, for example, and allow the tasks to move out of their original project sort order. The predefined sort options on the Sort menu are set to retain the outline structure. When you allow the sort not to retain the outline structure, the outlining tools in the Formatting toolbar are not available.

The task list in Figure 16.5 includes two inserted projects whose tasks have been sorted in start date order. A column for the Project field has been added to the table, to display the name of the source project for each task. The summary tasks and the project summary tasks have been temporarily hidden, and the outline indenting option has been turned off. You can change these outline display options on the View tab of the Options dialog box.

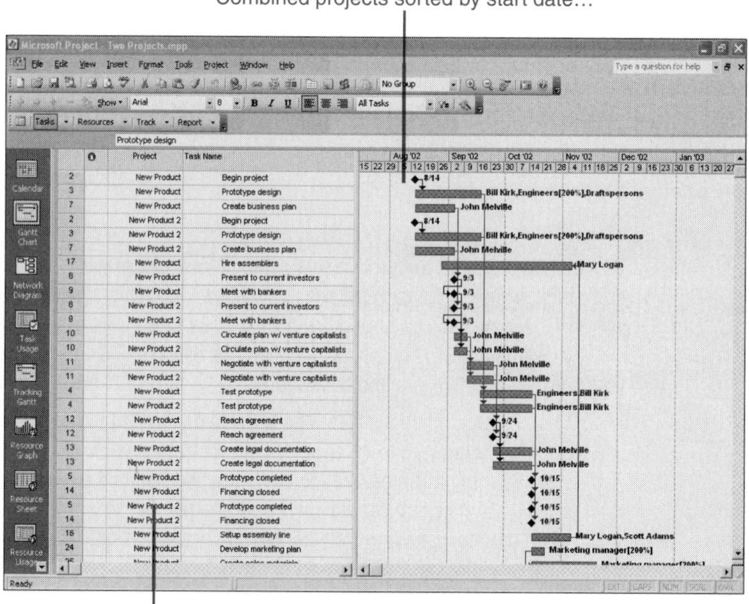

Figure 16.5
Sorting a file with inserted projects can make it easier to see when tasks from several projects are scheduled.

Note the duplication of task names in Figure 16.5. Most managers find that some common tasks occur in almost all projects of a similar type. If you are following good project management practices and creating project files from existing files or templates, you will undoubtedly have some repetition of task names in a combined master file. The inclusion of the Project column is one way to identify the source of each task.

TIP

If you have created and entered a task identification scheme of your own—for example, a work breakdown structure—you can display that information in the combined file, instead of or in addition to the Project file source name.

→ To learn about working with customized tables, **see** "Using and Creating Tables," **p. 840**.

→ For more information on creating and using custom fields, **see** "Customizing Fields," **p. 847**.

In addition to filtering and sorting, you can use a number of other formatting options, such as bar style formatting and layout commands, in the combined file. Individual inserted files are treated as summary tasks (with subtasks) in the combined file. You can also identify a critical path across all the combined files, instead of treating each inserted file as having its own, totally isolated, critical path.

To see a critical path across all projects and tasks in a combined file, select Tools, Options. On the Calculation tab, turn on the Inserted Projects Are Calculated Like Summary Tasks feature (shown in Figure 16.6). The files do not have to be linked in any way to use this feature.

Cross-project task dependencies are important if you are truly interested in managing the critical path. Otherwise, the critical path is simply displayed at the point where two projects just happen to converge. To truly appreciate the impact of changes to the project and, possibly, the critical path, task dependencies must be established.

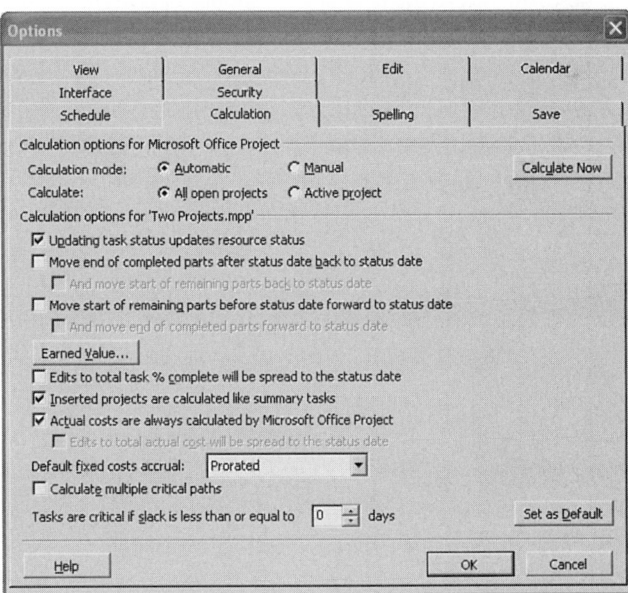

Figure 16.6
You can display a critical path across combined files by treating inserted files as summary tasks.

Creating Subprojects and Master Projects

There are advantages to managing a large or complex project in smaller, separate files: Computing speed, file sharing among co-workers, and faster printing and transmitting of smaller files are a few of them. When the time comes to review, analyze, and report on the plan across all the individual files, you can create a master project/subproject structure to combine the files of interest in one window. You can save this combined file and use it again later; you do not have to re-create it for each use. A further advantage of this approach is that the master project/subproject structure can be multi-tiered. This might be helpful in an organization that needs to combine projects at a departmental level, then at a functional level, then at a regional level, and finally at a national (or even international) level.

You can use two methods for combining files into a master/subproject structure. The first method—using the New Window command— was discussed earlier in this chapter, in the section "Displaying Tasks from Different Files in the Same Window." The following sections describe a second method for combining files—inserting files stored on disk into a new master project plan. Key master file issues, such as maintaining the combined file, removing a subproject, and linking between combined files, are also discussed in the following sections.

Combining Projects into One File

If a project that you want to combine with another is not already open, or if you want to insert a project at a specific point in a project, you select Insert, Project. To insert an entire project into another project, follow these steps:

1. Select the task row where the new project should be inserted. The existing task in that row will be moved down.
2. Choose Insert, Project to access the Insert Project dialog box (see Figure 16.7).

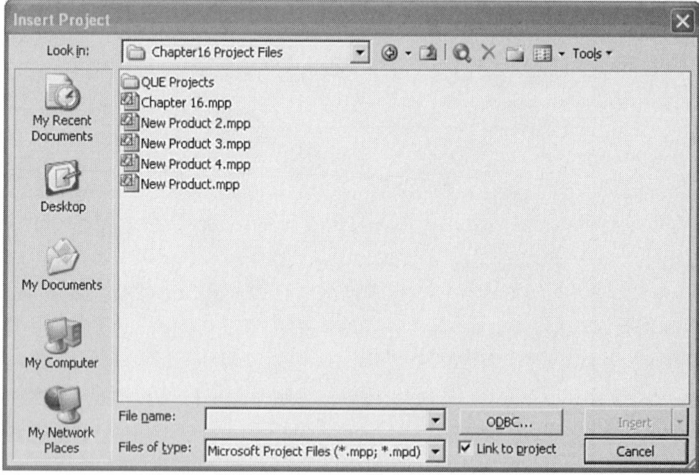

Figure 16.7
You can use the Insert Project dialog box to identify the file to be inserted into another.

3. Select the file to be inserted.

TIP

> If you want to insert multiple files at the same place in a master project file, click to select them in the order you want them displayed in the master file. To select multiple project files, select the first one and then extend your selection by holding down the Ctrl key while you select the other files. If you simply want to select a block of files that are all adjacent, use the Shift key to select the last file, to automatically select all the files between the first and last files you selected.

4. Use the Insert drop-down list on the Insert Project dialog box to select the Insert Read Only option to insert a read-only copy of the file. You can make changes to the source project in the master project, but you can't save changes back to the source copy. This is useful, for instance, if you want to allow a director or senior manager to see the effect of changes he or she would like to implement. That person cannot actually make the changes; he or she needs to discuss them with the individual project managers who are able to make changes in the source project. This way, project managers do not find that their projects change without their knowledge.
5. Create a link to the inserted project by choosing the Link to Project option. Changes to inserted and master files are also made to the other file, on a bidirectional basis. If the file is inserted as read-only, the update of the files from source project to master project works, but updates can't occur in the other direction. (Even if the files are inserted with full read-write capability, you still have the option of not saving changes and closing the files.)
6. Click OK when you are finished. The tasks of the inserted project are now available in the original file as if they had been entered there.

NOTE

> The ODBC button in the Insert Project dialog box allows you to insert a file that is stored in a database. This topic is covered in detail in Chapter 18, "Copying, Pasting, and Inserting Data with Other Applications." However, if you plan on using Project Professional and Server then the ODBC link will not apply.

WORKING WITH INSERTED PROJECTS

You can see information about an inserted project by choosing the Advanced tab in the Task Information dialog box. You access the dialog box by using the Task Information button in the Standard toolbar, or double-clicking the Project Summary Task that represents the inserted project. When you access the Task Information dialog box for a task that represents an inserted project, the title of the dialog box changes to Inserted Project Information, and the Advanced Tab displays details of the source project file. Notice in Figure 16.8 that the title bar indicates that this is an inserted project.

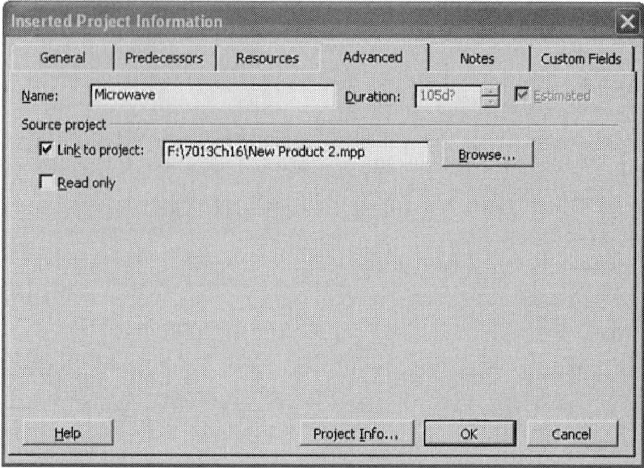

Figure 16.8
The Task Information dialog box for an inserted project displays information about the link to the source file and offers access to project information for that file.

You can choose whether to maintain a link with the individual source files. The Link to Project check box determines whether changes made in this file should be linked back to the original file. If it is checked, any content-related changes that you make to the new file are also made in the original source file. By default, there is a link between the inserted project and the original file that it came from. Regardless of your choice, any changes made to the formatting in the new window are not reflected in the source files. The obvious advantage of this is that you can make formatting changes in the new window for the purpose of printing reports for different audiences, without having those changes reflected in the original working file.

By default, files are opened as read-write, but you can change that to read-only. Select the Read Only check box if there is a link maintained and you prefer to protect the original source files. If the inserted file is set to read-only, the icon in the Indicators column of the Gantt Chart view shows an exclamation point and the message indicates that the file is read-only.

You can use the Browse button to change the link to another file or to restore the link when the file has been moved or renamed. (Upcoming sections in this chapter provide detailed information on moving, deleting, and renaming inserted projects.)

You can access the Project Information dialog box for the source file by clicking the Project Info button in the Inserted Project Information dialog box.

NOTE

> The reference to the location of the original source file is stored in the Subproject field for the inserted project task. If the Read Only check box is selected, Yes is stored in the Subproject Read Only field. You see these fields only if you add them to a table.

Project 2003 stores the relative path to linked or inserted projects. In previous versions of Project, the absolute path to these files was stored, causing users to save files to inconvenient locations simply to maintain links.

NOTE

> It's important to note that, when you combine project files by choosing Window, New Window or Insert, Project, these project files are only displayed together in one window—they are not linked to each other.

You can create inserted projects at any level of an outline, and you can insert a project into a project that is itself inserted into another project. Microsoft Project checks to be sure that no circular references exist within the levels.

Breaking a Large Project Apart by Using Inserted Projects

You can create inserted projects by moving tasks from a large project into new project files and then defining the new files as inserted projects. Some preparation is involved in making the move as easy and successful as possible.

If you move one or more tasks that are linked to tasks that will remain behind, you will lose the links and have to redefine them later. It is easier to copy the tasks that are going to become a new project file than cut them, save the copied tasks as a new file, insert the new project file, change the links, and then delete the original copied tasks.

To move tasks to a new project file, follow these steps:

1. Select the task IDs of the tasks that you plan to move. This ensures that all fields will be selected and that all relevant data will be copied. If the tasks to be moved include a summary and all the subtasks indented underneath it, you need only select the summary task.
2. Choose Edit, Copy Task (or press Ctrl+C) to copy the task data to the Clipboard.
3. Choose File, New to create a new project file. If the Prompt for Project Info for New Projects check box is checked on the General tab of the Options dialog box, the Project Information dialog box opens.

→ For more information on creating a new project file, **see** "Supplying Information for a New Project," **p. 56**.

4. With the Name field of the first task selected in the new file, choose Edit, Paste (or press Ctrl+V). The task data is copied.
5. Choose File, Save to save the new file. Fill in the dialog box to save the file and click OK.
6. Return to the original file by choosing the filename from the list at the bottom of the Window menu. Alternatively, you can press Ctrl+F6 until the project document reappears.
7. Select the task in the row below where the inserted task will be placed, and create the inserted project as described in the section "Working with Inserted Projects," earlier in this chapter.

Maintaining a library of subprojects allows you to incorporate the best practices of an organization and incorporate standard methodologies into all your projects. These linked methodologies can be previously completed projects, and they can also include the best lessons learned.

MAINTAINING INSERTED PROJECTS

16

You can replace an inserted project by changing the name in the Source Project area on the Advanced tab of the Task Information dialog box. You can use the Browse button to locate the file instead of typing it in. If you simply delete the filename, you sever the link between the two projects, and the inserted project task becomes a single task with the default one-day duration. If the new filename exists, it is used as the source project file instead of the one just replaced. If you type the name of the file to be inserted and Project can't find the file, a warning message appears, as shown in the title bar of Figure 16.9.

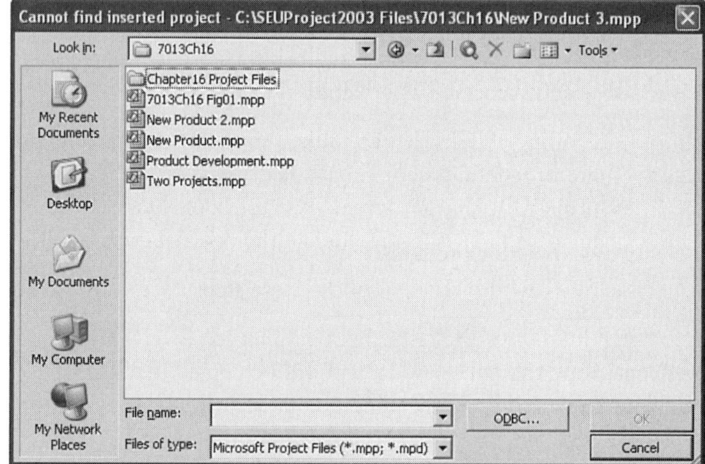

Figure 16.9
You need to re-identify an inserted project when the original is moved, deleted, renamed, or simply can't be found.

You need to be careful about moving or renaming projects that are used as inserted projects. When you open a project that contains an inserted project, if Microsoft Project can't find the file, it again displays the message shown in the title bar in Figure 16.9. To maintain the link, you would need to locate the file before proceeding.

CAUTION

You are not made aware of problems with linking to lost inserted project files until the outline for the file is expanded in the combined file. A combined file always opens collapsed down to a single summary line for each inserted project, even if the outline was expanded when the combined file was last saved and closed.

If you will be maintaining multiple subprojects rolled up into a master project, you should invest time into investigating how best to organize and catalog the repository of files. As with your desk filing cabinet or computer hard drive, creating the appropriate filing system can save a lot of time in organizing your files as well as in maintaining the linkages built into a master project.

IDENTIFYING TASKS THAT ARE INSERTED PROJECTS

In addition to the indicator for inserted projects in the Indicators column, you can use the Subproject File field, where the name of the inserted project is stored. You can design a table to display that field and thereby identify the tasks.

Each Subproject File field entry must contain a filename and extension that are separated by a period. Figure 16.10 shows a filter definition for displaying inserted projects by filtering the Subproject File field for entries that contain a period. You can use the *contains* test and enter a period as the value to look for.

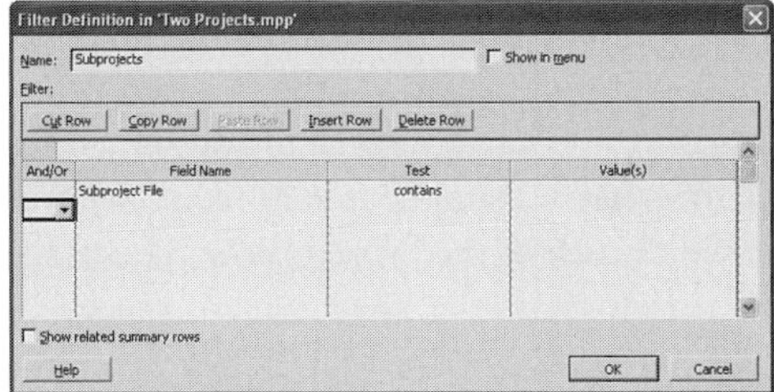

Figure 16.10
You can filter for inserted projects by searching the Subproject field for a period.

→ For more information on filter definitions, **see** "Creating Custom Filters," **p. 859**.

DELETING INSERTED PROJECTS

You delete an inserted project in much the same way as you delete a summary task. Simply select it and then press the Delete key on the keyboard, or right-click the task ID and choose Delete Task from the shortcut menu. You are warned about deleting more than one task, with the warning message shown in Figure 16.11. If you are using the Office Assistant, the warnings appear in the Office Assistant's question box rather than in the standard Windows dialog box.

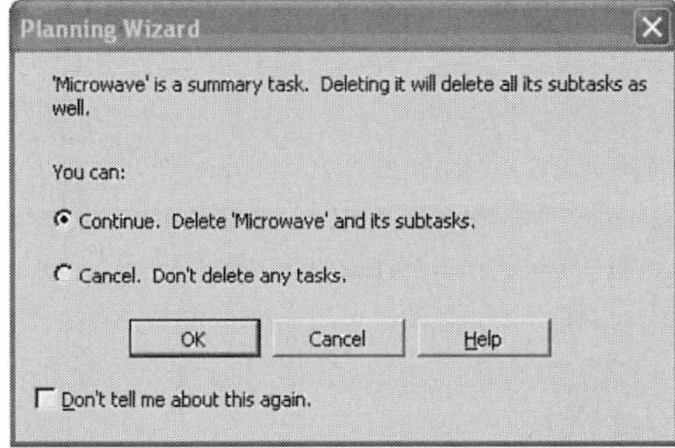

Figure 16.11
Deleting an inserted project deletes all the tasks that were part of that project.

Creating Links Between Tasks in Separate Projects

You can create two basic types of links between projects. In the first type, all the tasks of one project taken together are the predecessor or successor to a group of tasks in another project. For example, in the New Product project file, the design phase is probably handled by another department that is also using Microsoft Project. Many other tasks in the New Product project can't proceed until the design phase is complete. You could insert the entire project for the design phase and link it as you would link any other task.

A second kind of link occurs when a specific task in another project—not the project start or finish—needs to be linked to a specific task in the current project file. For example, in the design phase, there is a task called Prototype Completed. Although the design phase as a whole might not be complete, some sales and marketing tasks could begin when the prototype is complete.

Whichever situation you have, the method for creating the links is the same: Simply select both tasks and use the Edit, Link Tasks command or the Link Tasks tool on the Standard toolbar. If you have inserted a whole project into another project, you can easily expand the inserted project task list and select the tasks to be linked. You should use Window, New Window to display tasks from both projects together and then select the tasks to be linked. Alternatively, you can enter the full path of the project file and task ID in the Predecessors or Successors task fields, using this format:

drive:*directory**subdirectory**filename.ext**taskIDnumber*

For example, if the predecessor is Task 6 in the project file `productx.mpp`, which is stored in the directory `C:\Manufacturing\Development`, you would enter the following into the Predecessors field:

```
C:\Manufacturing\Development\productx.mpp\6
```

NOTE

> On networked computers, in Windows 95, 98, NT, 2000, or XP, it's not necessary to use a drive name; a network share can be used instead. The format in this case would be
>
> *sharename**directory**subdirectory**filename.ext**taskIDnumber*
>
> You can even store files on FTP sites and then insert them via the Insert Project dialog box, by pulling up the predefined FTP site under the drop-down list box for the Look In field.

Cross-links between files can use any of the standard task relationships (Finish-to-Finish, Finish-to-Start, Start-to-Finish, and Start-to-Start), and they can support lag and lead time.

→ To learn more about creating links between tasks, **see** "Understanding Dependency Links," **p. 177**, and "Entering Dependency Links," **p. 185**.

When a link is established, the name of the task it is being linked to appears in the task list, in gray text. The duration, start, and finish also display in gray. No other information is immediately available. If the task that is linked to has a duration, the taskbar appears in gray as well. If the task being linked to is a milestone, the milestone marker is gray. If you double-click the linked task, the project plan that contains the linked task opens. In the source project for the linked task, the task that was linked to from the destination project plan also appears in gray, and you can double-click it to return to the original project plan. If you access the Task Information dialog box for either of the two grayed tasks, you can view information about the task, but you can change only Note entries.

CAUTION

> Project allows you to enter a note about a grayed task, but the note you enter is not linked back to the original task.

NOTE

> When you create a link to a task in another project file, the External Task field is set to Yes. This means that you can create a filter for all tasks that have external links. This filter, combined with a table that includes the Predecessors and Successors columns, would provide a view of all external links and their sources.

For example, say you are using separate files for two new products in development. Suppose that design work for the second product prototype can begin when the prototype for the first product is finished. When the two tasks from separate files have been linked together, Project includes placeholder tasks in both files. The external successor task in the `First New Product` file would look as shown in Figure 16.12.

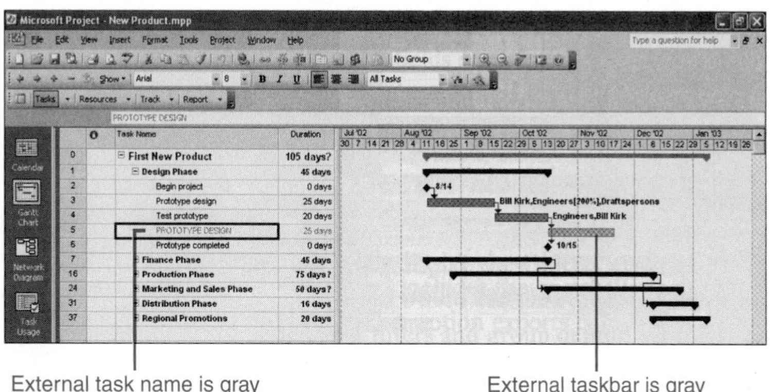

Figure 16.12
A predecessor or successor that refers to a task in another project creates a cross-linked task.

Notice the gray text of the task name Prototype Design. This task is only part of the `First New Product` file to the extent that it is a successor to the Prototype Completed task. If you double-click the Prototype Design task, the `Second New Product` file is opened, as shown in Figure 16.13. Notice the gray text of the first Prototype Completed task. This task is only part of the Second New Product plan to the extent that it is a predecessor to beginning the

Prototype Design task. If you double-click the gray Prototype Design task, you are returned to the `First New Product` file.

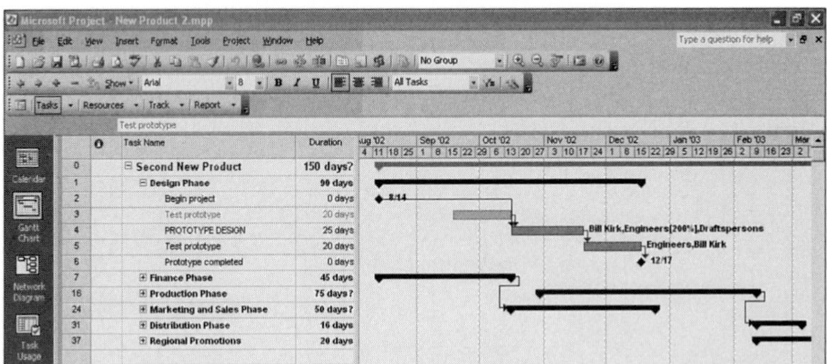

Figure 16.13
Grayed task names indicate cross-linked tasks and allow easy movement between files.

From here on out, any changes in the `First New Product` file that cause the Prototype Completed task to change will have an impact on the `Second New Product` file. Otherwise, the two project plans will function independently of each other.

When you open a file that has cross-linked predecessors, a Links Between Projects dialog box automatically appears if any changes have taken place to the external tasks. You can access this dialog box at any time by choosing Tools, Links Between Projects. You can use this dialog box not only to refresh any changes made to the external files but also to reestablish file locations or delete links. The Differences column shows what kind of changes have taken place. Notice in Figure 16.14 the full path is shown for the selected task in the title bar of the dialog box.

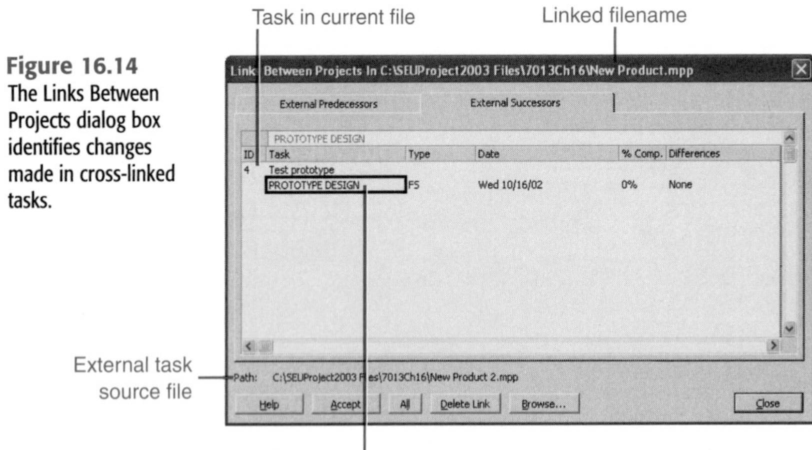

Figure 16.14
The Links Between Projects dialog box identifies changes made in cross-linked tasks.

If you create links that would cause a circular relationship between tasks—that is, one task acting as a predecessor and a successor of another—the dialog box in Figure 16.15 opens. You need to explore the relationships between the linked tasks and locate and remove the erroneous link.

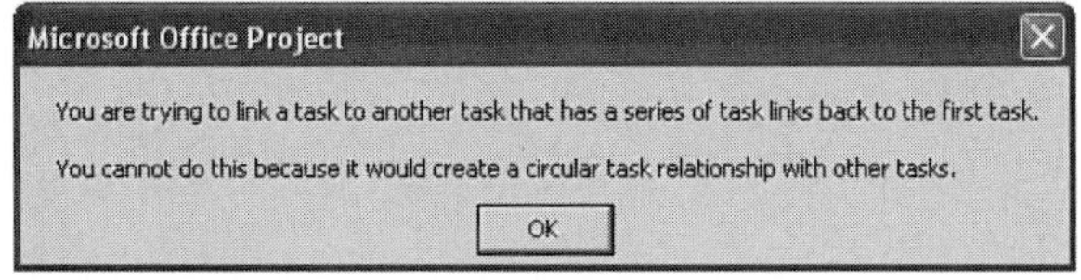
Microsoft Office Project
You are trying to link a task to another task that has a series of task links back to the first task.
You cannot do this because it would create a circular task relationship with other tasks.
OK

Figure 16.15
Project displays an error message if any cross-linked tasks create a circular relationship.

Sharing Resources Among Projects

It is not unusual to have several projects use the same set of resources. When this is the case, it's cumbersome to manage the same resources in several different project files. You can't easily see what each resource is doing for all projects. You might want to have Microsoft Project store the resource information in one file and only the assignment information in the project files. You do this by entering all resources in one project file (which might not even have any tasks) and by instructing the other project files to use the resources defined in the file with the resources.

If a number of projects share the same list of resources, you can open all the projects at the same time and view the allocation of resources across the projects. Microsoft Project warns you when a resource is overallocated because of conflicting assignments in different projects, and you can use the leveling command to resolve the resource overallocation by delaying tasks in different projects.

→ For more information on managing resource allocations, **see** "Strategies for Eliminating Resource Overallocations," **p. 417**.

Creating the Resource Pool

Any project file can be the one that contains the resource pool. If the resources typically work on many different projects, you can create a project file that has no tasks in it but that simply contains a list of the resources.

→ For more information on Project templates, **see** "Creating and Using Templates," **p. 103**.

Using the Resource Pool

You can define any project file to use the resources of another project file, by choosing Tools, Resources, Share Resources. If both files have resources defined in them at the time the link is established, the resource pool is enlarged to include all resources defined in both files. If the same resource is defined in both files and there is a difference in the definition between the two files, you must tell Microsoft Project which file takes precedence in settling definition conflicts. The Share Resources dialog box provides a check box for this purpose.

Maintaining a clean pool should be a significant concern to project managers and resource managers. Project's default option is for the pool to take precedence, and this should probably be the button of choice for every project link that is established. This way, each new sharer can be assured of having the most current resource data available. It will help prevent inconsistencies between projects that utilize the same set of resources.

After a sharing link is established, you can look at the Resource Sheet view in either file to see the complete list of resources, and you can change the resource definitions in either file. When you close the files, each includes a copy of the entire resource pool. In this way, you can open the project file that uses the resource pool independently of the file that actually contains the resources, if needed, to modify and manage that project file.

To enable a project file to use the resources of another file, follow these steps:

1. Open both project files: the one containing the resource pool and the one that is to share that pool. Make sure that the active project is the one that is to use the other project's resources.
2. Choose Tools, Resources, Share Resources to display the Share Resources dialog box (see Figure 16.16). Choose the Use Resources option button and use the From drop-down box for a list of currently open files from which you can choose.

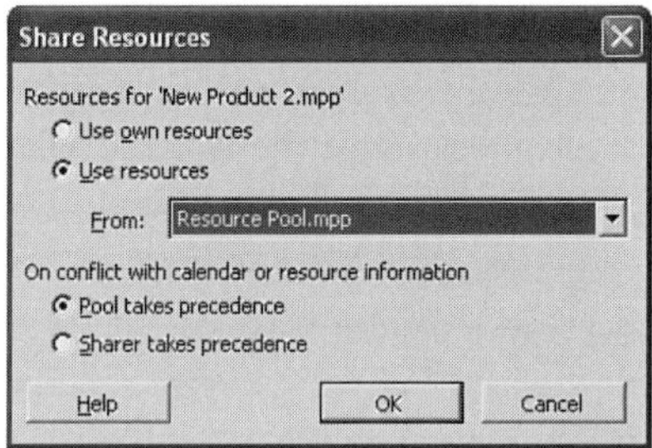

Figure 16.16
You can use the Share Resources dialog box to link to a resource pool in another project file.

3. Select the Pool Takes Precedence option button if you want conflicting definitions to be settled by the entry in the file that contains the resource pool. Select the Sharer Takes Precedence option button if you want resource definition conflicts to be settled by the entry in the file that uses the resource pool.
4. Click OK to complete the link.

If the file containing the resources is not open when you open a connected file that shares its resources, an Open Resource Pool Information dialog box opens (see Figure 16.17). You can choose to have Project open the resource pool as well as all other project files that use the resources.

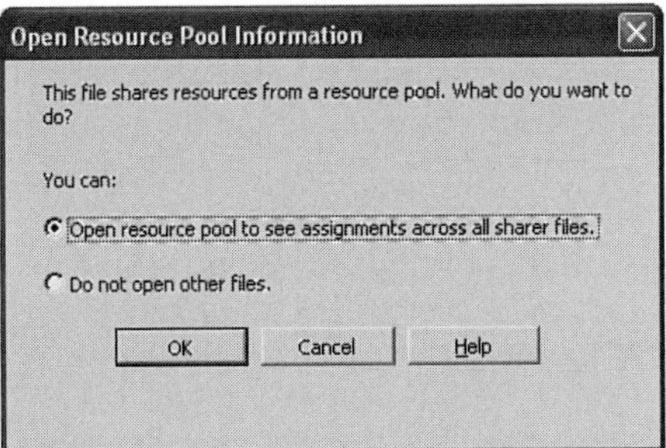

Figure 16.17 Microsoft Project offers to open the file that contains the resources.

16

The Open Resource Pool Information dialog box displays several different options (see Figure 16.18). If you choose the first option, to open the resource pool and see assignments across all sharer files, both files are opened and any changes made to the sharer file are immediately reflected in the pool. The pool file is said to be opened as read-only, but this is misleading. The pool can accept changes to resource assignment information, so it isn't read-only; however, it is locked to prevent other sharer files from making immediate changes to the pool.

The other option in the Open Resource Pool Information dialog box allows you to open and work on a project file without also opening the resource pool. This lowers the computing overhead and increases work speed.

CAUTION

If you open a shared file without also opening the pool and you make changes to the file, the changes are saved with the file, but the pool is not immediately updated. Your changes are not incorporated into the pool until the pool itself and all sharer files have been opened at one time. Options for opening the resource pool file are shown in Figure 16.18.

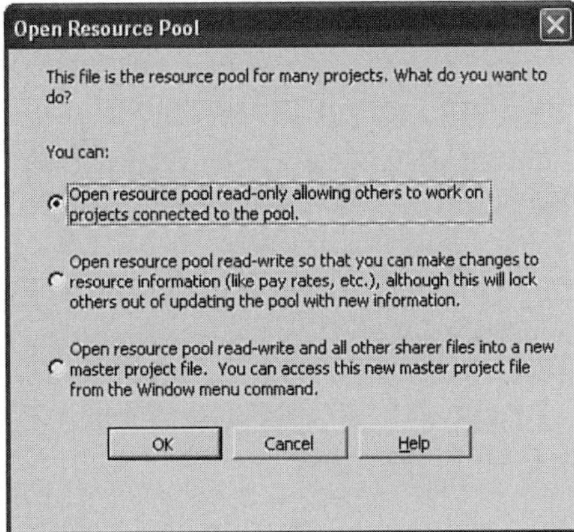

Figure 16.18 Access to and the behavior of the resource pool file are affected by how the pool was opened.

When you open the resource pool file directly, the option you choose on the Open Resource Pool dialog box determines the accessibility and updating behavior of the pool. The read-only option allows you to make changes and see the results immediately in a copy of the last-saved version of the pool file, but changes made in real-time by any other user are not reflected until the pool is closed and reopened. However, you can use certain commands to refresh the pool with current information while multiple users are working in it. Under Tools, Resources, choose the Update Resource Pool option to save changes to the stored resource pool, and then use the Refresh Resource Pool option to load a fresh copy of the pool into the open pool window. If these two options are not available (that is, they are grayed out), the file-sharing environment is such that updating and refreshing the pool are not necessary.

The second option for opening a resource pool file is to open the file as read-write. The descriptive text in the Open Resource Pool dialog box informs you that this option gives you complete editing control over the pool file but it completely locks out other users while you have the file open. You can use the third option—open the resource pool and all sharer files—to force the pool file to retrieve the latest saved versions of all attached files and essentially rebuild the pool.

TIP

It is good computing practice to periodically open the resource pool file and all sharer files, forcing the most up-to-date information into all files. This procedure also alerts you if files have lost or corrupted links.

After a project is set up to share another project's resource pool, if the resource pool is open in read/write mode, any changes you make to the resource pool while both files are open are recorded directly into the shared pool and are shared by both files immediately.

If you work with the dependent project file alone, however, and you make changes in the resource sheet of that project, the changes might not be saved back to the resource pool immediately (although you should be prompted to do so when saving the file). And if you merely add new resources with different names, the resources are added to the resource pool when the resource pool is next opened in read/write mode.

If you change the definition of the resource (for example, the pay rate, maximum units, or working days on the resource calendar), the changes might be lost when both files are loaded in memory together the next time. If you marked the Pool Takes Precedence option button in the Share Resources dialog box, the changes are lost if you try to make the changes in a dependent file; if you marked the Sharer Takes Precedence option button in the Share Resources dialog box, the changes are recorded in the resource pool. However, the Sharer Takes Precedence option is not used very often, and in the vast majority of cases, the Pool Takes Precedence option is the default.

TIP

For consistency, the resource pool should be the only file where underlying resource details are changed. Typically, one or two people in a company are made custodians of the resource pool, and they enter all changes to pay rates and other resource details. The sharer files should be connected to the pool, and the Pool Takes Precedence option should be selected.

SAVING MULTIPLE FILES IN A WORKSPACE

The pool and resource-sharing files can be saved simultaneously into a workspace file. This workspace file is assigned the default filename of `resume.mpw`. You can choose File, Save Workspace to save all open pool and sharer files together.

An easy way to open files attached to a resource pool is to open the pool file first and then open the Share Resources dialog box (by choosing Tools, Resources, Share Resources). The Share Resources dialog box presents a list of all sharing files. You open all sharing files by clicking the Open All button (see Figure 16.19). You can also open an individual sharing file by selecting the filename in the Sharing links area and clicking Open.

→ This is not to be confused with Shared Workspaces, which require Windows SharePoint Services to work. For more information on Shared Workspaces, **see** "Using Windows SharePoint Services and Shared Workspaces," **p. 628**.

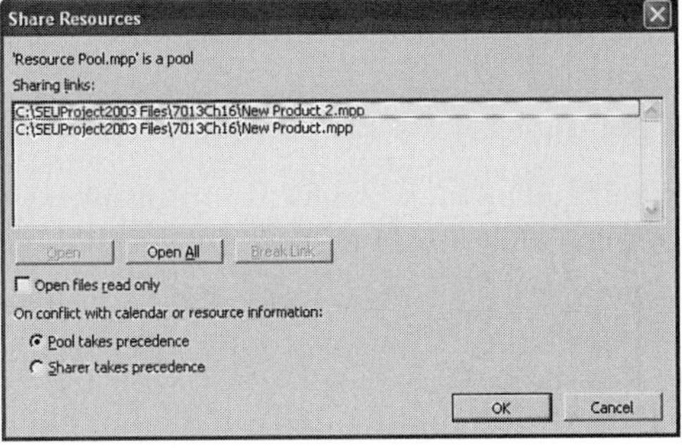

Figure 16.19 You can open all sharing files from within the Share Resources dialog box in the pool file.

DISCONTINUING RESOURCE SHARING

You can discontinue the sharing of resources at any time. To do so, simply open the file that uses another file's resources, open the Share Resources dialog box (by choosing Tools, Resources, Share Resources), and choose the Use Own Resources option button. The resources in the resource pool are then no longer available to the file. However, any resources that were assigned to tasks in the file are copied into the file's resource list and are saved with the file. Likewise, any resource in the file that was sharing the resource pool of another project is copied into the pool and remains there, even after sharing is discontinued.

To discontinue a project file's dependence on another file's resource pool, perform the following steps:

1. Open the file that is to become independent and use its own resources.
2. Make the file that is to use its own resources the active file window.
3. Choose Tools, Resources, Share Resources to open the Share Resources dialog box.
4. Choose the Use Own Resources option button.
5. Click OK to execute the new definition.

The message in Figure 16.20 confirms the removal of the connection between the two files.

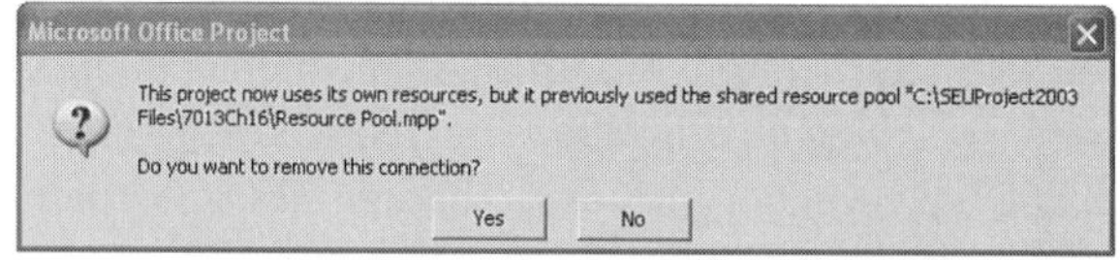

Figure 16.20
Project confirms that you want to remove the connection between a project file and a resource pool.

NOTE

You can also break a sharing link from the other direction: Open the pool file and display the Share Resources dialog box. As shown in Figure 16.19, a Break Link option is available.

Identifying Resource Pool Links

A resource-sharing connection is recorded in the file that contains the resource pool and in the file that uses the resource pool. The Share Resources dialog box displays linking information in both file types, and the layout of the dialog box tells you which of the two file types is active.

Figure 16.16 displays the Share Resources dialog box in a file that uses the resource list from another file. Contrast that illustration with Figure 16.19. As you can see, Project knows which file is acting as the pool file and changes the Share Resources dialog box to offer file link-management options.

TIP

When you first begin to experiment with inserted projects, cross-project links, and sharing resource pools, it would be worth your while to create a table that includes the following columns: External, Linked Fields, Predecessors, Successors, Subproject File, Subproject File Read-Only, and Notes. As you begin working with the files, you can see exactly what is happening and where Project is storing the information. Then you can change the column titles to abbreviations so that you can make the columns narrow and see more onscreen without scrolling.

➔ For more information on customizing tables, **see** "Using and Creating Tables," **p. 840**.

VIEWING RESOURCE LOADS WITHOUT SHARING A POOL

In a large organization, it might not be desirable to have multiple project managers attaching their files to a single resource pool. Performance can be affected, and other managers might be prohibited from making and saving changes to their files if someone has inadvertently opened all the sharer files. If your main reason for pooling is to summarize and report on resource assignments across multiple files, it is not necessary to maintain file links to a resource pool.

When two or more Project files have been consolidated, as discussed earlier in this chapter, Project can create a combined list of resources assigned to those files. Breaking the link to all underlying files causes Project to re-create a list of resources from all consolidated files. Resource names from each file are matched, and the assignments are totaled. Then the Resource Usage view, among others, shows the distribution of work by resource across all projects consolidated in the particular file.

To create this combined resource list, open the Task Information dialog box for the project summary line of each inserted project. Move to the Advanced tab and, in the Source Project area, clear the check box for the Link to Project option, as shown in Figure 16.21. Now the Gantt Chart view displays tasks renumbered consecutively; duplicate task IDs no longer exist. The individual files cannot be edited within this revised consolidation because the links no longer exist. You can create a separate consolidated file, including file links, to edit projects from this level.

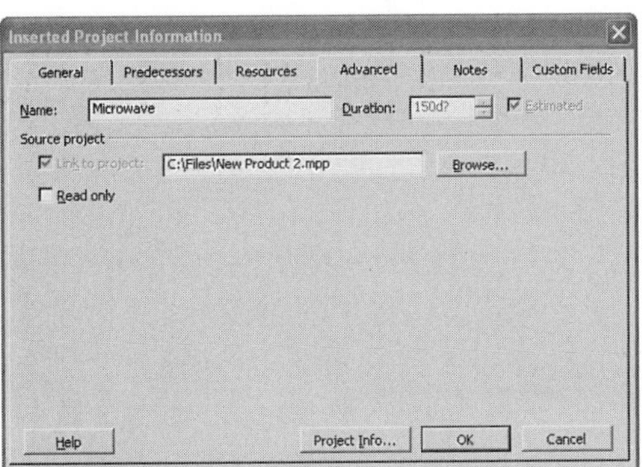

Figure 16.21
You can unlink consolidated files to create a combined resource list across projects.

TIP

> When using this method to create a consolidated resource list, you should still maintain a separate file that acts as a resource information repository. Designate someone to keep the resource detail information—pay rate, nonworking time, and so on—up-to-date in a single file. When updates are made, notify all project managers to open their Project files, link them to this resource file to bring down the most recent resource information, and then simply break the resource-sharing link and save their files.

Using Windows SharePoint Services and Shared Workspaces

If you have a server running Windows SharePoint Services, you can save your projects to it and take advantage of the many new features it offers. The Shared Workspace feature (shared with Microsoft Office 2003 applications) allows you to see other users' tasks (not to be confused with project tasks), documents, lists, and team member names, all from a task pane that is integrated into Project 2003. You can also check documents (projects) in and out from the workspace. Please note that this option does NOT require Microsoft Office Project Server and in fact cannot be used if you are using the Microsoft Office EPM solution (for example, Project Professional and Project Server). To activate the workspace features, you need to

16

1. Have access to a server that is running Windows SharePoint Services. You should also create a workspace and then enable permissions to the workspace.
2. Save a project to the server that is running Windows SharePoint Services. For example, create a new project, then in the Save As dialog (on the File menu) enter the URL to your server running Windows SharePoint Services in the File Name field, such as `http://sharepointserver:90/teamspace`.

When you click Save, Microsoft Project connects you to the Windows SharePoint Services-extended server where you can see other documents that have already been saved or workspaces that you have created; at this point, you can select a workspace, then enter a project name, and then click Save to finish the saving process. This is shown in Figure 16.22.

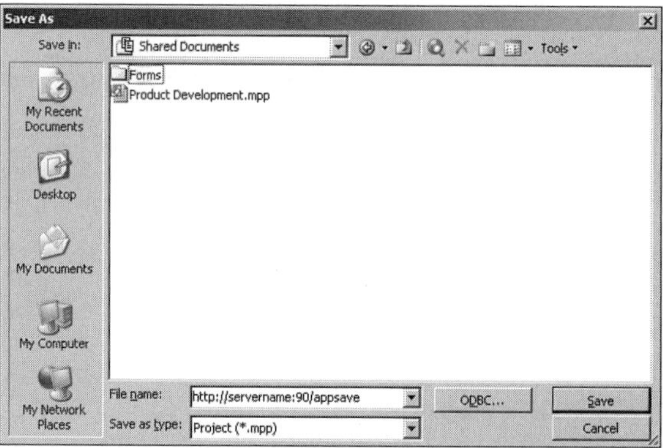

Figure 16.22
Saving tasks to a Project Workspace.

Once you have saved a project to the shared workspace on the server running Windows SharePoint Services, a number of menu items become available to you. On the Tools menu, the Shared Workspace option becomes active. Selecting this activates the Shared Workspace area. Additionally, on the File menu, the Check-out/Check-in and Versions menus become available.

In the Shared Workspace pane, you will be able to see a number of things, such as a list of other members of your group, whether they are online, if there are comments about documents, or even a list of documents that are also stored in the workspace.

You can check out projects from the common workspace and also create different versions of the projects. Should you choose to check in the project, you are prompted for comments that are saved with the version you are saving.

In the Versions dialog box, you can choose to open a given version, delete a version, view the comments, or restore a versioned project as the current project.

TROUBLESHOOTING

VIEWING TASK INFORMATION FROM MULTIPLE PROJECTS

When I choose Window, New Window, I can't tell which task is from which file, especially if I have sorted the tasks by their start dates. Can I change that?

You can modify the table that you are using so that it also displays the project filename, which is most likely just before or just after the ID number for the task. This way you can see the filename and the task ID together, so you can distinguish between files. To make this change, right-click a column heading and choose Insert Column. Then choose Project for the Field Name.

TURNING OFF RESOURCE SHARING

My project plan is sharing resources with several other plans. How do I make it stop sharing?

To fix this problem, open the file that uses another file's resources, open the Share Resources dialog box (by choosing Tools, Resources, Share Resources), and choose the Use Own Resources option button. Then, the resources in the resource pool are no longer available to the file. Remember that any resources assigned to tasks in the file are copied into the file's resource list and are saved with the file. Likewise, any resource in the file that was sharing the resource pool of another project is copied into the pool and remains there, even after sharing is discontinued.

CHAPTER 17

EXPORTING AND IMPORTING PROJECT DATA WITH OTHER FILE FORMATS

In this chapter

Exchanging Project Data with Other Applications 632

File Formats Supported by Microsoft Project 2003 632

Importing Project 2003 Data from Other Project Management Applications 636

Exporting Project 2003 Data to Older Versions of Microsoft Project 636

Using the Import/Export Wizard 637

Saving an Entire Project in a Database 640

Exchanging Selected Parts of a Project with Other Formats 649

Using Project 2003 as an OLE DB Provider 687

Troubleshooting 689

EXCHANGING PROJECT DATA WITH OTHER APPLICATIONS

There are many reasons you might find it useful to be able to share all or part of a Microsoft Project 2003 document with another software application. One common reason is to be able to prepare reports in other applications. Similarly, it is often useful to import data from other applications into Microsoft Project, especially to avoid retyping large amounts of data. The following scenarios illustrate some of the uses for Project's data-exchange capability:

- You might have a list of tasks or resource names in Excel that you want to use in a Project plan. You might also have a list of tasks in Outlook. It is faster and more accurate to import the data than to type it again in Project.
- You might want to analyze some of your Project data by using the special calculating power of Microsoft Excel.
- There might be others in your organization who want to query your project, but who don't have Project installed on their PCs. If the project is saved in a database format such as Access or SQL Server, you can work on it in Project and the others can use Access-aware applications to view the Project data details.
- You might prefer to publish your project on a corporate intranet or on the Internet, via Web pages, using Hypertext Markup Language (HTML) or eXtensible Markup Language (XML).

This chapter helps you choose the best method for exchanging data between a Microsoft Project 2003 project file and other software applications. As illustrated by the examples in the preceding list, you can transfer all the Project data or only a part of it. For small amounts of data, it is probably easier to copy and paste, using the Windows Clipboard. Chapter 18, "Copying, Pasting, and Inserting Data with Other Applications," describes how to copy and paste data between Project files and other file formats. For larger transfers, it is usually easiest to export and import data files as described in this chapter.

FILE FORMATS SUPPORTED BY MICROSOFT PROJECT 2003

You can import and export entire projects or selected sets of project data by using the File, Open and File, Save As menu commands. These commands allow you to read and write the project data in formats other than Project's native .mpp format. After providing an overview of the file formats supported by Microsoft Project 2003, this chapter examines the details of exporting and importing with each of the formats.

→ For information about using the File commands, **see** Chapter 4, "Managing Project Files," **p. 95**.

Microsoft Project supports three native formats that store all Project data, including views, tables, filters, groups, and field data. Additional formats are supported for exchanging selected data with other applications that don't read the Project native formats. Table 17.1 summarizes the file formats that you can use with Microsoft Project 2003. In general, if the format can handle the entire set of Project data, Microsoft Project creates copies of all its tables and fields in the new format. If only part of the Project data is to be exchanged, you need to use an Import/Export map to match Project fields with the fields in the other format.

NOTE

The file extensions referred to in Table 17.1 and the text are visible in Project's Open and Save As dialog boxes only if Windows is set to display file extensions.

TABLE 17.1 FILE FORMATS SUPPORTED BY MICROSOFT PROJECT 2003

File Format	Extension	Description
Native Formats		
Project	`.mpp`	This is the standard format for Project document files, and it is compatible with Project 2000/2002. It saves the complete set of project data. Project versions prior to Project 2000 cannot open these files.
Template	`.mpt`	Templates save standard, or *boilerplate*, information that you use frequently for projects. When a new project is created using the template, a new Project document is created.
Project Database	`.mpd`	This format is based on the Microsoft Access 2000/2002 file format. The entire project data set is saved in this format, including field data, views, calendars, and formatting. The files can be queried, opened, modified, and saved in either Microsoft Project or Microsoft Access.
Other Formats		
Project 98	`.mpp`	The Project 98 file format is used to save a project file to a version that is compatible with Project 98. Because of differences between Project 98 and 2003, certain features of the project file are lost in the 98 plan.
Microsoft Project Exchange (MPX) 4.0	`.mpx`	The MPX format is used to import data from older versions of Microsoft Project or from other project management applications. The MPX 4.0 format does not include the fields and features introduced in Project 98, 2000, 2002, or 2003. You can open an `.mpx` file in Project 2003, but you cannot save Project 2003 documents in `.mpx` format.

continues

17

Table 17.1 Continued

File Format	Extension	Description
Other Formats		
Microsoft Access	.mdb	The Microsoft Access 2000/2002 database format can be used to save all or part of a project's data. Any application that recognizes this format can open the file or query it for reports. An Import/Export map can be used with this format if you want to save only portions of the project.
Open Database Connectivity (ODBC)	N/A	ODBC databases are data storage sources that can be accessed by a wide variety of applications, both commercial software products and custom applications. You can store entire projects or selected project data in ODBC data stores. The use of an Import/Export map is optional.
Microsoft Excel Workbook	.xls	Project can export to the Microsoft Excel 5.0/95 format. You can export field data in this format but not project elements such as calendars and views. The resulting file can be opened directly as a workbook in Microsoft Excel or in any application that supports the Excel 5.0/95 format. Although you can read Excel 2002 data into Microsoft Project 2003, you cannot save data in the Excel 2002 format from Project 2003. An Import/Export map is required for exchanging data in this format.
Microsoft Excel PivotTable	.xls	This format is used for analyzing project data in an Excel PivotTable. You can export only selected field data to a PivotTable. You cannot import from an Excel PivotTable into Microsoft Project. An Import/Export map is required for exporting data in this format.
HTML	.htm	The HTML format is used to create Web pages to be viewed on the World Wide Web and corporate intranets. You can export selected field data to the HTML format, but not an entire project. You cannot import from HTML files into Microsoft Project. An Import/Export map is required for exporting data in this format.

File Format	Extension	Description
Other Formats		
XML	.xml	Another file format for Project 2003 is the XML format. This format is similar to HTML, and is complementary to HTML for publishing Project data to Web pages and for viewing on either the Internet or on corporate intranets. Unlike HTML files, however, XML files can be opened directly by Project 2003.
ASCII Text	.txt	This is a generic text format that is widely used for data transfers between applications and platforms. Field data is tab delimited. You can transfer field data for only a single Microsoft Project table in this format. An Import/Export map is required for exchanging data in this format.
Comma Separated Value	.csv	This is another generic text format that is widely used for transferring data between applications and platforms. Originally, field values were separated by commas, but now the format uses the default system list separator. You can transfer field data for only a single Microsoft Project table in this format. An Import/Export map is required for exchanging data in this format.

NOTE

The Project Workspace format, which has the extension .mpw, also appears in the list of file types in both the Open dialog box as Workspaces (*.mpw), and on the File menu as Save As Workspace. However, this is not really a data file format. It merely saves the *workspace settings* (that is, the names of the files that are open, not any field data), so that you can open all those files in the same window arrangement by simply opening the .mpw file.

The sections that follow examine all these file formats except the standard Project document (.mpp), Project template (.mpt), and Project Workspace (.mpw) types, which are covered in Chapter 4.

Most of the non-native formats require that you use an Import/Export map to define which field values in Project are to be associated with data locations in the other format. The creation and use of a map are described in detail with the first file format that requires it.

See the section "Creating Import/Export Maps for Access and ODBC Sources," later in this chapter.

Importing Project 2003 Data from Other Project Management Applications

In the past, the most comprehensive exchange of data between Microsoft Project and other products was through the MPX format. However, MPX has been replaced by the Microsoft Project Database format as the preferred vehicle for exchanging all project data. Project 2003 can open MPX files, but it cannot create or save files in MPX format.

To open a Microsoft Project 2003 file that was saved in MPX format, choose File, Open. After selecting the search directory in the Look In text box, the list of files you can open will include any MPX files in that directory, along with the rest of the Project files. To see just the MPX files, select MPX in the Files of Type list box. Select the MPX filename that you want to open and click the Open button. The MPX file will then be opened as a new Project 2003 (`.mpp`) project file.

Exporting Project 2003 Data to Older Versions of Microsoft Project

Project 2003 maintains backward compatibility with Project 2000 and 2002 by using the same file format. This means that you can save a Project 2003 file, and then open it, revise it, and save it in Project 2000/2002, and then reopen it again in Project 2003. In general, most Project 2003 data will be retained when the file is opened in Project 2000/2002; however, any new data fields that Project 2000 cannot understand simply remain hidden while the file is open in Project 2000.

NOTE

> Project 2003 uses a unique method of handling new and unknown data fields that may be included in upcoming releases of Microsoft Project. Instead of hiding the unknown data fields for backward compatibility, Project 2003 will display field names as Unavailable and field data as NA for data that comes from any future version.

To maintain backward compatibility between Project 2003 and Project 98, it is possible to use Project 2003 to both open and save project files in the native Project 98 format. When you attempt to save a project file in Project 98 format, the resulting file is stripped of any Project 2003 features that are not compatible with Project 98. You also see a dialog box that warns you of the potential for lost data.

To save a file in Microsoft Project 98 format, choose File, Save As. Select a save directory in the Look In text box, and then select Microsoft Project 98 in the Files of Type list box. Give your file a name and click the Save button.

TIP

> Because the file extension for a Project 98 file is the same as for a Project 2003 file (`.mpp`), you should use a unique naming system for Project 98 files. For example, `New Product-98.mpp` can be easily distinguished as a Project 98 project from its Project 2003 version, `New Product.mpp`.

USING THE IMPORT/EXPORT WIZARD

A helpful feature of Project 2003 is the Import/Export Wizard. This wizard launches automatically whenever you attempt to open or save a file that does not have the `.mpp` file extension. To demonstrate how the Import/Export Wizard functions, the following steps document what the Export Wizard shows when you attempt to save a file as an Excel workbook (`.xls`):

1. The first screen of the Import/Export Wizard is the Welcome page. If you are importing a file, Import Wizard is displayed on the title bar of the dialog box and if you are exporting a project file, the Export Wizard appears. There are no options for you to select—only an explanation of what this wizard can do. Click Next to continue or Cancel to stop the export procedure.
2. The second screen displayed is the Data page, which asks how you want to export the data. Generally, you can export data as a full project, selected data only, or some other option that is unique to the type of data you are exporting.

   As with most wizards in Microsoft software applications, you can click Back to return to the previous page, click Next to continue, or click Cancel to stop the exporting procedure.
3. If you chose to export selective data, the third screen is the Map page (see Figure 17.1). This page allows you to choose the type of map to use for exporting data. The choices are generally limited to creating your own map by selecting the New Map option, or using an existing map.

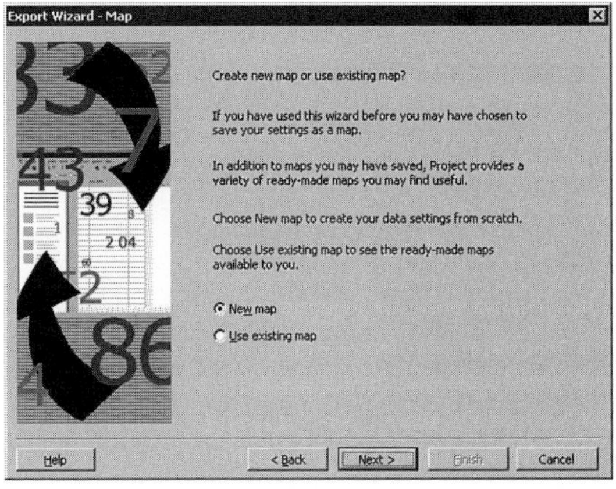

Figure 17.1
The Map page allows you to choose whether to use a new map or an existing map to export data.

4. If you choose the Existing Map option in the Map page, you see the Map Selection page (see Figure 17.2). Choose the existing map that you want to use to export your data and click the Finish button.

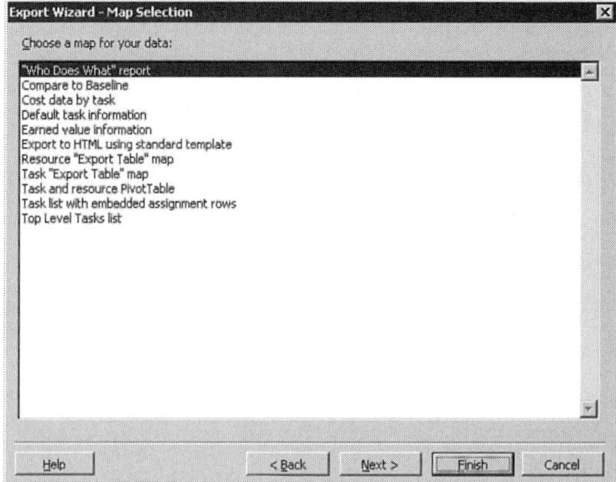

Figure 17.2
The Map Selection page lists all the predefined and custom maps for exporting data.

5. The next screen is the Map Options page, which allows you to select the type of data you want to export. The options generally include exporting tasks, resources, or assignments, or a combination of the three. One exception is that when you export project data to a text file (`.txt` or `.csv`), you can export only one of the three data types at a time.

   In addition to the data options to be selected, there may be additional options in the bottom half of the dialog box, depending on the file type.

6. The next screen is the Task Mapping page (see Figure 17.3), where you provide information that is used for mapping Project data into the receiving application. For example, you provide information on how to map the field names in Project with field names in the application that is receiving the exported data.

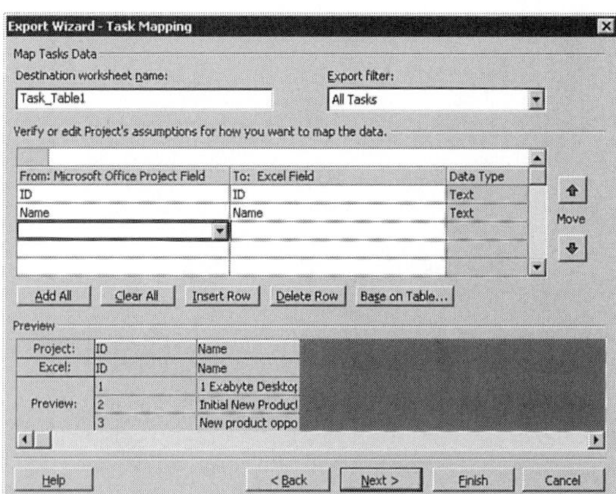

Figure 17.3
The Task Mapping page tells Project how to map your data to the application that is receiving the exported data.

7. The final screen of the Import/Export Wizard shows the End of Map Definition page. This page allows you to save your map, whether you created a new map or edited an existing map. To save the map, click the Save Map button. Otherwise, click Finish to export the data.
8. If you elected to save the map, you next see the Save Map dialog box (see Figure 17.4). Give the new map a name and click Save. You can use the Organizer button to copy one or more maps into the active Project file.

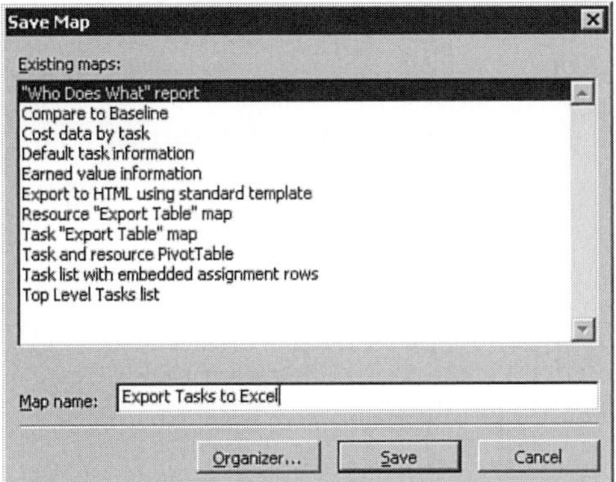

Figure 17.4
You use the Save Map dialog box to save a new or edited map.

You see additional wizard pages only when you are importing data. One of these is the Import Mode page (see Figure 17.5), which is used to tell Project how to import the data. Generally, if you have chosen to import partial data from a file such as an Excel workbook or an Access database, you will see this additional page as the fourth or fifth page in the wizard. You can choose to create a new file with the imported data or append the data to a project file that is already open in a project window. Finally, you can merge your data into an open project file, which overwrites tasks that match the key field you indicate to use for a merge.

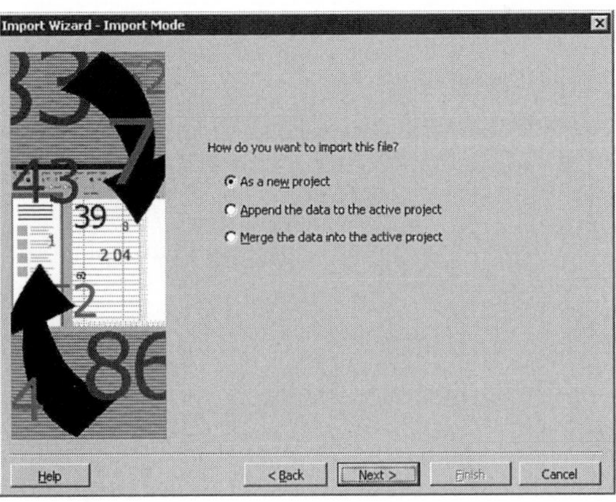

Figure 17.5
The Import Mode page is used only during an import operation, to determine how to import the data into a Project file.

SAVING AN ENTIRE PROJECT IN A DATABASE

To save an entire project in another format, select one of the database formats, such as the Microsoft Project Database format, the Microsoft Access Database format, or the ODBC format. In each of these formats, all aspects of the Project document can be saved, including all the field data, calendars, views, tables, filters, and format settings.

NOTE

> When you create a file in a foreign format, Project creates many new tables and fields in the external database to hold copies of the data from its internal tables and fields. Because of differences in naming conventions between Project and the database to which you are saving, the table names and field names in the database may be very different from the names you see in Project when you place fields in views or reports.

USING THE MICROSOFT PROJECT DATABASE FORMAT

When you use the Microsoft Project Database format, Project saves the entire project to a Microsoft Access 2002 database format, with the extension `.mpd`. This format has replaced the MPX format as the standard interchange format for project data. You can store multiple projects in the same `.mpd` file, which facilitates analysis of resources, tasks, or assignments that span many different projects. You can open individual projects from the `.mpd` file in Microsoft Project, in Microsoft Access, or in any application that supports the Microsoft Access format. You can query the `.mpd` file with any application that can query an Access database directly or an ODBC data source directly.

TIP

> To see a list of Project database files while using Access, go to the Open dialog box, type **`*.mpd`** into the File Name box, and press the Enter key. The file extension `.mpd` is not on the list of default data source extensions displayed by Access—nor is it on the list of options in the Files of Type pull-down list.

SAVING A PROJECT IN A MICROSOFT PROJECT DATABASE

When you save a project in Microsoft Project Database format, you have the choice of creating a new `.mpd` file that initially contains just one project or of adding the project to an existing `.mpd` file that may contain related projects that you want to keep together. When you open an `.mpd` file that contains multiple projects, you are asked to select the project that you want to retrieve.

You cannot save only selected parts of a project in Microsoft Project Database format; the entire project is saved, including all field data for tasks, resources, and assignments, plus all other information, such as views, formats, and calendars.

TIP

If you want to save selected parts of a project in a database format, save your project by using the Microsoft Access Database (`*.mdb`) file type and choose the Only Selected Data option on the second page of the Export Wizard.

TIP

To improve performance, Project's timephased assignment data is normally saved in a binary format, as a BLOB (binary large object) file, instead of in a table in the database. If you want the timephased assignment data to be available in a table in the database, you must choose Tools, Options and select the Save tab. Select the check box labeled Expand Timephased Data in the Database. Note that this is a project-level setting–it affects only the current project.

TIP

It's a good idea to give a project a title in the Properties dialog box before you start to save it to a database, especially when saving it to a database that already contains other projects. Project suggests the properties title as the name for the project you are saving during this process, and having that identifying name in place can help you avoid confusion when saving to a database.

To save a Project file as a new Microsoft Project database, follow these steps:

1. Choose File, Save As to display the Save As dialog box.
2. Select the location for the new database file in the Save In box.
3. Pull down the list of file types in the Save as Type list box and select Project Database (*.mpd). If there are any `.mpd` files in the location you have selected, they appear in the file list at this point. The extension on the project filename also changes to `.mpd`.

   In Figure 17.6, the project document was originally named `NewProduct.mpp`, but the extension is changed to `NewProduct.mpd` when the `.mpd` file type is selected. Because this is to be the name of the database, not just one project in the database, the user has added an "s" to the filename as `New Products.mpd`. An existing Project database named `Engineering Projects.mpd` appears in the file list.

TIP

When choosing the name for a new Project database, bear in mind that you might decide to store many project documents in the database. Unless you know that you will store only one project in the database, you should choose a generic name that will help you identify the current project you are saving as well as all the others that you will probably store in the same database file.

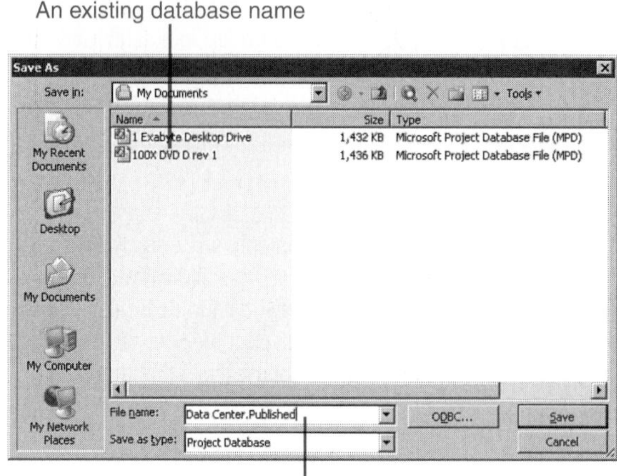

Figure 17.6
Selecting Project Database (*.mpd) as the file type changes both the list of files in the location and the extension on the default filename.

4. Supply the name for the database in the File Name text box. Note that this name does not necessarily have to match the name of the project; the database can potentially contain many projects. The default database name is the same name that is attached to the project file. To give the database a more general name, type in the new filename.
5. Click the Save button to start saving the data. The Export Wizard dialog box appears.
6. Click the Next button. The Project Definition dialog box appears (see Figure 17.7).

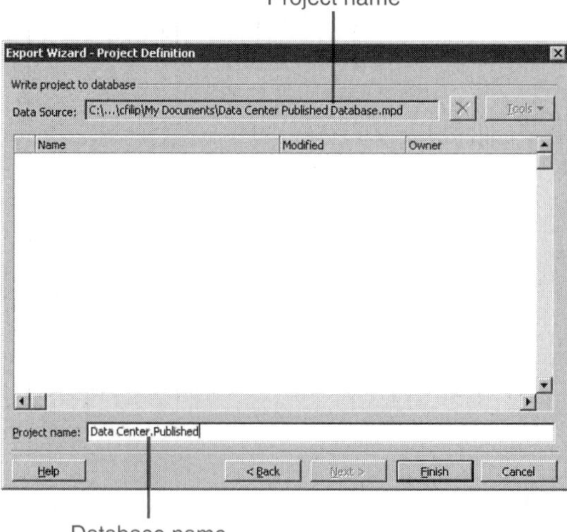

Figure 17.7
You must provide the Export Wizard with additional information before it saves a project as a database.

7. If you want to change the name of the project, type a new name in the Project Name text box. The project title appears as a default name for the project. The project title is maintained in the File Properties dialog box, on the Summary tab.

8. Click Save to begin creating the database. A Saving progress bar appears on the left of the status bar to let you know the file is being saved.

Saving a project in an already existing database requires a few additional steps:

1. Choose File, Save As to display the Save As dialog box.
2. Use the Save In box to select the location where the database file is stored.
3. Pull down the list of file types in the Save as Type list box and select Project Database (*.mpd). The Microsoft Project Database files that are already stored in that location are then displayed.
4. Choose the database name from the list. Note that the original project name in the File Name text box disappears and the database name replaces it. (You will restore the project's unique name in a moment.)
5. Click the Save button to start saving the project. The Export Wizard dialog box appears.
6. Click the Next button. The Existing Database dialog box appears. Because you are adding a project to an existing database, Project needs to know if you are replacing that database or just appending another project to those that are already stored there.
7. Click the Append option if you want to add this project to those that are already in the database. Also click the Append button if you want the project you are saving to replace another project that is already saved in the database. You have to give the new project the same name in the database as the project that it replaces and choose to overwrite the existing project in the database.

   Choose the Overwrite option if you want to remove all existing projects from the database and save only the new project in that file.

   Click the Cancel button if you want to back out of the process and leave the database file unchanged. If you choose Append or Overwrite, the Save to Database dialog box appears.
8. Review the names of other projects stored in the database file (see Figure 17.8). If you are replacing a project, select that project's name from the list. Otherwise, you can keep the default name of the new project or change its name by typing a new name in the Project Name list box.
9. Click the Finish button to begin saving the project in the database.

OPENING PROJECTS FROM A MICROSOFT PROJECT DATABASE

To open a project that was saved in a Microsoft Project Database, follow these steps:

1. Choose File, Open.
2. Select the location of the database file you want to open in the Look In box. The Microsoft Project Database files in that location are displayed, along with other project files that are stored there. If you want to see only project database files listed, choose Project Databases in the Files of Type box.

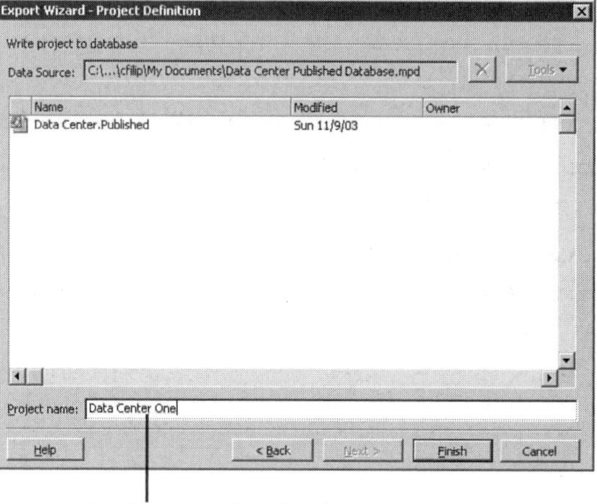

Figure 17.8
Project Data Center is the first project stored in this database. The user is preparing to save another project called Data Center One.

3. Choose the database name from the list and click the Open button. The Import Wizard dialog box appears.
4. Click the Next button. The Data Type dialog box appears.
5. Select the format of the data to be imported, and then click the Next button to continue. The Project Definition dialog box appears (see Figure 17.9).

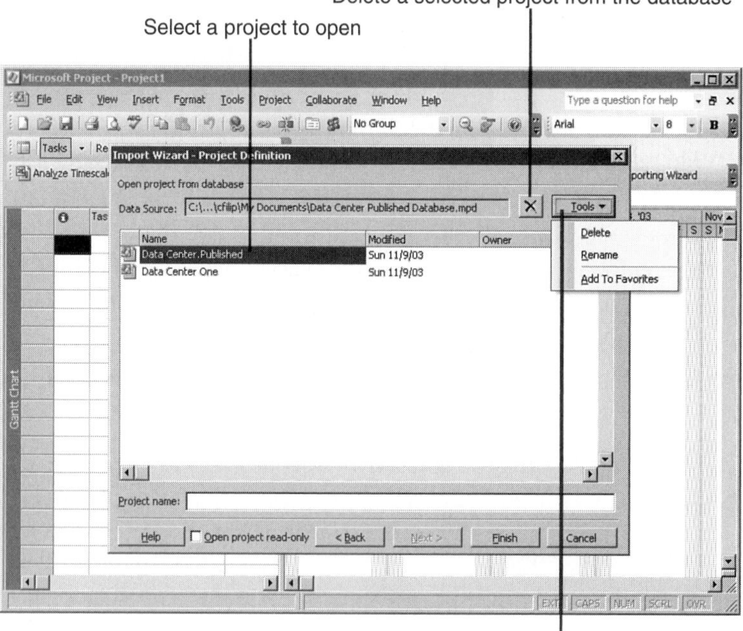

Figure 17.9
You can delete or rename projects while using the Import Wizard.

6. Select a project to open from the list of projects, and then click the Finish button to open the project.

NOTE

> Other buttons in the dialog box let you return to the previous dialog box and delete the selected project from the database. You can also use the Tools button to delete or rename the selected project.

If Project data has been changed by another application in the `.mpd` file, and then it is imported into Project 2003, Project attempts to determine which field was changed and makes appropriate adjustments to other data, which might rely on the changed field.

After opening and working with a project that is stored in an `.mpd` file, you can save your work as you would with any other file: Choose File, Save from the menu or click the Save button on the Standard toolbar. The project is saved in the database it came from, replacing the older version of the project.

17

CAUTION

> If you use the File, Save As command instead of File, Save, Project changes the extension of the project file to the default `.mpp` format. If you don't correct the name, the project is saved in a new standard project document instead of back into the database from which it came.

USING THE MICROSOFT ACCESS FORMAT

You can save an entire project in a standard Microsoft Access database, using the native Access 2000/2002 format. You must save all the project data when you choose to use the Microsoft Project Database format, but you can choose to save all or only selected parts of the project when you use the Microsoft Access format instead.

The steps for saving an entire project in the Access format are virtually the same as those used to save a Microsoft Project database. To save all of an open project document in a Microsoft Access 2000 database, follow these steps:

1. Choose File, Save As. Select the location for the new database file and select Microsoft Access Database (*.mdb) as the file type.
2. Supply a name for the new database, or select the name of an existing database. Click the Save button and the Export Wizard will appear.
3. Make all appropriate selections in the Export Wizard, and then click Finish to begin saving the project in the database.

OPENING PROJECTS FROM A MICROSOFT ACCESS DATABASE

You can open a project that was saved in a Microsoft Access database in the same way you open a project in a Project (`*.mpd`) database:

1. Choose File, Open from the menu to display the Open dialog box.
2. Select the location of the database file you want to open in the Look In box.
3. From the Files of Type list box, select Microsoft Access Database (*.mdb).
4. Choose the database name from the file list and click the Open button. The Import Wizard dialog box appears.
5. Click Next. The Data Type dialog box appears.
6. Select whether to open a full project, only selective data, or unmapped data.
7. Click Next. The Project Definition dialog box appears (see Figure 17.10).

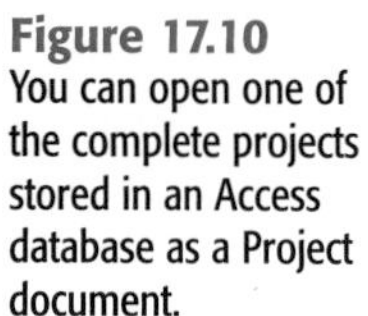

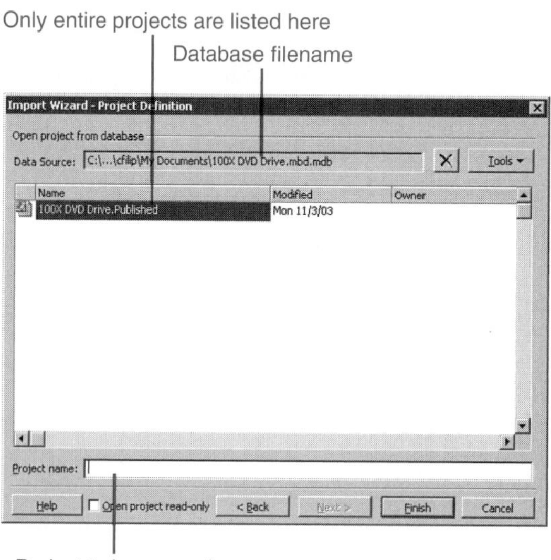

Figure 17.10
You can open one of the complete projects stored in an Access database as a Project document.

8. Select a project to open from the list of projects, and then click the Finish button to open the project.

CAUTION

If the database does not contain any complete project files (in other words, it contains only parts of one or more projects), you must create an Import map to import selected data from the tables in the database (see the section "Creating and Using an Import Map," later in this chapter).

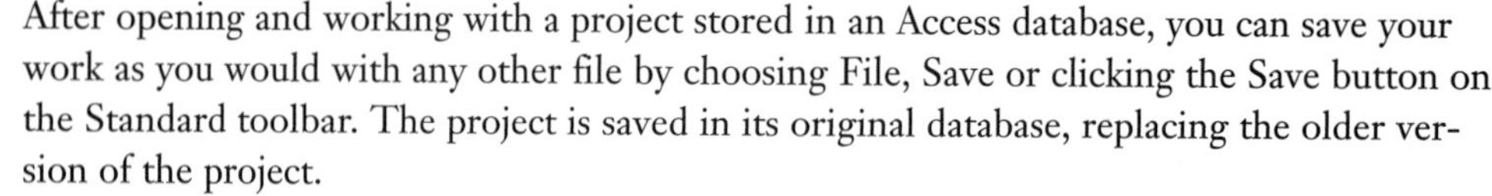

After opening and working with a project stored in an Access database, you can save your work as you would with any other file by choosing File, Save or clicking the Save button on the Standard toolbar. The project is saved in its original database, replacing the older version of the project.

> **NOTE**
>
> After saving or opening a project in a Project database or an Access database, you will find the project name in the list of recently used files at the bottom of the File menu. The list includes the database name in angle brackets, followed by a backslash, followed by the project name. For example, if you saved a project named `Product#24` in the `NewProducts.mpd` database in the `Projects` directory of your `E:` drive, you would see the following entry near the bottom of the File menu:
>
> ```
> <E:\Projects\NewProducts.MPD>\Product#24
> ```
>
> Clicking this entry in the file list opens the `Product#24` project from the database.

SAVING AND OPENING PROJECTS USING AN ODBC DATA SOURCE

You can store and retrieve project data with any ODBC-compliant data source, such as the following:

- Microsoft Access 2000/2002
- Microsoft SQL Server version 7.0 or higher
- Oracle Server version 8.0 or higher

ODBC database sources are ideal for customized applications that draw data and reports from many different enterprise-level databases. ODBC is not a file format; rather, it is a set of protocols, drivers, and instructions for storing the way to access and work with different data sources.

SAVING A PROJECT IN AN ODBC DATABASE

You can save a project in an ODBC database almost as easily as in any other format. There are a few additional steps involved in identifying an ODBC data source. The data source definition is not a database itself, but a reference, or pointer, to a database. You can create some databases in which to store a project on the fly. Others have to be created by server administrators. See your database administrator if you need help with the data sources that are available to you.

To save an entire project in an ODBC database, follow these steps:

1. Choose File, Save As.
2. Click the ODBC button in the Save As dialog box. This displays the Select Data Source dialog box (see Figure 17.11).
3. Choose either the File Data Source tab or the Machine Data Source tab to show the list of data sources that are already defined on the system. If you need to create a new Data Source Name, click the New button and complete the steps in the Create New Data Source Wizard.

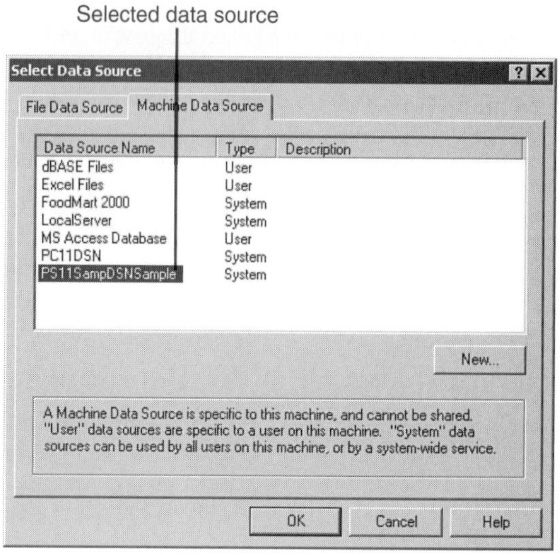

Figure 17.11
The Select Data Source dialog box lets you create a new data source definition or use an existing one.

NOTE

> If you are unfamiliar with how to create a new data source name (DSN), contact your database administrator for assistance.

4. Select a data source and then click OK.
5. If required by the data source you selected, enter your logon ID and password and then click OK. The Export Wizard dialog box appears.
6. Click the Next button. The Data dialog box appears.
7. Make sure the option to save a full project is selected, and then click the Next button. The Project Definition dialog box appears.
8. Provide the name you want to use for this project in the database.
9. Click the Finish button.

IMPORTING A COMPLETE PROJECT FROM AN ODBC SOURCE

To open a complete project from an ODBC database, complete the following steps:

1. Choose File, Open.
2. In the Open dialog box, click the ODBC button.
3. Select the tab (either File Data Source or Machine Data Source) that lists the data source you want to open.
4. Choose the data source and then click OK. The Project Definition page of the Import Wizard dialog box appears.
5. Select the project you want to open and click Finish.

NOTE

> You must be careful when importing a project from an ODBC source that was not originally created in Microsoft Project. The source database must have been carefully structured to parallel the database structure used by Microsoft Project.

NOTE

> After saving or opening a project in an ODBC data source, you will find the project name in the list of files at the bottom of the File menu. As with projects saved in Project or Access databases, the listing includes the ODBC data source name in angle brackets, followed by a backslash, followed by the project name. Clicking a listing opens the selected project.

17

EXCHANGING SELECTED PARTS OF A PROJECT WITH OTHER FORMATS

For some file formats, you are allowed to store only selected field values from a Project file. This is true for the Microsoft Excel format, the HTML format, and the text formats. In other instances, you simply might not want to save all of a project's information. For example, a colleague might ask you to provide an Access database that records just the task names, scheduled work, and actual work for a project, so that she can help estimate task work in a similar project.

When you save an entire project in a database, Microsoft Project automatically creates a standard set of tables in the database, with standard Microsoft Project database field names. If you save only part of a project's data to a database, you need to provide the name of the new or existing table(s) that will receive the data.

If you choose to save only parts of the project in one of the export formats, you must use an Export map to define which fields you want to export from Project and what you want to name the table or tables in which they will be stored. If you plan to change the values in the other format and then import the data back into Project, you must use that same map or a similar map as an Import map to tell Project where the imported data is to be inserted in the Project data structure.

WORKING WITH IMPORT/EXPORT MAPS

All Import/Export maps specify which tables and fields in a foreign data format will be matched with tables and fields in Microsoft Project's native format. A map allows you to define tables in the foreign format to match the data in Project's native tables. You can define the following tables in an Import/Export map:

- A task table for values that match Project's task fields
- A resource table for values that match Project's resource fields
- An assignment table for values that match Project's assignment fields

NOTE

You cannot import or export Project's timephased data by using Import/Export maps.

For each table in a map, you must specify the field name in Project and the corresponding data location in the foreign format. Option buttons make it very easy to add all Project fields to the table or to add the same set of fields that appear in one of the already defined tables in Microsoft Project.

For Export maps, you can choose to export a subset of the tasks or resources in the project by applying one of the predefined Project filters.

→ For more information about Project's predefined filters, **see** Chapter 19, "Using the Standard Views, Tables, Filters, and Groups," **p. 735**.

For import maps, you can choose how the imported data will fit into the open Project file. These are the options:

- You can place the imported records into a new Project document. Project creates a new `.mpp` document file with the field values you have selected. This file is a standard Project `.mpp` file that has no links to the source of the imported data; saving it does not update the source data.
- You can have the imported records appended to the tasks, resources, or assignments that are already in the open project. Project will add new tasks, resources, or assignments below the existing tasks, resources, or assignments.
- You can have the values in the imported records merged into the existing project to update the existing tasks, resources, or assignments. In this case, Project attempts to match the records to be imported with those that are already in the open document. When there is a match, the imported field values will replace the existing field values. In order for Project to match the records coming in with those in the current file, you must define one field as a key field to be used for matching records. For example, you could import resource names and standard rates to update the pay rates in the resource table. In this case, you would probably use the resource names as the key field to match records.

Import/Export maps are not file-format–specific; that is, if you design a map to export data to Access, you can use the same map to export data to an ODBC data source, to a text file, or to an Excel worksheet. However, the different file formats often convert non-text fields into different field types and different values. For example, if a resource is assigned eight hours of work on a task, the same export map would export those eight hours as the text value **`8 hrs`** to an Excel worksheet, and to an Access database as the number 480,000 (1,000 times the number of minutes in eight hours).

Furthermore, some maps export more data to one format than to another. For example, the Who Does What Report map exports more data to an HTML document than it does to an Access database (see the section "Using the Who Does What Report Map," later in this chapter).

NOTE

When you choose to save Project data in a non-Project format, Project modifies the options that are shown on the Import/Export map to match the format you chose. For example, if you choose Save As for an HTML format, and then you choose an Import/Export map that was originally designed for exporting to an Excel worksheet, the worksheet options are replaced by HTML options.

You must be very careful when using a map to import data into Project. A map designed for one database or worksheet might specify tables or fields that are not used in another data source. Always check the structure of the map before using it to import data.

Import/Export maps are saved in the `GLOBAL.MPT` file, rather than in the active Project file when you create them. You do not have to use the Organizer to rename a map. Rather, when you are editing a map, you can simply change its name. You must use the Organizer to delete a map.

→ For information on using the Organizer to delete objects such as Import/Export maps, **see** "Working with the Organizer and Global File," **p. 107**.

TIP

To share a map with other users, you can use the Organizer to copy the map into an open project file and then save the project. The other users can then open your project file and use the Organizer to copy the map into their `GLOBAL.MPT` files.

Reviewing the Predefined Import/Export Maps

Microsoft Project 2003 includes 11 predefined Import/Export maps for general-purpose use. Some are like predefined Project reports, views, or tables. The predefined maps are listed in Table 17.2. For those that are intended for a specific file format, Table 17.2 notes the intended file format.

TABLE 17.2 THE PREDEFINED IMPORT/EXPORT MAPS

Map	Description
Who Does What Report	Used to save an HTML table that lists resources and their task assignments.
Compare to Baseline	Used to export a table that lists all tasks with scheduled and baseline values.
Cost Data by Task	Used to export a table that lists task costs.
Default Task Information	Used to export or import the basic task fields that are included in the Task Entry table.
Earned Value Information	Used to export the task earned value fields.
Export to HTML Using Standard Template	Used to export basic task, resource, and assignment values to an HTML document.
Resource Export Table Map	Used to export all the fields in the predefined resource's Export table.
Task Export Table Map	Used to export all the fields in the predefined task's Export table.
Task and Resource PivotTable	Used to create Excel PivotTables for tasks and resources.
Task List with Embedded Assignment Rows	Used to export an HTML table of tasks and their assigned resources.
Top Level Tasks List	Used to export a table with data for tasks at the top outline level.

The following sections explain how these maps were created and how they can be used most effectively. All the predefined maps were designed for exporting selected data from Project to another file format. Some were designed with specific file formats in mind—for example, HTML or Excel PivotTables—but any map can be used to export to any of the formats. Maps generally work best, however, if they are used with the format for which they were designed.

Note that in all cases, the exported values for the duration and work fields are exported as text (not as numeric data), with the time unit attached as part of the text value, such as **`10d`**.

Although some maps are designed for exporting and some for importing, any map can be used for either operation. Be very careful, however, when using a map to import data into Project because the result might not be what you expect.

When you use an Import/Export map to exchange data with a file that has another format, the external file that supplies or receives the data is added to the list of recently used files at the bottom of Project's File menu. For example, after you export (save) data to an Excel worksheet named `TaskCosts.xls`, using the map named Cost Data by Task, you see the entry TaskCosts.xls (Cost Data by Task) on Project's File menu. Because clicking a file listing causes Project to open the file, clicking the listing would cause Project to import (open) the Excel file `TaskCosts.xls` and copy data into a Project document, using the Cost Data by Task map to determine which Project fields receive the imported data.

By default, Project's predefined maps all place imported data into a new Project document that is created on the fly. Therefore, clicking the file listing causes Project to create a new document that has the Excel data in it. You should close this new project file without saving it because the map was designed for exporting, not for importing, and the new project file is not a complete project file.

When imported data is placed in a new Project document, there is no harm done because you can simply close the new document. However, import maps can also be defined so that they append the imported data to the active file or merge the imported data into existing task or resource records, updating existing field values with the values stored in the external document. If the map named in the file listing is set to append or merge, clicking the file listing alters the data in the document that is active when you click the listing. If the active document has unsaved data in it, you could lose some or all of that data as a result of clicking the listing on the File menu.

CAUTION

> You should never open a foreign-format map file from the File menu's file list unless you're absolutely sure that you want that data imported. Even then, be sure you save the active document beforehand, just in case.

Using the Who Does What Report Map

The Who Does What Report map is best used to save an HTML table of resource assignments. The resulting table is named Who Does What and is similar to the Who Does What report you can print in Project by choosing View, Reports, Assignments, Who Does What. Like the Resource Usage view in Project, the HTML table lists resource names and task assignment names in the same column with the assignment names, indented under their resource names. There are columns for the Start, Finish, and Work field values for each assignment. The data for the Work field is text data (not numeric), with the unit "hours" appended as part of the text value.

Although this map works best when saving to HTML format, you can also use it to save to an Excel workbook or to one of the text file formats. When saving to Excel or one of the text formats, the resource rows are indistinguishable from the assignment rows because the assignments are not indented as they are in the HTML format. If you open the HTML document in Excel, however, the resources and assignments are formatted distinctively.

TIP

> When saving data to Excel or a text format, you should modify the Who Does What Report map and add the field named Assignment to the table to distinguish resource names from task assignment names. Rows in the list that are resources have No in the Assignment field, whereas rows for assignments have Yes. You could apply Excel's conditional formatting to bold the resource rows based on the value No being found in the Assignment column. See the section "Saving Project Data as an Excel Worksheet," later in this chapter, for more information.

If you attempt to use the Who Does What Report map to create a database table, Project doesn't include the associated assignment rows for each resource. To create database tables, you have to add to the map an additional table for the assignments and then link the tables on the resource names within the database application. (See "Working with Web-Enabled Project Data" later in this chapter for more details about the HTML format.)

USING THE COMPARE TO BASELINE MAP

You use the Compare to Baseline map to export a table named Baseline Comparison that lists all tasks, with their Start and Finish dates as well as their scheduled, baseline, and variance values for duration, work, and cost. This map works the same way for database, worksheet, and text formats.

USING THE COST DATA BY TASK MAP

You use the Cost Data by Task map to export a table named Task Costs that lists all the tasks (fixed cost, cost, baseline cost, cost variance, actual cost, and remaining cost) and their cost values.

USING THE DEFAULT TASK INFORMATION MAP

The Default Task Information map can be used to export or import the basic task fields that are included in the Task Entry table: ID, Name, Duration, Start Date, Finish Date, Predecessors, and Resource Names. This map works the same way with all file formats.

USING THE EARNED VALUE INFORMATION MAP

You use the Earned Value Information map to export the earned value fields for tasks to any of the file formats. It includes these fields: Task ID, Task Name, BCWS, BCWP, ACWP, SV, CV, Cost (EAC), Baseline Cost (BAC), and VAC.

→ For more information about earned value fields, **see** "Analyzing Progress and Revising the Schedule," **p. 555**.

USING THE EXPORT TO HTML USING STANDARD TEMPLATE MAP

You use the Export to HTML Using Standard Template map to export basic task, resource, and assignment values to an HTML document. The task table includes the ID, Name, Duration, Start, Finish, Resource Names, and % Complete fields. The resource table includes the ID, Name, Group, Max Units, and Peak (Peak Units) fields. The assignment table includes the Task ID, Task Name, Resource Name, Work, Start, Finish, and % Work Complete fields.

See the section "Working with Web-Enabled Project Data" later in this chapter for more details about the HTML format.

USING THE RESOURCE EXPORT TABLE MAP

You use the Resource Export Table map to export the fields that are included in the predefined resource's Export table. The resource's Export table is a fairly comprehensive set of 24 resource fields that covers the definition of the resource as well as scheduled, baseline, and tracking sums for work and cost for each resource.

USING THE TASK EXPORT TABLE MAP

You use the Task Export Table map to export nearly all the fields that are included in the predefined task's Export table. The 70+ fields that are exported include task definition fields; values for scheduled, baseline, and actual work, and values for cost, duration, start, and finish; and a large number of the user-definable text, cost, duration, number, and flag fields.

USING THE TASK AND RESOURCE PIVOTTABLE MAP

You use the Task and Resource PivotTable map to create an Excel document with two PivotTables that summarize the total cost of the resource assignments. Both PivotTables are organized by resource groups and within each group by resource names. The resulting Excel file contains four sheets in all:

- The Tasks sheet provides the data for the Task PivotTable and includes these columns: Resource Group, Resource Name, Task Name(s), Duration, Start, Finish, and Cost. If your project is outlined, there is a Task Name column for each outline level, and all summary task names for a subtask appear on the row for the subtask. The outline level 1 summary tasks are in the column named Task Name1, the outline level 2 summary tasks are in the column named Task Name2, and so forth.
- The Task PivotTable sheet shows for each resource group the tasks to which each resource in the group is assigned, along with the task duration, start, and finish. The cost for each assignment is the Data field in the PivotTable, and there are summary costs for each task and summary task, for each resource, and for each resource group.
- The Resources sheet provides the data for the Resource PivotTable and includes the Resource Group, Resource Name, Work, and Cost fields.
- The Resource PivotTable shows the work and cost totals for each resource group and each resource within a group. The totals are not broken down by task.

NOTE

If a project has more than two outline levels, Project creates the data sheets and the PivotTables, but it is not able to perform the layout of fields for the Task PivotTable, and that sheet therefore appears to be empty. You have to do the layout manually in Excel.

See the section "Exporting to an Excel PivotTable," later in this chapter, for more information about working with PivotTables.

USING THE TASK LIST WITH EMBEDDED ASSIGNMENT ROWS MAP

Use the Task List with Embedded Assignment Rows map to export an HTML table of tasks and their assigned resources. This map is best used to export a table that includes all the resource assignments for each task, as well as the Work, Duration, Start, Finish, and %

Work Complete fields for each assignment. All the information about exporting to Excel or Access, as mentioned earlier for the Who Does What Report map, applies to this map as well.

USING THE TOP LEVEL TASKS LIST MAP

You should use the Top Level Tasks List map to export a table that shows only the outline level 1 tasks. The fields include the Task ID, Name, Duration, Start, Finish, % Complete, Cost, and Work. This map works for all file formats.

CREATING IMPORT/EXPORT MAPS FOR ACCESS AND ODBC SOURCES

Creating an Import/Export map is fairly straightforward when you understand the process because Project does most of the work for you. To illustrate, we will first create a map to export selected cost data for tasks, resources, and assignments to an Access database. Then we will modify the same map to import a more limited set of data from the Access database. The same map could be used for an ODBC database as well.

CREATING AND USING AN EXPORT MAP

Export maps are easier to create than import maps because the Project field names are the source of the data, and you can create field names in the target format that are similar to the Project field names. When you create an Import map, the field names in the source format may not be as easy to relate to the field names in Project.

To create a map for exporting some of Project's cost data to an Access 2002 database, follow these steps:

1. Open the Project file whose data you want to export.
2. Choose File, Save As.
3. Select the directory location from the Save In list box.
4. In the Save as Type list box, select Microsoft Access Database (*.mdb).
5. If you are creating a new database, type its name in the File Name text box.

TIP

> If you are going to append data to an existing database, it is a good idea to create a copy of the database for testing while creating the new map. Then, when the map behaves as you want it to, you can use it to append to the intended database and you can delete the test database.

TIP

> In general, it is not wise to add partial project data sets to an Access database that already contains complete projects. Project does not let you add selective data to the tables it has already created in the database; therefore, you would have to create your own named tables to hold the data, which you might as well do in a special database that is dedicated to partial data sets.

6. Click the Save button to display the Export Wizard dialog box.
7. Click the Next button to display the Data dialog box.
8. Select the option to export only selective data, and then click the Next button. The Map dialog box appears.
9. Select the option to use a new map and click the Next button. The Map Options dialog box appears.
10. Select one or more types of data—tasks, resources, or assignments—to be exported. In Figure 17.12, you can see that all three types of data will be exported.

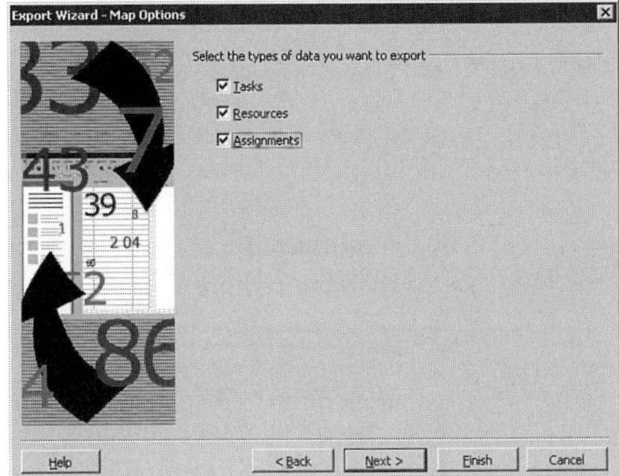

Figure 17.12 You use the Map Options page of the Export Wizard to determine which type of data tables will be created.

11. Click the Next button to display the Task Mapping dialog box.
12. Supply a descriptive name for the table in the Destination Database Table Name field.
13. If you want to limit the tasks that will be exported, use the list of filters in the Export Filter field to select a task filter. Any of the currently defined filters can be chosen. You cannot design a new filter at this point, as filters must be defined ahead of time. In Figure 17.13, you can see that the table to be created will be called Cost Summary by Task and that the All Tasks filter will be used.
14. Define the task fields that will be exported in the mapping table. You must list each of the Project fields that are to be exported in the column labeled From: Microsoft Project Field. You must create a name for the database field that will hold that data in the column labeled To: Database Field. The data type is filled in automatically, based on the Project field types.

    Click the list arrow in the first cell in the left column—the cell that displays the prompt (Click Here to Map a Field). The complete list of Microsoft Project task fields is displayed (see Figure 17.14).

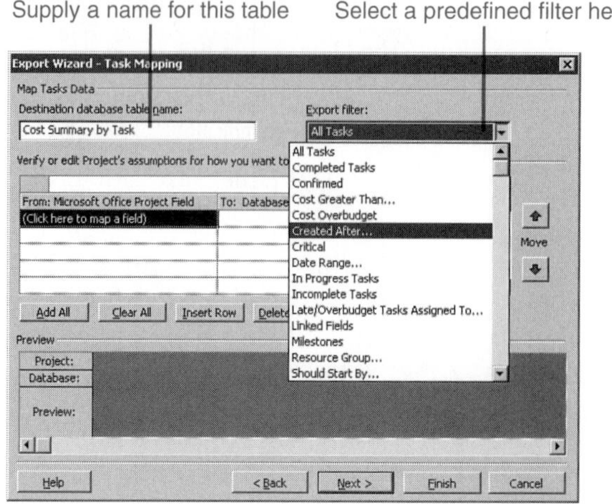

Figure 17.13
You use the Task Mapping page to name the task table in the destination database and to select an Export filter.

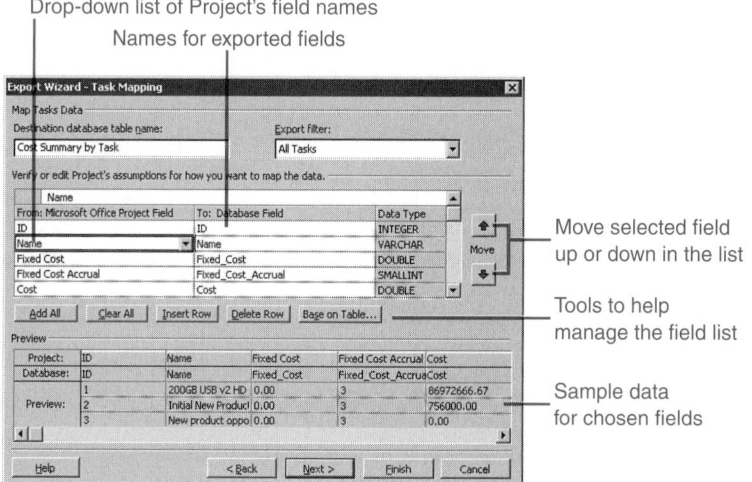

Figure 17.14
You use the Task Mapping dialog box to select a Project field name to be exported.

15. Select the fields to be exported from the list of Project fields, and press the Enter key after selecting each field. A default field name is inserted in the second column (for the exported database), and the field data type is automatically inserted in the third column. Below the mapping table, you should see a sample of the fields you have added and the data they contain.

    You can change the export field name to suit your tastes. Be sure, however, that you don't violate any field-naming rules for the format you are creating. For example, for an Access database, field names can't have leading spaces or include periods, exclamation points, or square brackets.

NOTE

When exporting to Access, you should leave in place the underscore word separators that Project supplies. Although Access accepts nonleading spaces in field names, the Microsoft Project procedure that creates the table for Access thinks that spaces are not allowed, and displays an error message indicating that illegal characters were used in a field name.

16. If needed, you can use several buttons to speed the process of managing the field mapping table (refer to Figure 17.14):
    - To move a field row in the list, select the row to be moved and use the Move arrows on the right side of the mapping table to move the row up or down in the list.
    - To insert all the task fields in Microsoft Project, click the Add All button.
    - To clear the mapping table, click the Clear All button.
    - To insert a blank row for a new field in the middle of the list, select the place where the row should be inserted and click the Insert Row button.
    - To remove a field row, select the row to be removed and click the Delete Row button.
    - To populate the mapping table with the same fields that are contained in one of the task tables in Microsoft Project, click the Base on Table button. The Select Base Table for Field Mapping dialog box appears (see Figure 17.15), with a list of all the currently defined task tables. Select the table you want to use and click OK. The field list is cleared from the mapping table, and the fields that are defined in the table you selected are inserted in the mapping table.

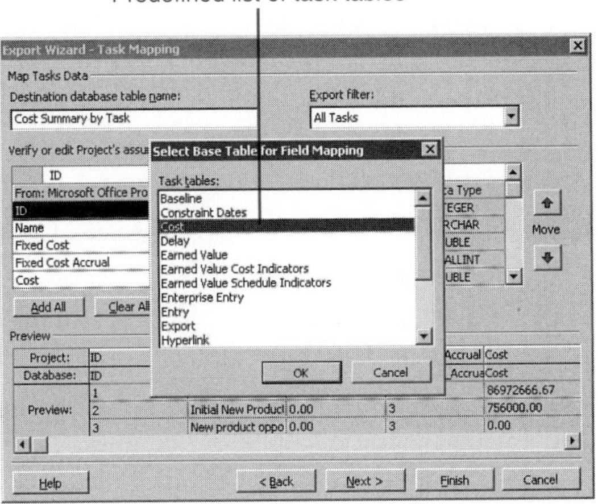

Figure 17.15
You can fill the mapping table with the fields defined in a Project table by using the Base on Table button.

17. When the task mapping table is completed, click the Next button to move on to the next table you have elected to include in the database export. In this example, the Resource Mapping page is displayed (see Figure 17.16). The table name is Summary by Resource. You fill in the fields by selecting the Cost table from the list displayed by the Base on Table button. (Note that you can also apply a resource filter to select a subset of the resource records to be included in the Export table.)

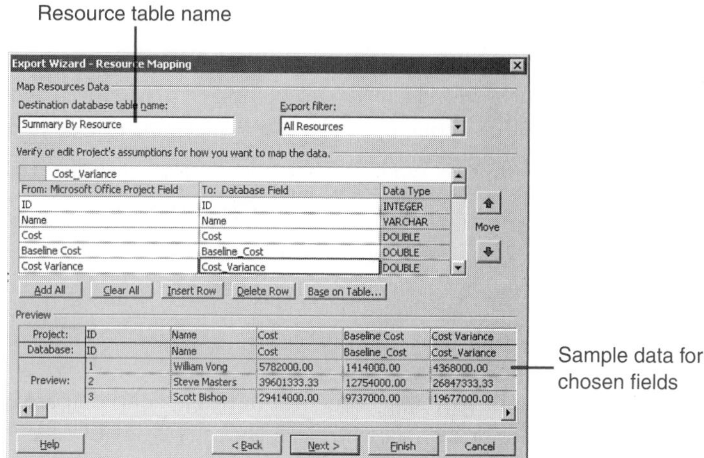

Figure 17.16
The resource mapping table is defined in the same way as the task mapping table.

18. Finally, if you are including assignment fields, click the Next button to display the Assignment Mapping page, and then repeat the process. The assignment records are the details that are combined for the task and resource cost summaries. Because there is no table in Microsoft Project for assignments (they only appear in the Task Usage and Resource Usage views and on certain forms), you cannot choose a table as a template for the fields to be included. Also, there are no filters for assignments. Both these options are dimmed on the Assignment Mapping tab.
19. When all the tabs are filled in, click the Next button. The End of Map Definition page appears.
20. Click the Save Map button to save the export map. The Save Map dialog box appears (see Figure 17.17).
21. Type a descriptive name for the map in the Map Name field and then click the Save button. You are returned to the End of Map Definition dialog box.
22. Click the Finish button to export the selected data to the database whose name you entered in the Save As dialog box in step 5.

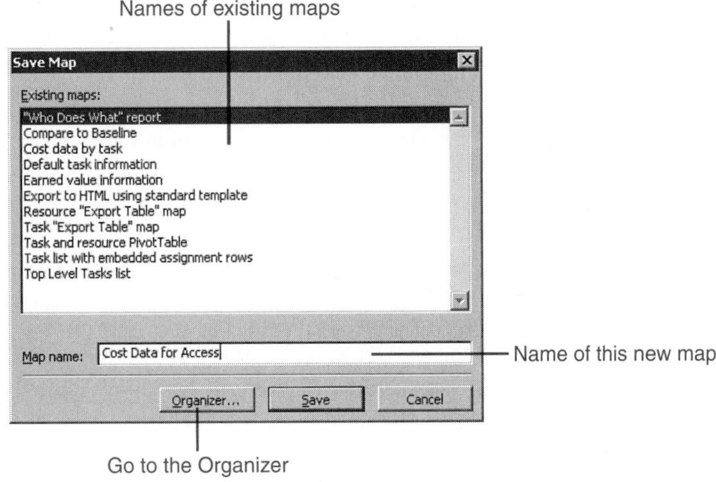

Figure 17.17
It is a good practice to save your map if you want to use it again in the future.

TIP

If you design a map for use with one file format—for example, with HTML—and then use the map to exchange data with an application of another format, such as Access, the results might be very different. For specialized maps it's a good idea to include the application name in the map name, as is done in the preceding example.

CREATING AND USING AN IMPORT MAP

When you want to import data into Microsoft Project from another source, you must either find a workable import map, or create one of your own. If the data was originally exported from Microsoft Project, you can use the same map for the import that you used for the export. Or, if you want to make slight changes, it is easy to edit the export map and then save it as a new import map.

The options for an import map are slightly different from those for the export map:

- The source tables are already defined (whereas you defined the target tables in the export map). For example, there may be many tables in the source database that have task information in them. You must choose the table that contains the task data you need. Similarly, you must identify the source tables that are appropriate for supplying resource or assignment fields.

  If you created the source by exporting fields from Project, it will be much easier to import the data back into Project from those same fields because the field names will be recognizable. If the source table was created by an application other than Project, the field names have to be matched with Project's internal fields.

- You cannot import only a portion of the records by using any of the Project filters. If you want only part of the records from the source, you have to filter the source first, to produce a new database, and then import the resulting tables into Project. Otherwise, it might be easier to import all the data into Project and then just delete the unwanted records.

- When importing, you can choose whether the imported data will be stored in a new project file or merged into an existing Project document. You can append the imported records to the records that already exist in a Project document. Or you can choose to merge the imported data by using it to update selected fields for tasks or resources that already exist.

To illustrate how to import from another file format, let's import from the cost database that was created earlier in this chapter, in the section "Creating and Using an Export Map."

If you intend to add the imported data to an existing Project document, you must open that project before starting the import process. Otherwise, it doesn't matter which project documents are open when you import because Project will create a new document. To import data by using a map, complete the following steps:

1. Choose File, Open, or click the Open tool.
2. Select the location of the data source in the Look In list box. If you are importing from an ODBC data source, click the ODBC button instead and select the data source in that dialog box.
3. In the Files of Type list box, select the format of the data source.
4. Choose the data source file from the file list and click the Open button. The Import Wizard dialog box appears.
5. Click the Next button to see the Data Type dialog box.
6. Select the option to import only selective data and then click the Next button. The Map dialog box appears.
7. Select the Use Existing Map option. If you want to create a new import map, select the New Map option, and then follow the same techniques outlined for creating an export map in the section "Creating and Using an Export Map." Click the Next button to display the Map Selection dialog box.
8. Select the map that you want to use to import the data. Be extremely careful when selecting a map, to be sure that it defines the way you want to import the data. Click the Next button to display the Import Mode dialog box.
9. Choose to import data as a new project to start a new Project file with the imported data. Or, choose Append the Data to an Existing Project to add the desired records after the records already in the project. Or, choose Merge the Data to an Existing Project to have Microsoft Project match incoming records with existing records and update the fields with the imported values.
10. Click the Next button. The Map Options dialog box appears.
11. Select the types of data—tasks, resources, or assignments—to import. Click the Next button.
12. The Mapping dialog box appears for the first type of data you selected in step 11.

13. Examine the Mapping dialog box for each type of data to be imported, to verify that the settings are correct. You should select the list of names in the Source Database Table Name field to verify that the appropriate table has been chosen for the type of data in each Mapping dialog box.

    Figure 17.18 shows the Task Mapping dialog box for the import map that is derived from the export map created earlier. The Source Database Table Name list is selected to show the tables in the source database.

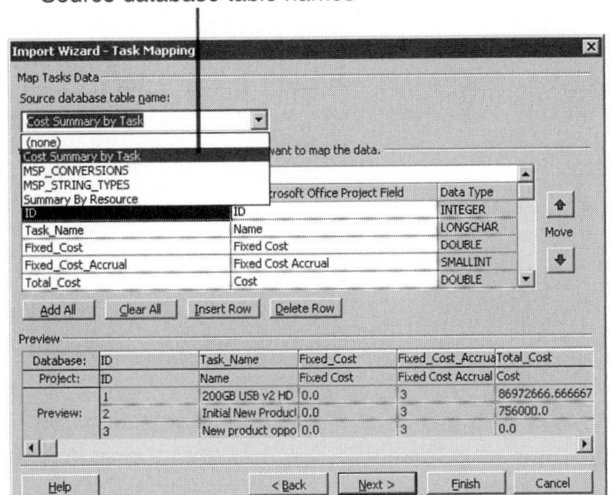

Figure 17.18
The map that you defined as an export map has a few different options when used as an import map.

NOTE

> The list of source database table names contains more tables than you explicitly defined in your export map. These extra table names have an `MSP_` prefix, and they are there to help the user decipher the data values that were exported.

14. Click the Next button and examine the Resource Mapping or Assignment Mapping dialog boxes to make sure the settings are correct.

15. If you choose to merge the imported data, the Set Merge Key button appears in the Task, Resource, and Assignment Mapping dialog boxes. You must select a merge key in each Mapping dialog box. Merge Key is a field that has identical values in both the existing Project file and the imported table. For example, the task ID field matches tasks as long as the task list has not been edited since the exported data was created. It would have been better to include the Unique ID field in the export because the Unique ID number doesn't change after a task is created and is a more reliable key field.

    After you have selected the key field, click the Set Merge Key button. The field name changes to MERGE KEY: *field name*. In Figure 17.19, the ID field has been selected as the Merge Key in the Task Mapping dialog box. If you need to change the Merge Key field, select the new key field and click the Set Merge Key button again.

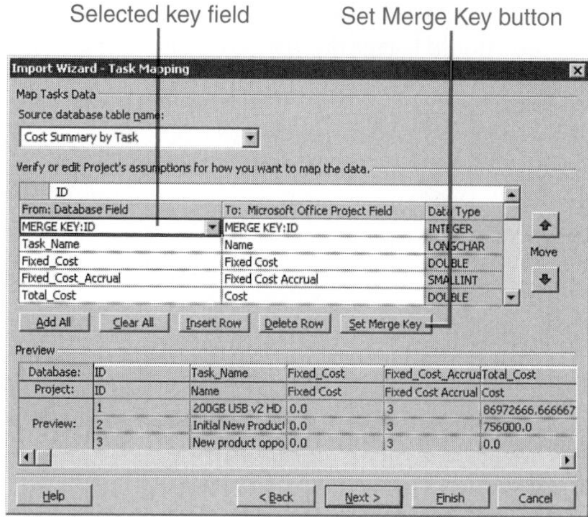

Figure 17.19
One field must be selected as the merge key field, to identify matching records when imported data is to be merged with existing data.

NOTE

> If you want to merge assignment data, you must use the Unique ID field for assignments.

16. Click the Next button to display the End of Map Definition dialog box. If you have made changes to the map and want to save the map by a new name, click the Save Map button.
17. Click the Finish button to import the desired data into your project.

Figure 17.20 illustrates the errors you may see in the mapping tables if you choose the wrong map. If the map names source fields that don't exist in the file you have started to open, the field name entries appear in red and have an `OUT OF CONTEXT:` prefix in the From: Database Field column.

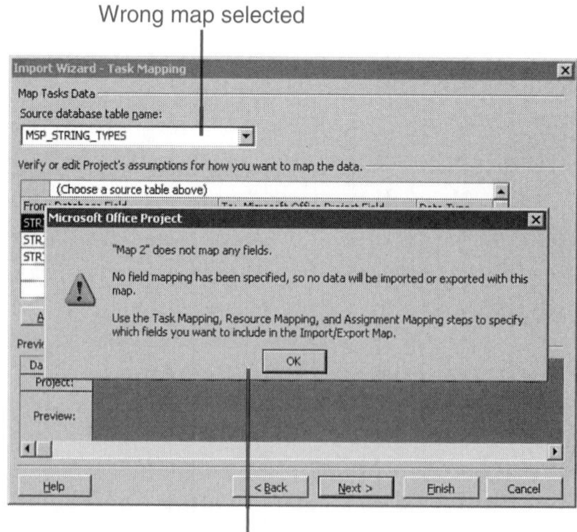

Figure 17.20
If you have chosen the wrong type of map to import data, you will see errors in the Resource Mapping dialog box.

If you don't see the imported data in Project after the import operation is finished, see "Missing Imported Data" in the "Troubleshooting" section at the end of this chapter.

WORKING WITH MICROSOFT EXCEL FORMATS

You can export field data to Microsoft Excel workbooks as worksheet data or as PivotTable data. Furthermore, you can import table data from Microsoft Excel workbooks, but not from PivotTables. When you export to Excel, Microsoft Project creates an Excel file in the Excel 5.0/95 format, which makes the data available to that version and all later versions of Excel. You can import from Excel documents that are saved in Excel 4.0 format or any later format, including Excel 2002.

When you create an Import/Export map that will work with the Excel format, a few options are different from those for creating an Import/Export map that will work with other formats:

- You can choose whether to export Project data by using the Project Excel Template or via an export map. The Project Excel Template exports a standardized set of Task, Resource, and Assignment fields, and it creates a separate worksheet for each type of data.
- You can choose whether to export field names as the first row of the worksheet. If you choose not to export field names, the field data goes in Row 1 of the worksheet and there are no column titles unless you add them later.
- You can instruct Project to include assignment rows such as those displayed in the tables of the Task Usage and Resource Usage views. The worksheet rows are not automatically outlined and indented in the Excel workbook as they are in Project.

  You can use Excel's Group and Outline command to group assignments under the task or resource, and this makes it possible to hide and display the assignment rows at will (as in Project). However, you will have to group each set of assignments by hand, and when the assignment rows are displayed, they are still not indented.

TIP

Before using Excel's Group and Outline command, remember to change Excel's default grouping direction. Choose Data, Group and Outline, Settings and then clear the Summary Rows Below Detail check box. This places the outline symbols for grouping (the plus and minus indicators) to the left of the task or resource name (like in an Assignment view), rather than at the bottom of the list of assignments in each group.

SAVING PROJECT DATA AS AN EXCEL WORKSHEET

You can use an Import/Export map you created for another format to export Project data to Excel. You might want to use an existing map, and then save it with a different name that indicates it is used for exporting to Excel. In the following example, the map for exporting to Excel is based on the Cost Data map developed previously in the section, "Creating and Using an Export Map."

To export Project data to an Excel workbook, follow these steps:

1. Open the Project file that you want to export.
2. Choose File, Save As to display the Save As dialog box.
3. Select the location for the new file in the Save In list box.
4. Change the Save as Type selection to Microsoft Excel Workbook (*.xls).
5. Type the name for the file in the File Name text box.
6. Click the Save button. Project displays the Export Wizard dialog box.
7. Click the Next button to display the Data dialog box.
8. If you choose to export selective data to Excel, click the Next button to display the Map dialog box.
9. Select the option Use Existing Map. If you want to create a new import map, select the New Map option, and then follow the same techniques outlined for creating an export map in the section "Creating and Using an Export Map." Click the Next button to display the Map Selection dialog box.
10. Choose a map and click the Next button. The Map Options dialog box appears.
11. Select the types of data—tasks, resources, or assignments—to be exported to Excel. Some options for Excel don't appear when maps are used for Access. Figure 17.21 shows the Map Options dialog box, with the settings from the Cost Data for Access map.

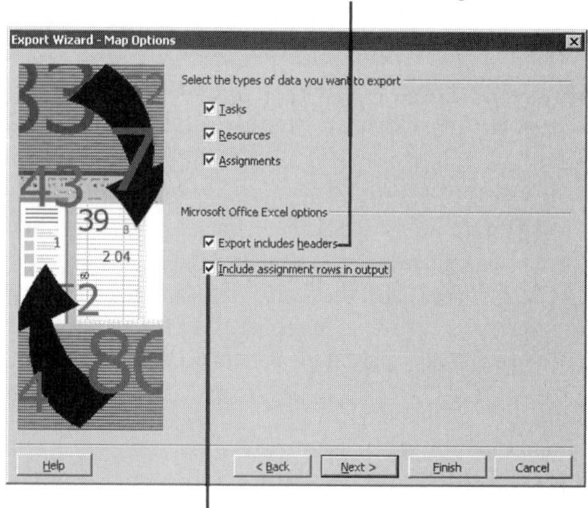

Figure 17.21
You can include assignment rows with task and resource data to identify which records are tasks or resources and which are assignments.

12. Select the check box labeled Export Includes Headers so that the first row of data on each sheet in the workbook will display field names as column headers. (If this option is not selected, there will be no label at the top of each column of data in the workbook.)
13. If you want tasks and resources to show details by assignment (as in the Task Usage and Resource Usage views), select the check box labeled Include Assignment Rows in

Output, and remember to include the field named Assignment so that you can distinguish assignments from tasks or resources.

CAUTION

> If you export the rows for the assignment details in a task mapping, the assignment rows will appear to be just additional tasks in the workbook that is created. If you then reimported that workbook back into Project, the resource assignments would indeed be listed as tasks, even if you included the Task Assignment field in the exported data. Similarly, exported assignment details in a resource mapping result in the assignments being treated as additional resources, and they cannot be imported back into Project satisfactorily.

14. Click the Next button to display the Task Mapping dialog box. Examine the task fields to be exported to Excel, to make sure the settings are correct. Notice the destination worksheet name that will be used for the worksheet that receives the task data.
15. Continue this process for the Resource Mapping and Assignment Mapping dialog boxes. Click the Next button to display the End of Map Definition dialog box.
16. Click the Save Map button. The Save Map dialog box appears.
17. Give the export map a unique name, to identify it for use with exporting to Excel, and click the Save button.
18. Click the Finish button to export the data to an Excel workbook.

When the exported data is opened in Excel, there is a worksheet for each of the tables that were defined in the export map in Project (see Figure 17.22). As specified in the export map, the field names appear in the first row of the worksheet, and the assignments for each resource are listed under the row for the resource.

CAUTION

> Be very careful about sorting. If you sort the rows in the worksheet, you will not be able to tell which assignments go with which tasks or resources.

The Data dialog box in the Import/Export Wizard includes the option Project Excel Template, which is for exporting data to Excel. This option exports data to Excel quickly, using a template or standard list of fields for task, resource, and assignment information. The standard task fields exported to Excel are ID, Name, Duration, Start, Finish, Predecessors, Outline Level, and Notes. The standard resource fields to be exported are ID, Name, Initials, Type, Material Label, Group, Email Address, Windows User Account, Max Units, Standard Rate, Cost Per Use, and Notes. The template exports the following assignment fields: Task Name, Resource Name, % Work Complete, Work, and Units.

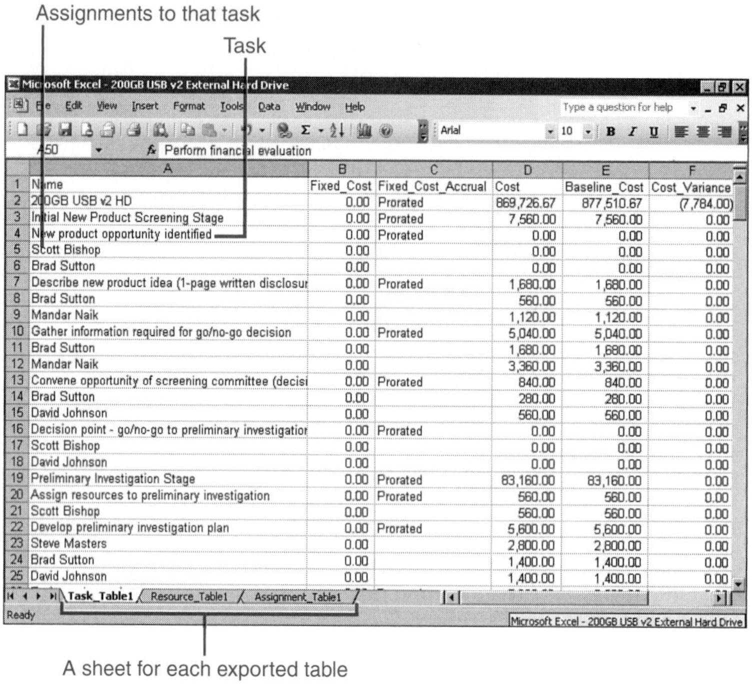

Assignments to that task

Task

A sheet for each exported table

Figure 17.22
The Excel workbook shows the Project data that was exported. The New Product Opportunity Identified task and its assignments are selected on the Task Table1 worksheet.

When you use the Project Excel Template option to export data to Excel, an Excel workbook is created that contains four worksheets, named Task_Table, Resource_Table, Assignment_Table, and Info_Table. The first three worksheets contain the type of data described by the worksheet name. The Info_Table worksheet contains general information about how to use the Project Excel Template. Figure 17.23 shows an Excel workbook that was created by using the Project Excel Template option and was then formatted by the user for ease of use.

For information on how to use the Project Excel Template to import Excel data into a Project file, see "Importing Project Data from the Excel Format," later in this chapter.

EXPORTING TO AN EXCEL PIVOTTABLE

Excel PivotTables summarize data in crosstab calculations, and they offer impressive flexibility for quickly changing the layout of the PivotTable. When you export to the Excel PivotTable format, the export map lets you choose the fields to be included for one or more of the three categories—tasks, resources, and assignments. A separate PivotTable is created for each category, and all these PivotTables are stored in the same Excel workbook. The save operation not only copies the selected data into Excel data sheets, but it also creates the PivotTables on separate worksheets that are based on the data sheets.

Figure 17.23
The Excel workbook shows the Project data that was exported by using the Project Excel Template option.

Microsoft Excel - 100X DVD Drive v2

	A	B	C	D	E
1	ID	Name	Duration	Start	Finish
2	1	New Product- 100X DVD Drive	772.d	4/21/2003 8:00	4/4/2006
3	2	Initial New Product Screening Stage	9.d	4/21/2003 8:00	5/1/2003
4	3	New product opportunity identified	.d	4/21/2003 8:00	4/21/200
5	4	Describe new product idea (1-page written disclosure)	2.d	4/21/2003 8:00	4/22/2003
6	5	Gather information required for go/no-go decision	6.d	4/23/2003 8:00	4/30/2003
7	6	Convene opportunity of screening committee (decision to pursue idea or	1.d	5/1/2003 8:00	5/1/2003
8	7	Decision point - go/no-go to preliminary investigation	.d	5/1/2003 17:00	5/1/2003
9	8	Preliminary Investigation Stage	59.d	5/2/2003 8:00	7/23/2003
10	9	Assign resources to preliminary investigation	1.d	5/2/2003 8:00	5/2/2003
11	10	Develop preliminary investigation plan	5.d	5/5/2003 8:00	5/9/2003
12	11	Evaluate the market	14.d	5/5/2003 8:00	5/22/2003
13	12	Analyze the competition	5.d	5/5/2003 8:00	5/9/2003
14	13	Technical Feasibility Analysis	22.d	5/14/2003 8:00	6/12/2003
15	14	Produce lab scale product	10.d	5/14/2003 8:00	5/27/2003
16	15	Evaluate internal product	5.d	5/28/2003 8:00	6/3/2003
17	16	Identify production process steps required for manufacture	7.d	6/4/2003 8:00	6/12/2003
18	17	Assess manufacturing capabilities	12.d	6/13/2003 8:00	6/30/2003
19	18	Determine safety issues	10.d	6/13/2003 8:00	6/26/2003
20	19	Determine environmental issues	12.d	6/13/2003 8:00	6/30/2003
21	20	Review legal issues	14.d	6/13/2003 8:00	7/2/2003
22	21	Perform financial evaluation	10.d	7/1/2003 8:00	7/14/2003
23	22	Develop risk analysis	5.d	7/15/2003 8:00	7/21/2003
24	23	Draft initial development stage plan	9.d	7/1/2003 8:00	7/11/2003
25	24	Conduct preliminary stage review decision	2.d	7/22/2003 8:00	7/23/2003

Task_Table / Resource_Table / Assignment_Table / Info_Table

Ready

Worksheets for task, resource, and assignment data

A worksheet for information about the template

To show how this works, let's export task and resource assignment costs to an Excel PivotTable. For this example, each record contains the name of a top-level task (a phase of the project), the name of a resource assigned to a task in that phase, and the scheduled cost of the assignment. The resulting PivotTable should display the data in a compact table that neatly summarizes the following items:

- The total cost for any phase of the project, along with the distribution of that cost among contributing resources, in dollar amounts and in percentage terms
- The distribution of cost for each resource in the different phases of the project

Creating a PivotTable such as this involves exporting the data and then fine-tuning the PivotTable in Excel to produce the results you want. The export operation creates only the simplest of PivotTables, but you can edit the PivotTable yourself to fine-tune the display of data.

To export Project data to an Excel PivotTable, follow these steps:

1. Open the Project file from which you want to export data.
2. Choose File, Save As.
3. Select the location for the new Excel file in the Save In list box, and provide a name for the file in the File Name text box.
4. Choose the file type Microsoft Excel PivotTable (.xls) in the Save as Type list box.
5. Click the Save button. The Export Wizard dialog box appears.

17

6. Click the Next button. The Map dialog box appears.
7. Choose New Map, and then click Next to display the Map Options dialog box.
8. In the Map Options dialog box, select one or more types of data you want to export to an Excel PivotTable, including tasks, resources, or assignments (see Figure 17.24).

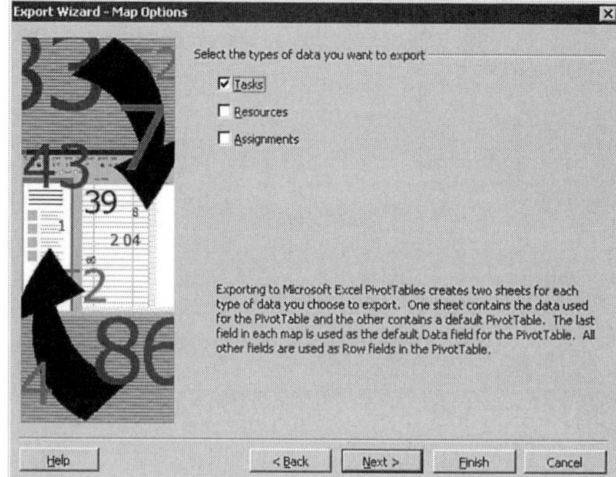

Figure 17.24
You can include tasks, resources, and assignments when exporting to a PivotTable, but each category will be a separate PivotTable in the resulting Excel workbook.

You can use only one category for each PivotTable. If you export fields from all three categories, you will produce three separate, unrelated PivotTables in the same Excel workbook.

9. Click the Next button to display the Task Mapping dialog box.
10. Type a name for the worksheet in the Destination Worksheet Name text box (see Figure 17.25).

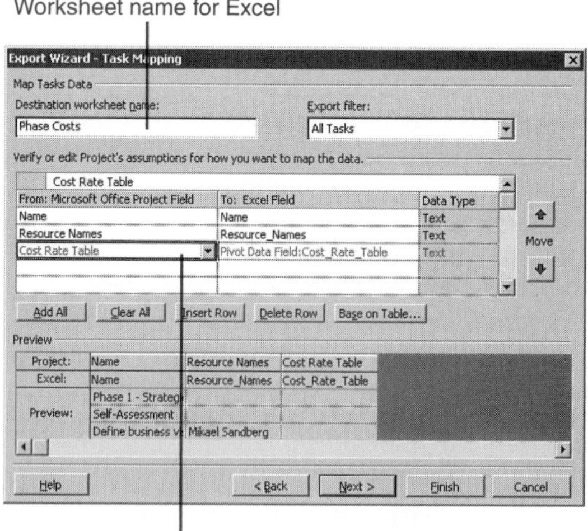

Figure 17.25
The last field in the mapping table appears in red, with the prefix Pivot Data Field:, to remind you that this field will be the calculated body of the PivotTable.

11. Choose the names of the Project fields you want to export in the From: Microsoft Project Field column. When you enter a Project field name, Project supplies the field name for the worksheet in the To: Worksheet Field column. Feel free to modify the worksheet field names.

    The last field entered in the mapping table is the field that Excel uses for the table data (that is, the calculated summary numbers in the body of the PivotTable). To remind you of this, Project displays the last field row in red, and it adds the prefix Pivot Data Field: before the export field name. If you edit the export field name, Project replaces the prefix, as long as it is the last field name row.

If the last field row is not red in your PivotTable map, see "Malfunctioning PivotTable Map" in the "Troubleshooting" section at the end of this chapter.

TIP

> If you plan to group the data in the PivotTable by major categories, with minor category details listed under them, put the major category fields above the minor category fields in the field mapping.
>
> Always make the field you want to be used for calculations the last field in the field mapping list. In this example, Cost is the last field listed because you want calculations based on its values to appear in the body of the PivotTable.

12. When the field map is completed, click the Next button. Repeat the process for any other data category tab you have chosen to use in the export.
13. Click the Next button to display the End of Map Definition dialog box.
14. Click the Save Map button. Give the new map a distinctive name, such as Excel – Export to Pivot Table, to identify it as a map to be used for exporting to an Excel PivotTable, and then click the Save button.
15. Click the Finish button to begin saving the exported data into an Excel PivotTable.

You can open Excel to see the data and PivotTable you have created (see Figure 17.26). You should see two sheets in Excel for each data category (tab) you exported. In this example, only the Task category is used, so you see a single pair of sheets. The first sheet contains the raw data you exported in a table; you could use this data to create a PivotTable on your own.

NOTE

> If you include the Task Name field in the Task Mapping list of fields, Project creates multiple Task Name columns in the worksheet—one for each outline level. For any subtask, the outline level 1 summary tasks will appear in the Task Name 1 column, the outline level 2 summary tasks will appear in the Task Name 2 column, and so forth (refer to Figure 17.26).

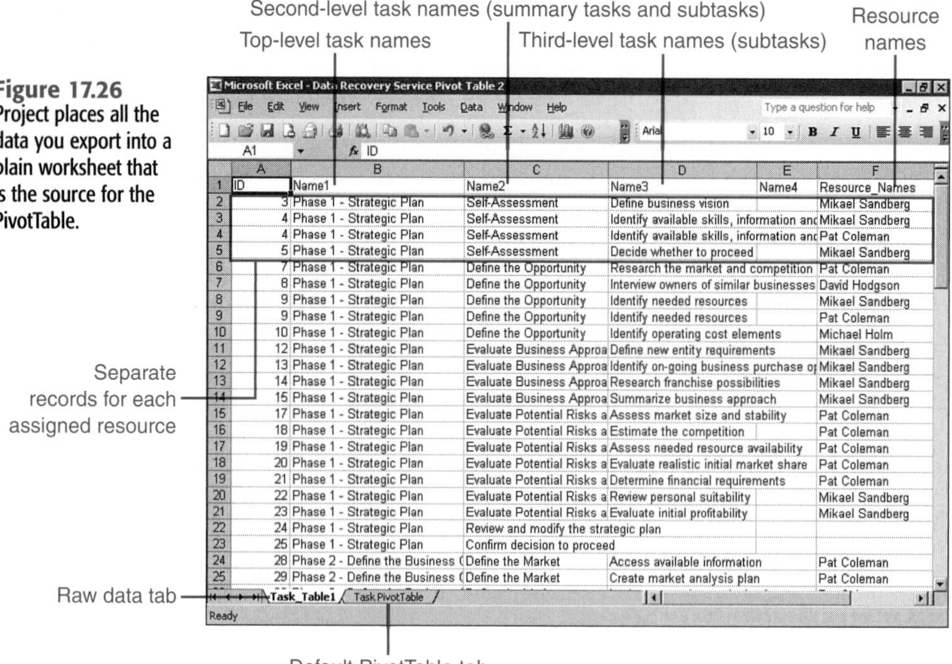

	A	B	C	D	E	F
1	ID	Name1	Name2	Name3	Name4	Resource_Names
2	3	Phase 1 - Strategic Plan	Self-Assessment	Define business vision		Mikael Sandberg
3	4	Phase 1 - Strategic Plan	Self-Assessment	Identify available skills, information anc		Mikael Sandberg
4	4	Phase 1 - Strategic Plan	Self-Assessment	Identify available skills, information anc		Pat Coleman
5	5	Phase 1 - Strategic Plan	Self-Assessment	Decide whether to proceed		Mikael Sandberg
6	7	Phase 1 - Strategic Plan	Define the Opportunity	Research the market and competition		Pat Coleman
7	8	Phase 1 - Strategic Plan	Define the Opportunity	Interview owners of similar businesses		David Hodgson
8	9	Phase 1 - Strategic Plan	Define the Opportunity	Identify needed resources		Mikael Sandberg
9	9	Phase 1 - Strategic Plan	Define the Opportunity	Identify needed resources		Pat Coleman
10	10	Phase 1 - Strategic Plan	Define the Opportunity	Identify operating cost elements		Michael Holm
11	12	Phase 1 - Strategic Plan	Evaluate Business Approa	Define new entity requirements		Mikael Sandberg
12	13	Phase 1 - Strategic Plan	Evaluate Business Approa	Identify on-going business purchase o		Mikael Sandberg
13	14	Phase 1 - Strategic Plan	Evaluate Business Approa	Research franchise possibilities		Mikael Sandberg
14	15	Phase 1 - Strategic Plan	Evaluate Business Approa	Summarize business approach		Mikael Sandberg
15	17	Phase 1 - Strategic Plan	Evaluate Potential Risks a	Assess market size and stability		Pat Coleman
16	18	Phase 1 - Strategic Plan	Evaluate Potential Risks a	Estimate the competition		Pat Coleman
17	19	Phase 1 - Strategic Plan	Evaluate Potential Risks a	Assess needed resource availability		Pat Coleman
18	20	Phase 1 - Strategic Plan	Evaluate Potential Risks a	Evaluate realistic initial market share		Pat Coleman
19	21	Phase 1 - Strategic Plan	Evaluate Potential Risks a	Determine financial requirements		Pat Coleman
20	22	Phase 1 - Strategic Plan	Evaluate Potential Risks a	Review personal suitability		Mikael Sandberg
21	23	Phase 1 - Strategic Plan	Evaluate Potential Risks a	Evaluate initial profitability		Mikael Sandberg
22	24	Phase 1 - Strategic Plan	Review and modify the strategic plan			
23	25	Phase 1 - Strategic Plan	Confirm decision to proceed			
24	28	Phase 2 - Define the Business (	Define the Market	Access available information		Pat Coleman
25	29	Phase 2 - Define the Business (	Define the Market	Create market analysis plan		Pat Coleman

Figure 17.26
Project places all the data you export into a plain worksheet that is the source for the PivotTable.

NOTE

> If you include the Resource Names field in the Task Mapping list of fields, Project creates a separate record for each resource name assigned to the task (refer to Figure 17.26).

The second sheet contains the default PivotTable that Project created (see Figure 17.27). You will almost always need to fine-tune the PivotTable that is created. Not only do you need to format things like column widths and the display of numbers, but you also need to adjust the layout of the PivotTable. Specifically, there are no column categories in the default PivotTable, but we want the resource names to appear as column headings. Also, there is only one calculation in the data area, and we want to show the percentage distribution in addition to the sum of the costs.

If the PivotTable sheet in your workbook is blank, see "Empty Exported PivotTable" in the "Troubleshooting" section at the end of this chapter.

NOTE

> For information on how to format Excel PivotTables, see Chapter 24, "Using PivotTables and PivotCharts," in *Special Edition Using Microsoft Excel 2003* by Patrick Blattner (published by Que).
>
> Also, there is an excellent section of Help articles in Excel 2002 on how to use PivotTables effectively. Look for the article on "Ways to Customize PivotTable Reports" in the Excel Help topics.

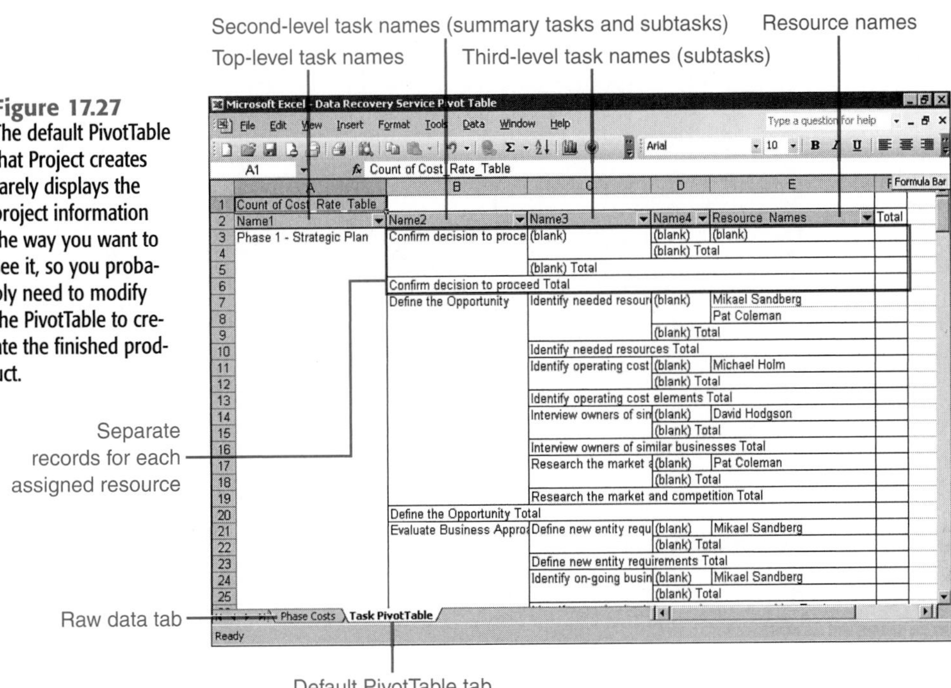

Figure 17.27 The default PivotTable that Project creates rarely displays the project information the way you want to see it, so you probably need to modify the PivotTable to create the finished product.

Figure 17.28 shows a sample of the finished PivotTable, after it is edited. The PivotTable in Figure 17.28 shows only the top-level tasks that are summary tasks (in other words, top-level tasks that do not summarize phases have been hidden). The resource names appear across column headings, with data for each resource in the column below its name. A second calculation has been added, to show the percentage of the phase costs attributable to the resource in that column. This figure also shows a few minor formatting changes (zero values are suppressed, decimals are removed, and so forth) that improve the readability.

IMPORTING PROJECT DATA FROM THE EXCEL FORMAT

You must be extremely careful when importing data from Excel into a Project file. You have to be sure that the data is mapped to the correct Project fields and that the data type is appropriate for those fields.

CAUTION

> As explained earlier in this chapter, if the Excel workbook was created by exporting tasks or resources from Microsoft Project, and if the option to include rows for resource assignments was selected, some of the rows in the workbook will be tasks (or resources) and others will be assignment details. Do not attempt to import data from a workbook such as this. Identify and remove the assignment details before attempting to import the data back into Project.

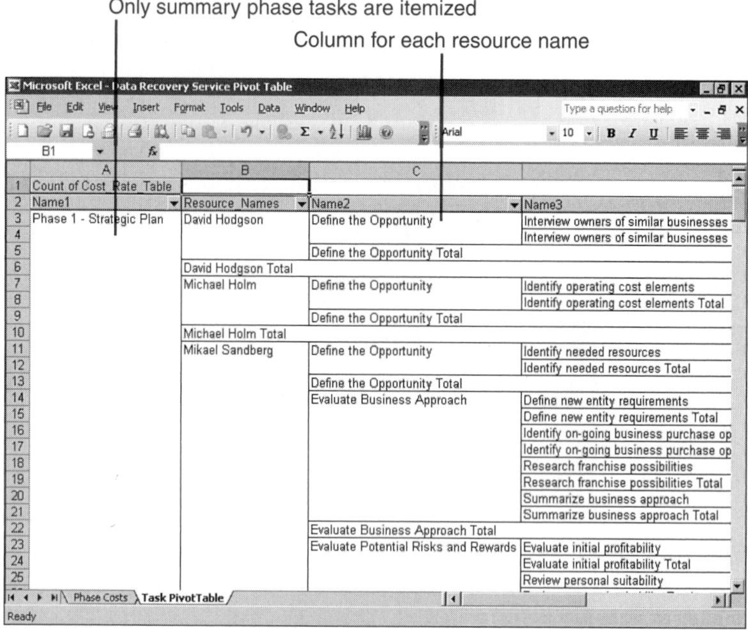

Figure 17.28
With task details suppressed and a few other formatting changes, the PivotTable is presentable.

The example that follows shows how to add a list of new employees to the resource sheet in a Project file. The list is stored in Sheet 1 of an Excel workbook. The names are to be added to the Resource data in the New Product Project file. The column headings are not exact matches for Project field names, and there are text entries in the overtime rate field, where Project expects to find only numbers. Figure 17.29 shows the data from the worksheet.

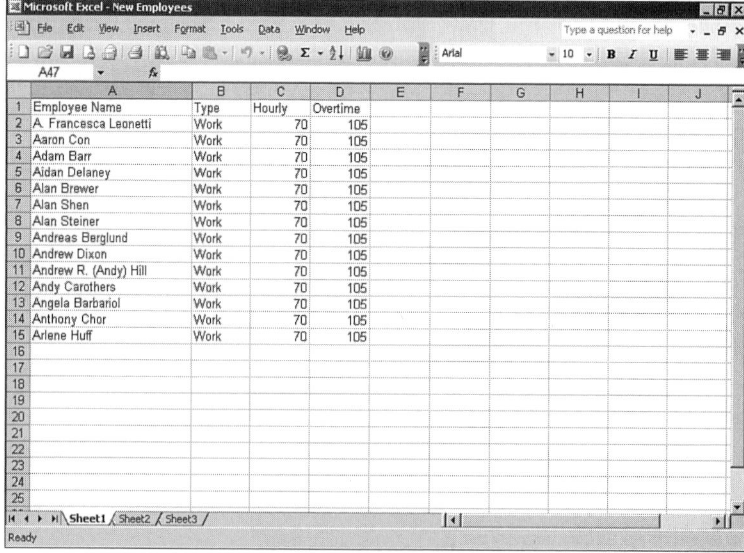

Employee Name	Type	Hourly	Overtime
A. Francesca Leonetti	Work	70	105
Aaron Con	Work	70	105
Adam Barr	Work	70	105
Aidan Delaney	Work	70	105
Alan Brewer	Work	70	105
Alan Shen	Work	70	105
Alan Steiner	Work	70	105
Andreas Berglund	Work	70	105
Andrew Dixon	Work	70	105
Andrew R. (Andy) Hill	Work	70	105
Andy Carothers	Work	70	105
Angela Barbariol	Work	70	105
Anthony Chor	Work	70	105
Arlene Huff	Work	70	105

Figure 17.29
The New Employees workbook contains new resources and their pay rates, which can be imported into Project.

To import the data from Excel into the Project file, follow these steps:

1. Open the Project file into which you want to import the data, unless you plan to have Project create a new document file for the imported data. Figure 17.30 shows the Resource sheet before the data is imported.

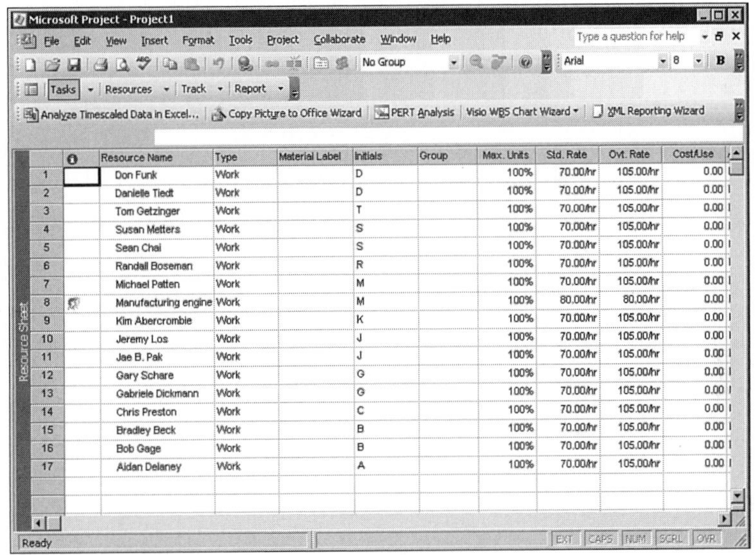

Figure 17.30
The current resource roster in the New Product Project file contains 17 names, including one material resource.

2. Although it is not necessary, it is wise to choose a view in Project that shows the data when it is imported. This is especially helpful if you're not sure what Project field names to use for some of the imported data. For example, in the Resource Sheet view, the employee's name should go in the column labeled Resource Name, but the actual name of that field is just Name. To see the real field name for a column, simply double-click the column heading for the field, to display the Column Definition dialog box, as is shown in Figure 17.31 for the column that is titled Resource Name.

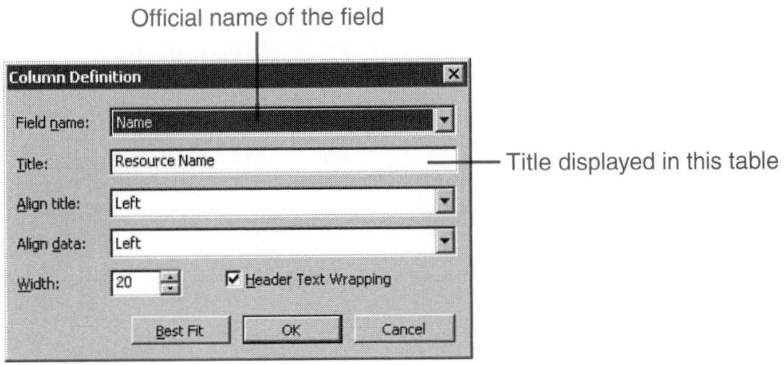

Figure 17.31
The column definition for the Resource Name column shows that the real name of the field is Name.

3. Choose File, Open to display the Open dialog box.
4. Use the Look In list box to select the location in which the Excel workbook is saved.
5. Change the Files of Type selection to Microsoft Excel Workbooks.
6. Select the Excel file from the file list and click the Open button. The Import Wizard dialog box appears.
7. Click the Next button to display the Map dialog box.
8. Select the New Map option and click the Next button. The Import Mode dialog box appears.
9. Select the option to append the data to an existing project. Click the Next button to display the Map Options dialog box.
10. Select Resources as the type of data to import. Make sure that the check box labeled Import Includes Headers is selected. If you don't check the Headers box, the map's field list will not display the Excel column headers (it will just number the columns). This would make it difficult for you to know which Excel column maps to which Project field (see Figure 17.32).

    Note that the option to import assignment detail rows is not available. Project has no way of knowing which rows are tasks (or resources) and which are assignment details.

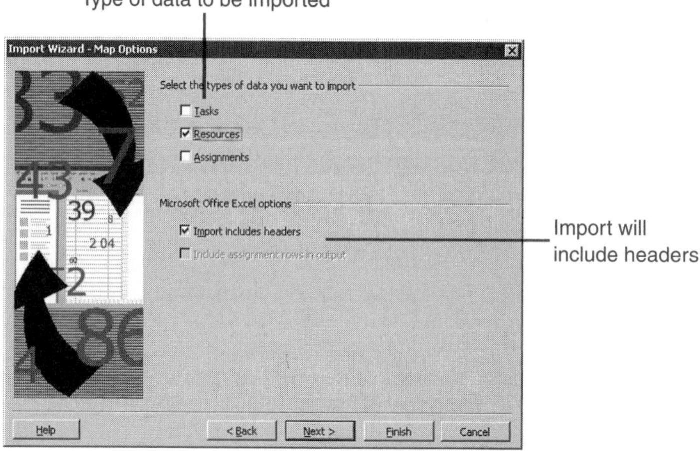

Figure 17.32
You need the headers to be imported, to help match the imported data with Project fields.

11. Click the Next button. The Resource Mapping dialog box appears.
12. Select the source worksheet name from the Source Worksheet Name list. In this example, the worksheet is named `Sheet1`.

    When the source worksheet is selected, Project fills the From: Excel Field column in the left side of the mapping table with the column headings from the worksheet. Project also attempts to find a matching field name from the project to display in the To: Microsoft Project Field column on the right side of the mapping table.

In Figure 17.33, Project is displaying the Excel field names but cannot locate a match in Project's Resource fields.

Column titles in Excel worksheet

Figure 17.33
Project cannot find a Resource field match for the fields found in the Excel worksheet.

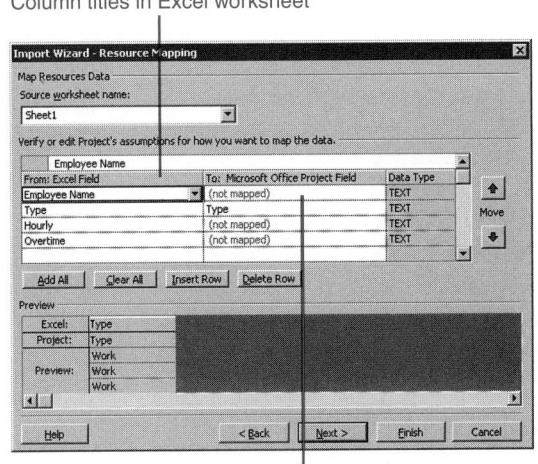

No matching Project field names found

13. Supply the correct field names in the To: Microsoft Project Field column of the mapping table for each field in the From: Excel Field column (see Figure 17.34).

Figure 17.34
You use the drop-down list of Project field names to select the correct field to receive the imported data.

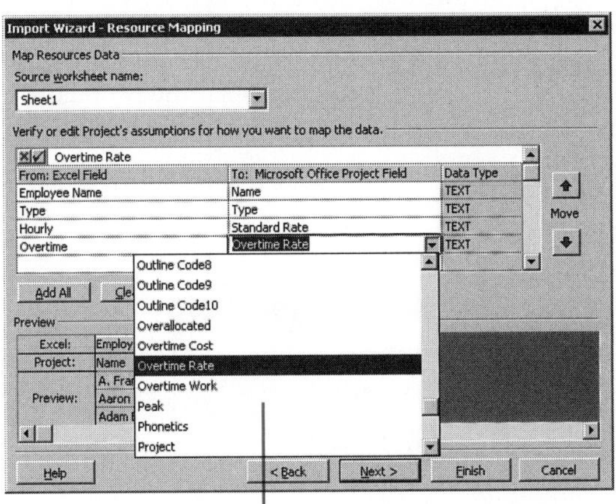

Drop-down list of field names

14. Click the Next button to display the End of Map Definition dialog box.

    If you want to save the map, click the Save Map button and give the map a unique name. Otherwise, click the Finish button to begin the import. Your data is appended to the end of the Resource Sheet list of resources (see Figure 17.35).

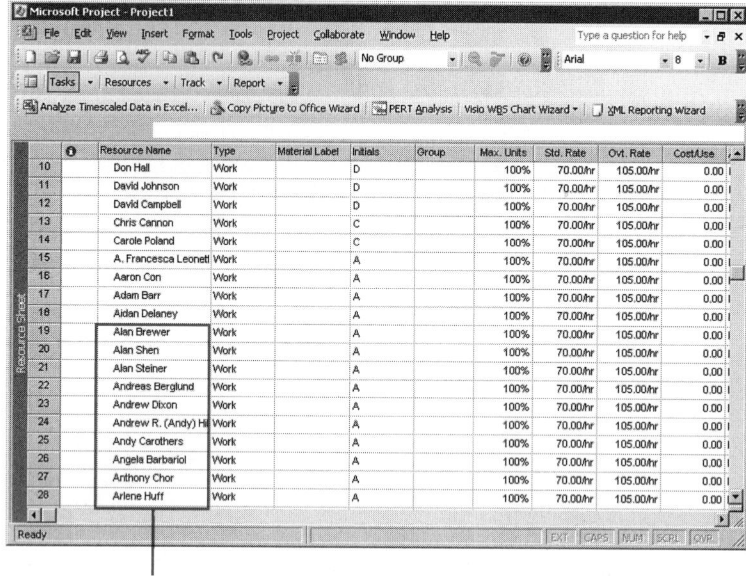

Figure 17.35
Project has appended the new resources to the resource list and skipped mismatched values in the Overtime Rate field.

If Project has a problem converting data that is being imported into a Task field, you might see a warning message. Project is not nearly as forgiving when importing Task data, as you can see in the error message shown in Figure 17.36 for a mismatched Duration value. If you see an error message while importing data into a project, select one of the following options:

- Click Yes to continue importing and to continue seeing error messages. You should generally choose this option, unless you know what the problems are and what corrective action you need to take in the Project file as a result.
- Click No to continue importing without seeing further error messages.
- Click Cancel to stop importing.

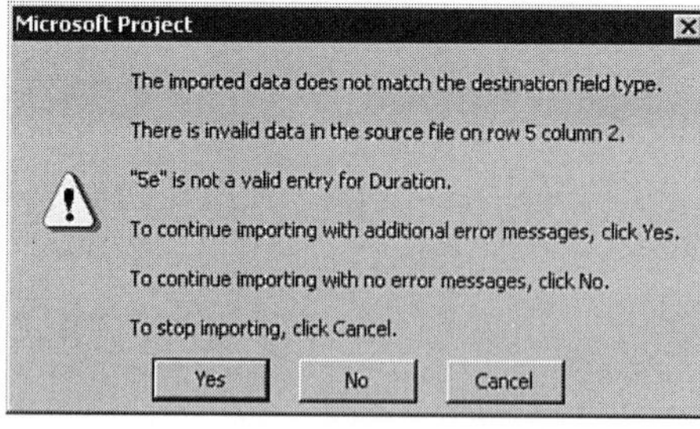

Figure 17.36
If there is a data mismatch during an import operation, Project warns you and lets you choose how to proceed.

CAUTION

> Mismatched data is not imported into Project, and the affected field in Project displays a default value. You need to find these holes in the data and manually supply the correct information.
>
> It's a good idea to jot down the source references in the warning message (refer to Figure 17.36). If you are importing a lot of data at once, the references can help you locate the problem in the source file so that you can determine where to look in the Project file to fill in the missing information.

If you prefer to begin a new project in Excel and then import it into a Project file, you can use one or both of the new Project Excel templates that ship with Project. When Project 2003 is installed, two Excel templates—`Microsoft Project Task List Import Template.xlt` and `Microsoft Project Plan Import Export Template.xlt`—are installed in the standard Office folder.

To begin a project in Excel, open Excel, and then click File, New and select one of the two Excel templates from the list. `Microsoft Project Task List Import Template.xlt` contains the same four worksheets (Task_Table, Resource_Table, Assignment_Table, and Info_Table) that are exported from Project to Excel when you select the Project Excel Template option in the Export Wizard. This template also contains the same fields that are exported from Project to Excel. `Microsoft Project Plan Import Export Template.xlt` is much simpler in content than the other template, with only two worksheets (Task_Table and Microsoft_Project) and seven fields (ID, Name, Duration, Start, Deadline, Resource Names, and Notes).

Create a new workbook by opening one of these two Excel templates, and then create your list of tasks, resources, and/or assignments, which can then be imported into Project. As you enter project data in Excel, be very careful about any data entered in a field that is a numerical field in Project, such as Duration, Work, Start, and Finish. Keep the following points in mind as you enter project data in an Excel template:

- Duration should be entered as a text value, and it must include your desired time unit, such as **`5d`**. Otherwise, your task durations will be set to 0 days.
- Work and units can be entered as numerical data, but Project assumes default measures of work (hours) and units (percentage). You can also enter work as text data, with your desired time unit included, such as **`40h`**.
- Cost rates are imported as hourly rates unless a `/` and another time unit are appended.
- Resource names cannot include commas, square brackets, or percent symbols.
- Setting predecessors in Excel is a very tricky process because they use the Project Task ID number and not Excel's row number. Therefore, predecessors are probably best entered after the data has been imported into Project.
- The default date format on the View tab of the Project Options dialog box sets the formatting for dates that are imported into Project. If you leave the Start and Finish fields blank in Excel, Project sets the current date as the start date for each task.

→ For information on time unit abbreviations, **see** "Entering Task Duration," **p. 132**.

A quick way to add a list of tasks into a Project file is to use the new Project Guide sidepane to the left of the project file. To import tasks from Excel into a project using the sidepane, complete the following steps:

1. In the Sidepane, click the List the Tasks in the Project hyperlink.
2. In the Excel section of the List Tasks pane, click the hyperlink Import Wizard from the Import Tasks (see Figure 17.37).
3. Follow the process previously outlined in this section to import tasks from Excel into Project.

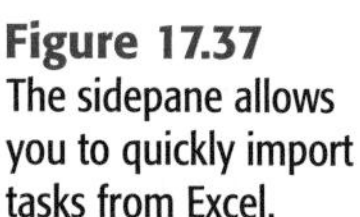

Figure 17.37
The sidepane allows you to quickly import tasks from Excel.

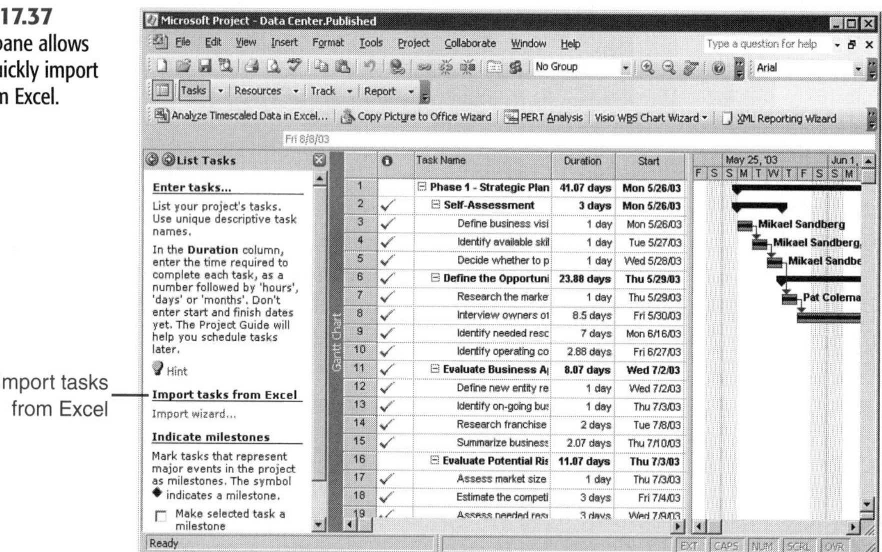

→ For additional information on using the Project Guide toolbar and the sidepane, **see** Chapter 2, "Learning the Basics of Microsoft Project," **p. 29**.

CAUTION

> When you are importing task start or finish dates, Project treats the imported dates as though you had typed them instead of letting Project calculate them. In other words, the tasks are assigned the soft constraint Start No Earlier Than (for fixed-start-date projects) or Finish No Later Than (for fixed-finish-date projects). You can reset these task constraints to As Soon As Possible or As Late As Possible after the tasks are imported into Project.

TIP

> If you are importing dates and there is no time of day attached to the source date, Project assigns the start time of the project to the Start field on each task and the time of midnight to the Finish field on each task. If there is a time of day attached to the date, Project keeps the time, unless it falls before the default start time or after the default end time (as defined on the Calendar tab of the Options dialog box); in this case, Project substitutes the default time of day.

WORKING WITH WEB-ENABLED PROJECT DATA

You can create pages for an intranet site or the Internet by exporting Project data to the HTML format, which is currently the standard format for Internet browsers. You can save Project data to the HTML format, but you cannot import Project data from the HTML format.

Another feature of Project 2003 is the ability to export project data in the XML format. XML is the standard language for describing and delivering data on the Web, just as HTML is the standard language for creating and displaying Web pages. The XML format is similar to HTML, and it is complementary to HTML for publishing Project data to Web pages and for viewing either on the Internet or on corporate intranets. Unlike HTML files, however, XML files can be imported by Project 2003 as well as exported.

To save a project to an XML file, follow these steps:

1. Open the project file from which you want to export data.
2. Choose File, Save As to display the Save As dialog box.
3. Select the directory for the new XML file in the Save In list box and give the new file a name.
4. Select the XML Format (*.xml) file format in the Save as Type list box and click the Save button. The project is then saved as an XML file.

When saving a Project file in XML format, the entire project file is exported to the file; you cannot export only selected data from the plan.

Unlike with HTML files, Project can import as well as export XML files. To import an XML file, follow these steps:

1. If you want to append or merge the XML data into a project, open the project file into which you want to import the data. Otherwise, you do not need to have a project open.
2. Choose File, Open to display the Open dialog box.
3. Select the directory from the Look In list that contains XML files, and then select the file you want to open.
4. Select the XML Format (*.xml) file format in the Files of Type list box and click the Open button. The Import Wizard dialog box is displayed.
5. Click the Next button to display the Import Mode dialog box.

6. Select whether you want to import the file as a new project, append the data to an existing project, or merge the data into an existing project.
7. Click the Finish button.

The XML file is imported into either a new project or your active project, depending on your choice in step 6.

WORKING WITH TEXT FILE FORMATS

Project supports two ASCII text formats: the tab-delimited and comma-separated value (CSV) formats. The Import/Export maps for both of these formats are almost the same as the Import/Export maps for Excel, but with one key difference. With Excel, you can import or export task, resource, and assignment data tables simultaneously. With text formats, you can import or export only one of those three data tables at a time.

EXPORTING PROJECT DATA IN THE TEXT FORMATS

To export a list of project milestones to a text file, follow these steps:

1. Open the project plan from which you want to export the milestones.
2. Choose File, Save As.
3. Select the directory for the new text file in the Save In list box.
4. Select the file format in the Save as Type list box. For a tab-delimited file, select Text (Tab delimited) (*.txt). This format places tab characters between each field of data in a record (with quote marks surrounding field values that contain commas) and separates the records with paragraph marks (that is, a carriage return and line feed).

   For a comma-delimited file, select CSV (Comma delimited) (*.csv). This format places commas between each field of data in a record (with quote marks surrounding field values that themselves contain commas) and separates the records with a paragraph mark.
5. Click the Save button. The Export Wizard dialog box appears.
6. Click the Next button to display the Map dialog box.
7. Select whether you want to use a new map or an existing map. Click the Next button, and the Map Options dialog box appears.
8. Select the type of data—tasks, resources, or assignments—you want to export. Project allows you to choose only one of the three data types (see Figure 17.38).
9. Leave the Export Includes Headers box checked so that the exported data will be labeled.
10. Check the Include Assignment Rows in Output box only if you want assignments to be included. Remember that assignments will be indistinguishable from tasks or resources unless you include the Assignment field to identify them.
11. Select a Text Delimiter from the drop-down list if you want to use either the space or comma as a delimiter instead of the tab character (which is the default).

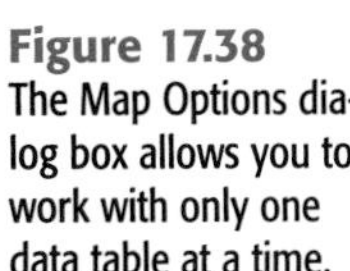

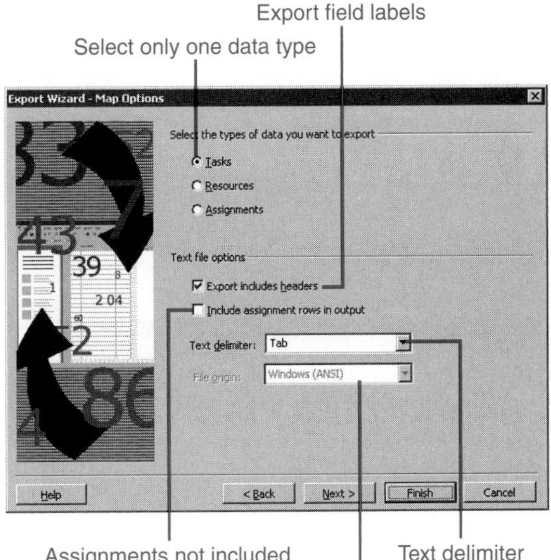

Figure 17.38
The Map Options dialog box allows you to work with only one data table at a time.

17

12. Click the Next button. The Mapping dialog box for your selected data type appears.

    In Figure 17.39 only two fields are to be exported—Task Name and Finish Date—and the Milestones filter has been selected. Notice that the Destination Table Name text box is not available for exporting or importing text-formatted data.

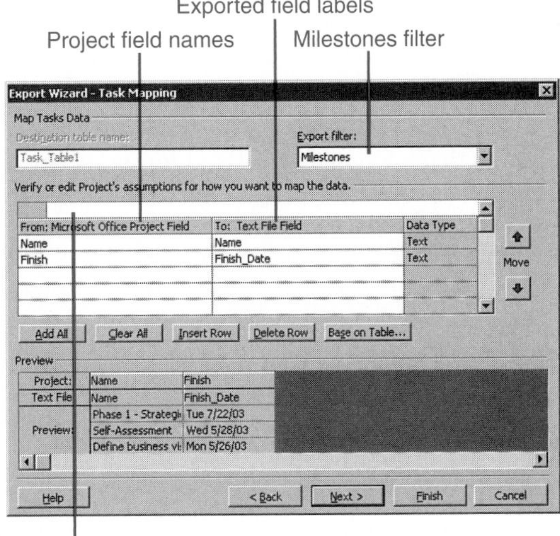

Figure 17.39
The Milestones filter limits the tasks that are exported to just those that are milestones.

13. When the map is complete, click the Next button to display the End of Map Definition dialog box.

14. If you want to reuse the map you just created, click the Save button. Give the map a unique name, such as Export Milestones to Text (txt), to identify it as a map used for exporting Milestones to a text file.
15. Click the Finish button to create the file.

The resulting text file can be opened and viewed in Notepad (see Figure 17.40) or any other text editor. It can also be imported into other applications that can import data from a tab-delimited text file.

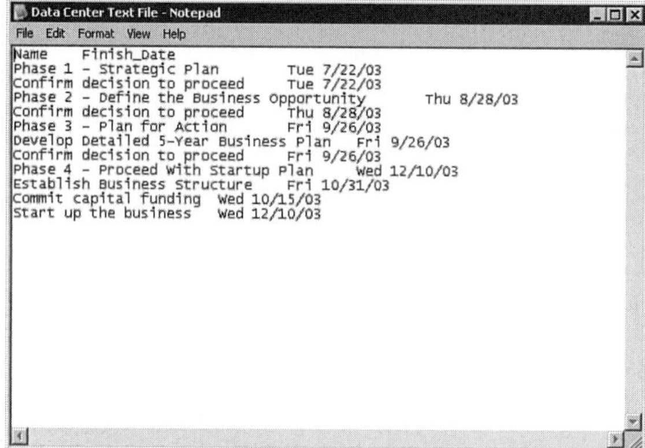

Figure 17.40
The New `Project.txt` file is opened in Notepad.

IMPORTING PROJECT DATA FROM THE TEXT FORMATS

Importing from a text file is similar to importing from an Excel workbook, except that you can import only one type of data at a time—you must import tasks, resources, and assignments separately. (See the previous section, "Importing Project Data from the Excel Format," for more information.) With text files, you are likely to encounter the same problems in matching field names that are found with Excel formats when the import source file was not originally exported from Project.

When importing from a text format, you have an additional option, which is grayed-out for exporting in Figure 17.38. You can use the File Origin text box to specify a different character set for the source data. The default is Windows (ANSI), but you can also select DOS or OS/2 (PC-8), or you can select Unicode. This maximizes your chances of importing the data correctly, knowing that text files may have originated in an OS/2 environment, or in an international environment where a text file might be created using Unicode as its character set.

IMPORTING A TASK LIST FROM OUTLOOK

Project 2003 has the ability to import a task list from Outlook. Because many people use Outlook to track their to-do lists of tasks, Project now makes it easy to import tasks directly from Outlook. Figure 17.41 shows a small list of tasks that has been entered into Outlook.

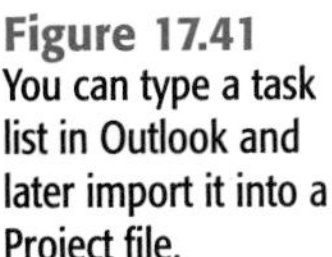

Figure 17.41
You can type a task list in Outlook and later import it into a Project file.

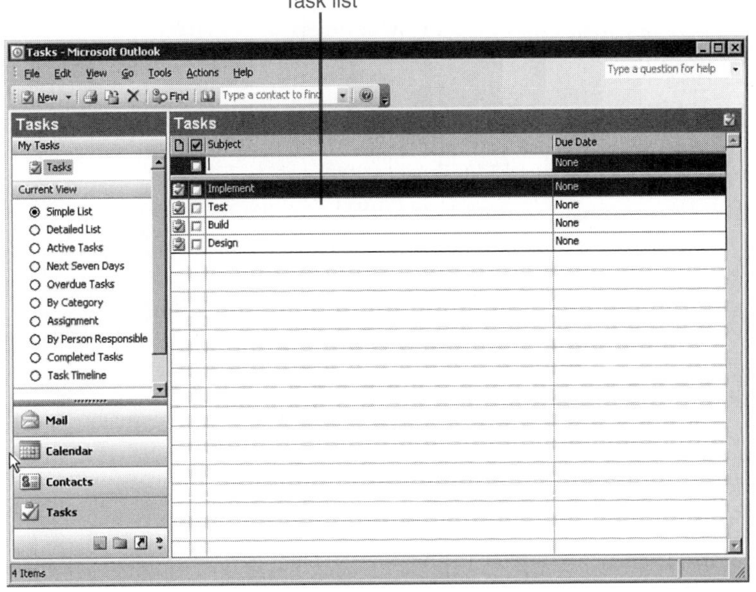

Figures 17.42 and 17.43 show the additional information that can be entered for each Outlook task, including notes and durations for each task. To add this information, double-click on the task and add the information.

Figure 17.42
The Task tab allows you to add notes for each task.

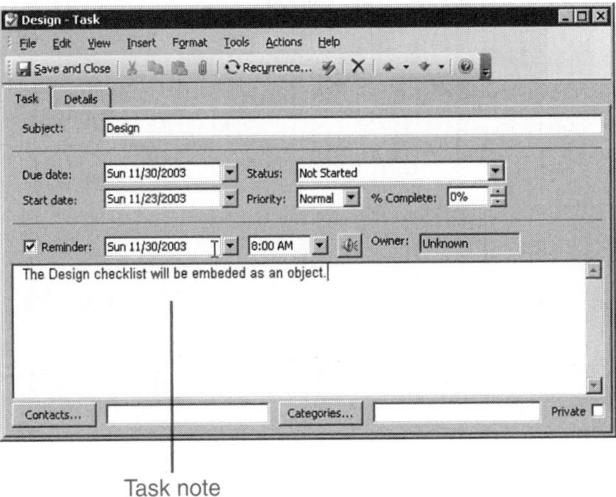

17

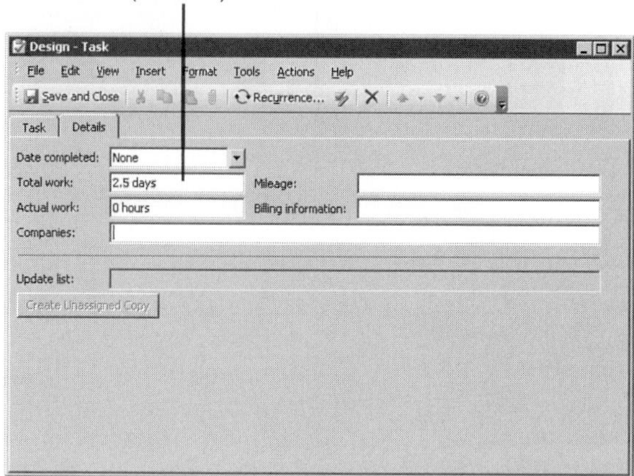

Figure 17.43
The Details tab for each task allows you to enter Total Work (a duration) for the task.

17

To import a task list from Outlook into a project, follow these steps:

1. Type your task information into the Tasks section of Outlook. Include start date, duration, due date, and notes, if appropriate.
2. Open a blank project or the project into which you want to import the tasks.
3. Click Tools, Import Outlook Tasks. The Import Outlook Tasks dialog box appears (see Figure 17.44).

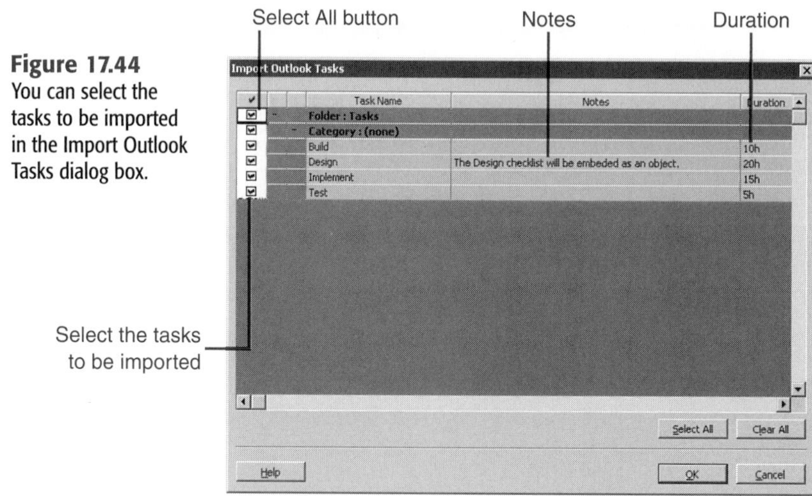

Figure 17.44
You can select the tasks to be imported in the Import Outlook Tasks dialog box.

4. Select the tasks you want to import by clicking the check box in the first column for each task. Click the Select All button to select every task in the list.
5. Click the OK button to import the Outlook tasks.

The Outlook tasks are imported into your Project file in alphabetical order (see Figure 17.45). At this point, you can drag the imported tasks into the proper sequence, set task dependencies and constraints, and so on. Note that Project ignored the start date for each task in Outlook while it imported the tasks. The start date for each imported task is set to the start date of the project.

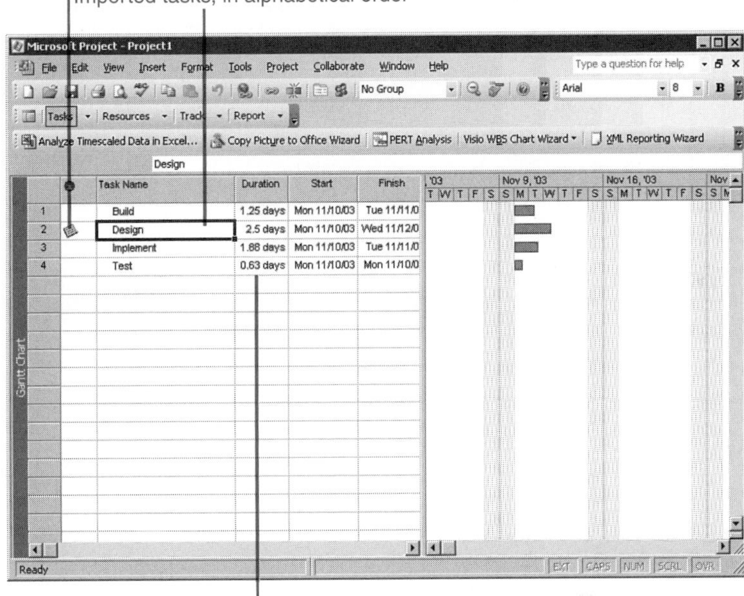

Figure 17.45
Tasks are imported from Outlook into the Project file, including a note and duration for each task.

USING MICROSOFT PROJECT 2003 AS AN OLE DB PROVIDER

Like Project 2000/2002, Project 2003 is a read-only OLE DB provider. This means you can read the current project data with another application; however, you cannot modify the Project data with the OLE DB client. For example, you can use Data Access Pages in Access 2002 to build dynamic reports that allow the viewer to drill down into the current project data, such as in Figure 17.46. This link is created entirely within the client application, such as in Microsoft Access.

The Project 2003 OLE DB provider contains additional project details, including the following:

- Calendar data and calendar exceptions
- Cost rates
- Custom fields, with graphical indicators, value lists, and custom outline code fields

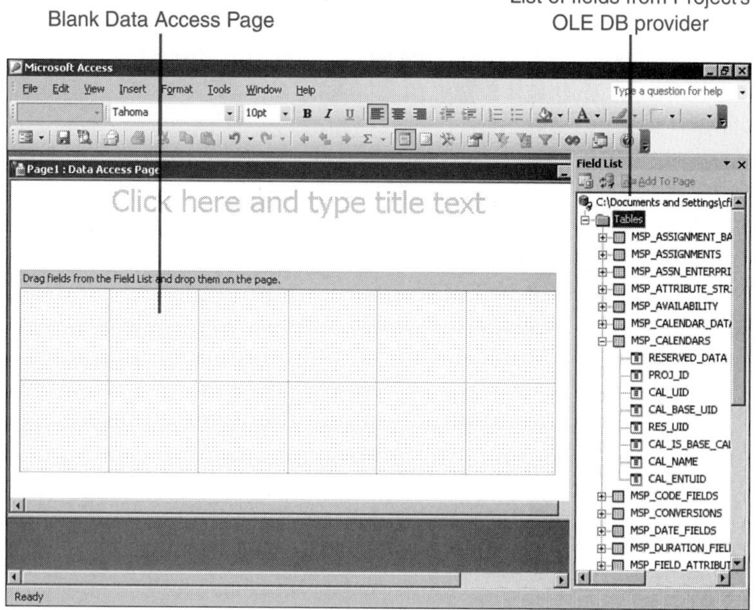

Figure 17.46
A new Data Access Page is being created in Access 2002, using Project's OLE DB provider.

17

- Resource availability
- Timescaled data for resources, tasks, and assignments
- Work Breakdown Structure (WBS) information

NOTE

For information about creating Data Access Pages, see Chapter 25, "Designing and Deploying Data Access Pages," in *Special Edition Using Microsoft Access 2002* by Roger Jennings (published by Que).

NOTE

Significant formatting issues are related to displaying Project data in other applications. For example, duration fields display the duration in minutes multiplied by 10 (for example, an hour will appear as 600) and work fields display the work as minutes multiplied by 1,000 (for example, an hour will appear as 60,000). The data has to be processed in order to provide a meaningful display for users.

→ A database technology that is similar to Data Access Pages is OLAP Cubes. For information about creating OLAP Cubes, **see** "Building OLAP Cubes and Updating Resource Tables," **p. 994**.

TROUBLESHOOTING

MISSING IMPORTED DATA

I imported data into Microsoft Project, but I can't see the data in Project. What have I done wrong?

Make sure you have used an appropriate import map. If the field names in the map don't exist or are mismatched with Project fields, you might not have imported any data. Also, make sure you are using the appropriate view or table. If you imported resource data and then used a task view, you would not see the data. Likewise, if the Project table in the current view does not include the fields you imported, you do not see the imported data.

MALFUNCTIONING PIVOTTABLE MAP

The last field row is not red in my PivotTable map, and it doesn't display the Pivot Data Field: prefix. Can I fix it?

Even though a map might be designed for exporting to a PivotTable, if you start the Save As command by choosing any format other than Microsoft Excel PivotTable, the map does not display the last field in red and generates a regular worksheet instead of a PivotTable. Of course, you can manually create a PivotTable based on the worksheet in Excel.

EMPTY EXPORTED PIVOTTABLE

After exporting project data to an Excel PivotTable, I find that the PivotTable sheet has no data in it. What's the problem?

Project cannot format an Excel PivotTable if there are more than eight fields in the data set. If the export map includes more than eight fields, Project exports the field data but is unable to create the initial PivotTable. However, you can use Excel's PivotTable Wizard Layout dialog box to place the fields in a PivotTable.

Remember that if you include task names, Project adds a field for each outline level that is used in the project; therefore, if a project has multiple outline levels, it's easy to exceed the maximum number of fields that Project can handle.

CHAPTER 18

Copying, Pasting, and Inserting Data with Other Applications

In this chapter

Copying Selected Data Between Applications 692

Linking Selected Data Between Applications 697

Working with Objects 703

Placing Objects into Microsoft Project 706

Placing Project Objects into Other Applications 719

Troubleshooting 729

COPYING SELECTED DATA BETWEEN APPLICATIONS

In Chapter 17, "Exporting and Importing Data with Other File Formats," you learned to export and import Project data in other file formats, using Project's Open and Save commands. You learned to exchange whole projects and to use Import/Export maps to work with selected blocks of data. In this chapter, you will learn how to exchange individual field values as well as objects between files, using the Copy and Paste commands and the Insert Object command. Both data that you paste into Project and objects that you insert into Project can often be linked to the original source, to enable you to update the Project document to show the most current values in the source file.

NOTE

> Unless you are very competent using VBA (Visual Basic for Applications) to write macros that send Project data to other applications, you will find that using Copy and Paste is the only easy way to copy Project's timephased data into other applications. Import/Export maps don't handle timephased data, and Project's timephased reports can only be sent to the printer or viewed onscreen in Project.

18

If you do not need to transfer all the information in a file (for example, you need just one or a few values from the source document), you can use the Windows Clipboard to copy and paste the data from one application's document (the source) to another application's document (the destination). Project can be the source or destination for exchanging data this way. You can simply paste a copy of the values or you can paste a permanent link that displays the current value from the source document but also can be updated on demand to display any changes in the source document.

When you are pasting Clipboard data into a table in Project, it is very important that you select the correct field(s) to receive the data. When you're importing files, the Import/Export map defines where the field data will be pasted. But with the copy and paste procedure, the paste location depends on where you click the mouse to make a selection just before you use the Paste command.

If you are pasting a single value, it's easy to select a recipient field that is appropriate for the value you are copying. If you are copying a block of two or more columns of values, however, you need to be in a table view in Project that has the appropriate columns next to each other to receive the block of copied values. Frequently, this means that you must define a custom table in Project to display the data field columns in the same order as the data that you are copying. When you paste the data into Project, you might also have to have a custom table displayed in the current view.

If you change the columns in the standard table for the current view and then find that you don't want the changes in all views that use that table, see "Restoring Standard Tables That Have Been Customized" in the "Troubleshooting" section at the end of this chapter. Also see "Efficiently Customizing a Table" in the "Troubleshooting" section for steps for creating customized tables.

The Excel worksheet in Figure 18.1 is laid out with fields for the resource names and the cost rates for each resource. The standard Entry table in the Resource Sheet view does not match this layout; it has five other columns between the Resource Name and the Standard Rate columns. Therefore, you should create a custom Entry table and hide those five columns to allow the data to be pasted correctly (see Figure 18.2).

Employee Name	Hourly	Overtime
Terry Uland	$15.00	$22.50
Myrta Hansen	$45.00	$67.50
Dave Erickson	$35.00	N/A
Roger Burnett	$25.00	$37.50
Benjamin Montanez	200/day	300/day
Charles Kirkpatrick	$30.00	$45.00
Renee Hensley	$20.00	$30.00
Marilyn Ray	65000/yr	$0.00
Ray Cobb	$20.00	$30.00
Gary Howard	$50.00	$75.00

Figure 18.1
To correctly paste this spreadsheet data, you need to create a custom table in Project, with columns laid out in exactly the same order as in the spreadsheet.

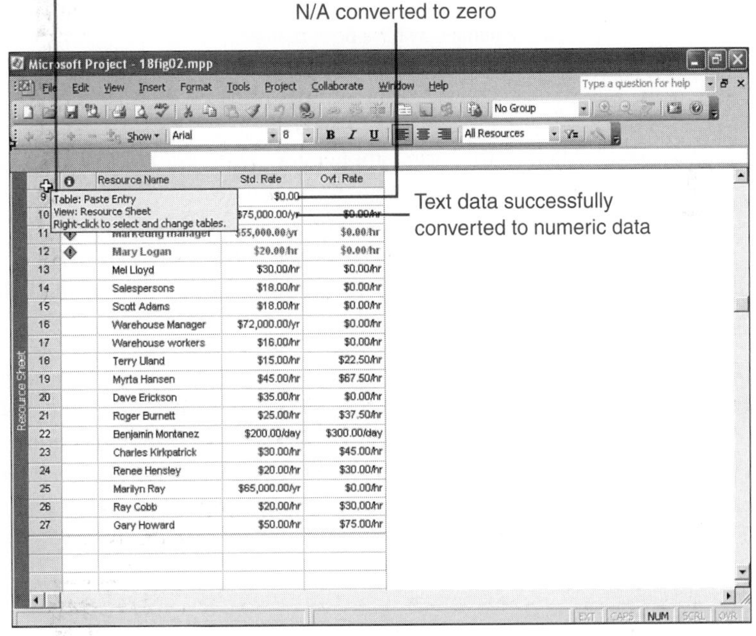

Figure 18.2
A custom resource table called Paste Entry can be created to accept the data pasted from the spreadsheet shown in Figure 18.1.

You must also be sure that the cell you select before executing the Paste command is the cell that should receive the upper-left cell of the pasted block. In Figure 18.2, the cell containing Terry Uland was selected before pasting.

COPYING DATA FROM OTHER APPLICATIONS INTO PROJECT

To copy data from another application into Microsoft Project, follow these steps:

1. Select the source data. You can select a single value or several values, as shown in Figure 18.1. If you select several values, be sure that the layout of the values matches the order of the values in the Microsoft Project table that will serve as the destination.

2. Place the data on the Clipboard by choosing Edit, Copy; by pressing Ctrl+C; or by clicking the Copy button on the Standard toolbar.
3. Activate Microsoft Project and select a view with a table that contains columns in the same order as the data you are copying, as shown in Figure 18.2.
4. Select the task or resource row and the first field in the table that is to receive the data. If you select blank rows, Microsoft Project creates new tasks or resources with the data you copy. If you select rows that already contain data, Project replaces the existing data with the newly copied data.

NOTE

> If you overwrite an existing resource, you are simply changing field values for that resource. Any tasks assigned to that resource are still assigned to it–even though the resource name may have been changed.

5. Paste your data into the target application by choosing Edit, Paste; pressing Ctrl+V; or clicking the Paste button on the Standard toolbar.

The paste operation places a static copy of the current value from the source document in the field that you selected. Microsoft Project does not automatically update this value if the value in the source document is changed.

If you select a field that does not support the data type you are importing, you see a pasting error message like the one shown in Figure 18.3. For example, the data from Figure 18.1 contained the text value N/A in cell D5 (the third row of the selection), and in Figure 18.3, Project says that it was unclear what to do with that value in the Overtime Rate field. The error message points out that the error was detected in ID 3 in the Overtime Rate column. The error dialog box offers you these option buttons:

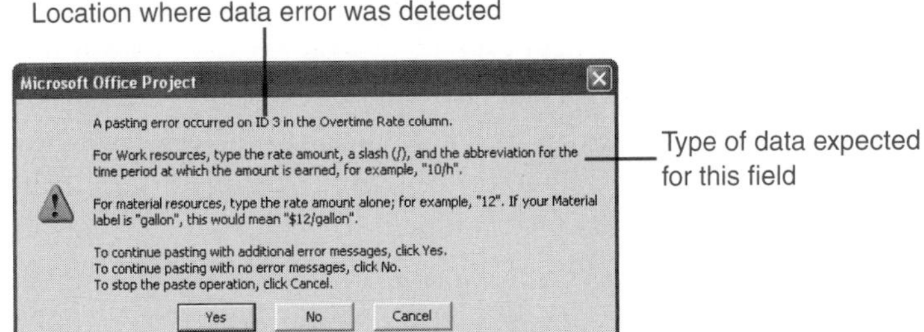

Figure 18.3
The pasting error message tells you where the error occurred and gives you clues about the type of data that is expected.

- **Yes**—If you want to continue pasting and continue receiving error messages, choose Yes. The mismatched value will be pasted into the cell, and Project will attempt to make sense of it.
- **No**—If you want to continue pasting but without having to deal with any more error messages, choose No.
- **Cancel**—If you want to stop the pasting operation, choose Cancel. Note that if you were pasting a block of values and several have already been pasted, canceling the paste operation would cause the pasted values to remain in the Project document, but no more values would be added.

CAUTION

Pasting dates into the Start or Finish fields for tasks creates soft constraints for those tasks (Start No Earlier Than constraints in projects scheduled using a start date, and Finish No Later Than constraints in projects scheduled using a finish date). You can change the constraint on the Advanced tab of the Task Information dialog box.

➔ For more information about removing constraints and the types of constraints, **see** "Working with Task Constraints," **p. 201**.

Copying Microsoft Project Data into Other Applications

To copy data from Microsoft Project to another application, follow these steps:

1. Select a view and apply a table that displays the data you want to copy to the other application.
2. Select the source data. You can select a single value, several adjacent values, whole rows or columns, or all cells in the table:
    - To select entire rows, click the ID number for the row or rows.
    - To select entire columns, click the column headers.
    - To select all cells in the table, click the Select All button above the ID numbers and to the left of the other column headers.
3. Place the data on the Clipboard by choosing Edit, Copy or by pressing Ctrl+C.

4. Activate the other application and select the location where you want to paste the data.
5. Choose Edit, Paste, or press Ctrl+V.

Figure 18.4 shows a block of data copied from the Resource Usage view into an Excel worksheet. Prior to the Copy operation, the Cost table in Project was modified to include the Assignment field. After the Paste operation in Excel, the user typed and formatted the heading at the top of each column in the worksheet. You can now do the final formatting on this worksheet by using the Assignment column to separate the rows that contain resource data from the rows that contain assignment data.

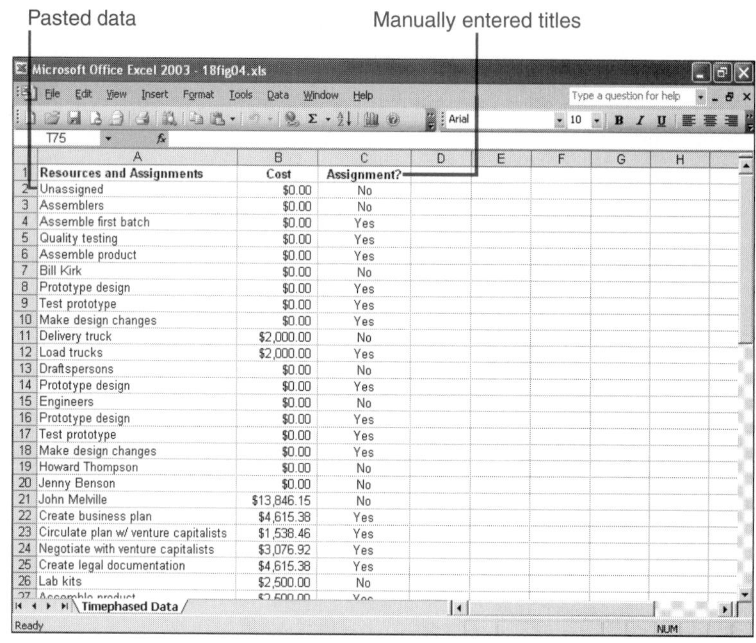

	A	B	C
1	**Resources and Assignments**	**Cost**	**Assignment?**
2	Unassigned	$0.00	No
3	Assemblers	$0.00	No
4	Assemble first batch	$0.00	Yes
5	Quality testing	$0.00	Yes
6	Assemble product	$0.00	Yes
7	Bill Kirk	$0.00	No
8	Prototype design	$0.00	Yes
9	Test prototype	$0.00	Yes
10	Make design changes	$0.00	Yes
11	Delivery truck	$2,000.00	No
12	Load trucks	$2,000.00	Yes
13	Draftspersons	$0.00	No
14	Prototype design	$0.00	Yes
15	Engineers	$0.00	No
16	Prototype design	$0.00	Yes
17	Test prototype	$0.00	Yes
18	Make design changes	$0.00	Yes
19	Howard Thompson	$0.00	No
20	Jenny Benson	$0.00	No
21	John Melville	$13,846.15	No
22	Create business plan	$4,615.38	Yes
23	Circulate plan w/ venture capitalists	$1,538.46	Yes
24	Negotiate with venture capitalists	$3,076.92	Yes
25	Create legal documentation	$4,615.38	Yes
26	Lab kits	$2,500.00	No

Figure 18.4
Three columns of data have been pasted from the Resource Usage view in Project, and the data is now ready for final formatting in Excel.

NOTE

To copy and paste the information contained in the timephased grid of either the Task Usage or Resource Usage views, you must follow a series of three steps. First, select the desired information in the table, and then copy and paste it to the destination application. Second, select the desired data in the timephased grid, matching the data in the grid with the appropriate rows in the table. You can then copy this information and paste it to the target application. Finally, type the column headings for both the table information and the timephased data in the target application.

If you want to keep your project's column headers when copying entire columns, see "Making Column Headers Appear When Pasting" in the "Troubleshooting" section at the end of this chapter.

LINKING SELECTED DATA BETWEEN APPLICATIONS

The copy operations described in the preceding section produce static copies in the destination document; the pasted copy of the data does not change if the source data changes. However, you can also paste a value from another application that is a *linked reference* to the data location in the source document. The linked reference can be updated to reflect changes in the value that is stored in the source document.

→ For information about using external dependency links, **see** "Creating Links Between Tasks in Separate Projects," **p. 618**.

LINKING MICROSOFT PROJECT DATA FIELDS TO EXTERNAL SOURCES

You can paste a link to an external data source into a Microsoft Project table. The external source can be another application (such as an Excel or Word file) or another Project document. For example, an Excel workbook could serve as the source for resource names and cost rates in a Project document. You could also link the constraint date for a task to a date in another file if you wanted the task to start or finish on that date.

To link Microsoft Project field values to values stored in other sources, follow these steps:

1. Select the source data (for example, a cell or range of cells in an Excel worksheet). You can select a single value or several values. If you select several values, be sure that the order of the values matches the order of the values in the table that you view when you paste the values into Microsoft Project.
2. Copy the data to the Clipboard.
3. Activate Microsoft Project and select a view that has a table with the columns arranged to match the order of the data you are copying.
4. Select the row in the table that is to receive the data.
5. Choose Edit, Paste Special. The Paste Special dialog box appears (see Figure 18.5).

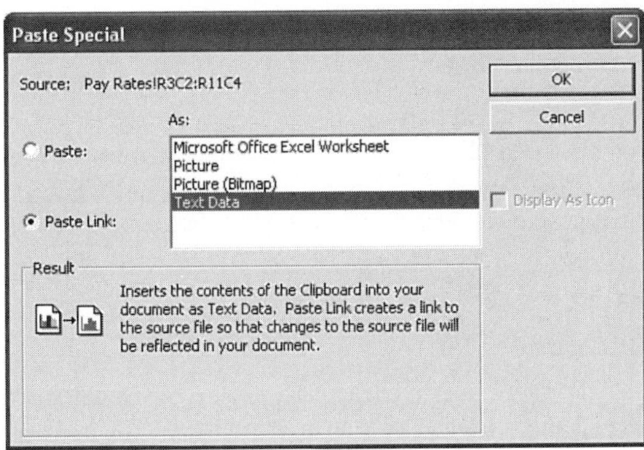

Figure 18.5
The Paste Special dialog box lets you specify the format for the data that will be pasted into the receiving file.

6. Select the Paste Link option.

18

TIP

> Choose the Paste Link option button before you select the format of the pasted data in the As box. Changing the link option can change the options in the As box.

7. In the As box, choose Text Data as the type of link if you want the data to become text in a table. Project attempts to convert text data into numeric data in a number field or into a date in a date field.

NOTE

> If you are in a Gantt Chart view, the Paste Special dialog box contains more options in the As box than if you are in the Resource Sheet view (as shown by the graphics options in Figure 18.5). You can choose the Worksheet or Picture options if you want to paste the data as a picture object in a graphic area. (See "Placing Objects into Microsoft Project," later in this chapter.) In the Gantt Chart view, for example, both those options would create a graphic object in the bar chart area of the view.

18

8. Click OK to establish the link. By default Project displays a small triangle in the lower-right corner of each cell that is linked to a source for its data. You can see the link indicators for the Name, the Standard Rate, and the Overtime Rate values in Figure 18.6. The resource names and their accompanying cost rate information are dynamically linked to the Excel worksheet in which the resource information is maintained.

Figure 18.6
Linked cells in a table view display a link indicator, a small triangle in the lower-right corner of the cell.

	Resource Name	Type	Material Label	Initials	Group	Max. Units	Std. Rate	Ovt. Rate	Cost/Use	Ac
1	Terry Uland	Work		T		100%	$15.00/hr	$22.50/hr	$0.00	Pr
2	Myrta Hansen	Work		M		100%	$45.00/hr	$67.50/hr	$0.00	Pr
3	Dave Erickson	Work		D		100%	$35.00/hr	$50.00/hr	$0.00	Pr
4	Roger Burnett	Work		R		100%	$25.00/hr	$37.50/hr	$0.00	Pr
5	Benjamin Montanez	Work		B		100%	$200.00/day	$300.00/day	$0.00	Pr
6	Charles Kirkpatrick	Work		C		100%	$30.00/hr	$45.00/hr	$0.00	Pr
7	Renee Hensley	Work		R		100%	$20.00/hr	$30.00/hr	$0.00	Pr
8	Marilyn Ray	Work		M		100%	##########	$0.00/hr	$0.00	Pr
9	Ray Cobb	Work		R		100%	$20.00/hr	$30.00/hr	$0.00	Pr
10	Gary Howard	Work		G		100%	$50.00/hr	$75.00/hr	$0.00	Pr

TIP

> Double-clicking a resource cell normally displays the Resource Information dialog box. Double-clicking a cell that is linked to an external source, however, opens the external source so that you can view or edit the source data. If you want to see the Information dialog box for the task, resource, or assignment that contains the linked cell, click the Information button in the Standard toolbar.

TIP

If you don't see the link indicator where it should be displayed, choose Tools, Options and select the View tab in the Options dialog box. Make sure that the OLE Links Indicators check box is selected.

If you attempt to paste a link with mismatched data, you receive an object linking and embedding (OLE) error message which states that the operation cannot be completed. Unlike with the regular Paste command, if there is a data mismatch while pasting a block of values, Project halts the operation and removes all values that were pasted in during that operation. These values are removed because a block of cells is considered one link. If one cell contains a mismatch, the entire paste link is ignored.

REFRESHING LINKED DATA IN MICROSOFT PROJECT

If you save a project file that contains linked values, Project saves the current values of the linked fields, along with the reference to the source for the value. That way, when you open a file with linked values, Project can display the most recent values.

When you open a Project file that contains links to other files, Project asks if you want to reestablish the links. If you do, Project can refresh the values in the linked cells with the current values in the source files (see Figure 18.7). If you select Yes, Project retrieves the current or saved values of each link's source. If you select No, Project opens the Project document and displays the last saved values for the linked cells. You can update the links later.

18

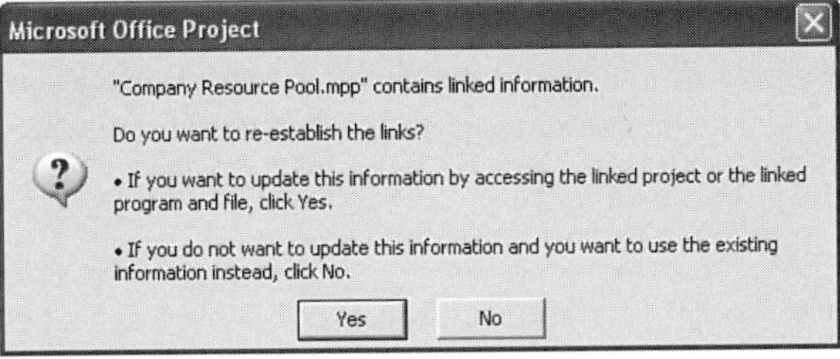

Figure 18.7 When opening a Project file with links to other files, you can have Project refresh the links or use the last values that were saved in the Project file.

You can update the linked values in a Project document at any time by using the Edit, Links command. The source application does not need to be open in order for the linked values to be refreshed. The Links dialog box lists all the external links in the current document (see Figure 18.8).

The Links list usually displays the path to the source, the document type of the source file, and the update status of each link. These three items are displayed in greater detail at the bottom of the dialog box for the selected link. If the filename and link reference are too long, the path to the source is truncated.

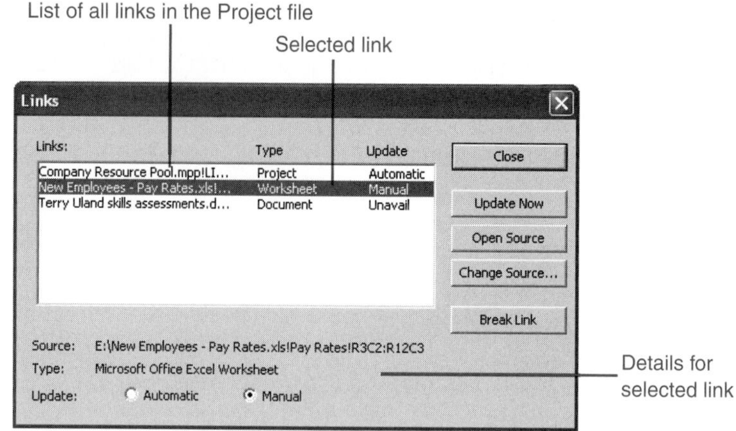

Figure 18.8
All external sources of linked data are identified in the Links dialog box.

In Figure 18.8, the selected item in the Links list shows the path to the file truncated (because it's too long for the display), but the details below show the filename (`New Employees - Pay Rates.xls`) and the location of the linked data within the file to be in the sheet named `Sheet1`, the cell range `R3C2:R12C3` (or `B3:C12`, in standard Excel range notation). The type is identified as Microsoft Excel Worksheet. The update status is Manual, which means that you must click the Update Now button to refresh the values in Microsoft Project.

If the update status is Automatic, and if the file is open in memory and supports automatic updating, changes in the source appear immediately in the Project document while it is also open in memory. Even if you select the Automatic update choice, some source applications don't support automatic updates, and the Update column at the top of the dialog box displays Unavail, as shown with the link to the `Terry Uland skills assessment.doc` source file shown in Figure 18.8. The update status is also shown as Unavail when the Project document has not been updated during the current editing session.

TIP

> If an object's Update field at the bottom of the dialog box has the Automatic button selected and you want to select the Manual button, do not make the change if the update status for the link in the list of links is unavailable. You should update the link with the Update Now button before you change the update method.

NOTE

> Notice in Figure 18.8 that there is just one link reference in the Links dialog box for the whole range of Excel cells that was pasted in the link operation. If you need to maintain each of the cells as separate links, you should copy and paste each of the cells individually.

To work with the links to external sources, follow these steps:

1. Choose Edit, Links from the menu to display the Links dialog box (refer to Figure 18.8).

TIP

If the Links command is dimmed, then the document has no linked values.

2. Select all the links that you want to refresh.
3. Click the Update Now button to refresh all the data links you have selected. The source for each link that you select is searched for the current values.
4. If you want to open the application document named in the selected link reference, click the Open Source button. You cannot select multiple links and click the Open Source button. You can have multiple linked source documents open simultaneously; however, you must open each of them individually. Other options in the Links dialog box include the following:
   - If you want to remove the selected link, click the Break Link button. The current value remains in the link location, but the reference to an external source disappears.
   - If you want to change the source of a selected link, click the Change Source button, and the Change Source dialog box appears (see Figure 18.9). Click the Browse button and choose another file to link to.

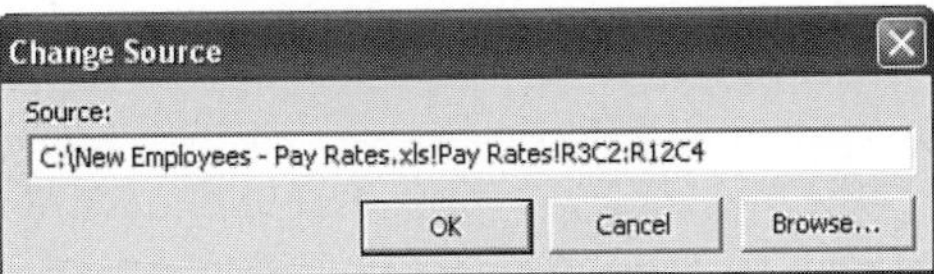

Figure 18.9
You can use the Change Source dialog box to redefine the link source.

TIP

Although you can browse through the directory of files to find the filename of a new source to link to, you might also need to indicate the location within the new source file to complete the change. For that reason, it is usually best to paste new links over the old ones instead of using this dialog box.

DELETING LINKS TO EXTERNAL SOURCES

As pointed out in step 4 in the preceding section, if you break the link to an external source, Project retains the current value that was linked but disassociates the value with the external source. Similarly, if you attempt to type over a field value that is linked to an external source, you are warned that the link will be lost, and you are offered the opportunity to proceed or to cancel the data entry. Choose No to abandon the editing change and preserve the link. If you choose Yes (to proceed with the change), the dynamic data exchange (DDE) link reference is lost. Fortunately, you can undo the change by using the Edit, Undo command.

To delete the data and its link to an external source, you can select the field whose link you want to remove and choose Edit, Clear, Contents (or press Ctrl+Delete). You are then asked to confirm the deletion.

CAUTION

> If you delete the link in a cell that is part of a block of linked values, the link for all cells in the block is removed—not just the link for the one cell. You can use the Edit, Undo command to restore the links.

IDENTIFYING TASKS OR RESOURCES WITH LINKS ATTACHED

You can filter task or resource tables to determine which tasks or resources use linked data from other sources. For either a task view or a resource view, you can choose the Linked Fields filter from the Filters drop-down list. To find the linked values, search for the links indicator in the lower-right corner of the cells.

PASTING LINKS TO MICROSOFT PROJECT DATA INTO OTHER APPLICATIONS

Both Microsoft Excel and Microsoft Word accept pasted links to individual data cells in Microsoft Project tables. If you want to copy a single linked value to one of these applications, you only have to display a table that has a cell for the value you want to use, select the cell, and use the Copy command. Then, in Word or Excel, you use the Edit, Paste Special command and use the Paste Link option to paste the data as text. If you want to copy a block of values, you should modify a table in Project so that the values you want to copy are adjacent to each other. Select the block and, as with a single value, use the Edit, Paste Special and Paste Link commands to paste the block of values in Word or Excel. The pasted block of data is a single entity in both applications, and when you update the links in the other application, all the values in the block are updated.

NOTE

> There are significant formatting issues related to displaying the Project data in other applications. For example, duration fields may display the duration in minutes, multiplied by 10 (an hour appears as 600), and work fields display the work as minutes, multiplied by 1,000 (an hour appears as 60,000). The durations may also be considered as text by the application as the unit can be copied with the value. The data has to be processed in order to provide a meaningful display for users.

Working with Objects

An *object* is a representation of data (usually a group of data or a special format for data) that is formatted by another application. The most frequent use of objects is to show graphic data (for example, Excel charts, artwork, PowerPoint slides, special displays such as the Network Diagram view or the Gantt Chart view from Microsoft Project) in an application that doesn't normally generate similar formats. You can also paste media formats such as sound files or video clips.

It is common to refer to the application that generates an object as the *server* application and the application that has the object pasted in it as the *client* application. The client document is also sometimes called the *container* document. These terms are used in the following discussion where they help clarify.

Pasting Objects

As with text data, you can copy data from an external application and paste it as an object in Project by using the Edit, Paste or Edit, Paste Special commands. For example, an Excel chart can be pasted into the Gantt Chart view. If you use the Paste Special command, the chart can be linked to the Excel document in which it was created. Like linked text data, a linked object can be updated automatically or manually, depending on the settings in the Links dialog box.

If the object is not linked, it is said to be *embedded* in the client document. An embedded object is stored entirely in the client document, and it cannot be automatically updated to show changes made in the original source document. Because the format is foreign to the client application, editing the object necessitates activating the application that created the object (the server application). After editing is finished and the server application is closed, the revised object still resides in the client application.

For example, if you paste an Excel chart into the Gantt Chart view as an object, either linked or embedded, the chart appears in the timescale area of the Gantt Chart view, along with the taskbars (see Figure 18.10). The Excel document in this instance would be the server, and the Project document would be the client or container.

After an object has been pasted, you can usually position and resize it within Project as if it were a piece of clip art. You can also edit many object formats directly from within Project, by double-clicking the object. If an Excel chart were pasted as a linked object, as in Figure 18.10, double-clicking the object would open Excel, with the chart open for editing. On closing Excel and saving any changes, the revised object would be visible in Project. If the chart in Figure 18.10 were embedded rather than linked, double-clicking would open the object for editing, and you would see Excel's menu bar and toolbars instead of Project's menu bar and toolbars (see Figure 18.11). However, you would still be working within Project. After making changes, click outside the object on the Project workspace to exit from editing mode and return to Project's menu bar and toolbars.

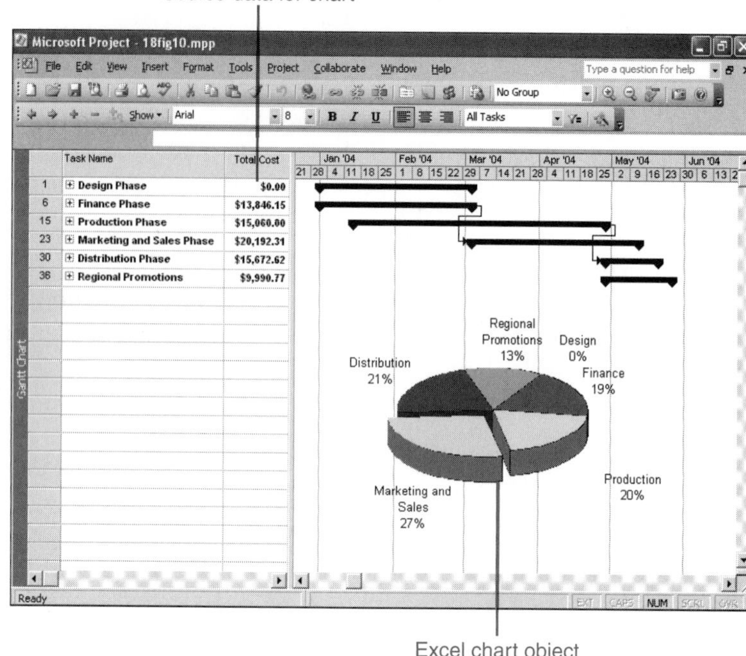

Figure 18.10
The Project data for each phase can be paste-linked into an Excel worksheet, and the data can be used to generate an Excel chart. The chart can then be paste-linked back to Project as an object in the Gantt Chart view.

18

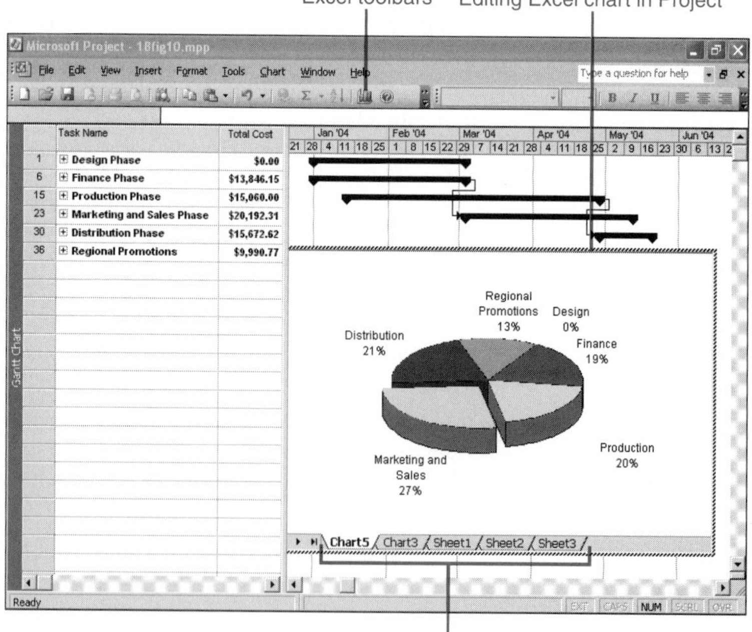

Figure 18.11
Double-clicking on an embedded chart object opens it for editing within Project, but with Excel's menus and toolbars.

NOTE

> If you are in editing mode, and you switch away from Project to another application, when you return to Project, Editing mode is maintained, and you can continue to edit the project.

If you paste a media object such as a video clip or sound file into the Gantt Chart view, it appears as an icon. Double-clicking the icon is typically how you run the video clip or sound file.

If Project is the source or server, and you paste copies of selected cells from the Gantt Chart view table into another application document as text, each row of task information becomes a row of ordinary text in the document. But if you copy the selection as an object, it is displayed as a graphic figure in the client document.

In Figure 18.12, the same Project task rows were pasted both as text and as a picture object into a Microsoft Word document. The task field text appears as an ordinary tab-separated list in Word. The picture of the tasks includes the Gantt Chart view table cells along with the taskbars and the timescale above the taskbars. See the section "Placing Project Objects into Other Applications," later in this chapter, for more options when placing Project objects in other application documents.

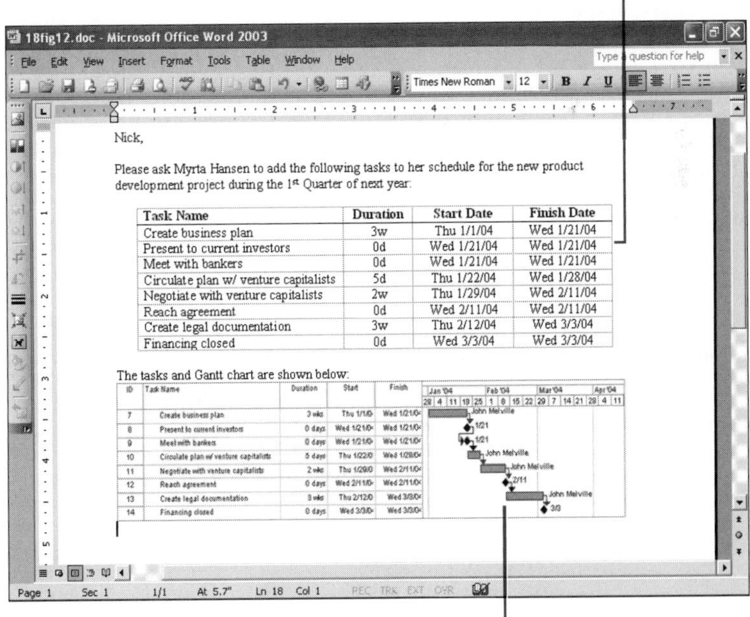

Nick,

Please ask Myrta Hansen to add the following tasks to her schedule for the new product development project during the 1st Quarter of next year:

Task Name	Duration	Start Date	Finish Date
Create business plan	3w	Thu 1/1/04	Wed 1/21/04
Present to current investors	0d	Wed 1/21/04	Wed 1/21/04
Meet with bankers	0d	Wed 1/21/04	Wed 1/21/04
Circulate plan w/ venture capitalists	5d	Thu 1/22/04	Wed 1/28/04
Negotiate with venture capitalists	2w	Thu 1/29/04	Wed 2/11/04
Reach agreement	0d	Wed 2/11/04	Wed 2/11/04
Create legal documentation	3w	Thu 2/12/04	Wed 3/3/04
Financing closed	0d	Wed 3/3/04	Wed 3/3/04

The tasks and Gantt chart are shown below:

Figure 18.12
A Microsoft Word document can show both pasted text and a Microsoft Project image in the same page.

INSERTING OBJECTS

You can place objects in a client document by using the Insert, Objects command. This command can insert an existing file that was created by another (server) application into the client document. The inserted object might be linked or it might be embedded.

The Insert, Objects command can also open a server application from within the client document, to let you create a new embedded object that exists only within the client document. For example, you can insert a new, blank Excel spreadsheet into a Project document and then enter whatever data you would like into the spreadsheet, using the Excel application's menu and toolbars. When you click on the Project workspace in the background, the object remains embedded in Project, and its data exists only in the Project document. Likewise, from within Word or Excel you could insert a Project object, such as a Gantt chart that you create on-the-fly. When you click outside the object, it remains embedded in the Word or Excel document.

PLACING OBJECTS INTO MICROSOFT PROJECT

You can paste or insert objects into Microsoft Project in four locations:

- In the graphics area of the Gantt Chart view
- In the Notes box of the Task, Resource, or Assignment Information Form views
- In the special task Objects box of the Task Form view or in the resource Objects box of the Resource Form view
- In the Header, Footer, or Legend of a view's Page Format dialog box

The following sections show how to use objects in each of these locations. The following sections go into detail about pasting, inserting, and working with objects in the Gantt Chart view. The remaining sections focus on the differences compared to placing objects in the Gantt Chart view.

PASTING OBJECTS IN THE GANTT CHART VIEW

The Gantt Chart view is the primary view for seeing a Microsoft Project file depicted graphically. You can enhance this view by pasting Project drawings (see Chapter 7, "Viewing Your Schedule") or objects from other applications into the timescale area. To paste an object into the Gantt Chart view, follow these steps:

1. Activate the source (server) application, and then select the source data and copy it to the Clipboard by using the Edit, Copy command.
2. Activate Microsoft Project (the client application) and display the Gantt Chart view.
3. Choose Edit, Paste Special to display the Paste Special dialog box (see Figure 18.13).
4. Choose Paste to embed the object or Paste Link to link it.

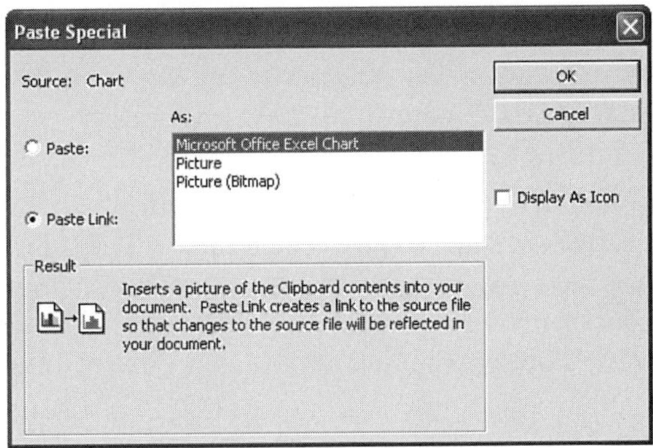

Figure 18.13 You can embed or link objects via the Paste Special dialog box.

5. In the As list, you might have an option that includes the server application's name. You might also have an option named Picture. These choices produce picture images that look similar. The option with the server application's name allows you to open the object in the server application—for instance, to edit or modify the object. The Picture option places in the Project document a picture of the object that cannot be edited in the client application.
6. Click OK to paste the image.

When the object appears in the Gantt Chart view, you can move and resize it. To move the object, click the object to select it, and then drag it to a new position. To resize the object, select it and then resize it by dragging its resizing handles to change its size. To remove the object, select it and press the Delete key.

TIP

> Resizing a picture object (whether it is linked or not) might cause the data in the object to appear distorted. This is because the resizing action can cause the horizontal and vertical dimensions to go out of proportion relative to one another. To resize a picture object so that the horizontal and vertical dimensions are in proportion, hold down the Shift key as you drag one of the object's corner handles.

CAUTION

> You can't undo resizing or deleting of an object. Be sure to save the Project document before experimenting with either of these actions.

TIP

> If you have more than one object placed in the Gantt Chart view, you can scroll through your objects by pressing the F6 key repeatedly until the first object is selected. Then press the Tab key to select other objects in that pane, one at a time.

→ For more information on working with objects in the Gantt Chart view, **see** "Adding Graphics and Text to Gantt Charts," **p. 247**.

INSERTING OBJECTS IN THE GANTT CHART VIEW

In the examples in the preceding section, the data in an object was created as part of a source (server) application document and was then copied and pasted into the target (client) application. You can also use the Insert Object command to place a linked or embedded copy of the entire source document into the client document as an object. Of course, embedding a source document in Project increases the Project document's file size, and the embedded document is cut off from updates to the original source document.

The Insert, Object command also gives you the option of creating an object without using an existing file. You can create a new object by using the formatting capabilities of server applications that support Microsoft OLE 2.0 or higher. The server application's interface opens from within Project, to allow you to create the new data. When you close the server, the object remains embedded in Project.

To insert an object, choose the Insert, Object command. Project displays the Insert Object dialog box (see Figure 18.14). The default option button is Create New, which allows you to create a new, embedded object, using one of the applications listed in the Object Type box. Choose Create from File if the data has already been created and saved to disk and you want to insert a linked or embedded copy of the source data.

18

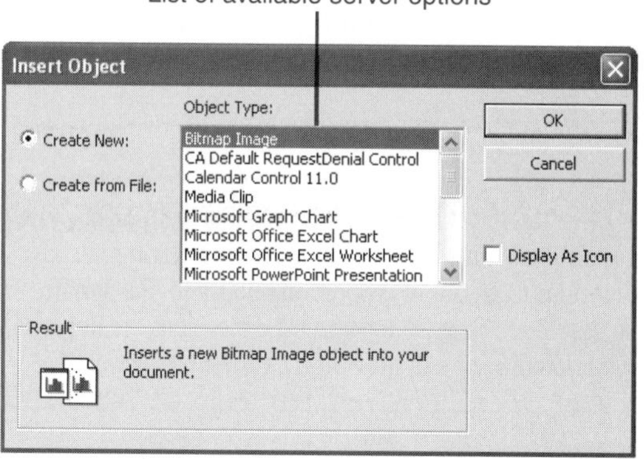

Figure 18.14
The Insert Object dialog box gives you the option of creating an object from scratch within a Microsoft Project file.

For example, suppose that you want to embed in the Gantt Chart view a new Excel worksheet object that shows budgeted (baseline) and current gross margin data for a project. To create this new worksheet object, you would follow these steps:

1. Display the Gantt Chart view in the top pane of the combination view.
2. Choose the Insert, Object command to display the Insert Object dialog box. It might take a little time for this dialog box to appear because Project must prepare a list of all the server applications on your system that support OLE 2.0 or higher.
3. Choose Create New (it is selected by default).

4. Choose the server application you want to use from the list that appears in the Object Type list. For this example, choose Microsoft Excel Worksheet.
5. Fill the Display as Icon check box if you want to see just an icon instead of the worksheet object in the Gantt Chart view. After the object is inserted, you can double-click the icon to display the object's contents. This is the best choice if there is little room for the object in the graphics area of the Gantt Chart view. For this example, fill the check box.

TIP

Even if you want the object to appear as a mini-worksheet in the Gantt Chart view, it is generally best to choose Display as Icon when you are initially inserting the object. If you choose Display as Icon, Project opens Excel in its own full-sized window, in which you can enter and format your Excel data. You then also have full access to all of Excel's features and toolbars. After the data has been entered and formatted, you can convert the object to display as a mini-worksheet. If Display as Icon is not selected, you have to create the object in a small window within the graphics area of the Gantt Chart view, and not all Excel menu commands are available there.

6. Click OK to insert the object. If you had selected the Display as Icon check box, Project opens Excel in a new window for you to create the worksheet.
7. Edit the spreadsheet to include the data and formatting that you want to appear in the Gantt Chart view.
8. When the worksheet is completed, choose File, Close and Return to *Filename* (where *Filename* is the name of the Project document in which you inserted the object). The icon for the object is then displayed in the Gantt Chart view (see Figure 18.15).

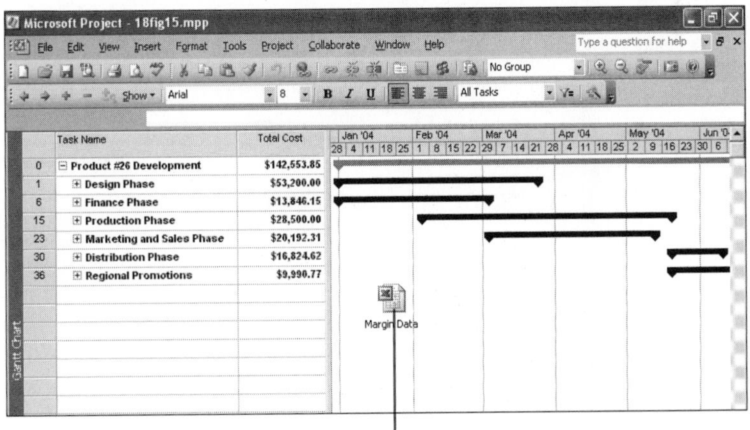

Figure 18.15
Relevant cost and gross margin data are shown in the Gantt Chart view as a worksheet object that is displayed as an icon.

After the object is embedded, you can double-click the icon to open or edit the data. You can also convert the object to display itself as a worksheet instead of an icon.

To convert the object by changing its display, follow these steps:

1. Click on the object icon to select it.
2. Choose Edit, Worksheet Object, Convert to display the Convert dialog box (see Figure 18.16).

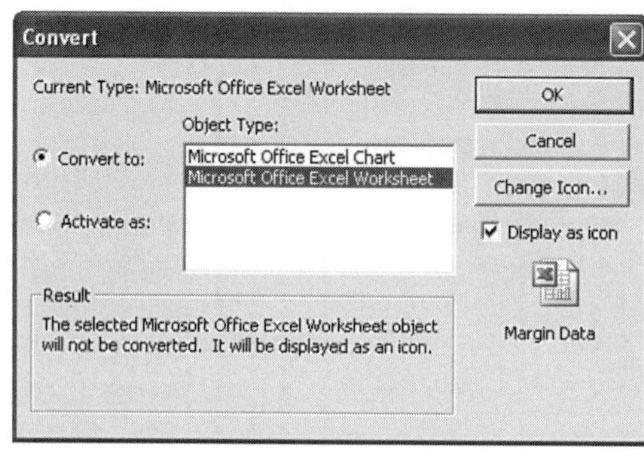

Figure 18.16
You can use the Convert command to change the display of an object from an icon to formatted data.

3. Clear the Display as Icon check box and click OK. The object appears as a small worksheet, as shown in Figure 18.17.

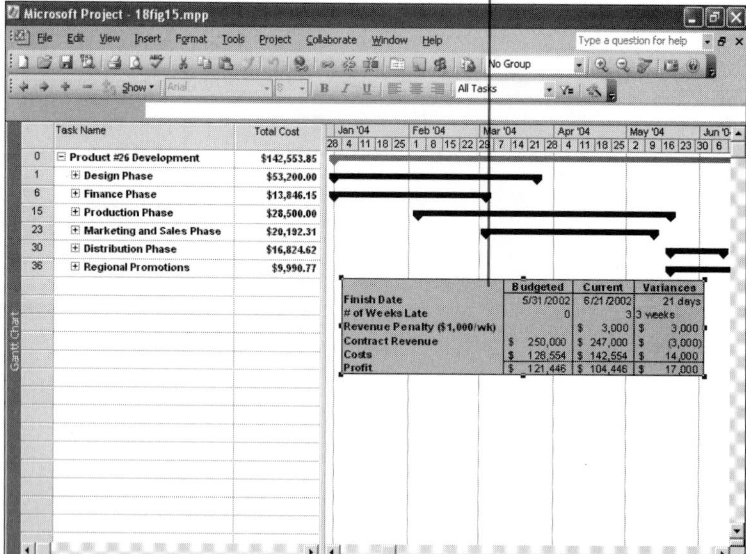

Figure 18.17
Relevant cost and gross margin data are shown in the Gantt Chart view as a worksheet object that is displayed as an icon.

The previous example shows how to create a new object by using the Insert, Object command. You can also insert an object into the Gantt Chart, using a file that already exists, by following these steps:

1. Display the Gantt Chart view in the top pane of a combination view.
2. Choose Insert, Object to display the Insert Object dialog box.
3. Choose the Create from File option. The File text box appears, with a Browse button beneath it, to help you select the filename (see Figure 18.18).

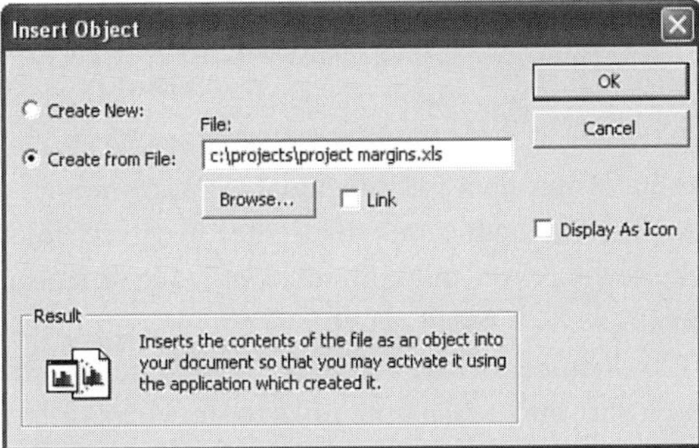

Figure 18.18
You can use the Insert Object dialog box to insert external document files as objects.

4. Either type the file's path and filename into the File box or use the Browse button to locate the file.
5. Select the Link check box if you want to insert a linked copy of the file's data. Leave the check box clear if you want to embed a copy of the file.
6. Select the Display as Icon check box if you want only an icon to appear in the Gantt Chart view.
7. Click OK to create the object.

18

To open or edit an object, you click the object to select it. At the bottom of the Edit menu, you see a submenu that is named for the object type. For example, the submenu for an object that originated as a worksheet might be titled Worksheet Object, and the submenu for a sound file might be titled Wave Sound Object. Depending on the format of the object, the submenu should contain one or more of these commands:

- **Edit**—This command opens the server application to allow you to edit the object. After editing, close the server application, and you are returned to Project.
- **Open**—This command is equivalent to the Edit command for text-based formats such as worksheets and documents. For media objects, this command displays a picture in the server application, plays the sound file, runs the video, and so on. Typically, the media object is not open for editing.

- **Play**—This command appears for some media objects, such as sound files and video. It plays the media data and then closes. For media objects, this is the default action when you double-click the object icon.
- **Convert**—This command appears only for some objects and can be used to change the Display as Icon choice for the object or to change the format of the object itself.

NOTE

> You can use the Edit, Links command to manage linked objects just as described in the section, "Refreshing Linked Data in Microsoft Project," earlier in this chapter.

PLACING OBJECTS IN THE NOTES FIELD

18

You can place objects in the Notes field for individual tasks, resources, or assignments (see Figure 18.19). The Notes field is the most obvious place to attach links to supporting documentation that is stored elsewhere on your computer, on your organization's network, or in an intranet folder. For example, you could insert into a note a group of objects, displayed as icons, that provide links to documents that define the scope, authorization, and budget for the project; or you could insert into a task note links to drawings or specifications for completing the task. By using links to external documents, you can provide reliable access to relevant documentation.

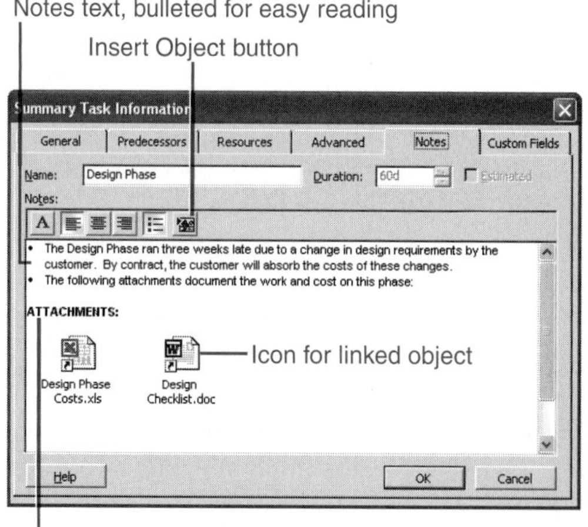

Figure 18.19
The Notes field can display embedded and linked objects as formatted data or as icons.

CAUTION

> If you insert objects in the Project Summary Task note, they will be lost if you later edit the note in the Comments text box on the File, Properties dialog box. When you click OK after editing the Comments box, you will receive a warning that objects will be lost if you change the note. You can then choose No to cancel the changes.

If you display links as icons, you do not increase the project file size by any substantial amount. If you display the linked object as formatted data, and especially if you embed the object, you may substantially increase the file size of the project document and thereby reduce the speed with which Project can open the file and process it. Furthermore, as the following Caution points out, a linked object in a note is not updated until you double-click the object to open the source document.

CAUTION

You will not find the linked objects you place in notes in the Links dialog box when you choose Edit, Links. The only way to update a linked object in a note is to double-click the object to open the source document.

Because linked objects in a note are not listed in the Links dialog box, if you change the filename or path to a linked object, you must delete the original link and place the object in the note again.

The only drawback to using the Notes field as a repository for links to supporting documentation is that there is no automatic way in Project to identify the notes that contain links to external documents. Although there is a filter called Tasks with Attachments, this filter displays all tasks with any type of text in the Notes field, whether those Notes contain any attachments or not. Thus, you have to find the links on your own.

TIP

Because there is no filter or indicator to tell you if a note contains an object, you should adopt the habit of placing a keyword such as `Attachments` just before the inserted or pasted objects in a note. Then you can create a custom filter to search the Notes field for notes that contain the text `Attachments`. You must place this keyword before any objects because the Find command stops searching a note when it encounters an object.

You can paste objects into a note by using the Paste or Paste Special commands on the shortcut menu for the Notes box. You can also insert objects in notes by using the Insert Object tool that is displayed above the Notes box (refer to Figure 18.19). If you paste objects, you can only embed them—there is no paste-link option within notes. If you insert them, however, you have the choice of embedding or linking most objects.

To paste an object into the Notes box, follow these steps:

1. Copy the object to the Windows Clipboard from within the server application.
2. Activate Microsoft Project, display an appropriate view, and select the task, resource, or assignment record whose note you want to paste into.
3. Click the Notes button on the Standard toolbar. The Notes tab of the Information dialog box is displayed, as shown in Figure 18.19.
4. Click in the Notes box at the location where you want to insert the object.

5. Right-click to display the shortcut menu and choose the Paste command, or choose the Paste Special command if it is available. Using the Paste command immediately pastes the object as a picture that cannot be opened by the server application after it has been pasted. If you are pasting a media object, such as a sound wave file, the Paste command pastes an icon, but the icon does not play the sound file. You need to use the Paste Special command for media objects.

   If you select the Paste Special command, the Paste Special dialog box (see Figure 18.20), which usually provides multiple formatting options in the As List box, appears:

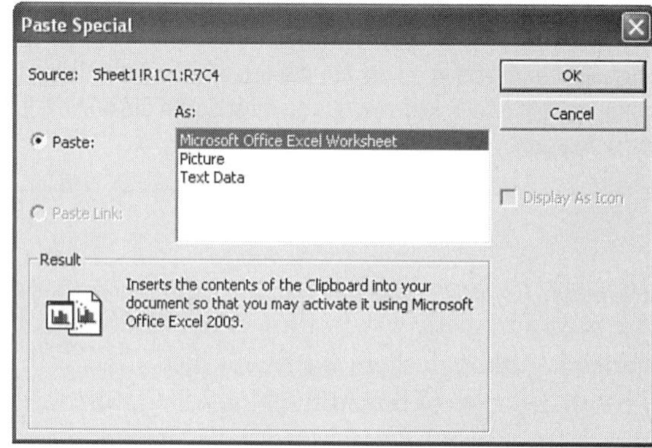

Figure 18.20
You can use the Paste Special dialog box to embed an object in different ways.

   - The Picture option is usually the equivalent of the Paste command's action—a picture of the data in its original format. For media objects, this is simply an icon that doesn't do anything.
   - If there is an option that contains the name of the object's format, such as Microsoft Excel Worksheet or Wave Sound, you can open the object by using the server application to view and edit (in the case of a worksheet) or to play (in the case of a media object).
   - If there is a Text option, the text that was copied to the Clipboard is pasted into the note as regular text.

6. If you chose the Paste Special command, select the format for the object in the As List box.
7. Click the OK button to paste the object.
8. If you want to resize the object, click the object to display the object's sizing handles, and then use the mouse to drag the sizing handles.
9. Click OK to save the note.

TIP

The Notes box in the Information dialog box cannot be enlarged, and you might find it too small for your tastes. You can increase the display size of task and resource notes (but not assignment notes) by viewing them in the Task Name Form view or the Resource Name Form view. These views can be displayed as full-screen views or in the bottom pane of a split window, under a task or resource view.

PLACING OBJECTS IN THE TASK OR RESOURCE OBJECTS BOX

Project has three standard task form views (the Task Form, the Task Details Form, and the Task Name Form views) that can display an Objects box, in which you can place objects that you want to associate with a task. Similarly, there are two standard resource form views (the Resource Form and the Resource Name Form views) that can display an Objects box for displaying objects that you associate with a resource. These forms are the only places you can view an Objects box onscreen. However, you can include the contents of the Objects boxes in custom reports (see Chapter 22, "Using and Customizing the Standard Reports").

You can paste objects in the Objects box by using either the Paste or Paste Special commands, and unlike with pasting notes, you can paste links to objects by using the Paste Special command. You can also use the Insert Object command to place embedded or linked objects in an Objects box.

Project also has a task Objects field and a resource Objects field. If you display the Objects field in a table, it shows the number of objects that are stored in the Objects box for that task or resource. The main usage of the Objects field is in filters, to identify tasks or resources that have objects in their Objects boxes. The standard filters Tasks with Attachments and Resources with Attachments select those tasks or resources whose Objects field have values greater than zero or whose Notes fields contain some text. You could make a custom filter to focus on just records that have objects stored in their Objects boxes.

In Figure 18.21, the Task Form view is displayed beneath the Gantt Chart view, with the Objects box displayed in the details area. The gross margin worksheet that was used in previous examples is displayed in the Objects box.

The table in the Gantt Chart has been modified to display the Objects field. It shows that there are two objects attached to this resource. You would use the scrollbar next to the Objects box to see the next object.

To paste an object into an Objects field, follow these steps:

1. In the source (server) application, select the object and copy it to the Clipboard.
2. Activate Project, and then display one of the task or resource form views, depending on the type of record into which you want to paste the object.
3. Choose Format, Details, Objects (or right-click anywhere outside a field box on the form and choose Objects from the shortcut menu).
4. Click in the Objects field at the bottom of the form to select it. A thick black border appears around the field, to indicate that it has been selected (see Figure 18.22).

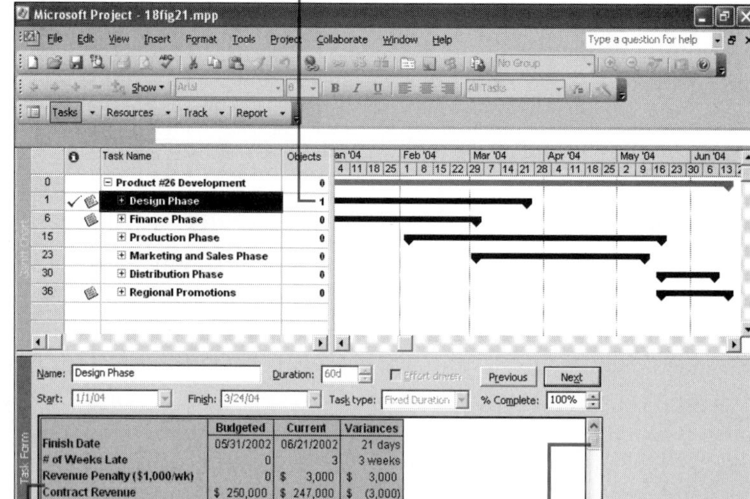

Figure 18.21
The Objects field displays objects that are attached to an individual task or resource.

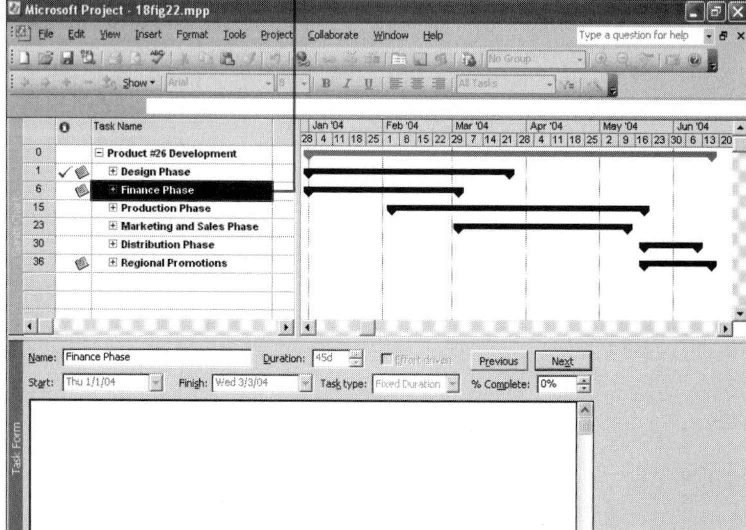

Figure 18.22
Remember to select the Objects field of the Task Form view before pasting or inserting objects into it.

5. Choose Edit, Paste Special from the menu, to display the Paste Special dialog box.
6. Choose Paste or Paste Link.
7. Choose the format option in the As list box.
8. Click OK to finish pasting the object.

To insert an object in the Objects box, select the Objects box and choose Insert, Object to display the Insert Object dialog box, and use the dialog box options as described previously for inserting objects in notes and in the Gantt Chart view.

You can place multiple objects in the Objects box. The first object you paste or insert appears immediately and is selected. When you place additional objects, they are inserted below the one that is currently selected and displayed. However, the selection does not change and the new object is not displayed. You can use the scrollbar or the down arrow to select and display the newly placed object.

TIP

> If you have multiple objects placed in an Objects box and would like to change the order in which they appear, you can use the Cut and Paste tools to move objects in the stack. Display the object to be moved and choose the Edit, Cut command. Then select the object after which you want to place the cut object and choose the Edit, Paste or Paste Special command. If the object being moved is not formatted as a simple picture object, you must use the Paste Special command to retain its format.

TIP

> The Objects box scrollbar does not scroll through a single object, even if it is too large for the area it is displayed in. If you can't see the entire object, increase the size of the form. If you still can't see the entire object, open it in the server application. You cannot resize the objects that are pasted in the Objects box. If the object is pasted as a picture and you can't see all of it, you are out of luck.

If you want to delete an object in the Objects box, scroll to display that object and press the Delete key. The object is then deleted from the document.

PLACING OBJECTS IN HEADERS, FOOTERS, AND LEGENDS

You can customize printed views and reports by placing graphics such as an organization's logo or a symbol for the project in the print header, footer, or legend area. In Figure 18.23, the running dog graphic has been inserted into the left header in the Gantt Chart Page Setup dialog box. This graphic represents the logo for this project. You can either paste a picture or insert a graphic file to create the object in this context, but you can only embed objects—you can't link them.

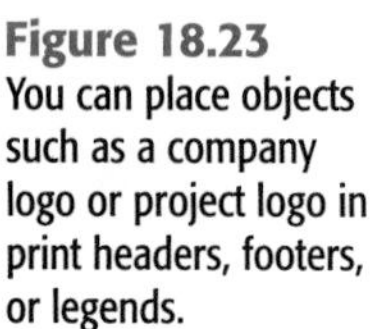

Figure 18.23
You can place objects such as a company logo or project logo in print headers, footers, or legends.

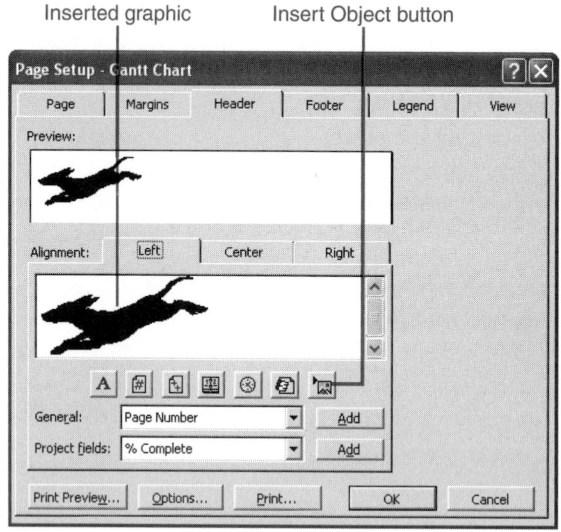

To place a graphic object in a view or report's header, footer, or legend, you must first display the Page Setup dialog box for the view or report. For views, you simply display the view and then use the View, Header and Footer command. You can also use the File, Page Setup command and then click the Header or Footer tab. To place a graphic object in a report, follow these steps:

1. Choose View, Reports to display the Reports dialog box.
2. Select the Custom box and click Select to display the Custom Reports dialog box (in which all reports are listed).
3. Select the report in the Reports list and click Setup.

NOTE

> **You cannot define a legend for any of the reports, and the Project Summary report doesn't even allow you to create a header or footer.**

When the Page Setup dialog box is active, follow these steps to embed a picture:

1. If you are copying a picture, select the picture in its source application and use the Copy command to place it on the Clipboard.

   If you are inserting a graphic file, you should create a copy of the graphic that is sized appropriately for the report. It can be awkward trying to resize pictures in the Page Setup dialog box.
2. Select the Header, Footer, or Legend tab, as appropriate.
3. Select the Left, Center, or Right tab to position the picture on the page.

   The customized area of a legend occupies only the left portion of the legend. The position tabs place the picture within that area of the legend.

4. If you are pasting a picture, right-click in the text box below the alignment tab and select the Paste command from the shortcut menu (or press Ctrl+V).

TIP

Although the Paste Special command might be available on the shortcut menu and it might offer to paste an object in the server application's format (which should let you edit the object from within the header, footer, or legend), you should be very wary of using this option. Server-formatted objects tend to be very unstable and can actually make the project file unstable as well. It is recommended that you use the Paste command and place only simple pictures in headers, footers, and legends.

If you are inserting a picture file, click the Insert Picture tool and browse to find the file. When the file is selected, click the Insert button to place the image in the tab.

5. If you want to resize the object, click it to display sizing handles and use them to change the size.
6. When the picture is embedded, click the OK button; or proceed to print by clicking the Print Preview or Print buttons.

PLACING PROJECT OBJECTS INTO OTHER APPLICATIONS

Microsoft Project has a number of distinctive graphical views that can be very effective when copied to the Clipboard and pasted into other applications. The views that can be copied include the following:

- All the Gantt Chart views
- The Network Diagram and Detailed Network Diagram views
- The Calendar view
- The Task Usage and Resource Usage views
- The Resource Graph view
- Any of the sheet views (such as the Task Sheet and Resource Sheet views)

NOTE

Project provides no facility for copying the Relationship Diagram view or any of the form views. To copy these views, you must use the Windows Print Screen command or a third-party screen capture program.

You can copy these views by using Project's Edit, Copy command or Edit, Copy Picture command. If you want to paste a linked object in the other application, or if you want to embed a Project object that can be edited, you must use the Copy command. If you want to paste an unlinked picture of a Project view, you use the Copy Picture command. The following descriptions compare the results you get when you use the different commands:

- If you want to paste a static, unlinked picture object, or if you need to create a GIF file to include in a Web page, you should capture the object by using the Copy Picture command. You can control precisely the date range to include in timescale views, and you can easily resize the image without seriously distorting fonts.
- If you want the object you paste to be linked to the source document in Project, you must capture the object by using the Copy command. You can paste the object as a linked picture object or as a linked Microsoft Project object. In practice there is very little difference between the two options. Both can be updated to show changes in the timescale data for the tasks that are included in the original picture, and you can double-click either type of object to open the Project document that is the source of the link. However, there are limitations to this object type:

  You can't change the tasks or resources that are included in the original picture without deleting the object and starting over.

  You have limited control over the date range that is included if the view contains a timescale. The Gantt Chart view in particular uses graphic elements that extend before and after the start and finish dates for tasks (for example, summary taskbars, linking lines, and bar text), and these often appear truncated in the final object.
- If you want total control over what is displayed in an object, capture the view by using the Copy command and paste it as an unlinked Microsoft Project object. The data can't be updated, and the entire project is embedded in the other application (thus increasing file size dramatically). But you have total control over what is displayed in the object image. You can change the view, use filters, change formats, and so forth.

18

USING THE COPY PICTURE COMMAND TO COPY A VIEW

Using the Copy Picture command is the best way to prepare a static picture object for insertion into other applications. It is also the only way to prepare a picture to be displayed by Web browsers (using the GIF format).

NEW Project 2003 introduces a new Copy Picture to Office Wizard to directly send the Project picture into PowerPoint, Word, or Visio. This wizard is detailed later in this chapter.

You need to prepare the view in Project before making the copy, although the options in the Copy Picture dialog box offer additional control over what will be included in the image. In preparing to copy the view, use these guidelines:

- Whatever view you plan to copy, it is best to set it up so that it is contained in one screen. You can capture larger areas, but it is more difficult to get the results you want as the image gets larger.
- If the view includes a table, you need to prepare the columns that are displayed and the rows that are selected. To prepare the table, you can use any of the following techniques:
  - Only the columns that are completely visible are included in the picture. Therefore, you should arrange the display of columns as you want them in the

picture. Also, you need to be sure that the vertical split bar is not covering any part of the rightmost column that you want to include in the picture.

  - The Copy Picture dialog box gives you the option of including just the rows that are visible on the screen or including only the rows that you have selected. If you want to include selected rows, select at least one cell in each row you want to include. To include all rows, click the Select All button in the upper-left corner of the table. If you select nonadjacent rows, the image will contain only the rows you selected.
  - Selecting a summary task row does not include its subtasks in the image; they must also be selected as well.

- If the view has a timescale, you get the best results by compressing the date range you want to include in the picture onto no more than two or three screens. However, you can create a picture that includes more screens of the timescale if you want, but the printed image can be no wider than 22 inches. You have to zoom out the timescale to get a very large date range into the image successfully.
- If you are copying the Task Usage or Resource Usage view, be sure that the cells in the grid are at least 100% of their normal size. Otherwise, even though the cells are large enough for the values on the screen, you might see many cells filled with pound symbols (#) in the image, indicating that the data can't be displayed. To fix the cell size, choose Format, Timescale and set the value in the Size box to 100% or greater.
- If you are copying the Calendar view, one of the Network Diagram views, or the Resource Graph view, Project includes only the current screen in the picture. Therefore, you should prepare the display that you want to fit onto one screen before capturing the picture.

The Copy Picture dialog box (see Figure 18.24) offers options that vary depending on the view you are copying. For all views, you have choices about the format in which the picture is rendered, including the following:

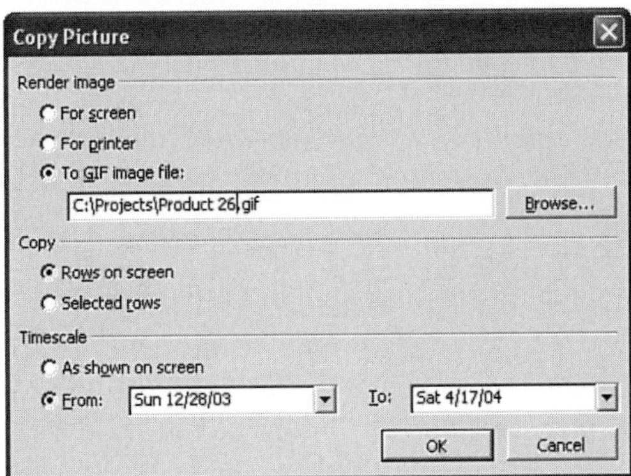

Figure 18.24
You can use the Copy Picture dialog box to tailor the image you copy—what it includes and how it is rendered.

- Choose the For Screen option if you are pasting the picture into another application simply to be viewed onscreen.
- Choose the For Printer option if you are pasting the picture into an application for printing. The format of the picture is determined by the printer you have selected in Project at the time that you save the picture. If you change printers before you print, you should copy the picture again.
- Choose the To GIF Image File option if you plan to use the picture in a Web page. The image is saved in a GIF-format file that most Web browsers can display with various controls. You must enter the path and filename for the file that is to be created. A Browse button is available that you can use to search the directory structure or search for a filename to replace.

If the view you are copying includes a table (for example, for the various Gantt Chart views, the Task and Resource Sheet views, the Task and Resource Usage views), you have the choice of including the following:

- Rows on Screen (only rows that are visible when you actually take the picture).
- Selected Rows (only rows in which you selected one or more cells before using the Copy Picture command).

18

If the view contains a timescale (which is true for the Gantt Chart views and the Task and Resource Usage views), you have the choice of the following:

- Using the dates as shown onscreen, which means that you can arrange the timescale onscreen as you want to see it in the picture, and then capture just that range of dates in a picture.
- Using a range of dates that you specify in the From and To date boxes.

TIP

> When you are selecting a date range with the Gantt Chart view, it's best to include at least one time unit before the From date and several time units after the To date. Many taskbars contain graphic elements that extend beyond the start and finish date of the task. This is especially true for bar text such as resource names that is displayed to the right of the taskbar. If you do not add extra time units to the date range, the data in the resulting picture might appear to be clipped off.

To copy the view to the Clipboard, follow these steps:

1. Set up the view you want to copy, using the guidelines listed earlier in this section.

2. Choose the Edit, Copy Picture command or click the Copy Picture button on the Standard toolbar to display the Copy Picture dialog box (refer to Figure 18.24).
3. Choose either For Screen, For Printer, or To GIF Image File. If you choose To GIF Image File, you need to supply the path and filename for the GIF file in the text box.
4. If you are in a table display, choose Rows on Screen or Selected Rows.

5. If there is a timescale in the display, select either As Shown on Screen or From and To dates. Remember to add an appropriate number of time units before the From or after the To selections, if necessary.
6. Click OK to save the picture.

The maximum size for a picture is 22 inches by 22 inches. If the number of tasks you select or the date range you specify for the timescale might create a picture greater than 22 inches in either direction, Project alerts you with the Copy Picture Options dialog box (see Figure 18.25), which offers the following options:

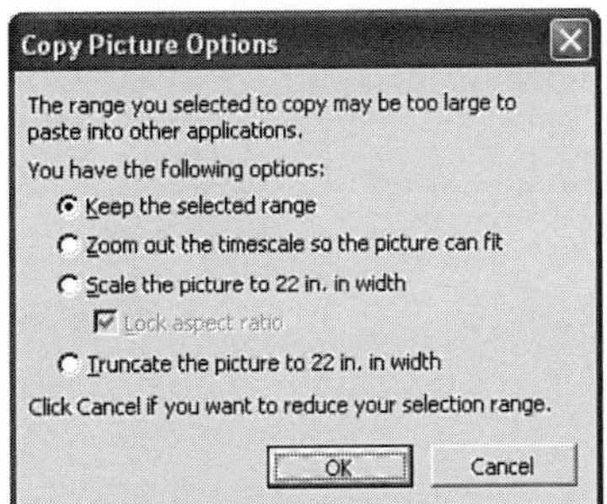

Figure 18.25 You must choose what to do when a picture is likely to be more than 22 inches in either dimension.

- Choose Keep the Selected Range if you want to try the picture anyway.
- Choose Zoom Out the Timescale So the Picture Can Fit if you want Project to automatically change the timescale units so that the date range fits within the maximum dimensions.
- Choose Scale the Picture to 22 Inches in Width if you want Project to compress the date range to fit within 22 inches, without changing the timescale units. Select the Lock Aspect Ratio check box to keep the proportions of the picture intact during scaling.
- Choose Truncate the Picture to 22 Inches in Width if you want Project to use only the date range and rows in the table that fit.
- Click Cancel to start the Copy Picture command over and change the date range.

In most cases, you get the best picture if you choose Cancel and manually adjust the timescale so that the picture will fit. It might save you time to choose Zoom Out the Timescale So the Picture Can Fit and paste the picture to see what timescale unit is needed. Then you can manually zoom out the actual timescale and capture the picture again.

When you switch to the application where you plan to paste the picture, select the location for the picture and use the Edit, Paste command (or press Ctrl+C). The Paste Special command is also available, but it produces the same end result (pasting the picture as a picture object).

The object appears with a border and resizing handles. If you drag the corner handles, the width and height of the object change proportionally.

Using the Copy Picture to Office Wizard

NEW Project 2003 introduces this new, easy way to copy a picture of your project data to an Office document (version 2000 or later), using PowerPoint, Word, or Visio. This wizard is called from the Analysis toolbar, which can be shown by selecting View, Toolbars, Analysis. Figure 18.26 shows the wizard's welcome page and the Analysis toolbar.

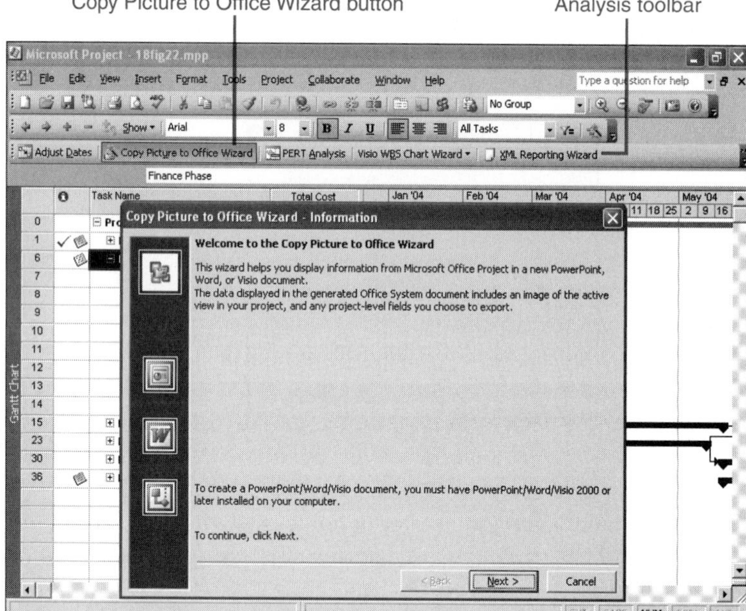

Figure 18.26
The Copy Picture to Office Wizard makes project data presentation very easy.

The wizard first lets you specify the outline level at which you want to detail your project (see Figure 18.27). Keeping the original outline level will use the current view to decide whether each summary task is collapsed or expanded. In this example, we didn't prepare the view before starting the wizard, so we decide to only show the first outline level.

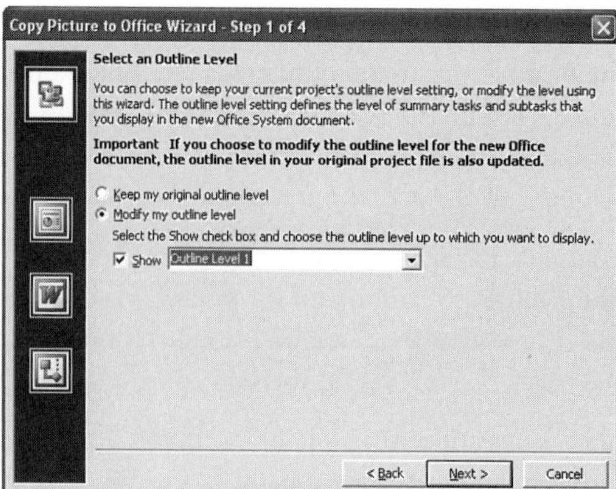

Figure 18.27
The Copy Picture to Office Wizard lets you select the outline level.

Next, the wizard lets you specify the rows and timescale limits of your image (see Figure 18.28). You can base your image on what you see on the screen, on a selection, or take all the rows. As with the Copy Picture command (described earlier in this chapter), the image size is limited to a printed height of 22 inches and a width of 22 inches.

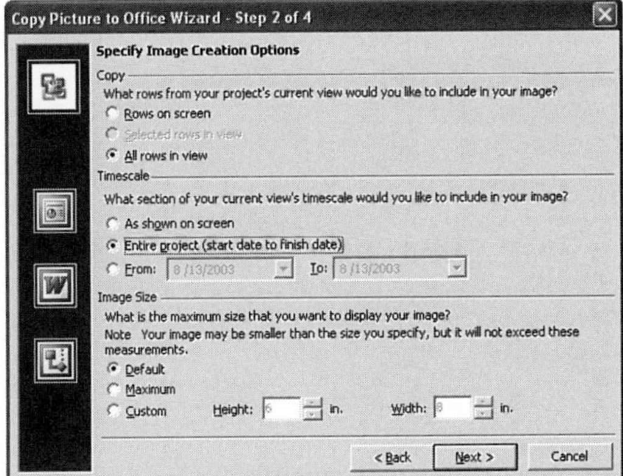

Figure 18.28
The Copy Picture to Office Wizard lets you select some dimensional parameters.

On the third step of the Copy Picture to Office Wizard, you are finally asked to select the target Office application, whether it's PowerPoint, Word, or Visio (see Figure 18.29). Office 2000 applications or later are required to interact with the wizard. When sending the picture to Word or Visio, you can also select the picture orientation as portrait or landscape. A preview button lets you view the results in Internet Explorer as a GIF image. You can save the picture at this point by right-clicking it and selecting Save Picture As.

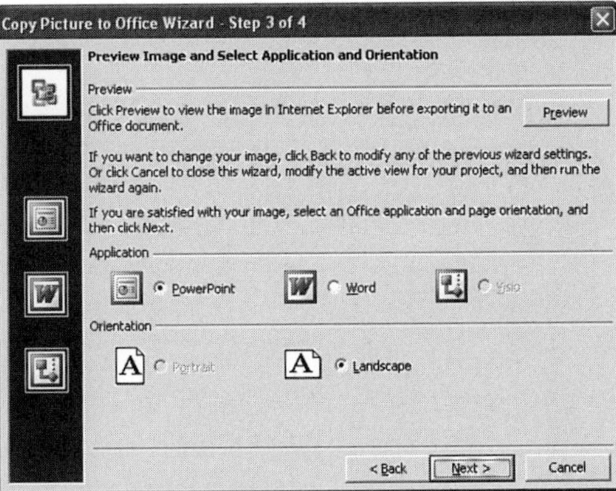

Figure 18.29
The Copy Picture to Office Wizard lets you select the destination of your picture.

On the last step, the wizard gives you an opportunity to export project-level data into a table that will be automatically embedded into the same document, making it easier to build your presentation (see Figure 18.30). Some fields are already selected from the general project info accessible through either the Project Information dialog box or the File Properties dialog box.

The wizard will use the current view to select which task-level fields will be included in the picture. Only full columns will be kept, as with a printout or with the Copy Picture command.

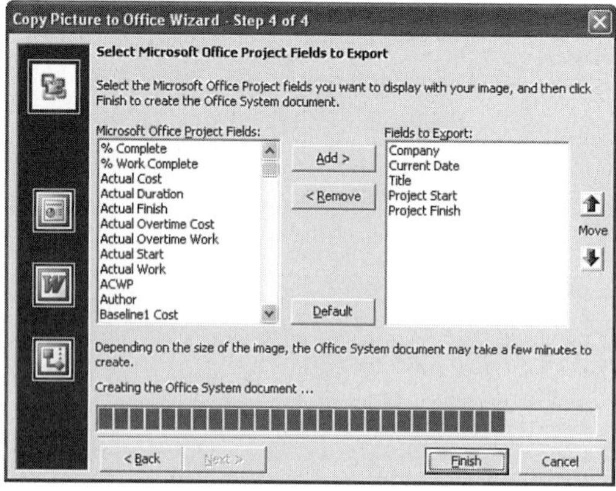

Figure 18.30
The Copy Picture to Office Wizard lets you select the project-level fields to include in the new document.

Figure 18.31 shows the results of using the Copy Picture to Office Wizard to import a picture into PowerPoint. Notice the project-level information in the table. The table is made up of individual data cells and you can modify the contents. The project picture is a graphic and you can apply any treatment to it the same way you would for any other graphic, including resizing, cropping, rotating, and modifying brightness and contrast.

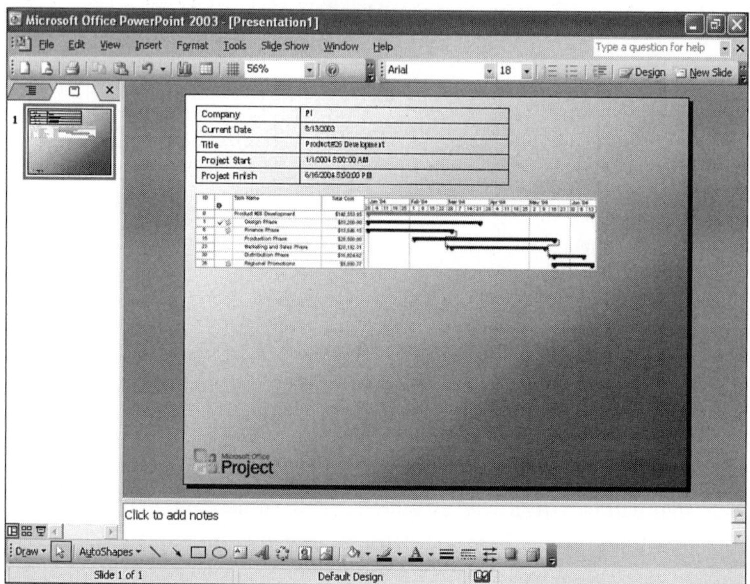

Figure 18.31
The Copy Picture to Office Wizard results in PowerPoint.

USING THE COPY COMMAND TO COPY A VIEW

When you copy a view to the Clipboard by using the Edit, Copy command, there is no dialog box with options for selecting what to copy. You must set up the screen exactly as you want the object to look when it is pasted into another application. The choices that you have all lie in the application where you paste the object by using the Edit, Paste Special command. Consider the following when making your choices:

- If you want the object to be linked, you can paste it as a linked picture or as a linked Microsoft Project object. Because the display is the same, you should choose the Microsoft Project object because it adds slightly less to the file size in the other application.
- If the object can be unlinked, you can use only the unlinked Microsoft Project object because the Copy Picture command produces better unlinked picture objects. The unlinked Microsoft Project object increases the file size in the other application by a considerable amount (by approximately the size of the Project document), but it gives you complete control over what is displayed in the other application.

To copy a view that will be pasted as a linked object, set up the view in Project to look the way you want it to look in the other application. Keep in mind that the Copy command generally copies only one screen (the exception is noted in the following list). Use the following guidelines to set up the view:

- If the view contains a table, only the columns that are visible on the screen are included, but all rows that you select are included. However, the rows must be adjacent, or you are only able to paste text instead of an object.
- If the view contains a timescale, the timescale in the object starts with the earliest start date of any of the selected tasks and includes one screen-width of the timescale. Therefore, you should scroll that earliest start date into view on your screen and compress the timescale to display exactly the date range you want covered in the object.
- When you copy the Network Diagram view or the Resource Graph view, the object includes only the current screen; therefore, you should make sure that the screen is exactly what you want in the object.
- The Calendar view can't be pasted as a linked object. You need to use the Copy Picture command to paste a Calendar object.
- If you copy the Task Usage view or Resource Usage view, the object includes only the table; the timephased data does not display or print. You must use the Copy Picture command if you want to display the Resource Usage view with its timephased data.

NOTE

If you are copying a view that will be pasted as an unlinked Microsoft Project object, the setup of the screen is not too important because you can open the object and manage the display by using the Project menu and toolbars.

When the view is prepared, you can copy the view by using the Edit, Copy command. Then, activate the other application to paste the object. To paste a linked Microsoft Project object, choose Edit, Paste Special to display the Paste Special dialog box (see Figure 18.32). Choose Paste Link to keep the link to the Project document, and then choose Microsoft Project Document Object from the list of format types in the As box. Leave the Display as Icon check box unchecked. Then click OK to finish.

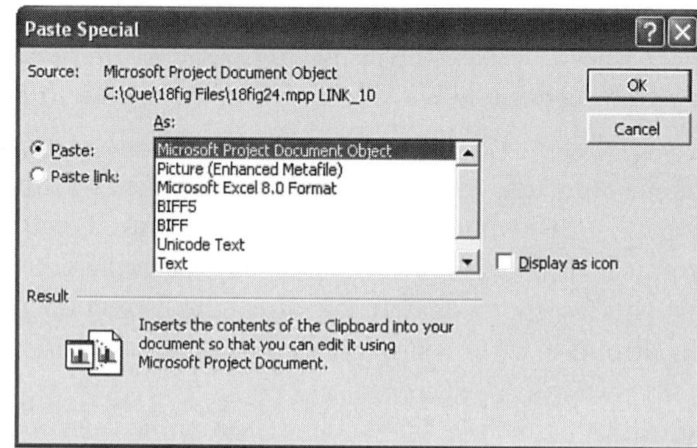

Figure 18.32 You can use the Paste Special dialog box to paste Microsoft Project objects into another application.

When you paste a linked Microsoft Project object, you can resize the object, but you can't change what is displayed inside it. If the object contains part of a Gantt Chart view, the timescale changes to reflect new dates when you update the link. You can resize the object by dragging the sizing handle at the lower-right corner so that the proportions remain unchanged. Otherwise, you might distort the fonts and graphic objects.

To paste the object as an unlinked Microsoft Project object, use the same commands listed previously, but select the Paste button in the Paste Special dialog box. The pasted object appears rather small (see Figure 18.33), and you can resize it if needed.

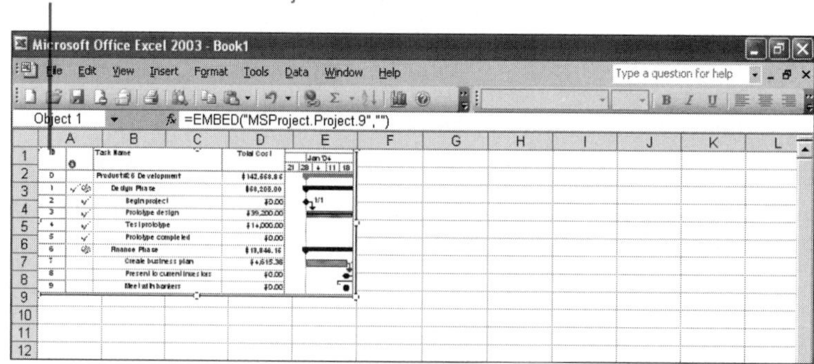

Figure 18.33 Immediately after being pasted into an Excel worksheet, an unlinked Microsoft Project object appears as a smaller size than most people want it to be.

To resize the unlinked object, follow these steps:

1. Double-click the object. Microsoft Project becomes the active application, and you see a portion of the view you copied.
2. Reactivate the destination application. You now see a thick gray border around the unlinked object.
3. Drag the resizing handles until you see the data in the view that you want shown in the object.
4. Click anywhere outside the object in the destination application. The thick gray handles disappear, and you see the object with the desired data displayed.
5. If the object contains a large area of whitespace below the data (as shown in Figure 18.34), click once on the object to select it, and then drag one of the resizing handles on the lower edge of the object to remove the whitespace.

Figure 18.34
You can remove extra whitespace by dragging one of the bottom resizing handles.

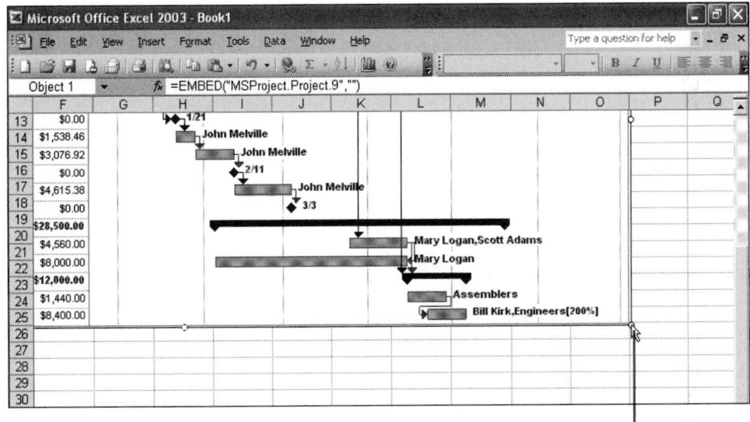

Drag one of the lower resize handles to remove this whitespace

TROUBLESHOOTING

MAKING COLUMN HEADERS APPEAR WHEN PASTING

I've copied and pasted both a table and timephased data from the Task Usage view into an Excel spreadsheet, but I can't get the column headers to appear automatically. What's wrong?

When you copy data from a Project view and then you do a standard Paste operation, the column headers from the table or timephased grid do not appear automatically. If you want to see the column headers after the paste operation, you must type them. If you want the column headers to appear automatically, you should consider doing a Paste Special and then pasting either a linked or an unlinked Microsoft Project object.

EFFICIENTLY CUSTOMIZING A TABLE

Before I paste data into Project from another application, I want to modify the columns in a standard table, but I don't want to permanently change the layout of the table. How can I do this?

The best way to make changes in a standard table is to make a copy of the table and customize the copy. The quickest way to do that is as follows:

1. Right-click over the gray-colored blank space above the row numbers (the Select All button) to display the Tables shortcut menu. Select More Tables to display the More Tables dialog box. The table you are viewing is selected.
2. Click the Copy button, and Project opens the Table Definition dialog box, with a copy of the table you were viewing.
3. Before modifying the table, give it a unique new name to distinguish it from the standard tables.
4. Make changes in the columns to be included in the table, and then click OK to save the table definition.
5. If you want to use this new table with other projects, click the Organizer button, copy the new table to your `GLOBAL.MPT` file, and then click Close.
6. In the More Tables dialog box, click Apply to view the new table design.

RESTORING STANDARD TABLES THAT HAVE BEEN CUSTOMIZED

I accidentally customized a standard table without making a copy of it first. How can I restore the standard table and keep the customized version as a new table?

You need to do three things: Rename the customized version of the table, apply the renamed table to the view you designed it for, and copy the standard version of the table from the Global template into the project. The quickest way to rename the table and apply it to its intended view is to follow these steps:

1. Display the view that contains the customized table.
2. Right-click the gray blank space above the row numbers (the Select All button) to display the Table shortcut menu.
3. Select More Tables to display the More Tables dialog box. The table name is highlighted.
4. Click the Copy button to have Project create a copy of the customized table in the Table Definition dialog box.
5. Rename the table with a unique new name to distinguish it from the standard tables.
6. Select the Show In Menu check box if you want the table to appear on the Table menu. Don't forget to delete the ampersand symbol (&) from the table name so that this copy does not have the same hotkey on the menu as the original table.

→ For more details about defining tables, **see** "Using and Creating Tables," **p. 840**.

7. Click the OK button to save the copy and return to the More Tables dialog box.

8. If you want to use this new table with other projects, click the Organizer button, copy the new table to your `GLOBAL.MPT` file, and then click Close.
9. Click the Apply button to display the new table in the active view.

To restore the original version of the standard table, follow these steps:

1. Be sure that there is no view open that contains the table name you plan to copy from the Global template.
2. Display the Organizer by choosing Tools, Organizer.
3. Select the Tables tab.
4. Select the name of the standard table that you want to restore from the list on the left (the list of tables in `GLOBAL.MPT`).
5. Click the Copy button to copy the table to the list of tables on the right (the list for the active project).
6. When Project tells you that the table already exists in the active project, click Yes to replace the table with the standard version from the template.
7. Click Close to close the Organizer.

Using and Customizing the Display

19 Using the Standard Views, Tables, Filters, and Groups 735

20 Formatting Views 775

21 Customizing Views, Tables, Fields, Filters, and Groups 833

22 Using and Customizing the Standard Reports 877

23 Customizing Toolbars, Menus, and Forms 921

CHAPTER 19

Using the Standard Views, Tables, Filters, and Groups

In this chapter

Exploring the Standard Views 736

Exploring the Standard Tables 757

Exploring the Standard Filters 761

Exploring the Standard Groups 770

Troubleshooting 773

EXPLORING THE STANDARD VIEWS

Views can be categorized in two different ways. The first logical breakdown of views is whether they display tasks or resources. All views focus on one or the other but not both. The next method of categorizing views is by their format. There are basically three different formats for views: sheets, forms, and graphs. Table 19.1 summarizes the predefined views, using these category breakdowns. The views marked with an asterisk must be accessed by choosing View, More Views (see Table 19.1).

TABLE 19.1 SUPPLIED VIEWS BY FORMAT AND FOCUS

View Type	Task Views	Resource Views
Graphical views	Calendar Gantt Chart (Bar Rollup*, Detail Gantt*, Leveling Gantt*, Milestone Date Rollup*, Milestone Rollup*, Multiple Baselines Gantt*, PA_Expected Gantt*, PA_Optimistic Gantt*, PA_Pessimistic Gantt*, Tracking Gantt) Network Diagram Descriptive Network Diagram* Relationship Diagram*	Resource Graph
Sheet views	Task Sheet* Task Usage PA_PERT Entry Sheet	Resource Sheet Resource Usage
Form views	Task Form* Task Details Form* Task Name Form*	Resource Form* Resource Name Form*
Combination views	Task Entry*	Resource Allocation*

The views listed with the Gantt Chart view are all based on a standard Gantt Chart view, except that they have different tables applied and the bars are formatted differently. See the section "Exploring the Standard Tables," later in this chapter, for a discussion of these different tables.

The combination views are two standard views that are displayed on the same screen. They provide a unique combination of information, and they are described at the end of this chapter.

The following sections describe each of the views, with all the task views first and then the resource views.

THE CALENDAR VIEW

In the popular Calendar view (see Figure 19.1), tasks are displayed in a familiar calendar format. Each task is displayed as a bar that spans the days and weeks during which the task is scheduled to occur. Many people can more easily visualize a project when they can see it displayed in this familiar format. This view can be very useful for reviewing a project plan, for editing a project after the initial design has taken place, and for printing.

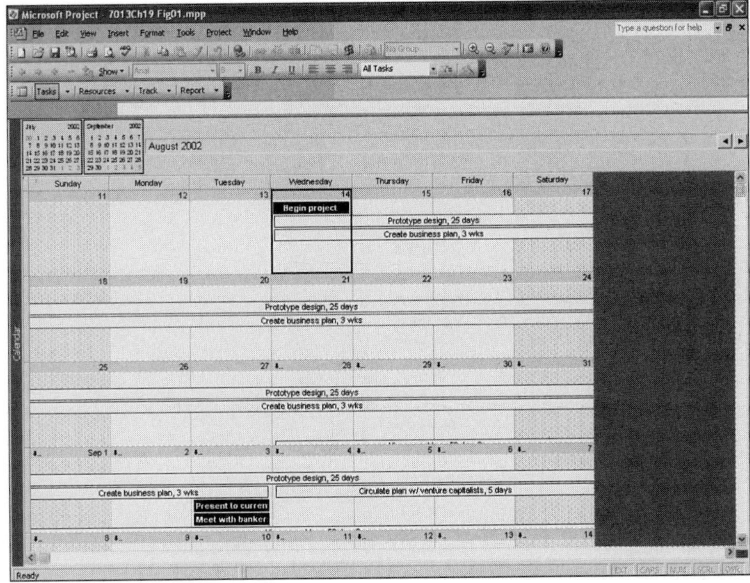

Figure 19.1
The Calendar view displays tasks in a familiar format as you view, edit, or print a project.

CAUTION

Although it's possible to create a project by using the Calendar view, it is not generally advisable to do so. Creating tasks in the Calendar view causes date constraints to be applied to the tasks.

→ To add tasks by using the Calendar view, **see** "Inserting Tasks in Calendar View," **p. 263**.

→ To learn more about constraints, **see** "Working with Task Constraints," **p. 201**.

Quite often, the calendar displays too many tasks at once, and it becomes difficult to see what you want. You can apply filters to hone in on particular categories of tasks—for example, tasks that are in progress, top-level tasks, or tasks that use a particular resource. This last type of filter is very helpful when you want to give each resource a list of his or her respective tasks. Filters are discussed at the end of this chapter.

THE GANTT CHART VIEW

The Gantt Chart view, one of the most popular project management views, is actually a task sheet on the left side and a bar chart on the right (see Figure 19.2). The chart is a list of tasks displayed as bars that overlay a timescale. The length of the bars is determined by the duration of the tasks. The placement of the bars on the timescale is determined by the start and finish dates of the tasks. Dependency lines are drawn to show the predecessor and successor relationships between tasks.

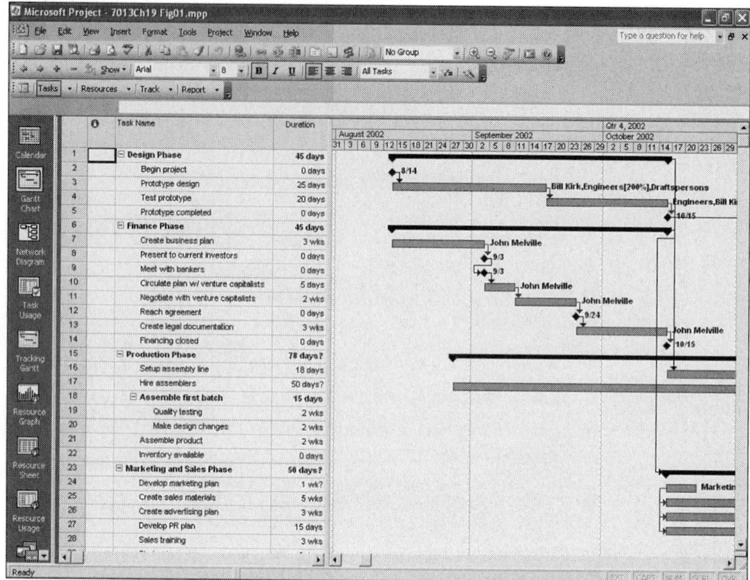

Figure 19.2
The Gantt Chart view draws bars on a timescale to show when tasks occur.

19

The Gantt Chart view is useful during many stages of a project. During the initial planning stages of a project, you can use this view to enter tasks, make determinations about dependency relationships, and even assign resources. After the initial planning phase, you will probably need to evaluate and adjust the schedule. The Gantt Chart view is useful in immediately displaying the effect of your efforts. After the project is underway, the Gantt Chart view offers a practical display of tasks that are in progress as well as those tasks that are behind or ahead of schedule.

The options for formatting the Gantt Chart view are so numerous that there is even a special automated tool, the Gantt Chart Wizard, which walks you through the process.

→ To learn more about how to format the Gantt Chart view by using the Gantt Chart Wizard, **see** "Using the Gantt Chart Wizard," **p. 801**.

The Rollup Views

Several of the views based on the Gantt Chart view are grouped together because they are all rollup views—information from detail tasks has been rolled up onto collapsed summary tasks. This is useful when the outline level for a detail task is collapsed but you would still like to see where that task falls along the summary task. The technique of using rollups is discussed in greater detail in Chapter 12, "Reviewing the Project Plan." This section describes the various predefined rollup views that are available, what information they provide, and how they are different from one another.

When choosing which rollup view to display, ask yourself what you would like to see along with collapsed summary tasks. These are your options:

- **Bar Rollup**—Colored boxes are drawn on the summary taskbar for each rolled-up task.
- **Milestone Rollup**—Diamonds appear on the summary task to show the milestones in time.
- **Milestone Date Rollup**—Milestones are represented by diamonds and dates on the summary tasks.

The rollup views use a field called Text Above. This field, which is visible on the Rollup table, offers a drop-down list with Yes and No as the options. When Yes is selected, the task name appears above the summary taskbar, rather than below it, which is the default. The rollup feature can also be enabled on an individual task by selecting that task, opening the Task Information dialog box, and checking the General tab option Roll Up Gantt Bar to Summary. You can also set Project to roll up all tasks and either show the rollups at all times or only when the summary tasks are collapsed. Select Format, Layout to set these features (see Figure 19.3).

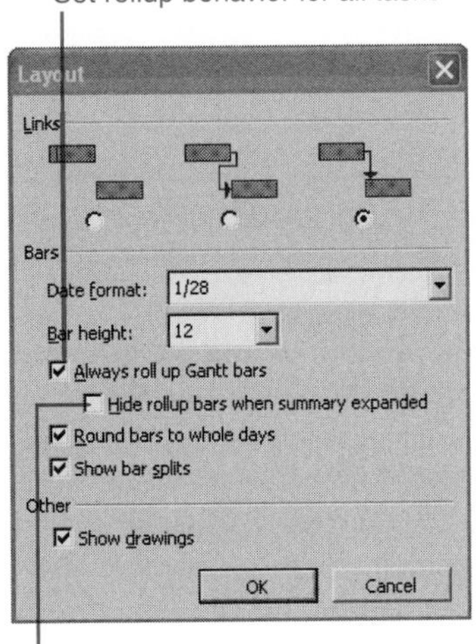

Figure 19.3
All tasks can be set to roll up to their summary tasks.

CAUTION

> Because rolled-up task names appear above the summary taskbar, there is an increased likelihood that the task names will overlap. You might need to increase the span of the timescale, shorten the task names, or be more selective about which tasks are rolled up.

THE BAR ROLLUP VIEW

If you roll up a task other than a milestone, the summary taskbar looks more like a task than a summary. This is useful when you want to highlight certain tasks when task details are not displayed. Figure 19.4 shows the rollup of the Prototype design task.

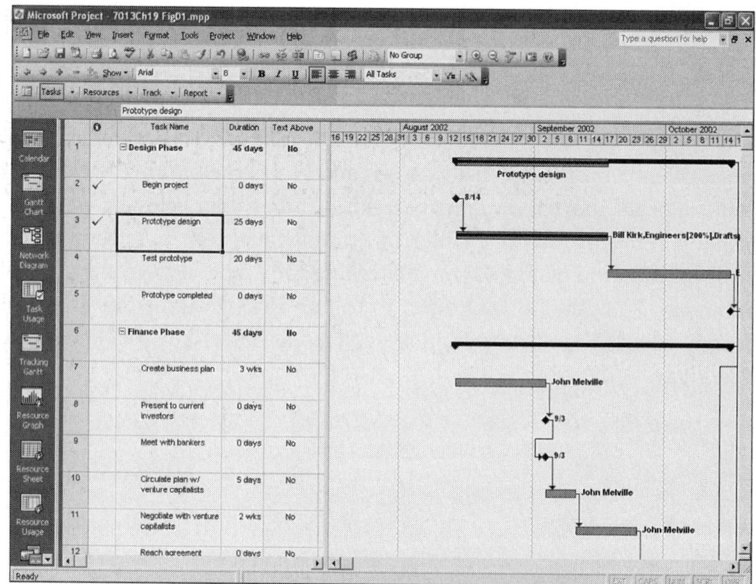

Figure 19.4
The Bar Rollup view allows you to emphasize specific task details in a collapsed outline.

THE MILESTONE ROLLUP VIEW

The Milestone Rollup view is similar to the Bar rollup view. As shown in Figure 19.5, when tasks are marked as Rolled Up, only the milestone task names are rolled up—not the dates. This view is useful for creating a summary display of only the specific project events—the milestones. If tasks (rather than just milestones) are rolled up, only a diamond shows for them on the summary taskbar, rather than a bar, as in the Bar Rollup view.

THE MILESTONE DATE ROLLUP VIEW

The Milestone Date Rollup view includes dates rolled up to summary tasks, along with names. Displaying dates on the chart eliminates the need to print columns of dates, which can reduce the number of pages to be printed. As shown in Figure 19.6, the names of the milestones appear above the summary taskbar and the date appears below it. A diamond appears on the end of the summary taskbar only if you roll up a milestone to it.

Senior management often uses milestone reports to review important dates in a project. Although they are helpful, such reports often encourage "management by exception," because only the significant planned and actual dates are reviewed. Although it is sometimes necessary, management by exception is not a preferred practice of project management because it affords little time to take corrective action. Often, troubled projects are identified only after a significant date slips, and there is no opportunity to get the project back on track.

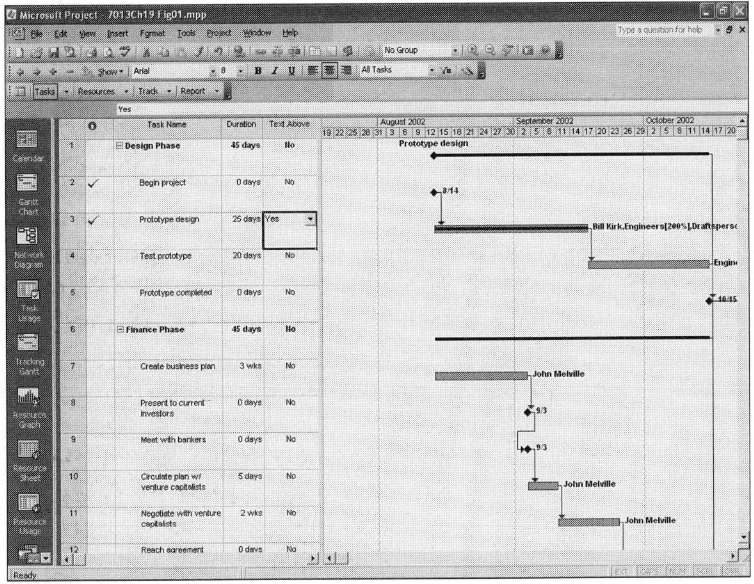

Figure 19.5
The Milestone Rollup view allows you to selectively place some rolled-up task names above the summary taskbar and some below it.

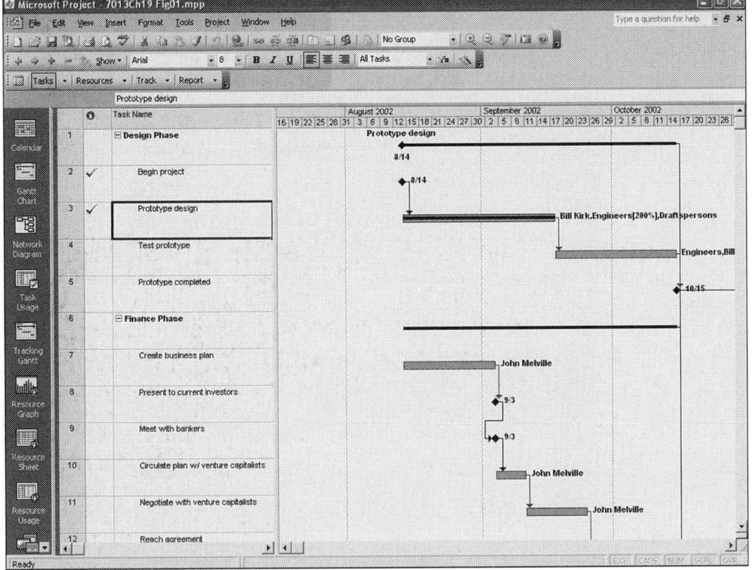

Figure 19.6
The Milestone Date Rollup view automatically puts names above the summary taskbar and dates below it.

19

THE SPECIALIZED GANTT CHART VIEWS

Following the same general format of the Gantt Chart view, the specialized Gantt Chart views have been specifically formatted to highlight certain project scheduling issues. One of the most useful views in Project is the Tracking Gantt view, in which you can see at a glance if your tasks are on their baseline schedules or how far they have slipped. The Leveling Gantt view is useful for examining and resolving resource overallocation problems. The Detail Gantt view shows task movement from leveling delays and remaining task slack.

THE TRACKING GANTT VIEW

The Tracking Gantt view is available on the View bar as well as the View menu. It is based on the standard Gantt Chart view but includes an additional gray bar, below the regular taskbar, with the baseline information (see Figure 19.7). Task progress is shown two ways: A solid color is shown on the scheduled taskbar—instead of the Gantt Chart view's black progress line—and the percentage complete value is shown on the right side of the bars.

The Tracking Gantt view is one of the most powerful views available to a project manager because it not only shows scheduled dates of tasks, but it shows actual and baseline dates, as well. With this formatting available, a project manager can easily review the past, present, and expected future status of project-related activities.

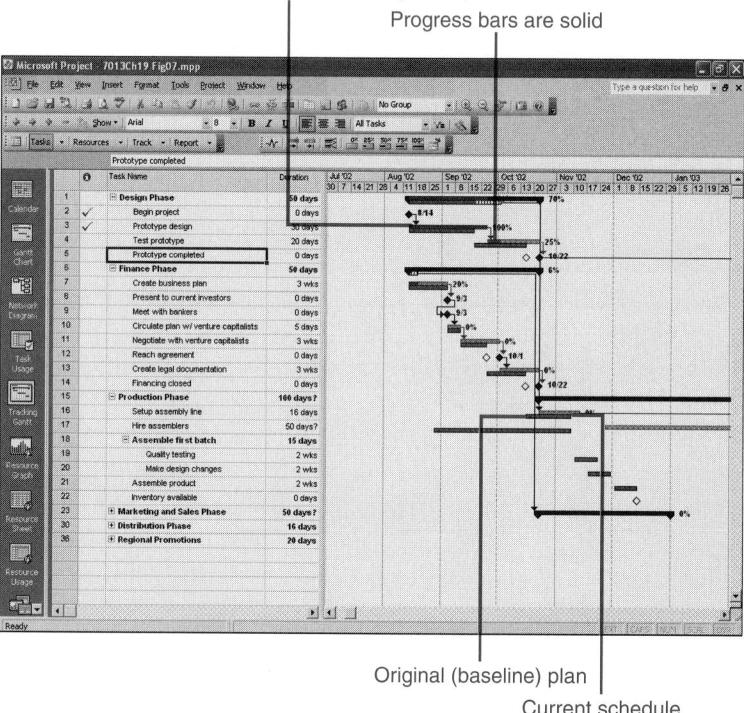

Figure 19.7
The Tracking Gantt view gives a snapshot of how the project is progressing.

CAUTION

The baseline bars are not displayed if the baseline has not been saved or has been cleared.

THE LEVELING GANTT VIEW

The left side of the Leveling Gantt view uses the Delay table, which includes the leveling delay field. This is where Project notes delays it calculates during automatic leveling, and where you can enter a delay in a task if a resource is too busy with other tasks. Several bars are included in this view for each task (see Figure 19.8). Extending to the left of each task is a very narrow bar that is drawn from the earliest date a task can start and shows any leveling delays on the task. Extending to the right of each taskbar is another very narrow bar that depicts *free slack* (that is, the amount of time a task can be delayed without delaying any other tasks). Using this bar, you can see how much a task can be delayed without causing a delay in another task. Colored bars show the task as currently scheduled. A dotted line shows where the task has been split as a result of leveling.

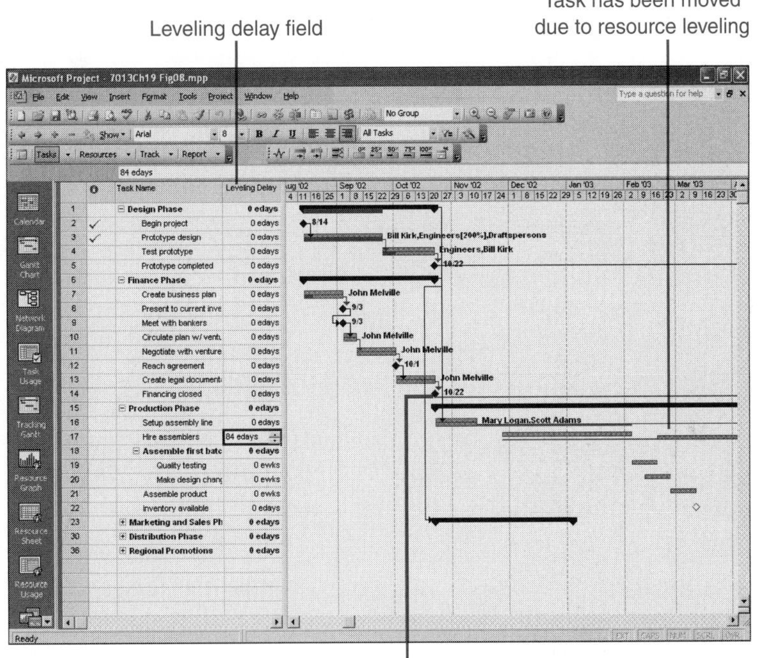

Figure 19.8
The Leveling Gantt view allows for the input of, and shows the effect of, delaying tasks.

→ To learn more about leveling a project, **see** "Resolving Overallocations by Delaying Assignments," **p. 440**.

THE DETAIL GANTT VIEW

The Detail Gantt view is very similar to the Leveling Gantt view in that it shows where delays have been created as a result of leveling, whether performed by Project through automatic leveling or by you through manual leveling. The Detail Gantt view (see Figure 19.9) does not show how the task was scheduled before it was delayed, as the Leveling

Gantt view does, but it includes text that shows the slack amount at the right side of the slack bars.

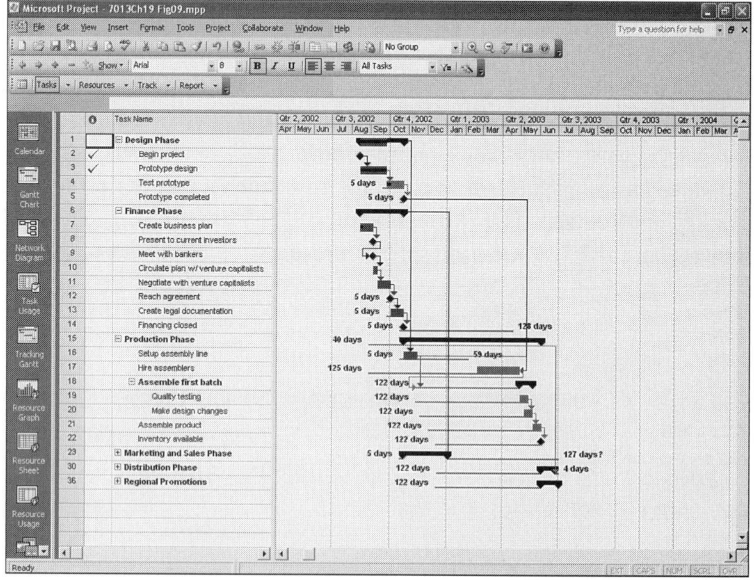

Figure 19.9
The Detail Gantt view is another tool for keeping track of tasks that have been delayed or that could be delayed, to resolve resource overallocations.

The Multiple Baselines Gantt View

Project 2003 can store 10 sets of baseline values for a single plan. The rescheduling of tasks over time is charted on the new Multiple Baselines Gantt view. The taskbars on this view are formatted to show the original baseline schedule, as well as the revised schedules stored in the Baseline1 and Baseline2 fields.

PERT Analysis Views

The PERT Analysis toolbar displays several special views that are associated with PERT analysis (which is the calculation of duration, using a weighted average of best-case, worst-case, and most-likely-case duration estimates). The easiest way to access these views is through the PERT Analysis toolbar. These views are not initially listed with the other views when you select View, More Views. You must first access them through the PERT Analysis toolbar, after which they display in the list of views.

→ To learn more about estimating durations, **see** "Project Extras: Letting Project Calculate Duration," **p. 171.**

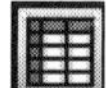

The PA_PERT Entry Sheet is the view where the user enters an optimistic estimation of duration, a pessimistic estimation of duration, and an estimate of the expected duration. The view is a sheet view that displays the PA_PERT Entry table. Project calculates the weighted average of the estimates and places the result in the Duration field.

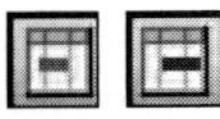

You can display three special Gantt Chart views by using the tools on the PERT Analysis toolbar. However, it is not a good idea to use these views because they roll up the best-case and worst-case estimates for tasks into estimates for the project in a statistically unsound fashion. As a result, they significantly exaggerate the best- and worst-case estimate of the duration of the project.

THE TASK RELATIONSHIP DIAGRAM VIEWS

Three views let you focus specifically on the linking relationships between tasks. The Network Diagram view and Descriptive Network Diagram view each display the entire project in a box-and-line format. The Relationship Diagram view focuses on a specific task and its immediate predecessors and successors. These views are described in the following sections.

THE NETWORK DIAGRAM VIEW

The network diagram, also referred to as a PERT chart or a logic diagram, is another graphical view of a project; it focuses on the dependency relationships between tasks. As shown in Figure 19.10, the Network Diagram view resembles a flowchart that has boxes (nodes) for the tasks. Lines are drawn to illustrate predecessors and successors. The display in Figure 19.10 was created using the Zoom Out tool in the Standard toolbar. By using the Network Diagram view, particularly during the design phase of a project, you can ensure that the project plan is flowing logically. This view is also useful when printed on a plotter and displayed on a wall; team members can easily view the plan and contribute project information.

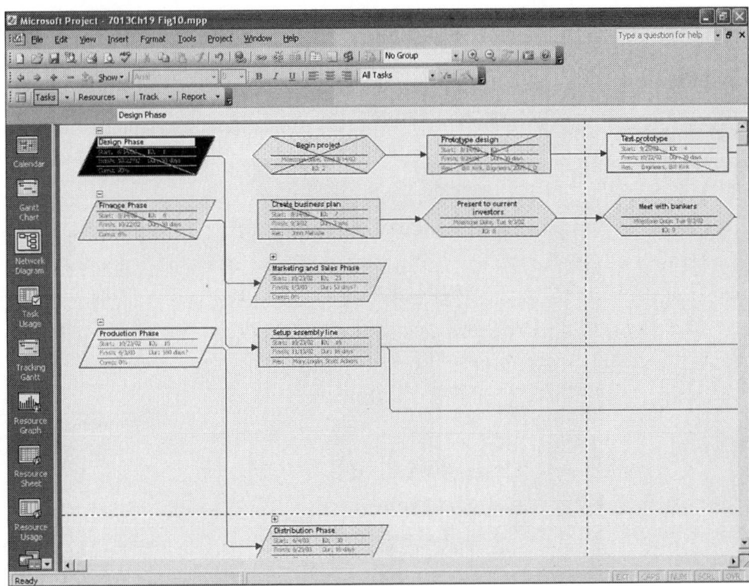

Figure 19.10
The Network Diagram view helps define the logic of predecessors and successors for the project plan.

If you move the mouse pointer close to a task node, Project zooms in to show a detailed view of that node. When you double-click a task node, the Task Information dialog box for that task is displayed. Outline symbols can be used to hide or display subtasks of summary tasks to see different levels of detail. The Network Diagram view can also be filtered to reflect only tasks that meet certain criteria. There is no timescale in the Network Diagram view, but you can reorder tasks according to time periods by selecting Format, Layout, and then choosing one of the options in the Arrangement box from among Top Down by Day, Week, or Month.

→ For additional information about the Network Diagram view, **see** "Working with the Network Diagram View," **p. 265**.

→ For detailed information on changing the Network Diagram view formatting, **see** "Formatting the Network Diagram View," **p. 807**.

The Descriptive Network Diagram View

The Descriptive Network Diagram view is almost identical to the Network Diagram view. This view also focuses on the dependency relationships between tasks. However, the boxes that make up the Descriptive Network Diagram view provide more detailed information regarding the tasks they represent. As shown in Figure 19.11, the Descriptive Network Diagram view illustrates the dependency relationships between tasks, and it provides additional information about those tasks. As with the Network Diagram view, if you move the mouse pointer close to the task node, Project zooms in to show a detailed view of that node. Outline symbols can be used to hide or display subtasks of summary tasks, and task filters can be applied.

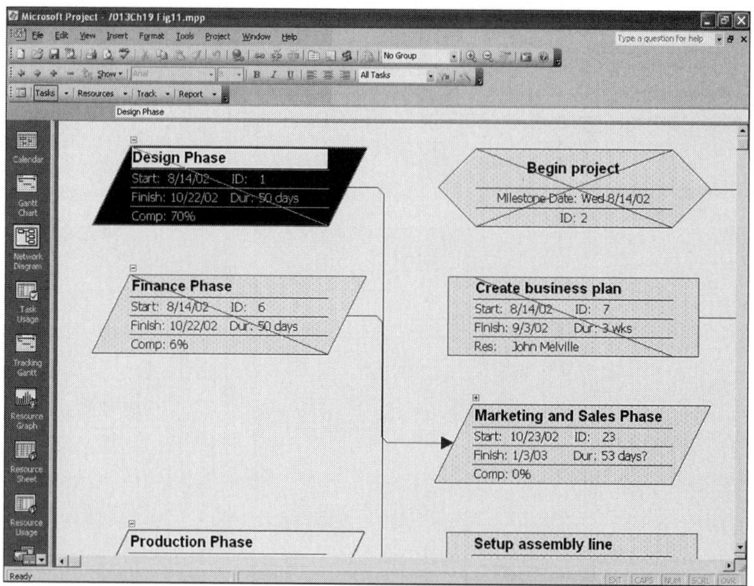

Figure 19.11 The Descriptive Network Diagram view provides additional task information for analyzing task dependencies.

THE RELATIONSHIP DIAGRAM VIEW

The Relationship Diagram view is a special kind of Network Diagram view. As shown in Figure 19.12, the Relationship Diagram view is typically displayed at the bottom of a task view. It shows only the immediate predecessors and successors for the task that is selected in the top pane. This is a very useful view when examining the task dependencies of the project, particularly when you're making sure that every task is linked and that the links all make sense. For example, in Figure 19.12, the dependencies for Task 18 are much clearer in the Relationship Diagram view shown in the bottom pane than in the Gantt Chart view in the top pane. The type of the relationship is also displayed in the Relationship Diagram view. Figure 19.12 clearly shows that each of the predecessors has a Finish-to-Start relationship with Task 18.

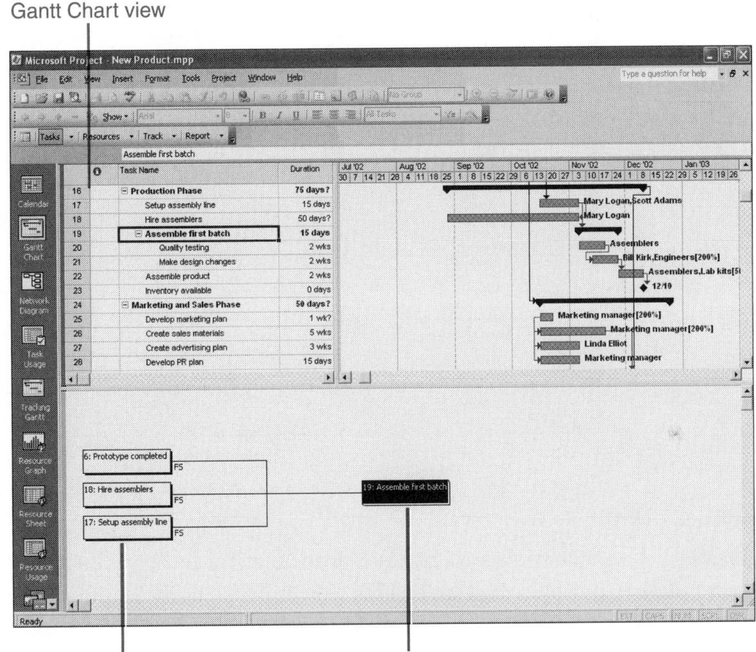

Figure 19.12
You can use the Relationship Diagram view to make sure that every task has at least one predecessor and successor and that all relationship links make sense.

➔ To learn more about working with task dependencies, **see** "Understanding Dependency Links," **p. 177**.

SHEET VIEWS FOR TASKS LISTS

Project classifies any view that focuses on task or resource information but does not include a graph as a sheet view. The task-oriented sheet views—Task Sheet view and Task Usage view—are described in the following sections.

THE TASK SHEET VIEW

The Task Sheet view has a spreadsheet format. Tasks are displayed in rows, and fields of information about those tasks are displayed in columns. The fields (columns) that are displayed are determined by the table that has been applied. (See the section "Exploring the Standard Tables," later in this chapter, for more details about tables.) This view is preferred by people who like working in a row-and-column format rather than with a form or with a graphical view. Figure 19.13 displays the Task Sheet view with the Entry table applied.

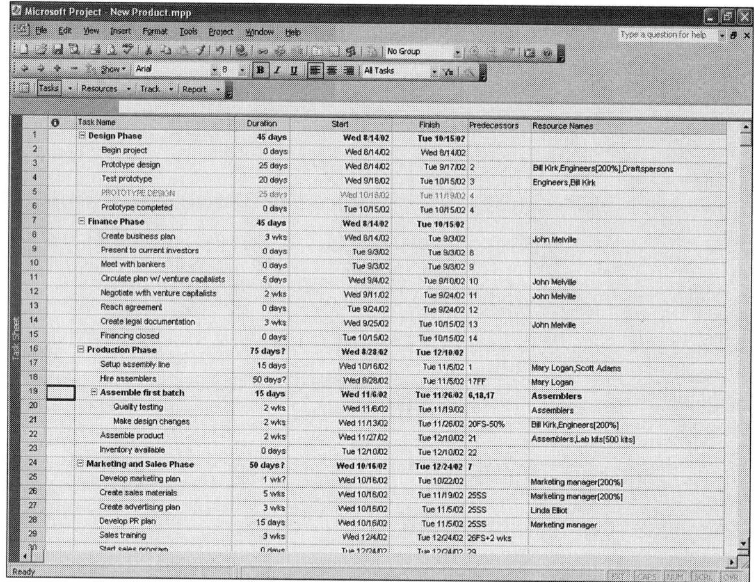

Figure 19.13
The Task Sheet view with the Entry table applied shows the same fields as a Gantt Chart view with the taskbars hidden.

THE TASK USAGE VIEW

The Task Usage view displays hours of work that are to be performed by each resource on each task, laid out on a timescale. This view is particularly helpful when you're checking resource assignments on each task. Additional rows of details, such as resource availability, can be added to the right side. As shown in Figure 19.14, Task 11 is a one-week task assigned to John Melville.

➔ The Task Usage view is primarily intended to be used for resource contouring. **See** "Contouring Resource Usage," **p. 348**.

FORM VIEWS FOR TASKS

Forms are another type of nongraphical view in Project. They focus on a single task or resource at a time and provide detail or drill-down information for each one. Forms are typically placed at the bottom of a split screen view, although they can be used as full-screen displays. The basic Task Form view and its variations—the Task Details Form view and the Task Name Form view—are described in the following sections.

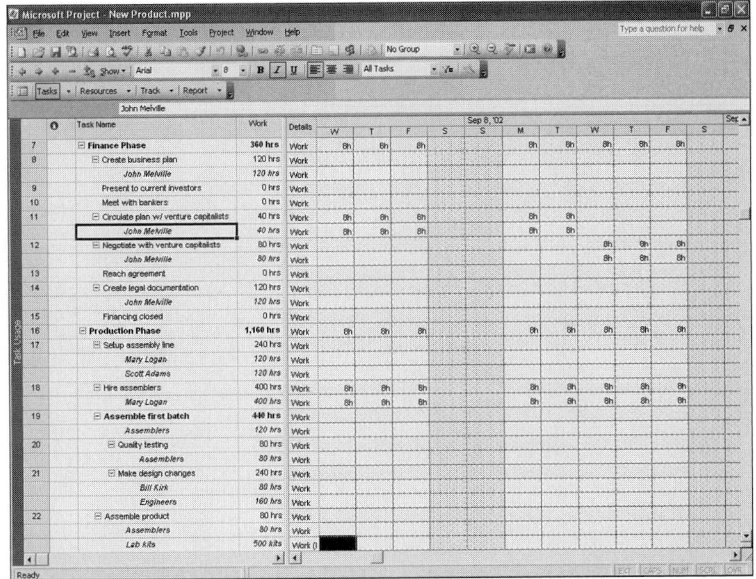

Figure 19.14
The Task Usage view displays exactly when work is scheduled to occur.

The Task Form View

The Task Form view presents basic information about only one task in a form format (see Figure 19.15). It is possible to see more information about one task in a form view than in a standard sheet view. The Task Form view is often used in the bottom pane to display more detailed information about the task selected in the top pane. To display the Task Form view in the bottom pane, be sure a task view is onscreen, then choose Window, Split. Project places the Task Form view in the bottom pane by default.

The bottom portion of the form itself can be set to display a variety of project details, such as predecessors and successors, resource schedule information, work hours, and cost. In a split view, you must make the form active before you enter or edit information or choose which details to display. You can click anywhere in the form or press the F6 key to move the Active View indicator onto the form. With the form active, you can choose Format, Details or right-click anywhere on the form itself to see the available detail options. It is also possible to create custom forms if the predefined forms do not meet your needs.

To display a form in a single-pane view, choose View, More Views, Task Form. Even though the task list is not visible, you can still move from one task to another by using the Previous and Next buttons.

➔ To learn how to enhance the Task Form view, **see** "Formatting the Task and Resource Form Views," **p. 817**.

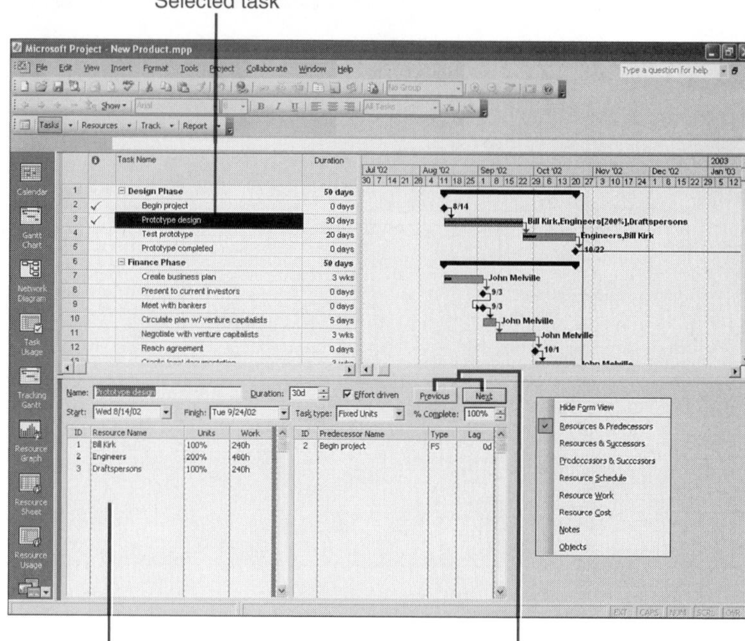

Figure 19.15
The Task Form view allows you to focus on one task at a time.

THE TASK DETAILS FORM VIEW

The Task Details Form view, shown in Figure 19.16, is similar in format to the Task Form view, but it shows more detail at the top of the form; in particular, the fields for Current, Baseline, and Actual Dates are shown. You could use this form for tracking the progress of tasks that are already underway. Constraints are also displayed on this form, making them more obvious. As with the Task Form view, the bottom portion of the Task Details Form view can display a variety of fields and can be opened as a full-screen view.

If the window has already been split, it probably displays the default Task Form view. You can replace the bottom view with the Task Details Form view. Make sure the form is active—click anywhere on the form, if necessary—before you choose View, More Views and then select the Task Details form.

THE TASK NAME FORM VIEW

The Task Name Form view is, as its name implies, a simple form that displays only the task name in the top portion of the form. The bottom portion of the form has the same formatting options as the Task Form view and the Task Details Form view. You access this view by choosing View, More Views, Task Name Form, and you can make it either a full-screen display or the bottom portion of a split window. The Task Name Form view is useful when it is used in the bottom pane of a combination view and you don't want to waste screen space on redundant information.

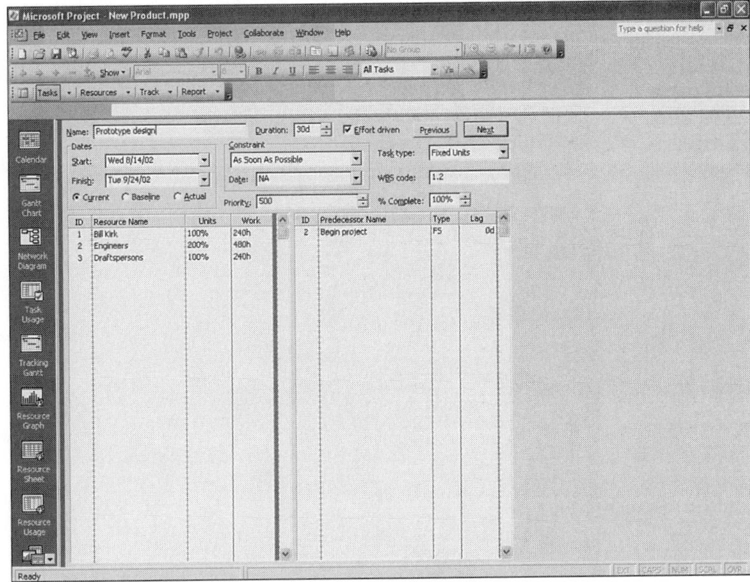

Figure 19.16
The Task Details Form view includes fields that are useful during scheduling and tracking.

Sheet Views for Resources

Two sheet views present resource information—the Resource Usage view and the Resource Sheet view. They are similar to their task sheet counterparts. The Resource Usage view displays a list of resources and their task assignments, which is like a restructured Task Usage view. The Resource Sheet view has a row-and-column format that is particularly convenient for entering and reviewing resource field values from the database. These two views are discussed in the following sections.

The Resource Usage View

The Resource Usage view, which you access through the main View menu or the View bar, is a sheet view that lists resources on the left and their allocation to tasks on a timescale on the right (see Figure 19.17). The allocation information on the right side can be set to display hours of work, hours of overallocated work, cost, available time, and other details. Resources are listed on the left, with the tasks assigned to them indented underneath. A symbol similar to the outline symbol in the task list allows you to hide or show the tasks that are assigned to the various resources. For example, in Figure 19.17 tasks for Scott Adams have been hidden; the plus symbol to the left of his name indicates that some information is not currently displayed.

A diamond-shaped icon with an exclamation point displays in the Indicators column for the resources that need to be leveled. When you point to this icon, a message displays, identifying the type of leveling setting that is required: day by day, week by week, and so on. This view is primarily used when resolving overallocation problems. It is particularly useful when displayed in a combination view, with the Gantt Chart view in the bottom pane to display the tasks assigned to each resource.

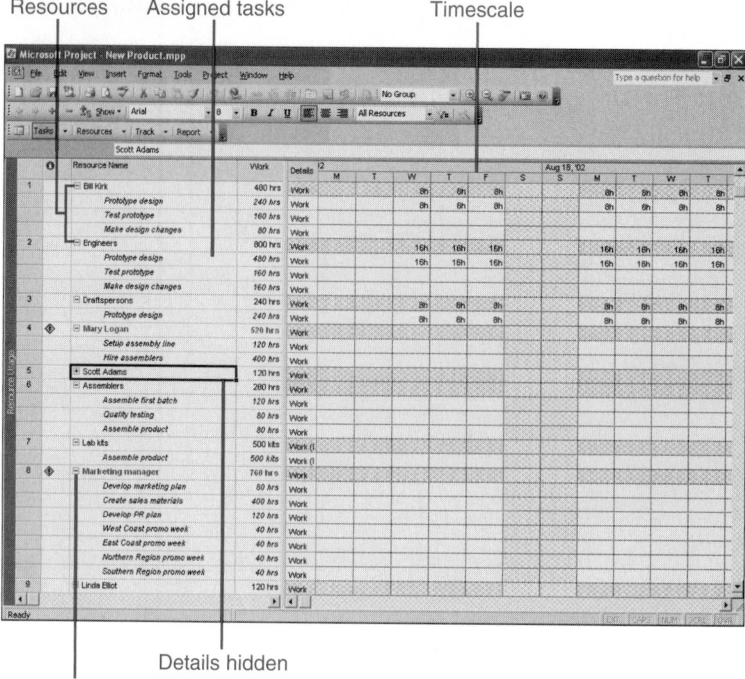

Figure 19.17
The Resource Usage view is helpful when resolving overallocation problems.

→ To learn more about resolving resource conflicts, **see** "Strategies for Eliminating Resource Overallocations," **p. 417**.

→ To learn about additional features of the Resource Usage view, **see** "Working with the Resource Usage View," **p. 410**.

19

The Resource Sheet View

The Resource Sheet view, shown in Figure 19.18, is a list of resource information that is displayed in familiar spreadsheet format. You access this view by choosing View, Resource Sheet, or by using the View bar, and you can use it to enter and edit data about both work resources and material resources. Each resource is in a row with fields of resource data in columns. The Indicators column displays an icon for overallocated resources. The fields that are displayed depend on the table that has been applied. (See the section "Exploring the Standard Tables," later in this chapter, for more details.) This view is most often used for creating an initial resource pool.

→ To learn more about setting up resources, **see** "Defining the Resource Pool," **p. 286**.

→ For additional information about how the Resource Sheet view can help you discover resource conflicts, **see** "Identifying Resource Overallocations," **p. 405**.

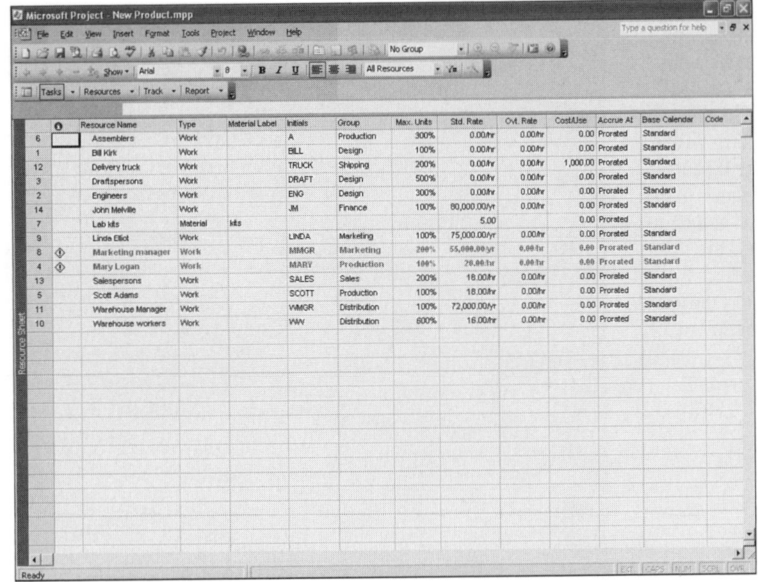

Figure 19.18
The Resource Sheet view provides a spreadsheet format for entering and editing basic resource data.

Form Views for Resources

Two form views focus on resources and their assignment details—the Resource Form view and the Resource Name Form view. The only difference between these two is the amount of detail at the top of the form. There is no Resource Details form that is similar to a Task Details form. As with task forms, resource forms are typically displayed at the bottom of a combination view. To create this combination, display a resource view first, such as the Resource Sheet view, and then choose Window, Split. The Resource Form view will open automatically in the bottom pane.

The Resource Form View

Displaying much the same information as the Resource Sheet view, the Resource Form view allows you to focus on one resource at a time (see Figure 19.19). This is the form that opens by default when a resource view is displayed and after the window is split. The information in the top portion of the Resource Form view is the same as in the Resource Sheet view. If a resource is selected in the Resource Sheet, then the details appropriate for that resource will be shown in the Resource Form View. The bottom portion of the form can be set to display a schedule of tasks to which the resource is assigned—the hours of work that are currently assigned, including overtime, costs associated with this resource, notes, and so on. You can find these choices by choosing Format, Details or by right-clicking the displayed form.

The Resource Name Form View

Similar to the Task Name Form view, the Resource Name Form view is a simple form that displays only the resource name in the top portion. You can format the bottom portion of this form to display a variety of fields about resources by choosing Format, Details.

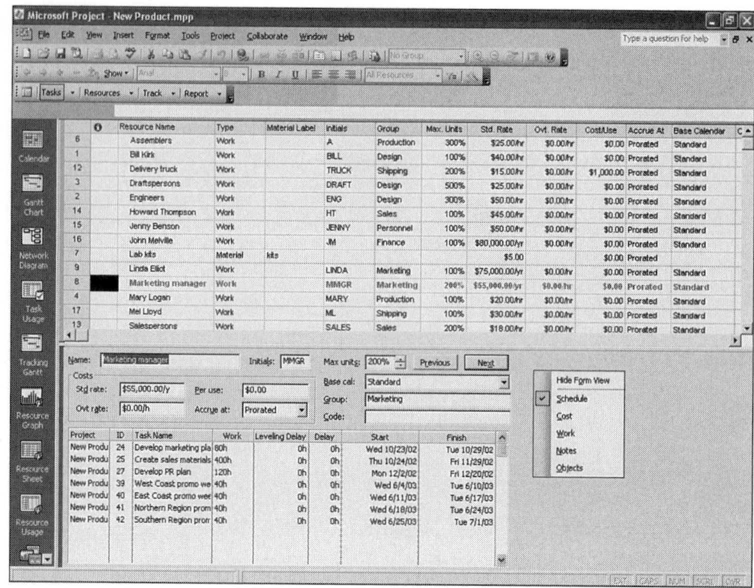

Figure 19.19
The Resource Form view displays both basic and detailed information about any resource. In this figure, the Resource Sheet is shown in the upper half of the screen and the Resource Form is displayed in the lower half of the screen.

THE RESOURCE GRAPH VIEW

The Resource Graph is a graphical view that displays resource allocation over time. It presents essentially the same information as the Resource Usage view, but in a graphical format. Found on the main View menu and on the View bar, it can be a single-pane view by itself, or it can be used as part of a combination view, in either the top pane or the bottom pane. Used in conjunction with the Go to Next Overallocation button on the Resource Management toolbar, it can be very useful in determining when resources are overallocated and by how much. For example, you can see in Figure 19.20 that, beginning the week of October 6, the marketing manager has way too much to do.

19

In traditional project management, the Resource Graph view is often referred to as a *resource histogram*. This view is frequently used to review the work allocation assigned to an individual resource.

→ For more information on viewing resource conflicts, **see** "Viewing Resource Overallocations," **p. 409**.

COMBINATION VIEWS

Some views in Project set up a split window when they are applied. These are known as *combination views* because they combine predetermined views in the top and bottom of the screen. Two combination views are supplied—the Task Entry view and the Resource Allocation view.

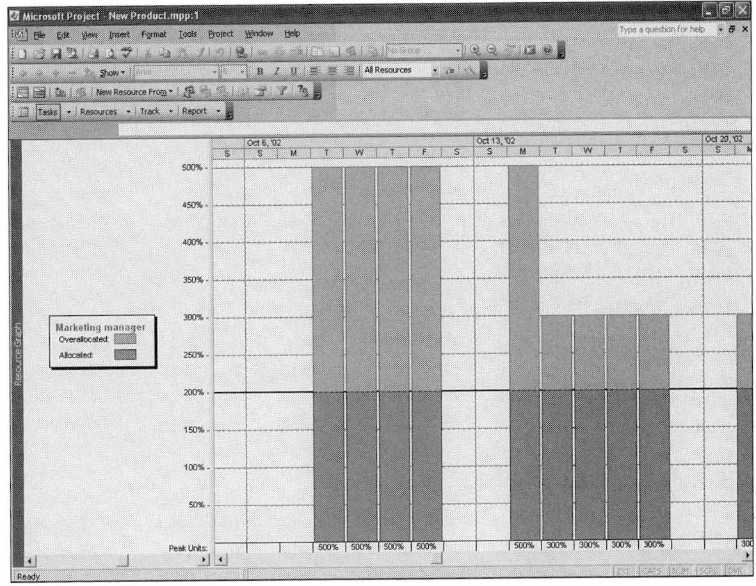

Figure 19.20
The Resource Graph view illustrates resource overallocations graphically on a timescale.

THE TASK ENTRY VIEW

The Task Entry view is a combination of two views—the Gantt Chart view in the top pane and the Task Form view in the bottom pane (see Figure 19.21). This is a useful view because you can see several different types of information at one time: tasks on a timescale at the top and detailed information about the selected task at the bottom. You can access this view in three ways: by choosing View, More Views; by clicking the Task Entry View button on the Resource Management toolbar; or by merely splitting the window by choosing Window, Split when a Gantt Chart view is active. The Task Form view is the view that opens by default when the window is split.

CAUTION

> The Task Entry View button runs the ResMgmt_TaskEntry macro, which displays the Task Entry view and applies the resource schedule details for the Task Form view in the bottom pane. The details selection remains in place every time the window is split, until a different details selection is applied.

THE RESOURCE ALLOCATION VIEW

The Resource Allocation view is another predefined combination view that uses views that have already been described: the Resource Usage view at the top and the Leveling Gantt view at the bottom (see Figure 19.22). As its name implies, the Resource Allocation view was designed for resolving resource overallocations. In the Resource Usage view in the top pane, you determine which resources are overallocated, during what period of time, and to what degree. In the Leveling Gantt view at the bottom, you can determine which tasks are assigned to that resource. With this information, you can make decisions about how to handle the overallocation. For example, in Figure 19.22, the top pane identifies the week of October 6 as a problem for the marketing manager. The bottom pane identifies the tasks that are assigned this manager. Each of these tasks requires the marketing manager's full attention, causing the overallocation. Having this information can help you make a wise decision about how to handle the problem.

➔ To learn more about resolving resource conflicts, **see** "Identifying Resource Overallocations," **p. 405**.

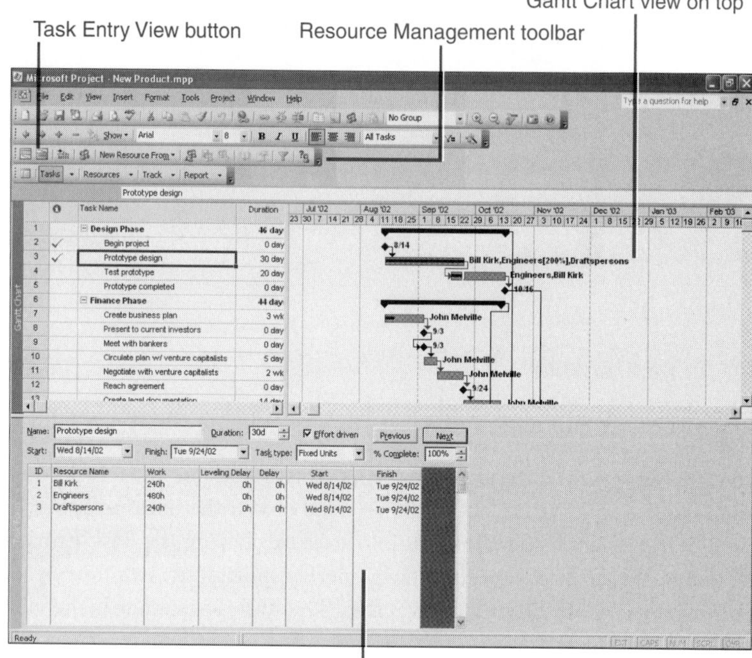

Figure 19.21
The Task Entry view offers several different perspectives on a project.

You can access the Resource Allocation view in two ways: either by choosing View, More Views or by clicking the Resource Allocation View button on the Resource Management toolbar.

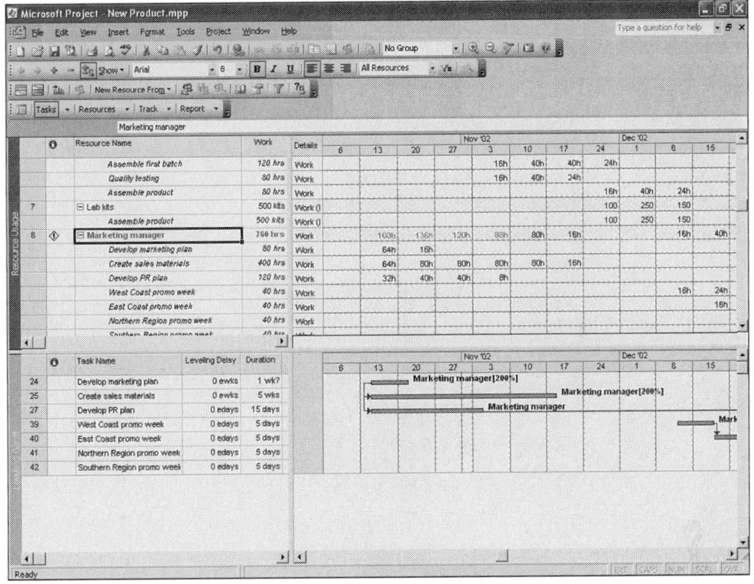

Figure 19.22
The Resource Allocation view shows when and by how much resources are overallocated, as well as what tasks the resources are assigned to during that time period.

EXPLORING THE STANDARD TABLES

In the sheet views, the fields (columns) that are displayed are controlled by tables. You can choose different tables by choosing View, Table, More Tables. If you are in a task view, the list of task tables is displayed. If you are in a resource view, a list of resource tables is displayed. When you access the More Tables dialog box, you can view either the task or resource list of tables by choosing the appropriate option button in the top-left corner of the dialog box. The most commonly used tables are listed on a cascading menu on the Table option of the View menu, as shown in Figure 19.23, but all tables are listed in the More Tables dialog box (see Figure 19.24). You can only apply tables, however, for the appropriate view format; that is, you can only apply a task table when you are in a task view.

19

You can customize and even create your own tables. The following sections describe each of the predefined tables that are included with Microsoft Project.

THE TASK TABLES

To access the task tables, display a task view, such as a Gantt Chart view, and choose View, Table. Then, you can access a table from the cascading list or by opening the More Tables dialog box. You can also edit, copy, and even create new tables in the More Tables dialog box.

Table 19.2 briefly describes all the predefined task tables. Table names that are marked with an asterisk (*) must be accessed by choosing View, Table, More Tables.

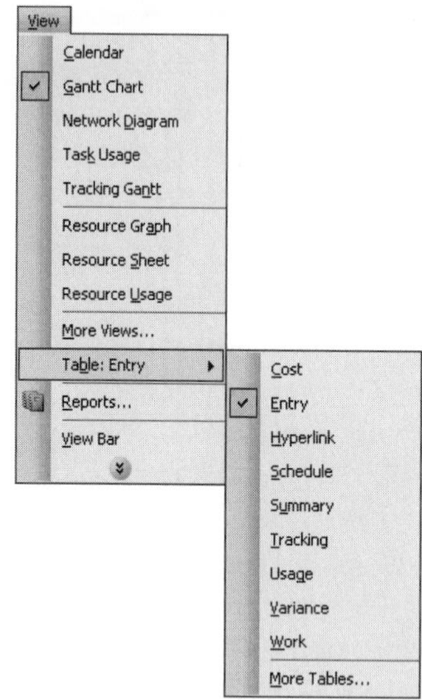

Figure 19.23
The commonly used tables are available under the View menu. You can choose More Tables to see the complete list of tables.

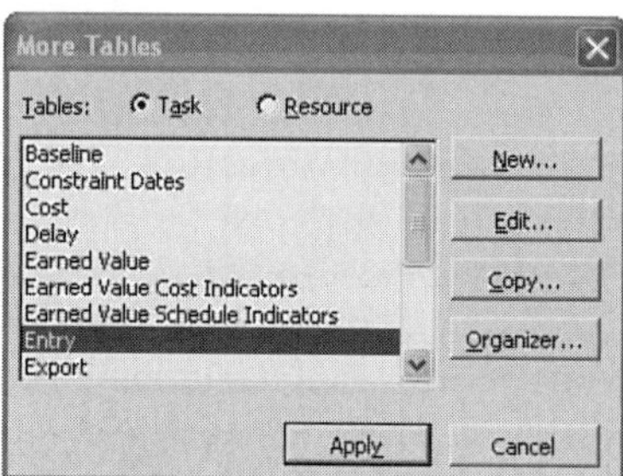

Figure 19.24
All tables are listed in the More Tables dialog box.

TABLE 19.2 THE PREDEFINED TASK TABLES IN PROJECT

Table Name	Recommended Use
Cost	This table shows how costs are varying from what you had originally planned.
Entry	This table is particularly helpful during the data entry stage, when you're creating a project. This is the Gantt Chart view default table.
Hyperlink	This table creates a hyperlink to another file, not necessarily a Project file.
Schedule	This table provides the calculated values of free slack and total slack so that you can tell how much a task can be delayed without it affecting related tasks or the project end date.

Table Name	Recommended Use
Summary	This table provides a summary of basic schedule and progress information.
Tracking	This table enables you to view or enter actual information on tasks as the project progresses.
Usage	This table provides information about the hours of work incurred for each task. It is the default table for the Task Usage view.
Variance	This table includes the calculated variance fields that summarize the difference between what was planned and what has actually happened in the project.
Work	This table is useful for identifying tasks that are requiring more effort than originally expected.
Baseline*	This table displays information about what you planned during the design phase of the project.
Constraint Dates*	This table is an invaluable tool for locating tasks that have had constraints applied, intentionally or accidentally.
Delay*	This table includes the leveling delay field, which you can use to see where delays have been imposed on a task, by you or by Project. This is the default table for the Detail and Leveling Gantt views.
Earned Value*	You use this table to compare actual progress against expected progress, based on work completed by resources, to predict whether a task will come in under budget, based on costs incurred thus far.
Earned Value Cost Indicators*	This table is based on the Earned Value table, but it includes more fields that are related to cost tracking.
Earned Value Schedule Indictors*	This table focuses on Earned Value schedule fields.
Export*	This table is designed for exporting to another application. It includes many standard and custom task fields.
PA_Expected Case*	In this table you can enter anticipated duration and schedule values for PERT analysis.
PA_Optimistic Case*	In this table you can enter best-case values for PERT analysis.
PA_PERT Entry*	This table combines best, worst, and expected duration values on one table.
PA_Pessimistic Case*	In this table you can enter worst-case durations for PERT analysis.
Rollup Table*	In this table you can control placement of the task name text for the rollup bar. It is the default table for the Rollup views.

NOTE

Comprehensive lists of fields included with supplied Project tables are documented in Project's online Help. From the Project screen, choose Help, Microsoft Project Help, and select the Contents tab. In the Reference area, choose Microsoft Project Reference. Follow the hyperlink in the right pane of Help to Views, Table, Filters, and Groups.

THE RESOURCE TABLES

When a Resource Sheet view is displayed, the columns are also controlled by tables. Only the resource tables are available when you are in a resource view. The most commonly used tables are available directly by choosing View, Table (see Figure 19.25); all resource tables are available when you choose View, Table, More Tables.

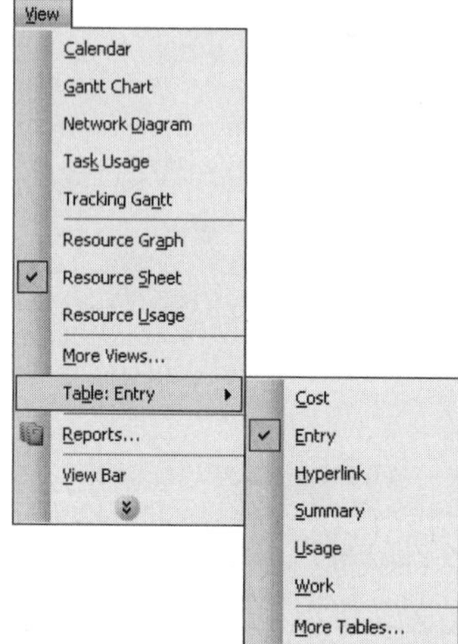

Figure 19.25 The resource tables are listed under the View menu when a resource view is displayed.

19

Table 19.3 briefly describes all the predefined resource tables. Table names that are marked with an asterisk (*) must be accessed by choosing View, Table, More Tables.

TABLE 19.3 THE PREDEFINED RESOURCE TABLES IN PROJECT

Table Name	Recommended Use
Cost	This table is helpful in determining which resources are the most and least expensive and which ones are overbudget and under-budget.
Entry	This table displays information about material resources as well as work resources that are usually gathered when the resource pool is being created. It is the default table for the Resource Sheet view.
Hyperlink	This table stores hyperlink references to a file on a computer, a network, an intranet, or the Internet.

Table Name	Recommended Use
Summary	This table provides a synopsis of information about each resource in a pool.
Usage	This table provides information about the quantity of resources that are being used, and it pinpoints which resources are being over- or underutilized.
Work	This table shows the progress of resources on their assigned tasks and compares it to planned work.
Earned Value*	This table shows calculated values that compare work and costs that were budgeted to what the work is actually costing. This table is for analysis only, not for entering or editing.
Export*	This table provides a vehicle for exporting a comprehensive set of resource information to other applications.
Entry—Material Resource*	This table focuses on material or consumable resources, such as lumber or concrete, and omits fields that apply only to work resources.
Entry—Work Resource*	This table focuses on work resources, such as individuals or facilities.

➔ To create your own custom table, **see** "Using and Creating Tables," **p. 840**.

Exploring the Standard Filters

As discussed previously in the chapter, tables are a central building block of Microsoft Project. They determine which columns of fields are displayed for tasks or resources. Filters are another major building block; they determine which tasks or resources are displayed, depending on criteria that you provide.

All the views except the Relationship Diagram view can have filters applied. Any view that can accept a filter can have one defined as part of the view: When the view is selected, the filter is automatically applied. All the standard views initially have the All Tasks or All Resources filters designated as part of the view definitions.

NOTE

> Any view in the bottom pane of a combination view cannot have any filters applied. The bottom pane is already being filtered by virtue of being the bottom pane, which is always controlled by what is selected in the top pane.

A filter helps you identify and display only the tasks or resources (depending on the view) that match one or more criteria. All other tasks or resources are temporarily hidden. If a filter is applied as a highlight filter, all tasks or resources are displayed, but those that are selected by the filter are displayed with highlight formatting features such as a different color, bold, italic, and underline, which you can define by choosing Format, Text Styles. Any filter can be applied as a highlight filter or a display-only filter. You define the criteria for a filter by specifying one or more field values that must be matched for a task or resource to be selected by the filter.

Filters have the following key characteristics:

- A *calculated* filter compares two or more values in the Project database, or it compares a database field to a value you enter manually in the filter definition. For example, a filter can compare the baseline cost to the total cost for a task, or it can compare the total cost to some value (such as $5,000) that you specify.
- *Interactive* filters prompt the user for a comparison value (or values) when the filter is applied. For example, the Using Resource filter asks the user to choose a resource name from a drop-down list.
- All filters can be applied to highlight tasks that meet the criteria, instead of hide those that don't match.

→ To learn more about highlighting specific groups of tasks or resources, **see** "Formatting Text Displays for Categories of Tasks and Resources," **p. 778**.

NOTE

Each filter on the Project, Filtered For menu that contains an ellipsis (…) is an interactive filter.

TIP

You can apply an existing filter by using the Filter list box on the Formatting toolbar.

A filter can do much more powerful work than perform one simple test. *Compound* filters incorporate multiple tests against the tasks to perform more complex filtering. The following tests can be included in filters:

- *Inclusive* filters use the And condition to require that all test conditions are met.
- *Exclusive* filters use an Or test to choose tasks that meet at least one test condition.
- You can evaluate groups of And/Or tests independently and combine the results with other groups of tests by using an And or Or condition between groups of tests. For example, the Using Resource in Date Range filter first finds all tasks that have a certain resource assigned, and then it tests both the start and finish dates for those tasks to find tasks that finish within a range of dates.

Applying a Filter to the Current View

To apply a filter to a view, you can choose Project, Filtered For or use the Filter tool on the Formatting toolbar. If the filter you want is on the Project, Filtered For menu (shown in Figure 19.26), you can select the filter name, and it will be applied immediately. If the filter is not on the Project, Filtered For cascading menu, you can choose More Filters and then select the filter name from the complete list of filters in the More Filters dialog box list (see Figure 19.27). You click the Apply button to apply the filter so that only tasks or resources that satisfy the filter appear. If you want to apply the filter as a highlight filter (so that filtered items are highlighted and all other items remain displayed), click the Highlight button instead of Apply.

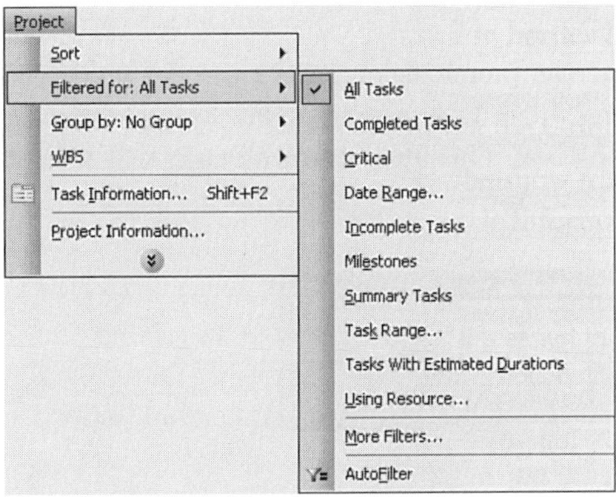

Figure 19.26
You can choose a filter from the cascading list on the Project, Filtered For menu.

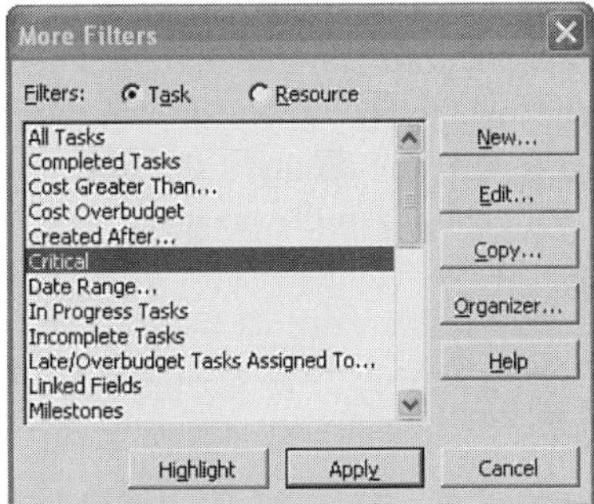

Figure 19.27
The More Filters dialog box lists all filters that are available for both tasks and resources.

NOTE

> You can apply filters as highlight filters by holding down the Shift key as you choose Project, Filtered For and select the filter name.

All Tasks

Another way to apply a filter to the current view is by selecting the filter name from the Filter tool on the Formatting toolbar (see Figure 19.28). When you select the filter name from the list, the filter is applied immediately. You cannot apply the filter as a highlight filter when you use the Filter tool.

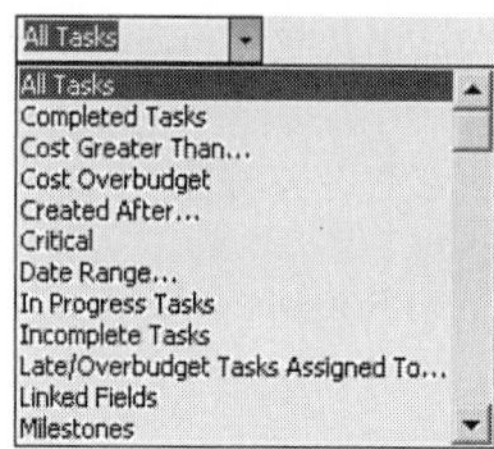

Figure 19.28
The Filter list box on the Formatting toolbar also provides access to filters.

When you apply an interactive filter, a dialog box appears, in which you must supply the values to be used for testing the tasks or resources. For example, Figure 19.29 shows the Using Resource filter dialog box. This filter selects all tasks that are assigned to the resource that you choose from the entry list.

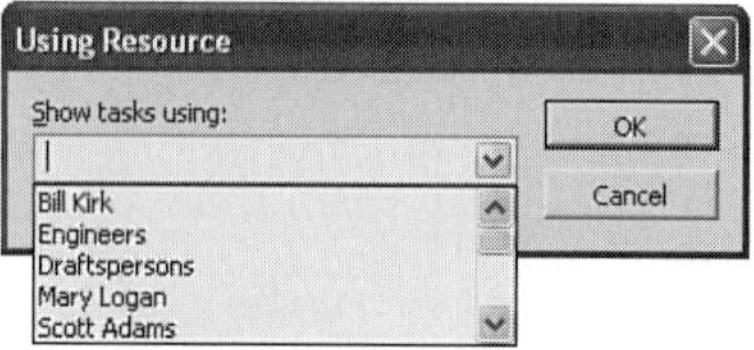

Figure 19.29
The Using Resource filter dialog box allows you to choose from a list of available resources.

When you apply a filter, all tasks or resources that satisfy the filter criteria at that moment are selected. If you change a value in a field, you might change how this value satisfies the filter criteria. The task or resource continues to be displayed or highlighted, though, because the filter criteria are evaluated only at the moment the filter is applied. You need to apply the filter again to see the effects of changes in the project.

NOTE

> You can reapply the filter by pressing Ctrl+F3. You can set a filter back to the default All Tasks or All Resources by pressing F3.

It is important to note that a filter is applied to the view that is currently being displayed and does not affect the list of tasks or resources on other views. For example, if you filter in the Gantt Chart view to see only critical tasks (by applying the Critical filter), and then you switch to the Tracking Gantt view, all tasks are displayed on the Tracking Gantt view, not just the critical tasks. An applied filter stays in effect on the view you applied it to until you remove it. After you have finished using a filtered view, you can remove the filter by selecting the All Tasks filter or the All Resources filter.

Using the Standard Filters

Not every view can be filtered, and there are other limitations to using filters. The following points summarize these limitations:

- You can apply only task filters to task views and only resource filters to resource views.
- You cannot apply a filter to a bottom pane view. The reason is that the bottom pane view is already filtered: It displays only the tasks or resources that are associated with the item or items selected in the top pane.
- The Relationship Diagram view cannot be filtered, but the standard filters are available for all other views.
- You cannot apply a highlight filter to a form. Using a filter as a highlight makes sense only for the views that display lists, because the purpose of a highlight is to make selected items stand out from the rest. Thus, only the views that contain tables can accept highlight filters.
- Each filter considers the entire set of tasks or resources for selection. You cannot use successive filters to progressively narrow the set of selected tasks or resources. For example, if you filter the task list to show milestones, and then you apply the Critical filter, you will see all critical tasks displayed, not just critical milestones. You must either create a filter, edit an existing one, or use the AutoFilter option to use more than one criterion at a time.

→ To learn how to create your own filters, **see** "Creating Custom Filters," **p. 859**.

DESCRIBING THE STANDARD FILTERS

The filters that are supplied with Microsoft Project provide standard selection criteria that are useful in many situations that you will encounter. You might never need to create your own filters. Tables 19.3 and 19.4 describe the standard task filters and resource filters, respectively.

All Tasks

Table 19.4 lists the filters that can be applied to task views. An asterisk (*) indicates that the filter is not found on the standard Project, Filtered For menu but is found instead on the More Filters menu. All filters are listed in the Filter tool on the Formatting toolbar as well. A filter name that is followed by an ellipsis (…) is an interactive filter.

19

TABLE 19.4 THE PREDEFINED TASK FILTERS IN PROJECT

Filter Name	Purpose
All Tasks	Displays all tasks.
Completed Tasks	Displays tasks that are marked as 100% complete.
Confirmed*	Displays tasks for which the requested resources have agreed to take on the assignment.
Cost Greater Than…*	Displays a prompt that asks for the cost to be used in a test for tasks that are greater than that cost.
Cost Overbudget*	Displays all tasks that have a scheduled cost greater than the baseline cost if the baseline cost is greater than 0.

continues

Table 19.4 Continued

Filter Name	Purpose
Created After...*	Displays a prompt that asks for a date to be used in a test for tasks that were created after that date.
Critical	Displays all critical tasks.
Date Range...	Displays a prompt that asks for a range of dates to be used in a test for tasks that either start or finish within that range of dates.
In Progress Tasks*	Displays all tasks that have started but have not finished.
Incomplete Tasks	Displays all tasks that have a percentage complete that is not equal to 100%.
Late/Overbudget Tasks Assigned To...*	Displays a prompt that asks for a resource name to be used in a test for tasks that are assigned to that resource, where the task's finish date is later than the baseline finish or the cost is greater than the baseline cost.
Linked Fields*	Displays all tasks that are linked to other applications.
Milestones	Displays all milestones.
Resource Group...*	Displays all tasks that are assigned to the specified resource group.
Should Start By...*	Displays all tasks that should have started but have not started by a date that the user supplies.
Should Start/Finish By...*	Prompts for a range of dates that are used to display tasks that should have started by the beginning date or should have finished by the end date.
Slipped/Late Progress*	Displays tasks where the finish date is later than the baseline or where the budgeted cost of work scheduled is greater than the budgeted cost of work performed.
Slipping Tasks*	Displays all tasks that are not finished and whose scheduled finish dates are later than the planned finish dates.
Summary Tasks	Displays all tasks that have subordinate tasks defined below them.
Task Range...	Displays all tasks that have ID numbers within a range that is specified by the user.
Tasks with a Task Calendar Assigned*	Displays all tasks that have been assigned task-specific calendars.
Tasks with Attachments*	Shows tasks that have objects attached, such as a graph or a note in the Notes field.
Tasks with Deadlines*	Displays all tasks that are assigned deadline dates that work in conjunction with a task's constraint.
Tasks with Estimated Durations	Displays all tasks where the duration has been marked as estimated, denoted by a ? after the duration.

Filter Name	Purpose
Tasks with Fixed Dates*	Displays all tasks that have constraints other than As Soon As Possible or that have already started.
Tasks/Assignments with Overtime*	Displays all tasks where overtime work has been assigned.
Top Level Tasks*	Displays all highest-level summary tasks.
Unconfirmed*	Displays all tasks for which the requested resources have not yet committed to the task.
Unstarted Tasks*	Displays all tasks that have not yet started. For example, the Actual Start field is still set to NA.
Update Needed*	Displays all tasks that have incurred changes, such as revised start and finish dates or resource reassignments, and that need to be sent for update or confirmation.
Using Resource in Date Range...*	Displays all tasks that use the resource that is named by the user, during the range of dates that is also supplied by the user.
Using Resource...	Displays all tasks that use the resource that is named by the user.
Work Overbudget*	Displays all tasks where the actual hours of work performed are greater than what was planned (the baseline work).

Table 19.5 lists the filters that are available for resource views. Again, an asterisk (*) marks filters that are not found on the standard Project, Filtered For menu but that are found instead on the More Filters menu.

19

TABLE 19.5 THE PREDEFINED RESOURCE FILTERS IN PROJECT

Filter Name	Purpose
All Resources	Displays all resources. This is the default filter.
Confirmed Assignments*	Displays resources who have confirmed their task assignments.
Cost Greater Than...*	Displays resources where the cost is greater than the amount specified by the user.
Cost Overbudget	Displays all resources that have a cost that is greater than the baseline cost.
Date Range...*	Displays resources who have tasks that are occurring during a range of dates that is specified by the user.
Group...	Displays all resources that belong to the group specified by the user (which have the same entry in the Group field).
In Progress Assignments*	Displays resources who have tasks that are being worked on. For example, the tasks have an actual start date but no actual finish.

continues

TABLE 19.5 CONTINUED

Filter Name	Purpose
Linked Fields*	Displays all resources with fields that are linked to other applications.
Overallocated Resources	Displays all resources that are overallocated—for example, resources that have too many hours of work assigned to them during some time period of the project.
Resource Range...	Displays all resources that have ID numbers within the range specified by the user.
Resources—Material	Displays consumable resources that are listed as Material in the Type field.
Resources—Work	Displays resources such as individuals or assets that are listed as Work in the Type field.
Resources with Attachments*	Displays resources that have objects attached or a note in the Notes field.
Resources/Assignments with Overtime*	Displays resources for whom some of the work assigned to is incurred as overtime.
Should Start By...*	Displays resources assigned to tasks that have not started, where the calculated start falls after a date specified by the user.
Should Start/Finish By...*	Displays resources assigned to tasks that have not started, where the start or finish of the task falls between a date range specified by the user.
Slipped/Late Progress*	Displays resources with tasks assigned, where the finish date is later than the baseline or the budgeted cost of work scheduled is greater than the budgeted cost of work performed.
Slipping Assignments*	Displays resources with tasks assigned that are not finished and whose scheduled finish date is later than the planned finish date.
Unconfirmed Assignments*	Displays resources with tasks assigned for which a commitment has not yet been made.
Unstarted Assignments*	Displays all resources assigned to tasks that have not yet started but that have been confirmed. For example, the Actual Start field is still set to NA.
Work Complete*	Displays resources assigned to tasks that are 100% complete.
Work Incomplete*	Displays resources assigned to tasks that have started but are not 100% complete.
Work Overbudget	Displays all resources with scheduled work that is greater than the baseline work.

USING THE AUTOFILTER FEATURE

The AutoFilter feature in Microsoft Project is very similar to the AutoFilter feature in Microsoft Excel. To turn on the AutoFilter feature, you can click the AutoFilter tool on the Formatting toolbar or choose Project, Filtered For, AutoFilter.

When it is enabled, the AutoFilter places a drop-down arrow at the top of each table column and creates a list of unique values in each column (see Figure 19.30). To filter that column, you choose an option from the drop-down menu. The column heading turns blue, to indicate that the column is filtered. You can apply a filter in this way to more than one column in order to perform successive filters. For example, in Figure 19.30 filters have been used to display only the tasks which are assigned to John Melville that are scheduled to last longer than one week.

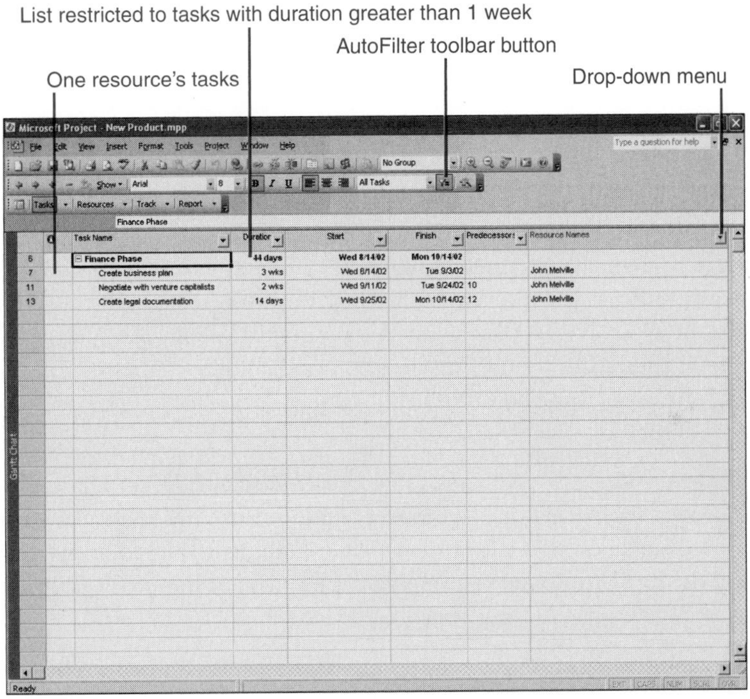

List restricted to tasks with duration greater than 1 week

AutoFilter toolbar button

One resource's tasks

Drop-down menu

Figure 19.30
The AutoFilter tool lets you easily narrow down a list of tasks or resources.

Project includes special options in some lists, depending on the field type. For example, the Duration field has AutoFilter options for values one week or less, more than one week, and so on. Date fields have options for ranges as well—such as this week, this month, and next month (see Figure 19.31).

Each of the drop-down menus also has a custom option that allows you to create and save a filter with more than one condition, using either an And or an Or condition (see Figure 19.31).

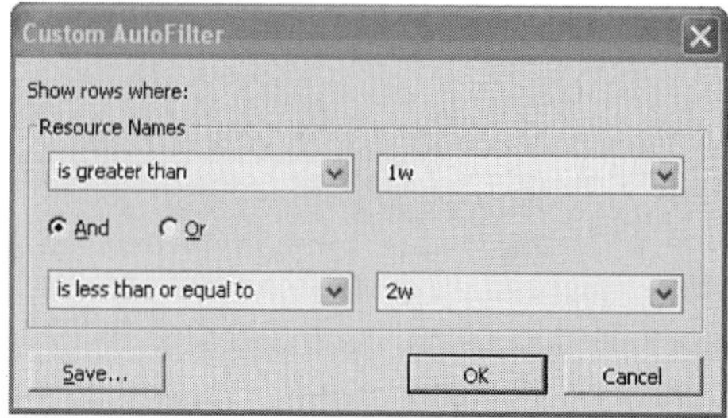

Figure 19.31
Multiple-condition tests can be saved with the Custom AutoFilter option.

➔ For additional information on creating your own specialized filters, **see** "Creating Custom Filters," **p. 859**.

NOTE

> The keystrokes that reapply the filter (Ctrl+F3) and set a filter back to the default All Tasks or All Resources (F3) also work with AutoFilter.

Exploring the Standard Groups

No Group

Another way to organize project information is to apply a *group* definition. Grouping allows you to, for example, create subtotals for numeric data or create a multiple-level, hierarchical structure of data based on some code such as the outline numbering. Applying a group definition rearranges the task or row information onscreen into a temporary outline structure, according to the values in specified Group By fields. In this way, grouping is similar to performing a multilevel sort. You can use the Show Subtasks, Hide Subtasks, and Show Outline Level drop-down list buttons on the Formatting toolbar to show or hide group details.

Group definitions also include value intervals for the Group By fields so you can control subgroup structure. Rolled-up values within subgroups are calculated and displayed on the group total lines. In Figure 19.32, the Cost table is displayed on the Resource Sheet view and the standard Resource grouping has been applied. A project manager could use this view to determine the cost contributions to the project by each level of resource pay rates.

Applying the Standard Groups

Groups, like tables and filters, are designed for task views or resource views, so there are two lists of group definitions. Most, but not all, views can have group definitions applied. The Calendar view and the Resource Graph view are two notable exceptions.

You can apply group definitions either by choosing the group name from the Group By tool on the Standard toolbar or by opening the Project menu and choosing Group By (see Figure 19.33). A cascading list of defined groups appears for you to choose from, or you can choose More Groups to create custom groups. To remove grouping from the view, you choose No Group from the definition list.

Figure 19.32
Applying a Group definition creates a new outline structure and displays rolled-up values.

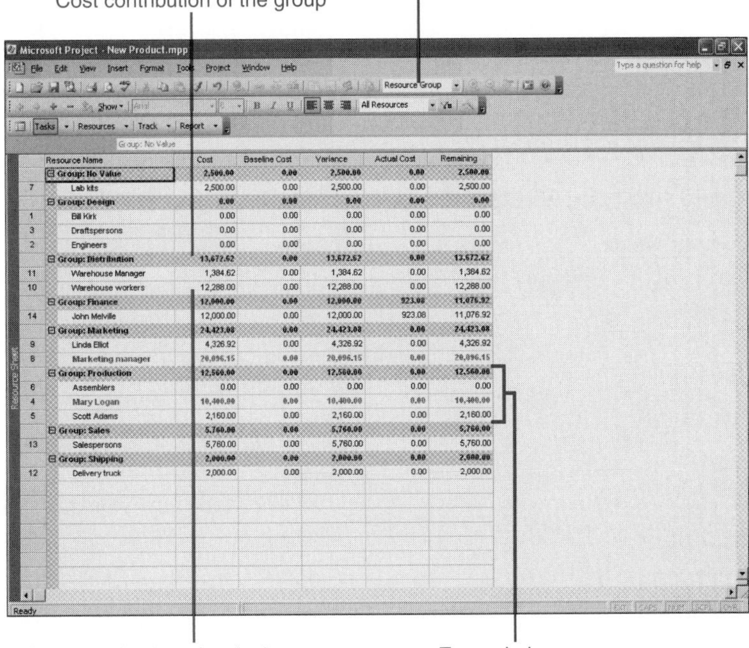

Figure 19.33
The list of group definitions is available under the Project menu.

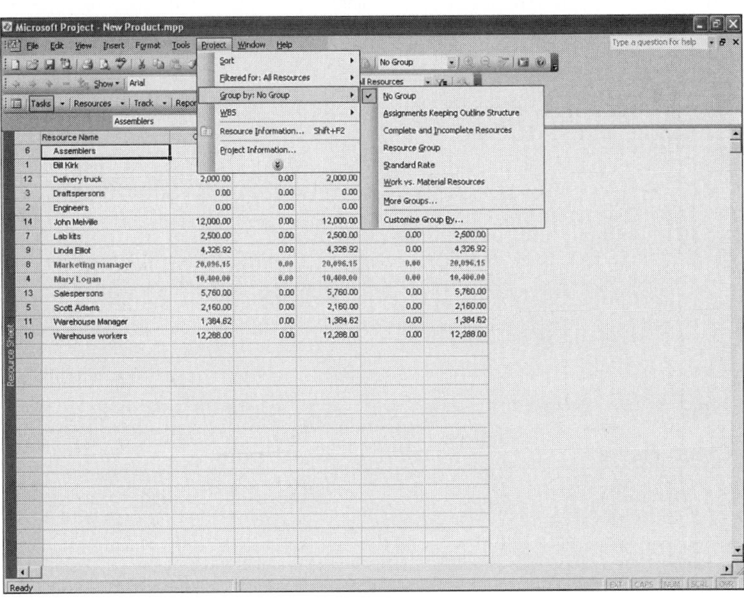

→ For information on techniques for creating custom group definitions, **see** "Creating Custom Groups," **p. 868**.

Describing the Standard Groups

Table 19.6 lists the group definitions that are available for task views. All groups are available either through the Group By button on the Standard toolbar or by choosing Project, Group By.

Table 19.6 The Predefined Task Group Definitions in Project

Group Name	Description
No Group	Removes the applied grouping.
Complete and Incomplete Tasks	Lists tasks not finished in the first group.
Constraint Type	Groups tasks in alphabetical order of constraint type.
Critical	Lists noncritical tasks first.
Duration	Based groups on each unique value in the Duration field.
Duration then Priority	Within the Duration groups, lists tasks lowest priority value first.
Milestones	Lists normal, non-milestone tasks first.
Priority	Groups tasks in Priority value intervals of 100.
Priority Keeping Outline Structure	Maintains outline structure when grouping by Priority values.
Status Request Pending	Lists tasks that do not currently require a status response from a resource first.

19

If a resource view is displayed, the group definition list changes to show only definitions that are applicable to resource data. Table 19.7 lists the group definitions that are available for resource views. One supplied group, Assignments Keeping Outline Structure, can be applied only to the Resource Usage view because it involves both resource and assignment fields. Another supplied definition, Resource Group, uses the group designations entered on the Resource sheet Entry table; do not confuse that group *field* with the Resource Group *definition*. All groups are available either through the Group By button on the Standard toolbar or by choosing Project, Group By.

Table 19.7 The Predefined Resource Group Definitions in Project

Group Name	Description
No Group	Removes the applied grouping.
Assignments Keeping Outline Structure	Groups resource assignments within the task outline structure.
Complete and Incomplete Resources	Lists resources who have not started their assigned work first.

Group Name	Description
Resource Group	Subtotals values based on the Group field entries on the Resource Sheet view.
Response Pending	Lists resources who need to respond to assignment requests last.
Standard Rate	Gives a breakdown of contributions by resource pay scales.
Work vs. Material Resources	Separates and summarizes the two types of project resources.

TROUBLESHOOTING

A Filter Is Not Limiting the Task List

I'm trying to create a filter to show tasks that start between two dates I specify. The filter criteria are set to find tasks with a start date greater than (date 1) and tasks with a start date less than (date 2). Why am I still seeing all my tasks?

Choosing And or Or is a common source of confusion. What you want to do is first select tasks that begin after date 1. Then, using the tasks that passed the first test, narrow the list further by restricting it with an And test. Change the And/Or test in the first column of the filter definition to And.

Filters Are View Specific, but Tables Are Not

In the Gantt Chart view, I filtered for slipping tasks and hid the Indicators column so that it wouldn't print. When I switch to the Tracking Gantt view, the Indicators column is hidden and I don't want it to be, but the filter is not applied and I want that. How are these views related to each other?

The views are independent of one another when you apply filters, but they both use the Entry table to display columns onscreen. An applied filter changes the display only for the view that is onscreen. If you change to another view and want to see it filtered as well, you must apply a filter to it, too. But when you modify a displayed table, you are actually changing the underlying definition of the table. The altered table then shows all views that use that table. To have different tables for different uses—for example, one for printing, one for edit and review—you can create and apply a custom table when needed. See Chapter 21, "Customizing Views, Tables, Fields, Filters, and Groups," for more information.

CHAPTER 20

Formatting Views

In this chapter

Using the Common Format Options in the Standard Views 776

Formatting the Gantt Chart View 790

Formatting the Calendar View 802

Formatting the Network Diagram View 807

Formatting the Task and Resource Form Views 817

Formatting the Resource Graph View 819

Formatting the Resource Usage View 826

Formatting the Task Usage View 829

Formatting the Sheet Views 830

Troubleshooting 830

Using the Common Format Options in the Standard Views

Views are basically broken down into three category types: sheets, forms, and graphical views. Views of the same type share similar customizing options. Sheet and graphical views all contain gridlines; therefore, you can use the Format, Gridlines command to change the appearance of the gridlines in all those views. Many graphical views also contain timescales, and you can also use the Format, Timescale command in those views. Use the Format, Text Styles command to change the font, size, and color of text in views.

Options on the Format menu change the look of the current view. Suppose you change the timescale on the Gantt Chart view to show months instead of days. Until you change the timescale again, you see this format for the timescale each time you display the Gantt Chart view. However, if you switch to another view that also has a timescale (for example, the Resource Usage view), you find that the timescale in that view does not show the changes that were made in the Gantt Chart view but instead reflects the way the Resource Usage view was last displayed.

Sorting the Tasks or Resources in a View

Sorting is especially relevant for views that display tasks or resources in a table or list layout. But you also can sort the order in which tasks or resources appear in the form views as you scroll with the Next and Previous buttons. You cannot sort the displayed items in the Relationship Diagram view, however.

Sorting enables you to arrange lists by a number of predefined fields, as well as a combination of up to three columns or fields that you specify. The predefined fields for sorting vary from one view to another. For example, in a resource view, predefined sort fields include By Cost, By Name, and By ID. The predefined fields in a task view include By Start Date, By Finish Date, By Priority, By Cost, and By ID. To sort the entries in a view, choose Project, Sort. A cascading menu appears, and it contains the predefined sort fields (see Figure 20.1). If you choose from one of these, the tasks or resources are sorted immediately, based on that one field and in ascending order. If you select the Sort By option, the Sort dialog box appears, offering more choices (see Figure 20.2).

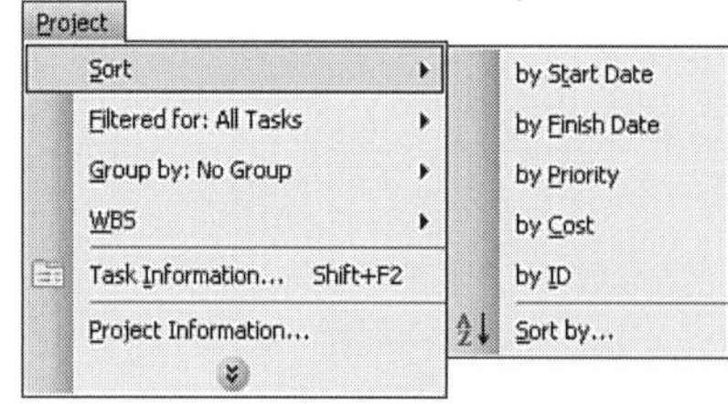

Figure 20.1
The cascading sort list offers easy access for sorting tasks or resources.

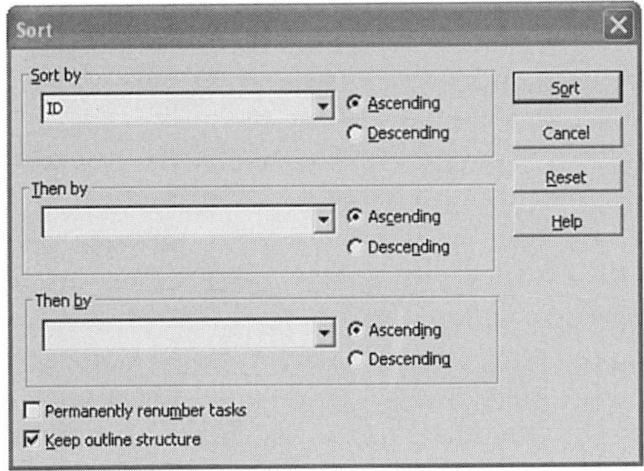

Figure 20.2
The Sort dialog box offers extensive options for sorting.

SELECTING THE SORT KEYS

In the Sort dialog box, you use the drop-down list in the Sort By area to select the major sort field, and then you can select the Ascending or Descending button to specify the sort order. If you want to further sort the list within the groups that are placed together by the first sort field, you can specify the two Then By fields, and indicate the sort order for each of these fields.

In addition to sorting on the predefined fields supplied with Project, you can also sort tasks or resources by custom fields, including outline and Work Breakdown Structure (WBS) codes you create. If a custom field has been renamed, both the generic field name and its alias appear in the sort key lists.

➔ For more information on creating and using custom fields, **see** "Customizing Fields," **p. 847**.

SELECTING THE SORT OPERATION

Although you can undo a sort, it is a good idea to save a project file before sorting, just in case. After you define the fields to sort by, you need to indicate whether you want the sorted tasks or resources to be permanently renumbered; they will be given new ID numbers. For task views, you can also choose to keep all tasks under their summary tasks but sort subordinate tasks within their summary task, by marking the Keep Outline Structure check box. To sort all tasks without regard for their position within an outline, clear this box.

For resource views, there is also a check box for sorting the resources by the projects to which they are assigned. This option is useful when you are using a pool of resources for more than one project.

➔ For more information on sharing a pool of resources, **see** "Sharing Resources Among Projects," **p. 621**.

To sort the list immediately, click the Sort button. To return the sort keys to the standard sort—by ID numbers only—click the Reset button. Note that clicking Reset does not display the original order of the list if Permanently Renumber Tasks was selected.

CAUTION

> Be careful with the Permanently Renumber option. If Project objects such as filters or macros address list items by their ID numbers, permanently renumbering them can have unexpected results.

FORMATTING TEXT DISPLAYS FOR CATEGORIES OF TASKS AND RESOURCES

Most of the views in Microsoft Project enable you to choose special formatting options for displaying text. You can differentiate categories of tasks or resources by the font, type size, style, or color of text used to display the data. For example, you can format names of critical tasks to be displayed in red or milestone task names to appear in italics. Text formatting also defines the appearance that highlight filters apply to items displayed selected by the filter.

→ For more information on highlight filters, **see** "Exploring the Standard Filters," **p. 761**.

To change the display of text for categories of tasks or resources in a view, choose Format, Text Styles. The Text Styles dialog box appears (see Figure 20.3).

NOTE

> If the Text Styles command doesn't appear in the Format menu, you can't change the text display in the current view. To change the text display for selected tasks or resources that don't fall into any particular category, see the section "Formatting Selected Text," later in this chapter.

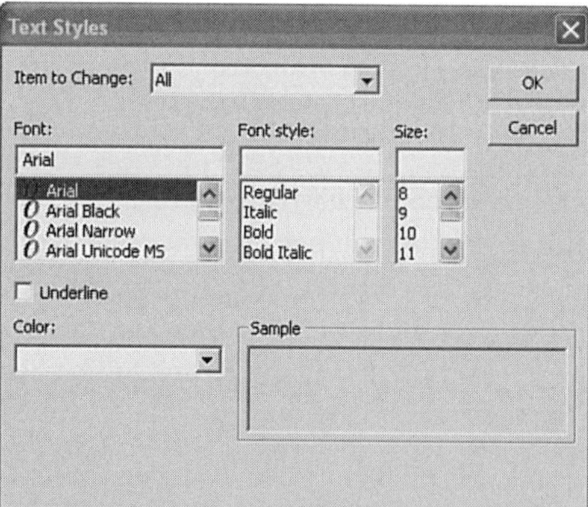

Figure 20.3
You can use the Text Styles dialog box to change text attributes for categories of tasks or resources.

20

CAUTION

> You cannot reverse text formatting changes by using Undo, and there is no Reset button. Regardless of how the changes were made—whether a style was changed, or formatting was manually applied—you must restore the original formatting manually.

SELECTING AN ITEM TO CHANGE

From the Item to Change drop-down list, choose the category you want to format. When a task or resource falls into two or more categories, some items in the list take precedence over others. The following are the task items, listed in descending order of precedence:

- Highlighted tasks
- Marked tasks
- Summary tasks
- Milestone tasks
- Critical tasks

If a Milestone task is also a Critical task, for example, the display is governed by the text format for milestones. If the same task is selected by a highlight filter, the task shows the Highlight task format rather than either the Milestone task or Critical task formatting. A highlighted task is a task that is selected when a filter is applied as a highlighting filter. Choose the Highlight option under Project, Filtered For to display all tasks or resources but apply special formatting to the ones that match the filter criteria.

TIP

> **You can choose to highlight tasks selected by a filter rather than hide tasks that weren't selected. To do so, press the Shift key while choosing a filter under Project, Filtered For. Alternatively, you can select Project, Filtered For, More Filters and use the Highlight button to apply a filter.**

Marked tasks have the logical value Yes in the Marked field of the Project database. You can use the Marked field to manually select tasks of interest without defining a filter or defining a custom field (or when there is no logical test that can be expressed for the filter).

Milestone tasks have the logical value Yes in the Milestone field. The Milestone field is set to Yes when you enter a duration of zero for a task, but you can designate any task as a Milestone task by checking the Mark Task as Milestone check box on the Advanced tab of the Task Information dialog box. You can also place the Milestone and Marked fields in a table for editing purposes.

→ For more information on adding fields to a table, **see** "Using and Creating Tables," **p. 840**.

The All item in the Item to Change drop-down list on the Text Styles dialog box enables you to easily make a change in all text categories at one time. For example, you might use the All item initially to set an overall font type or size. You can then override the font and size on individual categories. If you later choose the All category again, however, and make a change in the font or point size, any of your earlier manual changes are lost.

The items listed after All are specific to tasks or resources, depending on which type of view is currently displayed. After all, those type-specific text categories are items that are specific features of the active view. When the Gantt Chart view is the active view, for example, the first text items listed deal with tasks. After that, the item list includes general formatting options for the view. The following text style items are available for the Gantt Chart view:

- All
- Noncritical Tasks
- Critical Tasks
- Milestone Tasks
- Summary Tasks
- Project Summary Tasks
- Marked Tasks
- Highlighted Tasks
- Row & Column Titles
- Top, Middle, and Bottom (timescale tiers)
- Bar Text - Left
- Bar Text - Right
- Bar Text - Top
- Bar Text - Bottom
- Bar Text - Inside
- External Tasks

The following text style items are available for the Resource Usage view:

- All
- Allocated Resources
- Overallocated Resources
- Highlighted Resources
- Row and Column Titles
- Assignment Row
- Top, Middle, and Bottom (timescale tiers)

CHANGING THE FONT, STYLE, AND COLOR OF TEXT DISPLAYS

The Text Styles dialog box is similar in use and appearance to text formatting dialog boxes in other applications, such as Microsoft Word. You can use the Text Styles dialog box to change the assigned font, font formatting (that is, regular, bold, italic, and bold italic), point size, and color. A single style of underlining is also available in this dialog box. Click Reset to clear any previous formatting choices and return to the default settings for the style.

You use the Color drop-down list in the Text Styles dialog box to choose the color for the selected item's text. If you don't use a color printer, all the colors print as black with grayscale shading. The clear color option causes an item's text to be transparent in the display, although the row for the item still appears onscreen and on paper. Onscreen color provides useful visual clues even if you don't print in color.

FORMATTING SELECTED TEXT

You can make formatting changes to selected text items instead of to categories of styles. To do so, you use the Format, Font command and the Formatting toolbar to apply manual formatting. The choices that are available via the Format, Font command are the same as the choices in the Text Styles dialog box, except that you don't have a choice about what item to change. Changes that you make in this dialog box are made to any tasks that are *selected*, not to categories of tasks or resources.

The Formatting toolbar offers drop-down lists of common formatting options: font and point size; bold, italic, and underlined text; and left, center, and right alignments.

You can copy formatting by using the Format Painter button on the Standard toolbar. To use this button, select the task or resource that has the format you want to copy. Click the Format Painter button. The mouse pointer changes to a cross with a paintbrush attached. Select the tasks or resources to which you want to apply the format, and the formatting is automatically applied when you release the mouse button. Keep in mind that Undo is not available when you are using the Format Painter. If you change your mind about the format, you have to use the Formatting toolbar options or the Format, Font command to reset the changes you made.

NOTE

> **The difference between using Format, Text Styles and applying manual formatting is significant. With manual formatting, you are making changes to selected text only—not to categories of tasks or resources. When additional tasks or resources belonging to a certain category are added, formatting applied by using the Format, Font command, the Formatting toolbar, or the Format Painter are not taken into account.**

FORMATTING GRIDLINES

Gridlines add visual guides on tables and timescales. Many gridlines are drawn by default. Gridlines are drawn between the rows and columns of a table, between column titles, and between units on the timescale. You can add gridlines to views; for example, you can add gridlines between the bars in the Gantt Chart view. A very useful single gridline is the current date that appears by default on several views, including Gantt Chart views. 20

To format gridlines for the current view, choose Format, Gridlines, and the Gridlines dialog box appears (see Figure 20.4). (You can also access the Gridlines dialog box by pointing to any blank area of the Gantt Chart view and right-clicking. The Gridlines option appears on the shortcut menu.) The options in this dialog box vary, depending on the applied view; Figure 20.4 shows the Gridlines dialog box for the Gantt Chart view. Common gridlines are shown in Figure 20.5; in the figure, gridlines that are not displayed by default on the Gantt Chart view are marked with an asterisk (*).

Figure 20.4
You can change the way gridlines look by using the Gridlines dialog box.

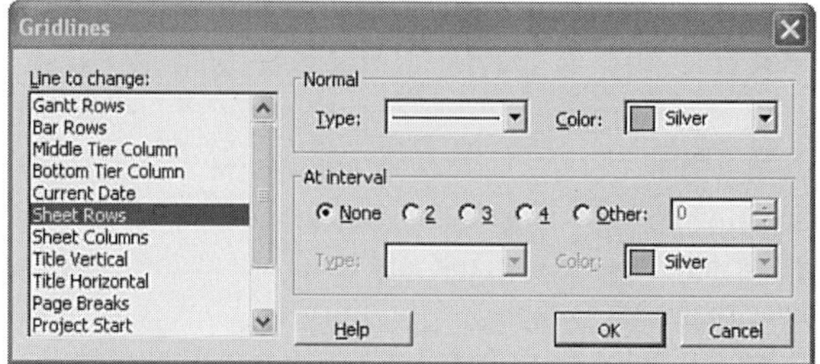

Figure 20.5
Gridlines can add clarity to a view.

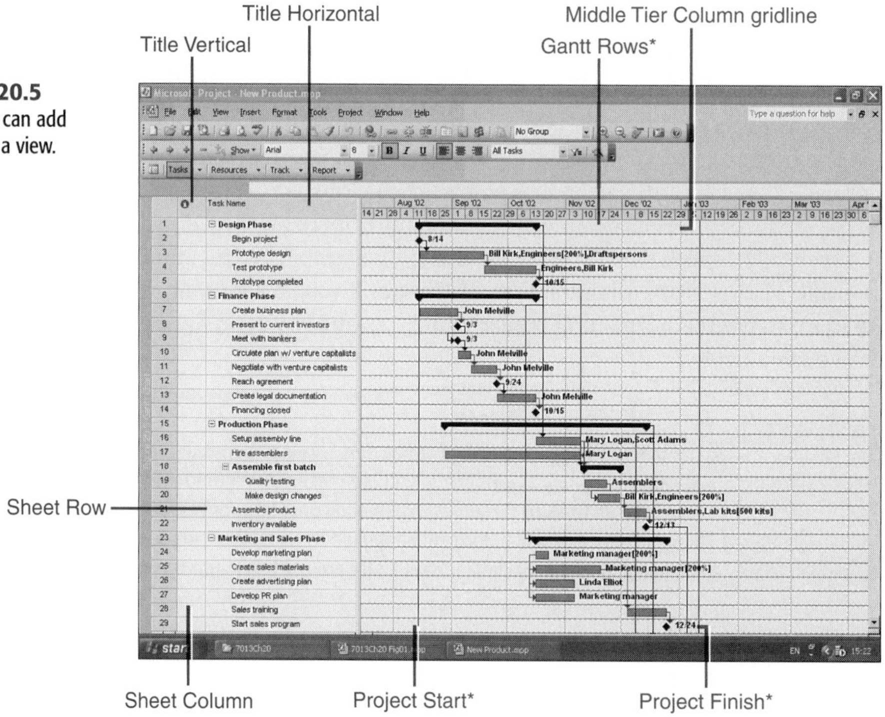

Title Horizontal
Title Vertical
Middle Tier Column gridline
Gantt Rows*
Sheet Row
Sheet Column
Project Start*
Project Finish*

From the Line to Change list in the Gridlines dialog box, choose the kind of gridline you want to change. The settings in the Normal section are applied to every line of the type that you choose, unless a selection in the At Interval section is also active (in which case, a different line and color appear at regular intervals). Only a few line categories can be given a distinguishing interval line type and color. Sheet Row and Sheet Column gridlines in table views, for example, can have intervals, and in the Gantt Chart and the Resource Usage views, rows and columns can have interval colors and line types.

You can use the Type drop-down list in the Normal section of the Gridlines dialog box to choose one of the five options (no line, solid, dotted, small dashes, and large dashes). Use the Color drop-down list section to choose a color. You can select the At Interval line type and color if you want a distinguishing line (if available). You can activate the At Interval Type and Color fields by choosing an interval: Choose 2 for every other row or column, or 3 or 4 for every third or fourth row or column. Or, you can choose Other and type the desired interval number.

USING THE OUTLINE OPTIONS

Views that list tasks (such as the Gantt Chart and Task Sheet views) can display tasks in ways that show information about their places in the outline structure. You can hide or display summary tasks, indent subordinate tasks to show their level in the outline, display outline numbers next to each task, and display summary tasks either with or without a special symbol to show that they have subordinate tasks.

➔ For more information on controlling the task outline, **see** "Outlining the Task List," **p. 154**.

To change the display of outlined tasks, choose Tools, Options. The Options dialog box appears. Click the View tab. The outline display default options are shown in Figure 20.6. Figure 20.7 shows the effects of each of these choices when they are marked.

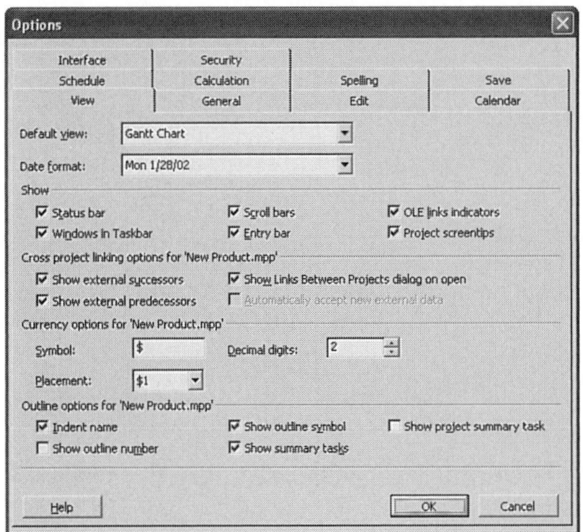

Figure 20.6
Options for displaying outline formatting appear on the View tab of the Options dialog box.

NOTE

Make sure you're in a view that can display outlines (for example, the Gantt Chart view or the Task Sheet view) before you access the Options dialog box. Otherwise, the Outline Options section won't be available.

In the View options dialog box, the Show Summary Tasks option is selected by default, so you see the summary tasks included in the list of tasks. If the Show Summary Tasks check box is not marked, the summary tasks do not appear in the list. If subtasks are hidden when you turn off the summary task display, those subtasks stay hidden. The outlining commands on the Formatting toolbar are not available when summary tasks are not shown. Hiding summary tasks is useful when you're applying filters or sorting a task list.

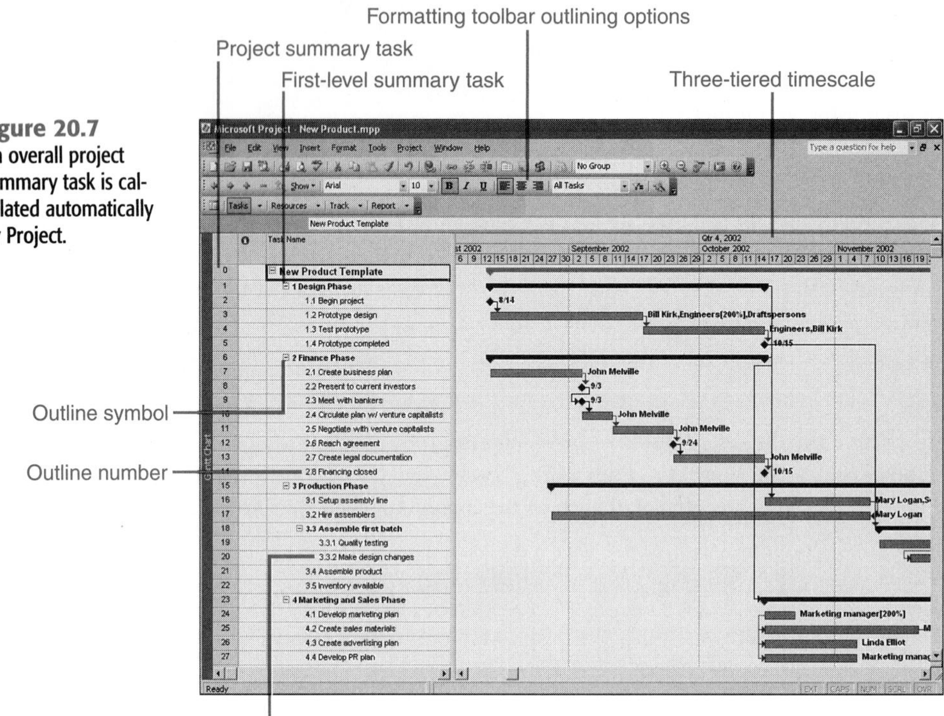

Figure 20.7
An overall project summary task is calculated automatically by Project.

If the Indent Name box is turned off, the indentations are removed and all tasks are aligned at the left margin.

A project summary task is a special task that summarizes and rolls up the entire project. You can choose the Project Summary Task option to display a project summary task at the beginning of the task list (with task ID number 0). This feature is particularly useful when you're consolidating projects.

➔ For information on techniques for consolidating projects, **see** Chapter 16, "Working with Multiple Projects," **p. 603**.

20

If the Show Outline Number check box is selected, each task name is preceded by an outline number that identifies each task's place in the outline. The outline numbering is in the so-called legal style, with each task number including the related summary task numbers. This is the same number you see for WBS codes in the Task Information dialog box on the Advanced tab, unless a custom WBS has been created. If the Show Outline Number check box is not selected, outline numbers are not displayed as part of the task list.

➔ For more information on WBS codes, **see** "Using Custom WBS Codes," **p. 163**.

If the Show Outline Symbol check box is selected, each summary task is preceded by a plus (+) or a minus (–) sign. A plus sign indicates that the summary task has subtasks that are not currently being displayed, and the minus sign indicates that all tasks under the summary task are showing.

TIP

When you are printing reports that include outlined tasks, you can save space by turning off the Indent Name option. If you do this, you should turn on the Show Outline Number option so that you can see your outline structure.

If you experience problems displaying the Outline Symbols then refer to the section "Missing Outline Symbols" in the "Troubleshooting" section at the end of this chapter.

FORMATTING TIMESCALES

Views that display timescales offer you the option of choosing the time units and the date formats for each level of the timescale display. Project 2003 provides three levels, or tiers, to the timescale.

To change the timescale, choose Format, Timescale. The Timescale dialog box appears (see Figure 20.8), with options for defining all three timescale tiers. A sample display area instantly previews what the timescale looks like as you select different options.

TIP

You can also access the Timescale dialog box by double-clicking anywhere timescale units are displayed or by right-clicking the timescale headings and choosing Timescale from the shortcut menu.

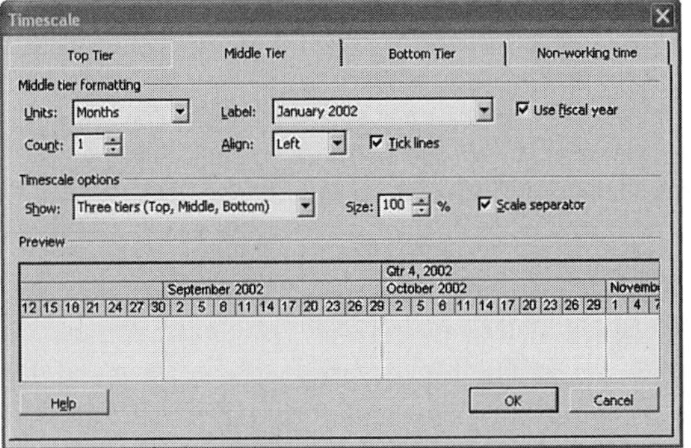

Figure 20.8
You can be very specific about how the timescale is displayed by using the numerous options in the Timescale dialog box.

TIP

You can also use the View, Zoom command to zoom in on a variety of predefined time periods, including the entire project.

20

CHANGING TIMESCALE TIERS

There are three tiers that can be displayed on the timescale—the top, middle, and bottom tiers. In the Timescale dialog box, there is an option to show one or more of these three tiers. If you choose to display a single line on the timescale, it will be defined by the bottom tier settings. Choosing to display two tiers will add the middle tier to the bottom tier display. You can also turn on all three tiers.

You can define the three tiers of the timescale separately, but they are defined within the same dialog box. The only requirements are as follows:

- **The units selected for a tier must be at least as large as the units selected for the tier beneath it.** Specifically, the time span of the lower scale unit, including the periods specified in the Count field, can't be longer than the timescale of the higher tier unit.
- **At least one tier must be displayed.** Project issues a Timescale Error message if you try to close the Timescale dialog box with all tiers hidden.

You can use the Units drop-down list in the Timescale dialog box to choose one of the time period options provided: Years, Half Years, Quarters, Months, Thirds of Months, Weeks, Days, Hours, or Minutes. To include more than one time period within each major unit, choose the Count text box and enter a number other than 1. To have a scale show fortnights (that is, two-week time periods), for example, you would select Weeks as the Units and 2 as the Count. To get the same effect, you could also select Days as the Unit and 14 as the Count. Keep in mind that the Label options are different for weeks and days, and this might influence which format you use.

NOTE

> If the tick lines that separate the units of the scales don't change in the sample area immediately after you change the count, you might need to select the Tick Lines check box twice to refresh the tick line display.

20

To choose the label to display in each major scale time unit, you use the Label drop-down list in the Timescale dialog box. The list of options is extensive and depends on the units selected for the display. You can use three basic types of labels for any of the time units:

- **The specific time period named, such as the year, quarter number, month name or number, and day number**—Many choices are available, including abbreviations, full or partial specifications, numbers, and words. Figure 20.9 shows a partial list of the options available for the Weeks unit.
- **The number of the time periods in the life of the project, starting from the beginning of the project or counting down from the end of the project**—These units are designated with either (From Start) or (From End) as part of the label definition. If the unit is Week 1 (From Start), for example, the time periods are labeled Week 1, Week 2, and so on, if you are counting from the beginning of the project. If you are counting backward from the end of the project, the time periods are labeled Week 40,

Week 39, and so on. This labeling scheme is useful in the early planning stages of a lengthy project, before specific start and finish dates are established, and when a project file is used as a template.

→ For more information on using a file as a project template, **see** "Creating and Using Templates," **p. 103**.

- **No label**—If for some reason you choose to have no label, Project allows you to display the timescale with tick marks only—no labels showing.

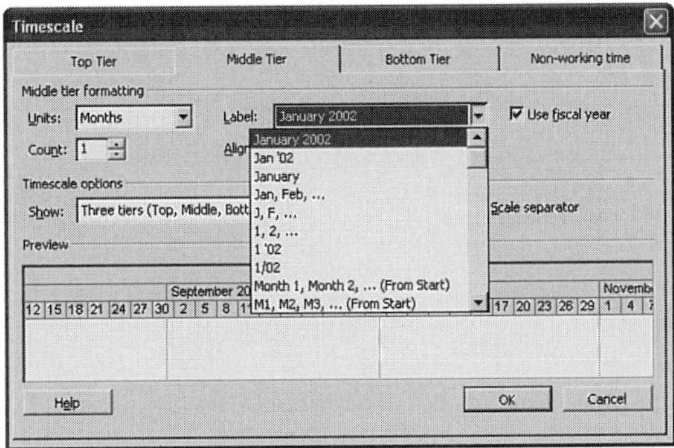

Figure 20.9
Labeling options vary depending on the time unit chosen.

You can center, left-align, or right-align the time unit labels by choosing from the Align drop-down list. Also, you must select the Tick Lines check box in order to display vertical separator tick lines between the larger time unit labels.

Additional settings are available for displaying and labeling periods in a fiscal year format. Each tier can reflect either calendar years (the default) or fiscal years. You must change the Fiscal Year Starts In option on the Calendar tab of the Options dialog box in order to change the month that begins the fiscal year (so that Quarter 1 covers the months used by your organization in its reports). Using the drop-down list, you can change from the default, January, to the month you want to use. If you choose a month other than January, you can select the Use Fiscal Year check box to indicate that you want to use the starting month for fiscal year numbering. Similarly, if you want the week—and the timescale labels—to begin on a day other than Sunday (the default), you must change the Week Starts On item.

COMPLETING THE TIMESCALE DEFINITION

The two options for Size and Scale Separator in the Timescale dialog adjust the overall look of the timescale. To change the width of the timescale units displayed, you choose the Size box and enter an adjustment percentage. For example, if the values in the Resource Usage view are too large to fit within the cells of the lowest displayed timescale units, type **`120`** or **`150`** to enlarge the unit space. Likewise, if you are happy with your timescale settings but you want to shrink the whole view so that more fits on the screen or on paper, you can choose a number smaller than 100%.

You can remove the horizontal line that separates the labels on the tiers. To do so, simply clear the Scale Separator check box.

After you enter all the changes, click OK to put the new timescale format in place. As with other formatting options, the timescale changes affect only the display of the view that was active when you changed the timescale. Each timescale view has its own timescale format.

CAUTION

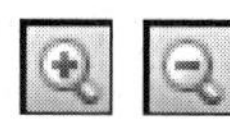

If you have customized your timescale settings, specifically the labels, when you use the Zoom In and Zoom Out buttons in the Standard toolbar or apply a Zoom setting from the View menu, you lose your customized settings.

CHANGING THE DISPLAY OF NONWORKING TIME

Base calendars in Project consist of working days, with default or nondefault work times, and nonworking days. You can use settings on the Nonworking Time tab in the Timescale dialog box to change the way nonworking calendar time is displayed on the Gantt chart. The choices on this tab are shown in Figure 20.10.

CAUTION

Don't confuse the shortcut menu available in the body of the Gantt Chart view with the shortcut menu for the timescale. The shortcut menu for the timescale provides a Change Working Time option that accesses the calendar and enables you to redefine what should be considered nonworking time. The shortcut menu for the body of the Gantt Chart view, on the other hand, provides a Nonworking Time option that simply changes the way nonworking time is displayed.

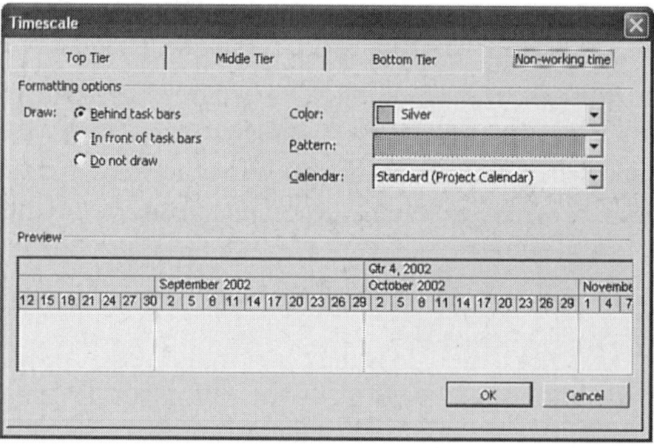

Figure 20.10
You can change or turn off the display of nonworking time on the Gantt Chart view in the Timescale dialog box.

You can choose the calendar for which you want the nonworking time displayed. The Standard calendar is used by default because it is the project's underlying calendar unless a different one has been designated via the Project, Project Information command. You can use the Calendar drop-down list if you want to select and display an individual's resource calendar or an alternative base calendar. The options in the Draw section of the Timescale dialog box determine the way the bars that span nonworking time (evenings and weekends, for example) are drawn. Nonworking time is shaded with a color and pattern of your choice. Whether this time is displayed depends on the timescale format. For example, you can't see nonworking days unless a tier in the timescale displays days or smaller units. But you will see, in zoomed-out settings, any complete weeks marked as nonworking time.

The options for where the shading is drawn include Behind Taskbars (the default), In Front of Taskbars (leaving a gap in the bars), and Do Not Draw. The Do Not Draw option effectively eliminates the shaded display of nonworking time altogether. Nonworking time is still displayed, but the display is no different from that for working time. Taskbars that span nonworking time simply look longer than you might expect from their duration values.

NOTE

> **Choosing the Do Not Draw nonworking time option does not change the Gantt Chart view to a five-day working week. Weekends are still shown—just not in a pattern or color.**

Choosing the display of nonworking time in front of the taskbars helps indicate that the tasks are not being worked on (over weekends, for example). The bars are longer not because the tasks' durations are longer but because they span nonworking time.

If you need to know how to change the Timescale spacing then refer to the section "Configuring Timescale Spacing" in the "Troubleshooting" section at the end of this chapter.

Using Page Breaks

A page break forces the start of a new page when you print the view but has no effect on the screen display, other than displaying an optional dashed line to indicate where the page break falls within the list. You can format the appearance of the page break line by using the Format, Gridlines command.

To force a page break in the views that permit it, select any cell in the row below the intended page break. This row will become the first row on the new page. Then choose Insert, Page Break. To remove a page break, select the row below the page break and choose Insert, Remove Page Break. To remove all page breaks from the view, select all tasks by clicking the Task or Resource Name column heading or by clicking the Select All square above the ID column, before choosing Insert, Remove All Page Breaks. 20

→ For more information on setting page breaks in views, **see** "Printing Views," **p. 493**.

The page breaks that you enter manually are honored by the Print command only if the Manual Page Breaks check box in the Print dialog box is marked. To print the report without using the manually inserted page breaks, clear the check box.

FORMATTING THE GANTT CHART VIEW

The Gantt Chart view is one of the most important presentations in project management reporting. Therefore, many format choices are available for this presentation. You can either format this view yourself or use the Gantt Chart Wizard.

FORMATTING THE GANTT CHART VIEW MANUALLY

The Format menu for Gantt Chart views includes the following options: Font, Bar, Timescale, Gridlines, Gantt Chart Wizard, Text Styles, Bar Styles, and Layout. The options Font, Timescale, Gridlines, and Text Styles are described in previous sections of this chapter. Refer to the appropriate sections for instructions on using these features. The following sections show several ways to change the look of the bar chart in the timescale section of the Gantt Chart view.

USING THE BAR STYLES OPTIONS

One way to change the display of the bar chart section of the Gantt Chart view is to choose Format, Bar Styles. The Bar Styles dialog box appears (see Figure 20.11).

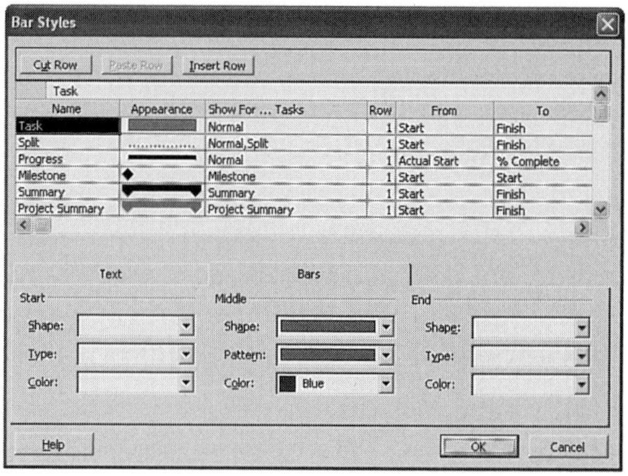

Figure 20.11
You can use the Bar Styles dialog box to change the display of categories of taskbars in the Gantt Chart view.

TIP

> You can also open the Bar Styles dialog box by right-clicking a blank spot on the timescale portion of the Gantt Chart view and choosing Bar Styles from the shortcut menu, or by double-clicking in the Gantt Chart view background.

The top half of the Bar Styles dialog box contains a definition table with rows for each of the bars and symbols that appear in the Gantt Chart view. The bottom half of the dialog box contains two tabs:

- The Bars tab has drop-down lists for specifying the formatted look of the bars and symbols. You can specify the way a bar looks at the start, the end, and in between. The second column in the table at the top of the dialog box displays a sample of the formatted look that you composed.

- The Text tab has options for adding text in various locations around the bars.

To insert a new bar definition within a table, select the row where you want to define the bar and then click the Insert Row button at the top of the dialog box. To delete a bar from the definition, select the row that defines the bar and then click the Cut Row button. You can paste this Cut definition into a new location by selecting the new location and clicking the Paste Row button.

TIP

> There is no Copy Row button; to copy a row, you need to use cut and paste. For example, to create a bar that closely resembles a bar already defined, cut the row to be copied and immediately paste it back to the same location. Then move to the location for the copy and paste the row again. A blank row is inserted, and a copy of the row that you cut is placed in the new position.

SUPPLYING THE BAR NAME

The first column of the definition table in the Bar Styles dialog box is used to enter a name for each bar type. The bar name can be anything you choose. This name is used only in the legend next to the bar symbol when the Gantt Chart view is printed. Type an asterisk (*) in front of the name if you don't want it to print in the legend.

DEFINING THE BAR APPEARANCE

The Appearance column in the Bar Styles dialog box shows what the bar or symbol looks like when the Bars palette definition is applied. You can change the look of the sample by using the Start, Middle, and End sections on the Bars tab at the bottom of the dialog box.

You can define the shape, type, and color of the start shape at the left edge of the bar, and you can define the end shape at the right edge of the bar. Use the Shape drop-down list to scroll the list for the shape you want. Choose the first option, which is blank, if you don't want a symbol to mark the start of the bar. Use the Type drop-down list to choose Dashed, Framed, or Solid. Select a color for the bar from the Color drop-down list.

In the Middle section, use the Shape drop-down list to view the options for the size and height of the bar itself. The list includes no bar at all, a full bar, the top half of a bar, a small bar in the center of the bar space, the bottom half of a bar, and heavy lines at the top, middle, and bottom of the bar space. You can apply a color and fill pattern or shading. The bar can show as an outline only, it can be solid, or it can have any one of nine fill patterns. These bar shapes can overlap. (See the section "Selecting the Row for the Bar," later in this chapter, for an explanation of how Project actually draws bars on the Gantt Chart view.)

TIP

> Bar colors can get lost when you're printing in black and white or when you're faxing a color printout. You should give at least one bar a patterned appearance to help distinguish critical from noncritical tasks.

You must select all the options described here for each bar or symbol that you place on the Gantt Chart view. Before choosing any options at the bottom of the Bar Style dialog box, make sure that the intended task type is selected at the top.

SELECTING THE TASKS THAT DISPLAY THE BAR

In the third column (Show For...Tasks) in the definition table, define the categories of tasks for which the bar should be displayed. When you click in this column, a drop-down list appears. You can choose a bar category from the drop-down list or type the category. If you want to use two or more task categories, separate the task categories' names with commas (or the list separator character specified under Control Panel, Regional Settings).

The Show For drop-down list contains a large number of task types:

- **Normal**—Normal tasks are tasks that are neither Milestone tasks nor Summary tasks. Thus, most tasks display this style.
- **Milestone**—Milestone tasks are identified in Project by the Milestone field, which is automatically set to Yes if a task has zero duration. You can also select the Mark Task as Milestone check box on the Advanced tab of the Task Information dialog box to treat a task as a milestone, and you can clear the box if you don't want a zero-duration task to be treated as a milestone.
- **Summary**—A summary task has one or more subtasks indented under it and is identified by the Yes entry in the Summary task field.
- **Critical**—Critical tasks are tasks on the critical path. Critical tasks are identified by Yes in the Critical task field, and that entry is determined by the task's slack. Normally, if slack is zero or less, the task is marked as critical, but you can change the cutoff point on the Calculation tab of the Options dialog box.
- **Noncritical**—Noncritical tasks are tasks that are not on the critical path—tasks with slack greater than that which defines a critical task.
- **Marked**—The Marked field lets you arbitrarily tag individual tasks for special formatting. You can add the Marked field to any task sheet and enter Yes for the tasks you want to tag.
- **Finished**—Finished tasks are tasks that have an actual finish date (that is, do not have NA in the Actual Finish field).
- **In Progress**—In Progress tasks are tasks that have an actual start date but no actual finish date.
- **Not Finished**—Not Finished tasks are tasks for which the Actual Finish date field contains NA. They include both Not Started and In Progress tasks.

- **Not Started**—Not Started tasks are tasks for which the Actual Start date field contains NA.
- **Started Late**—A Started Late task is a task whose scheduled start (they don't have to have actually started) is later than its baseline start.
- **Finished Late**—A Finished Late task is a task whose scheduled finish is later than its baseline finish.
- **Started Early**—A Started Early task is a task whose scheduled start date is earlier than its baseline start.
- **Finished Early**—A Finished Early task is a task whose scheduled finish is earlier than its baseline finish.
- **Started On Time**—A Started On Time task is a task whose scheduled start is the same as its baseline start.
- **Finished On Time**—A Finished On Time task is a task whose scheduled finish is the same as its baseline finish.
- **Rolled Up**—Rolled Up tasks are tasks that have the Rollup field set to Yes. You can set the Rollup field on the General tab of the Task Information dialog box by selecting the Roll Up Gantt Bar to Summary check box. Note that a summary task does not display rolled-up subtask dates unless the Show Rolled Up Gantt Bars check box on the Summary Task Information dialog is filled for the summary task.
- **Project Summary**—A Project Summary task has task ID number 0, which is displayed only if you select the Project Summary Task option on the View tab of the Options dialog box.
- **Group By Summary**—Group By Summary tasks are temporary tasks created by the Group By command that contain rolled-up values for a selected set of tasks.
- **Split**—Split tasks are tasks that have been split into two or more sections.
- **External Tasks**—External Tasks are "phantom" tasks that represent tasks in other projects that are linked as predecessors or successors to tasks in the current project.
- **Flag1...Flag20**—Flag tasks are tasks that have a custom Flag field set to Yes. You can add a Flag field to any task sheet for data entry.

20

Every task falls into one of the first three categories: Normal, Milestone, or Summary. You could use these three kinds of tasks in combination with the other types in the list to more narrowly define specific types of tasks—for example, you could call tasks Normal, Critical and Normal, Noncritical instead of just Normal (which includes both Critical and Noncritical tasks).

If a task falls into more than one category, it shows the formatting features of both categories (for example, Normal and Critical). If one formatting feature would overwrite another, the feature that is lowest in the definition table is applied last and remains visible in the display.

To select all tasks except the type that is named, you can place the word *Not* before the type name (for example, Not Summary, Not Milestone, or Not Rolled Up).

SELECTING THE ROW FOR THE BAR

Each task can have up to four distinct (that is, non-overlapping) bars drawn for it. Normally, you use only Row 1. That means there is only one row of bars for each task. If you define multiple bar styles that apply to a task, those styles are all drawn on that same row. The styles at the top of the table are drawn first, and any styles lower in the table that apply to the same task are drawn to overwrite them. If the overwriting bar is as large as the one it overwrites, it completely hides the overwritten bar. If it is smaller, you see them both. That's why the standard progress bar appears to be in the middle of the standard taskbar. The Progress style is on a lower row in the style table than the Task style, but two styles are both drawn to Row 1. Therefore, the progress bar appears to be on top of the taskbar.

If you want to show multiple styles for the same task side-by-side, you define them to occupy different rows. For example, if you wanted to see a bar for the task's early start and early finish dates, another bar for its late start and late finish dates, and a third bar for the scheduled dates, you could define a style for Row 1 that shows bars for the early start and finish dates, a style for Row 2 that shows bars for the late start and finish dates, and a style for Row 3 that shows the scheduled dates. You can define up to four rows for different styles for each task definition if you don't want the styles to overwrite each other.

DEFINING THE LENGTH OF THE BAR

The length and placement of every bar or symbol on the Gantt Chart are determined by entries in the From and To columns of the definition table at the top of the Bar Styles dialog box. You can use date fields or one of several measures of time (for example, Percent Complete, Total Slack, Actual Start). Choose an entry from the drop-down lists. The choices in the drop-down lists for these columns appear in the following list, with an explanation of how they are calculated:

- **Start and Finish**—The dates and times when a task is currently scheduled to start or finish.
- **Baseline Start and Baseline Finish**—The planned start and finish dates for a task that you save as part of the baseline. These fields contain NA if you have not saved the baseline (or if you have edited the field directly in a table).
- **Actual Start and Actual Finish**—The dates and times recorded for the start and finish of actual work on a task.(See more on these fields in the "Selecting a Progress Bar Style" section later in this chapter.)
- **Start1–Start10 and Finish1–Finish10**—There are 10 custom start and finish date fields that you can use to store additional task date information. When you save interim schedules, Project stores them in these fields. So, a style to show Interim Plan 1 would include a bar drawn from Start1 to Finish1.
- **BaselineStart1–10 and BaselineFinish1–10**—Project 2003 can store multiple baselines, which include Start, Finish, Duration, Work, and Cost fields for a task with each supplemental baseline. These date fields are similar in concept to the Start1–Finish1 fields described previously.

- **Deadline**—The date you entered as a deadline for a task (as opposed to defining a date constraint for the task), indicating when you want the task to be completed. It uses the same field as the From and To entries since the deadline date is a single point in time.
- **Preleveled Start and Preleveled Finish**—The scheduled start and finish dates for a task, just before the last resource leveling was performed.
- **Early Start and Early Finish**—Early Start is the earliest possible start date for a task, given the start of the project, the schedule for its predecessors, the calendar, and any constraints that may be imposed on the task. Early Finish is the earliest possible finish date for the task, given the task's Early Start date, its Duration, and its linking relationships.
- **Late Start and Late Finish**—Late Start is the latest start date for the task that would not delay the finish of the project. Late Finish is the latest finish date for the task that would not delay the finish of the project. If you define a Deadline date for the task, that date becomes the Late Finish date.
- **Free Slack**—Free Slack is a duration value and is the amount of time that a task can be delayed without affecting the schedule of any other task. In the Leveling Gantt view, the Slack style is drawn from the Finish to Free Slack—meaning that the bar starts at the task's finish date and is as long as the duration in the Free Slack field.
- **Negative Slack**—This is an amount of time that needs to be saved in order to avoid delaying any successor task. Negative Slack indicates that there is not enough time scheduled for the task. It is usually the From column value and is paired with the Start date in the To column.
- **Physical % Complete**—A field called Physical % Complete measures work progress against a stated goal, but does not affect duration or percentage-complete calculations. It is usually selected as the To value and paired with Actual Start as the From value.
- **Total Slack**—For fixed start date projects, Total Slack is the amount of time that a task's finish can be delayed (that is, scheduled for later) without delaying the finish of the project or causing a successor task's constraint to be violated. It is usually the To value and paired with the scheduled Finish date as the From value.

SELECTING A PROGRESS BAR STYLE

Progress bar styles are designed to show how much of a task has been completed. They should always be drawn from the Actual Start date. When a task is first created, the Actual Start and Actual Finish fields contain NA. As soon as you record that a task has started or finished, the NAs are replaced by the appropriate dates.

Many of the To field options for progress bars are the same as for other types of bars. A few fields warrant special discussion:

- **% Complete**—This field draws a progress bar whose length is proportional (as measured by % Complete) to the taskbar that is drawn from the task start to finish. In other words, if the task % Complete value is 40%, the progress bar is exactly 40% as long as the taskbar that's drawn from the task start to the task finish.

- **% Work Complete**—This field draws a progress bar whose length is proportional (as measured by % Work Complete) to the taskbar that is drawn from the task start to finish. This field is fairly straightforward. Normally, the task % Work Complete is the task actual work divided by the task total work.
- **Complete Through**—This field is the standard for normal tasks. Project adds the actual duration for the task to the actual start date to determine the end of the bar. Although Project maintains the Complete Through field internally, it is only available to you as a selection in the From and To columns of bar styles. You can't display it as text in any view.
- **Stop** and **Resume**—When you record actual work for a resource assignment, Project places the date and time when the actual work finished in the task Stop field and it places that same date and time in the task Resume field. You can select Resume in the To column to draw a progress bar that shows the earliest date when work needs to resume on any assignment. The Resume bar gives very little information about the overall progress of the task. You might find occasion to draw a bar from the Resume date to the scheduled finish of the task to show the span of time during which some work still needs to be done.
- **Summary Progress**—This field applies to summary tasks. Just as with normal tasks, the Complete Through progress bar adds the actual duration to the actual start date. Also like normal tasks, the % Complete bar is drawn to the exact proportion of the summary task duration that the % Complete field indicates. The % Work Complete bar compares the amount of completed and uncompleted work. The Resume bar uses the earliest Resume date of any subtask.

TIP

Choosing from the drop-down list for From and To requires a strong knowledge of what each of these dates represents. A complete description of Project database fields is available in the Reference section of online Help, under Help, Contents and Index.

20

PLACING TEXT IN A BAR CHART

The Text tab of the Bar Styles dialog box lets you specify field data to be displayed at the left, right, top, and bottom of the bar, as well as inside the bar. You can't type text in these areas yourself; you can only designate fields that contain text (including dates, durations, percentages, and other numeric values) to be displayed. Any custom fields you have defined and entered data into can also be displayed around the bars.

→ For more information on defining and using custom fields, **see** "Customizing Fields," **p. 847**.

One common modification made to Gantt Charts is to display resource initials, rather than full resource names, next to the tasks to which they are assigned. As shown in Figure 20.12, this change can produce a less-cluttered chart in the Gantt Chart view.

If you want to add text to taskbars then refer to the section "Adding Text to Taskbars" in the "Troubleshooting" section at the end of this chapter.

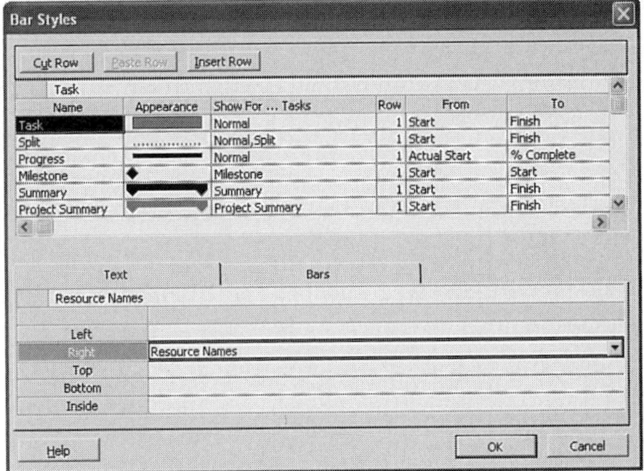

Figure 20.12
You can use the Text tab of the Bar Styles dialog box to place text from fields around the bars of the Gantt Chart view.

To select a field to be displayed beside a bar, select the bar row in the top of the Bar Styles dialog box, choose the Text tab, select one of the five rows for the desired text position on the bar, and select the name from the drop-down list. Click OK to accept the changes or click Cancel to close the dialog box without implementing the changes.

APPLYING MANUAL FORMATTING TO SELECTED BARS

You can choose to change the appearance of bars for only selected tasks instead of redefining a bar style. Choose Format, Bar to open the Format Bar dialog box, shown in Figure 20.13. Notice that this dialog box is essentially the same as the lower portion of the Bar Styles dialog box. The task definition portion is omitted because changes here are applied not to task types but only to tasks that you select before you open this dialog box.

For more information on changing the appearance of a taskbar refer to the section "Formatting the Taskbar" in the "Troubleshooting" section at the end of this chapter.

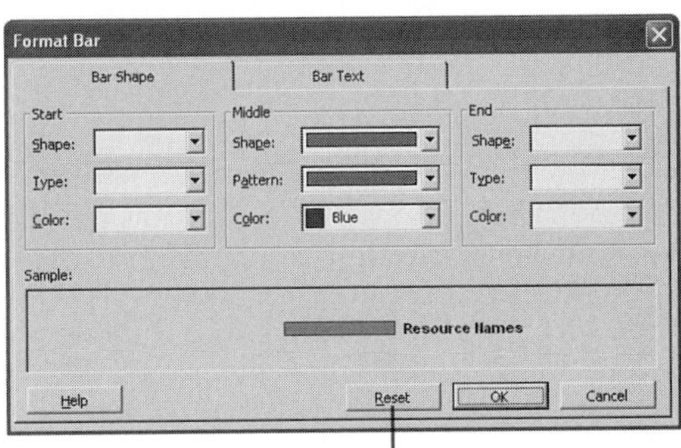

Return selected tasks to their default Bar Styles formatting

Figure 20.13
You can make selected taskbars stand out with formatting of their own.

Changes made in the Format Bar dialog box are considered to be manual formatting. There is no Undo operation available for these changes. To return a taskbar to its original formatting, you must select the modified tasks again and return to this dialog to reapply the standard settings. Project includes a Reset button in the Format Bar dialog box to make this step easy.

Changing the Layout of the Gantt Chart View

You can change the way bars are displayed in the Gantt Chart view by selecting Format, Layout. The Layout dialog box appears (see Figure 20.14). (You can also open this dialog box by right-clicking an open area on the timescale side of the Gantt Chart—not on a bar or timescale label—and choosing Layout from the shortcut menu.)

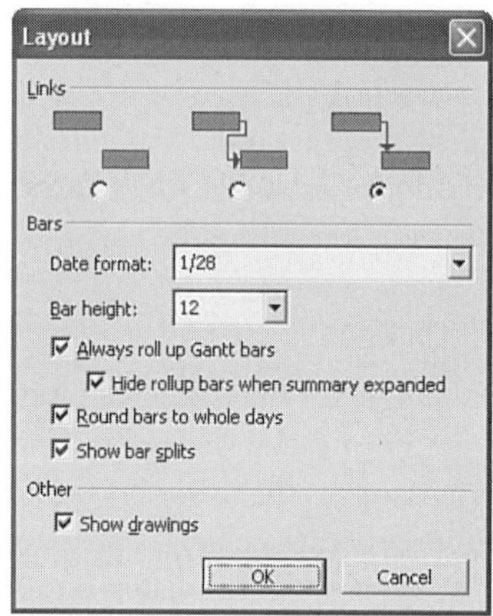

Figure 20.14
You can use the Layout dialog box to further define the appearance of taskbars in the Gantt Chart view.

The task linking lines can sometimes be distracting, particularly when the task list is sorted in non-ID order (for example, by Start date). You can turn off linking lines in the Links section of the Layout dialog box. You can also choose between two styles of lines: straight (the default setting)and rectilinear.

20

When dates are displayed as text around the bars, the Date Format option controls how the dates are displayed. You can choose an available format from the drop-down list. This doesn't change the default format for dates displayed elsewhere in the project, such as the Start or Finish fields. The first option on this list is Default, which returns you to the same format as specified on the View tab of the Options dialog box.

Use the Bar Height drop-down list to choose a vertical size for the bars. Sizes vary from 6 to 24 points, with a default of 12.

Project provides an easy method for designating that all tasks should be rolled up and represented on summary tasks. In the Layout dialog box, the Always Roll Up Gantt Bars option forces all tasks to behave as if the Roll Up Gantt Bar to Summary option in the Task Information dialog box has been turned on. When you select this option, milestone indicators and bars connecting subtask start and finish dates are drawn on the respective summary tasks.

The option Hide Rollup Bars When Summary Expanded eliminates the display of the summary bar itself when summary tasks are collapsed. The familiar black bar with down-pointing end shapes is not displayed under the rolled-up bars and markers. In addition, when summary tasks are expanded and the subtasks are visible, there are no rollup indicators drawn on the summary taskbars.

In Figure 20.15, the Layout options have been set to Always Roll Up Gantt Bars and to Hide Rollup Bars When Summary Expanded. Note the difference in the appearances of the bars for Summary Tasks 1 and 6.

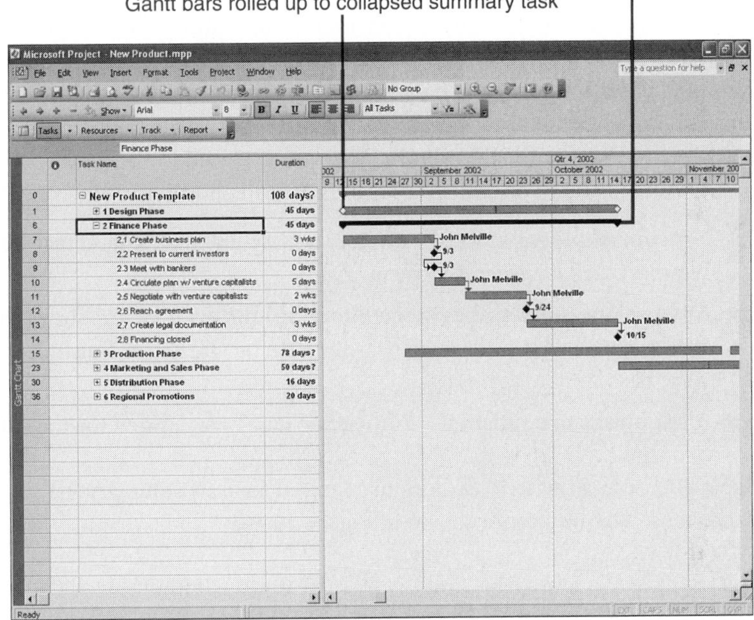

Figure 20.15
Summary tasks can show rolled-up markers for their subtasks.

The Round Bars to Whole Days option determines how tasks with a duration less than the time period in the lowest displayed timescale tier are displayed. For example, if a task with a duration of five hours is displayed in a Gantt Chart view with the bottom tier set to days and this box is not selected, then the bar displays a length of exactly five hours. If the Round Bars to Whole Days check box is selected, the bar extends to a full day. Only the display of the task is modified; the actual duration and calculated start and finish dates remain the same.

The Show Bar Splits check box instructs Project to change the display of tasks that have been split. If this box is not checked, the taskbar simply extends the duration of the task from start to finish, including the split. If this box is turned on, Project creates a gap in the bar for a split task and the split-off pieces are connected visually with a dotted line. The Show Drawings check box enables you to place graphics on the Gantt Chart.

→ For more information on including drawn objects on a Gantt chart, **see** "Adding Graphics and Text to Gantt Charts," **p. 247**.

A Bar Styles Definition Example

For summary tasks, you might find it useful to define styles that give a clear indication of the overall progress for the group of summarized subtasks. This would be helpful, for example, if you hid all subtasks to look at the big picture and just focused on the major phases of the project. Because summary tasks normally all look the same, no matter how many of their subtasks are completed, this customization would provide more information than the standard display. You could see at a glance which phases are completed, which are started but not finished, and which have not started yet.

If you want different summary task styles for different conditions, you must define a different style row for each condition that might occur. If all these custom styles are to be used for a single type of task (in this example, they will be applied to all summary tasks), the conditions would have to always occur in the same order over the lifecycle of the task. This is necessary so that the final condition for a task is placed lowest in the rows of styles, and will overwrite the earlier conditions. There are three conditions in the summary task lifecycle:

- **No subtasks have started**—Neither the Actual Start nor Actual Finish fields for the summary task have dates in them.
- **At least one subtask has started (and might even be finished), but not all subtasks are finished**—There is an actual start date but no actual finish date yet for the summary task.
- **All subtasks are finished**—Both actual dates are defined for the summary task.

Table 20.1 shows the style definitions required to draw summary bars representing changing conditions. The results are shown in Figure 20.16.

Table 20.1 Summary Task Progress Bar Styles

Task Name	Bar Appearance Start	Middle	End	Show For	Row	From	To
Summary: Not Started	Framed, dark gray	Gray bar, solid	Framed, dark gray	Summary	1	Start	Finish
Summary: Started	Solid, black	Gray bar, solid	Framed, dark gray	Summary	1	Actual Start	Finish
Summary: Finished	Solid, black	Black bar, solid	Solid, black	Summary	1	Actual Start	Actual Finish
Summary: Progress	None	Black bar, solid	None	Summary	1	Actual Start	Complete Through

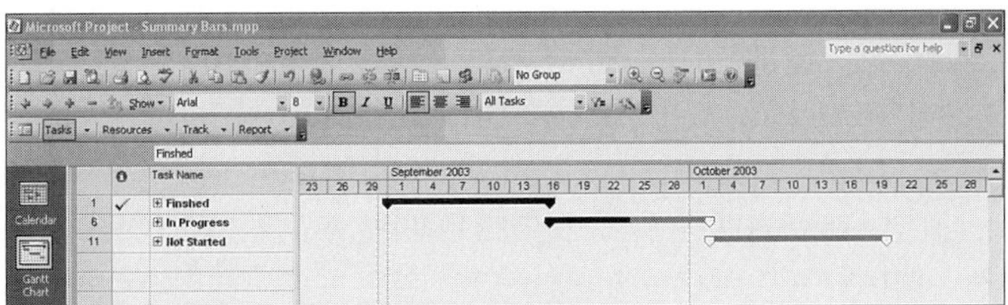

Figure 20.16
You can create multiple styles for a single Gantt Chart bar to apply formatting based on changing conditions.

USING THE GANTT CHART WIZARD

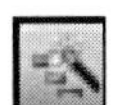

A wizard in Project makes formatting the bars in a Gantt chart extremely easy. The Gantt Chart Wizard walks you through the various formatting options, asking questions about how you would like to have the bars displayed. The options are basically the same as those covered in the previous section "Formatting the Gantt Chart View Manually," but the wizard takes you through the process step by step. To access the Gantt Chart Wizard, you can choose Format, Gantt Chart Wizard; use the Gantt Chart Wizard button on the Formatting toolbar; or choose Gantt Chart Wizard from the Gantt Chart shortcut menu (accessed by right-clicking any blank area of the Gantt chart).

CAUTION

Changes made via the Gantt Chart Wizard are applied to the Gantt Chart that is currently displayed onscreen. If you run the wizard on the supplied Gantt Chart view, the default formatting will be lost. Instead, it is recommended that you make a copy of the standard Gantt Chart and modify the copy. Choose View, More Views, Gantt Chart, and Copy. Then apply the copy and run the wizard.

When you start the wizard, you are presented with a welcome screen. Click the Next button to see the first set of choices (see Figure 20.17). As you make each choice, you are taken to the next appropriate step, depending on your choice. Simply choose the desired option, and then click the Next button to move to the next step. You can click Back, Cancel, or Finish at any time. If you are unsure as to the meaning of a particular option, click the Help button in the dialog box title bar and then click the option about which you have a question.

20

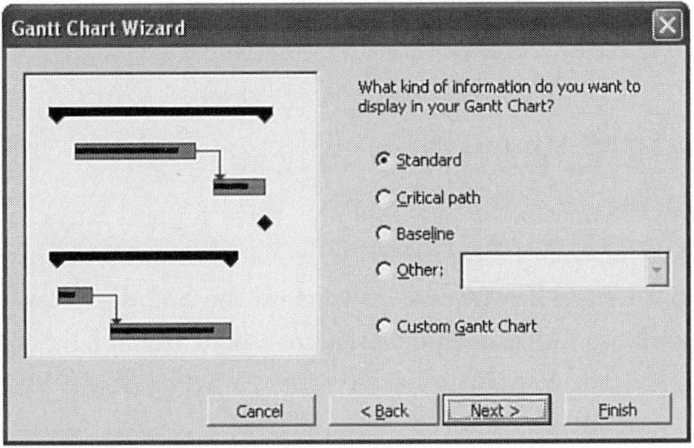

Figure 20.17
The Gantt Chart Wizard walks you through formatting options for the Gantt Chart view.

The first decision requires selecting the basic way that tasks are displayed. Your choice here acts as a starting point for setting up the format of the bars on the Gantt chart. The possible starting format options are as follows:

- **Standard**—This is the same as the default Gantt Chart. At any time you can run the wizard again and choose Standard to undo any changes you've made to a Gantt chart.
- **Critical Path**—When you select this option, critical tasks—that is, tasks that must be completed on time in order to meet the project deadline—are displayed in red. This is a helpful view to use when you're trying to reduce the total duration of a project (referred to as "crashing the schedule").
- **Baseline**—When this option is selected, two bars per task show the original and current schedules (similar to the supplied Tracking Gantt Chart view). This is an appropriate choice when you're tracking a project that is already underway.
- **Other**—This option offers a list of 13 predefined formats you can use as is or modify as desired.
- **Custom Gantt Chart**—This option offers the most extensive choices and walks through all choices for formatting, one step at a time. These options include choices for the colors, patterns, and shapes of Critical, Normal, Summary, and Milestone tasks. You also have options for adding bars for baseline information or slack and for placing text next to bars.

Regardless of your starting format, the wizard prompts you for the kind of text to display in and around the bars. Not all database fields are available via the drop-down lists in the wizard. There are custom choices that allow for distinct definitions of the text formats for Normal, Summary, and Milestone tasks.

The final wizard question asks whether the linking lines should be drawn to display dependency relationships between the taskbars. After you have made all your choices, click Finish, then Format It, and then the Exit Wizard buttons.

TIP

> If you are in doubt about the formatting you want on a Gantt Chart, or if you are unfamiliar with the extensive formatting options available, use the wizard as your starting point. After you exit the wizard, you can use the Bar Styles and Text Styles dialog boxes to tweak your design.

FORMATTING THE CALENDAR VIEW

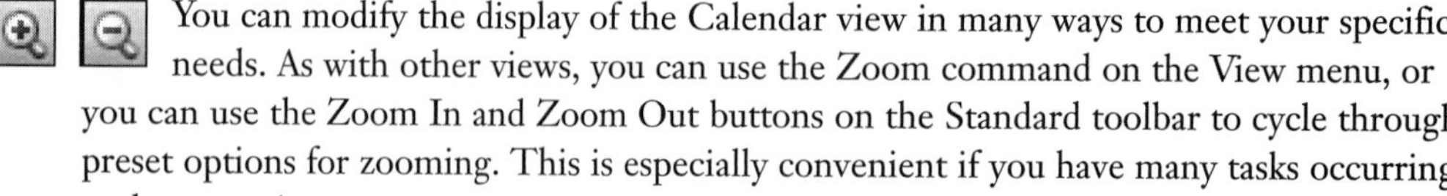

You can modify the display of the Calendar view in many ways to meet your specific needs. As with other views, you can use the Zoom command on the View menu, or you can use the Zoom In and Zoom Out buttons on the Standard toolbar to cycle through preset options for zooming. This is especially convenient if you have many tasks occurring at the same time.

You can change the height and width of the squares where the dates are displayed in a number of ways by using your mouse. If you use your mouse to point to any vertical line in the calendar, the mouse pointer changes to a double-headed arrow. Drag left or right to narrow or widen the column. Likewise, if you point to a horizontal line, the mouse pointer again changes to a double-headed arrow, indicating that you can drag up or down to make the date box taller or shorter (see Figure 20.18). This is particularly useful when you have more tasks on a given day than can be displayed at once.

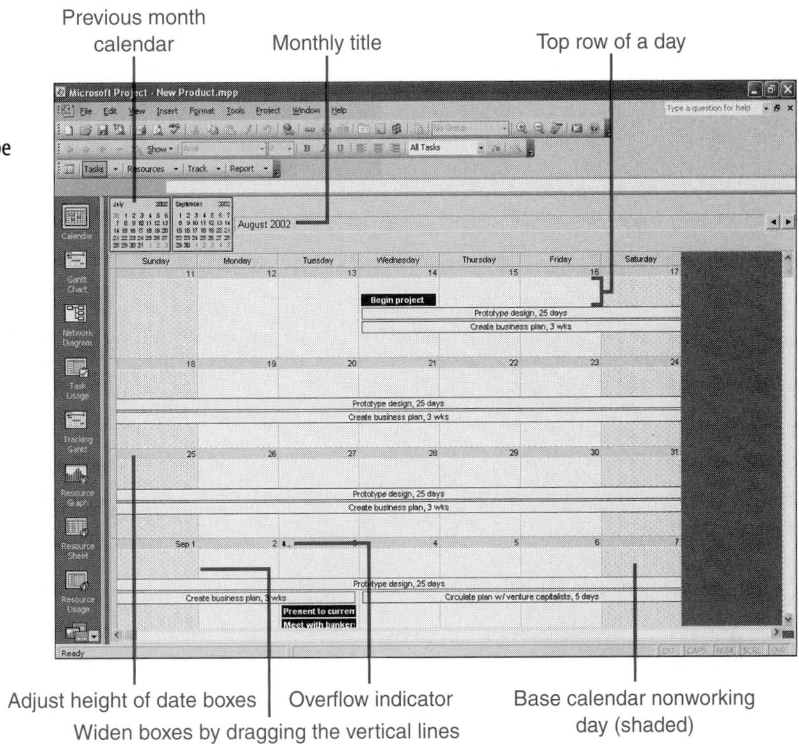

Figure 20.18 Date boxes on the Calendar view can be expanded to show more tasks per day.

The options that are available on the Format menu for the Calendar view include Timescale, Gridlines, Text Styles, Bar Styles, Layout, and Layout Now. The Text Styles and Gridlines options are the same as those discussed in previous sections of this chapter. The options Timescale, Bar Styles, and Layout are unique to the Calendar view and are discussed in detail in the following sections.

FORMATTING THE TIMESCALE FOR THE CALENDAR

You can display the Timescale dialog box by choosing Format, Timescale, or you can use the shortcut menu by right-clicking any spot other than a specific bar in the calendar portion of the view (not the headings). The Timescale dialog box, shown in Figure 20.19, has three tabs that offer choices for headings and titles, for additional data elements that can appear in the date boxes, and for applying shading on certain days.

Figure 20.19
Options in the Timescale dialog box for the Calendar view are very different from those for the Gantt Chart views.

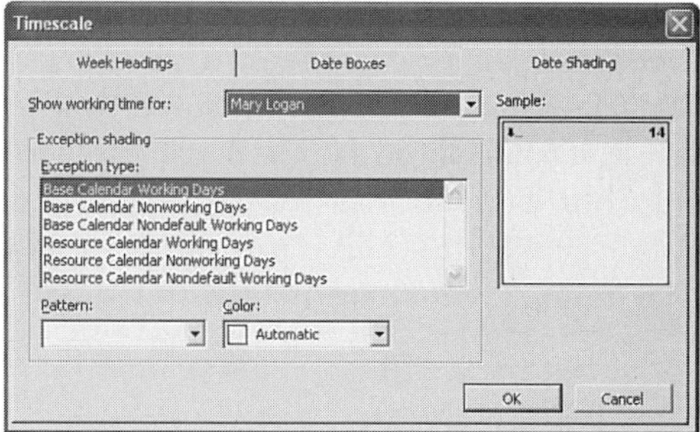

The Week Headings tab provides choices of labels for the month, for the days of the week, and for each week. In addition, you can choose to display a five- or seven-day week, and you can include small calendars for the previous and next months.

The Date Boxes tab enables you to place additional data elements in the top or bottom row of each individual date box. You can also apply patterns and colors for emphasis. The default setting omits a display for the bottom row and includes in the top row an overflow indicator and the date. The overflow indicator appears when all tasks that are scheduled to occur on a given day can't be displayed within the date box. When you print the calendar, overflow tasks appear on a separate page.

On the Date Shading tab (refer to Figure 20.19) you can shade a variety of categories of working or nonworking dates. In the Show Working Time For drop-down list, you can select a base or resource calendar as the starting point. Then choose an exception type, such as nonworking days or a resource's calendar, and apply a pattern and a color to make a visual distinction. A sample is displayed on the right as you make your choices.

To create Figure 20.20, the resource calendar for Mary Logan is used as the starting point. Mary's nonworking days have been formatted in horizontal stripes by defining the resource calendar nonworking time. The Using Resource... filter has been applied so that only Mary's tasks are displayed.

Selecting Calendar Bar Styles Options

As with the Gantt Chart view, with the Calendar view you have control over how the bars in the calendar appear, including text that can be displayed as part of the bars. You can access the Bar Styles dialog box by choosing Format, Bar Styles, or you can use the shortcut menu by right-clicking any spot other than a specific bar in the calendar portion of the view (not the headings). Then select the Bar Styles option. The Bar Styles dialog box appears (see Figure 20.21).

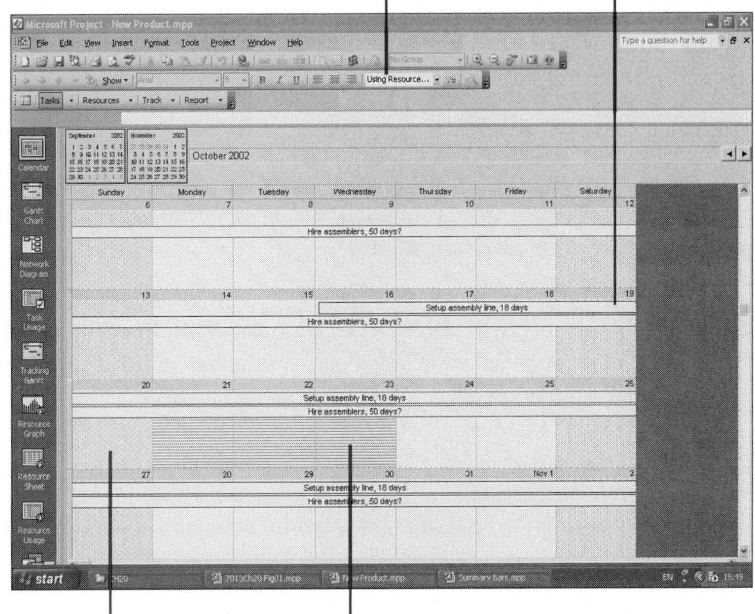

Figure 20.20
You can indicate working and non-working days on the Calendar view with options in the Date Shading tab of the Timescale dialog box.

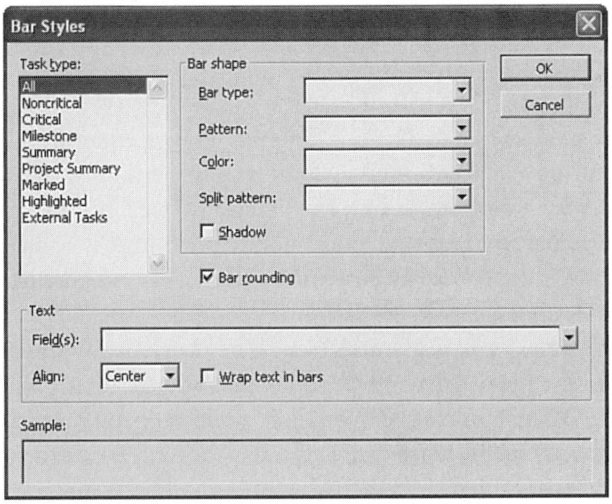

Figure 20.21
The Bar Styles dialog box offers choices for changing the display of taskbars in the Calendar view.

Bar Styles
Task type:
All
Noncritical
Critical
Milestone
Summary
Project Summary
Marked
Highlighted
External Tasks
Bar shape
Bar type:
Pattern:
Color:
Split pattern:
Shadow
Bar rounding
OK
Cancel
Text
Field(s):
Align: Center
Wrap text in bars
Sample:

20

First, select the type of bar you want to modify in the Task Type list box. Then use the drop-down lists in the Bar Shape area to modify the bar type, pattern, color, and split pattern for the bar. You can choose a bar or a simple line to represent a task's duration. If you choose a bar for the bar type, you can also apply a shadow for emphasis. You have a variety of choices for pattern and color. There are also choices of different displays for tasks that have been split.

The Bar Rounding check box deals with tasks whose durations are not a whole day (for example, durations of a half day or a day and a half). If the check box is left selected, the bar on the calendar is rounded to a full day.

In the Text area, you can choose the fields to be displayed in the bar either by typing in their names (separated by commas) or by choosing them from the Field(s) drop-down list. If you want to have more than one field listed on the bar and you are choosing from the drop-down list, make sure to deselect the field name and type a comma before selecting another field from the list. Otherwise, if you choose another field while the first field is still selected, the first field is replaced rather than added to. Field values can be centered, left-aligned, or right-aligned in the bars. When the text in a bar is long, it might be useful to check the Wrap Text in Bars check box. For all categories of tasks except All, a sample is displayed at the bottom of the dialog box, to show the effect of your choices.

CAUTION

Depending on your choices in the Bar Styles dialog box, you might see a warning message from Project's Planning Wizard, indicating that some of the calendar bars have different heights. The messages include instructions for how to reposition those bars.

SETTING THE LAYOUT OPTIONS FOR THE CALENDAR VIEW

The display order of tasks in date boxes is determined by settings in the Layout dialog box (see Figure 20.22). You can access the Layout dialog box either by choosing Format, Layout or by using the calendar shortcut menu. The default is Use Current Sort Order. The alternative to this is Attempt to Fit as Many Tasks as Possible (that is, without regard for sorting). The check box Show Bar Splits determines whether a task that has been split displays any differently than a regular task. By default, a split task shows a dotted outline during the portion of the task when work is not underway. The check box Automatic Layout specifies that the settings in the Layout dialog box are initiated automatically as tasks are edited, added, or deleted. When Automatic Layout is not selected, you must choose Layout Now from either the Format menu or from the calendar shortcut menu to apply the changes.

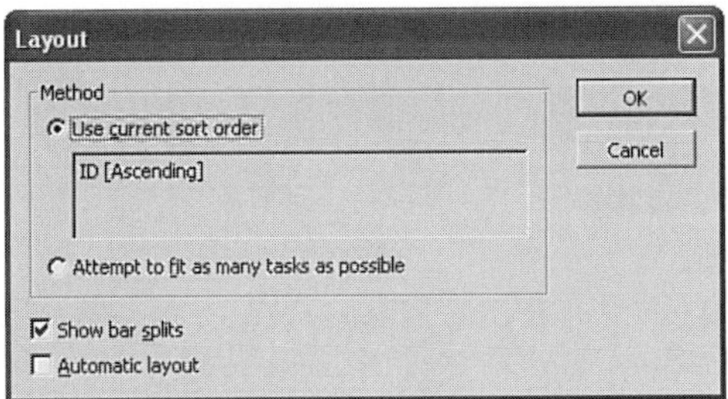

Figure 20.22
The Layout dialog box enables you to determine how and when tasks are sorted within each date box.

FORMATTING THE NETWORK DIAGRAM VIEW

The Network Diagram view, which is particularly useful in the planning phases, provides a look at a project's logic and flow. You can customize the Network Diagram view by changing the shape, size, and borders of the nodes; by creating named data templates that specify fields to display within each node; and by applying layout characteristics to task nodes. You can also change your perspective by zooming in or out to see more or less of the entire project and by applying a filter or grouping to the diagram. An overall description of the Network Diagram view is included in the section "Working with the Network Diagram View" in Chapter 7, "Viewing Your Schedule." The following sections discuss the extensive formatting and layout possibilities for the Network Diagram view.

The Format menu for the Network Diagram view contains the options Box, Box Styles, and Layout. You can also use the Zoom option on the View menu or the Zoom In and Zoom Out buttons on the Standard toolbar.

Notice that the Network Diagram view does not have a timescale displayed across the top of the view like the Gantt Chart view does. The diagram can move left, right, up, or down and still proceed "forward in time." For this reason, the Network Diagram view is very helpful in assessing the logical flow of the project and to review the sequencing of the tasks.

Using the Format menu to change the display of text is covered earlier in this chapter. The Zoom, Layout, and Layout Now commands are covered in previous sections but are summarized in the following sections for completeness. The Box Styles commands are covered in detail in the following sections.

USING THE BOX STYLES OPTIONS

You can customize the boxes that surround the nodes to display 10 node shapes, 4 border widths, and a variety of border colors. There are also options for background colors and patterns. Choose Format, Box Styles or double-click an open space in the Network Diagram view. The Box Styles dialog box appears (see Figure 20.23) and shows the formatting options for box styles, borders, and colors.

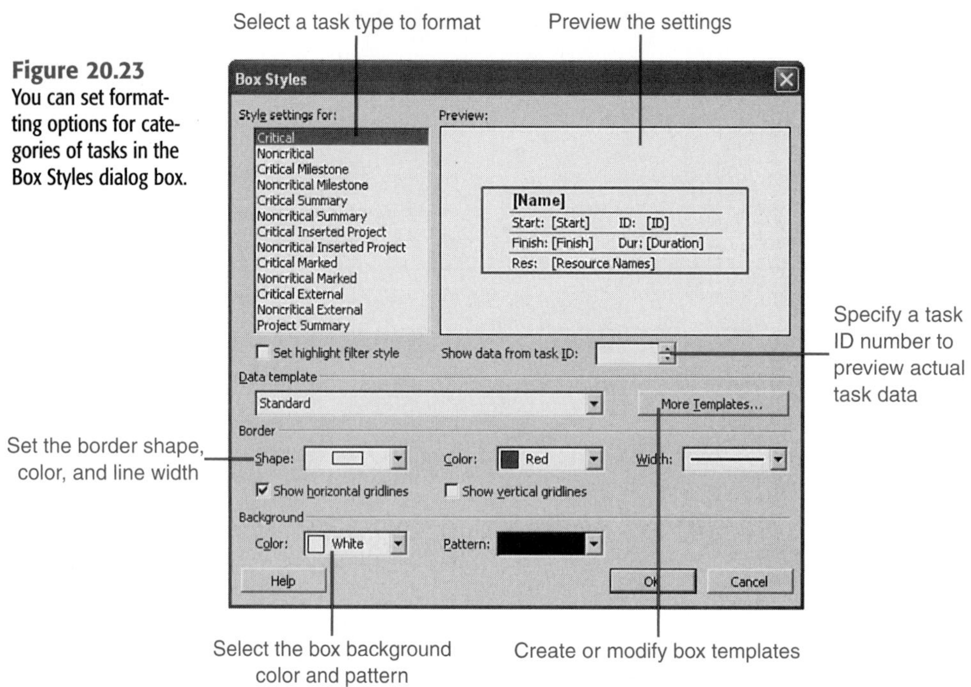

Figure 20.23
You can set formatting options for categories of tasks in the Box Styles dialog box.

The default box styles are assigned according to types of tasks. Critical tasks of any type, such as Milestone tasks or Summary tasks, are outlined in red and have white backgrounds. Noncritical tasks are outlined in blue and have aqua backgrounds. The default shapes are rectangles for normal tasks, four-sided parallelograms for summary tasks, and six-sided boxes for milestones.

By default, Project sets the formatting for boxes displayed in an applied highlight filter to be the same shape as nonhighlighted nodes but with the background color changed to yellow. You can turn on the Set Highlight Filter Style option to review or modify the highlight settings for node types.

Project provides 17 border colors that you can apply to shapes. If you have a color printer or plotter, the use of color can be an effective tool. With a grayscale printer, you can't distinguish one color from another; therefore, you need to change the border colors or box patterns to distinguish types of tasks.

You can set the Show Horizontal Gridlines and Show Vertical Gridlines options to view or suppress cell dividers in the node both onscreen and in printouts.

TIP

> To see how the style settings look with actual task information instead of the provided generic preview, enter a valid task ID number in the Show Data from Task ID entry box below the Preview area of the Box Styles dialog box.

USING DATA TEMPLATES FOR NETWORK DIAGRAM NODES

You can control the contents and the row and column layouts within each node by defining and applying data templates to the node types. Node definitions in a template include the following elements:

- Box cell layout of up to 16 cells in a 4-row×4-column grid
- Cell width sizing for all cells in a box
- Vertical and horizontal alignment settings for the contents of each cell
- Up to a maximum of three lines of text to be displayed in cells
- Descriptive labels inserted in front of data in each cell
- Font size, style, and color options for each cell
- Fields that appear in each of up to 16 cell positions
- Date formats for Network Diagram view displays

Initially, the contents and layout of boxes are defined by supplied templates. The standard template, which is used for normal critical and noncritical tasks, displays six fields of information in a 4-row×2-column grid: Name, ID, Start, Finish, Duration, and Resource Names. The Milestone template follows 3-row×1-column format and displays the task name, task ID, and start date. Summary tasks are assigned a third template, with six fields of information in a 4-row×2-column grid very similar to the Standard template: Name, ID, Start, Finish, Duration, and % Complete.

To create additional Network Diagram data templates for box formatting, follow these steps:

1. Choose Format, Box Styles to display the Network Diagram Box Styles dialog box.
2. In the Box Styles dialog box, click the More Templates button. The Data Templates dialog box appears, as shown in Figure 20.24.

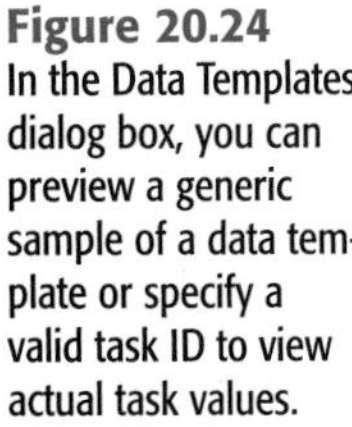

Figure 20.24
In the Data Templates dialog box, you can preview a generic sample of a data template or specify a valid task ID to view actual task values.

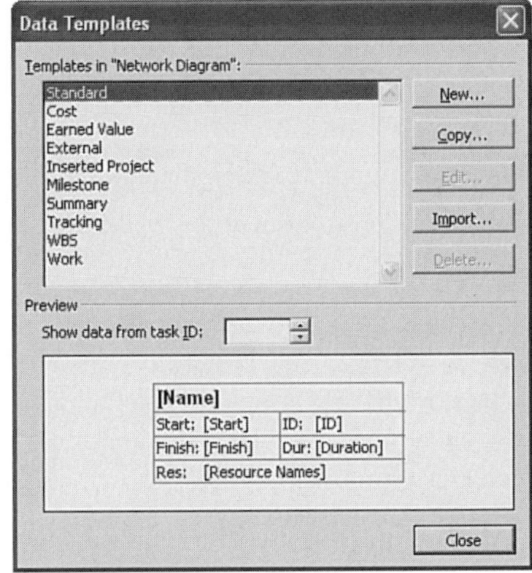

3. Click the Import button to bring up a box style template definition from within the current file or one that has already been created in another file. Any second file that is needed must already be open to allow this import to take place.
4. To create a new data template, click New. To use an existing template as a starting point, click Copy or Edit.

NOTE

> You cannot edit the supplied Standard data template. However, if the standard definition is close to what you want, you can make a copy of the Standard template and edit the copy.

5. Set the options for the new template in the Data Template Definition dialog box (see Figure 20.25).

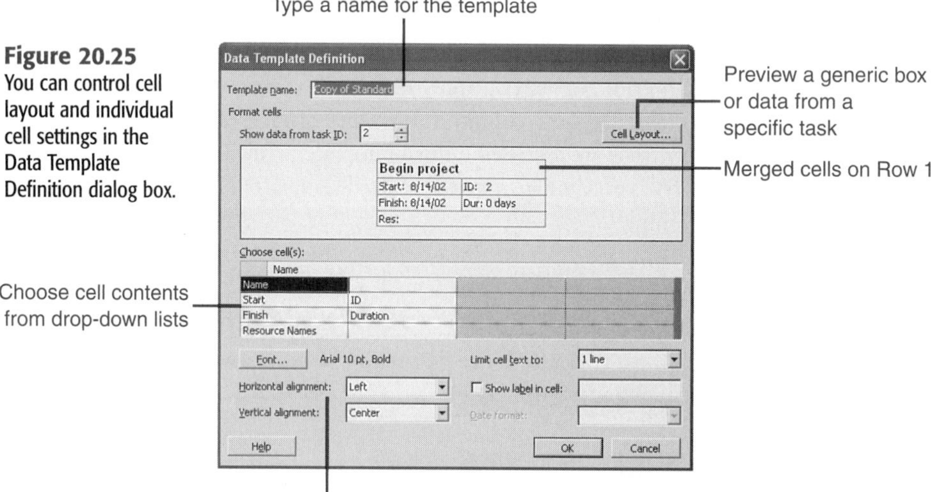

Figure 20.25
You can control cell layout and individual cell settings in the Data Template Definition dialog box.

20

6. Give the new template a name by typing in the Template Name entry area.
7. Click the Cell Layout command button to display the Cell Layout dialog box (see Figure 20.26).
8. In the Cell Layout dialog box, choose the number of rows and columns for the new diagram box. You can also expand or contract the setting for cell widths.
9. Also in the Cell Layout dialog box, make a selection for handling cells that are left blank. (In Figure 20.25, the standard data template contains a blank cell on Row 1, in Column 2. The Merge Blank Cells with Cell to the Left option is selected in the template definition, so the Name field appears to occupy two cells instead of one.)

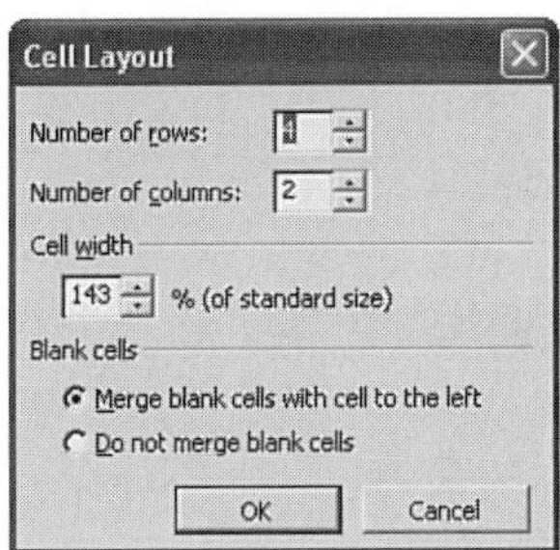

Figure 20.26
You can adjust the box grid and cell width in the Cell Layout dialog box.

10. Click OK when the cell layout is complete and you are ready to return to the Data Template Definition dialog box.
11. In the Data Template Definition dialog box, make selections for font, alignments, and number of text lines for each individual cell. Click each cell in the Choose Cell(s) area and make selections. Add a prefix label to any or all cells, and then select a date format for date cells if desired.

NOTE

> To select and change settings for more than one cell at a time, click and drag, Shift+click, or Ctrl+click to select multiple cells.

12. Click OK when you're finished with the template definition. Then click Close in the Data Templates dialog box.
13. In the Box Styles dialog box, apply data template settings to nodes by choosing a task type in the Style Settings For list and choosing a data template from the drop-down list.
14. Click OK when you're finished. Your changes are immediately reflected in the Network Diagram view onscreen.

Controlling the Network Diagram Layout

The layout in a network diagram is controlled by setting options in a Layout dialog box or by using the Layout Now command to force Project to refresh the display. After the general layout is defined and applied, you can apply task filters and group definitions to the diagram and hide tasks by collapsing summary tasks in the outline.

Selecting Layout Options

The Layout command on the Network Diagram Format menu controls the overall look and feel of the Network Diagram view, as opposed to the appearance and contents of individual network nodes. You can choose options for box layout order and spacing, style of box connection lines, color of linking lines, diagram background style and color, drawing of task progress lines, and whether the diagram is laid out automatically or you have manual control of the box placements.

To set layout options for the Network Diagram view, follow these steps:

1. Display the Layout dialog box shown in Figure 20.27 by displaying the Network Diagram view and choosing Format, Layout.

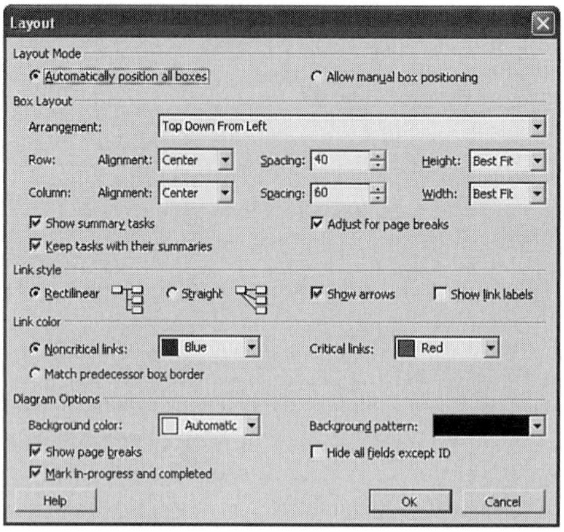

Figure 20.27
The overall Network Diagram view appearance is controlled by the Layout dialog box settings.

2. In the Layout Mode area, choose Automatically Position All Boxes to have Project maintain the onscreen layout or choose Allow Manual Box Positioning to allow click-and-drag movement of the boxes.
3. In the Box Layout area, use the drop-down lists and spinners to set row alignment, spacing, and height, as well as column alignment, spacing, and width. These settings are relative to those for other like elements; for example, a row alignment of Center places all boxes on a single horizontal row so that the box midlines form a straight line. Similarly, a column alignment of Left positions all boxes in a vertical column to display with left box edges aligned.

NOTE

Box sizes (height and width) might vary depending on the data template settings that are applied to box types. For more information, see the section "Using Data Templates for Network Diagram Nodes," earlier in this chapter.

4. The Arrangement drop-down list in the Box Layout area determines in what order Project draws the diagram. The standard, and default, arrangement is Top Down from Left. Figure 20.28 shows the Network Diagram view for the beginning of the plan, drawn in Top Down from Left order. Most network diagrams are drawn this way.

TIP

You can temporarily enlarge a box to more easily view its contents by moving the mouse pointer over the box and pausing.

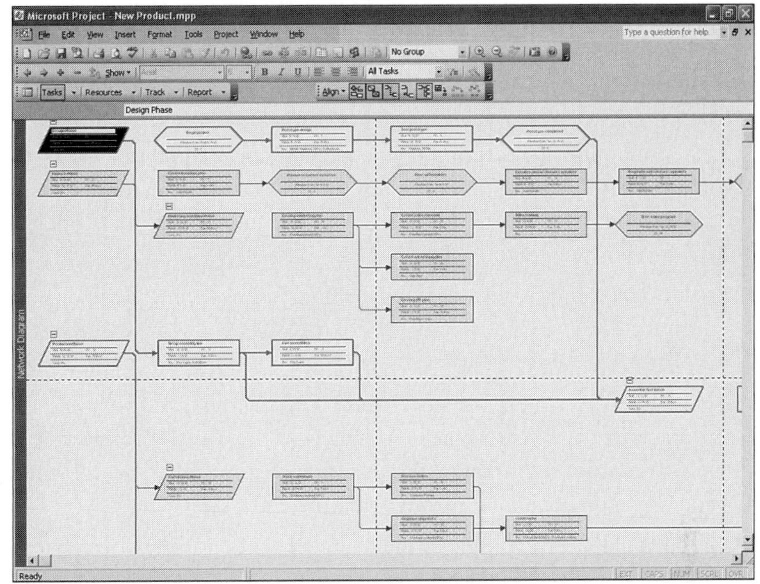

Figure 20.28
The standard diagram arrangement is Top Down from Left, with rectilinear linking lines and dotted page breaks displayed.

By comparison, Figure 20.29 illustrates how the top-left section of the Network Diagram view would look if the arrangement option of Top Down by Month was applied. This figure is set to a zoom percentage of 75% (see the section "Using the Zoom Command," later in this chapter). Each column of nodes represents a month in the project; within columns, boxes are in ID order.

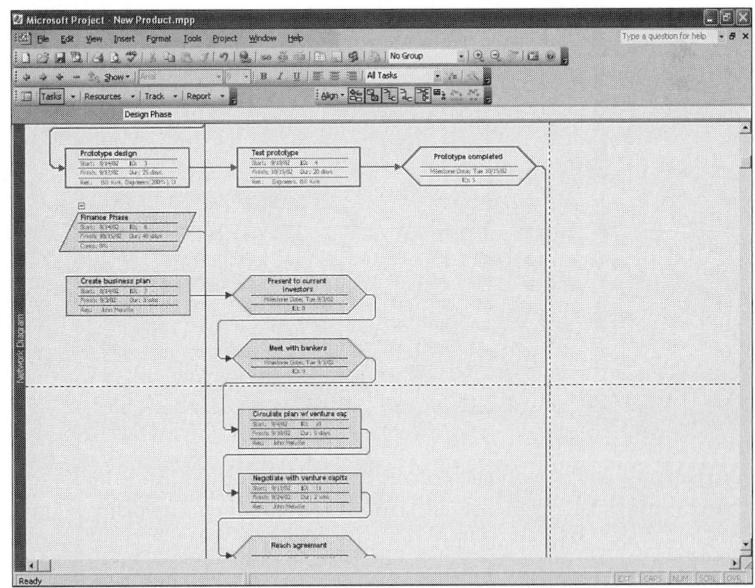

Figure 20.29
A Top Down by Month drawing of the Network Diagram view gives a good representation of the plan over time.

20

5. In the Box Layout area of the Layout dialog box, make selections to show summary tasks, to keep tasks with their summaries when changing the layout arrangement, and to adjust for page breaks so that boxes can't be split and printed partially on more than one page.
6. Choose options to determine whether lines between diagram boxes are straight or rectilinear (that is, squared). Choose Show Arrows to indicate successor direction between nodes, and choose Show Link Labels to include a small dependency type label (FS, SS, FF, SF) on each linking line.
7. Select color and pattern options for linking lines and for the diagram display background.
8. Two very helpful options are available at the bottom of the Layout dialog box. Show Page Breaks enables you to see onscreen how the printing lays out without having to go to Print Preview. Turn on the Mark In-progress and Completed option to draw a top left-to-bottom right diagonal line across boxes for tasks with some progress and an additional diagonal line through completed tasks.
9. You should use the Hide All Fields Except ID option if you're viewing and printing the overall structure of a plan and don't want to display any task details (see Figure 20.30).
10. Click OK after you have made all the needed selections.

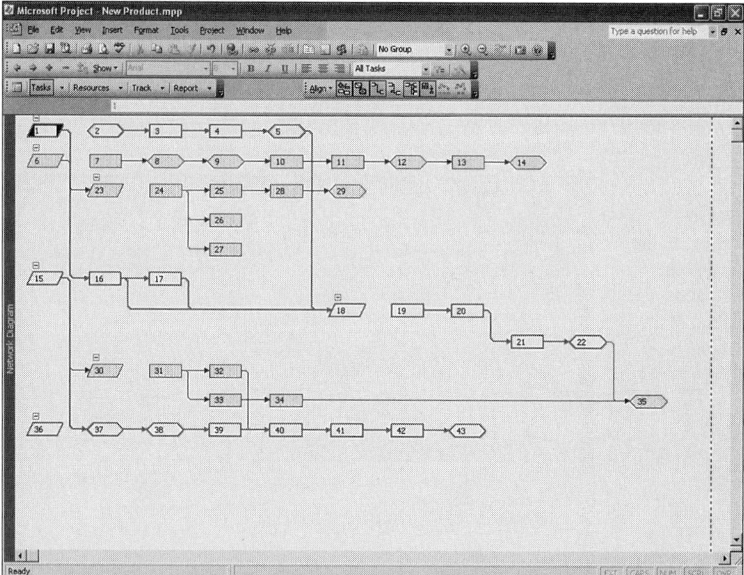

Figure 20.30
You can print a condensed schematic of the plan by hiding all fields except ID.

There is set logic behind each of the arrangement options in the Layout dialog box. When Top Down from Left is selected, Project redraws the Network Diagram view according to the following standard rules of node placement:

- Successor tasks are placed to the right of or below their predecessor tasks.
- Summary tasks are placed above and to the left of their subordinate tasks.
- Linked task nodes are connected with straight lines (or diagonal lines, if necessary), and an arrow is placed at the successor task's end of the line to indicate the direction of the relationship.

Other arrangement options apply similar rules.

Project includes a toolbar that is specific to Network Diagram view formatting. By using this toolbar, you can quickly apply many of the options in the Layout dialog box. Choose View, Toolbars, Network Diagram to turn the toolbar on (or off). Its buttons and their actions are described below in Table 20.2.

TABLE 20.2 THE NETWORK DIAGRAM TOOLBAR

Toolbar Icon	Tool Name	Action
Align	Align	If manual positioning has been turned on, you can use this tool to line up task nodes by their edges, centers, or midlines
	Hide Summary Tasks	Toggles on and off to hide summary tasks
	Show Progress Marks	Toggles to show (diagonal) progress marks on nodes
	Show Page Breaks	Toggles to show page breaks onscreen
	Show Link Labels	Toggles to show link labels (FS, SS, FF, SF) on lines connecting the nodes
	Straight Links	Displays task connecting links as Straight Links (toggles with rectilinear linking lines)
	Hide Fields	Hides all fields except task ID. It toggles with full node displays
	Layout Now	Instructs Project to redraw the screen and apply the format or manual position changes
	Layout Selection Now	Limits the application of changes to selected tasks only

20

CONTROLLING BOX PLACEMENT IN THE NETWORK DIAGRAM VIEW

If the Allow Manual Box Positioning option is turned on in the Layout dialog box, you can drag the boxes of the diagram around and reposition them to improve clarity. To reposition a node manually, place the mouse pointer over the edge of a node, hold until the mouse pointer shape changes to a four-pointed arrow, and then click and drag the border edge. You can also select the node and use Ctrl+arrow keys to move it. The manual positioning stays in place until Layout Now is executed, even if the file is closed and reopened later.

TIP

Hiding all fields except ID, as shown in Figure 20.30, is such a useful feature that it is accessible three ways: You can access it in the Layout dialog box, you can right-click on the diagram background, and you can click the Hide Fields button on the Network Diagram toolbar.

Any predefined or custom task filter can be applied to a Network Diagram view. After displaying the diagram, choose Project, Filtered For to apply one of the commonly used filters. Project 2003 provides the ability to apply group definitions to the diagram. Figure 20.31 shows the task nodes grouped into noncritical and critical task sections.

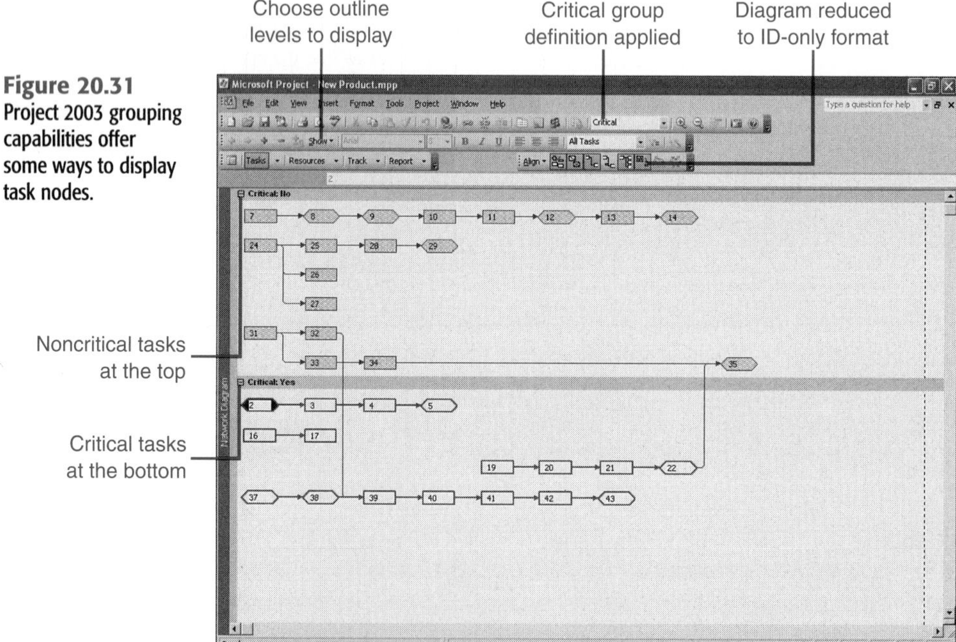

Figure 20.31
Project 2003 grouping capabilities offer some ways to display task nodes.

Show ▾ Another way to control the Network Diagram view display is to set the outline detail level to be displayed. The Show button on the Formatting toolbar enables you to choose what levels of subtasks are displayed. You can also collapse and expand individual summary tasks on the screen by clicking the + or – symbol above each summary task.

→ For more information on creating a task outline, **see** "Outlining the Task List," **p. 154**.

USING THE ZOOM COMMAND

When you are working in the Network Diagram view, it is often helpful to change the perspective—either pulling back to see the big picture or moving in closer for a more detailed view. This feature is especially useful when you manually move the nodes around to redesign a chart.

When you use the Zoom In and Zoom Out buttons, you are moved through the various preset zoom levels. When you use either the shortcut menu or the View menu, the Zoom dialog box appears. You can choose any of the preset zoom values or enter a value between 25% and 400% in the Custom text box.

FORMATTING THE TASK AND RESOURCE FORM VIEWS

Like the other forms, the Task and Resource forms can't be printed, and the formatting choices for them are limited. If a form is displayed as a full-screen view, you can view all tasks or resources with the form. You can use the Next and Previous buttons to move through the task or resource list. To display a Task or Resource Form view as a full-screen view, choose View, More Views, and select Task or Resource Form from the More Views dialog box.

You can create a split screen by choosing Window, Split; a form opens automatically as the bottom pane of a split screen. A form in the bottom pane of a split screen displays detailed information about the task or resource selected in the top pane.

REVIEWING THE FORMAT OPTIONS FOR THE FORM VIEWS

The Resource and Task forms have a limited number of format options. The Project menu provides a Sort option for both the Resource and Task Form views, and the Format menu provides a Details option that offers various entry field combinations that you can place at the bottom of the form.

When a form view is displayed full screen or as the top portion of a split screen, the Sort option changes the order in which resources or tasks appear when you use the Next and Previous buttons. If the form is displayed as the bottom portion of a split screen, applying a different sort order even when the form portion is active has no effect; in this case, the sort order applied to the top portion of the screen controls the behavior of the Next and Previous buttons on the form.

USING THE ENTRY FIELD OPTIONS

The Resource Form and the Task Form views have similar entry field detail options. The choices are available through Format, Details when a form is active on the screen. In the Resource Form view, the various tasks assigned to that resource are listed. Changing the details alters which fields about the tasks assigned are displayed. A Task Form focuses on information about the task, including the resources assigned. Therefore, changing the details in the Task Form view changes what resource information or what detailed task information is displayed about the selected task.

NOTE

> You can see a list of alternative formats for forms by right-clicking anywhere in a blank area of a form and choosing from the shortcut menu.

On the Task Form view, choose Format, Details, Resource Schedule to display fields for when work is scheduled as well as entry fields for imposing a delay either on the task itself or when the resource begins work on the task. Notice the columns named Leveling Delay and Delay (see Figure 20.32). The Leveling Delay field is a delay for the task itself, usually caused by applying resource leveling, and is the same field that appears on the Delay table on the Detail and Leveling Gantt Charts. The Delay field is a delay for the resource only. It shows delay if the resource does not start working at the beginning of the task.

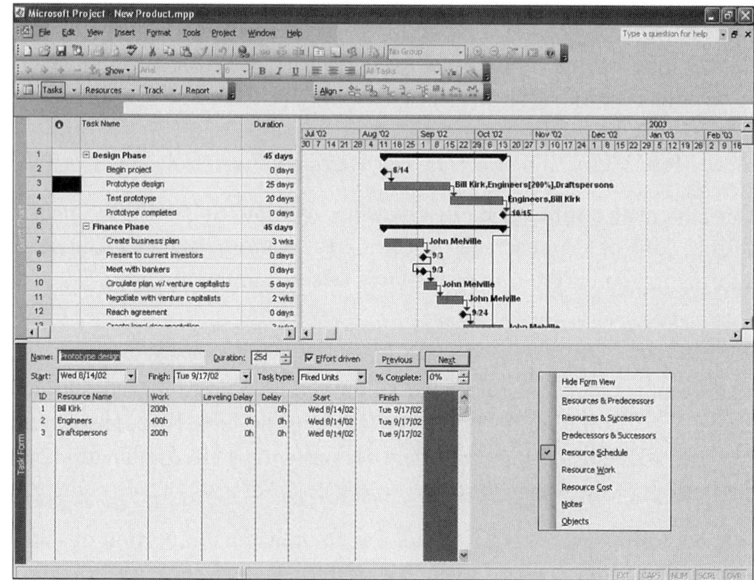

Figure 20.32
With a Task Form view active, you can choose Format, Details, Resource Schedule to display assigned resource scheduling information.

➔ To learn more about scheduling resource delays, **see** "Strategies for Eliminating Resource Overallocations," **p. 417**.

Other form details display additional entry detail fields, as summarized in Table 20.3.

TABLE 20.3 TASK AND RESOURCE FORM DETAILS

Task Form Detail	Resource Form Detail	Description
Resources & Predecessors	(Task form only)	Shows the default fields
Resources & Successors	(Task form only)	Focuses on upcoming tasks
Predecessors & Successors	(Task form only)	Shows the immediate links into and out of the task

Task Form Detail	Resource Form Detail	Description
Resource Schedule	Schedule	Shows the start, the finish, and any delays
Resource Work	Work	Shows the work fields for resources, including the Overtime field
Resource Cost	Cost	Includes Baseline, Actual and Remaining resource costs
Notes	Notes	Shows any notes entered, usually through the Task or Resource Information dialog box
Objects	Objects	Shows any OLE objects that are attached to the task or resource

FORMATTING THE RESOURCE GRAPH VIEW

The Resource Graph view shows values derived from the task assignments of one or more resources; these values are graphed along a timescale. To display the Resource Graph view, choose View, Resource Graph or click the Resource Graph icon on the View bar. Figure 20.33 shows a histogram, or bar chart (in the lower pane), for the allocated and overallocated task assignments for Mary Logan during the weeks of September 22 through November 10. The value displayed in this example is the peak units, or percentage of effort assigned during each time period (in this case, each week).

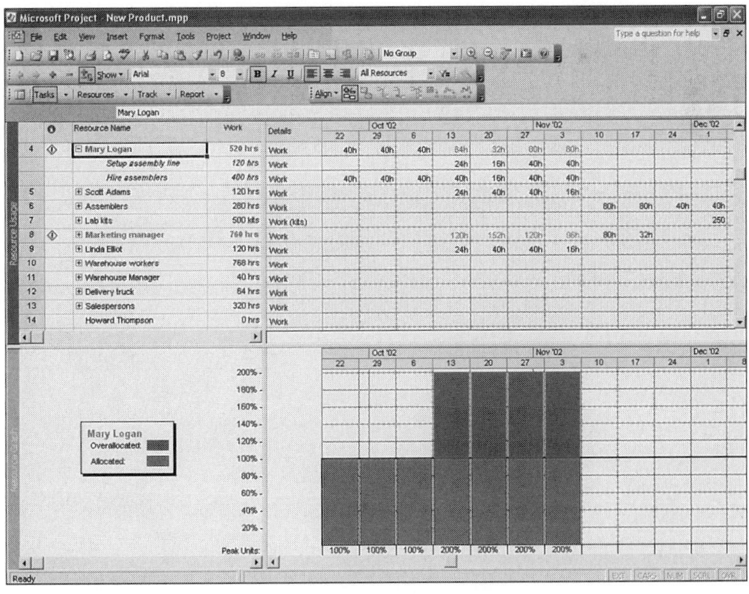

Figure 20.33 The Resource Graph view, showing peak units, can be displayed below the Resource Usage view.

→ For more information about resources that are overallocated, **see** "Understanding How Resource Overallocations Occur," **p. 402**.

You can use the graph to show the following measurements for a resource in a time period on each task:

- **Peak Units**—Highest assigned resource units in a time period
- **Work**—Amount of work assigned
- **Cumulative Work**—Running total of work assigned to date
- **Overallocation**—Work overallocation of the resource
- **Percent Allocation**—Percentage of effort currently allocated
- **Remaining Availability**—Effort, in hours, still available for assignments
- **Cost**—Cost of the assignments
- **Cumulative Cost**—Running total of cost contribution to date
- **Work Availability**—Total work availability (does not reflect assignments)
- **Unit Availability**—Total percentage availability (does not reflect assignments)

The graph can show these measurements for one resource, for a group of resources, or for the resource and the group together. The values can be shown for selected tasks or for all tasks during each time period.

If the Resource Graph view is displayed in the bottom pane below a task view, the displayed values are for one resource only. You can show values for this resource's assignment to the selected task or to all tasks during each period measured on the timescale. Figure 20.34 shows the assignment bars for Mary Logan, for all tasks during each month. This figure provides a quick glimpse of Mary's overassignment.

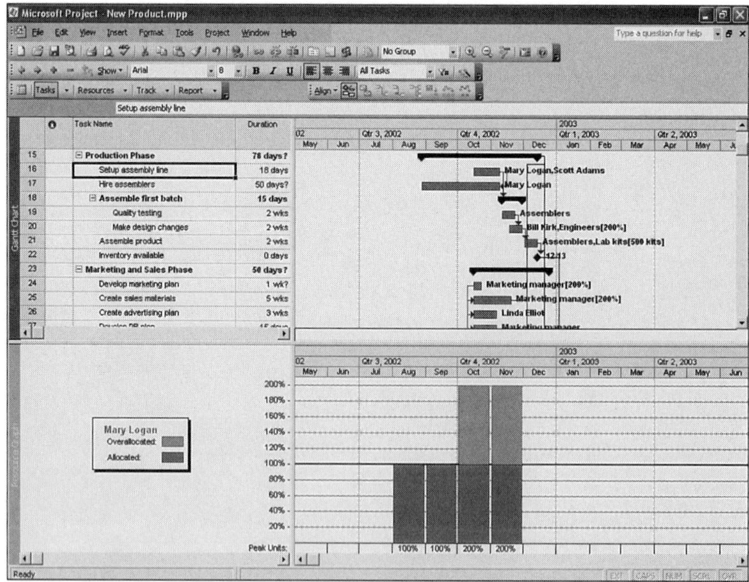

Figure 20.34
A Resource Graph view below a task view shows bars for all task work in that period for a single resource.

When the Resource Graph view is in the top pane or in the bottom pane but below a resource view, the values displayed are for all tasks and might be for one resource, for a group of resources, or for that one resource compared to the group of resources. If group data is displayed, the group is defined by the filter that is currently in use. For example, if the All Resources filter (the default filter) is in use, the data summarizes all resources for all tasks. Figure 20.35 shows the total costs associated with Mary Logan's task assignments, relative to the total costs of all resource assignments in the period.

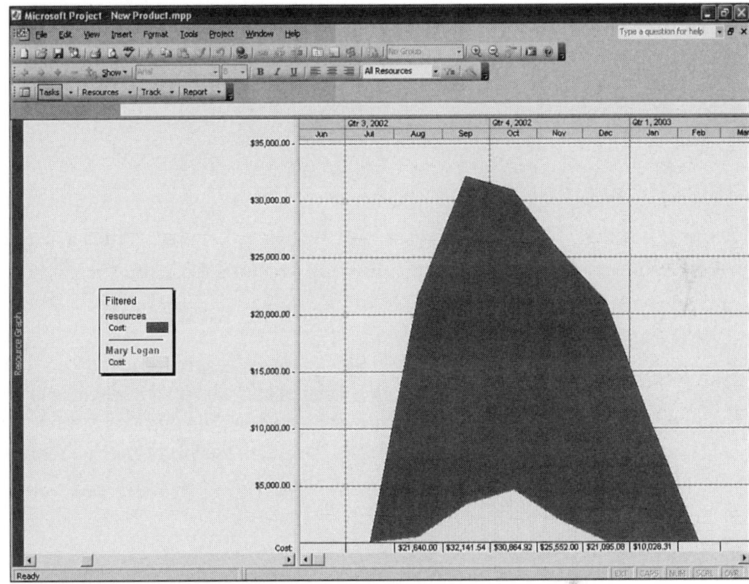

Figure 20.35 The Resource Graph view displays costs associated with a single resource compared to the costs of all other resources.

Table 20.4 summarizes the values displayed for different placement locations for the Resource Graph view.

TABLE 20.4 VALUES SHOWN IN THE RESOURCE GRAPH VIEW

Location of Graph	Group Value	One Resource Value
Top pane or bottom pane below a resource view	Value is for all tasks for all filtered resources	Value is for all tasks for the selected resource
Bottom pane below a task view	Value is for one resource but for all tasks	Value is for one resource but for only the tasks selected in the top pane

20

REVIEWING THE FORMAT OPTIONS FOR THE RESOURCE GRAPH VIEW

As with other views, the Zoom command on the View menu is available for the Resource Graph view and works as discussed previously in this chapter, to modify the timeframes that are displayed. Likewise, the Zoom In and Zoom Out tools on the Standard toolbar can be used in this view.

The Format menu for the Resource Graph view contains dialog box options described previously in this chapter for formatting the timescale (if the graph is not in a bottom pane), gridlines, and text styles.

The Bar Styles dialog box offers features that are unique to the Resource Graph. These features are discussed in the following section.

The Format menu also provides a Details option. The choices on this list of calculated values control what information is displayed in the timescale portion of the Resource Graph view. Because the Bar Styles dialog box options are based on these values, the Details options are described first in the following section.

SELECTING THE VALUES TO DISPLAY

Selecting Format, Details displays a list of choices of what values are calculated and graphed in the Resource Graph view. The following sections describe these choices.

NOTE

When Work is chosen in the Details dialog box, the unit (hours, minutes, or days) is determined by the Work Is Entered In option on the Schedule tab of the Options dialog box. The display of costs is determined by the Currency Symbol, Currency Placement, and Currency Decimal Digits choices on the View tab in the same dialog box.

DISPLAYING PEAK UNITS

The Peak Units option on the Format, Details menu measures the largest percentage of effort of a resource assigned at any moment during each time period on the graph. If the effort units exceed the available number as set in Maximum Units on the Resource Sheet view, the excess is shown as an overallocation. An availability line shows the number of units available.

Note that peak units are measured in *effort assigned*, not in work assigned. Therefore, peak units might mislead you when it shows an overallocation. Suppose a person is assigned full-time to two tasks during the same day. The peak units is 2, and because only 1 unit of a person is usually available per time period, the peak of 2 is displayed as an overallocation. If each of the two tasks is a one-hour task, however, the person should have no problem completing both tasks during the day.

The Peak Units measurement is very useful with multiple-unit resources in which the number of maximum units available is more than one. In these cases, the overallocation warning is more likely to be accurate.

DISPLAYING WORK

The Work choice on the Format, Details menu is measured in hours and is the number of units of each resource assigned to each task, multiplied by the duration in hours of the tasks per time period displayed. For example, say two programmers are assigned to work on a task that is estimated to take one 8-hour day. Project calculates this task to have 16 hours of work.

The amount of work to be done by the resource is determined by the number of units of the resource, the resource calendar, and the resource availability contour during the time unit. If the total work for the time period exceeds the available amount of resource hours, the excess is shown as an overallocation.

DISPLAYING CUMULATIVE WORK

Another choice on the Format, Details menu is Cumulative Work. This is a measurement of the total work for the resource since the beginning of the project. This running total includes the work during the time period shown.

DISPLAYING OVERALLOCATION

The Overallocation value on the Format, Details menu shows the overallocation of work for the resource for the time period. The Overallocation option shows just the amount of the overallocation—not any work hours that occurred during the normal work day. See the section "Displaying Work," previously in this chapter, for an explanation of how work is measured.

DISPLAYING PERCENT ALLOCATION

The Percent Allocation value on the Format, Details menu is a measurement of the allocated work versus the available work. The Percent Allocation shows the amount of work as a percentage of the amount available. See the previous section, "Displaying Work," for the way in which Work is measured.

DISPLAYING AVAILABILITY

The Remaining Availability value on the Format, Details menu is a measurement of the unallocated work for the resource during the time period. The Availability option shows the unused or unallocated work time that is still available. This is a useful option when you want to see who has some available time to work on tasks or to see if you are available when new tasks are assigned to you.

DISPLAYING COST

The Cost value on the Format, Details menu is the scheduled cost of the resource work during the time period. If the resource cost is to be prorated (as defined in the Cost Accrual field on the Costs tab of the Resource Form view), the costs appear in the time period when the work is done. If there is a per use cost associated with a prorated resource, that cost is shown at the start of the task. If the resource cost is to accrue at the start or end of the task, the entire cost appears in the graph at the start or end of the task.

DISPLAYING CUMULATIVE COST

The Cumulative Cost on the Format, Details menu display adds each period's cost to the preceding period's cumulative cost, to show a running total of costs. You can use this measurement to show total cost over the life of the project if you use only the group graph and include all resources in the group (see the section "Using the Bar Styles Dialog Box," later in this chapter).

DISPLAYING WORK AVAILABILITY

The Work Availability option on the Format, Details menu graphically presents the total number of hours a resource is available in a timeframe. This display is based on resource maximum units and the resource calendar. It does not reflect any work assignments that might exist in the period.

DISPLAYING UNIT AVAILABILITY

The Unit Availability option on the Format, Details menu reflects the same information as the Work Availability detail option, but the resource availability is expressed as percentages.

USING THE BAR STYLES DIALOG BOX

The Bar Styles dialog box enables you to specify what type of graph you would like to display (that is, Bar, Area, Step, Line, and Step Line graphs), if any, as well as how it should look. You can also use this dialog box to specify whether you want to see groups or just selected resource information. When the Resource Graph view is displayed, choose Format, Bar Styles to open the Bar Styles dialog box. A different Bar Styles dialog box appears for each of the value measurements just described. However, all these dialog boxes have the same layout and are used the same way. Figure 20.36 shows the Bar Styles dialog box for the Work value. As with all the Resource Graph view Bar Styles dialog boxes, this box has four main sections plus three options at the bottom of the box.

NOTE

The different areas of the Bar Styles dialog box that are available depend on the Details option that is set by choosing Format, Details.

The two top sections of the Bar Styles dialog box specify the display of overallocated amounts (if applicable), and the two bottom sections set the display of the allocated value up to the maximum available. The sections on the left side of the dialog box are for specifying the display of group data, and the sections on the right side are for specifying the display of one selected resource. Be aware that some of the values on the Details menu can display only two of the sections.

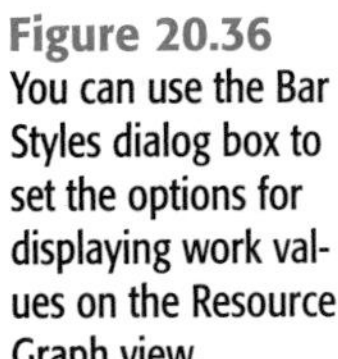

Figure 20.36
You can use the Bar Styles dialog box to set the options for displaying work values on the Resource Graph view.

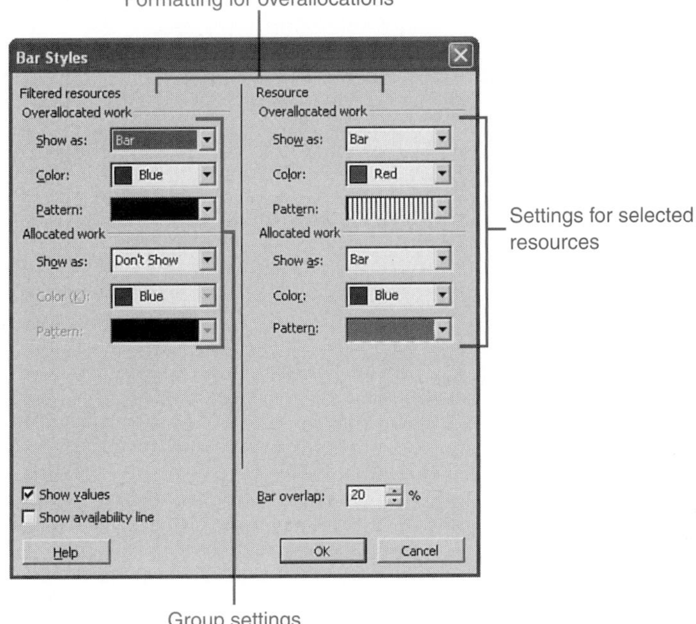

After the dialog box is closed, you might see sets of double bars, and each bar might have an upper and a lower segment. The upper segment is the overallocation measurement. The lower segment is the allocation up to the overallocation level. Where you see pairs of bars, the left bar is the group measurement, and the right bar is the selected resource measurement (note the similarity of the positioning of the bars to the positioning of options in the dialog box). Recall that the resource group is defined by the filter that is applied when the Resource Graph view is in the top pane or is displayed as a single pane. In this case, the group represents all resources because no filter has been applied.

In Figure 20.37, the bar on the right is the bar for the resource (Mary Logan), and the left bar is the bar for the group (all resources, in this case). The striped upper portion of the resource's bars are her overallocations. At the bottom of the graph, the work values are displayed in the time periods where the resource is allocated.

All these features are defined by the dialog box. (The graph in Figure 20.37 is defined by the settings in the dialog box in Figure 20.36.) The Show values box is selected so Project will display numeric data along with the bars. The bars overlap by 20% to show that they are paired.

The graph shading patterns are determined by the selections in the four sections of the dialog box. For each section, you choose three features that determine how the value is represented. Use the Show As drop-down list to choose the general format. Bar is the usual choice, but you can also use lines and areas. The Don't Show choice suppresses all representation of the value. You can select the Color of the image as well as fill the bar or area with a Pattern.

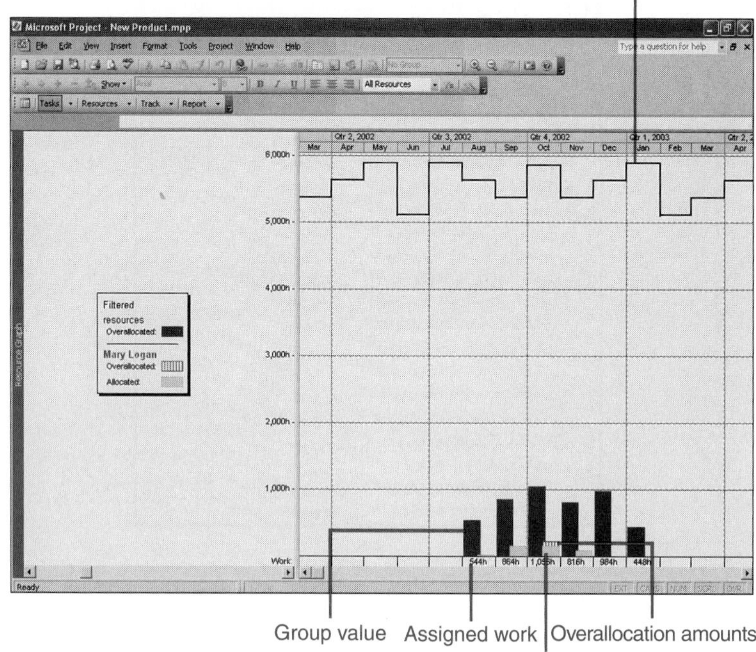

Figure 20.37 The Resource Graph view demonstrates overallocation of a single resource compared to the entire resource pool.

You manage what is graphed by choosing what to display or not to display in each of the four sections of the Bar Styles dialog box. If you want to display only the values for the selected resource, with no representation of the group values, you choose Don't Show from the Show As drop-down list for both sections on the left. If you want to show only the totals for all resources, you choose Don't Show for both sections on the right. When you choose Overallocation on the Format, Details menu, the Bar Styles dialog box has both of the bottom sections dimmed, to show that the sections are not needed. When you finish making changes, click OK to implement them or click Cancel to ignore them.

Formatting the Resource Usage View

The Resource Usage view shows the same data that is displayed in the Resource Graph view, except that the values appear as number entries in a grid under the timescale. Figure 20.38 shows the Resource Usage view above the Resource Graph view, to demonstrate the similarity of the data presented in these two views. In both views, the value displayed is scheduled Work.

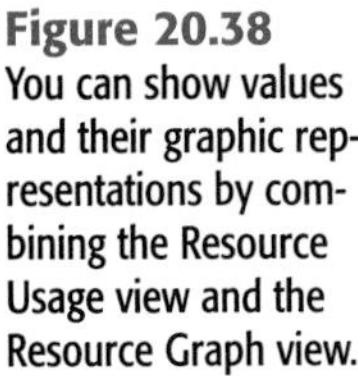

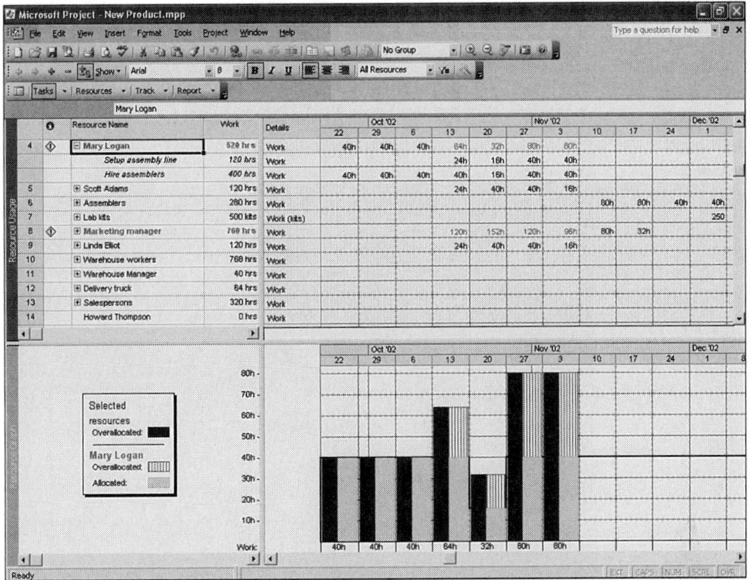

Figure 20.38
You can show values and their graphic representations by combining the Resource Usage view and the Resource Graph view.

The Format menu options for the Resource Usage view include text styles and formatting for fonts, gridlines, and the timescale. As with the other views, sorting is also available on the Project menu, and page breaks can be inserted by using the Insert menu. These topics are all covered previously in this chapter.

CHOOSING THE DETAILS FOR THE RESOURCE USAGE VIEW

The choices available by choosing Format, Details are some of the same value choices that are described in the "Formatting the Resource Graph View" section earlier in this chapter. You can select the value to display in the timescale grid by selecting one of these options.

If the Resource Usage view is placed in the bottom pane under a task view, the only resources that are displayed are resources assigned to the task that is selected in the top pane. The work value displayed next to a resource name is the total scheduled Work for that resource across all tasks during the entire project. A breakdown of other tasks assigned to that resource is displayed under the resource name. Figure 20.39 shows the Resource Usage view below the Gantt Chart view. The values in the usage table show work assigned to Mary Logan for all tasks during each time period. Scott Adams's work is also displayed because he and Mary are both assigned to the Setup Assembly Line task that is selected in the top pane.

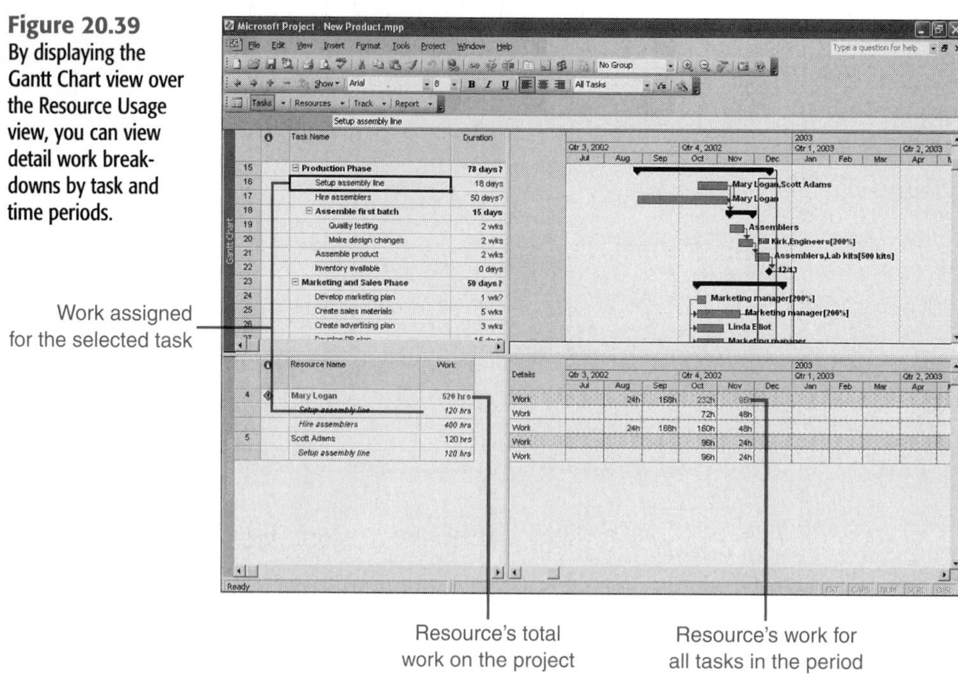

Figure 20.39
By displaying the Gantt Chart view over the Resource Usage view, you can view detail work breakdowns by task and time periods.

FORMATTING THE DETAIL STYLES IN THE RESOURCE USAGE VIEW

When the Resource Usage view is active, select Format menu option Detail Styles, and the Detail Styles dialog box appears (see Figure 20.40). In this dialog box, you can choose to display a wide variety of fields for each resource assignment. Each field will appear on its own row in the timescale table, and each might display a different font, background color, and pattern. From the Available Fields list on the left, select a field to be displayed and click the Show button. To prevent a field from being displayed, select it from the Show These Fields list on the right and click the Hide button. To rearrange the order in which the fields are displayed, click the Move Up and Move Down buttons on the right side of the dialog box. The Usage Properties tab contains options for how the detail data should be aligned and whether to display headings for the various columns and rows.

Figure 20.41 shows the addition of the Actual Work row for each task assigned to Mary Logan. Additional rows are useful when you're reviewing the Resource Usage view, and you can enter data into the time periods for many of the detail rows. For example, adding the Actual Work row would provide a handy place to enter actual hours when you are tracking progress on a project.

→ For more information on entering tracking data in a plan, **see** "Tracking a Project's Performance and Costs," **p. 528**.

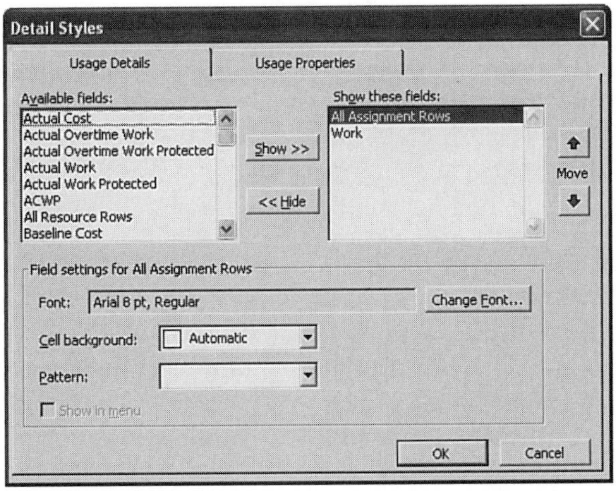

Figure 20.40
The Detail Styles dialog box offers many choices for how much detail to display in the timescale grid of the Resource Usage view.

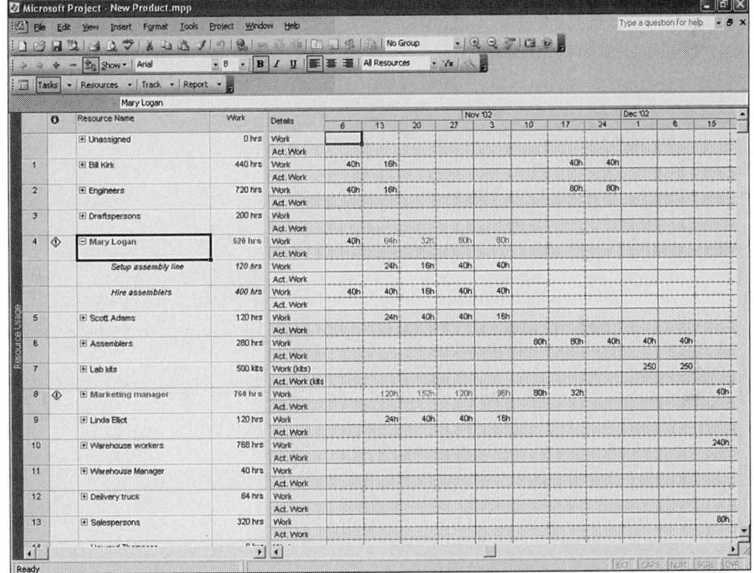

Figure 20.41
Adding extra rows to the Resource Usage view can make it a useful tracking tool.

FORMATTING THE TASK USAGE VIEW

The options for formatting the Task Usage view are identical to those for the Resource Usage view. The main difference between these two views is the focus. Whereas the Resource Usage view looks at the information from the perspective of the resource, the Task Usage view looks at each task, providing totals for various details and then a breakdown by each resource that is assigned to work on the task. As shown in Figure 20.42, the Prototype Design task has three resources assigned, and each resource has his own hours and costs. Work and cost totals for the task, the related summary task, and the project are also shown.

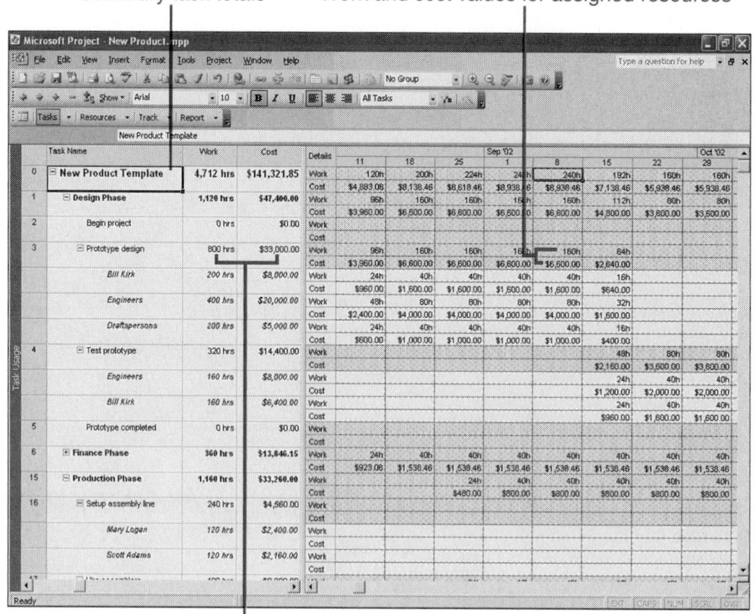

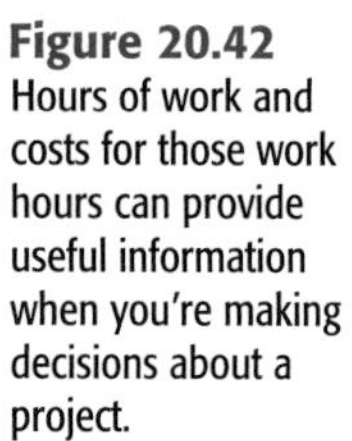

Figure 20.42 Hours of work and costs for those work hours can provide useful information when you're making decisions about a project.

FORMATTING THE SHEET VIEWS

The Task and Resource Sheet views display tables of field values for the list of tasks or resources. The columns that are displayed on sheet views depend on the table applied to the sheet. The Format menu for both the sheet views includes only options for changing font, gridlines, and text styles. The Project menu has options for sorting, filtering, and grouping, and the Insert menu offers a choice for inserting page breaks. (These features are discussed previously in this chapter.)

→ For more information on displaying table columns, **see** "Using and Creating Tables," **p. 840**.

TROUBLESHOOTING

MISSING OUTLINE SYMBOLS

I'm working on a project that has an outline, but my outline symbols on the formatting toolbar are grayed out. Why can't I use them?

The Show Summary Tasks option has been turned off. The outlining tools will display again if you select Show Summary Tasks from the View tab in the Options dialog box.

CONFIGURING TIMESCALE SPACING

I have set up my timescale exactly the way I like it, but the labels look a little crowded. Is there anything I can do to fix this, without changing the setup?

Yes, simply change the 100% in the Size text box on the Format, Timescale dialog box to a larger number. You might have to play with the number until you get the size right. Likewise, if your timescale is a little too big, change the Size number to 85% or 90% or whatever number gets the look you're after.

ADDING TEXT TO TASKBARS

I want to add text to the taskbars, but there's not enough room.

Add the text to a different row. You don't have to have a bar on the row; you can use it for text only.

To add the text to a different row, open the Bar Styles dialog box. Insert a row under the task type where you'd like to display text, such as under Normal, Noncritical. For Appearance, make the Start, Middle, and End shapes blank. In the Row column, choose or type **2**. Then, under the Text tab, set the text position as Inside and select the field to be printed.

FORMATTING THE TASKBAR

I would rather have information around the taskbars than in columns on the left. Can I make that work?

Yes. Add the text around the bars, as discussed in the section "Placing Text in a Bar Chart." Then create and apply a table that has only one column in it, or position the vertical divider bar on the Gantt Chart view so that only the leftmost column is visible. You have to print at least one column, but the information in the other columns can be placed around the taskbars and covered by the divider bar.

CHAPTER 21

Customizing Views, Tables, Fields, Filters, and Groups

In this chapter

Creating New Views 834

Using and Creating Tables 840

Customizing Fields 847

Creating Custom Filters 859

Creating Custom Filters with AutoFilter 867

Creating Custom Groups 868

Organizing Views and Other Custom Elements in Project Files 873

Troubleshooting 875

CREATING NEW VIEWS

Project provides more than 20 standard single and combination views. You can edit or copy standard views that are available on the View menu or in the More Views dialog box to create new views. If none of the standard views are close to meeting your needs, you can create a new view from scratch. To create a new view by editing an existing one, you use the same techniques you use to create a view from scratch. When you are familiar with the basics, copying and editing views is easy.

To create a new view, choose View, More Views. The More Views dialog box appears (see Figure 21.1).

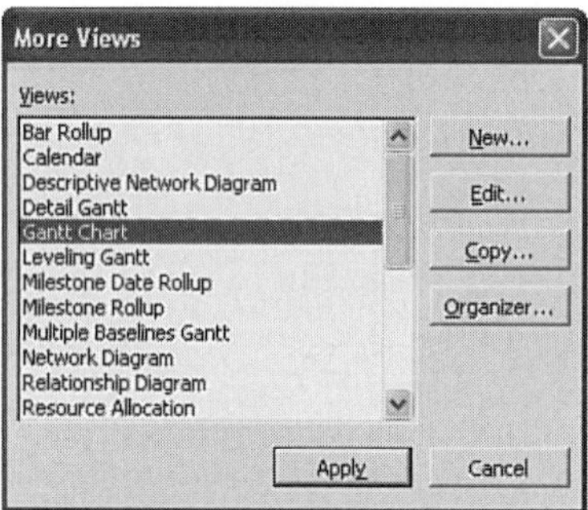

Figure 21.1
You can create new views or edit existing ones in the More Views dialog box.

In earlier chapters, you used this dialog box to change from one view to another. This section discusses three buttons on the right side of the dialog box: New, Edit, and Copy. You use the New button when you want to create a new view from scratch. You use the Edit button when you want to make changes to an existing view, overwriting the original. Finally, you use the Copy button when you want to make changes to an existing view but don't want to overwrite the original. The steps are the same whether you choose New, Edit, or Copy. For this example, choose New. The Define New View dialog box appears, as shown in Figure 21.2.

TIP

> If you want to preserve the standard views in their original form, use the Copy button rather than the Edit button and edit the copy of the view. You will then have both the original and the revised copies to use.

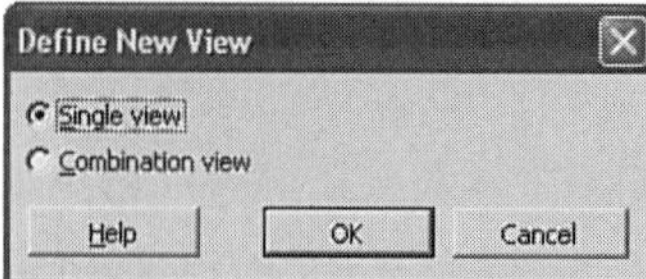

Figure 21.2
You can create a new view in the Define New View dialog box.

The new view can be a single-pane view or a combination view. As described in previous chapters, a combination view is simply a display of two views: one in the top pane and one in the bottom pane (see Figure 21.3). Two commonly used combination views are the Task Entry view (the Gantt Chart view over the Task Form view) and the Resource Allocation view (the Resource Usage view over the Leveling Gantt Chart view). When you often use two views in combination to perform standard tasks, it is advantageous to save the view combination for easy access. You can then make the new view be an option on the View menu. (See the section "Creating a Combination View," later in this chapter, for step-by-step instructions on how to do this.) Before you can create a combination view, you must create or determine which single-pane views you want to display.

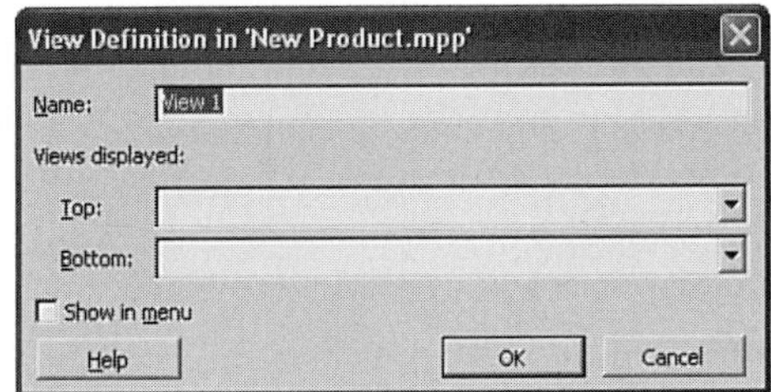

Figure 21.3
One form of the View Definition dialog box allows you to create combination views.

To create a new single-pane view, click the New button on the More Views dialog box. When the Define New View dialog box appears, choose Single View. The View Definition dialog box shown in Figure 21.4 appears.

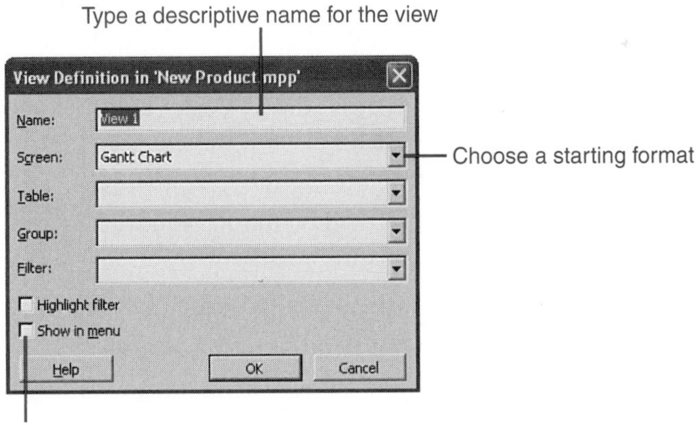

Figure 21.4
You can create a new single-pane view in the View Definition dialog box.

The View Definition dialog box has text boxes and check boxes for defining the following options:

- The name of the new view
- The basic screen or general view format used

- The table used (if the chosen screen uses a table)
- The group display setting to be used
- The filter that should be used, and whether it is a highlight filter or a limited-display filter
- Whether the new view name appears in the main View menu and on the View bar

NOTE

> If you copy an existing view, you cannot change the Screen option.

Entering the Name of the View

In the Name field of the View Definition dialog box, you should enter a name that readily identifies the features you are incorporating into the view. If the view is to appear on the View menu, you must select the Show in Menu check box at the bottom of the dialog box. You can designate a hotkey letter that can be used to select the view from the View menu. To do so, type an ampersand (`&`) before the chosen letter when you type the view name. When the view is displayed in the menu, this letter is underlined to indicate that this character is used to select the view. For example, if you enter `&Dependencies` in the Name text box, the Checking Task Dependencies view appears on the menu as Checking Task Dependencies; you can then type the letter `D` to select the view from the menu.

NOTE

> Try to make sure that you designate a letter that is not already used by another view. If you choose a letter that is already being used by another menu command, you will have to press the letter twice and press the Enter key to select the view.

Selecting the Starting Format

Microsoft Project provides a number of basic screens, which can be used alone or in combination to produce the standard views listed on the View menu and in the More Views dialog box. All views must use one of these basic, prefabricated screens.

You cannot change the screen assigned to one of the predefined views listed in the View menu. You can, however, create custom forms that resemble the basic screen formats.

→ For more information on creating custom forms, **see** "Using Custom Forms," **p. 950**.

These are the basic screen formats:

Calendar	Resource Sheet
Gantt Chart	Resource Usage
Network Diagram	Task Details Form
Relationship Diagram	Task Form
Resource Form	Task Name Form

21

Resource Graph
Resource Name Form
Task Sheet
Task Usage

You can modify some of these screens extensively to customize a view; some screens, however, can be changed only in limited ways. Format choices can be customized in varying degrees for each of the views, and format settings can be saved as part of a view.

➔ For more information on formatting, **see** Chapter 20, "Formatting Views," **p. 775**.

To specify the basic style for a new view, make the appropriate selection from the Screen drop-down list in the View Definition dialog box.

SELECTING THE TABLE FOR THE VIEW

If the screen you choose displays a table of field columns, you must identify the table to use in the view. To select a table, choose from the Table drop-down list in the View Definition dialog box. This list contains all the tables included in the More Tables menu for the screen type (that is, task or resource) that you have chosen. If you want to include a customized table, it must exist before you can use it in a view. See the section "Using and Creating Tables," later in this chapter, for more information.

SELECTING THE GROUP FOR THE VIEW

The Network Diagram view and all the views that display tables can also be displayed in groups based on selected fields. The group must have already been defined to be displayed in the Group drop-down list. A selection of No Group displays the tasks or resources in the view in sorted or ID order. See the section "Creating Custom Groups," later in this chapter, for more information.

SELECTING THE FILTER FOR THE VIEW

Every view has a filter attached, and the filter must be specified in the view definition. You need to select the Filter drop-down list in the View Definition dialog box to select one of the defined filters. In Figure 21.5, the Tasks With Fixed Dates filter is defined as a highlight filter for the view, which means that all tasks will be displayed, and tasks with fixed dates will be highlighted.

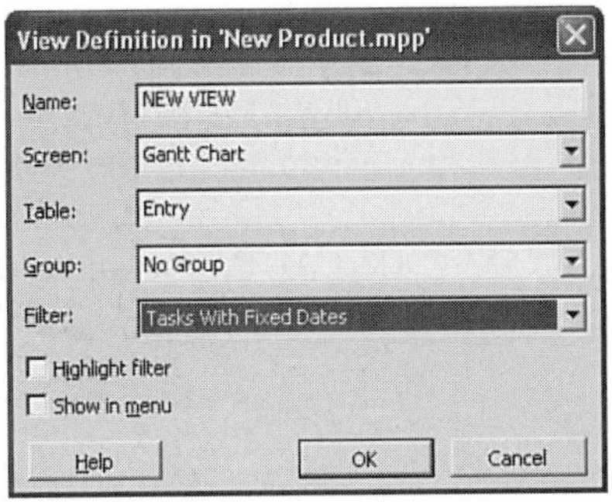

Figure 21.5
Choose a filter to complete the view definition.

A highlight filter shows all tasks or resources, and the ones that are selected by the filter are displayed with the highlight formatting (bold, italic, underline, and so on) that has been defined via the Format, Text Styles command for highlighted items.

If you want to apply a custom filter, you must first define the filter before you can use it in a view. See the section "Creating Custom Filters," later in this chapter, for more information.

NOTE

> The view definition cannot be "locked down." That is, you simply specify the starting points for the view. Then, when the view is displayed onscreen, you can make changes, such as applying another filter, to change the underlying view definition.

Displaying the View Name in the Menu

To display the view name in the View menu and on the View bar, mark the Show in Menu check box in the View Definition dialog box. All view names always appear in the More Views dialog box.

Saving the View Definition

When you have finished making selections in the View Definition dialog box, click the OK button to save your definition. You are returned to the More Views dialog box, where you can take one of the following actions:

- Click the Apply button to place the view onscreen immediately.
- Click the Close button to leave the current view onscreen but save the view you have just defined.
- Click the New, Copy, or Edit button to continue working with the list of views.
- Click the Organizer button to save the newly defined view to the global file. See the section "Organizing Views and Other Custom Elements in Project Files," later in this chapter, for more details.

If you want to change the screen type associated with a view, please refer to the section "Changing the Screen Type for a View" in the "Troubleshooting" section at the end of this chapter.

Creating a Combination View

If the new view is to be a combination view, the views for each pane must be defined before you can define the combination view. To define a combination view, access the More Views dialog box by choosing View, More Views. Click the New button to display the Define New View dialog box (refer to Figure 21.2). Then, select the Combination View button. The View Definition dialog box that appears is designed for defining a combination view (see Figure 21.6).

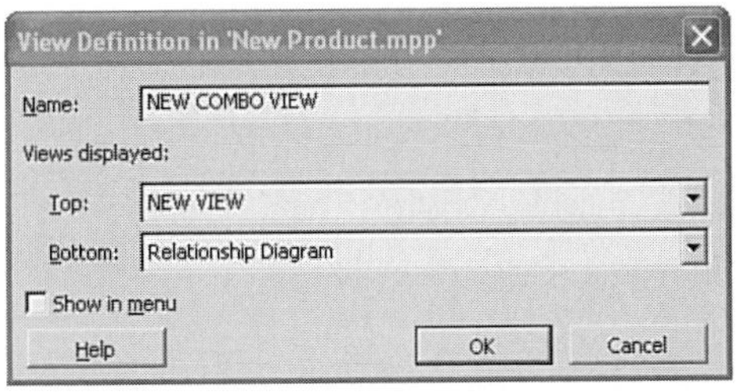

Figure 21.6
A combination view displays two single-pane views.

In the Name field of the View Definition dialog box, enter a name for the view. Include an ampersand (&) in front of a letter to designate a hotkey for the view when the name appears on the menu. From the Top drop-down list, choose the view to place in the top pane. All the single-pane views that have been defined are available here for selection. From the Bottom drop-down list, choose the view to place in the bottom pane. All the single-pane views can also appear in the bottom pane of a combination view. Select the Show in Menu check box if you want the view to appear on the View menu and on the View bar. Deselect this check box if you want the view to appear in the More Views dialog box only.

Figure 21.6 displays a definition for a new combination view that shows a customized Gantt Chart over the supplied Relationship Diagram view.

If you define a combination view that uses other customized views, and if these views use customized tables and filters you have defined, you must plan the order in which the customized components are developed. In other words, you must work from the bottom up. The following sequence shows the steps you'd take for a complex case:

1. Define all new tables that you plan to use. It doesn't matter whether their names appear on the View, Table menu.
2. Define any custom groups you might want to see. The group name does not have to appear on the Project, Group By menu, as long as it is a named group under More Groups.
3. Define any new filters you plan to use. These filters do not have to appear on the Project, Filtered For menu; appearing on the More Filters menu is sufficient.
4. Define the single-pane views you want to include in the combination view, using the appropriate basic screens. Assign to these individual views the tables, filters, and groups that you want the views to use.
5. Format each of the views with any special formatting options you prefer.
6. Define the combination view by selecting the names of the new customized views to be placed in the top and bottom panes. If you want to have this view directly available from the View menu, select the Show in Menu check box. The definitions you have created are then saved with the project file.

NOTE

> If you later decide that you want to use this view in another project file, you can copy it to a single project file or to `GLOBAL.MPT`—a template that makes views, tables, groups, and filters available to all project files. See the section "Organizing Views and Other Custom Elements in Project Files," later in this chapter, for more information.

*If you change or inadvertently modify an existing view, you can restore the original view—**see** the section "Restoring Standard Views" in the "Troubleshooting" section at the end of this chapter.*

USING AND CREATING TABLES

Tables are the building blocks of Microsoft Project that control which fields are displayed in sheet views. Through the manipulation of tables, you can determine the data displayed in each column, the width of the column, the alignment of the data within the column, the title that appears at the top of the column, and the alignment of the column title. A setting in Project 2003 allows column headers to wrap onto multiple lines. With the Table Definition dialog box, you can add new columns, delete columns, rearrange the order of columns, and make other changes in the definition of the table.

To change the display of a table, select View, Table and choose More Tables. The More Tables dialog box appears onscreen, with the currently displayed table highlighted (see Figure 21.7).

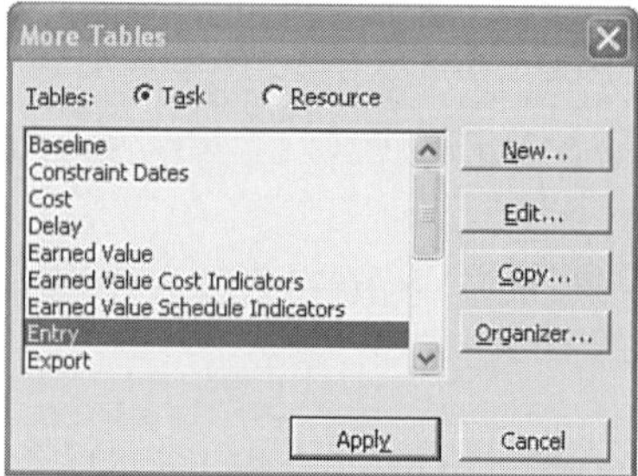

Figure 21.7
The More Tables dialog box offers choices for customizing tables.

You use this dialog box to perform the following procedures:

- Display a table that is not included on the main Table cascading menu. (Several task and resource tables are available only from this dialog box.)
- Create new tables, which can be based on existing tables.
- Change the features of any of the tables in the list box.
- Delete existing tables (through the Organizer).

The names of either task tables or resource tables appear in the list box in the More Tables dialog box, depending on the view that was active when you chose the More Tables command. To switch between task tables and resource tables, choose one of the options, Task or Resource, at the top of the dialog box.

To apply a table to the current view, choose the desired table from the list and click the Apply button. Note, however, that if the current view is a task view, you cannot display a resource table on this view.

To edit an existing table, choose the table from the list box and click the Edit button. If you want to create a new table that is similar to an existing table, select the original table from the list and click the Copy button. To create a new table from scratch, click the New button.

Whenever you click the New button, the Copy button, or the Edit button, the Table Definition dialog box appears. If you click New, the fields in the Table Definition dialog box are empty. If you click either Edit or Copy, the fields in the Table Definition dialog box contain the values for the table you selected from the list box. Figure 21.8 illustrates a dialog box for a copy of the Entry table. The explanations that follow also apply to editing and creating new tables.

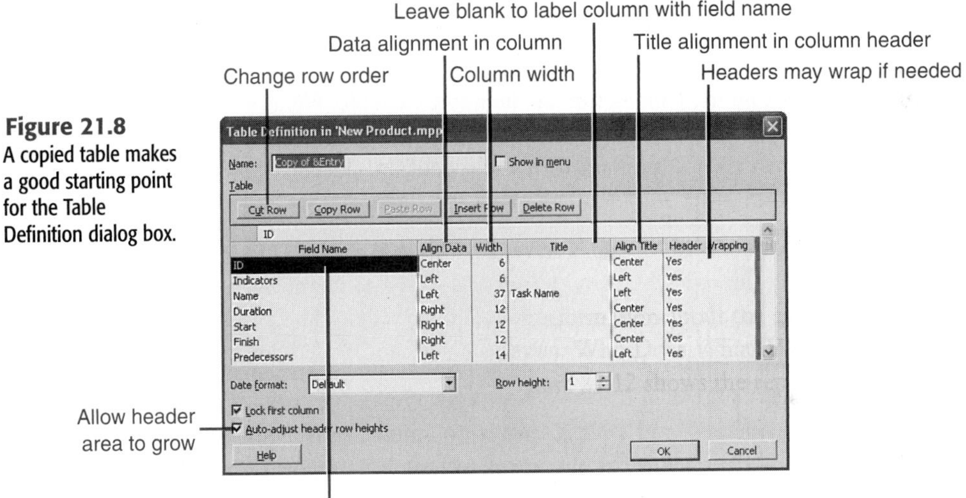

Figure 21.8 A copied table makes a good starting point for the Table Definition dialog box.

Entering a Table Name

When you create a new table or edit a copy of another table, you should supply a new name for the table. If the table name is to appear on the Table menu, use an ampersand (&) before any character in the name to indicate that this character is the hotkey used to select the table from the View, Table menu.

Adding and Changing the Columns in the Table

If you are creating a new table, click on a space in the Field Name column and access the drop-down list at the right side of the column, as shown in Figure 21.9. Choose a field by scrolling through the list and selecting the one you want.

If you want to add more fields, move the cursor down to the next blank row, using the scrollbar on the right side of the dialog box if necessary. To insert a field between the existing fields, select the row where you want to place the new field and click the Insert Row button to insert a blank row.

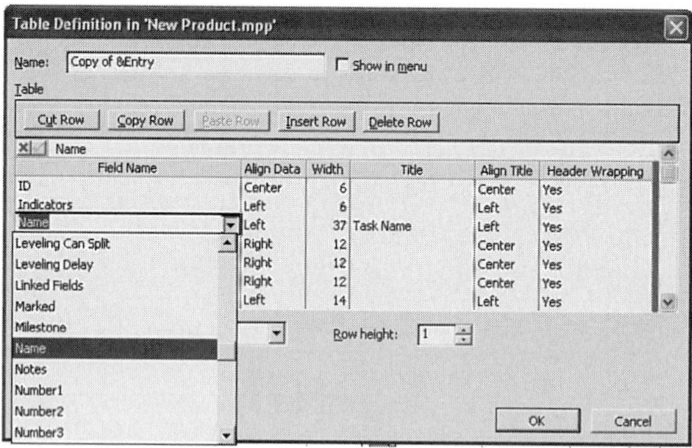

Figure 21.9
You can choose from the list of Project database field names to display columns in a table.

To remove a field from the table, select any item (for example, Field Name, Width) in the row that contains the field to be deleted and click the Delete Row button. To replace a field with a new field, select the Field Name entry for the old field and select the new field from the drop-down list. This removes the old field completely and replaces it with the new choice.

To rearrange the columns in the table, select the one you want to move and click the Cut Row button. Select the row where you want the cut row to be moved and then click the Paste Row button. You don't need to insert a blank row first. The pasted row will be inserted, with the existing row and all the rows beneath it moved down.

When you choose a name from the Field Name list, the default data Alignment (Right), field Width (10 characters), and Title Alignment (Center) for the field are supplied automatically. However, you can change the alignment to Left, Center, or Right by typing this specification or by selecting the alignment from the drop-down list. You can type a different value in the Width field if you want a width other than the default. Use the Title column to supply a column name if you want one that is different from the field name. Leave the Title column blank if you want to use the field name as the displayed column title. You can align the title of a column differently from the data displayed in the column; for example, you might want to center the title of a field over numeric data that is right aligned.

In Project 2003, you can use long column titles, also known as column headers; if you do, Project wraps long text within the title area. When a new field row is added, the default value for Header Wrapping is No (that is, off). Simply click in the Wrapping column for the field, and Project changes the setting to Yes. To turn wrapping off again, type **No** as the wrapping value. The drop-down list in the wrapping setting offers the choices Yes and No, but the definition table is too wide to see the drop-down arrow. You can use the arrow keys to move to the field or simply type **Yes** or **No** to cause Project to scroll the table to the left.

Another setting in Project 2003 affects how header rows wrap. The Auto-adjust Header Row Heights setting is on by default. This feature expands the header onto as many rows as needed when the column width is decreased. With this option turned off, header text may still wrap in a narrow column, but the header area won't automatically get deeper to accommodate all the text.

If you want to lock a column in a table so that it doesn't move when scrolling, ***see*** *the section "Freezing the First Table Column" in the "Troubleshooting" section at the end of this chapter.*

Completing the Definition of the Table

At the top of the Table Definition dialog box, the Show in Menu check box must be selected if you want the table to appear on the View, Table cascading menu (rather than just on the More Tables dialog box). If more table names are to be listed than can be shown on the cascading menu, the menu adds a scrolling feature at the bottom of the cascading list.

You should select the check box labeled Lock First Column if you want the first column of the table to remain onscreen at all times. As you scroll to the right in the table, the first column does not scroll out of view if this box is checked. However, the column cannot be edited when it is locked. In the standard sheet views, the first column is the task or resource ID. If the first column is locked, it displays on a gray background, as is typical with the ID column.

You can use the Date Format area of the Table Definition dialog box to specify the format for date fields in the table. If you leave the default entry in place, the date format selected through the Tools, Options command is used. You can select the drop-down list to display the other date format options you can elect to use. A change in the date format on a table does not change your default or the date format used in other views.

The normal row height in a sheet view is 1, which means that one row of text is displayed for each task or resource row in the table. If the row height is greater than 1, long text entries in any column of the table automatically wrap if the width of the column is insufficient to display them on one line. To change the number of text lines to be displayed for each task, choose Row Height and enter the appropriate number. This row height is an initial setting only and can be changed graphically onscreen.

Note that all rows start out the same height and that additional lines in cells take up space, even if they are blank. You can set individual rows to varying heights onscreen by dragging the row dividers up and down. To reset all rows to a consistent height, click the Select All button on the top left of the sheet before dragging a single row ID divider to the desired height.

Figure 21.10 shows the definition for a new table named Development, which displays tasks with ID, Indicators, Request Tracking Number (a custom text field), Name, Duration, and Start fields, as well as a custom text field with the title Comments. Note that the titles for several of the fields have been changed from the default field names.

21

TIP

If you intend to use descriptive text in the title of one of the custom fields (for example, Text1-30, Number1-20), you can assign that title to the field permanently so that anywhere you display the custom field, the assigned title, instead of the field name, is displayed. See the section "Naming Custom Fields," later in this chapter, for more information.

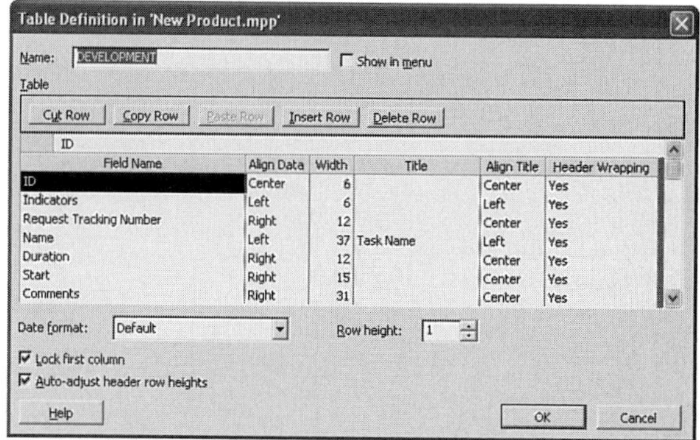

Figure 21.10
The table definition for parameters for the custom Development table.

Figure 21.11 shows the Development table (as defined in Figure 21.10) applied to the Task Sheet view.

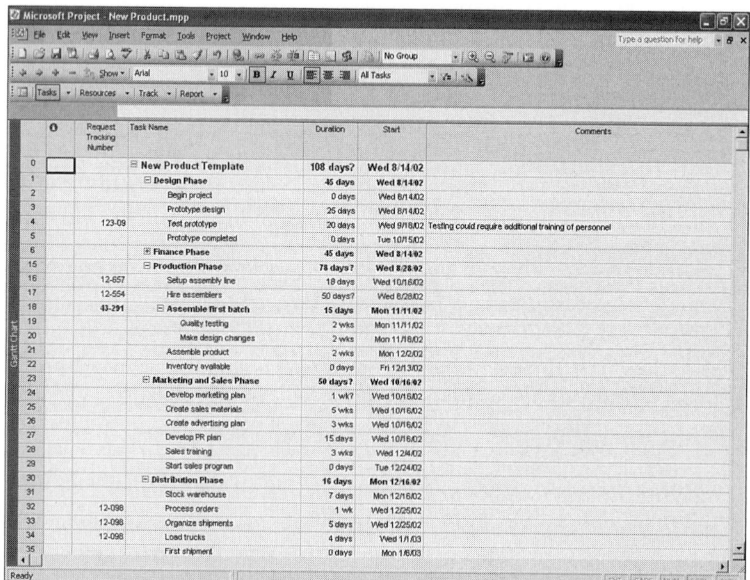

Figure 21.11
The Development table can be applied to the Task Sheet view.

TIP

A useful yet simple table is a table with only one field: the task ID. You can use this table in conjunction with a Gantt Chart that has the task names placed next to the taskbars for a completely graphical view.

CHANGING TABLE FEATURES FROM THE VIEW SCREEN

You can change most of the features you define in the Table Definition dialog box on the screen, without having to go through the View, Table command. You can access the Column Definition dialog box to insert, delete, or edit the definitions of columns directly in the table.

To change the definition of a column from the view screen, double-click the title of the column. The Column Definition dialog box appears, as shown in Figure 21.12, with the current column settings displayed in the selection fields.

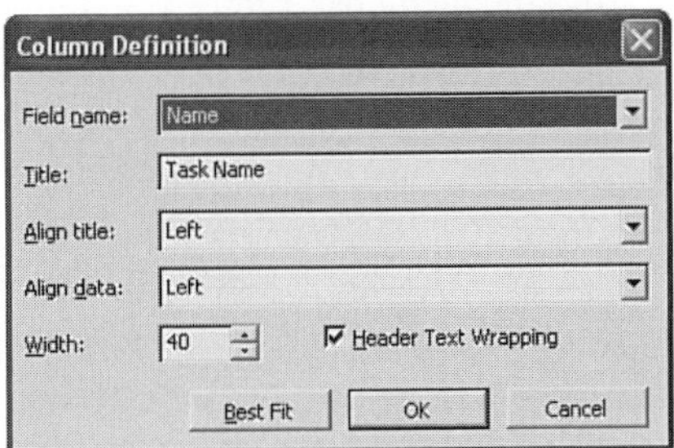

Figure 21.12
You can double-click on a column title to display the Column Definition dialog box.

To redefine a column, you can change the selections in any of the following entry fields:

- Choose Field Name to view the list of field names. Selecting a field from the list replaces the current column with the new field.
- Type a title if you want a text title, instead of the field name, to appear at the head of the column.
- Choose Align Title to change the alignment for the column title and Align Data to change the alignment for the data in the column.
- Allow long column titles to word wrap by selecting the Header Text Wrapping option.
- Choose Width if you want to set the width of the column manually. Enter the width in a number of characters. You also can click the Best Fit button to set the width to the widest entry in the column.

Complete the new definition of the column by clicking either OK or Best Fit. Click OK if you want to apply the new column definition, including the Width setting. Click Best Fit if you want Microsoft Project to calculate the width needed to fully display both the title and the longest data value that initially goes into the column. Clicking the Best Fit button closes the dialog box and applies the new definition, but with the calculated column width.

CAUTION

> Even if column header wrapping is on and the text is currently displayed on multiple lines, applying the best fit to the column causes the tile to be displayed on one long line. You then need to make the column more narrow to force the wrapping once again.

To insert a new column in the table, follow these steps:

1. Select the entire column that is currently located where the new column should be placed. (You Select a column by clicking on the column title.)
2. Either choose Insert, Column from the menu bar, right-click on the column title and choose Insert Column from the shortcut menu, or press the Insert key. Then select the values for the new column in the Column Definition dialog box.

The new column is inserted in front of the column that was selected. The selected column and all columns to its right are moved right one position in the table.

There are several methods for hiding columns:

- Right-click a column title and choose Hide Column from the shortcut menu.
- Select the entire column by clicking the title, and then choose Edit, Hide Column, or simply press the Delete key.
- Click the right divider line in the column heading and drag it to the left until it meets the left divider line.
- Open the table definition (that is, View, Table, More Tables) and delete the row that defines the column you want to remove.

All methods actually modify the underlying table definition. Hiding or deleting a column removes it from the table completely; dragging the column closed sets the column's width to zero.

How you retrieve a hidden column depends on the method used to remove it:

- If the Hide Column shortcut or Edit, Hide Column were used, you must reinsert the column into the table.
- Columns hidden by dragging with the mouse can also be opened by dragging. Move the mouse slowly from right to left, toward the title divider where the column is hidden. As soon as the mouse pointer changes to a vertical line with horizontal arrows, click and drag back to the right.

NOTE

> Project gives no indication that a column is hidden. You must remember which column, with what field data, is hidden and where.

- Open the table definition dialog box and reinsert a row for the removed column, or increase its width if it was hidden by dragging.

NOTE

> You cannot mix some hide and insert methods. That is, a column removed by using Hide Column can't be opened by dragging—because that column was removed from the table definition. You need to use Hide with Insert.

You can also change row heights onscreen by using the mouse. To change the row height, point to the bottom gridline in the first column (usually the ID column). When the mouse pointer changes to a double-headed arrow, drag up or down. This action adjusts the height for a single row or for multiple rows that are selected. To adjust all row heights at the same time, click the Select All area above the first column before adjusting the row height.

NOTE

> Be aware that changing row heights on a displayed table also changes the row heights in all other tables. Unlike column widths, unique row height settings aren't saved with the table definition.

The modified table is displayed whenever you select the same view, until you apply another table.

CUSTOMIZING FIELDS

Every project has its own characteristics and requirements for data storage. The custom fields in Project provide reserved spaces that enable you to use a project file as a central data repository for your plan.

Perhaps you have an internal code for identifying every task on a project. This might be a cost code, a work product code, or a code provided by a customer to facilitate information exchange. These codes might actually be alphanumeric descriptive text that doesn't fit a pattern. Costs might also be associated with the project that are not easily included in the resource or fixed-cost fields. It is also common to need to identify the status of a task as other than percentage complete, such as approved/not approved. Project provides a variety of custom fields and field types to accommodate storing these and other types of specialized data.

Project provides a set of custom fields for storing task information and another set for storing resource information. The names and lists of these fields are identical; the context of the use of a custom field (in a text-oriented view or a resource-oriented view) determines with which set you are working. Table 21.1 describes the custom fields that are available.

TABLE 21.1 CUSTOM FIELDS

Field Name	Field Data Description
Text1–Text30	Alphanumeric, up to 255 characters
Number1–Number20	Any positive or negative number
*Baseline1–Baseline 10 (multiple fields)	For capturing entire plans at intervals over time (including Cost, Duration, Start, Finish, and Work fields for each Baseline number)
Cost1–Cost10	Formatted number values
Date1–Date10	Any valid date value
Duration1–Duration10	Any valid duration value (for example, 5d)
Start1–Start10*	Any valid date value
Finish1–Finish10*	Any valid date value
Flag1–Flag20	Yes/No values
Outline Code1–Outline Code10	User-defined alphanumeric outline structures

* *Task Start/Finish fields*

Project uses task Start/Finish fields when you are saving interim schedule information for tasks. Similarly, the numbered Baseline fields allow you to capture complete plan snapshots (not just Start and Finish dates). You can use these fields for your own purposes only if you do not need them for baseline storage. Similar data can be stored in other custom fields.

NOTE

> The complete list of custom Project fields is available through online help. On the Help menu, select Contents and Index. In the Reference section, select Microsoft Project reference, and then select Fields Reference in the side pane.

Project enables you to create name aliases for the fields so that they consistently appear with descriptive field names anywhere you use them. Also, custom fields can calculate and store values according to formulas you create or import.

ACCESSING THE CUSTOM FIELDS

21

Custom field names appear in any drop-down list in which the predefined fields are accessible. For example, when you are inserting a new column on a table, the field choices for the column include all the custom field names, even if the fields have not yet been used for data storage.

Changes to a custom field, including changes to the field's name and rollup behaviors, are made in the Customize Fields dialog box. Choose Tools, Customize, Fields to display the dialog box shown in Figure 21.13.

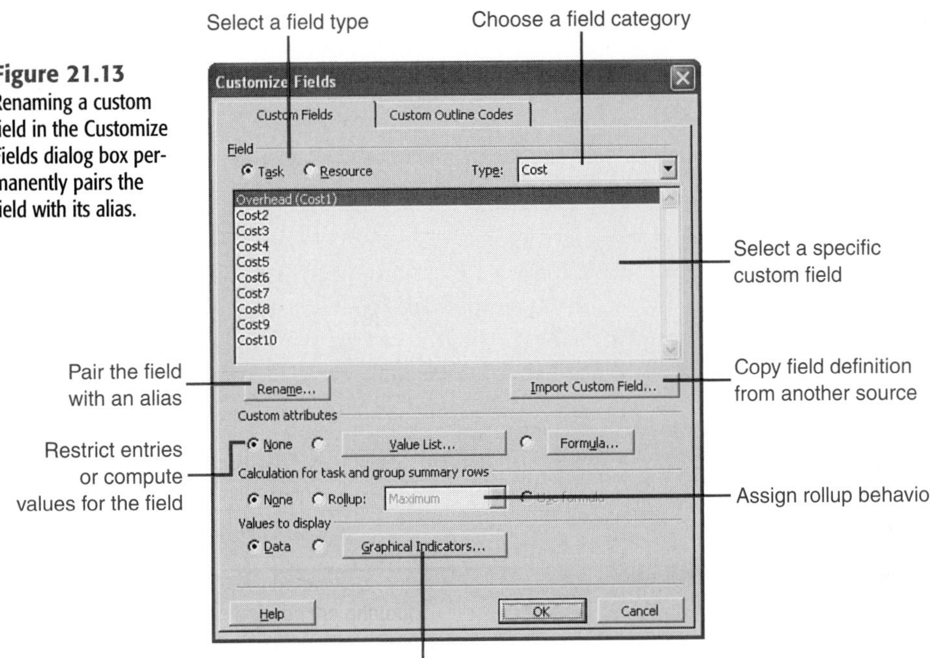

Figure 21.13
Renaming a custom field in the Customize Fields dialog box permanently pairs the field with its alias.

In the Customize Fields dialog box, custom field names are listed by type. To work with a particular field, select the general type (Task or Resource) first. Then use the Type drop-down list to select a particular category of custom field (for example, Text, or Number). When the list of available fields of that category appears on the left side of the dialog box, you can click on one field of interest to begin changing custom settings.

Naming Custom Fields

Typically, field names are shown as column headings. You can temporarily rename a field with a more descriptive label by editing the column definition. You might want the data in Text1 to be displayed under the heading Dept Code, for example. However, edits made on a single table stay with that table definition. If you later display Text1 in another table, it is again labeled Text1.

To avoid having to change the name labels for every display of a custom field, you can give the custom field an alias. To do so, click the Rename button in the Customize Fields dialog box and supply a more descriptive name for the field. In Figure 21.13, the Cost1 custom field has been renamed Overhead, and both labels (Cost 1 and Overhead) appear in the list of fields.

After an alias is established, any place the custom field is used—before or after the field is renamed—the new name label appears instead of the generic custom field name. The custom field name/alias pair appear together in drop-down field lists, as well. In Project 2003, custom fields with aliases are available for data entry on the new Custom Fields tab in the Task Information dialog box.

CREATING CALCULATED FIELDS

It is possible to create and apply calculations or formulas to fields in previous versions of Project without developing macro code. Data in custom fields can be derived from values in other fields in the project.

The Custom Attributes area of the Customize Fields dialog box enables you to specify value behaviors in custom fields. By default, all custom fields contain no entries and no formulas and can accept any valid entry for the field type. You can use the Value List option to restrict entries in a field to a specified list of values, as shown in Figure 21.14.

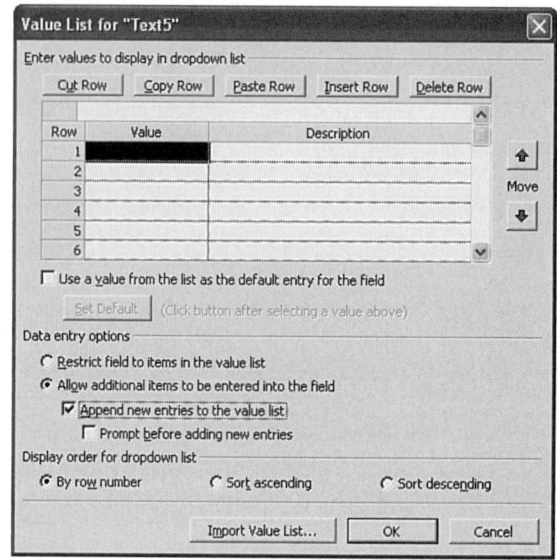

Figure 21.14
Users can be restricted to entering values from a predefined list, or the list can be allowed to grow.

In the Value List dialog box, you can enter acceptable values on as many rows as necessary, and you can add optional descriptions of the values to assist users in selection. Below the list you build is the option Use a Value from the List as the Default Entry for the Field. You can set the Data Entry Options section of the dialog box to Restrict Field to Items in the Value List to prohibit unacceptable field entries, or you can choose Allow Additional Items to Be Entered into the Field. You can also control the display order of the value list: by row number (the order in which the rows were entered), or in ascending or descending value order.

You can also use the Value List dialog box to import a list of values that exist in another project file. The supplying file must be open and the incoming data must be located in a corresponding field type (for example, cost into cost, text into text).

A powerful use of custom fields is the ability to define formulas for them that compute and populate values. Choosing the Formula option in the Custom Attributes area of the

Customize Fields dialog box brings up the Formula dialog box for the field, as shown in Figure 21.15. This dialog box might look familiar to users of other Microsoft applications such as Access.

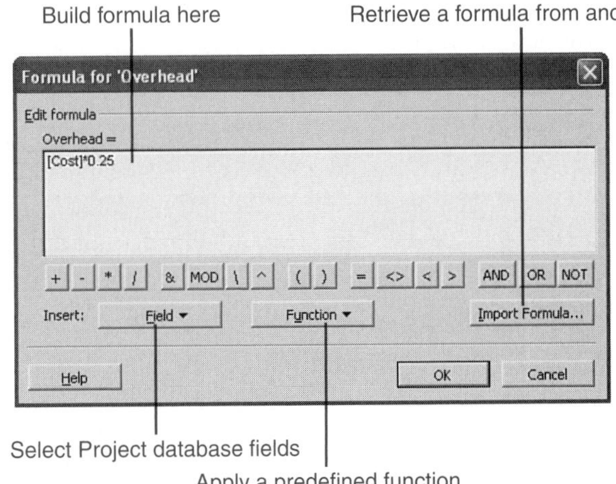

Figure 21.15
Formulas for custom fields can compute new values that are not provided in the Project database.

The formula in Figure 21.15 computes an overhead value for Cost1 that equals 25% of the task cost. A formula is built by typing directly into the Edit Formula area, by selecting fields and functions from the provided drop-down lists and operator buttons, or by choosing to import a formula that was previously created in another project file. The Insert Field drop-down list gives access to all the allowable Project fields. The fields are displayed in cascading menus of logical groups, such as date fields, number fields, and so on. The Function drop-down list displays all the possible predefined functions that can be used in custom field calculations. These functions are also displayed in cascading menus by groups, such as date/time functions and conversion functions.

NOTE

Do not include the equal sign (=) in the Edit Formula area. Project automatically adds it to any formula.

NOTE

You can access a detailed discussion of custom field formulas and available functions through online help. Click the Help button in the lower left of the Formula dialog box, or open the Help menu, and select Contents and Index. On the Index tab, search for *formula*, and choose Formula Dialog Box from the results.

To produce Figure 21.16, a customized cost table was created and applied to a Gantt Chart. The Project Cost column shows the normal total cost figure for each task, as calculated by Project. The Overhead column contains values generated by a formula for the Cost1 field and was renamed to the field alias, Overhead (refer to Figure 21.13). An additional cost field has been created: Cost2 has been renamed Cost with Overhead and assigned the simple formula [Cost] + [Overhead].

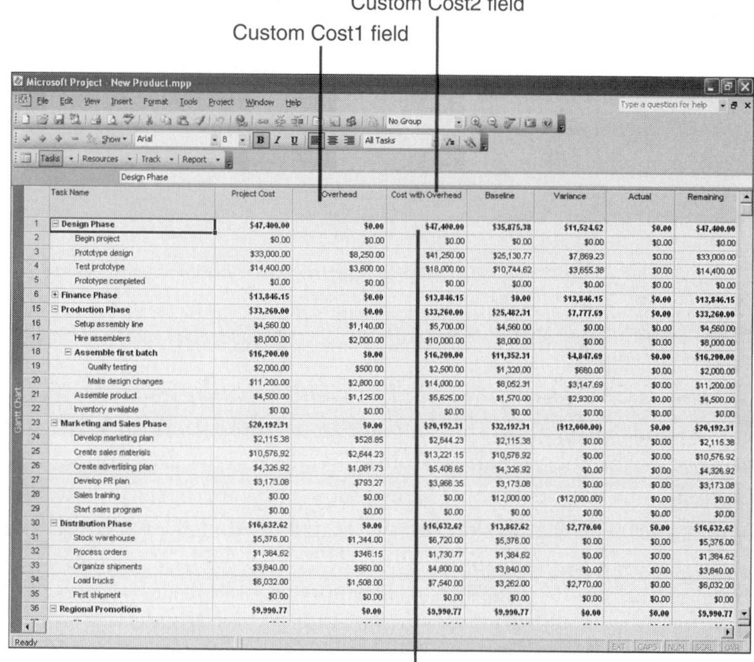

	Task Name	Project Cost	Overhead	Cost with Overhead	Baseline	Variance	Actual	Remaining
1	Design Phase	$47,400.00	$0.00	$47,400.00	$35,875.38	$11,524.62	$0.00	$47,400.00
2	Begin project	$0.00	$0.00	$0.00	$0.00	$0.00	$0.00	$0.00
3	Prototype design	$33,000.00	$8,250.00	$41,250.00	$25,130.77	$7,869.23	$0.00	$33,000.00
4	Test prototype	$14,400.00	$3,600.00	$18,000.00	$10,744.62	$3,655.38	$0.00	$14,400.00
5	Prototype completed	$0.00	$0.00	$0.00	$0.00	$0.00	$0.00	$0.00
6	Finance Phase	$13,846.15	$0.00	$13,846.15	$0.00	$13,846.15	$0.00	$13,846.15
15	Production Phase	$33,260.00	$0.00	$33,260.00	$25,482.31	$7,777.69	$0.00	$33,260.00
16	Setup assembly line	$4,560.00	$1,140.00	$5,700.00	$4,560.00	$0.00	$0.00	$4,560.00
17	Hire assemblers	$8,000.00	$2,000.00	$10,000.00	$8,000.00	$0.00	$0.00	$8,000.00
18	Assemble first batch	$16,200.00	$0.00	$16,200.00	$11,352.31	$4,847.69	$0.00	$16,200.00
19	Quality testing	$2,000.00	$500.00	$2,500.00	$1,320.00	$680.00	$0.00	$2,000.00
20	Make design changes	$11,200.00	$2,800.00	$14,000.00	$8,052.31	$3,147.69	$0.00	$11,200.00
21	Assemble product	$4,500.00	$1,125.00	$5,625.00	$1,570.00	$2,930.00	$0.00	$4,500.00
22	Inventory available	$0.00	$0.00	$0.00	$0.00	$0.00	$0.00	$0.00
23	Marketing and Sales Phase	$20,192.31	$0.00	$20,192.31	$32,192.31	($12,000.00)	$0.00	$20,192.31
24	Develop marketing plan	$2,115.38	$528.85	$2,644.23	$2,115.38	$0.00	$0.00	$2,115.38
25	Create sales materials	$10,576.92	$2,644.23	$13,221.15	$10,576.92	$0.00	$0.00	$10,576.92
26	Create advertising plan	$4,326.92	$1,081.73	$5,408.65	$4,326.92	$0.00	$0.00	$4,326.92
27	Develop PR plan	$3,173.08	$793.27	$3,966.35	$3,173.08	$0.00	$0.00	$3,173.08
28	Sales training	$0.00	$0.00	$0.00	$12,000.00	($12,000.00)	$0.00	$0.00
29	Start sales program	$0.00	$0.00	$0.00	$0.00	$0.00	$0.00	$0.00
30	Distribution Phase	$16,632.62	$0.00	$16,632.62	$13,862.62	$2,770.00	$0.00	$16,632.62
31	Stock warehouse	$5,376.00	$1,344.00	$6,720.00	$5,376.00	$0.00	$0.00	$5,376.00
32	Process orders	$1,384.62	$346.15	$1,730.77	$1,384.62	$0.00	$0.00	$1,384.62
33	Organize shipments	$3,840.00	$960.00	$4,800.00	$3,840.00	$0.00	$0.00	$3,840.00
34	Load trucks	$6,032.00	$1,508.00	$7,540.00	$3,262.00	$2,770.00	$0.00	$6,032.00
35	First shipment	$0.00	$0.00	$0.00	$0.00	$0.00	$0.00	$0.00
36	Regional Promotions	$9,990.77	$0.00	$9,990.77	$9,990.77	$0.00	$0.00	$9,990.77

Figure 21.16 You can add a calculated custom field to any task table.

Controlling Field Behaviors

For custom fields with values of any kind (text entries are not considered values), you need to take into account one more consideration when defining a field. The area in the Customize Fields dialog box labeled Calculation for Task and Group Summary Rows enables you to control custom field calculations for summary rows and for use in custom groups. By default, no value is entered on summary or group rows for custom fields. However, you can set the summary and group-level fields to use the formula set for the field, or you can set them to perform simple mathematical operations at the rollup level. The choices for math operations are Average, Maximum, Minimum, Sum, and Average First Sublevel. The Average First Sublevel option, which is applicable to grouping, prevents a field value from being carried up in the calculations from very detailed groups into less detailed groups. In Figure 21.17, the summary and rollup behavior for both custom fields is set to Use Formula, forcing Project to calculate every value instead of summing individual task values.

CREATING INDICATOR FIELDS

For issues of confidentiality, or to avoid raw data overload, you might choose to display graphic symbols in a custom field rather than display the actual data values. The bottom of the Customize Fields dialog box offers options for values to display for each customized field. By default, the actual keyed-in or computed values are displayed. You can substitute a variety of symbols for ranges of the actual values.

In the Customize Fields dialog box, click the Graphical Indicators button to display the Graphical Indicators dialog box. Figure 21.17 shows the Graphical Indicators dialog box set to display images instead of values for a third customized field, Cost3. This field has been renamed Overhead Indicators and contains the formula =[Cost1] to simply copy all values from Overhead into this Cost3 field. The test section of the Graphical Indicators dialog box lists the logical tests and test values for ranges of Cost3 (Overhead Indicators) data. As you can see in Figure 21.17, a low overhead value displays a flag; a medium overhead value displays a box; and a high overhead value displays a frowning face. Figure 21.18 illustrates the results of these settings.

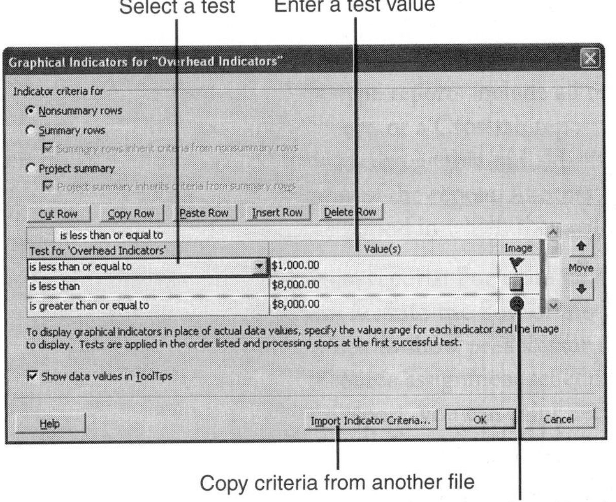

Figure 21.17
You can choose images from a predefined list and substitute them for actual values in custom fields.

TIP

> If you have already created a set of tests, values, and corresponding images in another project file—or even in another custom field within the same file—you can import those settings rather than re-create them. To do so, click Import Indicator Criteria on the Graphical Indicators dialog box.

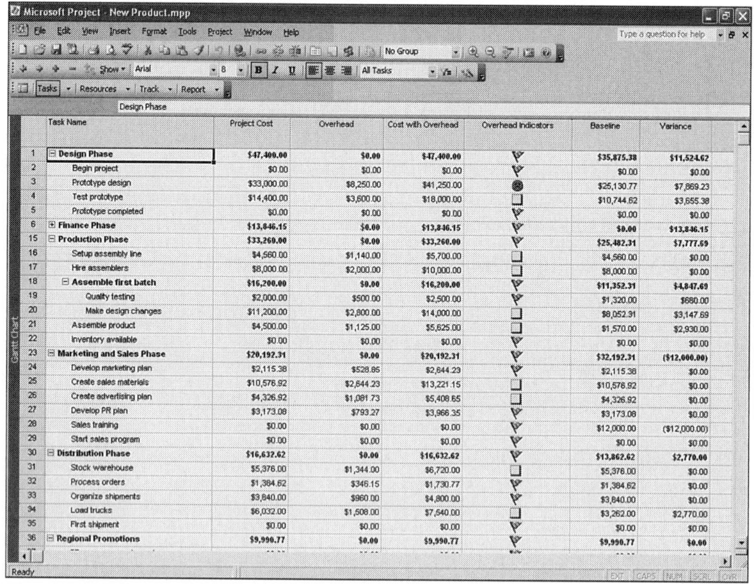

	Task Name	Project Cost	Overhead	Cost with Overhead	Overhead Indicators	Baseline	Variance
1	Design Phase	$47,400.00	$0.00	$47,400.00		$35,875.38	$11,524.62
2	Begin project	$0.00	$0.00	$0.00		$0.00	$0.00
3	Prototype design	$33,000.00	$8,250.00	$41,250.00		$25,130.77	$7,869.23
4	Test prototype	$14,400.00	$3,600.00	$18,000.00		$10,744.62	$3,655.38
5	Prototype completed	$0.00	$0.00	$0.00		$0.00	$0.00
6	Finance Phase	$13,846.15	$0.00	$13,846.15		$0.00	$13,846.15
15	Production Phase	$33,260.00	$0.00	$33,260.00		$25,482.31	$7,777.69
16	Setup assembly line	$4,560.00	$1,140.00	$5,700.00		$4,560.00	$0.00
17	Hire assemblers	$8,000.00	$2,000.00	$10,000.00		$8,000.00	$0.00
18	Assemble first batch	$16,200.00	$0.00	$16,200.00		$11,352.31	$4,847.69
19	Quality testing	$2,000.00	$500.00	$2,500.00		$1,320.00	$680.00
20	Make design changes	$11,200.00	$2,800.00	$14,000.00		$8,052.31	$3,147.69
21	Assemble product	$4,500.00	$1,125.00	$5,625.00		$1,570.00	$2,930.00
22	Inventory available	$0.00	$0.00	$0.00		$0.00	$0.00
23	Marketing and Sales Phase	$20,192.31	$0.00	$20,192.31		$32,192.31	($12,000.00)
24	Develop marketing plan	$2,115.38	$528.85	$2,644.23		$2,115.38	$0.00
25	Create sales materials	$10,576.92	$2,644.23	$13,221.15		$10,576.92	$0.00
26	Create advertising plan	$4,326.92	$1,081.73	$5,408.65		$4,326.92	$0.00
27	Develop PR plan	$3,173.08	$793.27	$3,966.35		$3,173.08	$0.00
28	Sales training	$0.00	$0.00	$0.00		$12,000.00	($12,000.00)
29	Start sales program	$0.00	$0.00	$0.00		$0.00	$0.00
30	Distribution Phase	$16,632.62	$0.00	$16,632.62		$13,862.62	$2,770.00
31	Stock warehouse	$5,376.00	$1,344.00	$6,720.00		$5,376.00	$0.00
32	Process orders	$1,384.62	$346.15	$1,730.77		$1,384.62	$0.00
33	Organize shipments	$3,840.00	$960.00	$4,800.00		$3,840.00	$0.00
34	Load trucks	$6,032.00	$1,508.00	$7,540.00		$3,262.00	$2,770.00
35	First shipment	$0.00	$0.00	$0.00		$0.00	$0.00
36	Regional Promotions	$9,990.77	$0.00	$9,990.77		$9,990.77	$0.00

Figure 21.18
A customized table can display both values and indicators for custom fields.

CREATING AND USING WBS CODE FORMATS

Many companies label and identify tasks by using some structure other than the task numbering system in a project file. A code field in Project automatically creates a numbered structure for your use. This code field is called *WBS*, which stands for Work Breakdown Structure.

By default, the WBS code is an exact duplicate of the project's outline numbers, but you can key in to the WBS field any number or letter combination that is suitable for your company. By creating a custom WBS structure, you can ensure that any user entries conform to the correct pattern.

➔ To learn about customizing WBS codes, **see** "Using Custom WBS Codes," **p. 163**.

CREATING AND USING CUSTOM OUTLINE FIELDS

You can create other coded numbering systems besides the automatic outline structure and custom WBS codes. Project provides 10 custom Outline Code fields. Different people in your organization might have different coding and reporting requirements. (For example, you might need to create a custom outline code field that is based on your organization's cost codes and sort the task list by that code when needed.) Multiple structures have typically been created in custom text fields. The limitation with using text fields for this purpose is the inability to control input so that it conforms to the outline code structure.

To create custom outline codes, you create a mask for the outline code field you plan to use. Unlike with calculated custom fields, Project doesn't populate the outline field with default codes—you must enter them manually.

Users can select a code for each task from a lookup table that you provide or they can type in outline codes—they can even create their own codes (which you can optionally require to conform to the mask). The lookup table guarantees that the code conforms to the mask, and it enables users to choose the correct codes by looking at descriptions for the codes in the lookup table.

The steps to creating custom outline structures are a combination of the steps used for customizing fields and those used for creating custom WBS codes. The actual definition of the outline takes place through the Customize Fields dialog box. Specifications for an outline code include sequence, values, and separators, just as in defining a custom WBS code.

CREATING AN OUTLINE MASK

To create a custom outline code mask, follow these steps:

1. Choose Tools, Customize, Fields to display the Customize Fields dialog box.
2. Select the Custom Outline Codes tab (see Figure 21.19).

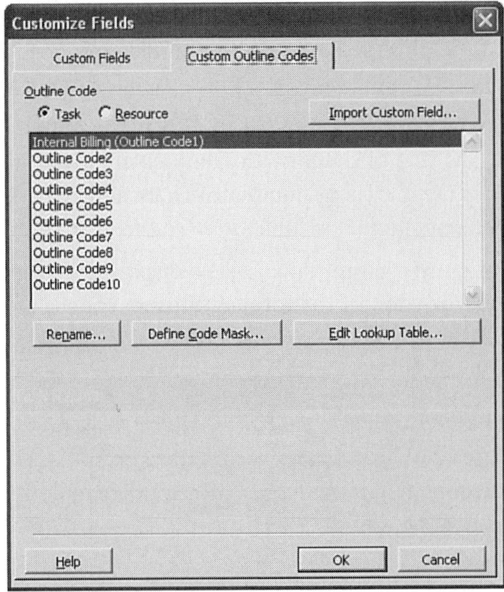

Figure 21.19
Begin creating an outline code mask by opening the Customize Fields dialog box and select the Custom Outline Codes tab.

3. Select one of the custom codes that appears in the list box.
4. Click the Rename button to assign the field an alias that will appear as the column heading. In the Rename Field dialog box that appears, type in the alias you want to use and click OK. In Figure 21.19, Outline Code1 has been renamed Internal Billing.
5. Click the Define Code Mask button to display the Outline Code Definition dialog box, in which you can create the mask (see Figure 21.20).

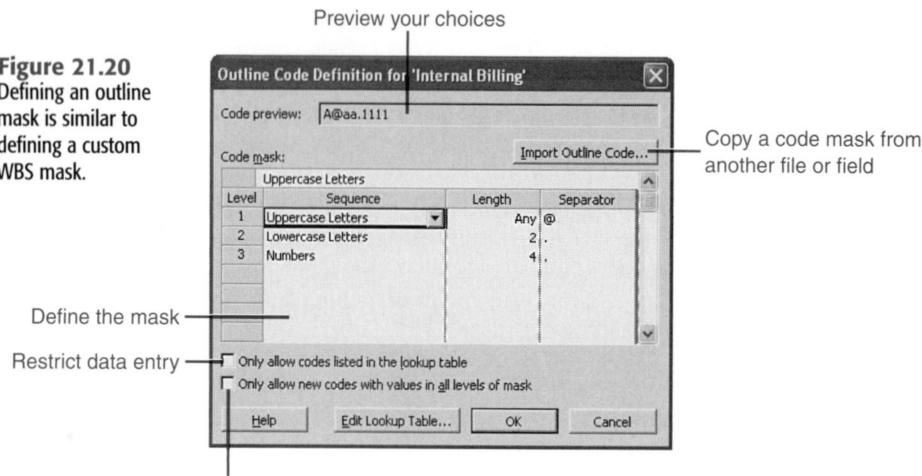

Figure 21.20
Defining an outline mask is similar to defining a custom WBS mask.

6. To create your own mask, click on the first blank row under the Sequence column in the Code Mask area of the Outline Code Definition dialog box. Use the pull-down arrow to choose Numbers, Uppercase Letters, Lowercase Letters, or Characters.
7. In the Length column, use the pull-down list to display the options for how many characters will be used for this part of the format. Choose Any if you want to be able to edit this part of the code and use a varying number of characters. Choose 1 through 10 to set a fixed number of characters for this section of the format.
8. In the Separator column, use the pull-down list to display the separator to use if another code follows this portion of the format. You can choose the period, hyphen, plus sign, or forward slash, or you can type in a symbol of your choosing.
9. Select the check box Only Allow Codes Listed in the Lookup Table if you want to disallow any codes except those you list in a lookup table.
10. Check the option Only Allow New Codes with Values in All Levels of Mask to force users to fill out codes completely if manual entries are being allowed.
11. Click OK to close the dialog box.

You might have previously created an outline code in another file or in another custom field in this file. Instead of creating an outline code from scratch, you can import an existing definition. To import an outline code definition, follow these steps:

1. On the Custom Outline Codes tab of the Customize Fields dialog box, click the Import Custom Field button to display the Import Outline Code dialog box (see Figure 21.21).
2. Select the Project name in the drop-down list of open projects. You are allowed to import a code within a project file from one custom field to another of the same type.
3. In the Field Type section, select Task, Resource, or Project to display the appropriate field names in the Field box.

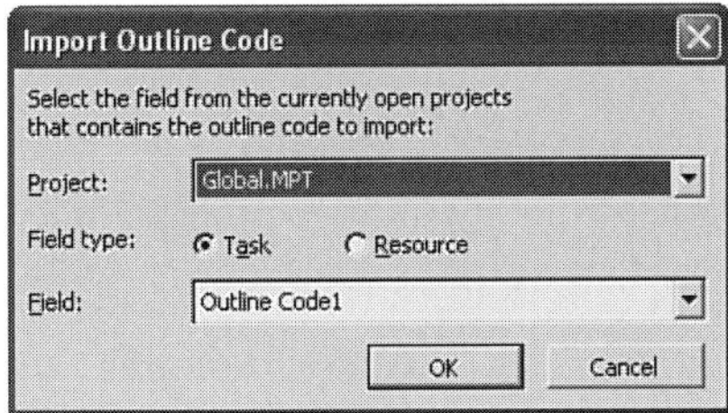

Figure 21.21
You can import an existing outline code mask from another file or from another field in the same file.

4. Select the field name in the Field drop-down list of custom fields.
5. Click OK.

Click OK in the Custom Outline Codes tab of the Customize Fields dialog box to complete the definition of the mask. If you already have the field displayed in the task view, you will see the new alias appear as the column heading.

CREATING AN OUTLINE CODE LOOKUP TABLE

You can define a value lookup table for users so that they can accurately enter the custom outline code. Basically, you type in an outline structure that fits your company's requirements. The steps for editing a lookup table are as follows:

1. Create an outline code mask.
2. In the Outline Code Definition dialog box, click Edit Lookup Table. The Edit Lookup Table dialog box appears, as shown in Figure 21.22.

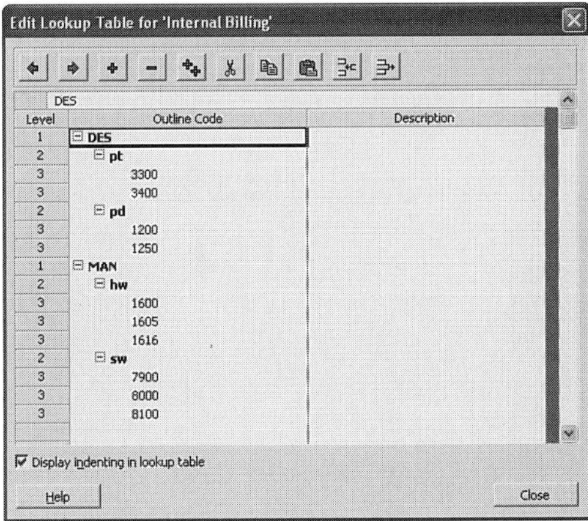

Figure 21.22
Your company's code structure can be reproduced in the outline code lookup table.

3. Type a list of valid entry codes in the Outline Code area. These entries are easiest to read and edit if the Display Indenting in Lookup Table option at the bottom of the dialog box is selected.

4. Use the right arrow and left arrow outlining buttons on the toolbar at the top of the dialog box to indent tasks to a higher-numbered level or outdent them to a lower-numbered level.
5. Use the standard Cut, Copy, and Paste buttons to assist in editing the outline code.
6. Type an optional description of the codes to assist users if desired.
7. Click Close when you're finished. If any typed entries do not conform to the outline structure created before you enter the Lookup Table area, a message warning is displayed, indicating that an entry does not match the mask.

USING CUSTOM OUTLINE CODES

Standard tables in Project do not include custom fields. You must modify a table to view the custom outline codes as well as other custom fields. See the section "Using and Creating Tables," earlier in this chapter, for more information.

In Figure 21.23, a copy of the Entry table has been modified to include the new custom outline code column that was renamed Internal Billing. Notice the drop-down list in the column; the outline code settings demand that the user choose values from the lookup table.

NOTE

> Outline codes you have defined are available for data entry on the Custom Fields tab of the Task or Resource Information dialog box.

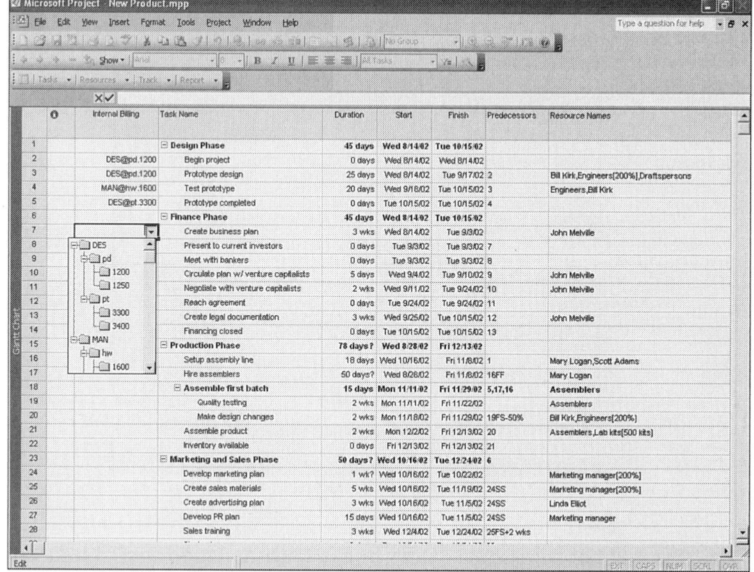

Figure 21.23
For this custom field, data entry is restricted to values from the outline code drop-down list.

Figure 21.23 shows the final results of several steps in the example described in this chapter:

- Rename Outline Code1 to Internal Billing (refer to Figure 21.19).
- Define the outline code (refer to Figure 21.20).
- Create the lookup table (refer to Figure 21.22).
- Display the Internal Billing code on the custom table (refer to Figure 21.23).

MANAGING CUSTOM FIELDS

After you have defined any custom field—text, numeric, cost, WBS, and so on—you should copy the field definition to the Global template to make it readily available for all your project documents that are based on the Global template.

CREATING CUSTOM FILTERS

Before you read this section, be sure to read the section "Exploring the Standard Filters" in Chapter 19, "Using the Standard Views, Tables, Filters, and Groups." This section builds on the information in that section by discussing how to create your own customized filters.

A good way to begin creating your own filters is to examine the definitions of the standard filters. To look at a filter definition, choose Project, Filtered For and select More Filters from the list that appears. Select a filter from the list (except the All Tasks filter or the All Resources filter) and click the Edit button. The Filter Definition dialog box appears. Figure 21.24 shows the Filter Definition box for the In Progress Tasks filter.

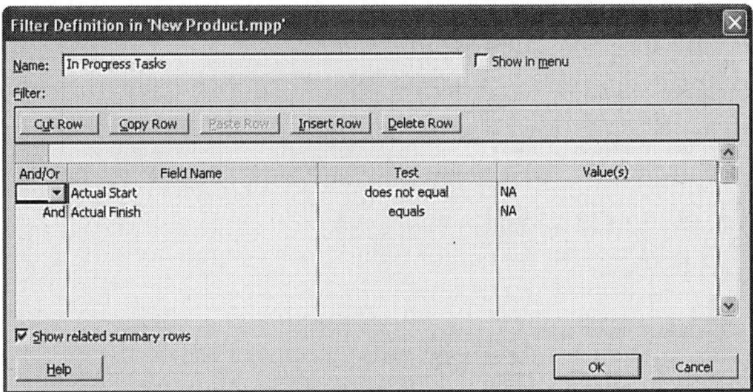

Figure 21.24
The In Progress filter definition sets criteria to display tasks that are already underway.

The In Progress Tasks filter applies two tests. The first test examines the Actual Start field to ensure that the value is *not equal* to NA (that is, a date has been entered, which indicates that the task has been started), and the second test examines the Actual Finish field to see whether the value is equal to NA (that is, the task has not finished). The logical operator And has been entered in the And/Or field, meaning that both the first and the second conditions must be met in order for a task to be selected.

Filters compare database fields to values you enter in the filter to values supplied by user input when the filter is applied or to values in other database fields. When multiple tests are combined with an And condition, all tests must be true; if multiple tests are combined with an Or condition, only one test must be true.

To define a filter, choose More Filters from the Project, Filtered For menu. If you want to create a new filter that is unlike any filter already defined, click the New button. Otherwise, select an existing filter name from the Filters entry list if you want to edit or copy an existing filter. If you edit an existing filter, the original definition is lost; start by creating a copy with which to experiment. Whether you click New, Edit, or Copy, the Filter Definition dialog box is displayed.

The following sections describe how to develop an overbudget filter that displays all tasks that are overbudget by at least $1,000.

A useful custom filter to create is one that will display only the detail tasks of the project, which are ones that are to be linked together and assigned to a resource. This filter actually removes from the view all the summary tasks and milestone tasks within the project. The custom filter is set for Summary Tasks=No and Milestones=No. This leaves only detail tasks.

When creating filters in Microsoft Project, in the Values field, you can choose values from a pick list.

Naming a Filter

You provide a name for the filter by typing a name in the Name field of the Filter Definition dialog box. If the filter name is to appear in the Filtered For menu, use an ampersand (`&`) before the letter that will be the hotkey. The check box labeled Show in Menu at the top of the dialog box must be selected in order for the filter name to appear in the menu and in the filter drop-down list on the Formatting toolbar.

To create an overbudget filter, enter the name as `Cost O&verbudget by 1000` (with *v* as the hotkey), and mark the Show in Menu box so that the filter is placed on the Filtered For menu (see Figure 21.25).

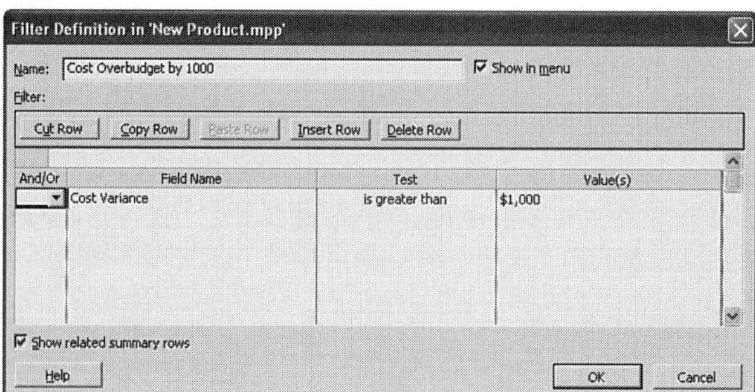

Figure 21.25
This is the completed Cost Overbudget by 1000 custom filter definition.

21

DEFINING FILTER CRITERIA

For each test to be imposed on the database, you must fill in a row of the Filter area in the Filter Definition dialog box. Each row must identify a field name, the nature of the test to be conducted in the field, and the value(s) to be looked for in the field. If multiple tests are to be imposed as part of the filter, the And/Or column must indicate the relationship of the criterion rows.

SELECTING A FIELD NAME

To select a field on which to filter, you need to type the field name or select a field name from the drop-down list. In the example shown in Figure 21.25, the field name is Cost Variance.

SELECTING A TEST

To select a test to use for the filter, you need to select the cell in the Test column and use the drop-down list to view the tests you can select. Then select the appropriate test or type the test phrase. In the example shown in Figure 21.25, the test is to be *greater than*.

Table 21.2 describes the items that can appear in the Test entry list.

TABLE 21.2 FILTER TEST OPTIONS

Test	Meaning
Equals	The field values must match the test value(s) exactly.
Does not equal	The field value must differ from the Value(s) column entry.
Is greater than	The field value must be greater than the Value(s) column entry.
Is greater than or equal to	The field value must be equal to or greater than the Value(s) column entry.
Is less than	The field value must be less than the Value(s) column entry.
Is less than or equal to	The field value must be equal to or less than the Value(s) column entry.
Is within	The field value must lie on or between the range of the Value(s) column entries. Two values are required.
Is not within	The field value must lie outside the range of the Value(s) column entries. Two values are required.
Contains	The field value must contain the string in the Value(s) column.
Does not contain	The field value must not contain the string that is in the Value(s) column.
Contains exactly	The field value must contain the exact string that appears in the Value(s) column.

Entering the Value(s) Column Entries

To enter the test value for a filter, you first select the cell in the Value(s) column. You have three options for specifying test values: Type a value for the test, include a prompt for interactive filters, or specify another database field name for calculated filters. The drop-down list for this column is used for calculated filters and contains the names of the fields, with each field name automatically enclosed in square brackets, as required by this type of calculated filter. In Figure 21.25, the value 1000 was typed in (numeric formatting is allowed but not required).

Completing the Filter Definition

To edit a filter definition, you use the Insert Row button on the Filter Definition dialog box to insert a blank row before the criterion row you have selected. You use the Delete Row button to remove a criterion row from the definition.

If the filter is to appear in the Filtered For menu, be sure that the Show in Menu check box is selected. Select the Show Related Summary Rows check box if you want the selected task's associated summary task(s)to also be displayed.

Click the OK button to complete the definition and return to the More Filters dialog box. Click the Apply button or the Highlight button to apply the filter immediately, or click Close to save the filter definition but not apply the filter at this time.

Using More Filter Criterion Tests

Defining tests requires some knowledge of the database fields, field types, and acceptable data values. This section illustrates various types of filter criteria. These samples should help you design almost any kind of filter.

Testing for Logical Values

Many of the fields in the Project database contain only the logical values Yes and No. For example, the Milestone field contains Yes for Milestone tasks and No for all other tasks. The standard filter for Milestone tasks looks for the value Yes in the appropriate field (see Figure 21.26).

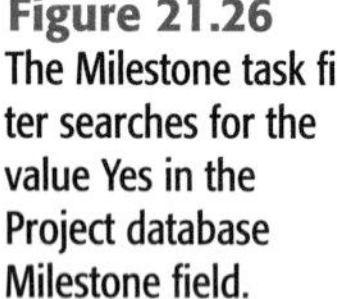

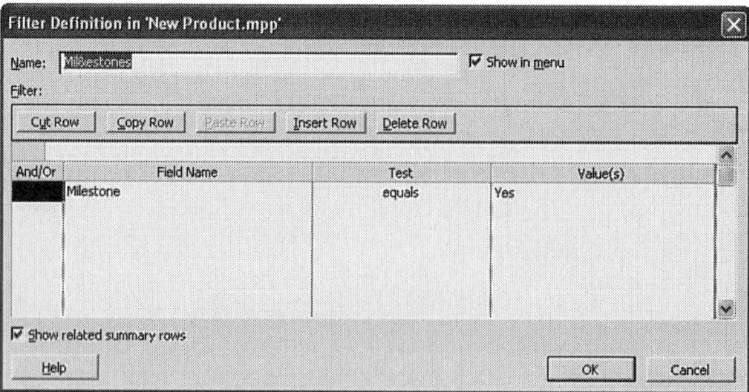

Figure 21.26 The Milestone task filter searches for the value Yes in the Project database Milestone field.

USING THE WITHIN AND NOT WITHIN TESTS

You use the Is Within test to look for values that lie within and include the upper and lower values in the Value(s) column. The Is Not Within test identifies values that fall outside a range of values. You enter the range of values being used in the test into the Value(s) column, with a comma separating the lower and upper values.

USING THE CONTAINS TEST

Some text fields (most notably Resource Names, Predecessors, and Successors) can contain lists of entries separated by commas. The Resource Names field contains the list of all the resources assigned to a task, and the Predecessors field contains a list of all the predecessors to the task. The Resource Names and Predecessors fields are really text fields. The Contains test examines the text to see whether a string of characters that is entered in the Value(s) column is contained within the field contents. The Contains test is useful when you want to locate all the tasks whose names include a specified string of characters. Figure 21.27 shows a filter that looks for the tasks whose names not only include the word *design* but other words as well, either before or after sales. Note that the match is not case sensitive.

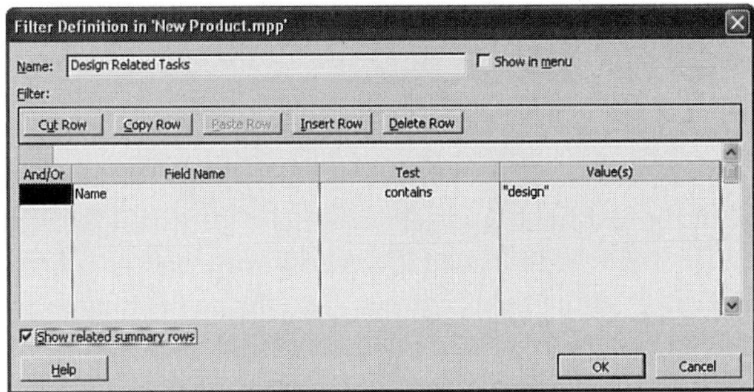

Figure 21.27
The Contains test is useful for character searches in filters.

The Contains Exactly test varies slightly, but significantly, from the Contains test. Contains Exactly is for use in fields with comma-separated lists and treats each item in the list as a separate entity. Thus, a Group... filter that uses `Contains` to search for the value "writer" would select all four resources listed in Table 21.3. But one that uses the `Contains Exactly` test and searches for "writer" would select all but writer extraordinaire.

TABLE 21.3 CONTAINS TEST GROUPS AND RESOURCES

Resource	Group
Robbie	writer
Robbie Smith	writer, instructor
Robbie Jane Smith	writer extraordinaire
Roberta Smith	writer, instructor

USING WILDCARDS IN A VALUE(S) STRING

You can search text field entries by using wildcard characters in the search string. You must use only the Equals or Not Equals test for strings that include wildcards. The wildcard characters in Microsoft Project are similar to wildcard characters used in DOS—the asterisk (*) and the question mark (?).

A wildcard can match any character that falls in the same place as the wildcard in the search comparisons. Therefore, the test string ab?d is matched by any single character in the third position, as long as the *a*, *b*, and *d* are in the right places. The asterisk represents any number of missing characters or no characters, whereas the question mark represents just one character. Here are some examples:

Test String with Wildcard	Possible Matches
f?d	f*a*d, f*b*d, f*c*d, f*d*d, f*e*d, f*2*d
f??d	f*in*d, f*or*d, f*oo*d, f*22*d
f*d	fd, f*a*d, f*ee*d, f*ormatte*d
f*	f, f*1*, f*122*, f*ind this text*
12-?06	12-*A*06, 12-*1*06, 12-*X*06
12-*06	12-*A*06, 12-06, 12-*abc0*06

If you want to search for a wildcard character (* or ?), you have to use the caret (^) symbol before it. For example, searching for `*^?*` would find all the records that contain a question mark somewhere in the text field. And searching for `*^^*` would find entries containing a caret symbol. Unlike in Excel, in Project, searching with wildcards for a field value that contains a string somewhere in the field requires a leading and ending asterisk. If you left off the leading and ending asterisks in the previous example, and searched for `^?`, Project would only display records that had a single character in them (a question mark).

USING INTERACTIVE FILTERS

An *interactive filter* is a versatile filter that searches for different values in a field from one time to the next. When an interactive filter is applied, Project prompts the user for input, and uses that input as the test value(s). This type of filter can be included on the Filtered for cascading menu and is automatically included on the filter drop-down list in the Formatting toolbar.

21

NOTE

> Each supplied interactive filter has an ellipsis (...) after its name in the Filter drop-down list on the Formatting toolbar.

You create an interactive filter by typing a message, enclosed in double-quotes and followed by a question mark, in the Value(s) column of the Filter Definition dialog box. When the filter is applied, the message is displayed in a dialog box as a prompt for the user, and the question mark causes Project to wait for the user to fill a blank that follows the message. For example, the message `"What words are you looking for in task names?"` is a suitable prompt. The entry in the Value(s) column of the filter definition would look like the entry in Figure 21.28.

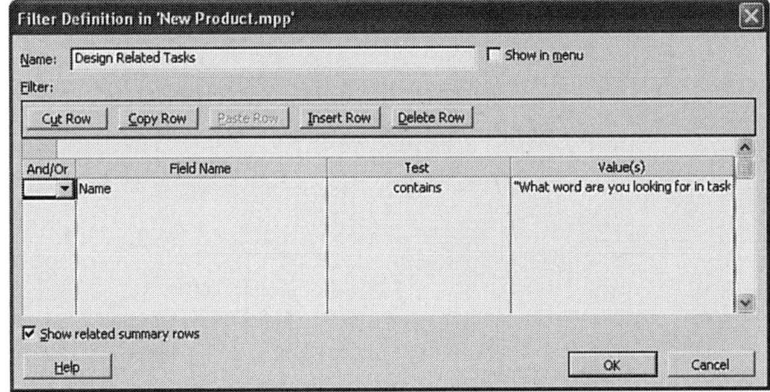

Figure 21.28
An interactive filter prompts the user for input each time it is applied.

When an interactive filter is run, one or more dialog boxes are presented for user input. In Figure 21.29, the Is Within test is being used, so two test values are required. The input area for both the beginning and ending filter dates are contained in a single dialog box. Figure 21.30 shows the dialog box that appears when the filter is applied.

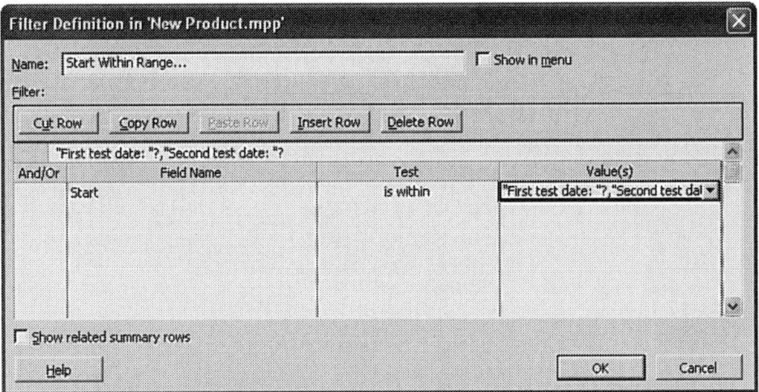

Figure 21.29
An interactive filter can prompt for more than one input value.

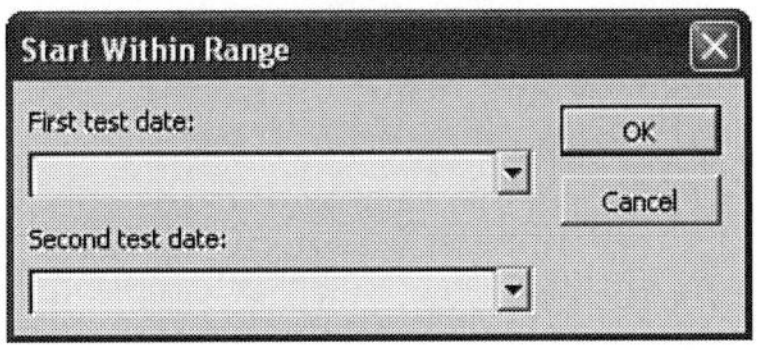

Figure 21.30
Two separate data entry areas can be included in a single dialog box.

Start Within Range
First test date:
Second test date:
OK
Cancel

21

Creating Calculated Filters

A *calculated filter* compares the value in one field of a task or resource with the value in another field for the same task or resource. For example, in our Overbudget filter, a task that is overbudget has a Baseline Cost field value that is less than the value in the Cost field. To filter overbudget tasks, the criterion needs to compare the Cost field with the Baseline Cost field (see Figure 21.31).

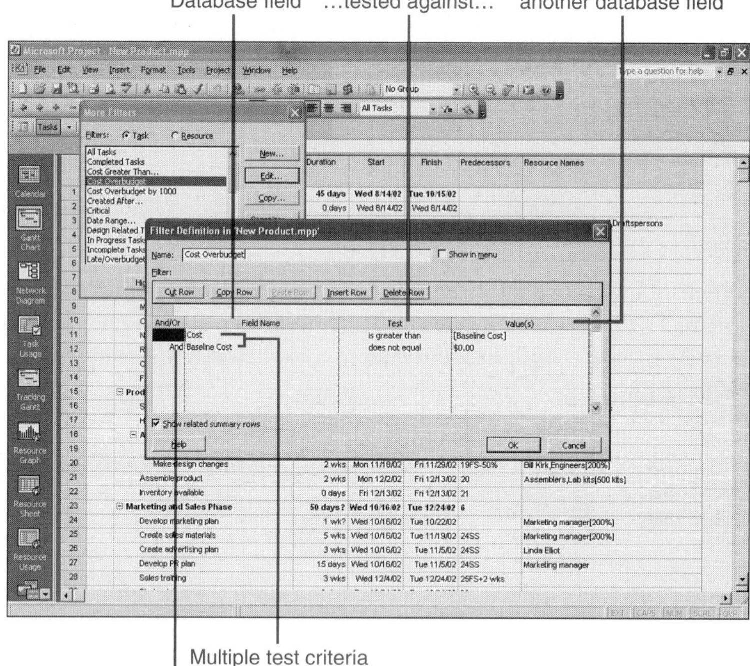

Figure 21.31
Calculated filters compare values in the Project database fields.

Creating Multiple Criteria Filters

If more than one test must be used to create a filter, each test is placed on its own row of the filter definition table. The first column (And/Or) is used to designate how each row is to be used with the results of tests above it. If it is necessary that the tests on both rows be satisfied in order to satisfy the filter, the operator And is placed in the And/Or column.

The Cost Overbudget filter shown in Figure 21.31 includes two tests. To be included in the filter results, a task's current cost must be more than the baseline cost for the task. But the filter also requires that the baseline cost must be greater than 0; this task must have a budget amount to be used for comparison.

If, however, passing *either* of the tests is sufficient to satisfy the filter, the operator Or is placed in the And/Or column. If the Or operator is placed in this column in Figure 21.31, all tasks with either a cost exceeding the planned amount or a positive baseline cost would be included.

If more than two rows are used to define a filter, the tests are evaluated from the top down. Therefore, the first two rows are evaluated by using the operator on the second first row, and then the third row test is added by using the operator on the third row, and so on—until all rows have been considered. For example, if And were replaced with Or in Figure 21.31, the filter would locate all tasks costing more than planned and then add to the results any tasks with a planned cost of zero.

You can group multiple criteria together to create more complex filters. For example, the Late/Overbudget Tasks Assigned To filter (shown in Figure 21.32) looks for tasks that are assigned to a resource (whose name is prompted for) and whose baseline has been set, as well as a finish that is later than planned or a cost that is greater than planned. The first two rows must both be met, and then either of the last two rows must be met.

To create a grouped series of criteria, you select an And or Or on a blank row between the two groups. Then you move to the next row, without entering any other criteria on the And/Or row. Notice the shaded row in Figure 21.32.

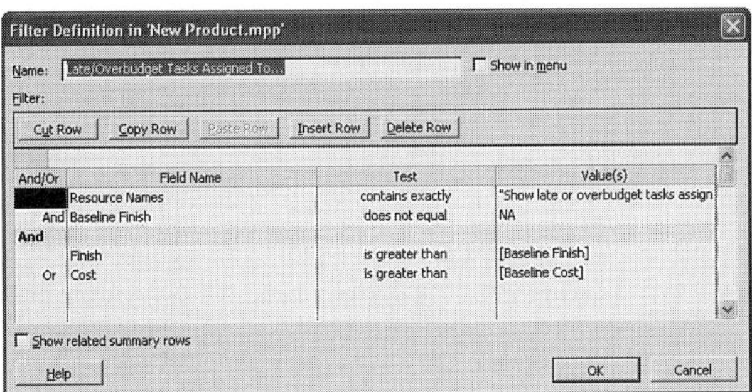

Figure 21.32
Entering a condition on a blank row creates separate groups of criteria.

CREATING CUSTOM FILTERS WITH AUTOFILTER

A very easy way to create a custom filter is by using the Custom option on the AutoFilter list. (Microsoft Excel users should recognize this feature.) First, turn on the AutoFilter feature by either choosing Project, Filtered For, AutoFilter or by clicking the AutoFilter button on the Formatting toolbar. This displays an AutoFilter drop-down list on each column heading. When you choose any of these lists, a menu appears, with a number of choices, including Custom. When you choose the Custom option, in this case from the Task Name field drop-down list, the dialog box in Figure 21.33 is displayed.

The first field is set to whatever column drop-down list you chose, and the test then depends on that field. For example, with a duration, or a start or finish date, the test is Equals, but the task name field's test is Contains. The drop-down list to the right of the field has a list of values from which you can choose, or you can type criteria as described in earlier sections. To add a second test against values in the same column, complete the second row, using either the And or the Or option. When you click OK, the filter is applied. If you want to modify the criteria the next time you access the Custom option from the AutoFilter drop-down list, the previous criteria will still be there.

Figure 21.33
The Custom AutoFilter dialog box helps you create a custom filter.

If the filter you create proves useful for future sessions, you can save it by using the Save button in the Custom AutoFilter dialog box. Clicking this button takes you to the Filter Definition dialog box described in earlier sections.

Creating Custom Groups

Grouping tasks or resources is yet another way to display project data to meet your needs. A key advantage to organizing lists in groups is the ability to display subtotals for numeric data in the groups. Timephased values in the usage views, such as Work Over Time, are automatically subtotaled by time period.

Project includes a number of predefined group definitions. The following sections focus on creating custom groups to meet your specific needs. The method for creating a custom group is very similar to creating a custom filter; the logic behind grouping is very similar to that behind sorting.

→ For a description of groups and their application, **see** "Grouping the Task and Resource Lists," **p. 467**.

Accessing Custom Groups

To define and format a custom group, you must first open the Group Definition dialog box. You need to choose Project, Group By, and then select More Groups from the cascading menu. First you need to choose between group types: Select either Task or Resource. Then you need to select an existing group name and click Edit or Copy to modify an existing group or to use a group as a starting point for the new group definition. To create a custom group from scratch, select New. The Group Definition dialog box is displayed, as shown in Figure 21.34.

Next, you can replace the generic Name, such as Group 1, with a descriptive name of your choosing. To have the group name appear in the Group By cascading menu, select the Show in Menu option. Finally, complete the group definition as described in the following section "Selecting Grouping Fields."

The Group Definition dialog box is also available directly from the Project, Group By cascading menu. This method is a shortcut to opening the dialog box and enables you to experiment with group settings without saving a named group. However, any group you create in this way is *temporary* in that Microsoft Project holds the definition under the name Custom Group. Custom Group is then displayed in the More Groups list, but you can't open it for editing while you're in the More Groups list. You must access this temporary definition via Customize Group By to name it and to save it. When the data is displayed and summarized as required, you choose Project, Group By, Customize Group By and select Save to name and permanently store the group definition.

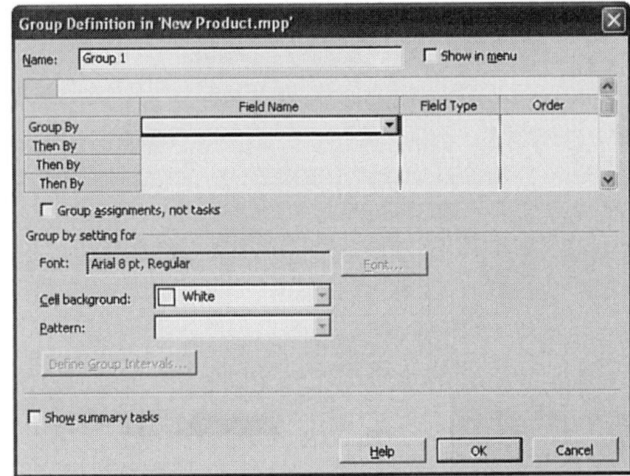

Figure 21.34
You can create and modify groups in the Group Definition dialog box.

Selecting Grouping Fields

The task or resource list can be grouped by up to 10 levels. You create groups by selecting one or more fields from the database to create an outlined group structure. Groups are defined from the top down; that is, the first field in the definition represents the broadest group. Additional grouping fields refine the categorized lists into increasingly more detailed groupings.

To create the group structure, access the Group Definition dialog box shown in Figure 21.35. Select one field name for the Group By line and a sort order for the field (that is, Ascending or Descending). For group refinements, move down one position and choose a Then By field (and its sort order). No preview area exists in this dialog box. Select OK when you are ready to return to the screen and view the results of your choices.

NOTE

Unfortunately, the word *group* has two different meanings in Project. Each resource can, and should, be designated as a member of a group; this is usually entered on the Resource Sheet view. But *group* also refers to the grouping feature. The supplied Resource Group grouping definition is one of the most useful starting points for other groupings. Usually it is clear by the context which use of *group* is intended.

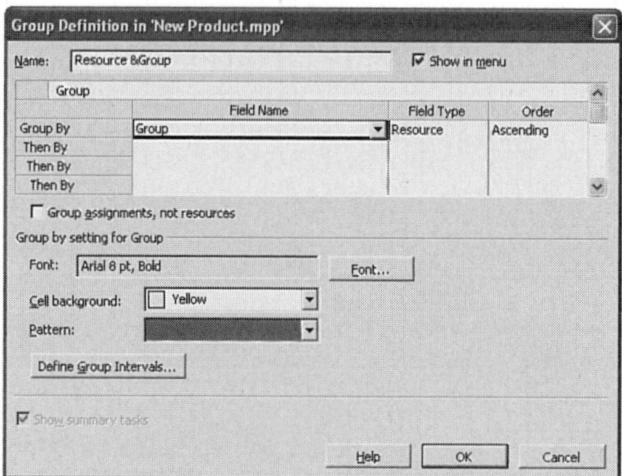

Figure 21.35
Choose levels of grouping and the group order in the Group Definition dialog box.

Defining Group Intervals

For some fields, the group interval is automatic. For example, if you're grouping on the Critical field, the only two possible values for Critical are Yes and No. In other fields, particularly date fields, the group intervals are created logically, but they might not match your requirements. In still other fields, such as costing data, a series of discrete or unique values exists, creating many groups with few entries in each.

The Group Definition dialog box includes an option to control how data is grouped. In the Group Definition dialog box, select a field name that is already specified on the Group By or Then By rows, and then click Define Group Intervals. The Define Group Interval dialog box appears, as shown in Figure 21.36. By default, every data type is set to be grouped on Each Value, from the earliest (or smallest) to the latest (or largest). The Group On drop-down list offers a choice of logical groupings for the data type. Date values can be grouped by intervals of minutes up to years; numeric data can be grouped in any intervals and can start the grouping in negative numbers; text values can be grouped only by each value or by the first few characters.

Figure 21.36
By default, unique values start new groups.

When you use the grouping feature, any numeric field displayed onscreen shows the group subtotals on the line with the group label. In Project 2003, any timephased numeric values, such as scheduled cost per time period, are also subtotaled in the appropriate time period.

Figure 21.37 shows the results of applying the Resource Group definition to the Resource Usage view. The timescale portion is formatted to show scheduled and cumulative costs within each month. Also, the new option Group Assignments, Not Resources is turned off by default in this grouping definition, so each task assignment for each resource can be displayed onscreen.

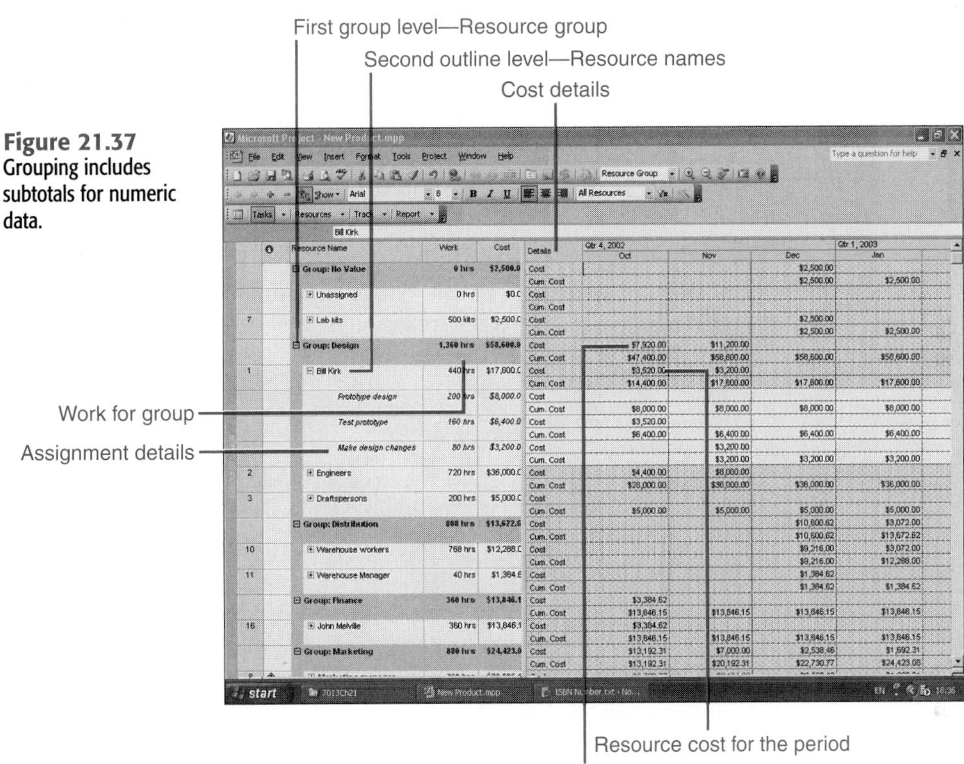

Figure 21.37
Grouping includes subtotals for numeric data.

> **TIP**
>
> You can't change the value rollup behavior of standard fields for group displays. To see, for example, the average value of a standard field for a group, you must create a calculated custom field (as described earlier in this chapter, in the section "Creating Calculated Fields") and use a simple formula to set the custom field equal to a standard numeric field. In the Customize Fields dialog box, you can set the Calculation for Task and Group Summary Rows Rollup option to Average.

FORMATTING GROUP DISPLAYS

In addition to specifying field group intervals, you can format the group displays. Each group displays the task or resource detail information, plus a summary bar for the group. Each group level has its own settings for font size, background color, and pattern.

TIP

> To avoid having the grouped display cluttered with multiple types of summary bars, be sure to turn off the Show Summary Tasks option.

Groups look, and in some ways act, like outlines. In Project 2003 the Show Outline Levels toolbar button makes it easy to collapse and expand the detail levels on a grouped view. In Figure 21.37, the groups are collapsed to Outline Level 2. The assignments for Bill Kirk can be displayed by clicking the plus sign next to his name. Figure 21.38 shows the same resource grouping, but Group Assignments, Not Resources is turned on in the grouping definition. Note that the resource names are not shown, so in Figure 21.38 only two outline levels are shown.

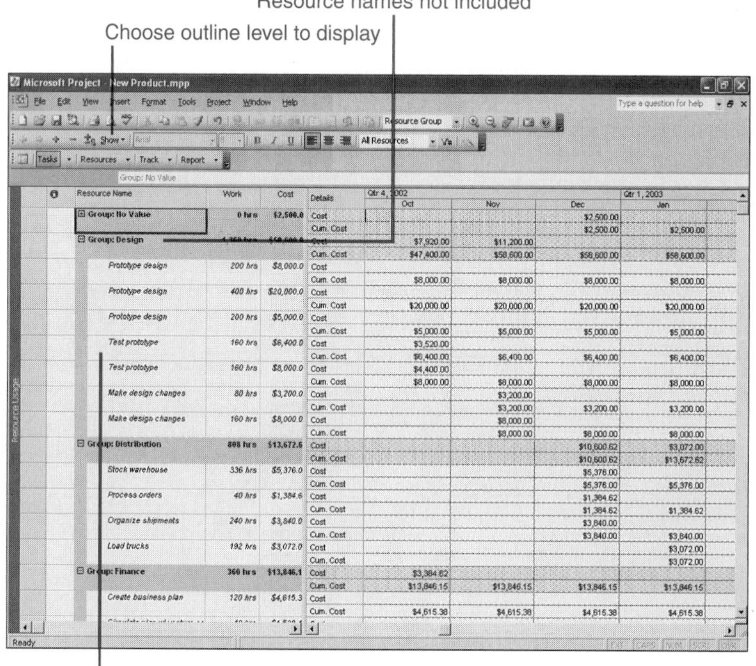

Figure 21.38 You use the Show Outline Levels button to hide group details.

SAVING CUSTOM GROUPS

Named custom group definitions are saved with a Project file. To make a group definition available to other files, you use the Groups tab in the Organizer, as described in the following section.

ORGANIZING VIEWS AND OTHER CUSTOM ELEMENTS IN PROJECT FILES

All the customized changes you make in a Project file—whether by defining views, tables, filters, groups, or format specifications—are saved as part of the current file. However, you can choose to make these customized elements available to other project files or to all projects by storing them in an underlying template. In Microsoft Project, the global template file is `GLOBAL.MPT`.

When you start Microsoft Project, `GLOBAL.MPT` loads with the project file. When you exit Project, all changes made to elements such as views are saved only with the project file. Customized views created for one project file are not directly available to other project files. If you save the view definition to the global file, however, these customized views can be made available across all project files that rely on that global file. This is also true for other customized objects, such as custom tables, filters, and field definitions.

To save view changes to the `GLOBAL.MPT` file, follow these steps:

NOTE

> **Views are the objects saved during this discussion, but the steps shown here are the same for all custom elements.**

1. Choose View, More Views and click the Organizer button.
2. The Organizer dialog box has tabs for each set of custom objects that can be copied between project files. The left side of the Views tab shows views that are available in the `GLOBAL.MPT` file, and the right side shows a list of the customized and modified views that are available in the current project file, along with any views that were used during this session of Project (see Figure 21.39). The other tabs follow the same format. Choose the tab that contains the customized objects (views, tables, filters, groups, and so on) that you want to copy.

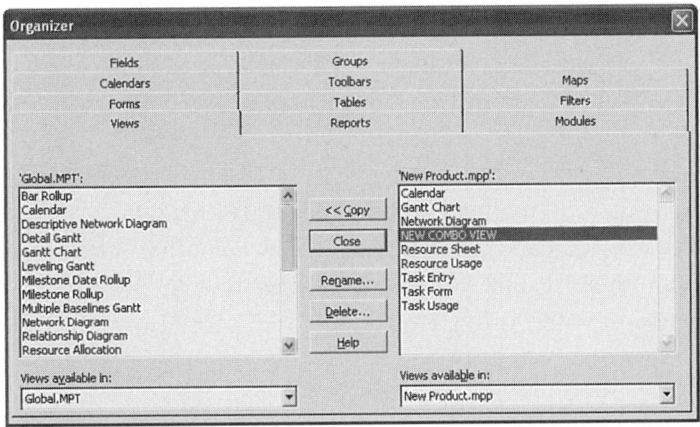

Figure 21.39
The Organizer helps you manage the storage of custom views, tables, fields, filters, groups, and more.

3. Select the view or views in the project file list that should also be in the GLOBAL.MPT file and click the Copy button. This copies these view definitions from the project file to the GLOBAL.MPT file.
4. The Cancel button changes to Close after the copy is performed. Click the Close button to close the Organizer when you are finished copying the view definitions.

NOTE

In the Organizer, when you display a list of elements from the open file, it does not mean all items in the list have been customized and need to be stored in the Global template. For example, any view that has been used during the current session of Project will appear in the Organizer list. There is no indication that the view has actually been modified. This is yet another reason to make and name copies of objects so that you know which ones are your creations.

If you save the customized views in the GLOBAL.MPT file, any time you create a new project based on that file (which is the default), those views will be available.

CAUTION

When you copy custom views to the GLOBAL.MPT file or to other Project files, be sure you copy any custom filters, groups, or tables that are part of the custom view.

You can also use the Organizer to rename and delete views from the GLOBAL.MPT file or from current project files. To delete a view, first select the view in the list from which it should be deleted. Choose Delete and answer Yes to confirm the deletion or No to cancel the deletion. The view is not available in either the GLOBAL.MPT file or in the current project file only—depending on which list was selected when the deletion was made.

Sometimes elements are saved with generic names (for example, View 1, or Group 1). To rename such an element, in the Organizer, select the object you want to rename, click the Rename button, and type in an appropriate new name.

NOTE

You cannot rename custom fields in the Organizer. Use Tools, Customize, Fields if you need to rename a custom field.

21

If you don't want to copy an element to the GLOBAL.MPT file but you want to use it in another project file, you can copy it from one file to another. First, be sure to open both files. Then, using the Organizer, choose both files from the drop-down lists at the bottom of the box—one on the left and one on the right. Choose the appropriate tab for the object you want and copy it.

TIP

> If you run a shared copy of Microsoft Project on a network, you might not be able to save custom elements in the `GLOBAL.MPT` file that is used by everyone. In that case, storing your modifications is a matter of computing practices. You might choose to set aside one project file to be used as a holding vessel for storing and retrieving your personalized elements. In that case, copy objects between two open files, not between an open file and the `GLOBAL.MPT` template.

You can access the Organizer in several ways. The most direct way is by selecting Tools, Organizer. However, most dialog boxes in which you can customize named elements have a button you can click to display the Organizer. For example, you can find such a button on the dialog boxes that appear when you select the following menu options:

- View, More Views
- View, Table, More Tables
- Project, Filtered For, More Filters
- Project, Group By, More Groups
- View, Reports, Custom

If you upgrade to Microsoft Project 2003 over an earlier version, the customized items in the old `GLOBAL.MPT` file are automatically incorporated into the new template, and you gain any of the new features of the new version of Microsoft Project. The new template does not completely overwrite the old; the two are merged.

TROUBLESHOOTING

RESTORING STANDARD VIEWS

I've modified a standard view by editing it and now I want to get back the original. What do I do?

Use the Organizer to copy the view definition you modified back into your project from the `GLOBAL.MPT` file. Be sure to rename the modified view first so that you don't overwrite your work.

CHANGING THE SCREEN TYPE FOR A VIEW

I want to change the basic screen type used for a view that I created. How can I make this happen?

Instead of copying an existing view, you must create a brand new view. Select View, More Views to create a new view definition. You might first want to choose Edit, to open the view you were copying so you can see the settings that were used. Then, you can create a new view and enter those settings in the new definition.

FREEZING THE FIRST TABLE COLUMN

I'm working in a table with many columns, and when I scroll to the right side of the table, the task names disappear. Is there any way to lock them in place?

Yes. You can edit the table and move the task name field to the very first column. Make sure the Lock First Column check box is selected. The only problem with this arrangement is that you can't move the cursor into the column for editing. You might want to edit your table in this way after your task names have been finalized.

CHAPTER 22

USING AND CUSTOMIZING THE STANDARD REPORTS

In this chapter

Understanding the Standard Reports 878

Customizing Reports 891

Creating Reports 894

Using the Common Customization Controls 896

Customizing Specific Report Types 899

Saving and Sharing Custom Reports 918

Troubleshooting 918

UNDERSTANDING THE STANDARD REPORTS

There will probably be circumstances when printing views from Microsoft Office Project doesn't give you the information you need or the format you'd prefer. The Gantt Chart view might not provide enough detail, or perhaps you'd like to see your project data in a text format instead of graphically. The reports in Project can provide the solution.

ACCESSING THE STANDARD REPORTS

The Reports command on the View menu provides access to the Reports dialog box, which lists six groups of report formats: Overview, Current Activities, Costs, Assignments, Workload, and Custom (see Figure 22.1). Together, the first five groups contain 22 predefined Project Summary, Calendar, Task, Resource, and Crosstab reports that are set up and ready to print. The last report category, Custom, allows you to access reports that are not available in the other five groups and create your own reports. Methods for creating and customizing reports are discussed later in this chapter.

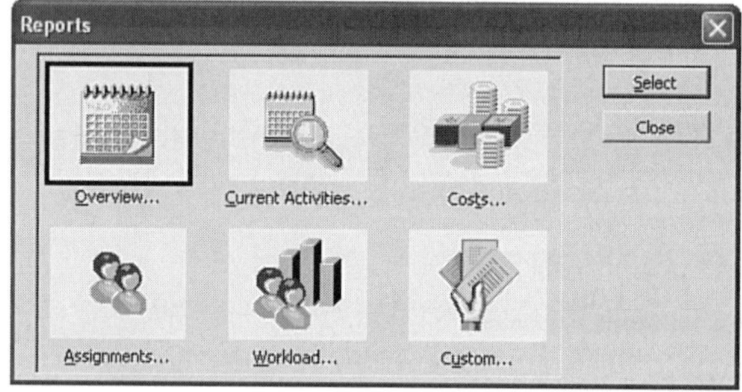

Figure 22.1
You can use the predefined reports to keep management and your project team informed of the status of all aspects of a project.

Report

You can also display reports by using the Project Guide toolbar. With the Project Guide toolbar displayed, click the Report button. In the Report bar, choose Select a View or Report. In the next pane, choose Print a Project Report. Finally, choose Display Reports.

To select one of the report categories, either double-click the category button or click the button once and then click Select.

After you select one of the category buttons in the Reports dialog box, another dialog box appears, showing the reports that belong to that category. For example, when the Overview Reports category is selected, the reports available in that category are shown (see Figure 22.2). To display one of these reports, you can either double-click the desired report icon or click it once and then click the Select button.

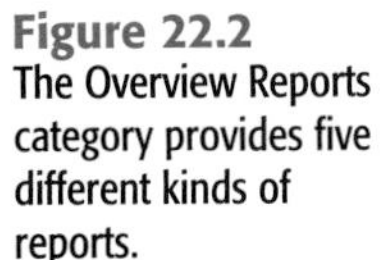

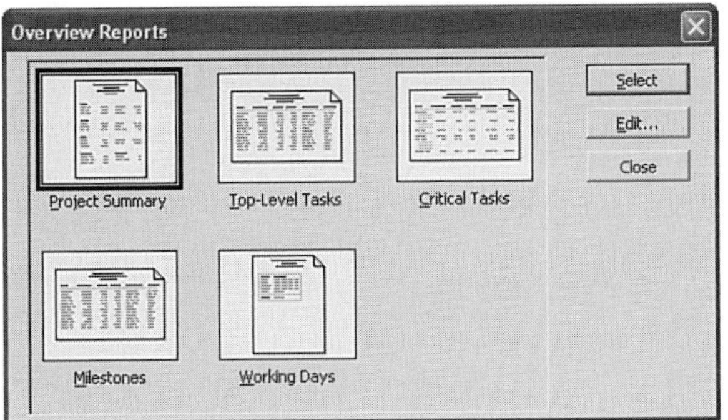

Figure 22.2
The Overview Reports category provides five different kinds of reports.

Most of the predefined reports available in Microsoft Office Project are variations of the four basic report types:

- **Task**—A report that lists all the tasks (or, optionally, only those selected by a filter) and might include various details about each task. You can add any of the task fields to this report by basing the report on a task table that includes the desired field.
- **Resource**—A report that lists all the resources (or, optionally, only those selected by a filter) and might include various details about each resource. You can add any of the resource fields to this report by basing the report on a resource table that includes the desired field.
- **Crosstab**—A report in table format that shows cost or work summaries by time period for the project's tasks or for its resources. You choose whether tasks or resources will be listed in the rows; whether columns will cover days, weeks, months, or other time periods; and which cost or work value you want summed up for each time period.
- **Monthly Calendar**—A monthly calendar that is similar to the Calendar view. This type of report is not included in the five predefined categories, but it can be used to create a new report.

The Task, Resource, and Crosstab reports are the primary types used for reports in the Overview, Current Activities, Costs, Assignments, and Workload categories displayed in the Reports dialog box.

The fourth report type, the Monthly Calendar report, can be used to create new reports, but there are no predefined examples of this type. There are also two unique predefined reports, the Project Summary report and the Base Calendar report, which are not based on any of the four report types previously mentioned.

When you select a report to display, you see the report, based on your active project, in Print Preview mode. To read the text of the report, you need to zoom in on the preview page by clicking the magnifying glass button on the toolbar to zoom in or positioning your mouse anywhere on the report. The mouse changes to a magnifying glass, and you can click to zoom in to that part of the report.

22

Common Report Elements

Most of the reports in Project have headers at the top. The information displayed in the header is based on the properties entered for the project. You choose File, Properties to add or modify this information. Headers most commonly contain the Title and Manager fields from the Properties information, as well as the current date, as set in the Project Information dialog box. The default setting for footers in most reports is the page number. Sometimes other fields are included in the header or footer as well.

TIP

> To change the header for a report, simply change the information stored in the Properties dialog box. For example, if you want the name of the project manager to appear in the header, choose File, Properties and then type the manager's name in the Manager field of the Properties dialog box.

In addition to standard headers and footers, there are common structural elements in most report definitions:

- **Period**—Select the time groupings for the information presented. Options include monthly, weekly, and quarterly.
- **Tables**—For Task and Resource reports, columns of information are printed, according to which named table has been specified in the report. If you create your own custom tables, they can also be used in reports.
- **Filters**—All tasks or resources will be included in the report, or the report can include only those that match select criteria.
- **Sort order**—Reports print tasks and resources in their ID order, or you can specify the sort order within the report definition.

As you explore and preview the predefined reports, look for the settings of these common elements. Later in this chapter, we'll discuss how to change these settings and customize the reports.

NOTE

> If you have modified the field list or column settings in the supplied Project tables, your changes are included in your reports. The examples given in this chapter are based on the default tables provided with Project.

→ For detailed information on the standard Project tables, **see** "Exploring the Standard Tables," **p. 757**.

→ To learn more about modifying standard tables, **see** "Using and Creating Tables," **p. 840**.

The Overview Reports Category

There are five supplied overview reports: Project Summary, Top-Level Tasks, Critical Tasks, Milestones, and Working Days (refer to Figure 22.2). These five reports are described in

Table 22.1. Together, these reports display summary data over the life of the project. They are useful as documentation for presentations to management after the initial design period has been completed, as well as status reports while the project is underway.

TABLE 22.1 REPORTS IN THE OVERVIEW CATEGORY

Report Name	Report Type	Best Use
Project Summary	(Not a standard report type)	Provides a snapshot of the project schedule and resource list details
Top-Level Tasks	Task	Focuses on major phases of the project instead of on individual tasks
Critical Tasks	Task	Shows the tasks that control the end date of the project
Milestones	Task	Focuses on the project turning points and deliverables
Working Days	(Not a standard report type)	Helps verify the base calendar working days and times

Three of the reports in the Overview category are based on the standard Task report type. Each provides a list of tasks, columnar information about those tasks as defined by the report's underlying table, and supporting details for the tasks, such as predecessor and successor information and resource assignments. If notes have been included in the project, they are printed along with the task list. An example of a task report in this category is the Critical Tasks report shown in Figure 22.3.

Two reports in this category warrant special discussion. The Project Summary report is not based on one of the four standard report types. It provides a printout of the highest-level project information—baseline, schedule, and actual values. The Working Days report prints the settings for the calendar you choose. In this type of report, standard working days and all exceptions—that is, nonworking days and days with altered work hours—are given in a summarized, noncalendar format.

THE PROJECT SUMMARY REPORT

The Project Summary report displays on one page the most significant project information. This report is useful for status meetings with a project team or senior management. Because the Variance and Remaining fields are calculated, this report is a good summary to have at the completion of the preliminary planning for a project, before work on the project actually begins.

The Project Summary report is a printed report of the Project Statistics dialog box. Although the format of the report is slightly different from the format of the dialog box, all the project elements displayed within the dialog box are included in the Project Summary report. If a project manager continually monitors project performance by utilizing project statistics, this report format provides a quick way of generating written verification of the current status of a project.

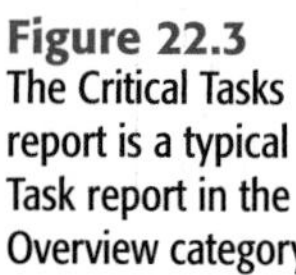

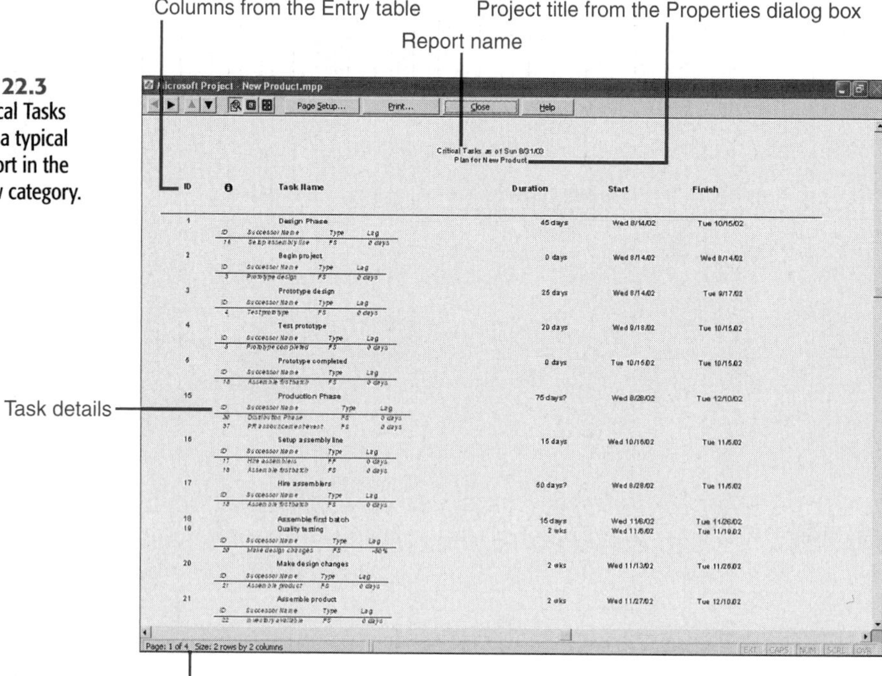

Figure 22.3
The Critical Tasks report is a typical Task report in the Overview category.

The Project Summary report has six sections: Dates, Duration, Work, Costs, Status (for both Tasks and Resources), and Notes (see Figure 22.4). The headings at the top of the report display the Title, Company, and Manager information if they were entered into the Properties dialog box for the project. The date displayed comes from the Current Date option in the Project Information dialog box. You can choose Project, Project Information to display the Project Information dialog box and adjust this date.

With the Project Summary report, you can make comparisons between what is currently scheduled, what the baseline indicates, and what actually happened.

The Task Status section displays the number of tasks not yet started, the number of tasks in progress, and the number of tasks completed in the project (see Figure 22.5). The number of overallocated resources is also shown. If Comments were entered on the Summary tab under the Properties dialog box, they appear in the Notes section.

THE WORKING DAYS REPORT

The Working Days report provides a list of the working and nonworking times for each base calendar used in a project. Using this report is an excellent way to verify that the appropriate working hours have been established and that holidays and other nonworking times are incorporated into a project. The information for each base calendar is printed on a separate page. Figure 22.6 shows information for a modified standard base calendar being used in this project.

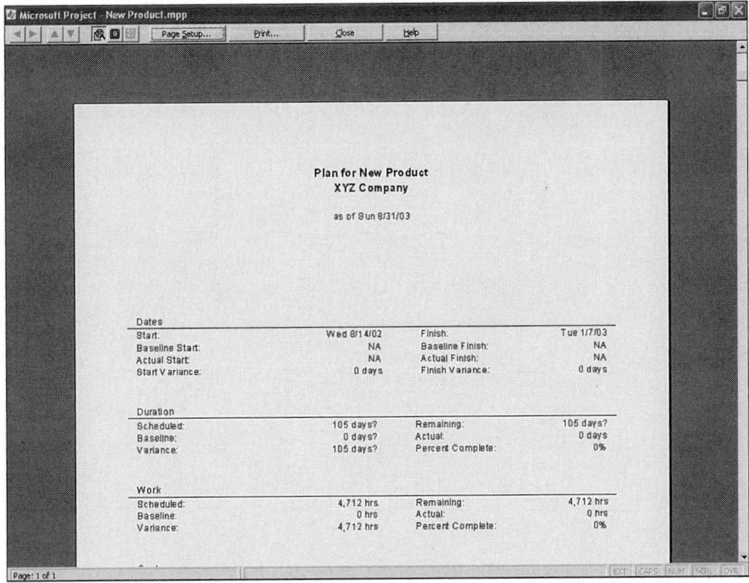

Figure 22.4
The top half of the Project Summary report displays the report headings, a comparison of dates, and durations.

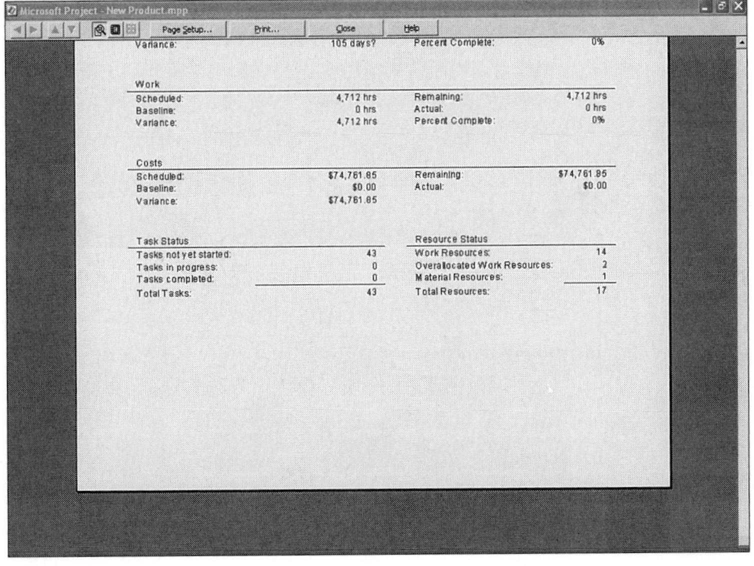

Figure 22.5
The bottom half of the Project Summary report compares work, costs, and the status of the tasks and resources.

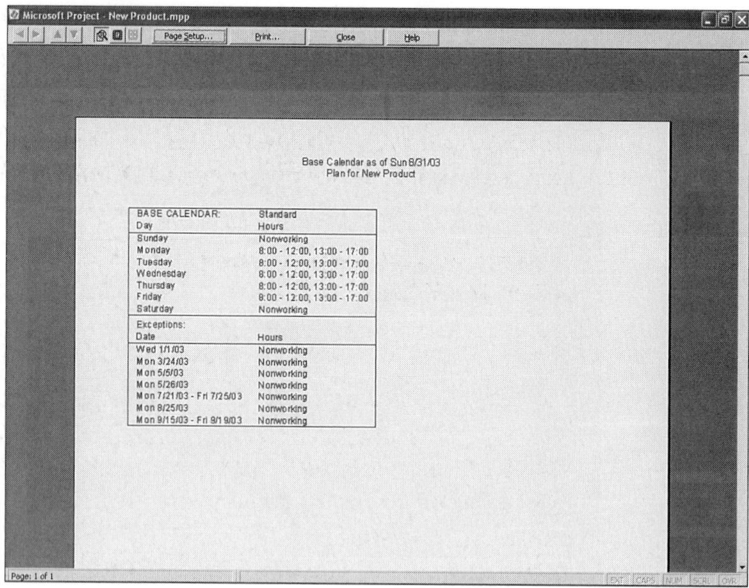

Figure 22.6
The Working Days report helps you verify the base calendars created for a project.

THE CURRENT ACTIVITIES REPORTS CATEGORY

The Current Activities category of reports focuses on tasks and provides a comprehensive status of the tasks as the project is under way. There are six reports in this category: Unstarted Tasks, Tasks Starting Soon, Tasks In Progress, Completed Tasks, Should Have Started Tasks, and Slipping Tasks (see Figure 22.7). Each of these reports is described in Table 22.2.

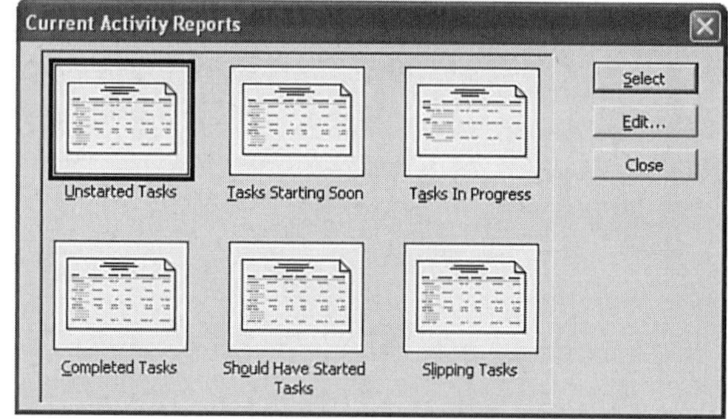

Figure 22.7
The Current Activity reports are useful primarily after a project has started; each focuses on specific groups of tasks.

TABLE 22.2 REPORTS IN THE CURRENT ACTIVITY CATEGORY

Report Name	Report Type	Best Use
Unstarted Tasks	Task	Focuses on tasks that have yet to start, making sure that materials are in place, resources are ready and available, and so on

Report Name	Report Type	Best Use
Tasks Starting Soon	Task	Shows tasks that occur within the range of dates entered by the user when the report is created
Tasks In Progress	Task	Shows which tasks are currently underway so progress can be checked
Completed Tasks	Task	Gives you a sense of accomplishment from seeing a list of tasks that have been finished
Should Have Started Tasks	Task	Provides a good reminder to update the status of tasks that have begun
Slipping Tasks	Task	Shows which tasks have started but are not scheduled to complete on time or within the duration that was originally planned

The Current Activity category of reports provides quick snapshots of project progress. You can use this type of report to get information on which tasks have yet to start (Unstarted Tasks), which tasks have finished (Completed Tasks), and which tasks have recorded some progress but are not yet finished (Tasks In Progress). The Tasks Starting Soon, Should Have Started Tasks, and Slipping Tasks reports provide tasks' status against their anticipated start and finish dates. They are good indicators of whether the project is generally on or off track. The Slipping Tasks report shown in Figure 22.8 is representative of this category.

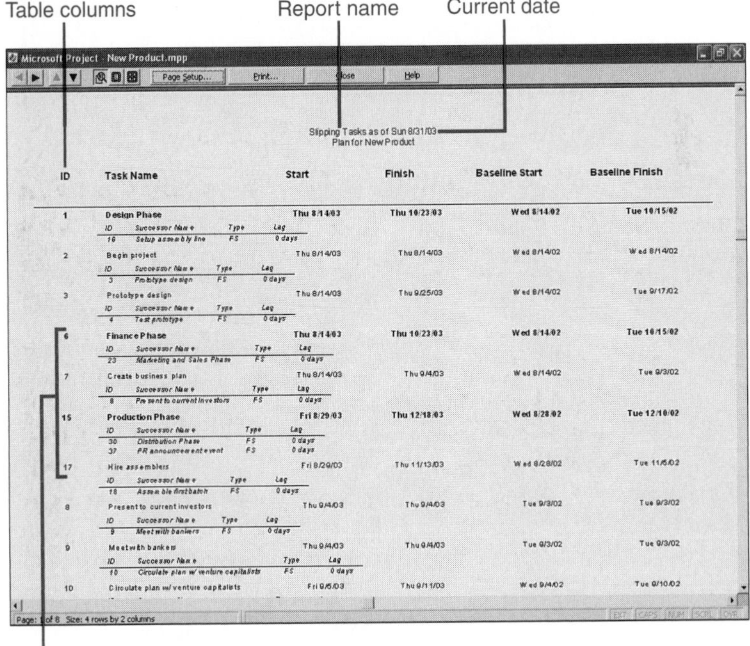

Figure 22.8
The Slipping Tasks report in the Current Activities category lists tasks that are not finishing as planned.

CAUTION

> Several of the supplied reports rely on project Baseline fields for comparisons. If you have added tasks after saving the baseline, make sure to update the baseline again for the tasks you added and any tasks that might be affected by adding the new tasks, to make sure that all relevant tasks are displayed in reports.

→ For more information on updating the baseline, **see** "Working with Project Baselines," **p. 522**.

THE COST REPORTS CATEGORY

Keeping accurate track of the project budget is a significant concern for most project managers. The five reports in the Cost Reports category—Cash Flow, Budget, Overbudget Tasks, Overbudget Resources, and Earned Value—provide a broad range of cost data that is essential when you're trying to stay within a budget for a project (see Figure 22.9). The reports are described in Table 22.3.

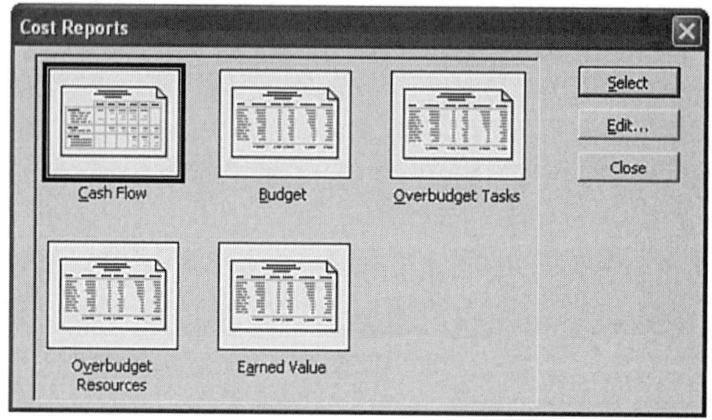

Figure 22.9
The reports in the Cost Reports category provide quick access to budget information.

TABLE 22.3 REPORTS IN THE COSTS CATEGORY

Report Name	Report Type	Best Use
Cash Flow	Crosstab (Task)	Shows the total amount of money required each week to finance the project, as well as the total cost for each task
Budget	Task	Shows tasks, sorted by total cost for each task, that are going overbudget based on actual information that has been entered
Overbudget Tasks	Task	Finds and sorts by cost variance the tasks whose actual, or scheduled, cost is higher than the baseline cost
Overbudget Resources	Resource	Pinpoints resources whose costs are higher than their baseline costs, typically because resources are working longer on tasks than was originally planned
Earned Value	Task	Uses data from the Earned Value table to compare the cost of what is actually happening on each task in the project to what you expected to happen

You can report on the anticipated expense over time by using the Cash Flow report, or you can see the current total budgeted amounts by task in the Budget report. The Overbudget Task report lists tasks that are currently running over their budgeted amounts, and the Overbudget Resources report shows resources that are currently reporting greater per-task expenses than originally planned. The Earned Value report derives its information from the fields in the Earned Value task table. The Earned Value report and the crosstab formatting of the Cash Flow report are discussed in this section.

Most of the reports in this category are based on the Cost table in Project. You can modify the table to hide the Fixed Cost Accrual field because it is not as crucial as the other fields in the table, especially when you're presenting status reports to senior management or a project team. To hide a field in a table, simply resize the field so that it doesn't show in the Gantt Chart view. When you are finished printing the report, you can resize the column so that it once again fits the text.

CAUTION

> Selecting a column and choosing Edit, Hide Column is the same as deleting the column in the table. You then have to edit the table definition or choose Insert, Column to add the column back.

Variance calculations usually compare baseline values to scheduled values. Therefore, most of the Cost reports require that a project baseline be set before you create the report. Also, unless you are costing a project purely on a fixed-cost-per-task basis, appropriate resource costing rates need to be entered.

→ For more information on setting the baseline, **see** "Working with Project Baselines," **p. 522**.

→ To learn about resource costing, **see** "Defining Costs," **p. 281**.

→ For a discussion of fixed costs for tasks, **see** "Assigning Fixed Costs and Fixed Contract Fees," **p. 396**.

THE CASH FLOW REPORT

The Cash Flow report shown in Figure 22.10 is an example of a Crosstab report type. The focus of this report is on task details taken from the Task Cost table. The report shows tasks in the first column and weekly periods of time in the remaining columns. The subsequent grid or spreadsheet that is created contains cost information. The cost information in this report is derived from resource usage costs and fixed costs associated with tasks. Tasks are displayed underneath their summary tasks. Each column (week) and row (task) is totaled at the bottom and right edges of the report.

THE EARNED VALUE REPORT

The Earned Value report is a cost-comparison tool that utilizes data from the Earned Value table. It allows you to compare the cost of what is actually happening on each task in the project to what you expected to happen. The Current Date field is used to calculate what costs have been incurred and what costs you expected to incur when you originally planned the project. The Actual Resource Costs and Fixed Costs fields are used to calculate the percentage complete of each task, as compared to what is entered in the % Complete database field. You can compare whether the estimated percentage completed matches the percentage completed of actual work done. For example, if a task is marked as 25% complete and the actual cost so far is $300, you can calculate whether $300 is equal to 25% of the originally planned cost—the cost expected to be incurred by today for this task.

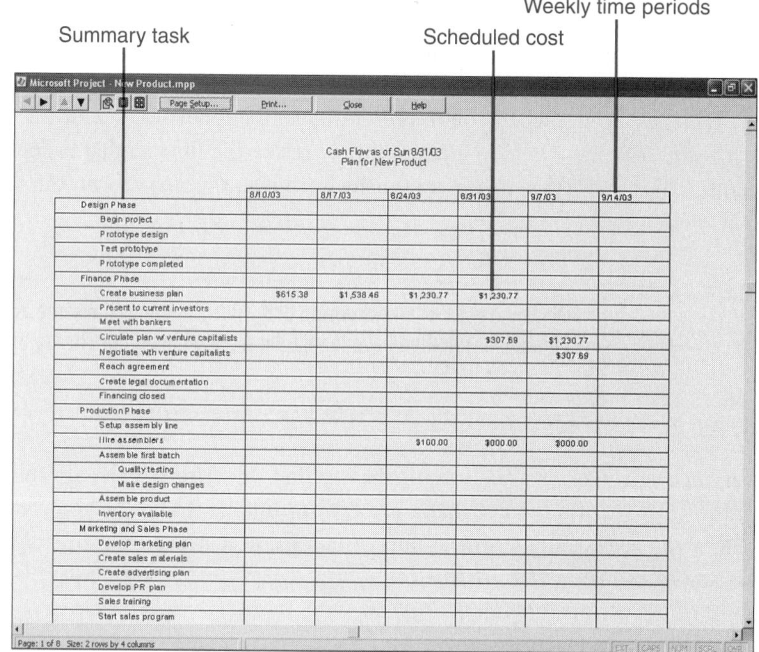

Cash Flow as of Sun 8/31/03
Plan for New Product

	8/10/03	8/17/03	8/24/03	8/31/03	9/7/03	9/14/03
Design Phase						
Begin project						
Prototype design						
Test prototype						
Prototype completed						
Finance Phase						
Create business plan	$615.38	$1,538.46	$1,230.77	$1,230.77		
Present to current investors						
Meet with bankers						
Circulate plan w/ venture capitalists				$307.69	$1,230.77	
Negotiate with venture capitalists					$307.69	
Reach agreement						
Create legal documentation						
Financing closed						
Production Phase						
Setup assembly line						
Hire assemblers			$100.00	$000.00	$000.00	
Assemble first batch						
Quality testing						
Make design changes						
Assemble product						
Inventory available						
Marketing and Sales Phase						
Develop marketing plan						
Create sales materials						
Create advertising plan						
Develop PR plan						
Sales training						
Start sales program						

Figure 22.10 The weekly costs depicted in the Cash Flow report are presented in the Crosstab report format.

NOTE

> Earned value analysis (EVA) was first developed by the U.S. Department of Defense in 1967 in response to contractors who often exaggerated their progress on cost reimbursable contract projects. EVA allows the consideration of various project elements–including scope, cost, and schedule measurements–in order to determine what value has been earned to date within the project life cycle.

→ For detailed information on EVA, **see** "Analyzing Performance with Earned Value Analysis," **p. 575**.

All normal tasks are displayed in an Earned Value report, sorted by their IDs. Summary tasks are not displayed in this report. Because the preview of this report is zoomed in, not all the columns of information are displayed in Figure 22.11.

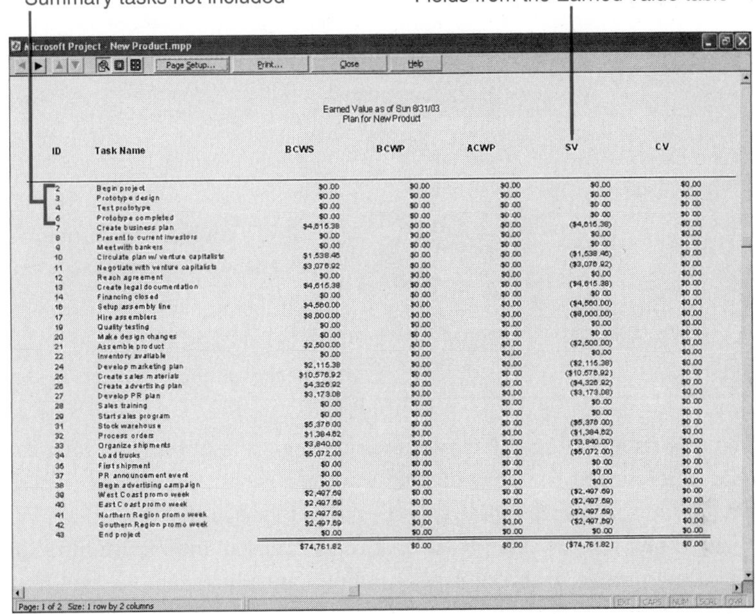

Figure 22.11
The Earned Value report allows you to precisely track progress of resource costs compared to percentage of work completed.

THE ASSIGNMENT REPORTS CATEGORY

The Assignment category of reports displays information about the assignment of resources to tasks. There are four reports in this category: Who Does What, Who Does What When, To-do List, and Overallocated Resources. Figure 22.12 shows the reports in this group, and Table 22.4 describes them.

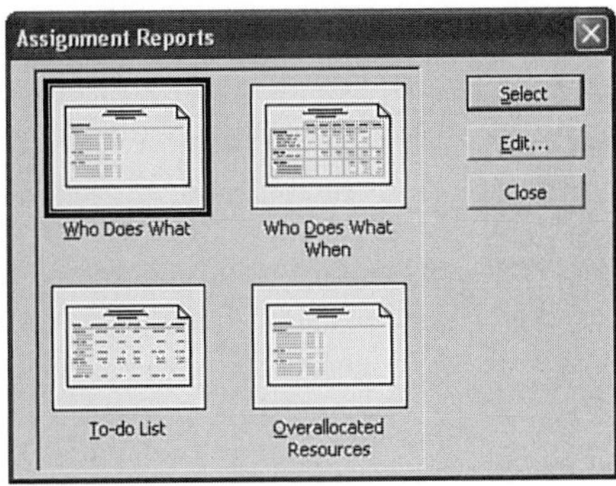

Figure 22.12
The Assignment reports category includes reports that focus on resources and what they are scheduled to do.

TABLE 22.4 REPORTS IN THE ASSIGNMENT CATEGORY

Report Name	Report Type	Best Use
Who Does What	Resource	Shows a comprehensive list of which tasks the resources working on the project are assigned to
Who Does What When	Crosstab (Resource)	Breaks down each resource's work assignments by day
To-do List	Task	Gives a chronological listing, by weeks, of tasks assigned to the resource specified when the report is generated
Overallocated Resources	Resource	Lists all resources that are assigned to more hours of work than the Max Units field specifies

The reports in the Assignment category focus on resources and their assignments. They offer different presentations of what work resources are assigned to perform and in what time periods. All work type resources are included in the Who Does What and Who Does What When reports. The To-do List report runs an interactive filter in which you choose which resource to focus on. A filter is automatically applied to the Overallocated Resources report; fully allocated and underallocated resources are not displayed in this report.

→ For more information on how Microsoft Office Project finds allocation problems, **see** "Identifying Resource Overallocations," **p. 405**.

→ For help in dealing with allocation problems, **see** "Strategies for Eliminating Resource Overallocations," **p. 417**.

TIP

> Using the by-day setting in the Who Does What When report can result in a long printed document. You should preview the report before printing it and consider restricting the printout to a time period that is shorter than the total project. After you decide on appropriate dates, enter them in the Timescale, From, and To boxes on Print dialog box.

THE WORKLOAD REPORTS CATEGORY

The Workload category of reports contains two Crosstab reports that display information about how resources are being used (see Figure 22.13). The reports focus on when and where resources are assigned, broken down by task or by resource, as summarized in Table 22.5.

Figure 22.13
The Workload reports show how many hours each week a task will be worked on.

TABLE 22.5 REPORTS IN THE WORKLOAD CATEGORY

Report Name	Report Type	Best Use
Task Usage	Crosstab (Tasks)	Displays the hours of work (or units of material) to which each resource is assigned, broken down by summary task and then detail tasks
Resource Usage	Crosstab (Resources)	Focuses on resources rather than tasks and shows the hours of work (or units of material) that resources are committed to during each week

When a project manager is juggling resources to accommodate overallocations or to speed up the project, Workload reports can be very useful in identifying resources that are not assigned to their full capacity. The Workload reports include numeric totals. Each week's hours are totaled at the bottom of the report; task and resource hours are totaled in the last column, at the far right of the report.

The Workload reports include both work and material resources in the display. Four additional resource reports are available in the Custom report category that allow you to focus on either work resources or material resources:

- **Resource (work)**—A list of all work-type resources
- **Resource Usage (work)**—Work-type resources and their weekly task assignments
- **Resource (material)**—A list of material-type resources
- **Resource Usage (material)**—Material-type resources and their weekly allocations

These reports are available by selecting the Custom icon in the dialog box that appears when you select View, Reports. The Custom category of reports is discussed extensively later in this chapter, in the section "Customizing Specific Report Types."

CUSTOMIZING REPORTS

Varying degrees of report customization are available in Microsoft Office Project, depending on the type of report. You can customize reports to change the way they look or the details of the information presented. You can start with an existing report and change the text formatting, the layout orientation, or the header and footer that appear when the report is printed. You can alter the details of the report by applying a different table or filter or by choosing a different sort order for the report.

For more information about modifying column widths in a report, refer to the "Troubleshooting" section titled "Changing Column Widths in a Report" at the end of this chapter.

The Custom category in the Reports dialog box allows you to customize any of the existing predefined reports or create your own reports. This section explores the range of options available to those who want to develop customized reports adapted to their project communication needs.

22

Customizing an Existing Report

In Microsoft Office Project you can customize an existing report or create a custom report by making a copy of an existing report and make changes to the copy.

You can customize an existing report in two places: from within the specific category in which the report is listed and from within the Custom category. (Earlier sections of this chapter describe the standard predefined reports.)

To change a report from within a specific category, double-click the category or click once on the category and then click Select. In Figure 22.14, the Assignment category has been selected and the Overallocated Resources report has been chosen. The Edit button in the Assignment Reports dialog box allows you to edit the contents of the report.

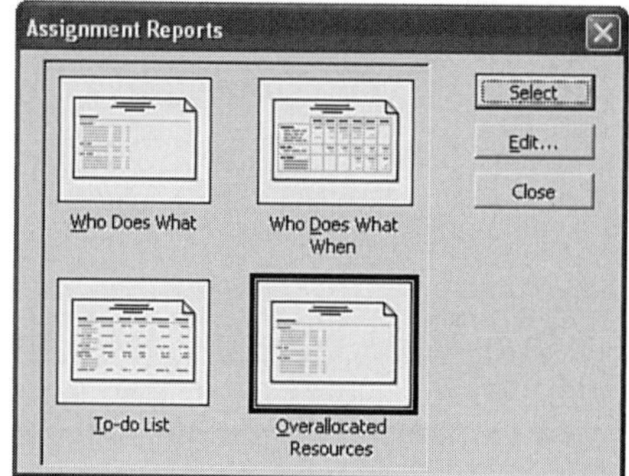

Figure 22.14 You can edit the content and level of detail while working in a category of reports.

Clicking the Edit button shown in Figure 22.14 displays a dialog box with the editing changes you are allowed to make. The choices in this dialog box depend on the type of report you are modifying. Figure 22.15 shows an example of this report definition dialog box for a Resource report.

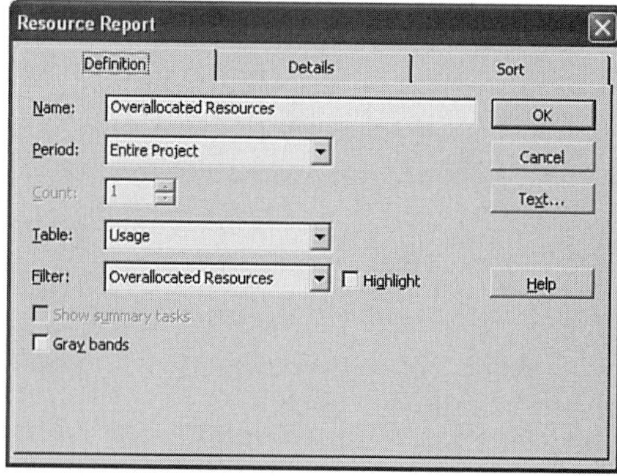

Figure 22.15 The choices displayed in the report definition dialog box vary depending on the type of report you are editing.

The editing choices listed in this dialog box are the same choices that would be available if you were editing the report through the Custom category (see the section "Customizing Specific Report Types," later in this chapter).

TIP

> It is recommended that you not customize the predefined reports, but instead make a copy of a report, using it as a basis for a new report. This way, the original report is left intact for you to use at a later time. If you have already made changes to a predefined report, see the section "Undoing Changes to a Predefined Report," in the "Troubleshooting" section at the end of this chapter.

Using the Custom Category of Reports

The Custom category can be used to make content and level-of-detail changes to reports. All reports available within Project can be accessed through this category, as shown in Figure 22.16.

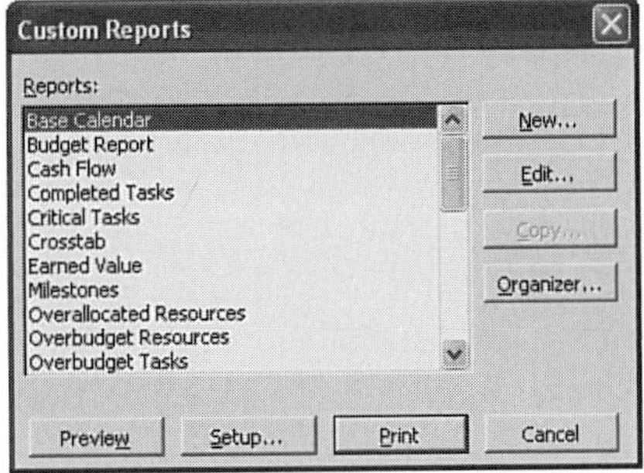

Figure 22.16
Open the Custom Reports dialog box to select a report to customize or to create a new report.

From the Custom category, you can do the following:

- **Preview a report before printing**—With the Print Preview screen activated, you have the opportunity to change the page setup before sending the report to the printer.
- **Set up the selected report before printing**—This is the same as the Page Setup function, which allows you to set up margins, headers, footers, and so forth.
- **Print one of the reports**—The selected report will print as it is currently defined.
- **Create a new report**—The design must follow one of the four report types: Task, Resource, Monthly Calendar, or Crosstab.
- **Edit a report that is either supplied by Project or that you create**—You can change such features as the table and filter used, the details that are shown (for Task and Resource reports), the column and row information (for Crosstab reports), the sort order for presenting the details (for reports other than Calendar reports), the text formatting used for parts of the report, and the use of border lines in the report. These changes become features of the named report.

- **Copy an existing report and make modifications in the new report**—When you do this, you can use both the original and the new copy when needed.
- **Access the Organizer to copy customized reports to or from the Global template**—The Organizer dialog box also allows you to delete reports from your Custom Reports list so you can keep your list current and uncluttered.

The New and Copy buttons in the Custom Reports dialog box function almost identically to the Edit button. However, the end result of using both New and Copy is a new report name that is added to the Custom Reports list. You use New to design a report from the ground up. You use Copy to use an existing report as a starting point for a new report. In both cases, editing begins at the Custom Reports dialog box.

After you've modified or created a report, you can print or preview the custom report directly from the Custom Reports dialog box by clicking either Print or Preview.

NOTE

> The Copy button is dimmed for the Base Calendar and Project Summary reports because these reports can be edited only for simple text-formatting changes.

Creating Reports

You can create a new report either by copying an existing report and making changes to the copy or by designing an entirely new report from scratch. Regardless of the method you choose to create a new report, after it is created, you use the same methods for customizing the new report. The following sections describe the steps you take to create a new report. Other sections in this chapter discuss customizing a report after it is created.

TIP

> Reports bring together many elements of Microsoft Office Project, particularly tables and filters. You should create and format your tables and create and test your filters before creating new reports that will incorporate these elements.

Creating a New Report Based on an Existing Report

One of the best and fastest ways to create a report is to start with one of the predefined Project reports that is similar to a report you need. By making a copy of the existing report, you take advantage of the features of that report, while leaving the original report unchanged for use in the future. Modifying a copy of an existing report is quick and convenient.

TIP

> It is recommended that you use one of the predefined reports as a basis for your new report, because most of the work in creating the report has already been done. If none of the predefined reports are similar to what you are looking for, you need to design a new report.

To copy an existing report, follow these steps:

1. Choose View, Reports.
2. Double-click the Custom category, or click it once and then click Select.
3. From the list in the Custom Report dialog box, choose the report you want to copy and then click the Copy button. The report definition dialog box for that report appears. The defined features in this report are identical to those of the original report. The only difference is that the report name is preceded by *Copy of*. For example, the Critical Tasks report would be renamed Copy of Critical Tasks.
4. In the Name box, enter a descriptive name for the report.
5. Complete the dialog box for the report type you have chosen to copy. Explicit instructions for making changes to the various types of Project reports are given later in this chapter.

Designing a New Report

Another method for creating a report is to design one from scratch. You should use this method if none of the existing predefined reports are similar to the report you need. You must use this method if you want to create a Monthly calendar report, because there are no predefined examples available for editing.

When you create a new report, you must select one of four report templates discussed earlier in this chapter: Task, Resource, Monthly Calendar, or Crosstab.

To create a new report, follow these steps:

1. Choose View, Reports.
2. Double-click the Custom category, or click it once and then click Select.
3. Click the New button. You should see the Define New Report dialog box (shown in Figure 22.17), with the four basic types of reports listed. Each new report must be modeled after one of these types.

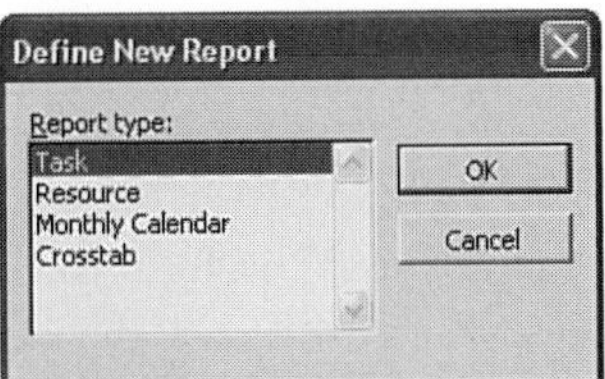

Figure 22.17
When designing a new report, choose one of these four report types.

4. Choose a type and click OK. The report definition dialog box for the report type you selected is displayed, with the default settings (see Figure 22.18). A default report name, such as Report 1, appears in the Name box.

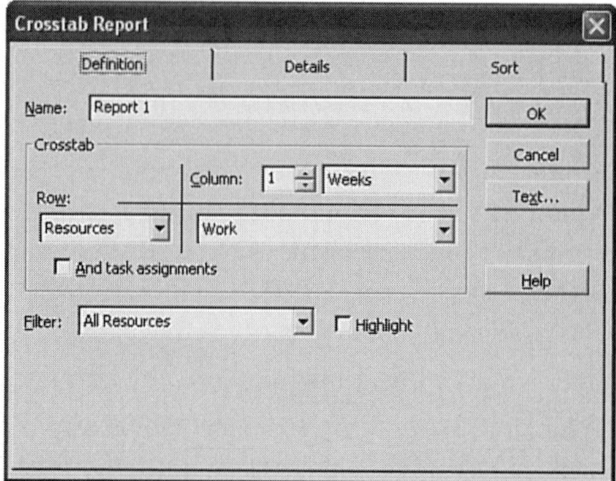

Figure 22.18
The Crosstab report options in the definition dialog box are not the same as the Task or Resource report options.

5. In the Name box, enter a descriptive name for the report.
6. Complete the dialog box for the report type you have chosen.

USING THE COMMON CUSTOMIZATION CONTROLS

With some custom options, the steps to make the changes are the same, regardless of whether you are changing an existing predefined report, a copy of a report, or a newly created report. You can change the way reports look by changing the text format, the page setup options, or the order in which the information is sorted. The following sections describe some of the common custom options.

CONTROLLING PAGE BREAKS IN A REPORT

You cannot put page breaks directly into a report. However, when a report is printed, Project normally maintains the manual page breaks you have inserted in a task or resource list. (Manual page breaks are added by using the Insert, Page Break command.) You can tell Project to ignore page breaks by clearing the Manual Page Breaks box in the Print dialog box (see Figure 22.19).

CHOOSING THE PAGE SETUP OPTIONS FOR A REPORT

While you're modifying a report, you might decide you'd prefer it to have different margins or to display a different header. These changes are controlled by the page setup. To access the page setup options from the Custom Reports dialog box, click the Setup button. If you are previewing the report, click the Page Setup button at the top of the preview screen. No matter how you access the Page Setup dialog box, the options you have are the same.

→ For additional information on how to change setup options, **see** "Changing the Page Setup," **p. 490**.

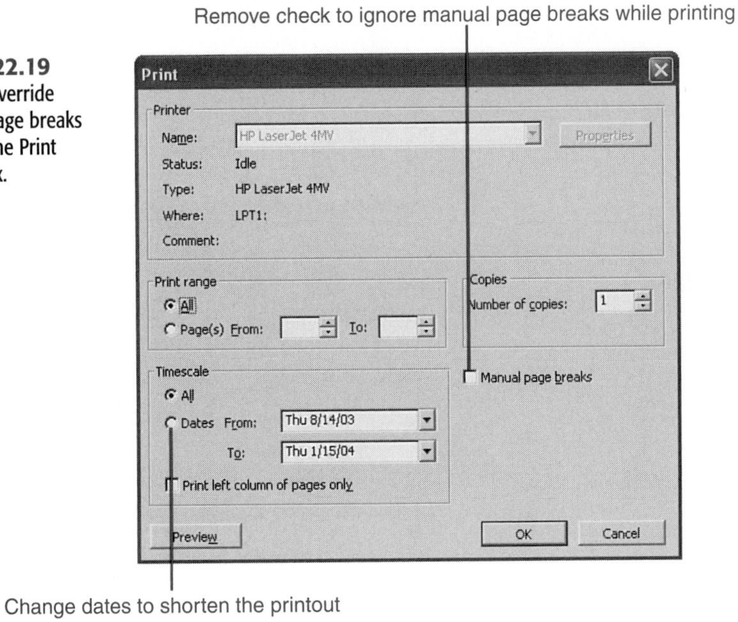

Remove check to ignore manual page breaks while printing

Change dates to shorten the printout

Figure 22.19
You can override manual page breaks through the Print dialog box.

FORMATTING TEXT IN A REPORT

Although some of the editing options differ from report type to report type, you can always format the way the text appears in the report. To do so, click the Text button in the report definition dialog box. If the dialog box has multiple tabs, the Text button appears on each tab. Note that the text styles are automatically displayed when you edit the Project Summary report, because this is the only option you can customize on that report. In Figure 22.20, the Overallocated Resources report is being edited.

The Text Styles dialog box allows you to select special formatting for categories of tasks or resources and for the detail information included on the particular report. The box resembles the dialog box that appears when you choose Format, Text Styles from the main menu. Use the Text Styles dialog box to make certain types of information stand out in a report by changing the size, font, or formatting of categories of text. Specific information choices depend on the type of report you are modifying. The default format of each category is 8-point type with no distinguishing characteristics, unless specified in parentheses. By default, all text in the report will be affected by your choices, unless you select a specific type of information in the Item to Change drop-down list.

There is no connection between the text format in a view and the text format in the corresponding report. When you're formatting text in a report, you need to format the text separately for each individual report and separately from the text format shown in the current view. For example, even if summary tasks are formatted as blue in the current Gantt Chart view, they will not appear in blue in a task report unless you select Summary Tasks in the Text Styles dialog box and apply the blue color.

Figure 22.20
You can click the Text button on any tab of a report definition dialog box to begin customizing the font styles used in a report.

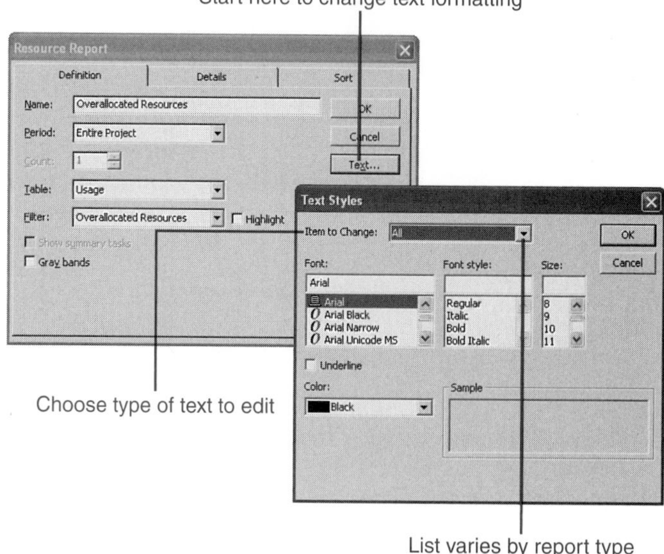

Changing the Sort Order for a Report

You can sort the order of the rows in all Task, Resource, and Crosstab reports. From the definition dialog box for any report, select the Sort tab to access the sorting options for the report. The Sort tab in the Crosstab Report dialog box (shown in Figure 22.21) looks similar to the Sort By dialog box that you open by using the Project, Sort, Sort By command. The options on the Sort tab allow you to sort by as many as three fields in the report. Each Sort By field can be sorted in ascending or descending order. The field used for sorting does not have to be included in the report itself.

When you're sorting the information in a report, there is no connection between the sort displayed in a view and the sort selected in a report. Therefore, you can print a report sorted by a specific field, such as Priority (for tasks) or Name (for resources) without affecting the task order in the current working view.

Figure 22.21
To change the sort order of the rows displayed in a report, use the controls on the Sort tab.

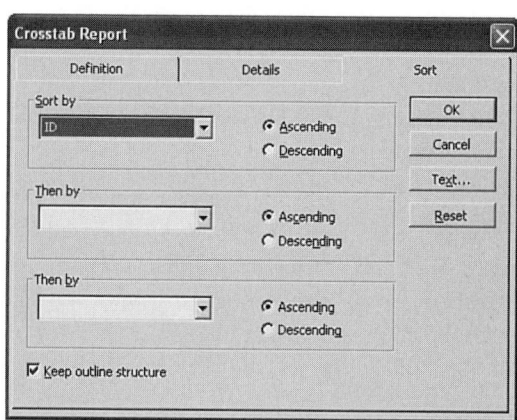

Collapsing Task Detail in a Report

Two settings affect the level or type of tasks that appear in Task, Crosstab, or Monthly Calendar reports: the outline level of the tasks and filters. If the outline is collapsed in the view when you print a report, the subordinate tasks that are hidden are not printed in the report. You must expand the outline before you print the report if you want all tasks to be displayed. However, the reports ignore any filter that might have been applied to the current view onscreen. You can select filters within the report definitions to be automatically applied, regardless of the filter that might or might not be applied to the active view. Note, however, that subordinate tasks hidden by a collapsed outline at the time the report is printed are not included in the report, even though the defined filter usually selects these tasks. Collapsing an outline overrides the filter.

→ To learn more about hiding or showing subtasks, **see** "Collapsing and Expanding the Outline," **p. 157**.

→ To learn more about filtering for specific tasks, **see** "Filtering the Task or Resource List," **p. 472**.

Customizing Specific Report Types

Of the five types of reports available in Microsoft Office Project (Task, Resource, Monthly Calendar, Crosstab, and Project Summary), the Task and Resource reports have the most options for customization. In each case, you can select the columns of information to be displayed, the filter to be applied, and the amount of supporting detail about the tasks or resources listed. The Crosstab reports allow you to select which task or resource detail you want to examine by given time period. Most of the Task, Resource, and Crosstab reports allow the addition of gridlines and gray bands.

The Monthly Calendar and Project Summary reports are very specific types of reports. Each is addressed separately in sections later in this chapter.

All reports allow you to use text formatting to modify the report for easier reading. You can edit reports to change the table and filter used and to change the details that are shown (for Task and Resource reports), the column and row information (for Crosstab reports), the sort order for presenting the details (for reports other than Calendar reports), and the use of border lines in the report.

Customizing the Project Summary Report

The Project Summary report is a specific predefined report listed under the Overview category, and it's the only one of its kind. You cannot copy this report. The only change you can make to the Project Summary report is to change the appearance of the text.

To change the formatting of the text for the Project Summary report, choose the report name from the Reports list in the Custom Reports dialog box. Then click the Edit button. The Report Text dialog box is displayed (see Figure 22.22). Use the Item to Change drop-down list to choose the text you would like to format. Change the formats for the project name, company name, manager name, and details. Click the OK button to return to the Custom Reports dialog box.

22

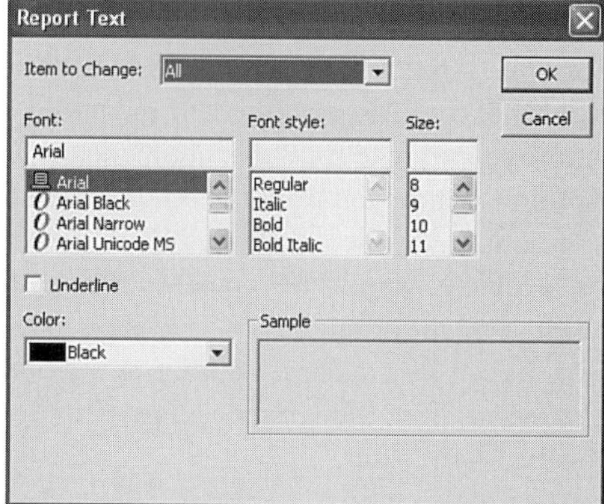

Figure 22.22
Use the Report Text dialog box to format text styles in Project Summary report.

The report in Figure 22.23 uses 14-point Times New Roman text for the project name, 12-point text for the company name, and 10-point text for the project manager name and details.

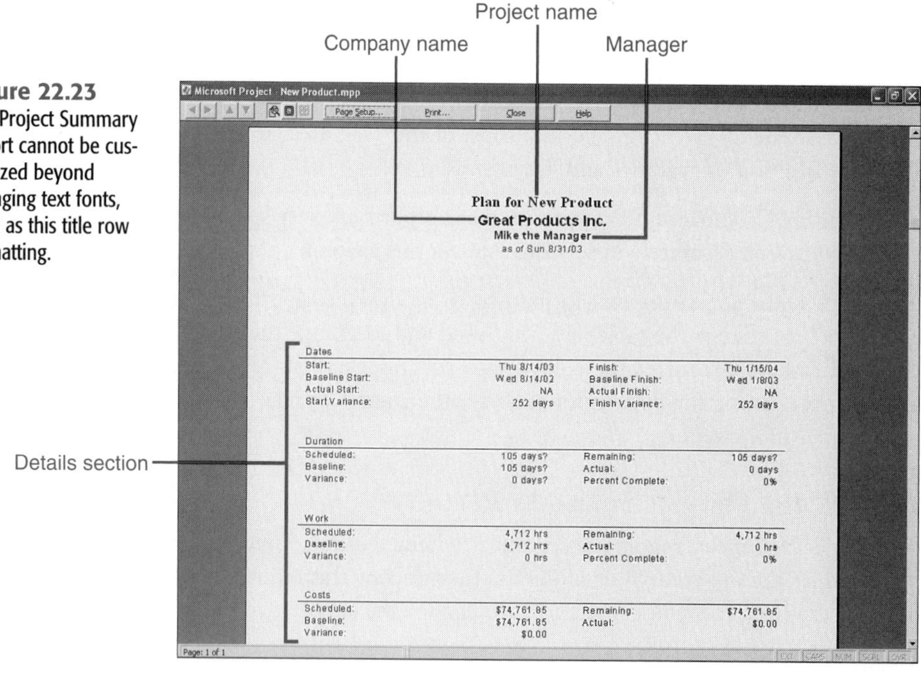

Figure 22.23
The Project Summary report cannot be customized beyond changing text fonts, such as this title row formatting.

Customizing the Calendar Reports

There are two Calendar reports: Working Days in the Overview category and Base Calendar in the Custom category. They are in fact the same report. Normally a report that is listed in one of the special categories is also listed in the Custom category. However, the Working Days report does not appear in the Custom category. Instead, the Base Calendar report is listed there. These reports show the working days, nonworking days, and work hours for each base calendar defined for the current file. Each base calendar is printed on a separate page.

The Base Calendar report cannot be copied, nor can you use its format when creating a new report. The only option in the Base Calendar report that can be changed is the text formatting for the calendar name and details of the report. To edit the Base Calendar report, choose Base Calendar from the Reports list in the Custom Reports dialog box. Then click the Edit button and make the desired changes to the text formatting. After making changes, close the Edit box to return to the Custom Reports list.

To print the Base Calendar report, choose Print or Preview.

Customizing Task and Resource Reports

The majority of the provided reports in Project create lists of tasks or resources, with supporting information included in the lists. List-type reports include all reports that are not the Project Summary report, any Calendar report, or a Crosstab report. As discussed earlier in this chapter, a Task or Resource report is based on a table of fields from the Project database. A filter can be applied to narrow the focus of the report. Another option lets you group the listed tasks or resources by the time period in which they will have activity.

You can add an array of supporting details to list reports. For example, in a Task list report, it might be important to show where each task fits into the flow of the project. You can turn on the options in the report definition dialog box to show predecessor and successor details for each task. Task reports can also include resource assignment schedules and work summaries for each task. Starting with a Resource report, you can print details about each resource's cost rates and any notes associated with the resource.

The two list-type Task and Resource reports are very similar, so the following sections discuss them together. Differences are described in the text.

Table 22.6 lists all the supplied Task reports, along with the underlying table of information used in the report, the applied filter, if any, and which supporting details are included in the report by default.

TABLE 22.6 PREDEFINED TASK REPORT SETTINGS

Report Name	Table Name	Filter	Default Details (If Any)
Budget Report	Cost	All Tasks	Show totals
Completed Tasks	Summary	Completed Tasks	None
Critical Tasks	Entry	Critical	None
Earned Value	Earned Value	All Tasks	Show totals
Milestones	Entry	Milestones	Task notes
Overbudget Tasks	Cost	Cost Overbudget	Show totals
Should Have Started Tasks	Variance	Should Start By...	Task notes; successors
Slipping Tasks	Variance	Slipping Tasks	Notes; successors
Task	Entry	All Tasks	None
Tasks in Progress	Entry	In Progress Tasks	Assignment schedule
Tasks Starting Soon	Entry	Date Range...	Assignment schedule
To Do List	Entry	Using Resource...	None
Top-Level Tasks	Summary	Top Level Tasks	Task notes
Unstarted Tasks	Entry	Unstarted Tasks	Task notes; assignment schedule

Table 22.7 summarizes the supplied Resource reports. The same key report definitions—underlying table of fields, applied filter, and supporting details included—are used in both Resource and Task list-type reports.

TABLE 22.7 PREDEFINED RESOURCE REPORT SETTINGS

Report Name	Table Name	Filter	Default Details, If Any
Resource	Entry	All Resources	None
Resource (material)	Entry-Material Resources	Resources—Material	None
Resource (work)	Entry-Work Resources	Resources—Work	None
Overallocated Resources	Usage	Overallocated Resources	Show totals; assignment schedule
Overbudget Resources	Cost	Cost Overbudget	Show totals
Who Does What	Usage	Resources—Work	Assignment schedule

There are other similarities between Task and Resource list-type reports. Tips and techniques discussed in the section "Using the Common Customization Controls" apply to both types of reports. Essentially, the differences in the reports lie in the choices of supporting details available: Task reports can include both task and resource details in the list; Resource reports focus on resource- and assignment-level details for the particular resource.

You can directly modify Project's existing list reports. The steps to customizing the predefined reports are described earlier in this chapter, in the section "Customizing an Existing Report." You can also copy and then modify reports, as discussed in the section "Creating a New Report Based on an Existing Report." You can choose to create a new Task or Resource report and provide your own report definition. See the section "Designing a New Report," earlier in this chapter, for detailed instructions on creating a new report.

In each of these three methods, you will open a dialog box to be used for editing the report. Figure 22.24 shows the dialog box used for editing a Task report. For both task and resource reports, this dialog box includes three tabs:

- **Definition**—This tab is for setting the overall report definition, such as table, filter, and time period grouping.
- **Details**—Beyond the basic report definition, a wide assortment of drill-down information can be printed. The Details tab provides different options for task and resource reports.
- **Sort**—You can use this tab to rearrange the list in an order that you prefer. (See "Changing the Sort Order for a Report," earlier in this chapter, for specific information.)

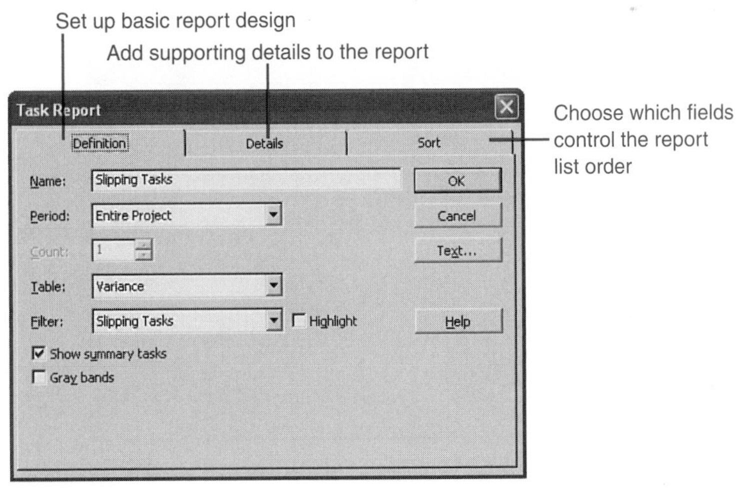

Figure 22.24
The report definition dialog box is named for the type of report being edited; this dialog box is called Task Report.

Changing the Definitions for a Custom Task List Report

You can select the Definition tab of the report editing dialog box to see the current settings for the basic content of the report (that is, the table, filter, and time periods). You have the option of grouping tasks or resources by time interval, but the default is to show the entire project with no intervals listed. To change the time period in the report, choose the Period box and choose Years, Half Years, Quarters, Months, Thirds of Months, Weeks, or Days. You also can indicate how frequent the interval should be. You use the Count box to indicate whether each list item (that is, task or resource) should be displayed every other interval, every third interval, and so on. For example, the time grouping might be useful if resources are paid every two weeks. In that case, you might want a list of the related task assignments grouped by pay periods. Specifically, you need to set Period to Weeks and also set the Count box to 2. Figure 22.25 shows an example of the settings for a biweekly grouping.

To change the columns of data to be displayed to the right of a line item in a report, select the Table box and choose one of the tables from the drop-down list. The Table drop-down list displays all the standard task tables, as well as any tables you have created by using the View, Tables command.

→ For a list of the standard task tables and the fields these tables display, **see** "The Task Tables," **p. 757**.

→ For help in creating your own custom tables, see "Using and Creating Tables," **p. 840**.

Any filter that has been applied to the view onscreen has no impact on the filter that is used with the report. To filter the report list, choose the Filter drop-down list and make a selection. Remember that if you want to use a custom filter, you must create it first by using the Project, Filtered For command. If you choose an interactive filter, the interactive prompt appears each time you print or preview the report. As shown in Figure 22.25, the interactive Using Resource... filter is run when this task report is created.

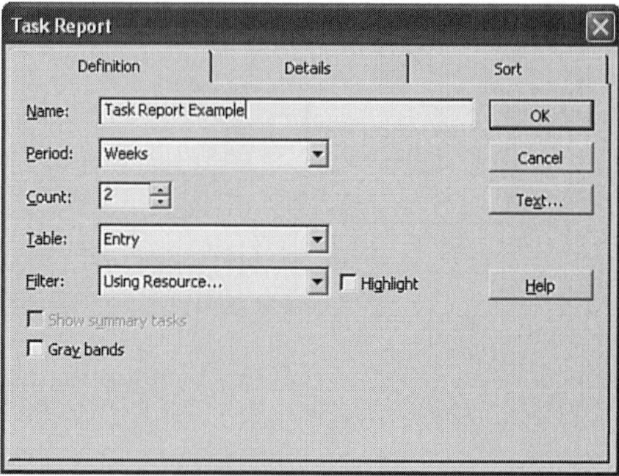

Figure 22.25 This Task report definition creates a biweekly listing of a single resource's tasks.

To use the filter as a highlight filter only, select the Highlight check box. List items that meet the filter criteria are shaded. To display only the filtered list of tasks or resources, clear this check box.

For more information about the use of filters in reports, please refer to the "Troubleshooting" section titled "Applying Filters to Reports" at the end of this chapter.

For Task reports, you can select the Show Summary Tasks check box if you want to have each detail task shown with its summary tasks. This is useful if the detail task names are general, similar, or duplicated within the same schedule. Having detail tasks associated with a descriptive summary task explains them more fully for the reader of the report. Resource list reports do not include this option.

You can select the Gray Bands check box if you want gray horizontal lines to separate the time periods.

Figure 22.25 shows the Task Report dialog box with customized Definition options. Figure 22.26 displays the resulting Task report.

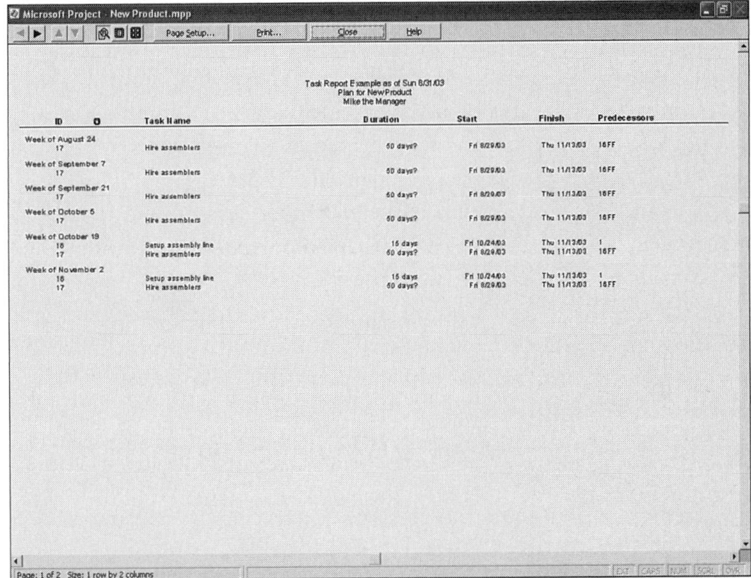

Figure 22.26
This preview of the customized task report for Mary Logan's tasks uses the settings selected in Figure 22.25.

CHANGING THE DETAILS FOR A CUSTOM LIST REPORT

Because the Project database tracks distinctly different task and resource fields, it's logical that there are differences in the types of supporting information available through Task and Resource reports. The Details tabs of the task and resource edit dialog boxes are where you decide what and how much specific information to include in your reports.

You can use some simple keystrokes to add details about tasks to a report. The Details tab of the Task Report definition dialog box (see Figure 22.27) includes several categories of details that you can select via check boxes. (Depending on the period indicated on the Definition tab, some of the detail options might not be available.) These categories are as follows:

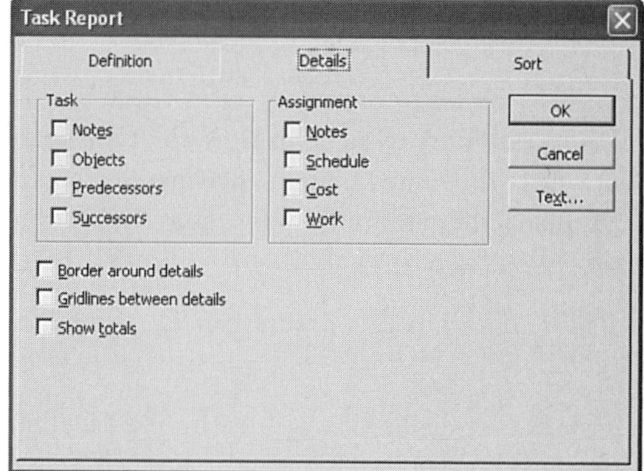

Figure 22.27
You can include additional information in a report by using the options on the Details tab of the Task Report dialog box.

- Under the Task heading, you can select any of four boxes:
    - Select Notes to include text you have entered in the Notes field for any of the tasks.
    - Select Objects if you want to include objects you have created using another Windows application, such as Microsoft Word or Excel.

→ For additional information on inserting objects, **see** "Placing Objects into Microsoft Project," **p. 706**.

    - Select Predecessors if you want to include a list of the predecessor task information under each task.
    - Select Successors if you want to include a list of the successor task information under each task.
- Under the Assignment heading, you can display many kinds of details about assigned resources by selecting any of the check boxes. Three fields always appear with the subcharts for the Schedule, Cost, and Work detail subcharts: Resource ID, Resource Name, and Units (of Resource Assigned). The following list shows the rest of the fields for each subchart:

Subchart	**Fields**
Notes	Assignment Notes
Schedule	Work (Scheduled Work) Delay Start (Scheduled) Finish (Scheduled)
Cost	Cost (Scheduled Cost) Baseline Cost Actual Cost Remaining (Scheduled Cost)
Work	Work (Scheduled Work) Overtime Work Baseline Work Actual Work Remaining Work (Scheduled)

If you choose two or three details for the subchart, Project combines the fields into one table if the report has landscape as the orientation in the Setup options. The Work field is not repeated if the Schedule and Work tables are combined.

- You can add notes to an assignment to keep track of information that is specific to that assignment, such as the rate of work or scheduling assumptions. Notes must be added in Task Usage or Resource Usage views. These notes are separate from and not related to the notes that are added to tasks or resources.
- If you want the detail subchart to be enclosed in border lines, select the Border Around Details check box.
- If you want to see gridlines between tasks, select the Gridlines Between Details check box.
- Select the Show Totals check box if you want to show totals at the bottom of the report for all columns in the table that contain numeric information.

TIP

When a report is displaying the details, it is easiest to read if a border surrounds the details; select the Border Around Details option to display the border.

Figure 22.28 shows the Cost details surrounded by a border for all the tasks in the project.

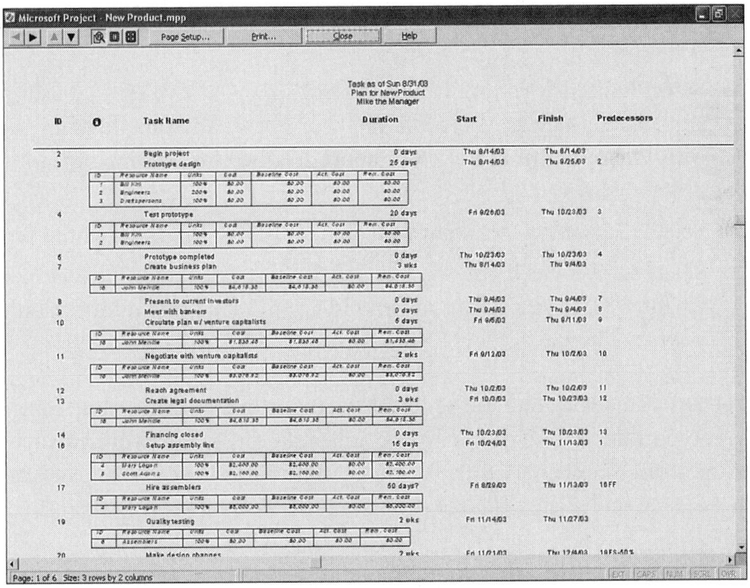

Figure 22.28
Task reports can be customized to show a subchart such as these cost details.

Changing the details included in a custom Resource report is much like changing details in a custom Task report. The Details tab of the Resource Report definition dialog box gives you many options. Figure 22.29 shows the Resource Report dialog box, with the Details tab selected and all the options at their default settings.

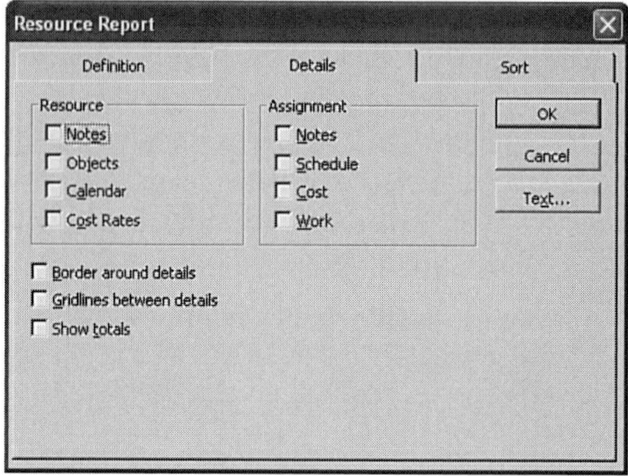

Figure 22.29
You use the Details tab of the Resource Report dialog box to select additional information that you want to appear in the report.

NOTE

Unless you selected the time period Entire Project on the Definition tab, the following check boxes on the Details tab are dimmed: Resource Notes and Objects; Assignment Notes, Cost, and Work; and Show Totals.

Under the Resource heading, you can select one of four boxes:

- Select Notes to include notes that you have entered in the Notes area for any of your resources.
- Select Objects if you want to represent data you have created using another Windows application, such as Microsoft Word or Excel. An example of an object might be a Microsoft Excel graph of work hours assigned for a group of resources assigned to a group of tasks.
- Select Calendar if you want to include resource calendars in the report.
- Select Cost Rates if you want to see the cost rate tables for each resource. Refer to Chapter 8, "Defining Resources and Costs," for more information on how cost rate tables are used.

The Assignment section in the Resource report includes the same four options as in the Task report details. Mark the Notes, Schedule, Cost, and Work check boxes to show details of the task assignments for the resource. The fields for each task assigned are the same as those listed under the resource details on the Task reports.

Remember that the assignment notes keep track of information that is specific to an assignment, such as the rate of work or scheduling assumptions. These must be added in Task Usage or Resource Usage views. They are a separate set of notes, not related to notes added to tasks or resources.

As with task list reports, you can add borders around resource details, use gridlines for easier viewing, and include totals for numeric columns in the report.

CHANGING THE TEXT FORMATTING IN A TASK OR RESOURCE REPORT

You can access the Text button from any of the tabs in the edit report dialog boxes. The Text Styles dialog box allows you to select special formatting for a category of tasks and resembles the Text Styles dialog box that you access by selecting Format, Text Styles from the main menu. You can use this dialog box to make certain types of information stand out in a report by changing the size, font, or formatting of categories of text.

To find out how to undo the changes in a predefined report, see the "Troubleshooting" section titled "Undoing Changes to a Predefined Report" at the end of this chapter.

The categories of text types available for special formatting in task reports are as follows:

- All (the default category)
- Noncritical Tasks
- Critical Tasks
- Milestone Tasks
- Summary Tasks (the default is bold)
- Marked Tasks
- Highlighted Tasks (shaded)
- Column Titles (the default is bold 9-point type)
- External Tasks
- Task Details (the default is italic 7-point type)
- Totals

The categories of text types available for special formatting in resource reports are as follows:

- All (the default category)
- Allocated Resources
- Overallocated Resources
- Highlighted Resources (shaded)
- Column Titles (the default is bold 9-point type)
- Resource Details (the default is italic 7-point type)
- Totals

The default format of each category is 8-point type with no distinguishing characteristics, unless another default is specified in parentheses.

You can find more specific information about formatting text in a report in the section "Formatting Text in a Report," earlier in this chapter.

22

Sorting Tasks in a Resource Report

The Sort tab on the Resource Report dialog box is identical for all custom reports. See the section "Changing the Sort Order for a Report," earlier in this chapter, for more information.

After you have made the custom changes you want, click OK on any of the dialog box's three tabs to return to the Custom Reports dialog box. From there, you can preview or print the report.

Customizing Crosstab Reports

Crosstab reports show cost amounts or work hours by task or resource in a grid format by selected time period. Table 22.8 lists the predesigned crosstab reports that are available for customizing and the data they include.

Table 22.8 Predefined Crosstab Report Settings

Report Name	Row Setting	Data Values
Crosstab	(Tasks or Resources)	None
Who Does What When	Resources	Resources—Work
Cash Flow	Tasks	Cost
Resource Usage	Resources	Work
Resource Usage (material)	Resources—Material	Work
Resource Usage (work)	Resources—Work	Work
Task Usage	Tasks	Work

You can customize a report either from the specific category the report belongs to or under the Custom category. From the Custom category list, select the Crosstab report you would like to customize and choose Edit, or make a copy. The Crosstab Report dialog box appears. There are three tabs in this dialog box: Definition, Details, and Sort. Not all options in the dialog box are available for all reports.

Changing the Definitions for a Custom Crosstab Report

You select the type of information to be displayed in a Crosstab report through the Definition tab of the Crosstab Report dialog box (see Figure 22.30). The Definition tab allows you to indicate whether you want to list tasks or resources down rows by selecting one of the two in the Row box.

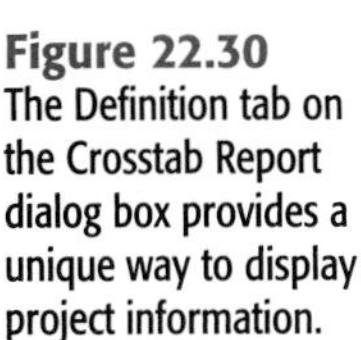

Figure 22.30
The Definition tab on the Crosstab Report dialog box provides a unique way to display project information.

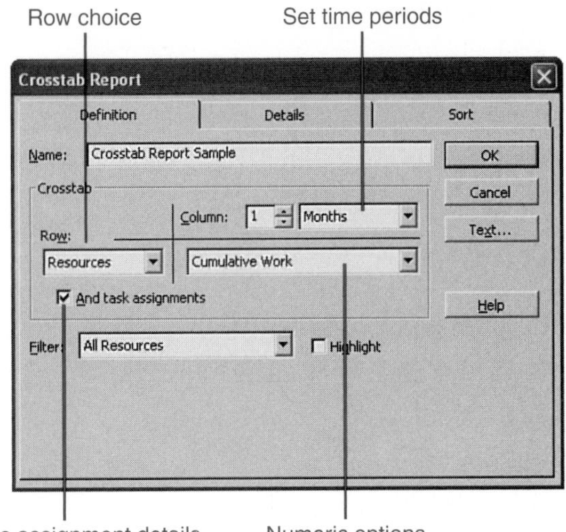

The information that is available for inclusion in the grid for the row information varies depending on whether you are working with tasks or resources. You can use the following options for tasks:

- Actual Cost
- Actual Overtime Work
- Actual Work
- ACWP (Actual Cost of Work Performed)
- Baseline Cost
- Baseline Work
- BCWP (Budgeted Cost of Work Performed)
- BCWS (Budgeted Cost of Work Scheduled)
- Cost (Scheduled)
- Cumulative Cost (Scheduled, Time-phased)
- Cumulative Work (Scheduled, Time-phased)
- CV (Cost Variance)
- Fixed Cost
- Overtime Work (Scheduled)
- Regular Work (Scheduled)
- SV (Schedule Variance)
- Work (Scheduled)

You can use the following options for resources:

- Actual Cost
- Actual Overtime Work
- Actual Work
- ACWP (Actual Cost of Work Performed)
- Baseline Cost
- Baseline Work
- BCWP (Budgeted Cost of Work Performed)
- BCWS (Budgeted Cost of Work Scheduled)
- Cost (Scheduled)
- Cumulative Cost (Scheduled, Time-phased)
- Cumulative Work (Scheduled, Time-phased)
- CV (Cost Variance)
- Overallocation
- Overtime Work (Scheduled)
- Peak Units
- Percent Allocation
- Regular Work (Scheduled)
- Remaining Availability
- SV (Schedule Variance)
- Unit Availability
- Work (Scheduled)
- Work Availability

After you select the information to appear in the Row and Column fields, you can also set the time period represented by each column in the grid with the Column section. Figure 22.31 shows a Crosstab report that lists monthly cumulative work by resources.

As with Resource and Task reports, you can select a filter for a Crosstab report. If you choose to list tasks as the row information, you are presented with a list of task filters in the Filter box. If you choose to list resources as the row information, you see a list of resource filters in the Filter box. Remember that if you want to use a custom filter, you must create it first, by using the Project, Filtered For command.

→ For additional information on creating your own filters, **see** "Creating Custom Filters," **p. 859**.

If you are listing resources in rows and want to include details on assigned tasks for each resource, select the And Task Assignments check box in the Crosstab Report dialog box. The box label changes to And Resource Assignments if you choose Tasks as the row information, and it lists all assigned resources for the tasks listed in the report. Figure 22.31 shows monthly cumulative work by resources, with task assignments included.

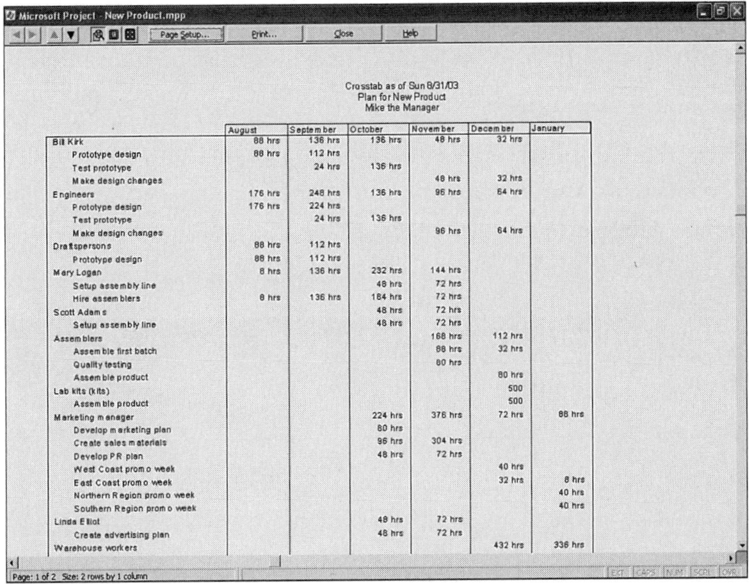

Crosstab as of Sun 8/31/03
Plan for New Product
Mike the Manager

	August	September	October	November	December	January
Bill Kirk	88 hrs	136 hrs	136 hrs	48 hrs	32 hrs	
Prototype design	88 hrs	112 hrs				
Test prototype		24 hrs	136 hrs			
Make design changes				48 hrs	32 hrs	
Engineers	176 hrs	248 hrs	136 hrs	96 hrs	64 hrs	
Prototype design	176 hrs	224 hrs				
Test prototype		24 hrs	136 hrs			
Make design changes				96 hrs	64 hrs	
Draftspersons	88 hrs	112 hrs				
Prototype design	88 hrs	112 hrs				
Mary Logan	8 hrs	136 hrs	232 hrs	144 hrs		
Setup assembly line			48 hrs	72 hrs		
Hire assemblers	8 hrs	136 hrs	184 hrs	72 hrs		
Scott Adams			48 hrs	72 hrs		
Setup assembly line			48 hrs	72 hrs		
Assemblers				168 hrs	112 hrs	
Assemble first batch				88 hrs	32 hrs	
Quality testing				80 hrs		
Assemble product					80 hrs	
Lab kits (kits)					500	
Assemble product					500	
Marketing manager			224 hrs	376 hrs	72 hrs	88 hrs
Develop marketing plan			80 hrs			
Create sales materials			96 hrs	304 hrs		
Develop PR plan			48 hrs	72 hrs		
West Coast promo week					40 hrs	
East Coast promo week					32 hrs	8 hrs
Northern Region promo week						40 hrs
Southern Region promo week						40 hrs
Linda Elliot			48 hrs	72 hrs		
Create advertising plan			48 hrs	72 hrs		
Warehouse workers					432 hrs	336 hrs

Figure 22.31
This Crosstab report shows monthly values for cumulative work by resource and their task assignments.

CHANGING THE DETAILS FOR A CUSTOM CROSSTAB REPORT

You add details to a custom Crosstab report by using the Details tab in the custom report dialog box, just as you do for Task and Resource reports. However, the details you add to a Crosstab report differ somewhat from those for Task and Resource reports because the type of information shown in a Crosstab report is primarily numeric rather than descriptive. Figure 22.32 shows the Details tab for a Crosstab report.

Figure 22.32
The Details tab of the Crosstab Report dialog box is notably different from the Task Report and the Resource Report dialog boxes.

The Details tab options are as follows:

- The Show section allows you to print row totals and column totals by checking the appropriate boxes. If both boxes are checked, an overall total is printed at the lower-right corner intersection of the row and column totals. If you chose to list tasks as the Row information, you have the option of showing summary tasks. If you select resources for the row information, the Summary Tasks option is unavailable. Summary task information includes information from all detail tasks, even if they are not displayed on the report (see Figure 22.33).

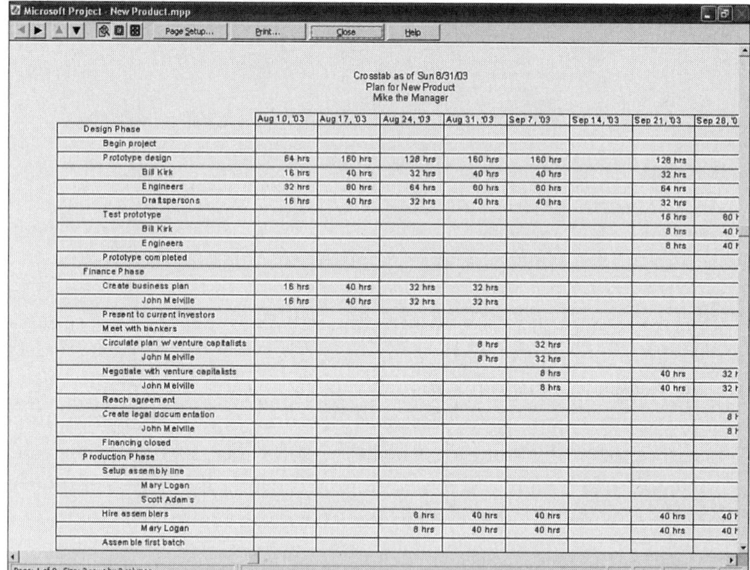

Crosstab as of Sun 8/31/03
Plan for New Product
Mike the Manager

	Aug 10, '03	Aug 17, '03	Aug 24, '03	Aug 31, '03	Sep 7, '03	Sep 14, '03	Sep 21, '03	Sep 28, '0
Design Phase								
Begin project								
Prototype design	64 hrs	160 hrs	128 hrs	160 hrs	160 hrs		128 hrs	
Bill Kirk	16 hrs	40 hrs	32 hrs	40 hrs	40 hrs		32 hrs	
Engineers	32 hrs	80 hrs	64 hrs	80 hrs	80 hrs		64 hrs	
Draftspersons	16 hrs	40 hrs	32 hrs	40 hrs	40 hrs		32 hrs	
Test prototype							16 hrs	80 h
Bill Kirk							8 hrs	40 h
Engineers							8 hrs	40 h
Prototype completed								
Finance Phase								
Create business plan	16 hrs	40 hrs	32 hrs	32 hrs				
John Melville	16 hrs	40 hrs	32 hrs	32 hrs				
Present to current investors								
Meet with bankers								
Circulate plan w/ venture capitalists				8 hrs	32 hrs			
John Melville				8 hrs	32 hrs			
Negotiate with venture capitalists					8 hrs		40 hrs	32 h
John Melville					8 hrs		40 hrs	32 h
Reach agreement								
Create legal documentation								8 h
John Melville								8 h
Financing closed								
Production Phase								
Setup assembly line								
Mary Logan								
Scott Adams								
Hire assemblers			8 hrs	40 hrs	40 hrs		40 hrs	40 h
Mary Logan			8 hrs	40 hrs	40 hrs		40 hrs	40 h
Assemble first batch								

Figure 22.33
A Crosstab report can show scheduled weekly work.

- You can show horizontal gridlines between tasks or resources by clicking the appropriate box in the Gridlines section.
- The Show Zero Values box allows you to show, or, for a cleaner look, suppress 0s for the grid box representing a time period when the time period's value is 0.
- You should select the Repeat First Column on Every Page option when the Crosstab report extends to more than one page horizontally and you want the row titles in the first column to repeat on every page.
- The Date Format box allows you to specify the date as it will appear along the top of the grid, representing the time period.

CHANGING THE TEXT FORMATTING AND SORTING IN A CROSSTAB REPORT

You can access the Text button on any of the tabs in the Crosstab Report dialog box. The Text Styles dialog box allows you to select special formatting and resembles the Format, Text Styles dialog box from the main menu. Use formatting to make certain types of information stand out in a report by changing the size, font, or formatting certain categories of text. The default format of each category is 8-point type with no distinguishing characteristics, unless specified in parentheses. You choose Item to Change to select the text you want to format. (The "Formatting Text in a Report" section, earlier in this chapter, covers specific steps to format the text.)

Remember that the text formatting you have altered in the view is not related to the text formatting in the report. You need to format the text separately for each individual Crosstab report and separately from the text format showing in the current view.

The Sort tab for the Crosstab Report dialog box is identical for all custom reports. See the section "Changing the Sort Order for a Report," earlier in this chapter, for more information.

After you have made the custom changes you want, click OK on any of the dialog box's three tabs to return to the Custom Reports dialog box. From there you can preview or print the report.

Customizing the Monthly Calendar Type Report

Microsoft Project offers the option of a Monthly Calendar report for those who want to report task information in a calendar format. This report is not available in any category except Custom, and it must be designed from scratch.

The Monthly Calendar report offers fewer formatting options than the Calendar view, but it can be customized to print any individual's resource calendar (which the Calendar view cannot do). You can customize the resource calendar for each individual resource through the Tools, Change Working Time command from the menu.

➔ For help with changing a resource's available time, **see** "Working Time," **p. 301**.

You access the Monthly Calendar report by clicking the New button from the Custom Reports dialog box. After that, select Monthly Calendar from the Define New Report dialog box and then click OK (see Figure 22.34).

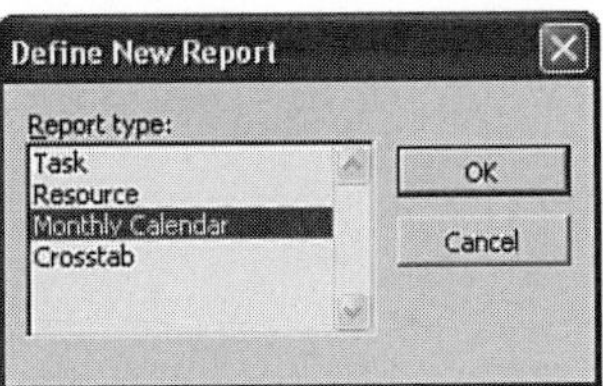

Figure 22.34
The Define New Report dialog box is the only place you can find the Monthly Calendar report.

The Monthly Calendar Report Definition dialog box offers choices for filtering, for choosing which base or resource calendar to display, and for displaying and labeling tasks (see Figure 22.35).

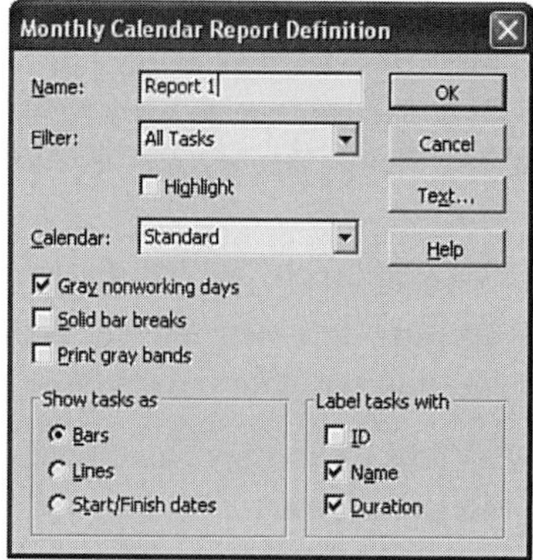

Figure 22.35
The Monthly Calendar Report definition dialog box differs from other report type dialog boxes.

You can choose any base or resource calendars to use for displaying the working and nonworking days on the report. The advantage of the Monthly Calendar report over the Calendar view is that it prints any individual's resource calendar, reflecting his or her working and nonworking days. To select the calendar to use for the report, choose the Calendar box and then choose one of the base or resource calendars from the drop-down list.

You can apply one of the filters from the Filter drop-down list to limit the tasks displayed. You might apply the Using Resource filter, for example, to print a calendar to distribute to a certain resource, showing the tasks and dates when the resource is scheduled to work on the project.

To make the filter a highlight filter only, select the Highlight check box. When you do this, all tasks are displayed, and the filtered tasks are displayed with the format chosen for highlighted tasks. If you select an interactive filter, the interactive prompt appears each time you preview or print the report.

The remaining options on the Monthly Calendar Report Definition dialog box allow you to regulate the display of the data, as follows:

- To distinguish working and nonworking days on the calendar, select the Gray Nonworking Days check box.
- If you decide to display bars for the tasks, you can choose to display breaks in the bars (from one week or month to the next) with dotted or solid lines at the bar ends. Select the Solid Bar Breaks check box if you want solid lines. For dotted lines, leave the check box unselected.
- Select the Print Gray Bands check box if you want a gray band to separate the dates in the list that is printed at the end for any tasks that couldn't fit onto the calendar display.
- To show tasks as bars or lines that stretch across the calendar for the duration of the task, select the Bars or Lines option. To show the scheduled start and stop dates for tasks on the calendar, select the Start/Finish Dates option.
- Mark the check boxes for ID number, Name, and Duration if you want to include these field values in the label for the task. You can use any combination of these three values.
- If more tasks are assigned on a day than will fit on the calendar, an asterisk is displayed beside the day number, and the unprinted tasks appear in a list at the end of the report. The list is sorted by date.

- Click the Text button to designate different text formats for parts of the report. You can select unique formats for different kinds of tasks (noncritical, critical, milestone, summary, marked, and highlighted) and for the labels in the calendar.

After you finish defining the Monthly Calendar report, click the OK button to return to the Custom Reports dialog box. You can then print or preview the report immediately or click the Close button to save the list of reports and print later.

Figure 22.36 shows an example of the settings in the Monthly Calendar Report Definition dialog box for a Monthly Calendar report filtered to show only the tasks assigned to Mary Logan. The report also is defined to use the resource calendar for Mary Logan. Figure 22.37 shows the resulting report, previewing the month of October 2002.

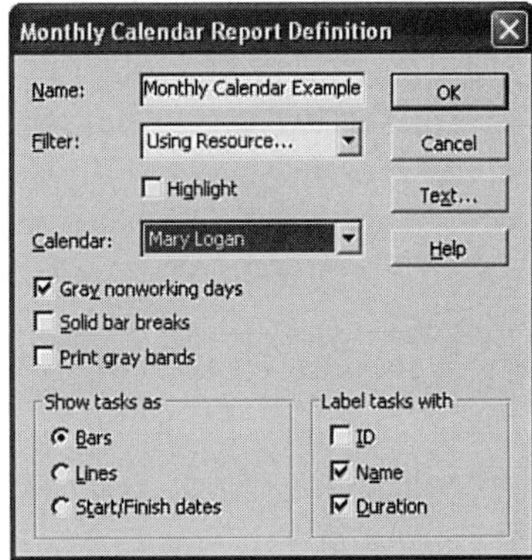

Figure 22.36
The Monthly Calendar report definition can be customized to filter for a particular resource and show her calendar.

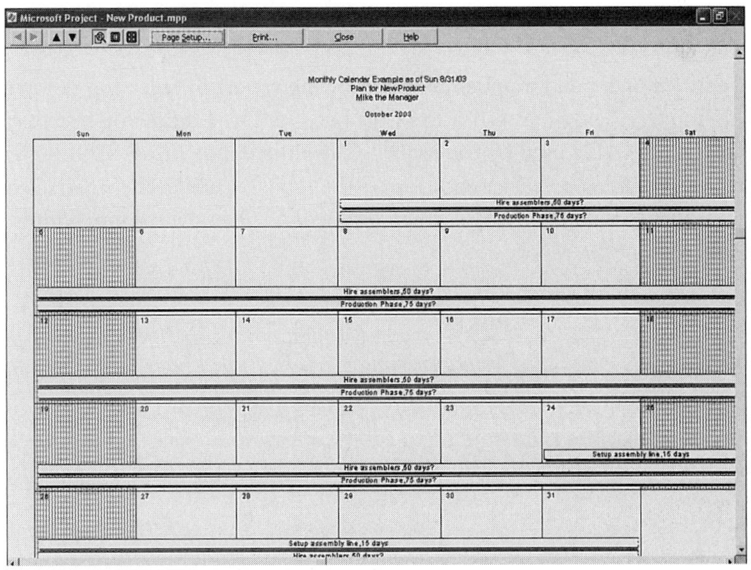

Figure 22.37
An individual resource is the focus of this Monthly Calendar report.

Saving and Sharing Custom Reports

All the report definitions are saved with the project file, so remember to save your file if you have customized reports—even if you have not changed the task or resource information. There is no option in Project to save the actual results of reports. They can only be printed or their definitions shared with other users. Special steps are required to be able to save or email report results. One method is to create a print-to-file driver for the printer selection. The steps to create this driver are beyond the scope of this book. A second method is to purchase and install a print-capture software program, such as Adobe Acrobat; see the application's manual for details.

For more information about sharing custom reports, please refer to the "Troubleshooting" section titled "Distributing Reports Based on Custom Tables" at the end of this chapter.

It is possible—and recommended—to make custom report definitions available to all your project files or to other people sharing the same copy of Microsoft Office Project. You must copy these reports into the global template file, `GLOBAL.MPT`, by using the Organizer. To do this, access the Organizer from the Custom Reports dialog box. All reports in the `GLOBAL.MPT` file are available to all users of Microsoft Office Project who share that `GLOBAL.MPT` file.

→ For additional information on the Organizer, **see** "Working with the Organizer and the Global File," **p. 107**.

Troubleshooting

Changing Column Widths in a Report

When I preview a report, several of the columns are too wide for the data being displayed. How can I reduce the width of the columns?

Identify which table supplies the data for the report by selecting the icon for the report in the Reports dialog box. Click the Edit button. The Edit dialog box that appears shows the name of the table used by the report. Close the dialog boxes. Choose View, Table (any possibly More Tables) to select and display the table on which the report is based. Then change the width of the columns on screen as needed. The new column widths will be used the next time you run the report.

Applying Filters to Reports

When I apply a task filter before running a report, Project ignores the filter and shows all the tasks anyway. What's the trouble?

Any filter that has been applied to the view has no impact on the filter that is used with the report. Instead of filtering the view, you should customize the report design to include the filter.

Distributing Reports Based on Custom Tables

I created a report based on a custom table and copied it into another user's file by using the Organizer. Now whenever she runs the report, she gets an error that says `table...on which it is based has been deleted.` *Did I do something wrong?*

When you use the Organizer to copy the custom report to another file, you must also copy the custom table used by that report to the other file as well. Without the custom table, the custom report has no data source.

If your report also requires a custom filter that you have created, be sure to copy that filter to the other file, too.

Undoing Changes to a Predefined Report

I've modified one of the existing Project reports. I want to keep my modified report, but I also want the original report to be available to use later. What should I do?

Access the Custom category of reports, by selecting View, Reports. Click the Copy button in the Custom Reports dialog box to make a copy of the report you modified, and then rename the copy. Then, by clicking the Organizer button in the Custom Reports dialog box, access the Global template. Copy the report from the Global template to your project file. You have now modified your report and have also reset the original report. For more information on using the Organizer and the Global template, see Chapter 4, "Managing Project Files."

CHAPTER 23

Customizing Toolbars, Menus, and Forms

In this chapter

Altering the Behavior of Personalized Menus and Toolbars 922

Customizing Toolbars 925

Customizing Menu Bars 941

Customizing Forms 949

Troubleshooting 960

Altering the Behavior of Personalized Menus and Toolbars

The toolbars and menus in Microsoft Project provide an efficient means for you to interact with the projects you design. Commands on both the toolbars and menus are organized to group together the tasks you perform most often. However, you may have discovered that although most of the toolbars and menus provide you with the commands you need, other commands might be unavailable or buried so deeply on a menu that they aren't convenient to use. Project provides a number of features that enable you to customize the user interface to make your work easier and more efficient.

Because people use a handful of commands frequently, other commands occasionally, and some commands not at all, Project, by default, personalizes menus and toolbars to display the most frequently used commands for easy access.

NOTE

> Microsoft uses a rather complex formula for determining when to promote and demote items from prominence in the personalized menus. The computation involves the number of times the application is launched and how many successive launches a given feature goes unused. As you use commands, the ones you use most frequently appear on the menu, and ones you don't use at all are suppressed. The end result is that what you use most frequently ends up on the abbreviated menus.

The personalized menus and toolbars are designed to increase your productivity. If you prefer to see the full set of toolbar icons and menu commands, you can double-click a menu title to see a full list of commands or you can permanently turn off the personalized menus and toolbars feature.

Adjusting the Behavior of Menus

If you want to see the full list of commands every time you click a menu, you can adjust the menu behavior in the Customize dialog box. To do so, right-click a menu or toolbar and choose Customize from the shortcut menu. In the Customize dialog box, click the Options tab (shown in Figure 23.1).

NOTE

> You can also gain access to the Customize dialog box by selecting Tools, Customize, Toolbars or View, Toolbars, Customize.

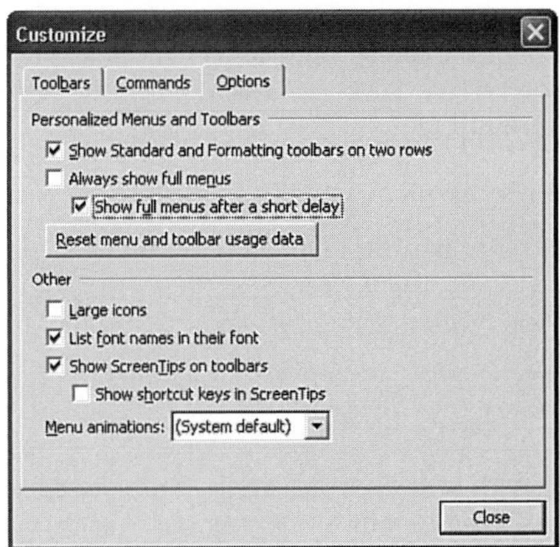

Figure 23.1
Personalized menus are turned on by default in Project.

Select the Always Show Full Menus option and click Close to turn off personalized menus. Making this change will affect the menu behavior in other Microsoft Office applications. You can also customize the items that appear on the Project menus (discussed later in this chapter, in the section "Customizing Menu Bars").

ADJUSTING THE BEHAVIOR OF TOOLBARS

When you first open Project, the Standard and Formatting toolbars are displayed at the top of the window (see Figure 23.2). You can use the *move handle* in front of each toolbar to move or adjust each toolbar. The mouse pointer changes to a four-headed arrow when the cursor is positioned on the move handle.

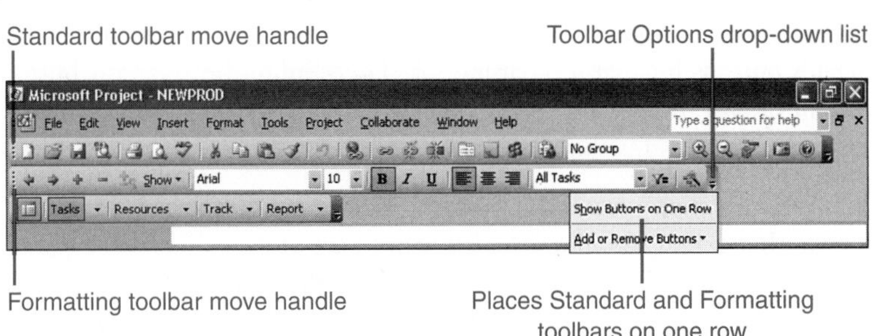

Figure 23.2
The Standard, Formatting, and Project Guide toolbars are displayed by default.

The Standard and Formatting toolbars are the most frequently used toolbars in Project. You can save some screen space by displaying these two bars on a single row. To do so, choose the Toolbar Options drop-down list at the right end of either toolbar and select Show Buttons on One Row. You can also find this setting in the Customize toolbar dialog box: Choose Tools, Customize, Toolbars and select the Options tab. Deselect the Show Standard and Formatting Toolbars on Two Rows check box.

23

NOTE

> The Show Standard and Formatting Toolbars on Two Rows setting is application specific. That is, having it set in Project does not change the appearance of the toolbars in the other Office programs.

Each toolbar displays a default set of buttons. The buttons you use most frequently are displayed on the toolbar; the buttons you use least frequently are hidden—hence the name *personalized toolbars*. Project also hides buttons if two or more toolbars are displayed on a single row and there isn't enough room to show all buttons for all bars.

NOTE

> If multiple toolbars are being displayed on a single row, you cannot drag one toolbar so far to the left that it completely covers the other toolbar on the same row.

You access the hidden buttons through the Toolbar Options drop-down list at the end of the toolbar (refer to Figure 23.2). If buttons have been hidden, when you select the Toolbar Options list, they are displayed at the top of the list. When you select a hidden button, that button is added to the toolbar and its associated action will be performed immediately. To make room for the button, however, one of the buttons that has not been used recently is placed on the More Buttons list.

QUICKLY CUSTOMIZING PERSONALIZED TOOLBARS

In addition to listing the active—but hidden—buttons, the Toolbar Options drop-down list also has an Add or Remove Buttons option that you can use to quickly customize a toolbar. When you pause over the Add or Remove Buttons option on a toolbar, a list of all toolbars sharing that row appears. When you click the name of a toolbar you want to customize, the default buttons for that toolbar appear. There might be an arrow button at the top or bottom of the list; if you click this, you can see additional toolbar buttons. Figure 23.3 shows the list of buttons for the Formatting toolbar in Project.

Buttons with check marks are from the default set of buttons associated with the toolbar. A button that is grayed out on the list is not part of the default set of buttons associated with the toolbar; it is a button that has been manually added to the toolbar through the Customize dialog box (the procedures to do this are discussed later in this chapter, in the section "Adding and Removing Command Buttons").

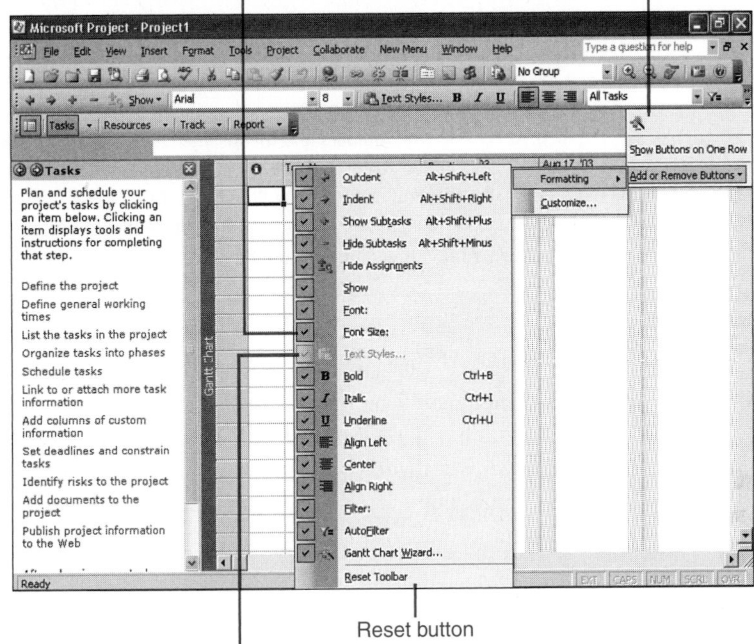

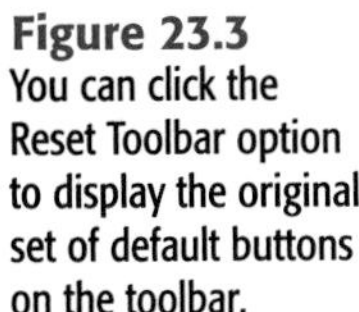

Figure 23.3
You can click the Reset Toolbar option to display the original set of default buttons on the toolbar.

CUSTOMIZING TOOLBARS

Buttons that are displayed on the toolbars provide shortcuts for executing menu commands. The menu commands that are used most frequently are attached to specific buttons and positioned on toolbars according to the types of tasks they perform. Microsoft has standardized its toolbars across applications so that tasks that are common to all applications remain constant in their presentation on toolbars. As a result, when you become accustomed to using toolbar buttons in one application, you recognize them in other applications. The Open button, for example, is available on the Standard toolbar of most Microsoft applications.

As you continue to work with Microsoft Project, you will find that some of the buttons on the toolbars are vital to the way you work, but you rarely use others. This is often determined by the type of work you do. In addition, you might find that there are tasks you perform frequently for which there are no toolbar buttons available. You can customize toolbars to remove the buttons you rarely use and replace them with buttons that help perform those tasks you do more frequently.

When you create simple macros to perform tasks you use most frequently, you can assign them to toolbar buttons. For example, if you were to create a simple macro designed to turn on the Project Summary task, you could assign a toolbar button to run the macro and include the button on a toolbar. After the macro is assigned to a toolbar, all you have to do is click the toolbar button to perform the function.

23

23

NOTE

In previous chapters, you may have created special views, tables, forms, or filters and found that they were stored as part of the project in which you created them. When you need to use them in another project, you have to copy them into the new project file or to the `GLOBAL.MPT` file. Customizing toolbars and menus is different because toolbars and menus are part of the application file rather than part of a project file. As a result, when you change the toolbars and menus, the changes are available to all projects you create or edit on your computer. They are automatically stored as part of the `GLOBAL.MPT` file. You can still copy them from the `GLOBAL.MPT` file to a project file when you want to include them in a file you are sending to someone else or when you want to copy them to a different computer. Otherwise, copying them is not necessary.

Reviewing the Built-in Toolbars

Microsoft Project 2003 includes 17 built-in toolbars, plus the menu bar, that group activities by type. Three of these toolbars—the Standard, Formatting, and Task Pane toolbars—appear by default when you start Microsoft Project. You can display any of the remaining toolbars as you need them. The new toolbars in Project 2003 include Compare Project Versions, Database Upgrade Utility, and Euro Currency Converter.

There are three default toolbars in Project:

- **The Standard toolbar**—This toolbar provides access to some of the main Microsoft Project features. Buttons on the left end of this toolbar are found on the Standard toolbars of other Microsoft applications. Buttons on the right end of the toolbar are specific to Microsoft Project.
- **The Formatting toolbar**—Buttons on this toolbar give you access to outlining features, filters, and text formatting features. Many of the buttons in the center of this toolbar are found on the Formatting toolbars of other Microsoft applications. Buttons on the left of this toolbar are frequently found on Outlining toolbars of other Microsoft applications. Project-specific buttons appear on the right end.
- **The Project Guide toolbar**—Buttons on this toolbar give you access to the features and functionality of the Project Guide. Commands on this toolbar help you define your project, work with tasks and resources, track progress, and report project information. The first button on this toolbar allows you to show/hide the task pane.

Fourteen additional toolbars are included with Microsoft Project:

- **The Collaborate toolbar**—This toolbar provides workgroup communication and enterprise project management information views (available with Microsoft Office Project 2003 Professional only).
- **The Custom Forms toolbar**—This toolbar contains many of the buttons needed to customize tasks or resource information entry screens.
- **The Drawing toolbar**—This toolbar provides access to graphic drawing tools for drawing figures and text boxes in the Gantt Chart view.

- **The Task Pane toolbar**—This toolbar displays a pane on the screen that contains shortcuts to common operations, such as opening and saving files and is consistent with other Microsoft applications.
- **The Resource Management toolbar**—This toolbar provides access to tools for resolving resource overallocations.
- **The Tracking toolbar**—This toolbar provides access to the commands that are necessary to track progress and reschedule work on uncompleted tasks.
- **The Visual Basic toolbar**—This toolbar displays buttons for recording, running, and editing macros.
- **The Web toolbar**—This toolbar displays buttons that activate your Web browser, keep a list of your favorite Web sites, and assist you in moving through Web pages.
- **The Analysis toolbar**—This toolbar provides button access to installed add-in programs.
- **The Compare Project Versions toolbar**—This toolbar helps you create a report comparing two Project files and then drill down to the specific information in the comparison report.
- **The Database Upgrade Utility**—This toolbar provides a tool that upgrades old version database projects into Microsoft Project 2003 format.
- **The Euro Currency Converter**—This toolbar provides tools to display project cost in multiple currencies.
- **The Network Diagram toolbar**—This toolbar displays analysis, viewing, and layout tools for use with the Network Diagram view.
- **The PERT Analysis toolbar**—This toolbar provides button access to the PERT estimating tools available in Project.

Many toolbar buttons are easy to identify, and their use is self-explanatory. The purpose of some buttons, however, is difficult to determine. To identify a button's function, you can point to it and pause briefly. The name of the button appears in the form of a ScreenTip.

DISPLAYING TOOLBARS

Project enables you to show and hide toolbars by using two different procedures. Perhaps the more efficient means is by selecting a toolbar from the Toolbar shortcut menu. Another way to select a toolbar is by using the View, Toolbars command. The procedures for displaying toolbars using both approaches are explained in the following sections.

The Toolbar shortcut menu contains a listing of all toolbars, as well as a command that lets you customize toolbars. To activate the shortcut menu, shown in Figure 23.4, position the mouse pointer over one of the visible toolbars and click the right mouse button. Notice in Figure 23.4 that the Standard, Formatting, and Project Guide toolbars have check marks next to them. These check marks indicate that the toolbars are currently displayed, or *active*. Other toolbars do not contain check marks, indicating that they are currently inactive.

23

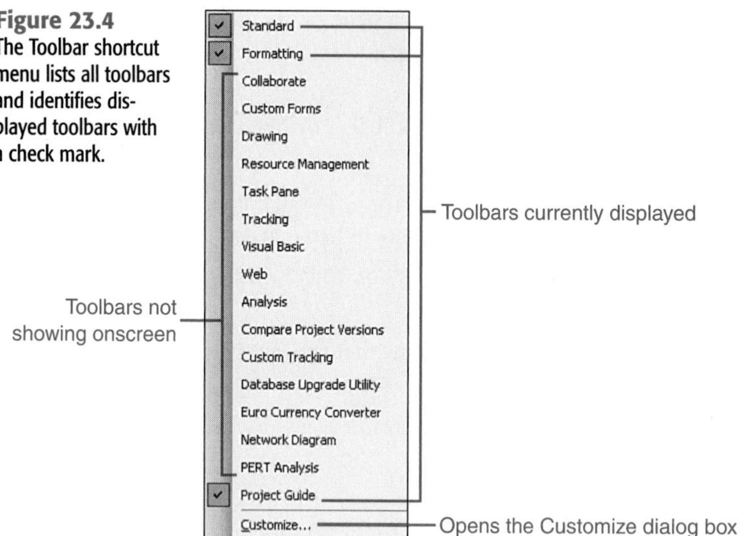

Figure 23.4
The Toolbar shortcut menu lists all toolbars and identifies displayed toolbars with a check mark.

Click on a toolbar name that isn't checked and Project will display the toolbar. If you click on a toolbar name that is already active, the check mark disappears, and the toolbar is then hidden.

As an alternative, you can show and hide toolbars by selecting View, Toolbars. The toolbar choices via this method are identical to those available through the previous Toolbar shortcut menu method.

Positioning Toolbars on the Screen

Most toolbars are set to position themselves at a docking location at the top of the screen. When a toolbar is displayed, you can move it from the top of the screen to a new position. Toolbars can be *docked* at the sides or bottom of the screen or *floated* in a small window of their own in the middle of the screen. Some toolbars have *combination boxes* (that is, buttons with a text box and an entry-list arrow). The Group drop-down box on the Standard toolbar and the Font drop-down box on the Formatting toolbar are examples of combination (or combo) boxes. When toolbars are docked on the sides of the screen, the combo boxes are not displayed.

To reposition a toolbar, click the move handle that appears on the left edge of the toolbar. As you drag the toolbar, it changes shape to fit the active position. When you have the toolbar placed where you want it, release the mouse button. Figure 23.5 shows a docked toolbar and a floating toolbar.

Notice that the floating toolbar has a title bar and a Close button. You can click the Close button to hide a floating toolbar or drag the title bar to dock it.

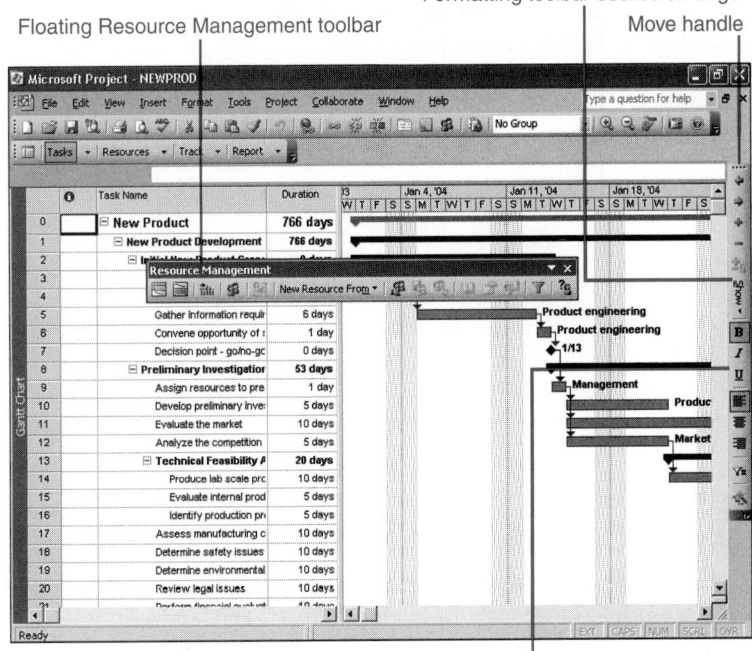

Figure 23.5 You can position toolbars onscreen to suit your taste.

TIP

> You can double-click the title of a floating toolbar to return it to its docked position.

Floating toolbars can be resized in the same way you resize other windows. When you position the mouse pointer on a border of the toolbar window, the mouse pointer changes to a double-headed arrow. Simply drag to resize the toolbar.

Using the Customize Dialog Box

Before you can create a new toolbar or customize an existing toolbar, you must display the Customize dialog box (see Figure 23.6). From the Customize dialog box, you can create new toolbars, add or remove buttons from any active toolbar, resize combo boxes, rearrange the order of the buttons on a toolbar, and establish toolbar options, such as activating the setting in which the Standard and Formatting toolbars share one row. The toolbar you want to customize must be active before you can customize it.

There are three ways to display the Customize dialog box:

- Right-click any toolbar and choose Customize from the Toolbar shortcut menu.
- Choose View, Toolbars, Customize.
- Choose Tools, Customize, and select Toolbars from the cascading menu.

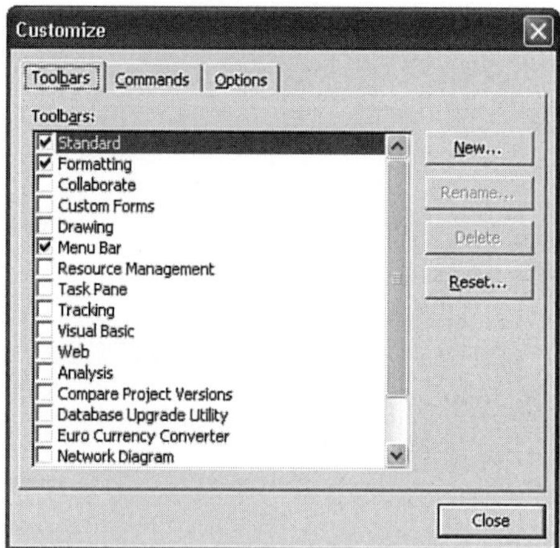

Figure 23.6
Open the Customize dialog box to create new toolbars or to change the buttons that appear on the existing toolbars.

The Customize dialog box has three tabs:

- **Toolbars**—You can choose to display or hide a toolbar by marking or unmarking the toolbar name. New toolbars can be created, renamed, or deleted, and toolbars you have customized can be reset to display their original buttons.
- **Commands**—You can use this tab to add a tool to a toolbar.
- **Options**—From this tab you can change the size of the toolbar buttons, control what is displayed in the toolbar button ToolTips, and control how the menus are animated.

TIP

When the Customize dialog box appears in front of toolbars you want to customize, you can drag the colored title bar of the Customize dialog box to move it to a different location.

ORGANIZING TOOLBAR BUTTONS

The Customize dialog box is the place to change your Project environment. With the Customize dialog box open, you can add, remove, and rearrange buttons on toolbars. You can also change the underlying button function, modify the button image, and place buttons into logical groups on the toolbars.

Before you can customize a toolbar, the toolbar you want to modify must be activated. You then need to access the Customize dialog box. From the Customize dialog box, choose the Commands tab (see Figure 23.7) to access the available commands.

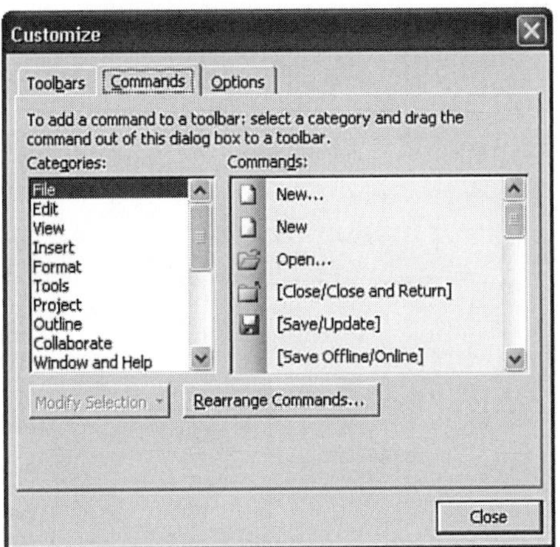

Figure 23.7 Choose the Commands tab in the Customize dialog box to see a categorized list of available commands.

The Commands tab displays a list of categories of commands on the left. Whenever you select a category, the corresponding commands appear in the list box on the right. In Figure 23.7, the File category is selected.

You use the Modify Selection button to change the actions performed by command buttons on the active toolbars. It is active when you select a command on a toolbar—not when the command is selected in the Commands list box. You can also activate Modify Selection by right-clicking a button on a toolbar, when the Customize dialog box is open.

Commands you add to the toolbars might or might not have corresponding icon buttons. Those that do not have icon buttons are displayed as text buttons.

Adding and Removing Command Buttons

When you want to add a command button to a toolbar or menu bar, you can simply drag the button from the Commands list onto the desired toolbar (see Figure 23.8). If you position the button between two existing buttons, the button drops into place, and existing buttons move to accommodate it. If there are too many buttons on the toolbar, those at the far right end begin to wrap to a new line for the toolbar while the Customize dialog box remains open. When you close the dialog box, Project hides the least-used buttons on the toolbar, to make room for the added buttons. It places the hidden buttons on the Toolbar Options drop-down list for that toolbar, as described in the section "Adjusting the Behavior of Toolbars," earlier in this chapter.

TIP

> Microsoft Project makes it easy to insert a button on a toolbar that executes a macro you have created. The category All Macros on the Commands tab of the Customize dialog box lists the macros in Project, including the ones you create. Simply drag the macro name to the desired toolbar. The name of the macro appears as a button on the toolbar. You can create an image for that button instead of having the macro name appear on the toolbar.

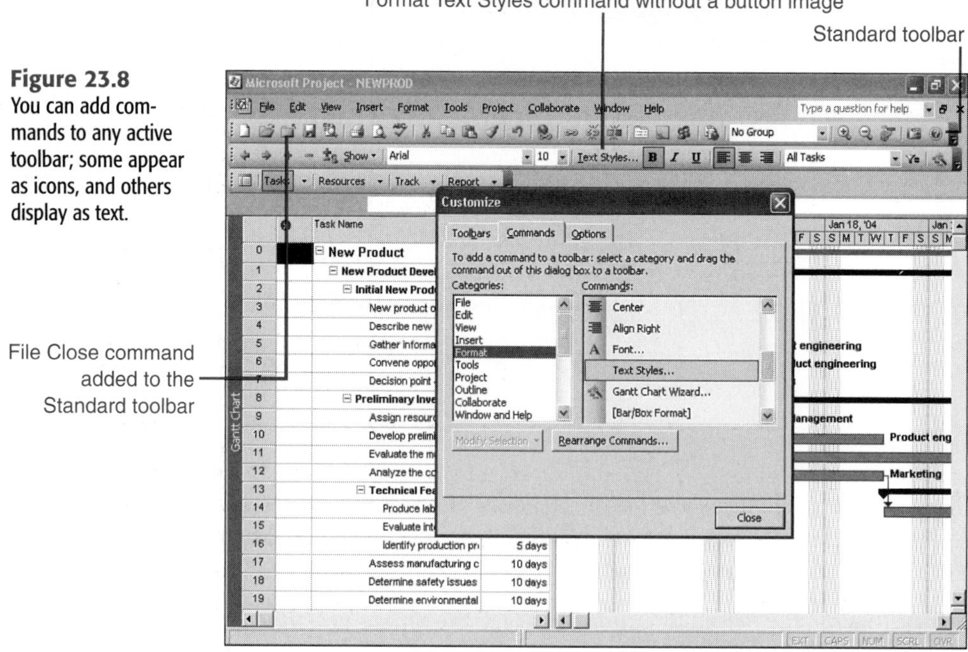

Figure 23.8
You can add commands to any active toolbar; some appear as icons, and others display as text.

→ For more information on creating your own customized command buttons, **see** "Customizing Command Buttons," **p. 936**.

*To learn more about removing a command button, **see** "Removing Toolbar Buttons" in the "Troubleshooting" section at the end of this chapter.*

→ To learn how to take advantage of macros in Project, **see** the chapter "Using Visual Basic with Project 2003" on the CD accompanying this book.

If you find that there are certain command buttons you never use, you can remove them from the toolbar to make room for other buttons. To remove a button from a toolbar, open the Customize dialog box, drag the button off its toolbar, and release it in the center of the screen, away from other toolbars.

REARRANGING COMMAND BUTTONS

The new Rearrange Commands dialog box allows you to quickly add, remove, and/or rearrange commands on toolbars and menu bars. To access the Rearrange Commands dialog box, click the Rearrange Commands button on the Commands tab of the Customize dialog box. Select the menu bar or toolbar you wish to alter, make your changes, and then click Close. Figure 23.9 shows the Rearrange commands dialog box with the File menu Controls listed.

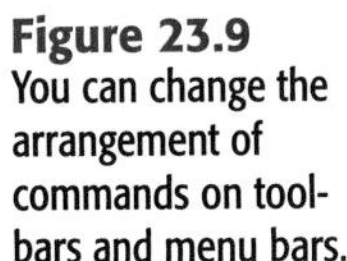

Figure 23.9
You can change the arrangement of commands on toolbars and menu bars.

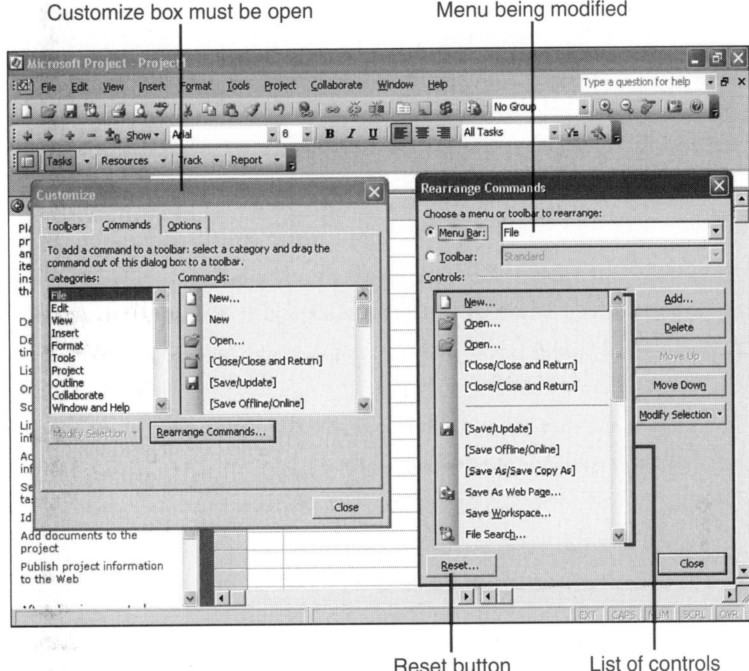

You can also rearrange the buttons on a toolbar by dragging them to different locations. To move buttons, the Customize dialog box must be open. When you select a button to move it, a heavy border indicates that the button is selected. As you move the button, the mouse pointer changes to a thick capital I.

When you want to move a button from one toolbar to another, you can use the procedures described in the previous section for removing and adding buttons. Or, you can simply drag the button from one toolbar to the other. When you move buttons from one toolbar to another, both toolbars must be displayed and the Customize dialog box must be open.

Grouping Command Buttons

Command buttons on toolbars are organized by groups. Vertical separator bars distinguish one group from another. To add a separator bar in front of the active command button, right-click the button that should begin the new group. A list of command-button display options appears.

To add a separator bar, click Begin a Group. A separator bar appears in front of the selected button. You can remove a separator bar from a button by right-clicking it on the toolbar and selecting Begin a Group again. A check mark in front of a modification option indicates that the option is active.

RESIZING COMBO BOXES

A combo box is a two-part box that combines a text box with a drop-down list arrow that can be used to select valid options. Combo boxes appear frequently in dialog boxes and on toolbars. For example, on the Formatting toolbar there are combo boxes for Font, Font Size, and Filter. You can change the width of the text box portion of a combo box while the Customize dialog box is open.

To increase or decrease the width of combo boxes, follow these steps:

1. Display the toolbar that contains the combo box and display the Customize dialog box. You can have any tab in the Customize dialog box active to resize a combo box.
2. Select the combo box in the toolbar. A heavy black border appears around the combo box, indicating that it is selected.
3. Position the mouse pointer over one side of the combo box. The mouse pointer changes to a dark two-headed arrow.
4. Drag the edge of the combo box to the desired size.
5. Repeat steps 2–4 for each combo box you want to resize.
6. Close the Customize dialog box.

CREATING NEW TOOLBARS

Sometimes the buttons you use most frequently are on several different toolbars. Instead of having four or five toolbars displayed, which reduces the space available on the screen to display your project document, you might want to have one or two toolbars that contain most (if not all) of the command buttons you use. At other times, you might want to customize an existing toolbar without affecting the original toolbar. Microsoft Project enables you to create new toolbars on which you can store the buttons you use most frequently, without affecting the buttons currently available on other toolbars.

When the toolbar you want to create contains many of the same buttons that are available on an existing toolbar, you can make a copy of the existing toolbar, give it a unique name, add the buttons you use most frequently, and delete any buttons you don't want on it. Alternatively, you can start with a blank toolbar and create a completely new collection of buttons.

CREATING A TOOLBAR BY COPYING AN EXISTING TOOLBAR

When an existing toolbar contains many of the buttons you want to include on your new toolbar, making a copy of the existing toolbar is a good starting point. Copying the existing toolbar reduces the number of buttons you'll need to place on the new toolbar.

You cannot create a copy of a toolbar from within the Customize dialog box. To copy a toolbar, you have to access the Organizer.

→ To learn how to copy and rename a toolbar, **see** "Managing Toolbars with the Organizer," **p. 947**.

After you create a copy of a toolbar, access the Customize dialog box and use the techniques outlined in the previous sections to modify the copied toolbar for your needs.

BUILDING A NEW TOOLBAR

Creating a new toolbar from scratch creates an empty floating toolbar window that you can fill with the command buttons.

To build a new toolbar, follow these steps:

1. Right-click any toolbar and choose Customize from the Toolbar shortcut menu, or choose View, Toolbars, Customize. The Customize dialog box appears.
2. From the Toolbars tab, choose New to open the New Toolbar dialog box. Project assigns a sequential number to each new toolbar and identifies the toolbar with a generic name, such as Custom 1.
3. Type the new toolbar name. Toolbar names must be unique and are limited to any combination of 51 characters and spaces.
4. Click OK.

The new toolbar name appears in the list on the Toolbars tab, and the new empty toolbar appears in the Project window (see Figure 23.10). Select the Commands tab and drag the desired buttons onto the toolbar to create the collection you desire. The toolbar enlarges as you add command buttons. As is true with all toolbars, you can dock the toolbar or leave it floating.

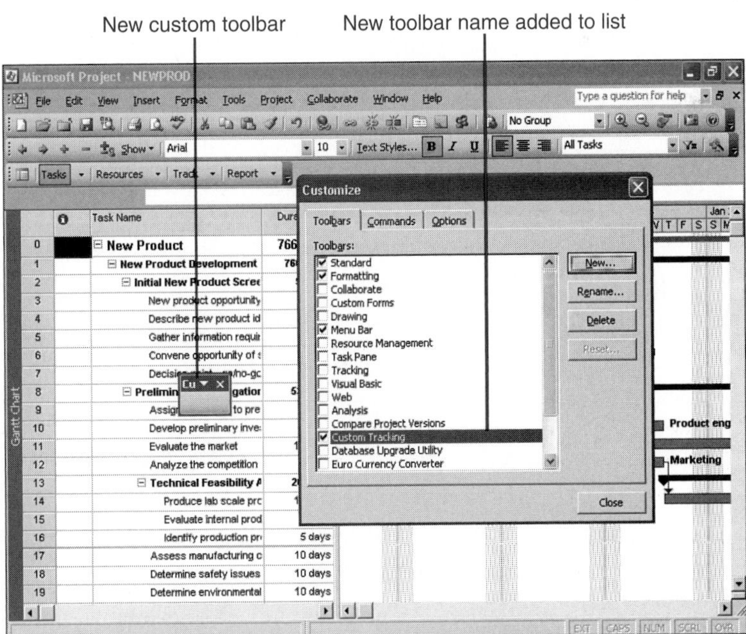

Figure 23.10
User-defined toolbars are initially displayed floating in the Project window.

Deleting a User-Defined Toolbar

Toolbars installed with the Microsoft Project software remain a part of the application even after you customize them. As a result, you can reset them but you cannot delete them. However, you can delete new toolbars you create, which are referred to as *user-defined*. To delete a user-defined toolbar, open the Customize dialog box, move to the Toolbars tab, select the toolbar to be removed, and click Delete.

NOTE

> If the Delete button is not active, you have selected a toolbar that was installed with the Microsoft Project software. Most of these toolbars can be reset but not deleted.

Restoring the Built-in Toolbars

Changes you make to the built-in toolbars as you customize might become out-of-date and might not fit every project you create. As a result, you might want to restore the default buttons to a toolbar. Microsoft Project includes a feature that makes restoring toolbars quick and easy.

CAUTION

> Resetting a toolbar removes *all* customized changes you have made to that toolbar—not just the most recent changes. If you reset a toolbar on which you have placed custom buttons, you lose the custom buttons. To avoid this, drag the custom buttons to another toolbar to preserve them.

To learn more about custom toolbar behavior, ***see*** *"Disappearing Custom Toolbars" in the "Troubleshooting" section at the end of this chapter.*

To restore the default set of command buttons to the built-in toolbars, open the Customize dialog box, move to the Toolbars tab, select the toolbar to be restored, and click Reset. Project will issue a warning that all customization is about to be lost; click OK to complete the procedure.

Customizing Command Buttons

Some of the commands that are available in the Customize dialog box have no button image associated with them. When such a command is added to a toolbar, only the name of the command is displayed. In addition, sometimes no command is available for a task you perform frequently, and it might be necessary for you to create a macro to record the steps of such a task. After you have created the macro, the name of the macro is listed on the Commands tab of the Customize dialog box. No button image is associated with the macro command. When the command is added to a toolbar, the name of the macro is displayed.

You can copy one of the available images to a command button that doesn't have an image, or you can design your own image for the command button by using the button display options.

ACCESSING THE BUTTON DISPLAY OPTIONS

To modify toolbar button images, you need to access the list of button display options. To see these options, you must first display the toolbar that contains the command button you want to change and then display the Customize dialog box. (The quickest way to display the Customize dialog box is to right-click any toolbar and choose Customize.) When you have the toolbar and dialog box displayed, choose one of the following methods to see the button display options list:

- Right-click the button you want to modify.
- Select the button you want to modify, and then select the Commands tab in the Customize dialog box and click the Modify Selection button.

CUSTOMIZING A BUTTON FACE

The Customize dialog box enables you to copy an existing button or access the Editor dialog box, where you can customize a button design. If another button carries a design that resembles the one you want to use on the new button, you can copy the design from the button to the Clipboard and then paste it on the blank button. Copying the design does not copy the functionality of the original button to the new button. After you paste the design on the blank button, you can modify the design to customize it for the new button. You can also create a design from scratch.

To change a button image, follow these steps:

1. If necessary, go to the Toolbars tab and display the toolbar that contains the button to be changed.
2. Right-click any toolbar and choose Customize from the Toolbar shortcut menu, or choose View, Toolbars, Customize. The Customize dialog box appears.
3. Right-click the button on the toolbar button you want to change. A heavy black border indicates that the button is selected, and the list of button display options appears. The following is a list of available options:

NOTE

> You can also click the Commands tab in the Customize dialog box and click the Modify Selection button to see the list of button display options.

   - Select Copy Button Image to put a copy of the selected button face on the clipboard.
   - Select Reset Button Image to immediately remove any previous editing applied to the selected button and return it to its original button face.
   - Select Edit Button Image to open the Button Editor and modify the selected button face.

- Select Change Button Image to choose a design from the Project image library and apply it to the selected button.

4. Close the Customize dialog box when you are finished changing the button face.

The option Paste Button Image becomes active on the Modify Selection list after an image has been copied; be sure to select another button and paste the new image onto it. The receiving button does not have to be blank; the existing face is replaced with the copied image.

Project contains a library of images you can apply to a button face instead of copying the face of a displayed button. Figure 23.11 shows the image library that is available in Microsoft Project.

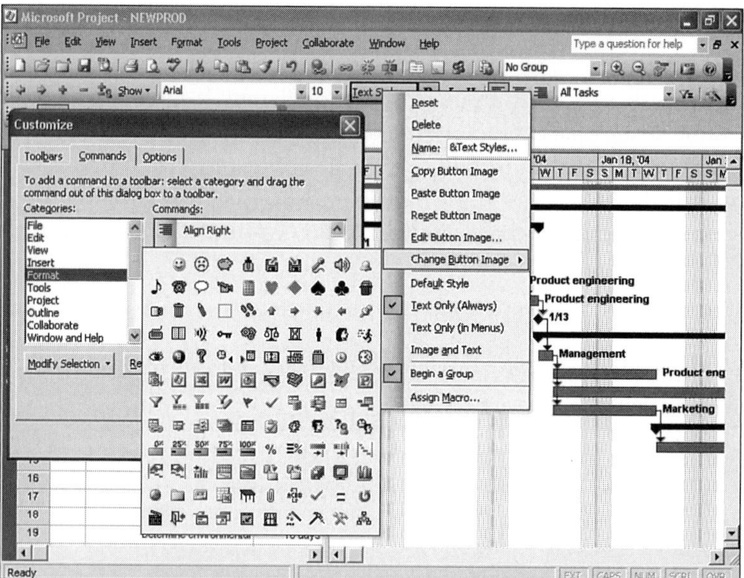

Figure 23.11 Select the Change Button Image option to display the list of images from the Project image library.

A third approach for changing a button face is to design your own image. When a command button has a blank button image, you can design your own image for it. You can also edit a button face after you choose a button image from the library or copy an image from another button; you might want to edit the picture. If the image was copied, changing the picture so that it differs from the design of a button used to perform a different task helps you identify both buttons. To edit the picture, you must use the Button Editor dialog box. The button design appears enlarged so that individual pixels can be identified in the Picture box. You can then change the location of each pixel in the image by using the mouse to achieve the desired design.

In Figure 23.12, the design assigned to the Paste button (on the Standard toolbar) is selected as the design for a new command button (Text Styles) on the Formatting toolbar, and you need to edit it so that it isn't confused with the Paste button.

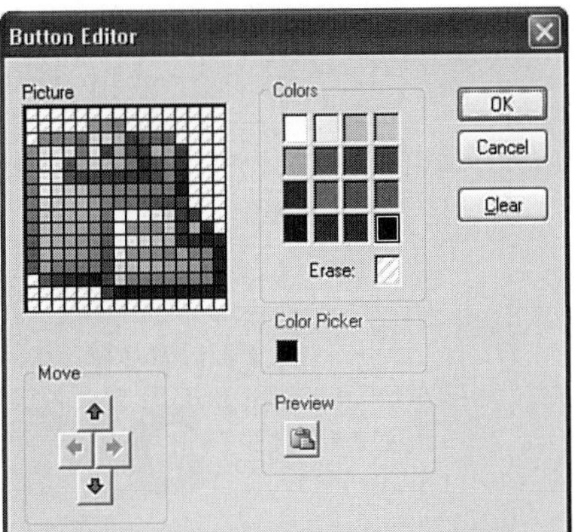

Figure 23.12
You use the Button Editor dialog box to create or modify a button image.

The Colors box in the Button Editor dialog box is a palette for selecting colored pixels for the design. The Move arrows help you position the picture on the button by moving it one row or column at a time. The Preview area shows how the current picture appears.

To change the picture, use any of the following techniques:

- To change the color of a pixel, click a color in the Colors box and then click the pixel, or drag the color across a group of pixels.
- To erase or clear pixels, select the Erase box and then click all pixels you want to clear, drag the pointer across pixels you want to clear, or click a pixel a second time to clear the existing color.
- To reposition the picture on the button, clear an area along the edge toward which you want to move the design and then click the desired move arrow button.
- To clear the picture canvas and start a new image from scratch, click Clear.
- To cancel changes and start over, click Cancel or press Esc.

When you are finished modifying the button, click OK, and the new design appears on the new button. Figure 23.13 shows the finished picture that will be assigned to the Text Styles button.

Changing the Actions of a Button

After you have added a command button to a toolbar or modified a button's image, you might decide to change the command associated with that button. The command that is executed when a button is clicked is identified in the Command drop-down list on the Customize Tool dialog box. Figure 23.14 shows the command for the Text Styles button on the Formatting toolbar.

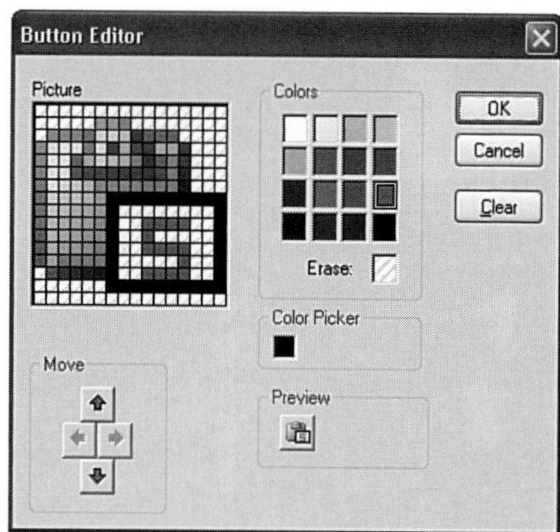

Figure 23.13
The finished picture for the Text Styles button is slightly different from the picture copied from the Paste button.

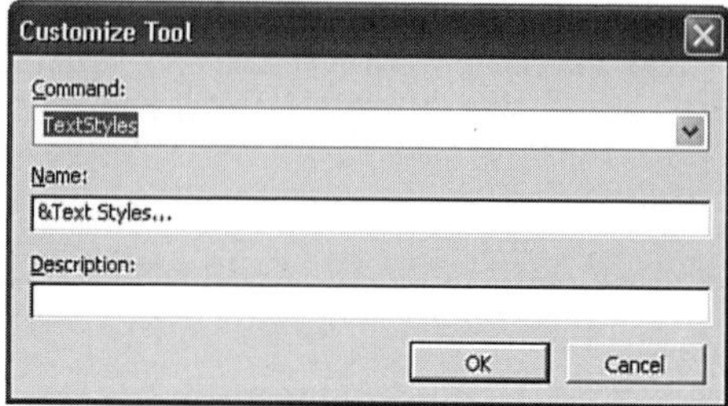

Figure 23.14
You can use Ctrl+click on a button to customize its behavior.

When you click the Command drop-down list, you see all the Microsoft Project commands (including forms and macros) that you can assign to a button. For example, to assign a Project add-in macro to a button, select the Macro command that displays the desired macro in double quotes from the Command drop-down list. Similarly, to designate the button to activate a custom form, you can choose the Form command that includes the desired form name in double quotes. Commands with names in double-quotes designate custom elements added to the Project environment.

To learn more about toolbar button behavior, ***see*** *"Strange Toolbar Button Behavior" in the "Troubleshooting" section at the end of this chapter.*

→ To learn more about macros and Microsoft Project, **see** the chapter "Using Visual Basic with Project 2003" on the CD accompanying this book.

You can access the Customize Tool dialog box directly from the Project window, without having to go through the Customize dialog box, by following these steps:

1. If you need to create a button (including a button for a macro), see the section "Adding and Removing Command Buttons," earlier in this chapter.
2. Press the Ctrl key and click the button you want to change. The Customize Tool dialog box appears.
3. Choose the Command drop-down list arrow and scroll through the commands to find the one you need. In Figure 23.15, a supplied macro name is selected. Commands are

listed in alphabetical order and are grouped by type on the list. As a result, you might have to scroll through the list to find the command you need.

4. Click OK.

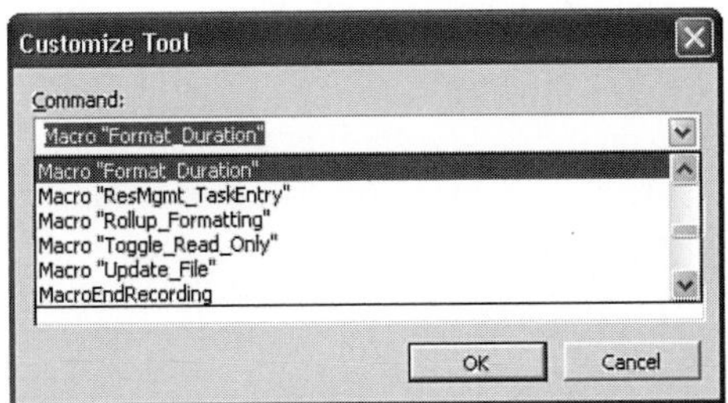

Figure 23.15
Macros automatically appear in the list of commands that can be assigned to a button.

23

Customizing Menu Bars

A *menu* is a collection of commands that pertains to a particular topic or action. So the File menu is a collection of commands that perform actions with documents—opening, closing, saving, printing, and so forth. Likewise, underneath a menu on the menu bar, there may be submenus. Any command that has a pointing triangle is considered a menu. In Figure 23.16, the complete Edit menu is active. Within the Edit menu are three other built-in menus—Fill, Clear, and Object.

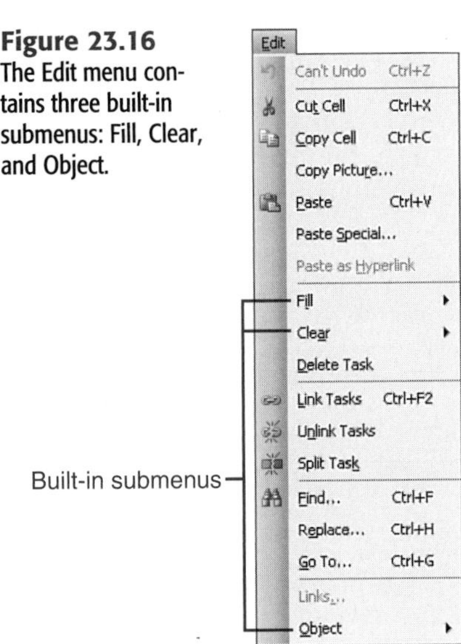

Figure 23.16
The Edit menu contains three built-in submenus: Fill, Clear, and Object.

A *command* is a specific action within an application; for example, Save As is a command. When describing a command, most people and reference books (such as the one you are now reading) typically identify a command by stating the menu followed by the command. So, although technically it is the Save As command, you will often see it referred to as the File, Save As command. Identifying the menu as well as the command simply provides additional clarity when referring to a command.

Project, like Office, treats the menu bar as just another toolbar. You customize a menu bar in much the same way you customize a toolbar—by dragging commands on and off the menu bar. You can create new menus, add commands to the menus, rearrange commands, and remove commands from the menus just as you do with the toolbars. By default, a menu bar is docked at the top of the screen, but like a toolbar, it can be moved and docked at the side or bottom of the screen, or it can be left floating in the middle of the screen.

The introduction of the personalized toolbars and menus feature in Project diminished the need to relocate commands to the tops of menus. By design, Project displays the commands you use frequently on the menu and hides the commands you rarely or never use. You can see the full list of commands by double-clicking the menu or by pausing on the menu to display the full list after a slight delay.

→ To prevent menus and toolbars from being personalized, **see** "Altering the Behavior of Personalized Menus and Toolbars," **p. 922**.

There are two main reasons for customizing a menu bar: to make commands buried too deep in the menu system more accessible and to create new menus. Customizing menus offers a wide range of possibilities. You might simply want to attach commands to existing menus. You can attach items such as frequently used views, tables, filters, and macros to existing menus quite easily. Specific procedures for adding elements such as views and tables to menus are included in the chapter in which they were created. Usually, such elements can be added to a menu by turning on a Show in Menu option in the item's definition.

NOTE

> Customized menus, like other toolbars, are different from elements such as views, tables, and filters because menus are part of the *application* file rather than a *project* file. As a result, changing them makes them available to all projects you create or edit on your computer. They are stored as part of the `GLOBAL.MPT` file that is used as a basis for all projects you create or open on your machine.

When you want to change the name of a menu bar item or create a new menu bar item, you are, in effect, creating a custom menu bar. The next few sections focus on editing items on existing menu bars and creating new menu bars.

To add commands to a menu, follow the steps outlined in the sections earlier in this chapter for adding commands to toolbars. The next few sections focus on customizing options that are unique to menus.

→ To learn more about the steps for altering the appearance of the toolbars and menus, or to add new commands to toolbars and menus, **see** "Customizing Toolbars," **p. 925**.

Adding New Menus to a Menu Bar

You can add a new menu either directly on a menu bar or as a submenu underneath a menu. To accomplish this, you must have the Customize dialog box displayed.

To add a new menu, follow these steps:

1. Right-click any toolbar and choose Customize from the Toolbar shortcut menu, or choose View, Toolbars, Customize. The Customize dialog box appears.
2. Select the Commands tab.
3. Scroll down the list of categories and select New Menu. The only option that appears in the Commands list is New Menu.
4. Drag the New Menu command to the place on a menu bar, or on an existing menu, where you want to insert the new menu (see Figure 23.17).

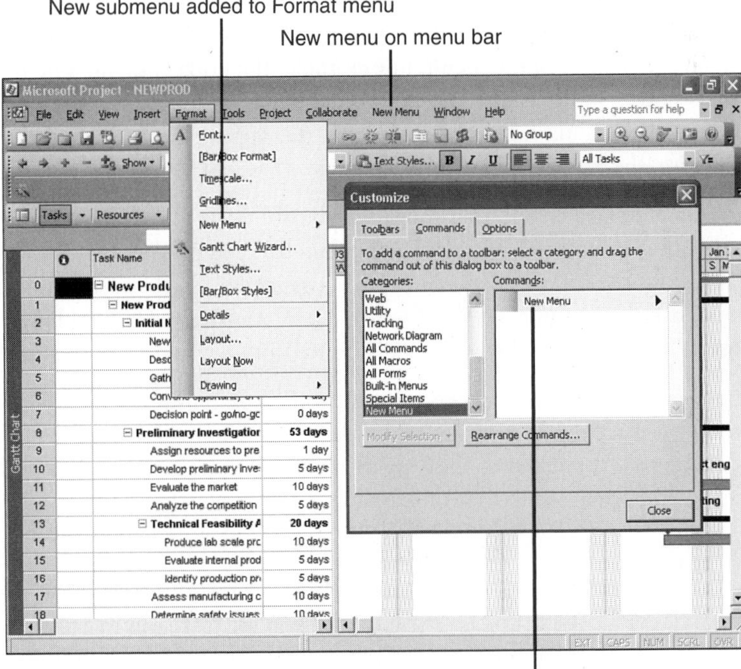

Figure 23.17
You can add new menus to the menu bar or inside existing menus.

- **Inserting a new menu directly on the menu bar**—When you drag the New Menu command to the menu bar, a thick capital I symbol appears on the menu bar. Release the mouse when this symbol is in the location on the menu bar where you want the new menu to appear.

- **Inserting a new menu within an existing menu**—Drag the New Menu command to the menu bar, next to the menu you want to place it under. When the list of commands on that menu appears, drag the mouse down to the exact position between the existing commands where you want the new submenu to appear. Release the mouse.

Renaming Menus and Commands

After you have added a new menu to a menu bar, you should name the menu and add commands to it. The Customize dialog box must be open to do this. To rename a menu, right-click the menu name to see the list of display options. In the Name text box, replace the default name with the name you want to use for the menu. Press Enter to accept the name change. To rename a submenu, click the main menu. Then right-click the newly inserted menu to change the name.

Most menus and commands have a keyboard hotkey that can be used to activate the menu or command via the keyboard instead of the mouse. These hotkeys are represented by the underscored letter in the menu. For example, the hotkey for the File menu is F. You designate a hotkey in the Name text box by using an ampersand (`&`) in front of the letter that is to be used as the hotkey. For the File menu, this appears in the Name text box as `&File`. Likewise, the Format menu name appears as `F&ormat` in the Name text box.

You should make certain that the letter you are using for a hotkey is not already being used by another menu or command. For a menu bar, you only need to look at the other menu names, not the commands underneath those menus. So if you are adding a new menu to the menu bar, the letters F, E, V, I, O, T, P, C, W, H are already used by the File, Edit, View, Insert, Format, Tools, Project, Collaborate, Window, and Help menus.

If you are adding a menu or command to an existing menu, you only need to look at the words on that specific menu to make sure you are not using duplicate letters. So if you are adding a new command to the Format menu, you only need to look at the words on the expanded Format menu to avoid duplicating hotkeys.

NOTE

> If you happen to set duplicate hotkeys within a menu, selecting the commands requires extra steps. For instance, if you have two commands on a menu that both have the letter *H* as the hotkey. Once you open the menu and press H, the first command from the top of the list with that hotkey is highlighted but does not execute a command, as it normally would. To perform that command, you must then press Enter. If you press H again, the second menu command with the hotkey H is selected. You have to then press Enter to execute the second command.

Adding Items to a Menu

You add items to menus by using the same basic techniques that you use to add buttons to toolbars. With the Customize dialog box open, simply select the category and item you want to add and drag it onto the menu bar. When you position the command between two existing commands, the new item drops into place. When you drag the item to a menu, a capital I indicates the position of the command. Figure 23.18 shows the Project Statistics command being added to a new menu. If you are adding items to an empty menu, there are no commands to use for positioning. If you pause over the menu name, a box appears, in which you can place the item.

23

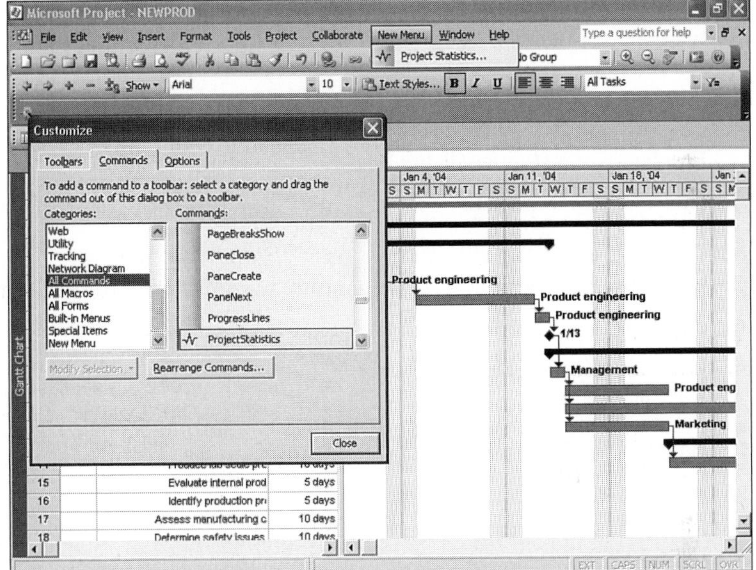

Figure 23.18
Add items to a new menu by dragging commands from the Customize dialog box.

The following are several different types of items you can add to a new menu bar:

- **Commands**—Any command can be added to a new or standard menu. You simply choose the command from either the category in which the command is listed or from the All Commands category listed toward the bottom of the list. All Commands is an alphabetical listing of every command in Project.
- **Built-in menus**—You can add other built-in menus to the new menu. If you choose the Built-in Menus category, a complete listing of menus that are installed with Microsoft Project appears.
- **Special items**—Many other items appear in menus besides commands and menus. These are often grouped in lists. For example, on the View menu you see lists of different types of views, and on the Window menu, you see a list of open project files.

Removing and Restoring Menus and Commands

If you no longer use a menu or a particular command, you can remove it from a menu bar or from within a menu. To remove menus or commands, perform the same steps you use to remove buttons from a toolbar—that is, simply drag them off the menu bar. The Customize dialog box must be open before you can remove menus and commands.

If you have customized a menu and removed some of the default commands from menus, you can restore the standard Project menus and commands to their original settings by restoring the menu bar.

CAUTION

Restoring the menu bar removes any custom menus you have created.

To restore the menu bar, follow these steps:

1. Display the Customize dialog box.
2. Select the Toolbars tab.
3. Choose Menu Bar from the list of toolbars.
4. Click Reset. A warning message appears, to confirm resetting the menu bar.
5. Click OK.
6. Close the Customize dialog box.

Moving Menus and Commands

NEW The new Rearrange Commands dialog box allows you to quickly add, remove, and/or arrange commands on toolbars and menu bars.

→ For more information on utilizing the Rearrange Commands dialog box, **see** "Rearranging Command Buttons," **p. 932**.

You can rearrange the order of the menu commands on the menu bar by dragging the menu name to a different location. You can also reorder the commands within a particular menu in the same way that you rearrange toolbar buttons. The Customize dialog box must be active for you to rearrange the order of the menus or commands.

When you select a menu or command name to move, a heavy border indicates that the name is selected. Hold and drag the name to its new location. As you move the name, the mouse pointer changes to a thick capital I. When the name is in the new location, release the mouse button.

Changing the Attributes of a Menu or Command

Each menu item has a set of attributes, or display options, that you can change. One of these options is the name that appears on the menu, discussed in the section "Renaming Menus and Commands," earlier in this chapter.

Another attribute is whether these items are separated into groups. Horizontal bars in the menus distinguish one group from another. The way you designate a group is by right-clicking the command that will be the first command in the group while the Customize box is open. The list of display options then appears on a shortcut menu. To add a horizontal separator bar, click Begin a Group. A check mark appears in front of the option to indicate that a separator bar has been added. You remove a separator bar from a menu item by selecting the item and removing the check mark.

To learn more about group box behavior, **see** *"Working with Group Boxes" in the "Troubleshooting" section at the end of this chapter.*

MANAGING TOOLBARS WITH THE ORGANIZER

Toolbars are global objects in Microsoft Project and are attached to the application in general rather than to a specific project. As a result, toolbars are stored as part of the `GLOBAL.MPT` file and are available for all projects you create, review, or edit. Changes you make to the various toolbars are also stored in the `GLOBAL.MPT` file.

→ To learn more about how useful the Global template is, **see** "The Global Template: `GLOBAL.MPT`," **p. 104**.

There might be times when you create a custom toolbar or edit an existing toolbar and want to copy it to another computer system, such as a laptop or a home computer. At other times you might want to include a special toolbar as part of a file you are sending to a coworker.

Toolbars that are attached to project files can't be displayed directly from the project. When you want to make a toolbar available on a different computer, you can copy it to a project and then, on the other system, copy it from the project into the `GLOBAL.MPT` file. The Organizer also provides options for renaming and deleting toolbars.

→ To learn all about how to work with the Organizer, **see** "Working with the Organizer and the Global File," **p. 107**.

To copy and rename a toolbar, follow these steps:

1. From the menu bar, choose Tools, Organizer. The Organizer dialog box appears.
2. Select the Toolbars tab in the Organizer. On the left side of the dialog box is the `GLOBAL.MPT` file; on the right side of the dialog box is the active Project file. Typically there are no toolbars listed in the active file.
3. Select the name of the toolbar you want to rename from the `GLOBAL.MPT` file, and then click Copy.
4. The toolbar name appears in the active file, listed on the right, as shown in Figure 23.19.

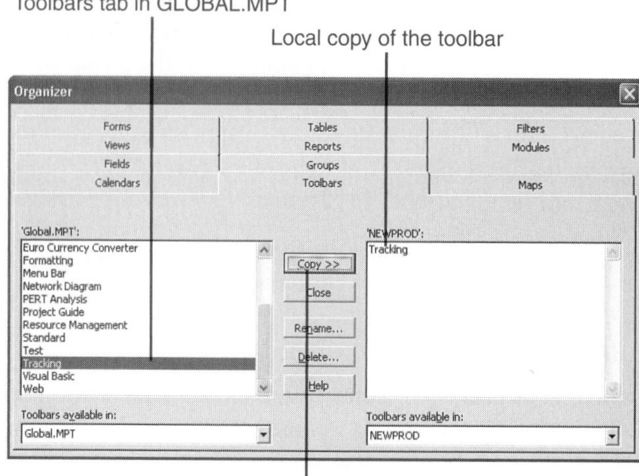

Figure 23.19
The Toolbars tab of the Organizer shows the named toolbars that are stored in the `GLOBAL.MPT` file.

TIP

> If the project file you want to use doesn't already appear above the box on the right side of the Toolbars tab on the Organizer dialog box, select it from the Toolbars Available In drop-down list.

5. Select the toolbar name you just made a copy of on the right (in your active file) and click Rename. The Rename dialog box appears.
6. In the Rename dialog box, type the new name for the copied toolbar and click OK (see Figure 23.20).

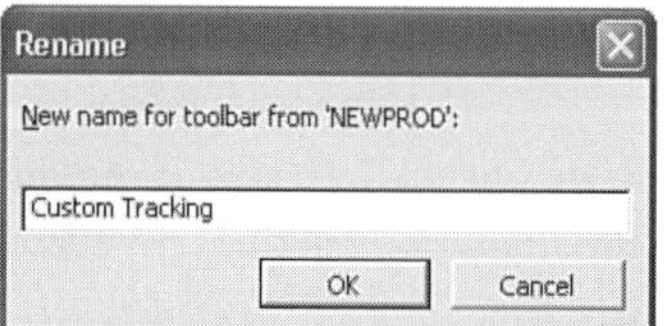

Figure 23.20
You should rename the local copy of the toolbar before customizing it to avoid confusion.

Make sure the name you type is not a name that is used by another toolbar. For example, if you copied the Tracking toolbar, you could rename the copy My Tracking or Custom Tracking to differentiate it from the original Tracking toolbar.

7. Close the Organizer.

Figure 23.21 shows that a copy of the Tracking toolbar has been renamed Custom Tracking and placed in the `NEWPROD.mpp` project file. You can move this file to another computer. On the second computer, you would reverse the process to use the toolbar: Copy Custom

Tracking into the `GLOBAL.MPT` file on the second system. The toolbar will then be available to all users of Project who share this version of the `GLOBAL.MPT` file.

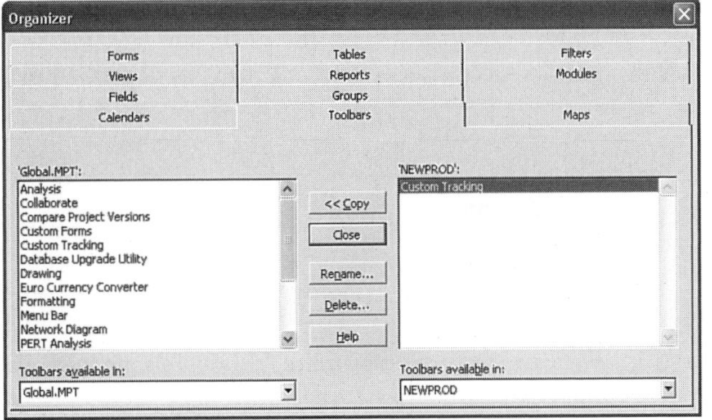

Figure 23.21
A toolbar copied into a project file must be copied into the `GLOBAL.MPT` template before it can be accessed.

Customizing Forms

Custom forms are pop-up data entry forms that resemble dialog boxes. These forms give you quick access to fields that might not be displayed on the current view. Using a custom form enables you to access a field that contains the information you need without changing views. This section identifies some of the features that are available for using custom forms and reviews the procedures for accomplishing these tasks.

Project provides a number of different forms that you can use to perform some of the most common tasks. You can, for example, use the Update Task form when you need to track the progress of a Project task. You can edit built-in forms by moving information around, but you can't add additional fields or delete fields. As a result, you might want to design your own custom forms. The Custom Form Editor, which is one of the server applications in Windows, is used to create custom forms.

Custom forms can be attached to toolbar buttons, to a menu, or to a hotkey. You cannot place a custom form in a pane and then use the form to scroll through the task list or resource list. The task(s) or resource(s) selected when you activate the form is affected by any entries you make. When you click the OK or Cancel button on the form, the form is removed from display.

Because you have to display a custom form for a selected task or resource, these forms are inappropriate as a primary vehicle for original data entry. To provide continued access to fields that are not included in a standard view, it would be most efficient to create a view that incorporates a custom table. You can then design and display the custom view in the Task Sheet view or the Resource Sheet view.

To learn more about using custom forms, ***see*** *"Making Your Custom Forms Work" in the "Troubleshooting" section at the end of this chapter.*

→ For guidelines on creating custom views, **see** Chapter 21, "Customizing Views, Tables, Fields, Filters, and Groups," **p. 833**.

Reviewing the Forms Supplied with Microsoft Project

Microsoft Project includes custom forms for both task and resource data. Each of these predefined forms is designed to accomplish a specific task, as described in Table 23.1.

Table 23.1 Custom Forms Supplied with Project

Form	Description
Task Data Forms	
Cost Tracking	Tracks the cost information for tasks and provides some progress information.
Earned Value	Examines project performance, utilizing planned, scheduled, and actual cost of work data.
Entry	Submits basic task information.
PERT Entry	Submits duration estimates—Optimistic, Expected, and Pessimistic.
Schedule Tracking	Tracks the duration and percentage completed and displays scheduled task dates and variances.
Task Relationships	Displays the list of predecessors and successors for the selected task(s).
Tracking	Tracks task duration progress.
Work Tracking	Displays duration and tracks actual work progress.
Resource Data Forms	
Cost Tracking	Displays cost information.
Entry	Submits basic resource information.
Summary	Displays the overall cost and work-tracking variances.
Work Tracking	Displays work-tracking information.

Like other elements in Project, forms are either task or resource oriented. For example, if a task-oriented view, such as a Gantt Chart view, is active onscreen when the Work Tracking form is opened, the form displays and accepts entries for the task work values. But if a resource view, such as the Resource Sheet view, is onscreen, the Work Tracking form displays resource work values that cannot be changed in the form. Some forms do not even open if the active view is the wrong type. Edits to the Summary form are allowed only if a resource view is active onscreen.

Using Custom Forms

The Custom Form dialog box in Project is attached to the Tools menu. To make a form more accessible, you might want to attach it to a toolbar button or a hotkey. Procedures for using the menus to access a form and for attaching forms to toolbar buttons and hotkeys are described in the following sections.

USING THE MENU TO DISPLAY A FORM

When you want to display or edit information for one task or resource, you select the task or resource before displaying the form. When you want to display or edit information for multiple tasks or resources, you select all tasks and resources before displaying the form. Remember that entries made to the form when multiple tasks or resources are selected affect all selected tasks or resources.

To display a custom form by using the menu, follow these steps:

1. Select the task(s) or resource(s) you want to edit.
2. Choose Tools, Customize, Forms. The Customize Forms dialog box appears (see Figure 23.22). If a task is selected, the task forms are listed. If a resource is selected, the resource forms are listed.

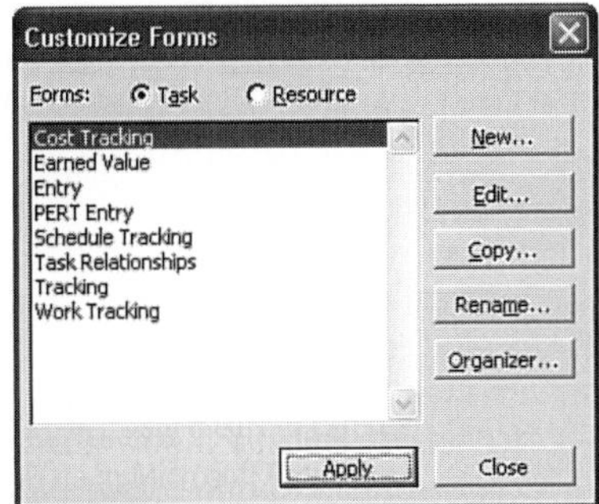

Figure 23.22
Task and Resource forms are available through the Customize Forms dialog box.

3. Select the desired form from the Forms list.
4. Click Apply.
5. Edit or view field values for the selected task(s) or resource(s).
6. Click OK.

ASSIGNING A HOTKEY TO DISPLAY A FORM

To make a form you use frequently more accessible, you might want to assign a hotkey to it. To assign a hotkey to a custom form, follow these steps:

1. Choose Tools, Customize, Forms to open the Customize Forms dialog box.
2. Select the form to which you want to assign to a hotkey from the Forms list.
3. Click Rename. The Define Custom Form dialog box appears (see Figure 23.23). You can use this dialog box to change the name of the form or to change the hotkey assignment.

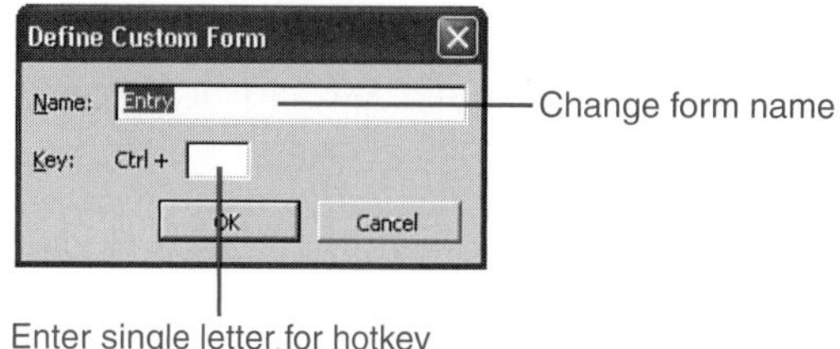

Figure 23.23
Use the Define Custom Form dialog box to rename a form or assign it a new hotkey.

23

4. Select the Key box and type the letter that you want to use to activate the custom form. This must be a single letter; numbers, the Alt key, and function keys cannot be used. When the user presses the Ctrl key with the letter designated here, the form will be displayed.

TIP

> The letters in a hotkey are not case sensitive, so it doesn't matter whether you type an upper- or lowercase letter in the Key box on the Define Custom Form dialog box.

CAUTION

> Be careful to avoid creating hotkeys that are already assigned to other tasks. The only keys available for assigning to forms are A, E, J, L, M, Q, T, and Y. When you try to use another reserved character in the Key box of the Define Custom Form dialog box, you are warned that it's reserved for use with Project and you are instructed to select a different character.

5. Click OK to save the key assignment.

To use the hotkey you have assigned to a form, first select a task or resource for which you want to display the form, and then press the hotkey combination.

Assigning a Toolbar Button to Display a Form

To assign a form to a toolbar button, you need to access the Customize Tool dialog box. You can access this dialog box directly from the Project window, without first displaying the Customize dialog box. To open the Customize Tool dialog box and assign a form to a toolbar button, follow these steps:

1. If you need to create a button to use to access a form, see the section "Adding and Removing Command Buttons," earlier in this chapter.
2. Press the Ctrl key and click the button you want to use to display the form. The Customize Tool dialog box appears (see Figure 23.24).
3. Select the Command drop-down list box and scroll the Form commands to find the form name you want to access through the toolbar button.

TIP

> To indicate the name of the form you want to access through the toolbar button, you can also type `Form "form name"` in the Command drop-down list box, where ***form name*** is the name that appears in the list of custom forms.

4. Choose the Description text box and type the description you want to display in the tooltip when you hover your cursor over the button
5. Click OK to save the button definition.

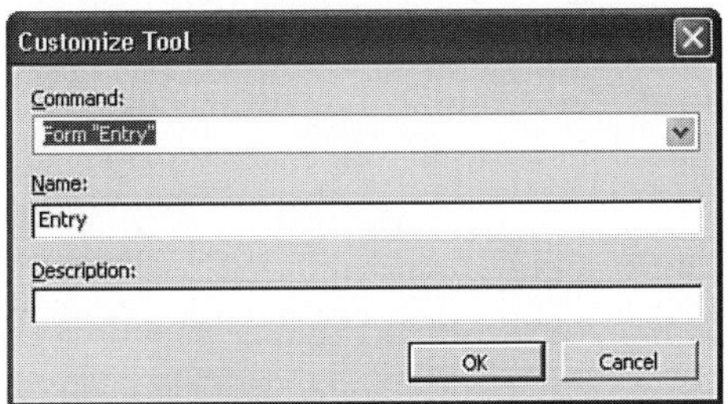

Figure 23.24
Open the Customize Tool dialog box to assign a form to a toolbar button.

After you assign a toolbar button to a form, select the task or resource and click the new button.

CREATING A NEW CUSTOM FORM

When the custom forms that come with Microsoft Project do not contain the fields of data and information you need, you can create your own custom form or modify an existing form so that it includes the fields you need. As with creating custom toolbars, you can create a new custom form by copying an existing form and modifying it to meet your needs, or you can create a new custom form from scratch.

The Custom Form Editor enables you to add fields to a custom form and modify the appearance of existing fields by sizing them or repositioning them on the form. You can also use the Custom Form Editor to set the placement of the form on the screen when you activate it.

When you create a form from scratch, the Custom Form Editor displays a small outline of a dialog box in the center of the screen (see Figure 23.25). A form is comprised of this dialog box area and a title bar for the form. Each custom form, by default, includes an OK button and a Cancel button. These buttons are positioned on the right side of the dialog box. You can select and add the other information that you need to the form.

When you create a new form by customizing a copy of an existing form, the existing form is positioned in the Custom Form Editor screen. Figure 23.26 displays a Copy of Entry form in the Custom Form Editor screen.

Figure 23.25 Initially, a custom form contains only the OK and Cancel buttons.

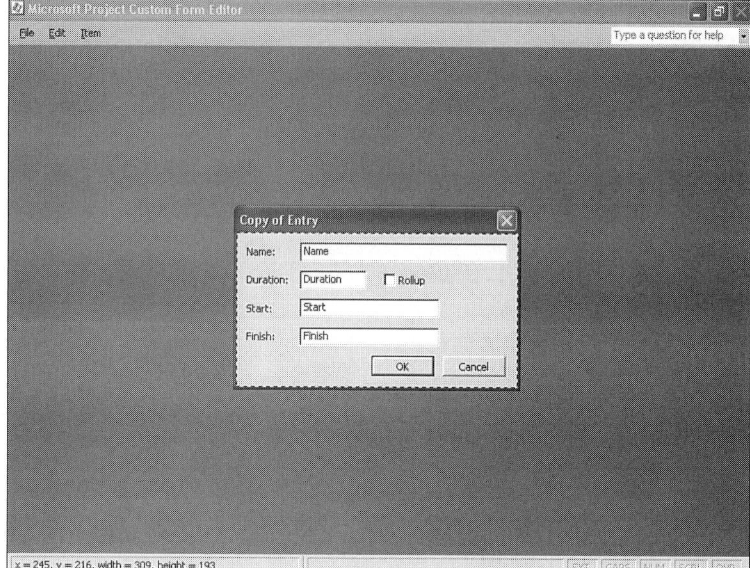

Figure 23.26 A copy of an existing form can be used to create a new form; the copy displays the existing form layout, which you can edit.

Opening a Form in the Custom Form Editor

Regardless of the approach you want to use to create a new custom form, you need to open the Custom Form Editor. To display the Custom Form Editor and modify a form, follow these steps:

1. Choose Tools, Customize, Forms. The Customize Forms dialog box appears.
2. Click New to create a new form, or select a form from the list and click Copy to base the new form on an existing form.
3. Type a name for the custom form in the Name field of the Define Custom Form dialog box.
4. Assign a hotkey letter in the Key field, if desired.
5. Click OK.

SIZING AND POSITIONING A CUSTOMIZED FORM

You can use the mouse to resize the form being edited by using the same procedures you use to size windows or other dialog boxes: drag the borders or corners of the box to any desired dimension within the Custom Form Editor window. To reposition the form in the window, drag the title bar until the form is properly positioned. To change the position or size settings for the form's dialog box, follow these steps:

1. Display the form in the Custom Form Editor window.
2. Select the dialog box outline by clicking once anywhere on the box, or choose Edit, Select Dialog.
3. Double-click the Form dialog box or choose Edit, Info to display the Form Information dialog box, as shown in Figure 23.27.

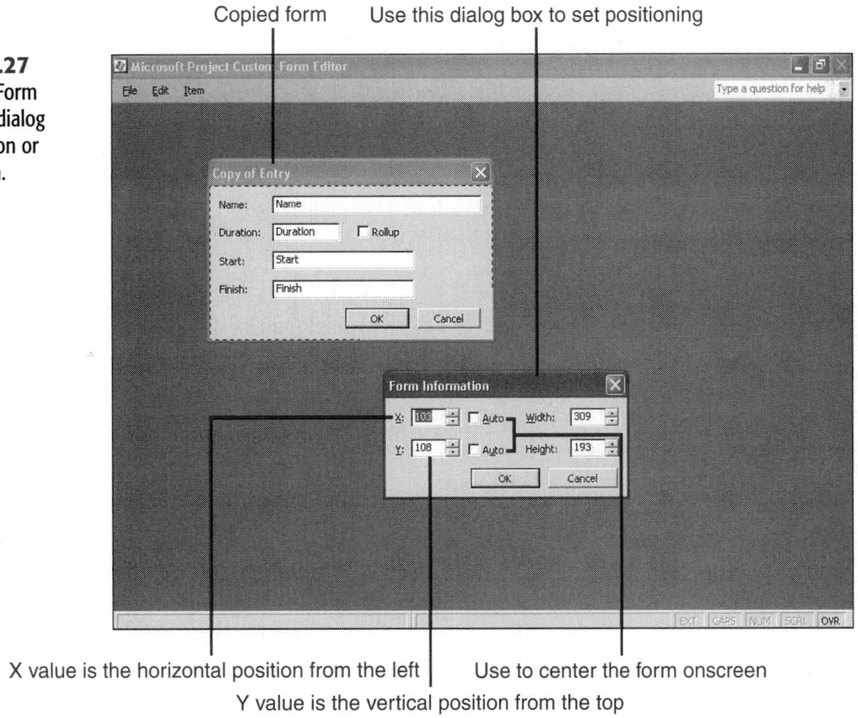

Copied form

Use this dialog box to set positioning

X value is the horizontal position from the left

Use to center the form onscreen

Y value is the vertical position from the top

Figure 23.27
You use the Form Information dialog box to position or resize a form.

4. Enter values in the X and Y text boxes if you want to manually set the horizontal and vertical positions of the form.

   The values in the X and Y boxes refer to the resolution values used in the screen display. A value of 1 in the X text box places the box at the left edge of the screen. A value of 100 places the left edge of the box 100 pixels from the left of the screen. If your screen resolution is 800 pixels wide, then a value of 400 would place the left edge of the box at the center of the screen. Similarly, the values in the Y box locate the top edge of the form relative to the top of the screen. Select the Auto check boxes to center the form on the Microsoft Project screen. The X and Y values can be set larger than the current display resolution (effectively having the box not shown on the screen when it is displayed).

5. Enter values in the Width and Height check boxes to set the dimensions of the form.

PLACING ITEMS ON A FORM

Examples of items that you might place on a form include fields with values from the database, text, borders, groups, buttons, and check boxes. Most forms automatically include OK and Cancel buttons. You can place additional items on forms by using commands from the Item menu. As you add each item, you should position it on the form, and you might need to adjust the size of the form to accommodate all form items. In the following activities, you will add items to the blank form pictured in Figure 23.25.

NOTE

> You might be accustomed to selecting multiple objects in drawing and graphics programs—for example, Microsoft PowerPoint—and choosing options to align them left, right, middle, and so on. There are no alignment features for items placed on a form in the Project Custom Form Editor. Furthermore, you cannot select more than one item at a time. You need to place each item individually and keep an eye on each item's X,Y coordinates to make sure it lines up with other items on the form.

PLACING TEXT ON A FORM

Text items are labels; they identify the information contained on a form. For example, to identify a resource name on a custom form, you would include the word *Resource* as a text item and place it beside the field resource Name.

When you add a text item to a form, a text box containing the word *Text* is outlined as a placeholder on the form. To replace the default word *Text* with the information you want to display on the form, select the word *Text* and type the desired label. The text placeholder is sized according to the width of the form. As a result, if the text you want to add to the form does not fit into the text placeholder, you need to adjust the size of the form, reposition items on the form, and drag the text placeholder to accommodate the message. After you complete the text entry, you can reposition, size, or even delete the text item. When the text item is positioned and complete, click a neutral area of the form to deselect the text item.

The position of a selected text item appears in the status bar. You can use these position indicators to position the text item, or you can double-click the text item to display the Item Information dialog box and specify an exact location for the item. You can also select the text item and then choose Info from the Edit menu.

Figure 23.28 shows the first text item that was added to the blank form. You can use the mouse to drag the item to another location.

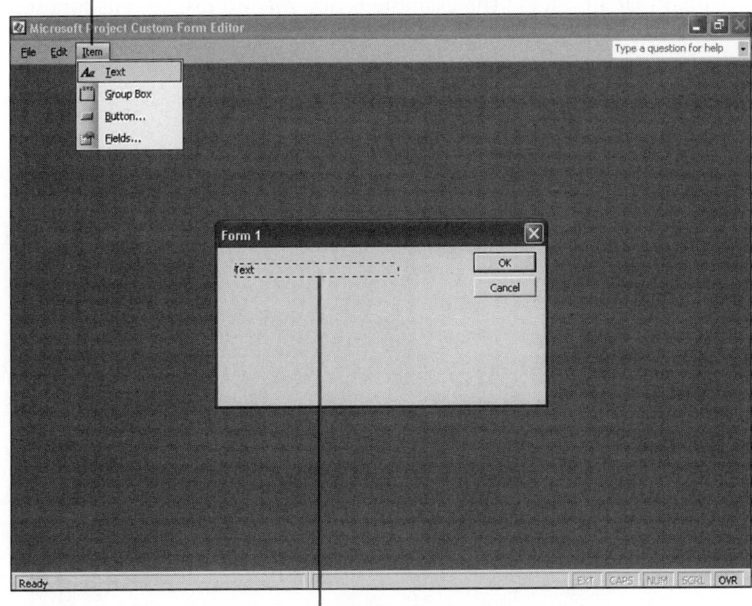

Figure 23.28
A new text item contains generic text that you can replace with more meaningful text.

23

PLACING FIELD VALUES ON A FORM

You can create custom forms to report information about a selected task or resource in an active project. To do this, you need to add a Field item to the form. Field items access project information and display it in the Customize Forms dialog box.

You can allow users to edit project file information directly by using the custom form. When you want to restrict editing, you can designate that the field be displayed as read-only. Reposition the field item or resize the display of a field item by using the same techniques used to reposition and size text items.

To add a field value item to a custom form, follow these steps:

1. Display the form in the Custom Form Editor window.
2. Choose Item, Fields. The Item Information dialog box appears.
3. Select a field from the Field drop-down list.

   Because the list includes fields of information contained in the project, placing a field in the form pulls the information from the project and reports the information for the selected task or resource each time you activate the custom form.
4. Choose Show as Static Text to make the data read-only, preventing users from editing that field in the form, if desired.

5. Click OK. The field item appears on the form as displayed in Figure 23.29. The field item that appears in the example is designed to display the duration of the selected task.
6. Reposition or size the field item as needed.

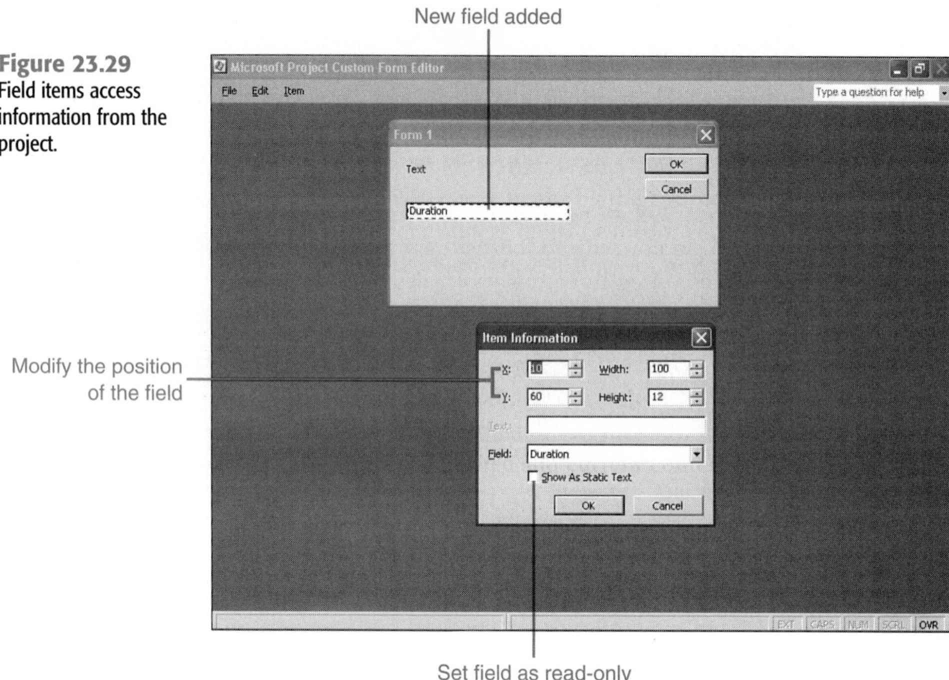

Figure 23.29
Field items access information from the project.

PLACING A GROUP BOX ON A FORM

Group boxes allow you to create sections on a custom form so that you can group related information. A group box is merely a formatting tool that provides a boundary line around fields on a form. You can then add fields to a form and place them inside the group box. The same basic procedures are used to add a group box to a form that you use to add a text item to a form.

You can then name the group box to summarize the relationship of the fields it contains. Enter the text that you want displayed at the top of the group box while the new group item is still selected, and then use the mouse to position the group box at the desired location. You might need to adjust the size of the form to accommodate a group box. Positioning a group box on top of existing items hides other items from view.

To add a group box to a custom form, choose Item, Group box in the Custom Form Editor. A new group box placeholder appears on the custom form and displays the default name Group, as shown in Figure 23.30. Add the desired items to the form and move them into the group box, positioning them as desired. Adjust the size of the group box as required.

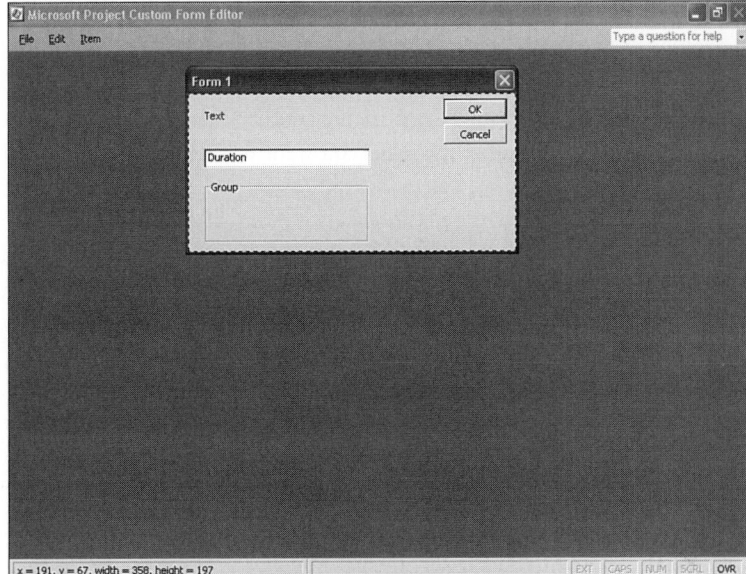

Figure 23.30
Group boxes provide visual orientation for form items.

PLACING BUTTONS ON A FORM

You can add two control buttons to a custom form: the OK button and the Cancel button. Each form can contain only one of each button, and they are added by default when you create a custom form. You can delete the buttons if desired, or you can move them to a new location on the form. If you add a new OK or Cancel button to a form that already contains these buttons, the editor simply replaces the original button with the added one. You use the same procedures to place a button on a form that you use to place other items on a custom form; that is, open the form in the Custom Form Editor window and choose Item, Button.

SAVING A FORM

To save the form and continue working on it, choose File, Save in the Custom Form Editor. When the form is complete, choose File, Exit to return to the Project screen. If unsaved changes exist when you try to exit the form, you are prompted to save the form again.

RENAMING, EDITING, AND COPYING CUSTOM FORMS

Forms you create are attached to the project in which they were created. Therefore, to use a form in another project, you need to copy the form to the other project or to your `GLOBAL.MPT` file. The Customize Forms dialog box provides access to the Organizer. Use the same techniques to copy custom forms to another project or the `GLOBAL.MPT` file that you use to copy views, tables, and other project-level elements. You can also use the Organizer to delete custom forms or rename them. The Customize Forms dialog box can be used to edit an existing form, to make a copy of a custom form, or to rename a form.

RENAMING CUSTOM FORMS

You can rename a custom form by using either the Customize Forms dialog box or the Organizer. To change the name of a form by using the Customize Forms dialog box, start by choosing Tools, Customize, Forms to display the Customize Forms dialog box. Then select from the Custom Forms list the form you want to rename and click Rename.

EDITING OR COPYING CUSTOM FORMS

You can edit an existing custom form when you need to add or remove items but don't want to create a completely new form. Editing an existing form places it in the Custom Form Editor window, and you can use techniques described earlier in this chapter to add and remove items. It might be better to make a copy of an existing form and experiment with your changes on the copy rather than jump straight to editing the only copy of a form.

To edit or copy a form, start by choosing Tools, Customize, Forms to display the Customize Forms dialog box. Click Copy or Edit, supplying a form name if needed, and the Custom Form Editor opens and displays the form for you to edit.

MANAGING FORMS WITH THE ORGANIZER

You create and save custom forms in the project file that is active when you create the form. You can use the Organizer to copy a custom form to another project file or to the `GLOBAL.MPT` file so that it's available for every project. You can also use the Organizer to delete or rename forms.

The Organizer is available through the Tools menu. You can also choose Tools, Customize, Forms to display the Custom Forms dialog box and then click on the Organizer button.

→ To learn more about the techniques and procedures you can use to rename, delete, and copy forms, **see** "Working with the Organizer and the Global File," **p. 107**.

TROUBLESHOOTING

REMOVING TOOLBAR BUTTONS

I can't remove a button from the toolbar. What am I doing wrong?

Be sure the Customize dialog box is open when you are adding or removing toolbar buttons. Otherwise, clicking the button automatically performs the commands of the macro that is attached to the button. When the Customize dialog box is open, Project knows you're working with the toolbars rather than issuing commands by using the toolbar buttons.

STRANGE TOOLBAR BUTTON BEHAVIOR

Sometimes when I click a toolbar button, the command doesn't execute—the Customize Tool dialog box opens instead. What's going on?

This happens when you have the Ctrl key held down while selecting a toolbar button. You might have been using the Ctrl key to select tasks or resources that are not next to each other. Be sure to let go of the Ctrl key before pressing a toolbar button.

DISAPPEARING CUSTOM TOOLBARS

I customized my toolbars at the office, but when I open a project on my system at home, the default toolbars appear. Where are my customized toolbars?

The toolbars you customized are attached to the application on the system you were using when you customized them. Actually, they are attached to the `GLOBAL.MPT` file on the system you used to do the customizing. To install them on your machine at home, you can copy your customized toolbars into an active project, copy that project to your home system, and then copy the toolbars into your home system's `GLOBAL.MPT` file.

To make all the items in the `GLOBAL.MPT` on your machine at work available on your machine at home, you need to copy the `GLOBAL.MPT` file on your machine at work to a disk and replace the `GLOBAL.MPT` file on your home system with the one you copied from the office computer.

WORKING WITH GROUP BOXES

When I move an item into a group box, the text box doesn't move with it. Is that really how it's supposed to work?

Yes it is. You have to move each piece of data and each item separately into a group box.

MAKING YOUR CUSTOM FORMS WORK

I created a custom form, but now I can't figure out how to use it. How can I make it work?

You can display the form from the Customize Forms dialog box by selecting the form and then clicking Apply. This, however, takes away the advantage of creating the form in the first place. Therefore, you will probably want to assign the custom form to a menu, to a hotkey, or to a toolbar button, to make accessing it more efficient.

Using Project Server and Project Professional

24 Introduction to Microsoft Office Project Server 2003 965

25 Enterprise Project Administration 985

26 Enterprise Project Management 1029

27 Enterprise Resource Management 1069

28 Enterprise Collaboration 1119

CHAPTER 24

Introduction to Microsoft Office Project Server 2003

In this chapter

Enterprise Project Management Using Project Server 2003 966

System Architecture and Requirements 968

Planning for Enterprise Information Sharing 970

Planning for Global Settings 975

Using Enterprise Global Settings 978

ENTERPRISE PROJECT MANAGEMENT USING MICROSOFT OFFICE PROJECT SERVER 2003

The concept of enterprise project management is a very popular trend in project management. Microsoft Project Server 2003, as did Project Server 2002, answers the needs for managing and reporting on projects and resources for an entire enterprise. Microsoft Project Server 2003 uses the underlying technology platform of the desktop project management software to create a way to view and manage resources and projects for full enterprise visibility. It includes supporting functions such as viewing and managing timesheets, status reports, issues, risks, and documents. All of these functions together help the portfolio management office (PMO) establish a full array of enterprise standards, processes, and reports.

24

NOTE

The terms program management office, project management office, or portfolio management office are interchangeable. For the purposes of this book, we use *PMO* to mean *portfolio management office*.

Key components of Microsoft Office Project Server 2003 include the following:

- Enterprise-level resource management that provides a single repository for all resources already assigned to projects or available for project assignment
- Enterprise-level portfolio management that enables project and resource modeling and analysis across groups of projects
- A broad security model for controlling access to, viewing of, updating of, and publishing of enterprise and detailed project information
- Advanced reporting capabilities
- Collaboration and global template capabilities that help standardize communication and enterprise processes for more accurate and consistent data

WHAT IS ENTERPRISE THINKING?

Enterprise-level project management is the management of projects, project resources, and the interrelationships between projects and resources, aggregated at the department, organization, or enterprise level.

This takes your organization from individual projects on the desktop with conflicting or duplicated information to full project enterprise visibility. Team members, executives, and managers will be able to see all or a subset of similar projects to better understand the scope of the work of their organization, and the way resources are being used. Because of this, the project manager and all members of the organization will need to start thinking more globally—how their project schedule and their management processes relate and contribute to the whole enterprise business picture.

Microsoft Office Project Server 2003 provides the base repository, user interface, and reporting tools required to enable enterprise-level project management. The project managers of an organization can put the full array of projects, grouped in various ways such as department or business solution, into a Project Server that allows all people to see the projects for portfolio analysis. Resource managers or functional managers can review how the resources assigned to those projects are used, and determine the organization's resource utilization on a global or project-by-project scale. The project manager and project team can use collaboration tools such as email, status reports, and a timesheet function, and can easily communicate status, issues, risks, and progress on a project. And finally, the entire project team can find project-related documents in one place, instead of searching around to find critical information to project success.

The organization, via the PMO or some other organization like PMO, will need to create or enhance current processes and procedures to fully implement the enterprise solution successfully. As with any repository, to use the data from Microsoft Project Server 2003 effectively requires planning roles, rules, and processes.

Reading Part VIII

Each of the chapters in Part VIII, "Using Project Server and Project Professional," about enterprise project management is targeted at the functions that you might perform in specific roles using Project Server 2003 as follows:

- This chapter focuses on enterprise thinking and an overall view of Project Server 2003. This will help you see how all the pieces of Project Server 2003 fit together from a portfolio manager's perspective.
- Chapter 25 describes functional system administration of Project Server 2003 for the PMO system administrator and others who need to know what settings are required to create the enterprise views your organization needs.
- Chapter 26 describes Project Web Access and Project Professional from a PMO and project manager's perspective.
- Chapter 27 describes how executives, resource managers, and project managers view and use the resource information that is available via Project Web Access and Project Professional.
- Chapter 28 describes how team members will use the document management and collaboration features of Project Web Access, including time tracking, status reporting, managing to-do lists, issues, risks, and document management.
- Under "Customizing and Administering Project Server Access" at `www.quehelp.com`, you can find information on how user administration and security are performed by the Project Server administrator.

This part of the book will also use the example of the Elkhart Software Company to illustrate many of the concepts of using the enterprise environment.

System Architecture and Requirements

This section provides the technical information you need to know before planning, deploying, and using Project Server 2003, including the following:

- Products associated with Microsoft Office Project Server 2003
- Software required in order to successfully install the Professional edition
- How the software works together to create the full functionality

System Architecture

The products that comprise Microsoft Office Project Server 2003 are shown in Figure 24.1.

24

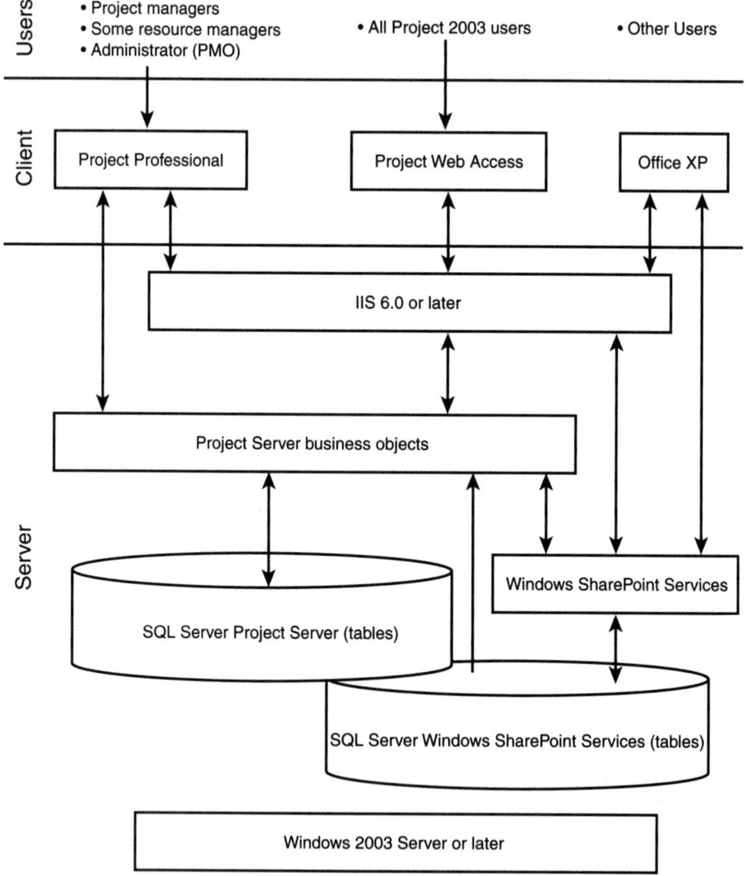

Figure 24.1
To be fully functional, Project Server 2003 requires companion products, as shown in this figure.

Resources and projects are stored in SQL Server through Microsoft Project Server. Other project collaboration data such as documentation, risks, and issues can be stored in the same SQL Server using Microsoft's Window SharePoint Services.

Together, Microsoft Project Server, Microsoft Windows SharePoint Services, and the SQL Server database are known as the Microsoft Project *repository* or *database*. The information stored in a Project Server 2003 repository can be accessed via Microsoft Project Professional or via Internet Explorer with a Microsoft Project Web Access license.

NOTE

> The workgroup functions of Microsoft Project Standard 2003 will no longer be available in versions after Project Server 2003 and are hidden in Project Server 2003. With that in mind, this section will focus on the enterprise coupling only and Standard will not be discussed.

Microsoft Office Project Server 2003 Software Product and Version Requirements

To plan the deployment of Microsoft Office Project Server 2003, you need to know in detail the release levels of all associated software. The following sections specify these software version requirements for each product that is required to run Project Server 2003.

NOTE

> The Microsoft Project Professional 2003 client and server components can both be installed on the same PC.

Client-Side Requirements

The following products must be installed on a user's system in order for the full Professional edition capabilities to be available to that user:

- Microsoft Windows 98, NT, 2000, Me, or XP
- Microsoft Project Professional 2003 (for project managers and administrators only)
- Internet Explorer 5.01 and above

NOTE

> Each user must have a Microsoft Project Web Access license to access the Microsoft Project Server 2003 repository.

- Microsoft Office XP (only for users who need to create Portfolio Analyzer views)
- Office Web Components (OWC)

NOTE

A version of OWC that allows users to read predefined views, but not create new views, ships on the Microsoft Project CD. If a user accesses Project Web Access to view certain views and doesn't have Office Web Controls installed, the OWCs are installed from the Project Server. Users who want to create views must have a licensed copy of Office XP installed on their system.

SERVER-SIDE REQUIREMENTS

The following products must be installed on a system that contains Project Server in order for the full Project Server 2003 edition capabilities to be available to that user:

- Microsoft Windows 2000 Server, Service Pack 1 (SP1) or above
- Microsoft SQL Server 2000, SP3 or later or MDSE with SP3
- Microsoft SQL Server 2000 Analysis Services, SP3 for OLAP reporting (Portfolio Analyzer functions)
- Microsoft Internet Information Server (IIS) 5.0 or above (IIS 6.0 is recommended for extended functions)
- Microsoft Project Server 2003

NOTE

You must use Microsoft Windows Server 2003 or later on the machine on which you have installed Windows SharePoint Services for using document management, issues, or risk features. Otherwise, Project Server 2003 does not require Windows 2003.

PREVIOUS VERSION COMPATIBILITY

For project publishing functions, Microsoft Project Server 2003 is compatible with Microsoft Project 2002. Furthermore, Microsoft Project Server 2003 is compatible with Microsoft Project Professional 2002. Microsoft Project Professional 2002 can publish projects to Project Server 2003 and Microsoft Project Professional 2003 can publish projects to Project Server 2002. Microsoft Project Server 2003 is not compatible with Project 2000.

PLANNING FOR ENTERPRISE INFORMATION SHARING

PMOs are responsible for planning the data, processes, and roles necessary to capture, report on, and analyze project and resource information in the enterprise. The goal of planning is to enable the gathering and reporting of the information the organization wants to use and report on.

A good place to start your planning is with business questions. When you know the questions that the business needs answered, you can determine which data is required from Microsoft Project Server 2003 to help answer those questions. Key business questions might be

- What is my organization's capacity for work?
- What skill bottlenecks exist in my organization?
- What would be the impact to other projects if we added this new project to our portfolio of projects?
- What is the cash flow for my projects?
- What is my portfolio of projects, and how do they meet our business imperatives?
- What would happen if I shifted the way projects are prioritized?
- What would happen if I added or removed resources that have specific skills?

Answering these questions requires that accurate, timely, and consistent information be available to the business leaders in an organization.

A business typically charters a PMO to establish and manage the planning, roles, rules, and processes associated with enterprise-level project management and the business questions your organization needs to have answered.

Planning Enterprise Roles and Group Responsibilities

The capabilities and functions of Microsoft Project Server 2003 are associated with a default set of user groups and roles. The variety of capabilities and roles can be overwhelming at first. Microsoft Project Server 2003 is most easily understood if thought of in terms of capability and group roles, as described later in this section. The list illustrates the correlation between the various capabilities or functions and the major user roles.

TIP

> The roles shown later in this section may or may not fit your current organizational language or operating structure. After reading through this chapter, you might want to consider your organizational structure in order to refine or improve the roles defined.

Keep the roles in mind as you are reading Part VIII. They will help you understand how the various capabilities are used and when and by whom they are used.

Microsoft Project 2003 predefines seven distinct Project users, known as groups:

Group	Roles
Administrators	Installing, configuring, and maintaining the Microsoft Project Server repository and suite of associated tools, supporting the user community, and managing Project Server 2003 databases
	Making changes to the enterprise global template
	Importing resources and schedules
	Creating portfolio analysis models
	Creating and managing views
	Checking in enterprise projects and resources if necessary

Group	Roles
Executives	Viewing and analyzing the enterprise project and resource information in the repository from a business perspective by using the Project Center and the Resource Center
Portfolio managers	Defining and deploying project management processes, standards, conventions, and tools
	Planning, defining, and entering enterprise project, resource, and task outline codes and custom codes
	Creating enterprise generic resources in the enterprise resource pool and assigning enterprise resource outline codes to them
	Creating enterprise project schedule templates
	Plan OLAP cube generation
	Viewing and analyzing the enterprise resource and project information from an organization perspective: uses Project and Resource Centers for analysis
Project managers	Using enterprise templates to quickly generate initial schedules
	Viewing and analyzing the enterprise resource information in the repository from a project perspective using the Resource Center
	Viewing and analyzing their project information in the repository using the Project Center
	Saving schedule versions in the Microsoft Project Server repository
	Using the enterprise resource pool via Enterprise Team Builder to assign project generic resource tasks to actual resources
Resource managers	Making sure information about each resource is kept up-to-date in the repository
	Reviewing resource assignments
	Performing resource analysis, modeling, and forecasting using the Resource Center and Portfolio Modeler
Team leads	Assisting resource managers and project managers with resource and project management
Team members	Entering data about their tasks' progress, status, issues, and risks into the repository via Project Web Access.
	Managing to-do lists

Each of the seven groups has unique responsibilities associated with setting up and using Microsoft Project Server 2003. The roles listed in the preceding list are the Microsoft Project Server 2003 defaults. In this book, all examples use the default roles and groups.

NOTE

It's important that you assign people to their proper groups. Keep in mind that people can hold multiple roles. For example, if someone holds both team member and team lead responsibilities, you should assign him/her to both groups.

PLANNING ENTERPRISE PROJECT MANAGEMENT PROCESSES

In addition to planning the roles that your organization needs, you need to define and implement the key project management processes and deliverables needed to support portfolio management. For example, many organizations are creating a front-door process for projects. The purpose of the front-door process is to make sure that a project does the following:

- Meets business objectives
- Has a viable business case
- Has viable schedules and plans
- Has a sponsor and customer
- Has an assigned priority
- Is not performing redundant work
- Has an architecture that conforms to corporate standards

Another key process that many organizations struggle with is the project progress tracking. Creating viable plans and schedules through a front-door process is a good start, but a month after a project begins, you need to think about some other issues: How much progress has been made? Is the project ahead of or behind schedule? Is it above or below budget? How is the project doing in terms of resources required and resources actually working?

Reporting accurate project progress information in a timely manner is a prerequisite for providing business leaders with the data required to manage the business. Microsoft Project Server 2003 provides the repository, user interface, reporting, and analysis mechanisms required to support all of these processes and more. However, Microsoft Project Server 2003 cannot improve an organization's project and portfolio management environment by itself. Each organization needs to establish or adjust the infrastructure mechanisms around Microsoft Project Server 2003 in order for the tool to truly benefit the organization.

PLANNING FOR ENTERPRISE PROJECTS

The project managers of an organization will create project schedules based on the standards and processes set up by the PMO. It is important that these projects are set up in some consistent fashion so that the data is accurate and reflects similarly across all projects. The best way to do this is to set up enterprise project schedule templates for the various kinds of projects in your organization. Resources should be consistently applied from the resource pool. The project managers need to consistently baseline, publish, and update their schedules as necessary. However, to make sure these schedules reflect the reporting needs of the organization, Microsoft Project Server 2003 uses project attributes, known as enterprise project outline codes, and the project manager will assign these project outline codes to each of their projects. When the enterprise project outline codes are assigned to projects, project data can be viewed and analyzed in a variety of ways, using the Project Center, Resource Center, and Portfolio Analyzer.

Planning for Enterprise Resources

The resource manager and/or the portfolio manager will establish the resources available as team members for projects. They will assign the attributes to each resource (such as rates, employee type, or skill set). Attributes are defined via enterprise resource outline codes. These resources are added to the resource pool, a repository of resources, available in the enterprise global area of Project Professional. The resource manager and/or portfolio manager will also help the organization decide if they want to use only actual resources or establish generic resources (such as a "programmer" or "tech writer" that can be assigned to a task prior to knowing who will actually work on it). Also, they would want to define whether local resources (resources added to a project schedule, but not from the resource pool) are acceptable to indicate contractors or temporary workers in the enterprise environment. They will need to define the processes around proposed (a resource that may possibly be used on the project) versus committed (the resource is definitely assigned to the project) resources on a project. They will also need to decide whether the enterprise should use resource calendars or some other way to account for a resource's non-project related time.

Reporting

The last item you want to consider is the kinds of reports you want to see. Although much of this will be discovered in your analysis meetings as you discuss enterprise project and resource outline codes, you will want to discuss the kinds of problems you want to be able to analyze so that you can decide what kinds of data and reports you need to create. Besides creating project or resource outline codes, you may also need to create custom codes to capture other data important to your organization. Some examples of how you might use enterprise outline codes or custom fields for reporting are

- If your organization wants to report on `resource` bottlenecks by skill (for example, programmer [Web, Visual Basic, and C++]) and location (for example, Seattle and Denver), you'll need to define an enterprise `resource` outline code for each resource skill and location, and then associate the enterprise `resource` outline codes with each enterprise resource. After project managers assign those resources to their schedules and begin to report actual work accomplished, you can use the enterprise resource outline codes to report on which types of programmer are most in demand, which are least in demand, what the demand peaks and valleys are, and so on, by location.

- If your organization wants to report on project schedule or budget performance by customer or sponsor, you need to define enterprise project outline codes that identify all possible customers and sponsors. Portfolio managers then assign each project a customer and sponsor from the list defined by the customer and sponsor enterprise project outline codes. When these projects are under way, you can group projects using those enterprise project outline codes.
- If your organization wants to report on project costs associated with capital and expense, and if you can assume that all labor costs within a certain project phase are either capital or expense, you can create enterprise resource custom fields that tag non-labor resources as either capital or expense. When projects are underway, you can generate custom reports by using the enterprise custom field information that provides all labor and non-labor capital and expense costs for the project. (Make sure that your custom reports meet the capital and expense business rules for your business rather than simply follow the pattern outlined in this example.)

PLANNING FOR GLOBAL SETTINGS

As described previously, you will need to plan for how you will view and manage the roles, processes, projects, resources, and reporting that will be used in your enterprise project management environment. One of the most important aspects of this is to plan your project and resource attributes, called enterprise outline codes in Project Server 2003. To do this, you may need a series of planning meetings with key people in your organization.

PLANNING PROJECT ATTRIBUTES

First, you will decide the attributes you want to assign to projects. Do you want to be able to report on projects by which department they belong to, which customer they belong to, or what project lifecycle they are currently in? Do you want particular data for each task in a project, such as status or associated cost center?

To establish a set of project and task attributes for your organization, you need to first determine all information that needs to be reported about projects and tasks.

For instance, Elkhart Software has offices in Denver and Seattle. Some projects are located in Seattle, and some in Denver. Elkhart Software also has multiple customers and several internal project sponsors to oversee the projects. Elkhart Software would therefore need to create three enterprise project outline codes: location (Denver and Seattle), customer (the customers), and sponsor (the sponsors). Elkhart Software additionally wants to be able to report on each project by priority and state. For each task, Elkhart Software has decided that they want to be able to report on each project's task billing code.

PLANNING RESOURCE ATTRIBUTES

To establish the set of resource skills and attributes for your organization, you need to first determine all information that needs to be reported about resources.

The most important resource attribute you will need to establish is the resource breakdown structure (RBS). This attribute establishes how managers can view their resources. For example, the RBS might be the organization or department a resource works in, such as IT, Operations, or Finance. The manager of the IT department may have views that allow them to view all IT personnel, but not those resources in Operations and Finance.

Another attribute might be the location of the resource. Let's consider an example in which Elkhart Software has offices in Denver and Seattle. Some resources are located in Seattle, and some in Denver. It would be useful to be able to attribute either Denver or Seattle to each enterprise resource so that managers can look at resource usage by role and location. Resource skills might include project manager, technical writer, system administrator, tester, trainer, and developer.

You can begin planning your enterprise resource definitions by determining what roles people have played on your project teams. You can refer to past and current projects, and create a list of skills that have been required on those projects.

When you have determined the skills needed by the organization, you might want to break down the definitions further. For example, instead of simply listing the skill *programmer*, you might want to have information on different types of programmers, such as Web, Visual Basic, and C++ programmers. Or, you could associate skill levels, such as junior and senior, with each skill. You might also want to consider skills that you might need in the future, not just the current ones.

→ You can also assign multiple skills to each resource. To learn more about this, **see** "Enabling Multiple Skills per Resource," **p. 1087**.

→ The way to enable the gathering and reporting of customized information for an organization is through outline codes and custom fields. For more information, **see** "Creating and Using Custom Outline Fields," **p. 854**.

Other Planning Considerations

Besides enterprise outline codes to help with analysis and reporting of project and resource data, you will want to consider the following other planning activities.

Plan for Consistent Project Schedules

Make sure all project managers in your organization use consistent methods and data input techniques to produce the project schedules. Using enterprise project schedule templates helps ensure that this happens. You will want to make sure they all use the enterprise calendar, which accounts for your company's holidays, and you will want to ensure that all schedules have the same custom fields if you are trying to collect special data for each task in a project (such as billing code or status for each task). You will additionally want to consider if you would like to use Versions. *Versions* are snapshots of projects and associated schedule data. By saving a project plan as different versions, a project manager can create several copies of the plan for internal project team use, while keeping at least one version, Published, available for external use.

PLAN FOR CONSISTENT VIEWS IN PROJECT PROFESSIONAL

Also, you might want to make all input consistent by setting enterprise views, Gantt Charts, timescale settings, and other preferred enterprise styles for viewing project schedules in Project Professional.

PLAN FOR MANAGING TIME REPORTING

You will need to decide how you would like to report time to capture actuals in your project schedule, and to capture timesheet data from your team members. You may want to

- Input actuals data directly into the project schedule and not use the timesheet application
- Use the timesheet application and allow project managers to decide whether they want to collect actuals based on % complete, total actual hours, or hours day-by-day
- Use the timesheet application, but ensure enterprise consistency by allowing project managers to capture data in only one of three ways: collect actuals based on % complete, total actual hours, or hours day-by-day
- NEW Use the timesheet application and capture actuals on a day-by-day basis for the entire enterprise, and lockdown time reporting periods so that team members cannot enter time except during actual periods. This is a new feature of 2003, and provides excellent auditing capabilities for your organization.
- NEW Add review and functional manager approval processes and functions to your timesheet processes. This is a new feature that allows someone other than the project manager to also review and approve timesheets.
- NEW Create a process for adjusting actuals and using the feature in Project Server 2003 for the adjustments. This would be used only with the new lockdown feature of 2003.

PLAN FOR COLLABORATION AND DOCUMENT MANAGEMENT

You will want to decide on how your project managers and their teams will want to use the collaboration and document features in Project Server 2003.

- Your organization will need to decide whether it wants to use status reports regularly to keep the project manager aware of task or project status apart from the task status updates recorded via time reporting.
- Your organization will want to decide whether it wants to use issues to help manage problems that occur in the course of a project.
- NEW You will want to decide whether you would like to use risk management for your projects to document and analyze possible jeopardy items or opportunities for your project. This is a new feature for Project Server 2003.
- NEW You might want to store and track all your project's documents using a document management method and the tool within Project Server 2003. New to this feature in Project Server 2003 is the capability to manage versions, and have check-in/check-out capabilities to ensure more document management integrity.

Plan for Roles, Security, and Views

Your organization will also need to plan for

- The roles you will use (project manager, portfolio manager, and so on)
- System access rules to Project Server 2003 based on those roles
- Access rules to the data stored and viewable in Project Server 2003 based on those roles (for instance, a team member should not be able to view resource rate information)

Using Enterprise Global Settings

When you are ready to use the Project Server 2003 environment, there are two places you will set up your data: Microsoft Office Project Web Access and Microsoft Office Project Professional. Project Web Access contains many of the global settings under the Admin tab, and the settings you choose are reflected mostly in Project Web Access views and functional pages. Some settings, however, will be reflected in Project Professional. Figure 24.2 illustrates the Home Page of Project Web Access.

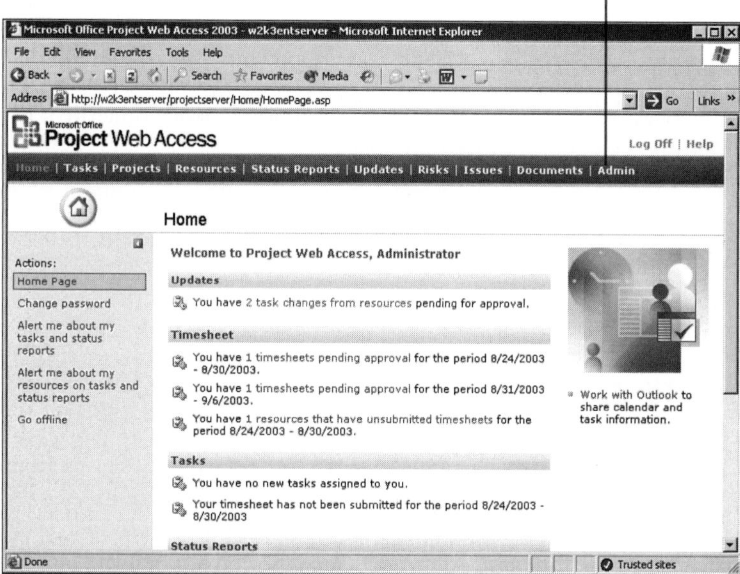

Figure 24.2 Project Web Access contains the Admin tab where you will set up global configurations.

You will also set up and use many enterprise features in Project Professional itself, especially Enterprise Global. You will enter the resource pool information in the Enterprise Global feature, and you will configure enterprise settings for Project Professional itself to help standardize your project schedule processes. Figure 24.3 illustrates the Project Professional interface.

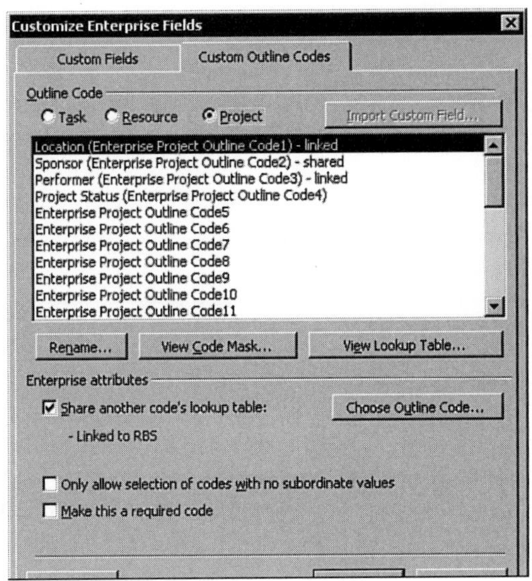

Figure 24.3 Project Professional contains the enterprise global template where you set up the resource pool and enterprise outline codes and custom fields.

USING ENTERPRISE PROJECT OUTLINE CODES TO CREATE PROJECT ATTRIBUTES

After you create a list of project attributes and their values, you will configure them in Project Professional using Enterprise Project Outline Codes. The Elkhart Software Company has decided to use the project attributes shown in Table 24.1.

TABLE 24.1 PROJECT ATTRIBUTES EXAMPLE

Project or Task Attribute	Value
Client	Internal
	IT
	Operations
	Finance
	Marketing
	Product Business Unit
	External
	Government
	Local
	State
	Federal
	Large Business
	Small Business
Location	Denver
	Seattle
	Los Angeles
	Atlanta
	Houston

Project Cycle	Active Postponed Closed Proposal
Status	Ahead of schedule On time Behind schedule 1 week Behind schedule 2 weeks or more

To enter the outline codes and their values, you will select Tools, Enterprise Options, Open Enterprise Global in Project Professional. You will use Custom Outline Codes tab and select the Project radio button.

To add project outline codes to projects themselves, so that you can start reporting on the project attributes, the project manager will enter the codes upon saving the project schedule the first time.

USING ENTERPRISE RESOURCE OUTLINE CODES TO CREATE RESOURCE ATTRIBUTES

After you create a list of resource attributes and their values, you will configure them in Project Professional using Enterprise Resource Outline Codes. The Elkhart Software Company so far has decided to use the project attributes shown in Table 24.2.

TABLE 24.2 RESOURCE ATTRIBUTE EXAMPLE

Resource Attribute	Value
RBS	IT Operations Finance Marketing Product Business Unit
Location	Denver Seattle Los Angeles Atlanta Houston

Skillset	IT
	  Programmer
	    C++
	    Visual Basic
	    Web
	  Database Analyst
	  Technical Writer
	  Manager

To enter the outline codes and their values, you will select Tools, Enterprise Options, Open Enterprise Global in Project Professional. You will use Custom Outline Codes tab and select the Resource radio button.

Two special resource outline codes require that you enter them as particular enterprise resource outline code numbers: the Resource Breakdown Structure (RBS) requires code 30, and enterprise resource multi–value (ERMV) codes require codes 20 through 29.

To add resource outline codes to resources themselves, so that you can start reporting on the resource attributes and easily view all resources by a particular skill set, the portfolio manager will enter the codes when adding resources to the resource pool.

To report on project or resource attributes, you will need to move the enterprise outline codes into Project Center and Resource Center views in Project Web Access.

Creating Consistent Project Schedules

The best way to create consistent project schedules is for project managers to follow similar processes and use standard data entry requirements when building project schedules. One of the best ways to facilitate this standardization is to use enterprise project schedule templates.

Using a Project Schedule Template

Project templates can greatly simplify the planning steps that project managers are faced with when starting a new project. With a project template, task names, task durations, linkages, work, and/or resource assignments can be predefined. Project managers can change them, but they give each project manager a quick and easy way to begin building a project schedule from a known starting point. Often these templates contain best practices learned from previous projects.

To open an enterprise template, select File, New. Under the Templates heading, select On My Computer. Select the Enterprise Templates tab in the Templates dialog box.

Using Project Versions, Including the Published Version

You may create versions if your organization would like to create different copies of your project schedule.

By default, Microsoft Project Professional establishes a system version called Published. Because the Published version is associated with features such as timesheet reporting (timesheets only show assignments from the Published system version), the Published version cannot be deleted from the system.

→ For information on creating new and deleting old versions of a project plan, **see** "Managing Project Versions," **p. 999**.

As a part of planning, the portfolio manager and others from a planning team need to decide what versions the organization may use. The Project Server administrator predefines the versions that are available to Microsoft Project Professional users. When versions are set up, all project information can be saved to any of the predefined versions.

The first time you save a project to the Project Server, you are prompted for a schedule name and version. If you save the project to a file, the project name and version are stored as part of the filename, separated by a period (for example, `Denver A.Published`). This provides backward compatibility (files can be saved with a filename such as `Denver A.Published.mpp` and opened with Microsoft Project 2000 or 2002), as well as a unique naming scheme.

Saving a project without changing the version overwrites any information that has already been saved in that version of the project. To save a different version type, click Save As and select a new type.

Versions other than the Published version are useful for a number of tasks, including the following:

- Performing full comparisons between versions of schedules, including added/deleted tasks and assignments, constraints, and other changes that are not saved in baselines
- Performing trend analysis between versions saved at regular intervals
- Performing what-if analysis on scenarios that the user might not want to make public or to affect the current or published version
- Following company approval cycles or project life cycles

Resources are included in a version, but they are not associated with versions. If enterprise resource pool information (for example, availability, calendars, outline codes) changes, the information is not retroactively applied to existing versions. Resource assignments, however, do reflect the version of the project to which they belong at the time the version was created.

In order to be active, cross-project links must occur between projects saved with the same version. For example, if you saved Project A as Version 1 and it is cross-linked to Project B, Project B must also be saved as Version 1. If it is not, the cross-project links become static or orphaned and do not update properly.

Creating Consistent Views in Project Professional

To help create standard processes and data entry in Project Professional, the portfolio manager may want to set up common views and formats. To do this, the administrator will open the enterprise global and change any global settings using the following general instructions:

- Select Tools, Enterprise Options, Open Enterprise Global in Project Professional.
- Select Tools, Options and review the default fields in the tabs being displayed. You might want to change items such as the Hours per day field on the Calendar tab.
- Select Format, Text Styles and change the color or format of how tasks items such as milestones, summary tasks, or critical path tasks display in projects. You would do that by selecting the item you would like to format in the Item to Change field drop down list in the Text Styles dialog box, then selecting your formatting changes to it.
- Create new views that are appropriate for the project managers in your enterprise. You might also add columns such as Work Actual Work or custom fields to the Enterprise

Gantt Chart while the Enterprise Global is open. Your project managers might be instructed to always use the Enterprise Gantt Chart to enter their schedule data, to ensure they enter the kind of data your organization requires.

CONFIGURING TIME REPORTING

Select the method of time reporting your organization wants to use and configure it for your organization.

If you choose not to use timesheets, in Project Web Access, select Server configuration, and under the Select heading select the features that you want to make available to users in the Project Web Access section. Select Deny for all task-related permissions. The timesheet will not display at all for your organization. You will decide how your organization will want to reflect task completion directly in your schedules.

If you choose to use timesheets but not lockdown the time periods, in Project Web Access, select Customize Project Web Access. Specify the default method of time tracking, and under the Lock Down Defaults, select either Allow Project Managers to Change the Default Method for Reporting Progress if a Different Method Is Appropriate for a Specific Project, or Force Project Managers to Use the Progress Reporting Method Specified Above for All Projects. The latter selection will set a standard time reporting method for all timesheets. However, to make sure resources can enter time without having locked down time periods, Select Non Managed Periods - Allow Project and Project Web Access Users to Update Actuals.

If you choose to use timesheets and lock down time periods, which will create an auditable time reporting method, in Project Web Access, select Customize Project Web Access. Under the Specify the Default Method for Reporting Progress on Tasks, select Hours of Work Done per Day or per Week: Resources Report the Hours Worked on Each Task During Each Time Period.

Also, under the Lock Down Defaults section, select Force Project Managers to Use the Progress Reporting Method Specified Above for All Projects. In the Time Period settings, select Managed Periods - Allow Only Project Web Access Users to Update Actuals During Open Periods. Set up the time periods in the displayed grid. You will continue to open and close time periods using this grid.

NOTE

> You must use the preceding method to configure Managed Timesheet Periods. Also, if you use this method, you cannot use any other method for time reporting other than Hours of Work Done per Day. You will not be able to use % Complete or Actual Work.

USING COLLABORATION AND DOCUMENT MANAGEMENT

To use the collaboration functions of status reports, issues, and risks, allow the permissions for groups to see the Status Reports page, Issues page, and Risks page in Project Web

Access. You will ensure that the permissions are set by selecting Project Web Access, Manage Users and Groups, and selecting the group to set its permissions. If you allow the permissions for groups to View Risks, View Issues, and View Status Report List, then resources will see the risks and issues for the projects to which they are assigned and will be able to respond to the status reports that project managers create. If you choose to use document management by allowing the View Documents permission, then the resources within the group you select can use the Documents page to access file folders with project documents.

MANAGING ROLES, SECURITY, AND VIEWS

To manage roles select Project Web Access, Manage Users and Groups. To manage security and create security templates, select Manage Security in Project Web Access. To create and modify views, such as the Timesheet view (the Tasks page), the Resource Center, the Project Center, or Portfolio Analyzer, select Manage Views in Project Web Access. Under "Customizing and Administering Project Server Access" at `www.quehelp.com`, you can find information on how user administration and security are performed by the Project Server administrator in Project Web Access.

CHAPTER 25

Enterprise Project Administration

In this chapter

System Administration 986

Project Web Access Administration 986

Managing Views 987

Building OLAP Cubes and Updating Resource Tables 994

Managing Project Versions 999

Database Administration and Management 1001

Project Professional Administration 1004

Managing the Enterprise Global Template 1007

Using Enterprise Outline Codes and Custom Fields 1010

Managing Enterprise Project and Resource Calendars 1018

Performing Enterprise Global Backup and Restore 1019

Importing Resources 1021

Importing Projects 1024

System Administration

Once you have planned how you want to configure your enterprise environment, you will need to implement the decisions your team made. This chapter introduces how to use Project 2003's administrative functions to configure and manage Project 2003.

The system administrator has to take an active role in Project 2003 for a couple reasons. The administrator must establish a Project server's users, groups, and security levels. Also, all the views in Project Web Access have to be created by the administrator, and the administrator must give specific groups of users rights to display those views. Unless otherwise specified, all functions described in this chapter require administrative rights to the Project server.

The role of system administrator has several functions, and may be performed by one person or several people depending on how your organization wants to set up and manage your enterprise environment. An administrator may exist in the PMO and establish the settings according to PMO standards and processes. You may also have an administrator that sets up and manages the users, groups, security and other overall system features. This chapter will discuss all administrative functions, but will focus on the major administrative functions from a portfolio management aspect, as well as all items related to Project Professional setup.

→ For detailed information about establishing users, groups, features, and security, **see** "Customizing and Administering Microsoft Project Server" on the CD accompanying this book.

This chapter discusses the administration from two perspectives: what you need to do for and within Project Web Access and what you need to do for and within Project Professional.

Project Web Access Administration

All administration functions to set up Project Web Access are under the Admin tab of Project Web Access. This tab will only display for those who have been given administration authority. Under this function you will set up

- Users of Project Web Access and their access rights.
- Overall organization data rights (called permissions) allowed for your enterprise.
- Groups for all of Project 2003, and their rights to data.
- Categories, which further define what kind of data the groups may access.
- Views, which define the format of the data for the groups and categories you define.
- How you want your Project Web Access pages to be formatted, such as for Gantt Bar format and group intervals. You will also be able to change the default menu and home page appearance.
- How you want to track actuals (time reporting) for your project schedules.
- How you want to set up email and Windows SharePoint Services.
- The OLAP cube, which sets update timeframes and range of data needed for the Portfolio Analyzer reporting view.

You will also perform some data management functions, such as checking in projects and resources, and deleting project tasks, status reports, resources, and projects from the database if needed.

USERS, GROUPS, AND PERMISSIONS

Users are set up in Project Web Access to establish their authorization into Project Web Access. Their usernames and other access information are established to help in the authorization. This is different than establishing them as resources for projects. That is done via the resource pool in Project Professional. Each user is then assigned to a group, such as project manager or administrator (although each user is assigned to the default group of team member).

NEW You can now integrate more easily with Microsoft Active Directory. Active Directory is a feature in Windows Server 2000 or Server 2003 that establishes security objects, such as users and groups for system networks. If your organization uses the Active Directory in Windows Server, Project 2003 now allows your organization to sync up the users and groups established in Active Directory to the users and groups in Project Server. This way, you only need to create security in one location: Active Directory. You can also use the Active Directory to sync up resources that you want to add to the resource pool.

Each of the groups established for the organization has permissions assigned to them. For instance, the project manager group permissions may be set so that project managers may view only their own projects in Project Center, but not others. At the same time, they may not be allowed to see Portfolio Analysis reporting or use the function called "delegate tasks." Each group, also, may be associated with a category which defines what set of data they may be able to view. For instance, the My Projects category may be set to allow project managers to view only the projects they own or are assigned to, or may be set to allow them to see all projects in the organization.

→ For detailed information about users, groups, categories, and security via permissions, **see** "Customizing and Administering Microsoft Project Server" on the CD accompanying this book.

MANAGING VIEWS

As the Project Server administrator, you are responsible for creating and modifying the Project Center, Resource Center, Timesheet, and Portfolio Analyzer views, as well as setting permissions for users to see these views.

The following sections provide information on creating and modifying Project Center, Resource Center, and Timesheet views.

→ For details on creating or modifying Portfolio Analyzer views, **see** "Creating a Portfolio Analyzer View," on the CD accompanying this book.

CREATING AND MODIFYING A PROJECT CENTER VIEW

To create a Project Center view, you need to select Admin, Manage Views, Add View and then select the Project Center radio button.

To modify a Project Center view, you need to select Admin, Manage Views and then select the Project Center view that you want to modify and click Modify View.

NEW In Project 2003, you now have the ability to copy an existing view to modify a view.

The functionality and options associated with creating and modifying a Project Center view are identical, except that the view's current configuration information is displayed when modifying a view.

For example, if you want to add the Location enterprise project outline code to the Project Work view, you need to perform the following steps:

1. In Project Web Access select Admin, Manage Views.
2. Select the Work view underneath Project Center and then click Modify View. The screen to add or modify a Project Center view is divided into sections, as shown in Figure 25.1:

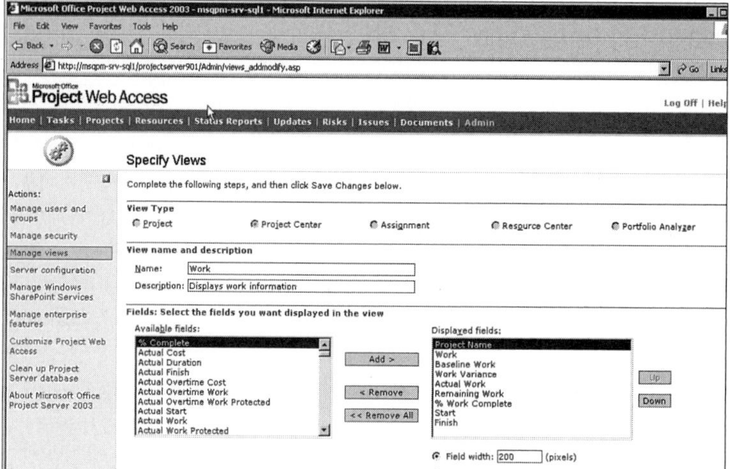

Figure 25.1
You need to enter the information required to create a new Project Center view.

- **View Type**—The view type is already set to the Project Center view when you are modifying a Project Center view. However, you need to select it if you are creating a new Project Center view.
- **View Name and Description**—The view name must be unique. Pick a name that describes either the type of view or the view's user(s), so that users can easily recognize the view in the Project Center screen. The Description field is accessible only to the administrator, and it can be used to define the view in more detail.
- **Fields**—This section consists of two panes. The pane on the right side defines the Microsoft Project fields that are currently defined for the View. The left pane contains the list of Microsoft Project fields that are available for use in the view but have not yet been included. You can move fields between panes by selecting fields and clicking the Add, Remove, or Remove All buttons.

NEW

- In the Field Width field just beneath the right pane, you can define the width you would like to display for the field to display in the view. The default is to allow Microsoft Project to automatically adjust the column width for the field.

NOTE

> Three fields—Project Name, Start, and Finish—are predefined for Project Center views and cannot be removed.

- After the desired fields have been added to the Project Center view, you can change the sequence in which the fields are displayed in the view by using the Up and Down buttons.
- The top field in the right pane when you are defining the view will appear on the far left in the Project Center view, the second field from the top in the right pane will appear second from the left, and so on, when the view is displayed.

NEW

- **Splitter Bar**—The Splitter Bar feature allows you to choose where you would like the splitter bar to appear in the view. You can change the default number pixels displaying in the field.
- **Gantt Chart Format**—The Gantt Chart Format section allows you to choose the type of Gantt Chart or custom Gantt Chart you want to use to display information. The default Gantt chart value is Gantt Chart (Project Center). You can change this value by selecting the drop-down list box and selecting an alternative Gantt Chart value.
- **Grouping Format**—The Grouping Format section allows you to associate a unique grouping format with different views. You might want to do this to provide visual cues for users about the view that is being used. The default grouping value is timesheet. You can change this value by selecting the drop-down list box and choosing an alternative grouping value.

NEW

- **Default Group, Sort**—You can select the default groups and/or sorting order you would like to appear on the view. The user may change the group or sort when they use the particular Project Center view, and press the Revert button on the Filter, Group, Search section of the screen to return to the default settings.

NEW

- **Outline Levels**—You can select the default outline levels for this view. This feature allows the administrator to set a view from summary level views to full level detail views.
- **Filter**—You can optionally specify filters to be applied to a view when you define the view. If you specify a filter, it is applied to the raw data before the view is displayed. For example, you could filter the view to display only projects in Denver. There are four components to each filter:

  Field—You can click the cell under the Field column header to see a drop-down list box of all fields that can be used as part of a filter.

Operator—You can click the cell under the Operator column header to see a drop-down list box of all the operators that can be used to test against the contents of the corresponding Field cell.

Value—This field specifies the value that is being tested by the operator.

And/Or—Up to three separate fields can be tested, if necessary, using logical And and Or operations. If you select And, the data must pass all tests for it to be excluded from the view. If you select Or, the data is excluded if any of the tests are passed. For example, if you specify Generic equals Yes And RBS equals USA.Denver, all resources that are both generic and have the location code USA.Denver are excluded. If you specify Generic equals Yes Or RBS equals USA.Denver, all resources that are either generic or have the location code USA.Denver are excluded.

- **Categories (Optional)**—You can control which users will be able to see and use the view by selecting and adding the desired categories. Users associated with categories that are defined as belonging to this view will then be able to see the view in the Project Center.

  The Categories section consists of two panes. The pane on the right side defines the categories that the view currently belongs to. The left pane contains the list of available categories. You can move categories between panes by selecting categories and clicking the Add, Add All, Remove, or Remove All buttons.

3. Select Enterprise Project Outline Code1 from the list of available fields. Click Add.
4. Select Enterprise Project Outline Code1 at the bottom of the list of displayed fields, and click the Up button as many times as necessary to move the code where you want it to display in the project view.
5. Click Save Changes.
6. In Project Web Access navigate to Project Center and make sure the Work view is selected.
7. Select the Filter, Group, Search tab, and from the Group By pull-down list, select Location. Your projects should now be grouped by location, as shown in Figure 25.2. Remember that your enterprise project outline codes may be named differently than the codes shown in the figure.

NOTE

> You can use the horizontal scrollbar at the bottom of the project list to find newly added enterprise project outline code. Remember that you can change the column placement by using the Up and Down buttons in the Modify Views page (where you add or modify fields within a view).

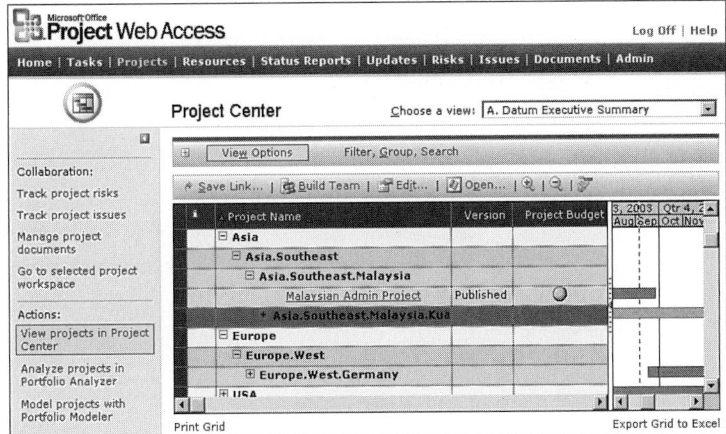

Figure 25.2
Data (Work, for example) will roll up in the way it is grouped.

CREATING OR MODIFYING A RESOURCE CENTER VIEW

Microsoft Project Web Access has one Resource Center view, called Resources Summary, installed and created by default in a standard implementation of the product set. You can create another Resource Center view by selecting Admin, Manage Views, Add View and then selecting the Resource Center radio button. As with the Project Center, you can copy an existing view to make modifications as well.

To modify a Resource Center view, you need to select Admin, Manage Views, and then select the Resource Center view that you want to modify and click Modify View.

The functionality and options associated with creating and modifying a Resource Center view are identical, except that the view's current configuration information is displayed when you are modifying a view.

To create or modify a Resource Center view, follow these steps:

1. Using Project Web Access, log on as the administrator and select the Admin tab.
2. Select Manage Views from either the main screen or the sidepane.
3. To add a new Resource Center view, select Add View, and then select the Resource Center radio button. To modify an existing Resource view, locate the view in the list, select the view, and click Modify. The screen to add or modify a Resource Center View is divided into the sections, as shown partially in Figure 25.3:
    - **View Type**—The view type is already set to the Resource Center view when you are modifying a Resource Center view. However, you need to select it if you are creating a new Resource Center view.
    - **View Name and Description**—The view name must be unique. Pick a name that describes either the type of view or the view's user(s), so that users can easily recognize the view in the Resource Center screen. The Description field is accessible only to the administrator, and it can be used to define the view in more detail.

25

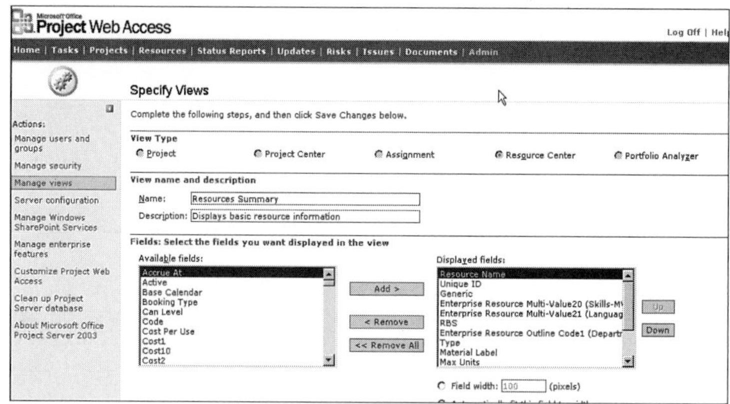

Figure 25.3
You need to provide the information required to create a Resource Center view.

- **Fields: Select the Fields You Want Displayed in the View**—This section consists of two panes. The pane on the right side defines the Microsoft Project fields that are currently defined for the View. The left pane contains the list of Microsoft Project fields that are available for use in the view but have not yet been included. You can move fields between panes by selecting fields and clicking the Add, Remove, or Remove All buttons.

- In the Field Width field just beneath the right pane, you can define the width you would like to display for the field to display in the view. The default is to allow Microsoft Project to automatically adjust the column width for the field.

> **NOTE**
> Two fields—Unique ID and Resource Name—are predefined for the view and cannot be removed from a Resource Center view.

After the desired fields have been added to the Resource Center view, you can change the sequence in which the fields are displayed in the view by using the Up and Down buttons.

The top field in the right pane when you are defining the view will appear on the far left in the Resource Center view, the second field from the top in the right pane will appear second from the left, and so on, when the view is displayed.

- **Grouping Format**—You use the Grouping Format section to provide visual cues for users about the view that is being used. The default grouping value is Views. You can change this value by selecting the drop-down list box and choosing an alternative grouping value.
- **Default Group, Sort**—You can select the default groups and/or sorting order you would like to appear on the view. The user may change the group or sort when they use the particular Resource Center view, and click the Revert button on the Filter, Group, Search section of the screen to return to the default settings.

NEW

- **Outline Levels**—You can select the default outline levels for this view. This feature allows the administrator to set a view from summary level views to full level detail views.
- **Filter (Optional)**—You can optionally specify filters to be applied to a view when you define the view. If you specify a filter, it is applied to the raw data before the view is displayed. See the four components for applying a filter in the Filter subsection of "Creating and Modifying a Project Center View," previously in this chapter.
- **Categories**—Individual users, like views, are linked to categories. If a user belongs to the same category as a view, that user has access to the view.

  The Categories section consists of two panes. The right pane defines the categories that the view currently belongs to. The left pane contains the list of available categories. You can move categories between panes by selecting categories and clicking the Add, Add All, Remove, or Remove All buttons.

NEW

- **RBS Filter**—When the administrator checks the box to implement this filter, the resources listed in a view will be limited to the resources below the RBS level of the user who is viewing the resource list.

4. Click OK to save the new or modified Resource Center view. Click Cancel to return to the Specify Views screen without making any changes.

MODIFYING A TIMESHEET VIEW

NEW In Project 2003, the Timesheet view allows you to enter other fields into the default columns already existing for the timesheet as displayed on the Project Web Access Tasks page. You can only modify the Timesheet view.

To modify the Timesheet view, you need to select Admin, Manage Views and then select the Timesheet view.

1. In Web Access select Admin, Manage Views.
2. Select the Timesheet view as shown in Figure 25.4, which is the last selection in the view list, and then click Modify View. The screen is divided into the sections described below:
   - **Fields**—This section consists of two panes. The pane on the right side defines the Microsoft Project fields that are currently defined for the View. The left pane contains the list of Microsoft Project fields that are available for use in the view but have not yet been included. You can move fields between panes by selecting fields and clicking the Add, Remove, or Remove All buttons.

     In the Field Width field just beneath the right pane, you can define the width you would like to display for the field to display in the view. The default is to allow Microsoft Project to automatically adjust the column width for the field.

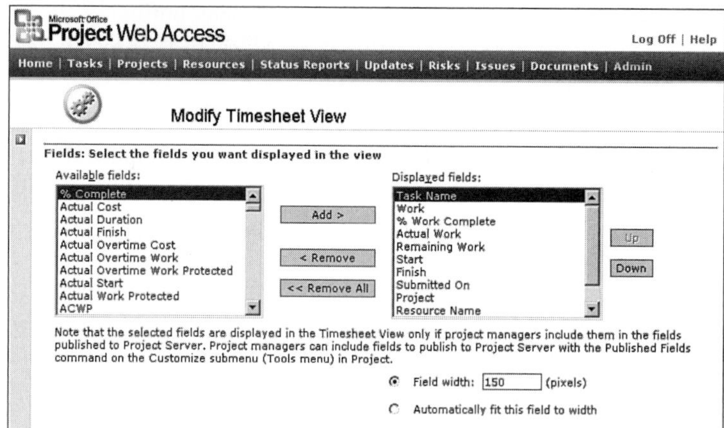

Figure 25.4
The Timesheet view allows you to add or remove fields on the Tasks page.

After the desired fields have been added to the Timesheet view, you can change the sequence in which the fields are displayed in the view by using the Up and Down buttons.

The top field in the right pane when you are defining the view will appear on the far left in the Timesheet view, the second field from the top in the right pane will appear second from the left, and so on, when the view is displayed.

- **Splitter Bar**—The Splitter Bar feature allows you to choose where you would like the splitter bar to appear in the view. You can change the default number pixels displaying in the field.

25

NOTE

> In order for the columns to appear in the timesheet on the Tasks page, project managers must add the new fields to their projects. This is accomplished by using Tools, Customize, Publish Fields in Project Professional. In the Customized Publish Fields dialog box, the project manager will move the fields needed into the tasks view, and publish their project schedule to the Project Server.

BUILDING OLAP CUBES AND UPDATING RESOURCE TABLES

Project Server uses Online Analytical Process (OLAP) technology to generate OLAP cubes and then stores the information in Extensible Markup Language (XML) for presentation and loading into the Project Center pages for the Portfolio Analyzer views. Also, Project Server updates the resource tables for viewing and reporting based on parameters you specify.

NOTE

OLAP databases are called *cubes* because they combine the analysis of data from several dimensions, such as project, resource, and time, with summarized data, such as work and availability.

OLAP is designed for ad hoc data reporting. It is a way to organize large business databases. OLAP cubes are organized to fit the way you retrieve and analyze data so that you can easily create the reports you need.

TIP

OLAP cubes generated by Microsoft Project can be used by other reporting tools. You can use the tutorial and online documentation (available on Microsoft's SQL Server installation CD) to familiarize yourself with OLAP cubes and XML blobs.

NOTE

All new projects saved to a Project server must be saved with the version Published first. That is, if you want to save a Draft version of a project schedule to the server, you must first save a Published version.

In addition, there is no way to exclude a project that has a Published version when generating an OLAP cube. Therefore, Draft schedules published to a Project server are included when OLAP cubes are generated. You can define an enterprise project outline code called Draft, with the attributes Yes and No, which you can use to filter out all draft versions when using the Portfolio Analyzer. Or you can use the Project dimension in the OLAP cube data to manually include or remove the specific projects that you're interested in analyzing.

When you create a Portfolio Analyzer view, you have the option to target the view to a Project Server OLAP cube on the current or a different server. You can also bind the Portfolio Analyzer view to one of several possible Project Server OLAP cubes. This flexibility allows you to create several Portfolio Analyzer views that point to a variety of OLAP cubes.

Each Portfolio Analyzer view data is as current as the OLAP cube it is bound to. The Project Server Administrator must schedule Project Server OLAP server cube updates. Although you can create multiple, different OLAP cubes, there are no utilities in Project Server to help you manage them or the Portfolio Analyzer views that bind to them. If you want to create multiple Project Server data cubes within a single Project Server instance, then the Project Web Access Administrator must manage cube regeneration using manual techniques.

TIP

You can use the Portfolio Analyzer view PivotTable Commands and Options dialog box (Data Source tab) to change the OLAP cube that the view is currently bound to.

BEFORE BUILDING AN OLAP CUBE OR UPDATING RESOURCE TABLES

Before creating an OLAP cube or updating resource tables, all the following must be true:

- The Microsoft Project Server must have Analysis Services installed as part of the SQL Server 2000 product installation.
- Enterprise-level project or resource outline codes must have been created and stored in the Enterprise Global file.
- Resources must have been added to the enterprise resource pool and assigned enterprise resource code values. For example, to be able to perform skill-based analysis using an OLAP cube, you must have defined a Skill enterprise resource outline code and assigned Skill values to the resources in the enterprise resource pool.
- All projects to be included in the update must have been created using enterprise resources, and the projects themselves must have been published to a Project server.

BUILDING AN OLAP CUBE AND UPDATING RESOURCE TABLES

If you open Project Web Access and select Admin, Manage Enterprise Features, Specify Resource and OLAP Cube Updates, you will notice that similar input screens are used for two different purposes:

25

- To generate an OLAP cube that provides the data used by the Portfolio Analyzer.
- To update resource data. Resource data, including resource availability data, is stored in tables in the Microsoft Project Server database. These tables, which need to be updated to get new data, are used by tools such as the Build Team from Enterprise tool in Project Professional. Note that building an OLAP cube automatically updates the resource table data.

To generate an OLAP cube, you need to perform the following steps:

1. Log on to Microsoft Project Web Access as the administrator and select Admin, Manage Enterprise Features, Specify Resource and OLAP Cube Updates.
2. Modify the parameters on the Updates to Resources and OLAP Cube screen, as shown in Figure 25.5.
3. Select the Yes radio button if you want an OLAP cube to be built when either the Update Now button is clicked or the scheduled time has expired. Select the No button if you just want to update the resource tables.
4. Enter the OLAP analysis server name. This is the name of the machine that hosts the analysis server. This option appears only if you are building an OLAP cube.
5. Enter a name for the OLAP cube, as well as a brief description. This option appears only if you are building an OLAP cube.
6. Enter the date range to be used when creating the OLAP cube. The Date Range section controls the scope of the project data that is included in graphs and OLAP cubes. This option appears only if you are building an OLAP cube.

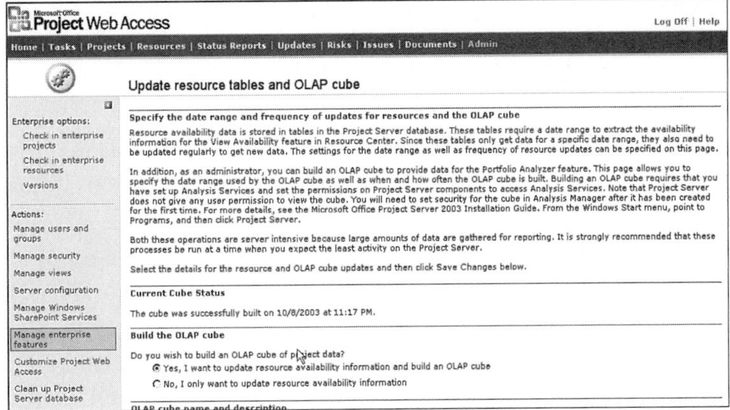

Figure 25.5 Creating an OLAP cube automatically updates the resource tables in a Project Server database.

The OLAP cube building process requires a starting date and an ending date from any of the three available Date Range options. You can select an option by marking the radio button next to one of the following options:

- **Use the earliest project start date and the latest project finish date**—This option provides a date range that spans the entire time period for all projects within a Project Server database. It selects the first date that any project starts and the last date that any project finishes.
- **Use the following date range at the time the cube is built**—This option provides a moving window across the project portfolio. The Values, The Next, and The Past define the width of the window as it moves across the data in time.

  If you choose this option, enter the number of time periods that will define the beginning and ending dates of the moving window. The time periods can be specified in days, weeks, or months. When the update process is executed, the start date is calculated from the date and time of the run and the value from the past. For example, if the update process runs on 6/1/2004 and the Past value is one month, the start date is 5/1/2004. Similarly, the ending date is calculated from the current date and time, with the Next value added to it.
- **Use the fixed date range specified below**—This option provides a fixed window across the project portfolio. The From and the To values define the width of the window. This date window does not move with time.

  With this option, both dates are selected from a calendar drop-down list box. You select the required date from the calendar or by typing it directly into the box.

25

CAUTION

Use the Fixed Date Range option with care. It is very easy for this date to be changed, then not changed back, and for data to be reduced without it becoming apparent. This can in turn affect business decisions that are based on the data.

7. Enter the date range to be used when updating the Resource Availability tables. The Date Range for Resource Availability section controls the scope of the resource data that is included in resource tables. This option appears if you are building an OLAP cube and if you are updating the resource tables.

   To update the resource availability tables, you need two dates: the starting date for update and the ending date. You can select from two options by marking the radio button next to the desired option:

   - Use the Following Date Range for Retrieving Resource Availability Information
   - Use the Fixed Date Range Specified Below

8. Enter the update frequency to be used for creating or updating an OLAP cube. The Update Frequency option appears if you are building an OLAP cube and if you are updating the resource tables.

   There are two ways of maintaining the update frequency of OLAP cube data:

   - **Scheduled**—If the Update Every radio button is selected, the frequency of the update is defined by the associated number of time periods, type of time period, and start date. First you need to select the elapsed time period between executions of the update process. The drop-down list box defines the number of time periods and whether the time period is days, weeks, or months. Next, you need to select the date and time for the first run in the Start Update On drop-down list boxes. The first run of the update process occurs on the date and time selected; the second and subsequent runs occur after the defined interval has elapsed.
   - **Update Now**—To update the OLAP cube immediately, select the Update Only When Specified radio button. In this case, the data is updated only when you navigate to this page and click Update Now.

     After you click the Update Now button, you need to wait for the OLAP cube to finish building before you attempt to access the data. This might take several minutes, depending on the number and size of projects and resources included in the OLAP cube. After you click the Update Now button, you can determine when the update process has completed by clicking the Refresh button on your browser. When the update process has completed, you receive the message "The cube was successfully built on *mm/dd/yy* at *hh:mm*" (or an error message) in the Current Cube Status section, as shown in Figure 25.5.

9. Click the Save Changes button to save the options selected and initiate any changes to the update frequency.

Although it might seem reasonable to assume that a higher frequency of data update is preferred, that is not often the case. Resource management tends to follow a cycle, as does updating of project plans. The update process should follow that process.

In many organizations this cycle is managed on a weekly basis. Timesheets are updated on a weekly basis, and project plans are updated to reflect the impact reported in the timesheets, together with any other changes on the same frequency. These updated plans are saved as the Published version of a project. Reporting and analysis need to be constant during this update cycle. A weekly update cycle should provide the timeliness necessary to analyze the data and to make informed business decisions.

Managing Project Versions

Microsoft Project 2003 gives users the ability to store multiple versions of a project plan. Each version is a complete copy of the plan at the time it was saved as a new version, and all the versions are stored on the Project server.

The Published version name is automatically created when Microsoft Project is installed, and cannot be renamed or deleted. Every project schedule saved to the Project server must have a Published version, and may have other versions.

The Project server administrator defines the versions other than Published that are available to the organization. Users can store copies of their plans in any of the available versions

To add a new version name for project managers to use, follow these steps:

1. Log in to the Microsoft Project server as an administrator.
2. Select Admin, Manage Enterprise Features, Manage Enterprise Project Versions. A list of all currently available versions is displayed, as shown in Figure 25.6.

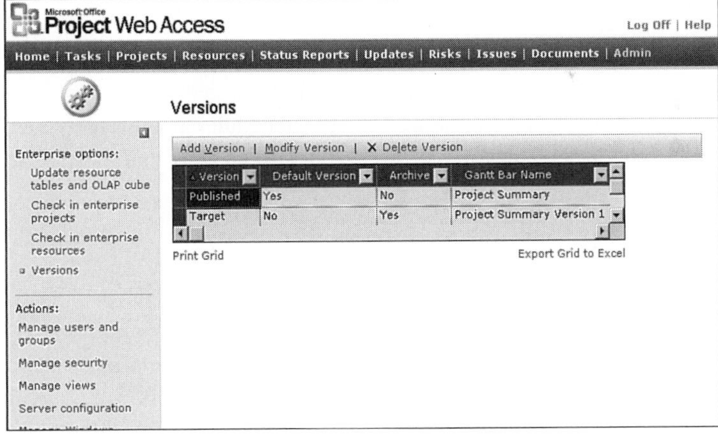

Figure 25.6
You can add, modify, or delete a project version.

3. To add a new version, click Add Version and fill in the following fields:
   - In the Version field, enter a unique, valid name for the new version. A valid version name cannot contain the characters / " : < > | , . ' ? * #.
   - In the Version Archived field, select either Yes or No. Archived project versions will not be updated with active Enterprise Global template or enterprise resource global data when they are opened; rather, they contain snapshot data from the

time the project version was saved. This might be useful to show cost information that utilizes the resource rate at the time of saving the plan rather than the resource rate currently available in the enterprise resource pool.

- In the Gantt Bar Name field, select a summary Gantt bar type for the new version.

NOTE

> You should consider formatting versions so that they can be easily identified by users. To do this, you can assign one of the six summary version bars available in Project Web Access to a version.
>
> A version named Draft, for example, can be assigned to Project Summary Version 3. If you do this, the Draft version's project summary bar will appear the same in all Gantt Chart views because the formatting for Project Summary 3 will be the same in all Gantt Chart views.
>
> Alternatively, depending on your corporate reporting requirements and the number of versions required to support them, you might choose to have different formats in different Gantt Chart views.

4. To keep the changes, click the Save Changes button. If you click Cancel, the changes are not made.

25

To modify a version, select the version to be changed and then select Modify Version, as shown in Figure 25.6. The parameters associated with modifying a version are identical to adding a new version, as described earlier in this section.

To delete a version, select the version to be deleted and then click Delete Version, as shown in Figure 25.6. For a version to be successfully deleted, there must be no project schedules currently saved with that version. If project schedules are currently saved with the version you are trying to delete, you are prompted with an alert that lists the associated projects.

→ For information on how versions work with cross-project links, **see** "Using Project Versions, Including the Published Version," **p. 981**.

Adding the Version Field to Views

Since Project 2002, which allows multiple versions, it is possible to have multiple lines in a view for a single project. Otherwise, you will see the same project listed twice, without knowing which project version you are viewing. To address this issue, the Version field has been added to the list of fields available when creating or modifying views.

TIP

> Add the Version field to all views that contain the Project Name field, to avoid confusion and misunderstanding.

DATABASE ADMINISTRATION AND MANAGEMENT

There are several administration functions you will perform in Project Web Access to clean up and keep the Project 2003 environment up-to-date.

CHECKING IN ENTERPRISE PROJECTS

Microsoft Project prevents users from overwriting each other's schedules by automatically checking out projects for the user if read/write access is requested.

While a project is checked out, other users can only read it—they can't modify it. A user can save a read-only file with a different filename or version, but he or she cannot overwrite the original file.

If a user does not correctly check a project back in, the administrator can force the project to be checked in. To force a check-in of a project, follow these steps:

1. Log in to a Project server as an administrator.
2. Select Admin, Manage Enterprise Features, Check-in Enterprise Projects. A list of all checked-out projects and who has them checked out appears. Two options, as shown in Figure 25.7, can be selected from this screen:
    - **Check-In**—The Check-In option resets the flag in the database so that the project is stored with checked-in status and is available for other users.
    - **Refresh**—The Refresh option refreshes the screen so that it is possible to confirm that requested actions have resulted in the expected responses.

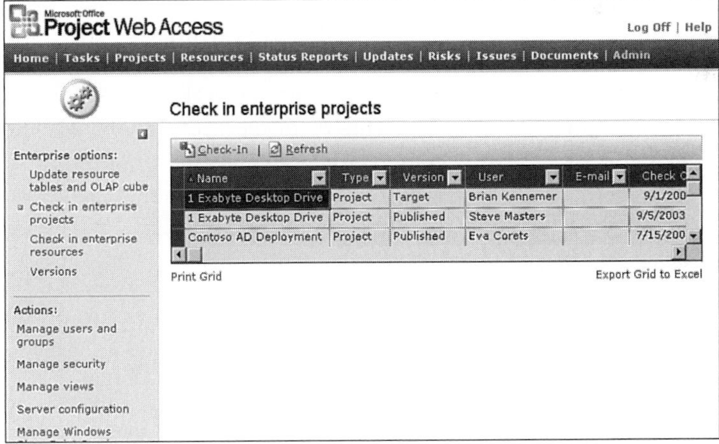

Figure 25.7
The administrator can force the check-in of an enterprise project.

3. Select the project you want to check in and select the appropriate action (Check-In or Refresh).

CAUTION

> Before Project checks in the project, a warning dialog box appears, asking for confirmation that the action is correct. If you check in a project that has been checked out, the user who has the project checked out will only be able to save changes to the database if he or she saves their checked-out project as a new project.
>
> You must exercise caution when forcing the check-in of an enterprise project. The administrator is strongly urged to investigate who has it checked out and have that person check it in whenever possible; otherwise, any data entered by the person who has the project checked out might be lost.

NOTE

> Project Managers can also check in projects they have checked out using Check in my projects in the side pane of Project Center.

Checking in Enterprise Resources

Microsoft Project prevents users from overwriting changes to the enterprise resource pool by automatically marking enterprise resources as checked out when the enterprise resource is opened for read/write access from the enterprise resource pool.

25

While an enterprise resource is checked out, other users can still add the checked-out enterprise resource to their projects and assign it to tasks; however, the other users can only read the enterprise resource's attributes (such as Max Units or Rates)—they can't modify them.

If a user does not correctly check a resource back in, the administrator can force the resource to be checked in. To force a check-in of a resource, follow these steps:

1. Log in to a Project Web Access as an administrator.
2. Select Admin, Manage Enterprise Features, Check-in Enterprise Resources. A list of all checked-out resources and who has them checked out appears. The two options available to the user are the same as for checking in enterprise projects, as described in the section "Checking in Enterprise Projects," earlier in this chapter.
3. Select the resource you want to check in and select the appropriate action (Check-In or Refresh).

CAUTION

> Before Project checks in the enterprise resource, a warning dialog box appears, asking for confirmation that the action is correct.
>
> You must exercise caution when forcing the check-in of an enterprise resource. The administrator is strongly urged to investigate who has it checked out and have that person check it in whenever possible; otherwise, any data entered by the person who has the project checked out might be lost.

CLEANING UP THE PROJECT SERVER DATABASE

You can remove tasks, status reports, projects, and resources from the database if needed. To clean up the database:

1. Log in to a Project Web Access as an administrator.
2. Select Admin, Clean Up the Project Server database. Select the radio button for the kind of cleanup you would like to perform, as shown in Figure 25.8.

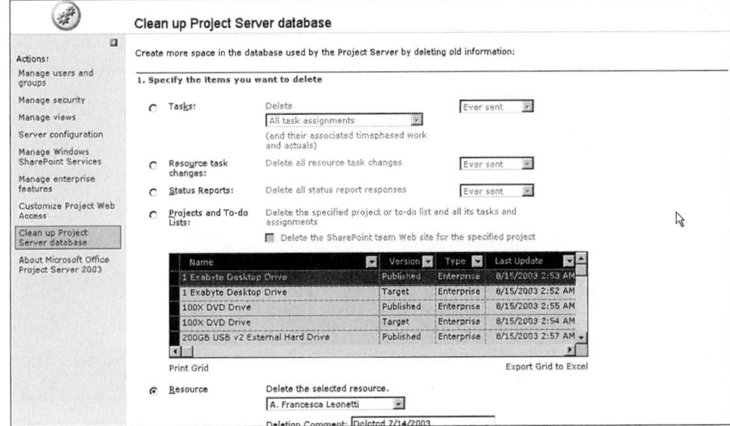

Figure 25.8
You can delete tasks, resource task changes, status reports, to-do lists, projects, and resources.

3. For Tasks, Resource task changes, and Status Reports, select the time ranges for the tasks or status reports you would like to delete. For projects and to-do lists:
   - Highlight the project or to-do list in the grid. You can only delete one project or to-do list at a time.

   NEW For resources:
   - Select the resource from the drop-down box. You can use the default comment, or enter a new comment about the resource deletion.

NOTE

> When you delete a resource, Microsoft Project changes the resource to a local resource in project schedules to which the resource has been assigned.

4. Press Delete. You will receive a warning message to ensure you want to continue with the deletion. Press Yes to continue.

Project Professional Administration

In Project Professional, you will have many administrative tasks to perform to set up the enterprise environment. The following sections discuss functions important for Project Professional administration, including logging in to Project Server, Managing the enterprise global (including creating enterprise custom codes and managing calendars), and importing projects and resources to the enterprise environment.

Logging in to Project Server from Project Professional

To set up the enterprise global and other enterprise configurations, you will need to make sure you are logged onto the Project Server. The following section describes how you log on to a Project Server from Project Professional.

➔ This section describes logging in to a Project Server from Project Professional 2003 only. For information on using Project Web Access to log in to the Project Server, **see** Chapter 28, "Enterprise Collaboration," **p. 1119**.

What you see when you bring up Microsoft Project Professional 2003 depends on how your user account is currently configured in Microsoft Project Professional:

- If your account is configured for manual connection (which is described later in this section), then you will be prompted to choose a Project Server account to log in to, as shown in Figure 25.9. Select your Project Server account and click Connect. Enter the password for your account and click Go to log in.

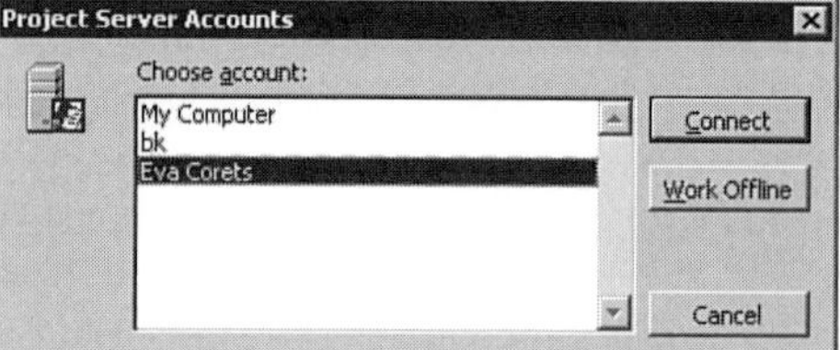

Figure 25.9 The Eva Corets account for the Project Server named projectserver on the default server is selected; this screen does not appear if you are using a Windows user account to log in to the Project Server.

- If your account is configured for automatic connection (which is discussed later in this section), then you will be prompted for a matching user ID and password. Enter the password for your account and click Go to log in.
- If no Project Server account has been established for you in the copy of Project Professional that you're using, you can only work offline. This section gives details on how to connect to a Project Server, using information provided to you by the administrator.

  If you work offline, enterprise features are not available to you, as shown in Figure 25.10.

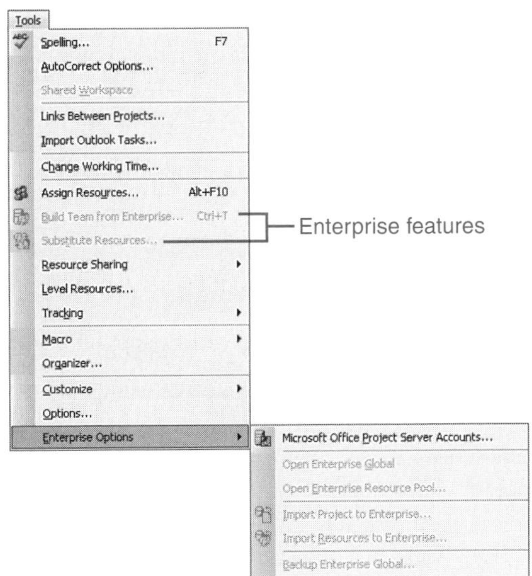

Figure 25.10 Notice that the enterprise features are grayed out, indicating that they are not available to you from Project Professional if you aren't logged in to a Project Server (that is, you are working offline).

You can use Project Professional without being logged in to a Project Server, but this is the same as using a copy of the Standard edition, with access to none of the enterprise features and none of the projects stored on the Project Server. Working offline is different from saving projects offline, which is useful when you won't have access to a Project Server (for example, when you are traveling).

To establish a new connection from your copy of Project Professional 2003 to a Project Server, you need the following information from your administrator:

- A valid user ID and password on the Project Server to which you are attempting to log in.
- Information about whether you should log in using a Windows user account or a Microsoft Project Server account.
- The Project Server's URL.

Follow these instructions to establish a connection between your copy of Project Professional and a Project Server, using the information provided to you by your administrator:

1. Bring up Project Professional and when you are prompted to choose an account, click Work Offline.

NOTE

> You don't have to be working offline to add a new Project Server account, but these instructions assume that you are working offline.

2. Select Tools, Enterprise Options, Microsoft Project Server Accounts. To add a new account, click Add and enter the information provided to you by the administrator, as shown in Figure 25.11. When you finish entering the required fields, including testing the connection to the Project Server, click OK.

   The following are the fields in the Account Properties dialog box:

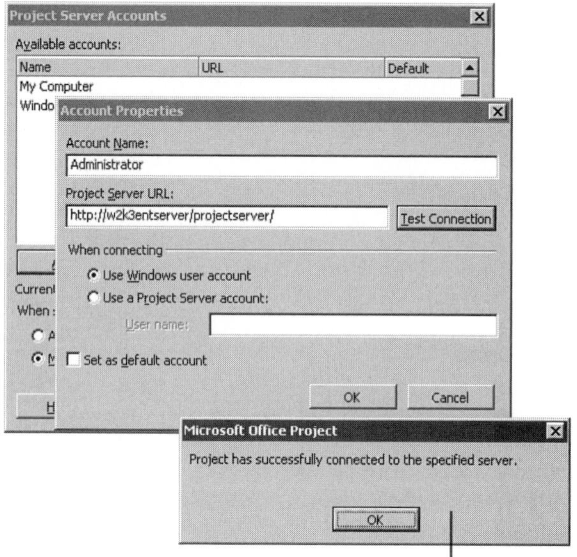

Figure 25.11
You need to enter the information shown to add a new Project Server account.

Account Name—This field is used for description purposes only. It is where defined account names are listed when you first log in to a Project Server (refer to Figure 25.9).

Microsoft Project Server URL—This is where you enter the Project Server URL provided by your administrator. After you enter the Project Server URL, you can verify the connection with the server by clicking the Test Connection button.

Account Type—This is where you specify whether the account you're adding is a Windows user account or a Microsoft Project Server account.

User Name—This is where you specify the login username provided by the administrator.

Default Account—This is where you indicate whether this is the default account for this copy of Project Professional. If this box is checked, then this account will already be selected each time you bring up Project Professional and are presented with the Choose Accounts screen (refer to Figure 25.9).

3. The final step in adding a new Project Server account is to establish whether you want to automatically or manually log in to the Project Server, as shown in Figure 25.12.

   The following are the fields in the Microsoft Project Server Accounts dialog box:

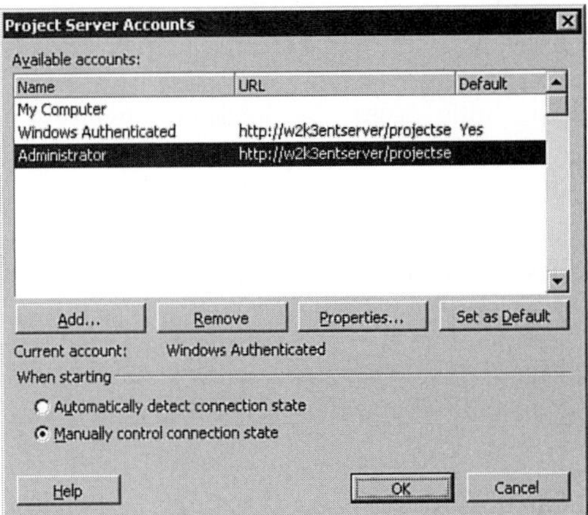

Figure 25.12
You can choose Automatically Detect Connection State to automatically log on to the project server using your default connection each time you bring up Microsoft Project Professional.

Add—You can click Add if you want to add another Project Server account.

Remove—To remove a project server account, select the account to be removed and click Remove. Note that the Remove button is grayed out (disabled) if you are currently logged in with that account.

Properties—You can click Properties to display the Project Server account's configuration information.

Set as Default—You can click Set as Default to set the currently selected Project Server account as the default account.

Connection State—If Manually is selected, you will be able to choose which Project Server account to log in to when you first load Project Professional. If you select Automatically, you will automatically log in to the default Project Server account when you first load Project Professional.

NOTE

After you add a new project server account, you need to exit and restart Microsoft Project Professional before you can log in using the new account.

MANAGING THE ENTERPRISE GLOBAL TEMPLATE

Previous versions of Microsoft Project, as well as the Standard edition of Microsoft Project 2002 and 2003, use a file called `GLOBAL.MPT` to store, manage, and share data items such as custom fields, views, filters, groups, reports, and calendars on a single computer. This section describes how Project 2003 extends the notion of a Global template for the enterprise and how to manage this new Enterprise Global template.

Understanding GLOBAL.MPT, the Enterprise Global Template, and the Enterprise Cache

When you start the Standard edition, GLOBAL.MPT loads into memory, along with any project file(s) that you are loading. When you exit the Standard edition, all changes made to GLOBAL.MPT data are saved with the project file only. This means that any changes made to a view, for example, are available to you only within that project file; they are not directly available to other project files. If you use the Organizer to save that view to GLOBAL.MPT, the changes are available across all projects that are tied to that GLOBAL.MPT file.

→ For details on the Organizer, **see** "Working with the Organizer and Global File," **p. 107**.

Project 2003 extends the availability of standardized project data to the enterprise by using three different global files:

- The traditional GLOBAL.MPT that is located in the user's profile folder. For example, a Windows 2000 user will find the GLOBAL.MPT file in the folder `c:\documents and settings\username\application data\microsoft\ms project\1033` (`1033` is the folder that is used if the user's language is set to American English).
- The Enterprise Global template is stored on the Project Server. The Enterprise Global template contains all the standardized data defined for the enterprise. This standardized data includes all the data items contained in the traditional GLOBAL.MPT file, plus new enterprise data items such as enterprise outline codes and custom fields.
- A cached global file that also resides in the user's profile folder.

When a user starts Project Professional but doesn't connect to a Project Server, Project uses the GLOBAL.MPT from the user's profile folder.

Each time a user starts Project Professional and there is an active connection to the Project Server, a fresh copy of the Enterprise Global template is transmitted to the user's computer, merged with the settings in the user's GLOBAL.MPT file, and stored in the global cache. Project Professional then uses this global cache file, which is also stored in the user's profile folder.

The automatic migration of data items stored in the Enterprise Global template to each user's local GLOBAL.MPT file each time a user loads Project Professional enables and facilitates the management of consistent enterprisewide data. For example, if an administrator wants to make a new macro, view, calendar, or report available to users, he or she simply puts the new data item into the Enterprise Global template, where it becomes available the next time each user loads Project Professional.

If the administrator later decides that the macro, view, or report needs to be updated or deleted, he or she can update the Enterprise Global template, and the enterprise data item is updated or removed the next time each user loads Project Professional.

The following examples illustrate how the Enterprise Global template affects a user's active session with Project Professional:

- **Example 1**—If a user starts Project Professional by selecting My Computer and Work Offline from the Microsoft Project Server Accounts dialog box, the `GLOBAL.MPT` file on the user's local computer is loaded, and Enterprise Global template data (for example, enterprise outline codes, custom fields) is not available to the user for that session.
- **Example 2**—If a user starts Project Professional by selecting a Project Server connection and Work Offline from the Microsoft Project Server Accounts dialog box (so there is no active connection to a Project server), the `GLOBAL.MPT` file on the user's computer is merged with the current global cache, if a global cache exists. This gives the user access to previously active Enterprise Global template data stored in the user's global cache, but that data might be outdated if changes have been made to the Enterprise Global template since the user last connected to the Project Server.

  In the Organizer, this mode is referred to as + Cached Enterprise.
- **Example 3**—If a user starts Project Professional by selecting a Project Server connection and clicking the Connect button from the Microsoft Project Server Accounts dialog box, or if the user opens a project plan from within Project Web Access, the global cache settings are compared to the Enterprise Global template content and updated as needed from the Project Server repository, and the updated global cache is merged with the local `GLOBAL.MPT` file to create a new global cache. This gives the user a refreshed version of the Enterprise Global template settings in his or her global cache.

  In the Organizer, this mode is referred to as + Non-cached Enterprise.

Each data item in the Enterprise Global template is prefixed with the word Enterprise, to distinguish it from data items stored in a user's `GLOBAL.MPT` file.

So what happens if data items from the Enterprise Global template and `GLOBAL.MPT` have the same name? If duplicates are found, the user is prompted to replace the local item, replace all items, rename the local item, or not open Project Professional.

TIP

> You should let users know not to start the names of the data items in their `GLOBAL.MPT` files with the word Enterprise if they want to avoid these conflicts.

MODIFYING THE ENTERPRISE GLOBAL TEMPLATE

There are two ways to change data in the Enterprise Global template:

- **Edit the Enterprise Global template directly**—If you have administrator privileges when you start Microsoft Project Professional and you're connected to an active Project Server repository, you can select Tools, Enterprise Options, Open Enterprise Global to open the Enterprise Global template and edit the data items as needed.

→ For details on editing enterprise outline codes in the Enterprise Global template, **see** "Using Enterprise Outline Codes and Custom Fields," **p. 1010** in this chapter.

NOTE

> A user will *not* see changes made to the Enterprise Global template data items until the Enterprise Global template is closed, and Project Professional is restarted on the user's computer.

- **Use the Organizer**—Depending on your user privileges, you may be able to make certain edits to your cached enterprise file. For example, you can use the Copy button to transfer data items between the active project plan and the cached or noncached enterprise file.

  Be aware that some actions, such as delete, are not permitted on Enterprise Global template data items. If you attempt to delete an Enterprise Global template data item from the cached enterprise file, Microsoft Project gives you an error message and prevents you from taking the delete action.

Working Offline with Enterprise Global Template Data

Enterprise Global template data items are loaded into your schedule only on demand (that is, when you actually use them). However, if there is a need to work offline with the Enterprise Global template data items available, there are three ways you can copy Enterprise Global template items into the local `GLOBAL.MPT` file:

- You can use the Organizer to move the desired data items from the Enterprise Global template to the local `GLOBAL.MPT` file.
- You can use Project Professional's File, Save As command to save a schedule loaded from an active Project Server session to an `.MPT` file.
- You can use Project Professional's File, Save Offline command to save a schedule loaded from an active Project Server session.

Using Enterprise Outline Codes and Custom Fields

When you want to apply a code to a task or resource, you use outline codes.

When you want to apply a code to a project, task, or resource and you want to apply the code consistently across all projects in the enterprise, you use enterprise outline codes.

Project provides 30 enterprise outline codes for use with projects, tasks, and resources. These are named Enterprise Project Outline Code 1, 2, 3, and so on; Enterprise Task Outline Code 1, 2, 3, and so on; and Enterprise Resource Outline Code 1, 2, 3,...29.

In addition, enterprise resources have a predefined outline code called the Resource Breakdown Structure (RBS) code. The RBS code can be any code that differentiates resources, but it should be reserved for the code value that is the most important, or most often used, throughout an organization. This is because the RBS code is built in to the

Team Builder, the Resource Substitution Wizard, and the Assign Resources dialog tools when filtering and selecting resources. For example, the RBS code could contain a resource's department or the organization structure and level that the resource works in.

→ The custom fields in Microsoft Project Standard 2003 enable you to store customized data in your schedule. For more information, **see** Chapter 21, "Customizing Views, Tables, Fields, Filters, and Groups," **p. 833**.

When you want to apply a custom field consistently across all projects, resources, or tasks in the enterprise, you use enterprise custom fields. The only difference between custom fields and enterprise custom fields is that enterprise custom fields are established for the entire enterprise, whereas custom fields are established for the local project only.

Portfolio managers define and create enterprise outline codes and custom fields, thus keeping their use consistent across the enterprise.

CREATING ENTERPRISE OUTLINE CODES

You create and change enterprise outline code fields in the Customize Enterprise Fields dialog box in the Enterprise Global template. Remember that only the administrator can open and edit the Enterprise Global template.

To configure enterprise outline codes, you need to log in to the Project Server from Microsoft Project Professional with administrator privileges.

→ For information on setting up a Microsoft Project Server Account **see** "Logging in to Project Server from Project Professional," **p. 1004**.

→ For information on how to add a user to the Administrator group, **see** "Defining Users and Groups" in the chapter "Customizing and Administering Project Server Access" on the CD accompanying this book.

NOTE

> **You must be working in the Enterprise Global in order for your enterprise outline codes to be permanently added to the Microsoft Project Server 2003 repository. If you aren't able to add enterprise outline codes because the data entry fields are disabled, then you don't have the Enterprise Global open.**

To create a custom enterprise outline code, follow these steps:

1. Select Tools, Enterprise Options, Open Enterprise Global.
2. Choose Tools, Customize, Enterprise Fields to display the dialog box shown in Figure 25.13.
3. Select the Custom Outline Codes tab.
4. Select the category of Outline Code you want to create (task, resource, or project).
5. Select the outline code field that you want to use (1 through 30, or in the case of enterprise resource outline codes, 1 through 29 plus RBS).
6. Click the Rename button to establish a new name for the code, and the dialog box shown in Figure 25.14 appears. Click OK after you enter the desired outline code name.

Figure 25.13
In this example, all resource skills are defined in one enterprise resource outline code field.

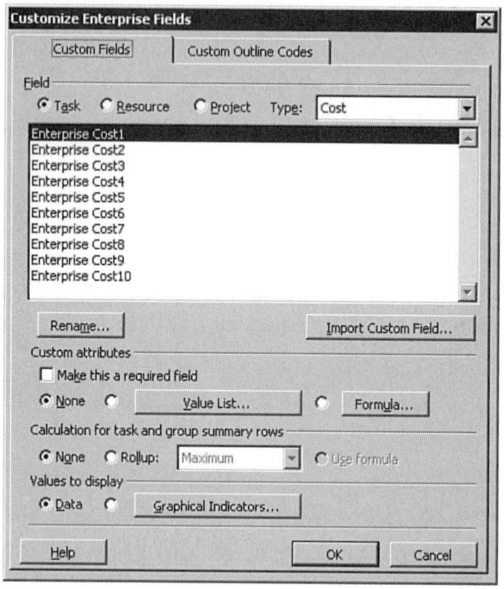

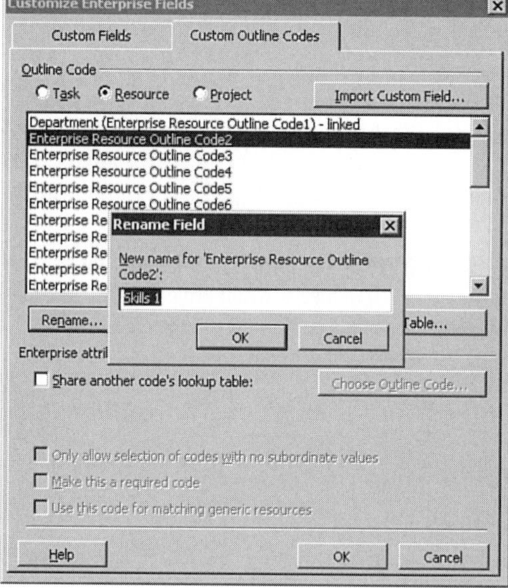

Figure 25.14
You can rename your enterprise resource outline codes.

7. Click the Define Code Mask button to display the Outline Code Definition dialog box shown in Figure 25.15. Remember to define a code mask for each level of outline code you define.

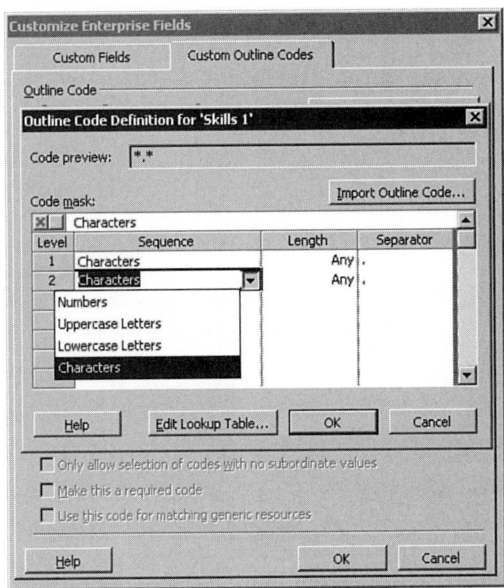

Figure 25.15
If you are defining the outline code to describe location with Level 1 as country and Level 2 as city, there must be two levels of code mask defined, as shown.

8. Click the Edit Lookup Table button to display the Edit Lookup Table dialog box shown in Figure 25.16, and enter your outline codes. For example, if you are defining a location outline code for state and city, your Level 1 code might be Colorado, and your Level 2 codes underneath Colorado might be Denver, Colorado Springs, and Boulder. Use the Indent and Outdent buttons to make codes subordinate to one another. Click Close to save the lookup table entries you have defined.

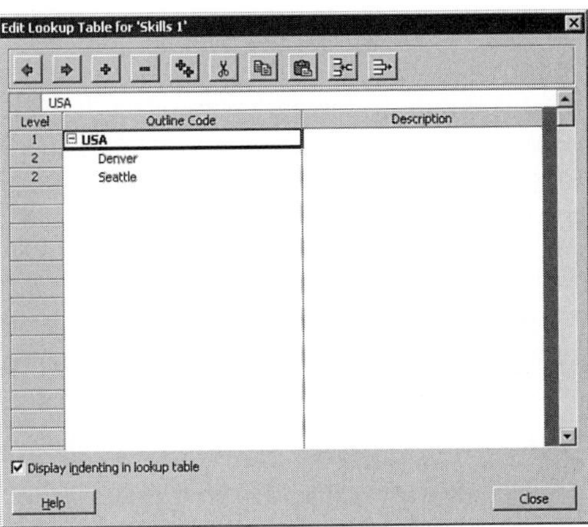

Figure 25.16
You use the icons at the top of the dialog box to manipulate the lookup table items that you've entered; hover over each icon to find out what it does.

9. Select the Share Another Code's Lookup Table check box and click the Choose Outline Code button if you want to have two outline codes share the same lookup table, as shown in Figure 25.17. You are then prompted to select the other outline code's field type and field name from pull-down lists. When outline codes are shared, changing the shared code's lookup table automatically changes the lookup table of the outline code that is referring to the shared code. You can click OK after you choose the outline code lookup table to share.

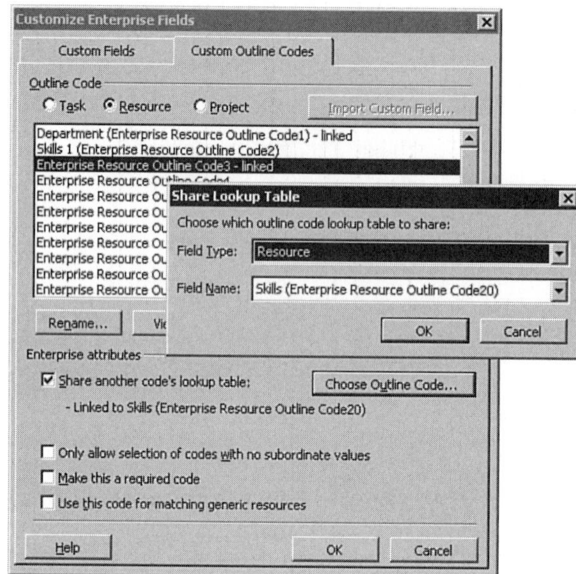

Figure 25.17
The Skills (Enterprise Resource Outline Code20) code is being shared with the location project outline code.

10. Select the Only Allow Selection of Codes with No Subordinate Values check box, as shown in Figure 25.18, if you want to force users to select the lowest level of detail in the outline code that you have defined. For example, if you have entered location codes with Denver and Seattle within the United States, then selecting this check box requires users to always select one of the cities (since the lowest level, the city, has no subordinate values).

11. Select the Make This a Required Code check box if you want to have Microsoft Project 2003 require a valid value before allowing the schedule to be saved or published to the Microsoft Project Server.

12. Select the Use This Code for Matching Generic Resources check box if you want to use this outline code as matching criteria for the Resource Substitution Wizard or matching criteria using the Team Builder from Enterprise function.

NOTE

> You see the Use This Code for Matching Generic Resources check box only if you are working with enterprise resource outline codes.

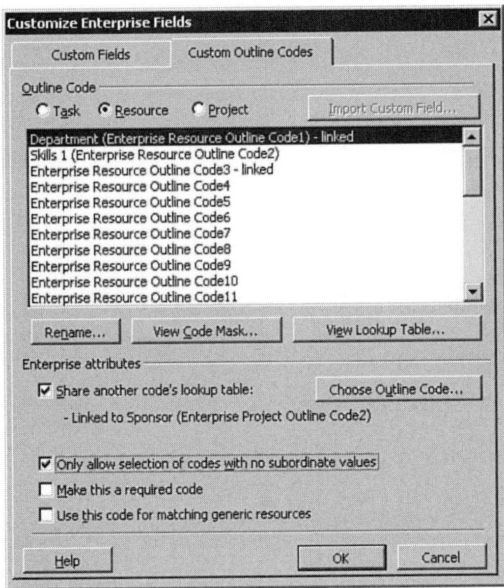

Figure 25.18
You can force users to select the lowest level of detail in the outline code.

13. When you are done building custom outline codes, click Close. You are returned to the Custom Enterprise Fields dialog. Click OK.
14. Save and exit the plan. Select the option Save and Check In Your Plan. Your outline code is now stored in the Enterprise Global and can be used for all projects that have access to the Microsoft Project Server to which you saved your plan.

25

NOTE

> You will need to exit and restart Microsoft Project to see any modifications to custom outline codes.

Enabling Proficiency Levels per Skill

Microsoft Project Professional supports using skill codes to designate skill proficiency levels. You might want to use this feature to distinguish between proficiency levels when performing resource substitution. For example, there might be times when any Visual Basic developer would suffice for an assignment, and there might be times when you want to specify that only a junior or senior Visual Basic developer should be assigned to a task.

To enable proficiency levels per skill, you need to set up your skill codes with the proficiency level as the lowest level of definition, as shown in Figure 25.19.

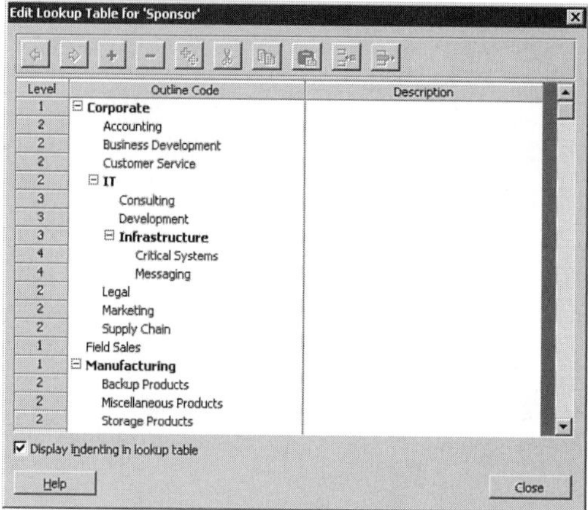

Figure 25.19
You can define your skill codes to have proficiency levels.

Microsoft Project Professional treats a resource that is assigned a skill code as having all levels of skill above and including the skill level assigned to. For example, if a generic resource is assigned the skill Developer.VB, the Resource Substitution Wizard will find any resource that matches either Developer.VB, Developer.VB.Senior, or Developer.VB.Junior. Likewise, if the generic resource is assigned the skill Developer, the wizard will find any resource that matches either Developer, Developer.VB, Developer.VB Senior, or Developer.VB.Junior.

NOTE

> **Make sure that the Only Allow Selection of Codes with No Subordinate Values check box in the Customize Enterprise Fields dialog box is not selected if you want to assign skill codes other than at their lowest level.**

ENABLING MULTIPLE SKILLS PER RESOURCE

Microsoft Project Professional supports assigning multiple skill codes to resources with a new feature called Enterprise Resource Multi-Value (ERMV) codes. Many resources have multiple skills. For example, a Visual Basic developer might also be a Web developer, and a technical writer might also be a tester. Enterprise Resource Multi-Value codes must use enterprise resource outline codes 20 through 29.

→ For more information **see** the "Enabling Multiple Skills per Resource" section in Chapter 27, "Enterprise Resource Management."

CREATING ENTERPRISE CUSTOM FIELDS

Enterprise custom fields are user-definable fields that can contain information that is unique to your organization's reporting needs. For example, to report on project status within the enterprise, you can set up an enterprise custom number field (perhaps ranking the value at 1 to 3), and have the status be automatically generated based on a formula, such as current end date – planned end date, earned value, and so on.

You create and change enterprise custom fields in the Customize Enterprise Fields dialog box in the Enterprise Global template. To create an enterprise custom field, follow these steps:

1. Select Tools, Enterprise Options, Open Enterprise Global.
2. Choose Tools, Customize, Enterprise Fields to display the Customize Enterprise Fields dialog box shown in Figure 25.20.

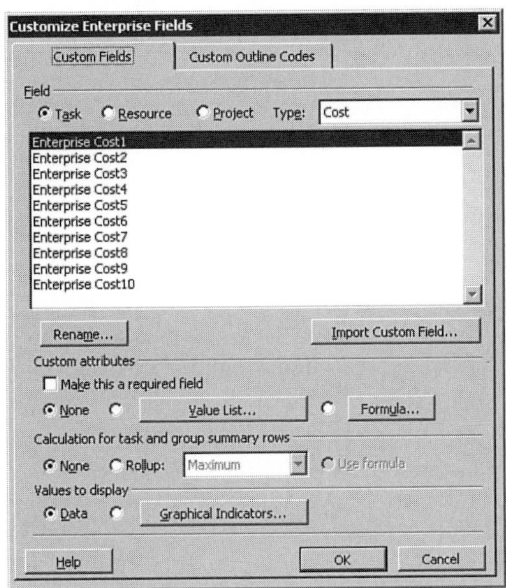

Figure 25.20
You need to be logged in as the administrator to see this screen.

3. Select the Custom Fields tab.
4. Select the category of custom field you want to create (task, resource, or project), and select the type (such as Text).
5. Select the custom field that you want to use.
6. Click the Rename button to establish a new name for the code, enter the new name for the custom field, and then click OK.
7. Select the custom attributes you want to associate with the field. You can select None, Value List, or Formula.
8. To create a formula for the field, click Formula to display the Formula dialog box, which is shown in Figure 25.21. Type the value name in the Value column, and type identifying text for that value in the Description column. You can add as many values as necessary. Select other options that are available in the dialog box as necessary to define the code. Click OK when you are done.
9. Build an enterprise custom field the same way you would a standard custom field. The only differences between enterprise custom fields and standard custom fields are the Required field and the fact that enterprise custom fields are available to all Enterprise Project users.

25

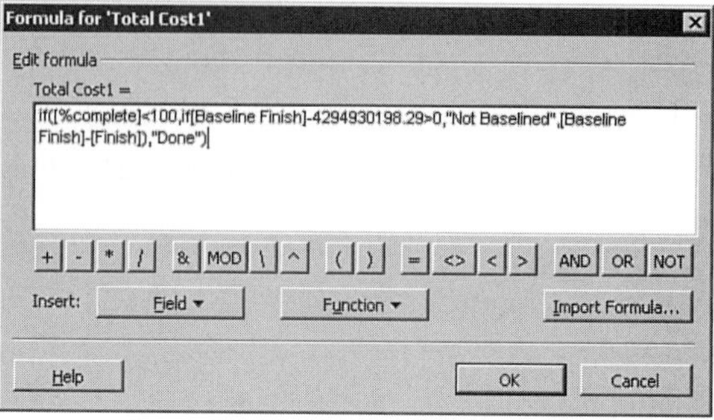

Figure 25.21
All users can see the results of this formula by displaying the Enterprise Project Text1 field column in their schedules.

➔ For more detailed instructions about creating custom fields and using the various custom field options, **see** "Customizing Fields," **p. 847**.

10. When you are done building custom fields, click Close. You are returned to the Custom Enterprise Fields dialog. Click OK.
11. Save and exit the plan. Select the option Save and Check In your plan. Your custom field is now stored in the Enterprise Global template and can be used for all projects that have access to the Microsoft Project Server to which you saved your plan.

MANAGING ENTERPRISE PROJECT AND RESOURCE CALENDARS

Enterprise project calendars are managed through the Enterprise Global template, and enterprise resource calendars are managed through the enterprise resource pool.

Enterprise project and resource calendars can be created only by users who have read/write access to the Enterprise Global template and the enterprise resource pool, but project managers have a variety of ways (described in the following sections) to modify existing project and resource calendars for their local projects without the changes finding their way back to the calendars stored in the Enterprise Global template. For this reason, we recommend that each organization define and document processes for ensuring that project and resource calendar information is updated in the Enterprise Global template and the enterprise resource pool.

As with other data stored in the Enterprise Global template, enterprise project calendars can be created by the administrator for use throughout an organization.

MANAGING ENTERPRISE PROJECT CALENDARS

When the Project server is first installed, it has one enterprise project calendar named the Standard calendar.

➔ You can create a new enterprise project calendar by opening the Enterprise Global template and selecting Tools, Change Working Time. **See** "Defining a Calendar of Working Time," **p. 76**, for details on how to add and configure a project calendar.

Every project saved to the Project Server must specify which enterprise project calendar it is using. All new enterprise calendars that you create in the Enterprise Global template are available to become the enterprise calendars for projects stored on the Project Server.

You can delete or rename project calendars by opening the Enterprise Global template, selecting Tools, Organizer, selecting the Calendar tab (make sure you are selecting the calendars in the Enterprise Global template), selecting the calendar to be deleted, and clicking the Delete or Rename button. You cannot delete or rename the Standard enterprise project calendar.

By default, project managers cannot create a new project, enterprise, or local calendars for their schedules. To allow project managers to create new local project calendars in Project Web Access, select Admin, Manage Enterprise Features, and place a check in the Allow Projects to Use Local Base Calendars check box, and then click Save Changes.

Even if project managers cannot create new project calendars, they can change the calendar options for their local schedules, allowing each project to define different calendar options than the selected enterprise project calendar.

Managing Resource Calendars

Enterprise resources are associated with two enterprise calendars: the enterprise project calendar and the resource's enterprise resource calendar.

When a new enterprise resource is created in the enterprise resource pool, it is automatically assigned to the Standard calendar, and an enterprise resource calendar is created from the Standard calendar for the resource. To assign an enterprise resource to a different calendar, you must manually select an enterprise calendar for the resource.

Tasks' durations and dates are calculated for an enterprise resource by combining the information from the resource's enterprise project calendar and the resource's enterprise resource calendar. If either calendar changes, the enterprise resource's assignments might change.

If a project manager alters an enterprise resource's resource calendar from within a project schedule, the project manager will receive a warning that all changes to enterprise resources will be lost. This means that as long as the project manager has the resource's schedule open, the changes he or she makes in the resource calendar will apply. Upon closing and reopening the project, the resource's calendar will revert back to the resource's enterprise resource calendar, and the project-specific calendar changes will be lost.

Performing Enterprise Global Backup and Restore

Like any other data, the Enterprise Global template can become corrupted, or it can be changed in error and then fail to recover. For these reasons, you need to back up your Enterprise Global template(s) on a regular basis. The next two sections describe how to back up and restore the Enterprise Global template.

Backing Up Enterprise Global Template Data

To back up an Enterprise Global template, you need to be logged in to Project Professional with sufficient privileges to perform the backups.

From within Project Professional, you select Tools, Enterprise Options, Backup Enterprise Global. A browse window prompts you to save the Enterprise Global template data to an external file. You also have the option to save this backup through an ODBC connection to a database. This method allows you to store several Enterprise Global templates in a central repository.

The default name for the backup file is `EntGlobalBackup`, but you will likely want to change this.

TIP

> Consider using a file-naming strategy that helps you easily identify the server name and last-used date of a particular Enterprise Global template. That way, you can use those files as starting points for changes to future global settings.

25

Restoring Enterprise Global Template Data

To restore an Enterprise Global template, select Tools, Enterprise Options, Restore Enterprise Global in Project Professional.

A dialog box asks you to select a server account user profile to use when performing the restore (the user profile must have the correct privileges). You can use the Browse button to locate the file to restore (see Figure 25.22).

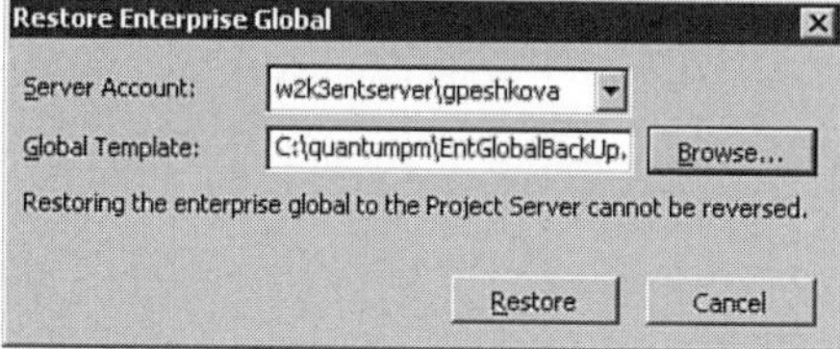

Figure 25.22
The Server Account list comes from the available server accounts defined for the PC you're using.

CAUTION

> Restoring the Enterprise Global template to a Microsoft Project Server cannot be reversed. Before clicking the Restore button, make a backup copy of the active Enterprise Global template so that you can recover the previous conditions if necessary.

IMPORTING RESOURCES

When Project Server is installed, there is only one resource stored within the database: the administrator.

The goal associated with importing resources is to quickly and easily have the enterprise resource pool populated with resources from existing schedules that have the appropriate codes (for example, skill codes) assigned to them. Here are some approaches that can be taken to accomplish this:

- Cut and paste resources from individual project plans into the checked-out enterprise resource pool, and edit each resource's enterprise codes manually. If you want to import many enterprise resources, this approach might be impractical.
- Use the Import Resources Wizard to edit the required enterprise resource codes manually as part of the import process. This is similar to the first option, in which you need to edit each resource's enterprise codes manually, except that in this case you edit them in the Import Resources Wizard instead of in the enterprise resource pool. If you want to import many enterprise resources, this approach might be impractical, too.

  The Import Resources Wizard cannot complete until all required enterprise resource codes for all resources being imported are resolved.
- Define all required enterprise resource outline codes and their values before you use the Import Resources Wizard. This is the best way to import large groups of resources because you are able to automate the resources and their required enterprise resource outline codes by using the Import Resources Wizard.

Before loading resources into the enterprise resource pool, you should consider the following (or you'll find yourself updating the Enterprise Global template and resource pool multiple times):

- What naming conventions has your organization adopted for the different resource types (for example, people might be last name, first name; material resource names might always start with the letters mat; external vendor names might always start with the letters xvend)? This is important because project managers must be able to find, identify, and select resources from the enterprise resource pool quickly and easily.
- What are the enterprise resource outline codes, and how are they associated with enterprise resources? For example, how many skill codes are there and how many are required? Or, what does the Resource Breakdown Structure (RBS) look like, and at what level are enterprise resources to be assigned to the RBS?
- How will you define and use generic resources?

CAUTION

> Do not underestimate the importance of planning *before* you import resources into the enterprise resource pool. After you import resources into the enterprise resource pool and assign them to tasks within projects, you cannot easily remove them.

Using the Import Resources Wizard

Although Microsoft Project can import resources from any .MPP file, you might want to create a single Microsoft Project plan that contains all the currently known resources. This project file, which does not need to contain any tasks, can then be imported by using the Import Resources Wizard.

In addition to importing resources, you might want to import each resource's enterprise outline codes. To accomplish this, you define outline codes and custom fields in the .MPP file that contains the resources to be imported, and you map those codes and fields to the enterprise resource codes and fields during the import process.

To use the Import Resources Wizard, follow these steps:

1. Prepare the input .MPP file with the list of resources that you want to import and their associated information (such as skills, location, cost, and maximum units) mapped to appropriate fields. For example, you might want to use Outline Code 1 in the .MPP file to map to Enterprise Resource Outline Code 1.
2. Start the Import Resources Wizard by selecting Tools, Enterprise Options, Import Resources to Enterprise.
3. Open the file containing the resources to be imported by clicking the Open from File button.
4. Navigate to the .MPP file, ODBC data source (that is, the schedule containing the resources might be stored in an existing Microsoft Project 2000 database), or Microsoft Project server file that you want to import. When you locate the file to import, select it and click Import.
5. Map local fields to enterprise fields, as desired. As shown in Figure 25.23, the field-mapping screen is divided into two columns. You use the column on the left to specify the outline codes you want to import, and you use the column on the right to specify the enterprise outline codes you want to import to.

   Note that any enterprise resource field defined as Required in the Enterprise Global template automatically appears in the Enterprise Resource Field column, marked Required.

   You can choose any field (whether it contains appropriate data or not) from the Imported Resource Field pull-down list, and then click Next. Then you can move forward with the wizard and resolve the code mapping later on.

   The Map column is automatically checked as each row of fields to map is added. If you decide you don't want to import a set of fields after defining them, you can prevent those specific fields from importing as mapped by removing the check mark from the Map field before continuing with the Import Resources Wizard.
6. The wizard examines the incoming resource names and outline codes, to determine whether there are duplicates of any errors (such as duplicate resource names or mismatched outline codes), as shown in Figure 25.24.

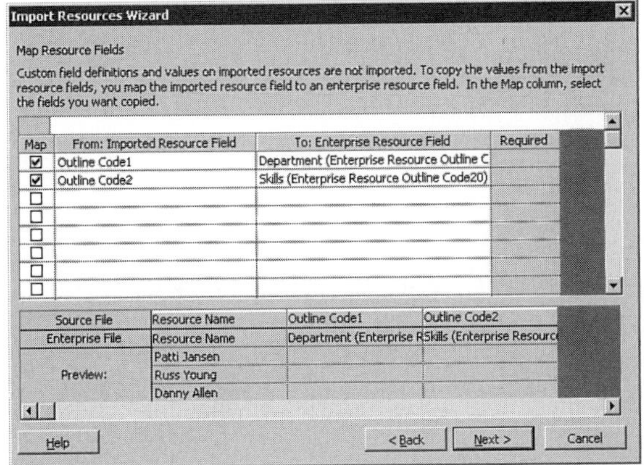

Figure 25.23
The Outline Code1 and Outline Code2 fields are mapped from an .MPP file to the Department and Skills Enterprise Resource Outline Code fields, respectively.

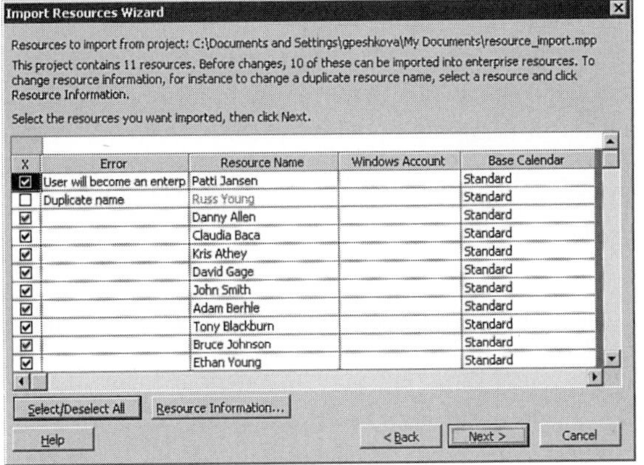

Figure 25.24
The second paragraph on the screen tells you how many resources are in the schedule being imported and how many are currently ready to be imported.

You can select a resource and click the Resource Information button to display and modify the enterprise data fields associated with the selected resource. Selecting a resource and clicking the Resource Information button displays the same Resource Information screen as in Project Professional, with the exception of the Working Time tab. Fields that are changed here and saved update the enterprise resource pool.

You use the Select/Deselect All button to choose the resources you want to import, or choose them individually by using the X column.

7. Resolve the errors and click Next to have the defined resources imported. Some errors are easier to resolve than others. For example, for duplicate names, you should leave the box in the X column unchecked. If you get an error such as Invalid Custom Field Value, make sure that the outline codes in the file you are importing from match the enterprise resource outline codes exactly.

TIP

After you have completed the resource import, you might want to validate the results by opening the enterprise resource pool and visually inspecting that the new resources and their enterprise outline codes have been added correctly.

IMPORTING PROJECTS

One of the requirements for taking full advantage of the Project Server environment is that all project schedules be stored in the Project Server database.

During the initial deployment of Microsoft Project 2003, however, a significant number of project schedules exist as .MPP files that need to migrate to a Project server. In addition, you might need to import project schedules from external vendors or other departments within your company, or you might want to import what-if schedules that users have built while not connected to the Project Server.

To help bring these schedules into a Project Server database, and to assist in ensuring that they conform to your Enterprise Global template requirements, Project Professional provides an Import Project Wizard.

Before you import project schedules into the Project Server, you need to do some planning and investigation to determine how and if the imported schedules adhere to your internal standards.

Your planning and investigation activities should answer questions like the following:

- Do the project plans adhere to your company standards for things such as Work Breakdown Structure (WBS), use of milestones, task linkages to produce a critical path, and assignment of resources to all tasks? If schedule standards are not adhered to, your organization's ability to use the various Portfolio Analysis views might be negatively affected.
- Do the incoming project plans contain actual work hours applied to tasks? If there are actual hours without resources or costs, various reports might not properly reflect total actual costs.
- Do the incoming project plans contain customizations such as Visual Basic for Applications programs, customized toolbars and menus, custom views or filters, and customized data fields? Such customizations can cause conflicts or require special handling when you consider the content of a Project Server's Enterprise Global template settings.
- Have you established versions within the Project Server environment? If you are importing experimental or what-if versions, you should save them with those designations.
- Do the incoming project plans have special project or resource calendars? If the imported project plan calendars conflict with the Project Server Enterprise Global template settings, you should decide how to treat this situation.

- Who will be the assigned project manager for the imported project plans? The person who does the actual import becomes the default project manager role for that project in the Project Server environment.

USING THE IMPORT PROJECTS WIZARD

Key functions performed by the Import Projects Wizard include the following:

- Enforcing valid values for all required fields
- Creating a copy of the project in the Project Server
- Publishing a project so that its data is available for modeling and analysis

These functions can all be performed outside the wizard, with the same results. The wizard simply makes the process easier to use and ensures that all steps are taken.

> **TIP**
>
> **You should import resources before importing the projects that use them so that you can use the resource-matching capabilities of the Import Projects Wizard.**

To import a project by using the Import Projects Wizard, follow these steps:

1. Within Project Professional, select Tools, Enterprise Options, Import Project to Enterprise. A Welcome screen appears. Click Next.
2. Select the file to be imported. You can do this either by navigating to the appropriate directory, using the browser (for .MPP schedules) or by clicking the ODBC button, selecting a data source from the list presented, and selecting a schedule from the list of schedules associated with the selected data source. After you select a file to import, click Import.
3. Enter information about the project that you are importing (see Figure 25.25).

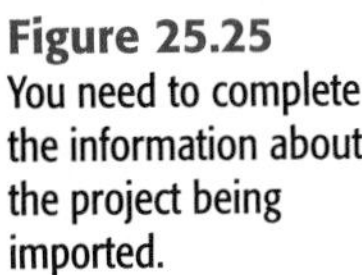

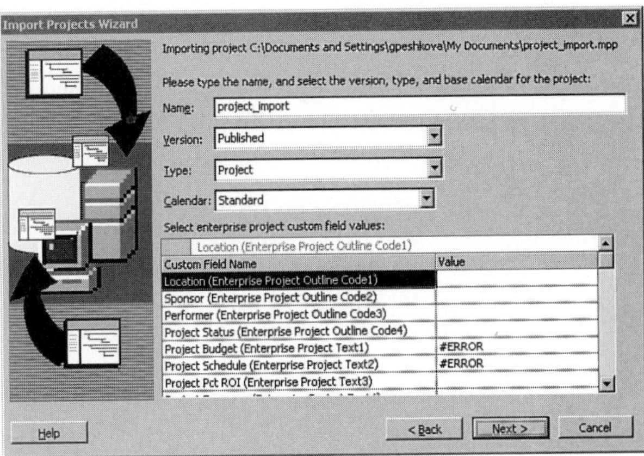

Figure 25.25
You need to complete the information about the project being imported.

You need to enter a unique name for the project. This should be a meaningful name so that it is easy to understand what the project is about.

Select the project's version. The drop-down list box shows all the versions available in the particular Project Server. Every project must be saved initially as a Published version. It is not possible to save a project plan to any other version if there is not already a Published version in the database.

You need to select one of two Type options: Project (the default) and Template. You choose Project to create a project schedule. You choose Template to create an enterprise template. Whichever you choose will be stored in the Project Server database.

You cannot click Next until all fields contain valid entries. If invalid data is entered (for example, if there is a check mark on a custom field, if the custom outline code can only contain values from the bottom of the structure, or if you have selected a version other than Published and the Published version doesn't exist yet), an appropriate error message appears, and you must reenter the data.

NOTE

The #ERROR shown in the figure is due to fields that are calculated and do not affect the import process.

25

NOTE

A required field has an * appended to its name in the Custom Field Name display.

4. If you are importing a schedule from a previous release of Microsoft Project, then you are prompted to map the base calendars in the project to enterprise calendars, or rename the base calendars.

   Mapping calendars can cause silent changes to calculated dates. This condition can occur if the calculated dates from the imported project plan depend on local calendar conditions that are *not* the same as in Enterprise Global template settings. A common example of this condition is when the imported project calendar does not contain a full list of holidays or other nonworking days, but the Project Server environment does consider these days. In that case, the imported project dates would be adjusted to not schedule work as per the enterprise calendar's nonworking days, therefore possibly lengthening previous task durations.

   Choosing an enterprise calendar will cause the schedule to use that base calendar as the project's base calendar.

   Renaming the imported projects calendar allows you to create a new enterprise calendar that is kept in your local enterprise global file, and is used by your projects exclusively.

CAUTION

> Your organization needs to determine the conditions, if any, under which a project can define and use its own local calendars. For example, is it acceptable in your organization for each project to establish standards such as working hours per day and holidays? If not, you'll want to publish and enforce (through process and review) how calendars are used in the enterprise environment.

5. The wizard detects the resources within the imported project plan and presents a decision screen, as shown in Figure 25.26.

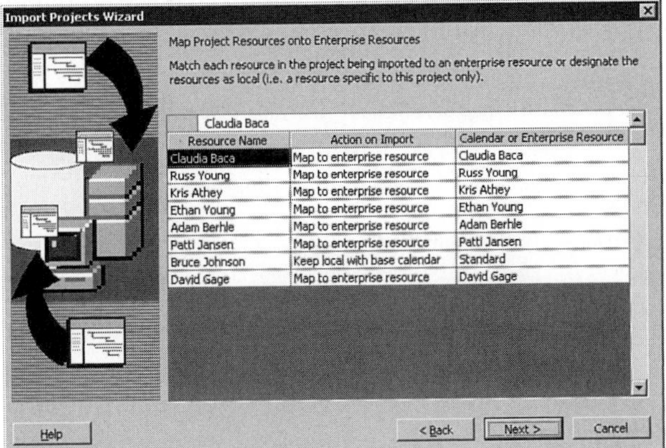

Figure 25.26
You can map resources from the imported project to enterprise resources.

You need to determine what action to perform for each resource in the schedule being imported. For each resource you need to decide what name to use. You can individually select and edit these names, which means you can change them before importing.

When each name is correct, you use the Action on Import column to control how each individual resource should be handled during import. Three possible actions can be taken:

- You can select Map to Enterprise Resource to specify that the resource is already in the enterprise resource pool. When this option is selected, you can choose which enterprise resource to map to from the pull-down list in the Calendar or Enterprise Resource column. When the project is loaded into a Project Server, each local resource will be replaced by the selected enterprise resource.
- You can select Keep Local with Base Calendar to keep the local resource (in the Resource Name column) as a local resource to the project. If this option is selected, you can choose which local calendar to apply to this resource from the pull-down list in the Calendar or Enterprise Resource column.
- You can select Import Resource to Enterprise to generate a new name in the enterprise resource pool. If a new resource is being imported and there are required values, you are prompted to enter the required values after the import process has started.

6. Click Next, and the wizard gives you the chance to remap incoming local data fields to enterprise fields, as shown in Figure 25.27.

Import	Task Name	Cost1	Number1
Enterprise	Task Name	Enterprise Cost1	Enterprise Number
Preview	Scope	0.00	0
	Determine project scope	0.00	0
	Secure project sponsorsl	0.00	0

Figure 25.27 You can automatically move localized data into appropriate enterprise fields.

7. Click Next, and the wizard gives you the opportunity to make changes to the imported tasks, as shown in Figure 25.28. Changes may be required if the wizard detects that there are errors in the enterprise custom field values for tasks.

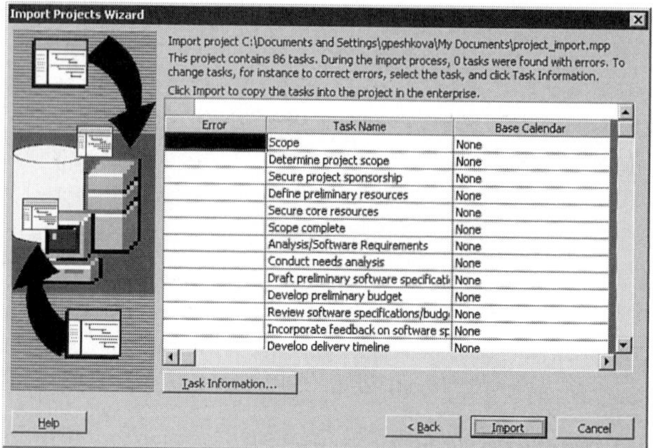

Figure 25.28 You can resolve enterprise custom field values for tasks.

View or modify task information by selecting a task and then clicking the Task Information button. You can also use this wizard screen to modify the base calendar for each task. You must correct any errors reported in the Error column before you can complete the import process.

CAUTION

> It is not possible to type in data at this point. Therefore, if the Enterprise Global template contains required custom fields, the source data for these fields must have been entered into a local custom field in the project plan before it can be entered into the Import Project Wizard.

8. Click Import, and the wizard reads the project plan into the Project Server repository and automatically saves it.
9. Click Import More Projects if you want to import another project plan.

CHAPTER 26

ENTERPRISE PROJECT MANAGEMENT

In this chapter

Using the Project Center Views 1031

Using Project Center Build Team 1036

Opening and Using Multiple Projects 1040

Check-in Projects from Project Center 1046

Using Administrative Projects 1047

Analyzing Enterprise Projects 1048

Using Enterprise Templates 1065

Working with Enterprise Versions 1066

Working with Enterprise Project Codes 1067

Chapter 24, "An Overview of Microsoft Office Project Server 2003," identifies several roles for users of Microsoft Project Professional, including project managers, portfolio managers and executives, and server administrators.

NOTE

> No matter what your role is, we recommend that you read all of Part VIII, "Using Project Server and Project Professional," to get a comprehensive understanding of the available features and capabilities.

Chapter 24 also reviews the general architecture of Project Server, Project Web Access, and Microsoft Project 2003 Professional. You should become familiar with those concepts before reading this chapter.

This chapter describes how project managers use the features and capabilities of Project Web Access and Project Professional 2003.

TIP

> In this chapter, we will generally refer to projects and resources from the sample database provided with the Microsoft Office Project 2003 installation media. Refer to the Project Server installation wizard for more details on installing and using the sample database.

NEW Each new feature of Microsoft Office Project 2003 is listed in Table 26.1, along with the project management functions that the feature supports. These and other features are described within this chapter.

TABLE 26.1 NEW MICROSOFT OFFICE PROJECT 2003 FEATURES FOR PROJECT MANAGERS

New Project Web Access and Project Professional Features	Project Management Functions
Revert	Restores the original Group and Filter conditions of Project Center views
Open multiple projects	Project Center allows you to open multiple projects within a single Microsoft Project session
Build team	Resources can be added to projects from the Project Web Access Project Center
Administrative projects	Manage non-project time with special Administrative projects
Self Check-in projects	Allows project managers to release database locks in case of problems

Using the Project Center Views

To use the Project Center, you must first log in to a Project Server using Project Web Access. When you are logged in to the Project Server, you find the Project Center by selecting the Projects main menu tab.

The Project Center provides access to project information, as defined by your administrator. For the purposes of this discussion, it is assumed that the Project Web Access administrator has granted you permissions to view project data for the entire organization.

You can access the Project Center from either Microsoft Project Web Access (by selecting Projects from the main menu) or from within Microsoft Project Professional (by selecting the menu sequence Collaborate, Project Center).

Six primary functions are associated with the Project Center:

- **View projects in Project Center**—The project views provide a high-level summary perspective of each project stored in the Project Server, so you can see and compare project progress, cost, variance, or other user-defined information at a glance. From the project views you can select and open individual projects to examine details, change the way projects are filtered and grouped, and change the type of data displayed in the view.
- **Analyzing projects in the Portfolio Analyzer**—The Portfolio Analyzer enables you to display and manipulate project and resource information from data stored in an OLAP cube. The OLAP cube contains a snapshot of all information associated with published projects (that is, projects of the version called Published), and is created and updated on a regular basis or an ad hoc basis by the administrator. The Portfolio Analyzer is useful for looking at and analyzing an organization's project and resource plan-of-record data.
- **Model projects with Portfolio Modeler**—The Portfolio Modeler allows you to simulate proposed changes to projects or resource assignments and view the impact of the changes, without affecting the actual project schedules. The Portfolio Modeler is useful for performing what-if analysis on projects and project teams.
- **Managing personal to-do lists**—You can manage personal to-do lists in the Project Center. To-do lists are useful for tracking personal tasks that don't require formal scheduling.
- NEW **Check in my projects**—If you are given permission by the Project Web Access administrator, you can now release database locks on projects that are left open due to network or other technology problems.
- NEW **Managing administrative projects**—Special projects can be created to track and manage activities not usually associated with projects that deliver goods or services. These administrative projects have special properties involving scheduling, resource usage, and actual work report through timesheets.

These topics are described in more detail in the following sections.

VIEWING PROJECT SUMMARY INFORMATION

You can use the project summary views when you want to get an overview of all projects stored in the Project Server, as shown in Figure 26.1.

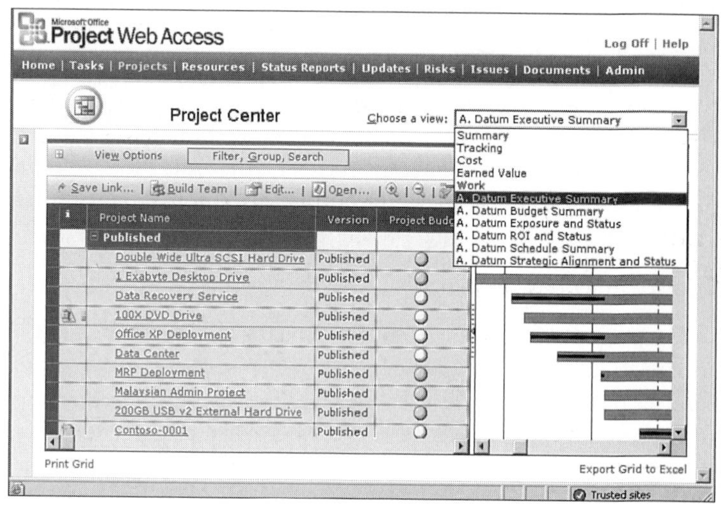

Figure 26.1
Select the Choose a View drop-down list to change summary views.

USING THE PROJECT CENTER'S VIEW TAB OPTIONS

You use the Project Center's View Options tab to refine the contents of the display. You can click on the View Options tab to see the list of View Options that are available, or you can click on the + and - icons on the left side of the tab to expand or collapse the View Options display.

There are three Project Center view options:

- **Show Time with Dates**—If the Show Time with Dates option is checked, time stamps are added to displayed dates.
- **Show To-Do Lists**—If the Show To-Do Lists check box is checked, to-do list items are included in the display.

- **Show Outline Levels**—This drop-down list allows you to quickly show project schedule work breakdown structure outline levels. This function is most appropriate when reviewing project details.

USING THE PROJECT CENTER'S FILTER, GROUP, SEARCH TAB

Select the Filter, Group, Search tab to display or hide the Project Center's filtering, grouping, and searching options. The following sections describe how Filter, Group, and Search work for Project Center views. Resource Center views behave in the same manner.

USING PROJECT CENTER FILTERS

You can use Project Center's Filter option to filter the project list. There are three options for filtering the project list:

- **Filter**—The Filter drop-down list box contains two options: All Projects and Custom Filter. If the Custom Filter option is selected (or the Custom Filter button is selected), the More Filters pull-down appears at the top of each column of schedule data.
- **Custom Filter**—The Custom Filter button provides the opportunity to use up to three criteria statements to filter the list of projects, as shown in Figure 26.2.

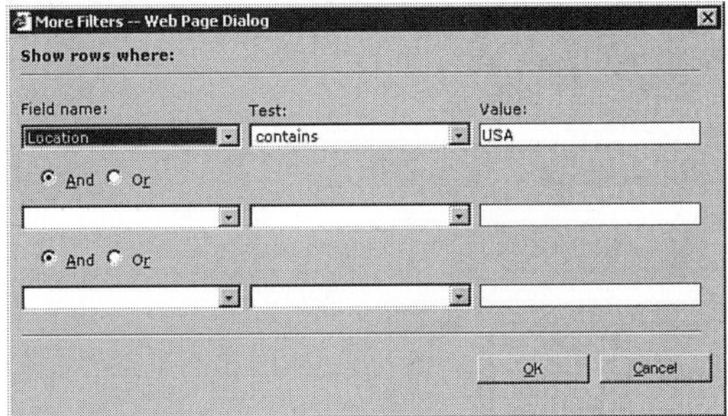

Figure 26.2 You can use custom filters to limit which projects are displayed.

- **Autofilter**—You check the Autofilter check box to have the standard Autofilter arrows appear at the top of each column in the Project Center view, and then click the Autofilter arrows to define and apply the Autofilters.

USING PROJECT CENTER GROUPS

26

You use the Group By function to sort the Projects in the Project Center into groups. The Group By function provides three drop-down list boxes, each of which defines a data field to group on. The Group By execution order is from left to right for each Group By field that is defined, with the results of each operation nested within the previous group's results for the listed projects.

Grouping projects by an Enterprise Global Project outline code can provide useful information. Suppose, for example, that you want to see projects grouped by project version and location. If the Location enterprise outline code has been added to one of your project views, you can group the projects by version then location by performing the following steps:

1. In Project Web Access, navigate to Projects tab and select the view that has the Location code added (in this example, the Location Enterprise Global code has been added to the A.Datum Executive Summary view).

NOTE

To group by a field, that field must be visible in the current view. If you want to group (or filter) a view with fields that aren't currently defined for the view, you need to have the Project Web Access administrator modify the view or create a new view for you.

→ For details on how to add Enterprise Global Project outline codes to views, **see** "Creating and Modifying a Project Center View," **p. 987**.

2. Select Filter, Group, Search tab. Select Versions from the Group By pull-down list. Select Location from the Then By list. Your projects should be grouped as shown in Figure 26.3.

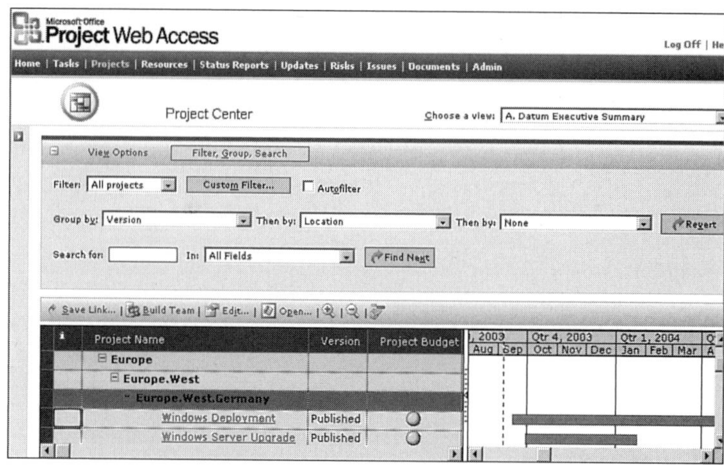

Figure 26.3 You can group the project view information by Enterprise Project outline codes (for example, Version and Location).

26

NEW

TIP

Revert—Click this button to restore the original Group and Filter conditions that were predefined for the active view by the Project Web Access administrator.

USING PROJECT CENTER SEARCHES

You use the Search For option to quickly locate projects by entering a text string to search for, and the fields in which you want to search for the text. After the search criteria are specified, you click Find Next to display each project that matches the search criteria.

As with the Group By function, the only fields available for searching are those that are defined as part of the current active view.

EDITING ENTERPRISE PROJECT INFORMATION

If you examine Figure 26.3, you can see a button icon called Edit. If the Project Web Access administrator has given you permission, then you can click this button to see a screen that allows you to modify the Enterprise Global code values of the selected project.

For example, your organization may have defined an Enterprise Global project code called Project Status that has the values Red, Yellow, and Green. The Edit function allows a project or portfolio manager to change the Project Status attribute to reflect the current status of the project.

→ For more information, **see** the section "Working with Enterprise Project Codes," later in this chapter.

Viewing Project Detailed Information

If you select a project name link from the Project Center summary views, you can see the details within the selected project as shown in Figure 26.4.

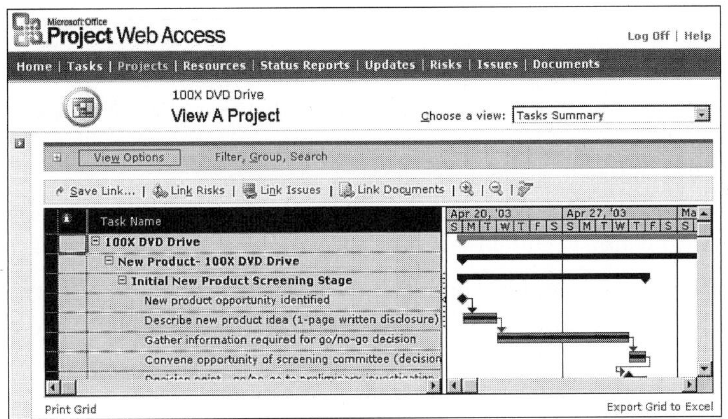

Figure 26.4
You can review project details with various views.

> **TIP**
>
> Use the Save Link function to set special navigation links so you can quickly return to frequently needed detail views.

Expanding and Contracting Details

Click the small + and – indicators to the left of project summary row text to expand or contract the selected section of the schedule. Then use the vertical and horizontal sliders at the right side and bottom edge of the detail window to see more schedule details.

Manipulating Columns and Rows

You can reposition displayed columns by using your mouse to drag and drop a column header to the left or right. Then you can resize the column width by using the mouse to drag and drop the right edge of a column boundary. If you double-click on the right edge of a column header boundary, the column width will expand or contract to fit the maximum width of data within that column.

You can also change the row height by using the mouse to drag and drop the lower boundary of a row. Every row within the schedule will expand or contract within this change.

LINKING RISKS, ISSUES, AND DOCUMENTS TO TASKS

As you examine project details, you can also relate individual project tasks to risks, issues, and other artifact documents. Use the Link Risks, Link Issues, and Link Documents functions to relate a task to this type of collaboration information. If a task has a linked Document, Issue, or Risk, then a graphic icon will appear within the information column that is marked with an "i" in the column header.

USING THE GANTT CHART

Use the Zoom-In, Zoom-Out, and Go-to-Task icons, positioned along the top of the view, to control the Gantt Chart display on the right half of the detail view. Then if you hover your mouse pointer over a particular Gantt Chart bar, an information pop-up will appear containing more data about the item.

You can reposition the vertical split boundary between the task details and the Gantt Chart parts of the display. Use your mouse to drag-and-drop the boundary, or double-click the vertical boundary to resize it to a column edge.

USING THE PRINT GRID OPTION

You can find the Print Grid option at the lower-left corner of the data-display window. If you click on this link, you are presented with a dialog allowing you to control the data and formats for information to be printed. You can select which columns to be output and the formats for each column to be printed.

USING THE EXPORT GRID TO EXCEL OPTION

Project Web Access 2003 also allows you to export the detailed data to a Microsoft Excel worksheet. You can find the Export Grid to Excel option at the lower-right corner of the data-display window. When you select this link, Microsoft Excel is started and the data details are automatically exported to Excel. The data is formatted into convenient outline groups, allowing you to interactively expand and contract the details as desired.

USING PROJECT CENTER BUILD TEAM

Project Web Access 2003 now has a new feature that allows you to attach resources to specific project schedules. You can use this convenient Project Center Build Team feature to add or remove resources from a project. This function works in a similar way to the Microsoft Project 2003 Professional menu Tools, Build Team from Enterprise.

→ The Project Center Build Team function attaches resources to a project but does *not* generally assign those resources to individual working tasks. **See** "Enterprise Resource Management," **p. 1069** for more details on using the Microsoft Project 2003 Professional functions to assign resources to tasks.

The following subjects are discussed within this section:

- **Build Team from list**—This set of functions allows you to manipulate the resources for the selected project.

- **Filter Enterprise Resources**—This is a special filtering mechanism that allows you search for those resources that match your filter criteria.
- **Change Booking Type**—You can establish whether a resource is attached to the project as either Committed or Proposed.
- **Availability**—You can examine resource availability to see if the resources you need actually have time to work on the project.

BUILD TEAM FROM LIST

When you open the Project Center Build Team function, you are presented with a screen with the following two list columns, as shown in Figure 26.5:

- **Filtered Enterprise Resources**—This shows the resources from the Enterprise Global Resource Pool. You can select one or more resources from this list.
- **Resource in the Project**—This shows those resources that are attached to the selected project. These resources become available for task-level assignments.

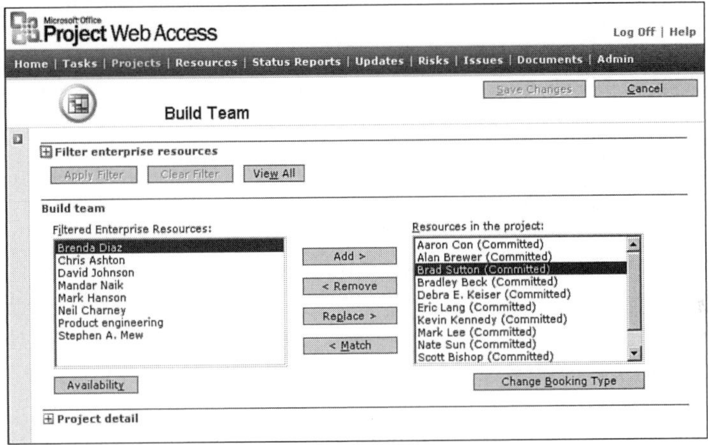

Figure 26.5 Use the Project Center Build Team function to see resources from the Enterprise Global Resource Pool and the selected project.

26

ADD, REMOVE, REPLACE, MATCH RESOURCES

You can manipulate which resources are attached to the project by using the following function buttons:

- **Add**—When you select one or more resources from the Filtered Enterprise Resources list, you can use the Add button to attach the Resources to the Project. The selected resources are then available for individual task assignments.
- **Remove**—If you select one or more resources from the Resources in the Project list, then you can use the Remove button to extract those resources from the project schedule. If those resources were assigned to project tasks, then they are completely removed from those working tasks.

- **Replace**—This function allows you to substitute an individual item selected in the Resources in the Project list with the resource selected from the Filtered Enterprise Resources list. The substitute resource is automatically assigned to any working tasks for the resource being replaced.
- **Match**—When you select an item from the Resources in the Project list, then click the Match button, the system automatically creates a filter and applies that filter to search the Enterprise Global Resource Pool. The resources matching the filter criteria are displayed within the Filtered Enterprise Resources list.

TIP

Use the Replace function to substitute actual resources from the Enterprise Global Resource Pool for Generic resources that were assigned to working tasks within the schedule.

CAUTION

If you attempt to remove or replace a resource that has previously reported Actual Work, the system will warn you that the resource cannot be removed from the project tasks. You must use Microsoft Project 2003 Professional manual resource manipulation techniques to substitute resources with reported Actual Work.

→ For details on how to change resource assignments, **see** "Assigning Resources to Tasks," **p. 365**.

FILTERING ENTERPRISE RESOURCES

26

When you select the Project Center Build Team function, you are presented with a screen allowing you to manipulate the resources for a given project. You can use the Filter Enterprise Resources function to search for resource matching your criteria.

For example, let's say you are a project manager who needs to find a resource who resides in the Central Iowa district of your company. You can use the Filter Enterprise Resources function, indicated by a small + sign, to enter search criteria to find a resource within the Enterprise Global Resource Pool. Refer to Figure 26.6.

The following steps illustrate the use of this feature:

1. You first click the + sign to open the Filter Enterprise Resources control table.
2. Select the Enterprise Outline code field and pick the RBS (Resource Breakdown Structure) item from the list.
3. Then select the USA.Central.Iowa from the Value drop-down list.
4. When you click the Apply Filter button the system automatically searches the Enterprise Global Resource Pool for resources that match your criteria. The results of that search are displayed within the Filtered Enterprise Resources list on the left side of the window.

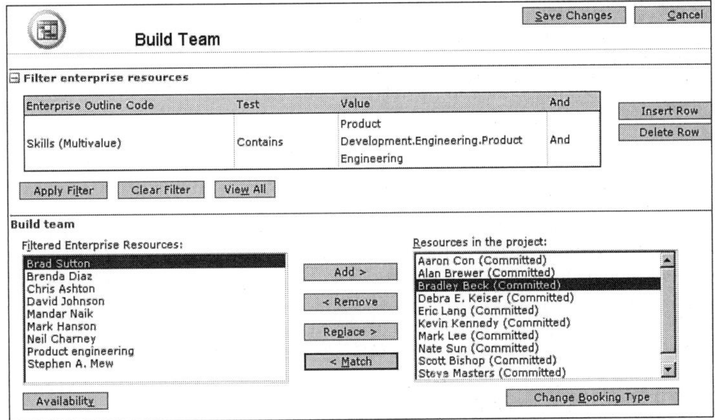

Figure 26.6
You can filter resources within the Project Center Build Team function.

TIP

> You can create complex filter criteria by adding more rows to the filter. You can also use the Match button to see different types of filter criteria the system automatically generates. You should experiment with this feature to understand how you can quickly search the entire Enterprise Global Resource Pool for resources you need.

CHANGE BOOKING TYPE

Microsoft Project 2003 Professional introduces a new feature that allows you to change the general booking condition of project resources. The following descriptions summarize this new feature:

- **Committed**—This default resource condition indicates that the individual resource is confirmed as a working resource for the selected project. Committed resources receive Task timesheet notices and can submit timesheet updates to the project manager.
- **Proposed**—This resource condition indicates that the selected resource is tentatively scheduled to work on project tasks. Proposed resources do not receive Task timesheet notices so they cannot submit actual work to the project manager.

The primary benefit of this Proposed "soft booking" type is to allow project managers to simulate the resource loading and cost impacts of selecting specific resources as part of the project team.

For example, say you are a project manager who is negotiating with resource managers to use certain resources for your project. You can use the Proposed condition for the resources to simulate the effects on your project and the workload on those resources. You then use the simulated "soft booking" analysis as a basis during your negotiations with appropriate staff managers. Once the resources are confirmed to work on the project, you can change the resource booking condition to Committed. This action enables Task timesheet assignments and updates.

CAUTION

> The booking condition for each resource is established for the entire project, not just for selected tasks. You cannot have a mix of Committed and Proposed conditions for a resource on different tasks within a specific project.

Viewing Resource Availability

The Project Center Build Team function also provides a quick link to view resource availability. You can select one or more resources from the Filtered Enterprise Resources and Resource in the Project. You can then click the Availability button to see a projection of time the resources can work.

For example, let's say you are a project manager who is trying to find appropriate resources to work on tasks within a project. You can use the Availability button within the Project Center Build Team function to get an overview of each resource workload. When you click the Availability button, a new window is displayed, allowing you to analyze each selected resource. You can examine overall availability and workload, in addition to viewing the daily details for each resource.

Opening and Using Multiple Enterprise Projects

NEW The Project Center now allows you to open and manipulate multiple projects within a single Microsoft Project 2003 Professional window. When you open multiple projects in this way, Microsoft Project creates a temporary composite project with all selected projects opened within the same window. This provides you several advantages for managing a group of projects:

- You can expand or contract the view of each open project, allowing you to inspect the details as needed.
- Tasks can be easily linked from one project to another, providing a logical association among project task activities.
- You can analyze the effects of changes across a group of projects to determine optimum scheduling conditions.

Open Multiple Projects from Project Center

If you want to open and edit multiple projects from a list shown in the Project Center, you simply select the projects and use the Open function as shown in Figure 26.7.

TIP

> If you want to pick multiple projects, hold down the Ctrl key on the keyboard while selecting the project row with the mouse. Each mouse click will select or clear an item from the project list.

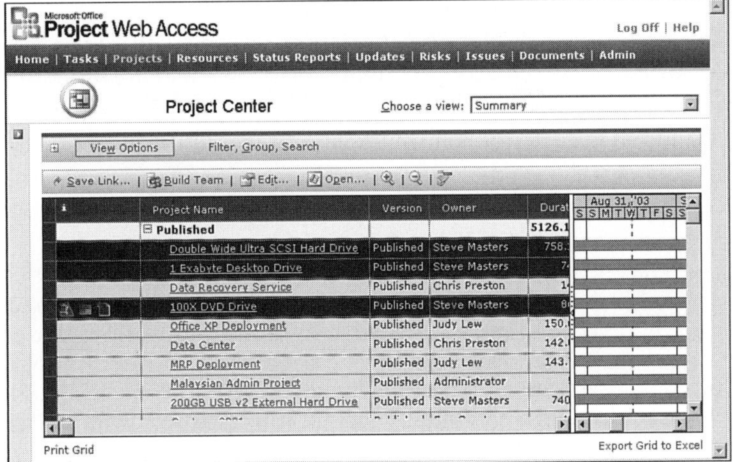

Figure 26.7
Use the Project Center to Open multiple projects for edit and review within Microsoft Project 2003 Professional.

You can also select multiple projects by using the Project Web Access Group and Filter functions to cluster projects within a header group. If you select the header group, all projects within that group will be selected.

After selecting multiple projects from the list, use the Open function to start Microsoft Project 2003 Professional with each project automatically opened.

CAUTION

Each project schedule will be opened with edit privileges unless another person has already opened a specific project. If a project has been previously opened, then that project will be opened as read-only within your Microsoft Project 2003 Professional session. Read-only projects are marked with an exclamation point within the graphical icon for the affected project. If a project is opened as read-only, then you cannot save changes, such as task links, made to that project.

If you select more than 10 projects to open then a caution window is displayed, as shown in Figure 26.8.

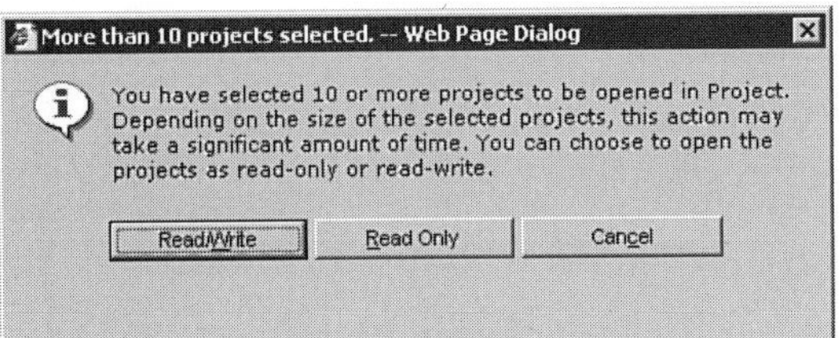

Figure 26.8
Caution message if opening more than 10 projects.

This caution message allows you to control how the projects are opened for Read/Write editing or just Read-Only review. If you open a large number of projects for Read/Write, then processing may take several minutes to check-out each project from the Project Server repository and deliver it to your Microsoft Project 2003 Professional session. Use the Read-Only mode if you are reviewing multiple projects and you do not want to save changes. If you select Cancel, then the projects are not opened and you are returned to the Project Web Access Project Center.

NOTE

> When you open multiple projects from Project Web Access Project Center, each project will be inserted into a temporary "master" project as if you had used the Microsoft Project 2003 Professional menu sequence Insert, Project. The system does *not* create a Master or Subproject relationship. When you exit Microsoft Project 2003 Professional, each opened project is saved as individual projects within the Project Server repository and the temporary "master" project is discarded. Task links across projects are retained if you chose to save changes for each affected project.

→ For detailed information on manually inserting projects, **see** "Creating Subprojects and Master Projects," **p. 612**.

OPEN OR DELETE PROJECTS FROM MICROSOFT PROJECT 2003 PROFESSIONAL

You can also use Microsoft Project 2003 Professional to open projects from the Project Server repository. Start Microsoft Project 2003 Professional and connect to Project Server, then use the menu sequence File, Open to see a list of projects stored within the Project Server repository. See Figure 26.9.

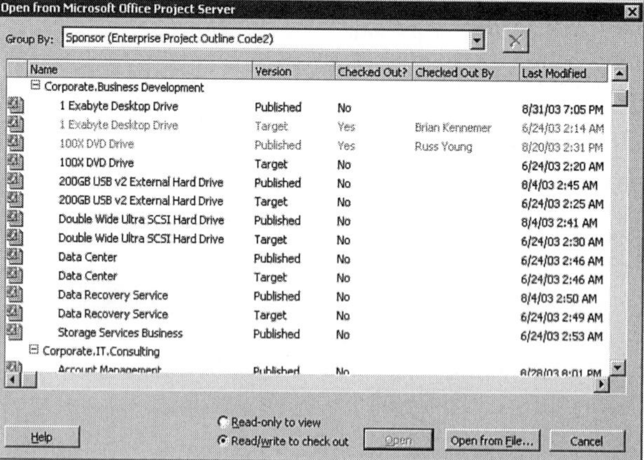

Figure 26.9 Use Microsoft Project 2003 Professional File, Open to see a list of projects stored within Project Server.

Use the Group By pull-down menu to organize projects based on the Enterprise Global Custom Project Codes associated with each project. See Figure 26.9. This display also shows who has checked-out projects and the last time each project was modified.

If you select a project from the list and use the mouse to click on the Permanently Delete Project button, shown as an X, then you are presented with a warning window. If you select Yes, then the project is permanently removed from the Project Server repository.

CAUTION

You should develop business processes to control when projects are permanently deleted from the Project Server database. A delete action will remove historical records of a deleted project and any associated resource assignments. The Project Web Access administrator can set permissions to control who has delete privileges.

➔ For detailed information on deleting projects and resources, **see** "System Administration," **p. 986**.

LINK TASKS ACROSS MULTIPLE PROJECTS

If you have opened multiple projects, you can create dependency links between tasks from one project to another. There are two methods for creating task links between projects:

- Use the typical Link Task function.
- Manually Key-in the task identifier as a predecessor or successor.

After tasks are linked from one project to another, you can see the results of those connections within the Project Web Access Project Center project detail views. See Figure 26.10.

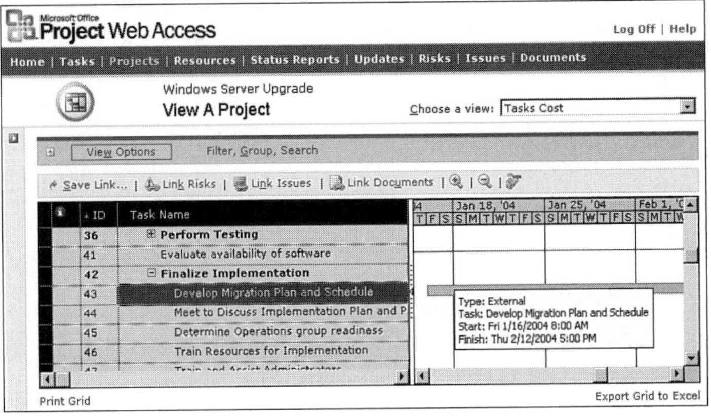

Figure 26.10
Project Center detail views show external project links in the Gantt Chart.

If you hover your mouse pointer over an externally linked task in the Gantt Chart, a pop-up information tip appears containing the task details.

USING THE LINK TASK FUNCTION FOR MULTIPLE PROJECTS

If you have used Project Web Access Project Center to open multiple projects, then you can easily link tasks between projects. Use the normal process whereby you select two tasks, one from each project, then apply the Task Link function.

You can inspect the cross-project task links by displaying the Predecessor and/or Successor columns within your project schedule. Cross-project task links use a special format to describe the links. See Figure 26.11.

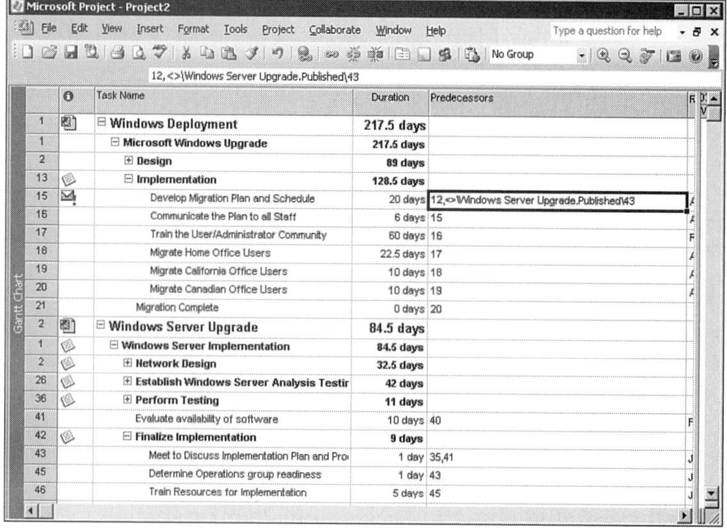

Figure 26.11
Cross-project task links within Microsoft Project 2003 Professional.

Although the format of this type of task link is unusual, the logical relationship remains the same, as if internal task links were created. Table 26.2 describes the format and meaning of this type of cross-project linked task as shown in the following example:

`Example: <>\Windows Server Upgrade.Published\43`

Table 26.2 Cross-Project Task Link Formats

Characters	Interpretation
`<>`	The project is located on the Project Server
`Windows Server Upgrade.Published`	The name of the project within the Project Server repository
`\43`	The task ID number of the linked task

This example can be interpreted to mean: Link to task number 43 within the project named Windows Server Upgrade.Published that is stored within the active Project Server database repository.

TIP

> You can manually key in this type of predecessor or successor if you know the exact task identifier and project name for the task to be linked. Use the menu sequence Tools, Links Between Projects to examine any external project task links.

NOTE

> Each time you open a project schedule that contains externally linked tasks, Microsoft Project temporarily opens the external project and uses the linked data to recomputed Start and Finish dates in addition to other information like Duration, Resource Units, and so forth.

MANUALLY KEY IN TASK IDENTIFIERS FOR MULTIPLE PROJECTS

You can also create cross-project task links by manually entering the appropriate phrase that points to a task within an external project.

Let's say there are two projects within your Project Server repository where you want to create special cross-project predecessor or successor relationships. You can use the Microsoft Project 2003 Professional menu File, Open for each project schedule. If you use the menu sequence Window, Arrange All you will see each project within a separate window.

After the project schedules are opened, then you can create cross-project task links by manually entering the project name and task number within the task ID column, as shown in the example within Figure 26.12.

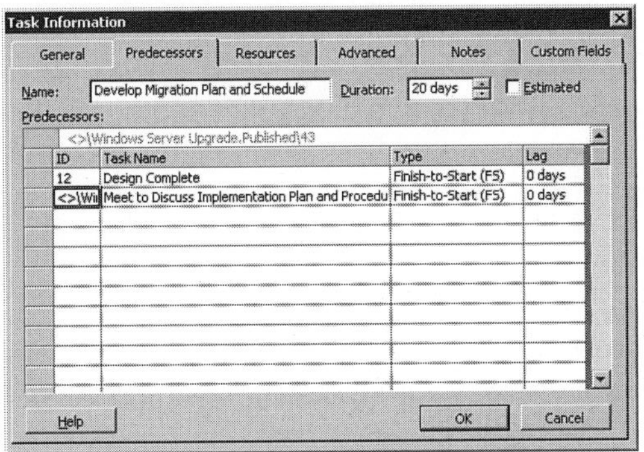

Figure 26.12
Manually entered cross-project task links within Microsoft Project 2003 Professional.

When you enter the character string in the format as shown in Figure 26.12, Microsoft Project automatically creates the cross-project task link and displays the connection within the Gantt Chart and other views.

If you later open a project schedule containing cross-project task links, you will notice that each externally linked task is displayed in a special color and/or font as defined within the menu sequence Format, Text Styles, and External Tasks. The default is a grayed-out task row that contains the appropriate text of the externally linked tasks.

CAUTION

> If you open a project with external task links and you delete such a link, the change is *only* reflected within the opened project. The deleted link does *not* take effect for the external project until that project is opened and saved.

➔ For more information on creating and using task links, **see** "Understanding Dependency Links," **p. 177**.

CHECK-IN PROJECTS FROM PROJECT CENTER

NEW The Project Center now allows project managers with permissions to "check-in" project schedules that may have become locked due to network or other failures. This new feature has the advantage of allowing project managers to correct problems that have occurred for projects they own, without disturbing the Project Web Access system administrators.

If the Project Web Access administrators have granted a project manager the appropriate permissions, then the project manager can use the Project Center menu Check in My Projects function. When this menu function is used, the project manager is presented with a screen to select a locked project they own and check-in to free the lock.

When you choose to check-in a project, the system issues a warning like the one shown in Figure 26.13.

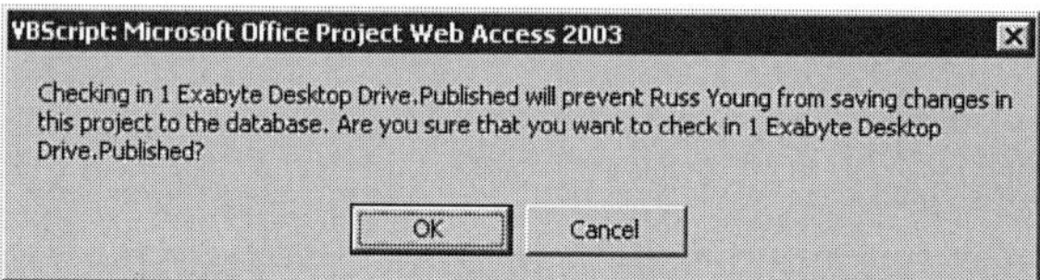

Figure 26.13 Check-in My Projects warning message.

If you proceed with the check-in action, then the database lock is released so the project schedule can be opened for edits.

26

CAUTION

If you check-in a project schedule that is being actively edited by another person, the system prevents that person from saving changes. See Figure 26.14.

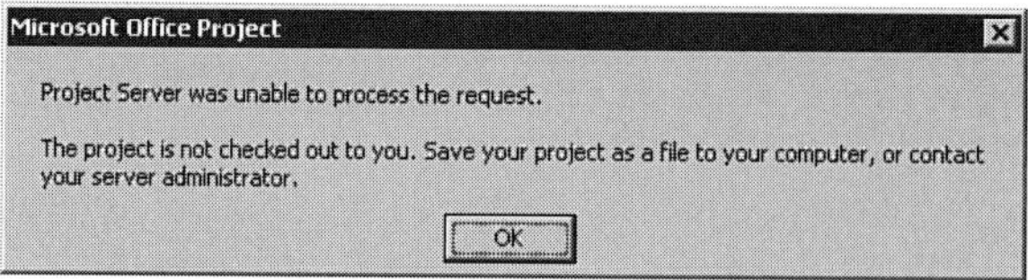

Figure 26.14 Error message after an attempt to save a project schedule that has been checked-in during an active edit session.

USING ADMINISTRATIVE PROJECTS

NEW The Project Center allows you to create and manage Administrative projects that are used to assign and track "non-project" activities outside the normal bounds of particular projects. The concept of non-working time, which was used within Microsoft Project Server 2002, is no longer used within Microsoft Office Project 2003. Administrative projects are now used to track this type of activity.

There are several advantages to using Administrative projects:

- All team members can use a common approach to report non-project time.
- Individual working projects can eliminate the need to include these types of activities within the Work Breakdown Structure (WBS).
- Administrative project resource assignment information is used during the calculation of OLAP cube data displayed within the Project Center and Resource Center Portfolio Analyzer views.

Administrative projects can be created using any of three strategies:

- Use the Project Web Access Project Center Manage Administrative Projects menu.
- Use the Microsoft Project 2003 Professional menu sequence File, Save As, Administrative Project check box.
- Load a predefined Administrative project template.

Each of these techniques creates a special type of project schedule that is designed to use particular administrative project scheduling and time-tracking methods. These special features can be summarized as follows:

- Tasks are defined as Fixed Duration, not Effort Driven, for scheduling.
- Project Web Access Tasks timesheet data always uses direct time entry, Hours of Work Done per Time Period, rather than %Complete or remaining work methods.
- Administrative projects appear at the bottom of the team member timesheet view.
- Administrative project tasks appear as categories selectable within the Notify Your Manager of Time You Will Not Be Available for Project Work.

Except for these special conditions, Administrative projects are developed and maintained like any other project schedule.

TIP

> Consider creating a standard business process whereby you name Administrative projects so they appear in certain locations within the Project Center summary views. For example, if you prefix all Administrative project names with "ZZ" they will automatically appear at the bottom of Project Center summary views. Also consider creating Enterprise Global Custom Project Codes that reflect the nature of Administrative projects, so people easily group and filter Administrative projects within various lists.

ANALYZING ENTERPRISE PROJECTS

Chapter 24 identifies several roles for users of Microsoft Project Professional 2003, including portfolio managers, project managers, resource managers, and executives.

This section describes how executives, portfolio managers, project managers, and others use Project Web Access Portfolio Analyzer and Portfolio Modeler functions to analyze project data and provide answers to business questions such as the following:

- Which resources are working on projects?
- Which resources are overloaded or have excess capacity?
- What happens to project delivery if we change resource assignments?
- How much actual work has occurred across a portfolio of projects?
- What are the predicted future costs of multiple projects within corporate initiatives?

Through Project Web Access, a user can see the project and resource information for which he or she has the appropriate permissions.

When reading about the Project Center analysis functions, keep in mind the following:

- Each view or report provides part of the information you need, so don't try to obtain all the information you need from a single view.
- You should look at the same data from a variety of perspectives to make sure that what you think the data is telling you is correct and/or reasonable. You should look for data that disproves any conclusion that you've come to. If you can't find any, then your conclusions might be right.
- Your job might be to have enough data to ask the right questions, rather than to answer those questions. For example, as an executive, you might use the portfolio modeler to determine that resource bottlenecks exist. It might fall to a portfolio manager, resource managers, and/or project managers to resolve the issue. Depending on your role, then, you might require access to the tools and data available in Microsoft Project Professional 2003 as well as the views in Project Web Access.
- Microsoft Project 2003 Professional and Project Web Access provide a great deal of power and flexibility in terms of data generation, capture, and analysis. You should use the information in this section as a place to begin your exploration.

The primary difference between the Portfolio Modeler and the Portfolio Analyzer is that the Portfolio Modeler provides a broad view of the portfolio data, whereas the Portfolio Analyzer provides the detailed data required to "slice and dice" the portfolio data to the level of detail required. Table 26.3 lists additional differences between the Portfolio Modeler and Portfolio Analyzer.

TABLE 26.3 PORTFOLIO ANALYZER AND PORTFOLIO MODELER COMPARISON

Comparison Area	Portfolio Analyzer	Portfolio Modeler
Data source	Portfolio Analyzer uses data from the selected SQL Server OLAP cube.	Portfolio Modeler gets data directly from the Project Server database.
Data currency	The data in a Portfolio Analyzer view is current as of the date and time the OLAP cube was generated.	The data in a Portfolio Modeler view is current as of the date and time the model was generated or refreshed.
Data specification	The data in a Portfolio Analyzer view always includes the Published version of all projects in the Project Server, as well as all resources in the enterprise resource pool, when the OLAP cube is generated.	You can specify which projects (and their versions) to include in a portfolio model. You can specify which resources to include in a portfolio model.
	You can specify date ranges for the data included in the Portfolio Analyzer.	You can specify different resource modeling options for each project included in the model (for example, you might choose to have all projects in the model be as-is, except for a new project to examine the impact of the new project on the current project portfolio).
Modeling tools	The SQL Server 2000 Analysis tools are available through Project Web Access.	The Analyze option in the Modeler is available through Project Web Access.

➔ **See** "Building OLAP Cubes and Updating Resource Tables," **p. 994**, for the parameters that are available when creating OLAP cubes, and **see** "Creating New Portfolio Models" **p. 1056**, for the parameters available when specifying portfolio models.

ANALYZING PROJECTS IN THE PORTFOLIO ANALYZER

The Portfolio Analyzer gives executives and managers easy access to summary information about the Published versions of projects and resources. The data can be grouped in a variety of ways, and the user can choose which data and which grouping to display in the view, by using PivotTable controls like those in Microsoft Excel.

Before you can look at a Portfolio Analyzer view, the administrator must first create the view.

NOTE

> The data and functionality available in each Portfolio Analyzer view depends on the data and options that the administrator has allowed when creating the view. Your ability to alter Portfolio Analyzer view also depends on having an Office 2003 family application installed on your system. The examples within this section assume you have sufficient privileges to modify view formats within the Portfolio Analyzer and that you have an Office 2003 family application installed on your computer.

To demonstrate the power and value of the Portfolio Analyzer, this section continues using the Microsoft-supplied sample database that can be easily installed by using installation wizard on the Project Server software media.

Let's assume you are an executive and you want to evaluate how projects are performing to projections within the Information Technology organization. You are particularly interested in workload projects versus budgeted work for projects during a certain fiscal quarter.

You can begin understanding how the projects are performing by using the project Web Access Project Center, Analyze Projects in Portfolio Analyzer function. When you select the view called IT Workload Comparison to Plan, you see a graphic chart similar to the one that appears in Figure 26.15.

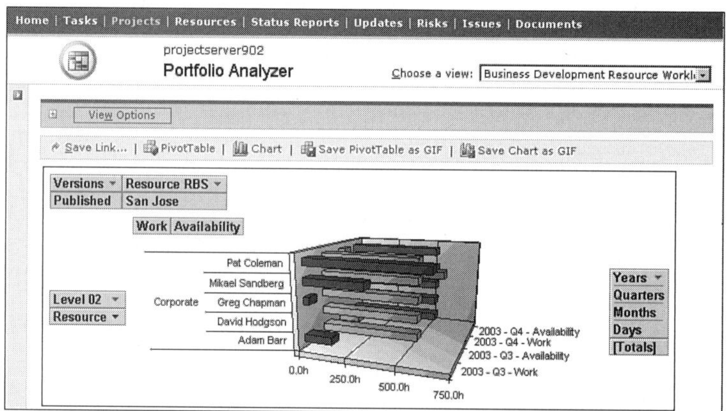

Figure 26.15
You can use the Portfolio Analyzer to examine portfolio data.

26

USING PORTFOLIO ANALYZER VIEWS

Before we begin understanding what the data in Figure 26.15 tells us, let's discuss various features available on this screen.

- **View Options**—If you have been given permission, you can use the Show Field List option, also shown in the toolbar, to manipulate the various data fields. The Show Toolbars option allows you additional controls to manipulate the display and export data to Microsoft Excel.
- **Save a Link**—Allows you to create a personal link so you can quickly return to the Portfolio Analyzer view.

- **PivotTable**—This button enables you to analyze information by sorting, grouping, filtering, and pivoting on data in a spreadsheet format, similar to Microsoft Excel.
- **Chart**—Charts graphically display information from the PivotTable.
- **Combination PivotTable and chart**—Data is presented in both a PivotTable and chart format. The data is the same for each view, so actions you take in one view immediately affect the other view content.
- **Save as GIF**—Allows you to save the graphical representation of the chart or pivot table into a graphic GIF file that can be inserted into another application like Microsoft Word or PowerPoint.
- **Drop-down lists**—You can control what data is shown by using the data field drop-down lists such as Versions, Resource Department, and Years, as shown within Figure 26.15. When you select a drop-down list, you can then click on the data options you want to view. When you click OK, the chart and/or pivot table views are immediately updated to include the data you chose.

CHANGING PORTFOLIO ANALYZER VIEW CONTENT

When you use the Portfolio Analyzer to view project information, you can manipulate certain viewing formats if the Project Web Access administrator has given you permission.

For example, if you start with a Portfolio Analyzer view like the one shown in Figure 26.15, then you can add or remove data fields. Follow these steps to show additional information within the IT Workload Comparison to Plan view:

1. Change the view so you see the PivotTable only.
2. Use the View Options tab to click the Show Toolbars button.
3. From the Toolbars buttons, click on the Field List item to display all of the defined data fields available for this OLAP cube. See Figure 26.16.
4. Now use the mouse to drag and drop the data item called Project Location to the area of the pivot table header called Drop Column Fields Here. This action adds the Project Location data to the pivot table and chart.
5. Close the Field List window so you can clearly see the new data display.
6. Next use the drop-down arrow on the Project Location group to set only the USA West item.

TIP

> Uncheck the All item at the top of the list to clear all settings, then use the + sign to expand the list so you can click the specific item(s) you want.

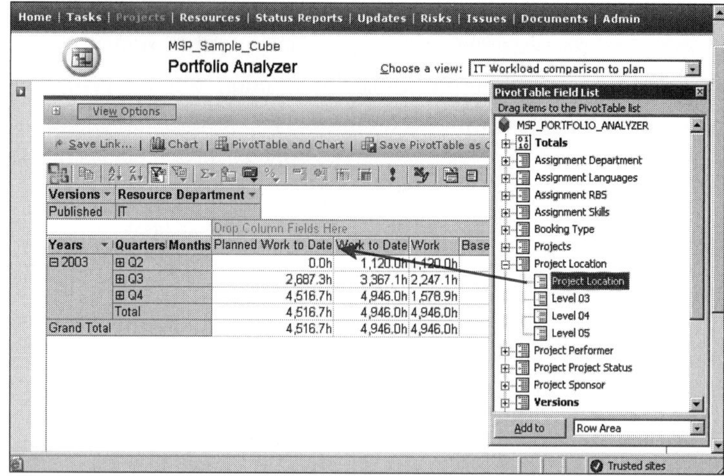

Figure 26.16
Use the Field List to add or remove data fields from a Portfolio Analyzer view.

7. Now manipulate the data fields to display only a single fiscal quarter. Your view should look something like Figure 26.17.

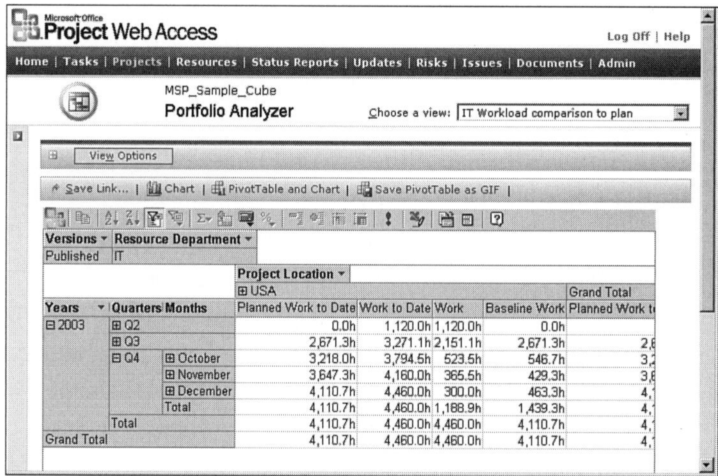

Figure 26.17
Manipulate the Portfolio Analyzer fields to show the information you need.

The pivot table data shown in Figure 26.17 allows you to better understand the workload characteristics of the projects within the Corporate Information Technologies group in the USA West sector. If you select the PivotTable and Chart viewing option, then you can see the graphic chart and numerical data within the same window as shown in Figure 26.18.

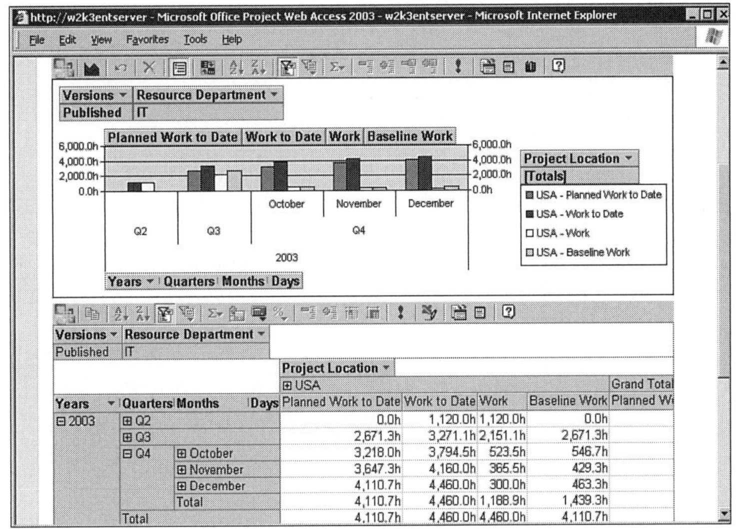

Figure 26.18
Use Portfolio Analyzer views to analyze complex project performance information.

TIP

Changes you make to the Portfolio Analyzer view information are not permanent. By default, the columns and viewing content are reset to the original format when you re-enter the Portfolio Analyzer functions. Use the Save Link function to create a shortcut that recovers the viewing format you modified.

USING PORTFOLIO ANALYZER TO ASSESS PROJECTS

Managers who have permission to view Portfolio Analyzer data can use the available views to assess how projects are progressing compared to projections. Access to this type of data is a powerful management tool that enables organization management to better predict problems in the future.

26

Let's return to the scenario we started at the beginning of this section: You are an organization executive who needs to determine conditions about Information Technology projects. We can use Figure 26.18 as a reference for our analysis.

So what are some of the conclusions or questions we can derive from reviewing data in Figure 26.18?

- The total Baseline Work of project in the IT USA West sector for fiscal quarter 4 in 2003 shows 1,439 hours. The total Work for the same period is 1,189 hours so projected work is lower than baseline for this quarter.
- The Work column shows a decreasing load from October, through November and December. This tends to indicate the organization will need more work to do as the year comes to a close. As the executive in charge, you should begin planning for more project activity or a staffing redistribution.

- The cumulative work in the Work to Date column is greater than the cumulated baseline work shown in the Planned Work to Date column. This tends to validate a general cost overrun from the expected baseline levels for the entire year.

TIP

> You can learn more about the calculations of each pivot table column if you click on the column header, for instance Planned Work to Date in Figure 26.18, then right-click with the mouse and select the Commands and Options menu item. Then you can examine the Calculations tab to see the column formula. Be careful not to accidentally corrupt these formulas.

- One key question from this analysis is, "Which projects are causing the overall workload overrun?" This clearly needs more investigation by using other Portfolio Analyzer views and various other Project Center views. Once you identify projects with problems, you probably need to discuss the issues with the project managers.
- Another key question is, "What projects will we assign people to work on near the end of the year?" If there are no other projects that need attention, then you probably need to redistribute staff to avoid real staff reductions.

Clearly, the Portfolio Analyzer views provide managers a great deal of information and ability to predict future problems. When problems are spotted early in the project or budget lifecycle, solutions can be determined before the problems turn into disasters.

Modeling Projects with the Portfolio Modeler

26

With portfolio modeling you can interactively simulate changes to projects or resource staffing and immediately view the impact of those changes on a group of projects without altering the actual schedules involved. This is known as *modeling* changes to schedules. See the section, "Transferring Portfolio Models to Actual Schedules," later in this chapter, for information on how to alter actual schedules to match results of modeling simulations.

NOTE

> For the purposes of this chapter, portfolio *modeling* is defined as creating information about a project schedule or group of schedules from data about those schedules. Applying user-controlled parameters to test the effect of the changes on the models can simulate changes to overall duration and resource usage.
>
> For example, one model might show the results (in terms of schedule duration and resource utilization) if Project ABC is the highest priority in the portfolio and the other projects are of lesser priority. A different model might show the results if Project XYZ is the same priority as the other projects in the portfolio.

Modeling different project and resource scenarios provides a fast and powerful way to find overallocated resources, determine the schedule feasibility of new projects, and identify the best staffing strategies to support projects across an organization.

You can use the Portfolio Modeler to answer questions such as

- What is the organization's work capacity within a specific calendar period?
- What resource bottlenecks are associated with multiple projects using the same resources?
- What is the effect on project schedules if resource skills are overused or underutilized?
- What is the impact to your project portfolio if you add a new project to the portfolio?

To answer these questions, you can use the following general approach to analyzing portfolios of projects:

1. Use the Project Center Tracking views and Grouping tools to review key metrics about each project within a portfolio list.
2. Create an "as-is" portfolio model that shows the current combined state of the projects within the portfolio list. With Portfolio Modeler models, you see each project as one line on a Gantt Chart; however, the Gantt bars are color-coded based on resource allocation over the calendar period. Use this model to determine if the projects within the portfolio model are likely to have schedule delivery or overallocated resources.
3. Create an "optimized" portfolio model to determine what happens to each project in the portfolio is changed restructure workloads on resources. *Optimized* means that the portfolio-modeling tool will substitute an available resource with matching resource attributes, from the model's resource pool, for an overallocated resource in the schedule.

NOTE

> **Optimizing the resources may cause each project's scheduled end date to be significantly delayed, because there may be resource bottlenecks across the portfolio of projects.**

4. Create variations of the project portfolio models, altering characteristics such as project priority, using resources within a set of projects, and so on.
5. Compare the results of the portfolio models to determine which projects need further detailed attention.
6. Discuss the modeling results with appropriate project managers to determine how the individual project details can be changed to better optimize project schedules and resource utilization.

You can access the portfolio modeling features by logging in to Microsoft Project Web Access, clicking Projects, and then selecting the Model Projects with Portfolio Modeler link.

Any existing portfolio models are listed on the initial Portfolio Modeler page, as in the Figure 26.19 examples.

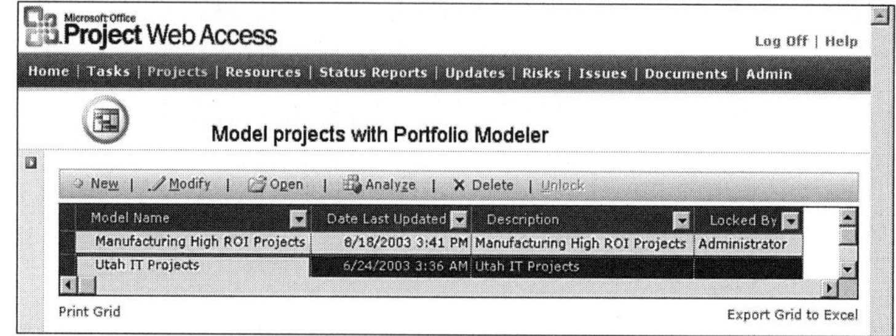

Figure 26.19
List of defined models within the Portfolio Modeler page.

From this screen you can add, open, modify, analyze, delete, or unlock portfolio models. Each of these functions is described in the following sections.

Creating New Portfolio Models

When you look at the list of projects by using a typical Project Center Gantt Chart views, you can see the current schedules for the each project. How viable are these schedules?

To find out how viable these schedules are from a resource allocation perspective, you can create a new portfolio model containing a set of projects you want to analyze.

To create the new portfolio model you need to follow these general steps:

1. Select the New tab on the Model Projects with Portfolio Modeler page, as shown in Figure 26.19.
2. Give your new model a name that implies the general purpose of the model and provide a description.
3. Select the projects to be included in the model, as shown in the Figure 26.20 example.

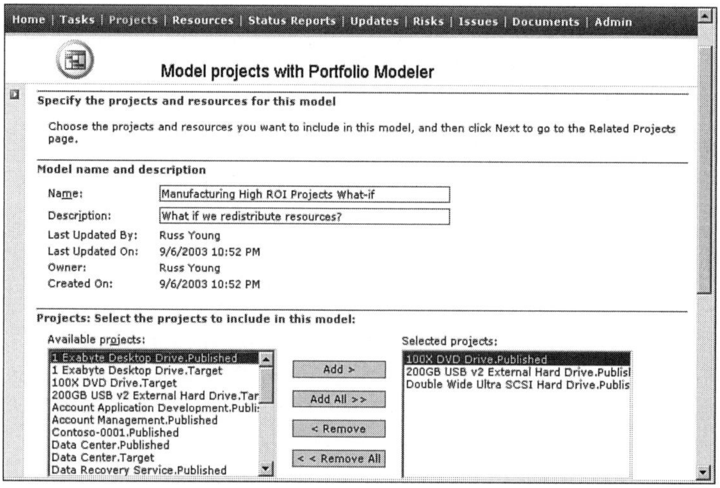

Figure 26.20
New portfolio model as "What-if?"

4. Then select how the model should consider resources.

   For some types of modeling, you need to choose from one of these three mutually exclusive ways to define the resources available to the modeler when creating the model:

   - **Include Resources in the Model's Projects**—This option limits the modeler's resource substitution to the list of resources already attached to the projects selected for the model.
   - **Include Resources at or below RBS Level**—This option limits the modeler's resource substitution to the list of resources associated with the specified RBS level, where RBS is the Resource Breakdown Structure.
   - **Include Resources Specified Below**—This option limits the modeler's resource substitution to the specific list of resources selected from the Enterprise Global Resource Pool.

5. After you have specified the projects and resources for the model, click the Next button at the bottom of the page.
6. As shown in Figure 26.21, the second step in creating a new portfolio model is to decide which, if any, additional related projects to include in the model.

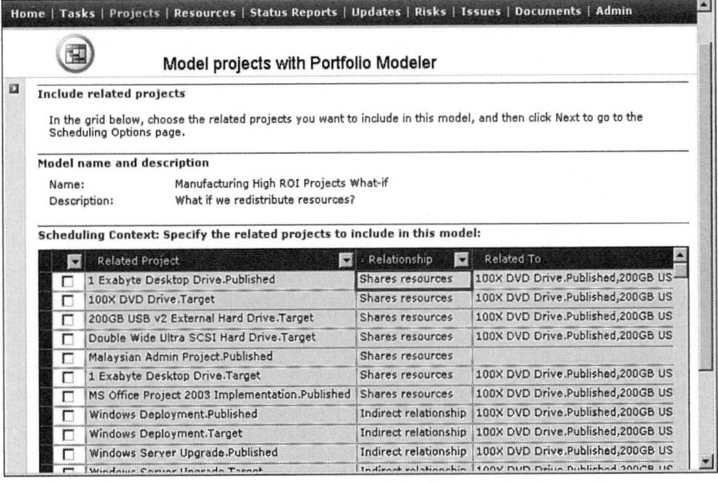

Figure 26.21
If you select additional projects, then the resource and schedule data from those projects will affect the projects within the model.

The Relationship column specifies whether the related project shares an external dependency (that is, projects with task links across projects) or shares resources with the projects in the Related To column. Click Next to continue defining the model.

7. Define the three scheduling options—Priority, Scheduling Options, and Start No Earlier Than Date—as shown in Figure 26.22. These options are described as follows:

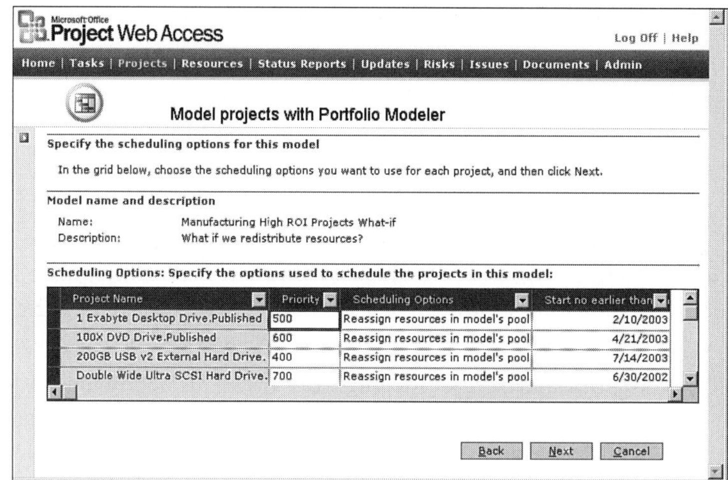

Figure 26.22
Choose the scheduling options for the model.

- **Priority**—Overallocated resources in higher-priority projects are substituted for first, where 1000 is the highest priority.
- **Scheduling Options**—The Scheduling Options define how the modeler is to use the resources available to the modeler. The four scheduling options and their definitions are as follows:

  Keep Dates and Assignments—Specifies that task start and end dates for resource assignments do not change when you create a model. This setting prevents the modeler from changing a project's resource assignments.

  Use Current Assignments—Specifies that resource assignments do not change; however, task start and end dates may change as the assigned workload is redistributed.

  Reassign Resources in Project—Specifies that the modeler can reassign resources within each project only. No resources from outside the project are used.

  Reassign Resource in Model's Pool—Allows the modeler to reassign resources, using any of the resources that you have included in the model's resource pool. The modeler uses RBS and other Enterprise Global resource codes for matching purposes.

  You can specify different scheduling options for each project in a model.
- **Start No Earlier Than Date**—Specifies the earliest date on which a project can begin for the model.

8. After you have selected the scheduling options for your model, click Next to create the model and return to the initial Portfolio Modeler screen.

You can now use the new model to analyze project performance and compare against other models you may create.

OPENING PORTFOLIO MODELS

To open an existing portfolio model, select the Project Center Projects tab, then Model Projects with Portfolio Manager. Next, select a model and click Open.

As shown in Figure 26.23, the opened model screen displays projects using color-coded Gantt Chart bars to identify the degree to which project resources are overallocated. The Gantt Chart bars can display red, yellow, or green to show the time periods where the total resource demand meets or exceeds the available capacity. For each time period

- **Green**—If the workload demand is less than the resource capacity, the bar is set to green.
- **Yellow**—If the demand exceeds the capacity by less than 10%, the bar is set to yellow.
- **Red**—If the demand exceeds the capacity by greater than 10%, the bar is set to red.

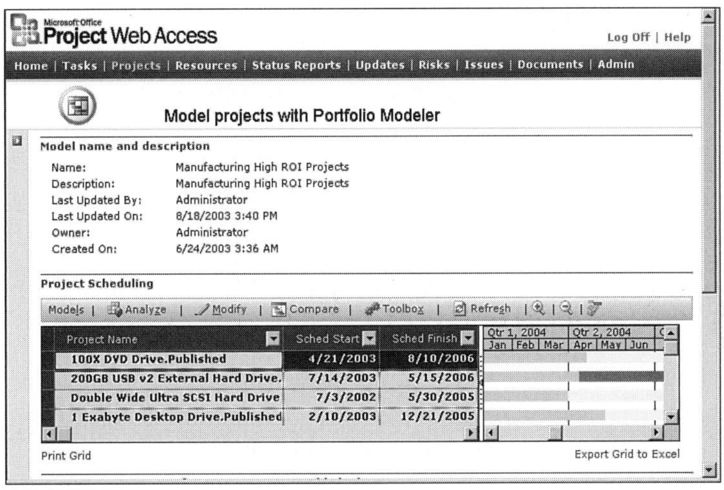

Figure 26.23 Example of Manufacturing High ROI Projects model showing resource overallocation Gantt Chart.

You can analyze or modify a portfolio model from the initial Model Projects with Portfolio Modeler screen, but you must open a model before you can use the Compare function or use the Model Property toolbox.

The Portfolio Modeler toolbox allows you to modify some of the model's parameters without going through all the screens associated with modifying a model. See the section, "Using the Portfolio Model Toolbox to Change Properties," later in this chapter, for details.

When you open a portfolio model, you see a portfolio model Gantt Chart and you also see a Resource Assignments chart, as shown in Figure 26.24.

26

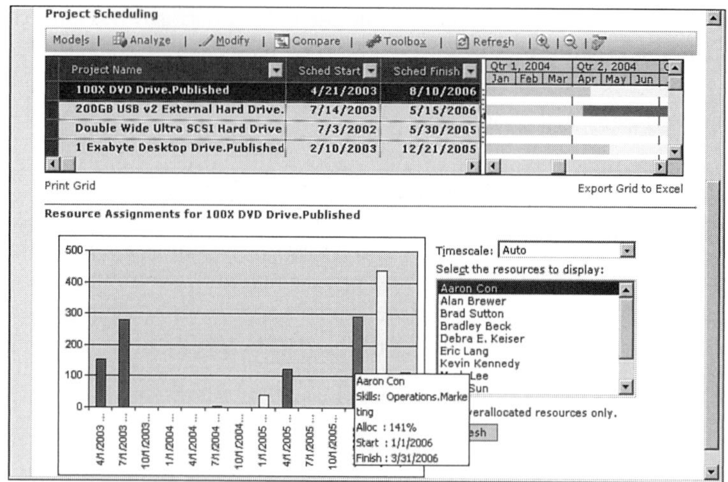

Figure 26.24
Analyze projects and resource allocation.

CAUTION

> **The Resource Assignments for Selected Project chart displays resource availability for one project only, the project selected in the Gantt Chart, and not for the portfolio of projects in the model.**

Each graphic bar in the Resource Assignments chart represents one resource or more resources, and the scale used on the chart's vertical axis represents the total number of work hours, based on the timescale.

The Timescale drop-down list box controls the units for each period on the graph. The options are Day, Week, Month, Quarter, Year, and Auto. The option that is selected defines the timescale at the bottom of the chart. The Auto option allows the Portfolio Modeler to determine which of the timescale options provides the best view and granularity.

If you use the mouse pointer to hover over graph bars in the Resource Assignments chart, a ScreenTip window displays detailed information about the resource represented by a graph bar, as shown in Figure 26.24.

The block representing each resource for a time period can appear in red, yellow, or green, to show the time periods where the demand for that resource meets or exceeds the resource's available capacity, usually the Max Units setting. The color coding is the same as the color coding used with the Portfolio Modeler's Gantt Chart.

Using the Portfolio Model Toolbox to Change Properties

The advantage of using the Portfolio Model Property toolbox is that you can bring up the toolbox while you have a model open, make changes to a project in the model, and then view the changes you have made immediately after you apply the changes. The disadvantage is that you can't modify all of a model's parameters with the toolbox.

To use the toolbox, open a portfolio model, select a project, and then click the Toolbox icon. Figure 26.25 shows the portfolio model parameters that can be changed via the toolbox. Each of these parameters is described in detail in the section "Creating New Portfolio Models," earlier in this chapter.

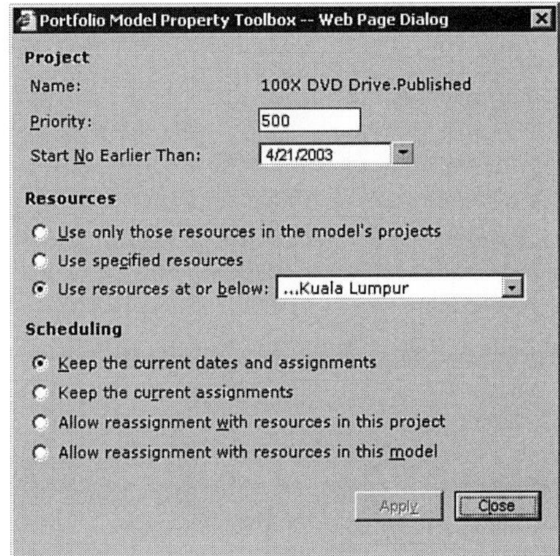

Figure 26.25
When you click the Toolbox icon, the Model Property Toolbox is displayed, prepopulated with the model's current parameter values.

Click Apply when you have finished making changes in the toolbox to see the changes applied to the open model.

COMPARING PORTFOLIO MODELS

After you create portfolio models, you often want to compare models to see what effects changes produce.

To compare models, you need to open a portfolio model and click the Compare icon. Figure 26.26 shows an example of two models selected for comparison.

NOTE

> The order in which the portfolio models are selected is the order in which they are displayed.

After you have selected the models to be compared and their order of display, click OK to see the portfolio models compared.

When you select individual projects within the compared models, you can see the resource workloads within the bar graph as shown in Figure 26.27. Select multiple resources from the list and click Refresh to view a composite graph with each selected resource.

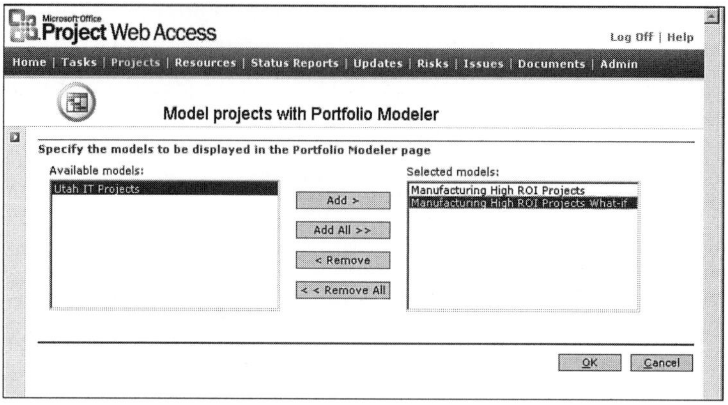

Figure 26.26
Two portfolio models are selected for comparison.

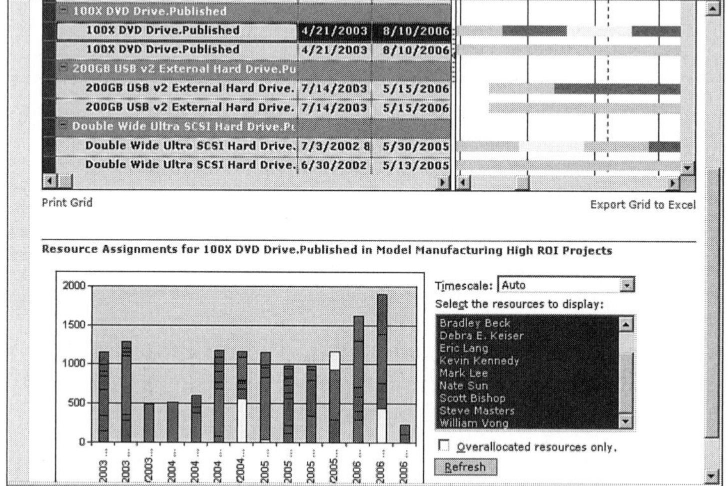

Figure 26.27
Review workload for multiple resources.

Figure 26.27 shows several resources that are overallocated for the indicated calendar times. Figure 26.28 shows how the comparison model used substituting new resources for those that were overloaded, so the workload has been redistributed. Notice how two new resources, without highlights in the list, have been selected to work in place of overloaded resources.

Modifying Portfolio Models

After you have created a portfolio model, you might want to change its parameters or create a new model, using the parameters of an existing model.

There are two ways to modify an existing portfolio model: by going through the Model Projects with Portfolio Modeler screens again or by using the Toolbox property (see the section "Opening Portfolio Models", earlier in this chapter).

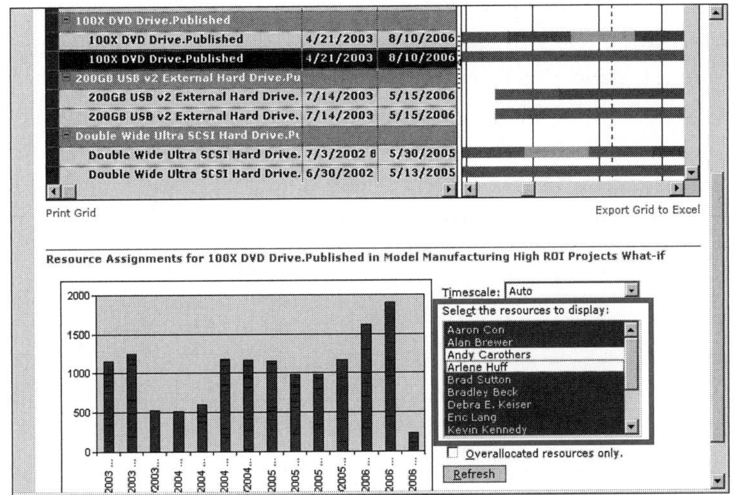

Figure 26.28 Workload can be redistributed to new resources.

The model-modification process prompts you with the same configuration screens that are used to create a model (see the section "Creating New Portfolio Models," earlier in this chapter), with the current parameters remembered.

You can modify the desired parameters as you move through the model definition screens to generate a model with the same name or a different name.

Using Portfolio Model Analyze Feature

You can use the Portfolio Modeler's Analyze feature to quickly and easily identify resource availability and bottlenecks for projects in a portfolio model.

26

NOTE

Don't confuse the Portfolio Modeler's Analyze feature with the Portfolio Analyzer (see the section "Analyzing Projects in the Portfolio Analyzer," earlier in this chapter).

Selecting a portfolio model and clicking the Analyze icon displays the details of the selected model. The model analysis screen provides useful information about the model you are working with. It also provides a chart that plots resource demand, capacity, and utilization for the entire model over time, and it tells you the scheduling options used per project to create the model.

The model analysis screen consists of four parts:

- **Model Name and Description**—This shows the name, description, owner, creation date, and last update.
- **Summary Statistics**—Summarizes statistics, with Shortest Schedule and Modeled Schedule for comparison.

- **The Demand/Capacity/Utilization Chart**—The Demand/Capacity/Utilization chart contains three separate line graphs, each line on the graph showing a cumulative value from the start of the model.
- **Model Scheduling Options**—This displays the scheduling parameters used to create the model for each project that is included in the model.

Use this information as the basis for discussion with project managers regarding detailed changes needed within affected project schedules.

Transferring Portfolio Models to Actual Schedules

Portfolio Modeler results are a starting point for making detailed changes to each project schedule. The project managers can use the general portfolio model information to change resources by using the Microsoft Project 2003 Professional Resource Substitution Wizard.

Table 26.4 compares the Portfolio Modeler and Resource Substitution Wizard tools.

→ For information on the Resource Substitution Wizard's scheduling options, **see** "Using the Resource Substitution Wizard," **p. 1110**.

Table 26.4 Comparison of Portfolio Modeler and Resource Substitution Wizard Scheduling Options

Portfolio Modeler Scheduling Option	Related Resource Substitution Wizard Scheduling Option	Differences Between Scheduling Options
Reassign Resource in Model's Pool	Resources in Pool	None. Both reassign resources from the resource pool you've established for the model or the wizard.
Keep Start/End Dates	Don't include the project when running the wizard	None. Both cause resource assignments and task start and end dates to not change.
Use Current Assignments	The Demand feature	None. Both cause resources assigned to tasks to not change; however, task start and end dates may change.
Reassign Resources	Use Resources in Project	None. Both reassign in Project resources within each project only. No resource substitutions occur from outside each project's resources.

REFRESH PORTFOLIO MODELER VIEWS

Project managers who have permissions to use the Portfolio Modeler functions can now use a new feature called Refresh to update model information. When you select this option, a caution window is displayed as shown in Figure 26.29.

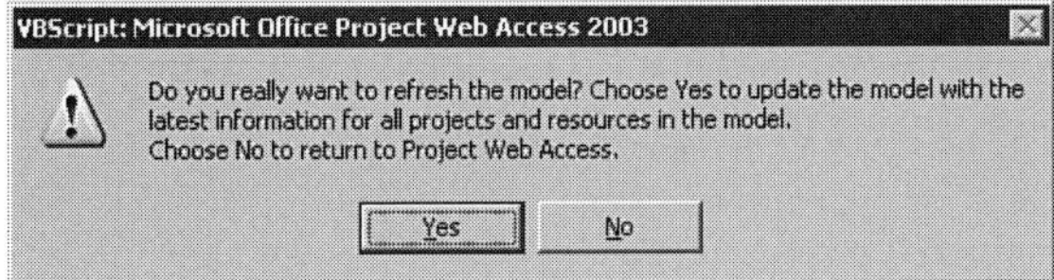

Figure 26.29
Caution message during Refresh action request.

If you select Yes then modeling conditions for the selected model are saved, recomputed, and updated to the Project Server database. This update involves opening the projects and resources within the model and using that information to recompute the entire model view.

NOTE

> The model refresh action is computer intensive and may take several minutes to complete the update. General Project Web Access users may see a system slowdown during the update timeframe.

USING ENTERPRISE TEMPLATES

Microsoft Project has provided schedule templates as an easy way for project managers to quickly create new schedules. With Microsoft Project Professional 2003, project managers can acquire and use enterprise templates from a Project server as well as project templates that are available on a user's personal file systems.

Project templates and enterprise templates are identical in terms of capability; their only difference lies in how they are stored and therefore how easy they are to maintain for all users in an organization. Personal project templates are stored as `.MPT` files on a computer's file system. Enterprise templates are stored on a Project server, and changes made to enterprise templates are automatically given to Professional edition users when they open the template.

CAUTION

> You can create and save your own local project templates with enterprise resources, generic resources, enterprise outline codes, and enterprise custom fields in them. If you do, be warned that as codes, fields, views, and resources are changed in the Enterprise Global template and the enterprise resource pool, those changes will most likely be updated in the enterprise templates but not in your local project templates.

Using enterprise templates along with the Resource Substitution Wizard, the Team Builder, or the Assign Resources dialog box is the quickest and easiest way to create a new schedule and add resources to tasks. All you have to do is open the enterprise template and you are ready to add the enterprise resources to the schedule and automatically assign the resource to the schedule's tasks.

→ If you need a new enterprise template, talk to your portfolio manager or administrator. If you are the portfolio manager or administrator and need detailed information on how to create enterprise templates, **see** "Managing the Enterprise Global Template," **p. 1007**.

To open an enterprise template, select File, New, select From My Computer, and then click the Enterprise Templates tab (see Figure 26.30).

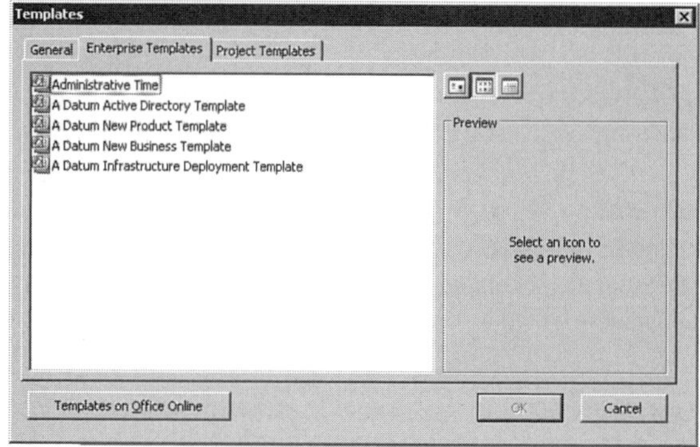

Figure 26.30 Select Enterprise Templates. If you don't see an Enterprise Templates tab, enterprise templates have not yet been saved to the Microsoft Project Server.

→ For more information about creating and using templates, **see** "Creating and Using Templates," **p. 103**.

26

WORKING WITH ENTERPRISE VERSIONS

By using Enterprise Project versions, you can create complete copies of a project schedule and label each copy with a unique version name. These versions can be for your internal use, or they can be made available to others in the organization for performing the following:

- Full comparisons between versions, including added and deleted tasks and assignments, constraints, and other changes not saved in baselines.
- Trend analysis between schedule snapshots taken at regular intervals.
- What-if analysis separate from the current (or published) version.

There is no limit to the number of versions that an organization can create; however, only versions that have been predefined by the administrator are available to project managers.

The first time a new project schedule is saved to a Project server, it must be saved with the system version called Published. This is because the Published version is associated with system features such as timesheet reporting (timesheets only show assignments from the Published version).

NOTE

> Because of its importance and the necessity for it to exist, the version Published is protected and cannot be deleted.

After the Published version of a project is saved, other versions of the project can also be saved. For example, if you have predefined a Test version and a What If version, then only those versions are available for use through Microsoft Project and Project Web Access. If the organization decides that a copy of each schedule in the organization should be saved at the end of each quarter, you can create Q1 2003, Q2 2003, Q3 2003, Q4 2003, and other versions, as necessary.

TIP

> Your organization might want to define several types of version definitions that reflect business processes. The Published version is the default production version when you save a project plan into the enterprise repository. You can also create versions such as Suspended, Preliminary, Pending Approval, and so on, as defined by the project approval and tracking processes established by your business.

You can view project versions in the Professional edition's Open File dialog box or at Project Web Access Project. When viewing projects at Project Web Access, you can sort, group, and filter by version.

Working with Enterprise Project Codes

Microsoft Project Professional uses enterprise project outline codes to enable the management of projects across an enterprise. When the enterprise project outline codes are assigned to projects, project data can be viewed and analyzed in a variety of ways, using the Project Center and the Resource Center.

Applying Outline Codes and Custom Fields to Projects

After the enterprise project outline codes and custom fields have been defined and entered into the Enterprise Global, project managers can assign those codes to individual projects.

To apply enterprise project outline codes to enterprise projects, follow these steps:

1. Select Project, Project Information to display the defined enterprise project custom fields, as shown in Figure 26.31.
2. Select the value for each Custom Field from the drop-down lists in the Value column, and then click OK.
3. When you are done, save the project to the Project server.

→ For more information about creating and using Enterprise Global project codes, **see** "Using Enterprise Outline Codes and Custom Fields" **p. 1010**.

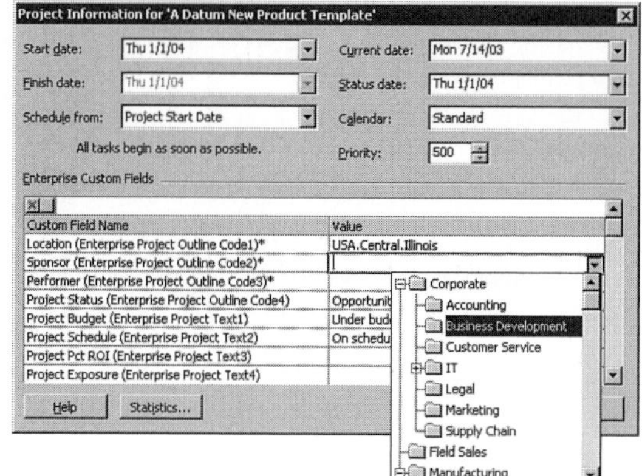

Figure 26.31
The * at the end of an enterprise custom field indicates that it is a required field.

26

CHAPTER 27

Enterprise Resource Management

In this chapter

An Overview of Enterprise Resource Management 1070

Managing Enterprise Resources in Resource Center 1072

Creating Custom Enterprise Resource Outline Code 1081

Working with Enterprise Resources 1090

AN OVERVIEW OF ENTERPRISE RESOURCE MANAGEMENT

This chapter describes how project and resource managers use the new features and capabilities of Project Professional 2003 to successfully manage resources available in an organization.

One of the biggest challenges of today's organizations is to ensure that the right resources are assigned to each project, and that all projects in the pipeline are properly staffed, taking into consideration project requirements, resources' skills, proficiency level, and availability.

With the release of Microsoft Project 2003, project and resource managers will notice a few significant changes in areas of resource management, such as

- Definition and management of a broad variety of types of resources, including designation of resources as Committed or Proposed, allowing resource managers more flexibility in establishing project teams.

- Substitution of generic resources is more accurate due to new Enterprise Global Outline Resource Codes that permit multiple selections to be assigned to a single code.

- Actual work numbers can be protected to prevent subsequent alteration of electronic records.

- Time spent by resource on administrative tasks can now be reflected in Administrative projects, allowing organizations to gain visibility into tasks that are non-project related, but essential for good management of the organization.

- Improved functionality for timesheets allows for better collaboration. New with Project 2003 is the introduction of multiple approvals for timesheets. Functional/resource managers now can review timesheets before the project manager will update the project schedules. Also, timesheets can now be locked so changes cannot be made to previously posted time data unless approved by a manager that has the authority to do so.

One of the most important aspects of Microsoft Project is that it provides enterprisewide visibility of projects and resources.

The Resource Center provides detailed information about resources stored in the enterprise resource pool. Managers can quickly view and analyze resource attributes, assignments, utilization, and availability.

NOTE

> Security rights and privileges apply to viewing and managing resources in Resource Center. If you can't see the Resource Center, please contact your manager and your System Administrator to determine if your security rights have been set properly.

The Resource Center can be accessed from either Microsoft Project Web Access (by selecting Resources tab) or from Microsoft Project Professional (by selecting Collaborate, Resource Center).

NOTE

> When accessing the Resource Center from Project Professional, you can only see the View Enterprise resource in the Resource Center displayed (as described in "Managing Enterprise Resources in the Resource Center," later in this chapter). To take advantage of all Resource Center's features and functionality, you must access the Resource Center from Project Web Access.

→ Remember that you must be successfully logged in to a Project server in order to access the enterprise features described in this section. For information on how to log in to a Project Server, **see** "Logging in to Project Server from Project Professional," **p. 1004**.

The System Administrator sets the permissions to see resource assignments in order for resource information to display.

NOTE

> By default, project managers can only see the View Resource Assignments, Adjust Actuals, and View Timesheet Summary options. When the project manager chooses these options, only resources that have been assigned to his/her project(s) will display.

To view the resources in Resource Center from Project Web Access, select Resource, and then View enterprise resources in Resource Center.

To view resources in Resource Center from Microsoft Project Professional, select Collaborate, then Resource Center.

Resource Center has only one predefined view named Resource Summary.

The views available to users in Resource Center depend on the user's specific authorization with Microsoft Project Server (granted by the System Administrator). The System Administrator has the ability to modify or create additional views by selecting Admin, and then Manage Views.

Depending on specific authorization with the Project Server and the role you perform in the organization, Resource Center enables you to perform up to six actions:

- View enterprise resources in Resource Center
- Analyze resource in Portfolio Analyzer
- View resource assignments
- Adjust actuals
- View timesheet summary
- Approve timesheets

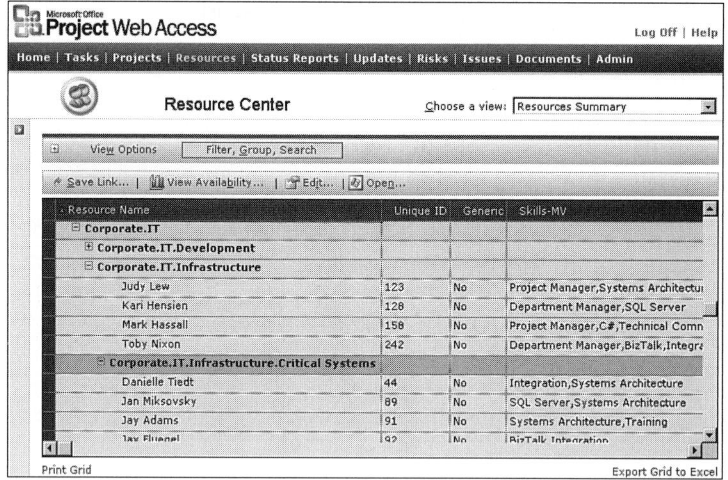

Figure 27.1 Resource Center will only display enterprise resources. Resources that are local to any of the project plans in the Project Server database will not be displayed in the Resource Center.

By default, the first action (View enterprise resources) is common and can be performed by both project and resource managers, while the rest can only be performed by resource managers.

NOTE

> The System Administrator has the ability to change the default views for specific users or groups in order to align these views with the roles and responsibilities of users within the organization.

MANAGING ENTERPRISE RESOURCES IN RESOURCE CENTER

27

In this view, users can perform the following functions:

- **Save Link**—This will create a link and add this view as a link in the sidepane, as shown in Figure 27.2.

  Once the link has been created, it will show up in the left sidepane, under a new heading: Saved Links. Once a link is created, a new option will also appear at the bottom of the left sidepane—Organize Your Saved Links. Selecting this option will open up a new window where users have the option of renaming the links (select Organize Your Saved Links, then Rename) or deleting links. Note that the deletion of a link is irreversible.
- **View Availability**—This will display the availability for a specific selected resource. Note that you can view the availability for a maximum of 30 resources at a time.
- **Edit Resource**—This displays resource details and enables users to change the attributes associated with this resource.

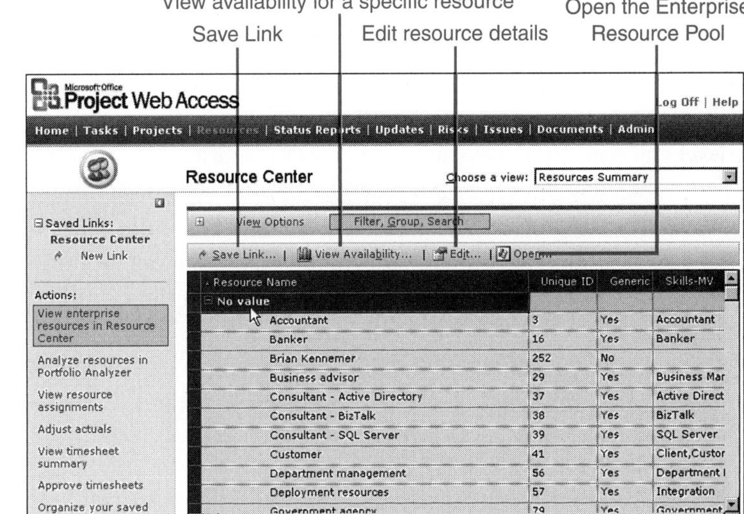

Figure 27.2
Functions that can be performed when viewing the Resource Center.

NOTE

> Only users with specific authorization with the Project Server can edit the details of resources. This is to prevent accidental alteration of resources details.

- **Open**—This opens the Enterprise Resource pool, enabling users to edit the resource attributes in the Global Enterprise Resource pool view.

CAUTION

> You have the option of selecting a single or multiple resources to be opened in Project Professional 2003 for editing. If you go back to Project Web Access and select additional resources to be opened, then the second group of resources will open with a new session of Microsoft Project Professional 2003. Make sure you treat each instance where you have Enterprise Global Resource Pool opened as a separate session. This means that you must save changes in both sessions for changes to occur.

Changes to the Enterprise Resource Global Pool will not be reflected immediately. You need to select Refresh in Project Web Access to view the updated information.

Using the Resource Center's View Options

You can use the Resource Center's View Options tab to refine the content of the data being displayed. By clicking in the View Options tab, you will see the list of View options available, or you can click the plus and minus sign icons at the left side of the tab to expand or collapse the View Options display. All of the Resource Center View Options are listed below, organized by View.

27

View Enterprise Resources

Under the View Enterprise Resources there are three options from which you can select to display the desired view:

- **Show Multi-valued Fields At**—From a drop-down box, you can select the outline level you want for the resource attributes to be displayed. To select all the outline levels select the value Bottom Outline Level.
- **Show**—You can select a second view from the value list of a drop-down menu. To select all outline levels, select the corresponding value from the drop-down list box. For example, if Level 2 is selected, any attribute that has three or more levels of detail will be excluded.
- **Show Time with Date**—This option adds the time, in the HH:MM:SS format, to the date in each of the appropriate date values when this box is checked. If the box is left unchecked, only the date is displayed.

View Availability

Under the View Availability there are three options from which you can select to display the availability of resources:

- **Include Proposed Bookings**—When this box is checked, the view will display all resources, committed and proposed. This will enable resource managers to fully understand the demand and be prepared to take appropriate actions.
- **Date Range**—You can specify the date range by either typing the date into the box or by selecting the date from the calendar that is displayed if the drop-down list box is selected.
- **Units**—You can select units of either days or weeks by using the drop-down list box and choosing the desired option.

After all the desired options have been selected, click on the Set Dates button to generate the graphic representing resource availability.

View Resource Assignments

Under the View Resource Assignments you will find:

- **Show Time with Date**—This option adds the time, in the HH:MM:SS format, to the date in each of the appropriate date values when the box is checked. If the box is left unchecked, only the date is displayed.
- **Show Summary Tasks**—This option will either show or hide (depending if the box is checked or not) all summary tasks, where summary tasks are defined as tasks that are marked with Yes in the summary field in Microsoft Project Professional.
- **Summary Rollup**—This option will either show or hide (depending if the box is checked or not) rolled up summary tasks. See definition of the summary tasks above.

- **Show To-do Lists**—By checking this box, you can see the contents of each resource's to-do lists added to the list of displayed tasks.
- **Administrative Tasks**—You can check the Administrative tasks check box if you want the Administrative projects time added to the list of displayed tasks for each resource.
- **Show (Outline Levels)**—This option is a drop-down list box. The user can select to restrict task displays that are at or above the specified outline level. For example, if Level 2 is specified, any task that is at level 3 or below in the Work Breakdown Structure will be excluded.

USING THE RESOURCE CENTER'S FILTER, GROUP, SEARCH TAB

You select the Filter, Group, Search tab to display or hide the Resource Center's filtering, grouping, and searching options.

The options associated with the Resource Center's Filter, Group, Search tab are identical to that of the Project Center, the only difference being that you are operating on resource data instead of project data.

→ **See** "Using the Project Center's Filter, Group, Search Tab," Chapter 26, **p. 1032**, for details on filtering, grouping and searching related to resources.

EDIT RESOURCE DETAILS VIEW

By selecting a resource from the initial Resource Center view and selecting Edit Resource Details, you can see and edit (if you have the appropriate permissions) the resource's enterprise resource outline codes, as shown in Figure 27.3.

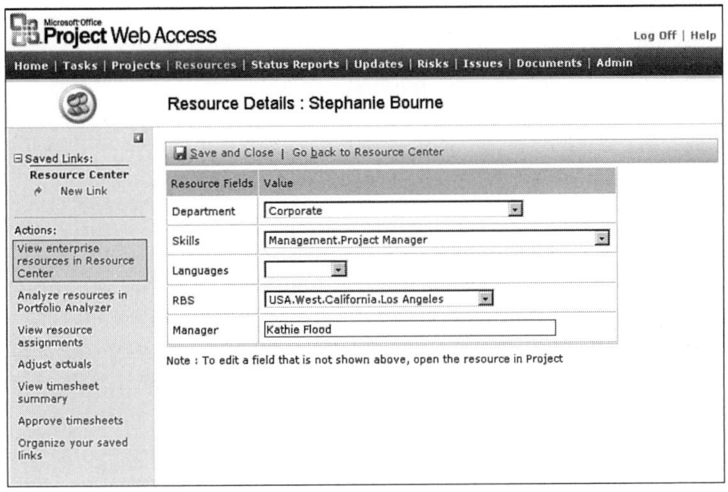

Figure 27.3
Use the Edit Resource Details screen to view and edit Enterprise resource outline codes.

You can have only one resource selected when you navigate to the Edit Resource Details screen. If you have more than one resource selected, you are prompted with an error message.

27

Resource Availability Views

Four predefined Resource Availability views are available from the Choose a View pull-down list:

- **Assignment Work by Resource**—The Assignment Work by Resource view, shown in Figure 27.4, displays assignment work by the resources that have been selected for this view, where *assignment work* is the total work currently defined for the resource(s) from all Published projects.

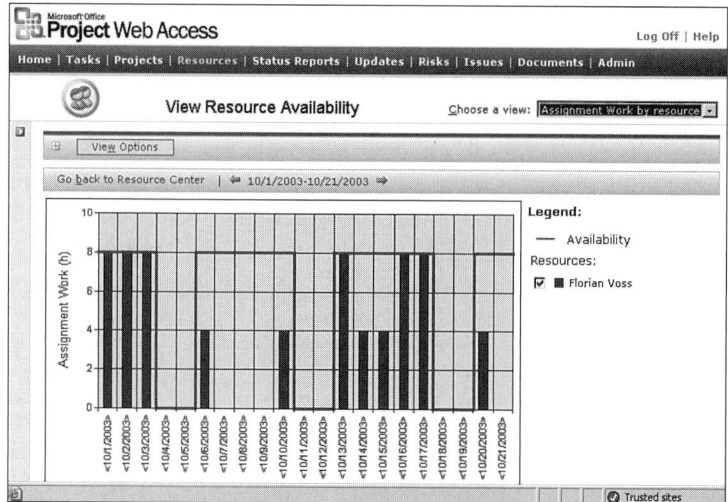

Figure 27.4 The Assignment Work by Resource view displays all the work currently defined for the selected resource(s) from all Published projects, by resource.

Resource capacity is shown on the graph, making it easy to determine whether and when the selected resources are under allocated or over allocated. Resource capacity is the total amount of effort that can be assigned to the resource without over allocation, and it is based on the resource's availability and resource calendar.

- **Assignment Work by Project**—The Assignment Work by Project view, shown in Figure 27.5, displays assignment work by the resources that have been selected for this view, but instead of the assignments displayed by resource (regardless of project), this chart shows the data by project. It could be more useful to look into the details of the assignments in order to understand the resource loading and timeline.

  Figure 27.5 shows the assignment work for Florian Voss, but this is difficult to know because the resource's name is not visible on the top of the display. You have to scroll down into the details section and expand the name field in the left pane.

- **Remaining Availability**—The Remaining Availability view, shown in Figure 27.6, displays the amount of time that the selected resource (Florian Voss) has available for work.

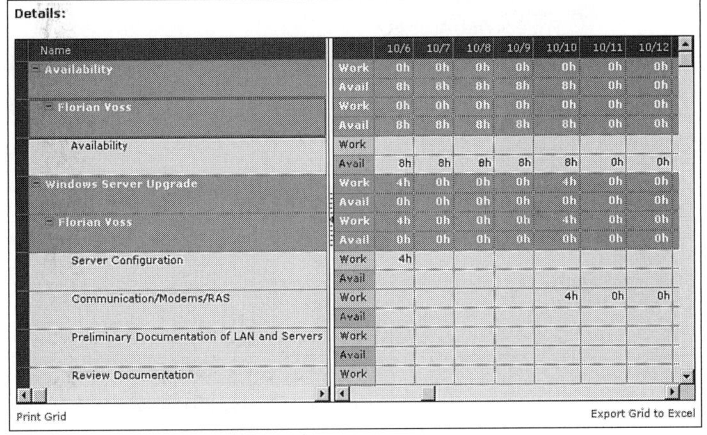

Figure 27.5 The Assignment Work by Project view displays all the work currently defined for the selected resource(s) from all Published projects, by project.

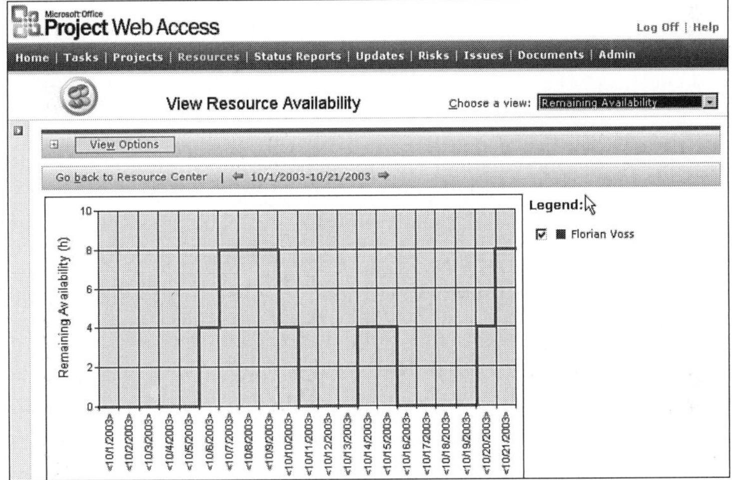

Figure 27.6 The Remaining Availability view displays the amount of time that the selected resource has available for work, over time.

- **Work**—The Work view, shown in Figure 27.7, displays the amount of work that the selected resource is assigned to do and over time, if applicable.

The Resource Center views provide ways for you to look at resource utilization across the enterprise. If you select the resource Florian Voss and click the View Availability button, for example, you can immediately see Florian's allocation displayed graphically, as shown in Figure 27.7.

Analyzing Resources in Portfolio Analyzer

If you navigate to Projects, Analyze Projects in Portfolio Analyzer, you get exactly the same view, and tools, as if you were in Web Access and selected Resources, Analyze Resources in Portfolio Analyzer.

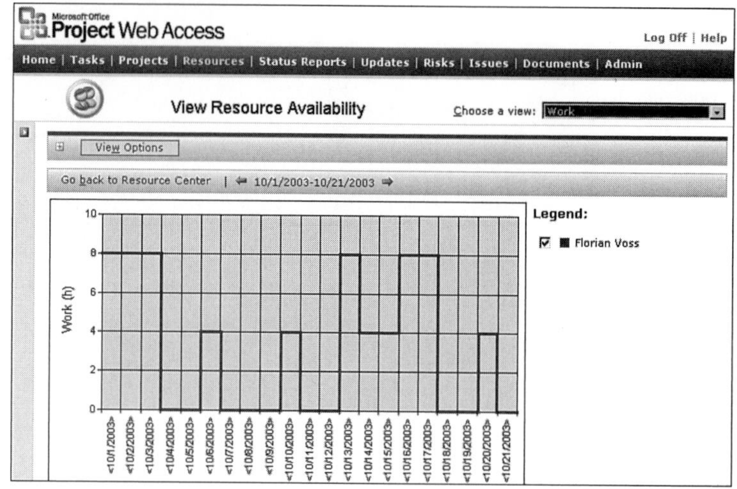

Figure 27.7
The Work view displays the amount of work that the selected resource (Florian Voss) is assigned to do.

→ For descriptions of the Analyze Projects in Portfolio Analyzer view, **see** "Analyzing Projects in the Portfolio Analyzer," Chapter 26," **p. 1049**.

VIEWING RESOURCE ASSIGNMENTS

The Viewing Resource Assignments screen is similar to Project's Task Usage view in that it displays details for each assignment (for example, task name, percentage of work complete) per resource, as shown in Figure 27.8. This view is useful for those who need access to this type of information but don't have access to Microsoft Project.

To view the resource assignments, you have the option of selecting all resources or only specific ones. This can be accomplished through Add/Remove Resources tab in the View Resource Assignment view. The screen will display two panes. The left pane is a scroll-down list from which you select the resources you wish to view the assignments for, and the right pane tells you what resources have been selected for display. You have the option of adding all resources, or removing all resources. Click the Apply button to set the parameters once your selection is complete.

After selecting a task, you can click the Link to Issues icon to navigate to the Issues page for the selected task. From the Issues screen you can create a new issue or create a link to an existing issue. After changes have been saved via the Save Changes tab, you can return to the Resource Assignments screen by selecting the Go Back to Assignments option.

After selecting a task, you can click the Link Documents icon to navigate to the Documents page for the selected task. From the Documents screen you can upload a new document, or you can link the task to an existing one. After changes have been saved via the Save Changes tab, you can return to the Resource Assignments screen by selecting the Go Back to Assignments option.

Resource assignments can be shown in either a Gantt chart format or a timesheet format. The Show Assignments Using section assumes a Gantt chart format, with items that are unique to a timesheet format.

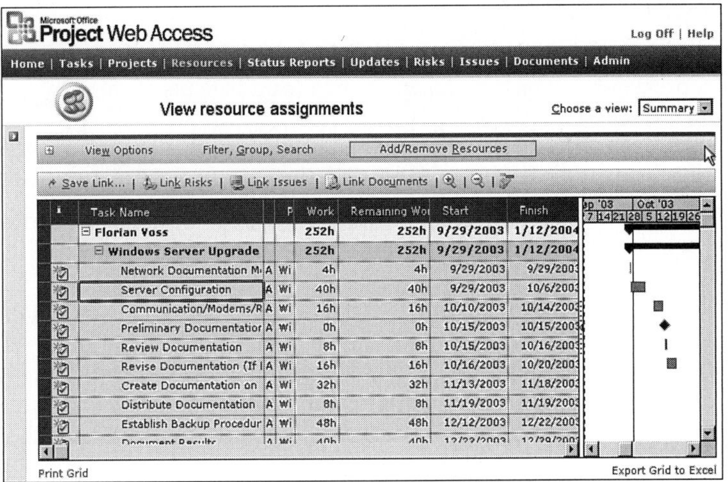

Figure 27.8
Assignments for the selected resource (Florian Voss) are grouped by resource, by project.

You have the option of displaying all assignments or restricting the view to current assignments, where current assignments are defined as those already in progress or that start within a specified number of days from the current date. The specified number of days is set by the administrator.

The assignments are displayed in a grouped structure of tasks by resource, by projects. Both generic and specific named resources are displayed.

For each resource within each project, the tasks are sorted in the same sequence in which they would be found in the project plan (by task ID). If you click on the Task Name column heading cell, the fields are sorted into alphabetically ascending sequence within project. If you click the cell again, the sort sequence is changed to alphabetically descending.

VIEWING RESOURCE ASSIGNMENTS IN TIMESHEET FORMAT

Resource assignment data can also be displayed in timesheet format, which shows the actual effort recorded against each assignment.

There are two differences between the Timesheet format view and the Gantt chart view:

- The standard Office Zoom buttons and the Go To option are replaced with start and end dates for the window in which timesheet data will be displayed (the date range and arrows that will move this window forward and backward in time). If these arrows are used, the date range is automatically set to two weeks and the dates in the View Options tab are updated.
- The Gantt Chart is replaced with a tabular report showing actual effort for each assignment. The data is displayed in the units specified in the View Options tab, and there are as many columns as there are units in the specified data range.

ADJUSTING ACTUALS

Project Web Access provides for a new feature that allows project managers to adjust actual work previously submitted. There are two main benefits of this new feature:

- Erroneous data can be adjusted and be prevented from propagating throughout the system.
- The Gantt Chart is replaced with a tabular report allowing the project manager to enter timesheet data for a person that cannot enter their own timesheet information.

Project managers use the Resource Center Adjust Actuals function to modify time data. By clicking on Add/Remove Resources tab, the project manager will select the individual resources for timesheet data adjustment. When you click on the Apply button, the timesheet data for the selected resource(s) is displayed for editing. Once the desired timesheet view is displayed, the project manager can then enter the corrected actual work for the appropriate dates. To complete this operation, you must click on the Update Actuals button to apply the changes to the project schedule; otherwise all changes will be lost. The changes are sent to the project manager for action as a normal project time update request, as shown in Figure 27.9.

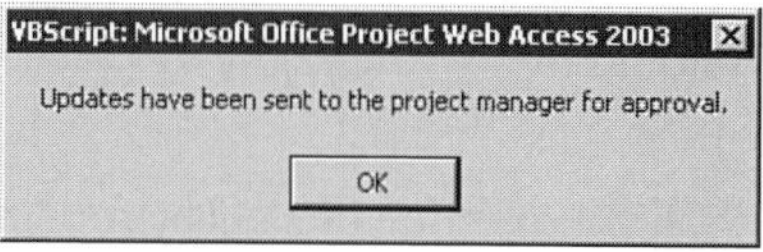

Figure 27.9 Corrected actual work for the date range is also being sent to the project manager for final approval

NOTE

> The Update Actuals function also alters the Actual Work Protected data in the date range for the affected task(s). This allows you to alter timesheets data even if the date range is closed for edits. The team member whose timesheet has been altered will see the new time entries in their personal timesheet view. You should create a business process to ensure timesheet data integrity is maintained.

VIEW TIMESHEET SUMMARY

When all projects are published, the team members will see their assigned tasks within their personal timesheet. Team members fill in the amount of time they spend on each project (including the Administrative projects tasks), and submit their time for regular timesheet updates.

APPROVED TIMESHEETS

Project Web Access 2003 now provides the ability for multiple people to approve timesheet information before the time data is updated to a project schedule. The benefit of this function is to distribute responsibility for timesheet approval to people other than the project manager(s).

After Project Web Access administration settings are complete, the home page of approvers (who may be project or resource managers, portfolio managers, or any other individual nominated to approve timesheets) will display messages indicating that there are timesheets awaiting approval. You can then accept or reject individual task timesheet rows submitted by the team members.

NOTE

It is up to the organization's senior and/or executive management to decide who has the authority to approve timesheets, and business processes should provide clear instructions in this regard.

The timesheet approver marks the tasks as Accept or Reject, as appropriate. As a timesheet approver, click the Save button to forward the accepted tasks to the project manager for update to the project schedule; rejected tasks will be returned to the timesheet submitter for revision.

Project Web Access 2003 also has a new feature to allow timesheet approvers to track the status of timesheets of team members within their direct supervision. A timesheet approver will see messages on their Home page indicating what timesheets have not yet been submitted.

This feature provides an improved method to determine which resources within an organization have not yet submitted their timesheets.

CREATING CUSTOM ENTERPRISE RESOURCE OUTLINE CODE

One of the goals of resource management is to synchronize resources and skill-set supply and demand with the project portfolio pipeline.

In Microsoft Project Professional 2003, enterprise resources are the people, equipment, and materials that a project manager can assign to tasks in project schedules.

Microsoft Project Professional provides a wide variety of capabilities that facilitate allocation and management of resources across the enterprise. This is done through allocation of certain attributes to enterprise resources. These attributes will enable managers to sort and filter data according to an organization's specific needs. They are set by applying outline codes to tasks or resources.

When you want to apply a code to a project, task, or resource, and you want to apply the code consistently across all projects in the enterprise, you use enterprise outline codes.

Project provides 30 customizable enterprise outline codes for use with projects and tasks, and 29 customizable enterprise outline codes for resources. These are named Enterprise Project Outline Code 1, 2, 3…30; Enterprise Task Outline Code 1, 2, 3…30; and Enterprise Resource Outline Code 1, 2, 3…29.

In addition, enterprise resources have a predefined outline code called the *Resource Breakdown Structure (RBS)* code. The RBS code can be any code that differentiates resources, but it should be reserved for the code value that is the most important, or most often used, throughout an organization. This is because the RBS code is built into the Team Builder, the Resource Substitution Wizard, and the Assign Resources dialog tools when filtering and selecting resources.

When you want to apply a custom field consistently across all projects, resources, or tasks in the enterprise, you use enterprise custom fields. The only difference between custom fields and enterprise custom fields is that enterprise custom fields are established for the entire enterprise, whereas custom fields are established for the local project only.

Portfolio managers define and create enterprise outline codes and custom fields, thus keeping their use consistent across the enterprise.

→ For information on setting up a Microsoft Project Server Account **see** Chapter 25, "Logging in to the Project Server from Project Professional," **p. 1004**.

→ For information on setting up the Enterprise Outline Codes, **see** Chapter 25, "Using Enterprise Outline Codes and Custom Fields."

NOTE

You must be working in the Enterprise Global in order for your enterprise outline codes to be permanently added to the Microsoft Project Server 2003 repository. If you aren't able to add enterprise outline codes because the data entry fields are disabled, then you don't have the Enterprise Global open.

To create a custom resource enterprise outline code, follow these steps:

1. Select Tools, Enterprise Options, Open Enterprise Global.
2. Choose Tools, Customize, Enterprise Fields to display the dialog box shown in Figure 27.10.
3. Select the Custom Outline Codes tab.
4. Select the category of Outline Code you want to create (task, resource, or project).
5. Select the outline code field that you want to use (1 through 30, or in the case of enterprise resource outline codes, 1 through 29 plus RBS).
6. Click the Rename button to establish a new name for the code, and the dialog box shown in Figure 27.11 appears. Click OK after you enter the desired outline code name.
7. Click the Define Code Mask button to display the Outline Code Definition dialog box shown in Figure 27.12. Remember to define a code mask for each level of outline code you create.

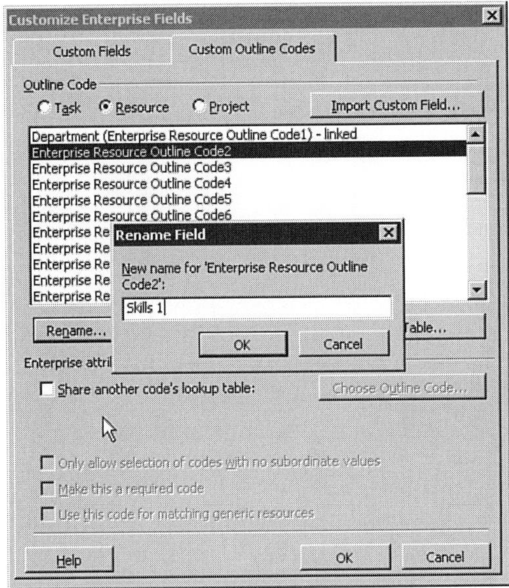

Figure 27.10
In this example, all resource skills are defined in one enterprise resource outline code field, which has been named Skills 1. You can also rename your enterprise outline codes.

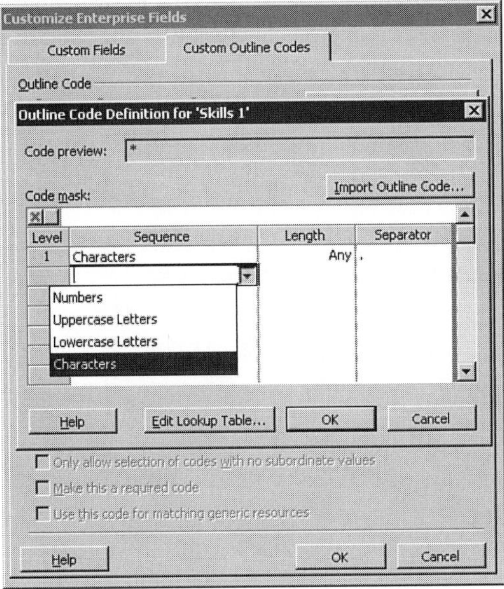

Figure 27.11
If you are defining the RBS outline code to describe location with Level 1 as state and Level 2 as city, there must be two levels of code masks defined, as shown.

8. Click the Edit Lookup Table button to display the Edit Lookup Table dialog box shown in Figure 27.12, and enter your outline codes. For example, if you are defining a location outline code for state or province, and city, your Level 1 code might be British Columbia, and your Level 2 codes underneath British Columbia might be Vancouver, Victoria, and Whistler. Use the Indent and Outdent buttons to make codes subordinate to one another. Click Close to save the lookup table entries you have defined.

27

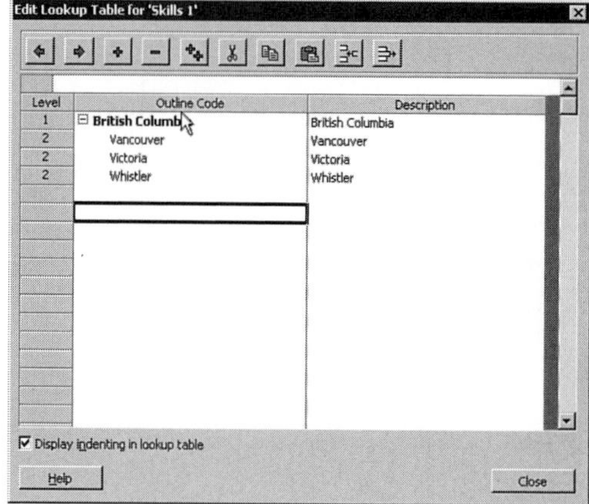

Figure 27.12
You use the icons at the top of the dialog box to manipulate the lookup table items that you've entered; hover over each icon to find out what it does.

9. Select the Share Another Code's Lookup Table check box and click the Choose Outline Code button if you want to have two outline codes share the same lookup table, as shown in Figure 27.13. You are then prompted to select the other outline code's field type and field name from pull-down lists. When outline codes are shared, changing the shared code's lookup table automatically changes the lookup table of the outline code that is referring to the shared code. You can click OK after you choose the outline code lookup table to share.

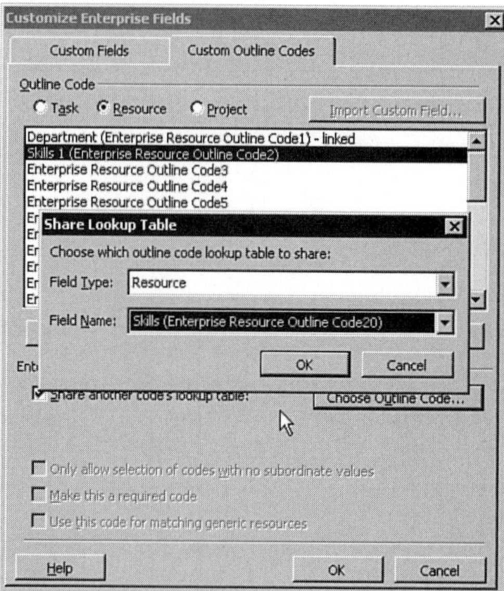

Figure 27.13
The Skills 1 code is being shared with the Skills outline code (Enterprise Resource Outline Code20).

27

10. Select the Only Allow Selection of Codes with No Subordinate Values check box, as shown in Figure 27.14, if you want to force users to select the lowest level of detail in the outline code that you have defined. For example, if you have entered codes with Denver and Seattle within the United States, then selecting this check box requires users to always select one of the cities (since the lowest level, the city, has no subordinate values).

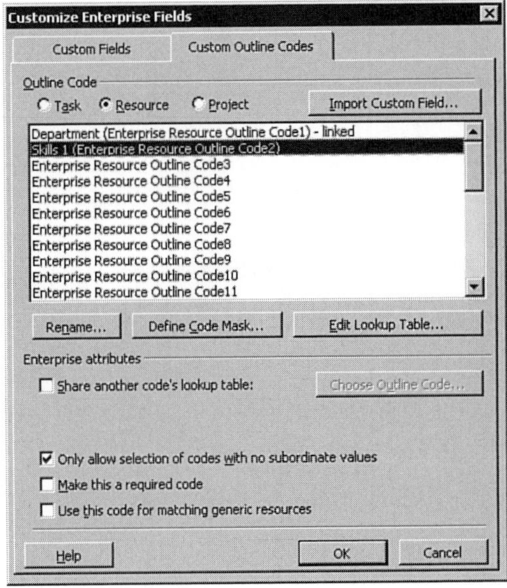

Figure 27.14
You can force users to select the lowest level of detail in the outline code.

11. Select the Make This a Required Code check box if you want to have Microsoft Project 2003 require a valid value before allowing the schedule to be saved or published to the Microsoft Project Server.
12. Select the Use This Code for Matching Generic Resources check box if you want to use this outline code as matching criteria for the Resource Substitution Wizard.

NOTE

You see the Use This Code for Matching Generic Resources check box only if you are working with enterprise resource outline codes.

13. When you are done building custom outline codes, click Close. You are returned to the Custom Enterprise Fields dialog. Click OK.
14. Save and exit the plan. Select the option Save and Check In your plan. Your outline code is now stored in the Enterprise Global and can be used for all projects that have access to the Microsoft Project Server to which you saved your plan.

27

NOTE

> You will need to exit and restart Microsoft Project to see any modifications to custom outline codes.

Enabling Proficiency Levels per Skill

Microsoft Project Professional supports using skill codes to designate skill proficiency levels (languages). You might want to use this feature to distinguish between proficiency levels when performing resource substitution. For example, there might be times when any German speaker would suffice for an assignment, and there might be times when you want to specify that only a junior or senior German speaker should be assigned to a task.

To enable proficiency levels per skill, you need to set up your skill codes with the proficiency level as the lowest level of definition, as shown in Figure 27.15.

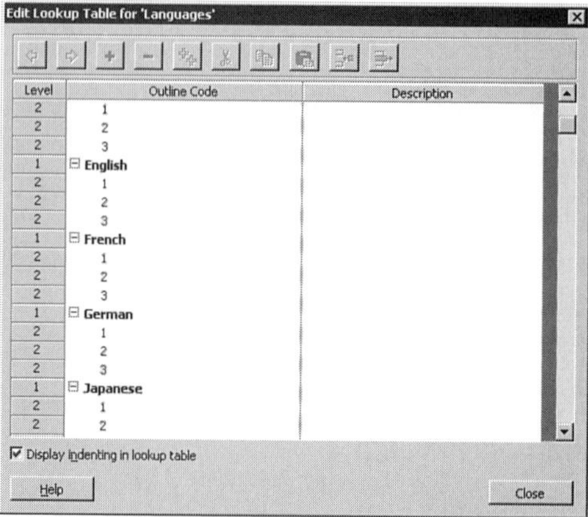

Figure 27.15 You can define your skill codes to have proficiency levels.

Microsoft Project Professional treats a resource that is assigned a skill code as having all levels of skill above and including the skill level assigned to. For example, if a generic resource is assigned the skill Developer.VB, the Resource Substitution Wizard will find any resource that matches Developer.VB, Developer.VB.Senior, or Developer.VB.Junior. Likewise, if the generic resource is assigned the skill Developer, the wizard will find any resource that matches either Developer, Developer.VB, Developer.VB Senior, or Developer.VB.Junior.

NOTE

> Make sure that the Only Allow Selection of Codes with No Subordinate Values check box in the Customize Enterprise Fields dialog box is not checked if you want to assign skill codes other than at their lowest level.

Enabling Multiple Skills per Resource

Microsoft Project Professional supports assigning multiple skill codes to resources. For example, a Visual Basic developer might also be a Web developer, and a technical writer might also be a tester. If a resource is associated with only one of his or her skills, the Resource Substitution Wizard will substitute that resource only for the one defined skill, possibly overlooking other valid resource assignment substitutions.

To enable multiple skills per resource, follow these steps:

1. Set up an initial skill code in one of the enterprise resource outline codes. Figure 27.16 provides an example of what the skill codes might look like.

   Notice in this skill code lookup table that multiple skills are defined in enterprise resource outline code 1 (Skill 1) and that skill proficiencies have also been defined.
2. After you have your initial skill code defined, create one or more additional skill codes and link each of them to the first skill code (refer to Figure 27.16).
3. Make sure you have each defined skill code's enterprise attributes set correctly. Figure 27.16 shows the attributes associated with the initial skill code, as well as with those associated with subsequent skill codes.

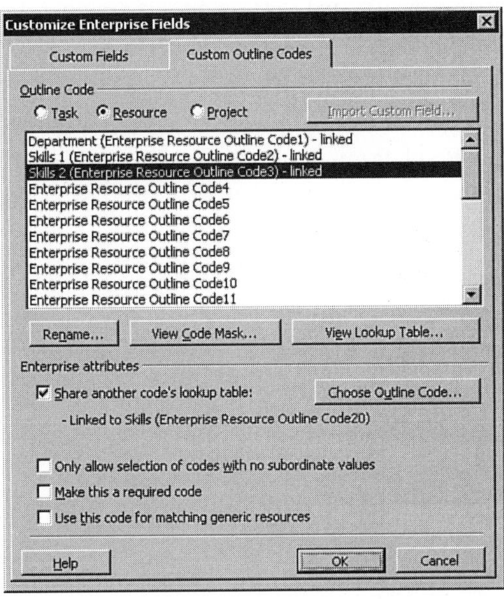

Figure 27.16 The initial and subsequent skill code's settings are required to get the Resource Substitution Wizard, the Team Builder, and the Team Assign dialog box to work correctly.

4. Assign skill codes to your resources, as appropriate.

➔ For more information **see** "Applying Outline Codes and Custom Fields to Resources," **p. 1096**.

27

NOTE

> Multiple skills and skill proficiencies are not mutually exclusive. That is, you can define skill codes with both features at the same time.

ENTERPRISE RESOURCE MULTI-VALUE FIELDS

In many cases, project and resource managers know what kind of skill-set and qualifications it takes to do the job, but it is also difficult to manually match the skill-set with a particular resource.

Because resources have more than one skill and also different levels of proficiency, Microsoft Project Professional introduced the multi-value fields that help project and resource managers to match skill-sets with resources.

MATCHING SKILL-SETS

From the home page, open up the Project Center view.

Move the cursor over the dark bar on the left side, highlight the project which you are interested in matching replacing resources, and select Open.

This project has resources already assigned to tasks. In this example, a resource manager will need to substitute a specific resource that is already assigned to a task with another resource that has a similar skill-set.

To do this, point the cursor over on the top menu bar and select the Tools function. From the drop down menu, select Build Team. A new dialog screen will open. The dialog screen shown in Figure 27.17 has three subsections: Filter Enterprise Resources, Build Team, and Project Detail.

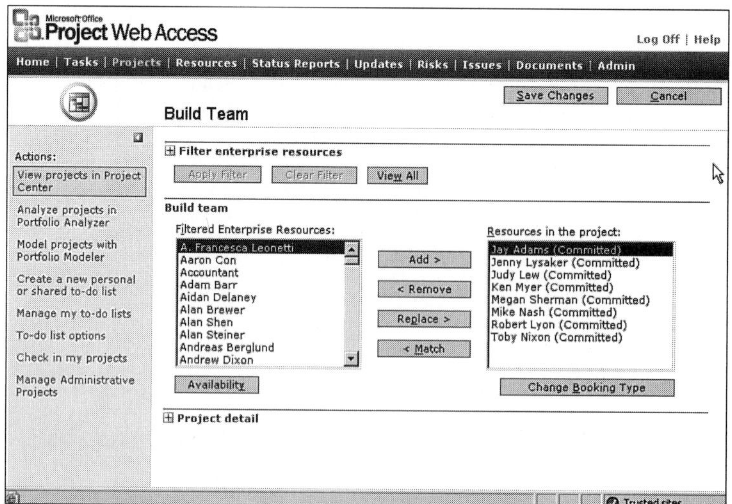

Figure 27.17 Resource managers don't need to have installed Microsoft Project Professional in order to access the Resource Pool and build team from Enterprise Global.

In the left pane there is a list of all enterprise resources. In the right pane there is a list of resources that may have been already assigned to the project team.

If you scroll down in the left pane, you will notice that resources that have already been assigned to the project team (and are now listed in the right pane) are grayed out.

In the previous example, let's assume that for a specific task, the project manager decides to add another person to work with the individual already assigned.

To do this, click on Tools, and then on Build Team. In the right pane, Project Team Resources, highlight the name of the person you want the skill-set to match and then click on Match. This action will trigger a filter to be activated. The filter that is being activated in the background by the Match button can be viewed in the expanded mode of the second section—Customize Filters.

NOTE

> Please note that Microsoft Project has automatically filled in boxes of this section. Values for these boxes are determined by values associated with those of selected resource.

Please note the values for these boxes:

1. Under the Field Name, the value is Skills (multivalue). That indicates that a search was performed, using the skill-set, for other resources with similar attributes to the initial individual assigned to the task.
2. Under the Test column, the value is set to contains.
3. Under the column Value(s), the value is set to match the skill set of the initially assigned resource.

Once you click on the Match button, in the left pane of the Build Team third section, the system will return only those resources that match the filter. The project manager now has the ability to add a new resource to the project team and assign that resource to the task together with the initially assigned resource.

There is also the case where a project or a resource manager will want to assign a resource based on different criteria, such as RBS. In this case, the Match criterion used will be RBS.

You can also use a combination of multiple filters. To do this, open the Build Team dialog box from the Tools menu and expand the second section, Customize Filters.

Select the value RBS in the first box underneath Field Name, as shown in Figure 27.18. In the next box under the Test column, select Contains, and in the last box, under the Value(s) column, select USA.West. In the second row, under the And/Or column, select And; then in the next box, under the Field Name, select Skills (multivalue). In the next box, under the Test column, select Contains, and in the last box, select Technical, IT, Systems Architecture.

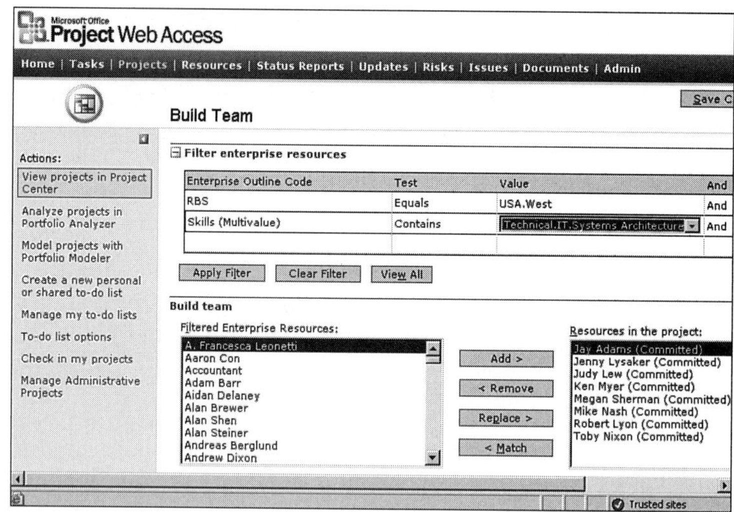

Figure 27.18
You can sort by a combination of multiple filters.

Click Apply Filter. Now, in the left pane of the Build Team section, you'll see a list of resources that satisfy both criteria: resources that are in the Western region and are also listed with skills under the System Architecture value.

NOTE

> Please note that selecting a value at a top level of the branch structure of a multi-value field and setting the Test value to Contains will return all resources that satisfy any of the criteria of the values under the branch. For example, selecting USA will return all resources in USA, no matter where they are located.

WORKING WITH ENTERPRISE RESOURCES

In Microsoft Project Professional 2003, enterprise resources are the people, equipment, and materials that a project manager can assign to schedules in order to get work done.

27

→ For more detailed information about the different types of resources available in Microsoft Project, **see** "Defining Resources and Costs" **p. 277.**

Microsoft Project Professional provides a variety of capabilities that enable the management of resources across an enterprise. The following is an overview of the key resource management elements in Microsoft Project Professional, each of which is described in more detail later in this chapter:

- **The enterprise resource pool**—All enterprise resources are stored in a repository on a Microsoft Project server called the enterprise resource pool. Portfolio or resource managers enter enterprise resources into the enterprise resource pool, and project managers can take them from the resource pool to add them to schedules. Each resource has skills, attributes, and availability that determine his or her appropriateness for specific project assignments.

- **Generic and actual resources**—Generic resources are useful for doing preliminary planning and for skill-based resource substitution. Actual resources represent each individual in an organization who can be assigned to work.
- **Local and enterprise resources**—Enterprise resources are available for assignment to any project in the enterprise by any project manager. In addition, project managers have the option of defining local resources, which are visible only to their own projects.
- **The Enterprise Resource Pool Wizard**—This wizard allows the user to add new resources to the enterprise resource pool from external sources quickly and easily.
- **Enterprise resource outline codes and custom fields**—Resources can be tagged with enterprise (project) outline codes that describe key attributes of the particular resource. These enterprise outline codes can be used later to provide a variety of reports on resource availability and utilization, or to assign resources to projects based on skills and availability. Enterprise custom fields are an extension of the custom fields' capabilities provided in earlier releases of Microsoft Project; they provide for standardized category definitions for grouping and reporting purposes.
- **The Enterprise Team Builder**—The Enterprise Team Builder allows a project manager to add resources to his or her project schedule quickly and easily. The project manager then has the option of assigning those resources to tasks manually or using the Resource Substitution Wizard to assign them to tasks automatically. Only resources assigned to a project are listed on the project's Resource Sheet view. You can run the Enterprise Team Builder as many times as you need to, in order to add resources to or remove them from a project schedule.

→ For information on the Enterprise Team Builder, **see** "Using the Project Center Build Team," **p. 1036**.

- **The Resource Substitution Wizard**—Resources can be automatically assigned to schedule templates based on matching enterprise outline codes between each generic resource's (in a schedule template) and actual resource's (in the enterprise resource pool) skills.

→ For details about the Resource Substitution Wizard, **see** "Using the Resource Substitution Wizard," **p. 1110.**

WORKING WITH THE ENTERPRISE RESOURCE POOL

Enterprise resources are stored in the enterprise resource pool, which provides a single repository for all enterprise resources and eliminates the scalability issues associated with resource pools from earlier versions of Project.

Whereas enterprise resource information is stored in the enterprise resource pool, enterprise, company, and department wide standard project information, such as the enterprise outline codes, is stored in the Enterprise Global.

NOTE

> The Enterprise Global template contains enterprise-level project and resource custom fields and view settings. The enterprise resource pool contains all other resource data.

After the enterprise outline codes and custom fields have been stored in the Enterprise Global template, you can associate them with enterprise resources by opening the enterprise resource pool and editing each resource's information sheet.

➔ For more information on outline codes, **see** "Applying Outline Codes and Custom Fields to Resources" **p. 1096**.

USING GENERIC AND ACTUAL RESOURCES

Generic resources are a type of resource that have been added to Microsoft Project Professional 2002 and have been kept in Microsoft Project 2003. A *generic resource* is a placeholder for a skill-set or role on a project, but it isn't associated with an actual person.

An *actual resource* in Microsoft Project Professional is a person in the company who can actually be put into a role on a project and complete assigned tasks.

USING ENTERPRISE GENERIC RESOURCES

Generic resources, like actual resources, can be stored in the enterprise resource pool (where they are available for assignment in other projects) or in a local project (where they are available to that project only). Storing generic resources in the enterprise resource pool ensures that the generic resources assigned to projects always have the same attributes and skills when assigned across multiple projects.

The Generic check box has been added to the General tab of the Resource Information dialog box for each resource defined in the enterprise resource pool. If the Generic check box is checked, the resource is generic, as shown in Figure 27.19.

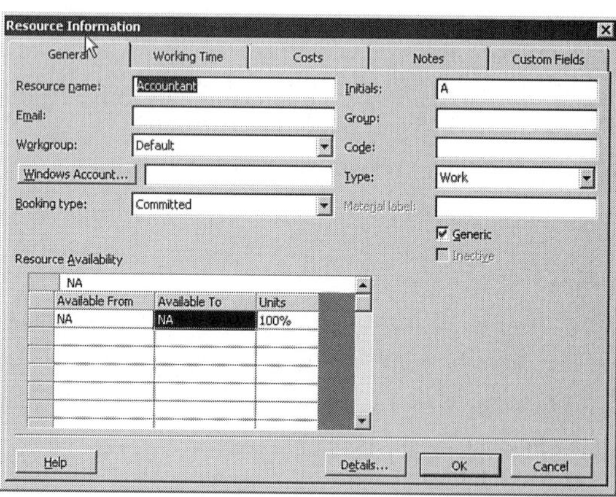

Figure 27.19 You can select the Generic check box to define a generic resource.

27

As shown in Figure 27.20, icons in the Indicators field in the Resources view specify whether a resource is local and/or generic.

➔ Generic resources need to be assigned enterprise resource outline codes to support skills-based resource replacement via the Resource Substitution Wizard, and to support the viewing of enterprise resource data by resource and skill. For more information about replacing generic resources with actual resources based on skill codes, **see** "Using the Resource Substitution Wizard," **p. 1110.**

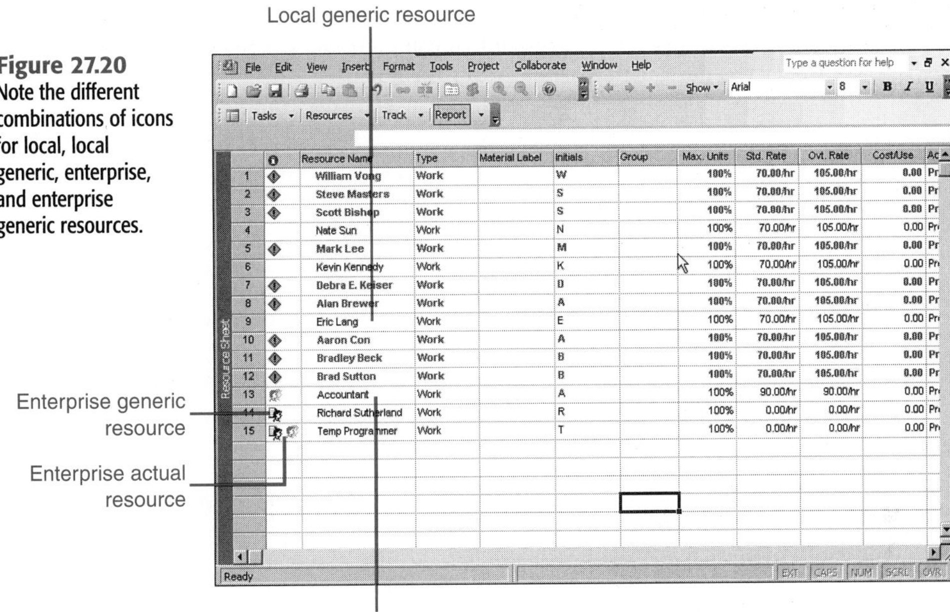

Figure 27.20
Note the different combinations of icons for local, local generic, enterprise, and enterprise generic resources.

Using Local Generic Resources

Local generic resources are similar to generic resources, but they are available only to the project plan in which they are defined.

NOTE

> A local resource has a head icon with a page behind it in the Indicators column. Don't confuse this icon with the two-heads icon in the Indicator column that indicates a generic resource.

Using Enterprise Actual Resources

Enterprise actual resources should be defined and created during an initial resource planning phase, after which the resources are available for assignment to projects across the enterprise. As with generic resource planning, creating a set of criteria for all enterprise resources ensures consistency and integrity with all enterprise resource allocation.

Using Local Actual Resources

Local actual resources are resources that represent actual human beings and that are defined in a single Microsoft Project schedule only. These resources are available to the project schedule in which they are defined, but to no others.

In an enterprise setting, it isn't recommended that a project manager use local actual resources because they defeat the purpose of being able to gather and analyze resource utilization and availability information at the enterprise level.

NOTE

> For most organizations, it is recommended that there be a process defined whereby project managers can request that new actual and generic enterprise resources be added to the enterprise resource pool or changed as necessary.

CREATING A NEW ENTERPRISE RESOURCE

You enter resources into Project so you can assign them to tasks in a project plan. You use the same procedure to create both generic and actual resources; the only difference is the selection of the Generic box in the Resource Details dialog box.

You can create resources from scratch or import them from a variety of sources, such as old projects or a Microsoft Outlook Contacts file. The following steps are necessary for adding a new resource to the enterprise resource pool:

1. Launch Microsoft Project.
2. Make sure you have the appropriate permissions. With Microsoft Project Professional's default group permissions, only the administrator, portfolio manager, and resource manager can add new resources.
3. Choose Tools, Enterprise Options, Open Enterprise Resource Pool. The Open Enterprise Resources dialog box, shown in Figure 27.21, appears. It lists all the enterprise resources that are currently in the Server database. Select the resources that you want to edit and click the Open/Add button. Click the Open/Add button without selecting any resources to enter just new resources.

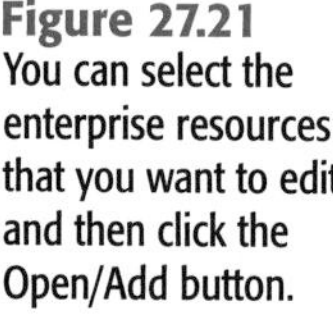

Figure 27.21
You can select the enterprise resources that you want to edit and then click the Open/Add button.

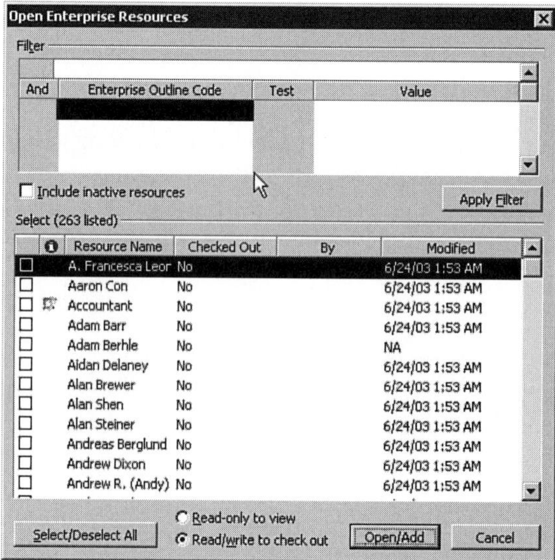

4. To modify a resource, right-click a resource's cell and select Resource Information from the pull-down menu. Use the dialog box shown in Figure 27.22 to modify the resource's details.

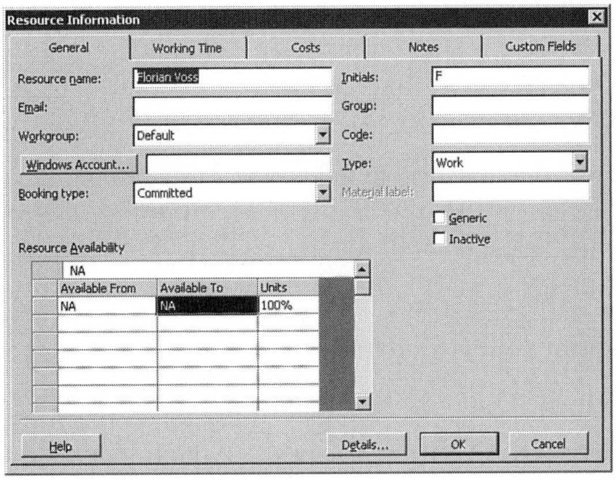

Figure 27.22
You enter new or changed resource information in the Resource Information dialog box.

5. On the General tab, fill in the appropriate information, and if the resource is to be a generic resource, select the Generic check box.
6. Select a collaboration method from the Workgroup drop-down list. The Default selection allows you to collaborate with this resource via the default method that has been set up by the system administrator. The Project Server selection allows collaboration to happen via the Project Server only. The E-mail Only selection permits collaboration information to only be sent in email messages. The None selection means that you do not want to collaborate with this resource.
7. Select the Custom Fields tab and assign the appropriate selections for each defined enterprise outline code and custom field, as shown in Figure 27.23. If there is an asterisk (*) at the end of an Enterprise Resource Outline Code, that asterisk indicates that it is a required field.

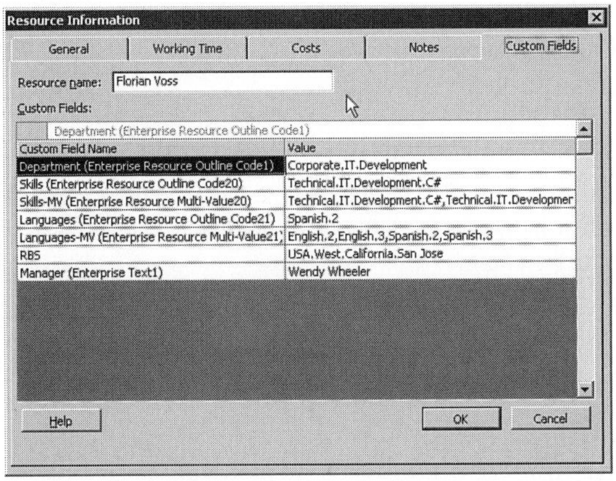

Figure 27.23
You can edit the custom Enterprise Resource Outline Codes in the Resource Information dialog box.

8. Save and close the enterprise resource pool.

TIP

> To make multiple resources generic, select more than one resource in the table, click the Task Information icon, select the Generic check box, and click OK.

APPLYING OUTLINE CODES AND CUSTOM FIELDS TO RESOURCES

After enterprise outline codes and custom fields have been entered into the Enterprise Global template and resources have been entered into the enterprise resource pool, the resources in the enterprise resource pool need to have the enterprise outline codes and custom fields assigned to them.

To apply enterprise outline codes to enterprise resources, follow these steps:

1. Select Tools, Enterprise Options, Open Enterprise Resource Pool.
2. Click the Select/Deselect All button to choose all the resources in the resource pool, then click the Open/Add button, as shown in Figure 27.21, to open the selected enterprise resources in a Resource Sheet view.
3. Assign the enterprise resource outline codes to the enterprise resources.

TIP

> One quick and easy way to assign outline codes to resources is to create a new Outline Codes view and table in the Enterprise Global template, where the columns in your new view include the enterprise resource outline codes. This way you can easily assign and maintain outline code information for every resource.

4. When you are done, save your work and exit the enterprise resource pool.

NOTE

> If you find that you cannot select enterprise resources to open in the enterprise resource pool, those enterprise resources might already be checked out. You can make sure that all enterprise resources are checked in by selecting Admin, Enterprise Options, and checking the enterprise resources in Web Access.

27

NOTE

> After enterprise resource outline codes and custom fields contents are established, you can edit them by selecting a resource and clicking Edit Resource Details in the Resource Center of Web Access.

WORKING WITH THE RESOURCE POOL IN MICROSOFT PROJECT WEB ACCESS

Microsoft Project 2002 introduced powerful resource management functions that allow resources to be selected and used from the Enterprise Global Resource Pool. Microsoft Project 2003 Professional extends the flexibility to attach resources to projects.

Project Web Access with Microsoft Office Project 2003 now contains a function that allows the project or resource manager to use the Project Web Access and Project Center to select team members from the Enterprise Resource Pool and attach those resources to a specific project.

Resource managers can now use Project Web Access search and replace features to find Enterprise Resources and substitute Actual resources for Generic resources within a project.

BUILD TEAM FROM ENTERPRISE GLOBAL RESOURCE POOL

This new feature allows project or resource managers to add or remove resources related to a specific project schedules. To access this feature from the Project Web Access, select Projects, then Build Team.

The Build Team dialog has several options as discussed in the next section.

ADD ENTERPRISE GLOBAL RESOURCES TO A PROJECT

You can use the Project Web Access Project Center Build Team function to add team members to a project.

Figure 27.24 You can add resources to a project from Enterprise Global Resource Pool in Project Web Access Build Team.

Resources are added to a project team by selecting the name from the left side and using the Add button to attach them to the project. This action alone does not assign resources to specific tasks; as a result of this action, team members are simply added to the resources within the project. Specific task work assignments are made within Microsoft Project 2003 Professional by selecting the resources that have been added to the project team.

NOTE

> The Add Team Member function relies on the Category settings that use the Resource Breakdown Structure (RBS) to determine which resources a project manager can add to a project team. The relative position of the project or resource manager to the team resources determines whether the project manager can add a resource to the project team. If the resource being added is not within the same RBS "branch" as the project or resource manager, an error message will be displayed informing you that you are not allowed to assign resources to the project.

Remove Enterprise Global Resources from the Project

There are three major conditions you should consider before removing resources from a project:

- Resources can be added to the project team, but are not assigned working tasks. When resources are simply a member of the project team but are not assigned to working tasks, then there is no overall effect caused by removing a resource from the project.
- Resources can be assigned to working tasks but no actual work has been recorded. There are several conditions that may be true for every resource assigned to a working task. You need to consider resource conditions such as resource units, resource work contour, planned versus baseline delivery dates, project costs, and so on.
- Resources may be assigned to working tasks and those resources may have already reported actual work for those tasks. Actual work may have be submitted for update but not yet posted to the project.

The Remove action extracts the indicated resource(s) from the project. If those resources are assigned to a working task, then the selected resources disappear from the project. If resources have reported actual work for the tasks, the actual work remains but the resource disappears from the task.

Replace a Resource with Another

The Project Web Access Built Team function also allows you to select resources from the left side of the selection dialog to replace resources within the project.

This feature allows you to do a general substitution of a resource within the project for one found in the Enterprise Resource Pool.

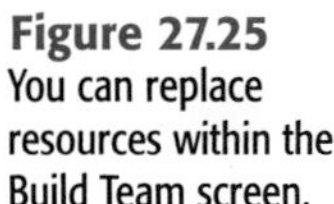

Figure 27.25
You can replace resources within the Build Team screen.

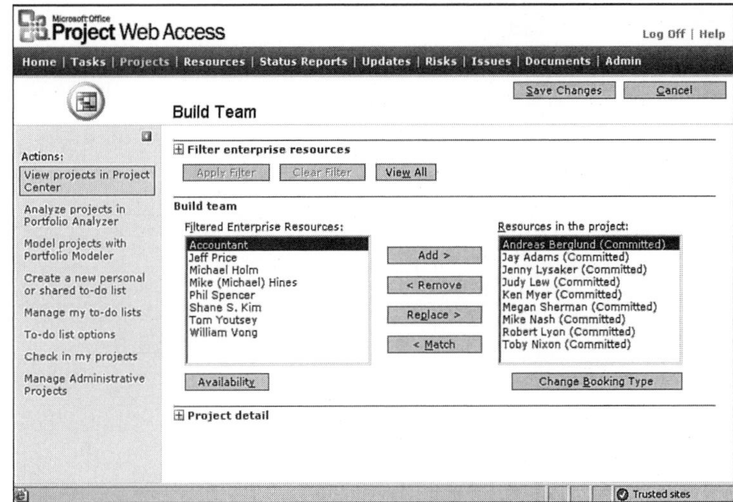

NOTE

When you substitute a resource that has actual values posted with another one, there are two things that will happen: First, Microsoft Project will add the new resource to the task, and second, it will protect the actual values posted by the substituted resource from being deleted. By doing that, you have a true picture of the assignments for a particular task: who has been working in the past and for how long, and who will be working the future.

MATCH ENTERPRISE RESOURCES

This function allows you to easily find resources within the Enterprise Global Resource Pool that match the characteristics of the resource you select from the right side of the dialog window. When you use the Match button, the system automatically uses the resource characteristics from the item on the right to search the Enterprise Global Resource Pool for resources that match those criteria.

NOTE

The Match function uses a combination of Enterprise Global Outline Resource Codes that you have established for your implementation. The Match function compares the codes marked with the Use This Code for Matching Generic Resources condition to find resources that equal all of the characteristics of each resource. Refer to information relating to Enterprise Global setup and configuration for more information.

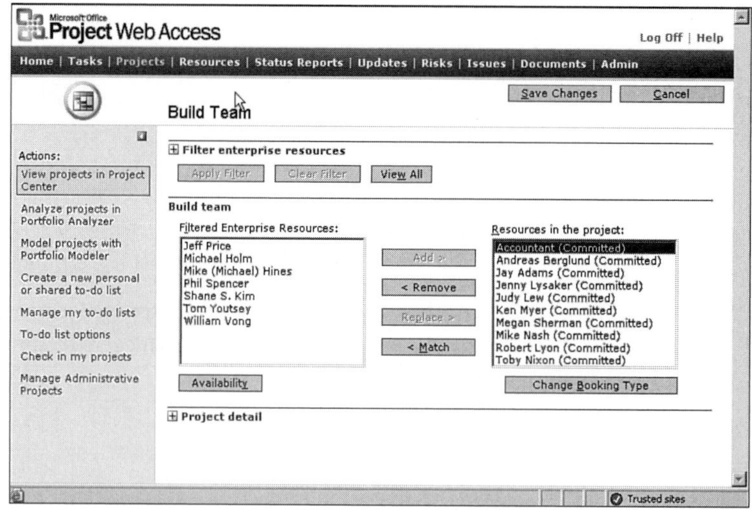

Figure 27.26
You can match resources within the Build Team screen and replace them as needed.

Filter Enterprise Resources

This function is similar in concept to the Match function, but the filter allows you much more flexibility to easily find resources that contain certain characteristics within the Enterprise Global Resource Pool.

Change Booking Type

The Change Booking Type option allows you to toggle between the default Committed condition and Proposed, as shown in Figure 27.27.

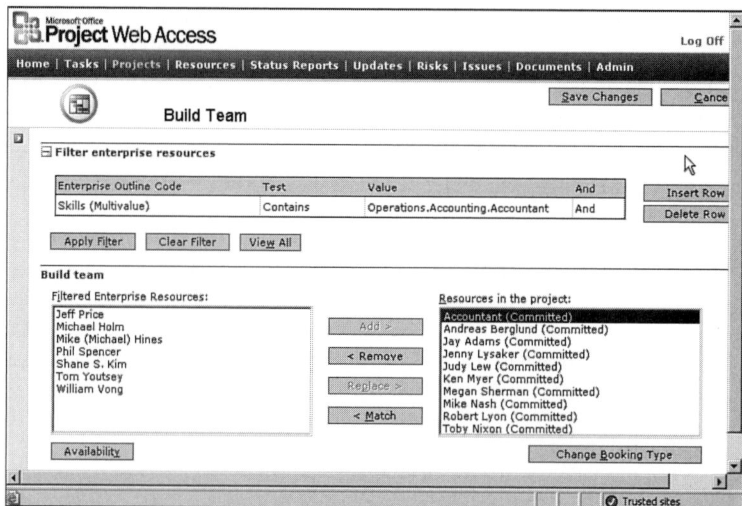

Figure 27.27
You can filter enterprise resources within the Build Team screen to easily find resources with certain characteristics and change the booking type for a resource within the Build Team screen.

The Booking Type allows resource managers to have an accurate representation of the demand for a particular skill-set or resource. This is particularly important when an organization is trying to synchronize the available resource with the project's pipeline and balance the supply with the demand.

PROPOSED VERSUS COMMITTED BOOKING

Microsoft Project 2003 has a new mechanism to designate status of resources as Committed (default option) or Proposed (optional). Key benefits to this feature include

- Proposed resources can be assigned to tasks without timesheet entries appearing on the resource Tasks list, and allow project and resource managers to simulate workloads while a project is still in the proposal lifecycle phase.
- Project and resource managers can use combinations of Committed and Proposed resource status to do what-if analysis when various projects are competing to use the same resources.
- Specific resources can be designated Proposed for one project and Committed for another. When a Proposed resource is switched to Committed within a project schedule, the resource will automatically receive task assignment messages the next time the project schedule is published.

The Proposed and Committed booking types can be used for Actual or Generic resources attached to project teams.

NOTE

Booking Type can only be applied for resources for an entire project schedule. It does not apply to individual tasks only.

Project Web Access 2003 and Microsoft Project 2003 Professional each have functions that allow project and resource managers to set the Proposed or Committed status for resources within a specific project schedule. This booking status can be easily toggled between Proposed and Committed with Project Web Access Project Center's Build Team function or Microsoft Project 2003 Professional.

CHANGING RESOURCE BOOKING TYPE IN MICROSOFT PROJECT 2003 PROFESSIONAL

The booking type can also be changed within Microsoft Project 2003 Professional functions. The project manager can simply toggle the booking type for each resource as needed.

VIEWING RESOURCE BOOKING STATUS WITHIN A PROJECT

The Booking Type column within the Build Team for Enterprise dialog can be used to inspect the booking status of resources. Figure 27.29 shows which team members are Committed and Proposed.

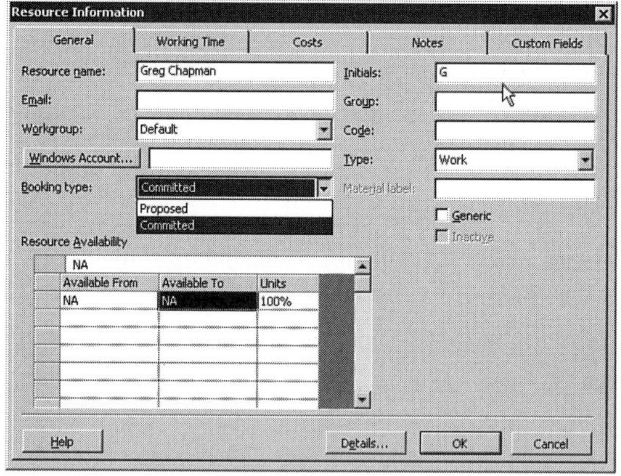

Figure 27.28
You can use the Resource Information dialog window to change the resource booking type.

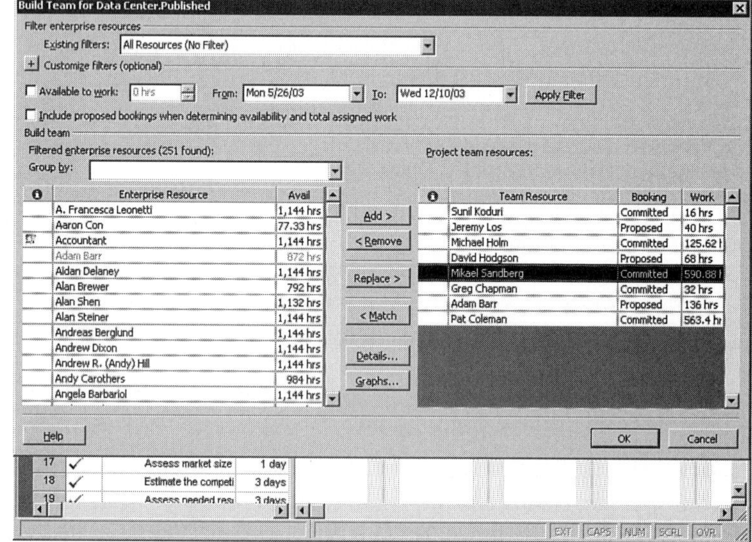

Figure 27.29
You can include proposed bookings when determining availability and total assigned work.

27

You can also use the Include Proposed Bookings When Determining Availability and Total Assigned Work check box to filter resources that are available to work on this project.

Working with the Resource Pool in Microsoft Project Professional

You can use the Team Builder to add resources from the enterprise resource pool to a schedule. When a resource is added to a schedule, you can assign the resources to tasks by using the Assign Resource dialog box.

Adding Resources to a Project Schedule

To use the Team Builder effectively, all enterprise resources must already be stored in the enterprise resource pool, and each resource must be assigned one or more enterprise outline codes or custom fields from the Enterprise Global template.

➔ If you don't know what the enterprise resource and project outline codes, custom fields, and generic resource names are for your organization, talk to your portfolio manager or administrator. If you are the portfolio manager or administrator and you need detailed information on how to plan, create, and use enterprise outline codes, **see** "Using Enterprise Outline Codes and Custom Fields," **p. 1010.**

For example, assume that you are a project manager and you are responsible for developing a preliminary schedule for a new software deployment project. The organization's portfolio manager has provided you with the following information:

- The enterprise generic resources that you need are already defined in the Enterprise Global template.
- The RBS Enterprise Outline Code indicates the location of the resources.
- Enterprise Project Outline Code 1 specifies the location of the project.
- Enterprise Project Outline Code 2 specifies the project's phase.
- The start date for your new project is January 2.
- You should save your schedule with the organization calendar.

Also, for the purposes of this example, assume that you built your project schedule using a project template called Software Development and you have made the following modifications to the project template as the basis for your preliminary schedule:

- You have added several system administration tasks.
- You have modified the effort or duration of each task in the schedule, based on your organization's estimation methods.
- You have modified each task's predecessors and successors, as appropriate.

The following steps show how you can use the Team Builder to add enterprise generic resources to your new preliminary schedule. Note that these same steps can also be used to add enterprise actual resources to a schedule.

1. With your schedule open, select Tools, Build Team from Enterprise. If more than 1,000 Resources are available for display, a prefilter dialog box automatically appears. You can use an existing filter or a custom filter to reduce the list of resources displayed.

➔ Because the schedule's resources aren't assigned to an enterprise calendar yet, you receive the warning "Enterprise Standard Calendars Are Needed," which you can ignore for now. **See** "Managing Enterprise Calendars," in Chapter 28 for information on using enterprise calendars.

NOTE

> If the Build Team for Enterprise option is unavailable, you are either not connected to Microsoft Project Server, you have opened your schedule in read-only mode, or you do not have a schedule open.

2. To replace the local resources in your project file with generic resources from the enterprise resource pool, first you should list just the generic enterprise resources in the Enterprise Resource list. To do this, expand the Customize filters, enter **`generic`** in the Field Name, enter **`equals`** as the Test, enter **`Yes`** as the Value, and click the Apply Filter button. You should see just the generic resources in the Enterprise Resource list, as shown in Figure 27.30.

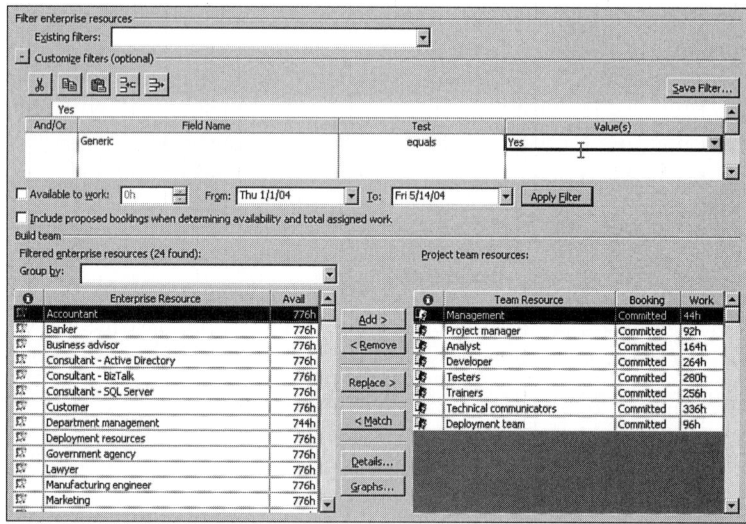

Figure 27.30
You can use the filter mechanisms to reduce or identify the attributes of the resources in the enterprise resource pool.

3. To perform the replace function, select the team resource named Project Manager, select the enterprise resource named Project Manager, and click the Replace button. Repeat this process to replace each team resource with its corresponding enterprise resource, as follows:

   Team Resource: Enterprise Resource

   Manager: Project Manager

   Analyst: Business Analyst

   Developer: Web Programmer

   Testers: Tester

   Trainers: Trainer

   Technical Communicators: Tech Writers

   Deployment Team: Operations

Your Software Development schedule is now populated with enterprise generic resources. Notice that you can't assign a resource to a task by using the Team Builder except by using the Replace function.

4. You can now save your schedule.

So far you've used the Filter, Add, and Replace features of the Team Builder. The following list describes all the features of the Team Builder, as shown in Figure 27.30:

- **Existing Filters**—This is a pull-down list of all filters currently available to you. You can create new filters by using the Save Filter button on the Customize Filter dialog box.
- **Customize Filters**—You can use Customize Filters to create and save new filters. This optional field is collapsed when you first enter the Team Builder. You can click the + button to expand this selection and display a grid with tools for building a filter. You can use the Apply Filter command to apply a filter to the list of enterprise resources, and then you can save your new filters by clicking the Save Filter button.
- **Available to Work**—You can use the Available to Work check box when you want to reduce the list of available resources to only those that have an amount of available time greater than or equal to the amount you enter, between the dates you specify. For example, if you need everyone on a project to be 100% available over a 6-month period, you enter **6mo** in the Available to Work field and then select the start and end dates that are assumed to be the start and end dates of the project.
- **Group By**—You can use Group By to organize the resources in the enterprise resource pool differently than the default alphabetical order. Because Contoso company has established the enterprise Resource Breakdown Structure (RBS) code to represent resource location, if you want to know who in the enterprise resource pool list is from Sacramento, you can enter **RBS** in the Group By field to group the enterprise resources by location.
- **Enterprise Resource**—The resources in this column on the left side of the dialog box are defined in the enterprise resource pool. You can select any of these resources to build a project team. The Avail column, next to the Enterprise Resource, shows how many hours each resource is available to work within the date and filter range criteria. Remember that other projects in Contoso company are using people from the same resource pool, so you might need to coordinate the selection of the resource for your project with the resource's manager. Notice that each generic resource has a small icon to the left of its name.

27

> **NOTE**
>
> With all the Team Builder resource lists, you can click and use Shift+click and Ctrl+click to select resources.

- **Team Resource**—The resources in this list are already assigned to the project or will be added to the project schedule when you click OK. The Work column shows how many hours each resource is assigned to work within the project's start and end dates.
- **Add**—You use the Add button to move a resource from the Enterprise Resource list to the Team Resource list. As you add resources to the project plan, the Work column reflects the load on those resources across all projects. This gives you an idea of how much work those resources are scheduled to perform for other projects in the enterprise.
- **Remove**—You use the Remove button to remove the selected member(s) from the Team Resources list. You are warned if the resource is assigned to tasks in the current project, and you cannot remove the selected member(s) until the resource(s) is no longer assigned to any tasks in the current project.
- **Replace**—You use the Replace button to replace the selected team resource with the selected enterprise resource. You can select only one team resource and one enterprise resource in order for the function to work. If the resource you are attempting to replace has actual hours reported within the project, a pop-up window appears, indicating that you must do the resource substitution by alternate means.
- **Match**—You use Match to find resources in the enterprise resource pool that meet the enterprise resource outline code criteria specified by the resource being matched. For example, if you have a resource named Tech Writer-French who has two enterprise resource outline codes—Tech Writer (Code1) and French (Code2)—and if both enterprise resource outline codes are marked as Use This Code for Matching Generic Resources in the Enterprise Global template, only resources in the enterprise resource pool that exactly match those two criteria will be displayed.

TIP

> If you have problems getting the Match function to work, look at the filter created in the Team Builder when you click the Match button. If, for example, your actual resources have skill levels per skill, you can either create a generic resource that matches each skill per skill level or you can create your own custom filters that find actual resources based on any combination of skill code and skill level.

- **Details**—You use the Details button to view the information sheet for the selected resource.
- **Graphs**—You use the Graphs button to view the availability graphs of the currently selected resources. This is a convenient way to visually determine the workload and availability for the resources you've selected. When you use this feature, you can inspect scheduled work or remaining availability for each person selected along a calendar time line. You can zoom to desired timescale increments, including every 15 minutes, hourly, daily, weekly, monthly, quarterly, biannually, and yearly resolutions.

After you have created a preliminary schedule using generic resources, you might want to ask the portfolio manager to turn your preliminary schedule into an enterprise template.

USING THE ASSIGN RESOURCES DIALOG BOX

Using the Assign Resources dialog box is a very quick and easy way to both add resources to a schedule and assign them to tasks. Because the Assign Resources dialog incorporates all the Team Builder menus and functions, it is how most project managers add enterprise resources to schedules and assign them to tasks.

TIP

> You can add actual enterprise resources to a schedule at any time while you're building a schedule. However, it is a good idea to wait until you are ready to apply resources to tasks. If you add actual resources to a schedule too early, those people might not be available when your project needs them because they are deployed on other projects. Therefore, you should use generic resources on tasks until you're sure the people you need will actually be available.

You need to transform the preliminary schedule to a detailed schedule by adding actual resources to the project and assigning them to tasks. To discuss how to do this, let's continue with the Software Development example. As the project manager, you are looking for project team members from Colorado who have the appropriate skills and are available hours for work for the duration of your project.

Follow these steps to complete the detailed schedule by using the Assign Resources dialog box:

1. Open your Software Development schedule by using Project Professional.

2. Bring up the Assign Resources dialog box by selecting the Assign Resources icon from the Standard toolbar, selecting Tools, Assign Resources, or pressing Alt+F10.
3. Click Add Resources, as shown in Figure 27.31. The pull-down menu provides three options:

CAUTION

> You should only use resources from the enterprise resource pool on a Project Server unless your portfolio manager permits other options. If you use resources that are not found within the enterprise resource pool, Project Server analysis reporting functions might reflect inaccurate data.

27

From Active Directory—You use this option to select resources from the Windows Active Directory that is maintained by your Windows domain system administrators.

From Address Book—You use this option when adding resources from a Microsoft Outlook address book.

Assign Resources

Task: Develop unit test plans using product specifications

Resource list options

Filter by:

All Resources | More Filters...

Available to work 0h

Add Resources

From Active Directory...

From Address Book...

From Project Server...

Resource Name	R/D	Units
		100%
Analyst		
Deployment team		
Developer		
Management		
Project manager		
Technical communicator		
Trainers		

Assign | Remove | Replace... | Graphs... | Close | Help

Hold down Ctrl and click to select multiple resources

Figure 27.31
By using the Assign Resources dialog box you can add resources to a schedule from an active directory, from an Outlook address book, or from a Microsoft Project server.

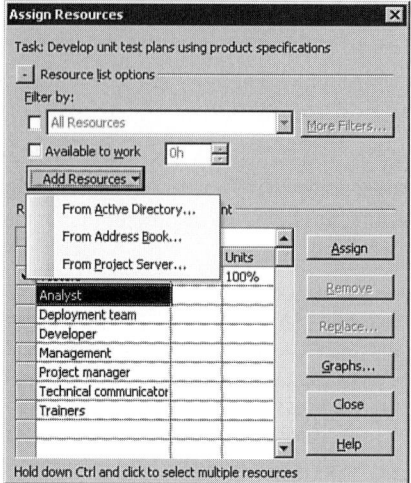

From Microsoft Project Server—You use this option to bring up the Team Builder, prepopulated with both resources in the enterprise resource pool and enterprise resources assigned to the project.

For this example, select the From Project Server option, as shown in Figure 27.31. That opens up the Team Builder screen, as shown in Figure 27.32.

4. Identify the enterprise resources that are from Colorado and that match skills with the enterprise generic resources in your schedule by selecting RBS from the Group By pull-down list, selecting one of the team resources, and clicking Match (see Figure 27.32).

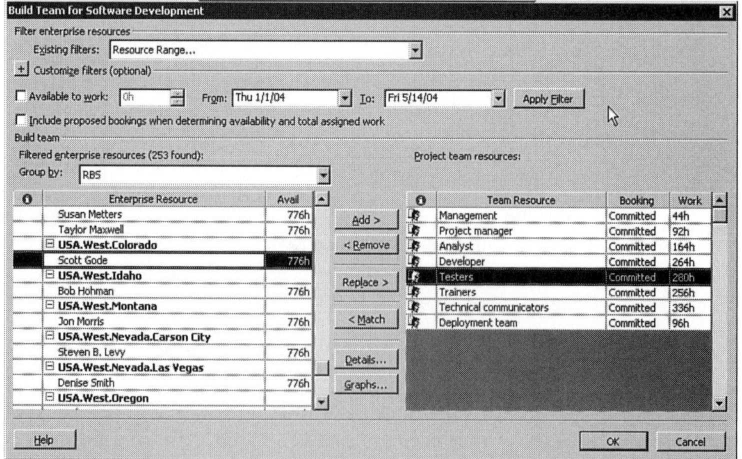

Figure 27.32
The Team Builder's features are all available from the Build Team dialog box.

5. As shown in Figure 27.32, in your enterprise resource pool, one Tester in Colorado has enough available hours. Replace the generic resource Tester with the enterprise actual resource Scott Gode by selecting Scott Gode from the Enterprise Resources column, selecting Web Programmer from the Team Resources column, and clicking Replace. Select and replace each of the remaining generic team resources.
6. You are done adding resources to your schedule, so return to the Assign Resources dialog box by clicking OK on the Team Builder screen.

Resources that are assigned to a task are automatically brought to the top of the list of the resource names, making it easier to manage long resource lists, as shown in Figure 27.33. You can also assign multiple resources to a task by using the same Assign Resources dialog box.

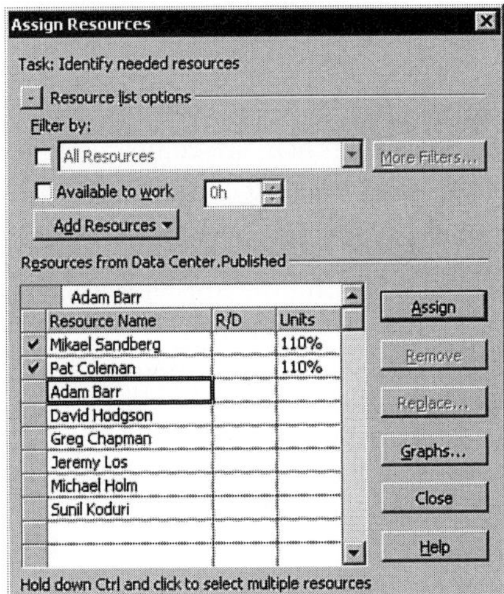

Figure 27.33
Assigning multiple resources to a task.

CAUTION

Be very careful when adding new local resources to a schedule. If a new local resource name exactly matches an enterprise resource name, you will have a hard time distinguishing between the two resources when you are using the Assign Resources dialog box. Also, data on local resources is not included in the views provided in the Project Center and the Resource Center.

TIP

To prevent accidental creation of local resources, open Microsoft Project Professional and select Tools, Options. Then select the General tab and uncheck Automatically Add New Resources and Tasks. Microsoft Project then prompts you when you attempt to add new resources to the local resource pool.

Your portfolio manager should provide you with the rules associated with using local resources for your organization.

So far you've used the Add Resources pull-down list and assigned resources by using the Assign Resources dialog box. The following are two other features of the Professional Edition's Assign Resources dialog box that are shown in Figure 27.33:

- **Resource List Options**—Expanding the resource list options by clicking on the + sign allows you to use preexisting and available to work filters to reduce the list of displayed resource names.
- **R/D**—You can request or demand that a resource not be substituted when using the Resource Substitution Wizard. See the section "Using the Resource Substitution Wizard," later in this chapter, for details.

USING THE RESOURCE SUBSTITUTION WIZARD

The Resource Substitution Wizard uses enterprise outline codes to match and replace generic resources with actual enterprise resources. You can think of this as a resource attribute matching function, where the attributes of generic resources (typically skills such as Tech Writer and capabilities such as Speaks French) are compared to those of actual resources in order to find a suitable substitution match.

In addition to assigning actual resources to tasks based on enterprise resource outline codes, the Resource Substitution Wizard can also "optimize" the allocation of resources across project schedules to minimize the duration of those schedules. If an actual resource is overallocated, the wizard looks in its resource pool for available resources with the same attributes to work the tasks.

There might be times, however, when you do not want an actual resource substituted. You can use the Assign Resource dialog box's Request/Demand field to control the Resource Substitution Wizard (see Figure 27.34).

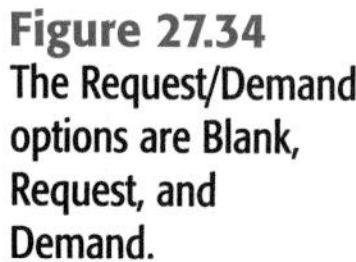

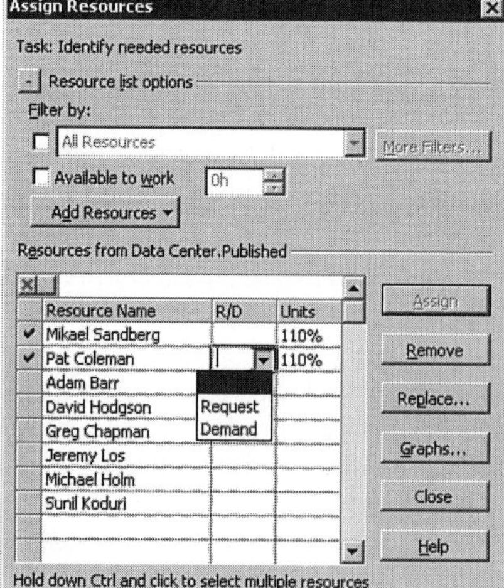

Figure 27.34
The Request/Demand options are Blank, Request, and Demand.

The Request/Demand field can be set to one of the following values for each resource on a task:

- **Blank**—By default the field is blank. This tells the Resource Substitution Wizard that it can freely substitute another resource for this one, as long as it meets the skill and availability criteria for the task.
- **Request**—You should choose Request to tell the Resource Substitution Wizard to keep this resource assigned to this task but allow the wizard to make a substitution if the resource is found to be overallocated.
- **Demand**—You should choose Demand to tell the Resource Substitution Wizard to keep this resource assigned to this task, even if it leaves the resource overallocated. You then have to level the resource yourself.

NOTE

Microsoft Project does not allow you to request or demand generic resources.

The primary advantage of using the Resource Substitution Wizard is that it is the fastest way to assign enterprise resources to the tasks in a schedule. If you use templates or project schedules that have generic resources assigned to all tasks, and those generic resources have skill codes defined, the Resource Substitution Wizard can quickly substitute actual enterprise resources for the generic resources.

The following are some Resource Substitution Wizard behaviors that you need to consider before using the wizard:

- The wizard substitutes for two or more generic resources on the same task, but it does not allow you to substitute two different actual resources for one generic resource that is allocated at 200%. For example, if you want two different Visual Basic programmers assigned to a task, you have to manually add the second Visual Basic programmer to the task.
- The wizard substitutes correctly for any resource unit value.
- If there are multiple enterprise resources that match an enterprise generic resource, the wizard substitutes using the first available actual resource that meets the criteria before moving on to the next available actual resource that meets the criteria. This might be fine for resources with skills such as tech writer or programmer, where resources are reasonably interchangeable; however, for skills such as project manager, where you most likely want the same project manager assigned to the entire project, it probably isn't appropriate.
- The wizard replaces overloaded resources with alternates (from the pool that you have specified) that have the right skills and are not overloaded. If you prefer to not replace resources, you should use the Request/Demand feature in the Assign Resources dialog box.

- The wizard does not level resources within schedules, although by optimizing resource allocation, it usually comes close. You should make it a practice to level resources within schedules after the Resource Substitution Wizard has applied resources to tasks.
- Although you might not mind the fact that the wizard assigned multiple different actual resources to testing tasks in the same project, you probably don't want to have multiple project managers assigned to the project management tasks. To resolve this, you might want to consider using the Team Builder's Replace function for project manager type tasks, locking those assignments in place. To do this, you use the Assign Resource dialog box's Request/Demand feature and then use the Resource Substitution Wizard to complete the substitutions.

Two things must be in place before you can use the Resource Substitution Wizard:

- Enterprise resource outline codes must have been assigned to the actual resources within the enterprise resource pool.
- You must have opened a schedule that has the following characteristics:

    All working tasks have generic or actual resources assigned to them.

    Each generic resource that is assigned to a task has enterprise resource outline codes attached.

Suppose that you have added some new tasks to Office XP Deployment schedule and have assigned the generic resource called Project Management to them.

You need to follow these steps to substitute an actual resource (Judy Lew, in this example) for the Project Management generic resource:

1. Open the Office XP Deployment. Make sure that the new tasks have been added to the schedule (Define final resources, in this example) and that the enterprise generic resource Project Management is assigned to these tasks.
2. Start the Resource Substitution Wizard by selecting Tools, Substitute Resources, Resource Substitution Wizard. Click Next on the welcome screen. All open schedules should be listed as part of the wizard's Step 1, as shown in Figure 27.35. Select only the projects needed for resource substitution, in this case Office XP Deployment, and then click Next.

TIP

> If you choose more than one project in which to substitute resources, you are actually asking the wizard to optimize resource assignments across all those projects. To avoid resource assignment confusion with the other projects, which might be underway, you should consider using the wizard to assign resources to your new schedule first and then optimizing resource assignments across projects as a later step.

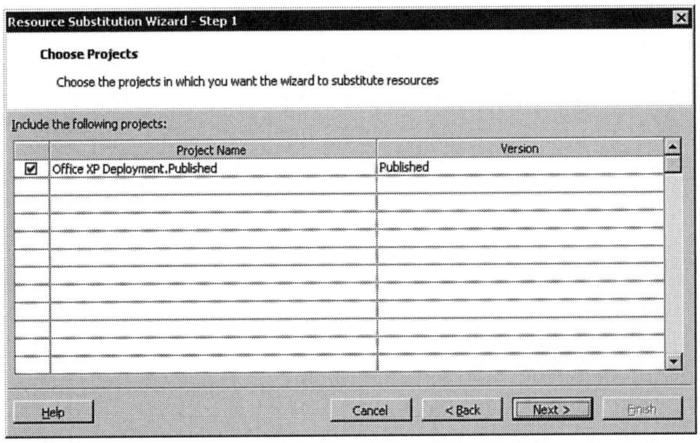

Figure 27.35
You can select the open project(s) in which you want to substitute resources by selecting the check box to the left of the project's name.

3. On Step 2 of the Resource Substitution Wizard, you need to identify the subset of resources from the enterprise resource pool that is to be considered during the resource substitution. As shown in Figure 27.36, for the Office XP Deployment project, you need to include resources at the RBS level of USA, specify a resource freeze horizon of the current date, and then click Next.

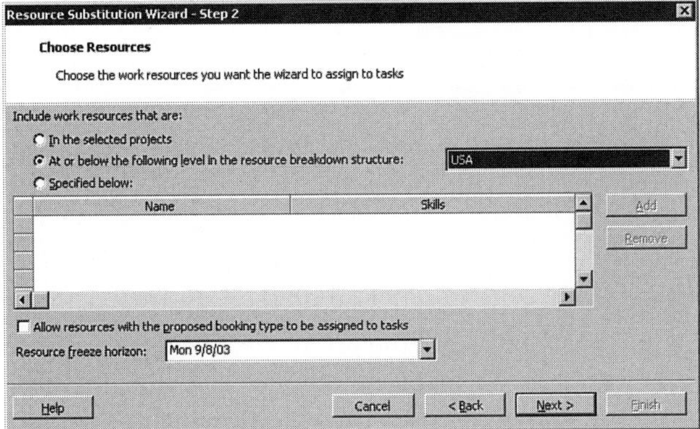

Figure 27.36
You can specify that only resources from a certain location are to be considered by the wizard for assignment to tasks.

You can choose from the following three options to specify the subset of resources to be used by the wizard:

In the Selected Projects—You can select this option to constrain the wizard to only substitute resources that are already in the selected projects. This option works well if your schedule(s) already contains all the enterprise actual resources you need.

At or Below the Following Level in the Resource Breakdown Structure—You can select this option to constrain the wizard to only substitute resources that are at or below the specified level in the RBS. This option allows you to limit the resources being considered for addition to your schedule by RBS code.

Specified Below—You can select this option to constrain the wizard to only substitute resources that you specifically select from the enterprise resource pool. If you select the Specified Below check box, you can click Add to bring up the screen shown in Figure 27.36. After you have added the desired resources to the schedule, click Next and continue with these steps.

The Resource Substitution Wizard considers only assignments made after the Resource Freeze Horizon date. If, for example, you established a Resource Freeze Horizon that is two weeks out, all resources would have two weeks to complete or hand off their current assignments before moving on to their new projects and/or assignments. If you are substituting resources for a new schedule only, then you can let the Resource Freeze Horizon default to the current date.

4. Step 3 of the wizard shows a list of related projects and their relationships, as shown in Figure 27.37. Because we are substituting resources for the Office XP Deployment project only, make sure that none of the related projects are selected, and then click Next.

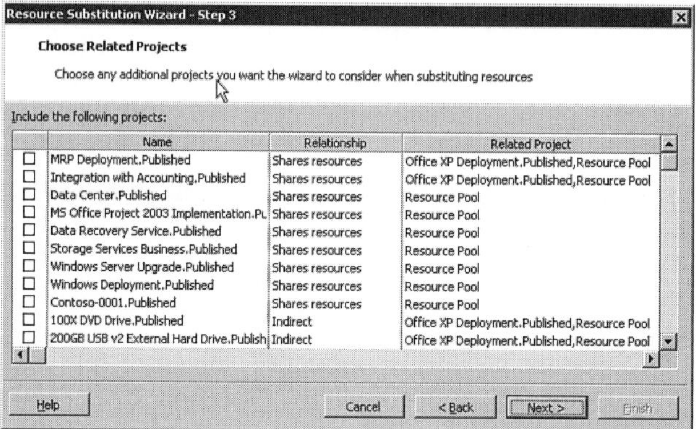

Figure 27.37
You should select none of the related Office XP Deployment projects because you want the wizard to substitute resources only in the Office XP Deployment.

Projects are considered related if the projects share any resources from the pool of resources that you've established for the wizard or if the projects have cross-project links active between them.

5. Step 4 of the Resource Substitution Wizard allows you to prioritize the projects you have selected and to establish the resource substitution options for each project being substituted for. You need to let the Office XP Deployment project's priority default to 500 (the priority doesn't matter because you are substituting for only one resource). Then choose Use Resources in Pool as the scheduling option (because the actual resource you want to substitute with, Judy Lew, is in the wizard's pool), as shown in Figure 27.38. When you are finished choosing scheduling options, click Next.

The priority field specifies which projects the wizard should substitute resources for first. The priority scheme used by the Resource Substitution Wizard is the same priority scheme used to prioritize tasks within a schedule: Priority numbers range from a low of 0 to a high of 1,000, with 500 as the default priority.

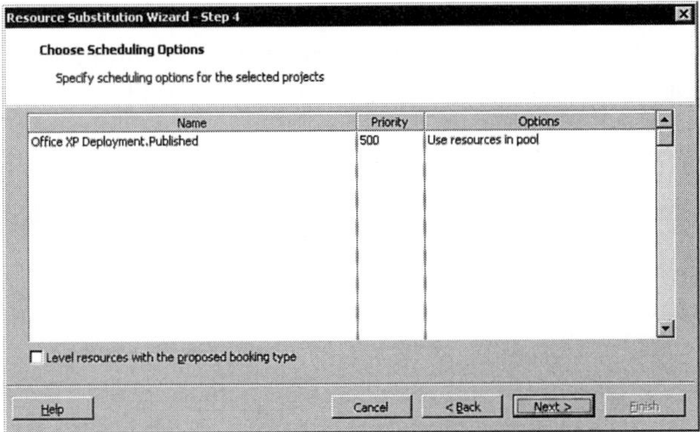

Figure 27.38 You can specify scheduling options for the selected projects.

The Options field specifies whether the wizard can substitute resources from the project only or from the pool of resources specified earlier. For the Office XP Deployment project example, the wizard's resource pool consists of all enterprise resources with an RBS of USA, as defined in Step 2 of the wizard.

NOTE

> The priority and options settings that you assign in the Resource Substitution Wizard are not recorded anywhere in the Project Server.

6. Step 5 of the Resource Substitution Wizard displays a summary of your configuration options so far, as shown in Figure 27.39. If you want to change one or more of these configuration items, click Back. In this example, these are the configuration items you want, so click Run. When the wizard finishes running, the Next button becomes available, and you need to click it to move to Step 6 of the wizard.

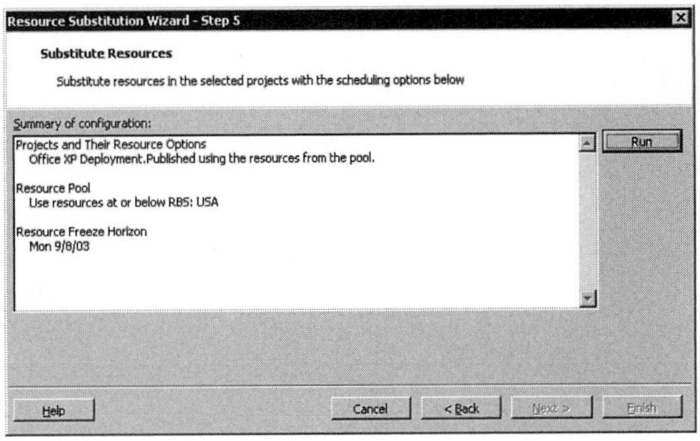

Figure 27.39 You can click Run if the summary of instructions is correct.

27

7. The wizard computes a substitution solution, as shown in Figure 27.40. If you are happy with these substitutions, you can click the Next button to accept the results. If you are not happy with the results, you can click Cancel to start over or Back to return to the previous step.

Resource Substitution Wizard - Step 6

Review Results

Review the resource substitution results. You can also sort, filter, and group the changes in a view to model them.

Task	Skill Profile	Assigned Resource	Requested Resource
Office XP Deployment.Published			
Office Deployment			
Analysis			
Identify Target Areas for Improvement			
Identify software improvements		Toby Nixon	Ken Myer
Identify support environment improvements/ac		Mike Nash	Jenny Lysaker
Design partners		Robert Lyon	Mike Nash
Review Current Market Solution Vendors			
Implementation partners		A. Francesca Leonetti	Mike Nash
Secure necessary architectural resources		Toby Nixon	Judy Lew
Design			
Draft Preliminary Infrastructure Design Do			

Help | Cancel | < Back | Next > | Finish

Figure 27.40
You can review the detailed results of the resource substitution in this screen.

8. As the last step you are prompted for how you want to save the results of the Resource Substitution Wizard, as shown in Figure 27.41. Here you have two options that are discussed further down.

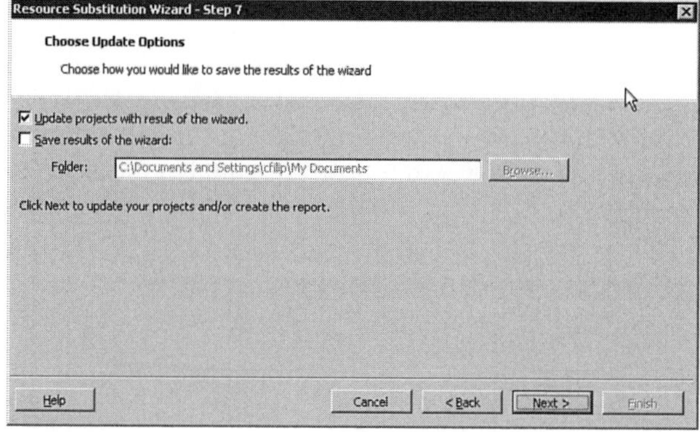

Figure 27.41
You can both update the projects with the results and save a report containing the results of the wizard.

Select Update Projects with Result of the Wizard if you want to have the Resource Substitution Wizard apply the recommended changes to all the projects that you selected. If you select Update Projects with Result of the Wizard, the wizard applies the resource assignment changes to each schedule but does not yet save the altered project plans.

Select Save the Results of the Wizard if you want to save a report of the results of the Resource Substitution Wizard to a file. Click the Browse button to specify the folder where you'd like to save the report file.

After you have selected options, click Finish.

When you are applying the substitution results, you might receive the confirmation dialog. This confirmation simply lets you know that you have modified the resource assignments for projects that have been published to the Project Server, and you will need to level and analyze the results of these changes before republishing them to the Project Server. If you get this message, click Yes to continue as shown in Figure 27.42.

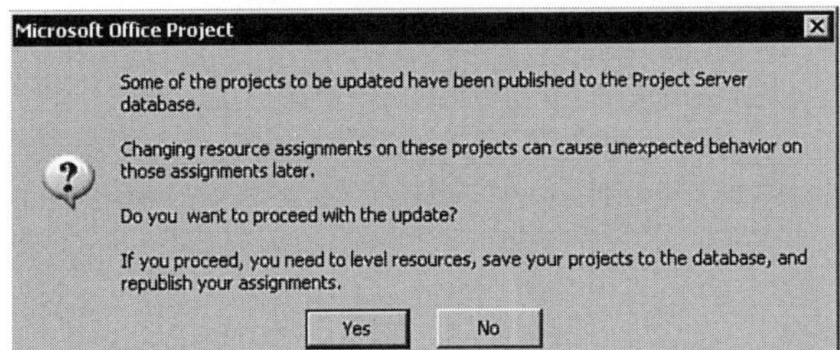

Figure 27.42
You might see this error when applying the Resource Substitution Wizard's results to the related project schedules.

9. Your Office XP Deployment project has been updated with the resource substitutions, but it has been neither saved nor published to the Project Server. You need to remember to save changed schedules after you inspect the results. For example, you might want to save these modified project schedules to a different version so they can be analyzed and/or approved.

CHAPTER 28

Enterprise Collaboration

In this chapter

Introduction to Enterprise Collaboration 1120

Using Project Web Access Tasks for Timesheets 1122

Updating and Revising Timesheets 1128

Using Project Status Reports 1129

Storing Project Artifact Documents 1133

Managing Risks 1135

Managing Issues 1137

Using Microsoft Outlook with Project Server 2003 1139

INTRODUCTION TO ENTERPRISE COLLABORATION

Chapters 24 through 27 describe how people across the organization use project and resource management functions within Project Web Access 2003. In this chapter, we discuss several Project Web Access collaboration features, including

- **Task Assignments for timesheets**—Project managers use techniques to inform team members they have working tasks.
- **Submitting Timesheets**—Team members submit timesheets for approval and update to project tasks.
- **Adjust actual time**—Using electronic timesheets to revise actual hours reported.
- **Reporting project status**—Use predefined status forms to get project status from team members.
- **Managing project documents**—That support overall project objectives.
- **Recording and managing risks**—Use electronic tracking methods to manage project risks.
- **Issues management**—That can be attached to individual project tasks.
- **Using Outlook to view tasks**—In a convenient format.

NEW

TABLE 28.1 NEW MICROSOFT OFFICE PROJECT 2003 FEATURES FOR ENTERPRISE COLLABORATION

New Professional Edition Feature	Project Management Functions
Multiple timesheet approvers	Allows staff and resources manager to review and approve timesheets before posting to projects
Timesheet lockdown periods	Provides time-data security to prevent changes
Risk management	Enables project managers to record and track progress to address risks
Outlook integration	Improves information exchange between Microsoft Outlook and Microsoft Project 2003 Professional

Project Server 2003 provides a robust environment supporting data storage and exchange so project teams can share information. Project data and associated documents are stored within the Project Server database repository and are managed by people who have access permissions to that data.

Project Web Access users can review, discuss, and exchange information about each project stored in the Project Server database repository. Each team member uses Project Web Access functions to review and update information like: timesheets, associated project documents, risks, issues, and status reports. All of this information is stored and managed through the set of functions found within Project Web Access as illustrated in Figure 28.1.

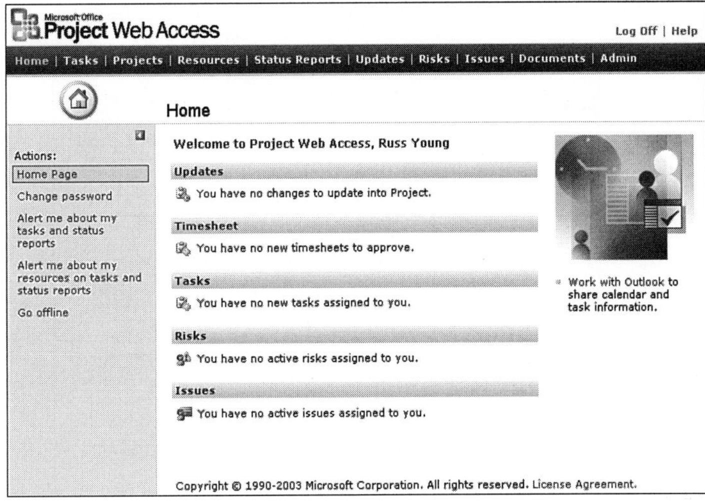

Figure 28.1
Project Web Access provides several collaboration functions such as Tasks, Status, Updates, Risks, Issues, and Documents.

Project managers use Microsoft Project 2003 Professional to develop work breakdown structures, assign team members to working tasks, and save project schedules into the Project Server database repository. Each time the project manager updates a project schedule, Project Server automatically manages information storage locations and transmits messages to team members and others who need to review updated project information.

Team members, project managers, and other Project Web Access users see the project information and can interact with the data using Project Server electronic collaboration techniques. As team members update project collaboration data, automatic messages are again transmitted to the subscribers so they can review the changes and stay informed about key project status and content.

The sections within this chapter give you more information about the key Project Server collaboration features and how to use the functions to manage project information.

➔ For information on Project Server architecture, **see** "System Architecture and Requirements," **p. 968**.

Understanding Enterprise Collaboration Flow

The Project Server architecture automatically creates and manages the internal data structures and information storage locations. When a project schedule is defined and stored within the Project Server 2003 database repository, the architectural components of Windows SharePoint Services are directed by Project Server to create the needed storage locations for that project.

Once the Windows SharePoint Services information stores are created, Project Web Access users are given access to that information based on their individual Project Server security permissions to a project. If the Project Web Access administrator changes user permissions, Project Server automatically directs Windows SharePoint Services to update permissions accordingly.

The flow diagram in Figure 28.2 illustrates these general principles.

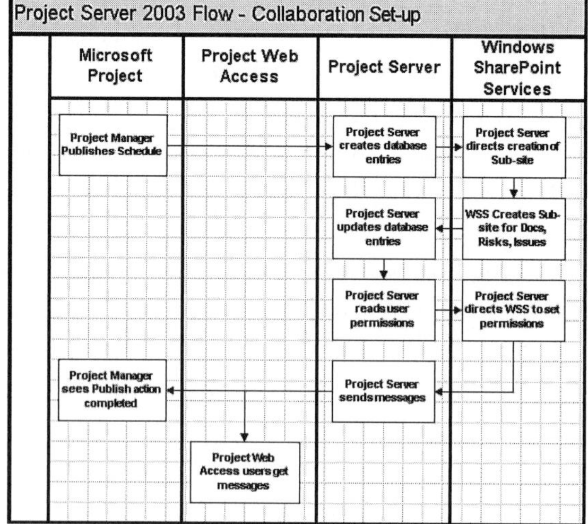

Figure 28.2 Project Server manages Windows SharePoint Services information stores.

Once the project schedule collaboration infrastructure is established, then Project Web Access users can view project data and use the collaboration features to share information.

Using Project Web Access Tasks for Timesheets

Project Server 2003 provides robust automated timesheet entry and update functions that allow team members to report time they spend working on tasks. Project managers can then use the reported time to automatically update individual tasks within a project schedule. Figure 28.3 depicts the general flow.

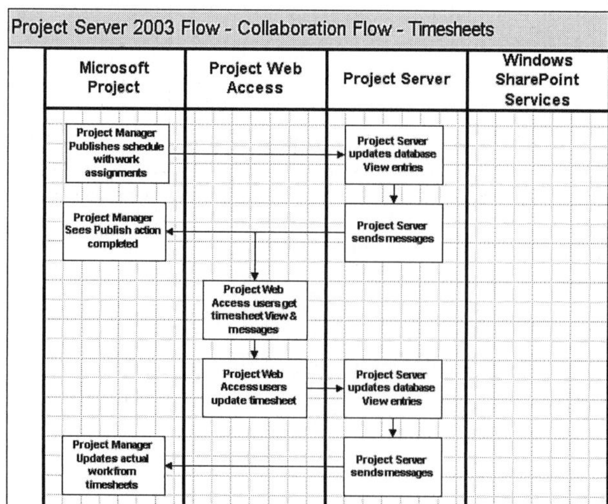

Figure 28.3 Project Server manages Timesheet flow.

28

If you trace the flow within Figure 28.3, you will see how Project Server sends task assignment messages to team members. As each team member updates his or her individual task assignments, Project Server records the reported time and sends a message to the project manager. The project manager can then direct the system to automatically update the project schedule tasks with the reported time.

The following sections describe more detail about time reporting and tracking functions within Project Web Access and Microsoft Office Project Professional 2003.

UNDERSTANDING TIMESHEETS

Timesheets allow project managers and team members to communicate assignments and progress on assigned tasks. This is communicated in the form of either a time entry for a given time period or as a percent complete assessment for a given time period. In both cases, an estimate of remaining effort is included to provide a complete picture of the progress being made on the assignment.

Project Web Access Timesheets provide a common form for this collaboration and communication of assignments, progress, and remaining effort. The interface supports three different generally accepted update methods:

- **%Complete and remaining effort**—The team member enters the %Complete value, from zero through 100%, and also enters any remaining work effort needed for specific tasks.
- **Hours worked for the time reporting period and remaining effort**—This allows the team member to generally report actual work and any remaining work for the entire report period. Time reporting periods can be for an entire week or longer periods, as established by the system administrator.
- **Hours worked per day and remaining effort for the time reporting period**—Team members can enter time for specific daily periods so the actual work is reported at a very detailed level.

NOTE

> The first two time tracking techniques have special effects when the project manager updates timesheet information into the project schedule. The reported actual work is loaded into the front end of the task start and finish duration timeline, according to the resource work contour settings for the task. The third time-tracking method provides the best time-entry resolution because the team members can show actual work on a daily basis.

NOTIFYING TEAM MEMBERS OF TASK ASSIGNMENTS

A project manager communicates assigned tasks to the team members by assigning individual resources to tasks within a project schedule, as shown in Figure 28.4.

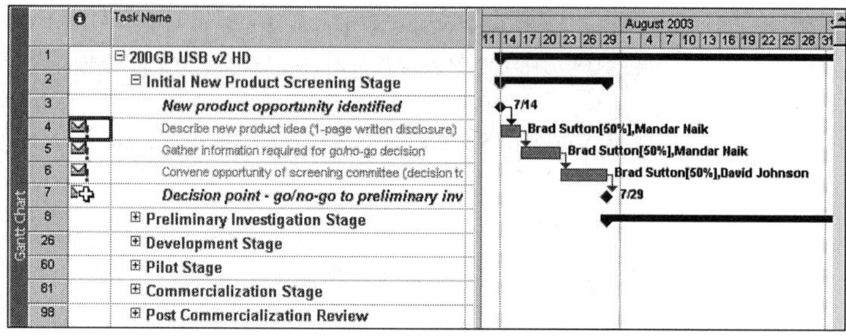

Figure 28.4
Project managers assign team members to tasks.

NOTE

Any time a task assignment is created or changed within a project schedule, a graphic icon will appear in the Indicators column for each affected task. The purpose of the icon is to alert the project manager that the marked tasks have resources assignments that should be sent to the team members.

→ For information on how to apply resources to tasks, **see** "Using the Assign Resources Dialog Box " **p. 1107**.

After resources have been assigned to tasks, the project manager uses the Project menu, chooses Collaborate, and then Publish to notify team members about their task assignments. Figure 28.5 shows the available menu options.

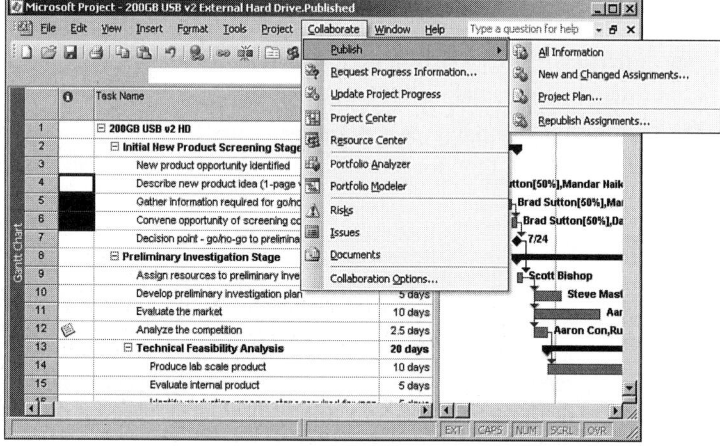

Figure 28.5
Project managers use Collaborate functions to notify team members of task assignments.

Each of the menu options is briefly defined as follows:

- **All Information**—Saves the tasks into the Project Server database repository and sends resource assignment messages to team members.

- **New and Changed Assignments**—Sends resource assignment messages to team members for those tasks that have been altered while the project schedule is open. This option has three suboptions:
  - **Entire Project**—Sends tasks assignment messages to the team for all changed tasks.
  - **Selected Items**—Sends tasks assignment messages to the team for only those tasks that were specifically selected.
  - **Current View**—Sends task assignment messages to the team for tasks that appear within the current filtered view of tasks.
- **Project Plan**—Saves the tasks into the Project Server database repository but does *NOT* send task assignment messages to team members.
- **Republish Assignments**—Re-sends all task assignments to all resources attached to the tasks.

The project manager has one additional Collaborate menu function to notify team members they should provide task progress. When you select the Request Progress Information menu, also shown in Figure 28.5, a new window appears that provides you with three task options as shown in Figure 28.6.

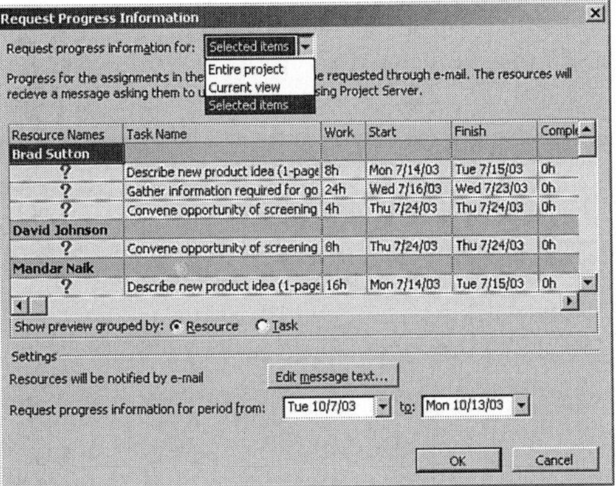

Figure 28.6 Project managers request progress information from the assigned team members using the Request Progress Information dialog.

- **Entire Project**—Sends tasks assignment messages to the team for all tasks.
- **Current View**—Sends tasks assignment messages to the team for only those tasks that appear in the filtered view.
- **Selected Items**—Sends tasks assignment messages to the team for specific tasks that have been selected.

Several of the Collaborate menu functions allow the project manager to use the Edit Message Text button to modify the assignment message before it is sent to the team members. Figure 28.7 shows an example of the default text that can be easily modified.

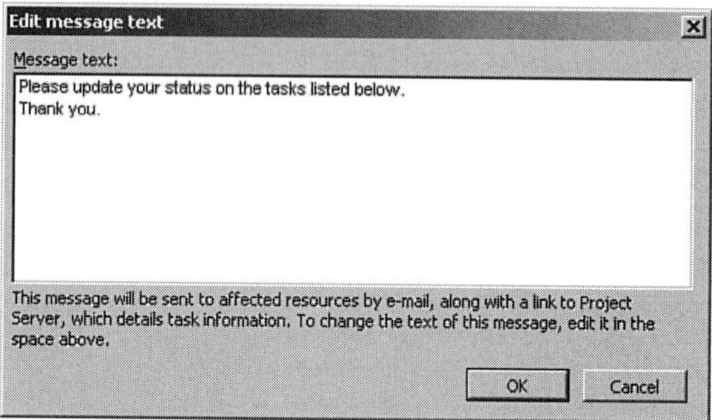

Figure 28.7 Project managers edit collaboration message text.

If email messaging is enabled within Project Server, each affected team member receives an email message when the project manager clicks the Send button. The task assignments are also saved to the timesheet tasks for each affected team member. Team members can use Project Web Access Tasks functions to review task assignments and submit time to the project manager.

Submitting Timesheets for Approval and Update

When a team member is assigned to work on a working task, they receive a message notifying them of their task assignments. Team members then use the Project Web Access Tasks page to see their assigned tasks and enter work progress to be submitted to the project manager for schedule updates. Figure 28.8 shows a typical example of a timesheet.

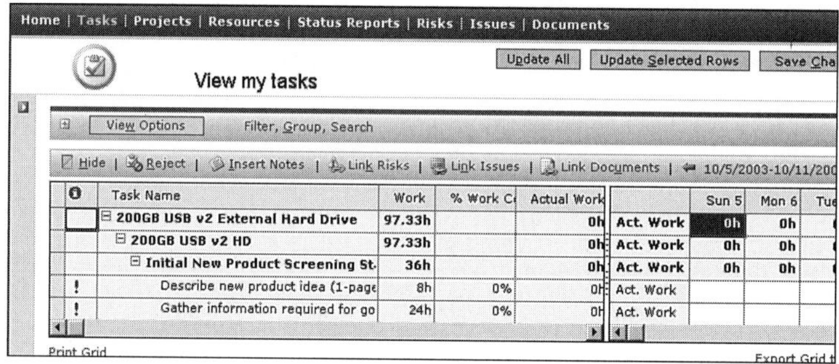

Figure 28.8 Team members see assigned tasks in a timesheet view.

Team members use the Tasks timesheet views to fill in the work effort spent on each task. Timesheet data entry is set by the Project Web Access administrator, who establishes one of the following timesheet modes:

- **%Complete**—Enter the percent complete on each task assignment worked and also provide an estimated remaining work for each task. Any adjustment to remaining work automatically recalculates the task %Complete based on the new total estimated effort.
- **Hours worked per time reporting period**—Enter the hours worked for each task assignment for the time reporting period and enter any remaining work estimate. %Complete will be recalculated based on the updated information.

- **Hours worked per day for the time period**—Enter actual hours worked per day for each assignment worked. If you enter a value for remaining work, the %Complete will be calculated based on the updated information.

➔ **See** the section "Understanding Timesheets" on **p. 1123** in this chapter for more information about timesheet entry modes.

➔ The Project Web Access administrator establishes Timesheet data formats and data–entry status methods. See Chapter 25 for more information about timesheet control settings.

Each team member can also supply notes that become attached to the task when the project manager updates the timesheet data into the project schedule. The added notes become part of the task comments when the timesheet data is updated. Follow these steps to add a note to a timesheet task:

1. Select the assignment row in the timesheet.
2. Click on Insert Note from the timesheet menu; refer to Figure 28.8.
3. Type in the comment text; see Figure 28.9.
4. Click OK to save the note text with the task.

Notes can be modified and added to as the assignment progresses, giving you a place to record ongoing communication regarding the task updates.

Figure 28.9
Team members attach notes to timesheet tasks.

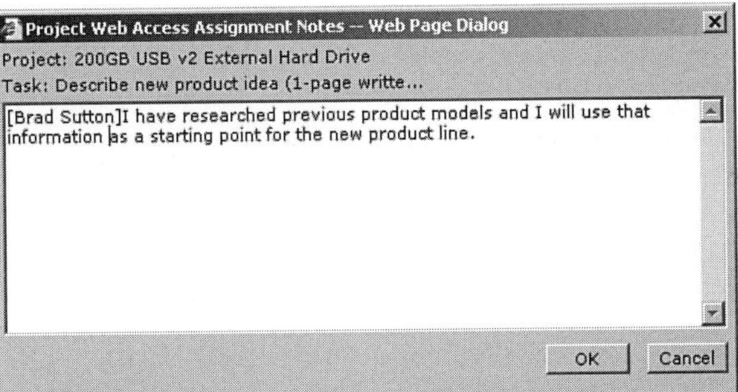

Once all timesheet work progress has been entered for the appropriate tasks, select Update all Rows from the top right corner of the Tasks page. Alternatively, you can submit individual task updates by first choosing specific rows in the timesheet and then clicking the Update Selected Rows button from the top right corner of the Tasks page.

TIP

> You can select multiple rows by using the Ctrl key or Shift key while picking tasks with the mouse.

Updating and Revising Timesheets

Project Web Access has several features that allow project managers to approve, update, and modify timesheets submitted by team members. This section describes those features so you can understand how timesheet data can be updated to tasks within project schedules.

Approving Timesheets Prior to Updating Schedules

Project Web Access 2003 now provides a new feature that enables staff managers to review timesheets before the information is updated into the project schedules. This new feature allows a manager to review submitted timesheets and either Accept or Reject each task entry.

Timesheet entries that are accepted are sent to the project manager for final update into the project schedule. Timesheet data that is rejected is returned to the team member for revisions and resubmission.

→ **See** "Approved Timesheets" on **p. 1080** in Chapter 27 for more information about approving timesheets before updating schedules.

Timesheet Lockdown Periods

Project Web Access 2003 now provides a new feature that allows the administrator to control time periods when timesheets can be updated. The purpose of this new feature is to prevent modifications or updates to timesheet information without the specific permissions to do so. The key benefit is to ensure that timesheet data is managed in a controlled way that is consistent with strong project and cost management principles.

Timesheet lockdown periods are controlled within the Project Web Access Admin functions under the Customize Project Web Access Tracking Settings menu. Figure 28.10 shows an example of how specific time periods can be Open or Closed for timesheet entry.

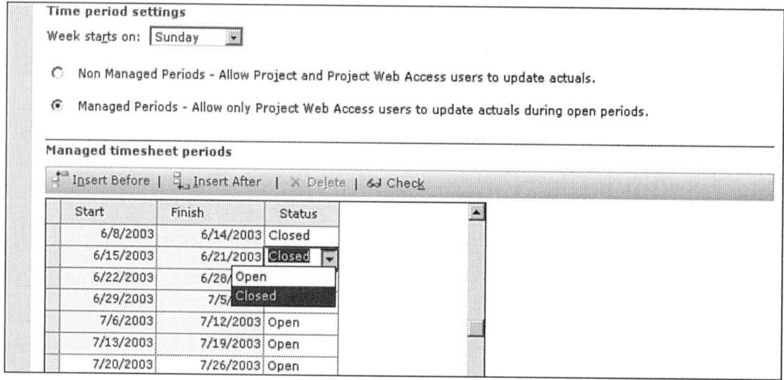

Figure 28.10
Project Web Access Admin settings to lock down timesheet periods.

Timesheet lockdown periods can only be enabled when the time-tracking setting is set to Hours Worked per Day for the Time Period. If you have selected another tracking mode and you also want to control locked out time periods, then you will see a warning message, as shown in Figure 28.11, when you attempt to save the time-tracking settings.

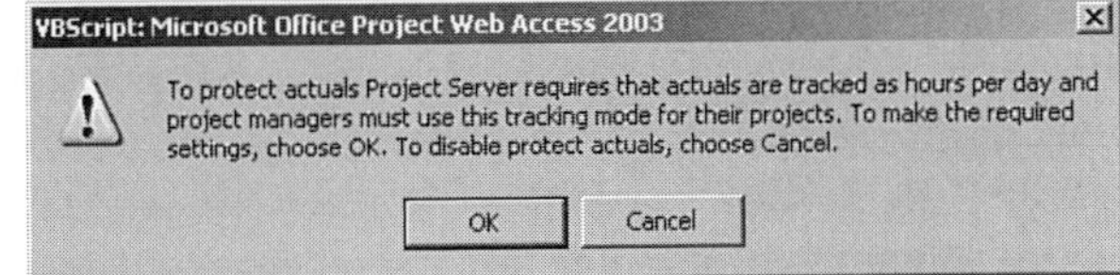

Figure 28.11 Warning message for setting locked time periods.

After the Project Web Access time lockdown periods have been established, team members are prevented from entering timesheet actual work for Time periods that are marked as Closed. When a team member examines his or her individual timesheet, they will see the Closed time periods grayed out for the locked date ranges. This prevents them from modifying data for those periods.

You can use this timesheet lockdown feature to freeze past timesheet submissions or lock out future timesheet periods. This allows you to create a moving window of time when timesheet entry is allowed.

TIP

> You should consider creating business processes to establish when timesheets can be submitted. Those processes should also address any need to modify timesheet data that falls within a Closed period.

Revising Timesheet Data

NEW Project Web Access 2003 now provides a new feature that allows staff managers to modify timesheet data after it has been submitted by team members. If you are a manager with appropriate Project Web Access permissions, then you can use the Adjust Actuals menu functions within the Resource Center.

There are two general approaches to revising timesheet data in Project Web Access. The Adjust Actuals function is used when Managed Time Periods is active and the timesheet period has been Closed. The second method permits team members to go back to the time period in question, make any revisions to the timesheet then resubmit the revised task updates. This method can only be used if the time period is still Open or Managed Time Periods is not active.

➔ **See** the section "Adjusting Actuals" on **p. 1080** in Chapter 27 for more information about adjusting timesheet actual work values.

Using Project Status Reports

Status reports provide a convenient forum for a workgroup to communicate with each other. These reports consist of the narrative dialog explaining what has occurred and the results seen in the project plans after updates have been applied. They can relate directly to a project or a workgroup effort across many projects.

Project Web Access provides a Web form that can be customized and formatted to fit the workgroup's requirements. These reports can be scheduled and assigned to team members for regular communication of status on a given project or group. Team members can also submit ad hoc reports independently. In addition, Project Web Access has the ability to combine status reports submitted by multiple team members into a consolidated report.

Figure 28.12 shows the logical flow of using status reports.

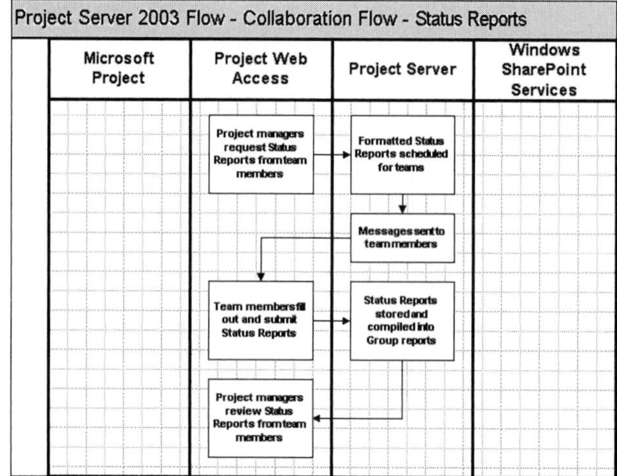

Figure 28.12 Project Web Access status report flow.

Requesting Status Reports

Project managers can request status reports from their team members by creating a requested report in Project Web Access.

The Report request is divided into four steps as shown in Figure 28.13.

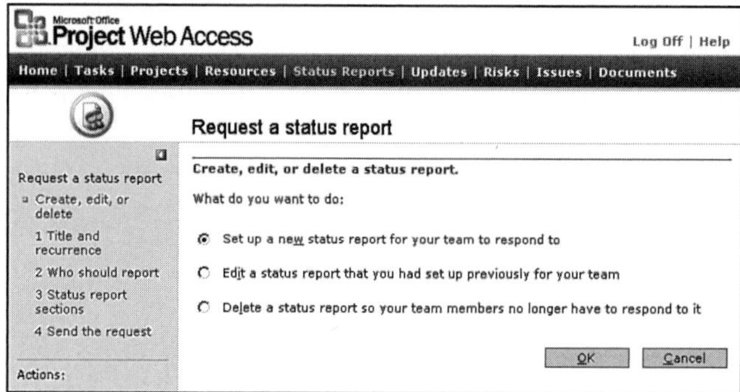

Figure 28.13 Create a new status report.

28

You can use the following steps to create a new status report:

1. Select Request a Status Report from the list on the Status Report page in Project Web Access.
2. Select the Set Up a New Status Report for Your Team to Respond To, and then select OK.
3. Next, fill in the title of the report and indicate how often it reoccurs with an initial beginning due date for the first report. Select Next to continue with the report creation.
4. Then select the resources who will submit a status report to you. The available resources appear on the left. Select a resource and click on the Add button between the lists. You can use the Ctrl Key to make multiple resource selections. When you add a resource to the report list, you can select whether to automatically merge their report into a combined Status Report. This selection is made by default. You have to clear the selection if you want to manually combine status reports.
5. Use the dialog box to format the major subsections of the report. The section titles and descriptions can be changed and new sections added by the requestor. After you format the report, click the Next button to finalize the report.

You can now either send the request out to the team listed in the report, save the report for further modification, or cancel the request. If you select Send then an alert message is transmitted to the team members so they can visit their Project Web Access home page to update the status reports.

SUBMITTING STATUS REPORTS

There are two ways to submit a status report:

- Respond to a scheduled status report request
- Submit an unsolicited status report

Scheduled status reports will appear on the Project Web Access home page as Status Report alert links. When you select an alert link, a Web form with editable sections will be displayed.

The report subsections are freeform text boxes that include some limited text formatting tools. There is also a tool that allows you to select a project task assignment from your timesheet.

Task titles and schedule information are selected by clicking the Insert Tasks from Timesheet button on the toolbar above the section. Your timesheet will appear at the top of the form that shows your task assignments, with selection boxes in the left column of the timesheet. Select the tasks you want to insert, select the section in the status report you want the tasks to go into, and then click on the Insert tool. Repeat this process for each section and remember to unselect the tasks after each insert. When you are finished, click done at the bottom of the page. You will then return to the report editor page.

After you enter text information, you can save the report for later submission or use the Send button to immediately deliver the report to the requesting manager.

Figure 28.14 illustrates an example of a status report that a team member is editing.

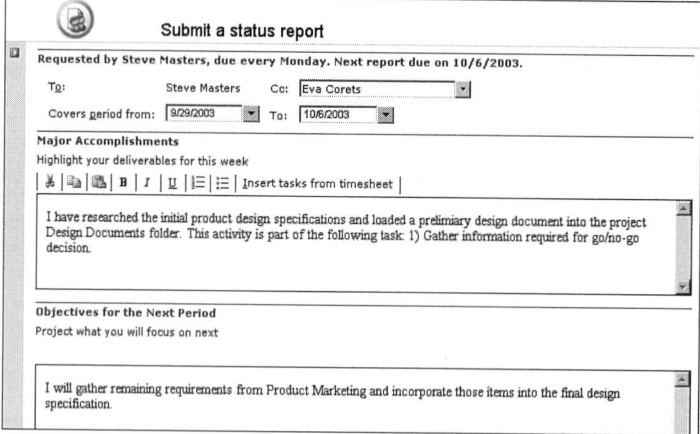

Figure 28.14
Team members provide status reports to project managers.

You can also submit an ad hoc status report by clicking the Submit an Unrequested Status Report link on the left side of the Submit a Status Report page. A new screen appears allowing you to name the report and declare the recipient for it. You can add various sections as you need, then use the Send button to transmit the report. The recipient will receive an email and also see a Status Report alert on their home page.

Compiling and Using Status Reports

Status report recipients receive an alert on their home page when a status report is submitted to them. They can also see who has submitted a requested report from the Status Reports page in Project Web Access.

To view and compile requested status reports, go to the Status Reports page. Select the requested report from the list of reports. A table displaying the requested submittal dates and the list of reporters will be displayed. Each date will indicate who has submitted a report by displaying a report icon for that team member row in the date column. A Team Report icon appears at the top of each column.

Select the icon for the individual team member to view that specific report. Select the team icon to compile and merge all individual submittals into a consolidated report for that date.

The table allows you to look at past reports and keeps history going back to the original request date when you created the request. Team members can also review past reports by selecting the Archive from the options on the Status Reports page.

When team members submit status reports to the project managers, those reports can be automatically compiled into composite reports for specific time periods.

Figure 28.15 shows how the project manager can view a composite report from the team members.

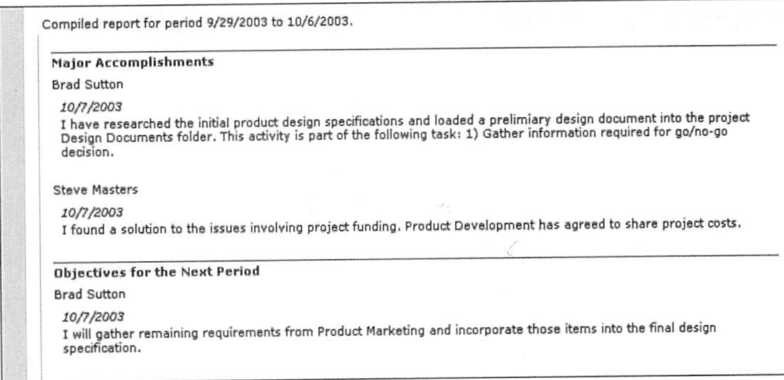

Compiled report for period 9/29/2003 to 10/6/2003.

Major Accomplishments

Brad Sutton

10/7/2003

I have researched the initial product design specifications and loaded a prelimiary design document into the project Design Documents folder. This activity is part of the following task: 1) Gather information required for go/no-go decision.

Steve Masters

10/7/2003

I found a solution to the issues involving project funding. Product Development has agreed to share project costs.

Objectives for the Next Period

Brad Sutton

10/7/2003

I will gather remaining requirements from Product Marketing and incorporate those items into the final design specification.

Figure 28.15
Project managers can review composite team status reports.

STORING PROJECT ARTIFACT DOCUMENTS

A document management facility within Windows SharePoint Services is created for each project when it is first created or imported into Microsoft Project Server. These libraries provide a repository for Project artifact documents that can include requirements, charters, specifications, illustrations, or any other material relevant to the project team's efforts on the project. The following sections describe the major features of Project Web Access document storage functions. Figure 28.16 depicts how project documents, risks, and issues are managed.

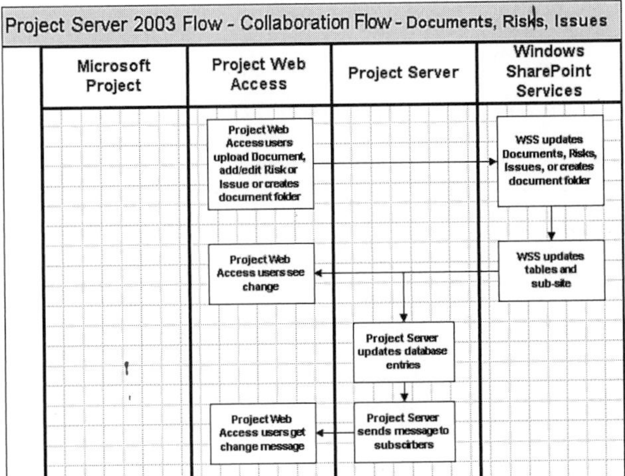

Figure 28.16
Project Web Access artifact management flow.

UNDERSTANDING DOCUMENT LIBRARIES

Document libraries allow you to store related information to your projects in organized groups. These groups or sublibraries are defined by you so that a "filing cabinet" concept can be instituted to hold all your related Project Documents. Figure 28.2 illustrates what happens when a project is published within the Project Server database repository.

→ **See** "Understanding Enterprise Collaboration Flow," **p. 1121** for more information about general Project Web Access collaboration.

USING DOCUMENT LIBRARIES

When you select Documents from the top menu bar in Project Web Access, you will see a list of Project Document Libraries.

Document libraries are grouped by either My Projects—those projects that have task assignments for you and other projects that you have permission to access—or the Public Documents Library, which contains general documents for the entire Project Server installation.

You can open a project document library by selecting a project link. The project document library page is displayed that shows subfolders for that library as shown in Figure 28.17.

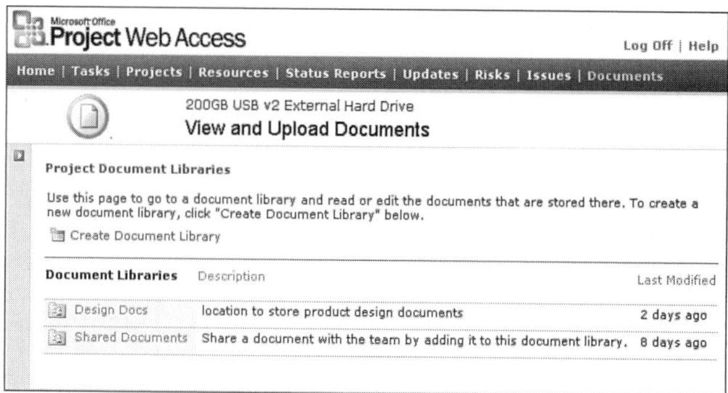

Figure 28.17
Project Document Libraries can have subfolders.

Graphical "folder" icons are displayed with the name and description of each folder. By default, each project library has a "Shared Documents" subfolder created for it. You can also add new subfolders to contain various documents related to a project.

You can easily open a subfolder by selecting an existing folder to view a list of documents stored within that library. The displayed list includes document names and other important information about each document.

Hovering the mouse pointer over the document name displays a pull-down list of options. You can view or edit the properties of the document, check out the document, edit the document using Microsoft Office, view the document version history, set alerts, and start a discussion about the document.

Selecting the document name opens the document for viewing in a Web-based facility.

LINKING DOCUMENTS TO TASKS

The natural lifecycle of projects often requires that document be related directly to working tasks within project schedules. Project Web Access 2003 allows you to link individual documents to specific tasks within a project schedule. These links are visible as a document icon in the indicator column when you view the schedule details within the Project Center.

Follow these general steps to link a document in a subfolder to a project task:

1. Go to the document subfolder for a project and select the Edit icon next to the document you want to link. You will see three hyperlink choices below the Status field in the edit form.
2. Choose the Select Project Tasks That Are Related to This Document link. A dialog box will appear with a list of tasks filtered for "My Tasks."
3. Select the related tasks by clicking the check box on the left side of the list adjacent to the task name. Click OK after you select the tasks.

The selected task names will then appear in the edit form below the Status field. Document icons also appear to the left of the selected tasks in Project Center detail views.

MANAGING RISKS

Project Web Access 2003 now provides a facility for defining and managing Risk management plans. This facility includes the ability to describe the potential risk areas of the project, the probability that risk will impact the project, any mitigation plan to minimize the potential risk, and the definition and triggering of contingencies if the mitigation is not successful. This feature provides all the basic elements of a risk management process, including responsible team member, risk manager, critical dates, and descriptive elements.

Use the Project Web Access Risk tab functions to create and manage risks for projects stored within the Project Server database repository. Selecting the Risks tab reveals a list of projects you have permissions to view. When you select a project name link, a set of risk management controls is presented as shown within Figure 28.18.

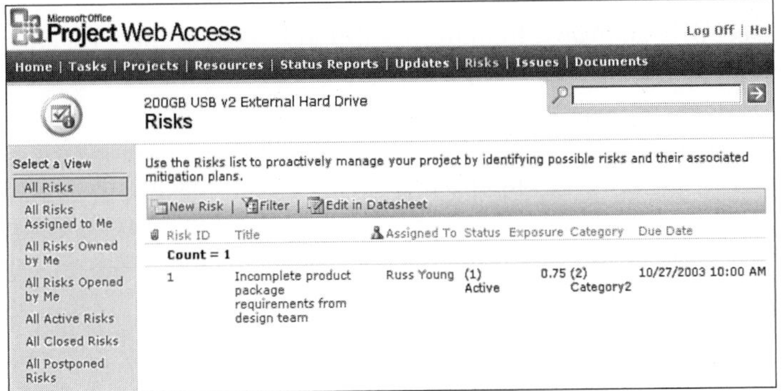

Figure 28.18
Project risks are managed within Project Web Access.

CREATING AND ASSIGNING RISK ITEMS

Navigate to the Risks Page from the top menu. The page will display a list of projects grouped by your projects and other projects (if you have permissions to view them). Use the following general steps to define a risk item:

1. Select the project that you want to create a Risk item for; the page will display a list of current risk items.
2. Select New Risk from the toolbar above the list. An edit form will display where you will fill in the relevant information about the risk. These elements are
   - **Title**—The title of the risk item (this is a required element).
   - **Assigned To**—The person who is responsible for managing this risk item.
   - **Status**—The risk item can be either Active, Postponed, or Closed.
   - **Due Date and Time**—Enter the expected or required resolution date for the risk item.
   - **Owner**—The person who has ownership of the risk item.
   - **Probability**—The probability that this risk item will occur. (This is a required element.)
   - **Impact**—A value from 1 to 10 that represents the severity of the effect this risk item will have on the project if it occurs. (This is a required element.)
   - **Cost**—The cost to the project if this risk item should occur.
   - **Description**—Outline that defines and describes the risk item.
   - **Mitigation Plan**—Describes the plan to handle the risk item and prevent it from occurring.
   - **Contingency Plan**—Describes the fallback plan if the risk item does occur.
   - **Trigger Description**—Describes the type of condition that would result in the Contingency Plan being implemented. This can be a date, a cost value exceeded, or other quantifiable measure within the Project data.
   - **Trigger**—The value to indicate the condition that would trigger the contingency plan.
3. Select Save and Close from the Toolbar at the top of the form after you enter all required information.

When a risk item is defined for a project a graphical icon is displayed adjacent to the project within the Project Center summary views. If a risk is attached to a specific working task then a graphical icon appears within the Project Center detail views. If you select a risk graphic icon then Project Web Access will open the appropriate project risk group for review and updates.

LINKING RISKS TO TASKS

Risks can be linked to tasks from two different views in Project Web Access.

- The first method is to select a Project View to see the detail schedule. Then you can select the Link Risk item from the toolbar at the top of the view.
- The second method is accomplished by navigating to the Risks page and either creating a risk item or editing and existing one.

Task linking selections can be found at the bottom of the creation or edit pages. Selections include affected tasks, triggers, mitigation tasks, contingency plan tasks, other risks, other issues, and documents. Clicking on any of these selections brings up a task dialog box with the project tasks.

Multiple tasks can be selected by checking the box to the left of the task name. Select OK to complete the link. Risk icons will then appear in the Project Center views for each linked task within a project. Clicking on the Risk icon navigates to the risk item linked to the task.

UPDATING AND CLOSING RISKS

Risk items' updates and status are provided by the responsible resource assigned to the item, the owner, or any team members who have access and the permissions to update the risk item. Navigating to a specific risk item and selecting the Edit icon to the left of the Risk Item Title allows you to provide updates. You can then edit the risk fields, change the status or assigned names, and generally modify the risk conditions. Select Save and Close after any updates or change in status to a particular risk item.

MANAGING ISSUES

Project Web Access 2003 provides a feature for defining and managing issues on each project in the repository. This facility includes the ability to describe the issue, categorize the impact of the issue, assign resolution to a resource, establish a due date, and set the status of the issue. Figure 28.19 is an example of issues that have been attached to a specific project.

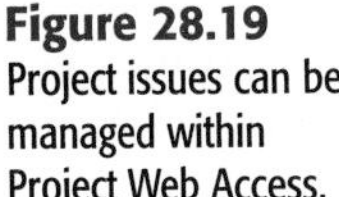

Figure 28.19
Project issues can be managed within Project Web Access.

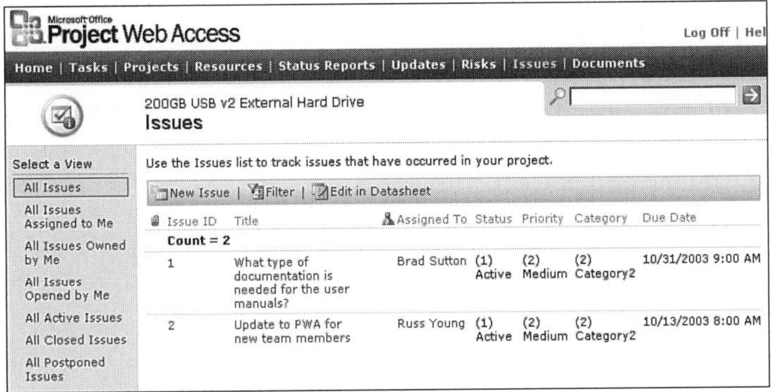

Creating and Assigning Issues

Navigate to the Issues page from the top menu. The page will display a list of projects grouped by your projects and other projects (if you have permissions to view them). Select the project that you want to create an issue for. The page will display a list of current issues. Select New Issue from the toolbar above the list. An edit form will display, where you will fill in the relevant information about the issue. These elements are

- **Title**—The title of the issue. (This is a required field.)
- **Assigned To**—Who is responsible for managing this issue.
- **Status**—The issue can be either Active, Postponed, or Closed.
- **Owner**—The person who has ownership of the issue.
- **Priority**—The importance of the issue. There are three possible levels: High, Medium, and Low.
- **Due Date and Time**—Enter the expected or required resolution date for the issue.
- **Discussion**—Outlines, defines, and describes the issue item.
- **Resolution**—Describes the end result of how the issue was resolved.

Select Save and Close from the Toolbar at the top of the form after you enter the required information.

Updating and Closing Issues

Issues are updated by the responsible resource assigned to the issue, the owner, or any team members who have access and the permissions to update issues. Updates are accomplished by navigating to the issue from the Issues page and selecting the Edit icon to the left of the issue title. Select Save and Close after any updates or changes in Status.

Linking Issues to Tasks

Issues can be linked to tasks from two different views in Project Web Access. The first method is to select a Project View to see the detail schedule. Select the Link Issues item from the toolbar at the top of the view.

The second method is accomplished by navigating to the Issues page and either creating an issue or editing an existing one. Task linking selections can be found at the bottom of the creation or edit pages. Selections include affected tasks, tasks that resolve the issue, other risks, other issues, and documents. Clicking on any of these selections brings up a task dialog box with the project tasks. Multiple tasks can be selected by checking the box to the left of the task name. Select OK to complete the link. Issues icons will appear in the Project views for the tasks selected and in the Project Center for each project. Clicking on the Issues icon will navigate to the issue linked to the task.

USING MICROSOFT OUTLOOK WITH PROJECT SERVER 2003

Team members' attention and focus on getting work done is the key to any project success. They need to collaborate with others and manage their work. They know it is important to keep the project manager up-to-date on their assignment progress (but it is not the main focus of their job) and they wish to spend as little time as possible doing so. Team members can use the Outlook integration feature of Microsoft Office Project 2003 to keep project managers updated. Figure 28.20 shows an example of how project tasks can appear in your Outlook Calendar.

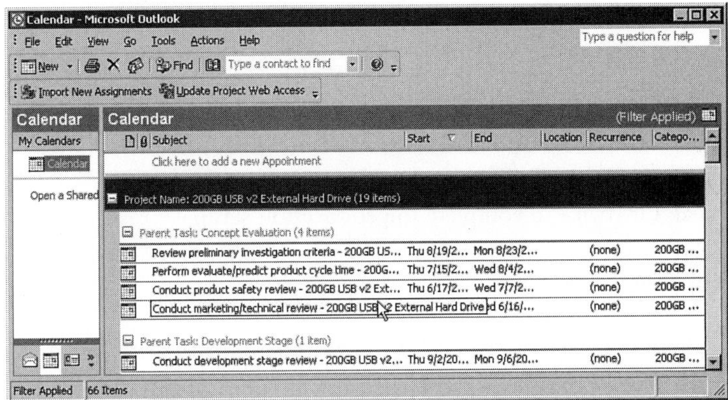

Figure 28.20
Project tasks appear within Outlook Calendar views.

SETTING UP OUTLOOK TO WORK WITH PROJECT SERVER

Before you can connect Project Web Access and Outlook, you must activate a COM Add-in on the workstation with Outlook. Make sure you are logged on as a local administrator, or that your Windows policies allow you to perform this installation. Follow these general steps to activate Outlook for Project Server:

1. Log on to Project Web Access as you normally would and navigate to the Tasks view.
2. Select View and Report Your Tasks from Your Outlook Calendar then click the Download Now button to download the Outlook add-in. If your security settings prompt you to accept ActiveX controls, click Yes.
3. When the File download dialog appears on the screen, select Open to begin installing the control.
4. Follow the instructions in the dialog to complete this process.

This installation only has to be performed once for each workstation using Outlook integration with Project Web Access.

SETTING THE URL FOR OUTLOOK TO CONNECT TO PROJECT SERVER

Outlook must have a valid connection to your Project Server installation before data can be shared between these applications. Use the following steps to create a connection between these software tools:

1. Open Outlook and select Tools from the menu.
2. Select Options from the list and click on the Project Web Access tab.
3. Within the option screen, select the Enter Login Information button toward the bottom of the dialog.
4. Enter the URL for your Project Server installation, such as `http://yoursevername/projectserver`. Be sure to click the Test Connection button to ensure Outlook can connect to Project Server.
5. If you use Windows Authentication to connect, select that option; otherwise, select Project Server Authentication and enter your Project Web Access username.
6. You can also schedule Outlook to automatically import your assignments to the Outlook Calendar and to automatically submit saved updates to Project Web Access on this screen.
7. Click OK twice to complete the connection setup.

Outlook is now ready to use with Project Web Access.

IMPORTING REVIEWING PROJECT TASKS IN CALENDAR VIEWS

Project task assignments are easily viewed and updated within Outlook by using the new Project Server toolbar menu items.

- **Import New Assignments**—Imports your assigned project tasks into your Outlook calendar. A list will appear with all new assignments from Project Web Access. Select OK to complete the task import.
- **Update Project Web Access**—Sends task updates to the appropriate project managers for timesheet updating.

If any of the new assignments are due in the current calendar period, reminders will appear. You can review and dismiss them individually or select Dismiss All to remove all reminders.

To review your tasks in the Outlook Calendar, select the Calendar view and use the following menu sequence to see Project assignments: View, Arrange by, Current View, Active Project-Related Appointment. Double-click an event to see details about the assignment.

SUBMITTING TIME WITH OUTLOOK

Assignments can be updated directly by using new Project Server menu controls within Outlook. To do this, select the Calendar view and set it to an appropriate timeframe to view the assignments. Double-click the assignment to view the assignment details. There are three tabs in this dialog. Select Project Web Access and maximize the frame to see your task timesheet, as shown in Figure 28.21.

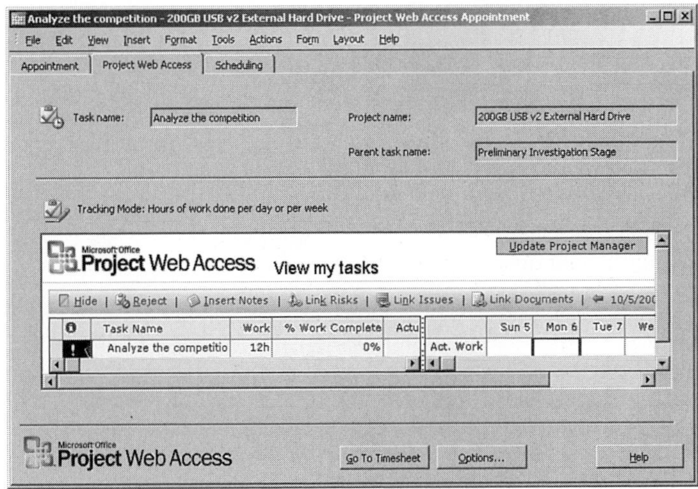

Figure 28.21
Review task details and submit time from Outlook.

Enter status on the task and then click the Update Project Manager button directly from this view to submit the work effort as a timesheet for the task. You can also use the Save Changes button and process all your task updates together. Then, when you are ready to update the project manager, select Update Project Web Access on the toolbar or from the Tools, Project Web Access menu.

INDEX

Note

Entries with the prefix CD: are located on the accompanying CD-ROM. For example, **CD:66–69** would be found on pages 66–69 of the CD-ROM chapters.

Symbols

& (ampersand), 839, 860, 944, CD:42

*** (asterisk), 52, 781, 864**

^ (caret), 52, 864

... (ellipsis), 864

- (minus sign), 233, 784

+ (plus sign), 233, 784

 # (pound sign), CD:25

? (question mark), 52, 864, CD:44

~ (tilde), 100

% (percent sign)
- % Complete field
  - progress bars, 795
  - tasks, 533
- % Work Complete field
  - assignments, 538
  - progress bars, 796
  - tasks, 535

3D View tab (Commands and Options dialog box), CD:83

24 Hour base calendars, 76

A

<A> tag, CD:20–21

abbreviations, 134–135

Access format. *See* .mdb file format

accessing Project Center, 1031

Account Name field (Account Properties dialog box), 1006

Account Properties dialog box, 1006

Account Type field (Account Properties dialog box), 1006

accounts, Project Server user accounts, CD:66–69

accrual methods, 285–286, 578

accrued costs
- accrual methods, 285–286, 578
- Cost Accrual field, 307
- defined, 285

actions (command buttons), 939–941

activating. *See* enabling

active split bars, 46

active toolbars, 927

actual cost of work performed (ACWP), 284, 578

Actual Costs Are Always Calculated by Microsoft Project calculation option, 541–543

Actual Duration field, 534

actual finish dates
- assignments, 537
- defined, 794
- tasks, 532–533

Actual Finish field
- assignments, 537
- tasks, 532–533

actual resources, 1091–1092
- enterprise actual resources, 1093
- local actual resources, 1093–1094

actual start dates
- assignments, 537
- defined, 794
- tasks, 532

Actual Start field
- assignments, 537
- tasks, 532

Actual Work field
- assignments, 537
- tasks, 535–536

actuals, adjusting, 1080

ACWP (actual cost of work performed), 284, 578

Add button (Team Builder), 1106

Add field (Microsoft Project Server Accounts dialog box), 1007

Add Group button, CD:68

Add Progress Line button (Tracking toolbar), 549

Add Progress Line tool, 561

Add Resources button (Assign Resources dialog box), 290

Add User button, CD:66
Add User screen (Project Server), CD:66–67
Adjust Dates tool, 227–228
Admin menu commands
Manage Enterprise Features, 996
Manage Views, 988, 991–993
administrators, 971
Administrative projects, 1047
Advanced Search pane, 32
ALAP (As Late As Possible) constraint, 202
alerts, 42–43
Align drop-down list (Timescale dialog box), 787
Align Title option (Column Definition dialog box), 845
Align tool, 815
All command (Clear menu), 128
All Information command (Collaborate menu), 1124
All Resources command (Filtered For menu), 410
All Resources filter, 317, 767
All Tasks filter, 765
Always Create Backup option (Save Options), 102
Always Roll Up Gantt Bars option (Layout dialog box), 161, 798
ampersand (&), 839, 860, 944, CD:42
Analysis toolbar, 927
Analyze Timescaled Data Wizard, 591–595
analyzing projects
earned value analysis, 575–577
actual cost, 578
controlling earned value calculation, 587–588
earned value, 577–578
Earned Value Cost Indicators table, 583–587
Earned Value Schedule Indicators table, 581–582
examining trends, 578
example, 579–582
Excel graphs, 590–595
planned value, 577
troubleshooting, 599
viewing, 589–590
Portfolio Analyzer
assessing projects with, 1053–1054
changing view content, 1051–1052
charts, 1051
compared to Portfolio Modeler, 1048–1049
drop-down lists, 1051
example, 1050
PivotTables, 1051
Save a Link option, 1050
Save as GIF option, 1051
view options, 1050
portfolio models, 1063–1064
projects, 1048
resources, 1048
Appearance column (Bar Styles dialog box), 791–792
application-level events, CD:63
applications
clients, 703
copying data between
blocks of values, 692–694
copying into other applications, 695–696
copying into Project, 694–695
single values, 692
timephased data, 692, 696
Windows Clipboard, 692
exporting data
Excel PivotTables, 668, 670–673
file formats, 632–635
Import/Export Wizard, 637–639
text files, 682–684
to older version of Project, 636
troubleshooting, 689
XML files, 681–682
importing data. *See also* Import maps
Excel format, 673–680
file formats, 632–635
Import/Export Wizard, 637–639
MPX format, 636
ODBC (Open Database Connectivity) sources, 648
Outlook task lists, 684–687
text files, 684
troubleshooting, 689
XML files, 681–682
inserting objects into, 719–720
linked data
creating, 697–699
defined, 697
deleting, 701–702
identifying, 702
link indicators, 699
pasting, 697–699, 702
refreshing, 699–701
restoring, 702
updating, 699–701
servers, 703
Apply Filter button (Team Builder), 1104
applying
filters, 318, 495, 762–764
Calendar view, 261–262
resource list filters, 370
groups, 770
work contours, 352
approving timesheets, 1128
Arc button (Drawing toolbar), 249
architecture of Microsoft Project Professional 2003, 968–969
Arrange All command (Window menu), 605
Arrow button (Drawing toolbar), 249
Arrow keys (task tables), 234
As Late As Possible (ALAP) constraint, 202
ASAP (As Soon As Possible) constraint, 202

Assign Resources command (Tools menu), 1107

Assign Resources dialog box, 289–291, 365–367, 1107–1110
displaying, 366
drag-and-drop, 376
features, 367–368
graphs, 372–373
modifying assignments, 377–379
removing assignments, 376–377
resource list filters, 369–371
resource unit assignments, 374–375

Assigned Calendar indicator, 353

assigning
calendars to tasks, 224–225
issues, 1138
resources, 26–27
risks, 1136

Assignment Delay field (Usage table), 446–447

Assignment Information dialog box, 344, 352, 390–391
Cost Rate Table field, 392–393
Notes field, 392–393
Work Contour field, 391–392

Assignment reports, 889–890

Assignment Units field, 325–329

Assignment view, CD:74

Assignment Work by Project view (Resource Center), 1076

Assignment Work by Resource view (Resource Center), 1076

Assignment Work field, 329

Assignment Work graph, 372

assignments, 360
adjusting actuals, 1080
Assign Resources dialog box, 365–367, 1107–1110
displaying, 366
drag-and-drop, 376
features, 367–368
graphs, 371–373
modifying assignments, 377–379
removing assignments, 376–377
resource list filters, 369–371
resource unit assignments, 374–375
assignment delay
Assignment Delay field (Usage table), 446–447
fixed-finish-date projects, 384–385
fixed-start-date projects, 382–384
Assignment Information dialog box, 390–391
Cost Rate Table field, 392–393
Notes field, 392–393
Work Contour field, 391–392
Assignment reports, 889–890
assignment units, 325
field format, 326
fixed consumption rates, 328
fractions, 328
material resource units, 328–329
maximum number of, 326
variable consumption rates, 329
work resource units, 326–327
availability of resources, determining, 402–404
components of, 322–324
consumption rates, 328–329
contouring, 440
Cost Rate tables, 392–393
delaying, 342–345, 440
individual assignments, 443–447
leveling delays, 324
tasks, 441–443
drag-and-drop, 376
driver resources, 355–357
extended working hours, 429–432
fixed contract fees, 396–399
fixed costs, 396–399
front-loaded contour, 324
hiding/displaying, 411
material resources
Material Resources field, 330
work formula, 333
modifying, 377–379
multiple resources, 333–334
nondriver resources, 355
notifying team members of, 1123–1126
notes, 393
overallocated resources
defined, 402
delayed assignments, 440–447
extended working hours, 429–432
filtering, 409–410
formatting display, 405
Go to Next Overallocation tool, 412
highlighting, 405
identifying, 405–409
increasing availability of, 410, 418–423
overtime, 423–428
reasons for, 403
reconciling, 406
reducing workload for, 419–421, 432
Resource Allocation view, 432–434
Resource Usage view, 410–411
sensitivity setting, 407–408
split assignments, 451–453
split tasks, 448–451
substituting underused resources for, 434–440
timephased details, 412–417
viewing, 409
overtime, 346–348, 385–387, 423–428
removing, 376–377
resource assignment fields
Assignment Units, 325–329
Assignment Work, 329
Material Resources, 330
Resource Name, 324–325
Work Resources, 329–330

resource availability graphs, 372–373
resource filters
applying, 370
Available to Work filter, 370–371
Group filter, 369
removing, 370
Resources – Material filter, 369
Resources – Work filter, 369
resource leveling, 419–421, 454–455
Automatic Leveling, 462
Clear Leveling dialog box, 462
Level Now dialog box, 459–463
priorities, 458–459
Resource Allocation view, 432–434
Resource Leveling dialog box, 455–459
resource substitution, 434–440
resource names, 324–325
Resource Substitution Wizard, 1110–1117
resource units, 374–375
slipping assignments, filtering for, 562
sorting, 463
for specific amounts of work, 375–376
split assignments, 451–453
split tasks, 345, 448–451
task calendars, 353–354
task duration for multiple resources, 357–358
task effort-driven setting, 364
Task Entry view
assignment delay, 382–385
overtime work, 385–387
step-by-step instructions, 379–381
Task Form view, 365
Task Information dialog box, 365, 393–394
Task table, 365, 395–396
task types
changing, 361–363
choosing, 335–338, 363
effort-driven tasks, 338–341
fixed-duration tasks, 335
fixed-unit tasks, 336
fixed-work tasks, 335
verifying, 361
Task Usage view, 365, 387–390
Team Builder, 1102–1103
Add button, 1106
Apply Filter button, 1104
Available to Work check box, 1105
Customize Filters field, 1105
Details button, 1106
Enterprise Resource list, 1105
Existing Filters list, 1105
Graphs button, 1106
Group By field, 1105
Match button, 1106
Remove button, 1106
Replace button, 1104–1106
Team Resource list, 1106
timephased assignments, 408
tracking
% Work Complete, 538
Actual Finish, 537
Actual Start, 537
Actual Work, 537
Remaining Work, 538
timephased Actual Work, 539
troubleshooting, 358, 399
viewing, 1074–1075, 1078–1079
approved timesheets, 1080–1081
Outlook, 1140
timesheet format, 1079
timesheet summary, 1080
work contours, 392
applying, 352
back loaded, 348–350
bell, 350
contoured, 351
documenting changes to, 352
double peak, 350
early peak, 350
example, 348–349
flat pattern, 348–350
front loaded, 348–350
late peak, 350
turtle, 351
work formula, 330–331
applying to existing assignments, 335
applying to new assignments, 331–334
work resources
work formula, 332
Work Resources field, 329–330

Assignments Keeping Outline Structure group, 772

asterisk (*), 52, 781, 864

Attach to Task button (Drawing toolbar), 250

attaching
hyperlinks
email hyperlinks, 150
to files/Web pages, 148–149
to new documents, 149
to resources, 150
to tasks, 147–150
notes
to projects, 146–147
to tasks, 142
objects
to dates, 250–252
to taskbars, 250–252, 274

attributes
commands, 946
menus, 946
projects, 979–980
resources, 980–981

auditing dependency links, 199–201

authentication, CD:72–73

Auto Save feature, 98–99

AutoCorrect command (Tools menu), 124

AutoCorrect, 124

AutoFilter, 769–770, 867–868

Autolink, 196–198

Automatic Leveling, 462

Automatic option (Resource Leveling dialog box), 456

Automatically Add New Resources and Tasks option (Options dialog box), 279, 308–309

automation, CD:28

availability of resources, 176
- Assignment Work graph, 372
- determining, 402–404
- enterprise resources, 1074–1077
- overallocated resources, increasing, 410, 418–423
- remaining availability, 823
- Remaining Availability graph, 372
- resource availability fields
  - Base Calendar, 300–301
  - Max Units, 297–298
  - Resource Availability, 298–300
  - Working Time, 301–302
- unit availability, 824
- viewing, 373, 1040
- work availability, 372, 824

Available to Work check box (Team Builder), 1105

Available to Work filter, 370–371

B

BAC (budget at completion), 586

back loaded work, 348, 350

backing up files
- Always Create Backup option, 102
- Enterprise Global template, 1019–1020, CD:35

background color (Web pages), CD:14–15

background images (Web pages), CD:16–17

backward-scheduled projects, 121

bar charts, formatting, 790
- bar appearance, 791–792
- bar length, 794–795
- bar names, 791
- bar styles definition example, 800
- bar styles options, 790–791
- Gantt Chart Wizard, 801–802
- layout, 798–799
- manual formatting, 797–798
- progress bar styles, 795–796
- rows, 794
- task types, 792–793
- text, 796–797

Bar command (Format menu), 797

Bar Height option (Layout dialog box), 798

Bar Rollup view, 739–740

bar styles
- Bar Styles dialog box, 804–806
  - Appearance column, 791–792
  - bar names, 791
  - Bars tab, 790
  - displaying, 790
  - From/To bar definition columns, 794–796
  - Resource Graph view, 824–826
  - Show For...Tasks column, 792–793
  - Text tab, 791, 796–797
- formatting, 804–806
- Resource Graph view, 824–826

Bar Styles command (Format menu), 790, 804

Bar Styles dialog box, 804–806
- Appearance column, 791–792
- bar names, 791
- Bars tab, 790
- displaying, 790
- From/To bar definition columns, 794–796
- Resource Graph view, 824–826
- Show For...Tasks column, 792–793
- Text tab, 791, 796–797

bar text (timescale), 242

Bars tab (Bar Styles dialog box), 790

Base Calendar field (resources), 300–301

base calendars, 76–78
- 24 Hour calendar, 76
- canceling changes to, 84
- copying between projects, 90–91
- copying to Global template, 84, 89–90
- creating, 82–83
- customizing, 901
- Define Working Times for Resources Wizard, 88
- editing
  - time formats, 81
  - working and nonworking days, 78–80
  - working hours, 80–81
- New Calendar Wizard, 86–87
- Night Shift calendar, 76
- printing, 91–92, 901
- resetting, 81–82
- saving, 84
- selecting, 78
- Standard calendar, 76

Baseline option (Gantt Chart Wizard), 802

Baseline table, 759

baselines
- clearing, 526
- copying, 528
- costs, 284
- defined, 522
- editing, 527
- fields, 522–524
- finish dates, 794
- interim plans, 525
- rebaselining, 524
- rolling up, 525
- saving, 522–526
- start dates, 794
- viewing, 527–528

Basic Search pane, 32

BCWP (budgeted cost of work performed). ***See*** **earned value analysis**

BCWS (budgeted cost of work scheduled), 577

behaviors
- custom fields, 852
- menus, 922–923
- toolbars, 923–924

bell work contour, 350
Best Fit option (Column Definition dialog box), 845
blank lines in macros, CD:41
Blank Project option (Task pane), 31
blocks of data, copying between applications, 692–694
<BODY> tag, CD:16
booking types, 1039–1040, 1100–1102
books, *A Guide to the Project Management Body of Knowledge*, 17
Border/Fill tab (Commands and Options dialog box), CD:83
borders, 499
bottom-up approach (task lists), 116
box styles, 807–808
Box Styles command (Format menu), 807
Box Styles dialog box, 807–808
breaking links, 626
breakpoints, CD:43–45
budget at completion (BAC), 586
Budget report, 886
budgeted cost of work performed (BCWP). *See* earned value analysis
budgeted cost of work scheduled (BCWS), 577
Build Team feature, 1036–1037
Build Team from Enterprise command (Tools menu), 1103
built-in templates, 104–105
Button Editor dialog box, 938–939
buttons
Assign Resources dialog box, 290
custom forms, 959
Customize dialog box, 937
Customize Fields dialog box
Define Code Mask, 855
Graphical Indicators, 853
Import Custom Field, 856
Rename, 849
Drawing toolbar
Arc, 249
Arrow, 249
Attach to Task, 250
Cycle Color Fill, 249
Draw, 248
Line, 249
Oval, 249
Polygon, 249
Rectangle, 249
Text Box, 249
Filter Definition dialog box, 862
Format Text Font, 504
Formatting toolbar, 156
Insert Project dialog box, 613
Inserted Project Information dialog box, 614
Outline Code Definition dialog box, 857
Print, 490, 512
Print Preview, 490, 509–511
Project Guide, 40–41
Resource Information dialog box, 308
Share Resources dialog box
Pool Takes Precedence, 622
Sharer Takes Precedence, 622
Use Own Resources, 625
Use Resources, 622
Standard toolbar, 613
Team Builder
Add, 1106
Apply Filter, 1104
Details, 1106
Graphs, 1106
Match, 1106
Remove, 1106
Replace, 1104–1106
toolbar command buttons, 930–931
actions, 939–941
adding, 931–932
attaching macros to, 931
button faces, 937–939
display options, 937
grouping, 933
moving, 932–933
removing, 931–932, 960
separator bars, 933
troubleshooting, 960
Tracking toolbar, 549–550
Zoom In, 494
Zoom Out, 494

C

calculated fields
creating, 850–852
formulas, 851
calculated filters, 762, 866
calculations
calculated fields
creating, 850–852
formulas, 851
calculated filters, 762, 866
calculation options
Actual Costs Are Always Calculated by Microsoft Project, 541–543
Edits to Total Task % Complete Will Be Spread to the Status Date, 543–544
Updating Task Status Updates Resource Status, 539–541
earned value, 587–588
resource costs, 282
schedules, 25
variances, 563–564
work, 330–331
Calculation for Task and Group Summary Rows area (Customize Fields dialog box), 852
Calendar command (View menu), 258
Calendar list box (Project Information dialog box), 59
Calendar reports, 901
Calendar view, 25, 258–259
adding tasks to, 263–265
combination views, 263
deleting tasks from, 265
displaying, 258

filters, 261–262, 737
finding tasks/dates in, 260–261
formatting, 802–803
bar styles, 804–806
layout options, 806
timescales, 803–804
linking tasks in, 265
print options, 507–508
restoring tasks in, 265
scheduled tasks, 259
scrolling, 260
task details, 262–263
zooming in/out, 261

calendars, 59, 136
base calendars, 76–77
24 Hour calendar, 76
canceling changes to, 84
copying between projects, 90–91
copying to Global template, 84, 89–90
creating, 82–83
Define Working Times for Resources Wizard, 88
editing, 78–81
New Calendar Wizard, 86–87
Night Shift calendar, 76
printing, 91–92
resetting, 81–82
saving, 84
scheduling with, 77–78
selecting, 78
Standard calendar, 76
Calendar view, 25, 258–259
adding tasks to, 263–265
combination views, 263
deleting tasks from, 265
displaying, 258
filters, 261–262, 737
finding tasks/dates in, 260–261
formatting, 802–806
linking tasks in, 265
print options, 507–508
restoring tasks in, 265
scheduled tasks, 259
scrolling, 260
task details, 262–263
zooming in/out, 261
defined, 108
enterprise project calendars, 1018–1019
enterprise resource calendars, 1019
environment options, 72–73
Days per Month, 68–69
Default End Time, 69–70
Default Start Time, 69–70
Fiscal Year, 70–72
Hours per Day, 68–69
Hours per Week, 68–69
extended working hours, 429–432
options, 70–73
Organizer, 88
task calendars, 176
assigning to tasks, 224–225, 354
creating, 223–226
scheduling with, 353–354

calling subroutines
with arguments, CD:54
without parameters, CD:52–53

Can Level field, 458

Cancel option (Copy Picture dialog box), 723

canceling base calendar changes, 84

caret (^), 52, 864

Case statement, CD:53–54

Cash Flow report, 886–887

categories, CD:70
custom views, CD:77
nonworking time categories, CD:93–94

Cell Layout dialog box, 810

Centered Mist Dark.html file, CD:14–16

Change Source dialog box, 701

Change Working Time command (Tools menu), 78, 429, 915

Change Working Time dialog box, 78–81, 429–430

changing. ***See also*** **editing**
booking type, 1100–1101
fill styles, 255–256
fonts, 257, 780
line attributes, 255–256
task type setting, 361–363
views, 47–48

charts
bar charts, 790
bar appearance, 791–792
bar length, 794–795
bar names, 791
bar styles options, 790–791
layout, 798–799
manual formatting, 797–798
progress bar styles, 795–796
rows, 794
task types, 792–793
text, 796–797
Portfolio Analyzer, 1051

Check-in Enterprise Projects command (Manage Enterprise Features menu), 1001

Check-in Enterprise Resources command (Manage Enterprise Features menu), 1002

checking in
projects, 1001, 1046
resources, 1002

checking spelling, 486

checklist for project management
management phase, 23–24
planning, 22–23
preliminary tasks, 22

choosing
task type, 335–336, 338
task type setting, 363
tracking methods, 546–549

cleaning up Project Server database, 1003

Clear Baseline command (Tracking menu), 526

Clear Baseline dialog box, 526

Clear command (Edit menu), 128, 702

Clear Leveling dialog box, 462

Clear Leveling Values Before Leveling option (Resource Leveling dialog box), 456

Clear menu commands
- All, 128
- Contents, 128, 702
- Entire Task, 128
- Formats, 128
- Hyperlinks, 128

clearing
- baselines, 526
- task lists, 128

client-side requirements (Microsoft Project Professional), 969

clients, 703

Clipboard, 692

Close button (Task pane), 30

closing
- Entry bar, 37
- issues, 1138
- Project Statistics dialog box, 62
- risks, 1137

Code field (resources), 307–308

codes
- outline codes, 471, 854
  - creating, 854–855
  - outline code lookup tables, 857–858
  - outline masks, 855–857
- WBS codes, 163, 471, 854
  - creating, 164–166
  - deleting tasks, 167
  - editing, 167
  - inserting tasks, 167
  - moving tasks, 167
  - renumbering, 168–169
  - saving, 170–171

Collaborate menu commands, 1124–1125

Collaborate toolbar, 926

collaboration, 983–984, 1120–1121
- documents, 1133
  - document libraries, 1134
  - linking to tasks, 1135
- flow diagram, 1121–1122
- issues, 1137–1138
- Microsoft Outlook
  - Project Server connections, 1140
  - setting up to work with Project Server, 1139
  - submitting time with, 1140–1141
  - viewing task assignments in, 1140
- planning, 977
- risks, 1135
  - assigning, 1136
  - closing, 1137
  - creating, 1136
  - linking to tasks, 1137
  - updating, 1137
- status reports, 1129
  - compiling, 1132–1133
  - requesting, 1130–1131
  - status report flow, 1130
  - submitting, 1131–1132
- task assignments, 1123–1126
- timesheets
  - approving, 1128
  - attaching notes to, 1127
  - lockdown periods, 1128–1129
  - revising, 1129
  - submitting for approval, 1126–1127
  - timesheet flow, 1122–1123
  - tracking methods, 1123

collapsing
- outlines, 157–158
- task detail, 899
- task list outline, 470–471

collections, CD:32

color
- text, 780
- Web pages, CD:14–15

Column command (Insert menu), 846

Column Definition dialog box, 126, 237–238, 845–847

columns
- creating, 841–843
- definitions, 845
- deleting, 238
- displaying, 236
- editing, 237–238, 841–843
- headers, 729, 842
- hiding, 238, 846
- inserting, 237–239, 846
- locking, 876
- moving, 1035
- redefining, 845
- retrieving hidden columns, 846–847
- width, 236–237

combination boxes (toolbars), 928

combination views, 246–247, 263
- creating, 838–840
- defined, 835
- Resource Allocation view, 755–756
- Task Entry view, 755

combining. *See* merging

combo boxes, 934

comma-separated value (CSV) files, 682–684

command buttons (toolbars), 930–931
- actions, 939–941
- adding, 931–932
- attaching macros to, 931
- button faces, 937–939
- display options, 937
- grouping, 933
- moving, 932–933
- removing, 931–932, 960
- separator bars, 933
- troubleshooting, 960

commands
- Admin menu
  - Manage Enterprise Features, 996
  - Manage Views, 988, 991–993
- attributes, 946
- Clear menu
  - All, 128
  - Contents, 128, 702
  - Entire Task, 128
  - Formats, 128
  - Hyperlinks, 128
- Collaborate menu
  - All Information, 1124
  - New and Changed Assignments, 1125
  - Project Plan, 1125
  - Republish Assignments, 1125

Customize menu
  Enterprise Fields, 1011, 1082
  Fields, 848
  Forms, 951
  Toolbars, 36
Debug menu, Toggle Breakpoint, CD:43
defined, 942
Edit menu
  Clear, 128, 702
  Copy, 694, 727–729
  Copy Picture, 722
  Copy Task, 129, 615
  Cut Task, 129
  Delete Task, 128, 265, 272
  Fill, 130
  Find, 235–236
  Go To, 260
  Hide Column, 846
  Info, 955
  Link Tasks, 187, 618
  Links, 699, 701
  Paste, 129, 615, 694
  Paste As Hyperlink, 148–149
  Paste Special, 697, 706
  Select Dialog, 955
  Split Task, 221
  Undo, 127, 702
  Unlink Tasks, 188
Enterprise Options menu
  Import Project to Enterprise, 1025
  Import Resources to Enterprise, 1022
  Microsoft Project Server Accounts, 1006
  Open Enterprise Resource Pool, 1094
File menu
  Exit, 959
  Page Setup, 497
  Print, 490, 512
  Print Preview, 490, 509–513
  Save, 99, 959
  Save As, 100, 645
  Save As Web Page, 102, CD:3
  Save As Workspace, 635
  Save Workspace, 102, 607, 625
  Send To, 486
Fill menu
  Down, 130
  Up, 130
Filter menu, Group, 1034
Filtered For menu
  All Resources, 410
  Overallocated Resources, 409
Format menu
  Bar, 797
  Bar Styles, 790, 804
  Box Styles, 807
  Detail Styles, 414, 828
  Details, 247, 413–414, 817, 822
  Font, 257, 781
  Gridlines, 776, 781
  Layout, 161, 252, 273, 739, 798, 806
  Text Styles, 472, 776–778
  Timescale, 245, 494, 785, 803
  Zoom, 245
Group By menu
  Customize Group By, 478
  More Groups, 478–479
  No Group, 315
  Work vs. Material Resources, 315
Help menu, What's This?, 36
Insert menu
  Column, 846
  Drawing, 248
  Hyperlink, 148
  New Task, 128, 264
  Objects, 706–708
  Page Break, 496, 789
  Project, 607, 612, 615
  Recurring Task, 138
  Remove All Page Breaks, 496, 789
  Remove Page Break, 496, 789
Item menu
  Fields, 957
  Group box, 958
Macro menu
  Record New Macro, CD:29
  Stop Recording, CD:29
Manage Enterprise Features menu
  Check-in Enterprise Projects, 1001–1002
  Manage Enterprise Project Versions, 999
  Specify Resource and OLAP Cube Updates, 996
moving, 946
Outline menu
  Indent, 156
  Outdent, 156
Programs menu, Microsoft Project, 30
Project menu
  Filtered For, 318, 495, 763, 859, 904
  Group By, 314–315, 478, 770–772, 868
  Sort, 310, 475, 610, 776
  Task Information, 263
  WBS, 164, 471
removing, 946
renaming, 944
Request Progress Information menu
  Current View, 1125
  Entire Project, 1125
  Selected Items, 1125
Resources menu
  Refresh Resource Pool, 624
  Share Resources, 621–622
  Update Resource Pool, 624
restoring, 946
Run menu, Run Sub/UserForm, CD:43
Send To menu
  Mail Recipient (As Attachment), 486
  Routing Recipient, 486
Settings menu, Printers, 490
Sort menu
  Sort By, 312, 610
  Sort By command, 475
Start menu, Programs, 30
Table menu, More Tables, 757, 760, 840
Toolbars menu
  Customize, 929
  Drawing, 248

Tools menu
  Assign Resources, 1107
  AutoCorrect, 124
  Build Team from Enterprise, 1103
  Change Working Time, 78, 429, 915
  Links Between Projects, 620
  Options, 65, 239, 783
  Organizer, 89, 109, 875, 947
  Resource Leveling, 443
  Resources, 621
  Substitute Resources, 1112
  Tracking, 524
Tracking menu
  Clear Baseline, 526
  Progress Lines, 560
  Save Baseline, 524
View menu
  Calendar, 258
  More Views, 47, 736, 834, 838
  Network Diagram, 267
  Reports, 91, 514, 878, 895
  Resource Sheet, 287
  Table, 236, 757, 760, 840
  Tables, 904
  Task Usage, 574
  Toolbars, 36, 927
  View Bar, 37
  Zoom, 261, 785
WBS menu
  Define Code, 164, 471
  Renumber, 169
Window menu
  Arrange All, 605
  Hide, 606
  Insert Project dialog box, 612–613
  More Windows, 604
  New Window, 607–608, 615
  Remove Split, 153
  Split, 246, 263, 605
  Unhide, 606
Worksheet Object menu, Convert, 710
Zoom menu
  Entire Project, CD:29
  Selected Tasks, CD:30

Commands and Options dialog box, CD:82

Commands tab (Customize dialog box), 930

committed booking, 1101

Committed booking type, 1039

common format options (views)
  sort options, 776–777
  text, 778–780

Compare Project Versions dialog box, 484

Compare Project Versions toolbar, 483, 927

Compare to Baseline map, 652, 654

comparing
  portfolio models, 1061
  project versions, 483–487

compatibility of file types, 97

compiling status reports, 1132–1133

Complete and Incomplete Resources group, 772

Complete and Incomplete Tasks group, 772

Complete status indicator, 558

Complete Through field (progress bars), 796

Completed Tasks filter, 765

Completed Tasks report, 885

compound filters, 762

compressing timescales, 469–470

configuring
  current date, 406
  macros, CD:28
  printers, 490
  time reporting, 983

Confirmed Assignments filter, 767

Confirmed filter, 765

conflicts, 216–217

Connection State field (Microsoft Project Server Accounts dialog box), 1007

consistent project schedules, 976

consistent project views, 977, 982–983

consolidated resources, 280

Constraint Date field (Task Information dialog box), 202–203

Constraint Dates table, 228–229, 759

Constraint Type field (Task Information dialog box), 202–203

Constraint Type group, 477, 772

constraints, 17
  ALAP (As Late As Possible), 202
  ASAP (As Soon As Possible), 202
  Constraint Dates table, 228–229, 759
  constraint indicators, 233
  creating with Schedule Tasks Project Guide, 207–208
  creating with Task Details form, 209
  creating with Task Information dialog box, 208
  creating with Task table, 208–209
  defined, 176, 201
  deleting, 216
  examples, 201
  finding, 214–216
  flexible/inflexible, 203–206
  FNET (Finish No Earlier Than), 203
  FNLT (Finish No Later Than), 203
  hard constraints, 212–214
  honoring, 212–214
  MFO (Must Finish On), 203
  MSO (Must Start On), 203
  Planning Wizard warnings, 210–212
  recurring tasks, 141
  resolving conflicts, 216–217
  reviewing, 214–216
  SNET (Start No Earlier Than), 203

SNLT (Start No Later Than), 203
soft constraints, 212–214

consumption rates
fixed, 294, 328
variable, 295, 329

containers, 703

contains condition (Find operations), 53

contains exactly condition (Find operations), 53

Contains Exactly test (filters), 861–863

Contains test (filters), 861, 863

Contents command (Clear menu), 128, 702

Contents tab (Properties dialog box), 64

continuous tasks, 135

contours (work)
applying to assignments, 352
back loaded, 348–350
bell, 350
contoured, 351
documenting changes to, 352
double peak, 350
early peak, 350
example, 348–349
flat pattern, 348–350
front loaded, 348–350
late peak, 350
selecting, 392
task calendars, 353–354
turtle, 351

contract fees, 396–399

contracting/expanding project details, 1035

Convert command (Worksheet Object menu), 710

Convert dialog box, 710

converting objects, 710

Copy command (Edit menu), 694, 727–729

Copy Picture command (Edit menu), 722

Copy Picture dialog box, 721–723, CD:22–25

Copy Picture to Office Wizard, 724–726

Copy Task command (Edit menu), 129, 615

copying
base calendars
between projects, 90–91
to Global template, 84, 89–90
baselines, 528
custom forms, 960
data between applications
blocks of values, 692–694
single values, 692
timephased data, 692, 696
Windows Clipboard, 692
formatting, 781
GLOBAL.MPT, 109
objects, 109–111, 254–255
into other applications, 695–696
into Project, 694–695
reports, 894–895
task names, 125
tasks, 129–130
toolbars, 947–948
views, 720–721
Copy command, 727–729
Copy Picture dialog box, 721–723
Copy Picture to Office Wizard, 724–726

corrective action, 556

Cost Accrual field (resources), 307

Cost Data by Task map, 652, 654

Cost Greater Than... filter, 765, 767

Cost option (Details menu), 823

Cost Overbudget filter, 317, 572–574, 765–767

Cost Per Use field (resources), 305

Cost Rate Table field (Assignment Information dialog box), 392–393

Cost Rate tables, 305–306, 392–393

Cost reports
Budget, 886
Cash Flow, 886–887
Earned Value, 886–888

Cost table, 283, 758, 760

Cost Tracking form, 950

costs, 278, 281
accrued costs
accrual methods, 285–286, 578
Cost Accrual field, 307
defined, 285
actual costs, 284
baseline costs, 284
budgeted costs, 284
calculation options, 541–543
Cost reports
Budget, 886
Cash Flow, 886–887
Earned Value, 886–888
Cost table, 283, 758, 760
Cost Tracking form, 950
current costs, 283
displaying, 482, 823
earned value analysis, 575–577
actual cost, 578
earned value, 577–578
Earned Value Schedule Indicators table, 581–582
examining trends, 578
example, 579–582
Excel graphs, 590–595
planned value, 577
Earned Value Cost Indicators table, 583
BAC (budget at completion), 586
CPI (cost performance index), 585
CV (cost variance), 584
CV% (cost variance percentage), 585
EAC (estimate at completion), 586
TCPI (to complete performance index), 586
VAC (variance at completion), 586

fixed costs
assigning, 396–399
defined, 281–282
documenting reasons for, 282
fixed contract fees, 396–399
reducing, 481–483, 596–597
resource costs
accrued costs, 307
calculating, 282
cost per use, 305
Cost Rate tables, 305–306
defined, 281
overtime rate, 304–305
standard rate, 303–304
scheduled costs, 283
total costs, 281–283
variance, 284, 571–572, 584–585

CPI (cost performance index) field, 585

crashing the schedule, 26, 480–481, 563

Create New Base Calendar dialog box, 82

Created After... filter, 766

criteria (filters), 315
Contains, 863
Contains Exactly, 863
Is Within/Is Not Within, 863
logical values, 862
table of, 861
test value column entries, 862
wildcards, 864

Critical filter, 473, 766

Critical group, 477, 772

critical milestones, 267

critical normal tasks, 267

critical options. ***See*** **environment options**

critical paths, 25–26, 480, 802

critical tasks, 25, 408, 480, 792, 881

Critical Tasks report, 881

cross-linked predecessors, 620

cross-project task links, 982
creating manually, 1045
Link Task function, 1043–1044

Crosstab Report dialog box, 910

crosstab reports
customizing
definitions, 910–912
details, 913–914
sort order, 915
text formatting, 914
definitions, 910–912
details, 913–914
sort order, 915
text formatting, 914

CSV (comma-separated value) files, 635, 682–684

cumulative costs, 824

cumulative work, 823

Current Activities reports, 884–886

current costs, 283

Current Date text box (Project Information dialog box), 59, 61

current dates, entering, 59–61, 406

Current View command (Request Progress Information menu), 1125

Custom Attributes area (Customize Fields dialog box), 850

Custom Enterprise Fields dialog box, 1011, 1017–1018, 1082

Custom Fields tab (Open Enterprise Resource Pool dialog box), 1095

Custom Form Editor, 953–956

Custom Forms toolbar, 926

Custom Gantt Chart option (Gantt Chart Wizard), 802

Custom Outline Codes tab (Customize Fields dialog box), 855–856

Custom Report dialog box, 893–895

Custom tab (Properties dialog box), 64–65

Customize command (Toolbars menu), 929

Customize dialog box, 35, 922, 929–930, 937

Customize Fields dialog box, 848–849
Calculation for Task and Group Summary Rows area, 852
Custom Attributes area, 850
Custom Outline Codes tab, 855–856
Define Code Mask button, 855
Graphical Indicators button, 853
Import Custom Field button, 856
Rename button, 849

Customize Filters field (Team Builder), 1105

Customize Forms dialog box, 951

Customize Group By command (Group By menu), 478

Customize Group By dialog box, 478

Customize menu commands
Enterprise Fields, 1011, 1082
Fields, 848
Forms, 951
Toolbars, 36

Customize Tool dialog box, 939–940, 952

customizing
command buttons
actions, 939–941
button faces, 937–939
display options, 937
commands, 944–946
Constraint Dates table, 228–229
fields, 847–848
accessing, 848–849
behaviors, 852
calculated fields, 850–852
enterprise custom fields, 974–975, 1010–1011, 1016–1018, 1067, 1081–1082, 1096
hyperlinks, 150–151
indicator fields, 853
managing, 859

naming, 849–850
outline codes, 854–859
WBS code formats, 854
filters
AutoFilter, 867–868
calculated filters, 866
creating, 859–860
definitions, 862
filter criteria tests, 861–864
interactive filters, 864–865
multiple filters, 866–867
naming, 860
forms, 949–950
assigning to toolbar buttons, 952–953
buttons, 959
copying, 960
Custom Form Editor, 953–956
display, 951
editing, 960
field values, 957–958
group boxes, 958, 961
hotkeys, 951–952
managing with Organizer, 960
renaming, 960
saving, 959
size, 955–956
text, 956
troubleshooting, 961
groups, 477–479
accessing custom groups, 868–869
display options, 871–872
group intervals, 870–871
grouping fields, 869
saving custom groups, 872
menus, CD:84
adding items, 945
attributes, 946
behavior, 922–923
custom sublevel menu choices, CD:85–86
custom top-level menu choices, CD:85
menu bars, 941–944
moving menus, 946
names, 944
removing menus, 946
outline numbers, 169
project properties, 64–65
Project Web Access
default home page appearance, CD:94
Gantt Chart formats, CD:92–93
grouping formats, CD:93
nonworking time categories, CD:93–94
notifications/reminders, CD:94–95
reports, 891
Calendar reports, 901
collapsing task detail, 899
column widths, 918
crosstab reports, 910–915
Custom Reports dialog box, 893–894
definitions, 904–905
details, 905–908
existing reports, 892–893
Monthly Calendar reports, 915–917
page breaks, 896
page setup options, 896
Project Summary report, 899–900
Resource reports, 901–909
sort order, 898, 910
Task and Resource reports, 901–909
text formatting, 897, 909
tables, 730
toolbars, 925–926
behavior, 923–924
combo boxes, 934
command buttons, 930–933, 936–941
Customize dialog box, 929–930
move handles, 923
personalized toolbars, 924
toolbar position, 928–929
views, 873–875, CD:74
categories, CD:77
default grouping, CD:76
fields, CD:75
filters, CD:76
Gantt Chart format, CD:75
grouping formats, CD:76
Portfolio Analyzer view, CD:77–84
splitter bars, CD:75
table selection, CD:75
WBS codes, 163
creating, 164–166
deleting tasks, 167
editing, 167
inserting tasks, 167
moving tasks, 167
renumbering, 168–169
saving, 170–171

cut and paste operations, importing resources with, 1021

Cut Task command (Edit menu), 129

CV (cost variance), 284, 571–572, 584–585

Cycle Color Fill button (Drawing toolbar), 249

D

data
copying between applications
blocks of values, 692–694
copying into other applications, 695–696
copying into Project, 694–695
single values, 692
timephased data, 692, 696
Windows Clipboard, 692
data fields
defined, 108
scrolling, 48–49
selecting, 50–51
linked data
creating, 697–699
defined, 697
deleting, 701–702
identifying, 702
link indicators, 699
pasting, 697–699, 702
refreshing, 699–701
restoring, 702
updating, 699–701
pasting
dates, 695
errors, 694–695
linked data, 697–699, 702
into other applications, 695–696
into Project, 694–695
timephased data, 692, 696

- sharing, 604, 632
  - combined resource lists, 627
  - files, 97, 632–635
  - reports, 918
  - resource pools, 621–626
  - shared workspaces, 628–629

Data Details tab (Commands and Options dialog box), CD:83

data fields
- defined, 108
- scrolling, 48–49
- selecting, 50–51

Data Format option (Table Definition dialog box), 843

Data page (Import/Export Wizard), 637

Data Template Definition dialog box, 811

Data Templates dialog box, 809–810

data templates. *See* templates

Database Upgrade Utility toolbar, 927

databases
- ODBC (Open Database Connectivity), 647–648
- OLAP (Online Analytical Process) cubes, 994–999
- OLE DB providers, 687–688
- Project Server database, 1003
- saving projects in, 640, 645–648

Date Boxes tab (Timescale dialog box), 804

Date Format option
- Layout dialog box, 798
- Options dialog box, 75

Date Range... filter, 766–767

Date Shading tab (Timescale dialog box), 804

dates
- attaching objects to, 250–252
- constraint dates. *See* constraints
- current dates, entering, 59–61, 406
- date formats, 75
- deadline dates
  - defined, 795
  - entering, 217–219
  - filtering, 219
  - missed deadlines, 220, 229
- finding, 243
  - Find command, 261
  - Go To command, 260–261
- finish dates, 176
  - actual finish dates, 794
  - baseline finish dates, 794
  - Actual Finish field, 537
  - defined, 794
  - early finish dates, 795
  - entering, 58–60
  - fixed-finish-date projects, 384–385
  - late finish dates, 795
  - preleveled finish dates, 795
- fiscal year, defining start of, 70–72
- formatting, 798
- including in headers/footers, 501
- OLAP (Online Analytical Process) date ranges, 997
- option settings, 68–69
- pasting, 695
- start dates, 176
  - actual start dates, 794
  - Actual Start field, 537
  - baseline start dates, 794
  - defined, 794
  - early start dates, 795
  - entering, 58–60
  - fixed-start-date projects, 382–384
  - late start dates, 795
  - preleveled start dates, 795
  - troubleshooting, 93–94
- status dates, 59, 61
- task tables, 239
- task-tracking fields, 532–533
- variances, 571

Day by Day sensitivity level, 407

Days per Month setting (Options dialog box), 68–69

deactivating. *See* disabling

Deadline Date field (Task Information dialog box), 217–219

deadline dates
- defined, 795
- entering, 217–219
- filtering, 219
- missed deadlines, 220, 229

Debug menu commands, Toggle Breakpoint, CD:43

Debug.Print command (?), CD:44

debugging macros, CD:42–43
- breakpoints, CD:43–45
- Immediate window, CD:43–45
- syntax checking, CD:43
- watches, CD:43–45

Decimal Digits setting (Options dialog box), 75

decimal points, 75

Default Account field (Account Properties dialog box), 1006

Default End Time setting (Options dialog box), 69–70

default grouping (views), CD:76

Default Start Time setting (Options dialog box), 69–70

Default Task Information map, 652, 654

Default View setting (Options dialog box), 73–74

defaults
- date formats, 75
- duration time units, 134
- printers, 490
- save format, 75
- views, 73–74

Define Code command (WBS menu), 164, 471

Define Code Mask button (Customize Fields dialog box), 855

Define Custom Form dialog box, 951–952

Define Group Interval dialog box, 478

Define New View dialog box, 834–835

Define Working Times for Resources Wizard, 88

Delay table, 759

delays, 440
- Delay table, 759
- delayed starts, scheduling, 342–345
- fixed-start-date projects, 382–385
- individual assignments, 443–447
- lag time, 180–181, 189–190
- lead time, 180–181, 189–190
- leveling delays, 324
- overlapping tasks, 180–181, 189–190, 441–443

delegating tasks, CD:69

Delete Task command (Edit menu), 128, 265, 272

deleting
- command buttons, 931–932
- commands, 946
- custom properties, 65
- dependency links, 185, 188, 198–199
- enterprise project calendars, 1019
- enterprise resources from projects, 1098
- filters, 370, 410, 474
- hyperlinks, 150
- inserted projects, 617
- linked data, 701–702
- menus, 946
- objects, 256
  - from Objects field, 717
  - Organizer, 111–112
- page breaks, 496, 789
- predecessor tasks, 189
- project versions, 1000
- projects, 1042–1043
- resources, 339, 376–377, 1106
- security templates, CD:71–72
- split bars, 47
- task constraints, 216
- task table columns, 238
- tasks, 128
  - Calendar view, 265
  - custom WBS codes, 167
  - Network Diagram view, 272
- toolbar buttons, 960
- user-defined toolbars, 936

dependency links, 177–178
- auditing, 199–200
- Autolink, 196–198
- cautions, 178
- creating
  - Entry table, 193–194
  - Link Tasks tool, 187
  - mouse, 194–196
  - Task Form view, 190–192
  - Task Information dialog box, 188–189
- defined, 176
- deleting, 185, 188, 198–199
- dependent tasks, 179–180
- editing, 187, 198
- Finish-to-Finish relationship, 183
- Finish-to-Start relationship, 182
- honoring, 212–214
- lag time, 180–181, 189–190
- lead time, 180–181, 189–190
- outlined projects, 185
- overlapping tasks, 180–181, 189–190
- predecessor tasks
  - choosing, 179–180
  - defined, 177
  - defining, 189
  - deleting, 189
- reversing, 227
- Start-to-Finish relationship, 183–184
- Start-to-Start relationship, 182
- successor tasks, 177–180
- summary tasks, 184–185
- tasks from different projects, 227
- troubleshooting, 226–227
- unrelated tasks, 178
- views, 199–201

dependent tasks, 179–180

Descriptive Network Diagram view, 746

designing reports, 895–896

Detail Gantt view, 743

detail headers, 463

Detail Styles command (Format menu), 414, 828

Detail Styles dialog box, 413, 828
- displaying, 414
- Usage Details tab, 415–416
- Usage Properties tab, 417

details (reports), customizing, 905–908

Details button
- Resource Information dialog box, 308
- Team Builder, 1106

Details command (Format menu), 247, 413–414, 817, 822

dialog boxes
- Account Properties, 1006
- Assign Resources, 289–291, 365–367, 1107–1110
  - displaying, 366
  - drag-and-drop, 376
  - features, 367–368
  - graphs, 371–373
  - modifying assignments, 377–379
  - removing assignments, 376–377
  - resource list filters, 369–371
  - resource unit assignments, 374–375
- Assignment Information, 344, 352, 390–391
  - Cost Rate Table field, 392–393
  - Notes field, 392–393
  - Work Contour field, 391–392
- Bar Styles, 804–806
  - Appearance column, 791–792
  - bar names, 791
  - Bars tab, 790
  - displaying, 790
  - From/To bar definition columns, 794–796
  - Resource Graph view, 824–826
  - Show For...Tasks column, 792–793
  - Text tab, 791, 796–797

Box Styles, 807–808
Button Editor, 938–939
Cell Layout, 810
Change Source, 701
Change Working Time, 78–81, 429–430
Clear Baseline, 526
Clear Leveling, 462
Column Definition, 126, 237–238, 845–847
Commands and Options, CD:82
Compare Project Versions, 484
Convert, 710
Copy Picture, 721–723, CD:22–25
Create New Base Calendar, 82
Crosstab Report, 910
Custom Enterprise Fields, 1011, 1017–1018, 1082
Custom Reports, 893–895
Customize, 35, 922, 929–930
Customize Fields, 848–849
  Calculation for Task and Group Summary Rows area, 852
  Custom Attributes area, 850
  Custom Outline Codes tab, 855–856
  Define Code Mask button, 855
  Graphical Indicators button, 853
  Import Custom Field button, 856
  Rename button, 849
Customize Forms, 951
Customize Group By, 478
Customize Tool, 939–940, 952
Data Template Definition, 811
Data Templates, 809–810
Define Custom Form, 951–952
Define Group Interval, 478
Define New View, 834–835
Detail Styles, 413, 828
  displaying, 414
  Usage Details tab, 415–416
  Usage Properties tab, 417
Edit Hyperlink, 150
Edit Lookup Table, 857–858, 1013, 1083
Export Wizard – End of Map Definition, CD:8
Export Wizard - Map, CD:10
Export Wizard – Map Options, CD:3–4, CD:11–13
Export Wizard – Task Mapping, CD:5–7
File Save, 607
Filter Definition, 859–862
Find, 20, 35, 50–53, 235
Font, 504
Form Information, 955
Format Bar, 797–798
Format Drawing, 251, 255
Formula, 1017
Graphical Indicators, 853
Gridlines, 781–783
Group Definition, 868–870
Import Outline Code, 856–857
Insert Hyperlink, 148–149
Insert Object, 708
Insert Project, 612
Inserted Project Information, 613
Item Information, 957
Layout, 161, 252, 273–274
  Calendar view, 806
  Gantt Chart view, 798–799
  Network Diagram view, 812–814
Level Now, 459–463
Links, 699–701
Links Between Projects, 620
Microsoft Project Server Accounts, 1006–1007
Monthly Calendar Report Definition, 915
More Filters, 763
More Groups, 478
More Tables, 757, 840
More Views, 47–48, 834, 838
Multiple Task Information, 131–132, 216
New Toolbar, 935
New Window, 608
Open Enterprise Resource Pool, 1094–1096
Open Resource Pool Information, 622
Options, 239
  Automatically Add New Resources and Tasks option, 279
  Calendar options, 72–73
  Date Format, 75
  Days per Month, 68–69
  Decimal Digits, 75
  Default End Time, 69–70
  Default Start Time, 69–70
  Default View, 73–74
  displaying, 65
  Duration Is Entered In, 73
  file-specific options, 66–67
  Fiscal Year, 70–72
  global options, 66
  Hours per Day, 68–69
  Hours per Week, 68–69
  Save Microsoft Project Files As, 75
  User Name, 73
  View tab, 783–784
Organizer, 947
Outline Code Definition, 855–857, 1012, 1082
Page Setup, 496–497
  Footer tab, 500–502
  Header tab, 500–502
  Legend tab, 503–504
  Margin tab, 499
  Page tab, 497–499
  View tab, 506–508
Paste Special, 697–698, 706, 714
Planning Wizard, 210–212
Print, 490–491, 512
Progress Lines, 560–561
Project Information, 57–58, 614
  Calendar list box, 59
  Current Date text box, 59–61
  displaying, 58
  Finish Date text box, 58–60
  priorities, 459
  Priority field, 59
  Start Date text box, 58–60
  Status Date text box, 59–61
Project Statistics, 61–62, 468–469, 565

Properties, 62–65
Rearrange Commands, 932–933
Recurring Task Information, 138
Rename, 948
Replace Resource, 377–378, 439
Reports, 91, 514, 878
Resource Assignment, 438–439
Resource Information, 288–289, 292–293, 698
  Base Calendar field, 300–301
  Code field, 307–308
  Cost Accrual field, 307
  Cost Per Use field, 305
  Cost Rate tables, 305–306
  Details button, 308
  Group field, 295–297
  Indicators field, 293
  Initials field, 295
  Material Label field, 295
  Max Units field, 297–298
  overallocated resources, 422–423
  Overtime Rate field, 304–305
  Resource Availability field, 298–300
  Resource Name field, 294
  Standard Rate field, 303–304
  Type field, 294–295
  Windows Account button, 308
  Working Time field, 301–302
Resource Leveling, 443, 455–459
Resource List Options, 290
Resource Sharing, 625
Risks: New Item, CD:91
Save As, 99–100, CD:3
Save Baseline, 524–525
Save Map, 639, CD:8
Save Options, 101
Save Workspace As, 102, 607
Share Resources, 622, 625–626
Sort, 312–313, 475–476, 776–777
Split Task, 221
Table Definition, 730, 841–844
Task Information, 131, 233, 246, 263, 336–337, 365, 613
  assigning resources with, 393–394
  deadline dates, 217–219
  General tab, 739
  Predecessors tab, 188–189
  task calendar assignments, 224–225
  task constraints, 208
Tasks Occurring On, 259
Text Styles, 472, 778–780
Timescale, 245, 470, 785–786, 803–804
  Align drop-down list, 787
  Date Boxes tab, 804
  Date Shading tab, 804
  Label drop-down list, 786
  Nonworking Time tab, 788–789
  Scale Separator box, 788
  Size box, 787
  Units drop-down list, 786
  Week Headings tab, 804
Updates to Resources and OLAP Cube, 996–998
Using Resource Filter, 764
Value List, 850
Versions, 629
View and Submit Issues, CD:89
View Definition, 835–838
WBS Code Definition, 164–166
WBS Renumber, 169
Zoom, 245, 261, 817

Dim statement, CD:39

disabling. ***See also*** **hiding**
  alerts, 43
  Auto Save, 99
  Autolink feature, 197
  Automatically Add New Resources and Tasks option, 309
  Project Server features, CD:84
  resource sharing, 625–626, 629
  SmartTags, 42

display values
  Resource Graph view
    cost, 823
    cumulative cost, 824
    cumulative work, 823
    overallocation, 823
    peak units, 822
    percent allocation, 823
    remaining availability, 823
    unit availability, 824
    work, 822–823
    work availability, 824
  Resource Usage view, 827

displaying
  alerts, 43
  Assign Resources dialog box, 366
  Bar Styles dialog box, 790
  baselines, 527–528
  booking status, 1101–1102
  Calendar view, 258
  Cost table, 283
  costs, 482, 823–824
  cumulative work, 823
  custom forms, 951
  detail headers, 463
  Detail Styles dialog box, 414
  Drawing toolbar, 248
  earned value analysis, 589–590, 599
  enterprise projects, 1032
  file extensions, 633
  full menus, 35
  graphs, 373
  groups, 871–872
  link indicators, 699
  Network Diagram view, 267
  Options dialog box, 65
  Organizer, 108
  outlines, 160–161
  overallocated resources, 409, 823
  page breaks, 496
  peak units, 822
  percent allocation, 823
  Project Guide, 41
  project information, 58, 1035–1036
  project-level statistics, 468–469, 565
  Project Statistics dialog box, 61

project summary tasks, 565, 784
remaining availability, 823
reports, 878–879
resource assignments, 411, 1078–1079
approved timesheets, 1080–1081
timesheet format, 1079
timesheet summary, 1080
resource availability, 1040
scheduled tasks, 259
tables, 757, 840
task assignments, 1140
task details, 262–263
task information, 629
task names, 126
task tables, 236–237
toolbar buttons, 937
toolbars, 36, 923–924, 927–928
unit availability, 824
variance, 599
versions, 1067
View bar, 37
view names, 838
windows, 606
work, 822–824

distributing
project plans, 486
reports, 919

divider bars, 47

docking toolbars, 928

documents, 56, 1133
containers, 703
environment options
calendar options, 72–73
date format, 75
days per month, 68–69
decimal digits, 75
default end time, 69–70
default save format, 75
default start time, 69–70
default view, 73–74
displaying, 65
duration time units, 73
file-specific options, 66–67
fiscal year, 70–72
global options, 66
hours per day, 68–69
hours per week, 68–69
user name, 73
HTML documents
background colors, CD:14–15
background images, CD:16–17
Gantt Chart images, CD:22–24
hyperlinks, CD:19–25
images, CD:17–18
publishing, CD:24
saving projects as, CD:3–8
title bar text, CD:18–19
troubleshooting, CD:24–25
viewing projects as, CD:9
libraries, 1134, CD:86
linking to tasks, 1036, 1135
management, 977, 983–984
Options dialog box
Calendar options, 72–73
Date Format, 75
Days per Month, 68–69
Decimal Digits, 75
Default End Time, 69–70
Default Start Time, 69–70
Default View, 73–74
displaying, 65
Duration Is Entered In, 73
file-specific options, 66–67
Fiscal Year, 70–72
global options, 66
Hours per Day, 68–69
Hours per Week, 68–69
Save Microsoft Project Files As, 75
User Name, 73
Project Information dialog box, 57–58
Calendar list box, 59
Current Date text box, 59–61
displaying, 58
Finish Date text box, 58–60
Priority field, 59
Start Date text box, 58–60
Status Date text box, 59–61
Project Statistics dialog box, 61–62
properties
contents, 64
custom properties, 64–65
general properties, 63
statistics, 63
summary information, 62–63
Properties dialog box
Contents tab, 64
Custom tab, 64–65
General tab, 63
Statistics tab, 63
Summary tab, 62–63
setting up, 56–57
calendar, 59
current dates, 59–61
days per month, 68–69
finish dates, 58–60
hours per day, 68–69
hours per week, 68–69
priorities, 59
project statistics, 61–62
properties, 62–65
start dates, 58–60
status dates, 59–61
SPS, CD:87–88

does not contain condition (Find operations), 53

does not equal condition (Find operations), 53

Does Not Equal test (filters), 861

double peak work contour, 350

Down command (Fill menu), 130

Draw button (Drawing toolbar), 248

Draw drop-down menu, 248

Drawing command
Insert menu, 248
Toolbars menu, 248

Drawing toolbar, 247–250, 926

driver resources, 355–357

drop-down lists, 1051

duplicate resource names, 294

Duration field (task tables), 120

Duration group, 477, 772

Duration Is Entered In setting (Options dialog box), 73

duration of tasks
calculating with Project, 171–174
continuous tasks, 135
default duration time units, 134
defined, 132
Duration field (task tables), 120
Duration group, 477, 772
duration inflation, 203
elapsed duration, 135–136
estimating, 132–133, 176
fixed-duration tasks, 335
multiple resources, 357–358
reducing, 597–598
selecting time units for, 73
summary tasks, 156
task-tracking fields
Actual Duration field, 534
Remaining Duration field, 535
time unit abbreviations, 134–135

Duration then Priority group, 772

E

EAC (estimate at completion), 586

early finish dates, 795

early peak work contour, 350

early start dates, 795

earned value analysis (EVA), 575–578, 888
actual cost, 578
controlling earned value calculation, 587–588
Earned Value Cost Indicators table, 583–589, 759
BAC (budget at completion), 586
CPI (cost performance index), 585
CV (cost variance), 584
CV% (cost variance percentage), 585
EAC (estimate at completion), 586
TCPI (to complete performance index), 586
VAC (variance at completion), 586
Earned Value form, 950
Earned Value Information map, 652–654
Earned Value report, 886–888
Earned Value Schedule Indicators table, 589, 759
SPI (schedule performance index), 582
SV (schedule variance), 581
SV% (schedule variance percentage), 582
Earned Value table, 759, 761
examining trends, 578
example, 579–582
Excel graphs, 590–595
planned value, 577
troubleshooting, 599
viewing, 589–590

Earned Value Cost Indicators table, 583–589, 759
BAC (budget at completion), 586
CPI (cost performance index), 585
CV (cost variance), 584
CV% (cost variance percentage), 585
EAC (estimate at completion), 586
TCPI (to complete performance index), 586
VAC (variance at completion), 586

Earned Value form, 950

Earned Value Information map, 652, 654

Earned Value report, 886–888

Earned Value Schedule Indicators table, 589, 759
SPI (schedule performance index), 582
SV (schedule variance), 581
SV% (schedule variance percentage), 582

Earned Value table, 759, 761

Edit Hyperlink dialog box, 150

Edit Lookup Table button (Outline Code Definition dialog box), 857

Edit Lookup Table dialog box, 857–858, 1013, 1083

Edit menu commands
Clear, 128, 702
Copy, 694, 727–729
Copy Picture, 722
Copy Task, 129, 615
Cut Task, 129
Delete Task, 128, 265, 272
Fill, 130
Find, 235–236
Go To, 260
Hide Column, 846
Info, 955
Link Tasks, 187, 618
Links, 699, 701
Paste, 129, 615, 694
Paste as Hyperlink, 148–149
Paste Special, 697, 706
Select Dialog, 955
Split Task, 221
Undo, 127, 702
Unlink Tasks, 188

Edit Points tool, 254

Edit Resource Details view (Resource Center), 1075

editing. *See also* changing
assignment-tracking fields
% Work Complete, 538
Actual Finish, 537
Actual Start, 537
Actual Work, 537
Remaining Work, 538
timephased Actual Work, 539
base calendars
time formats, 81
working and nonworking days, 78–80
working hours, 80–81
baselines, 527
custom forms, 960
custom WBS codes, 167
dependency links, 187, 198
Enterprise Global template, 1009–1010
enterprise resource details, 1075
groups, 478

hyperlinks, 150
objects, 711–712
outlines, 159, 187, 194, 201, 206
portfolio models, 1062–1063
Project Center views, 987–990
project information, 1034
project versions, 1000
recurring tasks, 142
reports, 892–893
resource assignments, 377–379
Resource Center views, 990–993
security templates, CD:70
tables, 841–843
task lists
clearing contents, 128
copying tasks, 129–130
deleting tasks, 128
Fill command, 130
inserting tasks, 128
moving tasks, 129–130
undoing changes, 127
task tables
columns, 237–238
date format, 239
task-tracking fields
% Complete, 533
% Work Complete, 535
Actual Duration, 534
Actual Finish, 532–533
Actual Start, 532
Actual Work, 535
Physical % Complete, 534
Remaining Duration, 535
Remaining Work, 535–536
timephased Actual Work, 536
tasks
Multiple Task Information dialog box, 131–132
Network Diagram view, 270
Task Information dialog box, 131
templates, 107–109
text, 257
work schedules, 388–390

editors

Custom Form Editor, 953–956
VBE (Visual Basic Editor)
Immediate window, CD:43–45
object browser, CD:36
opening, CD:35
Project Explorer, CD:35
Properties window, CD:36

Edits to Total Task % Complete Will Be Spread to the Status Date calculation option, 543–544

effort-driven tasks, 27, 338–341, 364

effort. *See* work

elapsed duration, 135–136

elapsed time, 441

ellipsis, 864

email

distributing projects plans via, 486
hyperlinks, 150
Microsoft Outlook
Project Server connections, 1140
setting up to work with Project Server, 1139
submitting time with, 1140–1141
viewing task assignments in, 1140

embedded objects. *See also* objects

converting, 710
editing, 711–712
headers/footers, 717–719
legends, 717–719
moving, 707
opening, 711–712
resizing, 703, 707, 729

enabling

alerts, 43
Auto Save, 98
AutoFilter, 769
Automatically Add New Resources and Tasks option, 309
multiple skills per resource, 1016, 1087
proficiency levels per skill, 1015–1016, 1086
Project Server features, CD:84
rollup views, 739

end accrual method, 286

End key (task tables), 234

End of Map Definition page (Import/Export Wizard), 639

end times, 69–70

enterprise actual resources, 1093

enterprise collaboration, 1120–1121

documents, 1133
document libraries, 1134
linking to tasks, 1135
flow diagram, 1121–1122
issues, 1137–1138
Microsoft Outlook
Project Server connections, 1140
setting up to work with Project Server, 1139
submitting time with, 1140–1141
viewing task assignments in, 1140
risks, 1135–1137
status reports, 1129
compiling, 1132–1133
requesting, 1130–1131
status report flow, 1130
submitting, 1131–1132
task assignments, notifying team members of, 1123–1126
timesheets
approving, 1128
attaching notes to, 1127
lockdown periods, 1128–1129
revising, 1129
submitting for approval, 1126–1127
timesheet flow, 1122–1123
tracking methods, 1123

enterprise custom fields, 1010–1011, 1081–1082

assigning to enterprise resources, 1096
assigning to projects, 1067
creating, 1016–1018
planning, 974–975

Enterprise Fields command (Customize menu), 1011, 1082

enterprise generic resources, 1092

Enterprise Global settings, 978
- project attributes, 979–980
- resource attributes, 980–981

Enterprise Global template, 104, 873–874, 926, 947, 1007–1008
- backing up, 1019–1020
- copying, 109
- copying base calendars to, 84, 89–90
- editing, 109, 1009–1010
- effect on user sessions, 1008–1009
- enterprise project calendar management, 1018–1019
- enterprise resource calendar management, 1019
- finding, 112
- restoring, 1020
- saving changes to, 873–875
- working offline, 1010

enterprise-level project management, 966–967, 971. *See also* enterprise projects; enterprise resources
- collaboration, 1120–1121
  - documents, 1133–1135
  - flow diagram, 1121–1122
  - issues, 1137–1138
  - Microsoft Outlook, 1139–1141
  - risks, 1135–1137
  - status reports, 1129–1133
  - task assignments, notifying team members of, 1123–1126
  - timesheets, 1122–1123, 1126–1129
- consistent views, 982–983
- document management, 983–984
- enterprise custom fields, 1010–1011, 1081–1082
  - assigning to enterprise resources, 1096
  - assigning to projects, 1067
  - creating, 1016–1018
  - planning, 974–975
- Enterprise Global settings, 978
  - project attributes, 979–980
  - resource attributes, 980–981
- enterprise outline codes, 1010–1011, 1081–1082
  - assigning to enterprise resources, 1096
  - assigning to projects, 1067
  - creating, 1011–1015, 1082–1085
  - matching skill-sets, 1088–1090
  - multi-value fields, 1088
  - multiple skills per resource, 1016, 1087
  - planning, 974–975
  - proficiency levels per skill, 1015–1016, 1086
  - RBS (Resource Breakdown Structure), 1010, 1082
- enterprise templates, 981, 1065–1066
- planning, 970
  - collaboration and document management, 977
  - consistent project schedules, 976
  - consistent views, 977
  - enterprise custom fields, 974–975
  - enterprise outline codes, 974–975
  - enterprise projects, 973
  - enterprise resources, 974
  - group responsibilities, 971–973
  - processes, 973
  - project and task definitions, 975
  - reports, 974–975
  - security, 978
  - skill and attribute definitions, 975–976
  - time reporting, 977
- processes, 973
- project versions
  - advantages of, 982
  - creating, 981
  - cross-project links, 982
  - defined, 976
  - opening schedules with, 982
  - Published version, 981
  - resources, 982
- reports, 974–975
- role management, 984
- security, 984
- time reporting, 983
- user roles and functions, 971

Enterprise Options menu commands
- Import Project to Enterprise, 1025
- Import Resources to Enterprise, 1022
- Microsoft Project Server Accounts, 1006
- Open Enterprise Resource Pool, 1094

enterprise outline codes, 1010–1011, 1081–1082
- assigning to enterprise resources, 1096
- assigning to projects, 1067
- creating, 1011–1015, 1082–1085
- matching skill-sets, 1088–1090
- multi-value fields, 1088
- multiple skills per resource, 1016, 1087
- planning, 974–975
- proficiency levels per skill, 1015–1016, 1086
- RBS (Resource Breakdown Structure), 1010, 1082

enterprise projects. *See also* enterprise-level project management
- analyzing, 1048
- booking types, 1039–1040
- Build Team feature, 1036–1037
- calendars, 1018–1019
- checking in, 1001, 1046
- deleting, 1042–1043
- filtering, 1030, 1033–1034, 1037–1038
- grouping, 1033–1034

linking tasks across
Link Task function, 1043–1044
manually, 1045
opening multiple, 1040–1043
Portfolio Analyzer
assessing projects with, 1053–1054
changing view content, 1051–1052
charts, 1051
compared to Portfolio Modeler, 1048–1049
drop-down lists, 1051
example, 1050
PivotTables, 1051
Save a Link option, 1050
Save as GIF option, 1051
view options, 1050
portfolio models, 1054–1055
analyzing, 1063–1064
comparing, 1061
creating, 1056–1058
modifying, 1062–1063
opening, 1059–1060
properties, 1060–1061
refreshing views, 1065
transferring, 1064
project information
editing, 1034
viewing, 1035–1036
resource assignment, 1037–1038
resource availability, 1040
searching, 1034
viewing, 1032

enterprise resource calendars, 1019

Enterprise Resource list (Team Builder), 1105

enterprise resource pool, 1090–1092

Enterprise Resource Pool Wizard, 1091

enterprise resources, 1090–1091. *See also* enterprise-level project management
actual resources, 1091–1092
enterprise actual resources, 1093
local actual resources, 1093–1094
adding to projects, 1097–1098
adjusting actuals, 1080
analyzing, 1048
applying custom fields to, 1091, 1096
applying outline codes to, 1091, 1096
booking type
changing, 1100–1101
proposed versus committed booking, 1101
viewing booking status, 1101–1102
building teams from, 1097
checking in, 1002
creating, 1094–1096
editing details, 1075
enterprise resource pool, 1090–1092
Enterprise Resource Pool Wizard, 1091
filtering, 1075, 1100
generic resources
defined, 1091
enterprise generic resources, 1092
local generic resources, 1093
importing, 1021–1023
matching, 1099
removing from projects, 1098
replacing, 1098–1099
resource assignments, 1074–1075
resource availability, 1074–1077
Resource Substitution Wizard, 1091
viewing, 1074, 1078–1079
approved timesheets, 1080–1081
timesheet format, 1079
timesheet summary, 1080

enterprise templates, 981, 1065–1066

Entire Project command
Request Progress Information menu, 1125
Zoom menu, CD:29

Entire Task command (Clear menu), 128

Entry bar, 37

Entry form, 950

Entry table, 193–194, 758–760

Entry—Material Resource table, 761

Entry—Work Resource table, 761

environment options (projects)
calendar options, 72–73
date format, 75
Days per Month, 68–69
decimal digits, 75
default end time, 69–70
default save format, 75
default start time, 69–70
default view, 73–74
displaying, 65
duration time units, 73
file-specific options, 66–67
fiscal year, 70–72
global options, 66
Hours per Day, 68–69
Hours per Week, 68–69
user name, 73

equals condition (Find operations), 53

Equals test (filters), 861

equipment as resources, 280

erasing Notes objects, 712

estimate at completion (EAC), 586

estimating task duration, 132–133, 176

Euro Currency Converter toolbar, 927

EVA. *See* earned value analysis

events, CD:62–63

Excel
earned value graphs, 590–595
exporting to, CD:58–61
PivotTables, 668–673
Task List Template, 118
worksheets
Import/Export maps, 665
importing project data from, 673–680
saving projects as, 665–668

exchanging data. *See* sharing data

exclusive filters, 762

Existing Filters list (Team Builder), 1105

Exit command (File menu), 959

expanding outlines, 157–158

expanding/contracting project details, 1035

Export Grid to Excel option, 1036

Export maps, 649
- cautions, 651
- Compare to Baseline, 652–654
- compatibility with Excel formats, 665
- Cost Data by Task, 652–654
- creating, 656–660, CD:5–8
- Default Task Information, 652–654
- defined, CD:3
- Earned Value Information, 652–654
- Export to HTML Using Standard Template, 654
- file location, 651
- HTML options, CD:10–13
- Resource Export Table Map, 652–654
- saving, CD:8
- tables, 649–650
- Task and Resource PivotTable, 652, 655
- Task Export Table Map, 652, 655
- Task List with Embedded Assignment Rows, 652, 655
- Top Level Tasks List, 652, 656
- Who Does What Report, 652–654

Export table, 759–761

Export to HTML Using Standard Template map, 654

Export Wizard, CD:3–13

Export Wizard – End of Map Definition dialog box, CD:8

Export Wizard - Map dialog box, CD:10

Export Wizard – Map Options dialog box, CD:3–4, CD:11–13

Export Wizard – Task Mapping dialog box, CD:5–7

exporting data
- to Excel, 668–673, CD:58–61
- Export maps, 649
  - cautions, 651
  - Compare to Baseline, 652–654
  - compatibility with Excel formats, 665
  - Cost Data by Task, 652–654
  - creating, 656–660
  - Default Task Information, 652–654
  - Earned Value Information, 652–654
  - Export to HTML Using Standard Template, 654
  - file location, 651
  - Resource Export Table Map, 652–654
  - tables, 649–650
  - Task and Resource PivotTable, 652, 655
  - Task Export Table Map, 652, 655
  - Task List with Embedded Assignment Rows, 652, 655
  - Top Level Tasks List, 652, 656
  - Who Does What Report, 652–654
- Export Wizard, CD:3–13
- to HTML, CD:3–8
- Import maps, 661–665
- Import/Export Wizard, 637–639
  - Data page, 637
  - End of Map Definition page, 639
  - Import Mode page, 639
  - Map Options page, 638
  - Map page, 637
  - Map Selection page, 638
  - Save Map dialog box, 639
  - Task Mapping page, 638
  - Welcome page, 637
- to older version of Project, 636
- text files, 682–684, CD:61
- troubleshooting, 689
- XML files, 681–682

extended working hours, 429–432

External Task field, 619

external tasks, 619, 793

F

fast-tracking projects, 183

FF (Finish-to-Finish) relationship, 183

Field Name field (Column Definition dialog box), 845

fields
- Account Properties dialog box, 1006
- adding to custom forms, 957–958
- assignment-tracking fields
  - % Work Complete, 538
  - Actual Finish, 537
  - Actual Start, 537
  - Actual Work, 537
  - Remaining Work, 538
  - timephased Actual Work, 539
- baselines, 522–524
- calculated fields, 850–852
- custom fields, 847–848
  - accessing, 848–849
  - behaviors, 852
  - calculated fields, 850–852
  - indicator fields, 853
  - managing, 859
  - naming, 849–850
  - outline codes, 854–859
  - WBS code formats, 854
- custom views, CD:76
- defined, 108
- Earned Value Cost Indicators table
  - BAC (budget at completion), 586
  - CPI (cost performance index), 585
  - CV (cost variance), 584

CV% (cost variance percentage), 585
EAC (estimate at completion), 586
TCPI (to complete performance index), 586
VAC (variance at completion), 586
Earned Value Schedule Indicators table
SPI (schedule performance index), 582
SV (schedule variance), 581
SV% (schedule variance percentage), 582
enterprise custom fields, 1010–1011, 1081–1082
assigning to enterprise resources, 1096
assigning to projects, 1067
creating, 1016–1018
planning, 974–975
External Task, 619
filters, 861
grouping fields, 869
indicator fields, 853
Microsoft Project Server Accounts dialog box, 1007
multi-value fields, 1088
Notes, 712–714
Objects, 715–717
outline fields
creating, 854–855
including in tables, 858–859
outline code lookup tables, 857–858
outline masks, 855–857
resource assignment
Assignment Units, 325–329
Assignment Work, 329
Material Resources, 330
Resource Name, 324–325
Work Resources, 329–330
resource fields, 292–293
Base Calendar, 300–301
Code, 307–308
Cost Accrual, 307
Cost Per Use, 305
Cost Rate tables, 305–306
Group, 295–297
ID, 293
Indicators, 293
Initials, 295
Material Label, 295
Max Units, 297–298
Overtime Rate, 304–305
Resource Availability, 298–300
Resource Name, 294
Standard Rate, 303–304
Type, 294–295
Working Time, 301–302
scrolling, 48–49
selecting, 50–51
Status, 557–558
Status Indicator, 557–558
Task Information dialog box
Constraint Date, 202–203
Constraint Type, 202–203
Deadline Date, 217–219
task tables, 235
Duration field, 120
Finish field, 120–123
ID field, 119
Indicator field, 120
Predecessors field, 123
Resource Names field, 123
Start field, 120–123
Task Name field, 120
task-tracking fields, 529–531
% Complete, 533
% Work Complete, 535
Actual Duration, 534
Actual Finish, 532–533
Actual Start, 532
Actual Work, 535
Physical % Complete, 534
Remaining Duration, 535
Remaining Work, 535–536
timephased Actual Work, 536
text fields, 150–151
timephased fields, 415–416
Usage table
Assignment Delay, 446–447
Leveling Delay, 444–445
Version field, 1000

Fields command
Customize menu, 848
Item menu, 957

File menu commands
Exit, 959
Page Setup, 497
Print, 490, 512
Print Preview, 490, 509–513
Save, 99, 959
Save As, 100, 645
Save As Web Page, 102, CD:3
Save As Workspace, 635
Save Workspace, 102, 607, 625
Send To, 486

File Save dialog box, 607

files. *See also* Enterprise Global template
backing up, 102
Centered Mist Dark.html, CD:14–16
exporting to, CD:61
filenames
including in headers/footers, 501
long filenames, 100
special characters, 100
formats, 96–97, 632–633
.csv, 635
displaying, 633
.htm, 634
.mdb, 97, 634, 645–646
.mdw, 102
.mpd, 97, 633, 640–645
.mpp, 97, 633
.mpt, 97, 103, 633
.mpw, 607, 635
.mpx, 633, 636
native formats, 632
.txt, 635
.xls, 634
hyperlinks, inserting, 148–149
merging, 607
Insert Project dialog box, 612–613
New Window command, 608
opening with macros, CD:61–62
options, 66–67
saving
Auto Save feature, 98–99
backups, 102
default location, 96–97

file type, 96–97
in HTML format, 102
password-protected files, 101
Read-Only files, 101
Read-Only Recommended files, 102
Save As dialog box, 99–100
workspaces, 102–103
searching for, 32
security, 100–102
sharing, 97
templates
built-in templates, 104–105
creating, 106–107
defined, 103
editing, 107
.mpt file extension, 103
opening, 104
version compatibility, 97

Fill command (Edit menu), 130

fill handles, 130

Fill menu commands
Down, 130
Up, 130

fill styles, 255–256

Filter Definition dialog box, 859–862

Filter menu commands, Group, 1034

Filtered For command (Project menu), 318, 495, 763, 859, 904

Filtered For menu commands
All Resources, 410
Overallocated Resources, 409

filters, 472–474, 761–762, 880
applying, 318, 495, 762–764
AutoFilter feature, 769–770, 867–868
calculated filters, 762, 866
Calendar view, 261–262, 737
compound filters, 762
criteria, 315
Critical, 473
custom filters
AutoFilter, 867–868
calculated filters, 866
creating, 859–860
definitions, 862
field names, 861
filter criteria tests, 861–864
interactive filters, 864–865
multiple filters, 866–867
naming, 860
Team Builder, 1105
custom views, CD:76
defined, 108
exclusive filters, 762
filter criteria tests
Contains, 863
Contains Exactly, 863
Is Within/Is Not Within, 863
logical values, 862
table of, 861
test value column entries, 862
wildcards, 864
highlight filters, 316, 472, 838
inclusive filters, 762
interactive filters, 762, 864–865
limitations, 764–765
macros, CD:56–57
multiple filters, 866–867
Project Center, 1030, 1033–1034, 1037–1038
refreshing, 474
removing, 410, 474
Resource Center, 1075
resource filters
All Resources, 317, 767
applying, 370
Available to Work, 370–371
Confirmed Assignments, 767
Cost Greater Than..., 767
Cost Overbudget, 317, 572–574, 767
Date Range..., 767
Group..., 317, 369, 767
In Progress Assignments, 767
Linked Fields, 702, 768
Overallocated Resources, 317, 409, 768
removing, 370
Resource Range..., 768
Resources with Attachments, 768
Resources—Material, 315–316, 369
Resources—Work, 369, 768
Resources/Assignments with Overtime, 317, 768
Should Start By..., 574, 768
Should Start/Finish By..., 574, 768
Slipped/Late Progress, 768
Slipping Assignments, 317, 562, 574, 768
Unconfirmed Assignments, 768
Unstarted Assignments, 768
Work Complete, 317, 768
Work Incomplete, 768
Work Overbudget, 572–574, 768
task filters, 473
All Tasks, 765
Completed Tasks, 765
Confirmed, 765
Cost Greater Than..., 765
Cost Overbudget, 765
Created After..., 766
Critical, 766
Date Range..., 766
In Progress Tasks, 766, 859
Incomplete Tasks, 766
Late/Overbudget Tasks Assigned To..., 766
Linked Fields, 766
Milestones, 473, 766
Resource Group..., 766
Should Start By..., 766
Should Start/Finish By..., 766
Slipped/Late Progress, 766
Slipping Tasks, 562, 766
Summary Tasks, 473–474, 766
Task Range..., 766
Tasks/Assignments with Overtime, 767
Tasks with Attachments, 766

Tasks with Deadlines, 219, 473, 766
Tasks with Fixed Dates, 215, 473–474, 767
Tasks with a Task Calendar Assigned, 226
Top Level Tasks, 570, 767
Unconfirmed, 767
Unstarted Tasks, 767
Update Needed, 767
Using Resource in Date Range..., 767
Using Resource..., 767
Work Overbudget, 767
troubleshooting, 773
view filters, 837–838
viewing, 1105

finalizing project plans, 486

Find command (Edit menu), 235–236

Find dialog box, 20, 35, 50–53, 235

Find What option (Find dialog box), 52

finding
critical path, 480
dates, 243
files, 32
Find dialog box, 20, 35, 50–53
GLOBAL.MPT, 112
resources, 20, 35, 50
task constraints, 214–216
taskbars, 243
tasks, 20, 35, 50
Calendar view, 260–261
Find command, 235–236

Finish Date text box (Project Information dialog box), 58–60

finish dates, 176
Actual Finish field
assignments, 537
tasks, 532–533
default finish dates, 121
defined, 794
entering, 58–60
fixed finish dates, 384–385, 403
variances, 571

Finish field (task tables), 120–123

Finish No Earlier Than (FNET) constraint, 203

Finish No Later Than (FNLT) constraint, 203

Finish-to-Finish relationship, 183

Finish-to-Start relationship, 182

finished tasks
defined, 792
finished early tasks, 793
finished late tasks, 793
finished on time tasks, 793

fiscal year, defining start of, 70–72

Fiscal Year setting (Options dialog box), 70–72

fixed consumption rates, 294, 328

fixed costs
assigning, 396–399
defined, 281–282
documenting reasons for, 282
fixed contract fees, 396–399

fixed duration, 26, 335

fixed finish dates, 384–385, 403

fixed start dates, 382–385

fixed-unit tasks, 336

fixed-work tasks, 335

flag tasks, 793

flat pattern (work), 348, 350

flex-time schedules, 77

flexible constraints, 203–206

floating toolbars, 928–929

FNET (Finish No Earlier Than) constraint, 203

FNLT (Finish No Later Than) constraint, 203

Font command (Format menu), 257, 781

Font dialog box, 504

fonts
changing, 257, 780
Font command (Format menu), 257, 781
Font dialog box, 504
headers/footers, 500

Footer tab (Page Setup dialog box), 500–502

footers
creating, 501–502
inserting objects into, 717–719
printing, 500–501
reports, 880
text alignment, 502–503
text formatting, 504, 506

For Each, Next statement, CD:40

Form Information dialog box, 955

form views
Resource Form view, 753
Resource Name Form view, 753
Task Details Form view, 750
Task Form view, 749
Task Name Form view, 750

Format Bar dialog box, 797–798

Format Drawing dialog box, 251, 255

Format menu commands
Bar, 797
Bar Styles, 790, 804
Box Styles, 807
Detail Styles, 414, 828
Details, 247, 413–414, 817, 822
Font, 257, 781
Gridlines, 776, 781
Layout, 161, 252, 273, 739, 798, 806
Text Styles, 472, 776–778
Timescale, 245, 494, 785, 803
Zoom, 245

Format Painter tool, 781

Format Text Font button, 504

formats (files), 96–97, 632–633
.csv, 635
displaying, 633
.htm, 634
.mdb, 97, 634, 645–646
.mdw, 102
.mpd, 97, 633, 640–645

.mpp, 97, 633
.mpt, 97, 103, 633
.mpw, 607, 635
.mpx, 633, 636
native formats, 632
.txt, 635
.xls, 634

Formats command (Clear menu), 128

formatting
Calendar view, 802–803
bar styles, 804–806
layout options, 806
timescales, 803–804
dates, 798
fonts, 257
footers, 504–506
Gantt Chart bar charts
bar appearance, 791–792
bar length, 794–795
bar names, 791
bar styles definition example, 800
bar styles options, 790–791
date format, 798
Gantt Chart Wizard, 801–802
layout, 798–799
manual formatting, 797–798
progress bar styles, 795–796
rows, 794
task types, 792–793
text, 796–797
gridlines, 781–783
group displays, 871–872
headers, 504–506
legend text, 504, 506
merged projects, 611
Network Diagram view
box placement, 815–816
box styles, 807–808
data templates, 809–811
layout options, 811–815
notes, 142–144
outlines, 160–161, 783–784
page breaks, 789
Resource Form view, 817–819
Resource Graph view, 819–821
bar styles, 824–826
display values, 822–824
format options, 821–822
Resource Sheet view, 830
Resource Usage view, 826–828
sort options, 776–777
Task Form view, 817–819
Task Sheet view, 830
Task Usage view, 829
taskbars, 831
text, 778–780
color, 780
copying formatting, 781
font, 780
global changes, 779
manual formatting, 781
milestones, 779
overallocated resources, 405
reports, 897, 909, 914
selected text, 781
timescales, 245, 785, 803–804
nonworking time display, 788–789
timescale definitions, 787–788
timescale tiers, 786–787
troubleshooting, 830–831
versions, 1000

Formatting toolbar, 35, 156, 411, 781, 926

forms
Cost Tracking, 950
custom forms, 949–950
assigning to toolbar buttons, 952–953
buttons, 959
copying, 960
creating, 953–954
displaying, 951
editing, 960
field values, 957–958
group boxes, 958, 961
hotkeys, 951–952
managing with Organizer, 960
renaming, 960
resizing, 955–956
saving, 959
text, 956
troubleshooting, 961
defined, 108
Earned Value, 950
Entry, 950
PERT Entry, 950
Resource Form view, 817–819
Schedule Tracking, 950
Summary, 950
Task Details, 209
Task Form view, 817–819
Task Relationships, 950
Tracking, 950
Update Project, 552–554
Update Tasks, 551
Word Tracking, 950

Forms command (Customize menu), 951

Formula dialog box, 1017

formulas
calculated fields, 851
work formula, 330–331
applying to existing assignments, 335
applying to new assignments, 331–334

forward-scheduled projects, 121, 403

free slack, 441, 743, 795

From Active Directory option (Add Resources dialog box), 1107

From Address Book option (Add Resources dialog box), 1107

From Microsoft Project Server option (Add Resources dialog box), 1108

front-door processes, 973

front-loaded contour resource scheduling, 324

front loaded work, 348, 350

FS (Finish-to-Start) relationship, 182

full menus, displaying, 35

functions, MsgBox, CD:42

Future status indicator, 558

G

Gantt Chart view, 32, 43, 232, 737–738, 1036. *See also* specialized Gantt Chart views
- bar charts
  - bar appearance, 791–792
  - bar length, 794–795
  - bar names, 791
  - bar styles definition example, 800
  - bar styles options, 790–791
  - layout, 798–799
  - manual formatting, 797–798
  - progress bar styles, 795–796
  - rows, 794
  - task types, 792–793
  - text, 796–797
- combination views, 246–247
- custom views, CD:75, CD:92–93
- date format, 798
- displaying, 246–247
- Draw drop-down menu, 248
- Drawing toolbar, 247–250
- Gantt Chart Wizard, 801–802
- indicator symbols, 44
- inserting objects into, 708–712
- objects
  - attaching to dates, 250–252
  - attaching to taskbars, 250–252, 274
  - copying, 254–255
  - deleting, 256
  - fill style, 255–256
  - hiding, 252
  - lines, 255–256
  - moving, 253
  - resizing, 253–254
  - selecting, 250
- pasting objects into, 706–708
- progress lines, 559–562
- project tracking, 550
- scrollbars, 45, 234–235
- splitting, 45–46
- tables, 44
- task information, 246
- task tables, 119, 232
  - columns, 236–239
  - date format, 239
  - displaying, 236
  - Duration field, 120
  - fields, 235
  - finding tasks in, 235–236
  - Finish field, 120–123
  - ID field, 119
  - Indicator field, 120
  - moving around in, 233–234
  - outlined task lists, 233
  - Predecessors field, 123
  - Resource Names field, 123
  - row height, 237
  - scrolling, 234–235
  - Start field, 120–123
  - subtasks, 233
  - summary tasks, 233
  - task indicators, 233
  - Task Name field, 120
- taskbars, 274
- text, 256–258
- timescales, 44–45
  - bar text, 242
  - finding dates in, 243
  - finding taskbars in, 243
  - formatting, 245
  - linking lines, 242
  - moving around in, 242–243
  - scrolling, 49, 243
  - taskbars, 50, 240
  - tiers, 244
  - zooming in/out, 245

Gantt Chart Wizard, 801–802

General drop-down list box, 501

General tab
- Commands and Options dialog box, CD:82
- Open Enterprise Resource Pool dialog box, 1095
- Properties dialog box, 63
- Task Information dialog box, 739

Generate WBS Code for New Task check box (WBS Code Definition dialog box), 166

generic resources, 281, 1092–1093

global options, 66

Global template, 104, 873–874, 926, 947, 1007–1008
- backing up, 1019–1020, CD:35
- copying, 109
- copying base calendars to, 84, 89–90
- editing, 109, 1009–1010
- effect on user sessions, 1008–1009
- enterprise project calendar management, 1018–1019
- enterprise resource calendar management, 1019
- finding, 112
- restoring, 1020
- saving changes to, 873–875
- working offline, 1010

Go To command (Edit menu), 260

Go to Next Overallocation tool, 412

goals of projects, 16

gold-plating, 583

Graphical Indicators button (Customize Fields dialog box), 853

Graphical Indicators dialog box, 853

graphical user interfaces. *See* GUIs

graphical views, 736
- Calendar view, 737
- Descriptive Network Diagram view, 746
- Detail Gantt, 743
- Gantt Chart. *See* Gantt Chart view
- Leveling Gantt, 743
- Multiple Baselines Gantt, 744
- Network Diagram, 745–746
- PERT Analysis, 744–745
- Relationship Diagram, 747
- Resource Graph, 754
- rollup views, 738–739
  - Bar Rollup, 740
  - enabling, 739

Milestone Rollup, 740
Milestone Date Rollup, 740–741
Text Above field, 739
Tracking Gantt, 742

graphs
Assignment Work graph, 372
earned value, 590–595
Remaining Availability graph, 372
Task Form view
bar styles, 824–826
display values, 822–824
format options, 821–822
formatting, 819–826
viewing, 373
Work graph, 372

Graphs button (Team Builder), 1106

Greater Than or Equal To test (filters), 861

Greater Than test (filters), 861

gridlines, 781–783

Gridlines command (Format menu), 776, 781

Gridlines dialog box, 781–783

Group box command (Item menu), 958

group boxes, 958, 961

Group By command (Project menu), 314–315, 478, 770–772, 868

Group By field (Team Builder), 1105

Group By menu commands
Customize Group By, 478
More Groups, 478–479
No Group, 315
Work vs. Material Resources, 315

group by summary tasks, 793

Group command (Filter menu), 1034

Group Definition dialog box, 868–870

Group field (resources), 295–297

Group filter, 317, 369

Group... filter, 767

grouping
enterprise projects, 1033–1034
fields, 869
resources, 295–297, 314–315, 1105
tasks, 495
toolbar buttons, 933

grouping formats (views), CD:76, CD:93

groups, 280, 297
applying, 770
creating, 479
custom groups
accessing, 868–869
display options, 871–872
group intervals, 870–871
grouping fields, 869
saving, 872
customizing, 477, 479
defined, 108, 475
displaying/hiding, 770
editing, 478
intervals, 478, 870–871
labels, filtering for, 320
Project Center, 1033–1034
Project Server, CD:68
resource groups
Assignments Keeping Outline Structure, 772
Complete and Incomplete Resources, 772
No Group, 772
Resource Group, 477, 773
Resource Pending, 773
Standard Rate, 773
Standard Rate group, 477
Work vs. Material Resources, 773
task groups
Complete and Incomplete Tasks, 772
Constraint Type, 477, 772
Critical, 477, 772
Duration, 477, 772
Duration then Priority, 772
Milestones, 477, 772
No Group, 772
Priority, 477, 772
Priority Keeping Outline Structure, 772
Status Request Pending, 772
views, 837
Web Access, 987

***A Guide to the Project Management Body of Knowledge*, 17**

GUIs (graphical user interfaces), 922
commands, 942, 946
forms
Cost Tracking, 950
custom forms, 949–961
Earned Value, 950
Entry, 950
PERT Entry, 950
Schedule Tracking, 950
Summary, 950
Task Relationships, 950
Tracking, 950
Word Tracking, 950
menu bars
adding menus to, 943–944
customizing, 941–942
menus
adding items to, 945
adding to menu bars, 943–944
attributes, 946
customizing, 922–923
defined, 941
moving, 946
removing, 946
renaming, 944
toolbars
active toolbars, 927
Analysis toolbar, 927
assigning custom forms to, 952–953
Collaborate toolbar, 926
combination boxes, 928
combo boxes, 934
command buttons, 930–933, 937–941, 960
Compare Project Versions toolbar, 927
copying, 934–935, 947–948
creating, 934–935
Custom Forms toolbar, 926
customizing, 923–941

Database Upgrade Utility toolbar, 927
displaying in one row, 923–924
displaying/hiding, 927–928
docking, 928
Drawing toolbar, 926
Euro Currency Converter toolbar, 927
floating, 928–929
Formatting toolbar, 926
managing with Organizer, 947–949
move handles, 923
Network Diagram toolbar, 927
personalized toolbars, 924
PERT Analysis toolbar, 927
positioning, 928–929
Project Guide toolbar, 926–927
renaming, 947–948
resizing, 929
Resource Management toolbar, 927
restoring, 936
Standard toolbar, 926
Task Pane toolbar, 927
Tracking toolbar, 927
troubleshooting, 961
user-defined toolbars, 934–936
Visual Basic toolbar, 927
Web toolbar, 927

H

hard constraints, 212–214

Header tab (Page Setup dialog box), 500–502

Header Text Wrapping option (Column Definition dialog box), 845

headers
- column headers, 729, 842
- creating, 501–502
- inserting objects into, 717–719
- printing, 500–501
- reports, 880
- text alignment, 502–503
- text formatting, 504–506

height
- rows, 237
- table rows, 847
- task name rows, 126

help, 39–40
- Planning Wizard, 42–43
- Project Guide, 38–41
- ScreenTips, 35, 38–39
- SmartTags, 41–42
- VBA (Visual Basic for Applications), CD:64
- What's This? feature, 36

Help menu commands, What's This?, 36

HREF attribute (<A> tag), CD:20–21

Hide Assignments tool, 411

Hide Column command (Edit menu), 846

Hide command (Window menu), 606

Hide Fields tool, 815

Hide Rollup Bars When Summary Expanded option (Layout dialog box), 161, 799

Hide Summary Tasks tool, 815

hiding
- groups, 770
- objects, 252
- Project Guide, 40–41
- resource assignments, 411
- rollup bars, 161, 799
- table columns, 846
- task table columns, 238
- toolbars, 36, 927–928
- View bar, 37
- windows, 606

highlight filters, 316, 472, 838

highlighting tasks, 472

histograms, 754

Home key, 234

honoring
- dependency links, 212–214
- task constraints, 212–214

hotkeys, 951–952

Hour by Hour sensitivity level, 407

Hours per Day setting (Options dialog box), 68–69

Hours per Week setting (Options dialog box), 68–69

HREF attribute (<A> tag), CD:20–21

.htm file format, 634

HTML (Hypertext Markup Language),
- <A> tag, CD:20–21
- <BODY> tag, CD:16
- documents
  - background colors, CD:14–15
  - background images, CD:16–17
  - Gantt Chart images, CD:22–24
  - hyperlinks, CD:19–25
  - images, CD:17–18
  - publishing, CD:24
  - saving projects as, CD:3–8
  - title bar text, CD:18–19
  - troubleshooting, CD:24–25
  - viewing projects as, CD:9
- saving files in, 102
- templates, CD:13
  - background colors, CD:14–15
  - background images, CD:16–17
  - Gantt Chart images, CD:22–24
  - hyperlinks, CD:19–25
  - images, CD:17–18
  - title bar text, CD:18–19
- <TITLE> tag, CD:18

Hyperlink command (Insert menu), 148

Hyperlink table, 758, 760

hyperlinks. *See also* links
- adding to HTML templates, CD:19–25
- attaching to files/Web pages, 148–149
- attaching to new documents, 149
- attaching to resources, 150

attaching to tasks, 147–150
in custom text fields, 150–151
deleting, 150
editing, 150
email hyperlinks, 150
Hyperlink table, 758–760
notes, 144

Hyperlinks command (Clear menu), 128

hyphen (-), 233

I

I-beam, 257

icons
inserted projects, 608
recurring tasks, 140

ID field, 119, 293

ID Only leveling order, 457

If, Then, Else statement, CD:41

images
icons
inserted projects, 608
recurring tasks, 140
including in headers/footers, 501
Web pages, CD:16–18

Immediate window (VBE), CD:43–45

Import Custom Field button (Customize Fields dialog box), 856

Import maps, 649
cautions, 651
Compare to Baseline, 652–654
compatibility with Excel formats, 665
Cost Data by Task, 652–654
creating, 661–665, CD:5–8
Default Task Information, 652–654
defined, CD:3
Earned Value Information, 652–654
Export to HTML Using Standard Template, 654
HTML options, CD:10–13
options, CD:10–13
Resource Export Table Map, 652–654
saving, CD:8
tables, 649–650
Task and Resource PivotTable, 652, 655
Task Export Table Map, 652, 655
Task List with Embedded Assignment Rows, 652, 655
Top Level Tasks List, 652, 656
variables, CD:13–14
Who Does What Report, 652–654

Import Mode page (Import/Export Wizard), 639

Import Outline Code dialog box, 856–857

Import Project to Enterprise command (Enterprise Options menu), 1025

Import Projects Wizard, 1025–1028

Import Resources to Enterprise command (Enterprise Options menu), 1022

Import Resources Wizard, 1021–1023

Import/Export Wizard
Data page, 637
End of Map Definition page, 639
Import Mode page, 639
Map Options page, 638
Map page, 637
Map Selection page, 638
Save Map dialog box, 639
Task Mapping page, 638
Welcome page, 637

important tasks, 480

importing data
Excel format, 673, 675–680
Import maps, 649
cautions, 651
Compare to Baseline, 652–654
compatibility with Excel formats, 665
Cost Data by Task, 652–654
Default Task Information, 652–654
Earned Value Information, 652–654
Export to HTML Using Standard Template, 654
file location, 651
Resource Export Table Map, 652–654
tables, 649–650
Task and Resource PivotTable, 652, 655
Task Export Table Map, 652, 655
Task List with Embedded Assignment Rows, 652, 655
Top Level Tasks List, 652, 656
Who Does What Report, 652–654
Import/Export Wizard
Data page, 637
End of Map Definition page, 639
Import Mode page, 639
Map Options page, 638
Map page, 637
Map Selection page, 638
Save Map dialog box, 639
Task Mapping page, 638
Welcome page, 637
MPX format, 636
ODBC (Open Database Connectivity) sources, 648
outline codes, 856–857
Outlook task lists, 684–687
projects, 1024–1028
resources, 1021–1023
text files, 684
troubleshooting, 689
XML files, 681–682

In Progress Assignments filter, 767

in progress tasks, 792

In Progress Tasks filter, 766, 859

inclusive filters, 762

Incomplete Tasks filter, 766

increasing availability of over-allocated resources, 410, 418–423

Indent button (Formatting toolbar), 156

Indent command (Outline menu), 156

Indent Name option (Options dialog box), 160, 784

indenting tasks, 156–157

independent text
- editing, 257
- fonts, 257
- text boxes, 256–258

indicator fields, 12, 853

indicator symbols, 44

indicators
- Assigned Calendar, 353
- constraint indicators, 233
- Earned Value Cost Indicators, 583–584
  - BAC (budget at completion), 586
  - CPI (cost performance index), 585
  - CV (cost variance), 584
  - CV% (cost variance percentage), 585
  - EAC (estimate at completion), 586
  - TCPI (to complete performance index), 586
  - VAC (variance at completion), 586
- Earned Value Schedule Indicators
  - SPI (schedule performance index), 582
  - SV (schedule variance), 581
  - SV% (schedule variance percentage), 582
- task indicators, 233

Indicators field (resources), 293

individual assignments, delaying, 443–447

individual resources, 280

inflation, 203

inflexible constraints, 203–206

Info command (Edit menu), 955

initializing variables, CD:39–40

Initials field (resources), 295

input boxes, CD:51–52

Insert Hyperlink dialog box, 148–149

Insert menu commands
- All Page Break, 789
- Column, 846
- Drawing, 248
- Hyperlink, 148
- New Task, 128, 264
- Objects, 706–708
- Page Break, 496, 789
- Project, 607, 612, 615
- Recurring Task, 138
- Remove All Page Breaks, 496, 789
- Remove Page Break, 496

Insert Object dialog box, 708

Insert Project dialog box, 612–613

Insert Row button (Filter Definition dialog box), 862

Inserted Project Information dialog box, 613–614

inserted projects
- creating, 615
- deleting, 617
- identifying, 617
- links, 613–614
- maintaining, 616–617
- managing, 614–615
- relative paths, 615
- replacing, 616
- viewing information about, 613

inserting
- hyperlinks, 148–149
- objects, 706
  - into Gantt Chart view, 708–712
  - into headers/footers, 717–719
  - into legends, 717–719
  - into Notes field, 144–146, 712–714
  - into Objects field, 715–717
  - into other applications, 719–720
- page breaks, 496
- recurring tasks, 138–141
- table columns, 846
- task table columns, 237–239
- tasks, 128
  - Calendar view, 263–265
  - custom WBS codes, 167
  - Network Diagram view, 270–271

interactive filters, 762, 864–865

interim plans, 525

Internet features. *See* Web pages

interrelationships, CD:28

interruptions, 176, 220–223, 228

intervals, 478, 870–871

Is Greater Than or Equal To test, 861

Is Greater Than test, 53, 861

Is Less Than or Equal To test, 861

Is Less Than test, 53, 861

Is Not Within test, 53, 863

Is Within test, 53, 861–863

issues, 1036–1138, CD:89–90

Item Information dialog box, 957

Item menu commands
- Fields, 957
- Group box, 958

Item to Change drop-down list (Text Styles dialog box), 779–780

iterative process model, 556

J-K

just-in-time scheduling, 179, 184

Keep Start/End Dates option (Portfolio Modeler), 1058

Keep the Selected Range option (Copy Picture dialog box), 723

keyboard
selecting objects with, 250
shortcuts, 49–51
sort keys, 777

keywords. *See* statements

L

Label drop-down list (Timescale dialog box), 786

labels
filtering for, 320
timescales, 786–787

lag time, 180–181, 189–190

late/delayed starts, scheduling, 342–345, 795

late finish dates, 795

Late/Overbudget Tasks Assigned To... filter, 766

late peak work contour, 350

Late status indicator, 558

layout
Calendar view, 806
Gantt Chart view, 798–799
Network Diagram view, 273–274, 811–815
page breaks
inserting, 496
manual page breaks, 516
printing, 495–496
removing, 496
viewing, 496

Layout command (Format menu), 161, 273, 739, 798, 806

Layout dialog box, 161, 252, 273–274
Calendar view, 806
Gantt Chart view, 798–799
Network Diagram view, 812–814

Layout Now tool, 815

Layout Selection Now tool, 815

lead time, 180–181, 189–190

Legend tab (Page Setup dialog box), 503–504

legends
creating, 503–504
inserting objects into, 717–719
text formatting, 504–506

length of bars (Gantt Chart), 794–795

Less Than or Equal To test, 861

Less Than test, 861

Level Assignment field, 458

Level Entire Project option (Resource Leveling dialog box), 456

Level From, To option (Resource Leveling dialog box), 456

Level Now dialog box, 459–463

Level Only Within Available Slack option (Resource Leveling dialog box), 456

Leveling Can Adjust Individual Assignments on a Task option (Resource Leveling dialog box), 457

Leveling Can Create Splits in Remaining Work option (Resource Leveling dialog box), 457

Leveling Can Split field, 458

Leveling Delay field, 444–445, 818

leveling delays, 324, 444–445, 818

Leveling Gantt view, 743

Leveling Order option (Resource Leveling dialog box), 456

leveling resources, 419–421, 454–455
Automatic Leveling, 462
Clear Leveling dialog box, 462
Level Now dialog box, 459–463
priorities, 458–459
Resource Allocation view, 432–434
Resource Leveling dialog box, 455–459
resource substitution, 434–440

levels in outlines, 159

libraries (document), 1134

Line & Fill tab (Format Drawing dialog box), 255

line attributes, 255–256

Line button (Drawing toolbar), 249

link indicators, 699

Link Tasks command (Edit menu), 187, 618, 1043–1044

Link Tasks tool, 187, 618

Linked Fields filter, 702, 766, 768

linking lines (timescale), 242

linking tasks. *See* dependency links

links. *See also* hyperlinks
breaking, 626
creating, 618–621
cross-project task links, 982, 1043–1045
dependency links, 177–178
auditing, 199–200
Autolink, 196–198
cautions, 178
creating with Entry table, 193–194
creating with Link Tasks tool, 187
creating with mouse, 194–196
creating with Task Form view, 190–192
creating with Task Information dialog box, 188–189
defined, 176
deleting, 185, 188, 198–199
dependent tasks, 179–180
editing, 187, 198
Finish-to-Finish relationship, 183
Finish-to-Start relationship, 182
honoring, 212–214

lag time, 180–181, 189–190
lead time, 180–181, 189–190
outlined projects, 185
overlapping tasks, 180–181, 189–190
predecessor tasks, 177–180, 189
reversing, 227
Start-to-Finish relationship, 183–184
Start-to-Start relationship, 182
successor tasks, 177–180
summary tasks, 184–185
tasks from different projects, 227
troubleshooting, 226–227
unrelated tasks, 178
views, 199–201

inserted projects, 613–614
linked data
creating, 697–699
defined, 697
deleting, 701–702
identifying, 702
link indicators, 699
Network Diagram view, 272–273
pasting, 697–699, 702
refreshing, 699–701
restoring, 702
tasks 265
updating, 699–701

linked lines, 274
notes, 144
relative paths, 615
resource pools, 626
troubleshooting, 616, 621

Links Between Projects command (Tools menu), 620

Links Between Projects dialog box, 620

Links command (Edit menu), 699–701

Links dialog box, 699–701

lists
organizing into groups. *See* groups
resource lists
creating, 287–292
merging, 627
pasting from another application, 318–320
sorting, 475–477
task lists
bottom-up approach, 116
Excel Task List Template, 118
Gantt Chart view, 118–119
importing, 684–687
level of detail, 27
milestones, 117
normal tasks, 117
summary tasks, 118
top-down approach, 116
WBS (Work Breakdown Structure), 116

local actual resources, 1093–1094

local generic resources, 1093

Lock First Column option (Table Definition dialog box), 843

lockdown periods (timesheets), 1128–1129

locking columns, 876

locking down time periods, 983

logging in to Project Server, 1004–1007

logical values, testing for, 862

long filenames, 100

long task names, 126

Look for Overallocations on an x Basis option (Resource Leveling dialog box), 456

Look in Field option (Find dialog box), 52

lookup tables, 857–858

M

Macro menu commands
Record New Macro, CD:29
Stop Recording, CD:29

macros
advantages of, CD:28–29
Case statement, CD:53–54
collections, CD:32
debugging, CD:42–43
breakpoints, CD:43–45
Immediate window, CD:43–45
syntax checking, CD:43
watches, CD:43–45

events
application-level events, CD:63
help, CD:64
list of, CD:63
Project_Open, CD:62–63

exporting data to Excel, CD:58–61
exporting data to text files, CD:61
filters, CD:56–57
input boxes, CD:51–52
message boxes, CD:52
methods, CD:33
modules, CD:37
object model, CD:32–33
opening files for writing, CD:61–62
properties, CD:32, CD:42
recording
for entire project, CD:29–30
for selected tasks, CD:30–32

recursion, CD:55–56
ResMgmt_TaskEntry, 755
subroutines, CD:31
calling with arguments, CD:54
calling without parameters, CD:52–53
main subroutines, CD:51

TaskSummaryName, CD:36–37
code listing, CD:37–38
creating, CD:37–38
For Each, Next statement, CD:40
If, Then, Else statement, CD:41
nested statements, CD:41
object properties, CD:42
Sub/End Sub statements, CD:38
user feedback, CD:42
variables, CD:38–40

testing, CD:29
TraceDependencies, CD:46

calling subroutines with arguments, CD:54
calling subroutines without parameters, CD:52–53
Case statement, CD:53–54
code listing, CD:47–50
filters, CD:56–57
input box, CD:51–52
main subroutine, CD:51
message box, CD:52
recursion, CD:55–56
variables, CD:50–51
views, CD:56–57
toolbar buttons, 931
troubleshooting, CD:33
user feedback, CD:33–34, CD:42
variables
defining, CD:38–39
initializing, CD:39–40
private variables, CD:50–51
public variables, CD:50–51
types, CD:38
VBA (Visual Basic for Applications), CD:31
VBE (Visual Basic Editor)
Immediate window, CD:43–45
object browser, CD:36
opening, CD:35
Project Explorer, CD:35
Properties window, CD:36
views, CD:56–57
when to use, CD:28
ZoomAll, CD:29–30
ZoomSelected, CD:30–32

Mail Recipient (As Attachment) command (Send To menu), 486

mail. *See* email

main subroutines, CD:51

Manage Enterprise Features command (Admin menu), 996

Manage Enterprise Features menu commands
Check-in Enterprise Projects, 1001–1002
Manage Enterprise Project Versions, 999
Specify Resource and OLAP Cube Updates, 996

Manage Enterprise Project Versions command (Manage Enterprise Features menu), 999

Manage Views command (Admin menu), 988, 991, 993

management (projects), 16
benefits of Project 2003, 18–19
corrective action, 556
custom fields, 859
custom forms, 960
earned value analysis, 575–577
actual cost, 578
controlling earned value calculation, 587–588
earned value, 577–578
Earned Value Cost Indicators table, 583–587
Earned Value Schedule Indicators table, 581–582
examining trends, 578
example, 579–582
Excel graphs, 590–595
planned value, 577
troubleshooting, 599
viewing, 589–590
Guide to the Project Management Body of Knowledge, A (italic), 17
guidelines, 19–21
inserted projects, 614–615
iterative process model, 556
management phase, 23–24
multiple projects, 604
planning phase, 22–23
preliminary tasks, 22
project constraints, 17
project goals, 16
Project Management Institute, 17
reviewing project status
assignment-level status, 574–575
progress lines, 559–562
project statistics, 565
Project Summary reports, 565
project summary tasks, 565–570
resource-level status, 573–574
slipping assignments, 562
slipping tasks, 562
Status field, 557–558
Status Indicator field, 557–558
task-level status, 570
variances, 563–564, 571–573
risks, 1135–1137
schedule revisions, 595–596
costs, 596–597
duration, 597–598
scope, 596
scheduling techniques, 24
calendar, 25
crashing the schedule, 26
critical paths, 25–26
critical tasks, 25
data entry, 24–25
resource assignments, 26–27
schedule calculations, 25
temporary nature of projects, 16
toolbars, 947–949
troubleshooting, 27

manual formatting
bar charts, 797–798
page breaks, 516
text, 781

Manual option (Resource Leveling dialog box), 456

Map Options page (Import/Export Wizard), 638

Map page (Import/Export Wizard), 637

Map Selection page (Import/Export Wizard), 638

maps
defined, 108
Export maps, 649
cautions, 651
Compare to Baseline, 652–654
compatibility with Excel formats, 665

Cost Data by Task, 652–654
creating, 656–660, CD:5–8
Default Task Information, 652–654
defined, CD:3
Earned Value Information, 652–654
Export to HTML Using Standard Template, 654
file location, 651
HTML options, CD:10–13
Resource Export Table Map, 652–654
saving, CD:8
tables, 649–650
Task and Resource PivotTable, 652, 655
Task Export Table Map, 652, 655
Task List with Embedded Assignment Rows, 652, 655
Top Level Tasks List, 652, 656
Who Does What Report, 652–654

Import maps, 649
cautions, 651
Compare to Baseline, 652–654
compatibility with Excel formats, 665
Cost Data by Task, 652–654
creating, 661–665, CD:5–8
Default Task Information, 652–654
defined, CD:3
Earned Value Information, 652–654
Export to HTML Using Standard Template, 654
file location, 651
HTML options, CD:10–13
Resource Export Table Map, 652–654
saving, CD:8
tables, 649–650
Task and Resource PivotTable, 652, 655
Task Export Table Map, 652, 655
Task List with Embedded Assignment Rows, 652, 655
Top Level Tasks List, 652, 656
Who Does What Report, 652–654

Margin tab (Page Setup dialog box), 499

margins, 499

marked tasks, 792

masks (outline), 855–857

master projects, 612–613

Match button (Team Builder), 1106

Match Case option (Find dialog box), 52

matching
enterprise resources, 1099
resources, 1106
skill-sets, 1088–1090

Material filter, 315–316

Material Label field (resources), 295

material resources
assigning, 328–329
Material Resources field, 330
work formula, 333
consumption rates
fixed, 294, 328
variable, 295, 329
defined, 280
Material Resources field, 330

Max Units field (resources), 297–298

maximizing windows, 606

.mdb file format, 97, 634
opening in Project 2003, 645–646
saving projects as, 645

.mdw file format, 102

memory, overcoming memory limitations, 604

menu bars
adding menus to, 943–944
customizing, 941–942

menus. *See also* commands
adding items to, 945
adding to menu bars, 943–944
attributes, 946
customizing, 922–923, CD:85–86
defined, 941
full menus, displaying, 35
moving, 946
removing, 946
renaming, 944

merged files, saving, 608

merging
multiple project files, 607
Insert Project dialog box, 612–613
New Window command, 608
resource lists, 627

message boxes, CD:52

messages
macro message boxes, CD:33–34, CD:42
notifications, CD:94–95
reminders, CD:94–95
workgroup messages, creating user accounts from, CD:69

methods, CD:33

MFO (Must Finish On) constraint, 203

Microsoft Access format. *See* .mdb file format

Microsoft Excel earned value graphs, 590–595

Microsoft Outlook. *See* Outlook

Microsoft Project command (Programs menu), 30

Microsoft Project Database format. *See* .mpd file format

Microsoft Project Exchange format. *See* .mpx file format

Microsoft Project Professional 2003. *See* Project Professional 2003

Microsoft Project Server Accounts command (Enterprise Options menu), 1006

Microsoft Project Server Accounts dialog box, 1006–1007

Microsoft Project Server URL field (Account Properties dialog box), 1006

Microsoft Project window. ***See*** **Project window**

Milestone Date Rollup view, 739–741

Milestone Rollup view, 739–740

milestones, 20, 44, 117
- advantages, 136
- creating, 137
- critical, 267
- defined, 792
- Milestone Date Rollup view, 740–741
- Milestones filter, 473, 766
- Milestones group, 477, 772
- Milestones report, 881
- Milestone Rollup view, 740
- noncritical, 267

Milestones filter, 473, 766

Milestones group, 477, 772

Milestones report, 881

minus sign (-), 233, 784

Missed Constraint indicator, 216

missing outline symbols, troubleshooting, 830

missing toolbars, troubleshooting, 52

mixed authentication, CD:72

mode indicator, 38

models. ***See*** **portfolio models**

Modify Selection button (Customize dialog box), 937

modifying. ***See*** **changing; editing**

modules, 108, CD:37

Monthly Calendar Report Definition dialog box, 915

Monthly Calendar reports, 915–917

More Filters dialog box, 763

More Groups command (Group By menu), 478–479

More Groups dialog box, 478

More Tables command (Table menu), 757, 760, 840

More Tables dialog box, 757, 840

More Views command (Views menu), 47, 736, 834, 838

More Views dialog box, 47–48, 834, 838

More Windows command (Window menu), 604

mouse
- copying objects with, 255
- creating dependency links with, 194–196
- creating tasks with, 125
- selecting objects with, 250

Move End of Completed Parts After Status Date Back to Status Date option, 545

Move Start of Remaining Parts Before Status Date Forward to Status Date option, 545–546

moving
- commands, 946
- menus, 946
- objects, 253, 707
- split bars, 47
- tasks, 129–130
  - custom WBS codes, 167
  - to new project files, 615
  - summary tasks, 170
- toolbar buttons, 932–933

.mpd file format, 97, 633
- opening in Project 2003, 643–645
- saving projects as, 640–643

.mpp file format, 97, 633

.mpt file format, 97, 103, 633

.mpw file format, 607, 635

.mpx file format, 633, 636

MsgBox function, CD:42

MSO (Must Start On) constraint, 203

multi-value fields, 1088

Multiple Baselines Gantt view, 744

multiple filters, 866–867

multiple projects. ***See also*** **Window menu commands**
- advantages, 604
- combined resource lists, 627
- enterprise projects
  - deleting, 1042–1043
  - linking tasks across, 1043–10445
  - opening, 1040–1043
- filtering, 610–611
- formatting, 611
- inserted projects, 613–614
  - creating, 615
  - deleting, 617
  - identifying, 617
  - maintaining, 616–617
  - managing, 614–615
  - relative paths, 615
  - replacing, 616
  - viewing information about, 613
- linking, 618–621
- managing, 604
- master projects, 612–613
- merging, 607
  - Insert Project dialog box, 612–613
  - New Window command, 608
- multiple windows
  - creating, 604
  - hiding/displaying, 606
  - tiling, 605–606
- resource pools
  - creating, 621
  - disabling resource sharing, 625–626
  - links, 626
  - maintaining, 622
  - opening, 622–624
  - refreshing, 624
  - resource sharing, 621–624
  - saving, 625
  - updating, 623–624
- sorting, 610–611
- split windows, 605

subprojects, 612–613
task dependencies, 611
views, 609
workspaces, 607

multiple resources, assigning, 333–334, 357–358

multiple skills per resource, 1016, 1087

Multiple Task Information dialog box, 131–132, 216

Must Finish On (MFO) constraint, 203

Must Start On (MSO) constraint, 203

N

Name field (resources), 294

names
custom fields, 849–850
custom filters, 860
custom forms, 960
filenames
including in headers/footers, 501
long filenames, 100
special characters, 100
Gantt Chart bar charts, 791
menus, 944
objects, 111
resource names, 294, 324
tables, 841
task names, 123
column width, 126
copying from other applications, 125
displaying long names, 126
entering, 124–125
naming conventions, 124
row height, 126
text wrap, 126
toolbars, 947–948
user names, 73
views, 836

native file formats, 632

navigating
Calendar, 260
Network Diagram view, 269–270
task tables, 233–234
Arrow keys, 234
End key, 234
Find command, 235–236
Home key, 234
Page Up/Page Down keys, 234
scrollbars, 234–235
timescale, 242–243

negative delay, 455

negative slack, 795

nested statements, CD:41

Network Diagram command (View menu), 267

Network Diagram toolbar, 927

Network Diagram view, 33, 265–267, 745–746
adding tasks to, 270–271
box placement, 815–816
box styles, 807–808
data templates, 809–811
deleting tasks in, 272
displaying, 267
editing task data, 270
formatting
box placement, 815–816
box styles, 807–808
data templates, 809–811
layout options, 811–815
layout options, 811–815
linked lines, 274
linking tasks in, 272–273
outlining, 269
rearranging task nodes, 273–274
scrolling, 269–270
selecting data in, 269–270
task types, 151–152, 267
toolbar, 815
zooming in/out, 267–268, 817

network shares, 618

New and Changed Assignments command (Collaborate menu), 1125

New Calendar Wizard, 86–87

New From Existing Project option (Task pane), 31

New From Template option (Task pane), 31

New Project Wizard, 85–86

New Task command (Insert menu), 128, 264

New Toolbar dialog box, 935

New Window command (Window menu), 607–608, 615

New Window dialog box, 608

Next Step button (Project Guide), 41

Night Shift calendar, 76

No Group command (Group By menu), 315

No Group group, 772

nodes (polygons), 254

noncritical milestones, 267

noncritical tasks
defined, 792
noncritical normal tasks, 267
noncritical summary tasks, 267

nondriver resources, 355

nonworking time
displaying in Gantt Chart view, 788–789
reporting, CD:93–94

Nonworking Time tab (Timescale dialog box), 788–789

normal tasks, 44, 117, 267, 792

not finished tasks, 792

not started tasks, 793

notes, 44
attaching to projects, 146–147
attaching to tasks, 142
attaching to timesheets, 1127
creating, 142–144
formatting, 142–144
hyperlinks, 144
inserting objects in, 144–146
Notes field
disadvantages, 713
erasing objects from, 712
inserting objects into, 712–714
resource assignments, 393

notifications, CD:94–95

numbers
custom outline numbers, 169
custom WBS codes, 163
creating, 164–166
deleting tasks, 167
editing, 167
inserting tasks, 167
moving tasks, 167
renumbering, 168–169
saving, 170–171
page numbers, printing, 499

O

object browser (VBE), CD:36

object model, CD:32–33

objects. *See also names of specific objects*
attaching to dates, 250–252
attaching to taskbars, 250–252, 274
converting, 710
copying, 109–111, 254–255
defined, 703
deleting, 256
Objects field, 717
Organizer, 111–112
editing, 711–712
embedded objects, 703
erasing from Notes field, 712
fill style, 255–256
hiding, 252
inserting, 706
into Gantt Chart view, 708–712
into headers/footers, 717–719
into legends, 717–719
into Notes field, 144–146, 712–714
into Objects field, 715–717
into other applications, 719–720
lines, 255–256
moving, 253, 707
opening, 711–712
polygons, 254
renaming, 111
resizing, 253–254, 703, 707, 729
selecting, 250, 269–270

Objects command (Insert menu), 706, 708

Objects field, 715–717

ODBC (Open Database Connectivity) databases, 647–648

ODBC button (Insert Project dialog box), 613

OLAP (Online Analytical Process) cubes, 994–999

OLE DB providers, 687–688

On Schedule status indicator, 558

Online Analytical Process cubes. See OLAP cubes, 994–995

online help. *See* help

Open a Project option (Task pane), 30

Open command (Resource Center), 1073

Open Enterprise Resource Pool command (Enterprise Options menu), 1094

Open Enterprise Resource Pool dialog box, 1094–1096

Open Resource Pool Information dialog box, 622

Open statement, CD:61–62

opening
enterprise templates, 981, 1066
files with macros, CD:61–62
multiple projects, 1040–1043
objects, 711–712
portfolio models, 1059–1060
projects
.mdb format, 645–646
.mpd format, 643–645
resource pools, 622–624
templates, 104
VBE (Visual Basic Editor), CD:35

Option Explicit statement, CD:39

options (projects)
calendar options, 72–73
date format, 75
Days per Month, 68–69
decimal digits, 75
default end time, 69–70
default save format, 75
default start time, 69–70
default view, 73–74
displaying, 65
duration time units, 73
file-specific options, 66–67
fiscal year, 70–72
global options, 66
Hours per Day, 68–69
Hours per Week, 68–69
user name, 73

Options command (Tools menu), 65, 239, 783

Options dialog box, 239
Automatically Add New Resources and Tasks, 279
Calendar options, 72–73
Date Format, 75
Days per Month, 68–69
Decimal Digits, 75
Default End Time, 69–70
Default Start Time, 69–70
Default View, 73–74
displaying, 65
Duration Is Entered In, 73
file-specific options, 66–67
Fiscal Year, 70–72
global options, 66
Hours per Day, 68–69
Hours per Week, 68–69
Save Microsoft Project Files As, 75
User Name, 73
View tab, 783–784

Options tab (Customize dialog box), 930

Organizer, 88, 107, 947
accessing, 875
calendars
copying between projects, 90–91
copying to GLOBAL.MPT, 89–90
custom form management, 960
deleting objects, 111–112

displaying, 108
modifying GLOBAL.MPT, 109
objects
copying, 109–111
types, 107–108
renaming objects, 111
toolbar management, 947–949

Organizer command (Tools menu), 89, 109, 875, 947

orientation (pages), 498

Other option (Gantt Chart Wizard), 802

Other Task Panes button (Task pane), 32

Outdent button (Formatting toolbar), 156

Outdent command (Outline menu), 156

outdenting tasks, 156–157

Outline Code Definition dialog box, 855–857, 1012, 1082

outline codes, 471, 854
creating, 854–855
enterprise outline codes, 1010–1011, 1081–1082
assigning to enterprise resources, 1096
assigning to projects, 1067
creating, 1011–1015, 1082–1085
matching skill-sets, 1088–1090
multi-value fields, 1088
multiple skills per resource, 1016, 1087
planning, 974–975
proficiency levels per skill, 1015–1016, 1086
RBS (Resource Breakdown Structure), 1010, 1082
including in tables, 858–859
lookup tables, 857–858
outline code lookup tables, 857–858
outline masks, 855–857

outline masks, 855–857

Outline menu commands, 156

outlined projects, 185

outlined task lists, 233

outlines, 117, 154
collapsing, 157–158
custom outlines, 169, 854
display options, 160–161
editing, 159, 187, 194, 201, 206
expanding, 157–158
formatting, 160–161, 783–784
indenting tasks, 156–157
levels, 159
outdenting tasks, 156–157
outline codes, 471
subtasks, 154–155
summary tasks, 154–156
symbols, 159
task duration, 156
task list outlines, 470–471

Outlook
Project Server connections, 1140
setting up to work with Project Server, 1139
submitting time with, 1140–1141
task lists, importing, 684–687
viewing task assignments in, 1140

Oval button (Drawing toolbar), 249

overallocated resources, 324. *See also* Resource Leveling dialog box
defined, 402
delayed assignments, 440
delayed tasks, 441–443
individual assignments, 443–447
displaying, 823
extended working hours, 429–432
filtering, 409–410
formatting display, 405
Go to Next Overallocation tool, 412
highlighting, 405
identifying, 405–409
increasing availability of, 410, 418–423
Overallocated Resources filter, 317, 409, 768
overtime, 423–428
reasons for, 403
reconciling, 406
reducing workload for, 419–421, 432
Resource Allocation view, 432–434
Resource Usage view, 410–411
sensitivity setting, 407–408
split assignments, 451–453
split tasks, 448–451
substituting underused resources for, 434–440
timephased details, 412–417
viewing, 409

Overallocated Resources command (Filtered For menu), 409

Overallocated Resources filter, 317, 409, 768

Overallocation option (Details menu), 823

overbudget filter, 860

overlapping tasks, 180–181, 189–190

overtime
assigning, 385–387
cautions, 346
overtime rate, 304–305
scheduling, 346–348, 423–428

Overtime Rate field (resources), 304–305

Overview reports, 880
Critical Tasks, 881
Milestones, 881
Project Summary, 881–882, 899–900
Top-Level Tasks, 881
Working Days, 881–882

P

PA_Expected Case table, 759

PA_Optimistic Case table, 759

PA_PERT Case table, 759

PA_PERT Entry Sheet, 744

PA_Pessimistic Case table, 759

Page Break command (Insert menu), 496, 789

page breaks
- creating, 496
- deleting, 789
- formatting, 789
- manual page breaks, 516
- printing, 495–496
- removing, 496
- reports, 896
- viewing, 496

Page Down key (task tables), 234

page setup, 496–497
- borders, 499
- footers
  - creating, 501–502
  - dates, 501
  - file names, 501
  - fonts, 500
  - images, 501
  - page numbers, 500
  - text alignment, 502–503
  - text formatting, 504–506
  - times, 501
  - total page count, 500
- headers
  - creating, 501–502
  - dates, 501
  - file names, 501
  - fonts, 500
  - images, 501
  - page numbers, 500
  - text alignment, 502–503
  - text formatting, 504–506
  - times, 501
  - total page count, 500
- legends
  - creating, 503–504
  - text formatting, 504–506
- margins, 499
- page numbers, 499
- page orientation, 498
- paper size, 498
- reports, 896
- scale, 498
- selecting pages to print, 512–513
- view options, 506–508

Page Setup command (File menu), 497

Page Setup dialog box, 496–497
- Footer tab, 500–502
- Header tab, 500–502
- Legend tab, 503–504
- Margin tab, 499
- Page tab, 497–499
- View tab, 506–508

Page Up key (task tables), 234

panes
- Advanced Search, 32
- Basic Search, 32
- Project Guide, 38–41
- Task pane, 30–32

paper size, 498

partially completed tasks, rescheduling, 544–546

password protection, 101

Paste As Hyperlink command (Edit menu), 148–149

Paste command (Edit menu), 129, 615, 694

Paste Special command (Edit menu), 697, 706

Paste Special dialog box, 697–698, 706, 714

pasting data
- column headers, 729
- dates, 695
- errors, 694–695
- linked data, 697–699, 702
- objects, 703–705
  - into Gantt Chart view, 706–708
  - into headers/footers, 717–719
  - into legends, 717–719
  - into Notes field, 712–714
  - into Objects field, 715–717
  - into Project, 694–695
  - into other applications, 695–696, 719–720
- resource lists, 318–320
- timephased data, 692, 696

paths, relative, 615

PDM (precedence diagramming method), 152

peak units, 822

Peak Units option (Details menu), 822

people as resources, 280

Percent Allocation option (Details menu), 823

percentage format (assignment units), 326

percentage lags, 190

percentage leads, 190

Permanently Renumber Tasks option (Sort dialog box), 777–778

permissions, 987

personalizing. *See* customizing

PERT Analysis toolbar, 927

PERT Analysis views, 744–745

PERT Entry form, 950

phases (summary tasks), 569–570

Physical % Complete field, 534, 795

PivotTables
- exporting to, 668–673
- Portfolio Analyzer, 1051
- troubleshooting, 689

placeholder resources, 281

planned value, 577

Planning Wizard, 42–43, 210–212

plans. *See* project plans

plus sign (+), 233, 784

***PMBOK Guide*, 17**

PMI (Project Management Institute) Web site, 17

PMO (portfolio management office), 966. *See also* enterprise-level project management; Project Professional 2003
- Administrative projects, 1047
- collaboration, 983–984
- consistent views, 982–983
- document management, 983–984

enterprise custom fields, 1010–1011, 1081–1082
assigning to enterprise resources, 1096
assigning to projects, 1067
creating, 1016–1018
planning, 974–975
Enterprise Global settings, 978
project attributes, 979–980
resource attributes, 980–981
Enterprise Global template, 104, 873–874, 926, 947, 1007–1008
backing up, 1019–1020
copying, 109
copying base calendars to, 84, 89–90
editing, 109, 1009–1010
effect on user sessions, 1008–1009
enterprise project calendar management, 1018–1019
enterprise resource calendar management, 1019
finding, 112
restoring, 1020
saving changes to, 873–875
working offline, 1010
enterprise outline codes, 1010–1011, 1081–1082
assigning to enterprise resources, 1096
assigning to projects, 1067
creating, 1013–1015, 1082–1085
matching skill-sets, 1088–1090
multi-value fields, 1088
multiple skills per resource, 1016, 1087
planning, 974–975
proficiency levels per skill, 1015–1016, 1086
RBS (Resource Breakdown Structure), 1010, 1082
enterprise project calendars, 1018–1019
enterprise projects
analyzing, 1048
booking types, 1039–1040
Build Team feature, 1036–1037
checking in, 1001, 1046
deleting, 1042–1043
filtering, 1030, 1033–1034, 1037–1038
grouping, 1033–1034
linking tasks across, 1043–1045
opening multiple, 1040–1043
planning, 973
project information, editing, 1034
project information, viewing, 1035–1036
resource assignment, 1037–1038
resource availability, 1040
searching, 1034
viewing, 1032
enterprise resource calendars, 1019
enterprise resources, 1090–1091
actual resources, 1091–1094
adding to projects, 1097–1098
adjusting actuals, 1080
analyzing, 1048
applying custom fields to, 1091, 1096
applying outline codes to, 1091, 1096
booking type, 1100–1102
building teams from, 1097
checking in, 1002
creating, 1094–1096
editing details, 1075
enterprise resource pool, 1090–1092
Enterprise Resource Pool Wizard, 1091
filtering, 1075, 1100
generic resources, 1091–1093
importing, 1021–1023
matching, 1099
planning, 974
removing from projects, 1098
replacing, 1098–1099
resource assignments, 1074–1075
resource availability, 1074–1077
Resource Substitution Wizard, 1091
viewing, 1074, 1078–1081
enterprise templates, 981
OLAP (Online Analytical Process) cubes, 994–995
creating, 996–999
requirements, 996
Portfolio Analyzer
assessing projects with, 1053–1054
changing view content, 1051–1052
charts, 1051
compared to Portfolio Modeler, 1048–1049
drop-down lists, 1051
example, 1050
PivotTables, 1051
Save a Link option, 1050
Save as GIF option, 1051
view options, 1050
portfolio models, 1054–1055
analyzing, 1063–1064
comparing, 1061
creating, 1056–1058
modifying, 1062–1063
opening, 1059–1060
properties, 1060–1061
refreshing views, 1065
transferring, 1064
processes, 973
Project Center views, 987–990
project management planning, 970
collaboration and document management, 977
consistent project schedules, 976
consistent views, 977
enterprise custom fields, 974–975
enterprise outline codes, 974–975
enterprise projects, 973
enterprise resources, 974
group responsibilities, 971–973
processes, 973
project and task definitions, 975

reports, 974–975
security, 978
skill and attribute definitions, 975–976
time reporting, 977
Project Server database, cleaning up, 1003
project versions
adding, 999–1000
advantages of, 982
creating, 981
cross-project links, 982
defined, 976
deleting, 1000
formatting, 1000
modifying, 1000
opening schedules with, 982
Published version, 981, 999
resources, 982
Version field, 1000
projects, importing, 1024–1028
reports, planning, 974–975
Resource Center views, 990–993
role management, 984
security, 984
system administration, 986–987
time reporting, 983
Timesheet views, 993–994

points (polygons), 254

Polygon button (Drawing toolbar), 249

polygons, 254

Pool Takes Precedence button (Share Resources dialog box), 622

Portfolio Analyzer
adding/modifying data, CD:79–82
assessing projects with, 1053–1054
changing view content, 1051–1052
charts, 1051
commands and options, CD:82–84
compared to Portfolio Modeler, 1048–1049
creating, CD:77–79
drop-down lists, 1051
example, 1050
graph types, CD:82
PivotTables, 1051
Save a Link option, 1050
Save as GIF option, 1051
view options, 1050

portfolio management office. *See* PMO

portfolio managers, 972

Portfolio Modeler, 1054–1055
accessing, 1055
analyzing portfolio models, 1063–1064
compared to Portfolio Analyzer, 1048–1049
comparing portfolio models, 1061
creating portfolio models, 1056–1058
modifying portfolio models, 1062–1063
opening portfolio models, 1059–1060
property toolbox, 1060–1061
refreshing views, 1065
transferring portfolio models, 1064

portfolio models, 1054–1055
analyzing, 1063–1064
comparing, 1061
creating, 1056–1058
modifying, 1062–1063
opening, 1059–1060
properties, 1060–1061
refreshing views, 1065
transferring, 1064

positive delay, 455

pound sign (#), CD:25

precedence diagramming method (PDM), 152

predecessor tasks
choosing, 179–180
cross-linked, 620
defined, 177
defining, 189
deleting, 189

Predecessors field (task tables), 123

Predecessors tab (Task Information dialog box), 188–189

predefined work contours, 392

preleveled finish dates, 795

preleveled start dates, 795

Preleveled taskbar, 464

previewing
print jobs, 490, 509– 513
reports, 893

Print button, 512

Print command (File menu), 490, 512

Print dialog box, 490–491, 512

Print Grid option, 1036

Print Preview button, 509–511

Print Preview command (File menu), 490, 509–513

printer setup, 490–491

Printers command (Settings menu), 490

printing, 490, 493
base calendars, 91–92
borders, 499
display enhancements, 495
filters, 495
footers
dates, 501
file names, 501
fonts, 500
General drop-down list box, 501
images, 501
page numbers, 500
Project Fields drop-down list box, 502
text alignment, 502–503
text formatting, 504–506
times, 501
total page count, 500
grouped displays, 495
headers, 500–501
dates, 501
file names, 501
fonts, 500
General drop-down list box, 501
images, 501
page numbers, 500

- Project Fields drop-down list box, 502
- text alignment, 502–503
- text formatting, 504–506
- times, 501
- total page count, 500
- legends, 503–504
- margins, 499
- number of copies, 513
- page breaks, 495–496, 516
- page numbers, 499
- page orientation, 498
- paper size, 498
- Print command, 490, 512
- Print Preview command, 490, 509–513
- printer setup, 490–491
- project-level statistics, 487
- reports, 514–515, 893
- scale, 498
- specific pages, 512–513
- specific panes, 494
- task lists, 170
- timescales, 494, 513, 516
- troubleshooting, 515–516
- view options, 506–508

priorities, 59, 458–459

Priority field (Project Information dialog box), 59

Priority group, 477, 772

Priority Keeping Outline Structure group, 772

Priority option (Portfolio Modeler), 1058

Priority, Standard leveling order, 457

private variables, CD:50–51

processes, 973

proficiency levels per skill, 1015–1016, 1086

program integrity, 103

program management office. *See* PMO

Programs command (Start menu), 30

Programs menu commands, Microsoft Project, 30

progress bars (Gantt Chart), 795–796

progress lines, 559–562

Progress Lines command (Tracking menu), 560

Progress Lines dialog box, 560–561

Project Center, 1031, CD:74. *See also* Portfolio Analyzer; Portfolio Modeler
- accessing, 1031
- Administrative projects, 1047
- booking types, 1039–1040
- Build Team feature, 1036–1038
- filters, 1030, 1033–1034, 1037–1038
- groups, 1033–1034
- multiple enterprise projects, opening, 1040–1042
- project check-in, 1046
- project information
  - editing, 1034
  - viewing, 1035–1036
- resource availability, 1040
- searches, 1034
- views, 987–990, 1032

Project command (Insert menu), 607, 612, 615

Project Database format. See mpd format, 640

project files. *See* files

Project Explorer, CD:35

Project Guide, 38–41
- Schedule Tasks Project Guide, 207–208

Project Guide toolbar, 492–493, 521, 926–927

Project Info button (Inserted Project Information dialog box), 614

Project Information dialog box, 57–58, 614
- Calendar list box, 59
- Current Date text box, 59–61
- displaying, 58
- Finish Date text box, 58–60
- priorities, 459
- Priority field, 59
- Start Date text box, 58–60
- Status Date text box, 59–61

project management, 16, 556–557. *See also* enterprise-level project management
- benefits of Project 2003, 18–19
- corrective action, 556
- earned value analysis, 575–577
  - actual cost, 578
  - controlling earned value calculation, 587–588
  - earned value, 577–578
  - Earned Value Cost Indicators table, 583–587
  - Earned Value Schedule Indicators table, 581–582
  - examining trends, 578
  - example, 579–582
  - Excel graphs, 590–595
  - planned value, 577
  - troubleshooting, 599
  - viewing, 589–590
- *A Guide to the Project Management Body of Knowledge*, 17
- guidelines, 19–21
- iterative process model, 556
- management phase, 23–24
- planning phase, 22–23
- preliminary tasks, 22
- project constraints, 17
- project goals, 16
- Project Management Institute, 17
- reviewing project status
  - assignment-level status, 574–575
  - progress lines, 559–562
  - project statistics, 565
  - Project Summary reports, 565
  - project summary tasks, 565–570
  - resource-level status, 573–574
  - slipping assignments, 562
  - slipping tasks, 562
  - Status field, 557–558
  - Status Indicator field, 557–558

task-level status, 570
variances, 563–564, 571–573
schedule revisions, 595–596
costs, 596–597
duration, 597–598
scope, 596
scheduling techniques, 24–27
temporary nature of projects, 16
troubleshooting, 27

***A Project Management Body of Knowledge Guide*, 471**

Project Management Institute Web site, 17

project management office. *See* PMO

project managers, 972

Project menu commands
Filtered For, 318, 495, 763, 859, 904
Group By, 314–315, 478, 770–772, 868
Sort, 310, 475, 610, 776
Task Information, 263
WBS, 164, 471

Project_Open event, CD:62–63

Project Plan command (Collaborate menu), 1125

project plans, 22–23
distributing, 486
enterprise-level project management, 970
collaboration and document management, 977
consistent project schedules, 976
consistent views, 977
enterprise custom fields, 974–975
enterprise outline codes, 974–975
enterprise projects, 973
enterprise resources, 974
group responsibilities, 971–973
processes, 973
project and task definitions, 975
reports, 974–975
security, 978
skill and attribute definitions, 975–976
time reporting, 977
outlining, 117
realigning, 479
cost reduction, 481–483
crashing the schedule, 480–481
critical path, 480
project versions, 483–487
reviewing
compressed timescales, 469–470
custom groups, 477–479
outline codes, 471
project-level statistics, 468–469, 487
resource groups, 477
sorting tasks, 475–477
spell check, 486
task filters, 472–474
task groups, 477
task list outline, 470–471
WBS (Work Breakdown Structure) codes, 471
spell checking, 486

Project Professional 2003, 966, 1030. *See also* enterprise-level project management
Administrative projects, 1047
Assign Resources dialog box, 1107–11010
collaboration, 983–984
consistent views, 982–983
document management, 983–984
enterprise custom fields, 1010–1011, 1081–1082
assigning to enterprise resources, 1096
assigning to projects, 1067
creating, 1016–1018
planning, 974–975
Enterprise Global settings, 978
project attributes, 979–980
resource attributes, 980–981
Enterprise Global template, 104, 873–874, 926, 947, 1007–1008
backing up, 1019–1020
copying, 109
copying base calendars to, 84, 89–90
editing, 109, 1009–1010
effect on user sessions, 1008–1009
enterprise project calendar management, 1018–1019
enterprise resource calendar management, 1019
finding, 112
restoring, 1020
saving changes to, 873–875
working offline, 1010
enterprise outline codes, 1010–1011, 1081–1082
assigning to enterprise resources, 1096
assigning to projects, 1067
creating, 1011–1015, 1082–1085
matching skill-sets, 1088–1090
multi-value fields, 1088
multiple skills per resource, 1016, 1087
planning, 974–975
proficiency levels per skill, 1015–1016, 1086
RBS (Resource Breakdown Structure), 1010, 1082
enterprise project calendars, 1018–1019
enterprise projects
analyzing, 1048
booking types, 1039–1040
Build Team feature, 1036–1037
checking in, 1001, 1046
deleting, 1042–1043
filtering, 1030, 1033–1034, 1037–1038
grouping, 1033–1034
linking tasks across, 1043–1045
opening multiple, 1040–1043
project information, editing, 1034
project information, viewing, 1035–1036

resource assignment, 1037–1038
resource availability, 1040
searching, 1034
viewing, 1032
enterprise resource calendars, 1019
enterprise resources, 1090–1091
actual resources, 1091–1094
adding to projects, 1097–1098
adjusting actuals, 1080
analyzing, 1048
applying custom fields to, 1091, 1096
applying outline codes to, 1091, 1096
booking type, 1100–1102
building teams from, 1097
checking in, 1002
creating, 1094–1096
editing details, 1075
enterprise resource pool, 1090–1092
Enterprise Resource Pool Wizard, 1091
filtering, 1075, 1100
generic resources, 1091–1093
importing, 1021–1023
matching, 1099
removing from projects, 1098
replacing, 1098–1099
resource assignments, 1074–1075
resource availability, 1074–1077
Resource Substitution Wizard, 1091
viewing, 1074, 1078–1081
enterprise templates, 981, 1065–1066
OLAP (Online Analytical Process) cubes, 994–999
Portfolio Analyzer
assessing projects with, 1053–1054
changing view content, 1051–1052
charts, 1051
compared to Portfolio Modeler, 1048–1049
drop-down lists, 1051
example, 1050
PivotTables, 1051
Save a Link option, 1050
Save as GIF option, 1051
view options, 1050
Portfolio Modeler, 1054–1055
accessing, 1055
analyzing portfolio models, 1063–1064
compared to Portfolio Analyzer, 1048–1049
comparing portfolio models, 1061
creating portfolio models, 1056–1058
modifying portfolio models, 1062–1063
opening portfolio models, 1059–1060
property toolbox, 1060–1061
refreshing views, 1065
transferring portfolio models, 1064
portfolio models, 1054–1055
analyzing, 1063–1064
comparing, 1061
creating, 1056–1058
modifying, 1062–1063
opening, 1059–1060
properties, 1060–1061
refreshing views, 1065
transferring, 1064
Project Center
accessing, 1031
Administrative projects, 1047
booking types, 1039–1040
Build Team feature, 1036–1038
filters, 1030, 1033–1034, 1037–1038
groups, 1033–1034
multiple enterprise projects, opening, 1040–1042
project check-in, 1046
project information, editing, 1034
project information, viewing, 1035–1036
resource availability, 1040
searches, 1034
view options, 1032
Project Center views, 987–990
project management planning, 970
collaboration and document management, 977
consistent project schedules, 976
consistent views, 977
enterprise custom fields, 974–975
enterprise outline codes, 974–975
enterprise projects, 973
enterprise resources, 974
group responsibilities, 971–973
processes, 973
project and task definitions, 975
reports, 974–975
security, 978
skill and attribute definitions, 975–976
time reporting, 977
Project Server database
cleaning up, 1003
logins, 1004–1007
project versions
advantages of, 982
creating, 981
cross-project links, 982
defined, 976
deleting, 1000
opening schedules with, 982
formatting, 1000
modifying, 1000
Published version, 981, 999
resources, 982
Version field, 1000
projects, importing, 1024–1028
Resource Center, 1070–1072
accessing, 1070–1071
Edit Resource Details view, 1075
filters, 1075

Open command, 1073
Resource Availability views, 1076–1077
Save Link command, 1072
View Availability command, 1072
View Availability view, 1074
View Enterprise Resources view, 1074
View Resource Assignments screen, 1078–1081
View Resource Assignments view, 1074–1075
Resource Center views, 990–993
Resource Substitution Wizard, 1110–1117
role management, 984
summary of features, 1030
system administration, 986–987
system architecture, 968–969
system requirements, 969–970
Team Builder, 1091, 1102–1103
Add button, 1106
Apply Filter button, 1104
Available to Work check box, 1105
Customize Filters field, 1105
Details button, 1106
Enterprise Resource list, 1105
Existing Filters list, 1105
Graphs button, 1106
Group By field, 1105
Match button, 1106
Remove button, 1106
Replace button, 1104–1106
Team Resource list, 1106
Timesheet views, 993–994
time reporting, 983
versions, 1066–1067

project schedules, 176–177
deadline dates
entering, 217–219
filtering, 219
missed deadlines, 220, 229
delays, 176
dependency links, 177–178
auditing, 199–200
Autolink, 196–198
cautions, 178
creating with Entry table, 193–194
creating with Link Tasks tool, 187
creating with mouse, 194–196
creating with Task Form view, 190–192
creating with Task Information dialog box, 188–189
defined, 176
deleting, 185, 188, 198–199
dependent tasks, 179–180
editing, 187, 198
Finish-to-Finish relationship, 183
Finish-to-Start relationship, 182
honoring, 212–214
lag time, 180–181, 189–190
lead time, 180–181, 189–190
outlined projects, 185
overlapping tasks, 180–181, 189–190
predecessor tasks, 177–180, 189
reversing, 227
Start-to-Finish relationship, 183–184
Start-to-Start relationship, 182
successor tasks, 177–180
summary tasks, 184–185
tasks from different projects, 227
troubleshooting, 226–227
unrelated tasks, 178
views, 199–201
duration estimates, 176
fast-tracking, 183
finish dates, 176
interruptions, 176, 220–223, 228
just-in-time scheduling, 179, 184
resource availability, 176
reviewing project status
assignment-level status, 574–575
progress lines, 559–562
project statistics, 565
Project Summary reports, 565
project summary tasks, 565–570
resource-level status, 573–574
slipping assignments, 562
slipping tasks, 562
Status field, 557–558
Status Indicator field, 557–558
task-level status, 570
variances, 563–564, 571–573
schedule revisions, 595–598
split tasks, 220–223, 228
start dates, 176
task calendars, 176
assigning to tasks, 224–225
creating, 223–226
task constraints
ALAP (As Late As Possible), 202
ASAP (As Soon As Possible), 202
creating with Schedule Tasks Project Guide, 207–208
creating with Task Details form, 209
creating with Task Information dialog box, 208
creating with Task table, 208–209
custom Constraint Dates table, 228–229
defined, 176, 201
deleting, 216
examples, 201
finding, 214–216
flexible/inflexible, 203–206
FNET (Finish No Earlier Than), 203
FNLT (Finish No Later Than), 203

hard constraints, 212–214
honoring, 212–214
MFO (Must Finish On), 203
MSO (Must Start On), 203
Planning Wizard warnings, 210–212
resolving conflicts, 216–217
reviewing, 214–216
SNET (Start No Earlier Than), 203
SNLT (Start No Later Than), 203
soft constraints, 212–214
troubleshooting
adjusted dates, 227–228
mouse and task links, 226–227
split tasks, 228
working times, 176

Project Server, CD:66
Assignment view, CD:74
authentication, CD:72–73
categories, CD:70
cleaning up, 1003
custom menus, CD:84–86
custom views, CD:74
categories, CD:77
default grouping, CD:76
fields, CD:75
filters, CD:76
Gantt Chart format, CD:75
grouping formats, CD:76
Portfolio Analyzer view, CD:77–84
splitter bars, CD:75
table selection, CD:75
enabling/disabling features, CD:84
groups, CD:68
logging in to, 1004–1007
Project Center view, CD:74
Project view, CD:74
Resource Center view, CD:74
security templates
creating, CD:71
deleting, CD:71–72
modifying, CD:70
SPS (SharePoint Services)
document libraries, CD:86
document management, CD:87–88
issues tracking, CD:89–90
risk tracking, CD:90–91
subwebs, CD:86
user accounts
creating from workgroup messages/status reports, CD:69
creating from workgroup updates/status reports, CD:569
creating when delegating tasks, CD:69
creating with Add User screen, CD:66–67

Project Statistics dialog box, 61–62, 468–469, 565

Project Statistics tool, 565

Project Summary report, 565, 881–882, 899–900

Project Summary Task option (Options dialog box), 784

project summary tasks, 565–570
creating, 566
defined, 793
displaying, 784
phases, 569–570
viewing, 565

Project Web Access. *See* Web Access

Project window, 32. *See also* views
Entry bar, 37
menu bar, 35
Project Guide, 38–41
ScreenTips, 38–39
status bar, 38
toolbars, 35–36
View bar, 37–38

projects, 56. *See also* management; project plans; project schedules; tracking
Administrative projects, 1047
analyzing, 1048
attaching notes to, 146–147
attributes, 979–980
backward-scheduled, 121
baselines
clearing, 526
copying, 528
defined, 522
editing, 527
fields, 522–524
interim plans, 525
rebaselining, 524
rolling up, 525
saving, 522–526
viewing, 527–528
Build Team feature, 1036–1037
calendars, 108, 1018–1019
checking in, 1001
combined resource lists, 627
constraints, 17
copying base calendars between, 90–91
defining, 975
distributing, 486
enterprise projects
booking types, 1039–1040
Build Team feature, 1036–1037
checking in, 1046
deleting, 1042–1043
filtering, 1030, 1033–1034, 1037–1038
grouping, 1033–1034
linking tasks across, 1043–1045
opening multiple, 1040–1043
project information, editing, 1034
project information, viewing, 1035–1036
resource assignment, 1037–1038
resource availability, 1040
searching, 1034
viewing, 1032
enterprise resources
adding, 1097–1098
booking type, 1100–1102
filtering, 1100
matching, 1099
removing, 1098
replacing, 1098–1099
environment options
calendar options, 72–73
date format, 75
days per month, 68–69
decimal digits, 75
default end time, 69–70
default save format, 75

default start time, 69–70
default view, 73–74
displaying, 65
duration time units, 73
file-specific options, 66–67
fiscal year, 70–72
global options, 66
hours per day, 68–69
hours per week, 68–69
user name, 73
forward-scheduled projects, 121, 403
goals of, 16
groups, 108
importing, 648, 1024–1028. *See also* Import maps; Export maps
inserted projects
creating, 615
deleting, 617
icons, 608
identifying, 617
links, 613–614
maintaining, 616–617
managing, 614–615
relative paths, 615
replacing, 616
viewing information about, 613
linking, 604, 618–621
master projects, 612–613
multiple instances of, 609
multiple projects
advantages, 604
filtering, 610–611
formatting, 611
linking, 618–621
managing, 604
merging, 607–608, 612–613
multiple windows, 604–606
sorting, 610–611
split windows, 605
task dependencies, 611
views, 609
workspaces, 607
New Project Wizard, 85–86
opening
.mdb format, 645–646
.mpd format, 643–645
organizing, 604
Portfolio Analyzer
assessing projects with, 1053–1054
changing view content, 1051–1052
charts, 1051
compared to Portfolio Modeler, 1048–1049
drop-down lists, 1051
example, 1050
PivotTables, 1051
Save a Link option, 1050
Save as GIF option, 1051
view options, 1050
portfolio models, 1054–1055
analyzing, 1063–1064
comparing, 1061
creating, 1056–1058
modifying, 1062–1063
opening, 1059–1060
properties, 1060–1061
refreshing views, 1065
transferring, 1064
Project Center
accessing, 1031
Administrative projects, 1047
booking types, 1039–1040
Build Team feature, 1036–1038
filters, 1030, 1033–1034, 1037–1038
groups, 1033–1034
multiple enterprise projects, opening, 1040–1042
project check-in, 1046
project information, editing, 1034
project information, viewing, 1035–1036
resource availability, 1040
searches, 1034
view options, 1032
project information
editing, 1034–1036
Project Information dialog box, 57–61
viewing, 1035
properties
contents, 64
custom properties, 64–65
general properties, 63
linking property values to project fields, 65
statistics, 63
summary information, 62–63
recording macros for, CD:29–30
resource pools
creating, 621
disabling resource sharing, 625–626
links, 626
maintaining, 622
opening, 622–624
refreshing, 624
resource sharing, 621–624
saving, 625
updating, 623–624
reviewing status of
assignment-level status, 574–575
progress lines, 559–562
project statistics, 565
Project Summary reports, 565
project summary tasks, 565–570
resource-level status, 573–574
slipping assignments, 562
slipping tasks, 562
Status field, 557–558
Status Indicator field, 557–558
task-level status, 570
variances, 563–564, 571–573
saving
as Excel worksheets, 665–668
as HTML documents, CD:3–8
.mdb format, 645
.mpd format, 640–643
ODBC databases, 647–648
as XML files, 681
spell checking, 486
statistics
displaying, 468–469
printing, 487
Project Statistics dialog box, 61–62, 468–469, 565
viewing, 565
subprojects, 612–613

templates. *See also* Global template
built-in templates, 104–105
creating, 106–107
defined, 103
editing, 107
.mpt file extension, 103
opening, 104
temporary nature of, 16
versions
adding, 999–1000
comparing, 483–487
deleting, 1000
formatting, 1000
modifying, 1000
Published version, 999
Version field, 1000
viewing as HTML documents, CD:9
workspaces, 607

proofreading project plans, 486

properties
portfolio models, 1060–1061
projects
contents, 64
custom properties, 64–65
general properties, 63
linking property values to project fields, 65
statistics, 63
summary information, 62–63
text boxes, 258
VBA (Visual Basic for Applications), CD:32, CD:42

Properties dialog box
Contents tab, 64
Custom tab, 64–65
General tab, 63
Statistics tab, 63
Summary tab, 62–63

Properties field (Microsoft Project Server Accounts dialog box), 1007

Properties window (VBE), CD:36

proposed booking, 1039, 1101

prorated accrual, 285

providers (OLE DB), 687–688

Public statement, CD:50

public variables, CD:50–51

Published version, 981, 999

publishing Web pages, CD:24

Q-R

Quartile Percentage button (Tracking toolbar), 549

question mark (?), 52, 864, CD:44

rate of consumption
fixed, 294, 328
variable, 295, 329

RBS (Resource Breakdown Structure) code, 1010, 1082

Read-Only files, 101

Read-Only Recommended files, 102

reading reports, 879

realigning project plans, 479
cost reduction, 481–483
crashing the schedule, 480–481
critical path, 480
project versions, comparing, 483–487

reapplying filters, 474

Rearrange Commands dialog box, 932–933

Reassign Resource in Model's Pool option (Portfolio Modeler), 1058

Reassign Resources in Project option (Portfolio Modeler), 1058

rebaselining, 524

reconciling overallocated resources, 406

Record New Macro command (Macro menu), CD:29

recording macros
for entire project, CD:29–30
for selected tasks, CD:30–32

Rectangle button (Drawing toolbar), 249

Recurring Task command (Insert menu), 138

Recurring Task Information dialog box, 138

recurring tasks, 137
constraints, 141
creating, 138–141
editing, 142
end dates, 139
icons, 140
linking, 141
start dates, 139
summary tasks, 139

recursion, CD:55–56

redefining table columns, 845

reducing
costs, 481–483, 596–597
duration, 597–598
scope, 596
workload for overallocated resources, 419–421, 432

references, linked
creating, 697–699
defined, 697
deleting, 701–702
identifying, 702
link indicators, 699
pasting, 697–699, 702
refreshing, 699–701
restoring, 702
updating, 699–701

Refresh Resource Pool command (Resources menu), 624

refreshing
filters, 474
linked data, 699–701
Portfolio Modeler views, 1065
resource pools, 624

Relationship Diagram view, 747

relationships
between tasks, 745–747
tracing with TraceDependencies macro, CD:46
calling subroutines with arguments, CD:54

calling subroutines without parameters, CD:52–53
Case statement, CD:53–54
code listing, CD:47–50
filters, CD:56–57
input box, CD:51–52
main subroutine, CD:51
message box, CD:52
recursion, CD:55–56
variables, CD:50–51
views, CD:56–57

relative paths, 615

remaining availability, displaying
Remaining Availability graph, 372
Remaining Availability option (Details menu), 823
Remaining Availability view (Resource Center), 1076

Remaining Duration field, 535

Remaining Work field
assignments, 538
tasks, 535–536

reminders, CD:94–95

Remove All Page Breaks command (Insert menu), 496, 789

Remove button (Team Builder), 1106

Remove field (Microsoft Project Server Accounts dialog box), 1007

Remove Page Break command (Insert menu), 496, 789

Remove Split command (Window menu), 153

removing. ***See*** **deleting**

Rename button (Customize Fields dialog box), 849

Rename dialog box, 948

renaming
custom forms, 960
enterprise project calendars, 1019
menus, 944
objects, 111
toolbars, 947–948

Renumber command (WBS menu), 169

renumbering custom WBS codes, 168–169

reordering tasks, 197, 273–274

Replace button (Team Builder), 1104–1106

Replace Resource dialog box, 377–378, 439

replacing
enterprise resources, 1098–1099
inserted projects, 616
resource assignments, 377–378
resources, 1104

Report button (Project Guide), 41

reports, 878
Assignment Reports category, 889–890
copying, 894–895
Cost Reports category
Budget report, 886
Cash Flow report, 886–887
Earned Value report, 886–888
creating
from existing reports, 894–895
from scratch, 895–896
crosstab reports, 910–915
Current Activities Reports category, 884–886
custom reports, 891
Calendar reports, 901
collapsing task detail, 899
column widths, 918
creating from existing reports, 892–895
creating from scratch, 895
creating with Custom Reports dialog box, 893–894
crosstab reports, 910–915
definitions, 904–905
designing, 895–896
details, 905–908
Monthly Calendar reports, 915–917
page breaks, 896
page setup options, 896
Project Summary report, 899–900
Resource reports, 901–909
saving, 918
sharing, 918
sort order, 898, 910
Task and Resource reports, 901–909
text formatting, 897, 909
defined, 108
designing, 895–896
displaying, 878–879
distributing, 919
editing, 892–893
filtering, 880, 918
footers, 880
headers, 880
Monthly Calendar reports, 915–917
nonworking time categories, CD:93–94
Overview Reports category, 880
Critical Tasks, 881
Milestones, 881
Project Summary, 881–882, 899–900
Top-Level Tasks, 881
Working Days, 881–882
period, 880
planning, 974–975
previewing, 893
printing, 490–491, 514–515, 893
Project Summary, 565
reading, 879
selecting, 878
sort order, 880
status reports, 1129
compiling, 1132–1133
creating user accounts from, CD:69
requesting, 1130–1131
status report flow, 1130
submitting, 1131–1132
tables, 880
Task and Resource reports
customizing, 901–909
definitions, 904–905
details, 905–908
sort order, 910
text formatting, 909

types of, 879
undoing changes to, 919
Workload Reports category, 890–891

Reports command (View menu), 91, 514, 878, 895

Reports dialog box, 91, 514, 878

Republish Assignments command (Collaborate menu), 1125

Request Progress Information menu commands, 1125

requesting
status reports, 1130–1131
user input, CD:51–52

Reschedule Uncompleted Work to Start option (Update Project form), 553–554

Reschedule Work button (Tracking toolbar), 549

rescheduling options, 544–546

resetting base calendars, 81–82

reshaping polygons, 254

resizing
combo boxes, 934
custom forms, 955–956
floating toolbars, 929
objects, 253–254, 703, 707, 729
polygons, 254

ResMgmt_TaskEntry macro, 755

resolving conflicts, 216–217

Resource Allocation view, 432–434, 444, 755–756

Resource Assignment dialog box, 438–439

resource assignments, 360, 365. *See also* resource scheduling
adjusting actuals, 1080
Assign Resources dialog box, 365–367, 1107–1110
displaying, 366
drag-and-drop, 376
features, 367–368
graphs, 371–373
modifying assignments, 377–379
removing assignments, 376–377
resource list filters, 369–371
resource unit assignments, 374–375
Assignment Information dialog box, 390–391
Cost Rate Table field, 392–393
Notes field, 392–393
Work Contour field, 391–392
assignment units, 325
field format, 326
fixed consumption rates, 328
fractions, 328
material resource units, 328–329
maximum number of, 326
variable consumption rates, 329
work resource units, 326–327
availability of resources, determining, 402–404
components of, 322–324
consumption rates
fixed, 294, 328
variable, 295, 329
contouring, 440
Cost Rate tables, 392–393
delaying, 342–345, 440
individual assignments, 443–447
fixed-finish-date projects, 384–385
fixed-start-date projects, 382–384
leveling delays, 324
tasks, 441–443
drag-and-drop, 376
driver resources, 355–357
extended working hours, 429–432
fixed contract fees, 396–399
fixed costs, 396–399
front-loaded contour, 324
hiding/displaying, 411
material resources, 330, 333
modifying, 377–379
multiple resources, 333–334
nondriver resources, 355
notes, 393
overallocated resources
defined, 402
delayed assignments, 440–447
extended working hours, 429–432
filtering, 409–410
formatting display, 405
Go to Next Overallocation tool, 412
highlighting, 405
identifying, 405–409
increasing availability of, 410, 418–423
overtime, 423–428
reasons for, 403
reconciling, 406
reducing workload for, 419–421, 432
Resource Allocation view, 432–434
Resource Usage view, 410–411
sensitivity setting, 407–408
split assignments, 451–453
split tasks, 448–451
substituting underused resources for, 434–440
timephased assignments, 408
timephased details, 412–417
viewing, 409
overtime, 346–348, 385–387, 423–428
removing, 376–377
resource assignment fields
Assignment Units, 325–329
Assignment Work, 329
Material Resources, 330
Resource Name, 324–325
Work Resources, 329–330
resource availability graphs, 372–373
resource filters
applying, 370
Available to Work filter, 370–371

Group filter, 369
removing, 370
Resources – Material filter, 369
Resources – Work filter, 369
resource leveling, 419–421, 454–455
Automatic Leveling, 462
Clear Leveling dialog box, 462
Level Now dialog box, 459–463
priorities, 458–459
Resource Allocation view, 432–434
Resource Leveling dialog box, 455–459
resource substitution, 434–440
resource names, 324–325
resource units, 374–375
sorting, 463
for specific amounts of work, 375–376
split assignments, 451–453
split tasks, 345, 448–451
task calendars, 353–354
task duration for multiple resources, 357–358
task effort-driven setting, 364
Task Entry view
assignment delay, 382–385
overtime work, 385–387
step-by-step instructions, 379–381
Task Form view, 365, 387–390
Task Information dialog box, 365, 393–394
Task table, 365, 395–396
task types
changing, 361–363
choosing, 335–336, 338, 363
effort-driven tasks, 338–341
fixed-duration tasks, 335
fixed-unit tasks, 336
fixed-work tasks, 335
verifying, 361
Task Usage view, 365
Team Builder, 1102–1103
Add button, 1106
Apply Filter button, 1104
Available to Work check box, 1105
Customize Filters field, 1105
Details button, 1106
Enterprise Resource list, 1105
Existing Filters list, 1105
Graphs button, 1106
Group By field, 1105
Match button, 1106
Remove button, 1106
Replace button, 1104–1106
Team Resource list, 1106
troubleshooting, 358, 399
viewing, 1074–1075, 1078–1079
approved timesheets, 1080–1081
timesheet format, 1079
timesheet summary, 1080
work contours, 392
applying, 352
back loaded, 348–350
bell, 350
contoured, 351
documenting changes to, 352
double peak, 350
early peak, 350
example, 348–349
flat pattern, 348–350
front loaded, 348–350
late peak, 350
turtle, 351
work formula, 330–335
work resources, 329–332

Resource Availability field (resources), 298–300

resource availability fields
Base Calendar, 300–301
Max Units, 297–298
Resource Availability, 298–300
Working Time, 301–302

Resource Availability table, 418

Resource Availability views (Resource Center), 1076–1077

Resource Breakdown Structure (RBS) code, 1010, 1082

Resource Center, 1070–1072, CD:74
accessing, 1070–1071
filters, 1075
Open command, 1073
Save Link command, 1072
views
creating, 990–993
Edit Resource Details view, 1075
modifying, 990–993
Resource Availability views, 1076–1077
View Availability view, 1072–1074
View Enterprise Resources view, 1074
View Resource Assignments view, 1074–1075, 1078–1081

resource costs
calculating, 282
Cost Accrual, 307
Cost Per Use, 305
Cost Rate tables, 305–306
defined, 281
Overtime Rate, 304–305
Standard Rate, 303–304

resource-driven tasks, 27

Resource Export Table map, 652, 654

resource fields, 292–293
Base Calendar, 300–301
Code, 307–308
Cost Accrual, 307
Cost Per Use, 305
Cost Rate tables, 305–306
Group, 295–297
ID, 293
Indicators, 293
Initials, 295
Material Label, 295
Max Units, 297–298
Overtime Rate, 304–305
Resource Availability, 298–300
Resource Name, 294
Standard Rate, 303–304
Type, 294–295

Workgroup, 308
Working Time, 301–302

resource filters
All Resources, 317, 767
applying, 370
Available to Work, 370–371
Confirmed Assignments, 767
Cost Greater Than..., 767
Cost Overbudget, 317, 572–574, 767
Date Range..., 767
Group..., 317, 369, 767
In Progress Assignments, 767
Linked Fields, 702, 768
Overallocated Resources, 317, 409, 768
removing, 370
Resource Range..., 768
Resources with Attachments, 768
Resources—Material, 315–316, 369
Resources—Work, 369, 768
Resources/Assignments with Overtime, 317, 768
Should Start By..., 574, 768
Should Start/Finish By..., 574, 768
Slipped/Late Progress, 768
Slipping Assignments, 317, 562, 574, 768
Unconfirmed Assignments, 768
Unstarted Assignments, 768
Work Complete, 317, 768
Work Incomplete, 768
Work Overbudget, 572–574, 768

Resource Form view, 753
formatting, 817–819
scheduling overtime, 425–426

Resource Graph view, 754
bar styles, 824–826
display values, 822–824
format options, 821–822
formatting, 819–821
bar styles, 824–826
display values, 822–824
format options, 821–822

Resource Group... filter, 766

resource groups, 477, 772–773

resource histograms, 754

Resource Information dialog box, 288–289, 292–293, 698
Base Calendar field, 300–301
Code field, 307–308
Cost Accrual field, 307
Cost Per Use field, 305
Cost Rate tables, 305–306
Details button, 308
Group field, 295–297
Indicators field, 293
Initials field, 295
Material Label field, 295
Max Units field, 297–298
overallocated resources, 422–423
Overtime Rate field, 304–305
Resource Availability field, 298–300
Resource Name field, 294
Standard Rate field, 303–304
Type field, 294–295
Windows Account button, 308
Working Time field, 301–302

Resource Leveling command (Tools menu), 443

Resource Leveling dialog box, 443, 455–459

Resource List Options button (Assign Resources dialog box), 290

Resource List Options dialog box, 290

resource lists
creating
Assign Resources dialog box, 289–291
Resource Information dialog box, 288–289
Resource Sheet view, 287–288
Task Form view, 291–292
filtering, 472–474
grouping, 477
pasting from another application, 318–320
sorting, 475–477

Resource Management toolbar, 412, 927

resource managers, 972

Resource Name field, 294, 324–325

Resource Name Form view, 753

Resource Names field, 123

Resource Pending group, 773

Resource Range... filter, 768

Resource reports
customizing, 901–903
definitions, 904–905
details, 905–908
text formatting, 909
definitions, 904–905
details, 905–908
sort order, 910
text formatting, 909

resource scheduling, 322. *See also* resource assignments
availability of resources, determining, 402–404
delays, 342–345, 440
individual assignments, 443–447
fixed-finish-date projects, 384–385
fixed-start-date projects, 382–384
leveling delays, 324
tasks, 441–443
driver resources, 355–357
extended working hours, 429–432
forward-scheduled projects, 403
nondriver resources, 355
overallocated resources
defined, 402
delayed assignments, 440–447
extended working hours, 429–432
filtering, 409–410
formatting display, 405
Go to Next Overallocation tool, 412
highlighting, 405
identifying, 405–409
increasing availability of, 410, 418–423
overtime, 423–428
reasons for, 403
reconciling, 406
reducing workload for, 419–421, 432

Resource Allocation view, 432–434
Resource Usage view, 410–411
sensitivity setting, 407–408
split assignments, 451–453
split tasks, 448–451
substituting underused resources for, 434–440
timephased details, 412–417
viewing, 409
overtime, 346–348, 423–428
rescheduling options, 544–546
resource leveling, 419–421, 454–455
Automatic Leveling, 462
Clear Leveling dialog box, 462
Level Now dialog box, 459–463
priorities, 458–459
Resource Allocation view, 432–434
Resource Leveling dialog box, 455–459
resource substitution, 434–440
split tasks, 345
task calendars, 353–354
task duration for multiple resources, 357–358
task types
choosing, 335–338
effort-driven tasks, 338–341
fixed-duration tasks, 335
fixed-unit tasks, 336
fixed-work tasks, 335
troubleshooting, 358
work contours
applying to assignments, 352
back loaded, 348–350
bell, 350
contoured, 351
documenting changes to, 352
double peak, 350
early peak, 350
example, 348–349
flat pattern, 348–350
front loaded, 348–350
late peak, 350
turtle, 351
work formula, 330–331
applying to existing assignments, 335
applying to new assignments, 331–334
work schedules, 388–390

resource sharing, disabling, 629

Resource Sheet command (View menu), 287

Resource Sheet view, 33, 287–288, 292–293, 752
Base Calendar field, 300–301
Code field, 307–308
Cost Accrual field, 307
Cost Per Use field, 305
Cost Rate tables, 305–306
formatting, 830
Group field, 295–297
ID field, 293
Indicators field, 293
Initials field, 295
Material Label field, 295
Max Units field, 297–298
Overtime Rate field, 304–305
Resource Availability field, 298–300
Resource Name field, 294
Standard Rate field, 303–304
Type field, 294–295
Working Time field, 301–302

Resource Substitution Wizard, 1091, 1110–1117

resource tables, 760–761

Resource Usage report, 891

Resource Usage view, 751
formatting, 826–828
overallocated resources, 410–411
print options, 507
project tracking, 550–551

Resource/Assignments with Overtime filter, 317

resources, 278. *See also* resource assignments; resource scheduling
adding to projects, 308–309, 339, 1037–1038
advantages, 278
analyzing, 1048
attaching hyperlinks to, 150
attributes, 980–981
availability of, 176
Assignment Work graph, 372
determining, 402–404
overallocated resources, 410, 418–423
Remaining Availability graph, 372
viewing, 373
Work graph, 372
booking types, 1039–1040
checking in, 1002
consolidated resources, 280
costs
accrued costs, 307
calculating, 282
cost per use, 305
Cost Rate tables, 305–306
defined, 281
fixed costs, 281
overtime rate, 304–305
standard rate, 303–304
total costs, 281
defined, 279
defining, 975–976
deleting, 1106
driver resources, 355–357
enterprise resource calendars, 1019
enterprise resources, 1090–1091
actual resources, 1091–1094
adding to projects, 1097–1098
adjusting actuals, 1080
applying custom fields to, 1091, 1096
applying outline codes to, 1091, 1096
booking type, 1100–1102
building teams from, 1097
creating, 1094–1096
editing details, 1075
enterprise resource pool, 1090–1092
Enterprise Resource Pool Wizard, 1091
filtering, 1075, 1100
generic resources, 1091–1093

matching, 1099
removing from projects, 1098
replacing, 1098–1099
resource assignments, 1074–1075
resource availability, 1074–1077
Resource Substitution Wizard, 1091
viewing, 1074
viewing assignments, 1078–1081
equipment, 280
extended working hours, 429–432
filters
All Resources, 317, 767
applying, 370
Available to Work, 370–371
Confirmed Assignments, 767
Cost Greater Than..., 767
Cost Overbudget, 317, 572–574, 767
Date Range..., 767
Group..., 317, 369, 767
In Progress Assignments, 767
Linked Fields, 702, 768
Overallocated Resources, 317, 409, 768
removing, 370
Resource Range..., 768
Resources with Attachments, 768
Resources—Material, 315–316, 369
Resources—Work, 369, 768
Resources/Assignments with Overtime, 317, 768
Should Start By..., 574, 768
Should Start/Finish By..., 574, 768
Slipped/Late Progress, 768
Slipping Assignments, 317, 562, 574, 768
Unconfirmed Assignments, 768
Unstarted Assignments, 768
Work Complete, 317, 768
Work Incomplete, 768
Work Overbudget, 572–574, 768
generic resources, 281
groups, 314–315, 1105
Assignments Keeping Outline Structure, 772
Complete and Incomplete Resources, 772
defined, 280, 297
Group field, 295–297
Resource Group, 477, 773
Resource Pending, 773
Standard Rate, 477, 773
Work vs. Material Resources, 773
importing, 1021–1023
individual resources, 280
leveling, 419–421, 454–455
Automatic Leveling, 462
Clear Leveling dialog box, 462
Level Now dialog box, 459–463
priorities, 458–459
Resource Allocation view, 432–434
Resource Leveling dialog box, 455–459
resource substitution, 434–440
matching, 1106
material resources, 280
naming, 294
nondriver resources, 355
overallocations, 324
defined, 402
delayed assignments, 440–447
extended working hours, 429–432
filtering, 409–410
formatting display, 405
Go to Next Overallocation tool, 412
highlighting, 405
identifying, 405–409
increasing availability of, 410, 418–423
overtime, 423–428
reasons for, 403
reconciling, 406
reducing workload for, 419–421, 432
Resource Allocation view, 432–434
Resource Usage view, 410–411
sensitivity setting, 407–408
split assignments, 451–453
split tasks, 448–451
substituting underused resources for, 434–440
timephased details, 412–417
viewing, 409
overtime, 423–428
people, 280
placeholder resources, 281
removing, 339, 1037–1038
replacing, 1104
resource fields, 292–293
Base Calendar, 300–301
Code, 307–308
Cost Accrual, 307
Cost Per Use, 305
Cost Rate tables, 305–306
Group, 295–297
ID, 293
Indicators, 293
Initials, 295
Material Label, 295
Max Units, 297–298
Overtime Rate, 304–305
Resource Availability, 298–300
Resource Name, 294
Standard Rate, 303–304
Type, 294–295
Working Time, 301–302
resource lists
creating, 287–292
filtering, 472–474
grouping, 477
pasting from another application, 318–320
sorting, 475–477
resource pools
creating, 286–292, 621
defined, 279
disabling resource sharing, 625–626
links, 626
maintaining, 622

opening, 622–624
refreshing, 624
resource sharing, 621–624
saving, 625
updating, 623–624
Resource reports
customizing, 901–909
definitions, 904–905
details, 905–908
sort order, 910
text formatting, 909
searching for, 20, 35, 50
sharing, 604
sorting, 310–314, 776
by ID number, 310
by name, 312–313
predefined fields, 776
Sort dialog box, 312–313
sort keys, 777
sort operation, 777
by type, 312–313
undoing sorts, 313
substituting, 434–440, 1110–1117
tables, 760–761
Task Sheet view, 830
Task Usage view, 829
versions, 982
viewing availability of, 1040
work resources, 280

Resources/Assignments with Overtime filter, 768

Resources button (Project Guide), 41

Resources command (Tools menu), 621

Resources – Material filter, 369, 768

Resources menu commands
Refresh Resource Pool, 624
Share Resources, 621–622
Update Resource Pool, 624

Resources with Attachments filter, 768

Resources – Work filter, 369, 768

reestablishing links, 699

restoring
commands, 946
Enterprise Global template, 1020
links, 702
menus, 946
tables, 730
tasks, 265
toolbars, 936
views, 875

Resume field (progress bars), 796

reversing dependency links, 227

reviewing
project plans
compressed timescales, 469–470
custom groups, 477–479
outline codes, 471
project-level statistics, 468–469, 487
resource groups, 477
sorting tasks, 475–477
spell check, 486
task constraints, 214–216
task filters, 472–474
task groups, 477
task list outline, 470–471
WBS (Work Breakdown Structure) codes, 471
project status
assignment-level status, 574–575
progress lines, 559–562
project statistics, 565
Project Summary reports, 565
project summary tasks, 565–570
resource-level status, 573–574
slipping assignments, 562
slipping tasks, 562
Status field, 557–558
Status Indicator field, 557–558
task-level status, 570
variances, 563–564, 571–573

revising
schedules, 595–596
costs, 596–597
duration, 597–598
scope, 596
timesheets, 1129

risks, 1036, 1135–1137, CD:90–91

Risks: New Item dialog box, CD:91

roles, 971, 984

rolled up tasks, 793

rolling up baselines, 525

Rollup table, 739, 759

rollup taskbars, 161–163

rollup views, 738–741

Round Bars to Whole Days option (Layout dialog box), 799

Routing Recipient command (Send To menu), 486

rows
Gantt Chart bar charts, 794
heights, 237, 847
moving, 1035

Run Sub/UserForm command (Run menu), CD:43

S

Safe Mode feature, 103

Save a Link option (Portfolio Analyzer), 1050

Save As command (File menu), 100, 645

Save As dialog box, 99–100, CD:3

Save as GIF option (Portfolio Analyzer), 1051

Save As Web Page command (File menu), 102, CD:3

Save As Workspace command (File menu), 635

Save Baseline command (Tracking menu), 524

Save Baseline dialog box, 524–525

Save command (File menu), 99, 959

Save Link command (Resource Center), 1072

Save Map dialog box (Import/Export Wizard), 639, CD:8

Save Microsoft Project Files As setting (Options dialog box), 75

Save Options dialog box, 101

Save Workspace As dialog box, 102, 607

Save Workspace command (File menu), 102, 607, 625

saving
- base calendars, 84
- baselines, 522–526
- custom forms, 959
- custom groups, 872
- custom WBS codes, 170–171
- files
  - Auto Save feature, 98–99
  - backups, 102
  - default location, 96–97
  - file type, 96–97
  - in HTML format, 102
  - password-protected files, 101
  - Read-Only files, 101
  - Read-Only Recommended files, 102
  - Save As dialog box, 99–100
  - workspaces, 102–103
- Import/Export maps, CD:8
- interim plans, 525
- merged files, 608
- projects
  - as Excel worksheets, 665–668
  - as HTML documents, CD:3–8
  - .mdb format, 645
  - .mpd format, 640–643
  - as XML files, 681
  - ODBC databases, 647–648
- reports, 918
- resource pools, 625
- versions, 1067
- views, 838
- workspaces, 102–103, 607, 625, 635

scale (pages), 498

Scale Separator box (Timescale dialog box), 788

Scale the Picture to 22 Inches in Width option (Copy Picture dialog box), 723

schedule performance index (SPI) field, 582

Schedule table, 758

Schedule Tasks Project Guide, 207–208

Schedule Tracking form, 950

schedule variance (SV) field, 581

schedule variance percentage (SV%) field, 582

scheduled updates (OLAP), 998

Scheduling Options (Portfolio Modeler), 1058

scheduling. *See* project schedules; resource scheduling

scope, 596

screen formats (views), 836–837

screen types, changing, 875

ScreenTips, 35, 38–39, 450

scrollbars, 49
- Calendar, 260
- data fields, 48–49
- Gantt Chart view, 234–235
- Network Diagram view, 269–270
- task tables, 234–235
- timescale, 45, 243

Search box (Find dialog box), 52

searching
- enterprise projects, 1034
- Find dialog box, 20, 35, 50–53
- for files
  - Advanced Search pane, 32
  - Basic Search pane, 32
- for resources, 20, 35, 50
- security templates
  - creating, CD:7
  - deleting, CD:7–8
  - modifying, CD:6
- task tables, 235–236
- for tasks, 20, 35, 50

security
- authentication, CD:72–73
- files, 100–102
- managing, 984
- password protection, 101
- planning, 978
- Safe Mode feature, 103
- security templates, CD:70–72

Select Dialog command (Edit menu), 955

Selected Items command (Request Progress Information menu), 1125

Selected Tasks command (Zoom menu), CD:30

selecting
- base calendars, 78
- data fields, 50–51
- objects, 250, 269–270
- reports, 878

Send To command (File menu), 486

Send To menu commands, 486

sensitivity setting, 407–408

separator bars, 933

sequencing requirements, 24

Series Groups tab (Commands and Options dialog box), CD:83

server-side requirements (Microsoft Project Professional), 970

servers. *See* Project Server

services, Windows SharePoint Services, 628–629
- document libraries, CD:86
- document management, CD:87–88
- issues tracking, CD:89–90
- risk tracking, CD:90–91
- subwebs, CD:86

Set as Default field (Microsoft Project Server Accounts dialog box), 1007

set statement, CD:40

Settings menu commands, Printers, 490

SF (Start-to-Finish) relationship, 183–184

Share Resources command (Resources menu), 621–622

Share Resources dialog box, 622, 625–626

shared workspaces, 628–629

SharePoint Services, 628–629
- document libraries, CD:86
- document management, CD:87–88
- issues tracking, CD:89–90
- risk tracking, CD:90–91
- subwebs, CD:86

Sharer Takes Precedence button (Share Resources dialog box), 622

shares (network), 618

sharing data, 604, 632. *See also* importing data; exporting data
- combined resource lists, 627
- files, 97, 632–635
- reports, 918
- resource pools
  - creating, 621
  - disabling resource sharing, 625–626
  - links, 626
  - maintaining, 622
  - opening, 622–624
  - refreshing, 624
  - resource sharing, 621–624
  - saving, 625
  - updating, 623–624
- shared workspaces, 628–629

sheet views, 748, 751–752

Should Have Started Tasks report, 885

Should Start By filter, 574, 766–768

Should Start/Finish By filter, 574, 766–768

Show Bar Splits option (Layout dialog box), 799

Show For...Tasks column (Bar Styles dialog box), 792–793

Show/Hide tab (Commands and Options dialog box), CD:83–84

Show Link Labels tool, 815

Show Outline Levels option (Project Center), 1032

Show Outline Number option (Options dialog box), 160, 784

Show Outline Symbol option (Options dialog box), 161, 784

Show Page Breaks tool, 815

Show Progress Marks tool, 815

Show Summary Tasks option (Options dialog box), 161, 783

Show Time with Dates option (Project Center), 1032

Show To-Do List option (Project Center), 1032

showing. *See* displaying

Size & Position tab (Format Drawing dialog box), 251

Size box (Timescale dialog box), 787

sizing
- combo boxes, 934
- custom forms, 955–956
- floating toolbars, 929
- objects, 253–254, 703, 707, 729
- polygons, 254
- task tables, 236–237

skills
- defining, 975–976
- matching skill-sets, 1088–1090
- multiple skills per resource, 1016, 1087
- proficiency levels per skill, 1015–1016, 1086

slack, 441

Slipped/Late Progress filter, 766, 768

Slipping Assignments filter, 317, 562, 574, 768

Slipping Tasks filter, 562, 766

Slipping Tasks report, 885

SmartTags, 41–42

SNET (Start No Earlier Than) constraint, 203

SNLT (Start No Later Than) constraint, 203

soft constraints, 212–214

Sort By command (Sort menu), 312, 475, 610

Sort command (Project menu), 310, 475, 610, 776

Sort dialog box, 312–313, 475–476, 776–777

sort keys, 777

Sort menu commands, Sort By, 312, 475, 610

sorting
- combined tasks, 610–611
- defined, 474
- reports, 880, 898, 910, 915
- resource assignments, 463
- resource lists, 475–477
- resources, 310–314
  - by ID number, 310
  - by name, 312–313
  - predefined fields, 776
  - Sort dialog box, 312–313
  - sort keys, 777
  - sort operation, 777
  - by type, 312–313
  - undoing sorts, 313
- tasks, 475–477, 495, 776–777

specialized Gantt Chart views
- Detail Gantt, 743
- Leveling Gantt, 743
- Multiple Baselines Gantt, 744
- Tracking Gantt, 742

Specify Resource and OLAP Cube Updates command (Manage Enterprise Features menu), 996

spell check, 486

SPI (schedule performance index) field, 582

split bars, 46–47, CD:75

Split command (Window menu), 246, 263, 605

Split Task command (Edit menu), 221

Split Task dialog box, 221

Split Task ScreenTip, 450

Split Task tool, 221, 450

splitting
- assignments, 451–453
- Gantt Chart view, 45–46
- tasks, 220–223, 228, 345, 448–451, 793
- views, 246–247, 263
- windows, 605

SPS. *See* SharePoint Services

SS (Start-to-Start) relationship, 182

Standard calendar, 76, 1018

Standard leveling order, 457

Standard option (Gantt Chart Wizard), 802

Standard Rate field (resources), 303–304

Standard Rate group, 477, 773

standard reports. *See* reports

Standard toolbar, 35, 926
- Format Painter tool, 781
- Link Tasks tool, 187, 618
- Split Task tool, 221
- Task Information button, 613
- Unlink Tasks tool, 188
- Zoom In button, 494
- Zoom Out button, 494

start accrual method, 285

Start Date text box (Project Information dialog box), 58–60

start dates
- Actual Start field, 532, 537
- default start dates, 121
- defined, 794
- entering, 58–60
- fixed-start-date projects, 382–384
- troubleshooting, 93–94
- variances, 571

Start field (task tables), 120
- dates, 123
- default start dates, 121
- default time of day, 122–123

Start menu commands, Programs, 30

Start No Earlier Than (SNET) constraint, 203, 1058

Start No Later Than (SNLT) constraint, 203

start times, 69–70

Start-to-Finish relationship, 183–184

Start-to-Start relationship, 182

started early tasks, 793

started late tasks, 793

started on time tasks, 793

starting Project, 30

state dates, 176

statements
- Case, CD:53–54
- Dim, CD:39
- For Each, Next, CD:40
- If, Then, Else, CD:41
- nested statements, CD:41
- Open, CD:61–62
- Option Explicit, CD:39
- Public, CD:50
- set, CD:40
- Sub/End Sub, CD:38

statistics
- displaying, 468–469
- printing, 487
- Project Statistics dialog box, 61–62, 468–469, 565
- viewing, 565

Statistics tab (Properties dialog box), 63

status bar, 38

Status Date text box (Project Information dialog box), 59, 61

status dates, 59, 61

Status field, 557–558

Status Indicator field, 557–558

status of projects, reviewing
- assignment-level status, 574–575
- progress lines, 559–562
- project statistics, 565
- Project Summary reports, 565
- project summary tasks, 565–570
- resource-level status, 573–574
- slipping assignments, 562
- slipping tasks, 562
- Status field, 557–558
- Status Indicator field, 557–558
- status reports, 1129
  - compiling, 1132–1133
  - requesting, 1130–1131
  - status report flow, 1130
  - submitting, 1131–1132
- Status Request Pending group, 772
- task-level status, 570
- variances
  - calculating, 563–564
  - cost variances, 571–572
  - date variances, 571
  - work variances, 572–573

status reports, creating user accounts from, CD:69

Status Request Pending group, 772

Stop field (progress bars), 796

Stop Recording command (Macro menu), CD:29

Straight Links tool, 815

Sub/End Sub statements, CD:38

submitting
- status reports, 1131–1132
- time with Outlook, 1140–1141
- timesheets for approval, 1126–1127

Subproject File field, 617

subprojects, 612–613

subroutines, CD:31
- calling with arguments, CD:54
- calling without parameters, CD:52–53
- main subroutines, CD:51

Substitute Resources command (Tools menu), 1112

substituting resources, 434–440, 1110–1117

subtasks, 154–155, 233

subwebs (SPS), CD:86

successor tasks, 177–180

Summary form, 950

summary information, entering, 62–63

Summary Progress field (progress bars), 796

Summary tab (Properties dialog box), 62–63

Summary table, 759, 761

summary tasks, 44, 118, 139, 154–156, 233
- critical, 267
- defined, 792
- linking, 184–185
- moving, 170
- noncritical, 267
- rollup taskbars, 161–163
- Summary Tasks filter, 473–474, 766

SV (schedule variance) field, 581

SV% (schedule variance percentage) field, 582

syntax checking (macros), CD:43

system administration, 986–987

system requirements, 969–970

T

tab-delimited text files, 682–684

Table command (View menu), 236, 757, 760, 840

Table Definition dialog box, 730, 841–844

Table menu commands, More Tables, 757, 760, 840

tables, 840–841
- applying to current view, 841
- columns
  - creating, 841–843
  - definitions, 845
  - editing, 841–843
  - headers, 842
  - hiding, 846
  - inserting, 846
  - locking, 876
  - redefining, 845
  - retrieving hidden columns, 846–847
- Constraint Dates, 228–229
- Cost, 283
- Cost Rate, 305–306, 392–393
- creating
  - columns, 841–843
  - names, 841
  - Table Definition dialog box, 843–844
- customizing, 730
- defined, 108
- definitions, 843–844
- displaying, 757, 840
- Earned Value Cost Indicators, 583–584, 589
  - BAC (budget at completion), 586
  - CPI (cost performance index), 585
  - CV (cost variance), 584
  - CV% (cost variance percentage), 585
  - EAC (estimate at completion), 586
  - TCPI (to complete performance index), 586
  - VAC (variance at completion), 586
- Earned Value Schedule Indicators, 589
  - SPI (schedule performance index), 582
  - SV (schedule variance), 581
  - SV% (schedule variance percentage), 582
- editing, 841
- Entry table, 193–194
- Excel PivotTables, 668–673
- fields, 50–51
- Gantt Chart view, 44
- naming, 841
- outline code lookup tables, 857–858
- reports, 880
- Resource Availability, 418
- restoring, 730
- Rollup, 739
- rows, 847
- task tables, 232
  - assigning resources with, 365, 395–396
  - columns, 236–239
  - date format, 239
  - displaying, 236, 757
  - Duration field, 120
  - fields, 235
  - finding tasks in, 235–236
  - Finish field, 120–123
  - ID field, 119
  - Indicator field, 120
  - moving around in, 233–234
  - outlined task lists, 233
  - Predecessors field, 123
  - Resource Names field, 123
  - row height, 237
  - scrolling, 234–235
  - Start field, 120–123
  - subtasks, 233
  - summary tasks, 233
  - task constraints, 208–209
  - task indicators, 233
  - Task Name field, 120
- views, 837

Tables command (View menu), 904

tags
- <A>, CD:20–21
- <BODY>, CD:16
- <TITLE>, CD:18

Task and Resource PivotTable map, 652, 655

Task Detail Form view, 750

Task Detail Name view, 750

Task Details form, 209

Task Entry view, 34, 45, 755
- resource assignments, 379
  - assignment delay, 382–385
  - overtime work, 385–387
  - step-by-step instructions, 379–381
- tasks, creating, 152–153

Task Export Table map, 652, 655

Task Form view, 33–34, 291–292, 749
- dependency links, creating, 190–192
- formatting, 817–819
- resource assignments, 365

task indicators, 233

Task Information button (Standard toolbar), 613

Task Information command (Project menu), 263

Task Information dialog box, 131, 233, 246, 263, 336–337, 365, 613
- assigning resources with, 393–394
- deadline dates, 217–219
- General tab, 739
- Predecessors tab, 188–189
- task calendar assignments, 224–225
- task constraints, 208

task links. *See* dependency links

Task List with Embedded Assignment Rows map, 652, 655

task lists
- bottom-up approach, 116
- clearing, 128
- copying tasks, 129–130
- custom WBS codes, 163
  - creating, 164–166
  - deleting tasks, 167
  - editing, 167
  - inserting tasks, 167
  - moving tasks, 167
  - renumbering, 168–169
  - saving, 170–171
- deleting tasks, 128
- dependency links, 177–178
  - auditing, 199–200
  - Autolink, 196–198
  - cautions, 178
  - creating, 187–196
  - defined, 176
  - deleting, 185, 188, 198–199
  - dependent tasks, 179–180
  - editing, 187, 198
  - Finish-to-Finish relationship, 183
  - Finish-to-Start relationship, 182
  - honoring, 212–214
  - lag time, 180–181, 189–190
  - lead time, 180–181, 189–190
  - outlined projects, 185
  - overlapping tasks, 180–181, 189–190
  - predecessor tasks, 177–180
  - reversing, 227
  - Start-to-Finish relationship, 183–184
  - Start-to-Start relationship, 182
  - successor tasks, 177–180
  - summary tasks, 184–185
  - tasks from different projects, 227
  - troubleshooting, 226–227
  - unrelated tasks, 178
  - views, 199–201
- editing, 127, 131–132
- Excel Task List Template, 118
- Gantt Chart view, 118–119
- hyperlinks
  - attaching to files/Web pages, 148–149
  - attaching to new documents, 149
  - attaching to resources, 150
  - attaching to tasks, 147–150
  - in custom text fields, 150–151
  - deleting, 150
  - editing, 150
  - email hyperlinks, 150
- importing, 684–687
- inserting tasks, 128
- level of detail, 27
- milestones, 117, 136–137
- moving tasks, 129–130
- Network Diagram view, 151–152
- normal tasks, 117
- notes
  - attaching to projects, 146–147
  - attaching to tasks, 142
  - creating, 142–144
  - formatting, 142–144
  - hyperlinks, 144
  - inserting objects in, 144–146
- outlines
  - collapsing, 157–158, 470–471
  - custom outline numbers, 169
  - display options, 160–161
  - editing, 159, 187, 194, 201, 206
  - expanding, 157–158
  - formatting, 160–161
  - indenting tasks, 156–157
  - levels, 159
  - outdenting tasks, 156–157
  - subtasks, 154–155
  - summary tasks, 154–156
  - symbols, 159
  - task duration, 156
- printing, 170
- recurring tasks, 137
  - constraints, 141
  - creating, 138–141
  - editing, 142
  - end dates, 139
  - icons, 140
  - linking, 141
  - start dates, 139
  - summary tasks, 139
- rollup taskbars, 161–163
- summary tasks, 118, 139, 156, 170
- task duration
  - calculating with Project, 171–174
  - continuous tasks, 135
  - default duration time units, 134
  - defined, 132
  - elapsed duration, 135–136
  - estimating, 132–133
  - time unit abbreviations, 134–135
- Task Entry view, 152–153
- task names, 123
  - column width, 126
  - copying from other applications, 125
  - displaying long names, 126
  - entering, 124–125

naming conventions, 124
row height, 126
text wrap, 126
Task Sheet view, 154
top-down approach, 116
undoing changes to, 127
WBS (Work Breakdown Structure), 116

Task Mapping page (Import/Export Wizard), 638

Task Name field (task tables), 120

Task pane, 30–32

Task Pane toolbar, 927

Task Range... filter, 766

Task Relationships form, 950

Task reports
customizing, 901–903
definitions, 904–905
details, 905–908
text formatting, 909
definitions, 904–905
details, 905–908
sort order, 910
text formatting, 909

Task Sheet view, 154, 748, 830

task tables, 119, 232
assigning resources with, 365, 395–396
Baseline, 759
columns
deleting, 238
displaying, 236
editing, 237–238
hiding, 238
inserting, 237–239
width, 236–237
Constraint Dates, 759
Cost, 758
date format, 239
Delay, 759
displaying, 236, 757
Duration field, 120
Earned Value, 759
Earned Value Cost Indicators, 759
Earned Value Schedule Indicators, 759
Entry, 758
Export, 759
fields, 235
finding tasks in, 235–236
Finish field, 120–123
Hyperlink, 758
ID field, 119
Indicator field, 120
moving around in, 233–234
outlined task lists, 233
PA_Expected Case, 759
PA_Optimistic Case, 759
PA_PERT Case, 759
PA_Pessimistic Case, 759
Predecessors field, 123
Resource Names field, 123
Rollup, 759
rows, 237
Schedule, 758
scrolling, 234–235
Start field, 120–123
subtasks, 233
Summary, 759
summary tasks, 233
task constraints, 208–209
task indicators, 233
Task Name field, 120
Tracking, 759
Usage, 759
Variance, 759
Work, 759

Task Usage command (View menu), 574

Task Usage report, 891

Task Usage view, 574–575, 748
formatting, 829
print options, 507
project tracking, 550–551
resource assignments, 365, 387–390

taskbars
adding text to, 831
attaching objects to, 250–252, 274
finding, 243
formatting, 831
jumping to, 50
missing taskbars, 274
rollup taskbars, 161–163
timescale, 240
troubleshooting, 274

tasks. *See also* task lists; task tables
adding, 263–265, 308–309
assigning resources to, 365
Assign Resources dialog box, 365–379, 1107–1110
assignment delay, 382–385
Assignment Information dialog box, 390–393
Cost Rate tables, 392–393
drag-and-drop, 376
for specific amounts of work, 375–376
modifying assignments, 377–379
notes, 393
overtime work, 385–387
resource availability graphs, 371–373
resource filters, 369–371
Resource Substitution Wizard, 1110–1117
resource units, 374–375
task effort-driven setting, 364
Task Entry view, 379–387
Task Form view, 365
Task Information dialog box, 365, 393–394
Task table, 365, 395–396
task type, 361–363
Task Usage view, 365, 387–390
work contours, 392
calendars, 136, 176
assigning to tasks, 224–225, 354
creating, 223–226
scheduling with, 353–354
combined tasks, 611
choosing type of, 335–338
constraints
ALAP (As Late As Possible), 202
ASAP (As Soon As Possible), 202
creating with Schedule Tasks Project Guide, 207–208
creating with Task Details form, 209

creating with Task Information dialog box, 208
creating with Task table, 208–209
custom Constraint Dates table, 228–229
defined, 176, 201
deleting, 216
examples, 201
finding, 214–216
flexible/inflexible, 203–206
FNET (Finish No Earlier Than), 203
FNLT (Finish No Later Than), 203
hard constraints, 212–214
honoring, 212–214
MFO (Must Finish On), 203
MSO (Must Start On), 203
Planning Wizard warnings, 210–212
resolving conflicts, 216–217
reviewing, 214–216
SNET (Start No Earlier Than), 203
SNLT (Start No Later Than), 203
soft constraints, 212–214
creating, 124–125, 975
critical tasks, 25, 408, 480, 792
custom WBS codes, 163
creating, 164–166
deleting tasks, 167
editing, 167
inserting tasks, 167
moving tasks, 167
renumbering, 168–169
saving, 170–171
deadline dates
entering, 217–219
filtering, 219
missed deadlines, 220, 229
defined, 116
delaying, 342–345, 441–443
delegating, CD:69
deleting, 128
Calendar view, 265
custom WBS codes, 167
Network Diagram view, 272
dependency links, 177–178
auditing, 199–200
Autolink, 196–198
cautions, 178
creating, 187–196
defined, 176
deleting, 185, 188, 198–199
dependent tasks, 179–180
editing, 187, 198
Finish-to-Finish relationship, 183
Finish-to-Start relationship, 182
honoring, 212–214
lag time, 180–181, 189–190
lead time, 180–181, 189–190
outlined projects, 185
overlapping tasks, 180–181, 189–190
predecessor tasks, 177–180
reversing, 227
Start-to-Finish relationship, 183–184
Start-to-Start relationship, 182
successor tasks, 177–180
summary tasks, 184–185
tasks from different projects, 227
troubleshooting, 226–227
unrelated tasks, 178
views, 199–201
dependent tasks, 179–180
duration
calculating with Project, 171–174
continuous tasks, 135
default duration time units, 134
defined, 132
duration inflation, 203
elapsed duration, 135–136
estimating, 132–133, 176
multiple resources, 357–358
summary tasks, 156
time unit abbreviations, 134–135
editing
Multiple Task Information dialog box, 131–132
Network Diagram view, 270
Task Information dialog box, 131
effort-driven tasks, 338–341, 364
exporting to Excel, CD:58–61
exporting to text files, CD:61
external tasks, 793
filters, 472–474
All Tasks, 765
Completed Tasks, 765
Confirmed, 765
Cost Greater Than..., 765
Cost Overbudget, 765
Created After..., 766
Critical, 766
Date Range..., 766
In Progress Tasks, 766, 859
Incomplete Tasks, 766
Late/Overbudget Tasks Assigned To..., 766
Linked Fields, 766
Milestones, 473, 766
Resource Group..., 766
Should Start By..., 766
Should Start/Finish By..., 766
Slipped/Late Progress, 766
Slipping Tasks, 562, 766
Summary Tasks, 473–474, 766
Task Range..., 766
Tasks/Assignments with Overtime, 767
Tasks with Attachments, 766
Tasks with Deadlines, 219, 473, 766
Tasks with Fixed Dates, 215, 473–474, 767
Tasks with a Task Calendar Assigned, 226
Top Level Tasks, 570, 767
Unconfirmed, 767
Unstarted Tasks, 767
Update Needed, 767

Using Resource in Date Range..., 767
Using Resource..., 767
Work Overbudget, 767
finding, 260–261
finished tasks, 792–793
fixed-duration tasks, 335
fixed-unit tasks, 336
fixed-work tasks, 335
flag tasks, 793
free slack, 441
Gantt Chart bar charts, 792–793
group by summary tasks, 793
groups, 495
Complete and Incomplete Tasks, 772
Constraint Type, 477, 772
Critical, 477, 772
Duration, 477, 772
Duration then Priority, 772
Milestones, 477, 772
No Group, 772
Priority, 477, 772
Priority Keeping Outline Structure, 772
Status Request Pending, 772
highlighting, 472
hyperlinks
attaching to files/Web pages, 148–149
attaching to new documents, 149
attaching to resources, 150
attaching to tasks, 147–150
in custom text fields, 150–151
deleting, 150
editing, 150
email hyperlinks, 150
important tasks, 480
in progress tasks, 792
inserting, 128
custom WBS codes, 167
Network Diagram view, 270–271
linking. *See* dependency links
marked tasks, 792
maximum length of, 69
milestones, 117, 136–137, 792
moving, 129–130, 167
Network Diagram view, 151–152
noncritical tasks, 792
normal tasks, 44, 117, 792
not finished tasks, 792
not started tasks, 793
notes
attaching to projects, 146–147
attaching to tasks, 142
creating, 142–144
formatting, 142–144
hyperlinks, 144
inserting objects in, 144–146
outlined task lists, 233
outlines
collapsing, 157–158
custom outline numbers, 169
display options, 160–161
editing, 159, 187, 194, 201, 206
expanding, 157–158
formatting, 160–161
indenting tasks, 156–157
levels, 159
outdenting tasks, 156–157
subtasks, 154–155
summary tasks, 154–156
symbols, 159
task duration, 156
predecessor tasks
choosing, 179–180
defined, 177
defining, 189
deleting, 189
priorities, 458–459
project summary tasks, 565–570
creating, 566
defined, 793
displaying, 784
phases, 569–570
viewing, 565
recording macros for, CD:30–32
recurring tasks, 137
constraints, 141
creating, 138–141
editing, 142
end dates, 139
icons, 140
linking, 141
start dates, 139
summary tasks, 139
relationships between
Descriptive Network Diagram view, 746
Network Diagram view, 745–746
Relationship Diagram view, 747
removing resources from, 376–377
reordering, 197, 273–274
rescheduling options, 544–546
restoring, 265
rolled up tasks, 793
scheduling, 24–27, 259
searching for, 20, 35, 50
slipping tasks, 562
sorting, 475–477, 495
combined tasks, 610–611
predefined fields, 776
sort keys, 777
sort operation, 777
splitting, 220–223, 228, 345, 448–451, 793
started early tasks, 793
started late tasks, 793
started on time tasks, 793
subtasks, 154–155, 233
successor tasks, 177–180
summary tasks, 44, 118, 139, 154–156, 233
defined, 792
linking, 184–185
moving, 170
rollup taskbars, 161–163
task assignments
notifying team members of, 1123–1126
viewing in Outlook, 1140
task details, 262–263
Task Entry view, 152–153
Task Form view, 817–819
task indicators, 233
Task Information dialog box, 131, 233, 246, 263, 336–337, 365, 613
assigning resources with, 393–394
deadline dates, 217–219

General tab, 739
Predecessors tab, 188–189
task calendar assignments, 224–225
task constraints, 208
task names, 123
column width, 126
copying from other applications, 125
displaying long names, 126
entering, 124–125
naming conventions, 124
row height, 126
text wrap, 126
Task reports
customizing, 901–909
definitions, 904–905
details, 905–908
sort order, 910
text formatting, 909
Task Sheet view, 154, 830
task type setting, 361–363
TaskSummaryName macro, CD:36–67
blank lines, CD:41
code listing, CD:37–38
creating, CD:37–38
For Each, Next statement, CD:40
If, Then, Else statement, CD:41
nested statements, CD:41
object properties, CD:42
Sub/End Sub statements, CD:38
user feedback, CD:42
variables, CD:38–40
total slack, 441
tracking fields, 529–531
% Complete, 533
% Work Complete, 535
Actual Duration, 534
Actual Finish, 532–533
Actual Start, 532
Actual Work, 535
Physical % Complete, 534
Remaining Duration, 535
Remaining Work, 535–536
timephased Actual Work, 536
types of, 267

Tasks/Assignments with Overtime filter, 767

Tasks button (Project Guide), 40

Tasks In Progress report, 885

Tasks Occurring On dialog box, 259

Tasks Starting Soon report, 885

Tasks with a Task Calendar Assigned filter, 226

Tasks with Attachments filter, 766

Tasks with Deadlines filter, 219, 473, 766

Tasks with Fixed Dates filter, 215, 473–474, 767

TaskSummaryName macro, CD:36–67
blank lines, CD:41
code listing, CD:37–38
creating, CD:37–38
For Each, Next statement, CD:40
If, Then, Else statement, CD:41
nested statements, CD:41
object properties, CD:42
Sub/End Sub statements, CD:38
user feedback, CD:42
variables
defining, CD:38–39
initializing, CD:39–40
types, CD:38

TCPI (to complete performance index), 586

Team Builder, 1091, 1102–1103
Add button, 1106
Apply Filter button, 1104
Available to Work check box, 1105
Customize Filters field, 1105
Details button, 1106
Enterprise Resource list, 1105
Existing Filters list, 1105
Graphs button, 1106
Group By field, 1105
Match button, 1106
Remove button, 1106
Replace button, 1104–1106
Team Resource list, 1106

Team Resource list (Team Builder), 1106

teams
building from enterprise resource pool, 1097
team leaders, 972
team members
notifying of task assignments, 1123–1126
responsibilities, 972

templates
built-in templates, 104–105
creating, 106–107
defined, 103
editing, 107
Enterprise Global template, 104, 873–874, 926, 947, 1007–1008
backing up, 1019–1020, CD:35
copying, 109
copying base calendars to, 84, 89–90
editing, 109, 1009–1010
effect on user sessions, 1008–1009
enterprise project calendar management, 1018–1019
enterprise resource calendar management, 1019
finding, 112
restoring, 1020
saving changes to, 873–875
working offline, 1010
Excel Task List Template, 118
HTML templates, CD:13
background colors, CD:14–15
background images, CD:16–17
Gantt Chart images, CD:22–24
hyperlinks, CD:19–25
images, CD:17–18
title bar text, CD:18–19
.mpt file extension, 103

Network Diagram view, 809–811
opening, 104
security templates
creating, CD:71
deleting, CD:71–72
modifying, CD:70

temporary nature of projects, 16

Test setting (Find dialog box), 53

testing macros, CD:29

tests (filters)
Contains, 863
Contains Exactly, 863
Is Within/Is Not Within, 863
logical values, 862
table of, 861
test values, 862
wildcards, 864

text
adding to custom forms, 956
adding to taskbars, 831
bar charts, 796–797
editing, 257
fonts, 257
formatting, 778–780
color, 780
copying formatting, 781
fonts, 780
global changes, 779
manual formatting, 781
milestones, 779
overallocated resources, 405
reports, 897, 909, 914
selected text, 781
headers/footers
aligning, 502–503
formatting, 504–506
independent text, 256
text boxes, 256–258
text fields, 150–151
text files, 682–684, CD:61
text wrap, 126

Text Above field (Rollup table), 739

Text Box button (Drawing toolbar), 249

Text Styles command (Format menu), 472, 776, 778

Text Styles dialog box, 472, 778–780

Text tab (Bar Styles dialog box), 791, 796–797

tiers (timescale), 244, 786–787

tilde (~), 100

tiling windows, 605–606

time
default end time, 69–70
default start time, 69–70
elapsed time, 441
extended working hours, 429–432
free slack, 441, 795
including in headers/footers, 501
lag time, 180–181, 189–190
lead time, 180–181, 189–190
negative slack, 795
nonworking time, 788–789, CD:93–94
reporting, 977, 983
submitting with Outlook, 1140–1141
task duration time units, 134
time formats, 81
time unit abbreviations, 134–135
total slack, 441, 795

timephased Actual Work field, 536, 539

timephased data
copying, 692, 696
editing, 412–417

timescale
bar text, 242
compressing, 469–470
finding dates in, 243
finding taskbars in, 243
formatting, 245, 785, 803–804
labels, 786–787
nonworking time display, 788–789
timescale definitions, 787–788
timescale tiers, 786–787
linking lines, 242
moving around in, 242–243
printing, 494, 513, 516
scrolling, 49, 243
spacing, 831
taskbars, 50, 240
tiers, 244
zooming in/out, 245, 494

Timescale command (Format menu), 245, 494, 785, 803

Timescale dialog box, 245, 470, 785–786, 803–804
Align drop-down list, 787
Date Boxes tab, 804
Date Shading tab, 804
Label drop-down list, 786
Nonworking Time tab, 788–789
Scale Separator box, 788
Size box, 787
Units drop-down list, 786
Week Headings tab, 804

Timesheet view, 993–994

timesheets
approving, 1128
attaching notes to, 1127
lockdown periods, 1128–1129
locking down time periods, 983
revising, 1129
submitting for approval, 1126–1127
time reporting, 977, 983
timesheet flow, 1122–1123
Timesheet view, 993–994
tracking methods, 1123

title bars, CD:18–19

<TITLE> tag, CD:18

to complete performance index (TCPI) field, 586

To-do List report, 890

Toggle Breakpoint command (Debug menu), CD:43

toolbars, 35–36
active toolbars, 927
Analysis toolbar, 927
assigning custom forms to, 952–953
Collaborate toolbar, 926
combination boxes, 928
combo boxes, 934
command buttons, 930–931
actions, 939–941
adding, 931–932
attaching macros to, 931

button faces, 937–939
display options, 937
grouping, 933
moving, 932–933
removing, 931–932, 960
separator bars, 933
troubleshooting, 960
Compare Project Versions, 483, 927
copying, 934–935, 947–948
creating, 934–935
Custom Forms toolbar, 926
customizing, 925–926
behavior, 923–924
combo boxes, 934
command buttons, 930–933, 936–941
Customize dialog box, 929–930
personalized toolbars, 924
toolbar position, 928–929
Database Upgrade Utility toolbar, 927
defined, 108
displaying, 36, 923–924, 927–928
docking, 928
Drawing, 247–250, 926
Euro Currency Converter, 927
floating, 928–929
Formatting, 35, 411, 781, 926
hiding, 36
managing with Organizer, 947–949
move handles, 923
Network Diagram, 815, 927
personalized toolbars, 924
PERT Analysis, 927
positioning, 928–929
Project Guide, 492–493, 521, 926–927
renaming, 947–948
resizing, 929
Resource Management 412, 927
restoring, 936
ScreenTips, 35
Standard toolbar, 35, 926
Format Painter tool, 781
Link Tasks tool, 187, 618
Split Task tool, 221
Task Information button, 613
Unlink Tasks tool, 188
Zoom In button, 494
Zoom Out button, 494
Task Pane toolbar, 927
Tracking, 549–550, 561, 565, 927
troubleshooting, 52, 961
user-defined toolbars, 934–936
Visual Basic, 927
Web, 927

Toolbars command
Customize menu, 36
View menu, 36, 927

Toolbars menu commands
Customize, 929
Drawing, 248

Toolbars tab (Customize dialog box), 930

tools. *See also* toolbars
Adjust Dates, 227–228
AutoFilter, 769–770
Edit Points, 254
Format Painter, 781
Link Tasks, 187
Organizer, 107
copying objects, 109–111
deleting objects, 111–112
displaying, 108
modifying GLOBAL.MPT, 109
object types, 107–108
renaming objects, 111
Split Task, 221
Unlink Tasks, 188

Tools menu commands
Assign Resources, 1107
AutoCorrect, 124
Build Team from Enterprise, 1103
Change Working Time, 78, 429, 915
Links Between Projects, 620
Options, 65, 239, 783
Organizer, 89, 109, 875, 947
Resource Leveling, 443
Resources, 621
Substitute Resources, 1112
Tracking, 524

Top Level Tasks filter, 570, 767

Top Level Tasks List map, 652, 656

top-down approach (task lists), 116

Top-Level Tasks report, 881

total costs, 281–283

total slack, 441, 795

TraceDependencies macro, CD:46
code listing, CD:47–50
filters, CD:56–57
input box, CD:51–52
main subroutine, CD:51
message box, CD:52
recursion, CD:55–56
subroutines
calling with arguments, CD:54
calling without parameters, CD:52–53
Case statement, CD:53–54
variables, CD:51–52
views, CD:56–57

Track button (Project Guide), 41

tracking, 520
assignment-tracking fields
% Work Complete, 538
Actual Finish, 537
Actual Start, 537
Actual Work, 537
Remaining Work, 538
timephased Actual Work, 539
baselines
clearing, 526
copying, 528
defined, 522
editing, 527
fields, 522–524
interim plans, 525
rebaselining, 524
rolling up, 525
saving, 522, 524–526
viewing, 527–528
calculation options
Actual Costs Are Always Calculated by Microsoft Project, 541–543

Edits to Total Task % Complete Will Be Spread to the Status Date, 543–544
Updating Task Status Updates Resource Status, 539–541
Gantt Chart view, 550
issues, CD:89–90
Project Guide toolbar, 521
rescheduling options, 544–546
Resource Usage view, 550–551
risks, CD:90–91
Task Usage view, 550–551
task-tracking fields, 529–531
% Complete, 533
% Work Complete, 535
Actual Duration, 534
Actual Finish, 532–533
Actual Start, 532
Actual Work, 535
Physical % Complete, 534
Remaining Duration, 535
Remaining Work, 535–536
timephased Actual Work, 536
timesheets, 1123
Tracking form, 950
tracking methods, 546–549
Tracking Setup Wizard, 547–549
Tracking table, 759
Tracking toolbar, 549–550, 927
Add Progress Line tool, 561
Project Statistics tool, 565
Update Project form
Reschedule Uncompleted Work to Start option, 553–554
Update Work as Complete Through option, 552
Update Tasks form, 551

Tracking command (Tools menu), 524

Tracking form, 950

Tracking Gantt view, 742

Tracking menu commands
Clear Baseline, 526
Progress Lines, 560
Save Baseline, 524

Tracking Setup Wizard, 547–549

Tracking table, 759

Tracking toolbar, 549–550, 927
Add Progress Line tool, 561
Project Statistics tool, 565

transferring portfolio models, 1064

trends in earned value, 578

triple constraint diagram, 17–18

troubleshooting
adjusted dates, 227–228
custom forms, 961
dependency links, 226–227
detail headers, 463
earned value fields, 599
filters, 773
formatting problems, 830–831
Global template, 112
importing/exporting, 689
links, 616, 621
macros, CD:33
print jobs, 515–516
project management, 27
resource assignments, 399
resource scheduling, 358
split tasks, 228
start times, 93–94
taskbars, 274
toolbars, 52, 960–961
views, 875
Web pages, CD:24–25

Truncate the Picture to 22 Inches in Width option (Copy Picture dialog box), 723

turning off. ***See*** **disabling; hiding**

turning on. ***See*** **displaying; enabling**

turtle work contour, 351

.txt file format, 635

Type field (resources), 294–295

Type tab (Commands and Options dialog box), CD:83

types, CD:38

U

Unconfirmed Assignments filter, 768

Unconfirmed filter, 767

Undo command (Edit menu), 127, 702

undoing changes
reports, 919
sort operations, 313
task lists, 127

Unhide command (Window menu), 606

Unit Availability option (Details menu), 824

units (assignment), 325
availability, displaying, 824
defined, 402
field format, 326
fractions, 328
material resource units, 328–329
maximum number of, 326
work resource units, 326–327

Units drop-down list (Timescale dialog box), 786

Unlink Tasks command (Edit menu), 188

Unlink Tasks tool, 188

Unstarted Assignments filter, 768

Unstarted Tasks filter, 767

Unstarted Tasks report, 884

Up command (Fill menu), 130

Update as Scheduled button (Tracking toolbar), 549

update frequency, 998

Update Needed filter, 767

Update Now option (OLAP), 998

Update Project form, 552–554

Update Resource Pool command (Resources menu), 624

Update Tasks button (Tracking toolbar), 550

Update Tasks form, 551

Update Work as Complete Through option (Update Project form), 552

Updates to Resources and OLAP Cube dialog box, 996–998

updates (workgroup), creating user accounts from, CD:5

updating
- issues, 1138
- linked data, 699–701
- resource pools, 623–624
- risks, 1137

Updating Task Status Updates Resource Status calculation option, 539–541

uploading documents, CD:88

Usage Details tab (Detail Styles dialog box), 415–416

Usage Properties tab (Detail Styles dialog box), 417

Usage table, 759–761
- Assignment Delay field, 446–447
- Leveling Delay field, 444–445

Use Current Assignments option (Portfolio Modeler), 1058

Use Own Resources button (Share Resources dialog box), 625

Use Resources button (Share Resources dialog box), 622

User Name field (Account Properties dialog box), 1006

user-defined toolbars
- creating from existing toolbars, 934–935
- creating from scratch, 935
- deleting, 936

user feedback, CD:33–34, CD:42

users
- administrators, 971
- authentication, CD:72–73
- executives, 972
- groups, 972–973
- names, entering, 73
- portfolio managers, 972
- project managers, 972
- Project Server user accounts
  - creating from workgroup messages/status reports, CD:69
  - creating from workgroup updates/status reports, CD:69
  - creating when delegating tasks, CD:69
  - creating with Add User screen, CD:66–67
  - groups, CD:68
- resource managers, 972
- requesting input from, CD:51–52
- roles, 971
- team leaders, 972
- team members, 972
- Web Access, 987

Using Resource Filter dialog box, 764

Using Resource in Date Range... filter, 767

Using Resource... filter, 767

V

VAC (variance at completion), 586

Value List dialog box, 850

variable consumption rates, 295, 329

variables
- defining, CD:38–39
- initializing, CD:39–40
- private variables, CD:50–51
- public variables, CD:50–51
- types, CD:38

variance, 284
- calculating, 563–564
- CV (cost variance), 571–572, 584–585
- date variances, 571
- displaying, 599
- SV (schedule variance), 581
- VAC (variance at completion), 586
- Variance table, 759
- work variances, 572–573

VBA (Visual Basic for Applications) macros
- advantages of, CD:28–29
- Case statement, CD:53–54
- collections, CD:32
- debugging, CD:42–43
  - breakpoints, CD:43–45
  - Immediate window, CD:43–45
  - syntax checking, CD:43
  - watches, CD:43–45
- events
  - application-level events, CD:63
  - help, CD:64
  - list of, CD:63
  - Project_Open, CD:62–63
- exporting data to Excel, CD:58–61
- exporting data to text files, CD:61
- filters, CD:56–57
- input boxes, CD:51–52
- message boxes, CD:52
- methods, CD:33
- modules, CD:37
- object model, CD:32–33
- opening files for writing, CD:61–62
- properties, CD:32, CD:42
- recording
  - for entire project, CD:29–30
  - for selected tasks, CD:30–32
- recursion, CD:55–56
- ResMgmt_TaskEntry, 755
- subroutines, CD:31
  - calling with arguments, CD:54
  - calling without parameters, CD:52–53
  - main subroutines, CD:51
- TaskSummaryName, CD:36–37
  - code listing, CD:37–38
  - creating, CD:37–38

For Each, Next statement, CD:40
If, Then, Else statement, CD:41
nested statements, CD:41
object properties, CD:42
Sub/End Sub statements, CD:38
user feedback, CD:42
variables, CD:38–40
testing, CD:29
TraceDependencies, CD:46
calling subroutines with arguments, CD:54
calling subroutines without parameters, CD:52–53
Case statement, CD:53–54
code listing, CD:47–50
filters, CD:56–57
input box, CD:51–52
main subroutine, CD:51
message box, CD:52
recursion, CD:55–56
variables, CD:50–51
views, CD:56–57
toolbar buttons, 931
troubleshooting, CD:33
user feedback, CD:33–34, CD:42
variables
defining, CD:38–39
initializing, CD:39–40
private variables, CD:50–51
public variables, CD:50–51
types, CD:38
VBA (Visual Basic for Applications), CD:31
VBE (Visual Basic Editor)
Immediate window, CD:43–45
object browser, CD:36
opening, CD:35
Project Explorer, CD:35
Properties window, CD:36
views, CD:56–57
when to use, CD:28
ZoomAll, CD:29–30
ZoomSelected, CD:30–32

VBE (Visual Basic Editor), CD:35
Immediate window, CD:43–45
object browser, CD:36
opening, CD:35
Project Explorer, CD:35
Properties window, CD:36

Verify Uniqueness of New WBS Codes check box (WBS Code Definition dialog box), 166

verifying task type setting, 361

Version field, 1000

versions, 1066
adding, 999–1000
advantages of, 982
comparing, 483–487
compatibility, 97, 970
creating, 981
cross-project links, 982
defined, 976
deleting, 1000
formatting, 1000
modifying, 1000
opening schedules with, 982
Published version, 981, 999
resources, 982
saving, 1067
Version field, 1000
viewing, 1067

Versions dialog box, 629

vertical divider bars, 47

View and Submit Issues dialog box, CD:89

View Availability command (Resource Center), 1072

View Availability view (Resource Center), 1074

View bar, 37–38

View Bar command (View menu), 37

View Definition dialog box, 835–836, 838

View Enterprise Resources view (Resource Center), 1074

View menu commands
Calendar, 258
More Views, 838
Network Diagram, 267
Reports, 91, 514, 878, 895
Resource Sheet, 287
Table, 236, 757, 760, 840
Tables, 904
Task Usage, 574
Toolbars, 36, 927
View Bar, 37
Zoom, 261, 785

View Resource Assignments view, 1074–1075, 1078–1081

View tab
Options dialog box, 783–784
Page Setup dialog box, 506–508

viewing. *See* displaying

views, 736. *See also names of specific views*
changing, 47–48
changing screen types for, 875
combination views, 246–247, 835, 838–840
consistent views, 982–983
copying, 720–721
Copy command, 727–729
Copy Picture dialog box, 721–723
Copy Picture to Office Wizard, 724–726
creating, 984
combination views, 838–840
Define New View dialog box, 834–835
filters, 837–838
groups, 837
More Views dialog box, 834
names, 836
screen formats, 836–837
single-pane views, 835–836
tables, 837
View Definition dialog box, 835–836
custom views, CD:74
categories, CD:77
default grouping, CD:76
fields, CD:75
filters, CD:76
Gantt Chart format, CD:75

grouping formats, CD:76
Portfolio Analyzer view, CD:77–84
splitter bars, CD:75
table selection, CD:75
defaults, 73–74
defined, 108
displaying name of, 838
formatting
Calendar view, 802–806
copying formatting, 781
Gantt View bar charts, 790–802
gridlines, 781–783
Network Diagram view, 807–816
outline options, 783–784
page breaks, 789
Resource Form view, 817–819
Resource Graph view, 819–826
Resource Sheet view, 830
Resource Usage view, 826–828
sort options, 776–777
Task Form view, 817–819
Task Sheet view, 830
Task Usage view, 829
text, 778–781
timescales, 785–789
troubleshooting, 830–831
macros, CD:56–67
naming, 836
organizing in Project files, 873–875
planning, 977
printing, 490, 493
borders, 499
display enhancements, 495
filters, 495
footers, 500–506
grouped displays, 495
headers, 500–506
legends, 503–506
margins, 499
number of copies, 513
page breaks, 495–496
page numbers, 499
page orientation, 498
paper size, 498
Print command, 490, 512
Print Preview command, 490, 509–513
printer setup, 490–491
scale, 498
specific pages, 512–513
specific panes, 494
timescales, 494, 513, 516
troubleshooting, 515–516
view options, 506–508
restoring, 875
rollup views, 738–739
Bar Rollup, 740
enabling, 739
Milestone Date Rollup, 740–741
Milestone Rollup, 740
Text Above field, 739
saving, 838
screen formats, 836–837
splitting, 46–47, 246–247, 263
troubleshooting, 875
vertical divider bars, 47
View bar, 37–38

Views menu commands, More Views, 47, 736, 834

Visual Basic Editor. *See* VBE

Visual Basic macros. *See* VBA macros

Visual Basic toolbar, 927

W

watches, CD:43–45

WBS (Work Breakdown Structure), 116, 471

WBS Code Definition dialog box, 164–166

WBS codes, 163
creating, 164–166, 854
deleting tasks, 167
editing, 167
inserting tasks, 167
moving tasks, 167
renumbering, 168–169
saving, 170–171

WBS command (Project menu), 164, 471

WBS menu commands
Define Code, 164, 471
Renumber, 169

WBS Renumber dialog box, 169

Web Access. *See also* Project Server
administration, 986–987
Assignment view, CD:74
collaboration. *See* enterprise collaboration
custom views, CD:74
categories, CD:77
default grouping, CD:76
fields, CD:75
filters, CD:76
Gantt Chart format, CD:75
grouping formats, CD:76
Portfolio Analyzer view, CD:77–84
splitter bars, CD:75
table selection, CD:75
customizing
default home page appearance, CD:94
Gantt Chart formats, CD:92–93
grouping formats, CD:93
nonworking time categories, CD:93–94
notifications/reminders, CD:94–95
documents, 1133–1135
groups, 987
issues, 1137–138
Microsoft Outlook, 1139–1141
permissions, 987
Project Center view, CD:74
Project view, CD:74
Resource Center view, CD:74
risks, 1135–1137
status reports, 1129
compiling, 1132–1133
requesting, 1130–1131
status report flow, 1130
submitting, 1131–1132
task assignments, notifying team members of, 1123–1126
timesheets
approving, 1128
attaching notes to, 1127
lockdown periods, 1128–1129

revising, 1129
submitting for approval, 1126–1127
timesheet flow, 1122–1123
tracking methods, 1123
users, 987

Web-enabled projects, 681–682

Web pages
background colors, CD:14–15
background images, CD:16–17
Gantt Chart images, CD:22–24
hyperlinks, 148–149, CD:19–25
images, CD:17–18
Import/Export map options, CD:10–13
publishing, CD:24
saving files as, 102
saving projects as, CD:3–8
title bar text, CD:18–19
troubleshooting, CD:24–25
viewing projects as, CD:9

Web toolbar, 927

Week Headings tab (Timescale dialog box), 804

Welcome page (Import/Export Wizard), 637

What's This? command (Help menu), 36

Who Does What report, 890

Who Does What Report map, 652–654

Who Does What When report, 890

width of columns, 126, 236–237

wildcards, 52, 864

Window menu commands
Arrange All, 605
Hide, 606
More Windows, 604
New Window, 607–608, 615
Remove Split, 153
Split, 246, 263, 605
Unhide, 606

windows. *See also* views
displaying, 606
hiding, 606
maximizing, 606
Microsoft Project, 32
Entry bar, 37
menu bar, 35
Project Guide, 38–41
ScreenTips, 38–39
status bar, 38
toolbars, 35–36
View bar, 37–38
splitting, 246–247, 263, 605
tiling, 605–606

Windows authentication, CD:72

Windows Account button (Resource Information dialog box), 308

Windows Clipboard, 692

Windows SharePoint Services, 628–629
document libraries, CD:86
document management, CD:87–88
issues tracking, CD:89–90
risk tracking, CD:90–91
subwebs, CD:86

Within test (filters), 861, 863

wizards
Analyze Timescaled Data Wizard, 591–595
Copy Picture to Office Wizard, 724–726
Define Working Times for Resources Wizard, 88
Enterprise Resource Pool Wizard, 1091
Export Wizard, CD:3–13
Gantt Chart Wizard, 801–802
Import Projects Wizard, 1025–1028
Import Resources Wizard, 1021–1023
Import/Export Wizard, 637–639
New Calendar Wizard, 86–87
New Project Wizard, 85–86
Planning Wizard, 42–43, 210–212
Resource Substitution Wizard, 1091, 1110–1117
Tracking Setup Wizard, 547–549

Word Tracking form, 950

work, 280
assigning
Material Resources field, 330
work formula, 332
Work Resources field, 329–330
assignment-tracking fields
% Work Complete field, 538
Actual Finish field, 537
Actual Start field, 537
Actual Work, 537
Actual Work field, 537
Remaining Work field, 538
timephased Actual Work field, 539
Assignment Work graph, 372
availability, displaying, 824
back-loading, 348, 350
calculating, 330–331
displaying, 822–823
extended working hours, 429–432
fixed-work tasks, 335
free slack, 441
front-loading, 348, 350
overtime
assigning, 385–387
cautions, 346
cost per use, 305
overtime rate, 304–305
scheduling, 346–348, 423–428
task-tracking fields
% Work Complete field, 535
Actual Work field, 535
Remaining Work field, 535–536
timephased Actual Work field, 536
total slack, 441
variances, 572–573
Work Breakdown Structure (WBS), 116, 471

work contours
- applying to assignments, 352
- back loaded, 348–350
- bell, 350
- contoured, 351
- documenting changes to, 352
- double peak, 350
- early peak, 350
- example, 348–349
- flat pattern, 348–350
- front loaded, 348–350
- late peak, 350
- selecting, 392
- turtle, 351

work formula, 330–331
- applying to existing assignments, 335
- applying to new assignments, 331–334

Work graph, 372
work resource units, 326–327
work schedules, 388–390
Work table, 759–761

Work Availability option (Details menu), 824

Work Breakdown Structure (WBS), 116, 471

Work Complete filter, 317, 768

Work Contour field (Assignment Information dialog box), 391–392

Work graph, 372

Work Incomplete filter, 768

Work option (Details menu), 822

Work Overbudget filter, 572–574, 767–768

Work Resources field, 329–330

Work table, 759, 761

Work view (Resource Center), 1077

Work vs. Material Resources command (Group By menu), 315

Work vs. Material Resources group, 773

workgroup fields, 308

workgroups, CD:69

working days, 78–80

Working Days report, 881–882, 901

working hours, 80–81

working offline, 1010

Working Time field (resources), 301–302

Workload reports, 890–891

Worksheet Object menu commands, Convert, 710

worksheets (Excel)
- Import/Export maps, 665
- importing project data from, 673–680
- saving projects as, 665–668

workspaces
- saving, 102–103, 607, 625, 635
- settings, 635
- shared workspaces, 628–629

write-reservation passwords, 101

X-Z

.xls file format, 634

XML (Extensible Markup Language), 681–682

Zoom command
- Format menu, 245
- View menu, 261, 785

Zoom menu commands
- Entire Project, CD:29
- Selected Tasks, CD:30

Zoom dialog box, 245, 261, 817

Zoom Out the Timescale So the Picture Can Fit option (Copy Picture dialog box), 723

zooming in/out
- Calendar view, 261
- Network Diagram view, 267–268, 817
- timescale, 245, 494

Zoom dialog box, 245, 261, 817
Zoom In button, 494
Zoom Out button, 494
ZoomAll macro, CD:29–30
ZoomSelected macro, CD:30–32

What's on the CD-ROM

The companion CD-ROM contains all the examples developed for the book, a third-party software library, and Web resources.

Windows Installation Instructions

1. Insert the disc into your CD-ROM drive.
2. From the Windows desktop, double-click the My Computer icon.
3. Double-click the icon representing your CD-ROM drive.
4. Double-click on `start.exe`. Follow the onscreen prompts to access the CD content.

NOTE

> If you have the AutoPlay feature enabled, `start.exe` will be launched automatically whenever you insert the disc into your CD-ROM drive.

License Agreement

By opening this package, you are also agreeing to be bound by the following agreement:

You may not copy or redistribute the entire CD-ROM as a whole. Copying and redistribution of individual software programs on the CD-ROM is governed by terms set by individual copyright holders.

The installer and code from the author(s) are copyrighted by the publisher and the author(s). Individual programs and other items on the CD-ROM are copyrighted or are under an Open Source license by their various authors or other copyright holders.

This software is sold as-is without warranty of any kind, either expressed or implied, including but not limited to the implied warranties of merchantability and fitness for a particular purpose. Neither the publisher nor its dealers or distributors assumes any liability for any alleged or actual damages arising from the use of this program. (Some states do not allow for the exclusion of implied warranties, so the exclusion may not apply to you.)

SPECIAL EDITION

USING®

Microsoft® Office

Project 2003

THE *ONLY* **PROJECT 2003** BOOK YOU NEED

Que crafted this book to grow with you, providing the reference material you need as you move toward Project proficiency and use of more advanced features. If you buy only one book on Project 2003, *Special Edition Using Microsoft Office Project 2003* is the only book you need!

- Understand project management concepts and the major phases of managing a project.
- Learn to navigate the screen display, scroll and select data, and select different views of a project.
- Learn how to specify the calendar of working days and hours, how to enter basic information about a project, how to specify the planned date for starting or finishing the project, and how to adjust the most critical of the default values that govern how Microsoft Project displays and calculates a project.
- Define and enter the tasks, milestones, and recurring tasks that must be completed to successfully finish a project.
- Define special conditions that govern the scheduling of tasks in a project, including specific deadlines and sequencing requirements for the tasks.
- Learn how to view the resources, costs, and task assignments in useful ways for auditing the project plan.
- Understand how executives, resource managers, and project managers view and use the resource information that is available via Project Web Access and Project Professional.
- Understand how team members will use the document management and collaboration features of Project Web Access, including time tracking, status reporting, managing to-do lists, issues, risks, and document management.
- Covers Microsoft Office Project 2003 Standard and Microsoft Office Project 2003 Professional.

Category	General Applications
Covers	Microsoft Office Project 2003
User Level	Intermediate—Advanced

que®

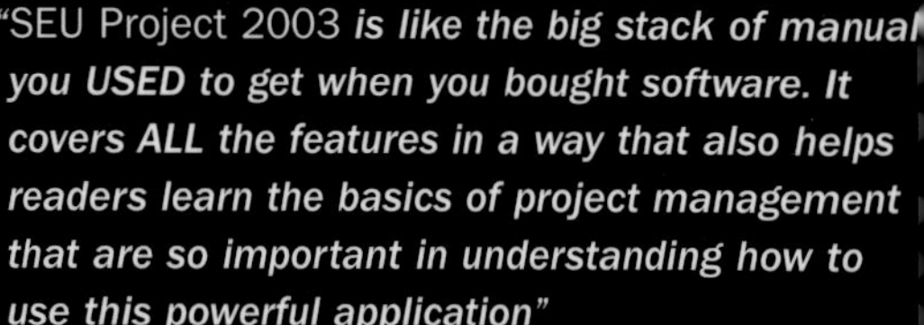

"SEU Project 2003 is like the big stack of manual you USED to get when you bought software. It covers ALL the features in a way that also helps readers learn the basics of project management that are so important in understanding how to use this powerful application"

—Brian Kennemer, Technical PM, QuantumPM

Tim Pyron is a Microsoft Project consultant and trainer. He is also the editor of Woody's Project Watch, http://www.woodyswatch.com, a free newsletter for Project users with a subscription of more than 40,000 readers. He has written seven books on all versions of Microsoft Project starting with Project 3.0. His most recent title includes *Special Edition Using Microsoft Project 2002*.

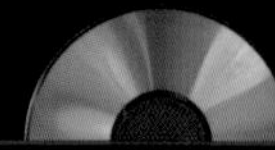

On the CD-ROM:

- **Source files**—Explore selected source files whil following along in the book or use them for experimenting on your own
- **Demonstration and Trial software**—Install additional project management tools such as EPK-Time, EPK-Portfolio, Milestones Project Companion Product, and PERT Chart EXPERT
- **Electronic content**—This entire book in Adobe's Portable Document Format (PDF) for fast and easy topic search
- **BONUS Chapters**—Read three additional Project chapters not seen in the book
- **Que's Special Edition Using Office Showcase**—Access four chapters from each of Que's other Special Edition Using Microsoft Office System 2003 titles absolutely FREE

inform

$39.99 USA / $57.99 CAN / £28.99 Net UK (inc. of

ISBN 0-7897-3072-3

www.quepublishing.c